The Dorling Kindersley

ILLUSTRATED
FAMILY
ENCYCLOPEDIA

VOLUME 2 · I-Z
Indian Ocean to *Zoos*

A DK PUBLISHING BOOK

LONDON, NEW YORK, MUNICH,
MELBOURNE AND DELHI

Senior Editor Jayne Parsons   **Senior Art Editor** Gillian Shaw

Project Editors
Marian Broderick, Gill Cooling,
Maggie Crowley, Hazel Egerton,
Cynthia O'Neill, Veronica Pennycook,
Louise Pritchard, Steve Setford, Jackie Wilson

Project Art Editors
Jane Felstead, Martyn Foote,
Neville Graham, Jamie Hanson,
Christopher Howson, Jill Plank, Floyd Sayers,
Jane Tetzlaff, Ann Thompson

Editors
Rachel Beaugié, Nic Kynaston, Sarah Levete,
Karen O'Brien, Linda Sonntag

Art Editors
Tina Borg, Diane Clouting,
Tory Gordon-Harris

DTP Designers
Andrew O'Brien, Cordelia Springer

Managing Editor Ann Kramer   **Managing Art Editor** Peter Bailey

Senior DTP Designer Mathew Birch

Picture Research Jo Walton, Kate Duncan, Liz Moore

DK Picture Library Ola Rudowska, Melanie Simmonds

Country pages by PAGE*One*: Bob Gordon, Helen Parker,
Thomas Keenes, Sarah Watson, Chris Clark

Cartographers Peter Winfield, James Anderson

Research Robert Graham, Angela Koo

Editorial Assistants Sarah-Louise Reed, Nichola Roberts

Production Louise Barratt, Charlotte Traill

First published in the United States in 1997.
This edition published in the United States in 2002
by DK Publishing, Inc.,
375 Hudson St., New York, NY 10014

A CIP catalogue record for this book is available from the Library of Congress

ISBN 0 7894 8865 5

Color reproduction by Colourscan, Singapore
Printed and bound in China by Toppan Printing Co. (Shenzhen) Ltd.

See our complete product line at www.dk.com

LIST OF MAIN ENTRIES
See index for further topics

POWER AND SPEED

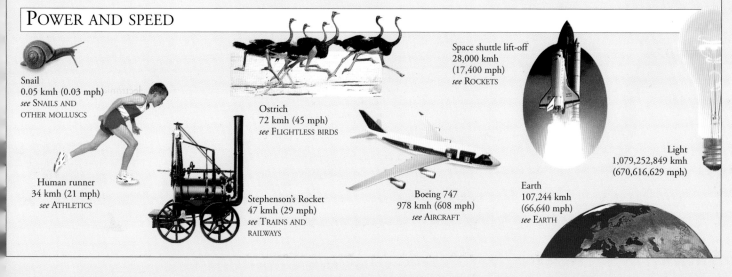

Snail
0.05 kmh (0.03 mph)
see SNAILS AND
OTHER MOLLUSCS

Human runner
34 kmh (21 mph)
see ATHLETICS

Ostrich
72 kmh (45 mph)
see FLIGHTLESS BIRDS

Stephenson's Rocket
47 kmh (29 mph)
see TRAINS AND
RAILWAYS

Boeing 747
978 kmh (608 mph)
see AIRCRAFT

Space shuttle lift-off
28,000 kmh
(17,400 mph)
see ROCKETS

Earth
107,244 kmh
(66,640 mph)
see EARTH

Light
1,079,252,849 kmh
(670,616,629 mph)

COMMUNICATION TIMELINE

490 BC
Marathon runner
see OLYMPIC
GAMES

Carrier pigeon
see BIRDS

18th century Sign language
see LANGUAGES

1840
Postage stamp
see STAMPS AND
POSTAL SERVICES

1837
Electric
telegraph
see TELECOMMUNICATIONS

1844
Morse code
see CODES AND
CIPHERS

1876
Bell telephone
see TELEPHONES

12th century Smoke signals | 1784 Mail coach | 1850 Pillar box | 1855 Printing telegraph | 1860 Semaphore and Pony Express | 1861 Postcards

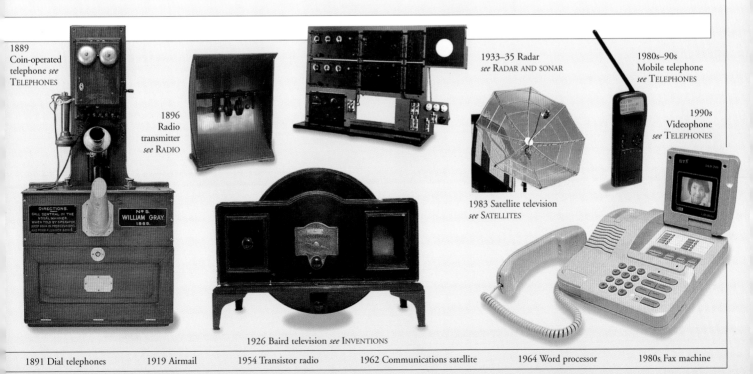

1889
Coin-operated
telephone *see*
TELEPHONES

1896
Radio
transmitter
see RADIO

1933–35 Radar
see RADAR AND SONAR

1980s–90s
Mobile telephone
see TELEPHONES

1990s
Videophone
see TELEPHONES

1983 Satellite television
see SATELLITES

1926 Baird television *see* INVENTIONS

1891 Dial telephones   1919 Airmail   1954 Transistor radio   1962 Communications satellite   1964 Word processor   1980s Fax machine

HOW TO USE THIS ENCYCLOPEDIA

THE FOLLOWING PAGES WILL HELP YOU get the most out of your copy of the *Dorling Kindersley Illustrated Family Encyclopedia*. The encyclopedia consists of three volumes. Volumes 1–2 contain nearly 700 main entries organized alphabetically, from Aboriginal Australians through to Zoos. To find the entry you want, simply turn to the correct letter of the alphabet.

If you cannot find the topic you want, then turn to Volume 3. This volume includes an index and gazetteer for the whole encyclopedia, which will direct you straight to the page you need. In addition, Volume 3 contains hundreds of reference charts, fact boxes, lists, and tables to supplement the information provided on the main entry pages.

MEASUREMENTS AND ABBREVIATIONS

Most measurements are supplied in both metric and imperial units. Some of the most common abbreviations used in the encyclopedia are shown below in **bold** type.

°C = degrees Celsius
°F = degrees Fahrenheit
K = degrees kelvin
mm = millimetre; **cm** = centimetre
m = metre; **km** = kilometre
in = inch; **ft** = foot; **yd** = yard
g = gram; **kg** = kilogram
oz = ounce; **lb** = pound
ml = millilitre; **l** = litre
pt = pint; **gal** = gallon
sq km (km²) = square kilometre
sq ft (ft²) = square foot
kmh = kilometres per hour
mph = miles per hour
mya = million years ago
BC = before Christ
AD = anno Domini (refers to any date after the birth of Christ)
c. = circa (about)
b. = born; **d.** = died; **r.** = reigned

THE PAGE LAYOUT

The pages in this encyclopedia have been carefully planned to make each subject as accessible as possible. Main entries are broken down into a hierarchy of information – from a general introduction to more specific individual topics.

Alphabet locators

Letter flashes help you find your way quickly around the encyclopedia.

Sub-entries

Sub-entries provide important additional information and expand on points made in the introduction.

This sub-entry explains how rainbows are caused by raindrops in the air.

Diagrams

Clear diagrams help explain complex processes and scientific concepts.

The diagram here shows how a raindrop splits sunlight into its constituent colours.

Introduction

Clear introductions are the starting point for each entry. The introduction defines and provides an overview of each subject.

In the main entry on COLOUR, the introduction explains that colours are different forms of light, and that sunlight contains light of many different colours.

COLLEGES see SCHOOLS AND COLLEGES • COLOMBIA see SOUTH AMERICA, NORTHERN

COLOR

A WORLD WITHOUT COLOR would be dull and uninspiring. Color is a form of light. Light is made up of electromagnetic waves of varying lengths. The human eye detects these different wavelengths and sees them as different colors. White light – like that from the Sun – is a mixture of all the different wavelengths. Objects look colored because they emit or reflect only certain wavelengths of light.

White light spectrum

Passing white light through a transparent triangular block called a prism separates the different wavelengths of light. The prism refracts (bends) each wavelength by a different amount, forming a band of colors called a white light spectrum, or visible spectrum. The seven main colors are red, orange, yellow, green, blue, indigo, and violet. Red has the longest wavelength and violet the shortest. Here, a convex lens combines the colors back into white light.

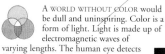

Rainbow

If it rains on a sunny day, you may well see a rainbow if you stand with your back to the Sun. A rainbow is a curved white light spectrum that forms when light is reflected and refracted by raindrops in the sky.

A rainbow at dawn

How a rainbow forms

The white sunlight passes through a raindrop, the raindrop acts like a tiny prism, refracting the light and splitting it up into its separate colors. The colors fan out and emerge as a spectrum. A rainbow is made up of spectra from millions of raindrops.

Sunlight
Colors refract again.
Spectrum
Light refracts.
Colors reflect off back surface.

Color and temperature

Objects at room temperature emit (give out) electromagnetic waves, but these waves are long for human eyes to see. Heating an object such as this steel bar, makes the waves short enough to be seen, and the bar begins to glow. As the bar's temperature rises, it glows with different colors.

Steel bar at 1,170°F (630°C)

Steel bar at 2,790°F (1,532°C)

Spectroscope

An instrument called a spectroscope is used to analyze the light emitted by hot substances. Inside the spectroscope, a prism or diffraction grating (a glass slide scored with fine lines) splits light from a glowing substance into its component wavelengths.

Light source
Diffraction grating

Emission spectrum

Each chemical element gives out a unique range of light wavelengths when heated. Seen through a spectroscope, these wavelengths appear as a set of bright lines on a dark background. This is the element's emission spectrum. A compound's emission spectrum is a combination of spectra from the elements that make up the compound.

Emission spectrum of a sodium flame
Sodium flame

Cone cells

At the back of the eye are special cells called cones that enable humans to see colors. There are three types of cones, called red, green, and blue cones. Each type of cone is sensitive to a different range of light wavelengths. White light stimulates all three types of cones.

Cone cells

Sensitivity of red cones *Sensitivity of green cones* *Sensitivity of blue cones*
Visible spectrum
Sensitivity of cone cells in the human eye

Red hot and white hot

As the steel bar gets hot it emits more and more of the visible spectrum. At about 1,170°F (630°C), it is "red hot" and emits light from the red end of the spectrum. At about 2,790°F (1,532°C), it is the "white hot" bar emits the entire white light spectrum.

Glowing white
Glowing red
Visible spectrum

Hot stars

The color of a star gives a clue to its age. To the naked eye, most stars look white, but their true colors can be seen through a telescope. Young stars are hot and glow with white light. Older stars are relatively cool and glow red or orange.

A cluster of young stars

Joseph von Fraunhofer

The German physicist Joseph von Fraunhofer (1787–1826) became interested in the nature of light while training as a mirror maker and lens polisher. His training enabled him to make spectroscopes of great precision. From 1814–17, he used them to make the first scientific study of the Sun's emission spectrum.

Munsell color system

Describing colors exactly using words alone is not easy. To avoid confusion, manufacturing industries use standard color-identification systems. The Munsell system is used to specify colors for dyes and pigments. It defines a color by its value (brightness), its chroma (strength), and its hue (position in the spectrum).

Color matching systems

Graphic designers use swatches of color cards to match the colors in their work with those available from printers. The designer supplies the printer with the reference number of the color, so the printer knows exactly what is wanted.

Each color has a reference number.

226

Labels help to identify images.

Natural history data boxes

On the natural history pages, data boxes summarize essential information about a key animal featured in the entry. The box contains information about the animal's size, diet, habitat, lifespan, distribution, and scientific name.

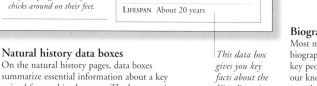

act as rudders.
Strong chest muscles pull down the wings.
Penguin rises through the water to break through the surface.
Huddling reduces heat loss.
emperor penguins carry chicks around on their feet.

KING PENGUIN

SCIENTIFIC NAME *Aptenodytes patagonica*

ORDER Sphenisciformes

FAMILY Spheniscidae

DISTRIBUTION Islands and ocean north of Antarctica

HABITAT Coasts and open sea

DIET Fish and squid

SIZE Length, including tail 95 cm (37.5 in)

LIFESPAN About 20 years

This data box gives you key facts about the King Penguin.

Biography boxes

Most main entry pages have biography boxes that tell you about key people who have contributed to our knowledge of the subject. The encyclopedia also has single-page entries on the life and work of more than 50 major historical figures.

This biography box describes the work of the physicist Joseph von Fraunhofer.

Headings

The topic headings enable you to see at-a-glance which subjects are covered within the main entry.

The heading Colour matching systems *refers to the way designers use reference numbers to match the colours on their work to the colours of printers' inks.*

INDEX

Volume 3 contains an index and a gazetteer. The index, which comes first, lists all the topics mentioned in the encyclopedia and the pages on which they can be found. The gazetteer follows on, with references to help you find all the features included on the maps.

• page numbers in **bold** type (eg Knights and heraldry **495-6**) show that the subject is a main A–Z entry in Volumes 1–2.
• page numbers in plain type (eg armour 69) send you to sub-entries, text references, and the reference section.
• grid references (eg Cremona Italy 475 C3) are letter-number combinations that locate features on maps.

This two-page entry discusses the main types of primate.

Running head

There is an A–Z running head at the top of most pages to help you find important topics that are not main entries within the encyclopedia.

Illustrations

Each main entry is heavily illustrated with models, photographs, and artworks, adding a vibrant layer of visual information to the page.

This annotation tells you how different colours can be produced by mixing red, green, and blue light.

Annotation

The illustrations are comprehensively annotated to draw attention to details of particular interest and to explain complex points.

The running head on PRINTING tells you that although there is no main entry on primates, you can find the topic on MONKEYS AND OTHER PRIMATES.

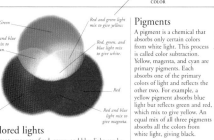

Colored lights

Different amounts of red, green, and blue light can be mixed to form light of any other color. This process is called color addition. Unlike paints, red, green, and blue are the primary colors of light. Equal amounts of any two primary colors give a secondary color (yellow, cyan, or magenta). When all three primaries are mixed in equal amounts, white light is produced.

Color television
The principle of adding colored lights is used in color television. The screen is covered with tiny strips that glow with red, green, or blue light. They are so small that, at normal viewing distance, the human eye cannot tell them coming from them. By adjusting the intensity of these three colors, the sensation of any other color is produced.

Image is formed by tiny glowing strips.

Painting with dots
Pointillism is a style of painting in which an artist uses thousands of tiny colored dots to build up a picture. When viewed close up, the colors of the individual dots are clearly visible. Like the colored strips on a television screen, the dots are too small to be seen from farther away. When viewed from a distance, the dots seem to merge, giving areas a single color.

Pigments

A pigment is a chemical that absorbs only certain colors from white light. This process is called color subtraction. Yellow, magenta, and cyan are primary pigments. Each absorbs one of the primary colors of light and reflects the other two. For example, a yellow pigment absorbs blue light but reflects green and red, which mix to give yellow. An equal mix of all three pigments absorbs all the colors from white light, giving black.

Color printing
To print a color picture, three single-color images are printed on top of each other – one in cyan, one in magenta, and one in yellow. Each picture is made up of tiny colored dots. The dots overlap and absorb the right wavelengths of light to give all the other colors required. A black image is then added to make the picture sharper.

Picture is made up of tiny ink dots.

Mixing paints
Paints are pigments mixed with water or oil. Any color except white can be made by mixing the three primary pigments. Mixing paints has the effect of evenly mixing the pigments, and absorbing more of the white light spectrum.

Scattering and interference

Two other processes, called scattering and interference, can remove colors from the spectrum. Interference occurs when light from two sources meets and combines. In scattering, some parts of the spectrum are briefly absorbed by particles of matter and then radiated out again in all directions.

Soap bubble
When white light strikes a soap bubble, it reflects off both the inner and outer surfaces of the bubble. The reflected light rays interfere, canceling out some colors but making others appear bright.

Interference creates a pattern of bright colors and dark bands.

Blue sky
Sunlight includes all the colors of the spectrum. The sky appears blue during the day because blue air molecules in the atmosphere scatter light from the blue end of the spectrum in all directions.

Using interference
Stress is a force that can stretch or bend objects. Engineers shine light through plastic models of their designs to test their ability to withstand stress. The plastic molecules make the light rays split up and interfere. The interference patterns show the points of greatest stress.

High stress

Thomas Young

The English doctor and physicist Thomas Young (1773–1829) carried out many experiments to prove that light travels in waves. He realized that colors are light waves of different lengths and that interference effects occur where light waves meet and combine. Young also investigated color vision. In 1801, he proposed that the human eye contains three types of color sensors (now called cone cells), sensitive to blue, red, and green light.

Reflecting colors

Objects have color only when light falls upon them, because colors do not exist in total darkness. An object that appears one color in white light may look different when illuminated by colored light. The yellow pot in this sequence of pictures appears yellow only in white light.

White light
The yellow pot reflects the red and green parts of the white light spectrum, but absorbs the blue part.

Red light
The yellow pot reflects red light, and therefore appears red when illuminated by red light.

Green light
When illuminated by green light, the yellow pigment reflects the green light and appears green.

Blue light
When only blue light is available, the yellow pot absorbs the blue light, making it look black.

FIND OUT MORE   DYES AND PAINTS   EYES AND VISION   LIGHT   PHOTOGRAPHY   PRINTING   TELEVISION

Find out more

The Find Out More lines at the end of each entry direct you to other relevant main entries in the encyclopedia. Using the Find Out More lines can help you understand an entry in its wider context.

On COLOUR, the Find Out More line directs you to the entry on PRINTING, where there is a detailed explanation of the colour printing process and how printing presses work.

PRINTING'S Find Out More line sends you to CHINA, HISTORY OF, which lists ancient Chinese inventions, including printing.

Timelines

An entry may include a timeline that gives the dates of key events in the history or development of the subject.

The PRINTING timeline stretches from the printing of the first books in ancient China to the computerization of modern printing.

COLLECTION PAGES

There are more than 70 pages of photographic collections, which follow main entries and provide a visual guide to the subject. They are organized under clear headings.

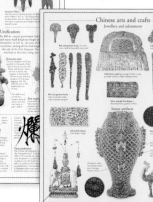

The entry on the history of China is followed by a collection page showing Chinese jewellery and ornaments.

CONTINENT AND COUNTRY PAGES

The encyclopedia contains entries on all the world's continents and countries, each containing a detailed map. Continent entries focus on the physical geography of the region; country entries provide information about the society and economy of the country. Below is the single-page entry on the Netherlands

The country's flag appears by its name.

Locator map
A small map in the top left-hand corner of the page shows you where the region lies within a continent or in relation to the rest of the world.

Map of Netherlands' position in Europe.

The introduction defines the region and provides an overview to the entry.

Compass points north

Scale bar

Scale bar and compass
Each map has a scale bar that shows how distances on the map relate to actual miles and kilometers. The compass shows you which direction on the map is north (N).

Grid reference
The numbers and letters around the map help you find all the places listed in the index.

The index gives Amsterdam's grid reference as C4, so you can find it on the map by locating the third square along (C) and the fourth square down (4).

Population density
A population density diagram shows how many people there are to every square mile or square kilometer.

The Netherlands is a very densely populated country

KEY TO MAP

- International border
- Disputed border
- Road
- Railroad
- International airport
- Lake
- Seasonal lake
- River
- Canal
- Waterfall
- ● Capital city
- ◉ Major town
- ● Minor town
- ▲ Spot height (feet)
- ▼ Spot depth (feet)

NETBALL *see* BALL GAMES

NETHERLANDS

ALSO CALLED HOLLAND, the Netherlands straddles the deltas of five major rivers in northwestern Europe. The Dutch people say they created their own country because they have enclosed about one-third of the land from sea, swamps, and marshland with earth barriers, or dikes, and drained the water from it. Despite being one of the most densely populated countries in the world, the Netherlands enjoys high living standards. Amsterdam is the official capital, although the government is based at The Hague.

NETHERLANDS FACTS
CAPITAL CITY Amsterdam (seat of government The Hague)
AREA 37,330 sq km (14,413 sq miles)
POPULATION 15,800,000
MAIN LANGUAGE Dutch
MAJOR RELIGION Christian
CURRENCY Euro
LIFE EXPECTANCY 78 years
PEOPLE PER DOCTOR 385
GOVERNMENT Multi-party democracy
ADULT LITERACY 99%

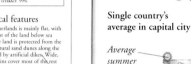

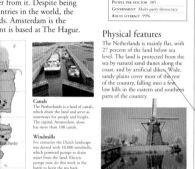

Physical features
The Netherlands is mainly flat, with 27 percent of the land below sea level. The land is protected from the sea by natural sand dunes along the coast, and by artificial dikes. Wide, sandy plains cover most of the rest of the country, falling into a few low hills in the eastern and southern parts of the country.

Canals
The Netherlands is a land of canals, which drain the land and serve as waterways for people and freight. The capital, Amsterdam, alone has more than 100 canals.

Windmills
For centuries the Dutch landscape was dotted with 10,000 windmills, which powered pumps to drain water from the land. Electric pumps now do this work in the battle to keep the sea back.

Climate
The Netherlands has mild, rainy winters and cool summers. In winter northerly gales lash the coast, damaging dikes and threatening floods. Frosts sometimes freeze canals.

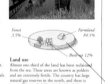

Land use
Almost one-third of the land has been reclaimed from the sea. These areas are known as polders and are extremely fertile. The country has large natural gas reserves in the north, and there is some offshore oil drilling in the North Sea.

Farming and industry
The Dutch economy is one of the most successful in Europe. Most imports and exports travel through Rotterdam, the world's biggest port. In addition to high-tech sectors such as electronics, telecommunications, and chemicals, the Netherlands has a successful agricultural industry. Productivity is high, and products such as vegetables, cheese, meat, and cut flowers are significant export earners.

Amsterdam
The Dutch capital is built on 70 islands, linked by about 500 bridges, which span its many canals. The best way to get around is by bicycle, and around 750,000 people cycle to school or work each day. Today, Amsterdam is a busy centre for tourism and diamond trading.

One of Amsterdam's many canals

People
The Dutch see their society as the most tolerant in Europe, with relaxed laws on sexuality, drugs, and euthanasia. The country has a long history of welcoming immigrants, often from former Dutch colonies. Most of these people are now assimilated as Dutch citizens. However, members of the small Turkish community, which makes up just one per cent of the population, do not enjoy full citizenship.

Street scene, Amsterdam

1,083 per sq mile (418 per sq km)

89% Urban 11% Rural

Dutch tulips

FIND OUT MORE | CANALS | DAMS | EMPIRES | EUROPE | EUROPE, HISTORY OF | EUROPEAN UNION | FARMING | NETHERLANDS, HISTORY OF | PORTS AND WATERWAYS

601

Country file
On each country page there is a fact box containing key details about the country, such as its population, capital city, area, currency, political system, and main language and religion. Other categories of information include:

Literacy – the percentage of people over 15 years old who can read and write.
People per doctor – a rough guide to the availability of medical facilities.
Life expectancy – how long an average person can expect to live.

Climate
A climate diagram gives details of rainfall levels and temperatures in the country, region, or continent.

Average summer temperature — *Average winter temperature* — *Average rainfall*

Single country's average in capital city

Average summer temperature — *Average winter temperature* — *Average rainfall*

Regional average is the average of all capital cities on map

Concise explanation of the country's main physical characteristics.

Land use
The land-use diagram tells you how much of the country's total land area is taken up by, for example, woodland, agriculture, and urban developments such as villages, towns, and cities.

Most of the land in the Netherlands is used for farming.

Urban/rural split
A small diagram shows the percentage of people living in urban (built-up) areas and rural (country) areas.

The majority of people in the Netherlands live in urban areas.

REFERENCE PAGES
Volume 3 of the Encyclopedia contains an illustrated reference section with essential facts, figures, and statistical data, divided into the five main strands described here.

International world
This strand contains a double-page map showing all the countries of the world, and data on the world's population, economy, and resources.

History
The history strand features a timeline of key historical events, stretching from 40,000 BC to the present day, together with the dates of major wars, revolutions, battles, and great leaders.

Living world
The centrepiece of this strand is a detailed guide to the classification of living things, supported by lists of species in danger, and many other facts about the natural world.

People, arts, and media
This strand is crammed full of information about television, theater, music, art, philosophy, architecture, literature, dance, and much more besides.

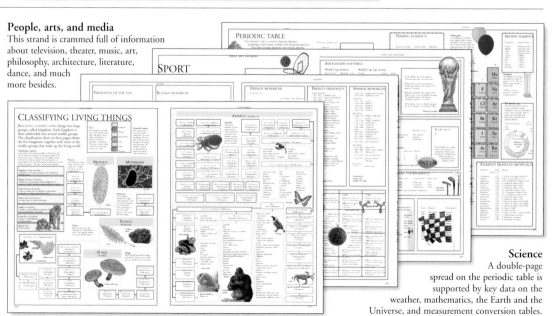

Science
A double-page spread on the periodic table is supported by key data on the weather, mathematics, the Earth and the Universe, and measurement conversion tables.

INDIAN OCEAN

BOUNDED BY AFRICA to the west, Australia and Indonesia to the east, and Asia to the north, the Indian Ocean is the world's third largest ocean. In the south it merges with the Southern Ocean that extends right around the globe. Unlike the Atlantic and Pacific, it has no natural outlet to the north, although the Suez Canal at the northern tip of the Red Sea links it with the Mediterranean Sea. Monsoon winds bring flooding to the Indian subcontinent and Southeast Asia.

Physical features

The currents of the Indian Ocean change direction spectacularly according to the monsoon winds. Between February and March, a strong current flows southwest along the coast of Somalia, changing direction completely between August and September. In the Bay of Bengal, the current flows clockwise in February, and counter-clockwise in August.

INDIAN OCEAN FACTS

AREA	28,350,000 sq miles (73,426,000 sq km)
AVERAGE DEPTH	12,762 ft (3,890 m)
GREATEST DEPTH	24,441 ft (7,450 m), Java Trench
NUMBER OF ISLANDS	5,000
LARGEST ISLAND	Borneo
SMALLEST COUNTRY	Singapore
POPULATION	1,000,000

Ocean islands
There are estimated to be more than 5,000 islands in the Indian Ocean. Many, such as the Seychelles and the Maldives, are coral atolls, where beautiful beaches and a warm climate attract increasing numbers of tourists.

Monsoon
During the northern winter, cool, dry winds blow over the ocean from the northeast. In summer, the wind direction changes and southwesterly winds blow north from the ocean, bringing heavy monsoon rains to coastal areas. Although farmers depend on these rains, they often cause serious flooding.

Strait of Malacca
Lying between the Indonesian island of Sumatra and the Malay Peninsula, the shallow Strait of Malacca is one of the main trade routes at the eastern end of the Indian Ocean, effectively providing a link with the Pacific Ocean. Malacca in Malaysia and Singapore are the two leading ports.

Salt
Around the shores of the Indian Ocean, particularly in India and the Middle East, people extract salt from the seawater. They channel water into shallow enclosures called pans and allow it to evaporate in sunshine, leaving crystals of pure salt that can be collected, packaged, and sold. Oceans are salty because minerals dissolved from rocks by rivers are washed into them.

Salt panning, Karachi, Pakistan

I

Maldives

The Maldives is a tiny Asian republic in the Indian Ocean, just southwest of Sri Lanka. It consists of 1,190 small coral islands, only 202 of which are inhabited. People have lived here for 2,300 years. Today the islanders live from fishing and growing coconuts. However, tourism is the principal source of income on the bigger islands.

MALDIVES FACTS

CAPITAL CITY Male

AREA 116 sq miles (300 sq km)

POPULATION 286,000

MAIN LANGUAGES Dhivehi, Sinhala, Tamil

MAJOR RELIGION Muslim

CURRENCY Rufiyaa

Reef protection
Many of the coral islands in the Indian Ocean have an average height of 6 ft (1.8 m), and are at risk of suffering serious storm damage, especially during the monsoon season when waves can break over them. To help give some protection, many islanders build a sturdy seawall around their island to act as a barrier against the water.

Stone and concrete walls

Tourism
Maldivians prefer to keep tourists away from the villages where they live and many of the main luxury hotels have been built on some of the uninhabited islands. The islands are popular with divers, who like to explore the coral reefs and their shoals of brightly colored tropical fish.

Seychelles

The Seychelles is an independent African country that sprawls over 150,000 sq miles (400,000 sq km) of the Indian Ocean northeast of Madagascar. Of the 115 islands, 32 of them, where the majority of the population live, are formed from granite rock, and the rest are low, isolated outcrops of coral.

SEYCHELLES FACTS

CAPITAL CITY Victoria

AREA 176 sq miles (455 sq km)

POPULATION 79,300

MAIN LANGUAGES Creole, English, French

MAJOR RELIGION Christian

CURRENCY Rupee

Wildlife
The isolated position of the Seychelles has permitted the evolution of many unique species of plants and animals, including the coco-de-mer palm, which produces the world's heaviest seed pods, and unique varieties of orchid, giant tortoise, gecko, chameleon, and "flying fox" – a type of fruitbat. Several reserves have been set up to protect this natural heritage.

Tea picking in Victoria

People
Most Seychellois are of mixed African and European origin. About 90 percent of them live on the island of Mahé. The people enjoy some of the highest living standards in Africa. Tea, fish, and dried coconut, are the main exports; however 90 percent of foreign earnings now come from tourism.

Mauritius

Dominated by the peaks of former volcanoes, the African country of Mauritius lies 1,200 miles (2,000 km) off the southeastern coast of Africa. It consists of Mauritius Island itself and a few smaller islands several hundred miles to the north. Mauritius is densely populated. More than half the people are Hindu Indians; most of the rest are Creoles and Chinese.

MAURITIUS FACTS

CAPITAL CITY Port Louis

AREA 718 sq miles (1,860 sq km)

POPULATION 1,200,000

MAIN LANGUAGES English, French, Creole, Hindi, Bhojpuri, Chinese

MAJOR RELIGIONS Hindu, Christian, Muslim

CURRENCY Rupee

Other islands

Most other islands in the Indian Ocean are very small. Of special note are the atolls of the Aldabra group, where giant tortoises still roam in the wild. Christmas Island, an Australian territory near Java, is so-called because a British seaman sighted it on Christmas Day in 1643.

Mayotte
The French island of Mayotte forms part of the Comoros Islands. It covers an area of 144 sq miles (374 sq km) and has a population of about 142,000. People grow ylang-ylang and vanilla for export.

Sugar
The main cash crops are tea and cane sugar, which makes up 30 percent of the country's exports. Textiles and tourism are also thriving industries. Mauritius belongs to the Indian Ocean Commission, which seeks to promote trade.

Molasses

Sugarcane   *Raw cane juice*

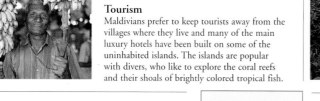

Education
Mauritius has a well-educated workforce, and hopes to become an independent financial center. About 1,800 students are enrolled at the University of Mauritius, founded in 1965. The university specializes in research on agriculture and sugar technology.

Réunion
The island of Réunion is a self-governing overseas department of France. It has an area of 969 sq miles (2,510 sq km). Most of the 706,300 people are French Creoles. The mountains get heavy rainfall.

Fishing
Although the fishing industry is not as developed in the Indian Ocean as it is in the Atlantic and North Pacific oceans, the total annual catch is about 3,703,728 tons (3,360,000 tonnes). Most of the fish are caught by onshore fishermen. There are few areas of shallow seas where fish may breed.

Fishermen on the Maldives

FIND OUT MORE   CORAL REEFS   FARMING   FISHING INDUSTRY   ISLANDS   OCEANS AND SEAS   PORTS AND WATERWAYS   TRADE AND INDUSTRY   VOLCANOES   WINDS

INDONESIA

THE LARGEST archipelago in the world, spread over 3,000,000 sq miles (8,000,000 sq km) of ocean, Indonesia is made up of 13,670 islands. The country was a Dutch colony from the 1700s to independence in 1949. Military rule dominated for more than 30 years until public protests forced an end to the General Suharto regime in 1998, leading to democratic elections. In 1999 East Timor, a former Portuguese colony annexed by Indonesia in 1975, voted for independence. The ensuing transitional process has been very turbulent.

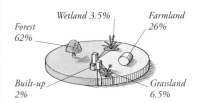

Wetland 3.5% Farmland 26%
Forest 62%
Built-up 2% Grassland 6.5%

Land use

Although much of Indonesia's land is mountainous and forested, rice is grown on terraces cut into the hillsides. Animals graze on the pastures of Irian Jaya. Forestry and logging are important businesses.

Tropical rain forest

Lush tropical rain forests cover nearly two-thirds of Indonesia's land. Elephants and tigers live in the forests of Sumatra, as well as rare animals such as the Komodo Dragon, a lizard. As many as 100 different tree species can be found in one hectare. Logging has destroyed large areas of rain forest. In 1997 smog from forest fires created a regional health hazard.

Physical features

Lying between the Pacific and Indian Oceans, the Indonesian islands are volcanic, forested, and mountainous. There are five main islands: Sumatra, Java, Kalimantan, Sulawesi, and Irian Jaya, part of New Guinea.

Islands

In addition to the five main islands there are thousands of smaller ones; about half are uninhabited. Rich in marine life, the coral reefs that surround the islands are popular with divers. Tourists are drawn to the palm-fringed beaches, rain forests, and striking volcanoes.

Krakatoa

Indonesia's position on the meeting of two of Earth's plates means it is prone to earthquakes and volcanic eruptions. Indonesia has 400 volcanoes; 100 are active. Krakatoa, a volcanic island near Java, had a major eruption in 1883, blowing the island apart.

78°F (26°C)   78°F (26°C)

70 in (1,775 mm)

Regional climate

Tropical monsoons between December and March bring humidity and heavy rains to Indonesia. Java and the Sunda Islands have a dry season between June and September. Mountains are cool.

Jakarta

The modern metropolis of Jakarta is Indonesia's capital and the largest city in Southeast Asia, with a population of 10,800,000. A trading center for 2,000 years, it was used by the Dutch as a hub for the spice trade. Colonial buildings are overshadowed by tall skyscrapers, a sign of the growing economy.

Jakarta's glittering skyscrapers tower over the residential area.

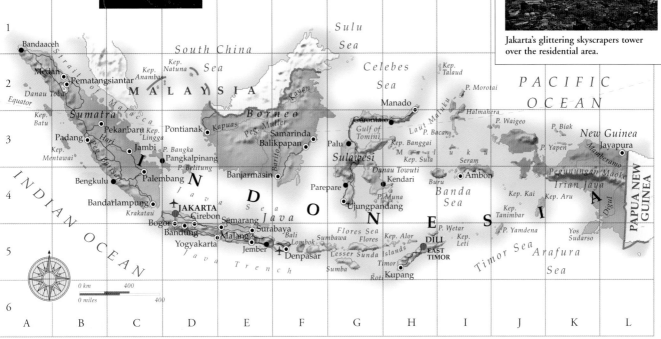

People

Indonesia has the world's fourth largest population. About 60 percent of Indonesians live on the crowded main island of Java. The majority are Muslims descended from the first Malay settlers, but society is diverse, with about 360 ethnic groups speaking more than 250 different languages.

306 per sq mile
(118 per sq km)

40%
Urban

60%
Rural

Minangkabau
The Minangkabau live in the hills of central Sumatra. They are Muslims, but, unusually, the Minangkabau are matriarchal – property and family names descend through the mother's line, and women have authority.

Leisure

The Indonesians retain many traditions of music, dance, painting, wood- and stone-carving, and textile crafts. Elaborate puppet theatres are popular in Java. Badminton is the main international sport.

Gong-chimes are struck with a padded hammer.

Dancing
Elaborate dance routines, accompanied by large *gamelans*, are a feature of life in Java and Bali, and are popular tourist attractions. Colorful dance dramas often tell stories derived from Hindu mythology. The Ramayana ballet is performed by moonlight outside the 9th-century Hindu Ramayana Temple at Yogyakarta.

Gamelan
A common form of music in Indonesia is the *gamelan*, which contains bowed and wind instruments with gongs, gong-chimes, drums, and rattles. The orchestra has up to 40 players.

Farming

About 46 percent of Indonesia's labour force works in farming, which is the main economic activity. As well as rice, farmers grow cassava, palm nuts, maize, sugar-cane, and potatoes on the fertile volcanic soils. Cash crops include coffee, rubber, and tea.

Whole dried nutmeg

Nutmeg on plant

Grated nutmeg

Spices
The islands of Maluku, formerly known as the Moluccas, are Indonesia's famed "Spice Islands". Nutmeg is the principal cash crop, and cardamom, chillies, cumin, cinnamon, coriander, star anise, and ginger are grown.

Rice
Indonesia ranks third in world rice production. The country has been self-sufficient since 1984, mainly due to an intensive rice-planting program. Farmers are encouraged to grow many varieties of high-quality rice in irrigated fields or on hillside terraces, some of which are about 2,000 years old.

Food

Rice and the many unique Indonesian spices form the basis of all meals. Fiery hot chillies, nuts, and coconut milk are used freely in cooking, and are often used to make a sauce, served with meat or fish dishes. Fried rice is a popular dish, easily adapted to contain meat, fish, or vegetables.

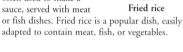

Fried rice

Communications

Spanning four time zones and separated by vast expanses of sea, the Indonesian islands need good communications. A state shipping company links the islands, several of which are also served by air.

Oil and gas
The country's economic backbone since the 1870s, oil and gas make up one-quarter of export and domestic earnings. Huge gas supplies are exported in liquid form. Oil output is declining.

Satellite telephones
Indonesia was one of the first countries in the world to install satellite communications. Because of the difficulties involved in linking so many islands with cables, a satellite telephone system was installed. This enables messages to be relayed via orbiting satellites.

Industry

Indonesia has vast mineral reserves and ranks highly in gold and tin production worldwide. Manufacturing is being encouraged to diversify the country's economy.

Batik printing block

Batik-decorated cloth

Tourism
More than five million tourists flock to Bali, Sumatra, and Java every year. The Balinese have worked hard to promote their island, and enjoy high numbers of visitors, who come for the beautiful scenery, colorful street life, and golden beaches.

Batik
First developed in Java more than 1,000 years ago, *batik* is a technique of dyeing cloth. A design is drawn on cotton and painted over with a dye-proof substance, such as hot wax or rice paste. When the cloth is dipped in dye, the waxed parts remain white. *Batik* textiles are made into scarves and wrap-around garments called *sarongs*.

Shipping
Indonesia owns more than 2,300 ships, many of which are used for transporting timber, oil, and gas. Ports are being expanded to improve trade links.

 FIND OUT MORE   ASIA, HISTORY OF   CORAL REEFS   DANCE   FARMING   ISLAM   MUSIC   OIL   SHIPS AND BOATS   TELECOMMUNICATIONS   TEXTILES AND WEAVING   VOLCANOES

INDUSTRIAL REVOLUTION

MORE THAN 200 YEARS AGO, changes took place in industry that transformed society and altered the way goods were made. The changes, which began in Britain in about 1760, are known as the Industrial Revolution. They included the use of water and steam power, the invention of new machinery, increased coal and iron production, the introduction of factories, the growth of towns, and a revolution in transportation. Industrialization also created new types of work and new social groups. By 1850, the Industrial Revolution was spreading to the rest of the world.

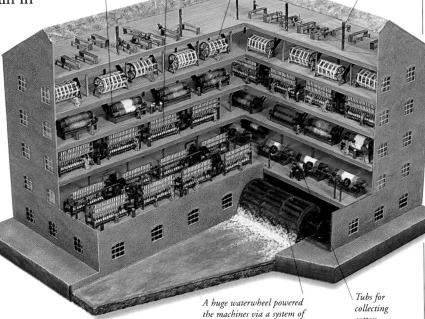

Carding machines separated cotton fibers.

Water-driven spinning frames produced cotton thread.

Reeling and winding machines wound the cotton onto bobbins.

A drive shaft took power from the waterwheel to machines in the factory.

A huge waterwheel powered the machines via a system of unguarded cogs and wheels.

Tubs for collecting cotton

An early 19th-century cotton mill

New technology

The textile industry was the first to be mechanized. In the 1700s, new water- or steam-driven machines replaced the old spinning wheels. This change meant that cloth, particularly cotton, could be produced faster than ever before.

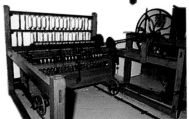

The spinning jenny
James Hargreaves, an English weaver, invented the spinning jenny in 1764–67. Worked by one person, it consisted of a frame and a number of spindles that spun several threads at once.

The water frame
As the name suggests, the water frame was a spinning frame powered by water. It replaced the spinning jenny and was used in the first factories.

Factories

People used to make goods in their homes, but the invention of new machinery took manufacturing into factories. The first factories were cotton mills, and the factory owners employed huge numbers of people to operate the machines. Most employees worked 16 hours a day, six days a week, and were subjected to harsh discipline. The work was hard and sometimes dangerous, but for the first time, workers received regular wages.

Child labor
Factory owners employed children in mills and mines because they could enter cramped spaces and their small hands could operate delicate machinery. Dangerous conditions meant that many children died.

New industrial towns

As industrialism increased, new towns sprang up around coal mines and factories. Many people arrived from the countryside in search of work. Living conditions in the new towns were dreadful, with poverty, overcrowding, poor sanitation, and illness. After the 1850s, urban conditions began to improve.

Transportation

A revolution in transportation was stimulated by the need to move raw materials and finished goods cheaply and quickly. A network of canals was built beginning in 1760 to carry coal, iron, and steel to and from the new industrial centers. However, by the 1840s, one of the greatest achievements of the industrial age had appeared – the railroads.

"Puffing Billy"

Iron bridge
In 1779, the world's first iron bridge was built across the Severn River, England.

Severn Gorge, between Wales and England

Railroads
After the ironmaster Abraham Derby discovered how to smelt iron cheaply, using coke rather than charcoal, the way was clear for the mass production of iron. The world's first public railroad opened in 1825, linking the coal mines of Darlington with the port of Stockton, England. By the 1870s, there were 15,500 miles (25,000 km) of railroad track in Britain alone.

Social change

The Industrial Revolution transformed society. It created a new social group, the industrial waged, working class. A new army of industrial workers sprang up including railroad workers, dockers, textile workers, engineers, and factory girls. Industrialization also produced a new, wealthier, middle class. The separation of work from home had profound effects. For the first time, and for the middle classes only, the home became a place of peace and leisure.

New products

As mass production increased in factories, new goods became available. Cheap cotton clothing was the first product to be made completely by machinery. Soaps, dyes, and iron goods became widespread. However, many of the industrial processes were harmful to the workers' health.

Iron goods
Developments in the iron industry meant that cast iron could be molded into any shape, from pots and pans to iron bed frames and machine parts.

Soap
The growing textile industry stimulated a demand for soap and bleach. When a process was invented that turned table salt into baking soda, soap could be mass produced.

Matches
The first friction matches were produced in the 1830s. To make the matches, women dipped splinters of wood into white phosphorus, a flammable chemical. As the phosphorus ate away the skin of their faces, many suffered "phossy jaw."

Gas lighting
Coal provided steam for new machinery, and heated coal produced a combustible (burnable) gas. By 1850, gas lamps were common in the streets of most towns and cities, and in the wealthier homes.

Middle classes
The middle classes included merchants and industrialists. Middle-class men worked as managers and owners in industry, middle-class women remained at home, living lives of enforced idleness. Some of these women began to work with the poor and needy, or fight for women's rights.

Satin- and lace-trimmed hat

Mother-of-pearl buttons

Silk bow and a lace collar

Silk parasol

A middle-class girl's dress was usually made of delicate material, such as silk, or had a lot of handiwork on it, such as a lace collar.

Kid leather high-heeled boots

Working classes
Most working people lived lives of relentless drudgery in the early years of the Industrial Revolution. Men worked long hours in the new industries, and women had a double burden of work both inside the home, and outside in the mills and factories.

Cotton mob-cap

Two wool shawls for warmth

Thick wool shirt

Thick calico skirt

A factory girl's clothing had to be warm and long-lasting. It was often made of cheap material, such as wool or cotton.

Hobnailed leather boots

Popular protest

The early years of the Industrial Revolution were hard for the workers. Social unrest increased as different groups fought for improvements in working conditions. Some, such as the Luddites, attacked the new machines that were taking away their jobs and skills. Labor unions, which emerged after 1824, sought better working conditions and workers' rights.

Cooperative movement
The followers of this early political and social movement challenged the competitiveness of the new industrial society. They argued instead for cooperation and a form of socialism, or common ownership. In 1844, the movement established Britain's first cooperative shop, in Lancashire, England.

Timeline

1709 Abraham Darby uses coal to smelt iron ore.

1733 John Kay develops flying shuttle, which speeds up weaving.

1764–67 Spinning jenny is invented.

Spinning, c.1900

1761 Bridgewater canal links coal mines to Manchester.

1768 Richard Arkwright develops a water-driven spinning frame.

1769 James Watt improves the steam engine.

1789 Steam-powered loom introduced.

1830s Industrial Revolution underway in Belgium and the US.

1833 Factory Act prohibits children under nine from working in cotton mills to allow time for schooling.

1842 Coal Mines Act bans women and children from mines in England.

Robert Owen
Born in Wales, Owen (1771–1858) was an early socialist. His book *A New View of Society* (1813) argued for cooperation instead of competition in society. His ideas led to the the first Cooperative Shop, in Rochdale, England, which sold fresh food on a non-profit basis. He also set up one of the first trade unions, and created model working communities in Lanark, Scotland, and New Harmony, USA.

FIND OUT MORE   CITIES   EUROPE, HISTORY OF   TRANSPORT, HISTORY OF   UNITED KINGDOM, HISTORY OF

INDUS VALLEY CIVILIZATION

ON THE BANKS of the Indus River in modern-day Pakistan, one of the world's earliest civilizations grew and flourished between c.2700 and 1750 BC. The civilization was centered at the cities of Mohenjo-daro and Harappa, each of which contained about 40,000 people. Large public buildings, built of mud bricks, show that the civilization was prosperous. We know little about the day-to-day life of Indus Valley inhabitants, except that they traded with Sumeria and may have practiced an early form of Hinduism. The mysterious collapse of their civilization after 1750 BC may have been caused by invasions or a natural disaster.

Mohenjo-daro

Indus Valley cities were planned and built on a grid pattern. They had broad main roads and narrow lanes. Drains carried away the household waste. All the houses were built around central courtyards. During the day, people lived and worked in these courtyards.

The great granary
Some scholars think that the Indus Valley people used the granary as a bank – it was a secure store of wealth for the merchants and rulers of the city.

The granary had wooden 150-ft (46-m) walls and roofs running the length of the building.

The bathhouse was one of Mohenjo-daro's biggest and most important buildings.

Small baths are in buildings near the bathhouse.

The central bath may have been used for religious purposes, such as the ritual cleansing before ceremonies.

The citadel is the raised area that contains the important public buildings, such as the bathhouse and the great granary. The higher ground makes the area easier to defend.

The citadel, Mohenjo-daro

A stupa, or Buddhist shrine, was built much more recently than the ancient city of Mohenjo-daro. The original main temple of the Indus Valley people may be hidden beneath the stupa's mound.

Weights and measures
Like most ancient civilizations, the Indus Valley people developed a system of weights and measures. As a result, trade became easier and goods could be valued for tax purposes.

Ancient script

Archaeologists have found stone seals in a script unlike any other ancient form of writing. When long texts are found, scholars can often decipher them – but the Indus Valley inscriptions are very short, so their meaning remains a mystery.

Unicorn

Indus script

Seals
The Indus people used seals to show ownership. Each seal is carved with the image of an animal, such as a unicorn, and an inscription.

Religion

Little is known about the Indus religion. The importance of water, shown by the existence of the bathhouse, has led some scholars to link it with later Hinduism. Various statues have been found that may represent gods and goddesses.

Head-dress

Goddess figures
Most of the statuettes found in the Indus cities have headdresses and jewelry, indicating they were probably goddess figures.

Priests
This steatite (soapstone) statue is the most well-known object found at Mohenjo-daro. It has a serene expression that suggests it might be a statue of a priest or one of the Indus Valley gods.

Crafts

Indus people were skilled potters and metalworkers. They made fine painted vessels, terra-cotta statues, and beautiful gold jewelry. They also learned how to blend copper and tin to produce bronze.

Terra-cotta animals, Mohenjo-daro

Bull

Pig

Gold jewelry, Harappa

FIND OUT MORE   ASIA, HISTORY OF   BRONZE AGE   CITIES   GUPTA EMPIRE   HINDUISM   MAURYAN EMPIRE

INFORMATION TECHNOLOGY

THANKS TO information technology, you can enjoy the fantasy world of a virtual reality game, and make friends with people on the other side of the world via the Internet. Information technology (IT) is the use of computers to handle, store, process, and transmit information. The key to information technology is software: sets of instructions called programs that tell computers what to do. Software can be used to design magazines and forecast the weather, and may even one day enable computers to think like humans.

Programs enable processing of information.

Programs

Computers cannot work without programs. A program is a sequence of simple instructions that tells a computer how to perform a specific task, such as adding up a list of numbers or printing a document. The programs that make a computer work are called software.

Computer languages

A computer can process information only when it is in the form of binary numbers, which are made up of the digits 0 and 1. It is difficult to write a computer program in this form, so programmers write their instructions in special codes called computer languages. The computer then translates the instructions into binary numbers, which it can understand.

Alan Turing

British mathematician Alan Turing (1912–54) made important advances in the theory of computers. He was the first to propose that computers might one day be able to "think" – that is, perform a task in an identical way to a human.

Software applications

The software that controls a computer's essential functions is called its operating system. All other software programs are called applications. They include word processing, which helps you write letters and documents, and multimedia, which combines text, pictures, video, music and animation into one.

A spreadsheet shows a grid of columns and rows on the screen.

Illustrator can change the colors in the photograph.

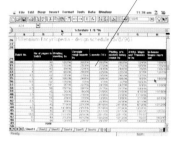

Spreadsheet

A spreadsheet is a software application that performs calculations on a table of numbers, such as sums of money or dates. Businesses use spreadsheets to display financial accounts, forecast sales figures, and plan work schedules.

Computer graphics

Illustrators can use software to produce computerized images called graphics. Graphics software enables an illustrator to create entirely new images on-screen, or to alter images fed into the computer with a scanner.

Desktop publishing (DTP)

Designers of books, newspapers, and magazines arrange the pictures and text on each page, using desktop-publishing software. DTP also allows editors to correct the text on-screen.

Computer simulation

Given the correct information and programs, powerful modern computers can simulate real-life situations, such as flying an airplane, maneuvring the space shuttle, or exploring the ocean depths. Computer simulation is used for research, education, training, and entertainment.

Handheld control unit

Virtual reality

One form of computer simulation is called virtual reality . A computer creates 3-D images and sounds that seem almost real. Using a headset and a handheld unit, the user can move around in and interact with this "virtual" world, created by the computer.

Virtual reality game

Headset makes player feel part of computer-generated scene.

Virtual reality kit

Trackball mouse

Speaker

Headset

Keyboard

Handheld control unit

Computer modeling

Meteorologists use simulations called computer models to forecast changes in the weather. Using information gathered by weather stations, a computer creates a realistic model of a complex weather pattern, such as a hurricane, and then predicts how it will develop. Many scientists use computer modeling to test their theories.

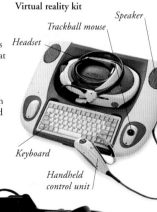

Tracking sensor detects horizontal and vertical movement and sends this data to the controlling computer.

Earphones supply stereo sound.

Small screen in front of each eye gives a sense of depth and realism.

Virtual reality headset

Information superhighway

The information superhighway is a planned communications network that will use the optical fibers of the telephone line to bring a huge choice of services to people's homes. Using the latest multimedia software, a special terminal – like a combined television and computer – will allow users to access the Internet, watch interactive television and movies, play games, listen to music, and even do their shopping from their own homes.

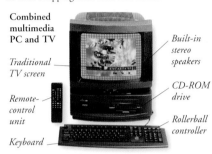

Combined multimedia PC and TV

Traditional TV screen

Remote-control unit

Keyboard

Built-in stereo speakers

CD-ROM drive

Rollerball controller

Artificial intelligence

The ability of a computer to think for itself is called Artificial Intelligence (AI). Some computers can already assess their own performance and work out ways to improve it. However, many people believe that computers can never be truly intelligent, because they can only follow instructions. AI research has so far produced neural networks and speech synthesizers.

Braille keyboard and special software for visually-impaired user

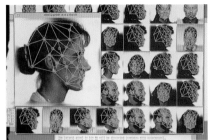

Face-recognition program

Neural networks

One area of research into artificial intelligence uses circuits that work in a similar way to the nerves (neurons) in the brain. These circuits, called neural networks, can learn to do simple tasks, such as recognizing human faces.

AI for disability

Some people with disabilities use computers to help them communicate. Computers called speech synthesizers can recognize spoken words or produce speech from text typed in. Braille keyboards, voice recognition, and special software are all used by visually-impaired people.

Internet

The Internet is a global network of computers linked together by the telephone system. Once your computer is connected to the Internet, you can send and receive electronic mail (e-mail), exchange views in newsgroups (groups of Internet users with shared interests), and browse information on the World Wide Web – a collection of information "pages" held by museums, governments, businesses, colleges, universities, and individuals.

Internet communication

Text, pictures, sound, and other information is sent across the Internet from computer to computer in the form of binary digits, or bits. The bits are coded in a type of computer language called a protocol, and sent as tiny "packets" of data.

Packets are addressed and sent to the correct destination via the Internet.

Binary digits

Receiving computer reassembles the packets.

If the route is busy, the packets find another way to reach their address.

World Wide Web

Information is stored on the Internet at linked sites called pages. The pages can be thought of as a web of information that spans the globe. Web pages are viewed with software called a browser. By clicking on a certain part of a page with a mouse, the user can visit other pages holding related information.

E-mail

Letters typed on a computer can be sent quickly, easily, and cheaply across the Internet using e-mail. Each Internet user has a unique e-mail "address," so that they can receive mail from other users. Mail is sent and received through a large computer called a server.

Personal computer (PC)

Computer splits picture into packets of data.

Server

Receiving

PC modem

Server modem

Receiving

Sending

Sending

Telephone line carries modem signal.

E-mail message typed into PC is sent as binary data to the modem.

Modem

A modem is a device that converts binary computer data into a varying electrical signal and sends it along the telephone line.

Server's modem converts signal back into binary data.

Server

A server is a powerful computer that routes out-going e-mail to the correct Internet address, and holds incoming messages in a "mail box" until the user wishes to open it.

John Von Neumann

The Hungarian-born mathematician John Von Neumann (1903–57) was the first to suggest that the program needed to operate a computer should be stored in its memory. He also devised a way of making a computer create random numbers – a vital function in many modern software applications.

Timeline

1960s The US military links up all its large computers, forming a network known as ARPANET.

Late 1970s Users can now interact with computer data by clicking on icons and windows on the screen with a mouse.

1981 The first IBM personal computers using MS-DOS become available.

Microsoft's Bill Gates

1980s ARPANET becomes the Internet, as the US military withdraws from the network, and it is used increasingly by universities and colleges.

1984 Apple Macintosh computers, using software produced by American Bill Gates's Microsoft company, become increasingly popular.

1985 First CD-ROMs appear.

1990s Dramatic increase in people using the Internet.

1994 RISC (reduced instruction set computing) allows for faster microchips.

2001 A web server the size of a match-head is produced.

FIND OUT **MORE** | **BRAIN AND NERVOUS SYSTEM** | **COMPUTERS** | **ELECTRONICS** | **NUMBERS** | **TECHNOLOGY** | **TELECOMMUNICATIONS** | **TELEPHONES**

INSECTS

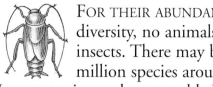

FOR THEIR ABUNDANCE and diversity, no animals can match the insects. There may be as many as a million species around the world. Insects are invertebrates and belong to the group called arthropods, the only arthropods that can fly. Many have a complex life cycle. Wherever they exist, they have a huge ecological impact as herbivores, hunters, decomposers, plant pollinators, and disease carriers. They are in turn food for predators, against which they have evolved some remarkable defenses.

Field digger wasp
This parasitic wasp paralyzes its prey, such as a fly, and takes it back to its nest for its grubs to eat. Its paralyzing sting is located on the tip of its long abdomen.

The thorax is in three segments and bears the legs and wings.

The head carries feeding apparatus and sense organs.

Fly
The exoskeleton, or cuticle, of flies, like that of all insects, is fragile and lightweight, giving the flies flexibility, but also making it easier for predators to pierce them with a bite or sting.

Breeding

Insects normally reproduce by mating, attracting one another first with scents, displays, vibrations, or other signals. The male's sperm is transferred into reproductive organs containing eggs in the female's abdomen. The female lays the fertilized eggs, often burying them in soil, or attaching them to a surface such as a leaf.

Adult mayfly

Mayflies
Breeding is all a mayfly does during the last stage of its life. As soon as it turns into an adult, it has just a few hours to find a mate and reproduce before it dies.

Parent bugs
Most adult insects leave their young to fend for themselves. Some bugs and earwigs look after their young offspring and try to protect them.

Parent bug with young

Insect features

Adult insects have a head, a thorax, and an abdomen, each composed of segments. They also have six jointed legs modified for walking, jumping, digging, or swimming. All parts are enclosed in an exoskeleton.

The abdomen contains most of the internal organs.

Hard wings form a protective case for the other pair.

Cardinal beetle

Eyes
The huge eyes of this dragonfly, like those of most insects, contain hundreds of units, each with its own lens. Together, the units make up a composite image.

Antennae
Reaching their maximum length in longhorn beetles, the antennae of insects are used to sense the shape and texture of objects and to detect scents and tastes.

Mouthparts
An insect's mouthparts include mandibles (hard jaws), maxillae (secondary jaws), and a labium (lower lip) for sucking fluids. This lacewing has large mandibles for biting.

Wings
The wings of flying insects are delicate membranes supported by veins. Most insects have two pairs of wings, and in beetles one pair is hard.

Life cycles

Different stages exist in the life of an insect between hatching and adulthood. Some insects undergo a dramatic change called complete metamorphosis. Other insects start out as wingless nymphs, then grow in steps, molting their old cuticles before becoming mature adults.

Incomplete metamorphosis
Though it lives underwater after hatching, a young damselfly, or nymph, resembles the adult that flies. After several "steps," the final nymph surfaces, breaks out of its cuticle, and unfurls its new wings.

Complete metamorphosis
Young butterflies, bees, flies, and beetles are totally different from their parents. Eggs hatch into larvae. Later, the larvae pupate, when their tissues reform into the shape of an adult.

1 A female butterfly, in this case a swallowtail butterfly, lays an egg on the leaf of a suitable food plant.

2 A larva, called a caterpillar, hatches out of the egg and starts to feed on the plant immediately.

3 The caterpillar grows and develops, molting its skin several times as it does so.

4 At last it stops eating and turns into a chrysalis, or pupa. It may secure itself to a plant.

5 Inside the pupal cuticle, the insect transforms into an adult butterfly and then emerges.

A nymph crawls up a stem out of the water.

The cuticle splits along the back.

The adult damselfly gradually breaks free.

Blood is pumped into the wings.

The adult reaches its full size.

This adult damselfly is about 1.75 in (4.5 cm) long.

I

Habitats

Insects abound in most of the world's habitats, even the seemingly inhospitable. Though they reach their greatest diversity in the humid tropics, teeming numbers of them also exist in grassland and woodland, both among the vegetation and hidden away under the soil. Land and air are their true domains, but some species live in water for all or part of their life.

Tropical caves
Among the extreme environments occupied by insects are deep tropical caves. In the darkness, hordes of specialized scavengers, among them beetles and cockroaches, sift through bat droppings on the cave floor.

Scarab beetle

Deserts
Securing food and water in deserts and other dry places requires special effort. Scarab beetles dig underground shelters for their larvae, which they supply with ample food – balls of dung rolled from camel or buffalo droppings.

Nests
Many insects make homes from objects in their environment. The most accomplished builders are social insects such as wasps, bees, ants, and termites, which build communal nests. Wasp colonies create beautiful "paper" nests of chewed wood pulp.

The queen wasp lays one egg at the bottom of each cell.

The small entrance controls the temperature and humidity.

Water
A few insects, such as diving beetles and water boatmen, spend all their life in freshwater. Many more live there as nymphs or larvae, crawling along the bottom or in plants. Caddis fly larvae carry their own covering of debris for protection against enemies.

This covering is made of leaves stuck together with silk.

Caddis fly larva

As the larva grows, it makes its case longer.

Paper wasp's nest

Cross-section of a paper wasp's nest

A species of gryloblattid

Snowfields
Tiny wingless insects live in the intense cold and harsh winds of mountain peaks. Gryloblattids live on minute fragments of food blown up on the ice from lower altitudes. Antifreezing substances in their body fluids stop them from seizing up in the freezing conditions.

Feeding

Insects eat virtually all types of organic matter. Few plants are safe from attack by larvae or adults, and insects play a major ecological role in breaking down plant and animal remains. Some insects are specialized feeders, such as many weevils, which attack human foodstuffs; others, such as cockroaches and bush crickets, eat anything.

Nectar feeders
The energy-rich nectar of flowers lures pollinating insects such as butterflies, bees, flies, and beetles. As they feed, the insects get dusted with pollen, which they transfer from flower to flower.

Hunters
Some insects are fierce hunters. They have strong jaws for biting or piercing their prey with poison-filled probes. Some, such as mantids, use stealth to snatch passing prey; others actively seek out and chase their victims.

Mantid grasps a fly with its front legs.

Wood borers
The larvae of insects such as the furniture beetle gnaw tunnels through timber. They need to eat a large amount to get enough nourishment, because wood is very indigestible.

Furniture beetle

Parasites
Parasitic insects eat the living tissue and body fluids of larger animals. They live either on or in their host or, as in this bloodsucking fly, land on the skin to feed. In addition to damaging their host directly, they also pass on diseases such as malaria and sleeping sickness.

Piercing, sucking mouthparts

Weta raises its spiny legs.

Defense

Both adult insects and their young are food for a host of predators, including other insects, spiders, lizards, birds, and mammals. They are not without their own means of defense and escape. Some actively threaten or counterattack the enemy; others are designed to avoid being detected in the first place.

Attack
Some insects drive off enemies with squirts of poison, blows, bites, or stings. Among the most formidable weapons are the jaws of soldier ants, like this one from Venezuela. Squadrons of ants attack intruders and often fatally injure them.

Stripes like those of a wasp

Mimicry
The hoverfly is one of a number of insects that avoid attack because they look like more aggressive species. Because of its similarity to a wasp, the hoverfly fools many predators into leaving it alone.

Leaf insect

Camouflage
A blend of shape and color can make an insect extremely difficult to spot in its natural habitat. Amid dense foliage, the leaf insects of tropical forests have almost perfect camouflage.

Threat
Aggressive postures and alarming noises can be enough to ward off enemies. The wetas – large cricketlike insects of New Zealand – raise their spiny hind legs and drop them with a crackling sound.

FIND OUT MORE   ANIMALS   CAMOUFLAGE   ECOLOGY   EVOLUTION   FLIGHT, ANIMAL   FLOWERS   NESTS

Insects

Beetles, wasps, ants, and bees

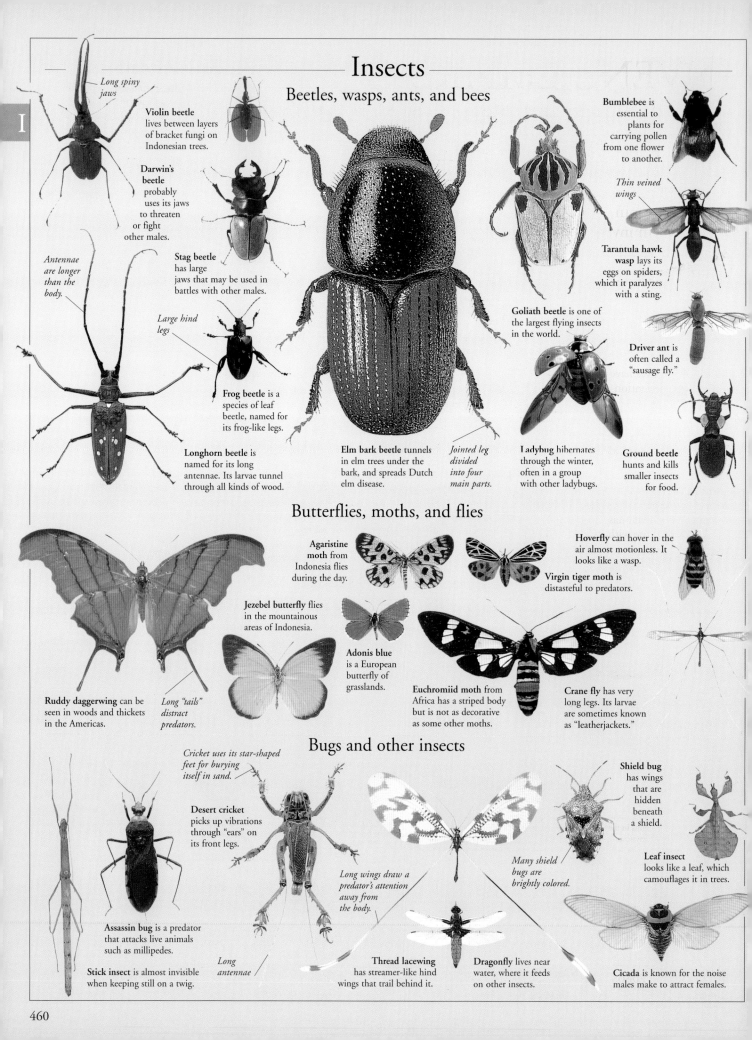

Long spiny jaws

Violin beetle lives between layers of bracket fungi on Indonesian trees.

Darwin's beetle probably uses its jaws to threaten or fight other males.

Stag beetle has large jaws that may be used in battles with other males.

Antennae are longer than the body.

Large hind legs

Frog beetle is a species of leaf beetle, named for its frog-like legs.

Longhorn beetle is named for its long antennae. Its larvae tunnel through all kinds of wood.

Elm bark beetle tunnels in elm trees under the bark, and spreads Dutch elm disease.

Jointed leg divided into four main parts.

Bumblebee is essential to plants for carrying pollen from one flower to another.

Thin veined wings

Tarantula hawk wasp lays its eggs on spiders, which it paralyzes with a sting.

Goliath beetle is one of the largest flying insects in the world.

Driver ant is often called a "sausage fly."

Ladybug hibernates through the winter, often in a group with other ladybugs.

Ground beetle hunts and kills smaller insects for food.

Butterflies, moths, and flies

Agaristine moth from Indonesia flies during the day.

Jezebel butterfly flies in the mountainous areas of Indonesia.

Adonis blue is a European butterfly of grasslands.

Hoverfly can hover in the air almost motionless. It looks like a wasp.

Virgin tiger moth is distasteful to predators.

Euchromiid moth from Africa has a striped body but is not as decorative as some other moths.

Crane fly has very long legs. Its larvae are sometimes known as "leatherjackets."

Ruddy daggerwing can be seen in woods and thickets in the Americas.

Long "tails" distract predators.

Bugs and other insects

Cricket uses its star-shaped feet for burying itself in sand.

Desert cricket picks up vibrations through "ears" on its front legs.

Shield bug has wings that are hidden beneath a shield.

Many shield bugs are brightly colored.

Leaf insect looks like a leaf, which camouflages it in trees.

Long wings draw a predator's attention away from the body.

Assassin bug is a predator that attacks live animals such as millipedes.

Stick insect is almost invisible when keeping still on a twig.

Long antennae

Thread lacewing has streamer-like hind wings that trail behind it.

Dragonfly lives near water, where it feeds on other insects.

Cicada is known for the noise males make to attract females.

INVENTIONS

AN INVENTION is something created by human effort that did not exist before. Most are useful to society or industry, and simplify the way things are done. Inventions range from the simple, such as the safety pin, to the complex, such as the television. An invention can come from the work of an individual or the work of a team. Human civilization is founded on a host of inventions, from the stone tools of prehistoric people to the robots of today.

Making life easier

Most people's lives have been improved by inventions, particularly during the 20th century. For example, the development of computers has led to global communications via the Internet, jet engines have provided a faster means of transport across the world, and the tractor has transformed agriculture. In the home, inventions such as the refrigerator have made preserving food easier, while the microwave oven has proved invaluable to those with busy lifestyles.

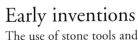

The wheel
The wheel is probably the most important invention of all time. Today wheels are found in almost all machines. The first wheel was used by potters to help shape clay in Mesopotamia, more than 5,000 years ago. Wheels were then fitted to carts, revolutionizing transport.

Archimedes' screw
In about 200 BC, Greek scientist and mathematician, Archimedes (c.287–212 BC) invented a water-lifting machine incorporating a screw-like mechanism. This device is still used in irrigation schemes in some countries, and is the basis of drill bits and kitchen mixers.

Early inventions

The use of stone tools and weapons, such as bows and arrows, in prehistoric times gave people greater mastery over their environment. When they settled as farmers, the plough (c.3000 BC) greatly improved crop production. Around the same time, the wheel revolutionized transport. The alphabet (c.1500 BC) was also a milestone in civilization, becoming the basis of the written language.

Handle is turned to lift water.
Model of Archimedes' screw
Water moves up the tube.

Home
Many inventions have improved life in the home. For example, the invention of electrical appliances provided cheap, clean lighting and the power to run devices which make cleaning, cooking, and washing easier. Less housework meant women could work outside the home for the first time.

Scanning coil sweeps electron beams across screen.

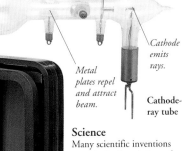

The cathode screen is coated with powder that glows when struck by cathode rays.

Anode hole creates beam of electrons.

Metal plates repel and attract beam.

Cathode emits rays.

Cathode-ray tube

Science
Many scientific inventions provide the foundations of the technologically based society we live in today. For example, electronics took off after the forerunner of the modern TV receiver tube, the cathode-ray tube, was invented in 1892. Also, medical inventions have helped to improve diagnosis and treatment.

Industry
The steam engine and spinning jenny were two key inventions that set in motion the Industrial Revolution in the 18th century. Factories improved their productivity following Henry Ford's introduction in 1913 of the moving assembly line. By the late 1960s, the development of the microprocessor ushered in the modern electronics industry.

Electron guns emit beams that strike red, green, and blue phosphorous on to screen to give colour picture.

Colour television tube

Kellogg brothers

Today's flourishing cereal industry has its origins in the inventive mind of US physician John Harvey Kellogg (1852–1943), and the business skills of his brother William Keith (1860–1951). John Harvey developed cereals such as cornflakes as part of a vegetarian diet for his patients. His brother founded the Kellogg company in 1906 to sell John's inventions.

W. K. Kellogg

J. H. Kellogg

Inventors

Some people invent when there is a need for something, prompting the saying "necessity is the mother of invention". Others invent when they have a sudden flash of inspiration, and to make money. Today, more inventions are the result of organized research by a team, rather than by one person.

Patents

To prevent other people copying and profiting by their inventions, inventors must register a patent. This gives the inventor the sole right to make and sell the invention. The patent also details why the invention is new and original. Inventors have to register patents in as many countries as they can afford.

Patent for zip fastener

FIND OUT MORE

EDISON, THOMAS • ELECTRONICS • FOOD • INDUSTRIAL REVOLUTION • INFORMATION TECHNOLOGY • MEDICINE, HISTORY OF • TECHNOLOGY • TRANSPORT, HISTORY OF

Inventions
Home and leisure

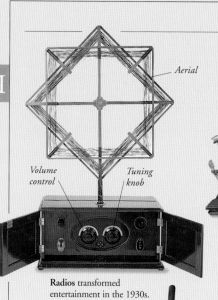

Aerial

Volume control   *Tuning knob*

Radios transformed entertainment in the 1930s.

The tea maker, invented in 1904, was one of many gadgets that helped save time around the house.

Tape recorders developed after the invention of magnetic tapes in the 1930s.

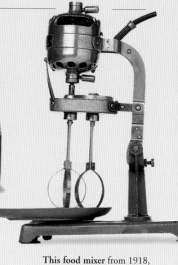

This food mixer from 1918, was driven by an electric motor.

Pop-up toasters were first introduced in 1926. Ready-sliced bread appeared in 1930.

Ice box

Compartments to keep foods separate.

Electric refrigerators began to appear in 1913.

Key pad

Electronic calculators became popular across the world by the early 1970s.

The television was invented by John Logie Baird in 1926. This one is from the 1950s.

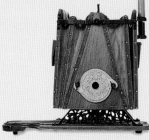

This vacuum cleaner dates from the early 20th century.

Ballpoint pen, invented in 1938.

Personal stereos first went on sale in 1979.

Compact disks were first launched in 1982.

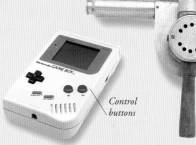

Control buttons

Computer games were played throughout the 1980s.

Hair dryers were first sold for personal use in 1920.

Science and industry

Supporting frame   *Spring*

Probe

Transistors, invented in 1947, are still used in electronic devices.

Pacemakers, invented in the 1960s, control heartbeats.

Filament

Audion tubes, invented in 1906, amplified radio signals.

Ruby crystal

Lasers were developed in the 1960s for a variety of electronic uses.

Printed circuit boards were patented in 1943.

Parking meters were first introduced in 1935.

IRAN AND IRAQ

A REGION OF inhospitable, rugged mountains and barren, rocky desert, Iran and Iraq both lie within the area known as the Middle East in southwestern Asia. Border disputes and rivalries between these strongly Muslim countries resulted in a damaging war between 1980 and 1988. As with many other Middle Eastern countries, oil has brought great wealth to Iran and Iraq, enabling them to provide higher living standards for their people. However, Iraq has suffered economic hardships as a result of the Gulf War (1990–91).

Physical features

Mountains dominate the north, west, and south of Iran and the east of Iraq. Much of the rest of the region is vast, uninhabited desert. Iran's Caspian Sea coast is green and fertile, and southern Iraq has marshland.

90°F (32°C)   -43°F (6°C)

8 in (193 mm)

Regional climate

Iran and Iraq have very hot, dry summers, but winters are much colder and harsher in Iran than in Iraq. The region's annual rainfall is low, and fresh water is scarce.

Elburz Mountains

In northern Iran, the Elburz Mountains rise from the Caspian Sea. Winds blowing south from the Russian Federation bring rain to the northern slopes, which are covered in forest and farmland. Sheltered from the rain-bearing winds, the southern side of the mountains is arid and infertile. The highest point is Mount Damávand at 18,605 ft (5,671 m). Snow is common, and there are ski resorts east of Tehran.

Iranian plateau

Closed in by the Zagros and Elburz Mountains to the west and north, Iran's vast central plateau consists of two great deserts, the Dasht-e Kavir and the Dasht-e Lut. Lying at about 2,950 ft (900 m) above sea level, these barren, rocky deserts are uninhabited because of the almost total lack of water.

Kurds

There are about 25 million Kurdish people. They live in Kurdistan, a mountainous region that straddles the borders of Turkey, Syria, Iraq, and Iran. Their fight for self-government has been put down repeatedly with much bloodshed. Forced to leave Iraq after the Gulf War, many Kurds became refugees.

Iranian Kurds cooking food

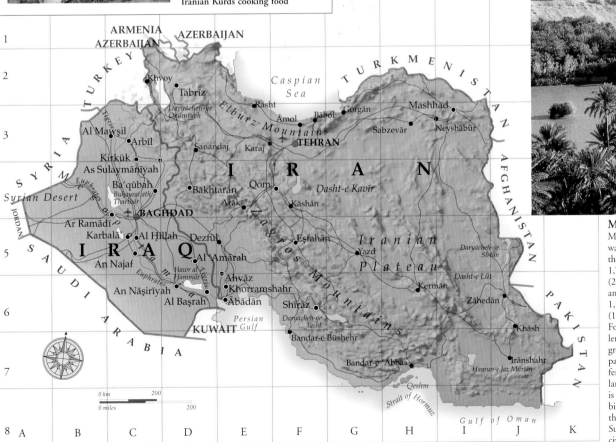

Mesopotamia

Most of Iraq's water comes from the Euphrates, 1,700 miles (2,753 km) long and the Tigris, 1,150 miles (1,850 km) long. For much of their length, these two great rivers run parallel. The fertile strip of land between them is Mesopotamia, birthplace of the ancient Sumerian civilization.

Iran

Bordered by Afghanistan to the east, Iraq to the west, and former Soviet republics to the north, Iran was called Persia until 1935. For years the country was ruled by shahs, or kings, but, in 1979, when Ayatollah Khomeini (1900–89) deposed the last shah, the country became an Islamic republic. The modern Iranian government rules according to strict Islamic laws.

Tehran

Iran's capital lies in the foothills of the Elburz Mountains. Tehran contains parks, art galleries, and museums, as well as one of the world's largest bazaars. The city was modernized by the last shah and the Shahyad Monument commemorates 2,500 years of shah rule.

Shahyad Monument, built in 1971

Mosques

All mosques (Muslim places of worship) have at least one tower, (minaret), from which the faithful are called to prayer five times a day. Mosques are also often ornately decorated with abstract designs and inscriptions from the Koran, the holy book of Islam.

14th-century Friday mosque, Kerman

Carpet woven from Iranian wool

Persian carpets

Iran has been famous for its handwoven rugs and carpets since the 13th century. With rich, dark colors and traditional patterns, they are the country's second largest export.

Tehran carpet traders

Farming

Although farming employs about 33 percent of the Iranian workforce, the lack of water means that only 11 percent of the land can be cultivated. Underground irrigation channels called *qanats* are used to transport water to farming areas. Wheat, barley, and rice are the main crops. Sheep are raised for wool and meat.

Wind separates the wheat grain from the chaff.

IRAN FACTS

CAPITAL CITY	Tehran
AREA	636,293 sq miles (1,648,000 sq km)
POPULATION	67,700,000
MAIN LANGUAGE	Farsi
MAJOR RELIGION	Muslim
CURRENCY	Rial
LIFE EXPECTANCY	69 years
PEOPLE PER DOCTOR	1,250
GOVERNMENT	Islamic republic
ADULT LITERACY	77%

Iraq

Iraq is one of the strongest military powers in the Middle East. Under Saddam Hussein (b.1937), who became president in 1979 with dictatorial powers, it began to dominate its neighbors, but a stalemate in the war with Iran, and the foiled annexation of Kuwait (1990–91), reduced its strength. It is now attempting to rebuild its shattered economy. Iraq is a strongly Islamic country.

Food

People in Iraq eat lamb, chicken, or fish with vegetables and chick peas, served with rice and *khubz* (pita bread). Popular dishes are stuffed vine leaves called *dolma* and *quozi,* grilled lamb stuffed with rice and spices.

Oil

Iraq has huge reserves of oil and gas. Before the Gulf War, oil accounted for more than 95 percent of the country's export earnings. However, following the United Nations' ban on the sale of Iraqi oil to member states, Iraq now has a poor economic situation and is faced with the task of rebuilding its oil industry destroyed in the war.

Baghdad street trader selling bread

IRAQ FACTS

CAPITAL CITY	Baghdad
AREA	169,235 sq miles (438,320 sq km)
POPULATION	23,100,000
MAIN LANGUAGE	Arabic
MAJOR RELIGION	Muslim
CURRENCY	Dinar
LIFE EXPECTANCY	59 years
PEOPLE PER DOCTOR	1,667
GOVERNMENT	One-party dictatorship
ADULT LITERACY	56%

Farming and industry

Agriculture employs about 12 percent of the workforce, but does not produce enough crops to supply the country's needs. Trade bans imposed after the Gulf War limited imports, leading to food shortages. Only about eight percent of Iraq's workers are engaged in manufacturing, mainly in food processing.

View of mosque with a decorative minaret

Baghdad

Iraq's capital on the banks of the Tigris River has been an important Arab city since AD 752. An industrial and cultural center its old, narrow streets with bustling markets contrast sharply with its modern buildings. There are many mosques, and monuments to President Hussein.

Marsh Arabs

The Tigris and Euphrates join to form the Shatt-al-Arab, which is surrounded by marshland. This area is home to the Marsh Arabs, who live in reed houses built on artificial islands made of reeds and mud. They are threatened by plans to drain the marshes.

FIND OUT MORE

ASIA, HISTORY OF   DESERTS   FARMING   ISLAM   ISLAMIC EMPIRE   LAW   MOSQUES   OIL   PERSIAN EMPIRES   SUMERIANS   TEXTILES AND WEAVING

IRELAND

THE REPUBLIC OF IRELAND occupies two-thirds of the island of Ireland in the Atlantic Ocean off the west coast of the United Kingdom. The rest of the island, the six counties of Northern Ireland, chose to remain part of the United Kingdom when, in 1922, the Republic voted for independence. The Republic is a member of the European Union and has efficient farming and food-processing industries. Electronic goods account for 25 percent of all exports. The political reunification of the island is a key goal of the Republic.

IRELAND FACTS

CAPITAL CITY	Dublin
AREA	27,155 sq miles (70,280 sq km)
POPULATION	3,700,000
MAIN LANGUAGES	English, Irish Gaelic
MAJOR RELIGION	Christian
CURRENCY	Euro
LIFE EXPECTANCY	76 years
PEOPLE PER DOCTOR	455
GOVERNMENT	Multiparty democracy
ADULT LITERACY	99%

Physical features

Central Ireland consists of a fertile plain, punctuated by lakes, peat bogs, and undulating hills. Low mountains rise to the south, west, and southeast. The west coast has deep inlets and bays. The Shannon is the longest river in the British Isles.

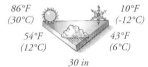

Connemara
Hundreds of beautiful lakes and peat bogs are typical of the wild scenery of Connemara in western Ireland. The spectacular peaks of the Twelve Bens mountain range were carved out by glaciers in the last Ice Age.

Emerald Isle
Ireland's abundant rainfall produces fresh green fields, giving it the nickname of the "Emerald Isle." The land is used for grazing dairy cattle and growing crops. Ireland is famous for its butter and cheese, and for horses and horseracing.

86°F (30°C) 10°F (-12°C)
54°F (12°C) 43°F (6°C)
30 in (762 mm)

Climate
The warm waters of the Gulf Stream provide Ireland's mild, damp climate. Ocean winds bring the country plenty of rain, especially along the west coast.

Wetland 1%
Barren 3.5%
Farmland 80.5%
Forest 14.5%
Built-up 0.5%

Land use
Ireland's most important natural resources are its fertile farmland and peat, used for fuel and gardening. There are oil reserves off the coast.

Farming and industry
Ireland has one of the fastest-growing economies in Europe. Traditional industries such as hand-cutting peat compete alongside a new, rapidly expanding high-tech sector. Recently, the strength of the economy has reversed a historical trend of emigration. Eight percent of the workforce farms.

Dublin
Dublin is a lively center of commerce, social activity, and cultural heritage. Christchurch Cathedral was restored in the 1870s, and is one of Dublin's finest landmarks, alongside Trinity College, Dublin Castle, and the Custom House.

Christchurch Cathedral

People
Ninety-five percent of the population of Ireland is Irish and 93 percent is devout Roman Catholic. The church plays a key role in society, although the younger Irish question its strict policies on birth control, divorce, and abortion. Long-standing, bitter, conflict exists between Catholics in southern Ireland and Protestants of Northern Ireland.

People crossing Dublin's Ha'penny Bridge

139 per sq mile (54 per sq km)

59% Urban 41% Rural

Stacking peat to dry in County Galway

FIND OUT MORE CHRISTIANITY COAL ENERGY EUROPE EUROPE, HISTORY OF EUROPEAN UNION FARMING GLACIATION IRELAND, HISTORY OF TRADE AND INDUSTRY

IRELAND, HISTORY OF

THE RICH CELTIC influence of Ireland distinguishes it from its neighbor, England, but its history has been dominated by struggle with that country. The English invaded Ireland in 1171. At first their rule was weak, but, by the 17th century, English control was complete. However, the religious differences between the Protestant English and Roman Catholic Irish led to long-lasting tensions. In 1921, the island was divided: the Catholic counties of the south, west, and east were given self-government; the northern, mainly Protestant counties remained part of the United Kingdom.

The Celts excelled at metalwork.

Celtic gold boat

Celtic Ireland
Around 600 BC, Celtic people from central Europe settled Ireland. Celtic craft and design – especially metalwork – have influenced Irish art ever since.

St. Patrick
In 432, a missionary named Patrick landed in Ireland. By 631, Patrick had converted the whole country to Christianity. For the next 300 years, Ireland enjoyed a golden age of arts and scholarship, which was centred on the monasteries. Irish missionaries set out to convert other parts of Europe.

Book of Kells
One of Ireland's most famous monasteries was built by the brilliant missionary, St. Columba, at Kells. It housed an outstanding 8th-century illuminated manuscript of the Latin Gospels.

Illuminated initial from the *Book of Kells*

Brian Boru
Ireland lacked strong government, and in the 8th century, Viking invaders started to settle along the coast. In 1002, Brian Boru, king of Munster, made himself High King of all Ireland. In 1014, he defeated the Vikings at Clontarf. Brian lost his life in the battle, but ended the Viking threat to Ireland.

English rule
In 1155, Pope Adrian IV gave the lordship of Ireland to his English ally Henry II. Henry's invasion in 1171 marked the start of eight centuries of English rule, though initially this was restricted to a small area. From the 1600s, religious differences and the ascendancy of the wealthy Protestant English over the Catholic Irish worsened Anglo-Irish relations.

Battle of the Boyne
In 1690, the Protestant William of Orange took the throne of the Catholic James II of England after defeating him in battle. Northern Irish Protestants still celebrate this victory with a march on July 12 – Orangeman's Day

Great Famine
In 1845, the potato crop – the main food of the Irish peasantry – failed. Over the next four years, one million people died of starvation, and more than 1,600,000 emigrated to the USA. Meanwhile, landlords were still demanding their starving tenants pay rent on their lands.

Potatoes were blighted by an airborne fungus.

Modern Ireland
In 1921, Ireland was divided into two parts: six Protestant counties in the north and 26 Catholic counties in the rest of the country. In 1922, the 26 counties formed a free state within the British Empire. The Free State achieved independence in 1937 and changed its name to Eire.

General Post Office, Dublin, a symbol of the Easter Rising

Easter Rising
On Easter Monday, 1916, militant republicans staged an uprising in Dublin and occupied the General Post Office. One of the leaders, Patrick Pearse, proclaimed Ireland an independent republic from the GPO's steps. The British soon crushed the rebellion, and executed 14 of its leaders. This caused a wave of sympathy among the people, and resistance to British rule increased.

Northern Ireland
In 1921, British and Irish political leaders signed the Anglo-Irish Treaty in which six counties in Ulster remained within the United Kingdom. Ulster's Protestant local government practised anti-Catholic policies, which led to civil rights protests and violence in 1968. The British government posted troops to Northern Ireland to keep order. They have remained to the present day.

Mural in Belfast, Northern Ireland

Mary Robinson
In early 1991, Mary Robinson (b.1944) became the first-ever woman president of the Republic of Ireland. As a lawyer, Robinson had campaigned for civil and women's rights. As president, she spoke up for the disadvantaged in Irish society. In 1997 she went on to become the UN High Commissioner for Human Rights.

Timeline
c.461 Death of St. Patrick. Ireland's religious conversion is complete.

795 Vikings first sail to Ireland.

1171 Henry II of England invades Ireland.

1607–41 Scottish and English Protestants colonize province of Ulster.

1690 William of Orange defeats James II; Protestant Ascendancy begins.

1801 Act of Union unites Ireland and England.

1845–48 The Great Famine.

1916 Easter Rising.

1921 Partition; Northern Ireland is formed.

1922 Irish Free State formed; war between supporters and opponents of Partition.

1973 Ireland joins European Union.

FIND OUT MORE   CELTS   CHRISTIANITY   EUROPE, HISTORY OF   MONASTERIES   UNITED KINGDOM, HISTORY OF

I

IRON AND STEEL

OUT OF THE 70 or so metals that exist on Earth, iron is the most important. It is used more than all the other metals put together – some 600 million tons every year. It is used to build many things, from bridges, skyscrapers, and ships to cars, bikes, and tools. However, iron is not generally used in its pure state, but in the form of its alloy, steel. The presence of traces of carbon in this alloy makes it hard, strong, and tough. Steel also contains smaller amounts of other metals, producing a range of alloy steels with different properties.

Iron ore
The main raw material for making iron is iron ore. There are two main iron-ore minerals, hematite and magnetite. Hematite is named after its blood-red color; magnetite is so called because it is naturally magnetic.

Hematite

Iron smelting
Iron is produced when the ore is heated with coke and limestone in a blast furnace. The coke acts both as fuel and as a chemical agent to remove oxygen from the ore, leaving the metal. The limestone absorbs impurities in the ore and forms a layer called slag.

Adding iron ore to furnace

Cast iron
The iron made in the blast furnace, called pig iron, contains many impurities. Nevertheless, it is sometimes used to make metal castings. This cast iron, which contains up to four percent carbon, is strong, but brittle.

Traces of carbon in cast iron

Iron cross-section

Built using cast iron

Eiffel Tower, France

Steel refining
Most pig iron produced is sent for further processing, or refining. Refining removes many of the impurities from the iron, especially the carbon. The result is steel. The most common refining method is called the basic oxygen process. A high-speed jet of oxygen is blasted into molten pig iron and burns out the impurities.

Steel is poured into ingot molds and taken to be shaped.

Ladle containing molten steel

Scrap iron is tipped into the converter.

Molten pig iron is poured into the ladle ready for transfer to converter.

Manufacturing steel

The converter is filled with molten pig iron, scrap, and additives. Oxygen is blown in, causing a violent chemical reaction.

Containers holding molten pig iron from the blast furnace

Shaping steel
Once refined, steel is usually cast into huge ingots, which are then shaped further. This is done using a variety of methods, such as rolling and forging. In rolling, the reheated ingot is passed between heavy rollers. In forging, the ingot is hammered or squeezed by powerful machines.

Steel cross-section showing small traces of carbon

Henry Bessemer
In 1856, English engineer Henry Bessemer (1813–98) invented the first process for producing steel cheaply. His method involved blowing air through molten pig iron in a converter. The air blast burned out carbon and other impurities in the iron.

Types of steel
There are basically two main types of steel – carbon steel and alloy steel. The properties of carbon steel depend on the percentage of carbon it contains, while the properties of alloy steel are based on the nature of the other alloying metals added to it.

Stainless steel products   **Steel chain**

Carbon steel
The most common steel, mild steel, is a carbon steel containing up to about 0.25 percent carbon. Other carbon steels, with carbon contents up to 1.5 percent, are stronger and harder, but more brittle.

Mild steel car body

Stainless steel
This is one of the most widely used of all alloy steels. It contains about 18 percent chromium and 8 percent nickel. Both of these metals resist rusting and staining and impart this property to steel.

Rust
When iron or steel is exposed to damp air, it soon becomes covered with a reddish-brown film called rust. Rust is a hydrated iron oxide, formed when iron is attacked by oxygen and moisture in the air. Protective paints applied on some surfaces can prevent rust from forming.

Rust on an abandoned car

FIND OUT MORE   BRONZE AGE   BUILDING AND CONSTRUCTION   CARS AND TRUCKS   CHEMISTRY   COAL   INDUSTRIAL REVOLUTION   METALS   SHIPS AND BOATS

ISLAM

IN THE 7TH CENTURY AD, a new faith appeared in the world. This faith was revealed to the prophet Muhammad and its name is Islam, an Arabic word meaning "submission to the will of God." Believers in Islam are called Muslims. They believe in one God, Allah, who is eternal and created the Universe. They also believe that Allah sent a series of prophets to explain his wishes and to tell people how to live their lives. The most important prophet was Muhammad.

The Qur'an

The sacred book of Islam is called the Qur'an. Muslims believe that the Angel Gabriel, acting as Allah's messenger, dictated it to Muhammad, and it was later written down by the prophet's followers. The Qur'an reveals Allah's will for humankind. All Muslims study the Qur'an, and its text is often copied in longhand using beautiful calligraphy.

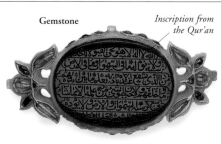

Gemstone

Inscription from the Qur'an

Shading shows worldwide distribution of Muslims. Islam is the second largest world religion.

The Islamic world

The center of the Islamic world is Mecca, in the Arabian peninsula. From here, in the 7th and 8th centuries, the faith spread quickly, until much of the area from Spain in the west to the Indus River in the east was converted. Islam has continued to expand, and there are now about 750 million Muslims in the world.

Pillars of Islam

There are five duties that every Muslim must obey. These are known as the five Pillars of Islam. The first is Shahadah, the sincere declaration of faith that there is "no other God but Allah and that Muhammad is his prophet." The second, Salat, commands Muslims to pray five times a day. The third pillar, Zakah, is the gift of money to the poor. The fourth, Sawm, is to fast during Ramadan. The final pillar, Hajj, is the duty to make the pilgrimmage to Mecca.

The Kaaba is the holy shrine in the Great Mosque at Mecca.

Muslims walk seven times counter-clockwise round the Kaaba.

Hajj

Every Muslim who can afford it and who is well enough has an obligation to make the pilgrimage to Mecca, in Saudi Arabia, the birthplace of Muhammad. Each year, during the twelfth month of the Muslim year, more than two million Muslims visit Mecca. Many save up for years to make the journey. It is the most important event in their lives.

Salat

Five times each day, Muslims stop whatever they are doing, face the direction of Mecca, and pray. Men go to prayers at the mosque at midday on Fridays, but at other times may pray in any clean place; women usually pray at home. Before following the sequence of prayer positions, a Muslim must carry out a washing ritual.

An imam (priest) begins his prayer by raising his hands to his ears and making a declaration of faith.

The imam bows down from the waist, hands on knees, reciting a prayer.

This prayer mat has a built-in compass showing the direction of Mecca.

Jihad

The Qur'an says that Muslims should oppose anyone who rejects the faith, if necessary by means of armed struggle. The term "jihad" (the Arabic word for "struggle") means striving to spread the Islamic way of life, sometimes through a "holy war." Jihad can also take other forms, such as learning, good works, and self control.

Medieval conquests spread the Islamic faith.

This is known as the Sujud position.

He prostrates himself with his forehead, nose, palms of hands, knees, and toes touching the ground.

After a few moments sitting up on his knees, the imam returns to the Sujud position.

At the end of the set of prayers, the imam turns his face to the left and then to the right.

Muslims may pray kneeling on a woven carpet, straw mat, or clean ground.

Festivals

Muslims celebrate several important events in Muhammad's life. These include the prophet's birthday (Mawlid al-Nabi) and the Night of Power (Laylat al Qadr), which commemorates the night when Muhammad received the Qur'an from the angel Gabriel. The Night of the Journey (Laylat al-Mi'raj) celebrates the night when Muhammad was taken up to heaven. The two most important festivals are Id al-Fitr and Id al-Adha.

Celebrations for Id al-Fitr include music and dancing for these Muslims, in Cameroon, Central Africa.

Id al-Adha

This festival takes place during the twelfth Muslim month, which is the pilgrimage month of Dhul-Hijjah. It marks the sacrifice of Abraham, who was prepared to sacrifice his son Isaac to God. At the last minute God told him to give a ram instead. Muslims traditionally sacrifice a sheep or goat and give one third of the meat to the poor.

Id al-Fitr

The ninth month of the Islamic year is Ramadan, the month of fasting. The end of Ramadan is celebrated by Id al-Fitr. This festival begins with a light meal and a meeting at the mosque for prayers, at which thanks are given for a successful fast. After prayers there are parties, at which people eat special cakes and candies, and exchange presents and cards. Before the festival, people give money to the poor so that everyone can join in the celebrations.

Whirling dervishes

Dervishes are members of mystical Islamic sects called Sufi that developed during the 12th century. There are various orders of dervishes, but they are best known for a prayer ritual in which they perform an ecstatic whirling dance, aiming to induce a trance and a direct experience of God.

Daily life

Islam affects the whole of a Muslim's life – everyday conduct, art, ethics, laws, and government. The Qur'an gives guidelines for all aspects of life and stresses the importance of the family. Family members are expected to care for one another, and the elderly are regarded as heads of the family. Marriages are usually arranged. It is traditional for women to stay at home to look after the house, but increasingly Muslim women go out to work. Women often cover their heads out of doors.

Verses from the Qur'an

Arabic script

Ornamental border decorates verses.

Halal food

According to the Qur'an, food that Muslims are allowed to eat is called halal. Products that come from animals that eat other animals are forbidden, as is meat from pigs. Other meats are halal when they are slaughtered correctly. All fish, fruit, grains, and vegetables are halal, too.

Education

Every Muslim must understand the text of the Qur'an because its teachings are part of everyday life. Education is therefore very important in Islam. Mosques traditionally contain a school and pupils learn to read the Qur'an in its original Arabic.

Branches of Islam

Islamic fundamentalists at a protest in Iran, carrying posters of Ayatollah Khomeini

Islam has two main branches: Sunni and Shi'ah. After the death of Muhammad, his followers chose Abu Bakr as their leader. Umar, Uthman, and Ali (Muhammad's son-in-law) were chosen in turn after Abu Bakr. But one group of Muslims thought they should be led by Muhammad's descendants.

They broke away, choosing the descendants of Ali as leaders. This break-away group are known as the Shi'ahs, and the group that remained are Sunni Muslims.

The crescent is associated with special acts of devotion to God.

This Shi'ah standard bears the names of God, Muhammad, and Ali.

Islamic fundamentalism

Some Muslims have turned their backs on the influence of modern Western society in favor of traditional Islamic values. They are known as Islamic fundamentalists.

Sunni and Shi'ah

Sunnis make up the larger of the two groups of Muslims. Their name derives from an Arabic word meaning "authority." The Shi'ah Muslims, who make up about 10 per cent of the Islamic population, live mainly in Iran and Iraq. Their leaders are known as ayatollahs. The two groups have separate theologies, legal systems, and ways of performing their rituals.

FIND OUT MORE CRUSADES · FESTIVALS · HOLY LAND, HISTORY OF · ISLAMIC EMPIRE · MOSQUES · MUHAMMAD · OTTOMAN EMPIRE · RELIGIONS · SIGNS AND SYMBOLS · WRITING

ISLAMIC EMPIRE

IN THE 8TH CENTURY, Arabian conquerors ruled a massive empire that stretched from Spain to China's borders. The Arab rulers had a mission to spread Islam, a religion whose powerful message was of equality, and whose followers are called Muslims. Under Muslim rule, people from many different lands worshiped one God, spoke a common language, and had one holy book. It was a time of wealth and learning: palaces, mosques, and universities were built in large Islamic cities, and within them knowledge was pursued by the world's most learned scholars.

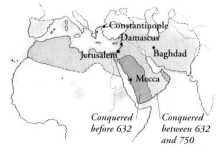

Spread of the empire c.750
The Arab conquest was speedy. Within a century of Muhammad's death, Arabs had defeated the Persian and much of the Byzantine empires. There were many converts to Islam, but the conquerors also tolerated other religions.

Early dynasties

Religious leaders, known as caliphs, ruled the empire. During the reign of the fourth caliph, two rival branches of Islam formed – the Sunni and Shi'ah. After the fall of the (Sunni) Umayyad and Abbasid dynasties, the (Shi'ah) Fatimid dynasty took over, using local rulers to keep order. This division ended the idea of one supreme caliph ruling a single empire.

Umayyads and Abbasids
The aristocratic Umayyad caliphs had a luxurious lifestyle. The Abbasid dynasty resented this and eventually seized power. Their best-known caliph, Harun al-Rashid (766–809), featured in the classic *A Thousand and One Nights*.

Royal escape, A Thousand and One Nights, 1898 edition

Capital cities

Muslim cities always have a central mosque and bazaars (covered markets). The first Muslim capital was Mecca, Muhammad's birthplace and Islam's holiest city. In 752, the Abbasids founded Baghdad, which, within 50 years, had become the largest city in the world.

Damascus
Before the Abbasid dynasty built Baghdad, the Islamic capital was at the ancient city of Damascus. The Umayyads built a Great Mosque in marble, and decorated it with mosaics.

Umayyad mosque, Damascus

Science

Astronomers hung their astrolabes from their belts.

Star map and the Zodiac

Islamic science brought together many branches of knowledge. At the college in Baghdad, scholars translated books from ancient Greece, Persia, and India into Arabic. Scientists observed and measured the natural world. Mathematicians invented algebra (from the Arabic *al-jabr*). The Arabic system of numbers is used worldwide today.

Astronomy
Muslims led the world in astronomy – they built many observatories and perfected the use of the astrolabe. Arabian nomads used the stars to navigate through the desert.

Alidade (movable pointer) is at the center.

Persian astrolabe *Circumference is marked off in degrees.*

Ginger

Coriander

Cardamom

Medicine
Islamic doctors absorbed and followed ancient Greek theories, but also formulated many of their own. Long before Europeans they knew for example that blood circulates around the body. They stressed the importance of a healthy diet and understood the healing power of herbs and plants.

Ibn Sina
The Islamic Empire's greatest philosopher and scientist, Ibn Sina (980–1037), was born in Bukhara in modern Uzbekistan. He was an exceptionally good doctor who was known to Europeans as Avicenna. His *Canon of Medicine* is one of the most highly regarded books in medical history.

Canon of Medicine, 1400s

Timeline

632 Muhammad dies. Four of his close companions succeed him in turn as caliph. Islamic Empire begins.

634–650 Muslims conquer Middle East.

650 Qu'ran is written.

661–750 Umayyad caliphate (dynasty) rules. They make Damascus their new capital.

670–708 Muslims attack and then conquer North Africa.

Cinnamon

711–721 Muslims conquer Spain.

732 Muslim conquest turned back in France.

750–880 The Abbasid dynasty rules the Islamic empire.

909 The (Shi'ah) Fatimid dynasty captures North Africa. Muslim territories split up and are ruled under separate leaders for the first time.

1055 Seljuk Turks begin to control the Islamic Empire.

FIND OUT MORE   ARCHITECTURE   ASIA, HISTORY OF   EMPIRES   ISLAM   MEDICINE, HISTORY OF   MUHAMMAD   PERSIAN EMPIRE   SAFAVID EMPIRE   SCIENCE, HISTORY OF

ISLANDS

DOTTED OVER THE OCEANS OF THE WORLD are millions of islands. Some islands are no bigger than rocks, but others are vast landmasses – Greenland, for example, covers 0.85 million square miles (2.2 million square kilometers). An island is an area of land smaller than a continent that is surrounded by water. Islands may be created when the sea rises or the land sinks, drowning valleys to leave only the highest ground above sea level. Islands may also form when ocean-floor volcanoes, built up by the lava from successive eruptions, emerge above water.

How a coral island forms

Coral polyps are tiny sea creatures that live in colonies in tropical oceans. A coral reef is an underwater ridge formed from the remains of dead coral. A reef may form around the exposed summit of an underwater volcano. If the volcano sinks, it may leave behind a ring-shaped island called an atoll.

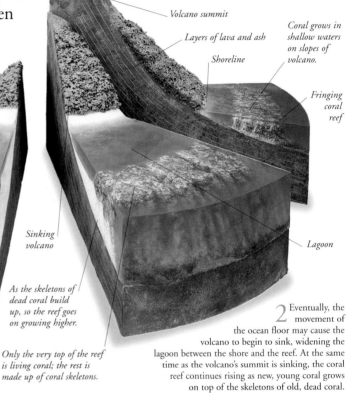

1 Over time, volcanic eruptions may build an ocean-floor volcano so high that its summit emerges above the surface of the water, forming an island. In warm tropical waters, a fringing reef of coral may begin to grow along the shoreline.

Volcano summit

Layers of lava and ash

Shoreline

Coral grows in shallow waters on slopes of volcano.

Fringing coral reef

Reeftop becomes colonized by vegetation.

Only tip of volcano is visible.

4 Eventually, the volcano's summit is completely submerged, leaving only the coral reef. The reef begins to form a ring-shaped island called an atoll as it is covered first by sand and then by vegetation.

Lagoon gradually fills with sand.

Sinking volcano

Lagoon

As the skeletons of dead coral build up, so the reef goes on growing higher.

2 Eventually, the movement of the ocean floor may cause the volcano to begin to sink, widening the lagoon between the shore and the reef. At the same time as the volcano's summit is sinking, the coral reef continues rising as new, young coral grows on top of the skeletons of old, dead coral.

3 The volcano goes on sinking, and the coral continues to grow. As the lagoon expands even more, small outcrops of new coral appear within the lagoon. In places where the coral is growing particularly rapidly, the tops of the reef begin to dry out.

Growing reef stays above the water as the volcano sinks.

Only the very top of the reef is living coral; the rest is made up of coral skeletons.

Volcanic islands

The Hawaiian Islands are a chain of volcanoes formed above a "hot spot" – that is, a place where hot, molten rock burns through the Earth's crust. The Hawaiian chain is slowly growing longer as the movement of the ocean floor shifts each volcano along, and a new volcano erupts over the hot spot.

The islands of Java and Bali

Island arcs
Where two pieces, or plates, of the Earth's crust collide, molten rock escapes and creates a long arc of volcanic islands. Java, Bali, the Philippines, and Japan are all part of the same giant island arc.

Drowned lands

Many large islands form when the movement of the Earth's crust causes the land to sink. This is how Britain became an island, and how the Isle of Wight was separated from mainland Britain.

Satellite image of Isle of Wight, Britain

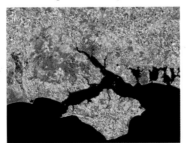

Eyot
Where a large river flows over broad, flat floodplains, the river channel may split up into several smaller channels. If the river carries a lot of sediment, such as sand or mud, it may deposit the sediment as sandbars or mud banks between the channels. Small islands called eyots (or aits) form as the sandbars and mud banks dry out.

Eyot in the River Seine, France

Cyclades Islands form an archipelago

Archipelago
Sea levels rise locally as land sinks or globally as an era of warmer climates melts the polar ice caps and increases the amount of water in the oceans. When this happens, low-lying coastal lands are drowned. A new coastline is formed, fringed with tiny islands that are the summits of former hills and mountains. These island clusters are known as archipelagos.

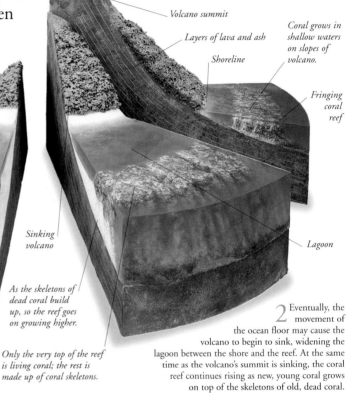

FIND OUT MORE   COASTLINES   CONTINENTS   CORAL REEFS   EARTH   ISLAND WILDLIFE   OCEAN FLOOR   ROCKS AND MINERALS   VOLCANOES

ISLAND WILDLIFE

ISOLATED LOCATIONS and the lack of large predators, competitors, and disease has allowed the evolution of a unique range of wildlife on many islands. Island habitats vary greatly, from the ice and rock of Greenland to the tropical rain forests of Borneo. Island floras and faunas are fragile ecosystems, easily upset by foreign invaders and freak weather conditions. Some islands possess unique species found nowhere else (endemics); other remote islands are inhabited by species from otherwise extinct groups (relicts).

Islands

Continental islands such as Borneo became separated from larger landmasses. Their wildlife is similar to that of the mainland. Oceanic islands, such as Fiji, are more remote and are either coral reefs or volcanic in origin. Their flora and fauna are often very varied. Sulawesi, for example, has wildlife of Asian and Australasian origin, as well as an animal unique to the island – the babirusa.

Colonization

In 1883, a volcanic eruption destroyed all life on the island of Krakatoa. Since then the process of recolonization – the establishment of plants and animals in a new environment – has been studied. Colonizers crossed 25 miles (40 km) of water. First came ferns and algae. After 40 years, there were forests, 29 bird species, two geckos, one python, one monitor lizard, insects, bats, and rats.

Dense vegetation cover provides homes for many animals.

Moorea, French Polynesia

Mammals

Large carnivorous mammals are found only on large islands that have a large population of prey. Many isolated islands have large herbivorous mammals that are often unique to that island. Madagascar is home to lemurs such as the aye-aye that live nowhere else in the world. The anoa dwarf cow lives only on Sulawesi. On very remote islands, bats are often the only mammals because they arrived by flying.

Long toe to get bugs out of bark

Aye-aye

Plants

The fertile volcanic soil of oceanic islands provides ideal growing conditions for plants. Some plants, such as coconut palms, are widely distributed around many islands, others are unique to specific islands. For example, the Canaries are home to 500 species of endemic plants, including ancient dragon trees. Madagascar has seven species of baobab tree; the African mainland has only one.

Seeds are spear-shaped and stick in ground where they land.

Red mangrove

Colonizing seeds

Seeds reach remote islands carried on wind or water currents, and on the feet or in the guts, of birds. The coconut has a tough outer shell that protects the inner kernel during long ocean journeys. The first plant to become established on oceanic islands is often the red mangrove. Its seeds start to germinate before they drop from the parent plant and are ready to take root where they land.

Baobab tree

Coconut

Giant tortoise

Reptiles

Most reptiles are good swimmers and easily colonize close islands or float on driftwood to more distant ones. Fijian iguanas are related to those in America; their ancestors are believed to have rafted on vegetation across the Pacific. Tuataras live on islands off the New Zealand coast; they resemble lizards, but they are actually relicts from the far distant past. Relicts are ancient animals that survive on isolated islands long after their relatives are extinct elsewhere.

Giants and dwarves

Different conditions on islands compared with the mainland can affect the size of animals. Giant tortoises grow large because of the lack of large predators in the Galápagos Islands. On Chappell Island, near Australia, black tiger snakes also grow larger than normal. They feed on mutton bird chicks that exist for a brief period only. The snakes get big as they eat many chicks at once to build up reserves for the rest of the year. Island dwarfs also exist where food or other resources are limited.

Tuatara

Strong legs help when excavating burrows.

Invertebrates

Invertebrates have colonized many islands. They arrived by rafting on vegetation, by flying, or by being carried on the wind. Larger species such as the Pacific robber crab cannot migrate. However, its larvae hatch from eggs laid in the sea and drift on the ocean currents to colonize islands thousands of miles away.

Large claws used to climb palms and sever coconuts.

Robber crab

Birds

Many islands are rich in bird life because flight enables birds to colonize islands easily. Strong fliers, such as frigate birds, are often the first birds to arrive. But with no natural predators, many island birds, such as the New Guinea cassowary, became flightless. Introduced species pose a threat to these birds, which lack a means of defense or escape. For example, feral dogs often kill New Zealand kiwis.

Frigate bird

FIND OUT MORE CONTINENTS • CRABS AND OTHER CRUSTACEANS • FLIGHTLESS BIRDS • FRUITS AND SEEDS • ISLANDS • MONKEYS AND OTHER PRIMATES • PIGS AND PECCARIES • REPTILES

ISRAEL

ISRAEL IS A LONG, NARROW COUNTRY, lying between the Jordan River and the Mediterranean Sea. Although it is a new nation, founded in 1948 as a homeland for the world's Jews, Israel is also a very old country. Previously called Palestine, it was a home for Arabs for about 1,400 years, before which it was a Jewish land for about 1,700 years. Since 1948, Israel has fought several wars with its Arab neighbors. Relations are tense with renewed outbreaks of fighting, despite frequent peace talks. Israel receives financial help from the US.

ISRAEL FACTS	
CAPITAL CITY	Jerusalem
AREA	7,992 sq miles (20,700 sq km)
POPULATION	6,200,000
MAIN LANGUAGES	Hebrew, Arabic
MAJOR RELIGIONS	Jewish, Muslim, Christian
CURRENCY	Shekel
LIFE EXPECTANCY	79 years
PEOPLE PER DOCTOR	217
GOVERNMENT	Multiparty democracy
ADULT LITERACY	96%

Physical features

Israel stretches south through the Negev Desert to Elat on the Red Sea. The green Plain of Sharon runs along the coast, while inland, parallel to the coast, is a range of hills and uplands with fertile valleys to the west and desert to the east.

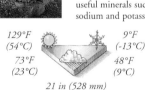

Negev Desert
In Hebrew, the word Negev means "arid land." Like many other deserts, the Negev is not completely lacking in life. Much of it is covered by scrub; when rain comes, it springs into life with a carpet of wildflowers. Large areas are now being irrigated for farming.

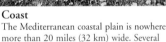

Dead Sea
The Dead Sea lies between Israel and its eastern neighbor, Jordan. It is a vast lake 46 miles (74 km) long and 10 miles (16 km) wide. At 1,300 ft (400 m) below sea level, it is also the lowest point in the world. It is so salty that nothing can live in it – and even non-swimmers cannot sink. The water contains useful minerals such as sodium and potassium.

Coast
The Mediterranean coastal plain is nowhere more than 20 miles (32 km) wide. Several rivers flow through the region, fertilizing the soil. It contains fine, sandy beaches, popular with vacationers. In the north are cliffs with beautiful caves and grottoes.

129°F (54°C) 73°F (23°C)   9°F (-13°C) 48°F (9°C)
21 in (528 mm)

Climate
Israel has hot, dry summers, and mild winters when most of the rain occurs. Rainfall varies from 1 in (25 mm) per year in the southern Negev to 43 in (1,088 mm) in parts of Galilee.

Jerusalem
Dating back more than 3,000 years, Israel's capital, Jerusalem, is a cultural and religious center for Jews, Muslims, and Christians. The Western wall of Herod's temple is sacred to Jews, the Dome of the Rock is a Muslim holy place, and the Church of the Holy Sepulchre marks the site of Jesus' crucifixion. The modern city is home to half a million people.

Desert 43.5%
Forest 5%
Farmland 29.5%
Grassland 20.5%
Built-up 1.5%

Land use
Almost half of Israel is desert, but irrigation has enabled large areas to be reclaimed as farmland. The country has valuable mineral resources in the Dead Sea area, and reserves of copper ore and gold.

The Dome of the Rock

473

People

More than 80 percent of Israelis live in high-rise apartment buildings. The majority of people are Jewish, but there are about 800,000 Palestinians, who are Muslim. Most Israelis work a six-day week.

Jewish people
Some Jews have always lived in Israel, but the majority moved to the country after World War II (1939–45). Sephardic Jews from the Middle East and the Mediterranean are in the majority, but Ashkenazi Jews, from central Europe, dominate politics and business. Women enjoy equal opportunities and serve in the army. Orthodox Jews keep the Sabbath, from Friday night to sunset on Saturday.

790 per sq mile (305 per sq km)   **91% Urban**   **9% Rural**

Leisure

Israelis enjoy sports such as soccer, tennis, basketball, and badminton. On the coast, Israelis swim, surf, sail, and water-ski. Scuba diving is popular in Elat. People like to listen to jazz, rock, and pop music, and attend folk festivals.

Jewish festivals
There are many Jewish festivals, when families spend time together. The annual Israel Festival is a three-week cultural extravaganza, including circus and theater shows.

Dead Sea mud
Many of the minerals in mud from the Dead Sea have medical properties. Special soaps and creams are sold worldwide to treat skin complaints and arthritis.

Dead Sea mud cosmetics

Farming

Only about 30 percent of Israel's land can be used for growing crops. Lack of water is a constant problem, and irrigation is a necessity. Most of the crops are grown on the fertile coastal plain, where vineyards and citrus groves are plentiful.

Sprinklers water the crops.

Crops
Farming accounts for about five percent of exports. Almost half of Israel's food is grown on *kibbutzim*, places where several families live and work together, sharing everyday tasks such as cooking and cleaning. Cash crops include citrus fruit, pomegranates, grapes, roses, and carnations.

Roses are grown for cut flowers.

Irrigation
Israeli farmers rely heavily on efficient irrigation to water their crops, which would otherwise die in the heat. Computerized irrigation has enabled parts of the desert to be cultivated, supporting specialized agriculture.

Pomegranate

Citrus fruits

Food

Kosher food, prepared according to Jewish religious dietary laws, is eaten by Orthodox Jews, but many Israeli restaurants serve a variety of foods including eastern European, Russian, Austrian, and German dishes. *Falafel* is a well-known Israeli food – balls made from chickpeas, herbs, and spices, and fried in oil, served with *tahini*, a paste of sesame seeds, and pita bread.

Tahini   *Falafel*

Pita

Transportation
Israel has good highways. Bus services are efficient and the railroad system is being expanded. Freight travels by rail or boat from the Mediterranean ports of Hefa and Ashdod, and Elat in the Gulf of Aqaba. Tel-Aviv-Yafo has the main airport.

Hefa port

Industry

Israel has a diverse manufacturing economy. Tel Aviv-Yafo is the center of the country's industry, which is concentrated in electronics, engineering, plastics, chemicals, textiles, and food processing. Tourism is growing steadily.

Diamonds
Cutting and polishing diamonds is a major Israeli industry. The uncut stones account for 16 percent of total imports. Cut stones make up about 22 percent of exports. The only other major diamond-cutting countries are India and the Netherlands.

Mining
Copper, gypsum, limestone, and a small amount of oil and gas are mined, especially in the Negev. Factories like these around the Dead Sea extract potash, magnesium, and bromine, used for photography and in dyes and anesthetics.

Palestinians

In 1948, when Israel was created, many Palestinian Arabs left the country, leading to a conflict between Jews and Palestinians that would last many years. About 800,000 Palestinians remained in Israel. In 1967, Israel occupied the Palestinian territory of the Gaza Strip. Land negotiations continue over Gaza, Jericho, and the West Bank.

Tensions still exist between Jews and Muslims

FIND OUT MORE   ASIA, HISTORY OF   CHRISTIANITY   CRYSTALS AND GEMS   DESERTS   FARMING   HOLY LAND, HISTORY OF   ISLAM   JUDAISM   ROCKS AND MINERALS

ITALY

BORDERED BY THE ALPS in the north, the boot-shaped peninsula of mainland Italy stretches about 500 miles (800 km) into the Mediterranean Sea. An agricultural society for centuries, Italy has recently emerged as a major industrial power. The country's wealth, best farmland, and industry lie mostly in the north. By contrast, the south is arid, and farming and industry are on a smaller scale. Italy includes the Mediterranean islands of Sicily and Sardinia.

ITALY FACTS

CAPITAL CITY Rome
AREA 116,320 sq miles (301,270 sq km)
POPULATION 57,300,000
MAIN LANGUAGE Italian
MAJOR RELIGION Christian
CURRENCY Euro
LIFE EXPECTANCY 78 years
PEOPLE PER DOCTOR 169
GOVERNMENT Multiparty democracy
ADULT LITERACY 98%

Physical features

Mountains dominate the Italian landscape, from the lakes and valleys of the Alps and Dolomites in the north, to the Apennines that run down the southern peninsula. South of the Alps is the fertile valley of the Po River. Italy is prone to earthquakes and has active volcanoes, such as Vesuvius, Stromboli, and Etna.

Sicily
The largest island in the Mediterranean Sea, Sicily is mainly mountainous. The highest point is Mount Etna at 10,930 ft (3,332 m), an active volcano that towers over the town of Catania. The economy thrives on farming and tourism. Sicily's warm climate, beautiful beaches, and ancient ruins attract increasing numbers of visitors each year.

Apennine Mountains
Extending for about 860 miles (1,400 km) from the northwest to the southwest tip and across the sea into Sicily, the Apennines form the backbone of Italy. The highest point is Mount Corno at 9,560 ft (2,914 m).

Climate
Southern Italy has hot, dry summers and mild winters. In the north, the summers are cooler, especially in the hills and mountains, and the winters colder and wetter. The Po Valley tends to be foggy in winter, and snow covers the Alps. The Adriatic coast suffers from strong, cold winds, such as the *bora*.

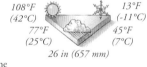

108°F (42°C)   13°F (-11°C)
77°F (25°C)   45°F (7°C)
26 in (657 mm)

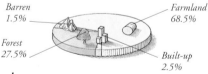

Barren 1.5%   Farmland 68.5%
Forest 27.5%   Built-up 2.5%

Land use
Most of Italy is cultivated or used as pasture for grazing sheep on grassy mountain slopes. The most fertile area is the broad, flat Po Valley in the north of the country. Italy has very few mineral resources and imports most of its oil products.

Map grid references and labels:

A B C D E F
SWITZERLAND · AUSTRIA · ALPS · FRANCE
Aosta · Lake Maggiore · Bolzano · Alto Adige · Dolomites · Trento · Belluno · Udine · SLOVENIA
Bergamo · Monza · Brescia · Vicenza · Treviso · Trieste
Novara · Milan · Verona · Mestre · Venice
Turin · Cremona · Padova · Gulf of Venice
Alessandria · Piacenza · Parma · Mantova · Ferrara · Po · Po Delta
Genoa · Reggio nell' Emilia · Modena · Ravenna
Savona · La Spezia · Bologna
Golfo di Genova · Viareggio · Forlì · Rimini · Adriatic Sea
San Remo · Pisa · Arno · Prato · SAN MARINO
Ligurian Sea · Livorno · Toscana · Florence · Arezzo · Ancona
Isola d'Elba · Siena · Lago Trasimeno · G H
Arcipelago Toscano · Grosseto · Perugia · Assisi
ITALY · Terni · Ascoli Piceno · Corno Grande 9,554ft
Viterbo · L'Aquila · Pescara · Pianosa
VATICAN CITY · ROME · Frosinone · Isole Tremiti
Sassari · Olbia · Foggia · Bari · Strait of Otranto
Alghero · Nuoro · Benevento · Ofanto · Altamura
Oristano · Sardinia · Arbatax · Naples · Salerno · Taranto · Brindisi
Iglesias · Isola d'Ischia · Sorrento · Potenza · Lecce
Cagliari · Isola di Capri · Golfo di Salerno · Golfo di Taranto · Otranto · Gallipoli
Tyrrhenian Sea · Cosenza · Crotone
Mediterranean Sea · Ustica · Isole Eolie · Stromboli · Catanzaro · Ionian Sea
Salina · Lipari · Vulcano
Trapani · Palermo · Messina · Reggio di Calabria
Isole Egadi · Cefalù · Monte Etna 10,958ft
Marsala · Sicily · Catania
Sicilian Channel · Caltanissetta · Agrigento · Augusta
Pantelleria · Caltagirone · Siracusa
Ragusa
Isole Pelagie (Italy) · Linosa · Gozo · VALLETTA · Mediterranean Sea
Lampione · Lampedusa · MALTA

0 km 100 / 0 miles 100

Rome
Founded about 2,500 years ago on seven hills near the Tiber (Tevere) River, Rome is one of the world's finest cities. Ancient ruins are visible beside modern office buildings, fashionable shops, and Renaissance palaces, all of which are part of daily life for the three million inhabitants. Rome is also the home of Italy's democratic government.

Piazza di Spagna

People

Most Italians are Roman Catholics. Italy has few ethnic minorities and few racial tensions, but there is conflict between the wealthy north and poorer south. In the 1950s and 1960s, a weak economy forced many Italians to find work abroad.

505 per sq mile (195 per sq km) | 67% Urban | 33% Rural

Family life
Most Italians live at home before marriage. Life revolves around the extended family. Several generations often live close together, able to help each other and share childcare and meals.

Colosseum, Rome

Industry

Italy has few natural resources, but its skilled workforce transforms imported raw materials into sophisticated manufactured goods. Major exports include cars, electronic and electrical goods, clothing, shoes, and textiles. Italy is famous for the style and innovation of its product design.

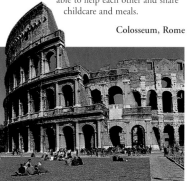

Tourism
Italy's magnificent towns, varied and scenic countryside, ancient Roman ruins, buildings, paintings, and sculptures lure millions of tourists each year. Tourism plays a vital role in the country's economy.

Design
The Italians' flair for design is apparent in their cars and clothes. The fashion houses of Milan, Rome, and Florence rival those of Paris, and designer names such as Benetton, Gucci, and Armani are famous throughout the world. Italian clothes and shoes are widely exported.

Shoes made by Gucci

Leisure

Italy's three great passions are soccer, fast cars, and opera. Italians also enjoy skiing, sailing, and volleyball. Horse racing is a popular spectator sport.

Carnival
Every spring most Italian towns and villages celebrate *carnevale*, a festival at which people dress in bright costumes and wear masks. The most famous *carnevale* is held in Venice.

La passeggiata
In the early evening, many Italians like to take a stroll – *passeggiata* – in the square, or *piazza*, or through the streets, talking to friends or stopping for a cup of coffee or a glass of wine. Covered footpaths called colonnades make a stroll possible even if the weather is bad.

Farming

Italy's countryside is dotted with small family-run farms producing a variety of crops, such as grain, fruit (especially grapes), and vegetables. Italy is also a leading producer of olives and olive oil.

Grapes
Italy is the world's largest wine producer. Grapes grow everywhere, but the best wine, such as Chianti, comes from the north. Sicily produces Marsala, a dessert wine.

Food and drink

The two traditional Italian foods are pizza with a variety of toppings, and pasta, a type of dough made with flour and water and served with a sauce, often as a first course. In the north, where rice and corn are grown, people also eat a rice dish called risotto, and polenta, a savory corn side dish. Meals are eaten with wine or, in the north, beer.

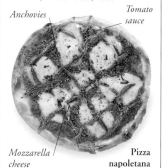

Anchovies

Tomato sauce

Mozzarella cheese

Pizza napoletana

Vatican City State

The Vatican City in the center of Rome is the world's smallest independent state. It is the world center of the Roman Catholic religion, and the Pope is the head of state.

St. Peter's Basilica
More than 50,000 people can worship in St. Peter's, which is the largest and most important Christian church in the world.

VATICAN CITY STATE FACTS

CAPITAL CITY Vatican City

AREA 0.17 sq miles (0.44 sq km)

POPULATION 1,000

MAIN LANGUAGES Italian, Latin

MAJOR RELIGION Christian

CURRENCY Euro

San Marino

Perched in the northern Apennines, San Marino was founded in the fourth century AD and is the world's oldest republic. Each year San Marino has a famous Grand Prix.

Tourism
San Marino's main source of income comes from the two-and-a-half million tourists who visit the country each year.

SAN MARINO FACTS

CAPITAL CITY San Marino

AREA 24 sq miles (61 sq km)

POPULATION 26,900

MAIN LANGUAGE Italian

MAJOR RELIGION Christian

CURRENCY Euro

Malta

Lying midway between Europe and Africa, the islands of the Maltese archipelago were ruled by foreign powers until independence in 1964. The main income is tourism.

Grand Harbor
Valletta's Grand Harbor is a busy modern port. Its rapid development was due to its position on the trade route between Africa and Europe.

MALTA FACTS

CAPITAL CITY Valletta

AREA 124 sq miles (320 sq km)

POPULATION 389,000

MAIN LANGUAGES Maltese, English

MAJOR RELIGION Christian

CURRENCY Maltese lira

FIND OUT MORE CHRISTIANITY DESIGN EUROPE EUROPE, HISTORY OF EUROPEAN UNION FARMING FESTIVALS ITALY, HISTORY OF ROMAN EMPIRE VOLCANOES

ITALY, HISTORY OF

ONCE THE CENTER of the great Roman Empire, Italy has been disunited and divided for most of its history. Most of the Italian cities were independent of each other, and foreign powers ruled large parts of the country. Some of the cities, such as Venice, Florence, and Bologna, became powerful in their own right. Because of their wealth, Spanish, German, and French armies fought for control of Italy's great cities for centuries. It was not until 1861 that Italy became a single, united country, free of foreign control. Today, Italy is at the forefront of the European Union.

End of the Roman Empire
In the 5th century, Germanic tribes overran the Roman Empire. Italy was taken over by the Ostrogoths, many of whom soon converted to Christianity and adopted Roman customs.

Mausoleum of Theodoric, Ostrogoth ruler of 6th-century Italy, Ravenna

Italian city states
While other European countries, such as Spain and France, were gradually united during the 14th and 15th centuries, Italy remained a patchwork of small warring states. The south of the country was ruled by Spain, the center by the Pope in Rome, and the north consisted of various rich republics and monarchies.

Cosimo d'Medici

Medici family
This family took over the Republic of Florence in 1434 and ruled it for almost 300 years. Florence became one of Europe's richest cities, and the Medici family grew very powerful.

Venice
This coastal city made its wealth from seaborne trade. Its galleys carried much of the eastern Mediterranean trade, while its merchants traded as far afield as China.

Ruler's palace, Venice

United Italy

In 1860–61, the previously disunited states of Italy came together to form a united country under King Victor Emmanuel II of Piedmont. In 1866, the Austrians were thrown out of Venice, and in 1870 the Pope lost control of his lands around Rome. For the first time in centuries, Italy was free of foreign control.

Cavour
Count Cavour (1810–61), prime minister of Piedmont from 1852, was a strong believer in Italian unification. Through clever diplomacy, he overcame all the potential enemies of unification and proclaimed a united Italy in March 1861.

Piedmont
Venetia
Tuscany
Papal States
Rome
Sardinia
Kingdom of the Two Sicilies

Sardinia

United 1860

United 1870 **Unification of Italy**

Garibaldi
In May 1860, the Italian patriot Giuseppe Garibaldi (1807–82) sailed from Genoa with 1,000 volunteer soldiers called red shirts. His plan was to overthrow the kingdom of Naples and Sicily and to unite it with the rest of Italy. He then tried to invade Rome, but was prevented from entering the city. He is remembered as one of the founders of modern Italy.

Modern Italy
In 1946, Italy voted to become a republic. Despite frequent changes in government and a weak political leadership, Italy has become one of the leading industrial powers in Europe. The country is a world leader in fashion and design, producing a range of high-quality goods from household items to sports cars. In 1957, Italy helped establish the European Economic Community – now known as the European Union – by organizing the Treaty of Rome. Italy remains a prominent member of the Union.

Ferrari sports car

Fascism

In 1922, Benito Mussolini became prime minister of Italy. He was leader of the Fascist Party, an anti-socialist group believing in strong government and national pride. The Fascists encouraged the arts, but led Italy unprepared into World War II.

The Flight of the Swallows by Giacomo Balla

Timeline

410 Visigoths under their leader Alaric destroy Rome.

476 Invading Goths depose the last Roman emperor.

1271 Merchant Marco Polo leaves Venice for China.

Towers of Bologna

1434 Medicis rule Florence and employ Renaissance artists.

1494–1559 France and Spain fight for control of Italy.

1796 Napoleon Bonaparte invades Italy.

1852 Count Cavour becomes prime minister of Piedmont.

1860–61 Italy united as one nation under the leadership of Piedmont.

1870 Rome joins the rest of Italy and becomes the capital.

1914–18 Italy fights with Allies in World War I.

Benito Mussolini, 1883–1945

1922 Mussolini takes power.

1940 Italy sides with Germany in World War II.

1943 Italy surrenders.

1945 Mussolini is executed.

1957 Italy becomes founder member of European Union.

FIND OUT MORE

EUROPE, HISTORY OF

EUROPEAN UNION

GOVERNMENTS AND POLITICS

HOLY ROMAN EMPIRE

MEDIEVAL EUROPE

RENAISSANCE

ROMAN EMPIRE

WORLD WAR I

WORLD WAR II

JAPAN

FOUR PRINCIPAL ISLANDS, Hokkaido, Honshu, Kyushu, and Shikoku, and more than 3,000 smaller ones off the east coast of Asia make up Japan. They stretch about 1,200 miles (1,900 km) into the Pacific Ocean and its "ring of fire," where the Earth's plates collide, making the country vulnerable to earthquakes and erupting volcanoes. Most Japanese live on Honshu, the largest island, and enjoy high living standards. Japan's booming economy is a global phenomenon, and its future lies in new technology for the 21st century.

JAPAN FACTS

CAPITAL CITY	Tokyo
AREA	145,869 sq miles (377,800 sq km)
POPULATION	126,700,000
MAIN LANGUAGE	Japanese
MAJOR RELIGIONS	Shinto, Buddhist
CURRENCY	Yen
LIFE EXPECTANCY	81 years
PEOPLE PER DOCTOR	526
GOVERNMENT	Multiparty democracy
ADULT LITERACY	99%

Physical features

Japan's main islands are mountainous, and about 90 percent of the land is covered in forest. There are 16,566 miles (26,505 km) of coastline, breaking into fertile plains inland. On Honshu, the volcanic Japanese Alps separate the snowy west coast from the warmer east.

Ryukyu Islands

Okinawa forms part of the Ryukyu chain of over 100 islands. Their coral reefs and beaches attract many visitors, and more than one million people have settled in the area.

Hokkaido

Japan's second largest island, at 30,303 sq miles (78,485 sq km), Hokkaido is a rural, forested area where wild bears roam. Winters are long and snowy. Only about five percent of Japanese people live on this northerly island, including the Ainu, who were the first people to settle in Japan. Fewer than 20,000 survive today, keeping their own culture, language, and religion.

Mount Fuji

Known as Fuji-san in Japan, Mount Fuji is the country's highest peak at 12,389 ft (3,776 m). Located near the Pacific coast of central Honshu, the perfectly symmetrical volcanic cone can be seen from a great distance. Mount Fuji is regarded as a sacred symbol of Japan, and thousands of pilgrims climb to its crater every year.

Climate

Japan's climate varies from north to south. Hokkaido is covered in snow for four months of the year, while the southern islands enjoy a tropical climate. Honshu has humid summers and cold winters with snow; Kyushu and Shikoku have long, hot summers and mild winters. Rainfall is high.

100°F (38°C)   -11°F (-24°C)
77°F (25°C)   41°F (5°C)
57 in (1,460 mm)

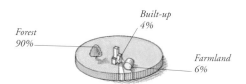

Built-up 4%
Forest 90%
Farmland 6%

Land use

Flat land for growing crops or raising livestock is scarce in Japan. Forested mountains cover some of Hokkaido, but more than half of Japan's grain is grown on the island's fertile plains. Lack of space has required buildings to be built close together, especially in cities.

Tokyo

The world's most densely populated city, Tokyo is home to 31,000,000 people. Most live in its sprawling concrete suburbs, commuting to the crowded center on the extensive train networks. All Japan's major companies have headquarters in Marunouchi, the central state-of-the-art district that leads the world in business and banking. Here, shiny modern office buildings stand side by side.

Tokyo's skyscrapers

Map labels:
Kurile Islands. Administered by Rus. Fed., claimed by Japan.
La Perouse Strait
Wakkanai
Sea of Okhotsk
Kurile Islands
Rebun-tō
Rishiri-tō
Kunashir
Iturup
Shikotan
Abashiri
Kitami
Habomai Is.
Asahikawa
Nemuro
Otaru
Sapporo
Obihiro
Kushiro
Chitose
Tomakomai
Hokkaidō
Okushiri-tō
Hakodate
Fukushima
Seikan Tunnel
Aomori
Hachinohe
Morioka
Akita
Honshū
Sea of Japan
JAPAN
Sendai
Sado
Niigata
Fukushima
Kōriyama
Iwaki
Toyama
Hitachi
Kanazawa
Nagano
Mito
Oki-shotō
Dōzen
Fukui
Biwa-ko
TOKYO
Kawasaki
Chiba
Tottori
Mt. Fuji
Yokohama
Matsue
Nagoya
Hamada
Okayama
Kōbe
Kyōto
Okazaki
Tsushima
Hiroshima
Kurashiki
Osaka
Hamamatsu
Shimonoseki
Yamaguchi
Wakayama
Iki
Matsuyama
Tokushima
Kitakyūshū
Shingū
Fukuoka
Kōchi
Sasebo
Ōita
Shikoku
Nagasaki
Nakamura
PACIFIC OCEAN
Gotō-rettō
Kumamoto
Amakusa-shotō
Kyūshū
Miyazaki
Kagoshima
Tanega-shima
Ōsumi-shotō
Yaku-shima
East China Sea
Amami-Ō-shima
Tokuno-shima
Ryukyu Islands
Okinawa
Naha
Korea Strait

0 km 200
0 miles 200

J

People

Ethnic Japanese make up 99 percent of the population. More than three-quarters of the people live in overcrowded urban areas. Most families have lots of consumer goods. Japan has a low birth rate, and around one-fifth of its population is elderly.

| 872 per sq mile (337 per sq km) | 79% Urban | 21% Rural |

Children
Japanese children have long school days that include a half-day on Saturdays and sometimes extra evening classes. They are expected to work hard and respect their elders. Young people are cherished and have a special Children's Day.

Leisure

The Japanese spend many hours at work but are encouraged to relax. There are many traditional activities and festivals throughout the year, including colorful religious street processions, the tea ceremony, and spring blossom-picking.

Sports
People enjoy traditional Japanese sports, such as karate and judo. Baseball is the most popular player and spectator sport, and work stops during the All Japan Schools tournament. Business executives often play golf or tennis.

Bonsai
The Japanese love nature and many are skilled in the art of bonsai, growing miniature trees. Junipers, maples, and pines grow up to 2 ft (60 cm) tall and survive for years.

Farming

The average Japanese farm is just 3.3 acres (1.2 hectares), but Japan grows much of what it needs to support its large population. Half the land is devoted to rice cultivation. Sheep graze on mountain slopes.

Tuna fish

Fishing
Japan has one of the world's largest fishing fleets, and its annual fish catch accounts for 15 percent of the total global catch. About 15,000 people work at Tokyo's fish auction, where restaurateurs use sign language to bid. Fish are processed on board ship.

Rice
Despite the shortage of arable land, Japan ranks highly in world rice production, with 14,578,000 tonnes (13,225,000 tons) each year. Fertilizers and modern machinery help farmers grow good-quality rice and use every piece of land. Most paddies lie in the south.

Food

Rice and fish form the basis of most Japanese cooking. On average, each person eats 66 lb (30 kg) of fish a year. People use chopsticks to eat their meals, which are attractively presented on black lacquer dishes with attention to color and detail. Raw fish, called *sashimi*, is eaten with vinegared rice, called *sushi*.

Chopsticks

Rice

Marinated raw fish

Industry

Japan has become an industrial giant, over the past 50 years, manufacturing high quality goods ranging from huge oil tankers to tiny electronic components. Traditional industries, such as coal-mining, steel, and fine arts, are profitable, but their importance has decreased with the success of the export-led economy.

Electronics
Japan is a world leader in the production of high-tech electronic consumer goods such as personal stereos, televisions, computers, cameras, and computer games machines. More than 50 percent of the world's robots are made in Japan.

Motor industry
Cars, motorcycles, and trucks are Japan's largest exports. Toyota, Nissan, and Honda are household names throughout the world. Japan is the leading motorcycle manufacturer.

Honda motorcycle has a top speed of 120 mph (190 kmh).

Work ethic
The Japanese have a long work week, and lots of time is spent entertaining clients after work. Very often, people are employed by the same company for all their working lives. In return, employers look after their staff, providing housing and healthcare. Most workplaces begin the day with physical exercise and loyalty declarations.

Transportation

Trains and planes are the way most Japanese travel. Crowded streets, expensive road tolls, and lack of parking spaces hamper the use of cars in the cities. Bicycles are popular for short journeys.

Bullet Train
Traveling at speeds of 130 mph (210 kmh) or more, Japan's *Shinkansen*, or "Bullet Train," is one of the fastest trains in the world. Railroads cover the entire country, and tunnels and bridges link the country's main islands, providing access to remote regions.

Air traffic
Japan's air route between Tokyo and Chitose, on Hokkaido, is one of the busiest in the world. Tokyo has two large airports. Environmental protests delayed the opening of Narita City airport, 41 miles (66 km) north of the capital, for 20 years. It finally opened in 1978.

| FIND OUT MORE | AIRPORTS | BALL GAMES | CARS AND TRUCKS | EARTHQUAKES | ELECTRONICS | FARMING | FISHING INDUSTRY | JAPAN, HISTORY OF | MOUNTAINS AND VALLEYS | TRAINS AND RAILROADS |

JAPAN, HISTORY OF

THE ISLAND NATION OF JAPAN has a long history of imperial rule, beginning in the 4th century when many small kingdoms unified. In the 6th century, Japanese emperors adopted the Chinese imperial system of government. However, their rule weakened until, in the 12th century, warrior leaders called shoguns seized power and made the emperors mere figureheads. In 1868, the patriotic samurai abolished the shogunate and reinstated the imperial family. Over the next 50 years, Japan opened up to western influences. It modernized, expanded, and was then all but destroyed in World War II. However, Japan has recovered to become an economic superpower.

Ainu people
The Ainu are racially different from Japanese, who over centuries forced them to the northern island of Hokkaido. Most now live by fishing and farming.

Chinese influence

China influenced the history of Japan. By the 7th century, Japanese society had adopted Buddhism, Chinese script, Confucianism, a new calendar, a new legal system, and many architectural and artistic techniques from T'ang China.

Nara
Japanese emperors built their first capital at Nara (Heijo-kyo) and based its design on the Chinese capital, Chang'an. As Japan's religious and political center from 710 to 794, Nara had splendid architecture, particularly visible today in its Buddhist temples.

Great Buddha, Todaiji, Nara

Kyoto

In 794, Kyoto (Heian-Kyo) replaced Nara as Japan's capital. Japan was moving away from Chinese influences, and Kyoto became the center of purely Japanese artistic and cultural developments. Kyoto declined as a political and cultural force in 1185 when the rule of the shoguns (military dictators) began. From 1338, the Ashikaga shoguns based their court there and revived Kyoto as a cultural center. Their elegant temples and villas survive today.

Court culture
Kyoto's court was a place of artistic merit. Courtiers excelled at poetry writing and painting. One noblewoman, Murasaki Shikibu, wrote *The Tale of Genji* (11th century), one of the world's first novels.

Prince Genji visiting ladies

Kiyomizu Temple (meaning pure water) was built close to mountain streams.

Kondo, or main hall

Stilted platform commands a view over the city.

Kiyomizu Temple, established in 798

Tokugawa
In this period (1603–1868), centuries of civil unrest ended. The Tokugawa shoguns made strict laws that ensured peace. Swords became less functional and more lavishly decorated. In 1641, the shogun closed Japan to the outside world to prevent foreigners from destabilizing the country.

Tokugawa-period court sword

Warrior centuries

By 1300 the weak Ashikaga shogunate was losing control over the provinces. The fall of Kamakura was followed by anarchy in the late 1400s to 1603, which was known as the Era of the Nation at War. During the unrest, the missionary, St. Francis Xavier (1506–52) arrived in Japan, and converted 100,000 Japanese to Christianity. Fearful of a takeover, Toyotomi Hideyoshi (1536–98) expelled all missionaries, and in 1596 he ordered the crucifixion of 26 Christians.

Civil war
In the Era of the Nation at War, feudal lords seized control of vast tracts of land. In the late 1500s, the first of Japan's three greatest military leaders – Oda Nobunaga (1534–82) – restored order. Oda was followed by his general, Hideyoshi, who reunified Japan. Tokugawa Ieyasu (1542–1616), who followed Hideyoshi, founded the dynasty that was to last into the modern age.

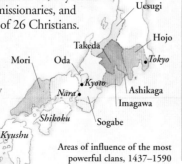

Hokkaido

Honshu

Uesugi

Hojo

Takeda

Tokyo

Mori   Oda

Kyoto

Ashikaga

Nara

Imagawa

Shikoku   Sogabe

Kyushu

Areas of influence of the most powerful clans, 1437–1590

Japanese art

As Chinese influence waned, Japanese art developed a unique style. In the Momoyama period (1573–1616), artists preferred extravagant displays of craftwork and color. Subject matter included court life, the seasons, and the military.

Decorated 17th-century fan

Lacquerware
China and India developed the art of lacquer. From China, lacquering traveled to Korea, and from there to Japan. Once in Japan, lacquer artists invented a stunning lacquering technique using gold powder.

Dragon design

Lacquer screen

J

Meiji Restoration

Commodore Perry's expedition, 1853

In 1853, Commodore Perry of the US Navy sailed into Tokyo Bay. Western powers then forced the shogun to open up the country. In 1868, afraid of Japan's loss of independence, rebel samurai defeated the shogun's army, restored Emperor Meiji as the figurehead of a new government, and moved the capital to Tokyo.

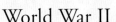

The British-built Tyre was Japan's first locomotive.

Industry

After 1868, Japan experienced rapid industrialization. The Meiji government developed modern industries, such as shipbuilding. The building of new railroads was particularly important – they unified Japan and helped trade and industry grow.

Tyre locomotive, 1870

Expansion

Japan competed with China and Russia to gain territory. This rivalry led to the Sino-Japanese War (1894–95) and the Russo-Japanese War (1904–5). Japan won both conflicts, and gradually expanded into China and the Pacific area.

China and Russia wars

After their speedy victory over China, Japan took over Taiwan as a colony. Ten years later, after the Japanese victory over the Russians at Tsushima, Japan gained recognition as a world power and took control of valuable Russian ports in Manchuria (China). In 1911, Japan finally annexed Korea.

Russian warship   *Japanese torpedo boat*

Battle of Tsushima, 1905

World War II

By the spring of 1942, Japan had conquered Malaya, Thailand, Burma, Hong Kong, the Philippines, the Dutch East Indies, and parts of China. But by 1945, Japan was losing ground, and suicide missions flew against American ships in a desperate attempt to avoid defeat. Japan surrendered after the atomic bombing of Hiroshima and Nagasaki.

Hiroshima

On August 6,1945, an American B-29 plane dropped an atomic bomb on Hiroshima. About 200,000 people died, either from the blast itself or the fallout afterward. Three days later, a second atomic bomb destroyed most of Nagasaki and killed an estimated 140,000 people.

Hiroshima, August 1945

Kamikaze means "Divine Wind."

Kamikaze, or suicide pilots

Pollution

Industrial development brought problems. During the 1960s, air, water, and soil pollution caused deaths and illnesses. Companies responsible were forced to pay compensation to victims, and new laws improved the environment. Nuclear waste is still transported worldwide by Japanese ships.

Waste carrier *Akatsu Maru* leaving for Europe

Modern Japan

Japan's industry suffered during World War II, but since 1945 it has made a remarkable recovery by developing new products and markets. Car manufacturing has expanded, and high-tech consumer goods are exported.

Wealth and leisure

As Japan has become wealthier, leisure industries have expanded rapidly. By 1989, leisure accounted for 28.8 percent of a family's budget. Sports – including golf, aerobics, skiing, and baseball – have become increasingly popular, as have cultural activities, such as concerts. Travel is now common, and more Japanese visit foreign countries than ever before.

Golf driving range

Economic prosperity

The Japanese economy grew so rapidly in the 1950s and 1960s that people often spoke of an economic miracle. This "miracle" was, in fact, produced by good industrial relations, high education levels, and the use of modern equipment.

Datsun 240 Z

Handheld computer plugs into mobile phone to access Internet.

Mobile Internet

Timeline

1192 First shogun assumes power.

1274 Kublai Khan attacks Japan, but is driven back by storms.

1336 Ashikaga shoguns (Muromachi) rule.

1543 Influx of Portuguese traders opens the way for Christian missionaries.

1549 Missionary St. Francis Xavier lands in Japan.

1603 Beginning of Tokugawa shogunate.

Noh mask

1641 Tokugawa shoguns expel all Europeans (except Dutch merchants confined to an island off Nagasaki).

1853–54 Commodore Matthew Perry sails into Tokyo; isolation ends.

1868 Meiji Restoration.

1912 Korea annexed.

1912 Meiji dies.

1930s Japanese expansion into China.

1955 Start of fast economic growth.

Emperor Hirohito

Hirohito (r.1926–1989), known since his death as the Showa ("enlightened peace") emperor, ruled through World War II and in the years of rapid change afterward. His reign was turbulent and his political power was limited, but Hirohito helped unite the nation during years of war and peace.

FIND OUT MORE · ARCHITECTURE · ASIA, HISTORY OF · KUBLAI KHAN · SAMURAI AND SHOGUNS · WORLD WAR II

JAZZ

JAZZ IS ONE OF THE GREATEST, most exciting musical developments of the 20th century. It began in the southern United States, where musicians blended elements from ragtime, blues, and spirituals with West African rhythms. Its earliest form, Dixieland, was played by small groups; by the 1930s, big bands were playing rearranged orchestrations called swing. Later developments have marked a return to smaller groups of players, and experiments in combining jazz with classical and rock music.

GRAND OPENING OF
Dixie Park,
On Easter Sunday, Mar. 27, 1910.

ADMISSION TO PARK · 15 CTS.

Minstrel shows were once part of the New Orleans music scene.

New Orleans
Jazz had its roots in New Orleans, a busy seaport with a cosmopolitan population. Jazz was first performed by black musicians, but because of racism it became widely popular only when played by white musicians. Riverboats, which carried bands for entertainment, and the development of commercial sound recording, helped spread the sounds of jazz.

Modern jazz quartet

Jazz band
The main features of jazz are strong rhythm, improvised melodies, and syncopation. It can be played by single performers or by large bands or orchestras. Small groups of musicians are common: three, four, or five players, usually but not always including a rhythm section (drums, bass, and/or piano), and a trumpet, saxophone, or singer as the lead.

Improvisation
Jazz players improvise, or vary, melodies so that each performance sounds fresh and different, though based on the same musical structure.

Syncopation
Rhythm is a key part of jazz music – players may shift the beat of a melody unexpectedly (a technique called syncopation) and use the beat as the driving force of the music.

The roots of jazz
Jazz developed from a combination of many musical styles. An important element was the African traditions that slaves took to America and kept alive in their work songs, such as strong rhythm, and melodies that singers could vary with each performance. Slaves who converted to Christianity mixed Christian songs with their own harmonies. Ragtime and the blues were also key elements.

Blues musician, 1902

Ragtime
In about 1900, ragtime music emerged in New Orleans, St. Louis, and Memphis. It was played on the piano with a steady bass beat and a syncopated melody. The best-known composer was Scott Joplin (1868–1917).

Scott Joplin

Ella Fitzgerald
American Ella Fitzgerald (1918–96) was one of the all-time great jazz singers. She was known for her rich, deep voice and sang with big bands in an elegant, relaxed style. She was also a great "scat" singer – a style in which the vocalist sings meaningless syllables to an improvised tune.

Blues
Black musicians invented the blues, a musical style that expresses deep, sad feelings. Early musicians knew hundreds of songs, which they sang while playing the banjo, guitar, or harmonica.

Types of jazz
There are many varieties of jazz, including boogie-woogie, swing, bebop (a fast style, with interesting harmonies), and cool, a more relaxed style typified by the trumpeter Miles Davis (1926–91). Jazz has also influenced classical composers and rock and pop musicians, who use blues harmonies in their work.

ELLINGTON AT NEWPORT

Swing
Big bands appeared in the 1920s. Their leaders, such as "Duke" Ellington (1899–1974), composed, arranged, and wrote down their music, which was known as swing. Tightly syncopated rhythms gave swing a typically bouncy style.

Free jazz
In the 1960s, saxophonist John Coltrane (1926–67) broke away from the conventions of jazz and formed a quartet to explore new sounds and techniques. For example, he experimented with ways to achieve harmonic richness.

JOHN COLTRANE GIANT STEPS

John Coltrane

High-kicking move

Jazz dance is sometimes fast and showy.

Jazz dancer

Jazz dance
Exuberant dance styles go hand-in-hand with the rhythms and lively melodies of much jazz music, especially swing or bebop. Jazz dance moves have influenced other modern dance forms.

FIND OUT **MORE**   DANCE   MUSIC   MUSICAL INSTRUMENTS   ROCK AND POP   SLAVERY

JELLYFISH, SEA ANEMONES AND SPONGES

Translucent dome, or bell, of jellyfish

THESE PRIMITIVE ANIMALS have lived in the oceans for more than 550 million years. They are all invertebrates – animals without backbones. Jellyfish and sea anemones belong to a group of animals called the Coelenterata, which also includes corals. Most have tentacles and poison-loaded stinging cells, which they use to kill their prey. Sponges belong to a group of animals called the Porifera. They live in all waters from the ocean depths to shallow lakes. There are soft sponges, such as natural bath sponges, and hard ones with silica skeletons.

Thick tentacles

Mouth lies below center of bell.

Upside-down mangrove jellyfish

Tentacle of Portuguese man-of-war releases stinging cells.

Stinging tentacles
Jellyfish tentacles contain special cells. Each cell has a projecting hair and contains a coiled poisonous thread called a nematocyst. If an animal touches the hair, an explosive release of the nematocyst is triggered, injecting the prey with paralyzing toxins. Other types of nematocysts release sticky threads or coil around prey.

Jellyfish
Two cell layers separated by firm jellylike material make up the body of a jellyfish. The body is dome-shaped, like a delicate gelatinous umbrella, and is called a medusa. Its beauty, however, is deceptive; an array of trailing tentacles hides a battery of stinging cells that can capture and immobilize prey. The tentacles feed the prey through the mouth into the digestive cavity.

Polyps break away to form new medusae.

Polyp multiplies to form a stack of small saucer-shaped polyps.

Life cycle of a jellyfish
Common larger jellyfish produce both sperm and eggs. The eggs are fertilized in the female medusa. These turn into larvae that escape and settle on rocks. Each larva turns into a polyp that multiplies by producing a stack of smaller polyps. One by one the polyps separate into new free-swimming medusae.

Polyp of jellyfish

Movement
A jellyfish swims by lifting the sides of its bell to suck up water below. Then, by contracting the bell, water is squirted backward, pushing the jellyfish forward. If the bell stops opening and closing, the jellyfish will sink.

Jellyfish with bell contracted

Moon jellyfish

Sponge
Sponges are among the most simple multi-celled animals known. They are like vase-shaped sieves, with porous body walls, supported by a "skeleton" of hard minerals or protein fibers. Water enters the sponge through the body wall and passes out through a central opening.

Central opening

Tube sponge

Feeding
Most sponges are filter feeders. Their cells have projections that beat and draw water through their body walls. Special cells lining the walls filter out small food particles suspended in the water.

Sponge releasing sperm

Reproduction
Sponges reproduce asexually by growing and budding and sexually by producing sperm, which is carried to other sponges on water currents to fertilize their eggs. The eggs become larvae, settle on rocks, and grow into new sponges.

Sea anemone
Sea anemones have soft bodies consisting of a stout, muscular column ending in a basal disk. The disk produces a sticky cementlike substance that secures the anemone to the seabed or rock. Stinging tentacles form a circle around a central mouth that opens into the digestive cavity. The sea anemone uses its tentacles for defense and to catch prey. Although often beautiful in color and shape, some anemones are aggressive predators and even cannibals. They escape attack by floating, burrowing, or rising from the seabed.

Basal disk

Tentacles have trapped a fish.

Strawberry anemone

Body column

Feeding
Sea anemone tentacles are armed with stinging cells that fire on contact to paralyze prey. Even small fish are caught and pushed through the mouth into the stomach. Inside, enveloped by sheets of tissue that release enzymes, the flesh of the prey is broken down and digested by cells lining the stomach.

Tentacles have pulled fish inside to be eaten.

Symbiosis
Sea anemones have a range of mutually beneficial, or symbiotic, relationships with other animals. Clown fish are covered in mucus for protection from the tentacles of anemones in which they hide. The anemones in turn, are protected by the fish. Cloak anemones hitch a ride on the back of a shell occupied by a hermit crab. The anemone protects the crab in exchange for food.

Clown fish hiding in tentacles of a sea anemone.

MANGROVE JELLYFISH

SCIENTIFIC NAME	*Cassiopeia sp.*
PHYLUM	Coelenterata
CLASS	Scyphozoa
ORDER	Rhizostomeae
DISTRIBUTION	Marine Caribbean
HABITAT	Shallow, tropical mangrove bays
DIET	Small organisms
SIZE	Length: up to 12 in (30 cm)
LIFESPAN	Several years

FIND OUT MORE | ANIMALS | CORAL REEFS | FISH | MARSH AND SWAMP WILDLIFE | OCEAN WILDLIFE | POISONOUS ANIMALS | SEASHORE WILDLIFE

JESUS CHRIST

J

IN ABOUT AD 30, a young Jewish man began to preach in Palestine that he was the son of God, the Messiah, or anointed one, that Jewish writings had described. Many people accepted his message and his following grew rapidly. The Jewish authorities resented his work, and he was arrested and crucified by the Roman governor of Palestine in about AD 33. Within a century, his message had spread throughout Asia Minor and into Europe, becoming tolerated throughout the Roman Empire in 313. Today, Christianity, the religion that grew from his teachings, is one of the world's great religious faiths.

Early life
Jesus was born in Bethlehem in what is now the Israeli-occupied West Bank. He trained as a carpenter. The Bible says that his mother, Mary, was a virgin when she gave birth. In his early 30s, he gave up work and devoted his time to preaching and healing.

Five loaves and two fish were all that Jesus had to feed the five thousand.

Parables
In order to get his message understood, Jesus often used parables, or stories with a meaning. One of the most famous was the parable of the sower, in which Jesus compared his words to the seeds cast by a man sowing corn. Some seed falls on stony ground and withers away; some falls on good soil, where it flourishes.

Seed was sowed by throwing it onto the land.

Sower's bag and seed

Jesus's work

For three years, Jesus preached his message in Palestine. He gathered 12 local men to support him; they became known as the Apostles, from a Greek word meaning a person sent, or chosen. Jesus declared the need for people to repent of their sins and to believe and follow him. Within three years, his preaching, and his ability to heal the sick, brought him a considerable following throughout Palestine. His wider group of followers became known as disciples.

Apostles
The 12 apostles of Jesus were local men who worked ordinary jobs, such as fishing and farming.

Miracles
According to the Bible, Jesus used miracles to prove that he could conquer adversity and suffering. On one famous occasion, he is said to have provided enough food for a gathering of 5,000 people, although only a few loaves of bread and two fish were available.

John the Baptist
At the time of Jesus's birth, many Jews, including John the Baptist, Jesus's cousin, were expecting the coming of the Messiah. John prepared the way for Jesus, prophesying his coming and baptizing him in the Jordan River.

Sermon on the Mount
Throughout his ministry, Jesus preached sermons to his disciples and the many people who followed him. The most famous was the Sermon on the Mount, in which Jesus summed up the main beliefs of the Christian religion and told his followers how people should lead their lives.

Mary Magdalene
Mary was one of the most ardent of Jesus's followers. Jesus cured her of "demons" (probably a physical illness), and she accompanied him and helped him in Galilee. Mary witnessed Christ's crucifixion and burial. Three days later, he appeared to Mary, and told her that he was ascending to heaven.

Death

After three years preaching, Jesus was arrested by the Roman authorities who governed Palestine at that time. He was tried by the Roman governor Pontius Pilate, tortured, and crucified.

Last Supper
Just before he was arrested, Jesus ate supper with his disciples. He broke bread and drank wine with them, asking them to remember him and to continue his work. Christians still celebrate the Last Supper in the ceremony of the Mass, or Eucharist, when they share bread and wine, believing it to represent Jesus's body and blood.

Crucifixion
Jesus was put to death by crucifixion – being nailed to a wooden cross – a common form of punishment in the Roman Empire. His followers believe that three days later he rose from the dead.

JESUS CHRIST

c.4 BC Born to poor parents in Bethlehem.

c.AD 30 Begins ministry, preaching and healing the sick.

33 Arrested, tried, and crucified by Roman authorities in Jerusalem.

33 St. Paul and other followers of Jesus begin to spread the Christian message; Christians are persecuted in the Roman Empire.

65–75 St. Mark writes his Gospel, the earliest surviving record of the life of Jesus.

313 Christianity receives official tolerance in the Roman Empire.

 FIND OUT MORE   CHRISTIANITY   CHURCHES AND CATHEDRALS   MONASTERIES   RELIGIONS   ROMAN EMPIRE

JOHNSON, AMY

ONE OF THE GREAT pioneers of aviation, Amy Johnson showed that women could succeed in a man's world. When she learned to fly in June 1929, Amy Johnson became one of the world's first women pilots. Her flying instructor said she would only be taken seriously as a pilot if she did something remarkable, like fly to Australia. And so, in April 1930, she took off on a 19-day flight halfway around the world. In spite of bad weather, breakdowns, and crash landings, she arrived in Australia. She also landed in the record books: for this and other flights she is remembered as one of the great aviators.

Early life
Amy Johnson was born in 1903 in the English port of Hull, where her parents worked in the fishing industry. She went to college and then took a secretarial course. But she did not want any of the office jobs that were open to women in the 1920s.

Learning to fly
Johnson overcame a great deal of prejudice to learn to fly. Flying was a male occupation and there were few flying clubs that accepted women. But she persevered, and first flew solo in June 1929. At the end of the year, she had gained an aeronautical engineer's license.

Flight to Australia
Amy Johnson covered the 9,950 miles from London to Australia in 19 days, landing in Darwin on April 24, 1930. On the way she coped with jungle landings, sandstorms, and damage to the aircraft.

Equipment
As a solo pilot, Johnson had to take equipment to cover every eventuality. She took a flying suit and helmet, but wore khaki shorts for most of the flight. To defend herself, she took a gun. Her first aid kit doubled as a repair kit for the aircraft.

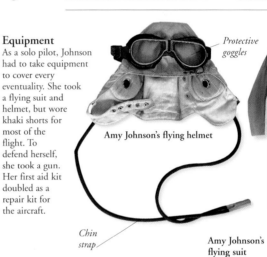

Protective goggles

Amy Johnson's flying helmet

Chin strap

Amy Johnson's flying suit

The route
Johnson's plan was to avoid flying over open sea where her chances of survival would be much less if she crashed. She therefore flew southeast over mainland Europe and Asia before turning south to fly down the Malay Peninsula and hop from island to island along Indonesia. The final stretch of the flight was the most hazardous, because it involved flying across the exposed Timor Sea.

Gypsy Moth
The airplane Johnson chose for her flight was a secondhand Gypsy Moth, one of the most popular small aircraft of the day. She had it fitted with extra-large fuel tanks for long-distance flying. Its canvas wings got damaged en route and she mended them with tape.

Overnight bag containing first aid and repair equipment

Landing at Darwin
When Johnson took off from London's Croydon Airport she was unknown. As her flight progressed, newspapers and radio began to report on her epic flight. By the time she climbed down from her plane in Darwin, she was an international heroine.

Later life
The great flight made Amy Johnson world famous. The British *Daily Mail* newspaper gave her $16,000 to go on a publicity tour, and she made many speeches and media appearances around the world. Songs were written about her and her amazing flight. However, Johnson found all this publicity very strenuous and suffered a nervous breakdown as a result.

Marriage
Johnson married a fellow pilot, James Mollison, and this seemed an ideal match. They made several long-distance flights together. But the couple were not suited. Their marriage soon broke up and Johnson went back to her solo flying career.

Disappearance
In 1940, Amy Johnson began to work flying planes from factories in Scotland to air force bases in the south of England. In January 1941, a plane she was piloting from Prestwick, near Glasgow, crashed into the Thames Estuary. Her body was never found.

AMY JOHNSON

1903 Born in Hull, England.

1929 Learns to fly at the London Airplane Club; makes first solo flight and gains engineer's license.

1930 First woman to fly solo from England to Australia.

1933 Flies east to west across the Atlantic with James Mollison.

1936 Sets new record on return flight from Cape Town to London.

1940 Joins war effort, piloting planes from factories to air force bases.

1941 Dies when plane crashes in Thames Estuary.

FIND OUT MORE   AIRCRAFT   AIRPORTS   EXPLORATION   FLIGHT, HISTORY OF   WOMEN'S MOVEMENT   WORLD WAR II

JUDAISM

THE FIRST OF THE GREAT world religions to teach belief in one God, Judaism emerged in about the 13th century BC. Its followers are called Jews. At the core of Judaism is the Torah, the sacred text that God, or Yahweh, revealed to the prophet Moses and the ancient Israelites. Because they were chosen to receive this revelation, the Jews look upon themselves as God's chosen people, with the responsibility of bringing God's message to the rest of humanity. Jews also look forward to the time when God will send his Messiah, who will usher in an age when all Jews will be united in Israel and God's rule on Earth will begin.

Origins

The ancient leaders Abraham, Isaac, and Jacob were the first to worship one true God and are the founding fathers of Judaism. The Bible tells how their descendants, the Israelites, were conquered by the Egyptians and made to work as slaves in Egypt. Moses led the Israelites to freedom and received the Torah, or written law, from God.

The Ten Commandments
On Mount Sinai, God gave Moses the Ten Commandments. This event is celebrated today in the festival of Shavuot when the story of Moses is read in the synagogue. Jews stay up at night reading the Torah to show they are ready to receive the word of God again.

Jews around the world

Today there are some 14.5 million Jews worldwide. Most are descended from one of two main ethnic groups. Ashkenazi Jews have their origin in central and eastern Europe. Their traditional language is Yiddish. The majority of Jews in the US are Ashkenazi Jews. The other group is the Sefardi Jews, who came originally from Spain and Portugal.

Jerusalem, the capital of Israel, was the center of the ancient Jewish kingdom.

Shading shows worldwide distribution of Jews. Judaism is the sixth largest world religion.

Israel
The Jews have a long history of living in many different countries and suffering persecution. In 1948, the modern state of Israel was established as a permanent homeland. Supporters of Israel, who are known as Zionists, hoped that Jews would be able to live and worship there peacefully.

Branches of Judaism
Orthodox Jews follow closely the traditional Jewish way of life. They include groups such as Hasidic Jews (above), who wear traditional clothes and study only religious subjects. Non-Orthodox, or Reform Jews, have become part of wider society and adopted Western dress while still observing Jewish law.

Sacred texts

The Jewish Bible is called the Tenakh. It contains 24 books, written by different authors, that were collected in the 10th century. The first five books make up the Torah. There are also books of the Prophets and texts such as the Psalms and the Proverbs. A body of writing containing teachings, commentaries on the Bible, and learned debates is called the Talmud.

The ark of the covenant
The Torah scrolls are kept in the ark of the covenant. This ark is a cabinet covered by a curtain in the synagogue wall that faces toward Jerusalem. The original ark of the covenant held the Ten Commandments while the people of Israel journeyed from Egypt to the Promised Land.

Embroidered mantle

The crown symbolizes the Torah as the crowning glory of Jewish life.

A ribbon binds the scrolls.

Handles support the Torah scroll because it is too sacred to touch.

The lion is a symbol of the tribe of Judah.

The scrolls of the Torah

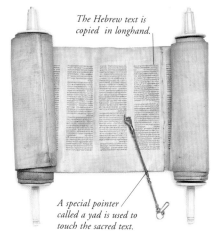

The Hebrew text is copied in longhand.

A special pointer called a yad is used to touch the sacred text.

The Torah
This collection of books is at the core of Judaism. It contains a series of 613 commandments that are God's instructions to the people of Israel. For religious Jews, these instructions are binding. The Torah scrolls are kept covered by an embroidered mantle or in a sturdy container.

Guidance of God
In the Torah, God has revealed teaching about himself, his purposes, and how he wishes his people to obey him in every part of their lives. An important part of worship is reading the Torah aloud in the synagogue. At Simchat Torah, the yearly cycle of readings from the Torah comes to an end and begins again.

Holy days and festivals

The Jewish year begins in the fall with the New Year Festival of Rosh Hashanah. Ten days later comes the Day of Atonement, or Yom Kippur. This is the holiest day in the Jewish calendar; Jews spend it praying, fasting, and seeking God's forgiveness. Other festivals occur during the year. Many commemorate events in Jewish history, such as the Israelites' escape from Egypt, the giving of the Ten Commandments to Moses, and the destruction of the first and second temples in Jerusalem.

Pesach

The spring festival of Passover, or Pesach, commemorates the time when the Jews left their captivity in Egypt and returned to Israel. Jews believe that God punished the Egyptians by killing their firstborn sons, but he passed over the houses of the Israelites. This gives its name to Passover; on that day Jews eat a ritual meal called the Seder.

Lettuce for the food eaten in slavery.

Egg symbolizes new life.

Seder plate

Herbs represent spring.

A decorated cloth covers the matzah.

Bitter horseradish represents the misery of slavery.

Shankbone of lamb recalls lambs killed at the first Passover.

"Pesach" is the Hebrew word for Passover.

Nut and fruit paste

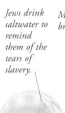

Jews drink saltwater to remind them of the tears of slavery.

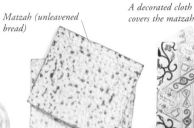

Matzah (unleavened bread)

Sukkot

The harvest festival of Sukkot commemorates the way God provided for the Jews as they wandered in the wilderness on their way to the Promised Land. Jews weave palm leaves into a lulav and may build festive huts to symbolize the tents that gave them shelter. Work is restricted and the festival ends with a time of joy called Rejoicing of the Torah, or Simchat Torah.

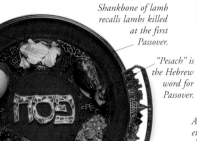

Lulav made of woven palm leaves

At Sukkot, a lulav and an etrog are carried around the temple seven times.

A citrus fruit called an etrog is a symbol of the heart.

Hanukkah

The festival of lights, Hanukkah is an eight-day long midwinter festival that is marked by the lighting of candles. It celebrates the dedication of the temple of Jerusalem after it was recaptured from an enemy army in 164 BC. Like several other festivals in the Jewish religious year, Hanukkah reminds Jews of God's faithfulness to his people in the past.

Daily life

The home and the family are important in Judaism, and there are many rules to guide behavior. For Orthodox Jews in particular, these rules affect every aspect of daily life, from getting up in the morning when the hands are ritually washed, to going to bed at night, when prayers are said. Other rules concern food and dress.

Menorah, nine-branched candlestick

On Friday, after sunset, the woman of the household lights the Sabbath candles.

Kosher food

Jews must eat food that is kosher, or fit to eat. Animals that do not have cloven hoofs and chew the cud are forbidden, as are birds of prey and sea creatures without fins and scales. Animals that Jews eat must be slaughtered according to specific rules.

Sabbath

The weekly day of rest – from dusk on Friday to after dark on Saturday – commemorates the way God rested after the creation. On the Sabbath, Jews dress in their best clothes, and do not cook, work, or use transportation. They light the Sabbath candles and walk to the synagogue.

Worship

The synagogue is the place for community prayers, readings from the Torah, and learning about the faith. On weekdays there are three prayers for morning, afternoon, and evening; on the Sabbath and on festivals there are longer services. When a Jewish boy reaches 13, a ceremony in the synagogue called Bar Mitzvah marks his coming of age.

Jewish men wear skull caps at prayer.

A tefillin contains prayers.

Rabbi

Rabbis were originally teachers and they devoted themselves to studying the Torah. Today, rabbis play a leading role in worship and take spiritual care of their community, like the leaders of other religious faiths.

Anti-semitism

For centuries, the Jews existed without their own state and were often treated as second-class citizens. In some cities, Jews were forced to live in cramped areas known as ghettos. Pogroms – organized campaigns of persecution or killing – have marked Jewish history. The worst example is the Holocaust.

A mob assaults a Jew in front of soldiers in Russia, 1881.

FIND OUT MORE

EUROPE, HISTORY OF   FESTIVALS   HOLOCAUST   HOLY LAND, HISTORY OF   ISRAEL   JESUS CHRIST   RELIGIONS   WORLD WAR II

KANGAROOS AND OTHER MARSUPIALS

IN AUSTRALIA, NEW GUINEA, and the Americas, there is a group of mammals that is not found anywhere else in the world. These are the 266 species of marsupials, or pouched mammals. Marsupials include the familiar kangaroos and koala, as well as numbats, bandicoots, wombats, possums, and wallabies from Australia, and the American opossums. In contrast to other mammals, marsupial young undergo little development in their mother's uterus before being born. Instead, female marsupials have a marsupium, or pouch, into which the young crawl and complete their development.

Ears swivel to hear sounds in all directions.

Strong tail aids balance when leaping and standing.

Reproduction

Marsupials differ from other mammals in the way they reproduce. After a male and female mate, the fertilized egg develops in the female's uterus for about 30 days. The young is then born, but is tiny at birth; for example, a red kangaroo weighing about 60 lb (27 kg) gives birth to a single young weighing just 0.03 oz (800 mg). The newborn has a mouth and well-developed forelimbs, but is otherwise like an embryo. It continues to develop in its mother's pouch for 6–11 months, feeding on her milk.

Claws

Red kangaroo

Red kangaroo

The red kangaroo is the largest of all marsupials. Males are reddish-brown in color, and may be twice the size of females, which are bluish-gray. They have powerful back legs and long feet adapted for hopping. Like many other marsupials, red kangaroos are largely nocturnal, resting by day under shady trees, but they are also active on cooler winter days. They graze mainly on grass, but also feed on the foliage of shrubs by leaning forward on their forelimbs and balancing on their tail.

Mob of eastern gray kangaroos feeding

Mobs
Red and gray kangaroos and wallabies live in groups called mobs. A mob is a social grouping of 10 or more individuals, including a mature male, a few younger males, females, and their young. Sometimes, a larger mob containing hundreds of kangaroos may form at a good feeding site.

Boxing
Within a mob a male kangaroo may gain control over one or more females so he can mate with them. Sometimes other males challenge for access to these females. The competing males stand upright on their hind legs and link forearms in an attempt to push each other to the ground. If this does not resolve the battle for supremacy, they box, hitting each other violently with their forepaws, and kicking out with their hind feet, until one of them submits.

Thick stomach skin prevents excessive damage during boxing.

Females can be pregnant, with a joey in the pouch and one out, at the same time.

Eastern gray kangaroo with joey

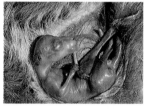

Life cycle of a kangaroo
1 After birth, the blind, naked kangaroo struggles through the fur on its mother's abdomen to reach her pouch and attach itself to her teat.

2 The baby kangaroo, or joey, is now about five months old. No longer attached to the teat, the joey can stick its head out of the pouch, but still depends on its mother for milk.

3 After a year, the joey leaves the pouch and feeds mainly on vegetation. It still occasionally sticks its head in the pouch to suckle, and some joeys return to the pouch if threatened.

Leaps and bounds
Kangaroos and small wallabies move in a distinctive manner, using their powerful hind legs and large feet like springs to hop from one feeding area to another. The long tail helps them balance. A kangaroo covers 3–6 ft (1–2 m) with each leap when moving slowly; this increases to 30 ft (9 m) when traveling at high speed. Because kangaroos cannot move their back legs separately, they are unable to walk.

Kangaroos may travel at speeds of up 31 mph (50 kmh) when leaping.

Kangaroo pushes off ground with large back feet.

Tail is raised to act as a counterbalance when leaping.

Back legs are extended forward, ready to touch down.

Eastern gray kangaroo hopping

Doria's tree kangaroo

Curved claws

Tree kangaroo
Close relatives of kangaroos and wallabies, tree kangaroos live in the tropical forests of NE Australia and New Guinea. They have long, strong forelegs, shortened hind feet, and a long tail. They are good climbers, using their claws to grip and tail to balance. They feed on leaves and fruit, and can travel rapidly from tree to tree in search of food.

K

Tasmanian devils

The largest carnivorous marsupial, the Tasmanian devil resembles a stocky terrier-sized dog. It is found only on the island of Tasmania, off the coast of Australia. It was probably given the name "devil" because of the eerie whine it makes. The Tasmanian devil shelters by day in wombat holes or hollow logs, coming out at night to hunt for food. It catches prey such as snakes, lizards, and small mammals, but most of its diet consists of carrion.

Keen sense of smell is used to hunt for food.

Powerful jaws and sharp teeth are used to eat meat, fur, skin, and bones.

Virginia opossum

Opossums are American marsupials that live mainly in South and Central America. The cat-sized Virginia opossum is the largest of the 75 species, and is the only one in North America. It has litters of 10 or more young, up to three times a year in warmer regions. When threatened, the Virginia opossum pretends to be dead ("playing possum") in order to avoid attack.

They forage in trees and on the ground for fruit, insects, eggs, and small vertebrates.

A prehensile tail and grasping hands and feet enable them to climb well.

Numbat

The numbat lives in the forests of western Australia; it is the only Australian marsupial fully active in the day. It feeds on ants and termites, turning over old logs in search of their nests. The numbat rips open the nest with its front legs and extracts the insects with its long, sticky tongue.

It uses its long snout and foreclaws to root around in the soil for food.

Long-nosed bandicoot

Mostly rabbit-sized or smaller, bandicoots are very active, nighttime foragers that move in a galloping fashion. Like other bandicoots, the long-nosed bandicoot uses its strong, clawed forelegs to dig for insects, other invertebrates, seeds, fungi, and plant roots in the soil. Bandicoots breed throughout the year. Females have a litter of 2–5 young, which develop in their mother's pouch for about 50 days.

Koalas

Koalas live in the tops of trees in eucalyptus woods in eastern Australia. They feed, breed, and sleep in the trees, rarely descending to the ground. They spend up to 18 hours each day resting and sleeping in the forks of trees, apparently to save energy. Koalas have an opposable thumb and toe that help them to grip tree trunks. They climb by grasping the trunk with their sharp front claws, bringing up their back legs in a series of jumps. Females have a single young that leaves its mother's pouch after seven months.

Eucalyptus leaves provide all the food and water that a koala needs, so it rarely has to drink.

Young are carried on mother's back for a few months after they leave the pouch.

Feeding

Koalas have a very specialized diet, eating the leaves of only 12 out of 100 species of eucalyptus trees. An adult koala eats about 2.5 lb (1.1 kg) of leaves each day, and can store them in its cheek pouches. Koalas are adapted to extract the most out of the leaves, which are not very nutritious, by having a very long intestine in which the leaves can be fully digested.

Common wombats

Common wombats are shy, burrowing marsupials from southeastern Australia. They emerge from their burrows at night, and travel up to 2 miles (3 km) in search of roots, grasses, and fungi. Wombats lead a solitary life except when they mate. Females give birth to a single young that stays in the pouch for six months. The pouch opens at the rear to stop it from filling with earth as the wombat burrows.

Burrows are rarely shared, but often form part of a large network.

Wombats have sharp, strong incisors for gnawing through tough vegetation.

Burrows

Wombats are rapid, powerful diggers. They use their strong front legs and large claws to dig networks of burrows up to 100 ft (30 m) in length. By resting in their burrows during the day, wombats keep cool in summer and warm in winter. They sometimes emerge to sunbathe in small hollows that they scrape out near the burrow.

RED KANGAROO

SCIENTIFIC NAME	*Macropus rufus*
ORDER	Marsupialia
FAMILY	Macropodidae
DISTRIBUTION	Throughout inland Australia, excluding the extreme north, extreme southwest, and east coast
HABITAT	Dry grassland and scrub, often near dense vegetation that can provide shelter; semidesert regions
DIET	Grasses and other short plants
SIZE	Males: height, up to 6 ft 6 in (2 m); weight 180 lb (82 kg)
LIFESPAN	12–18 years

FIND OUT MORE ANIMALS AUSTRALIAN WILDLIFE GRASSLAND WILDLIFE MAMMALS NESTS AND BURROWS NOCTURNAL ANIMALS RAIN FOREST WILDLIFE

KHMER EMPIRE

ONE OF THE MOST important civilizations in Southeast Asia, the Khmer Empire was ruled from the 9th to the 15th centuries by godlike kings. They glorified themselves and their people with magnificent building projects. Angkor, the royal capital of the Khmers, was founded in 802 by Jayavarman II. People flocked to the city from all over the region. In the 12th century, Angkor's masterpiece, Angkor Wat, was built. Shortly afterward both city and temple were destroyed by the Chams, but they were rebuilt by Jayavarman VII within 50 years.

Extent of the empire
Angkor, the capital of Khmer culture, was in present-day Cambodia. At the peak of its power, the empire stretched from the South China Sea to the Gulf of Siam (modern Thailand) and included all of what is today Cambodia, eastern Thailand, Vietnam, and Laos.

Angkor Wat was used as a royal shrine.

The five towers represent Mount Meru – the home of the Hindu gods.

Religion

Buddhist head, Angkor Thom

Most Khmer kings were Hindu, therefore many of Angkor Wat's sculptures are monuments to Hindu gods. Some of the kings were actually thought to be god-kings. The Hindu Suryavarman II believed himself to be an incarnation of the Hindu god Vishnu, while his Buddhist son, Jayavarman VII, believed himself to be a reincarnation of the Buddha.

Grassy areas were once moats.

Outer walls represented mountains at edge of the world.

Angkor Wat
Angkor Wat is the greatest Khmer temple and was the largest religious building in the world for centuries. Built of stone – a material reserved for the gods – it took about 50,000 workers just over 40 years to complete in the reign of Suryavarman II (1113–50). Legend has it that the temple was not built by humans but by the Hindu god Indra, who came to Earth to create it. Reliefs include scenes of Hindu gods, the Khmer people at war, and royal processions.

Elephants support the Khmer infantry.

Elephants
The Khmers, believing that elephants had great religious significance, captured them and trained them for war service and parades. One famous regiment included about 200,000 elephants.

Bayon
Historical events, life at court, and parades are carved around the walls of the Bayon, the last great Khmer temple built at Angkor. Suryavarman II's son, Jayavarman VII, built the Bayon in c.1200 to commemorate a resounding victory over the neighboring Cham people, who had destroyed Angkor in 1177.

Farming and foodstuffs
The Khmers' success was due to their advanced farming techniques, which allowed them to feed the large number of people who lived within the temple palaces. Engineers built networks of channels that – apart from containing fish – irrigated rice fields and fruit trees in the dry season. Harvests were abundant and the empire became the richest in Southeast Asia.

Rice

Mango

Carp

Decline
The neighboring Siamese (Thai) people attacked Angkor in 1431. This, combined with the cost of maintaining the monuments, led to the great city's decline, and Angkor was abandoned shortly afterward. Over centuries, jungle vegetation covered the temple and Angkor became known as the "Lost Capital." In 1861, it was rediscovered by French naturalist Henri Mouhot.

Temples were carved with dancers, animals, and birds.

Engraving of the central tower, Angkor Wat, 1875

Jayavarman VII
The heroic Jayavarman (1181–1219) was leader of the Khmers. After the destruction of Angkor by the Cham people, Jayavarman led a successful counterattack, and encouraged his people to rebuild Angkor. During his long life he constructed a new temple, the Bayon, to commemorate his triumphs. The massive stone faces carved on the outside walls of the temples represent Jayavarman and are also meant to resemble the Buddha. Jayavarman changed the state religion from Hinduism to Buddhism.

FIND OUT MORE   ARCHITECTURE   ASIA, HISTORY OF   BUDDHISM   HINDUISM   FARMING, HISTORY OF

KING, MARTIN LUTHER

IN THE LONG FIGHT of black Americans for equal rights, one man stands out for his great commitment to racial equality. Martin Luther King, Jr. was a Baptist Church minister whose Christian faith informed his work. He believed in nonviolent protest as a way of obtaining change, and led many sit-ins, marches, and voter registration campaigns. King was an inspired speaker, whose words gave hope to millions. His assassination in 1968 dashed many of those hopes.

Civil rights movement

Black Americans were given equal rights under the US Constitution, but were still treated as second-class citizens in many southern states. Local state laws denied black Americans the right to vote or go to integrated schools. Black and white people were segregated (kept apart) and even had to sit in different seats on buses. Black protests led to a growing civil rights movement in the 1950s and 1960s. King emerged as the charismatic leader of this movement.

Bus boycott
On December 1, 1955 Rosa Parks, a black woman, refused to give up her seat on a bus to a white man in Montgomery, Alabama and was arrested for violating the city's segregation law. Black residents, led by King and Rev. Ralph Abernathy, encouraged a boycott of the city's buses that led to their desegregation.

Sit-ins
One tactic of civil rights campaigners was to stage sit-in demonstrations in segregated restaurants and other public places. In 1960, King was arrested at a segregated lunch counter in an Atlanta department store. He was sent to prison and was released only after the intervention of the Democratic presidential candidate, John F. Kennedy.

Malcolm X
Many black people disagreed with King's aim of full integration of black and white, preferring black separatism. Their leader was Malcolm X, who was a member of the Black Muslim movement led by Elijah Muhammad. He later converted to orthodox Islam and took up the cause of racial unity. He was assassinated in February, 1965.

Freedom rides
In 1961, black and white civil rights protesters defied state segregation laws by traveling together on segregated buses. The government sent in national guardsmen to protect the riders. This led to increased racial tension and activity by the racist Ku Klux Klan, which carried flaming crosses in marches in the South.

Early life
Martin Luther King, Jr. was born in Atlanta, Georgia on January 15, 1929. King's father was a prominent Baptist minister, inspiring his son to follow him into the church to study theology. King was awarded his doctorate of theology in 1955.

Little Rock
In 1957, the governor of Arkansas refused to admit nine black children to the all-white Little Rock Central High School. President Eisenhower sent 1,000 paratroopers and 10,000 national guardsmen to protect the children as they went to school.

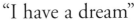

"I have a dream"
On August 28, 1963, King led the historic March on Washington to demand civil rights reform. More than 200,000 marchers heard his words: "I have a dream that one day this nation will rise up and live out the true meaning of its creed: 'We hold these truths to be self-evident, that all men are created equal.'"

Birmingham jail
King went to jail many times for his beliefs. During a period in jail in Birmingham, Alabama, in spring, 1963, he wrote an eloquent letter outlining his philosophy of nonviolent protest. He was inspired in this policy by the Indian leader Mohandas K. Gandhi's nonviolence campaign against British rule in India, the movement known as satyagraha (devotion to truth).

Assassination
The last years of King's life were marked by increasing disputes with more radical black leaders who disagreed with his nonviolent approach. In April, 1968, he visited Memphis, Tennessee to offer support to striking city sanitation workers; he was assassinated at the motel where he was staying on April 4. Protest riots broke out in most major US cities.

MARTIN LUTHER KING

1929 Born in Atlanta, Georgia.

1951 Receives Bachelor of Divinity degree.

1954 Becomes pastor of Baptist Church in Montgomery, Alabama.

1960 President of the Southern Christian Leadership Conference; sent to prison for his part in a sit-in in Atlanta.

1963 Spells out his doctrine of nonviolent protest; leads march on Washington.

1964 Awarded Nobel Peace Prize.

1968 Assassinated in Memphis, Tennessee.

FIND OUT MORE   HUMAN RIGHTS   SLAVERY   SOCIETIES, HUMAN   UNITED STATES, HISTORY OF

KINGFISHERS AND HORNBILLS

THE KINGFISHER FAMILY includes some of the world's most brightly colored birds. Many kingfishers feed on fish, but forest kingfishers, which include the kookaburra, live in dry places and eat insects, snakes, and even small birds. Kingfishers hunt by watching for small animals from a convenient perch, or by hovering over water until they see food, then diving down to catch it. Hornbills are bigger and more powerful than kingfishers. Some feed entirely in the treetops on fruit, but others spend a lot of time on the ground, feeding on anything edible they can find.

Belted kingfisher
This is one of the only two species of kingfisher that live in North America. It makes a loud rattling call often when it is flying. It breeds as far north as Alaska, and winters further south, some birds as far south as Panama.

Kingfishers

There are about 90 species of kingfishers. A few live in Europe and the Americas, but they are most common in Africa, Asia, and Australia. Kingfishers are fast fliers, and they are often seen speeding low over the water from one perch to another. All kingfishers nest in holes. Those that live near water peck burrows in riverbanks, while forest kingfishers nest in tree holes.

The kingfisher carries its prey to a perch and strikes it on a branch before swallowing it.

The kingfisher uses its wings to flap its way out of the water.

Clear membrane covers the eyes underwater.

Kookaburra
This Australian bird is the world's largest kingfisher. It is more than 16 in (40 cm) long from beak to tail. It lives in forests and scrub, and is known for its loud call, which sounds like crazy laughter.

Grooves in the face give good forward vision.

Sharp-edged beak holds slippery prey.

Water runs off the kingfisher's waterproof plumage.

Fishing
About two-thirds of kingfishers, including this common kingfisher, live near water and feed on fish and other water animals. They catch their food by diving straight in, or by hovering and then making an attack. Once they have caught something in their beak, they carry the prey to a perch or to their burrow.

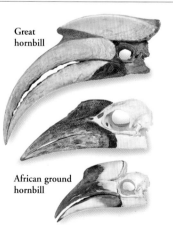

Great hornbill

African ground hornbill

White-billed pied hornbill

Hard shield, or casque, covers the top of the beak.

Trumpeter hornbill
This medium-sized hornbill lives in southern Africa. Like most other hornbills, it has a long tail, strong feet, and a patch of bare skin around its eyes. It also has a loud call that sounds like a mixture between a crying baby and a badly tuned trumpet.

Partly joined front toes

Long, rounded tail has banded feathers.

Protecting the young
Hornbills nest in tree holes and they protect their young in a remarkable way. When the female is about to lay her eggs, she enters the nest and the male makes a mud wall to seal her in. He passes food through a small hole in the wall.

Hornbill beaks
A hornbill's beak is not as heavy as it looks because it contains lots of air spaces that reduce its weight. The shield, or casque, above it is also hollow. The main function of the casque is probably as an ornament during courtship.

Hornbills

There are nearly 50 species of hornbills, and the largest are more than 4 ft (1.2m) long. These birds get their name from their huge downward-curving beaks. They live in the forests of Africa and Asia. When they fly, their wings make a loud whooshing sound.

COMMON KINGFISHER

SCIENTIFIC NAME	*Alcedo atthis*
ORDER	Coraciiformes
FAMILY	Alcedinidae
DISTRIBUTION	Europe, North Africa, Asia, and Indonesia
HABITAT	Rivers, streams, canals, and drainage ditches
DIET	Small fish
SIZE	Length: 6.5 in (16 cm)
LIFESPAN	About 5 years

FIND OUT MORE   AUSTRALIAN WILDLIFE   ANIMAL BEHAVIOR   BIRDS   NESTS AND BURROWS   SEABIRDS   WOODPECKERS AND TOUCANS

KITES

THE FIRST FLYING MACHINE was a kite, flown about 3,000 years before people took to the air. A basic kite consists of a frame and covering material. Launched and held in the air by the upward push of the wind currents on its underside, a kite is controlled from the ground. Kites have had many uses: the Chinese used them to estimate the position of the enemy in war; in 1752, American scientist Benjamin Franklin hung metal from a kite to prove the electrical nature of lightning. Today, kite flying is both a popular pastime and a competitive sport.

History of kite flying

The Chinese were flying kites long before the first recorded reference to a wooden bird kite, in 500 BC. Gradually kites became popular in other Asian countries, such as India, where often they had religious significance. By the time kite flying spread to medieval Europe, the Chinese were building kites big enough to carry people into the air.

An 18th-century Indian painting of kite flying

Types of kites

There are several basic kite shapes, but for each shape there are hundreds of different designs. Most kites can be made cheaply from sticks and paper. Some need a tail to help them fly in a stable position, but tails, ribbons, and color are used mostly for decoration.

Flat kites
Simple flat kites are the oldest design. They are made from a framework of thin sticks tied together, covered with paper or fabric.

Box kites
Made of a frame containing squares or triangles of paper or fabric, box kites are stable fliers. They have been used to carry weather forecasting instruments.

Delta kites
The wings of a delta kite are supported by spars or rods. The wing span makes it fast and easy to maneuver, ideal for stunt or fighter kites.

Airfoil kites
Made of fabric, an airfoil kite is inflated by the wind. Wing-shaped inflatable kites have a different name – parafoils.

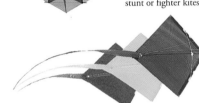

Stunt kites
Stunt kites are used for displays. They can be flown singly or stacked together to create a spectacular kite train.

Making kites

Kites can be simple structures made from paper and sticks. They are frequently more complex, made from silk or other light materials. Bright, colorful designs are often used to adorn kites.

How to fly a kite

Before launching a kite, find an open space where there is a strong breeze, such as a gently sloping hill where the wind blows upward. Avoid buildings and trees (which block the wind), roads, and electrical poles and wires. Launch the kite as shown here.

The diamond-shaped Malay kite has an angled surface to help it stay on a stable course.

Kite may fall as it gets near ground.

Equipment

In addition to the actual kite, you need a flying line and a reel to store it on. Flying lines must be strong enough to hold the kite, but light enough to let it fly, such as nylon fishing line. Reels can be simple, or handle-shaped to make them easier to hold. Stunt kites require strong hand grips.

Kite festivals

In many Asian countries kite festivals are popular. There is also a serious competitive sport in which fighting kites compete for air space.

Reels

Hand grips

Handles

Hold kite at arm's length.

1 Hold the kite in one hand and the reel of line in the other, with your back to the wind.

In light winds, give gentle tugs on the line.

Twist reel to let line out.

2 As the kite catches the wind, release it. Gradually allow more line out to let the kite rise.

Hold reel sideways to pay out line quickly.

3 If the kite veers left or right, let out more line to stabilize it. Add a tail to balance an unstable kite.

Pull in line with free hand.

Keep reel upright.

4 Retrieve the kite by winding in the line. In stronger winds, walk toward the kite.

FIND OUT MORE | AIR | ELECTRICITY | FESTIVALS | FLIGHT, ANIMAL | FLIGHT, HISTORY OF | FRANKLIN, BENJAMIN | WINDS

Kites

Traditional kites

Thai Pakpo is made from paper and bamboo.

Chinese centipede is a traditional Chinese kite, consisting of circular kites joined together in a train led by a dragon's head.

Japanese Edo has a classic Japanese design.

Simple kites

Parrot's wings bow and the tail flexes.

Della Porta is rectangular with a long loop tail for stability.

Cat is a variation on the hexagonal-shaped kite.

Box kites

Classic box kite is made up of two square cells.

Professor Waldorf is an early multicellular kite.

Nova lacks the stability of a two-celled box, but handles well.

Star is a two-celled structure supported by three spars.

Single-celled kite

Tri-star has two triangular sections.

Fighters and stunt kites

Grandmaster is a modern version of the traditional Indian fighter.

Tukkal is an Indian fighter made from paper and bamboo.

Hawaiian team kite is a delta-winged stunter.

Bamboo spine held in place by gold foil

Skynasaur aerobat flies in a range of winds without turning fast.

Traditional Indian fighter has appliqued colored tissue paper.

Flexifoil uses the wind to give it shape during flight.

KNIGHTS AND HERALDRY

Prick or goad

Miniature spur

KNIGHTS WERE WARRIORS ON HORSEBACK in medieval Europe. In wartime from the 11th to the 15th century, they were the foundation of any ruler's army, and in peace they helped keep local order. During the Middle Ages knights rose in status and wealth to form part of a European ruling class. Each knight was expected to lead an ethical life and to obey the Code of Chivalry. Knights developed a great sense of their own importance, which was reflected in an obsession with heraldry — the formation of distinguishing coats-of-arms. After 1500, the introduction of new weapons, such as the cannon, and new military methods diminished the knights' importance.

Iron stirrup

Specialized warriors

Rulers paid knights for their services with valuable gifts of land. The people on the land worked for the knights in return for protection. The first knights were sometimes men of humble origin, but in time they became a group of warrior-governors.

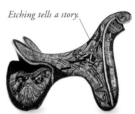

Etching tells a story.

Horseback advances
Spurs helped mounted knights control their horses in battle. Stirrups and high-backed saddles – used to help knights stay mounted – also came into use between the 8th and 11th centuries. During this period, the knights' importance increased.

Wooden etched saddle

Code of Chivalry

Medieval knights followed the ideals of the Code of Chivalry and demonstrated prowess (bravery, strength, and skill), largesse (generosity), loyalty, piety, and courtesy. This code attempted to civilize what was really a primitive activity – war.

Christian knight
Churchmen encouraged new knights to fight non-Christians, but never to harm Church property or unarmed people.

Courtly love
Minstrels' tales, or romances, helped shape the Code of Chivalry, and many knights believed that romantic love inspired great deeds – as in the French *Roman de la Rose*, and the many stories about Britain's King Arthur.

Scene from *Roman de la Rose*, 1487

Knights
The knight's prime duty was to fight. After 1300, his armor became increasingly elaborate, expensive – and heavy. A suit could weigh as much as 55 lb (25 kgs) and fit snugly. One medieval poet called the knight "a terrible worm in an iron cocoon."

Falling plates allowed more air to reach the face.

Lance rest

Small plates on gauntlet gave freedom of movement to the hand.

Plates above and below the knee allowed movement without exposing the hose beneath.

The sole was left exposed so shoe did not skid.

Tournaments

Originally, knights used mock battles to train. These training sessions turned into a dazzling medieval spectator sport – the tournament – with teams of opposing knights. Single combat between champions was called jousting and was fought using various weapons. Victory often resulted in fame and riches.

Tournament, 15th century

Heraldry

Tournament crowds identified their heroes by their coat-of-arms, a personal combination of patterns (devices) displayed on surcoats, shields, and horse draperies. In live battle, the coat-of-arms helped knights tell friend from foe and enabled the official observers, known as heralds, to record any great feats.

Art of blazonry
From around 1140, heralds were experts in blazonry (the recording and regulating the devices used in coats of arms). One rule in blazonry is that where there are two coats of arms, they can be "quartered". From 1250, French and English heralds kept records, called rolls. The rolls are used to check the family history.

Jar with two coats-of-arms, quartered

Squires
Squires were young men who served a kind of apprenticeship to become knights. The word comes from the French *escuyer*, meaning "shield-carrier". A squire might enter a knight's service at 14, where he would learn arts of combat and chivalry, and become a knight at around 21. As a "knight bachelor", he would look for a heiress to marry, to finance his career in arms.

Pel

Squire at the pel, or practice post

FIND OUT MORE — ARMS AND ARMOR • EUROPE, HISTORY OF • MEDIEVAL EUROPE • NORMANS • SAMURAI AND SHOGUNS • WARFARE

Heraldry collection

Personal

Pope Sixtus V's coat of arms, Rome

Arm badge worn by the servant of a knight, François de Lorraine

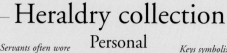

Servants often wore a livery badge.

Keys symbolize entrance to the Kingdom of Heaven.

Pope Urban VIII's coat of arms, St. Peter's, Rome

Stemmata belonged to important citizens.

Stemmata, or stone-carved coats of arms, are often seen on public buildings in Tuscany, Italy.

Crown indicates a royal person.

Arms of Maximillian I (r.1493–1519) of Austria

Coat of arms of the Medici family, art patrons, Florence

Pope Pius II's coat of arms, Tuscany, Italy

Pope Clement X's coat of arms, Rome

Organizations

Crest

Supporters are heraldic animals.

Metropolitan Police Force, London, UK

Scales of justice

Magistrates' Association coat of arms, UK

RATIONE ET CONSILIO

Shield, or escutcheon, is the most important part of any coat of arms.

NATION SHALL **SPEAK PEACE** **UNTO NATION**

British Broadcasting Company coat of arms, UK

Motto

RESPICE MISERICORDIAM

Royal Society for the Prevention of Cruelty to Animals coat of arms, UK

Crest is the sun.

Supporters are hawks.

Worshipful Company of Spectacle (eyeglass) Makers, England, 1629

Geographical

Swedish "lesser" coat of arms is not as ornate as the "greater" coat of arms, but it is still used as the symbol of Sweden's royal family.

Spanish dish showing arms of Castile and Léon

Bohemia

Moldova

Silesia

PRAVDA VITEZI

Coat of arms of the modern Czech Republic

The inscription reads "truth victorious."

FLUCTUAT NEC MERGITUR

Symbol of the city of Paris

One of the 17 *contrada* **(district) symbols,** Siena, Italy

Shields and weapons often featured arms. This 15th-century wooden shield has the city of Prague arms on it.

KOREA, SOUTH AND NORTH

SOUTH AND NORTH KOREA together form a peninsula between the Yellow Sea and the Sea of Japan in East Asia. They were one single country until 1948, when South Korea separated from communist North Korea. In 1950, North Korea invaded the south, leading to the Korean War, which devastated South Korea's economy. In the following years, however, South Korea bounced back. In 2000, leaders from the two nations met for the first time since 1953.

SOUTH KOREA FACTS

CAPITAL CITY	Seoul
AREA	38,232 sq miles (99,020 sq km)
POPULATION	46,800,000
MAIN LANGUAGE	Korean
MAJOR RELIGIONS	Buddhist, Christian
CURRENCY	South Korean won
LIFE EXPECTANCY	75 years
PEOPLE PER DOCTOR	769
GOVERNMENT	Multiparty democracy
ADULT LITERACY	98%

South Korea

At the southern tip of the Korean peninsula, South Korea is one of the most successful of the Pacific Rim "tiger" economies. The country has strong trade links with Japan, the US, and, more recently, China.

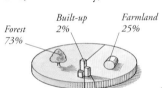

Forest 73% | **Built-up 2%** | **Farmland 25%**

Land use
Most of South Korea's farmland lies in the west and south and is under permanent cultivation. There is only a small amount of pasture land, mainly on mountain slopes.

People
More than 99 percent of the people are Koreans whose ancestors settled in Korea thousands of years ago. Family life is central to Korean society. Women play a traditional role, and it is not respectable for married women to work.

1,228 per sq mile (474 per sq km)

80% Urban 20% Rural

Economy
Once a mainly rural society, South Korea has become highly industrialized since the Korean War, due to a reconstruction program. The country is one of the world's leading shipbuilders and it is a major producer of cars and electronics.

Seoul
South Korea's capital since 1394, Seoul was devastated during the war, but has been rebuilt and expanded. It is now home to 11,100,000 people – nearly one-quarter of the total population. The 1988 Olympic Games were held in Seoul.

Seoul's public transport all runs to one timetable.

Forest in Soraksan National Park

Forests
More than two-thirds of South Korea is covered in thick, temperate forest, much of which cloaks the mountain slopes in the east and south. The stunning scenery and blaze of fall color attract many tourists to the country's national parks.

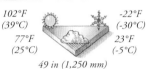

Mountains
Two ranges of mountains dominate South Korea. The T'aebaek-Sanmaek range runs down the east coast, while the Sobaek-Sanmaek lies in the south.

T'aebaek-Sanmaek Mountains

102°F (39°C) | -22°F (-30°C)
77°F (25°C) | 23°F (-5°C)
49 in (1,250 mm)

Climate
Seasons are distinct. Winters are very cold and dry while summers are humid with heavy rains. The island of Cheju has a warm climate.

North Korea

Communist North Korea is isolated from the outside world, both politically and financially. North Korea has rich mineral resources, but lacks the money to exploit them. The economy is currently weak, leading to food shortages.

Collective farming
Agriculture is carried out mainly by collective farms, each run by about 300 families. Floods wrecked harvests between 1995 and 1996.

NORTH KOREA FACTS

CAPITAL CITY	Pyongyang
AREA	46,450 sq miles (120,540 sq km)
POPULATION	24,307,000
MAIN LANGUAGE	Korean
MAJOR RELIGIONS	Traditional beliefs, Ch'ondogyo
CURRENCY	North Korean won

FIND OUT MORE ASIA, HISTORY OF CITIES FARMING FORESTS GOVERNMENTS AND POLITICS MOUNTAINS AND VALLEYS PACIFIC OCEAN SHIPS AND BOATS TRADE AND INDUSTRY

KUBLAI KHAN

KUBLAI KHAN WAS one of the most powerful emperors the world has known. As leader of the great Mongol Empire, he overthrew the powerful Song dynasty of southern China, placing China under foreign rule for the first time. Under Kublai's rule, China prospered and trade developed with Europe and the rest of Asia. By the time of his death in 1294, Kublai Khan had truly earned the title of Great Khan, the greatest of the Mongol chieftains.

Early life
Kublai Khan, the grandson of Mongol leader Genghis Khan, was born in 1215. He was educated by Confucian scholars, and established himself as a war leader when a young man. In 1248, his older brother, Mongo, became Khan. Mongo died in 1259, and a fight to succeed him broke out between Kublai and a cousin. Kublai won, and in 1260 became Great Khan.

Conquests

Kublai Khan's greatest achievement was the conquest of China. When he became Great Khan in 1260, the Mongols controlled only China north of the Yellow River. After almost two decades of warfare, Kublai conquered the Song Empire in the south, taking control of the entire country by 1279. The Mongols ruled China until they were driven out in 1368.

Xanadu •
Cambaluc (Beijing) •

Empire of Kublai Khan

Kamikaze
Kublai Khan made two unsuccessful attempts to invade Japan. The first, in 1274, was called off after a storm forced the Mongols back to port in Korea. The second, in 1281, ended in disaster when a typhoon, known to the Japanese as the kamikaze, or divine wind, destroyed the Mongol fleet.

Kublai Khan's army, Indonesian carved relief

Southeast Asia
In five separate incursions between 1257–92, Mongol forces under Kublai Khan moved south from China into Burma, northern Thailand, and Annam (now northern Vietnam). An expeditionary force of the Mongol navy even visited the Indonesian island of Java in 1292–93. Although the Mongols did not actually conquer Southeast Asia, the area was under their firm control for more than a century.

Yüan dynasty

The Mongols were foreigners, but their rule was accepted by most of China. Kublai founded a new ruling dynasty – the Yüans – and encouraged trade by removing restraints on merchants, formerly subject to heavy taxation. He did much to improve the administration of the country, and built a new imperial capital at Cambaluc, now known as Beijing.

Communications
Kublai Khan encouraged economic prosperity and improved communications in his vast empire by building or improving canals, and by creating roads. He also established post offices for mail. The Mongols controlled the ancient silk route (Silk Road) between Europe and China, and enabled traders from Europe to travel safely to China.

Social changes
Kublai Khan made many changes to Chinese society. He reintroduced civic government based on merit to run the country, recruiting scholars from many different nations as his staff, but excluding Chinese. Many members of the old Chinese civil service retired. Kublai also prepared a standardized code of law, built up the Chinese education system, and developed the use of paper currency.

Early Chinese paper banknote

Covering of mats

Single oar propels boat.

Eye for boat to "see"

19th-century model of a Chinese riverboat

Marco Polo

The Venetian merchant Marco Polo (1254–1324) went to China in the 1270s. He stayed for 17 years, serving as an official in the civic government. On his return to Europe in 1295, he wrote *Travels*, giving Europeans a first glimpse of the Mongol Empire.

Arts
Arts and culture prospered under the Yüan dynasty. The writing of fiction flourished, as did the theater, where many new plays were produced. Craftsworkers made distinctive blue and white porcelain, a skill that was perfected by the potters of the Ming dynasty.

Porcelain vase with dragon motif

Xanadu
Kublai Khan built a luxurious palace at Xanadu (now called Shantou). The palace is immortalized in a poem by Samuel Coleridge.

Manuscript of Coleridge's poem, *Kubla Khan*

KUBLAI KHAN

1215 Birth of Kublai Khan.

1257 First Mongol incursion into Annam (northern Vietnam).

1260 Kublai becomes Great Khan.

1274 First attempt to invade Japan.

1275–95 Marco Polo works for Chinese government.

1279 Kublai completes conquest of Song China.

1281 Kamikaze destroys Mongol invasion fleet in Japan.

1292–93 Mongol fleet visits Java.

1294 Death of Kublai Khan.

FIND OUT MORE

ASIA, HISTORY OF   CHINA, HISTORY OF   EMPIRES   EXPLORATION   MONGOL EMPIRE   POTTERY AND CERAMICS

LAKE AND RIVER WILDLIFE

THE FRESHWATER habitats on land may be tiny in volume compared with the oceans, but the many lakes, ponds, and rivers are home to a huge variety of wildlife. Plants take root in the soft soil and provide food and shelter for many different animals: air-breathing animals that enter the water from the surroundings, and truly aquatic creatures, which spend all their time in the water. Together, they show all manner of adaptations to underwater life, including ways of making shelters and of coping with fast currents or murky conditions.

Lake contains cold, clear water from mountain streams.

L

Lakes and rivers

Along the course of a typical river, there is a variety of freshwater habitats. Different water conditions in lakes and rivers – for example, flow rate, depth, turbulence, clarity, and temperature – suit different wildlife species.

Wonder Lake near Mount McKinley, Alaska

Hippos stay in the water to keep cool in the hot African sun.

Mammals

Only a few species of mammals, such as river dolphins, spend their whole life in freshwater. Many others enter the water to feed, and some of these are excellent swimmers. The steep banks along rivers make good burrow sites for rodents such as water voles.

The otter uses its muscular tail for moving and steering through water.

Otters
Sleek-bodied river otters dive in search of fish. They propel themselves with their tails and webbed hindfeet. Otters have thick waterproof fur and can close their nostrils and ears when swimming.

Beavers
Beavers use rivers and lakes for refuge rather than feeding. They build "lodges" for themselves in the water from piles of timber that they cut from waterside bushes.

Hippopotamus
A hippopotamus typically spends the day resting in a lake or a river. It emerges at dusk to graze on the land. Weighing up to 3 tons, this heavy animal can dive and swim with ease.

Birds

Many species of birds are closely associated with lakes and rivers. Some are able to dive underwater; others paddle over the surface, wade through the shallows, flit about at the water's edge, or fly close to the water to snatch fish.

Flamingos
Long legs enable flamingos to wade through the edges of lakes, sifting the water for small food items. Some African lakes are home to more than a million birds.

Grebe
Skillful swimmers, grebes paddle over the surface of lakes. In a flash they will twist and disappear, barely making a ripple as they dive to catch a fish.

The wagtail bobs its tail as it forages for insects.

Gray wagtail
The gray wagtail often nests along the banks of fast-running upland streams. It perches on rocks to snatch waterside insects.

Reptiles and amphibians

Though few species spend their entire time in water, a great many reptiles and amphibians never stray far from rivers and lakes. Turtles, crocodiles, frogs, and newts are all closely associated with water. Many snakes, lizards, and toads also readily enter rivers to feed, take shelter, or deposit their eggs.

Nile crocodile
Like the hippopotamuses, which sometimes share their habitats, Nile crocodiles lurk in the water with only their nostrils and eyes exposed. They seize unsuspecting mammals that come down to the river to drink.

Newt tadpole swims from its egg.

Tadpoles
The larvae of newts and other amphibians are fully aquatic. The tadpoles have gills for extracting oxygen from the water and large tails to help them swim.

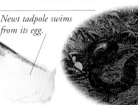

Anaconda
The most massive of all the snakes, the South American anaconda hunts its prey in rivers and pools, and snatches animals at the water's edge. It kills large prey by crushing it in its coils.

Crocodiles kill their prey by dragging it underwater and holding it there until it drowns.

Sharp teeth are replaced continuously.

Strong claws

L

Fish

Rivers and lakes all over the world are, above all, the domain of fish. Totally adapted to an aquatic life, fish have internal gills for taking in oxygen from the water, and a series of fins with which to propel themselves about. They abound in all types of freshwater habitats.

This freshwater catfish is from South America.

Catfish
These fish live at the bottom of rivers and lakes, where they avoid midstream currents but are surrounded by sediment-laden water. They probe the riverbed for food, using their long, sensitive feelers.

Cichlid
Cichlids are a large group of often colorful fish. They live mostly in tropical lakes and rivers. Unusually for fish, many look after their eggs and young (fry). Some let the fry shelter in their mouths when danger threatens.

Trout
The trout represents the typical strong-swimming freshwater fish. With its streamlined body and powerful fins, it can hold its own in the fastest river currents. It also thrives in the calm waters of lakes. Trout often rise to the surface to feed on insects.

Black spots on the trout's back help it blend in with the riverbed.

A piranha's short, broad jaws are very powerful.

Piranhas
These deep-bodied fish live in South American rivers. Some feed on plant matter, but a few, such as these red-bellied piranhas, have razor-sharp teeth for cutting flesh. Hunting in schools, they may attack and devour animals much bigger than themselves. Even these carnivorous piranhas eat meat only when their normal food of fruit and nuts is in short supply.

Invertebrates

A host of invertebrate animals inhabit lakes and rivers. Among them are insects and their larvae, shellfish, shrimps, and crayfish. A great many invertebrates simply float in the water or crawl around on the riverbed, but some have elegant adaptations which help them swim.

Water boatman
The water boatman uses its long hind legs as paddles. It spends all its life in water, swimming upsidedown in a hunt for crustaceans, tadpoles, fish fry, and the larvae of other insects.

Leeches
Leeches are parasitic, worm-like creatures. They attach themselves to fish and other animals that enter the water, and feed on their blood.

Great pond snail
Although it resembles a land snail, this plant-eating pond dweller cannot survive for long out of water. It lays jellylike eggs, often on the underside of waterlily leaves.

Plants

Without vegetation to provide food and shelter, animal life in lakes and rivers would be less diverse. Many plant species grow only in and around water, either rooted in the water-logged sediment and soil or floating on the surface.

Stiff stalks keep the flowerheads above water.

Leaves have a waxy surface, so water runs off them easily.

After flowering, each flower becomes a fruit that develops underwater.

Alder tree roots take in water.

Waterlily
Sprouting up from the bed of a pond or slow-flowing river, waterlilies unfurl their round leaves flat on the surface of the water, where they make convenient floating platforms for frogs and other wildlife. The flowers poke into the air, and attract flying insects to feed on and pollinate them.

Stalks are soft and flexible so they bend in the water.

Plants
Some plants rooted to the riverbed remain wholly underwater, their leaves, stems, and roots providing shelter for invertebrates and fish. The long, branched roots of alder trees keep the soil of riverbanks from being washed away.

Reeds
The shallow edges of lakes and rivers often have a dense green fringe of plants, such as reeds, growing out of the water. The roots of the plants are submerged, but the stems and flowers may rise more than 3 ft (1 m) into the air.

Algae
Simple plants called algae are an important source of food for the wildlife of most lakes and rivers. Floating clumps of algae can form on still or slow-flowing water.

FIND OUT MORE AMPHIBIANS BIRDS FISH INSECTS LAKES MAMMALS PLANTS RATS AND OTHER RODENTS REPTILES RIVERS

LAKES

A FIFTH OF THE WORLD'S fresh water is contained in lakes – large bodies of inland water. Some of the water that fills lakes comes from rainfall, but most lakes are fed by rivers. Lakes usually lose water through a river outlet, but some lakes, such as Great Salt Lake in Utah, lose water by evaporation, leaving the lake salty. Lakes are geologically temporary features, lasting at most a few hundred thousand years. Lake Baikal in Siberia is one of the few exceptions as it is already 25 million years old. Lakes are useful for drinking water supplies, for generating electricity, and for field irrigation.

Types of lakes

The shape of a lake usually depends on how and where it forms. The biggest lakes tend to be those created by glaciation, such as the Great Lakes of North America, or by earth movements, such as Lake Baikal, Siberia.

Artificial lakes

Artificial lakes or reservoirs are created to control a river, store water, or provide water pressure for hydroelectric power. Lake Nasser, behind the Aswan High Dam on the Nile River, is the largest in the world.

Artificial lake

Glacial erosion lakes

Glaciers scoop out U-shaped valleys and ice-eroded hollows that may be dammed by moraine (glacial deposits) when the ice retreats. Long "ribbon" lakes may fill the valley floor while small, circular lakes or tarns may fill the hollows. Ice sheets may also leave behind huge hollows that later fill with water, like the lakes of Kuopio, Finland.

Ribbon lake

Circular tarn lake

Glacial deposition lakes

Ice sheets leave behind moraines, glacial deposits that can dam smaller lakes. Glaciers may also leave behind ice or flowtill, which later melts to form little hollows; these fill with water to form lakes known as "kettles."

Glacial till lake

Volcanic lakes

Lakes may form as rainwater collects in the crater of an extinct or dormant volcano such as Crater Lake in Oregon. A lake may also form when the lava flow from a volcano dams a river, such as the Sea of Galilee in the Middle East.

Crater lake

Lava-dammed lake

Tectonic lakes

The movement of the Earth's crust can create large lakes. A downfold in the Earth's crust can create a giant basin. A rift valley (a block of land sinking between tectonic plates) can make a troughlike lake, such as Lake Nyasa in Africa. Landslides, too, can dam a river to create a lake.

Rift valley lake

Landslip lake

River and marine lakes

When a river erodes through the neck of a meander – a curve in the course of a river – and cuts it off, it may form a lake, called an oxbow lake, in the old bend. A lake may also be formed when the ocean builds up a bar of sand on the coast that dams up a lagoon.

River

Cut-off river meander

Oxbow lake

The life of a lake

A few lakes have lasted many millions of years, but most lakes last just a few thousand years. They eventually clog up with sediment dumped by rivers, or dry up as rainfall dwindles. Marshes, bogs, and swamps are often the remnants of old lakes, clogged with vegetation and silt.

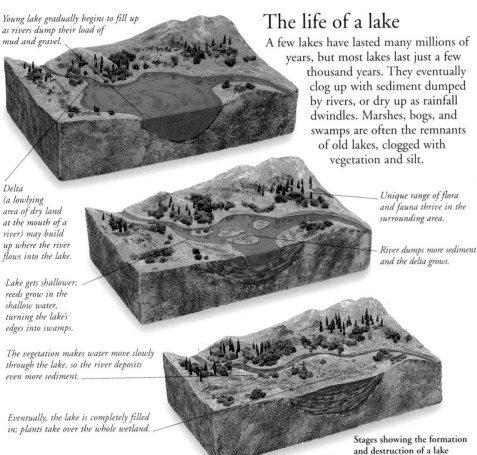

Young lake gradually begins to fill up as rivers dump their load of mud and gravel.

Delta (a lowlying area of dry land at the mouth of a river) may build up where the river flows into the lake.

Lake gets shallower; reeds grow in the shallow water, turning the lake's edges into swamps.

The vegetation makes water move slowly through the lake, so the river deposits even more sediment.

Eventually, the lake is completely filled in; plants take over the whole wetland.

Unique range of flora and fauna thrive in the surrounding area.

River dumps more sediment and the delta grows.

Stages showing the formation and destruction of a lake

The world's greatest lakes

The biggest lake in the world is so big it is called a sea – the Caspian Sea in Asia. It covers an area of 143,236 sq miles (370,980 sq km). The deepest lake is Lake Baikal in Siberia, at a depth of 1.06 miles (1.7 km).

Saltwater lakes

In dry areas, many rivers drain into enclosed lakes. The intense water evaporation under the desert sun concentrates inflowing salts, making the water salty. Such lakes as Great Salt Lake, Utah, or the Dead Sea in the Middle East, dry out into salt flats or playas.

Jerusalem

Dead Sea evaporates

FIND OUT MORE   CONTINENTS   DAMS   ELECTRICITY   FOSSILS   GLACIATION   LAKE AND RIVER WILDLIFE   OCEANS AND SEAS   RIVERS   VOLCANOES

LANGUAGES

WHETHER TALKING OR writing, we communicate with each other by using language: a system by which sounds or signs convey objects, actions, and ideas. Language is one of the things that made the growth of civilization possible. Because people could speak, they were able to pass on knowledge. Having developed over thousands of years, languages adapt constantly to reflect the changing needs of their users: new words, such as "internet," enter the vocabulary all the time, and grammar, the rules that govern the use of language, also changes.

The world's languages
There are at least 4,000 speech communities (people who speak the same language) around the world. About 90 per cent are in danger of dying out. On the North American continent alone, 100 languages have fewer than 300 speakers each.

About 750 languages are spoken in Papua New Guinea.

Families

By identifying similar words or structures that occur in different languages, we can see that many languages are related, and probably developed from the same ancestor. For instance, Russian is similar to many languages in Europe and Central Asia. People in these areas perhaps adopted the language of nomads who migrated from southern Russia 6,000 years ago. Scholars also group languages into families, by comparing the languages as they are used today.

The languages spoken in Africa reflect that it was once heavily colonized.

The major languages
Almost half the world's people speak the 10 most widespread languages. Many of these languages originated in Europe, but spread around the world as Europeans colonized other countries. For example, the Portuguese spread their language to Brazil.

Key: millions of speakers

◎	Arabic:	170m	◎ Portuguese:	160m
◎	Chinese:	1,000m	◎ Russian:	270m
◎	English:	1,400m	◻ Spanish:	280m
◎	French:	220m	◻ Hindi:	400m
			◎ Others	

Noam Chomsky

Influential US linguist Noam Chomsky (b.1928) argued that we are born with the ability to speak a language. He suggested that some very general aspects of grammar are built into every human mind, no matter what the nationality.

Speech

Nobody knows how human speech evolved from animal grunts. Although humans can make a vast range of sounds, most languages use fewer than 40. Usually, sounds are only meaningful when joined as words. Even then, a listener may not understand a word without hearing the whole sentence.

Dialects
A dialect is a variation of the pronunciation of a spoken language. Sometimes a dialect becomes a language in its own right: Spanish, Italian, and French were once all dialects of Latin.

Gypsies around the world speak a dialect that mixes a local language with Romany, the gypsy language.

Sign and body languages

There are other forms of language as well as speech and writing. Gestures can also communicate and emphasize the spoken word. Banging the table with an angry fist is a crude example; much more subtly, a conductor uses a baton to control a whole symphony orchestra.

Arms folded, a barrier to ideas

Body language
Even when we are trying hard to control what we say, our bodies may communicate our inner feelings. In this picture, the woman who has folded her arms is signaling that she does not want to hear what she is being told.

Sign languages
People who have hearing or speech difficulties may communicate with others by a variety of sign languages that use hand gestures or finger spelling.

US manual alphabet

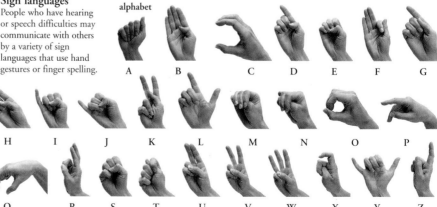

A B C D E F G
H I J K L M N O P
Q R S T U V W X Y Z

FIND OUT MORE   CODES AND CIPHERS   EDUCATION   GENETICS   SIGNS AND SYMBOLS   SOCIETIES, HUMAN   WRITING

LASERS AND HOLOGRAMS

Microchips etched by NdYAG laser

A LASER BEAM CAN CUT through steel as easily as a knife cuts through butter. A laser is a device that produces a powerful beam of light. The word "laser" stands for Light Amplification by Stimulated Emission of Radiation. All lasers produce coherent light. Coherent light is very pure, which means that all the light waves have the same wavelength, they are all "in step" with one another, and they are all traveling in exactly the same direction. Laser light can be used to create three-dimensional photographs called holograms.

Laser beam rapidly etches letters and numbers into surface of chip.

How a laser works

The heart of a laser is a material called a lasing medium. The lasing medium is given energy, usually by an electric current or by light from a device called a flash tube. The atoms of the lasing medium absorb the energy and then give it out again as waves of coherent light. The light reflects back and forth between two mirrors, becoming more and more intense, until it emerges from one of the mirrors (which is only partly reflective) as a laser beam.

Theodore Maiman

In 1953, US physicist Charles Townes (b. 1915) invented a device called a maser that produced microwaves. In 1960, his fellow US physicist Theodore Maiman (b. 1927) used the principles of Townes's device to build a laser. Maiman's laser used a ruby crystal as the lasing medium.

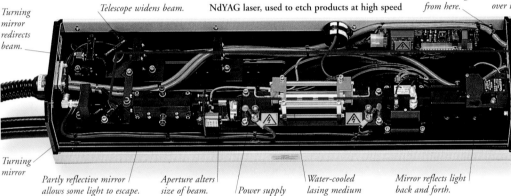

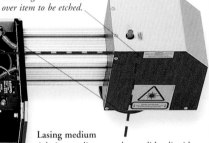

Turning mirror redirects beam.

Telescope widens beam.

NdYAG laser, used to etch products at high speed

Beam emerges from here.

Scanning head moves over item to be etched.

Turning mirror

Partly reflective mirror allows some light to escape.

Aperture alters size of beam.

Power supply

Water-cooled lasing medium

Mirror reflects light back and forth.

Lasing medium
A lasing medium may be a solid, a liquid, or a gas. This laser uses an artificial crystal containing the element neodymium (Nd).

Applications of lasers

Lasers have many uses, because they produce a powerful beam of uniform light that will not spread out over long distances and that can be directed very precisely. Lasers are used to read supermarket bar codes, play compact discs, guide weapons, and send signals along optical fibers.

Metal cutting
A powerful infrared laser beam can generate enough heat to cut through metals or to weld (join) them together by melting them.

Laser surgery
Surgeons can control lasers with great precision to burn away cancer cells or delicately trim the lens of an eye to improve a person's sight.

Light show
Laser beams always follow a straight line, so they can be used to produce stunning visual effects at rock concerts and other special events.

Holograms

Holograms are photographs that appear three-dimensional (3-D). This effect is produced by taking a photograph using two different sets of light waves from a laser beam. Holograms have many uses because they allow people to see an object from different angles.

Hologram of radar dish

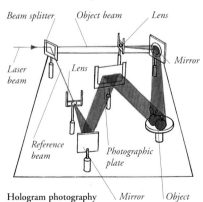

Beam splitter

Object beam

Lens

Laser beam

Lens

Mirror

Reference beam

Photographic plate

Hologram photography

Mirror

Object

Making holograms
To make a hologram, a laser beam is split into two parts, one called an object beam and the other a reference beam. Only the object beam reflects off the object that is to be photographed. Both beams strike a plate of photographic film, where they interfere (combine) and create a 3-D-looking image.

FIND OUT MORE
ELECTRONICS ENERGY LIGHT METALS PHOTOGRAPHY SOUND RECORDING WEAPONS X RAYS AND THE ELECTROMAGNETIC SPECTRUM

LAW

THE LAW can be defined as the rules and standards that administer all aspects of society. They regulate the government of the state, the relationship between the government and individuals, and the conduct of individuals toward each other. The police and the courts are usually responsible for enforcing the law. Throughout history, in different parts of the world, laws have been codified in many different ways, but the law is a fundamental element of all societies.

Lawmaker, Hammurabi

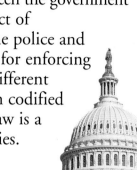

Hammurabi code
The earliest surviving law code was drawn up by Mesopotamian ruler Hammurabi (1792–1750 BC). It contains 282 laws, with headings such as Family, Labor, Personal Property, and Trade. His codes were engraved on a stone pillar.

Justice
Courts aim to administer the law according to generally accepted principles that are seen as fair and just. In US law, for example, it is accepted that a person is innocent until proven guilty, and that he or she has a right to legal representation.

Scales of Justice show that justice weighs opposing evidence.

The US Capitol is the site of the Senate and House of Representatives. The Supreme Court is nearby.

Early law

Every society's code of law has been gathered over several centuries, often incorporating many elements of law codes of earlier societies. Most Western societies have inherited legal principles from Imperial Rome. Emperor Justinian (c. 483–565) codified more than 1,000 years of Roman law. His code was written in Latin, which is still the language of law in the western world.

Legislation

In democratic societies, new laws are formulated and passed by governments. Legislation, or law-making, is a complex process. Firstly, legal advisers are responsible for drafting the wording of the law. Provisional laws are scrutinized and debated by the legislative assembly and, as a result, may be amended and altered. When they are finally accepted, they are known as statute laws.

Capitol, Washington DC, US's lawmaking center

Types of law

Many people are familiar with criminal law; famous cases are highly publicized, and courtroom dramas on film and television are very popular. However, the law deals with every aspect of life, from traffic offenses to mass murder. Governments are ruled by constitutional and international laws. The actions of individuals are regulated not only by criminal law, but also family law and civil law. Civil law embrace special areas such as taxation, property, inheritance, and medical law.

Sinking of Greenpeace's *Rainbow Warrior* by France led to legal proceedings.

International law
These laws govern the relationship between states, as well as regulating international organizations and multinational corporations. The United Nations has the power to use international law against a nation or individuals who are committing acts of aggression. International law is also used to resolve disputes between nations and international organizations.

Constitutional law
A nation's constitution is a set of political principles by which a state is governed, and constitutional law is a body of rules and practices that are laid down based on these principles. In some countries, such as Great Britain and France, the constitution is unwritten, but the United States of America has a written constitution. It was signed in 1787, at the end of the War of Independence. Its first Ten Amendments guarantee certain basic rights, for example the right of the individual to bear arms and to enjoy freedom of religion and freedom of speech. These rights are the foundation of US law.

The Declaration of Independence laid the foundation for the American constitution.

Criminal law
Criminal laws impose obligations on all members of society not to do certain things that are considered an offense against both society and an individual. Acts of violence, such as assault and murder, and crimes against a person's property, such as theft, are the most obvious examples. However, criminal law also deals with minor misdemeanors such as failure to pay parking fines, traffic offenses, and public disorder.

Suspect with crime number

Civil law
This branch of the law deals with claims by individuals that another has injured their property, person, or reputation, or failed to carry out a legal obligation (contract). These claims can range from minor disputes between neighbors to complex cases involving international corporations. Civil law also covers day to day events such as buying or selling a house.

Some people may choose to take legal advice when buying or selling a property.

Family law
Relationships between couples, parents and children, and within families are all governed by family law. The most common areas of dispute resolved by family lawyers are divorce settlements, and the question of custody of, and access to, children. Family law can also safeguard the rights of children against violent or neglectful parents.

Lawyers often consider the needs of a couple's children as a high priority in divorce cases.

L

Law and society

Every society has evolved a system of rules and regulations, but legal systems are not always the same worldwide. For example, in parts of the Islamic world the law is based on religious principles, while in some tribal societies the right to judge offenders is hereditary, passing from chief to chief. Whatever system is applied, laws are a vital tool in the regulation and ordering of society. If laws are consistently disregarded and broken, a state of chaos may result.

This British car driver obeys the law by wearing a seat belt.

Sultan Hasan Mosque, Cairo, Egypt

How law affects us

The law can affect many aspects of daily life. Refraining from violence and theft are obvious ways of avoiding breaking the law. Many routine, everyday actions, such as driving a car, also make legal demands on individuals. For example, in many countries it is a legal requirement to wear a seat belt while driving. If a person chooses to disregard these laws, he or she will be breaking the law and, if caught, be liable to prosecution.

Religious law

Some Islamic countries are governed by the Sharia ("The Path"), a system of Islamic law that was formulated in medieval times. The law code is taken directly from the teachings of the Qur'an and the prophet Muhammad. Like Western law, Sharia regulates the individual's relations with family, neighbors, and the state, and it also rules each person's relationship with Allah (God). Many Islamic countries adopted Western law codes in the 19th century, and confined the use of Sharia to family law.

Courtroom

In most cases, the application of the law involves verbal discussion and argument between trained and qualified lawyers. This normally takes place in a courtroom. English-speaking nations use the "adversarial" system in which the prosecution puts forward arguments against the accused, which are rebutted by the defense. An impartial third party – a judge, and sometimes a jury – reviews the arguments and makes a final decision as to guilt or innocence. Hearings are normally open to the public.

The judge is an official who controls the court proceedings and has the authority to hear cases in court, and pass sentences.

A clerk of the court is a legally qualified assistant to the judge, responsible for the administration of the courtroom, for legal research, and for advising the judge on points of law.

Evidence

Legal trials normally involve the examination of evidence. This may be spoken evidence given by witnesses, who are then cross-examined by lawyers. It can be written evidence, which is the most common in civil cases. In some criminal trials, the evidence might be an actual object such as a murder weapon, or scientific data, for example, blood samples.

Witness box

Judge's bench

The recorder records, and later transcribes, everything that is said in court. Recorders may use a stenograph (a machine that types in shorthand) or a tape recorder.

The jury is a body of randomly selected men and women (usually 12) chosen to attend the trial, review the evidence, and make a judgment. In the US, most people between the ages of 18 and 70 are eligible for jury duty.

The defense team represents the accused in criminal trials. They must rebut the arguments of the prosecution and defend the innocence of their client. In many courts the accused will sit with their lawyers unless called to the witness box.

The prosecution represents the State, which brings the case against the accused in criminal trials. The prosecution is responsible for proving guilt.

Law reports

Members of the public are allowed into the courtroom in most criminal trials. The family of the accused and representatives of the press are given priority.

Legal teams assist lawyers by carrying out research and interviewing witnesses before the trial.

FIND OUT MORE   AMERICAN REVOLUTION   BABYLONIAN EMPIRE   CRIME   GOVERNMENTS AND POLITICS   HUMAN RIGHTS   ISLAM   POLICE   RELIGION   UNITED NATIONS

LEAKEY FAMILY

Louis Leakey

Mary Leakey

Richard Leakey

ONE FAMILY HAS DONE more than any other to unravel the early development of the human race and the history of our fossil relatives, the hominids. Working in Africa, the husband-and-wife team of Louis and Mary Leakey, and their son Richard, found fascinating evidence of human ancestors, showing that the continent was home to three different stages of human ancestry. There is still controversy about how these ancestors were related, but without the Leakeys, that debate could not have taken place.

The family
Louis Leakey (1903–72) was born in Kabete, Kenya. He grew up among the local Kikuyu people, and became interested in the culture and archaeology of the area. In 1936, he married his second wife, Mary (1913–96), who also became a celebrated archaeologist. Louis specialized in fossilized human remains, while Mary studied the stone tools made by our ancestors. Their son Richard (b. 1944) is a noted archaeologist and conservationist.

Olduvai Gorge

Louis and Mary Leakey spent more than 20 years excavating the Olduvai Gorge, south of the Serengeti Plain in Kenya. It yielded some remarkable finds. They found many animal bones, together with stone tools made by hominids who lived millions of years ago. Both Mary and Richard discovered hominid bones of immense importance in the gorge, establishing the area as one of the most important archaeological sites in the world.

Homo habilis
In 1961, Louis Leakey discovered some hominid remains. These were of a species that was later named *Homo habilis* (or "handy man"), so-called because he used primitive tools. *Homo habilis* is two million years old. Louis and Richard Leakey both argued that *Homo habilis* is an ancestor of modern humans, or *Homo sapiens.*

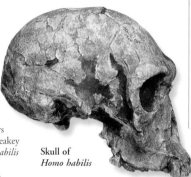

Skull of *Homo habilis*

Laetoli

In 1978, Mary Leakey made a dramatic discovery: the fossilized footprints of three hominids, preserved in volcanic ash at Laetoli, southwest of Olduvai. The footprints proved that *Australopithecus* walked upright at least 3.6 million years ago, earlier than scientists had previously suspected.

Footprints, found at Laetoli

Louis and Mary examine "Zinj".

Zinjanthropus
In 1959, Mary discovered the remains of a human skull. She named the creature *Zinjanthropus*. "Zinj" turned out to be 1.75 million years old, thus tripling the time it was known that hominids had lived on Earth. It was some time before it became clear that "Zinj" was not a direct human ancestor but an *Australopithecus*, a prehuman hominid from a parallel line of evolution.

Skull of "Zinj"

Pronounced ridge above the eyes

Archaeological tools used for unearthing fossil remains

Rock hammer

Chisels

Equipment for delicate work

Lake Turkana

Richard Leakey carried on his parents' work, making important discoveries at Lake Turkana, Kenya, and other sites in East Africa and Ethopia. He has found remains of *Homo habilis* dating from 1.88 million years ago.

Turkana boy
In 1984 Richard made one of his most important discoveries: the almost complete skeleton of a young male *Homo erectus* (upright man), a close ancestor of modern humans.

Kenyan affairs
In 1989, Richard Leakey became Kenyan National Parks director of wildlife management. He fought against the poaching of elephants and rhinoceroses for their tusks, and tried to reform the corrupt management of the parks. This brought him into conflict with the government of President Moi. Richard formally entered politics in 1997, serving in government until 2001.

LEAKEY FAMILY

1903	Louis Leakey born in Kabete, Kenya.
1913	Mary Nicol born in London.
1936	Louis's first marriage ends and he marries Mary.
1944	Richard Leakey born.
1959	Mary discovers "Zinj" at Olduvai Gorge.
1961	Louis discovers *Homo habilis* at Olduvai Gorge.
1972	Richard discovers *Homo habilis* at Lake Turkana.
1972	Louis Leakey dies.
1978	Mary discovers Laetoli footprints.
1996	Mary Leakey dies.

FIND OUT MORE   ARCHAEOLOGY   EVOLUTION   FOSSILS   HUMAN EVOLUTION   PREHISTORIC PEOPLE

LEONARDO DA VINCI

PAINTER, DRAFTSMAN, SCULPTOR, inventor, scientist, anatomist, architect: Leonardo da Vinci had many skills. He was born in 1452 during the golden age of the Italian Renaissance in art and architecture, and made his name as a painter, producing a series of masterpieces for rich patrons in Italy and later France. His restless mind led him to explore every area of scientific and artistic research; his notebooks record many inventions that show him to be outstanding in the scope of his knowledge.

Early life
Leonardo was born in Vinci, a hill village near the Italian city of Florence, in 1452. His father, Piero, was a legal clerk and his mother was a peasant. In 1466, he moved to Florence and became apprenticed to Andrea del Verrocchio, a prominent Florentine artist. He was soon pursuing artistic work on his own.

The artist
Leonardo was a uniquely gifted artist who produced paintings of matchless beauty and complexity. Yet, as the Renaissance art historian Giorgio Vasari relates, he "envisaged such subtle, marvellous, and difficult problems that his hands, while extremely skillful, were incapable of ever realizing them." As a result, few of his paintings were ever completed. Those that were finished are not very well preserved today, because Leonardo constantly experimented with new pigments and materials, many of which did not have a permanent effect.

The Virgin and Child
Before he began to paint a picture, Leonardo would draw a detailed sketch, known as a cartoon, so that he could work out the composition in advance. The finished picture of *The Virgin and Child with St. John the Baptist and St. Anne*, if it was ever completed, has never been found, but the cartoon gives a good idea of what it might have looked like.

Mona Lisa

In about 1503, Leonardo began to paint a portrait of a local Florentine woman, believed to be Lisa Gherardini, the wife of a wealthy merchant. The portrait, known as the *Mona Lisa*, now hangs in the Louvre gallery in Paris. Its subject's mysterious smile makes it one of the world's most famous paintings.

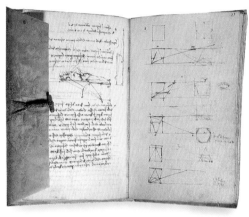

Perspective sketches
Throughout his life, Leonardo made detailed notes on the art of painting. These writings are collected together in his book, *Treatise on Painting*. In 1492, he wrote a lengthy piece on perspective, investigating the way space and distance are perceived by the eye. On the pages shown above, he illustrates his method for transferring a figure onto the sides of a curved vault, a revolutionary technique that was later called *trompe l'oeil* (paintings that "deceive the eye").

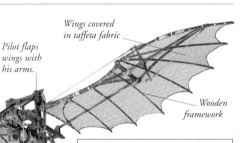

Wings covered in taffeta fabric

Pilot flaps wings with his arms.

Wooden framework

The inventor
Leonardo was a skilled scientist and inventor. Throughout his life, he drew designs for flying machines, weapons, mathematical puzzles, and musical instruments. He invented a centrifugal pump and a diving suit. He designed buildings and fortifications, and built military canals and collapsible bridges for use in wartime.

Flight
Using his observations of birds in flight, Leonardo designed a flying machine powered by human muscles. Although the wood-and-canvas machine was technically clever, it would never have flown because of the weight of materials required to build it.

Anatomy
Leonardo was fascinated by the workings of the human body, which he saw as a machine. He dissected more than 30 bodies, studying them in order to solve mechanical problems.

War and warfare
Although he considered war a "beastly madness," Leonardo devised several war machines. He drew designs for a scythed chariot and for an early tank, with guns around its rim. He also claimed to have invented a machine that fired lethal missiles, which, as they exploded, showered the enemy with deadly fire.

LEONARDO DA VINCI

1452 Born in Vinci, near Florence.

1466–72 Apprenticed to Andrea del Verrocchio in Florence.

c.1482 Moves to Milan and works for the Duke of Milan.

c.1485–88 Draws design for a tank.

1492 Investigates linear perspective.

c.1497 Paints *The Last Supper* at a monastery in Milan.

1498–99 Draws cartoon of *The Virgin and Child.*

1500 Returns to Florence.

c.1503–06 Paints the *Mona Lisa.*

c.1515 Accepts invitation from King Francis I to settle in France.

1519 Dies in France.

FIND OUT MORE   ART, HISTORY OF   FLIGHT, HISTORY OF   INVENTIONS   PAINTING AND DRAWING   RENAISSANCE

LIGHT

WITHOUT LIGHT, you would not be able to read this page. It is light that enables us to see the world around us. Light is a form of energy called electromagnetic radiation, which travels as invisible waves. Our most important source of light is the sun, but light can also be produced artificially using electricity or fire. Lenses and mirrors enable us to use light to form images and to see tiny or distant objects.

Light source

Any object or substance that emits light is called a light source. The light source in a flashlight is a thin metal wire in the bulb called a filament. When you turn on the switch, an electric current makes the filament glow white hot. A curved mirror behind the bulb directs the light out as a bright beam.

Atoms of filament vibrate faster.

Vibrating atoms emit rays of light.

Filament
A lightbulb filament is usually a coil of tungsten wire. When the bulb is switched on, the filament heats up to around 3,600°F (2,000°C). Atoms of all substances vibrate. As the filament heats up, the atoms gain extra energy and vibrate faster. Eventually they give out this extra energy as light.

Bulb filament glows white hot.

Light bounces off mirrored surface.

Incandescence

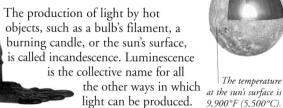

Glowing flame

The production of light by hot objects, such as a bulb's filament, a burning candle, or the sun's surface, is called incandescence. Luminescence is the collective name for all the other ways in which light can be produced.

The temperature at the sun's surface is 9,900°F (5,500°C).

Bioluminescence
Fireflies have special chemicals inside their bodies that react together and produce light. This process is called bioluminescence.

Fluorescence
In a type of luminescence called fluorescence, substances absorb light energy briefly and give it out again. Some laundry detergents contain fluorescent chemicals to make clothes look brighter.

Fluorescent laundry detergent

Electroluminescence
Some streetlights use electroluminescence to make light. Electricity is passed through a gas in a tube. The electrical energy causes the gas atoms to emit light.

Streetlight

Polarized light

The rays of light from a source such as a bulb vibrate in many different planes (directions). Some materials, called polarizing filters, allow rays vibrating in one plane only to pass through them. Light in which all the rays vibrate in the same plane is called polarized light.

Light rays

Second filter cuts out remaining rays.

Filter cuts out rays vibrating in every plane except one.

Polarized light

"Lenses" are polarizing filters.

Sunglasses
On a sunny day, the bright glare from the ocean and other reflective surfaces makes you squint. Sunglasses use polarizing filters adjusted to the correct angle to cut out the rays causing the unpleasant glare, but allow other rays to pass through.

Liquid crystal display (LCD)
In a calculator's LCD, strips of a substance called liquid crystal are held between two polarizing filters. Pressing the calculator's keys makes the liquid crystal change the direction in which light rays passing through the display vibrate. The filters block the light in some places, but not in others, forming numbers on the display.

Augustin Fresnel

The French physicist Augustin Fresnel (1788–1827) carried out experiments to prove that light travels as waves and investigated polarized light. He also invented a type of lens in which the surface is cut into a series of concentric ringed steps. This type of lens (now called a Fresnel lens) is especially good for concentrating light into a strong beam. Fresnel lenses are used in lighthouses, searchlights, and car headlights.

Rays of light in the early morning

Speed of light

Light travels through space at 186,287.5 miles/s (299,792.5 km/s). This is the ultimate speed limit – nothing can travel faster. Light travels more slowly in different substances: in water, for example, it travels at about 140,000 miles/s (225,000 km/s), and in glass at about 124,000 miles/s (200,000 km/s). Light always travels in straight lines called rays, but its direction can be deflected by objects in its path.

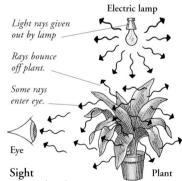

Electric lamp

Light rays given out by lamp

Rays bounce off plant.

Some rays enter eye.

Eye

Plant

Sight
A houseplant does not produce light. It is only visible to us because light rays from another source – such as the sun or an electric lamp – bounce off the plant and into the eye. Inside the eye is a lens that forms an image similar to the image formed in a camera. Cells at the back of the eye sense the image and pass information to the brain.

L

Matter and light

A material's appearance depends on the way the particles of matter inside it respond to light. A clear or milky material allows light to pass through it, and is said to be either transparent or translucent. An opaque material will absorb or reflect light, making it dull or shiny. When light hits an opaque object, it casts a shadow, which is an area where light does not reach.

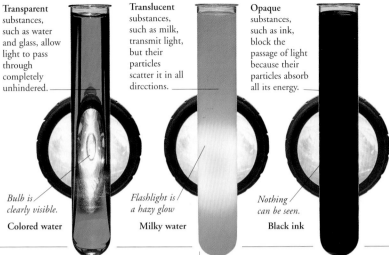

Transparent substances, such as water and glass, allow light to pass through completely unhindered.

Bulb is clearly visible.

Colored water

Translucent substances, such as milk, transmit light, but their particles scatter it in all directions.

Flashlight is a hazy glow

Milky water

Opaque substances, such as ink, block the passage of light because their particles absorb all its energy.

Nothing can be seen.

Black ink

Hero of Alexandria

The first comprehensive study of the reflection and refraction of light was *Catoptrics*, written by Hero (1st century AD), a Greek inventor and mathematician who lived in Alexandria, Egypt. Hero also invented various pneumatic (air-powered) machines, and a steam-powered engine. In geometry, he devised a formula (still known as Hero's formula) for calculating the area of a triangle.

Refraction and reflection

If you rest a pen in a glass of water, the part of the pen below the surface appears to bend. This is caused by refraction – a process in which light entering a transparent material at an angle bends, or refracts. When light strikes a shiny material, however, it simply bounces off the surface. This process is called reflection. Mirrors and lenses work by reflection and refraction.

Light refracts as it passes through water, glass, and air.

Plastic pen

Pen appears to bend.

Pen looks as though it is split in two.

Mirrors

A mirror is a surface. Parallel light rays striking a plane (flat) mirror will reflect off it at the same angle. Like lenses, curved mirrors cause light either to come together at a focus or to spread out. Convex and concave mirrors may form images and are used in many devices, including huge telescopes.

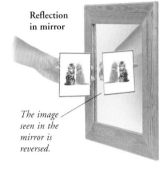

Reflection in mirror

The image seen in the mirror is reversed.

Concave mirror

A concave mirror, curves inward. When parallel light rays strike a concave mirror, they converge to a focus. A concave mirror can make an object look larger or smaller, depending on the object's distance from the mirror.

Concave mirror

Convex mirror

Convex mirror

Parallel light rays diverge when they strike an outward-curving convex mirror. A convex mirror can make an object look smaller. A car's rearview mirror gives a wide view, but makes other vehicles look farther away than they really are.

Lenses

A lens, such as a magnifying glass, is a curved piece of transparent material that changes the direction of light rays passing through it by refraction. Lenses can be used to form images of objects. They occur in cameras, eyeglasses, telescopes, microscopes, and projectors.

Convex lens makes stamp look larger.

Magnifying glass

Convex lens

A convex lens curves outward. Parallel light rays passing through a convex lens will converge (come together) at a point called the focus. Convex lenses can make an object look larger or smaller depending on the distance of the object from the lens. They are used in eyeglasses for farsightedness.

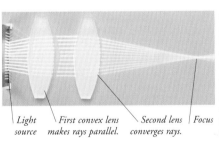

Light source

First convex lens makes rays parallel.

Second lens converges rays.

Focus

Total internal reflection

If a light ray enters a material at a shallow enough angle, it may be refracted so much that it does not emerge from the material, but is reflected inside it. Such total internal reflection is the reason light can travel along the length of a narrow glass bar. This principle is used in optical fibers, which are thin glass threads that carry laser light in telecommunications links.

Light ray

Prism focuses light.

Light ray strikes end of bar at steeper angle and escapes.

No light escapes.

Shallow angle

Glass bar

Concave lens

A concave lens is bowl-shaped and curves inward. When parallel light rays pass through a concave lens, they diverge (spread out). Concave lenses make objects look smaller than they really are. This type of lens is used in eyeglasses to correct nearsightedness.

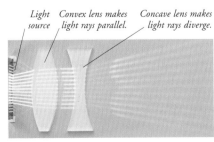

Light source

Convex lens makes light rays parallel.

Concave lens makes light rays diverge.

Timeline

c.500,000 BC Fire used as lighting in cave dwellings.

1792 William Murdock, a Scot, invents gas lighting.

c.1815 Augustin Fresnel, a French physicist, shows that light travels as waves.

1849 Fizeau shows that speed of light is 315,000,000 m/s.

1864 James Clerk Maxwell proves that light is electromagnetic radiation.

1879 Edison and Swan invent the light bulb.

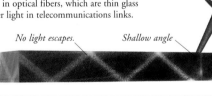

Edison's bulb

1905 Einstein shows that light consists of particles.

1939 Fluorescent lamps first demonstrated

1999 New bulbs invented to last for 100,000 hours.

2000 Princeton scientists break the light barrier.

FIND OUT MORE   COLOR   EINSTEIN, ALBERT   ENERGY   EYES AND VISION   LASERS AND HOLOGRAMS   MICROSCOPES   NEWTON, SIR ISAAC   TELESCOPES   X RAYS AND THE ELECTROMAGNETIC SPECTRUM

LINNAEUS, CAROLUS

CAROLUS LINNAEUS, ALSO KNOWN as Carl von Linné, was a Swedish botanist, naturalist, and doctor who was one of the first people to try to catalog the immense variety of life in an organized way. To do this, he devised a system of scientific names using Latin, which was at the time the international language of science and learning. His system proved so simple and effective that it is still in use today.

Early life
Linnaeus was brought up in southern Sweden. He was fascinated by plants from a very early age, and was encouraged to study medicine by a local doctor who shared his interest in medicinal herbs. After receiving his degree, he became a university lecturer in botany.

Linnaeus as a young man

Traveling scientist

European travel played an important part in Linnaeus's achievements as a scientist because it enabled him to see plants and animals from many different habitats. Starting in 1732, he traveled throughout much of Europe, including the Arctic, but he also made a point of visiting the botanical gardens in Europe's great cities, where plants from far-off places were grown for scientific study. This gave him a broad insight into the variety of life on Earth.

Flora Lapponica

Lapland journey
In 1732, Linnaeus went on a three-month expedition to Lapland. This was one of the most important events in his life. Despite the difficult conditions during his explorations, he made detailed records of everything he found, and published them in a book called *Flora Lapponica* (The Plants of Lapland). This book established his reputation as a botanist, and paved the way for important works that were to follow.

Working abroad
In 1735, Linnaeus went to college in Holland to advance his medical career. There he met a rich merchant, George Clifford, who owned a garden of exotic plants. Linnaeus identified and classified these plants. He also traveled to England and visited the Physic Garden at Chelsea, London, where medicinal plants are grown.

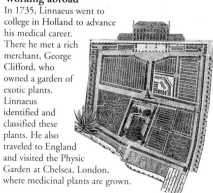

Botanist

Linnaeus was interested in almost every aspect of the living world, but botany, the study of plants, was his great love. In the early 1740s, after his stay in Holland, he returned to Sweden, where he became a professor of medicine, then of botany. In 1753, his book *Species Plantarum* (Species of Plants) appeared. It is still the most important book on plants ever published.

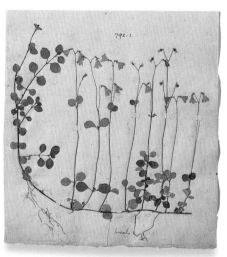

Classification
Linnaeus's greatest contribution to science was his system of two-part Latin names, or binomials. He devised them to simplify the confusing jumble of plant names that existed in his time, but their coverage slowly grew to include all living things. Today, they are an essential part of biological classification.

Later life
By the time he had reached his fifties, Linnaeus was one of the most respected scientists in the world. In 1761, he was given the Swedish rank of nobleman, and by the time he died in 1778, he had written nearly 200 scientific books. After his death in 1778, Linnaeus's influence continued. His way of identifying living things has proved invaluable in showing how different species are related.

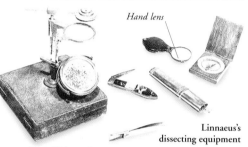

Hand lens

Linnaeus's dissecting equipment

Classifying plants
Linnaeus devised a new way of classifying plants. He called it his *Methodus sexualis*, or sexual method, because it was based largely on dissecting flowers to determine their male and female parts. Today, botanists no longer use this system, but it was an important first step in classifying plants in a logical way.

Genera Plantarum, with Linnaeus's own notes

Cataloges of life
In 1737, Linnaeus published *Genera Plantarum* (Types of Plants), one of his first great works of classification. This and his other books classified everything from plants and animals to types of rocks. His huge work *Systema naturae* (The System of Nature) was the largest of these books. It was constantly growing, and many editions were published.

CAROLUS LINNAEUS

1707 Born at Råshult, southern Sweden.
1727 Enters University of Lund.
1732 Expedition to Lapland.
1735 First edition of *Systema Naturae*.
1736 Visits England.
1741 Appointed Professor of Medicine at Uppsala.
1742 Appointed Professor of Botany at Uppsala.
1753 *Species Plantarum* published.
1778 Dies in Uppsala.

FIND OUT MORE · BIOLOGY · PLANTS · SCIENCE, HISTORY OF

LIONS AND OTHER WILDCATS

WILDCATS ARE SKILLED predators. They usually stalk their prey, dash from close range, and kill by biting the neck or head. There are 36 species of wildcats, ranging from the black-footed cat, weighing 5 lb (2.2 kg), to the tiger, weighing up to 620 lb (280 kg). Lions, tigers, jaguars, leopards, and snow leopards are called big cats and can roar; smaller cats can only purr. Many wildcats have been hunted to the point of extinction, some for their fur, others for preying on farmers' cattle.

Teeth

Wildcats have sharp teeth and powerful jaws, which equip them to eat flesh. The small, pointed incisors grip prey; large, curved canine teeth tear flesh; and sharp-edged cheek teeth (carnassials) cut through hide and muscle.

Features of a wildcat

Wildcats have powerful bodies and long tails for balance. They have sharp, curved claws that are used both to seize and hold prey and to defend themselves. They have quick reflexes and excellent eyesight and hearing. Although they spend most of their time on the ground, wildcats are good climbers. Most wildcats are solitary creatures.

Broad head

Flexible back

Sandy-colored coat

Claws (except those of the cheetah) retract into a protective sheath to protect them from unnecessary wear.

Strong, muscular body

Lioness

Large paws

Long tail for balance.

Lioness grips buffalo around neck and bites throat.

Lions

Lions are the most powerful of all carnivores. They live mainly in Africa, but a small number survive in India. The males are about a third larger than females, known as lionesses. Males have manes that darken with age from a sandy color to black. Manes help males look larger to impress females and intimidate rival males.

Shaggy mane

Roaring

The roar of the lion is one of the most characteristic sounds of the African night. It is heard at dawn and dusk, rarely during the day. Roaring is a means of marking territory and serves as a warning to other lions to keep away. All the big cats can roar.

African lion

Hunting

Lions live in grasslands where they hunt zebras and other animals. Lionesses do most of the hunting, usually at dusk, and stalk their prey before launching an attack from close range. They leap on the animal, drag it to the ground, and bite its neck to kill it. Hunting is often communal, with one group of lionesses driving the prey toward another group lying in ambush. Male lions move in on the lionesses' kill and eat first.

Pride of lions

Lions are social animals and live in prides – family groups of several females and their young in loose association with a male. The females give the pride stability and strength. The male regards the pride as a means of satisfying his needs, with the least exertion to himself. He mates with all the females, who give birth every two years to 2–6 cubs after 110 days' gestation. The cubs are reared communally by the females.

Lion

Lionesses rear cubs for 18 months and teach them how to hunt.

Cub

Flehmen

Flehmen is part of a courtship pattern in which a male lion licks the female's urine, raises his head, and pulls back his upper lips to expose his teeth. He then inhales air over a taste and smell organ in his mouth that enables him to identify females ready to mate. Flehmen is also linked to territorial behavior.

The lips are drawn back and the teeth exposed.

Tigers

There are eight varieties of tigers. They live in an area ranging from India through Southeast Asia to Siberia, Manchuria, and Indonesia. The Siberian tiger is the largest wildcat; males stand up to 43 in (110 cm) at the shoulder and weigh up to 620 lb (280 kg). Loss of habitat and reduction of its natural prey have sharply reduced tiger populations.

Reproduction

Tigresses mate every few years from about 3 years of age. The female comes into heat for 3–7 days and a pair mates many times during this period. After about 3½ months' gestation, 2–6 cubs are born. They are blind for the first 10 days. The mother suckles them for 8 weeks. Only 1–2 cubs in each litter survive.

Sumatran tiger with cubs

Indian tiger in undergrowth

Cubs stay with mother for 2–3 years.

Camouflage

The striking pattern of dark stripes on the contrasting tawny base color acts as effective camouflage to conceal the tiger in its grassland surroundings.

Territory

Tigers have individual territories, varying in size according to the terrain and quantity of prey. They mark out their territories by shredding tree bark and spraying urine. Female territories are small at 10 sq miles (26 sq km); male territories are larger and incorporate those of several females. A tiger may have several dens within its territory.

Sumatran tiger scratching tree

L

Leopards

Leopards live in much of Africa, southern Asia, and the Middle East; in fact they are more widely found than any other wildcat. Most leopards live in forests, but some live in grassland and woodland savannahs. They are excellent climbers, their long tails help them keep their balance. They sleep, rest, and watch for prey from the branches of trees. Their coat varies from pale yellow to black and is covered with spots, providing effective camouflage against the light and shade of their surroundings.

Leopard roars to warn scavengers.

Leopard keeps a firm hold of the impala with its large paws and claws.

The impala is wedged into the fork of the tree to prevent hyenas, jackals, and other scavengers from eating it.

Female leopard with cub

Hunting

Leopards normally hunt at dusk or dawn and prey on many animals, including deer, medium-sized antelope, baboons, and warthogs. They stalk their prey or lie in ambush on a branch overhanging a game trail. Leopards kill their prey by biting the throat or the back of the head. They are strong, agile animals and can easily carry prey of their own weight into a tree.

Reproduction

Leopards reach sexual maturity by 2½–3 years. The male is attracted by the smell of the female's urine when she is in season. They mate and stay together for a week. After a 3½-month gestation period, the female gives birth to 2–3 cubs in a rock crevice or dense thicket. The cubs are weaned by 3 months and independent by 2 years.

Cheetahs

With their long legs, small heads, and light build, cheetahs are the fastest animals on land. They can run at speeds of up to 62 mph (100 kmh). Female leopards usually live alone. Males often live in groups of 4–5 animals, typically brothers, that may stay together for life. In Africa, only 9,000–12,000 cheetahs remain because they cannot withstand change in their habitat and because they are susceptible to certain viruses transmitted by domestic animals.

Small head

Cheetah running at full speed

Male cheetahs often hunt together in small groups.

Long legs

Hunting

Cheetahs hunt by day, when other predators are resting. They prey on small antelope and gazelles, relying on their superior speed to run them down. They maintain high speed only for short distances and give up when they get tired.

Habitat

Most wildcats live in forests, but they have adapted to live in habitats as diverse as deserts, wetlands, grasslands, and mountains. The sand cat, for example, lives in deserts and can get all the water it needs from its prey. It has thick pads on its feet so it can move fast over soft sand. The fishing cat lives in wetlands and has learned to hunt by flipping fish out of the water.

Forest cats

Forest cats often have coats of stripes and spots that help them blend in with the light and shade of the forest. The margay and clouded leopard can hang upside down from branches and run down trunks headfirst.

Jaguar in the rain forest

Mountain cats

Thick coats and dense underfur help wildcats to withstand cold mountain conditions. Camouflage is also important, especially for cats active by day. The snow leopard's coloration, for example, blends well with the gray rocks and snow of the mountains of central Asia.

Snow leopard in the snow

Small wildcats

Serval

Servals are agile creatures with narrow heads and long legs. They live in well-defined territories in lightly wooded areas and the savannahs of sub-Saharan Africa. They hunt mainly at dusk, listening for the movement of lizards and rodents such as the mole rat.

Large, erect ears

Very long legs

Caracal

Caracals, also called desert lynxes, live in the semi-arid areas of Africa and India. They prey on animals such as birds, rodents, and small antelopes. They are good at leaping, and catch birds nesting in low branches; they may even leap into the air to seize birds on the wing. They can turn their ear tufts to communicate with rivals or mates.

Black ear tufts

European wildcat

The European wildcat is believed to be the ancestor of the domestic cat. It lives in habitats ranging from forest to open grassland over most of Africa, western Europe, and Asia. It hunts on its own or in pairs, preying chiefly on rodents and birds.

Striped fur

Bobcat

The bobcat, or bay lynx, from North America, has adapted to live in high mountains, marshlands, forests, and deserts. At night it preys on rabbits, hares, and rodents. Males defend vast territories of up to 39 sq miles (100 sq km), and females an area half this size.

Short, stumpy tail

LION

SCIENTIFIC NAME	*Panthera leo*
ORDER	Carnivora
FAMILY	Felidae
DISTRIBUTION	Africa south of the Sahara, and the Gir Forest in India
HABITAT	Open grasslands and lightly wooded savannas
DIET	Carnivorous, preying on animals such as wildebeest, zebras, antelope, and gazelles. A group of lionesses will even tackle a buffalo. If very hungry, lions will also attack rhino calves
SIZE	Height at shoulder 2 ft 6 in (0.8 m); weight 450 lb (204 kg)
LIFESPAN	15–16 years

FIND OUT MORE

AFRICAN WILDLIFE   ASIAN WILDLIFE   CAMOUFLAGE AND COLOR   CATS   CONSERVATION   MOUNTAIN WILDLIFE   NORTH AMERICAN WILDLIFE   RAIN FOREST WILDLIFE

Wildcats

Grassland cats

Shaggy mane makes male appear much larger than he really is.

Pumas also live in the mountains. They are powerful and can jump 23 ft (7 m) in a single leap.

Lions are the largest and most powerful of the grassland predators.

European wildcats are now very rare in Europe. In Britain, they live only in Scotland.

Servals can leap up to 10 ft (3 m) into the air to catch birds on the wing.

Cheetahs rely on their tremendous speed to run down their prey.

Mountain cats

The snow leopard's coat gets paler in winter to provide better camouflage.

Snow leopards live in the mountains of central Asia at heights of up to 18,000 ft (5,500 m).

Geoffroy's cats live at high altitude in the Andes.

Forest cats

Leopards' coat markings camouflage them very well, both in trees and on the ground.

Black panthers are a melanistic, or all black, version of the leopard.

Lynxes use their ear tufts to communicate – their tails are too short for this purpose.

Tigers, the largest members of the cat family, are poor climbers, but good swimmers.

Jaguars, the largest and stockiest of the South American cats, are good tree climbers.

Leopard cats live in the forests of Southeast Asia, and prey on small mammals and birds.

Bobcats get their name from their short, "bobbed" tails.

Margays spend most of their time in trees, and hunt at night for nesting birds.

Ocelots have been hunted extensively for their beautiful fur.

Ocelots hunt on the forest floor, but may also pounce from branches.

Wetland cats

Fishing cats scoop fish from the water with their paws.

Jungle cats live in marshes and in dense wetlands.

Desert cats

Ear tufts

Sand cats live in the Sahara and the deserts of western Asia. They sleep by day in burrows.

Caracals kill rodents and even small antelope.

LIQUIDS

WHEN YOU SPILL A DRINK, it spreads out into an irregular puddle. None of the drink is lost, it simply takes on a different shape. This is because the drink is a liquid – a form of matter with a definite volume but no fixed shape. A liquid is made up of tiny vibrating particles of matter, such as atoms and molecules, held together by forces called chemical bonds. Water is by far the most common liquid on Earth.

When a liquid flows, its particles tend to cluster together as drops.

Properties of liquids

A liquid forms random shapes when it is allowed to flow freely. It also takes the shape of any container it is placed in. It is difficult to compress a liquid, because the forces between its particles prevent them from coming too close together.

A flowing liquid has no regular shape.

Liquid particles
A liquid's particles are able to move past one another, which is why a liquid can flow.

Surface tension

The attraction between a liquid's particles produces a force, or tension, across the liquid's surface that causes it to behave like a stretched "skin." Surface tension pulls drops and bubbles into spheres. Mercury has much stronger forces between its particles than water, so it has greater surface tension and forms more rounded droplets.

Water   Mercury

Meniscus
A liquid's surface forms a curve called a meniscus where it meets the walls of its container. Liquids with weak bonds between their particles, such as water, cling to the walls and curve upward. Those with strong bonds, such as mercury, pull away from the walls and curve downward.

Water droplet   Mercury droplet

Viscosity
A liquid's viscosity is a measure of its ability to resist flowing. It results from friction between the liquid molecules as they try to slide past one another. Thick, viscous liquids such as black molasses have a lot of friction between their molecules; runny liquids such as clear honey have less friction and a lower viscosity.

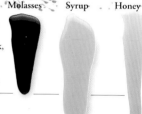

Molasses   Syrup   Honey

Water

Each water molecule contains two hydrogen atoms linked to one oxygen atom. Above its boiling point (212°F, 100°C), water takes the form of a gas called steam. Below its freezing point (32°F, 0°C), water becomes a solid called ice. Water dissolves many substances, such as salt and sugar, to form solutions.

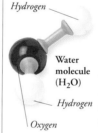

Hydrogen
Water molecule (H₂O)
Hydrogen
Oxygen

Boiling point

Heating a liquid gives more energy to its particles and makes them vibrate faster. At a certain temperature, called the boiling point, all the particles have enough energy to break free of their bonds and bubbles of gas form rapidly throughout the liquid. Each liquid has its own specific boiling point.

Evaporation
Below its boiling point, a liquid may slowly change to a gas by evaporation. At the liquid's surface, a few particles at a time gain sufficient energy to escape into the air as a gas. Water evaporates from laundry on a clothesline because its molecules gain extra energy from the sun and the wind.

Freezing
As a liquid cools, its particles lose energy and the bonds between them get stronger. At a temperature called its freezing point, the liquid becomes a solid. Impurities can lower the freezing point. For example, seawater, which contains salt, freezes at a much lower temperature than pure water.

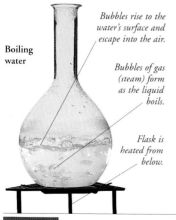

Boiling water

Bubbles rise to the water's surface and escape into the air.

Bubbles of gas (steam) form as the liquid boils.

Flask is heated from below.

Hydrometer
A liquid's density is often given relative to the density of water. This "relative density" is measured with a device called a hydrometer. The higher the hydrometer floats in the liquid, the more dense it is. Glycerine has a relative density of 1.3, meaning that it is 1.3 times more dense than water. Turpentine has a relative density of 0.7.

The relative density of water is 1.

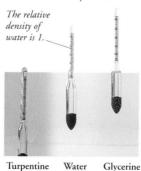

Turpentine   Water   Glycerine

Ice
Most substances contract when they freeze, because their particles grow closer together. Water, however, expands as it freezes into ice, because its molecules spread out. This is why a drink sometimes rises out of the bottle as it freezes.

Frozen juice

Orange juice is mostly water.

Osmosis
When two solutions of different concentration are separated by a semi-permeable membrane (a porous barrier), liquid will flow from the weaker solution to the more concentrated one. This process is called osmosis. When you soak dried fruit, the fruit swells up as it absorbs water by osmosis through the walls of the fruit cells.

Dried fruit

Dried fruit after soaking in water

FIND OUT MORE

ATOMS AND MOLECULES   FRICTION   GASES   MATTER   OCEANS AND SEAS   SOLIDS

LITERATURE

LITERATURE IS A WORK of art in words. It is writing that carries strong and lasting value through beauty or emotional power. At its heart, literature offers the reader important insights into the nature of human feelings and desires. The oldest form of literature is oral poetry, which was handed down by word of mouth and only later put into writing. Other forms include plays, novels, and short stories. Letters, journalism, speeches, and diaries can also be literature if they are especially well written.

What is literature?
Literature expresses the writer's thoughts, hopes, and fears. But not everything that is written is literature. Writing is literature only if it is well written and of lasting interest to people from many societies and different generations. Sometimes writers try to use literature to change the world in which they live, by protesting against injustice and influencing the opinions of people or governments.

Most modern literature is printed in bound books

Oral literature
Long before written literature, people recorded their myths and stories in poems, told by successive generations. Each storyteller added new details so the tales grew richer with every telling.

Costume design for Scheherazade

One Thousand and One Nights
This is a collection of folktales that were once told by storytellers in Middle Eastern bazaars. In medieval Europe, the tales were written down and linked by the story of Scheherazade, a queen whose husband threatens to kill her. She enchants him by telling him stories for 1,001 nights until he spares her life.

Greek helmet

Iliad
The *Iliad* is an ancient Greek poem, one of the most famous ever written. It was probably composed orally before 800 BC. It tells of the war fought by Greece and Troy over Helen, the most beautiful woman in the world.

Epics and sagas
Epics are long poems telling the stories of legendary heroes, their adventures and great deeds. They often record a culture's most precious traditions and beliefs. Sagas are prose epics written about the lives of famous men and women in medieval Iceland.

Beowulf
The Old English epic *Beowulf* was written c. AD 700. It tells of the hero Beowulf, who kills two monsters, Grendel and Grendel's mother, but is finally slain by a dragon.

Themes of literature
Writers use their work to explore key themes that concern them and their readers. Throughout history and in every language, some themes are always present: love, death, morality, religious truth, and human loyalty. They can be explored through high-spirited comedy or bleak tragedy. Often, writers pick up themes, subjects, or styles from other writers and develop them further.

Pilgrim from the Tales

Illuminated page, *The Canterbury Tales*

Chaucer
Geoffrey Chaucer (c.1343–1400) was one of the great figures of English literature. His most famous work, *The Canterbury Tales* (1387–1400), is a set of intertwined stories told by a group of pilgrims traveling to Canterbury. Chaucer borrows themes from European literature and English folktales and turns them into a richly varied series of poems. Some are comic, others serious. They have remained popular for 600 years.

Scenes from *Faust*

Faust is confronted by the devil.

Goethe
Johann Wolfgang von Goethe (1749–1832) is a central figure of German literature. He wrote poems, novels, and plays. His most famous literary work is a poetic drama, *Faust*, which is based on the medieval legend of a magician who sells his soul to the devil. Goethe uses the story to explore themes of sin, redemption, and the nature of art.

Dante
The Italian poet Dante Alighieri (1265–1321) was born in Florence. His masterpiece, *The Divine Comedy*, depicts the poet visiting Hell, Purgatory, and Paradise in a dream. The poem discusses the philosophical and religious questions of the day.

Book of Kings
For 1,000 years, the *Book of Kings (Shah-nameh)* has been the central achievement of Persian literature. The work of Firdausi (c.935–c.1020), it tells the story of the kings of Persia from mythical times. The many battles and fights against monsters it describes have made it a favorite source for modern Iranians.

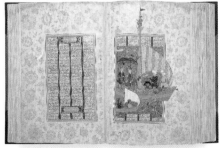

Book of Kings

Rise of the novel

Novels are prose narratives presented in book form. Since the 18th century, they have become the most important literary form in the Western world. Their popularity derives from their amazing variety. Novels can be minutely detailed pictures of ordinary life or outrageous fantasies. They can explore realistic characters who reflect human problems, or tell simple exhilarating tales.

Windmills at La Mancha

Still from the film, *Sense and Sensibility,* 1995

Jane Austen
One of the first novelists to focus closely on the lives of ordinary people was the English writer Jane Austen (1775–1817). In novels such as *Sense and Sensibility* (1811), she wittily portrays the behavior of men and women searching for happiness in love and marriage.

Miguel de Cervantes
The Spanish writer Miguel de Cervantes (1547–1616) published *Don Quixote* from 1605–1615. The hero confusedly thinks he is a knight. In his madness, he attacks windmills, aided by his squire Sancho Panza. The book's popularity enabled Cervantes to write professionally.

Leo Tolstoy
The novels of Count Leo Tolstoy (1828–1910) include *War and Peace* (1863–69), set during the Napoleonic Wars, and *Anna Karenina* (1873–77), in which a married woman falls in love with a dashing soldier. The novels combine studies of Russian life with perceptive analyses of the characters' motives.

A samovar (tea urn) is part of Russian domestic life.

John Steinbeck
John Steinbeck (1902–1968) wrote about the hard life of the rural American poor. His most famous novel, *The Grapes of Wrath* (1939), follows a family who leaves the barren lands of Oklahoma to start a new life on the richer soil of California. Steinbeck won the Nobel Prize for Literature in 1962.

Still from the film *The Grapes of Wrath,* 1940

Short stories
The most successful short stories are very tightly plotted and carefully written. Often they hinge on a single powerful event. In *The Metamorphosis* (1916), by the Czech writer Franz Kafka (1883–1924), a man wakes to find he has become a giant cockroach. Short stories often have a shocking ending. In 1841, the American writer Edgar Allen Poe (1809–49) published *The Murders in the Rue Morgue,* in which the killer turns out to be an orangutan.

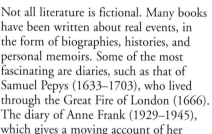

Nonfiction

Not all literature is fictional. Many books have been written about real events, in the form of biographies, histories, and personal memoirs. Some of the most fascinating are diaries, such as that of Samuel Pepys (1633–1703), who lived through the Great Fire of London (1666). The diary of Anne Frank (1929–1945), which gives a moving account of her persecution by the Nazis during the World War II, has been read by millions.

Wild Swans
This book by Jung Chang (b.1952) recounts China's troubled recent history, as seen through the eyes of three generations of the author's family. It was published in 1991.

Popular culture

Many books do not try to explore deep truths about life, but satisfy the reader's desire to escape reality into a world of high adventure, fantasy, horror, or romance. Part of the writer's craft lies in giving a new twist to a familiar theme, such as crime detection or espionage.

Boris Karloff

Magnifying glass

Red roses symbolize romance.

Horror
Since the 19th century, horror novels such as *Frankenstein,* published in 1818 by English author Mary Shelley (1797–1851), have exploited people's fear of monsters, ghosts, and the supernatural.

Crime
Ever since Arthur Conan Doyle (1859–1930) wrote about Sherlock Holmes, stories of crime and detection, or "whodunnits," have been hugely popular. Readers can try to solve the crimes for themselves, and marvel as the detective unravels the truth.

Romance
People often dream about finding perfect love, and popular romances show that dream coming true. The hero or heroine must overcome many obstacles and misunderstandings, before winning the heart of his or her loved one.

Timeline

Before 400 BC The epic poem *Mahabharata* is written in India. It is the longest poem ever composed.

c. 1000 AD The world's first novel is *The Tale of Genji* by Lady Murasaki, of the imperial court in Japan.

From the film *Mahabharata*

1100s The *Rubaiyat* is written by the Persian poet Omar Khayyám.

1580–1612 William Shakespeare (1564–1616), the greatest British dramatist, writes his plays.

1719 Daniel Defoe (1660–1731) writes *Robinson Crusoe,* the first successful natural style novel.

1852 *Uncle Tom's Cabin* by American Harriet Beecher Stowe (1811–96) features slavery.

1864 First science fiction story, *Journey to the Center of the Earth* by Frenchman Jules Verne (1828–1905), is published.

1958 Nigerian writer Chinua Achebe (b.1930) publishes *Things*

Fall Apart, which charts Africa's journey from tradition to modernity.

1993 Toni Morrison (b.1931) wins Nobel Prize for Literature, the first African American woman to do so.

Toni Morrison

FIND OUT MORE   BOOKS   CHILDREN'S LITERATURE   DRAMA   LANGUAGE   PAPER   POETRY   PRINTING   WRITING

LIZARDS

BASKING IN THE SUN allows lizards to absorb its rays. Many lizards do this because they are cold-blooded reptiles and need heat to activate their bodies. There are more than 3,000 species of lizard and they live in most parts of the world. They vary in size from tiny chameleons, which can sit on a match head, to huge Komodo dragons. Not all lizards are sun-lovers; many have adopted nocturnal rain forest lifestyles or have adapted to live in caves.

Features of a lizard

Lizards belong to the same group of scaled reptiles as snakes. Unlike snakes most lizards have legs, moveable eyelids, ears, and a notched rather than a forked tongue, but there are exceptions. Some lizards, such as glass lizards, have small legs or none at all, and are thought to be more highly evolved than lizards with legs. Some small skinks, such as coconut skinks, have a clear spectacle over their eyes instead of eyelids. Monitor lizards have forked tongues and the Borneo earless monitor lizard lacks ears. Many lizards have a third, or pineal eye, used to monitor radiation levels when basking in the sun.

L

Folds of scaled skin

Five toes with sharp claws

Eyed lizard

Worm lizards

There are about 100 types of worm lizard. They are related to true lizards, but belong to a different group of animals called the Amphisbaenia. They have ringed bodies and either no legs or just a front pair. They burrow in sand or leaf litter and feed on invertebrates. The largest worm lizard also eats carrion and small reptiles. They live in the tropics, except for one species that lives in Greece.

Black and white worm lizard

Adaptation to habitat

Lizards live in most environments from seashores to mountains, and from deserts to rain forests. Forest lizards such as chameleons can camouflage themselves and some have prehensile tails for climbing. Geckos have special toes to climb smooth surfaces. Marine iguanas have glands to excrete excess salt, and many mountain lizards are black to maximize heat absorption.

Rain forest lizards

Lizards live in all parts of the rain forest from the canopy down to the leaf litter. Rain forest lizards are agile climbers with long toes and claws. Most are green or brown for camouflage. "Flying geckos" and "flying lizards" do not actually fly, but have evolved a means of gliding downwards from high trees.

Sulawesi flying lizard

Desert lizards

Desert lizards obtain all their water from food and the early morning dew. They usually have flattened bodies and are pale brown in color. Many are unusual in appearance, such as Australian frilled lizards, bearded dragons, thorny-backed molochs, and American horned toads, which are lizards despite their name.

Claws | *Spikes on skin* | **Bearded dragon**

Feeding

Lizard jaws and teeth are strong and can crush hard prey such as snails. Some eat insects, some eat larger animals and carrion, and others eat only plants. Many insectivorous lizards, such as some geckos, ambush their prey at night when they are attracted to lights; others, including chameleons, stalk and capture their prey with their long, sticky tongues.

Turret eyes can swivel in any direction.

Flap-necked chameleon

Fly has just been captured. *Chameleon shoots out tongue at high speed.*

Movement

Lizards' legs join the body at the side so they have a twisting motion when they run. Some legless lizards move in jumps by flicking their tail. "Flying lizards" glide downwards using flaps of skin on their sides, legs, and tails that slow and aim their descent. Basilisks, also called "Jesus lizards", have long toes that enable them to run over the surface of water. Gecko feet are covered in tiny lamellae that help them grip smooth surfaces.

Tokay gecko

Reproduction

Some lizards lay leathery-shelled eggs in leaf litter or sandy holes. The eggs are left to incubate, and the young break out by using a special egg tooth. Other lizards are live bearers giving birth to fully formed infants in membranous sacs. A few species are parthenogenetic and exist only as females, producing offspring without a mate.

Defence

Lizards have evolved many ways of defending themselves. Horned lizards squirt blood from their eyes, crocodile skinks make loud screeching noises, and blue-tongued skinks stick out their bright blue tongues. Many lizards can shed their tails voluntarily; tensing the muscles suddenly breaks off the tail, which is left wiggling to confuse predators. Chameleons change color to camouflage themselves, and many geckos are secretive by nature.

Soft-shelled eggs

Sand lizards with clutch of eggs

Australian frilled lizard

These lizards are found throughout northern Australia and southern New Guinea. If threatened, they try to scare off attackers by erecting a large fan of skin supported by bones. The frill is also used in territorial disputes between rival males.

Frill of skin

EYED LIZARD

SCIENTIFIC NAME	*Lacerta lepida*
ORDER	Squamata
FAMILY	Lacertidae
DISTRIBUTION	Spain, Portugal, southern France, northwestern Italy, and North Africa
HABITAT	Dry scrubland, vineyards, and olive groves
DIET	Insects, smaller lizards, nestling birds, small mammals, and fruit
SIZE	Length 2 ft 7 in (0.8 m)
LIFESPAN	Up to 14 years (in captivity)

FIND OUT MORE | CAMOUFLAGE AND COLOR | DESERT WILDLIFE | EGGS | ISLAND WILDLIFE | RAIN FOREST WILDLIFE | REPTILES | SEASHORE WILDLIFE

Lizards
Carnivores and scavengers

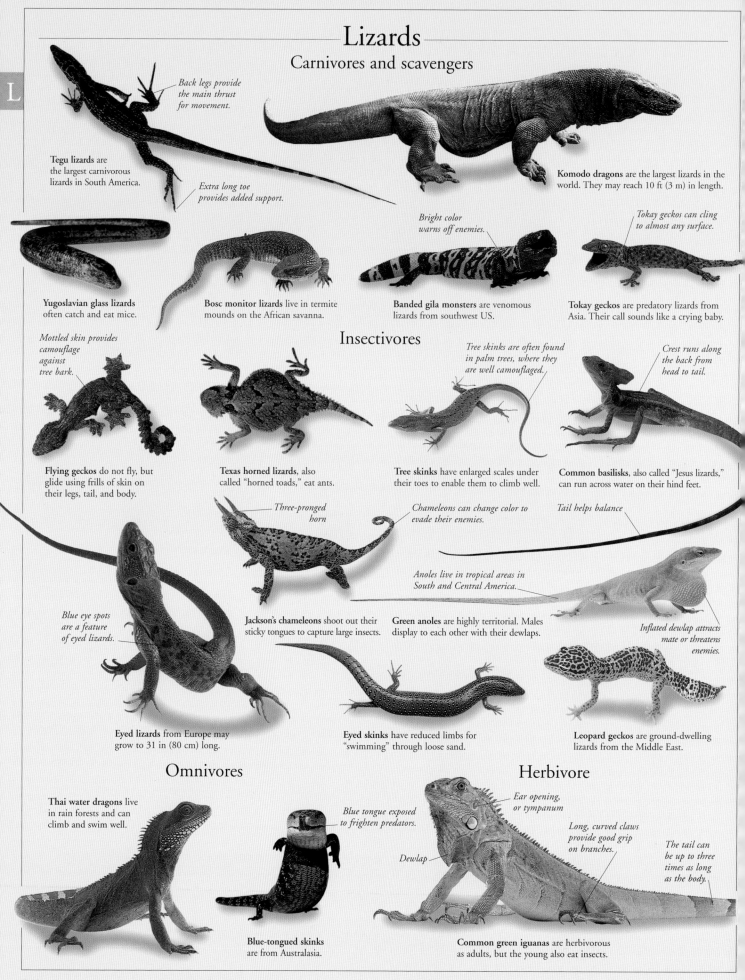

Back legs provide the main thrust for movement.

Tegu lizards are the largest carnivorous lizards in South America.

Extra long toe provides added support.

Komodo dragons are the largest lizards in the world. They may reach 10 ft (3 m) in length.

Bright color warns off enemies.

Tokay geckos can cling to almost any surface.

Yugoslavian glass lizards often catch and eat mice.

Bosc monitor lizards live in termite mounds on the African savanna.

Banded gila monsters are venomous lizards from southwest US.

Tokay geckos are predatory lizards from Asia. Their call sounds like a crying baby.

Insectivores

Mottled skin provides camouflage against tree bark.

Tree skinks are often found in palm trees, where they are well camouflaged.

Crest runs along the back from head to tail.

Flying geckos do not fly, but glide using frills of skin on their legs, tail, and body.

Texas horned lizards, also called "horned toads," eat ants.

Tree skinks have enlarged scales under their toes to enable them to climb well.

Common basilisks, also called "Jesus lizards," can run across water on their hind feet.

Three-pronged horn

Chameleons can change color to evade their enemies.

Tail helps balance

Anoles live in tropical areas in South and Central America.

Blue eye spots are a feature of eyed lizards.

Jackson's chameleons shoot out their sticky tongues to capture large insects.

Green anoles are highly territorial. Males display to each other with their dewlaps.

Inflated dewlap attracts mate or threatens enemies.

Eyed lizards from Europe may grow to 31 in (80 cm) long.

Eyed skinks have reduced limbs for "swimming" through loose sand.

Leopard geckos are ground-dwelling lizards from the Middle East.

Omnivores

Thai water dragons live in rain forests and can climb and swim well.

Blue tongue exposed to frighten predators.

Blue-tongued skinks are from Australasia.

Herbivore

Ear opening, or tympanum

Long, curved claws provide good grip on branches.

Dewlap

The tail can be up to three times as long as the body.

Common green iguanas are herbivorous as adults, but the young also eat insects.

L

LUNGS AND BREATHING

EVERY ONE OF THE BODY'S CELLS needs oxygen in order to release energy from food. The release of energy, known as aerobic respiration, produces a waste product called carbon dioxide that is exhaled when we breathe. Breathing pumps air in and out of the lungs. Inside the lungs, an exchange takes place: oxygen moves from the air into the blood and carbon dioxide from the blood into the air. The lungs, and air passages linking the lungs to the outside of the body, make up the respiratory system.

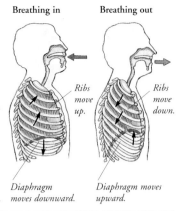

Breathing in **Breathing out**

Ribs move up. *Ribs move down.*

Diaphragm moves downward. *Diaphragm moves upward.*

Breathing
Although the lungs do not have muscles of their own, our breathing is nevertheless controlled by muscles. Air is pumped in and out of the lungs by the action of the intercostal muscles situated between the ribs and by the diaphragm between the chest and abdomen.

Lungs

The two lungs are spongy, pink organs lying in the chest, protected by the rib cage. Below the lungs is a sheet of muscle called the diaphragm. An airway called the bronchus enters each lung and branches repeatedly to form smaller bronchi, which themselves branch into very fine airways called bronchioles.

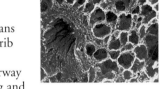

Alveoli
The bronchioles end as tiny air sacs called alveoli. It is through the alveoli that oxygen enters, and carbon dioxide leaves, the blood. There are over 600 million alveoli in the lungs.

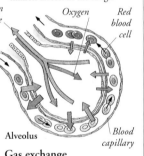

Carbon dioxide *Oxygen* *Red blood cell*

Alveolus *Blood capillary*

Gas exchange
Each alveolus is surrounded by a network of blood capillaries. Oxygen from the air dissolves in the moisture lining the alveolus and passes into the blood. Carbon dioxide passes from the blood into the alveolus.

Cartilage ring *Trachea (windpipe)*

Bronchiole is the smallest branch of the bronchi. It ends in alveoli.

Bronchus is one of two main branches of the trachea; it divides into smaller bronchi.

Respiratory system

Air enters and leaves the respiratory system through the nasal cavity and mouth. The air goes down the pharynx (throat), passes through the larynx (voice box), and into the trachea (windpipe). The trachea divides into two main bronchi, which carry the air into the lungs, where oxygen is absorbed into the blood.

Vocal cords

Larynx (voice box)

Cartilage ring helps keep trachea open during breathing.

Trachea carries air to and from lungs.

Right lung

Pulmonary artery carries oxygen-poor blood into lung.

Pulmonary vein carries oxygen-rich blood away from lung.

Tertiary bronchus

Left lung cut open to show internal structure.

Aorta *Spine*

Esophagus carries food to stomach.

Primary bronchus is branch of trachea.

Secondary bronchus branches out of primary bronchus.

Larynx

The larynx links the throat to the trachea. It is made of pieces of cartilage, one of which you can feel as a triangular lump called the Adam's apple in the front of your neck. The upper piece of cartilage forms a flap called the epiglottis, which blocks the entrance to the larynx when you swallow food. Stretched between the pieces of cartilage at the base of the larynx are the vocal cords.

Coughing and sneezing
Coughing clears mucus and dirt from the trachea, and sneezing clears the nose. For both actions, you take a deep breath and muscles squeeze your lungs. Your vocal cords suddenly open and air rushes upward, dislodging particles.

Vocal cords open.

Epiglottis
Vocal cord
Thyroid cartilage
Adam's apple
Trachea

Vocal cords
The vocal cords are pairs of membranes in the larynx. When fully or partially closed, the vocal cords vibrate and generate sounds as air passes over them.

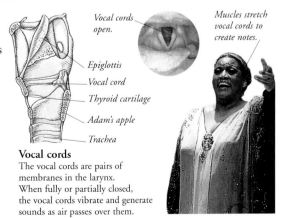

Muscles stretch vocal cords to create notes.

People yawn when resting or tired.

Yawning
When you yawn, you breathe in deeply with your mouth wide open. This ventilates the lungs, expelling "stale" air and replacing it with fresh air.

FIND OUT MORE DIGESTION • FIRST AID • GASES • HEALTH AND FITNESS • HEART AND CIRCULATORY SYSTEM • HUMAN BODY • MUSCLES AND MOVEMENT • SKELETON

M

MACHINES, SIMPLE

A MACHINE IS A DEVICE that makes a job easier to do. Most of the machines in our daily lives are complex devices made up of a combination of simpler machines such as pulleys, levers, and gears. Machines that increase a force, or "effort," applied to them are said to give a mechanical advantage. Other machines change the size, direction, or speed of a movement.

Inclined plane

A slope that reduces the effort needed to lift a load forms a simple machine called an inclined plane. A shallow slope reduces the effort more than a steep one, but the slope is longer, so the load must travel farther.

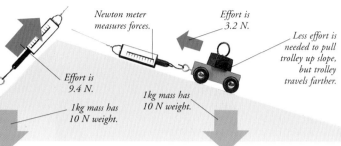

Newton meter measures forces.

Effort is 3.2 N.

Less effort is needed to pull trolley up slope, but trolley travels farther.

Effort is 9.4 N.

1kg mass has 10 N weight.

1kg mass has 10 N weight.

Inclined planes

Lever

A rod that moves on a pivot, or fulcrum, is called a lever. A force (the effort) applied to one part of a lever moves another part with a larger or smaller force (the load) over a different distance. This mechanical digger uses levers to move soil from place to place.

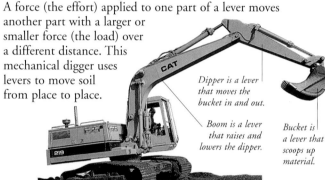

Dipper is a lever that moves the bucket in and out.

Boom is a lever that raises and lowers the dipper.

Bucket is a lever that scoops up material.

Class one levers

A lever in which the fulcrum lies between the effort and the load is called a class one lever. Pliers consist of two identical class one levers with the same fulcrum.

Effort

Fulcrum

Load

Class two levers

A load between the fulcrum and the effort produces a class two lever. A nutcracker is a pair of class two levers. The load is the force required to crack the nut.

Fulcrum

Effort

Load

Class three levers

A class three lever has the effort between the fulcrum and the load. Kitchen tongs consist of two class three levers.

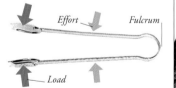

Effort

Fulcrum

Load

Effort and load

On an inclined plane, the effort is the force needed to pull an object up the slope. The load is the weight of the object being lifted. These forces are measured in units called newtons (N).

Screw

A screw is a shaft with a spiraling inclined plane, called a thread, wrapped around it. Turning the screw makes it move forward with a greater force than the effort used to turn it. As the screw turns, objects are pushed away or pulled up the thread. This clamp uses a screw to hold an object tightly onto a work surface.

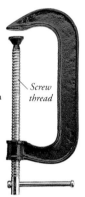

Screw thread

Mechanical advantage

A machine's mechanical advantage is calculated by dividing the load by the effort. The shallow slope above gives an advantage of 3.13 (10 ÷ 3.2), while the steep slope gives only 1.06 (10 ÷ 9.4).

Spiral staircase

A staircase is a type of inclined plane that makes it easier to lift your body to the top of a building. Wrapping the stairs around a shaft to form a spiral staircase saves space. The steeper the stairs, the less turns it takes to climb them, but the more force you need to apply on each step.

Christopher Polhem

Swedish inventor Christopher Polhem (1661–1751) contributed much to our understanding of machines. He wrote over 20,000 articles on engineering and many other subjects, and was one of the first to see the potential of using machines to replace human labor.

Machine elements

Inside most complex machines, a number of simple machines and other mechanical parts link together to control, transmit, or change force and motion, so that the larger machine can perform a specific task.

Flywheel is a heavy disk that rotates at a constant speed and ensures that a machine runs smoothly.

Crank is a rod linked to a rotating shaft that changes circular motion into to-and-fro motion.

Cam-follower

Worm gear

Cam is an irregularly shaped wheel that moves a rod called a cam-follower to and fro as it rotates.

Bevel gear

Spur gear

Gears are toothed wheels that alter the size of a force, or the speed or direction of motion.

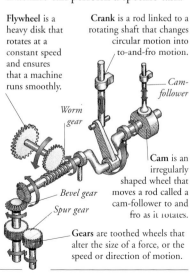

Block and tackle

A block and tackle is a device for lifting heavy loads. It consists of a rope (the tackle) passing over a pulley wheel (the block), and changes the direction of pull on the rope.

Multiple pulley arrangements

A rope looped around a number of pulleys becomes a force magnifier. When the rope is pulled, the load moves a shorter distance than the rope, reducing the effort needed to lift it. The more loops of rope there are, the more the effort is reduced.

Wheel and axle

A wheel fixed to a central shaft forms a machine called a wheel and axle. When the axle turns, the wheel rim turns with less force but travels a greater distance. Turning the wheel rim moves the axle a shorter distance, but with more force.

Engine turns axle, rotating wheel and moving vehicle.

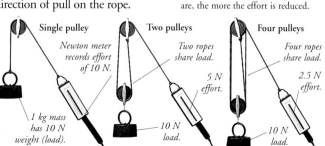

Single pulley

Newton meter records effort of 10 N.

1 kg mass has 10 N weight (load).

Two pulleys

Two ropes share load.

5 N effort.

10 N load.

Four pulleys

Four ropes share load.

2.5 N effort.

10 N load.

FIND OUT MORE ENGINES AND MOTORS   FORCE AND MOTION   FRICTION   TECHNOLOGY

MAGELLAN, FERDINAND

FERDINAND MAGELLAN, A PORTUGUESE sailor employed by Spain, was the first person to sail westward across the Atlantic and Pacific Oceans. He did this because the Spanish wanted to find a route to the rich Spice Islands (now the Moluccas) in southeastern Asia, which were unclaimed by any foreign power. Although it was not Magellan's original intention, one of his ships continued the voyage westward, eventually arriving back in Europe. By completing this remarkable voyage, its crew became the first people to sail all the way around the world.

Early life
Magellan was born into a noble Portuguese family in about 1480. He served as a page in a royal household and then worked in India for Francisco de Almeida, the first Portuguese viceroy (governor) in India. In 1513–14, he worked for the Portuguese in Morocco, but was accused of financial irregularities and lost the favor of the king of Portugal. The king rejected Magellan's proposal to reach the Spice Islands by sailing a westerly course across the Atlantic Ocean.

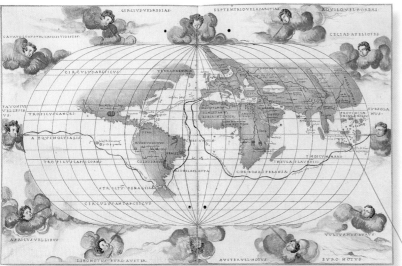

Map of the *Vittoria*'s route

Circumnavigation
In 1517, Magellan took his plan for a journey to the Spice Islands to Charles V of Spain, who provided him with five ships and about 265 men. Magellan set sail from Seville in September 1519. In November 1520, he entered the Pacific and sailed west toward Asia. He reached the Philippines in 1521, where he was killed. Some of his men got back to Spain in 1522.

The Moluccas in Southeast Asia were Magellan's goal when he set off on his westward voyage around the world

Mutiny
While Magellan was spending the winter of 1520 at San Julian at the tip of South America, some of his crew tried to mutiny. One ship was wrecked, and two more were lost. Later, one ship deserted Magellan and returned to Spain.

East Indies

In 1494, Pope Alexander VI divided the then unclaimed world of America and Asia between Spain and Portugal. West of the dividing line was land claimed by Spain; east was territory claimed by Portugal. But the Moluccas in the East Indies, with their rich spice crops, remained unclaimed. To reach these islands, Magellan had to sail west across the Pacific. Magellan named this ocean the Pacific (peaceful), because its waters were so calm after the turbulent Atlantic.

Cinnamon

Nutmeg

Ginger

Strait of Magellan
In October 1520, the two lost ships reappeared, reporting that they had found a channel between the mainland and the island of Tierra del Fuego. Magellan set sail with his three remaining ships and, on October 21, entered the channel, now called the Strait of Magellan. By November 28 they had become the first Europeans to sail into the Pacific.

Death of Magellan
On March 6, 1521, Magellan reached the Mariana Islands. Ten days later, he made landfall in the Philippines. At Mactan, on the island of Cebu in the Philippines, Magellan intervened in a local war, but was killed in a skirmish on April 27. His crew decided to continue on toward Europe without him.

The Vittoria
In April 1521, after Magellan's death, his lieutenant, Sebastián del Cano, took command, setting sail with just two ships. One ship, the *Trinidad,* then sailed across the Pacific to Panama, leaving the other, the *Vittoria,* to sail on around the world. In September 1522, the *Vittoria* returned to Spain.

FERDINAND MAGELLAN

c.1480	Born in Portugal.
1505–12	Serves in India.
1513–14	Serves in Morocco but loses the favor of Portugal's king.
1517	Approaches the king of Spain with proposal to sail to the Spice Islands.
1519	Sets sail from Seville.
1520	Sails into the Pacific Ocean.
1521	Killed in the Philippines.
1521	Under the command of del Cano, the remaining two ships load with spices in the Moluccas.
1522	The *Vittoria* returns to Spain.

FIND OUT MORE   MAPS AND MAPPING   EXPLORATION   SPAIN, HISTORY OF

MAGNETISM

SAILORS USED MAGNETIC compasses to navigate the world's oceans at least 1,000 years ago, but the true nature of magnetism puzzled people for many centuries. Magnetism is an invisible force that comes from objects called magnets. The area around a magnet that is affected by it is called its magnetic field.

Magnet

A magnet has two points, called a north pole and a south pole, where its magnetism is strongest. Lines of magnetic force loop around the magnet from pole to pole.

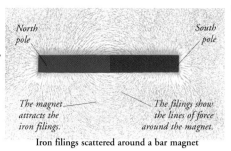

The magnet attracts the iron filings.

The filings show the lines of force around the magnet.

Iron filings scattered around a bar magnet

Magnetic Earth

The Earth itself acts like a giant bar magnet, with a magnetic field and two magnetic poles. These poles are found near the Earth's geographical north and south poles. The Earth's magnetism is probably caused by the movement of molten iron at the Earth's core.

Magnetite

The rocky mineral magnetite, which contains iron, is naturally magnetic. Early sailors used a piece of this rock suspended from a string as a magnetic compass. Magnetite is also called lodestone, which means "guiding stone."

Compasses line up with the Earth's magnetic field.

Compass

A compass is a navigational device containing a small, free-moving magnet called a "needle." The needle is attracted by the Earth's magnetism. It swivels on a pivot until one end points to the Earth's magnetic north pole and the other end points to the magnetic south pole.

Magnetic forces

When two magnets are placed pole to pole, a force acts between them. Different poles (a north and a south) pull each other together. This is attraction. Similar poles (two north or two south) push each other apart. This is repulsion.

South pole → ← *North pole*

Magnetic attraction

North pole ← → *North pole*

Magnetic repulsion

Maglev train

A maglev (magnetic levitation) train hovers above the track, supported by a strong force of repulsion between magnets on the train and the track. Other magnets pull the train along the track.

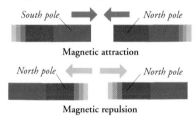

Magnetic materials

When placed within a magnet's force field, some materials turn into magnets themselves – either briefly or permanently. These materials are said to be magnetic.

Magnets will attract iron and some other metals.

Domains in a magnetic material

Domains in a magnet

Non-magnetic materials, such as plastic and cloth, cannot be picked up by magnets.

Magnetic domains

Inside a magnetic material are tiny regions of magnetism called domains, all pointing in different directions. Their effects cancel out, so there is no overall magnetism. In a magnet, the domains all point the same way. Their effects combine to give a strong magnetism.

This steel rod is magnetized by stroking it with a bar magnet.

Magnetism in space

The Earth's magnetic field stretches more than 37,000 miles (60,000 km) out into space. In addition to affecting objects on the planet's surface, the Earth's magnetism also affects electrically charged particles such as electrons and protons emitted by the Sun. The other planets in the Solar System also have magnetic fields, as does the Sun itself.

Geographic north

Magnetic north

Earth's magnetic field

Magnetic south

Geographic south

Lines of force

Magnetic induction

Placing a magnet near a magnetic material causes the material's domains to line up and point in the same direction, turning it into a magnet. This is magnetic induction. The effect is usually temporary, but some materials, such as steel, stay permanently magnetized.

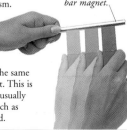

William Gilbert

The study of magnetism was pioneered by William Gilbert (1544–1603), an English doctor and physicist. He suggested that the Earth's magnetism is best understood by thinking of the Earth as a huge bar magnet. Gilbert was also the first to use the term "magnetic pole."

Aurora

The Earth's magnetic poles pull electrically charged particles from the Sun into the atmosphere. As the particles strike atoms or molecules in the air, colored light is emitted in a dazzling display called an aurora.

Solar prominence

Occasionally, disturbances in the Sun's magnetic field allow huge streams of hot gas to erupt from the Sun's surface. Such eruptions are called solar prominences. They can be up to 62,000 miles (100,000 km) high.

FIND OUT MORE   EARTH   ELECTRICITY   ELECTROMAGNETISM   FORCE AND MOTION   X RAYS AND THE ELECTROMAGNETIC SPECTRUM

MALAYSIA AND SINGAPORE

THE 13 STATES of Malaysia are split into two distinct parts. Most people live in Malaya, a long peninsula of mainland Southeast Asia containing 11 states, with the island of Singapore at its southernmost tip. The two remaining Malaysian states of Sarawak and Sabah occupy the northern part of the island of Borneo. Sandwiched between them is Brunei, one of the richest countries in the world. Malaysia, Singapore, and Brunei are all former British territories; Malaysia and Singapore gained independence in the 1960s, and Brunei in 1984. Since then, their economies, particularly Malaysia's, have developed at a dramatic rate.

Mountains and forests
Large areas of Sabah and Sarawak are dominated by mountains that are covered with forest and jungle. In some places the vegetation is so dense that the terrain is virtually impenetrable. The Rajang River loops through Sarawak, interrupted by spectacular waterfalls.

Physical features

A central mountain chain in the Malay Peninsula divides fertile plains in the west from a narrow coastal belt in the east. Singapore is largely flat and is built-up, making it almost a single city-state. Sabah and Sarawak have swampy coastal plains and are separated from the Indonesian part of Borneo by rugged, heavily forested mountains. The interior of Brunei is covered with humid tropical rain forest.

Plural societies

Like other Southeast Asian countries, Malaysia, Singapore, and Brunei are plural societies. The term describes people who live together, but keep their own culture, language, and way of life. Kuala Lumpur is home to a cosmopolitan mix of people, including Malays, Chinese, Indians, and various indigenous groups.

People waiting at a bus stop, Kuala Lumpur

Cameron Highlands
Located in Penang state on the Malay Peninsula, the Cameron Highlands rise about 4,000 ft (1,200 m) above sea level. The fresh, cool air and magnificent views have made them one of the best-known resorts in Asia. The soil is rich, and the Highlands have become the center of Malaysia's tea-growing industry.

Regional climate
Malaysia, Singapore, and Brunei have a tropical climate that is hot and humid all year round. They are vulnerable to seasonal monsoon winds, which can cause dramatic differences in the distribution of rainfall. The coolest areas are the mountains, high ground, and the seashores affected by ocean breezes.

81°F (27°C)   81°F (27°C)

95 in (2,403 mm)

Sarawak Chamber
Lubang Nasib Bagus, also known as the Sarawak Chamber, is the world's largest single cave. The chamber forms part of a large cave system in Gunung Mulu National Park, and measures about 2,300 ft (700 m) long, 980 ft (300 m) wide, and more than 230 ft (70 m) high.

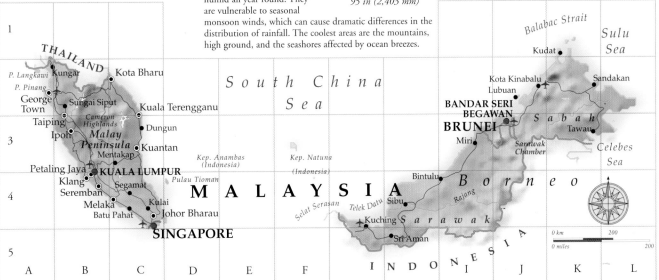

Malaysia

One of the most dynamic countries in Southeast Asia, Malaysia has experienced tremendous economic growth in recent years. While the timber, oil, rubber, and tin industries are still predominant, Malaysia has encouraged manufacturing, which now accounts for over two-thirds of exports. As a result, urban areas are rapidly expanding, although 43 percent of the population still live in rural areas, mostly in the Malay Peninsula. Only about 19 percent lives in Sabah and Sarawak. Malaysia's 13 states are ruled by sultans and governors, from which a new king is chosen every five years.

People

Malays and other indigenous people form about 60 percent of Malaysia's population. Chinese traders settled in the country from the 1400s onward, and later, during the British colonial period, many Indian and Chinese people were brought in as workers. These Perenakan (Malaya-born) Chinese formed their own society, a mixture of Chinese and Malay cultures, and now make up 30 percent of the population. They control much of Malaysia's business and are richer than the Malays, causing some tension.

Wealthy Perenakan women

MALAYSIA FACTS

CAPITAL CITY	Kuala Lumpur
AREA	127,317 sq miles (329,750 sq km)
POPULATION	22,200,982
DENSITY	175 per sq mile (68 per sq km)
MAIN LANGUAGE	Malay
MAJOR RELIGIONS	Muslim, Buddhist, Chinese faiths, Hindu, Christian
CURRENCY	Ringgit
LIFE EXPECTANCY	72 years
PEOPLE PER DOCTOR	2,000
GOVERNMENT	Multiparty democracy
ADULT LITERACY	88%

Kuala Lumpur

Malaysia's capital city began as a mining camp at the junction of two rivers. Its Malay name literally means "muddy meeting place." Today, it is a bustling city, with many modern high-rise buildings and traditional temples. One of the most elaborate buildings is the railroad station. The city is home to more than 1,500,000 people. A new capital is being built at Putrajaya, a high-tech development near Kuala Lumpur.

Railroad station

Sepak raga

Among Malaysia's traditional sports is *sepak raga*, which is played with a *raga*, or ball, woven from strips of rattan. Rattan comes from the reedy stems of certain species of palm trees that are extensively grown in the country. In the game, players try to pass the ball by kicking or heading it, but must not use their hands. The player who lets the ball touch the ground is the loser. Another popular game is *main gasing*, played with spinning tops made from hardwood and carefully placed lead weights.

Kites

Malaysia's national pastime is flying kites, known as *wau*, which was introduced from China. An international festival is held in Kelantan every June, in which the object is to keep one's kite flying as high and as long as possible.

Experienced kiteflyers can make their huge, brightly colored kites perform spectacular maneuvers.

A tea shoot, or flush

Tea

Malaysia's hot, wet climate is ideal for growing tea, and 6,613 tons (6,000 tonnes) are produced every year. Most tea grows in plantations, particularly near the Cameron Highlands. Tea-pickers, usually women, collect the young, tender shoots, called flushes, in large baskets, which they carry on their backs. New shoots appear every few days and must be dried quickly for the best flavor.

Dried tea leaves

Palm oil

Malaysia leads the world in the production of palm oil, which comes from the fruit of the oil palm tree. The oil is mainly used for cooking and is exported around the world for use in the manufacture of margarine, ice cream, and soap. This industry has reduced Malaysia's dependence on rubber.

Rubber

Malaysia is the world's second largest producer of natural rubber. Rubber trees were introduced from Brazil in 1876 and are now grown in large plantations on the slopes of the Malay Peninsula. Workers collect latex in a cup or halved coconut as it oozes from cuts made in the trees' bark. The latex is then sent to a local factory where it is mixed with water and acid to make rubber sheets that are hung up to dry.

Electronics

The electronics industry, developed since the 1970s to broaden Malaysia's economic base, is now its most profitable. Malaysia is one of the world's largest producers of disk drives for computers, and one of the leading manufacturers of integrated circuits. Japan is a key trading partner, often exchanging finished products for raw materials, such as oil and gas.

Proton cars

More than 150,000 Proton cars are produced every year. First made in 1985, they are the most popular cars in Malaysia and are exported to Indonesia, Singapore, and the UK. Such is the Proton's success, that a second car model was launched in 2000.

Singapore

In 1819, Sir Stamford Raffles (1781–1826) set up a British trading post in Singapore, formerly known as Temasek, which enabled the island to be a free trade center for the East Indies. Now, it boasts a successful export-led economy and tourist trade. One of the world's most densely populated countries, Singapore has a myriad of traditional cultures and buildings along with towering skyscrapers and modern stores.

Chinatown
Nearly 78 percent of the population is Chinese. Chinatown, in Singapore City, is a colorful, busy area where traditional cultures flourish. The district is a popular tourist attraction, offering authentic Chinese foods, ancient crafts, and ornate temples.

Laws
The government of Singapore keeps strict control over the media and, in urban areas, littering, chewing gum, eating on trains, and smoking in public are forbidden. Punishments are severe and Singapore has a very low crime rate.

Golf
Singapore is known for its golf courses and has developed specialized golf vacations. The facilities are enjoyed both by people on business and local golfers. It is common for games to go on well into the evening.

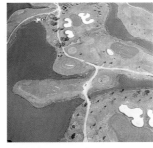

Financial center
Since the 1960s, Singapore has been one of the leading financial centers of eastern Asia. It has secured huge foreign investment in establishing manufacturing and electronics industries. The many banks and the stock exchange generate about one-quarter of the country's wealth alone. Singapore's economic future is predicted to be in high-tech industries.

Orchids
Land for farming is scarce in Singapore, but the country has several orchid nurseries. At the Mandai Garden, the largest commercial orchid nursery in Singapore, exotic and rare flowers are intensively cultivated for export using the latest technology. The orchids are prized for their beauty and color and are flown to Japan, Europe, Australia, and the US.

The orchid is Singapore's national flower.

SINGAPORE FACTS

CAPITAL CITY	Singapore
AREA	239 sq miles (620 sq km)
POPULATION	3,600,100
MAIN LANGUAGES	Malay, Chinese, Tamil, English
MAJOR RELIGIONS	Buddhist/Taoist, Muslim
CURRENCY	Singapore dollar

Singapore harbor
Over 25,000 ships dock at Singapore harbor every year, making it one of the busiest ports in the world. Tankers bring crude oil from the Middle East to be refined and shipped out to neighboring east Asian countries. Most of Malaysia's export trade flows through the port.

Mass transit
About 800,000 passengers a day travel on the Mass Rapid Transport System, a highly efficient train that runs partly underground. It was created to relieve congested roads. Car drivers must bid at auction for the right to buy new cars, and must pay to enter the city during rush hour. Singapore also has rail links with Malaysia.

Brunei

The tiny state of Brunei is an Islamic monarchy. Massive offshore reserves of oil and natural gas have made it extremely wealthy. As a result, the small population enjoys free education, healthcare, and pensions, and pays no income tax. Only about 15 percent of the land is farmed, since Brunei is mostly rain forest. Rice, tropical fruit, and cassava are the main crops.

Sultans
Brunei is a monarchy, ruled since 1967 by the sultan Hassaal Bolkiah. He is one of the world's richest men, believed to be worth US$25 billion. Recently, the sultan built a lavish royal palace in the capital, Bandar Seri Begawan. The city also houses Southeast Asia's largest mosque, named after Bolkiah's predecessor, Omar Ali Saifuddien. A popular tourist site, it has its own lagoon.

BRUNEI FACTS

CAPITAL CITY	Bandar Seri Begawan
AREA	2,228 sq miles (5,770 sq km)
POPULATION	328,000
MAIN LANGUAGES	Malay, English
MAJOR RELIGION	Muslim
CURRENCY	Brunei dollar

Mineral wealth
Huge offshore oil reserves were discovered in Brunei in 1929. Recent estimates say there are at least 40 years' worth of natural gas and 25 years of oil reserves left. Much of Brunei's mineral income is invested.

FIND OUT **MORE** | ASIA, HISTORY OF | CARS AND TRUCKS | ELECTRONICS | EMPIRES | FLOWERS | ISLAM | KITES | MONEY | OIL | PORTS AND WATERWAYS | TRAINS AND RAILROADS

MALI EMPIRE

M

ONE OF THE WEALTHIEST medieval African kingdoms was that of the Mali. Founded in c.1235 in West Africa by a great warrior-king, Sundiata, the empire reached its peak in the 14th century under Sundiata's descendent, Mansa Musa. Mali wealth came from gold mines and trans-Saharan trade, and helped the empire dominate surrounding peoples, such as the Songhai. In the 1400s, the Songhai began to attack the overgrown Mali Empire and eventually conquered it.

Extent of empire 1300s
Trade routes across the Sahara
Tombouctou
Gao
Djénné
Extent of empire 1200s

Extent of empire
At its height in the 14th century, the Mali Empire covered a large part of what is now Senegal, Gambia, Guinea, and the Republic of Mali. The city of Djénné, and the Songhai cities of Tombouctou and Gao on the Niger River became major trading centers. Tombouctou was particularly famous for its trade in gold. The gold was mined in the Niger and Senegal river valleys and exported to North Africa across the Sahara Desert.

Mansas

Mansa Musa

Mansa Musa

Mansa, or "king of kings," was the title used by all Mali's rulers. Sundiata (r.1235–1255), the first mansa, was a member of a tribe ruled by ancient Ghana. Sundiata overthrew Ghana (which was 500 miles, or 800 km, northwest of modern Ghana), established his empire there, and converted to Islam.

Mansa Musa

Kankan Musa, better known as Mansa Musa (r.1312–37), was Mali's greatest ruler, as famous for his piety as for his military successes. After conquering Tombouctou, Gao, and Walata, he established new schools, colleges, and libraries in Tombouctou, and made it a center for Islamic learning.

The Catalan map of Charles V (1375) depicting the Mali Empire

Architecture

The 14th-century Great Mosque in Djénné is the world's largest surviving dried-mud building. Every year, after the rainy season, local people gather together to replaster it by hand. While on a pilgrimage in the 14th century, Mansa Musa met the Spanish scholar and architect As-Saheli and persuaded him to go to Mali. When As-Saheli arrived at the important trading town of Tombouctou, he introduced "burned" bricks as a new building material for important buildings, such as mosques and palaces.

Spires decorated with ostrich eggs, the symbol of fertility and fortune
Protruding beams

Great Mosque at Djénné

Pilgrimage to Mecca

In 1324–25, Mansa Musa made a pilgrimage to Mecca. This pilgrimage was so lavish it made Mali famous throughout the world. When he passed through Egypt, Mansa Musa distributed so much gold – possibly as much as 1.5 tons – that he devalued the metal and depressed the local gold market for years afterward.

Camel driver

Caravans
Camel caravans of up to 10,000 transported Mali's goods across the Sahara. They could cover 200 miles (350 km) of desert in a week.

Trade

As well as spreading Islam, Arab traders also developed caravan routes across the Sahara. These routes linked northern African towns, such as Fez and Cairo, with western towns, such as Djénné. The wealth of sub-Saharan empires depended on controlling these trade routes, which Mali did between 1235 and c.1400.

Djénné
Traders transported goods along the Niger River to and from Djénné. The town was also on a caravan route going south. It became a marketplace for northern African goods going to southern forest kingdoms, such as Benin.

Modern market day, Djénné, Mali

Ibn Battuta

In 1325, the Moroccan writer, jurist, and diplomat Ibn Battuta (1304–77) went on pilgrimage to Mecca. Over 29 years he covered 75,000 miles (120,000 km) in 44 countries. His last journey was to the Mali Empire where he visited the court of Mansa Sulayman, praised Mali piety, but saw little of the famous Mali gold.

Timeline

1235–55 Sundiata rules Mali, after subjugating Ghana Empire.

1255 Sundiata's eldest son, Mansa Oulin, seizes power. Decades of struggle over the succession follow.

1298 Sundiata's general, Sakura (1285–1300), seizes power.

1300 Saharan robbers murder Sakura.

African figs

1312–37 Mansa Musa rules.

1324–25 Mansa Musa's pilgrimage to Mecca.

c.1320–40 Mali Empire reaches its peak.

1336–58 Reign of Mansa Sulayman (Mansa Musa's grandson).

1352 The Arab traveler Ibn Battuta stays in the old Mali capital of Niani for nine months.

c.1400 Gao rebels against Mali overlords; empire begins to decline.

1468 Songhai Empire takes over Mali Empire.

FIND OUT MORE — AFRICA, HISTORY OF • BENIN EMPIRE • ISLAMIC EMPIRES • ISLAM • SONGHAI EMPIRE

MAMMALS

MAMMALS ARE a very complex and diverse group of animals, which includes the largest creatures on Earth. They are remarkably flexible, and through adaptations they are able to live in all regions of the world except the Antarctic continent. Mammals are characterized by having hair, a backbone, mammary glands with which they feed their young, and a particular articulation of the lower jaw. They are warm-blooded, which means they have a constant internal body temperature and do not have to adjust to the temperature of their immediate surroundings.

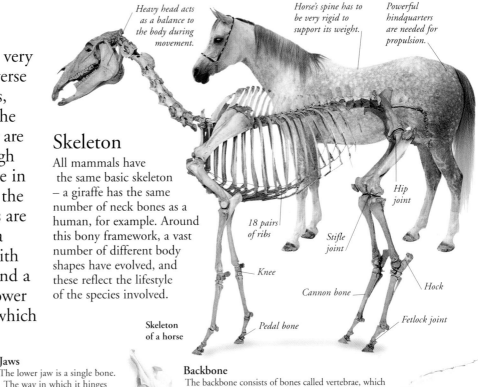

Heavy head acts as a balance to the body during movement.

Horse's spine has to be very rigid to support its weight.

Powerful hindquarters are needed for propulsion.

Skeleton

All mammals have the same basic skeleton – a giraffe has the same number of neck bones as a human, for example. Around this bony framework, a vast number of different body shapes have evolved, and these reflect the lifestyle of the species involved.

18 pairs of ribs

Hip joint

Stifle joint

Knee

Cannon bone

Hock

Skeleton of a horse

Pedal bone

Fetlock joint

Jaws
The lower jaw is a single bone. The way in which it hinges with the skull is one of the evolutionary features that differentiates mammals from reptiles. The upper jaw does not move.

Chimpanzee skull

Backbone
The backbone consists of bones called vertebrae, which hinge against one another and act as a flexible support for the rest of the skeleton. The spinal cord – the main highway of the central nervous system – runs through the backbone.

Shoulder blades are attached here.

Hips attach to sacrum (fused vertebrae).

Backbone of a red fox

Teeth

Most mammals have four different types of teeth: incisors, canines, premolars, and molars. The way in which they develop differs depending on diet and lifestyle. The skull, small at birth, grows quickly, and, in order for teeth that fit fully grown jaws, mammals typically have two sets – milk and adult.

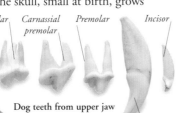

Molar *Carnassial premolar* *Premolar* *Incisor*

Dog teeth from upper jaw

Canine

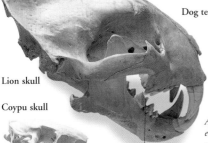

Lion skull

Coypu skull

Carnassials

Carnivore teeth
Most carnivores have large canines to catch and grip prey. Their last upper premolar and first lower molar are arranged to shear against each other like scissors and are called carnassials.

African elephant molar

Asian elephant molar

Rodent teeth
Rodents' incisors keep growing and have hard enamel on only the front. The teeth wear down from behind, keeping them sharp. Rodents have a gap between their incisors and premolars. They can seal off their mouths while gnawing inedible substances.

Elephant teeth
Elephants eat coarse food, and their teeth wear down very quickly. They have three premolars and three molars in each quarter, but use only one at a time. As one becomes worn out, the next one slides into place.

Hair

This is one of the key features that sets mammals apart from other animals. Some mammals, such as the musk ox, are obviously hairy, while others appear to have no hair at all. Elephants have only a sparse covering, while whales have just tiny whiskers when they are young. Most of the hair of armadillos and pangolins has been replaced by scales.

Hedgehog unrolling

Asian short-clawed otters

Protective hair
Most of a hedgehog's hairs have become thickened and stiffened to form spines. They are pointed at the outer end and form a rounded bulb under the skin. If threatened, a hedgehog will roll into a tight ball, erecting its prickly spines, which point in all directions.

Waterproof hair
Otters have thick underfur that is kept dry by the dense guard hairs of their outer coats. Otters have to groom regularly, and seagoing species often have to wash the salt from their coats in freshwater.

Long, stiff whiskers

Sensitive hairs
A cat's whiskers are stiff hairs that project mainly from its face around the mouth, eyes, and cheeks. They are highly sensitive, and a cat can use them to avoid objects and judge the size of openings in total darkness.

M

Temperature control

Some mammal species keep their temperatures at the same level. Others allow their temperatures to vary considerably, and save energy by hibernating in the winter or by going into a very deep sleep at other times. Their temperature may fall almost to the freezing point, and their metabolic rate slows down.

Keeping cool
Elephants have a high volume in relation to their surface area and can become too hot. To lose heat, they flap their large ears, which have prominent veins at the back. The blood leaving the ears is 66.2° F (19° C) cooler than the blood entering.

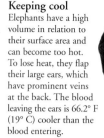

Large blood vessels

Elephant's ear

Sweat glands
Primates, such as monkeys and apes, have sweat glands all over their skin. The sweat evaporates, and this process cools the animals. Dogs have sweat glands only on the soles of their feet. To help keep cool, they pant to allow their saliva to evaporate.

Heat loss
Many small bats have difficulty keeping warm because their wings consist of a large area of uninsulated skin from which they lose heat. When at rest, they save energy by allowing their body temperature to fall to that of their surroundings.

Red fox

Arctic fox

Size
Arctic foxes live in the cold far north. They are smaller than other foxes, such as the red fox, which lives in temperate climates and therefore need to eat less. In winter, when it is really cold, red foxes can forage less often and stay curled up in their warm dens instead.

Surface area
Polar bears have a low surface-to-volume ratio. (The larger the animal the smaller its surface area in relation to its volume.) This means they are able to conserve heat better than the smaller brown bears, which live in warmer climates.

Brown bear

Polar bear

Scent glands

Most mammals live in a world dominated by smell, and scent is very important for transmitting various items of information. Scent glands can be found in many different places on mammals – on the cheeks of cats, under the tails of badgers, under the chins of rabbits, and on the heels of deer. Scent can also be deposited in many different ways.

Communication
Some mammals, such as hyenas, leave traces of scent to pass on information to others of their species. They paste scent on stems of grasses, from which it may be possible to tell their sex, sexual status, and diet.

Identification
A badger uses a gland under its tail to deposit scent on the other members of its social group. The rest of the social group do the same, and a composite scent is built up. This is a sort of family smell, and strangers can be readily recognized.

Establishing Dominance
Dwarf mongooses use scent from glands in their cheeks to pass on information about their social status to other members of their pack. This helps them to establish dominance.

Reproduction

The most common form of mammalian reproduction is placental reproduction. After a successful mating, the embryo is attached to the mother's uterus via the placenta, through which it absorbs nutrients from its mother and expels waste products. This placenta that forms the main part of the afterbirth, which is expelled immediately after the birth of the baby mammal.

Cat giving birth

Kittens are born deaf and blind.

Domestic cats usually have four or five kittens in a litter.

1 After nine weeks' gestation, the kittens are pushed down the birth canal and expelled into the outside world.

2 The mother licks the membrane away from the kitten, which stimulates it to take its first breath.

3 The mother eats the placenta, which was expelled with the kitten. In the wild, it would attract predators.

4 The mother licks and dries all her kittens repeatedly. They will begin to suckle from her within an hour of birth.

Parental care
Female mammals feed their young on milk excreted from their mammary glands, but parental care does not stop there. For some species, such as gorillas, parental guidance, teaching, and protection can go on for many years.

Delayed implantation
Grey seals come on land to give birth and mate once a year. Their gestation period is less than 12 months, so the embryo floats, unattached to the mother, for some months after mating.

Monotremes
Monotremes, such as the platypus, lay eggs. The platypus incubates the eggs in a nest and, after they hatch, feeds the young on milk that runs from mammary glands onto the mother's fur.

Marsupials
While in the mother's uterus, a marsupial embryo lives mainly on a yolk sac. It is born premature after about 12 days and follows a trail of saliva left by the mother, crawling through her fur to her pouch, where it starts to drink milk from a nipple.

Wallaby and young

FIND OUT MORE ANIMALS ANIMAL BEHAVIOR KANGAROOS AND OTHER MARSUPIALS MONKEYS AND OTHER PRIMATES RATS AND OTHER RODENTS REPRODUCTION SKELETON SKIN, HAIR AND NAILS

Mammals

Rusty-colored patch gives this wallaby its name.

Red-necked wallaby is a marsupial, and carries its young in its pouch.

Koala is an Australian marsupial that lives on eucalyptus leaves and spends much of its time asleep.

Spotted hyena is the second largest carnivore in Africa.

African elephant is the largest land mammal. Its nose and top lip form a trunk.

Defensive spines

Sumartran rhinoceros is the smallest rhino and very rare. It lives in Southeast Asia.

Huge paws

Stripes camouflage the tiger in long grass and forests.

Short-beaked echidna from Australia is a mammal that lays eggs.

Common raccoon has dextrous front paws with which it feels for food in water.

Indian tiger is on the verge of extinction in the wild.

European mole is adapted to an underground lifestyle and is a capable digger.

European rabbit is a lagomorph that lives in large social groups.

Common weasel is one of the smallest carnivores, but can single-handedly catch and kill prey larger than itself.

Camel can survive for long periods using the fat stored in its hump.

Antlers are shed and regrown every year.

Reindeer is the only deer to have a furry nose, which allows it to forage comfortably in the snows of the Arctic.

Hollow hairs contain air, which traps body heat.

Zebra's stripes may confuse predators.

Dromedary lives in the desert areas of North Africa and southwest Asia.

Broad feet prevent the camel from sinking into the desert sand.

Long legs keep the dromedary's body high off the ground in the cooler air.

Ring-tailed lemur evolved on the island of Madagascar and occurs nowhere else.

Western lowland gorilla is one of three gorilla sub-species – the largest living primates.

Common zebra lives in family groups led by a stallion.

Polar bear is the largest land carnivore and one of seven species in the bear family.

Manatee is a herbivorous sea mammal related to elephants.

Meerkat belongs to the mongoose family. It lives in social groups in the Kalahari Desert.

Gorillas sleep in trees and bushes.

529

MANDELA, NELSON

M

IN THE STRUGGLE by black South Africans to get rid of the policy of apartheid, Nelson Mandela stands out above all others. His work with the African National Congress and his constant campaigning for the rights of black people eventually led to his imprisonment. For 27 years Mandela was kept in prison, refusing offers for his release except on his own terms. The South African government finally set him free in 1990. In 1993, he won the Nobel Peace Prize with white leader F W de Klerk for their work in bringing peace and reconciliation to their country. The following year, he was elected president of the country that had imprisoned him.

Early life
Nelson Mandela was born the son of a Xhosa chief in Mvezo, Transkei, in 1918. He went to local schools, and then to Healdtown, the top school for black children. He then studied at the University College, Fort Hare, before studying law at Witwatersrand University. Once qualified, he practiced law in Johannesburg.

African National Congress

The African National Congress (ANC) was founded in 1912 to protect and advance the interests of black people in South Africa. As a young man in Johannesburg, Mandela met civil-rights activist Walter Sisulu, who introduced him to the ANC and was to become a lifelong friend. Mandela became active in the ANC's Youth League and joined the ANC executive branch in 1950. Mandela traveled widely in South Africa for the ANC, championing its ideal of a free, multiracial, democratic government.

Mandela and Sisulu

Sharpeville
On March 21, 1960, South African police opened fire on a demonstration against the pass laws in the township of Sharpeville, southwest of Johannesburg. Sixty-nine Africans were killed and nearly 400 wounded. A state of emergency was then declared across South Africa, which faced widespread international criticism for the shootings.

Burning his pass
Every black African had to carry a pass book at all times that restricted access to white-only areas. Along with many others, Mandela refused to carry his pass, joined protests against these unjust apartheid laws, and demonstrated publicly by burning his own pass.

Imprisonment

In 1961, the ANC was banned and its leaders arrested. At first Mandela evaded capture, but he was finally caught and jailed for five years. While in prison, he was charged under the Suppression of Communism Act for organizing sabotage and trying to cause revolution. In June 1964 he was sentenced to life imprisonment. He spent much of the time in a maximum security prison on Robben Island but was moved in 1985 to a Cape Town hospital and then to a less secure prison.

Boycotts
Around the world, antiapartheid campaigners boycotted South African produce, such as fruit and wine, in protest against apartheid and Mandela's imprisonment. The boycotts, which included a complete ban on sporting links, did much to persuade the apartheid government to release Mandela and negotiate with him.

President
After his release from prison, Mandela began negotiations with the South African government to abolish apartheid and introduce multiracial government. Free elections were held in April, 1994, resulting in an overwhelming victory for the ANC. The following month, Mandela became the first black president of South Africa. The new government began the long and difficult task of modernising and stabilising the country.

Mandela and de Klerk

Winnie Mandela
In 1961, Mandela married Winnie Mdikizela, his second wife. While he was in prison, she campaigned tirelessly for his release and for the ANC. However, some of her own political activities attracted considerable controversy, and after his release from prison in 1990, the couple separated and later divorced in 1996.

Fruit from South Africa

Freedom
On February 2, 1990, South African president F W de Klerk lifted the ban on the ANC. Nine days later Nelson Mandela walked out of Victor Verster prison, near Cape Town, after 27 years behind bars. His release was greeted by celebrations all over the world.

NELSON MANDELA

1918 Born, son of a chief of the Xhosa people, Transkei province.

1944 Joins the Youth League of the ANC.

1950 Becomes part of the ANC's executive.

1961 Imprisoned for his leadership of the ANC.

1964 Sentenced to life imprisonment for trying to cause revolution.

1990 Released from prison.

1994 Becomes South Africa's first black president.

FIND OUT MORE

AFRICA, HISTORY OF   GOVERNMENTS AND POLITICS   HUMAN RIGHTS   SOCIETIES, HUMAN   SOUTH AFRICA   SOUTH AFRICA, HISTORY OF

MAORIS AND POLYNESIANS

FROM ABOUT 1300 BC, peoples from Southeast Asia began an epic journey across the uncharted waters of the Pacific, settling the scattered island archipelagos. They took seeds and livestock with them and soon established small farming communities. From about the 9th century AD, groups of settlers began to reach the large islands of New Zealand, where over several centuries they evolved the unique Maori culture.

Map showing settlement of the Pacific

Hawaii
New Guinea Islands
Marshall Islands
Kiribati
Marquesas Islands
Solomon Islands
Samoa
Vanuatu
Fiji
Tahiti
Tonga
Cook Islands
Easter Island
Australia
New Zealand

Settlement of the Pacific

Peoples from New Guinea reached the island of Fiji in about 1300 BC. They then made their way, via Samoa and Tonga, into Polynesia. They reached the Marquesas Islands in about 200 BC, and from there traveled vast distances to Hawaii, Easter Island, and New Zealand.

Polynesians

The Polynesians lived by farming tropical fruits such as yams, breadfruit, and taro, and raising pigs and chickens. They supplemented their diet with fish. Until Europeans arrived in the 18th century, the Polynesians had no knowledge of metal, but they were expert craftsworkers in wood, stone, bone, and shell. Today, many islanders continue the traditional agricultural life.

Religion

Polynesians worshiped many deities in elaborate temple complexes, or *marae*. Their lives were ruled by the idea of "taboo": certain practices, people, or things were considered to be sacred, and any crimes against them were punished. Their religious and political rulers, or chiefs, were protected by the rules of taboo, and were therefore extremely powerful.

Wood carving of Polynesian god

Navigation

The Polynesians sailed the Pacific in canoes, navigating by the position of the Sun and stars. Stick charts, which used cowrie shells to indicate the positions of the islands and sticks to represent the currents, were used as maritime maps.

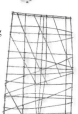

Easter Island statues

On Easter Island, at the eastern edge of Polynesia, the people carved massive statues that stood on raised platforms called *ahu*. It is not known why these statues were made, but they are thought to have religious significance. The statues, many as high as 40 ft (12 m), were actually carved in stone quarries. Once finished they were transported using a combination of sleds, trestles, ropes, and sheer strength, and then levered up to their final position.

Measuring a statue on Easter Island

Maoris

The warlike Maoris of New Zealand lived by fishing, farming, and hunting. They decorated their bodies with tattoo designs to enhance their appearance and provide camouflage in times of war. The Maoris resisted the British colonization of their island in the 19th century, and a series of bloody wars followed. Peace was reached by 1880.

Rafters lead down to figures of other ancestors around the walls.

The poutokomanwa supports the ridge pole.

The koruru represents the head of the ancestor.

Maoris today

Today, Maoris account for about 10 percent of the population of New Zealand. There is still a great deal of resentment between the Maoris and the government. For many years the Maoris felt that the 19th-century peace treaties signed with the British had not been honored, and fought for ancestral lands that had been taken by colonists. In 1995 the British crown apologised to the Maoris, and the 1998 Waitangi Tribunal ordered a return of lands. The Maoris continue to protect their language and culture.

Maihi represents the ancestor's arms.

Raparapa are the ancestor's fingers.

Meeting house

The focus of Maori village life is the meeting house, a large wooden building elaborately carved with curved shapes and spirals. It often symbolizes the body of a specific ancestor: the ridge pole is the ancestor's spine, while the rafters represent the ribs. The meeting house is a place for official business, communal decisions, weddings, funerals, and other rituals. The square, or *marae*, in front of the meeting house is sometimes used for open-air debates.

Tatau *(door)*   Whakamahau *(porch)*   Matapihi *(window)*

Maori society

Maori society was divided into many tribes, and warfare between them was common. Many still uphold these tribal traditions. The All Blacks rugby team's *haka* dance, performed on rugby fields across the world, is a legacy of the Maori war dance and is a gesture of aggression and defiance.

FIND OUT MORE

ART, HISTORY OF   COOK, JAMES   HOUSES AND HOMES   MYTHS AND LEGENDS   NAVIGATION   NEW ZEALAND   NEW ZEALAND, HISTORY OF   POLYNESIA   SOCIETIES, HUMAN

MAPS and MAPPING

THROUGHOUT HISTORY, maps have been used to survey and record territory, plot routes, and reflect our knowledge of the world's geography. Many of the principles used in modern mapping were laid out by classical Greek geographers, such as Ptolemy. Over time, new discoveries in mathematics, astronomy, and space technology have transformed mapmaking.

Map by Italian Enrico Martello, c.1470 showing area around Mediterranean.

Early maps

The first map was made in Babylon in about 2500 BC. Mapmaking was revolutionized in the 15th century by explorers, who increased their knowledge of the size and geography of the globe.

Map projections

Cartographers (mapmakers) use different projections to show the spherical surface of the Earth on a flat piece of paper. All projections involve some distortion of the globe. Cartographers must therefore choose projections that best suit the purpose of the map.

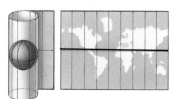

Cylindrical

In this projection, the Earth's sphere is "unwrapped" from a cylinder onto a flat surface to make a rectangular shape. The lines of longitude and latitude are shown as a regular grid of straight lines. Visually the Earth's surface becomes more distorted toward the poles. The most common world map is Gerardus Mercator's projection, which was devised in 1569.

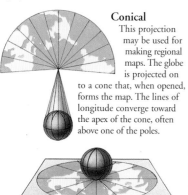

Conical

This projection may be used for making regional maps. The globe is projected on to a cone that, when opened, forms the map. The lines of longitude converge toward the apex of the cone, often above one of the poles.

Azimuthal

In this projection, the image gives the impression of looking at the Earth from space. The surface of the globe is projected onto a flat sheet, which touches the globe at the point that lies at the center of the map. Because distortion increases as you move away from the center of the map, this projection is often used for mapping polar regions.

Key/Legend

● Capital city
◉ City
○ Town
— Road
— Railroad
⌇ Lakes and rivers
⌇ Country boundary
✈ Airport

Compass point indicates magnetic North.

Relief represents the height of the land. Different techniques, such as contour lines or colors, are used to give accurate height readings.

Map of Iberia, Western Europe

Lines of latitude are a series of horizontal lines that represent distances north and south from the Equator.

Lines of longitude are grids of vertical lines that join the poles at each end of the Earth's axis to show east-west distances.

The scale bar shows the relationship between distance on a map and the corresponding distance on the Earth's surface.

Parts of a map

Most maps use a similar range of symbols, known as conventions, that are instantly recognizable. The main conventions used – colors, different kinds of type, and symbols – are explained in the key or legend.

Types of maps

Maps are used for different reasons, and their style varies according to their purpose. Some are used to find a route, others record settlements and land division. Satellite maps record landscape features of parts of the Earth's surface.

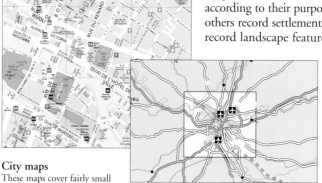

City maps

These maps cover fairly small areas such as towns and cities. Most people use these maps to find individual streets, railway stations, and hospitals, as well as particular places of interest such as parks, museums, and churches.

Road maps

One of the most frequently used map is the road map. Different kinds of roads are indicated by color and width of line, so it is possible to see instantly what is a highway and what is a minor road.

Satellite maps

Satellites orbiting the globe are used to observe and record the Earth's surface. By using remote sensing equipment, they can pick up energy from human settlements, rocks, water, and vegetation, and translate it into images. Satellite images are used to create highly accurate maps.

FIND OUT MORE ASTRONOMY COLUMBUS, CHRISTOPHER EXPLORATION MAGNESTISM NAVIGATION SATELLITES SPACE EXPLORATION TRAVEL

MARSH AND SWAMP WILDLIFE

THE SALT- AND FRESHWATER wetlands of the world provide some of nature's finest havens for wildlife. These areas where shallow, still, or slow-moving water mingles with emergent vegetation are commonly called marshes and swamps, and act as a crossroads between land and aquatic habitats. The animals that live here are adapted to exploit food opportunities, avoid danger, move around easily in their habitat, and cope with changes in water levels. Saltwater wetlands undergo daily changes in water level with the ebb and flow of the tides, and freshwater wetlands undergo changes throughout the year as the water table rises and falls Some even dry out completely.

Marshes and swamps

Wetlands often develop on coastal flats, alongside rivers, lakes, and estuaries, and in inland depressions where water cannot quickly drain away. They vary according to terrain, water conditions, and climate. Marshes are areas of poorly drained land; swamps are areas of permanently waterlogged ground, often overgrown. Other types of wetlands include upland peat bogs, low-lying flood meadows, mangrove swamps, salt marshes lining river mouths, and dense reed beds.

Reeds often grow at the water's edge.

Water lilies provide perches for some animals.

Many animals lurk below the water's surface.

Okavango delta, Botswana

Mammals

Mammals that live in marshes and swamps swim or wallow regularly, or can move over flimsy vegetation and soft mud without sinking. They range in size from tiny harvest mice that cling to reed stems, to giants such as hippos and rhinos. Wetlands are havens for mammals such as tigers, jaguars, and otters, threatened elsewhere, because humans hunters have difficulty in this terrain.

Large nose, or proboscis, of male may reach 3 in (7.5 cm) in length.

Proboscis monkey
Saltwater flooding and the changing tides make a mangrove swamp a hostile environment for most ground-based mammals, but tree-dwelling monkeys can climb the branches of the mangroves, well above the rising water. The strange-looking proboscis monkey feeds mainly on mangrove leaves around the coast of Borneo.

Sitatunga antelope
The sitatunga of tropical Africa is more at home in wetland habitats than any other antelope. It can swim well, even in deep water, and easily copes with walking over treacherously swampy surfaces. Flexible joints in its feet mean the antelope can splay out its long hooves, and so spread its weight on soft ground.

Webbed toes make movement in water easier.

Capybara
The wetlands of South America are the home of the capybara – the largest of the world's rodents. Family groups of capybara spend most of the time in and around water. They are good swimmers, and submerge themselves in water to avoid enemies, leaving just their eyes and nostrils poking above the surface.

Birds

Large beak

Very sensitive eyes allow kingfisher to see when it dives below water.

Marshes and swamps are ideal habitats for birds. The mixture of open water, muddy shallows, and emergent vegetation provides feeding opportunities for many birds, including waterfowl, waders such as redshanks, and aerial predators. The dense vegetation also provides a safe place for birds, such as reed warblers, to roost. Many birds fly from other habitats into marshy areas, but few dry-land predators will tread through water to follow them.

Malachite kingfisher
This is a common waterside bird across most of tropical Africa. It perches on reeds, mangroves, and other swampland plants to scan the water below for signs of prey. On sighting a small fish or dragonfly larva near the surface, the kingfisher dives down to snatch the unwary victim in its bill.

Bittern is well camouflaged in the reeds.

European bittern
Reedy European marshes are the home of the bittern, a wading bird whose narrow-striped plumage provides excellent camouflage against surrounding reeds. When the bird senses danger, it raises its long, sharp bill upward, to accentuate its camouflage and make it almost impossible to detect.

Amphibians

Both tropical and temperate freshwater wetlands are ideal habitats for amphibians. Frogs, toads, salamanders, and newts relish the part-land, part-water environment. Few amphibians can tolerate saltwater habitats because of their permeable skin.

American bullfrog
Well-known for its deep, loud croaks, the American bullfrog is suited to life in wetlands. Webbed feet help it swim, and eyes on the top of its head allow it to see when submerged in water. It spends its time in and out of the water and eats various prey, including smaller frogs.

Large ear drum enables bullfrog to hear well.

Long legs for leaping

M

Reptiles

Marshes and swamps are some of the best places to see reptiles in tropical regions. Crocodiles and turtles often bask in the sunshine at the water's edge, and freshwater and saltwater wetlands also harbor lizards, such as green iguanas. Venomous and non-venomous snakes are common predators in swamps, where they slither through the vegetation or swim across the shallow water.

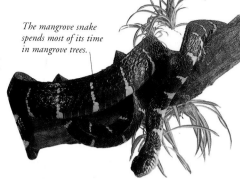

The mangrove snake spends most of its time in mangrove trees.

Mangrove snake

The beautifully patterned mangrove snake patrols the mangrove swamps of Southeast Asia. It spends most of the day draped over a branch of a mangrove tree. Later in the day it descends to hunt among the branches and foliage for birds and their nests, which it raids for their young. It bites its prey and injects venom through grooved fangs. Sometimes it moves right down to the mud to snatch other prey.

Caiman can lie hidden below water while still able to see and breathe.

Strong teeth seize and chew prey.

Spectacled caiman

Although smaller than crocodiles and alligators, the caimans of South America can still grow to nearly 10 ft (3 m) in length and are large enough to carry off a full-grown capybara in their many-toothed jaws. In the vast wetlands of the Brazilian Pantanal, the spectacled caiman is still the most common large predator, despite the severe reduction of its population by hunters.

Snapping turtle

Lurking unseen on the swamp bed among aquatic vegetation, the snapping turtle of North and South America is a patient, but fearsome predator. As soon as any suitably sized prey such as fish, frogs, waterbirds, or rodents draw too close, the turtle shoots its head forward with lightning speed and clamps its jaws shut around its victim.

Invertebrates

Wetlands are home to a huge diversity of invertebrates. Insects and spiders live on plants; crustaceans and the larvae of insects such as mosquitoes live in water; and worms and shellfish remain buried in mud. They feed on plants, debris, or hunt each other. They themselves provide food for many larger marsh and swamp animals.

Great raft spider

This large spider – females may be nearly an inch (2 cm) long – lives in marshy areas of Britain. It hunts in the vegetation at the water's surface. It lures small fish by tapping the water with its front legs, then lunges to attack them with its fangs.

Fish

Fish aims jets of water at insects to knock them off leaves.

The dense vegetation, fluctuating water levels, and often oxygen-poor water of marshes and swamps have created many adaptations in the fish that live there. For example, freshwater angelfish have flattened bodies to slip easily among the stems of underwater plants. Lungfish bury themselves in mud when pools dry up, while Siamese fighting fish can breathe air from the surface if the water becomes stagnant.

Archer fish

In the mangrove swamps of Southeast Asia, archer fish may pick up insects from the surface of the water. Even insects resting on leaves are not safe. The archer fish can spit a precisely aimed jet of water up to 3.3 ft (1 m) high to knock unsuspecting prey down into its jaws.

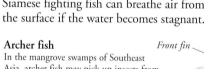

Mudskippers

Mudskippers live in mangrove swamps. When the tide retreats, they do not need to travel with it. Stiff front fins act like legs and enable them to move around on the mud. As long as their skin remains moist, they are comfortable out of water.

Front fin

Mottled skin for camouflage

Emperor dragonfly

This large dragonfly lives in wetlands in Britain. Males are normally bright blue and females green. On summer days adults hunt back and forth over pools, chasing other flying insects. If their homes dry up during a drought, emperor dragonflies migrate long distances to search for new breeding sites.

Its normally bright color has faded after preservation.

Plants

Pitcher plants contain enzymes to digest their prey.

Plants that thrive best in marshes and swamps are those adapted to growing in soggy soil and capable of efficiently transporting air from the leaves to the oxygen-starved, submerged roots. Most wetland plants are non-woody, such as low-growing herbs and mosses and tall, narrow-stemmed reeds and papyrus. Some large woody plants do grow in wetlands, including willows, swamp cypress, and mangroves.

Pitcher traps insects.

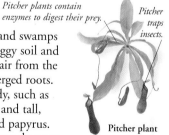

Pitcher plant

Carnivorous plants

These meat-eating plants obtain nutrients from insects' bodies in addition to making food by photosynthesis. They are common in bogs and marshes where it is hard to extract nutrients from soil. Pitcher plants, sundews, and flytraps have special devices to trap or ensnare their prey.

Mangroves

Tropical shores are often lined with mangrove swamps. Mangroves can tolerate being submerged in saltwater up to their stems. The leaves secrete excess salt, and parts of the roots project above the swamp mud to absorb oxygen directly from the air when the tide is out.

Fiddler crab

Holes dotted across the bed of a mangrove swamp are the burrows of fiddler crabs. When the seawater retreats, the crabs emerge to scoop edible morsels from the mud. Males use only their smaller claw for feeding. The other claw, hugely enlarged and vividly colored, is mainly for display. The male waves it at females, signaling he wants to mate, and brandishes it to ward off other males from territory. He uses it as a weapon if a rival does not back down.

Huge right pincer of male

Reeds

Tall, thin-stemmed reeds grow closely together in shallow water to form dense beds at the edges of lakes. As old plants decay and trap sediment, the base of the reed bed builds up until it rises above the water level. Eventually, the bed dries out, and new plants colonize the former marsh.

FIND OUT MORE AMPHIBIANS CARNIVOROUS PLANTS CROCODILES FISH GRASSES, RUSHES AND SEDGES HERONS, STORKS AND FLAMINGOS PHOTOSYNTHESIS REPTILES SNAKES

MARX, KARL

ACROSS EUROPE, the Industrial Revolution created huge differences in wealth between capitalists, who owned the factories and took the profit, and workers, who produced the wealth. The German philosopher Karl Marx created a radical new plan to end this system. With the rallying cry of "Working men of all countries, unite!" he set out a theory of history that made economics the driving force of every event. He believed that a class struggle would break out between capitalists and workers, and that workers would one day construct a classless, communist society. Marx's ideas were ignored during his lifetime, but have had an enormous impact on the history of the 20th century.

Early life
Marx was born into a German-Jewish family in the Rhineland town of Trier in 1818. He studied at Bonn and then Berlin, where he took law but was more interested in history and philosophy. Marx became strongly critical of religion and the luxurious life of the upper classes.

The Communist Manifesto

In 1848, Marx and Engels wrote The Communist Manifesto. Opening with the words: "The history of all hitherto existing society is the history of class struggles," the book describes communism and urges workers to overthrow the bourgeoisie – those who possess capital and property – and take power themselves. The manifesto was hugely influential in the development of communism.

Das Kapital

Marx's lifelong work was a study "to lay bare the laws of motion of capitalist society." The first volume of *Das Kapital* was published in 1867; two more volumes appeared after his death. In *Das Kapital*, Marx set out to explain why working people are exploited in capitalist societies. He predicted that capitalism would fail, giving way to a classless communist society.

Title page of *Das Kapital*

Marx in London
Marx lived in Germany in 1848, but was charged with high treason and, eventually, fled to London. There he spent the rest of his life in poverty, supported by money from Engels and income from journalism. He devoted his life to studying capitalism.

19th-century London Street

1848 Revolutions
In 1848 revolutions broke out in many European countries. They occurred independently of each other, but had much in common, as discontent against rulers erupted in the streets. The revolutions were quickly crushed, but they gave Marx hope that a full-scale communist revolution would soon break out.

Revolutionaries fighting on the streets of Vienna

Friedrich Engels
Engels (1820–95) was born in Germany but spent much of his life working in his father's textile business in Manchester, England. There he became interested in the conditions of working people, and used his considerable wealth to support Marx in his writing and research. After Marx's death, he edited and had published the final two volumes of *Das Kapital*.

The First International

The First International Working Men's Association was established by Marx in 1864 to further his ideas and to coordinate revolutionary activities around the world. After disagreements between Marx, who favored strong central control, and the anarchist Mikhail Bakunin (1814–76), who favored local power, the First International dissolved itself in 1876.

The Paris Commune
After the defeat of France in the war with Prussia in 1871, the citizens of Paris refused to accept the entry of German troops into the city. They rose in revolt and set up a government, or Commune, based on France's revolutionary government of 1792. They were put down with great severity. Many of the Communards were influenced by Marx's ideals, and the defeat of the Commune was a bitter blow to communists everywhere.

Death of Marx
Tired, dispirited, and plagued by ill health, Marx wrote a steady stream of books and articles in his later life. He died in March 1883; his much-loved wife and daughter both died before him. Marx was buried in Highgate Cemetary in North London.

Memorial to Marx

KARL MARX

1818 Born in Trier, Rhineland.

1835–41 Studies in Bonn and Berlin.

1842 Works as a newspaper editor in Cologne.

1843 Marries Jenny von Westphalen.

1848 Writes *The Communist Manifesto* with Friedrich Engels.

1849 Flees to London, where he spends most of the remaining years of his life.

1864 Forms the International Working Men's Association, known as the "First International".

1867 Publishes the first volume of *Das Kapital*.

1883 Dies in London.

FIND OUT MORE | COLD WAR | EUROPE, HISTORY OF | GOVERNMENTS AND POLITICS | INDUSTRIAL REVOLUTION | RUSSIAN REVOLUTION | SOCIETIES, HUMAN | SOVIET UNION | TRADE AND INDUSTRY

MATHEMATICS

WE ARE ALL MATHEMATICIANS, because we all use numbers in our daily lives. The study of numbers, shapes, and quantities is called mathematics. People invented mathematics long ago to help them count and measure things, survey land, and construct buildings. Mathematics is an essential tool for understanding the world around us. Today, scientists use it to test their theories, engineers use it to design new machines and structures, and businesses use it to monitor their sales and income. There are many different branches of mathematics, including geometry and statistics.

2-D shapes around the home

Polygons, such as squares and triangles, are flat shapes with three or more straight sides.

Squares

Triangle

Hexagon

Circles

Rectangles

3-D shapes around the home

Pyramid

Cone

Cylinder

Cubes

Spheres

Polyhedra, such as cubes and pyramids, are solid shapes with polygons as faces.

Geometry

The branch of mathematics that studies the properties of shapes, points, lines, curves, surfaces, and angles – and the relationships between them – is called geometry. Geometry classifies shapes into two main groups: flat shapes, such as squares and circles, and solid shapes, such as cubes and spheres.

Flat shapes
Shapes that have length and width but no depth are said to be two-dimensional (2-D). They have an area but no volume. They may have straight sides, such as squares and triangles, or curved sides, such as circles.

Solid shapes
Spheres and cubes are solid shapes, because they have depth as well as length and width. Solid shapes are said to be three-dimensional (3-D). Solid shapes take up space, so they have a volume. They also have a surface area.

Angles

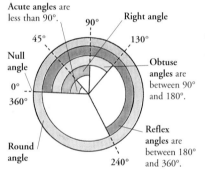

Acute angles are less than 90°.

90°

Right angle

45°

130°

Null angle

0°
360°

Obtuse angles are between 90° and 180°.

Reflex angles are between 180° and 360°.

Round angle

240°

Types of angle
Angles are measured in units called degrees (°). An angle of 0° is a null, or zero, angle. The angle between the lines that meet at a corner of a square is 90°, and is called a right angle. One complete turn of 360° forms a round angle.

An angle is a measure of how much an object turns, or the amount of rotation between two lines that meet. A clock's hands, for example, move through various angles as time passes. The minute hand makes one complete turn every hour; the hour hand, one turn every 12 hours.

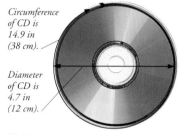

Circumference of CD is 14.9 in (38 cm).

Diameter of CD is 4.7 in (12 cm).

Pi (π)
If you divide the circumference of any circle by the circle's diameter, the result of the calculation will always be about 3.14. This number expresses the ratio of the circumference of a circle to its diameter, The ratio is exactly the same for every circle. It is called pi, after one of the letters of the Greek alphabet, and is normally written as the symbol π.

Symmetry
A line drawn down the middle of your face divides your face into two halves that look like mirror images of each other. Shapes with this property are symmetrical. The dividing line is called a line of symmetry – some shapes have two or more lines of symmetry.

Symmetrical numbers

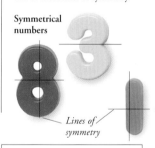

Lines of symmetry

Right-angled triangles

A right-angled triangle is a triangle in which two of the sides meet at an angle of 90°. Engineers, mathematicians, and scientists use such triangles to find heights or lengths. There are two ways of doing this. Knowing the lengths of two sides of a right-angled triangle, you can find the length of the third using Pythagoras's theorem, named after the Greek philosopher Pythagoras (ca.550–ca.500 BC). Trigonometry uses the angles of a triangle to find the lengths of its sides.

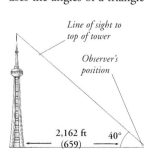

Line of sight to top of tower

Observer's position

2,162 ft (659)

40°

Trigonometry
A right-angled triangle's angles are directly related to the lengths of its sides by three special ratios called the tangent, sine, and cosine. A person 2,162 ft (659 m) from a tower and looking up at an angle of 40° to see its top can use trigonometry to find its height. The distance multiplied by the tangent of 40° (0.839) gives a height of 1,814 ft (553 m).

Side B is 3 units long, so its square is 9 units².

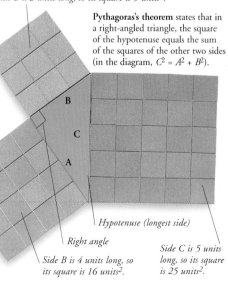

Pythagoras's theorem states that in a right-angled triangle, the square of the hypotenuse equals the sum of the squares of the other two sides (in the diagram, $C^2 = A^2 + B^2$).

B

C

A

Hypotenuse (longest side)

Right angle

Side B is 4 units long, so its square is 16 units².

Side C is 5 units long, so its square is 25 units².

Euclid

Euclid (ca.300 BC), a Greek mathematician, was one of the founders of geometry. His 13-volume book *Elements* studied the geometries of all the major shapes and outlined the key mathematical theories of the time. It was used as a school text until the 20th century.

M

Algebra

Substituting letters or symbols for unknown numbers, and using equations (statements that two things are equal) is called algebra. In this equation, a banana represents an unknown number. The banana's value is clearly 4. Algebraic equations involve variables (numbers that can change their values) and constants (those that stay the same).

+ 2 = 6

What is the value of the banana?

Functions

A function is an equation that relates two or more variables. In the function C = (F - 32) x 5 ÷ 9, the variables C and F represent temperatures on the Celsius and Fahrenheit scales. The function makes it easy to calculate that 80°F is equivalent to just under 27°C (C = [80 - 32] x 5 ÷ 9).

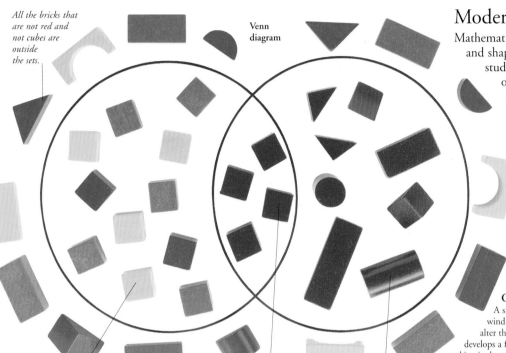

All the bricks that are not red and not cubes are outside the sets.

Venn diagram

Set containing all the bricks that are cubes

Where the sets overlap, all the bricks are red cubes.

Set containing all the red bricks

Modern mathematics

Mathematics is about more than just numbers and shapes. Much of modern mathematics studies the relationships between groups of items called sets. Other important areas include logic, which is used to test new mathematical ideas, and chaos, which studies the behavior of unpredictable systems.

Sets

The items in a set may be numbers, objects, or even ideas. The relationships between the members of different sets can be shown on a Venn diagram, named after John Venn (1834–1923), a British mathematician. This simple Venn diagram of different-shaped colored bricks shows a set of red bricks and a set of cube-shaped bricks. Bricks that are red cubes are found where the sets intersect, or overlap.

Chaos

A small disturbance in wind or temperature can alter the way the weather develops a few days later, making it almost impossible to make accurate long-term weather forecasts. In principle, even the flapping of a butterfly's wings could affect the weather. The sensitivity of "chaotic" systems, such as the weather, is often called the butterfly effect.

Can a flapping butterfly change the weather?

Statistics

The word "statistics" has two meanings: it refers not only to collections of numbers called data, but also to the the science of analyzing data. The study of statistics enables mathematicians to calculate trends in collections of data. Graphs display the data visually, making the trends easier to understand. Data can also be split into different categories and shown on a bar graph or a pie chart.

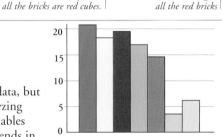

Bar graph
A bar graph displays collections of data or different quantities as columns against a vertical scale. The height of the columns shows the size of the quantities. Without the scale, the graph would be meaningless.

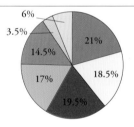

Pie chart
On a pie chart, different quantities are represented by different angles within a circle. The larger the quantity, the larger the angle, and the greater the area of the circle it occupies.

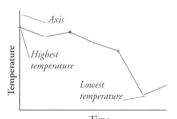

Line graph
The change of a variable quantity over a period of time can be shown as a line graph. This graph records temperature on the vertical axis, while time runs left to right along the horizontal axis.

Probability

When you toss a coin, there is an equal chance of throwing heads or tails. Probability is the study of the chances of events occurring. The chance of throwing a head is said to be a probability of one-half (0.5). Using probability, statisticians can take data gathered from a small sample of items and make guesses about a much larger number of similar items.

Tossing a coin

Timeline

30,000 BC "Tally marks" are made on bones to represent numbers.

ca.2300 BC The first proper number system is devised in Mesopotamia.

ca.500 BC Geometry is used in mathematical proofs in Greece, India, and China.

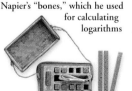

Napier's "bones," which he used for calculating logarithms

ca. AD 1000 Arab mathematicians use algebra as well as geometry.

1614 Scottish mathematician John Napier invents logarithms.

1660s Englishman Isaac Newton and Konrad Liebniz, a German, publish key works on mathematics.

1980s US mathematicians develop chaos theory.

FIND OUT MORE | BUTTERFLIES AND MOTHS | HEAT AND TEMPERATURE | MONEY | NEWTON, SIR ISAAC | NUMBERS | PHYSICS | WEATHER | WEIGHTS AND MEASURES

MATTER

EVERY OBJECT AND SUBSTANCE that exists in the Universe is made up of matter – including the air we breathe, the water we drink, the ground we walk on, and even our own bodies. Scientists define matter as anything that occupies a space. All matter is made up of tiny particles called atoms and molecules. Forces called chemical bonds combine the particles in different ways to form many different types of matter.

Mass and density

The mass of an object is the amount of matter it contains. Mass is measured in units called kilograms (kg). An object's density shows how concentrated the matter is. Density is calculated by dividing the object's mass by its volume. A wooden block has a greater volume than a lead block of the same mass, because lead is more dense, with particles packed more closely together.

Lead is 11 times more dense than wood.

The two blocks have the same mass, so the pans balance.

Lead   Wood

States of matter

Most substances can exist as a solid, a liquid, or a gas – together, these are known as the three states of matter. The state of a substance depends upon the way its particles are arranged, how much energy they have, and the strength of the bonds between them.

Changing state

A substance may change its state if its temperature rises or falls sufficiently. When heated, solids change to liquids by melting, and liquids change to gases by evaporation. When cooled, gases change to liquids by condensation, and liquids change to solids by freezing. The change of a solid directly into a gas (and vice versa) is called sublimation.

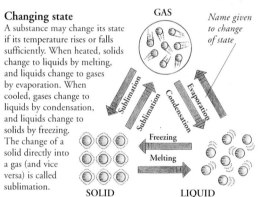

Name given to change of state

GAS

Sublimation · Sublimation · Condensation · Evaporation

Freezing

Melting

SOLID   LIQUID

The air is made up of a mixture of gases, such as oxygen and nitrogen.

Gas
The bonds between the widely spaced particles of a gas are very weak, or nonexistent, meaning that a gas will spread out to fill any available space.

The water cascading down the cliff is a liquid.

Liquid
Liquid particles have more energy and are spaced a little farther apart than solid particles. The flexible bonds between them enable the liquid to flow.

The rocks that make up the cliff are solids.

Solid
The particles of a solid are packed tightly together. The bonds between the solid particles are stronger and more rigid than those between liquid particles.

Plasma
Extreme heat or a powerful electric current can split up the atoms of a gas and form plasma – a mixture of charged particles called electrons and ions. Plasma is often called the fourth state of matter. It forms in lightning and in stars, and can be created using a device called a plasma ball, in which a strong current passes through low-pressure gases.

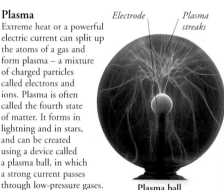

Electrode   *Plasma streaks*

Plasma ball

Conservation of matter

Matter is always conserved during a chemical reaction, which means that the atoms of the reacting materials (the reactants) are not destroyed, but rearranged to form new materials (the products). The combined masses of the reactants are the same as the combined masses of the products.

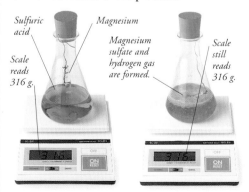

Sulfuric acid

Magnesium

Magnesium sulfate and hydrogen gas are formed.

Scale reads 316 g.

Scale still reads 316 g.

Before the reaction   After the reaction

Matter and energy
Scientists have discovered that when the nucleus, or center, of an atom splits into two smaller nuclei during a nuclear reaction, there is a tiny loss of mass. The scales in the picture show that mass is lost when a uranium nucleus splits to form nuclei of barium and krypton. According to the German physicist Albert Einstein (1879–1955), the missing mass is converted into energy. Einstein showed that mass and energy are effectively the same thing, which is why scientists today prefer to use the term "mass-energy."

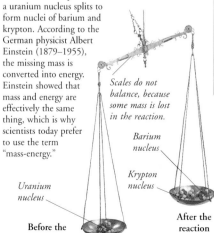

Scales do not balance, because some mass is lost in the reaction.

Barium nucleus

Krypton nucleus

Uranium nucleus

Before the reaction   After the reaction

Living matter
Animals and plants are often referred to as living matter. Like rocks, air, and water, living organisms are made up of atoms, but they are different from nonliving forms of matter because they can grow, move, reproduce, and react to their environment.

Toucan

Vacuum
A total absence of matter is called a vacuum. It is impossible to obtain a perfect vacuum. Pumping air out of a container produces a near vacuum, but some air molecules will always remain inside. When scientists refer to a vacuum, they usually mean a space with very few atoms in it. The closest thing to a true vacuum is the space between stars.

FIND OUT MORE   ATOMS AND MOLECULES   EINSTEIN, ALBERT   GASES   LIQUIDS   NUCLEAR POWER   SOLIDS

MAURYAN EMPIRE

IN C.322 BC, a young nobleman and great warrior, Chandragupta Maurya, overthrew the foreign governors installed in western India by Alexander the Great. Chandragupta and his successors then formed the Mauryan Empire by uniting almost all of India, Afghanistan, and what is now Pakistan as one great nation for the first time. The empire reached its height under its greatest ruler – Chandragupta's grandson, Asoka, who introduced Buddhism to India.

Origins of the empire

When Alexander and a battle-weary army took over what is now the Punjab, his conquest lasted only a few years. From a base in Pataliputra, Chandragupta seized the neighboring kingdom of Magadha and pushed westward through Alexander's lands in the Punjab.

Alexander the Great

The pillar at Sarnath showing the four lions, India's emblem

Asoka

In 261 BC, Asoka conquered the southern state of Kalinga. Thousands of people were killed during the battle. This enormous loss of life turned Asoka against violence forever. He converted to Buddhism and devoted his life to governing peacefully. The empire reached its peak under Asoka's rule.

Fragment of the sixth pillar of edict

Edicts of Asoka
Asoka had many of his edicts (sayings) inscribed on rocks, in caves, and on pillars that were specially built all over India. These inscriptions advise a life of toleration, nonviolence, simplicity, and vegetarianism. They describe the emperor, who once wrote that "All men are my children," as striving for the well-being of his subjects.

Governing the empire

The Mauryan government was well organized. A civil branch dealt with births and deaths, immigration, manufacturing, industrial arts, trade, and tax collection. A justice system prescribed severe punishments for lawbreakers. Governors administered each region. The two emperors that came before Asoka held the system together with an army of 700,000 men and a secret police force that sent spies all over the empire.

Part of stupa gateway

A yaksi, or female nature spirit

The yaksi guards treasure hidden under tree roots.

Religious tolerance

Asoka used an idea called "dharma" (the principles of right thinking), instead of conquest, to hold his empire together. He encouraged a policy of religious tolerance among his nobles and civil servants, and this policy helped him unite an empire that contained people of different religious beliefs.

Buddhism in the Mauryan Empire
Buddhism became a major religion during the Mauryan period, and many craftworkers began to create beautiful religious items, particularly from steatite. These include reliquaries (containers for sacred relics) and symbols that were central to Buddhist ideas, such as the Wheel of Law. The spokes of the wheel symbolize rays of light, or enlightenment, shining from the Buddha.

Wheel of Law

Steatite casket

Steatite is a type of soapstone.

Casket contains crystal reliquaries and coins.

Steatite reliquary

Stupas
Asoka sponsored the building of many Buddhist shrines, or stupas. These were places of pilgrimage for Buddhists, and the carvings inside them inspired prayer and meditation. Most have been rebuilt, but the entrance gates of the Great Stupa at Sanchi are from the Mauryan period.

Timeline

322 BC Chandragupta Maurya founds the Mauryan Empire.

c.301–269 BC Reign of Bindusara, Chandragupta's son. He conquers parts of the Deccan, southern India.

269–232 BC The Mauryan Empire reaches its height under Asoka, Chandragupta's grandson.

261 BC Asoka conquers the kingdom of Kalinga.

Carving of the Buddha

Crystal reliquary

184 BC The empire collapses when Brihadnatha, the last emperor, is killed by a rival dynasty.

c.250 BC Asoka builds Buddhist stupas and erects pillars bearing inscriptions.

FIND OUT MORE   ALEXANDER THE GREAT   BUDDHISM   BUDDHA   GUPTA EMPIRE   INDIA, HISTORY OF

MAYA

SOME 2,000 YEARS AGO, the remarkable Mayan culture began to emerge in Central America. The peak of this culture – its Classic period – was between 300 and 900. The Maya were a sophisticated people and had skilled astronomers and mathematicians. They developed a writing system and built spectacular cities, such as Palenque and Tikal, whose ruins still tower over the rain forest today. The Maya traded with the Mesoamericans of central Mexico, worshiped a large group of gods, and performed religious rituals based on their calendar. They survived in the region until the Spaniards arrived in the 1500s.

Palenque Tikal

Rituals

The Maya conducted special rituals on particular dates in the calendar, and many of these involved the king. Blood-letting, or human and animal sacrifice, were common in the rituals because the Maya believed that sacrificial blood nourished their gods. The victims were often prisoners of war or orphans.

Blood-letting
This stone lintel from Yaxchilan temple shows the lord Shield Jaguar and his wife Lady Xoc carrying out a royal blood-letting ritual. Mayan rulers thought their blood was of the highest status, so shedding it, as Lady Xoc is doing by threading a thorny rope through her tongue, was a way of satisfying the gods and proving royal lineage.

This glyph says "He is letting blood."

Shrunken head on the king's headdress

Beaded necklace with image of Sun God

This glyph says "She is letting blood."

The name of "Lady Xoc"

Jaguar-pelt sandals

The name of "Shield Jaguar"

The torch indicates this ritual probably took place at night.

Traditional headdress

Scrolls on Lady Xoc's cheeks and lips represent the blood she sheds to feed the gods.

Thorn-lined rope that Lady Xoc pulls through her tongue

Blood-stained paper in a woven basket

Temples

Mayan cities always had a ceremonial center, where the people built stepped pyramids and placed sacred temples on top of them. This was thought of as a way of getting closer to the gods, who were often connected with the sky. At the same time, they removed the rituals from the eyes of ordinary people.

Palenque
This lowland city grew in influence in the 7th century under its greatest leader, Pacal. The king adorned the city with a large palace and several pyramid temples. He extended his power over the surrounding area by military raids and marriage alliances.

Glyphs

The Maya developed a system of writing using signs, called glyphs. Glyphs were used for recording the many dates and festivals of the complex Mayan calendar, which was based on the movement of the sun. Glyphs were also used to write the names and dates of the Mayan rulers. Many of the glyphs were pictorial – they were pictures used to represent ideas. For example, a glyph of a shield and a club together meant "war."

People

At the top of Mayan society there was a lord, or king. Below him there were nobles, who were high-ranking farmers, merchants, and priests. Below them were commoners, who were farm workers, hunters, or craft workers. Lowest of all were slaves – men and women who had been taken prisoner in war and who did the hardest work, such as building.

Mayan lord

Cloth given as tribute

Lords
This vase, from c.700, shows a Mayan lord with tributes, or gifts, given to him by subject (conquered) peoples.

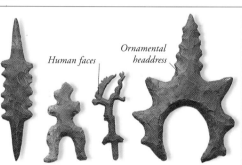

Flint carvings
These carvings were highly prized and were often buried with the dead. They were made by flaking away the flint to leave a silhouette. Typical subjects were human faces, figures of the gods, and mythical creatures.

Human faces

Ornamental headdress

Hunter

Deer

Hunting
Mayan men hunted game in the Yucatan Peninsula to supplement their diet of vegetables. Hunters called this area the "land of turkey and deer" for this reason.

Food basket

Terra-cotta figure

Farming
Peasant women, such as the one represented in this figure, grew most of the food on terraced hillside farms or in forest clearings. Their main crops were corn, squash, beans, and chilies.

Timeline
2000 BC–AD 300 This period begins with a rural economy and ends with the rise of the Mayan cities.

300–550 Early Classic period: city states develop in the Mexican lowlands.

550–900 The Late Classic period: art and architecture flourish in the Mayan cities. The population rises and agriculture becomes more intensive to support the population.

Terra-cotta frog pot

900 onward Mayan cities decline, and other Mesoamerican peoples, such as the Toltecs and later the Aztecs, begin to dominate the area.

FIND OUT MORE

AZTECS   CENTRAL AMERICA, HISTORY OF   INCAS   MESOAMERICANS   PYRAMIDS

MEDICINE

MEDICINE IS A SCIENCE that aims to prevent or treat the disorders that affect the human body. These range widely, from minor injuries, such as a sprained ankle, to life-threatening conditions, such as heart disease. The skill and knowledge of doctors and nurses, as well as major advances in modern diagnostic techniques, surgery, and drugs, have made medicine highly effective. Today, more people live in good health, for longer than ever before.

Diagnosis

Patients are not always able to describe the symptoms of their illness.

Identifying the cause of an illness and prescribing the appropriate treatment is called diagnosis. It requires great skill from the doctor, and involves a number of stages. After listening to a description of the symptoms, the doctor examines the patient, for example checking heart beat or blood pressure. Samples may be sent for testing, before a doctor finally decides on a course of treatment, or refers the patient to a specialist at a local hospital.

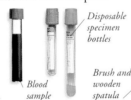

Disposable specimen bottles

Symptoms and signs
Symptoms are the indications of an illness noticed by a patient and described to the doctor. Symptoms include pain, bleeding, or a rash. The doctor considers these factors with any signs of disease that he or she notices, to formulate a diagnosis.

Tests
Doctors use a range of diagnostic tests to help them make an accurate diagnosis. They may take samples of blood, urine, mucus, feces, vomit, or pus. The samples are put in labeled tubes and sent for testing at a laboratory.

Blood sample

Brush and wooden spatula

Diagnostic kit
Tongue depressor

Nasal speculum

Mirror

Laryngeal mirror

Ophthalmoscope

Laryngoscope head

Otoscope head examines inside ear.

Doctors

By law, a medical doctor must complete a period of training before he or she is qualified to diagnose and treat patients. This involves a minimum three years of study, followed by work as a trainee in a hospital. In most countries, a national register lists those doctors who are qualified to practice; doctors can be dropped from the register for malpractice.

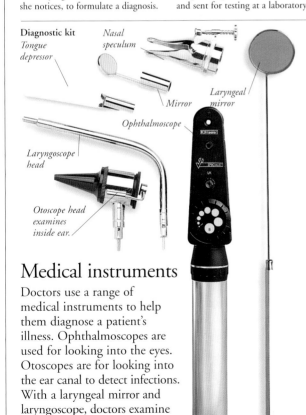

Medical instruments

Doctors use a range of medical instruments to help them diagnose a patient's illness. Ophthalmoscopes are used for looking into the eyes. Otoscopes are for looking into the ear canal to detect infections. With a laryngeal mirror and laryngoscope, doctors examine the throat and trachea.

Branches of medicine

Medicine has many branches, and no one doctor can be an expert in all of them. Some doctors are general practitioners (GPs); the first contact for most patients, they have a broad understanding of most conditions. When necessary, a GP refers patients to specialists in a wide range of fields, from orthopedics to psychiatry.

M

Orthopedics
Orthopaedics deals with diseases and injuries of bones, joints, muscles, ligaments, and tendons. Orthopedic surgeons treat a range of conditions, including broken bones.

Broken leg in cast

Pediatrics
The study of the growth and development of babies and children, and the treatment of diseases experienced in childhood, is called pediatrics.

Psychiatry
The diagnosis and treatment of emotional and behavioral problems, and mental illness, is called psychiatry. Psychiatrists use counseling, drugs, and in some cases electroconvulsive therapy (ECT) to help patients.

ECT

Eczema

Dermatology
This is the study of the skin, hair, and nails, including treatment of conditions such as skin cancer, acne, warts, and eczema.

Gynecology
Gynecology is concerned with the woman's reproductive system. It deals with pregnancy and childbirth, and also disorders such as menstrual problems or infertility.

Pregnant woman

Neurology
Neurologists treat disorders of the brain and nervous system – conditions such as muscular dystrophy and Parkinson's disease.

Brain

Christiaan Barnard

South African surgeon Christiaan Barnard (1923–2001) performed the world's first heart transplant operation at Groote Schuur Hospital, Cape Town, in 1967. The patient survived for just 18 days, but Barnard's pioneering operation introduced a procedure that is now carried out routinely in hospitals around the world.

Surgery

Surgery is a branch of medicine that involves cutting into the body to treat a disease or an injury. Surgeons carry out procedures, called operations, in operating rooms. An operation may be minor, such as the removal of a skin blemish, or major, such as a heart by-pass operation that takes many hours.

Surgical instruments

Suture scissors

Scalpel

Retractor

Artery forceps

Forceps

Metzenbaum scissors

Oxygen cylinder on trolley

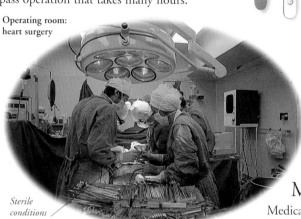

Operating room: heart surgery

Sterile conditions

Surgical instruments
These are the instruments used during operations. They include scissors for cutting tissue and trimming stitches; scalpels, used for cutting; retractors, which hold tissue apart; and artery forceps, used to clamp blood vessels.

Anesthetics
Anesthetics are drugs used to relieve a patient's pain during surgery. The drugs can be injected or inhaled. Local anesthetics numb only the affected part of the body; general anesthetics render the patient unconscious.

Patrick Steptoe and Robert Edwards

British gynecologist Patrick Steptoe (1913–88) and physiologist Robert Edwards (b.1925) developed the technique of *in vitro* fertilization (IVF), which helps infertile women have babies. IVF involves removing an egg from the mother, and then fertilizing it with sperm and returning the fertilized egg to the mother's uterus. The first baby conceived by IVF was Louise Brown, born on July 25, 1978, in England.

Patrick Steptoe

Robert Edwards

Medical technology

Medical technology advanced rapidly during the 20th century. Imaging techniques, such as X rays and PET scans, allow a disease to be diagnosed without having to cut open the patient. With sophisticated surgical equipment, doctors carry out increasingly complex treatments, curing more diseases and keeping more patients alive.

PET scan of healthy brain

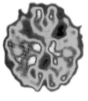

PET scan of brain with Alzheimer's disease

PET scan
PET (positron emission tomography) scanners investigate activity in the brain. They detect radiation given off by the brain and produce an image. They are used to locate tumors and diagnose epilepsy.

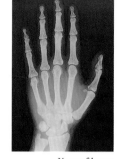

Endoscope image of vocal chords

Vocal chords are close together.

Endoscope
Doctors look inside the body using an endoscope – a long, flexible tube of optical fibers. Some fibers carry light into the body; others carry an image back to the doctor on a video screen.

X ray of bones in hand

X rays
An X ray is radiation used to take photographs of bones and teeth. As X rays pass through a patient's body, they are absorbed by bone but not by softer tissues. Detected by photographic film, this produces a shadowy image of the inside of the body.

Alternative medicine

Alternative medicine is the collective term for therapies that take a different approach to curing illness from orthodox medicine. Some, such as acupuncture, are ancient; others, such as homeopathy, date from the 19th century. Some therapies are now used instead of, or in addition to conventional medicine.

Homeopathy
Homeopaths give patients dilute forms of natural substances that, if undiluted, would produce symptoms of the disease in healthy people. This is believed to boost the body's natural defense system and its healing abilities.

Homeopathic remedies

Reflexology
Reflexology is based on the theory that each part of the foot is linked to a specific area of the body. By massaging and manipulating the foot, reflexologists aim to stimulate the body into healing itself or relieving pain.

Big toe is connected with top of head and brain.

Region of foot that governs diaphragm and solar plexus.

Reflexology

Part of the foot thought to be connected with the heart.

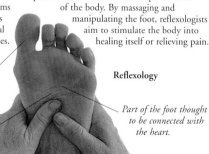

Part of the foot thought to be responsible for base of spine.

Area thought to be linked with bladder.

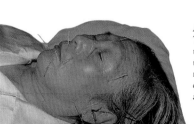

Acupuncture
This ancient Chinese therapy involves treating disease by sticking needles in the skin at particular points, called meridians. Insertion of the needles controls the flow of Qi (vital energy) along meridians, restoring good health.

Patient undergoes acupuncture for facial paralysis.

FIND OUT MORE   DISEASES   DRUGS   FIRST AID   HEALTH AND FITNESS   HEART AND CIRCULATORY SYSTEM   HOSPITALS   HUMAN BODY   MEDICINE, HISTORY OF   PLANT USES

MEDICINE, HISTORY OF

RECORDS OF PHYSICIANS treating the sick stretch back more than 4,500 years. However, for most of this time doctors had little scientific knowledge and relied mainly on superstition and herbs. Medical science as we know it began 300 years ago, when a flowering of knowledge helped doctors understand how the body works, and innovations, such as immunization, helped cure its ills. Today, medical advances save more lives than ever before, but treatment can be expensive – and many of the world's poorest people cannot afford it.

Prehistoric medicine

Buried skeletons provide hints about prehistoric medical treatment. In a procedure called trepanning, early surgeons drilled their patients' skulls, perhaps thinking this would let diseases escape. Archaeologists have found skulls that show partial healing, so not all patients died after the operation.

Trepanned skull, 2000 BC

Ancient Greece and Rome

Greek doctors learned surgery by treating war wounds, but blamed the gods for any failures. Ancient Romans improved public health with clean water supplies and sewer systems.

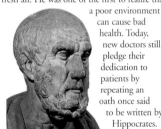

Hygieia   *Asclepius*

Asclepius and Hygieia
The Greek god of medicine, Asclepius, may have actually been a real physician 3,200 years ago. The Romans worshiped both him (as Aesculapius) and his daughter, Hygieia, whose name gives us the word "hygiene."

Greek sculpture

Egyptian cures
Ancient Egyptians founded the first medical school 2,500 years ago. Our knowledge of Egyptian medicine comes from the Ebers Papyrus, a scroll containing 700 remedies – some of which are still used.

Qing-dynasty needles

Ancient Egyptians thought that raw garlic cured tapeworms.

Garlic

Acupuncture
Chinese physicians began using acupuncture around 2500 BC. Acupuncturists aim to ease pain and cure disease by pushing tiny needles into the body. Today, western scientists accept that acupuncture stops pain, but they cannot explain why.

Acupuncture needles and mahogany case

Four humors
A Greek surgeon named Galen (129–199) believed incorrectly that human beings were in good health only when they had a perfect balance of their bodily fluids – their "four humors." The humors (blood, phlegm, choler, and melancholy) corresponded to physical build and certain ailments. This idea dominated medicine for 1,400 years.

Melancholy   *Blood*

Choler   *Phlegm*

Four Humors

Hippocrates
Greek physician Hippocrates (c.460–370 BC) separated medicine from magic. His treatments included diets, purgatives, baths, and fresh air. He was one of the first to realize that a poor environment can cause bad health. Today, new doctors still pledge their dedication to patients by repeating an oath once said to be written by Hippocrates.

Islamic medicine
Religion was a powerful force in the Arab world. The holy books of Islam contain rules about hygiene and diet. Galen's ideas about the four humors strongly influenced early Islamic medicine, but in the 13th century, the Arabs advanced medical knowledge when the physician Ibn-an-Nafis (1210–88) made important discoveries about the circulation of the blood.

Modern Turkish baths, Istanbul, Turkey

Islamic medicine recognized that cleanliness was an important part of maintaining good health.

Medieval medicine

For 1,000 years in medieval Europe, doctors trusted religion, astrology, and Galen's teachings. Even during the Renaissance, there was widespread ignorance about illness and its treatment.

Anatomy theater, Padua University

Medical schools
There were few medical schools in medieval and Renaissance Europe. The 16th-century medical faculty at Padua University, Italy – where Galileo lectured – has the world's earliest surviving anatomy lecture hall.

Wise women
For most people the only source of medical help was a "wise woman." These neighborhood healers cured illnesses using traditional herbal remedies, such as coltsfoot. However, when universities began to educate doctors, most excluded women, despite their knowledge.

Coltsfoot, used to treat coughs

M

Scientific Revolution

Smellie's short forceps c.1746

From the 17th century, medicine benefited from a new spirit of investigation and observation that revolutionized all sciences. This is known as the Scientific Revolution. One of the most important breakthroughs was the discovery, by the English physician William Harvey (1578–1657), that the heart pumps blood continuously around the body.

Immunization
By infecting a boy with a mild disease (cowpox) in 1796, English physician Edward Jenner (1749–1823) gave him immunity (protection) from the deadly smallpox. Developments of Jenner's method now keep us safe from many previously fatal diseases.

Jenner performs the first vaccination.

Childbirth
Until the 1700s, pregnancy often ended in death for mother and baby. Hungarian Ignaz Semmelweis (1818–65) showed that lack of cleanliness killed the mothers – and improved hygiene saved eight out of 10 lives. To help save babies' lives during a long delivery, a Scottish doctor named William Smellie (1679–1763) developed special forceps.

Pain control
Before anesthetics were invented, surgery was a painful ordeal. American dentist William Morton (1819–68) showed that patients who inhaled ether vapor became unconscious and did not feel the surgery.

Early anesthetic equipment

Mental illness

Strait-jacket

Treatment of mentally ill people used to consist of chaining them up in cells to control their "madness." In the 1700s, hospitals abolished these cells and chains. Psychotherapy started more than a century later, when the Austrian doctor Sigmund Freud (1856–1939) began talking to patients about their disturbing thoughts.

In the 1800s, straitjackets were used instead of chains.

Straitjacketed patient, c.1818

Joseph Lister
English surgeon Lister (1827–1912) learned of germs from Louis Pasteur (1822–95). In 1865, Lister realized that he could prevent wound infection by killing germs in operating rooms, so he developed antiseptic (rot-preventing) surgery. His idea reduced the death rate following operations by two-thirds.

Modern medicine

In the 20th century, medical knowledge developed more quickly than ever before. The control of infectious diseases meant that children in the developed world born in the 1990s can now expect to see 25 more birthdays than children born in 1900. Through a better understanding of how our bodies work, scientists devised new drugs, new ways of detecting illness, and new treatments, which now make our lives healthier as well as longer.

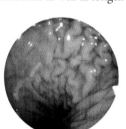

Endoscope view of stomach

Drug treatment
Originally drugs, such as penicillin, came from a natural source, such as a mold. Modern scientists can now produce a wide range of artificial (synthetic) drugs, including antibiotics.

Medical imaging
The discovery of X-rays in 1895 allowed doctors to get a clear picture of a patient's bones without surgery. In the 1950s, doctors perfected the first flexible endoscope (an instrument for examining the inside of the body without using a scalpel). Doctors developed an early version of this instrument – a tube and a candle – in the 18th century.

Medical research
Research has led to the invention of many diagnostic and imaging tools. One of the most useful modern research tools is the CAT (computerized axial tomography) scan. This machine allows doctors to view the brain in sections, making diagnosis of brain disease or damage much easier and treatment quicker.

CAT scan

Eye drop dispenser

Tablets and capsules

Rediscovery of traditional cures
Initially, 20th-century medicine rejected all ancient herbal remedies. However, the medical establishment has recently re-examined their usefulness, and traditional cures are now sometimes used with modern medical practices. One American company has even tried to patent (own) the turmeric poultices used in India for minor wounds.

Turmeric powder, traditionally used in poultices

Timeline

1st century AD Roman Aulus Celsus (25 BC–AD 50) writes one of the first medical textbooks.

12th century In Europe, monastery hospitals improve medical treatment.

1163 Church forbids monks to practise surgery; for the next 600 years, barbers act as surgeons.

1543 Flemish anatomist Andreas Vesalius (1514–64) publishes the first accurate pictures of the human body.

The narcotic opium comes from poppies.

Poppy seeds

1849 Elizabeth Blackwell is first US woman to gain medical degree.

1854 John Snow (1813–58) links clean water and good health.

1860s Pasteur discovers germs.

1921 Insulin treatment is developed for fatal diabetes.

Syringe

1928 Bacteriologist Alexander Fleming discovers penicillin.

1953 John Gibbon Jr performs cardiac surgery with his heart-lung machine.

1960 John Charnley (1911–82) invents replacement hip joint.

1979 Mass immunization frees the world of smallpox.

1986 "Keyhole surgery" invented.

2001 Significant breakthroughs are made in treatments for incurable illnesses such as cancer and HIV.

FIND OUT MORE | BLACK DEATH | DRUGS | FREUD, SIGMUND | GALILEO GALILEI | HEART AND CIRCULATORY SYSTEM | ISLAMIC EMPIRE | MEDICINE | PASTEUR, LOUIS | SCIENCE, HISTORY OF | VESALIUS, ANDREAS | WITCHES AND WITCHCRAFT

Early medicine
Ancient drugs

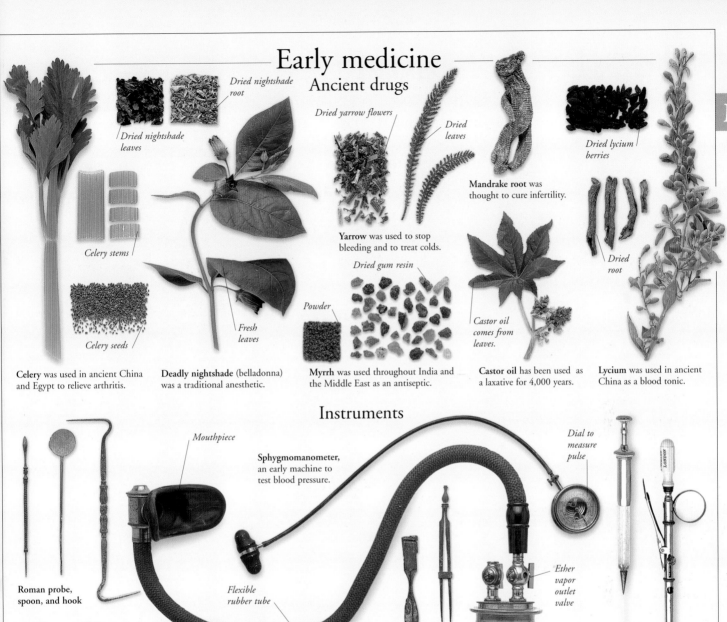

Dried nightshade root

Dried nightshade leaves

Dried yarrow flowers

Dried leaves

Mandrake root was thought to cure infertility.

Dried lycium berries

Celery stems

Celery seeds

Fresh leaves

Powder

Dried gum resin

Castor oil comes from leaves.

Dried root

Celery was used in ancient China and Egypt to relieve arthritis.

Deadly nightshade (belladonna) was a traditional anesthetic.

Myrrh was used throughout India and the Middle East as an antiseptic.

Castor oil has been used as a laxative for 4,000 years.

Lycium was used in ancient China as a blood tonic.

Instruments

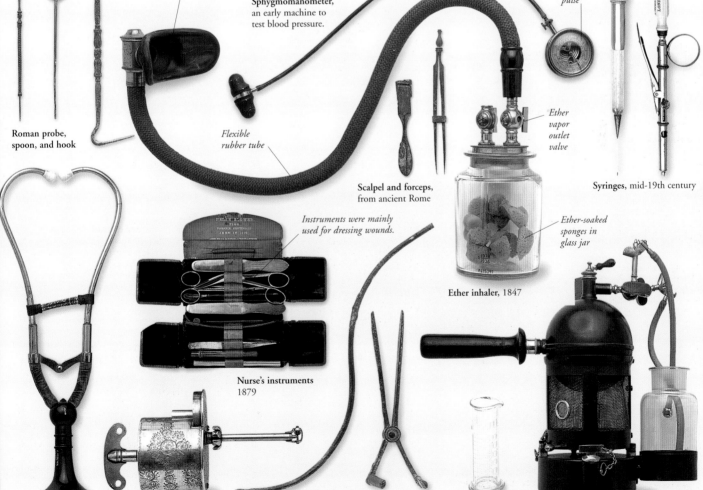

Mouthpiece

Sphygmomanometer, an early machine to test blood pressure.

Dial to measure pulse

Roman probe, spoon, and hook

Flexible rubber tube

Ether vapor outlet valve

Scalpel and forceps, from ancient Rome

Instruments were mainly used for dressing wounds.

Syringes, mid-19th century

Ether-soaked sponges in glass jar

Ether inhaler, 1847

Nurse's instruments 1879

Laënnec's stethoscope, 1855.

Dental drill was run by clockwork, 1864.

Ancient Roman catheter and speculum have a similar design to the modern instruments.

Minim measure, to measure medicine

Antiseptic carbolic steam spray, designed by the surgeon Lister

MEDIEVAL EUROPE

THE MEDIEVAL PERIOD IN EUROPE, also known as the Middle Ages, lasted roughly from 1000 to 1500. It was the time between the obscurity of the Dark Ages and the intellectual flowering of the Renaissance. There was an expansion of trade during this period, and a population explosion followed by the formation of many towns. People were still governed by kings, but the powerful Catholic church dominated Europe's culture. Medieval Europe was a time and place of contrasts: the finest religious art was being created, yet most people lived lives of desperate poverty.

Sovereigns and the state

In most medieval countries, the sovereign – usually a man – owned all the land. He also tried to control the church, claiming that he got his power directly from God. This claim often brought church and state into conflict.

Frederick II
A gifted lawgiver and soldier, the Holy Roman Emperor Frederick II (1194–1250) was also a religious skeptic. He quarreled with the Pope, who excommunicated him for refusing to go to the Holy Land on a crusade. When Frederick finally arrived in the Holy Land in 1228, he claimed Jerusalem by diplomacy and without any bloodshed.

St. Louis
Louis IX (r.1226–70) of France was a pious king who governed his fellow Christians peacefully, but was intolerant of non-Christians. His first crusade to the Holy Land was unsuccessful, and he returned to follow peaceful policies at home. In 1270 he began a crusade against the Muslims in northern Africa. He died of the plague at Tunis.

Eleanor of Aquitaine
Wife of two kings – Louis VII of France and Henry II of England – and mother of two others, Eleanor (1122–1204) was one of the most powerful women of her time. She went on a crusade in 1147 and gave Henry II extensive French lands when they married. She played a key role in English government during the reign of her son Richard I.

Bishops and the church

One of the strongest forces in Europe, the church was ruled by a network of archbishops and bishops, headed by a pope. These educated men believed that they were responsible for the souls of the people and that they could supervise all human affairs – even those of kings.

Monasteries
Monks and nuns lived a life apart, giving up their personal possessions and leading lives of chastity. But they still played a vital part in medieval society, providing many services today run by the government – such as education, healing, and care of the poor and needy.

Becket is carried to heaven by angels.

Becket is killed by one of King Henry II's knights in Canterbury Cathedral.

Reliquaries were special caskets used to house saints' bones or other relics. This 12th-century example depicts the murder of St. Thomas Becket, the English Archbishop of Canterbury (1118–70).

Churchmen
In medieval Europe, the eldest son of a rich family inherited all his father's property. The younger sons often "took holy orders" and made careers in the church. Many became bishops, gaining considerable power. Rulers often appointed churchmen to positions of power in the state. These appointments gave the church a chance to influence state affairs.

Peasants' revolts

Europe's population fell dramatically after the Black Death. Peasants had to work harder, but were not paid higher wages. This caused peasant uprisings in France (1358) and England (1381), both of which were ruthlessly crushed.

Wat Tyler is attacked. *Richard II*

Wat Tyler and the Peasant's Revolt
Tyler and the peasants marched to London to ask Richard II to lift the poll tax. Tyler's first meeting with the king was successful – the king promised to lift the tax – but at their second meeting, a scuffle broke out and Tyler was killed.

How people lived

Most people lived in the country and worked the land. They gave a share of their produce to a local lord in return for protection and a home. Life expectancy was much shorter than it is today. Because of frequent and unpredictable Black Death epidemics, death was seen as a malicious joker ready to take anyone at any time.

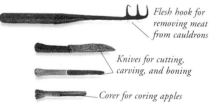

Flesh hook for removing meat from cauldrons

Knives for cutting, carving, and boning

Corer for coring apples

At home
Ordinary families lived in small huts that often had only two rooms: one for animals and another for people. Food was prepared in cauldrons using simple utensils. Times were hard in the winter, since food could not be preserved. A bad harvest meant that people starved the following winter.

Billhook for maintaining hedges

Sickle for cutting crops

Trowel

On the land
People worked hard on the land. The horse-drawn plow prepared the ground for cultivation, but there were no other labor-saving machines. Everything from digging to cutting crops and shearing sheep was done by hand.

Towns and trade

Towns, mainly based around markets or ports, flourished because of an increased interest in trade and a growth in population. By the 14th century, some 70 towns in northern Europe had formed the Hanseatic League to monopolize trade in the area.

Money
Coins became common in medieval Europe because there was so much trade. Gold coins were issued for the first time since the 7th century. Merchants used small balances like this to weigh the coins to make sure the precious metal they contained hadn't been removed.

Town walls
Most medieval towns were fortified with high stone walls and strong gatehouses. These kept out bandits in peacetime and enemy soldiers in war. Carcassone, France, still has its medieval walls.

Medieval science

Medieval European science relied on the writings of the ancient Greeks and Romans. Europeans had not yet developed a scientific method that resulted in new discoveries, as was happening in the Islamic world. There were advances in some areas, however: medieval engineers developed and built grand structures such as the great Gothic cathedrals.

Blakene astrolabe

Book of Hours

Man

Woman

Zodiac signs

The astrolabe was an Arab invention developed to measure the altitude of the Sun, Moon, and stars. It came to Europe via trade routes and helped astronomers navigate at sea.

Parts of the body were thought to be ruled by the signs of the zodiac, as this 14th-century manuscript shows.

Medicinal herbs
Medieval physicians relied on herbs to make medicines, ointments, and poultices. Modern scientists have analyzed the plants and found that they contain healing substances. Sage, for example, contains acids that are effective against colds; lavender contains an oil that is effective against burns and stings.

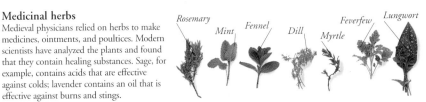
Rosemary *Mint* *Fennel* *Dill* *Myrtle* *Feverfew* *Lungwort*

M

Medieval art

Most medieval art was commissioned by the church to decorate cathedrals and monasteries. Many of the buildings were in a style called "Gothic," marked by dramatic, pointed arches. Within the buildings, Gothic painters used vivid, lifelike colors, but were not realistic.

Old Testament figures

Sculpture
Cathedrals were decorated with statues of the Holy Family, Bible scenes, saints, and bishops. Large-scale figures, such as these at Chartres, became the hallmark of the Gothic style.

Architecture
Medieval masons built fine stone houses as well as churches. This one was built in Lincoln, England, for a 12th-century Jewish merchant. The rounded doorway arch shows it is in the "Romanesque" style that was popular before the Gothic style.

Manuscript illumination
In the monasteries, monks copied the text of the Bible and other Christian books in longhand. They adorned the text with beautiful illustrations and illuminated important letters (that is, painted them with bright colors and gold leaf).

Stained-glass windows
Scenes from the Bible were brought to life in the vivid stained-glass windows in churches and cathedrals. The pictures were created with small pieces of colored glass joined together using strips of lead. These examples come from the superb Chartres Cathedral in France – one of the wonders of the medieval age.

The Blue Virgin Window shows Christ turning water into wine.

The South Rose Window

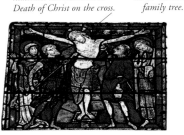
The Redemption Window illustrates the Passion and Death of Christ on the cross.

Tree of Jesse shows Christ's family tree.

Clothing
Peasants wore simple clothes made of wool – loose smocks for the body, and hose or stockings for the legs. Richer materials, such as linen, velvet, and finer wool fabrics, were available to merchants and the nobility. Boots and shoes were made out of leather, as were accessories, such as belts and bags.

Felt hat
Straw hat
Laces, or "points"
Short wool jacket
Linen shirt
Leather flask, or "costrel"
Wool "split" hose
Leather working boots
Laborer

Bailiff
Peaked felt hat
Doublet
Pewter buttons
Linen lining
Stirrups
Leather boots

Merchant
"Borrelais" hat
Wool coat
Eating knife
Long wool jacket
Mid-calf leather boots
"Joined" hose

Linen head wrap
Townswoman
Linen shift
Prayer beads
Wool stockings with leather garters
Over sleeves
Wooden clogs, or "pattens"

FIND OUT MORE BLACK DEATH CHURCHES AND CATHEDRALS CRUSADES EUROPE, HISTORY OF FEUDALISM FRANCE, HISTORY OF HOLY ROMAN EMPIRE MEDICINE, HISTORY OF NORMANS

MEITNER, LISE

SOME OF THE MOST important discoveries in nuclear physics were made by Lise Meitner, a woman who often had to struggle to get the research facilities she needed. In spite of facing prejudice as a woman and a Jew, she published more than 130 scientific papers in a long career in Austria, Germany, and Sweden. Many of her discoveries were made with her colleague, physicist Otto Hahn (1879–1968). These included nuclear fission, the process that forms the basis of nuclear power and atomic weapons. She gained many awards for her work, including the Ferni Award in 1966.

Early life
Lise Meitner was born in 1878 in Vienna, Austria. While she was growing up, her heroines were the British nurse Florence Nightingale and the French physicist Marie Curie. As a young woman, she persuaded her father to pay for a private tutor to prepare her for university. She went to the University of Vienna, and received her doctorate in 1906.

Radioactivity

In 1896, French physicist Henri Becquerel (1852–1908) discovered radioactivity (the rays that are emitted from certain substances). Meitner's work made a huge contribution to the understanding of radioactivity. During her time in the laboratory, she was often unwell, as she frequently came into contact with dangerously radioactive substances and mercury vapor.

Woman physicist

In the early 20th century it was unusual for a woman to become a physicist, and Meitner endured a great deal of prejudice. At Berlin University, where she was a professor from 1926 to 1933, she worked in an old workshop, because women were not allowed in the main building. Male colleagues tended to ignore her and discuss work with Hahn only.

Worktable and equipment used by Lise Meitner and Otto Hahn in experiments leading to the discovery of nuclear fission.

Protactinium
In 1907, Meitner went to work at Berlin University. In 1917, she moved to Berlin's Kaiser Wilhelm Institute to work with Otto Hahn. The next year, she and Hahn discovered an important form of an element named protactinium. The name means "before actinium" because the element actinium is produced when the atoms of protactinium decay radioactively.

Spectroscope used to measure beta radiation

Lise Meitner and Otto Hahn worked as equals, but Meitner was subjected to much prejudice.

Nuclear fission
In 1938, Meitner made her most important contribution to nuclear physics. She realized that nuclei of the element uranium could be made to split into two smaller fragments. The process, which she called "fission," released a great deal of energy. This energy has been used in nuclear power stations and nuclear weapons. Meitner refused to be involved in the creation of nuclear weapons.

Letter announcing the discovery of protactinium

Exile in Sweden

In 1938, Meitner, a Jew, was forced to flee Nazi Germany to avoid persecution. Another great scientist, Danish physicist Neils Bohr, helped her escape and find research facilities at the University of Stockholm, Sweden. She continued her research with her nephew, Otto Frisch, who was also in exile in Sweden.

Interpreting fission
While Meitner was in Sweden, Hahn continued their work in Germany, bombarding atoms of uranium with particles called neutrons. Hahn found traces of the element barium in the experiments, but did not know why they were there. Meitner found the answer. She realized that each uranium atom had split in two fragments, one of which was barium.

Notes on fission by Lise Meitner

Hahn–Meitner Institute
In 1959, a research institute was founded in Berlin in honor of Meitner and Hahn. Its original aim was to carry out research into nuclear physics, chemistry, and mathematics. Scientists there have also done research on materials science and the future of solar power.

LISE MEITNER

1878 Born in Vienna, Austria.

1906 Receives doctorate from the University of Vienna.

1907 Travels to Berlin to attend a lecture, and ends up staying for more than 30 years.

1918 With Otto Hahn, discovers a form of the element protactinium.

1926 Becomes a professor at the University of Berlin.

1938 Flees Nazi Germany and moves to Stockholm, Sweden.

1939 With Otto Frisch, publishes a paper explaining nuclear fission.

1949 Becomes Swedish citizen.

1968 Dies in Cambridge, England.

 FIND OUT MORE   CURIE, MARIE   NIGHTINGALE, FLORENCE   NUCLEAR POWER   PHYSICS

MESOAMERICANS

WONDERFULLY RICH CULTURES flourished in ancient Mesoamerica – the middle part of the Americas, today known as Mexico, Belize, Guatemala, and Honduras. The Toltecs, Mixtecs, and Huaxtecs were separate groups, but with many things in common. They all worshiped the same group of gods, practiced human sacrifice, developed writing, and played a similar ball game. Their finest achievements are their stone temple-pyramids and superb sculpture and pottery, but they never developed the wheel, and did not use bronze or iron. They were at their peak from 900, but perished when Spanish invaders arrived in Mexico in the early 1500s.

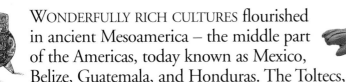

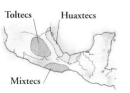
Toltecs   Huaxtecs
Mixtecs

M

Ball game

This "game" had great religious and political significance to the Mesoamericans, and losers were often sacrificed to the gods. Players had to hit a small rubber ball through a high opening on the side of a court by using hips, elbows, and knees – but no hands or feet.

Ballplayer
Players were usually noblemen. They dressed in special protective garments to play, all of which were padded – including the thick leather belt. The padding cushioned the player from the impact of the hard rubber ball, which often traveled at high speed.

Ball court, Chichen Itza

Ball court
The Mesoamericans built large ball courts in many of their city centers. The playing area was widened at either end, making a shape like a capital "I."

Circular stone markers

Codex illustration of a ball court

Hacha
When the ballplayers started a game, they hung ceremonial heads from their belts, which were known as "hachas," or axes. The Mesoamericans used a stone head such as this to mold the hacha.

Belt mold
Mesoamerican craft workers used greenstone molds to make protective belts for the ballplayers. They wrapped a strip of wet leather around the mold and left it to dry. When they removed the leather, the workers stuffed it with a padding material similar to cotton called kapok

Image of toad on the belt symbolizes Earth.

Toltecs
The Toltecs came from Tollán, near modern Tula, Mexico. They were a warlike people, and conquered several Mexican cities between 900 and 1100. Most of their wealth came from trade in volcanic glass.

Tollán
The great Toltec capital had a central precinct, that contained a market and a temple-pyramid. Most Toltec art was military in style. For example, the pyramid columns are in the form of soldiers.

Warriors
Some pottery figures have a butterfly breastplate, that helps identify them as warriors.

Funerary urn

Tripod vase

Crafts
Skilled Toltec potters decorated their work in relief with painted designs, as on this funerary urn. The tripod vase features images of Quetzalcoatl, the feathered serpent god also worshiped by the Aztecs.

Jewelry was worn by the upper classes.

Mixtecs
The Mixtecs were based in the northern Oaxaca mountains in c.1200 and were known for their metalwork. They were also warlike, conquering nearby cities, and resisted the mighty Aztecs in the 15th century.

Gold ring
Gold pendant

Huaxtecs
The Huaxtecs were trading people who reached the peak of their civilization between 900 and 1450. Their traders traveled all around the Gulf of Mexico and up into the central highlands. Their craftsworkers were excellent stone sculptors.

Headdress shows this figure had high status.

Hands over the womb show this deity may be a fertility goddess.

Huaxtec deity in stone

FIND OUT MORE | AZTECS | CENTRAL AMERICA, HISTORY OF | MAYA | OLMECS

METALS

SINCE EARLY TIMES, metals have played a key role in shaping human civilization, and the extraction and working of metals is still a vital industry in the modern world. All metals are elements. Metals provide us with strong, long-lasting materials for use in construction, engineering, transportation, and manufacturing.

Shaping iron on an anvil

Metalworking

One of the reasons metals are so useful is that they are relatively easy to shape, whether they are cold, hot, or molten. They can be hammered over an anvil, rolled out into sheets, or stretched out into tubes and wires. Other techniques include casting (pouring molten metal into a mold) and forging (pressing a hot metal into shape using a huge metal block).

Welding

Metal parts can be joined by welding. The edges of two metal pieces are melted with a gas flame or a powerful spark of electricity called an electric arc. The molten metals fuse together and form a strong joint as they cool.

Electric arc melts metal.

Metallic bonds

Metal atoms are held together by forces called metallic bonds. All atoms contain negatively charged particles called electrons. In metals, some of the electrons break free from their atoms to form a common pool of electrons called an electron gas. The free-moving electron gas binds the metal atoms firmly together in a strong metallic bond.

Electrons move freely between atoms.

Properties of metals

Most metals are hard and dense and conduct heat and electricity well. They are solid at room temperature (68°F, 20°C), and generally have much higher melting and boiling points than nonmetal elements. Iron, for example, melts at 2,795°F (1,535°C), while the nonmetal nitrogen has a melting point of -346°F (-210°C).

Molten iron is poured into a mold.

Casting iron

Semimetals

Some elements, such as germanium and silicon, are called semimetals because they have some of the properties of metals and some of nonmetals. They are also known as semiconductors, which means that they conduct electricity only under certain conditions. They are ideal for use in electronic components, such as microchips, in which electric current has to be carefully controlled.

Silicon chip

Microchip

Mercury

Mercury is the only metal that is liquid at room temperature. Its silvery color and the fact that it flows easily earned mercury the name quicksilver. It is used in thermometers, barometers, and batteries.

Top of nail is exposed to air.

Rust flakes off surface of nail.

Rust forms as iron reacts with oxygen in air and water.

Iron nail in water

Rust

If iron is exposed to air and water, its surface will corrode and form a flaky material called rust. Most metals corrode in air and water. Corrosion can be prevented by giving the metal a protective coating.

Ores

Only a few metals occur naturally in their pure state. Most are locked up within rocks and minerals called ores. A metal can be extracted from its ore by heating the ore or passing a powerful electric current through it.

Copper ore (chalcopyrite)

Types of metals

Some metals are highly valued for their appearance; others are valued for their usefulness. However, most of the "metal" objects that we encounter in our daily lives are actually metal mixtures called alloys.

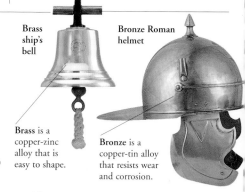

Brass ship's bell

Bronze Roman helmet

Brass is a copper-zinc alloy that is easy to shape.

Bronze is a copper-tin alloy that resists wear and corrosion.

Silver

Gold

Tin

Lead pellets

Platinum

Precious metals

Gold, silver, and platinum are often used in jewelry. They are known as precious metals because their rarity, beauty, and durability make them more expensive than base metals, such as iron, which are commonly available.

Poor metals

Some metals, such as aluminum, tin, and lead, are known as poor metals because they are weaker than most metals and melt more easily. Despite their name, they are very useful, and they are widely used in alloys. Lead and tin, for example, form the alloy solder, which is used to link electronic components.

Alloys

An alloy is a mixture of two or more metals. Alloys have different properties from the pure metals they contain. Copper and tin are weak metals, but when mixed together they form the strong alloy bronze. Some alloys contain nonmetals: steel, for example, is a mixture of iron (metal) and carbon (nonmetal).

| FIND OUT MORE | ATOMS AND MOLECULES | BRONZE AGE | ELECTRONICS | ELEMENTS | IRON AND STEEL | MIXTURES AND COMPOUNDS | ROCKS AND MINERALS | ROMAN EMPIRE |

MEXICO

A LINK BETWEEN the US and the Spanish-speaking countries of Central America, Mexico lies within the continent of North America. Before Spanish conquerors arrived in the Americas in the 1500s, Mexico had several thriving civilizations of its own, including the Maya and Aztec empires. Spectacular ruins of their buildings still survive and many Mexicans have Aztec and Mayan ancestors. Mexico has great mineral wealth, but, because it has one of the world's fastest growing populations, unemployment is high, its economy is shaky, and millions live in poverty.

M

Physical features

Mexico's varied landscape includes deserts, grasslands, tropical forests, swamps, and snow-capped volcanic peaks. Two parallel mountain chains, the Sierra Madre Occidental and Oriental, dominate the country. The most fertile land is found on the central plateau between them.

Sierra Madre
The two chains of the Sierra Madre, or mother range, form barriers in the east and west of Mexico. The western range has dormant, smoking volcanoes, notably Popocatépetl. Mexico's tallest peak is Citlatépetl, at 18,700 ft (5,700 m).

Sonoran Desert
Straddling the border between Mexico and the US, the dry Sonoran Desert, at 120,000 sq miles (310,000 sq km), is one of the largest in the world. Here, at Pinacate National Park, west of Nogales, the desert is littered with some of the world's largest cacti, the giant saguaro, which can grow up to 60 ft (18 m) tall.

117°F (47°C) 25°F (-4°C)
61°F (16°C) 55°F (13°C)
29 in (747 mm)

Climate
The climate varies according to height. The north is mostly arid, but can be bitterly cold in the mountains. The south and coasts are hot and humid with the most rainfall.

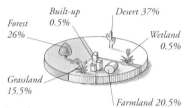

Built-up 0.5% Desert 37%
Forest 26% Wetland 0.5%
Grassland 15.5% Farmland 20.5%

Land use
About 40 percent of Mexico's land is so arid that few people live there, and it cannot be farmed. The once abundant rain forests have been cleared to make way for urban growth.

Mexico City

The world's second most populated city, Mexico's capital has 20,899,000 residents. The city lies on the site of the old Aztec capital, built in the 1300s. Mexico City sits below two high volcanoes, a position resulting in earthquakes, and air pollution from trapped urban smog.

Presidential palace

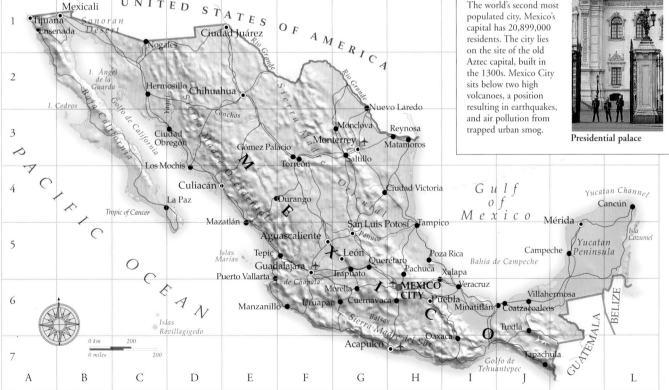

551

M

People

Mexico's population is set to increase by more than half by 2050. More than one-third of the people are under the age of 14. Poverty is a problem for many Mexicans, and several generations of one family often live together. Most people are *mestizos*, of mixed European and Native American descent.

| 134 per sq mile (52 per sq km) | 75% Urban | 25% Rural |

Native Americans
About 20 percent of Mexico's people are Native Americans. Tarahumara Indians live in the Sierra Madre region of Chihuahua. They are known for their brightly colored textiles, which are made and taken to market by the women.

Leisure

Sports and festivals are the favorite leisure activities for Mexicans. Spanish sports such as bullfighting are popular, as are rodeo events called *charreadas*. Soccer matches draw huge crowds.

Day of the Dead
At the beginning of November, Mexicans celebrate the Day of the Dead. During this festival, influenced by ancient Aztec traditions, death is not mourned, but celebrated. On the Day of the Dead, the streets are decorated with flowers, and skeletons made of papier-mâché are everywhere.

Papier-mâché skeleton

Festivals
Mexicans celebrate more than 120 fêtes and festivals every year, many of which are religious Roman Catholic celebrations. Some are national holidays. The Guélaquetza annual dance in Oaxaca is a colorful event that dates back to pre-Columbian times.

Farming

More than one-fifth of Mexicans work in agriculture, but only one-fifth of the land is used for growing crops. Water is scarce and, in some areas, all irrigation is artificial. Some farmers work under the *ejido* system, by which government-owned land is allocated to them; they work it and keep the profits.

Corn

Avocado

Chili peppers

Green pepper

Crops
Coffee, tomatoes, fruit, and vegetables are grown for export, while sugarcane, corn, and wheat feed the Mexican farmers' families. Avocados, green peppers, and chilies are also home-grown foods. Citrus fruits grow well in Mexico's warm climate.

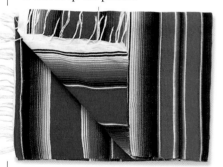

Textiles
Monterrey, Mexico's ninth largest city, is a center for textile weaving. Cotton is grown as a cash crop on the farms around the city. Traditional brightly colored patterns are still chosen, but now most garments are machine-made.

Food

Mexico has introduced many foods to the world, including avocados, chocolate, corn, tomatoes, and vanilla. *Tortillas*, or corn pancakes, are eaten like bread or made into snacks called *tacos* and filled with *guacamole*, a thick, spicy sauce made from onions, tomatoes, red peppers, and avocados.

Guacamole

Beer   Tortillas

Industry

Oil and silver production are Mexico's largest industries, but the service sector, including tourism, employs the most people. Car assembly, steel, textiles, food products, and breweries are important businesses.

Shrine for making sacrifices.

Tourism
Fine beaches and spectacular ruins lure nearly 20,000,000 visitors to Mexico every year. Impressive Mayan temple-pyramids such as Chichén Itzá were built strategically on the Yucatan Peninsula and are now World Heritage archaeological sites.

Silver brooch

Silver
Mexico is one of the world's largest producers of silver. The metal is mined at Durango, in the center of the country, where it was discovered by Spanish settlers in the 16th century. Mexico also has reserves of gold, lead, and tin.

Oil
Mexico ranks highly in world production of oil, which accounts for one-quarter of the country's total export earnings. Most of the oil is drilled from offshore wells in the Gulf of Mexico and along the Atlantic coast. Oil revenues have been used partly to finance an extensive industrialization program to boost Mexican business. Fluctuations in oil prices caused economic problems in the 1990s.

Maquilladoras
Many US companies have set up assembly plants in northern Mexico around the Rio Grande. Known as *maquilladoras*, they have attracted US investment because labor costs are less than in the US.

MICROSCOPES

MILLIONS OF TINY PARTICLES that play vital roles in our lives would go unobserved without the help of microscopes. A microscope magnifies small objects to reveal details invisible to the naked eye. The simple microscope uses one lens, capable of magnifications of between 70 and 250 times. Compound microscopes use a combination of two lenses and can produce magnifications of up to 2,000 times the size of the object being viewed. Electron microscopes use beams of electrons instead of light; they can magnify by hundreds of thousands of times.

Compound microscopes

The compound microscope uses two lenses (an objective lens and an eye-piece) and gives a much greater power of magnification than the simple microscope. It was the use of the compound lens that led to the discovery of cells.

Robert Hooke

English scientist Robert Hooke (1635–1703) was responsible for improving the early compound microscope, and also introduced the term "cell" to biology. He was a versatile scientist, who devised a spring for watches and an early telegraph system, as well as discovering how elastic objects stretch. Following the fire of London in 1666, he also designed several of London's most prominent buildings.

Simple microscopes

Dutch scientist Antoni van Leeuwenhoek's (1632–1723) simple microscope consisted of a single convex lens held between two metal plates. The eye had to be placed close to the lens to see the object placed on a pin. Using different lenses produced different magnifications.

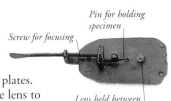

Pin for holding specimen

Screw for focusing

Lens held between two plates

How a simple microscope works

A simple microscope, such as a magnifying glass, consists of one convex lens that bulges outward and bends light inward. Seen through the convex lens, the object appears as a magnified and upright image.

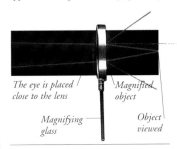

The eye is placed close to the lens

Magnified object

Magnifying glass

Object viewed

Magnified images

Forms of life such as the dust mite, which surround us but that the human eye cannot see, are made visible by the use of a microscope. Under a microscope, a shaft of hair can be matched to an individual, identified by the DNA present in the hair.

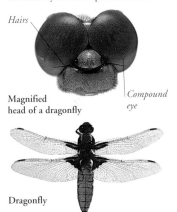

Hairs

Magnified head of a dragonfly

Compound eye

Dragonfly

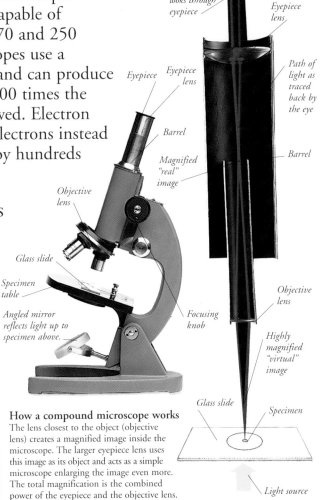

Observer looks through eyepiece

Eyepiece lens

Path of light as traced back by the eye

Eyepiece

Eyepiece lens

Barrel

Barrel

Magnified "real" image

Objective lens

Objective lens

Glass slide

Specimen table

Focusing knob

Highly magnified "virtual" image

Angled mirror reflects light up to specimen above.

Glass slide

Specimen

How a compound microscope works

The lens closest to the object (objective lens) creates a magnified image inside the microscope. The larger eyepiece lens uses this image as its object and acts as a simple microscope enlarging the image even more. The total magnification is the combined power of the eyepiece and the objective lens.

Light source

Petrograph microscopes

A petrograph microscope is used to study the make-up of rocks (petrology is the study of the composition of rocks). It uses polarized light to identify the minerals in thin sections of rocks.

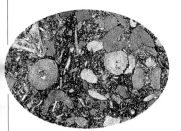

Black marble seen through petroscope

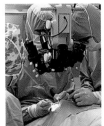

Microscopic surgery

One of the latest developments in surgery is microscopic surgery. An endoscope (optical fiber) is inserted into the patient. The surgeon can see the operation through the fiber optic and microscope.

Binocular microscope

Binocular microscopes

Using two eyes provides depth to the images perceived. Binocular microscopes, with two separate instruments fastened together, provide microscopic vision for both eyes and allow for detailed study of an image.

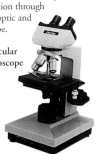

Electron scanning microscopes

Electron scanning microscopes can magnify extensively without losing the clarity of the image. Electrons are reflected off the surface of the specimen, producing a fluorescent image on a screen. This is photographed showing the surface in great detail.

Electron scanning microscope image of pollen

Electron scanning microscope

FIND OUT MORE

ATOMS AND MOLECULES   CELLS   FLOWERS   GLASS   LIGHT   INVENTIONS   MEDICINE   SCIENCE, HISTORY OF   TELESCOPES

MICROSCOPIC LIFE

A MICROORGANISM is a life-form that is too small for the human eye to see unaided. This usually means that it is less than 0.04 in (1 mm) in size. Microorganisms include protozoa, bacteria, fungi, algae, and viruses. The two main groups into which micro-organisms are divided are the protist and moneran groups. Some protists, such as the brown algae called kelp, can grow to more than 164 ft (50 m) in length, but most are microscopic, with the smallest measuring only 0.00000001 mm^3 in volume.

Protists

Protozoa, algae, and microscopic fungi are all protists – they belong to the Protista kingdom of organisms. Most protists are uni-cellular organisms, and their cell structure is similar to that of plants and animals. Some protists are multicellular, but their structure is simpler than that of higher organisms. There are up to 120,000 species of protists.

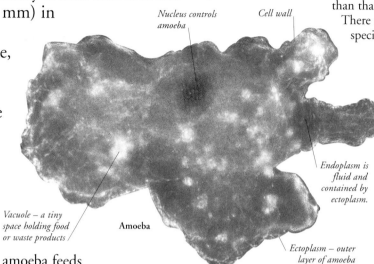

Nucleus controls amoeba

Cell wall

Endoplasm is fluid and contained by ectoplasm.

Vacuole – a tiny space holding food or waste products

Amoeba

Ectoplasm – outer layer of amoeba

Protozoa

There are more than 50,000 protozoa. They live in water and water-based liquids such as blood, and use tails, hairs, or tentacle-like extensions to move around. All protozoa are uni-cellular. Amoebas are a type of protozoan, but, unlike other protozoa, do not have tough external shells, or organs, such as tails or hairs, for movement. The amoeba is controlled by a single nucleus, which functions like a brain.

How an amoeba feeds

1 Amoebas move by pushing the more rigid part of their body, the ectoplasm, against the more fluid part, the endoplasm.

2 When an amoeba meets a possible food item, such as another protist, it slowly envelops the prey with its entire body, and sucks inward.

3 The food is then drawn toward the center of the cell, where the nutrients are dissolved. Any waste products are expelled.

Single-cell algae

Algae are plant-like organisms that generally obtain their food through photosynthesis. Most are unicellular, but some are multicellular and look very much like true plants. A highly diverse group of microorganisms, the most plant-like are green algae, and it is from these that plants are thought to have evolved.

Diatoms, single-cell algae

Microscopic fungi

Although mushrooms and toadstools are often large, many other types of fungi are microscopic. Fungi do not obtain their food from photosynthesis. Instead, they produce minute, thread-like structures called hyphae. The fungi use the hyphae to absorb food from the surface on which they are growing.

Microscopic fungi grown by termites in their nest

Slime molds

Although similar to fungi, slime molds are categorized separately. Many slime moulds acquire a fan-like shape as they flow over the surface on which they grow, such as damp, decaying logs. As the slime mold expands, it absorbs other microorganisms and bits of decaying plant material. Like fungi, slime molds reproduce by producing spores.

Slime mould

Plankton

Billions of tiny plants and animals float in sea- and freshwater; together, they make up plankton. The smallest plankton, phyto-plankton, are microscopic algae and bacteria. Phytoplankton forms the first link of the food chain in water and is eaten by predatory protists and zooplankton, which is composed of the young of marine animals such as crabs and shrimps.

Marine zooplankton

Monerans

The kingdom Monera includes organisms such as bacteria, which live in the air, on land, and in water. Most monerans are unicellular, but some are multicellular and resemble fungi. Monerans are divided into two groups: bacteria and blue-green bacteria; many are parasites.

Bacteria

Bacteria are often classified by their shape. Some, such as *Bacillus subtilis*, are rod-shaped; others are spherical or curved. In some species, individual cells are joined together to form long chains.

Actual size is magnified by 10,000.

Bacillus subtilis

Reproduction

Bacteria usually reproduce by splitting in two. This process is called binary fission. The two new bacteria are called daughters. Bacteria, such as *Klebsiella*, reproduce this way; and create a massive increase in population.

Bacteria has divided in two.

Multiplied by more than 100.

Bacteria has now multiplied by about 30.

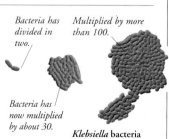

***Klebsiella* bacteria**

Blue-green bacteria

Until recently, blue-green bacteria were thought to be a type of algae. Now they are classified as a type of bacteria. They occur in a wide range of habitats, and when conditions are right they can multiply rapidly, causing "blooms" on lakes and in the sea.

"Bloom" forms green surface on lake

Viruses

Viruses, such as rubella which causes German measles, belong to a group of disease-producing organisms. Each virus is made from a length of nucleic acid surrounded by a protein coat. Viruses are inactive chemicals that show no sign of life until they invade a host. Once they have infected their host, they can reproduce in great numbers. Viruses can cause allergic reactions in the host cell, as well as causing it physical damage when they burst free from it.

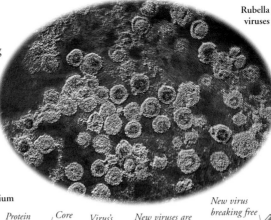
Rubella viruses

Rubella viruses erupting from cell

Reproduction

Viruses reproduce by inserting their nucleic acid, or genetic material, into that of a host cell and forcing the cell to produce more viruses. Almost every species of bacterium is parasitized by one or more viruses. These viruses are also known as bacteriophages.

Virus invading a bacterium

Virus's nucleic acid · Virus · Bacterium

Protein head · Core · Tail

Virus's nucleic acid

New viruses are formed inside the bacterium.

New virus breaking free

Reproduction of a virus

1 The virus's nucleic acid is stored in a head made of protein. The head sits on a core with a tail. When a bacterium is found, the virus imbeds its tail in the cell wall.

2 The tail of the virus contracts, pulling the core downward. All of the nucleic acid contained in the virus's head is injected into the bacterium.

3 The nucleic acid from the virus joins with the bacterium's nucleic acid and forces it to produce more viral nucleic acid. The cell is then forced to make protective proteins for the virus's survival.

4 After about half an hour, the bacterium bursts open, releasing another generation of viruses. By this time, the virus has been replicated 300 times, and the host cell has been damaged.

Antony van Leeuwenhoek

Microorganisms were unknown until the 1670s, when a Dutch merchant, Antony van Leeuwenhoek (1632–1723) started recording observations he made, using microscopes that he built. The study of "animalcules," as he called microorganisms, was only one of his many discoveries using a microscope.

Microbial diseases

Like most other organisms, humans are prone to attack by microorganisms, such as protists and viruses. These microbes, as they are called, can cause the host to become sick or can even kill it. Microbes injure their host in a number of ways. Some bacteria produce poisons, while protists can cause an allergic reaction in the host.

Salmonella causes food poisoning in humans.

These bacteria can occur in milk, meat, and eggs.

Salmonella enteridis

Protozoan diseases

Worldwide, more people have died from protozoan attacks than have died in war. In Africa, the protozoan *Trypanosoma brucei* causes sleeping sickness, which can weaken the human immune system and result in death.

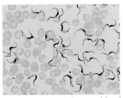
Trypanosomes in human blood

Fungal diseases

Only a few fungi infect humans. *Trichophyton soudanese* causes ringworm. Fungal infections are called *tinea* and are named after the part of the body they infect. For example, athlete's foot is called *tinea pedis*.

Trichophyton soudanese

Bacterial diseases

Many species of bacteria live in the digestive tracts of animals. Most bacteria are harmless, but some, such as those that cause cholera, typhoid, and *Salmonella* infections, can be fatal.

Viral diseases

Every year, thousands of people die from the results of viral infections, such as influenza, rabies, HIV, and yellow fever. Vaccines are available for many of the more common viruses, such as chickenpox, smallpox, and polio.

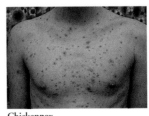
Chickenpox

Symbiotic microorganisms

Some microorganisms are essential to the life of their host: the two have a symbiotic relationship. For example, algae called zooxanthellae, live inside corals. They can photosynthesize and convert sunlight into carbohydrates on which the coral feeds. Other microorganisms live in the guts of animals, including humans, and aid the digestion of food.

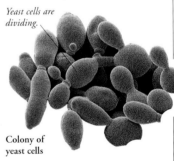
Zooxanthellae algae (yellow in color) live inside the coral polyps.

Coral packed with zooxanthellae algae

Microorganisms in food

The bacterium commonly called yeast (made up of single-celled organisms) is central to the fermentation process needed to make bread, beer, and wine. Other useful bacteria are used to refine crude oil or to preserve foods, such as milk and butter. Even the holes in Swiss cheese are caused by carbon dioxide-releasing bacteria.

Yeast cells are dividing.

Colony of yeast cells

AMOEBA

SCIENTIFIC NAME *Amoeba proteus*

ORDER Amoebida

FAMILY Gymnamoebidae

DISTRIBUTION These single-cell protists are found throughout the world wherever there is water

HABITAT Amoebas need to live in water – in ponds, puddles, or even in the digestive systems of animals

DIET Minute particles of organic matter and other microorganisms

SIZE 0.004–0.08 in (0.1–2 mm)

LIFESPAN Maximum of 1 month

FIND OUT MORE

CELLS · CORAL REEFS · DISEASES · GENETICS · MICROSCOPES · MUSHROOMS AND OTHER FUNGI · OCEAN WILDLIFE · PARASITES · PHOTOSYNTHESIS

MIGRATION, ANIMAL

SEVERAL HUNDRED BILLION animals are on the move at any one time, making journeys from one place to another called migrations. Migrating animals include insects, fish, amphibians, reptiles, birds, and mammals, including humans. They find their way using innate knowledge, familiar landmarks, the Earth's magnetic field, or the position of the Sun, Moon, and stars. Animals migrate to find food, to alleviate overcrowding, or to reproduce. Some animals migrate every year; others migrate only when their surroundings force them to.

To reproduce

An important reason for migration is to find a place where there is enough space, food, and suitable weather to raise a family. In the oceans, mammals, such as whales and seals, may migrate to warm water to have their young. Some species of fish also migrate between feeding and breeding grounds.

Gray whale
Many large whales feed in cold polar waters where there is plenty of food, but migrate to warmer areas in the tropics to breed. The gray whale travels from the Arctic to the coast of California.

Salmon have strong muscles and are powerful swimmers.

Elvers

Salmon
Young salmon hatch in rivers and streams and spend some years there before swimming to the ocean. After feeding and growing for several more years, they follow chemical clues in the water to find their way back to the river where they were born. They often have to leap up waterfalls as they fight their way upstream. After laying their eggs, they die.

Eels
Born in the Sargasso Sea southeast of Bermuda, eels migrate to rivers in North America and Europe to feed and grow. The young eels, called elvers, may wriggle over land to reach their feeding grounds.

Escaping the weather

Animals may migrate to escape freezing winters or hot summers. They return when the weather is more favorable. If animals stayed in one place, there would be too much competition for food, space, and places to breed. Seasonal migrations can be short, such as up and down a mountain.

Each bird flies in the slipstream of the bird in front to save energy.

Spiny lobster
As many as 100,000 spiny lobsters may migrate each fall, walking along the seabed in single files of up to 60 individuals. The lobsters stay in contact by touching each other with their antennae.

Snow goose
Snow geese breed in the Arctic summer, but migrate south in winter to the Gulf of Mexico. They fly in a "V" formation in order to save energy for the long journey.

Bogong moth
These moths migrate up the Australian Alps for the hot summers. They sleep in cracks in the rock until it is cooler.

Looking for food

If the food supply in a location changes regularly every year, animals make regular annual migrations to tap new supplies. When conditions vary from year to year, migrational patterns are irregular.

Locusts
Migratory swarms of locusts occur where suitable habitats are scarce and there is overcrowding. The locusts gather in large groups and grow longer wings and wider shoulders. They migrate up to 1,980 miles (3,200 km) a year.

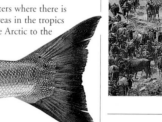

Wildebeest
On the plains of East Africa, wildebeest migrate to find fresh grass and water. They can sense water up to 60 miles (100 km) away and follow the seasonal movement wet weather. The herds are under constant danger of attack from predators such as lions and hyenas.

Long-distance travelers

The distances traveled by animals on migration often run into several thousand miles each year. These long journeys use up huge amounts of energy, and birds may double their weight before setting off.

Arctic tern
This bird migrates farther than any other bird. It flies from one end of the globe to the other and back again each year – a round trip of more than 31,000 miles (50,000 km).

Monarch butterfly
These butterflies migrate up to 2,500 miles (4,000 km) every fall, from Canada to Mexico and California, to hibernate in mountain forests. They, or their offspring, then make the return trip.

Northern fur seal
Female northern fur seals migrate some 3,100 miles (5,000 km) from their breeding grounds in the north to spend the winter in warmer water. They return in the spring.

| FIND OUT MORE | AFRICAN WILDLIFE | ANIMAL BEHAVIOR | HIBERNATION | POLAR WILDLIFE | TRAVEL | WHALES AND DOLPHINS |

MINOANS

ON THE ISLAND OF CRETE in the Aegean Sea, an advanced civilization emerged around 2500 BC – Europe's first empire. These people, who were traders, became known as the Minoans, after the legend of the wealthy King Minos of Crete. The Minoans built huge palaces on Crete, and decorated them with paintings and luxury items. Scholars have deciphered only part of their writing. In 1450, the Minoans were conquered by the warlike Mycenaeans from Greece.

Spread of the Minoan Empire
From their homeland on Crete, the Minoans dominated the Aegean Sea from 2000 to 1450 BC. The settlements were mainly coastal, and the most important – Knossos, Mallia, Phaistos, and Zakros – were built around large palaces.

Skylight allowing light into the palace

Throne room

Bull jumping may have taken place in the central courtyard.

Olive trees grew in the courtyard.

Wooden pillars were painted red and blue.

Knossos
The largest of the Minoan palaces, Knossos, was built c.1900 BC, then rebuilt 200 years later after being destroyed, either by war or an earthquake. The huge, richly decorated complex may have been a religious center and a base for trading, as well as a home for the local ruler. The palace is arranged around a central courtyard and contains rooms for many different purposes – royal apartments, ceremonial chambers such as the throne room, shrines, workshops, and dozens of storerooms.

Bull jumping
In this sport, which possibly had religious significance, young men and women took turns somersaulting over the back of a bull.

Pottery
The storerooms at Knossos were full of earthenware jars, (pithoi), some 6 ft (2 m) tall. These jars stored oil and wine.

Bird

Snake

Flounced skirt

Religion
Many hilltops and all the palaces contained shrines, where the Minoans made offerings of food and drink to the gods. Several different deities were worshiped, including a god of animals and the hunt. Bulls were also believed to be sacred. The most important deity was a goddess of the Earth and fertility.

Snake maiden
Archaeologists have found many images of this goddess, wearing the typical costume of a Minoan woman. She sometimes carries snakes in her hands, and sometimes has them twined around her body. Minoans probably saw her as a guardian of the home, and also as a deity who would encourage fertility and promote good harvests in the fields.

Trade
The Minoans traded using a circular route around the Mediterranean, from Crete to Egypt, then to Palestine, and back to Crete via Cyprus. They exported pottery, metalwork, and food. They imported raw materials, such as copper and precious stones.

Grapes

Olives

Thera
A volcanic eruption on nearby Thera in 1470 BC was once thought to have caused the end of the Minoan Empire. Research now shows that invaders from mainland Greece, known as the Mycenaeans, wiped out the Minoans.

Timeline
2500 BC Trading settlements begin to expand on th island of Crete.

1900 BC First Cretan palaces are built; Minoans begin to trade and build up overseas links.

1800 BC Writing begins on Crete as Minoan scribes develop the Linear A script.

1700 BC Cretan palaces are destroyed by fire, possibly during wars between different Cretan states. The palaces are rebuilt.

1550 BC Cretan civilization at peak.

1500 BC Linear B script (a way of writing an ancient form of Greek) starts to be used.

1470 BC Eruption on island of Thera.

1400 BC Knossos falls after Crete is overrun by invaders from the Greek mainland, the Mycenaeans. At the same time, the mainland Mycenaean palace civilization expands, as does Mycenaean trade in the Mediterranean.

FIND OUT MORE | EUROPE, HISTORY OF | GODS AND GODDESSES | GREECE, ANCIENT | WRITING

MIXTURES AND COMPOUNDS

WE CANNOT SEE the salt in the ocean, but we know it is there because the water tastes salty. The salt and water form a mixture called a solution. Salt and water themselves are compounds – substances that contain elements bound strongly together by a chemical reaction. In science, a mixture is a combination of elements or compounds mingled loosely together. Mixtures are much easier to separate into their component parts than compounds.

The crystals break up into tiny particles that spread throughout the liquid.

After a few seconds, the crystals have dissolved completely in the water.

Solutions

Potassium permanganate crystals dissolve rapidly when they are dropped into water. The two substances are soon indistinguishable because they form a uniform mixture called a solution. In a solution, particles of a solid (the solute) are completely intermingled with the particles of a liquid (the solvent). A solution is said to be concentrated if it contains a large amount of solute, and dilute if it contains only a small amount.

Crystals of potassium permanganate

Suspensions and colloids

When muddy water is left to stand, the mud settles and the water becomes clearer. Muddy water is a suspension – a mixture of solid particles hanging in a liquid. The mixture eventually separates because gravity makes the particles sink to the bottom. A colloid is a mixture of tiny particles of matter dispersed evenly throughout a solid, liquid, or gas. The particles are too small to be separated by gravity and too large to dissolve, so they stay suspended in the main substance.

The two substances are evenly mixed.

Eventually, the solid lead iodide particles settle out.

Suspension of lead iodide in potassium iodide

Aerosols are solid or liquid particles suspended in a gas.

Smoke (aerosol of ash in air)

Gels consist of solid particles suspended in a liquid.

Shaving foam (air in liquid soap)

Types of colloids
The particles in a colloid can be gas bubbles, droplets of liquid, or tiny solid pieces. Colloids include aerosols, gels, emulsions, and foams. Fog, for example, is an aerosol of water particles in air. Colloids are also known as dispersions.

Foams are colloids of gas particles dispersed evenly throughout a liquid or solid.

Emulsions are mixtures of liquid particles suspended in another liquid.

Hair gel (solid fat in water)

Emulsion paint (liquid pigment in oil)

Separating mixtures

Pouring coffee through a filter is a familiar way of separating a mixture: the filter separates the grounds from the liquid coffee, making it more drinkable. Other separation methods include decanting, centrifuging, distillation, and evaporation. Decanting, the simplest method, involves pouring liquid from the top of a denser liquid or solid sediment.

Decanting oil from vinegar

Oil is less dense than vinegar.

Filter paper

Residue of coffee grounds

Liquid coffee filtrate

Filter
A porous barrier called a filter is used to separate a mixture of large solid particles in a liquid. The filter allows the small liquid particles (the filtrate) to pass through, but holds back the larger solid particles (the residue).

Centrifuge
A centrifuge is a machine that separates mixtures by spinning them very fast in test tubes. Denser substances sink to the bottom and separate out. Centrifuges are used to extract dense blood cells from blood plasma.

Mixture is held in test tubes.

Overhead view of centrifuge

Distillation
A process called distillation can be used to separate a liquid from a mixture. The mixture is heated until the liquid boils and turns into a gas. The gas is then forced into a tube called a condenser, where it cools to form a pure liquid.

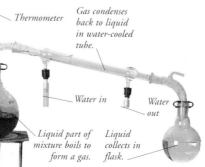

Thermometer

Gas condenses back to liquid in water-cooled tube.

Water in

Water out

Liquid part of mixture boils to form a gas.

Liquid collects in flask.

Evaporation
Heat can separate a liquid from a mixture by evaporation. In hot climates, this method is often used to obtain salt from seawater. Shallow pools called salt pans are dug out on the beach and filled with seawater. The water evaporates in the warm sun, leaving salt crystals behind.

M

M

Tongs hold glowing steel wool.

Some of the iron chloride that forms turns immediately into a gas.

This reaction, like many others, needs heat to start if off, so the steel wool is first heated in a flame.

Chlorine is a reactive gas, so the reaction is vigorous.

Gas jar of chlorine

By the end of the reaction, the tangle of steel wool has changed into lumps of iron chloride.

Making compounds

Compounds can be formed only during chemical reactions. For example, the elements iron and chlorine react vigorously together to form the compound iron chloride, in which the particles of iron and chlorine bind tightly together. Compounds often have very different properties from those of the elements they contain. Iron is a hard, magnetic, silvery metal, while chlorine is a reactive green-yellow gas. However, the compound they form – iron chloride – is a crumbly, orange-brown solid that is non-magnetic and fairly unreactive.

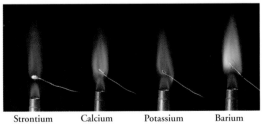

Sampling molten iron in a blast furnace

Separating compounds
Compounds can only be broken apart by chemical reactions. Most metals have to be extracted from naturally occurring compounds called ores. In a blast furnace, the metal ore iron oxide (a compound of iron and oxygen) is heated with coke that contains carbon. The heat of the furnace causes a chemical reaction in which the carbon removes the oxygen from the iron ore, leaving behind molten iron metal.

Structure of compounds

Inside a compound, the particles of different elements are bound together by forces called bonds, which form during chemical reactions. Covalent compounds contain atoms linked together into groups called molecules. In ionic compounds, electrically charged particles called ions link up to form a structure called a lattice.

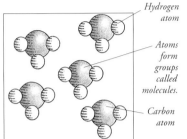
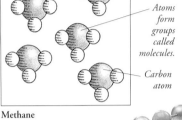

Hydrogen atom

Atoms form groups called molecules.

Carbon atom

Methane

Covalent compounds
At normal temperatures, covalent compounds, such as methane, form liquids, gases, or soft solids. They are poor conductors of electricity, and have low boiling and melting points, because there are only weak bonds between the molecules of these compounds.

Ionic compounds
Inside ionic compounds, such as sodium chloride (common salt), strong bonds hold the ions of the different elements firmly together. Ionic compounds form hard, brittle solids. They have high boiling and melting points, and are good conductors of electricity when molten or in solution.

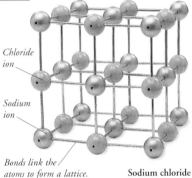

Chloride ion

Sodium ion

Bonds link the atoms to form a lattice.

Sodium chloride

Justus von Liebig
The German chemist Justus von Liebig (1803–73) made many advances in the study of carbon-based compounds. He established a teaching laboratory in 1839 and devised standard procedures such as distillation for separating and analyzing mixtures and compounds. He was one of the discoverers of chloroform, and also pioneered the development of artificial fertilizers.

Chemical analysis

There are many ways to analyze a mixture or compound to find out what it is made of and how much of each ingredient it contains. These techniques are used to check food and medicine for purity, test air and water samples for pollution, and examine blood and urine for signs of disease.

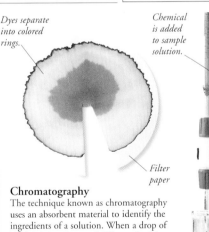

Dyes separate into colored rings.

Chemical is added to sample solution.

Filter paper

Flame tests
If a metallic element is present in a substance, it can be identified with a flame test. A clean wire is dipped into a powder of the substance and then put into a flame. Different metals burn with flames of different colors, so the flame's color identifies the metal. Fireworks use metal compounds to produce colored sparks.

Strontium   Calcium   Potassium   Barium

Chromatography
The technique known as chromatography uses an absorbent material to identify the ingredients of a solution. When a drop of black ink (a mixture of different dyes) is placed in the center of a filter paper, the ink spreads out to form rings of different colors. The dyes in the ink are absorbed by the paper at different rates, depending on the size and shape of their molecules.

Chemical reaction changes color of sample solution.

Burette

Mass spectrometry
The ions of each element have a different mass. A mass spectrometer uses this fact to analyze unknown substances. It changes the atoms of an unknown substance into ions, and separates them according to their mass. It then produces a graph, called a mass spectrum, that shows the proportions of each element present.

Titration
The concentration of a solution can be found by titration. The sample reacts with a chemical whose concentration is known. When the reaction is complete, a color change occurs. The amount of the chemical needed to bring about this color change enables chemists to calculate the concentration of the sample.

FIND OUT MORE   ATOMS AND MOLECULES   CHEMISTRY   COLOR   ELEMENTS   GASES   LIQUIDS   MATTER   OCEANS AND SEAS   ROCKS AND MINERALS   SOLIDS

MONASTERIES

M

A MONASTERY IS HOME to monks, people who have chosen to live apart from society, devoting their lives to religion. Most organized religions have monasteries, especially the Christian and Buddhist traditions. As well as being a church or temple, a monastery is where monks live and work. Nuns, women who choose to follow a religious life, normally live in convents.

The nave, at the western end of the church, is where lay people worship.

The choir, at the eastern end of the church, is where monks worship.

Parts of a Christian monastery

At the heart of a Christian monastery is the church, where the monks or nuns gather for worship at set times every day. It also contains the buildings in which the monks or nuns live – including rooms for eating, bathing, sleeping, and studying. Some monasteries also have accommodations for guests.

Monks spend many hours of each day in the monastery church, attending eight services from midnight to early evening before bed. The words of many services are chanted, not sung. This music is called plainsong.

The chapter house is where the monks meet to discuss the business of the monastery. The monks eat together in the refectory, while one of them reads from a religious book.

The cloister is a covered walkway within the monastery.

The cloister garth is a courtyard used for rest and relaxation.

Refectory

The garden provides produce for the monks' table. Monasteries also often have outlying farms where livestock is raised.

Life in a monastery

Prayer dominates monastery life. In medieval Europe, monasteries also provided education, and monks wrote books, composed music, or healed the sick. Today, monks and nuns still teach, or help the poor or homeless.

Gatehouse

Storeroom

Rosemary

Bay leaves

Produce

In the Middle Ages, a monastery was self-sufficient, producing all its own food. Monks became skilled farmers and gardeners. Today, they make all sorts of produce for sale.

Honey made to raise money for monastery.

The dorter, or dormitory, is where monks sleep. In some orders, there is more privacy, with a small area partitioned off for each person.

The infirmary, or hospital, is housed in a separate building to reduce the risk of spreading infection.

Herb gardening

Many different herbs were grown in the gardens of medieval monasteries. Aromatic plants such as bay, rosemary, and garlic were used to flavour the monastery's food and to make medicines and ointments for healing the sick.

Monks and nuns

Life in a monastery or convent follows strict rules. Monks and nuns vow to obey their spiritual leader and to give up personal property and relations with the opposite sex.

Novices

In their first years of monastery life, monks and nuns are called novices. During this training period, they make sure they can live by their religious vows.

Buddhist monk

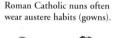

Roman Catholic nuns often wear austere habits (gowns).

Eastern monasteries

Monasteries play a large part in many eastern religions. In Buddhist countries, young men often spend a short time as a monk as part of their normal education. The Hindu, Taoist, and Jain faiths all have strong monastic traditions.

Monastic caves

Monks and nuns deny themselves comforts they would have as lay people. Few led a harsher life than the monks of St. Antoine, Lebanon, who lived in caves in cliffs.

Caves of the order of St. Antoine

FIND OUT MORE | BUDDHISM | CHRISTIANITY | CHURCHES AND CATHEDRALS | HINDUISM | MEDICINE, HISTORY OF | MEDIEVAL EUROPE | RELIGIONS

MONET, CLAUDE

IN 1874, A PAINTING WAS exhibited that gave its name to a revolutionary movement in art. The painting was *Impression: Sunrise* and the artist, Monet, became the most famous Impressionist painter. Monet found new ways of painting what he saw. Instead of working in a studio, he liked to take his easel into the open air. He, and artists such as Renoir and Degas, developed a loose, rapid style of painting that was completely unlike the smooth, highly finished style then fashionable among artists. Painting was never the same again.

Impressionism

Monet and his friends did not like the pictures that were shown at the Salon, France's yearly painting exhibition. So in 1874, Monet and a group of 29 other artists put on their own exhibition. Many of the paintings were small canvases painted in the open air. The artists used loose brushstrokes and many dabs of pure color – hallmarks of what is now called the Impressionist style. At first people thought the pictures looked "unfinished," but they are now among the most popular paintings in the world.

Impression: Sunrise, 1872
Monet included this view of the French port of Le Havre in the exhibition of 1874. A critic, Louis Leroy, wrote an article attacking the painting, which he thought too sketchy to be shown as a finished work. Leroy called his article "Exhibition of the Impressionists," meaning the term as an insult. But the name stuck, and it is now used to describe the work of Monet and his friends.

Changing light
Monet was fascinated by light. He painted several groups of pictures of the same subject, showing how the colors varied with the changing light. In 1892–93, he painted a series of pictures of Rouen Cathedral, France. He worked quickly, on as many as 14 different paintings in one day, building up heavy layers of paint that seemed to imitate the thickness of the stone itself.

Two paintings of Rouen Cathedral

Early life
Claude Monet was born in Paris in 1840, but his family moved to the town of Le Havre in Normandy when he was five. There he learned to paint, producing pictures of his family and local scenes, and portraits of the people of Le Havre.

From Normandy to Paris
As a young man in Le Havre, Monet met the landscape painter Eugène Boudin (1824–98). Boudin painted in the open air, and he persuaded Monet to do the same. Monet enjoyed this experience and realized that he wanted to be an artist. In 1859, he went to study art in Paris, where he met the painter Camille Pissarro (1830–1903) and other artists who became his friends.

Berthe Morisot
Berthe Morisot (1841–95) was the first female member of the Impressionist group. She was born into a rich French family and had private lessons in painting and drawing. But she rejected the conventional style of her teachers and decided to paint like the Impressionists. Morisot specialized in gentle paintings of family life and seascapes painted in delicate brushstrokes.

Monet's palette

Painting outdoors
In the early 19th century, artists usually sketched out of doors, but painted their finished pictures in the studio. Monet was one of the first to paint entire, finished canvases in the open air. He took his easel everywhere – the beach, fields, railroad stations – and had a boat made into a floating studio so that he could paint along the Seine River.

Canopy shelters the deck.

Windows all around cabin

Monet's floating studio

Giverny
In 1883, Monet moved to Giverny, in northwestern France. He created a beautiful garden around his house, and built a pond in which he planted water lilies. For the next 25 years, this garden was his favorite subject, and he painted the lily pond again and again. He was fascinated by the colors of the flowers, the effects of light on the foliage, and the reflections in the pond water. Many of the water lily paintings were huge, so Monet built a special studio in which to work.

Monet at Giverny

Water lilies

CLAUDE MONET

1840	Born in Paris.
1845	Moves to Le Havre.
1859	Returns to Paris to study.
1874	Exhibits in First Impressionist Exhibition.
1876–78	Paints at Gare St. Lazare railroad station, Paris.
1883	Retires from Paris to Giverny.
1892	Begins series of paintings of Rouen Cathedral.
1900	Paints by the Thames River in London.
1908	Works on water lily paintings; starts to lose his eyesight.
1926	Dies at Giverny.

FIND OUT MORE   ART, HISTORY OF   COLOR   CHURCHES AND CATHEDRALS   FRANCE   LIGHT   PAINTING AND DRAWING   PICASSO, PABLO

MONEY

YOU CANNOT EAT MONEY, WEAR IT, or live in it, but people need it to feed, clothe, and house themselves. People use money to pay for the things they want to buy – it is a means of exchange that works as long as the buyer and the seller both agree on the value of the paper, metal, or plastic used to pay. Money works as a standard of value, allowing one to see how much goods are worth. It also provides a store of wealth more convenient than other things of value, such as property. Before money was invented, people used barter, swapping one item for another.

Gold standard
Each country has its own money, or currency. So governments need a standard way of judging how much a nation's currency is worth, to work out exchange rates from one currency into another. In the 20th century, many Western governments measured the value of a currency according to the value of gold and a nation's gold reserves. Various systems existed, which all related the value of a banknote to a precise weight of gold. The gold standard system ended in the 1970s; now the value of currency depends on the market.

17th-century banknote, Sweden

Serial number

Australian dollars

Credit card

Types of money
The most familiar forms of money are coins and banknotes, also known as cash. Much of the money stored in a bank exists not as piles of notes, but as data stored in computers. To spend it, people use checks and plastic credit or debit cards.

Coins
The first coins were made in Lydia, Turkey, c.600 BC. Early coins were made of precious metal. Today, they are more likely to be made of a common metal, like aluminum.

Banknotes
They may be only pieces of paper, but banknotes are accepted as valuable because of the sum they represent. They first appeared in China in the 11th century and in Europe six centuries later.

Check

Payee's name written here

Ten pence

One penny

Tiny computer

Credit card
With a credit card, a person can buy something and pay for it later. The cards are issued by banks, credit companies, and large stores, and can be used in most shops. Each month, the company sends a total bill to the cardholder. Cardholders must repay the debt promptly, or will owe interest (extra money) on the balance.

Smart cards can now make and record payments.

Two pence

Twenty pence

Five pence

Fifty pence

Pound coin

Modern British coins

Gold and silver mix

The lion's head, an emblem of the Lydian kings.

Lydian coins

Check guarantee card

Checks
A check is a written instruction to a bank to pay money to someone. For security reasons, they are often unusable without proper identification.

The origins of money
The earliest records of money being used come from ancient Mesopotamia (modern Iraq) some 4,500 years ago. Payments were made with weighed amounts of silver. Since then, weighed amounts of metal have been used as money in many places worldwide.

Weight
Weighing the precious metal showed how much a person had and what it was worth.

Mesopotamian weight

Price list
This clay tablet contains a price list written in Mesopotamia in the 19th century BC. It expresses prices in terms of shekels and minas, the standard weights of the time. One shekel of silver would buy twelve mina of wool, ten mina of bronze, three measures of barley, or three measures of sesame oil.

First designs show the main pictures and words that appear on the note.

Design for the lines, shades, and colors, meant to discourage forgers.

Anti-forgery elements such as security thread are often added to the paper used to make the banknotes.

Printing inks are mixed specially, giving the exact colors required for the note. This is another process that makes forgery difficult.

Printing inks

Making banknotes
To reduce the chance of forgery, the process of making banknotes is shrouded in secrecy and production is made as complicated as possible. The design includes many fine details hardly noticeable at first glance, and special inks and papers not used in ordinary printing.

Burnisher smooths the flat surfaces

Burin used to cut design into intaglio plate.

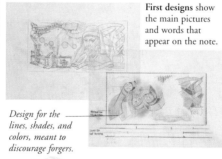

Printing
Three printing processes are used: one for the background, one for the main design, and another for the serial number. One process, intaglio, makes the ink stand slightly raised up from the paper – another indication that the note is genuine.

Finished specimen note

Banks

Most people store their money with a bank, which keeps an account of how much money each customer deposits. People gain access to their money through cash machines, teller transactions, or by writing checks. Banks may provide interest when a certain amount of money is kept in the account, but will charge customers who borrow money. Banks also provide financial services such as pensions, mortgages, and insurance policies.

Bankers, Italy

Early banks

Banks were set up about 3,000 to 4,000 years ago in Babylon as a secure place for customers' money. By 600 BC, there were banks in China; later, in ancient Rome, banks offered investment and foreign exchange services. Banking declined in medieval Europe because the Church disapproved of money-lending for profit. But in the 15th and 16th centuries, important banks were set up in Italy, providing financial services all over the Mediterranean.

M

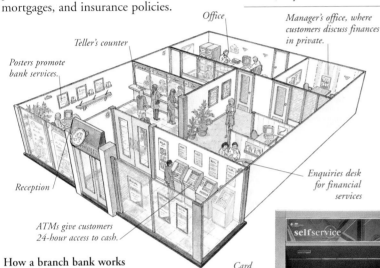

Office

Teller's counter

Manager's office, where customers discuss finances in private.

Posters promote bank services.

Reception

ATMs give customers 24-hour access to cash.

Enquiries desk for financial services

How a branch bank works

Large banks have branches in suburban towns. Tellers serve customers through bulletproof glass panels. They can cash checks, using money kept in drawers beneath the counter, and inform customers about their accounts using a terminal connected to the bank's central computer. Customers can also buy foreign currency for trips overseas. Most of the money is kept in vaults behind massive steel doors.

Card inserted here

Panel for keying in PIN

ATMs

Automated teller machines (ATMs) allow customers to take money from their accounts even when the bank is closed. Customers insert a plastic card and key in a personal identification number (or PIN). The machine is connected to a computer that contains information about the amount of money in each person's account.

Bank vault | Reinforced door | Security guards

Security

An armored truck delivers banknotes to a bank, where they are stored in vaults for safekeeping. These are strong rooms, built for maximum security, and are usually equipped with time locks. At the end of a working day, all the cash at the counter tills is counted and returned to the vaults.

Deposit box

Safety deposit boxes

Banks keep their cash in strongrooms. For a fee, they also keep a customer's valuables, such as share certificates, in strong boxes in the strongroom.

Stock markets

People who want to invest in a company buy shares. Stock is the money raised by the company as a result of selling its shares. Major centers of financial trading, such as London, New York, and Tokyo, have stock markets where shares in companies are bought and sold.

How the exchange works

Rather than buy shares directly from a company, investors deal with brokers who are based at the stock exchange. Dealers work out the share prices by balancing the shares on offer with the current demand. Investors hope to buy shares before they rise in value and to sell them when the price is at its height, but it is usually difficult to predict exactly when this will be. Increasingly, brokers rely on computers to keep in touch with prices worldwide.

Screens show up-to-date share prices.

Broker at work on the hectic floor.

New York Stock Exchange

Fort Knox

The greatest gold reserves in the world are held at the US Depository in Fort Knox, Kentucky. Since 1936, the bulk of the US's gold has been stored there. The gold is kept in steel and concrete vaults, enclosed in a large, bomb-proof building with massive walls. Electronic alarm systems, closed-circuit television, and armed guards provide extra protection.

Company	Price	Weekly change +/-
Gordon Properties	44	-2
JCP Interiors	69	-1
O'Neill Group	162	+7
Shaw Associates	121	+5
Thomson PLC	46	+2

Stocks and shares

The value of shares goes up and down. Prices are published daily in the newspapers so that people can see the value of their investments. The current price is printed along with the amount the share gained or lost during the day.

Inflation

Inflation devalues money, because when prices rise, people need to spend more to buy the same amount of goods. For example, if inflation in the US is running at 10 percent per year, then a shopping cart filled with $30-worth of food in year one will cost $33 in year two. Governments try to control inflation; if it gets out of control, money becomes worthless.

FIND OUT MORE GOVERNMENTS AND POLITICS GREAT DEPRESSION SOCIETIES, HUMAN TRADE AND INDUSTRY UNITED STATES OF AMERICA

World banknotes

Captions identify denominations of currency and year issued

Africa and Europe

Austria, Belgium, Finland, France, Germany, Greece, Ireland, Italy, Luxembourg, Netherlands, Portugal, Spain
5, 10, 20, 50, 100 euros (2002)

Denmark
100 kroner (2001),
200 kroner (1992)

Poland
50, 200 zlotych (1994)

Switzerland
10 francs (1995),
20, 50 francs (1994)

Kenya
100 shillings (2001),
200 shillings (2000)

Zimbabwe
5, 10 dollars (1994)

South Africa
10 rands (1993),
50 rands (1992)

Gambia
5, 25 dalasis (2001)

Egypt
5, 100 pounds (2001)

The Americas

Asia and Australia

Venezuela
10,000 bolívares (2000),
20,000 bolívares (1999)

Chile
1,000 pesos (1994),
10,000 pesos (1992)

Japan
1,000, 5,000 yen (1993)

Indonesia
10,000 rupiahs (1992),
20,000 rupiahs (1995)

Mexico
100, 200 pesos (2000)

Colombia
5,000 pesos (1995),
10,000 pesos (1994)

Australia
10 dollars (1993), 20 dollars (1994)

India
500,1000 rupees (2000)

Canada
5 dollars (1986), 10 dollars (1989),
20 dollars (1991)

United States
5, 10 dollars (2000), 20 dollars (1998)

Singapore
2 dollars (2000), 50, 100 dollars (1999)

North Korea
1, 5, 50 won (2000)

MONGOL EMPIRE

FOR CENTURIES, the Mongols lived a nomadic life on the steppes, or grasslands, of Asia. Suddenly, during the 13th century, they erupted onto the world stage. Led by Genghis Khan, the Mongols carved out a vast empire that stretched across Europe and Asia. They were ruthless soldiers, reducing every city they conquered to ashes. Yet they gave their empire a century of peace. Trade flourished along the Silk Road between China and Europe, and China was united after years of division. Their empire was short-lived, and broke up with the death of Kublai Khan in 1294.

Foundation of the empire

In 1206, a kuriltai (assembly) of Mongol tribes met and proclaimed Temujin, leader of the Mangkhol tribe, supreme ruler "of all who dwell in tents of felt." They gave him the name Genghis Khan, "prince of all that lies between the oceans." By 1279, they ruled an empire that stretched from central Europe along the ancient Silk Road to the Pacific Ocean.

Genghis' empire

Yurts
The Mongols lived in yurts, or gers (tents). They were made of skins and handwoven cloth stretched over a wooden frame, and easy to dismantle.

Mongol archer carried a bow and about 30 arrows.

Mongol shield made of wood and leather

Mongol warriors
The Mongols were skilled and agile horsemen, able to cover more than 100 miles (160 km) a day. They rode small horses that were bred to withstand the intense cold and were capable of short bursts of great speed. Their mounted archers were only lightly armed. They used bows and arrows that could pierce an enemy's armor.

Fighting
The Mongols were devious and clever in battle, stampeding riderless horses into the enemy lines to confuse them, and tying stuffed sacks onto horses to make their armies look bigger than they were. A favorite tactic was to pretend to withdraw, luring the enemy into an ambush.

Genghis Khan
Genghis Khan, or Temujin as he was then known, was born in Mongolia in about 1167. As a young man he became a fearsome chief. After his election as supreme leader of the Mongols, he led his armies to victory across Asia. He died in China in 1227, but his death was kept secret until his son could succeed him.

Mongol conquests
At first the Mongol armies overran northern China, capturing Beijing in 1215. They then conquered most of Central Asia and Persia. Later campaigns took them west into Hungary and Poland, south into Egypt and India, and east toward Java and Japan.

Mongol knife set

Ivory chopstick

Steel-bladed knife

Leather sheath

Mongol warrior's boots
Leather stitched to uppers for decoration and extra strength.

Tough leather uppers

Mongol warriors sack Kiev.

The sacking of Kiev
In 1240, Mongol armies reached the great Russian city of Kiev. They burned the city to the ground, and killed or mutilated every person. Six years later, a Papal envoy on his way to see the Mongol leaders reported that only 200 of Kiev's houses were left.

Tamerlane
In the early 14th century, Mongol power decreased. But in 1369, Timur "Leng" (the lame), known as Tamerlane (1336–1405), made himself ruler of Samarkand in Central Asia and began to recreate the Mongol Empire. He conquered most of Central Asia, but died before he could invade China.

Timeline
1206 Temujin proclaimed Genghis Khan at a Mongol tribal assembly.

1211 Mongols begin invasion of northern China.

1229 Ogodei, son of Genghis, is elected Great Khan.

Genghis Khan, ruler of the Mongols 1206–1270

1240 Mongols overrun Russia and advance into Hungary and Poland.

1241 Death of Ogodei halts Mongol invasion of Europe.

1258 Mongols capture Baghdad.

1260 Egyptians defeat Mongols at Ain Jalut; Kublai Kahn becomes fifth and last Great Khan.

1279 Kublai Khan finally conquers southern China and founds Yuan Dynasty.

 FIND OUT MORE   ARMS AND ARMOR   ARMIES   ASIA, HISTORY OF   CHINA, HISTORY OF   WARFARE

MONGOLIA

THE RULERS of Mongolia once dominated China, central Asia, and eastern Europe. Today, this landlocked country north of China is a remote, sparsely populated place, with a mainly agricultural economy that is steadily becoming more industrialized. Mongolia has vast mineral reserves, and manufacturing is growing. Dominated by China for many years, Mongolia became an independent communist state in 1924. It is now a multiparty democracy.

Physical features

Mongolia is a high plateau, ringed by mountains to the north and west, and by the cold semidesert and desert of the Gobi in the south. Much of the eastern side of the plateau is dry, open grassland. There are lakes and forests in the northwest.

Ulan Bator

Once a small country town called Urghat, Mongolia's capital, now called Ulan Bator, was transformed into a major city by its communist rulers. It is the country's political, cultural, and industrial center, producing processed foods and textiles.

Choghin Temple in the Buddhist Gandan Monastery, Ulan Bator

Gobi Desert

The Gobi Desert covers about one-third of the country and has an area of 401,500 sq miles (1,040,000 sq km), making it the fourth largest desert in the world. The Gobi is arid sand or rock and is the site of a discovery of fossil bones and dinosaur eggs.

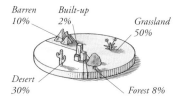

Barren 10% Built-up 2% Grassland 50% Desert 30% Forest 8%

Land use

Much of the Gobi is barren, surrounded by steppe (dry grassland), where animals can graze. In wetter areas, farmers grow grains, such as millet, oats, and wheat.

Altai Mountains

The eastern arm of the Altai Mountains separates Mongolia from Russia in the north and China in the southwest. The average height ranges from 6,600–1,000 ft (2,000–3,000 m); the Altai's highest peak in Mongolia is Najramdal Uur at 14,350 ft (4,374 m).

Climate

Mongolia is dry and windy with short, mild summers and long, severe winters when temperatures plummet. The country is prone to violent earthquakes.

72°F (22°C)   -22°F (-30°C)
63°F (17°C)   -15°F (-26°C)
8 in (208 mm)

4 per sq mile (2 per sq km)   59% Urban   41% Rural

People

Khalkha Mongols form the largest ethnic group. Mongolians are traditionally nomads, but their numbers are steadily declining as people give up their *yurts* (tents) and move to houses in the towns. Mongols are skilled equestrians. Many people are Buddhists.

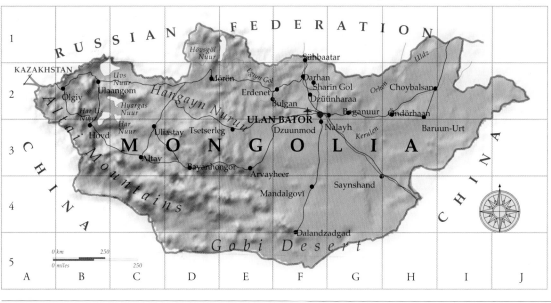

Farming and industry

Many Mongolians still work as animal herders, although there are large state-run farms that produce grain. Harsh winters ravaged livestock in 2000–01. Industry is concentrated around Ulan Bator and is dominated by wool, food processing, and animal hides. Coal is mined in Darhan and Choybalsan.

FIND OUT MORE   ASIA   ASIA, HISTORY OF   BUDDHISM   CHINA, HISTORY OF   DESERTS   FARMING   GOVERNMENTS AND POLITICS   MONGOL EMPIRE   MOUNTAINS AND VALLEYS

MONGOOSES AND CIVETS

RENOWNED FOR ITS ability to kill snakes, the Indian mongoose will tackle a full-grown cobra. It is one of 38 species of mongooses, belonging to a group of carnivorous mammals that includes civets, genets, the fossa, and binturong (or bear-cats). Mongooses live in southern Europe, southern Asia, and much of Africa. They range in size from the Indian mongoose, measuring 4 ft (1.22 m) long, including the tail, to the dwarf mongoose, which is only 12 in (30 cm) long. Meerkats, or suricates, are a type of mongoose living on the dry, open plains of Africa.

Bands of dark fur

Thick, coarse hair

Long, bushy tail

Short legs

Long claws

Narrow snout

Banded mongoose

M

Features of a mongoose
Mongooses have slender bodies, long, coarse hair, bushy tails, short legs, and claws that cannot be retracted. Most mongooses are gray, gray-brown, or lightly speckled; the banded mongoose is distinguished by dark stripes across its body. Mongooses spend most of their time on the ground, but are very agile and can climb and swim quite well. Most species reach sexual maturity by 18–24 months, and the females give birth to 2–8 young.

Narrow snout

Long claws

Termite mound

Meerkat keeps a lookout for any sign of danger.

Thick, dense fur

Feeding
Mongooses eat small mammals, birds, lizards, insects, fruit, roots, and bulbs. The crab-eating and marsh mongooses live close to water and feed on crustaceans, frogs, and fish. The marsh and banded mongooses also feed on bird and crocodile eggs, which they smash on the ground and then eat.

Banded mongoose with egg

Mongooses and snakes
The larger mongooses, such as the Indian gray mongoose, often kill snakes. They are no more immune to snake bites than other animals, but rely on their quick reactions and agility to avoid being bitten. They sieze the snake behind the head and hang on until it dies.

Indian mongoose attacking a cobra

Family groups
The banded and dwarf mongooses and the meerkat all live in family groups, and are very sociable. Meerkats live in groups of up to 30 animals. Each animal has specific duties to enable the group to work together. Sentries keep a lookout from a high point for predators, and bark a warning to the rest of the group if danger threatens. Females remain close to the nest and take care of the young, while hunters go in search of food.

Burrows
The banded and dwarf mongooses and the meerkat live in burrows that they either dig themselves, or take over from other animals, such as termites. At dawn they emerge from their burrow to sun themselves. Sentinels are posted to warn of impending danger. They usually stay near their burrows so they can dive to safety if danger threatens. Birds of prey are among mongooses' chief enemies; if one of a group is attacked, the others leap to its defense.

A disused termite mound taken over by meerkats

Meerkat emerges from hole in termite mound.

Solitary mongooses
Most mongooses, such as the white-tailed, Indian, and marsh mongooses, are solitary, nocturnal animals. The marsh mongoose lives among reeds or long grass bordering swamps and rivers. It is a good swimmer, and preys on waterfowl, small mammals, frogs, fish, and insects.

Marsh mongoose

Civets
Civets are weasellike in appearance. They are solitary, nocturnal creatures, mostly living in forests. The African civet favors more open country, hiding by day, often in an abandoned aardvark or porcupine burrow, and hunting at night. It has good senses of hearing, sight, and smell. Civets are omnivores, preying on rodents, small mammals, birds, lizards, frogs, and locusts, as well as eating eggs, berries, fruit, and even carrion.

Coarse hair

Back legs are longer than front legs.

Patterned coat helps camouflage the civet in the forest.

African civet

Musk
Civets secrete a strong-smelling, oily fluid, called musk, from well-developed scent glands under the tail. Musk is in demand for the perfume industry. In parts of Africa – for example, Ethiopia and Zanzibar – civets are kept in captivity, and the musk removed several times each week.

BANDED MONGOOSE

SCIENTIFIC NAME	*Mungos mungo*
ORDER	Carnivora
FAMILY	Viverridae
DISTRIBUTION	Africa south of the Sahara
HABITAT	Savannas close to water
DIET	Lizards, snakes, frogs, birds' eggs; will also break open elephants' droppings to obtain dung beetles
SIZE	Body: up to 18 in (45 cm) long; tail: up to 12 in (30 cm) long
LIFESPAN	Up to 11 years

FIND OUT MORE

AFRICAN WILDLIFE   ANIMALS   ANTS AND TERMITES   GRASSLAND WILDLIFE   MAMMALS   NESTS AND BURROWS   NOCTURNAL ANIMALS   SNAKES

MONKEYS AND OTHER PRIMATES

MONKEYS BELONG TO a group of animals called primates. Most primates live in trees, but some live on the ground. They have grasping fingers, long arms, and forward-looking eyes. Monkeys have tails, but apes are tailless and include gibbons, orangutans, gorillas, and chimpanzees. There are two main groups of primates. The higher primates, or anthropoids – monkeys, apes, and humans – all have large brains and a high level of intelligence. The lower primates, or prosimians, are less intelligent and include the lorises, tarsiers, lemurs, bushbabies, and pottos.

Features of a monkey

Monkeys and other primates have large brains and are quick to learn. They have forward-looking eyes and strong fingers. Their fingers and toes usually have flat nails. Most primates have an opposable thumb that can be pressed against the fingers to grasp and manipulate objects; some also have a similar big toe. Some primates have a prehensile tail that can be wrapped around a branch. It acts as an extra limb.

Fur-covered body

Large eyes

Long arms

Capuchin monkey

Five long, grasping fingers

Prehensile tail acts as a fifth limb and aids balance.

Chimpanzees

Our closest relative, the chimpanzee, occupies the forests and savannas of central Africa. Chimps are highly intelligent and sociable, and live in groups of up to about 60 animals with a complex, ever-changing hierarchy. They spend most of the time on the ground, but each night they build a nest to sleep in, up to 100 ft (30 m) above the ground.

Grooming sessions often last for about an hour.

Chimps climb trees to search for food.

Social grooming

Chimps comb each other's fur with their fingers and pick out lice and dirt. Grooming is an important social activity and helps strengthen family ties and friendships.

Feeding

Chimps eat mainly plant food, including leaves, flowers, and fruits such as wild figs. They also prey on other animals, including small antelope and bush pigs. Some even kill other primates, such as the red colobus monkey. Several chimps chase the prey toward others that are waiting to block its escape.

Communication

Chimps have developed a body language with a large range of facial expressions. They use expressions as well as sounds to communicate a range of emotions.

Curiosity, apprehension, or sullenness (if accompanied by a puzzled expression) are shown by protruding lips.

Upper lip covers teeth in a happy playful face.

Playing

Young chimps spend much of their time playing together. They wrestle, chase each other, and swing through the trees. Play is important because it teaches youngsters about chimp society and how to survive in the forest. Chimps stay with their mothers until reaching full maturity at about 13 years of age. The older offspring help take care of their younger siblings.

Chimp using a twig to "fish" for termites

Toolmaking

Next to humans, chimpanzees are considered the most intelligent of the primates. They can learn to understand simple sign language and are adept at using "tools." They use long twigs to extract termites from their mounds, a wad of leaves to soak up water from tree hollows, and rocks to crack nuts. They have even learned to use sticks and stones as weapons against rivals and enemies.

Anger is shown by baring the teeth; if combined with certain postures and calls, it acts as a warning to rivals.

Dian Fossey

American zoologist Dr. Dian Fossey (1932–1985) devoted her life to studying the mountain gorilla, of which only a few hundred survive. She learned to imitate the sounds and gestures that gorillas make and was able to communicate with them in their own "language."

Gorillas

The mountain gorilla lives in the highlands of Rwanda. It forages on the ground for wild celery, berries, and bamboo shoots. The lowland gorilla lives in the rain forests of equatorial Africa. It is the largest of all the primates; a mature male may weigh up to 330 lb (150 kg) and reach 5.5 ft (1.7 m) tall when standing upright. Despite their massive size and strength, gorillas are seldom aggressive. They live in family groups of 10–20 animals, led by a dominant male.

Silverbacks are mature male gorillas whose backs have turned a silvery-gray color with age. The dominant male of the family group is always a silverback.

Chest beating

A male gorilla intimidates rivals by beating his chest. He starts with a loud roar followed by a series of hoots. He then waves handfuls of leaves or uproots bushes and hurls them into the air. Finally, he rises to his full height and beats his chest with the cupped palms of his hands.

Orangutans

Orangutans are solitary apes that live in the rain forests of Borneo and Sumatra. They live in treetops and, except for the adult males, rarely descend to the ground. Their short legs contrast with their very long arms, which may span 7 ft (2.1 m). Males are larger than females, with longer hair and large cheek pouches. Females give birth once every four years to a single young with whom they develop a strong bond.

Mothers suckle their young for up to five years.

Sleeping

Female orangutans and their young make a nest each night in which to sleep. The nests are made by the orangutan pulling vegetation around herself and weaving it together for support and padding. Adult males are too heavy for a nest and sleep on the ground.

Long, thick hair

Durian fruit

The fruit is rich in protein and carbohydrates.

Mangosteens

Feeding

Orangutans feed mainly on plants, such as leaves and nuts, but they also eat insects and their eggs. Their favorite food is fruit, particularly the fruit of the durian for which they search far and wide. They use their strong hands and large front teeth to open tough-skinned fruits, such as mangosteens.

Red howler monkey

Howler monkeys, such as the red howler, have exceptionally loud calls that carry over a long distance. At dawn and dusk, the forest echoes to the male's loud booming call. He may be joined by other members of the group. Howlers live in troops of up to 30, in treetops. They have a prehensile tail that they can wrap around a branch and use as an extra limb. They can hang upside down by their tails.

Baboons

Baboons generally live on open savannas, in large groups of up to 100 animals. They forage for almost anything they can find, from insects to lizards and other small animals. Given the opportunity, baboons will also kill larger animals, such as hares and young gazelles. The mandrill, the most brightly colored of all primates, lives in the forests of West Africa.

Huge canine teeth can inflict a severe wound.

Olive baboon

Threat display

Baboons have long, dagger-like canine teeth that can deliver a vicious bite. They bare their teeth to warn off opponents and intimidate rivals and enemies.

Black and white colobus monkey

The leaf-eating colobus monkeys live in the treetops of African rain forests, rarely descending to the ground. Colobus live in small family troops and follow a regular route through the trees from their sleeping area to their feeding place. The male's distinctive call, echoed by the other members of the troop, is a feature of the African rain forests.

Coat of black-and-white hair fans out when they leap.

Golden lion tamarin

This tiny monkey, found only in the Atlantic coastal forest of southeast Brazil, is one of the most brightly colored of all primates. Females normally give birth to twins, which the male and older offspring help nurture. They feed on fruit, flowers, nectar, tree sap, and small vertebrates. Destruction of the rain forest has brought the golden lion tamarin close to extinction. Breeding these monkeys in captivity began in 1970 to save them and eventually return them to the wild.

Golden mane

Tamarins differ from most primates in not having opposable thumbs.

Gibbons

Gibbons live in family groups, consisting of a mated pair and their young. They are highly territorial. They call to each other, large sacs in their throats amplifying the sounds. With their long arms, fingers, and toes, and their light build, gibbons move swiftly through the trees, swinging hand over hand, a method of movement known as brachiation. In this way, gibbons can span spaces 23 ft (7 m) wide. There are nine species of gibbons; the largest is the siamang.

Gibbon grasps branch with its left hand.

Gibbon twists its body around so it can then change its grip to its right hand.

Gibbon grasps branch with right hand, lets go with left hand, and continues along its way.

Long tail helps balance.

Ring-tailed lemur

Lemurs are primitive primates found only on the island of Madagascar. There are 21 species. Ring-tailed lemurs live in the forest but spend a lot of time on the ground. They live in groups of 5–30 animals, presided over by a dominant female. Males mark their territories by impregnating their tails with scent from special glands and raising them high in the air to waft the scent toward rivals.

Tail is longer than body.

Throat sac

Right arm has been lifted up to branch.

Right arm of gibbon hangs by its side, but will be raised to grip branch when changing hands.

Siamang

CHIMPANZEE

SCIENTIFIC NAME *Pan troglodytes*

ORDER Primates

FAMILY Pongidæ

DISTRIBUTION Africa, from Sierra Leone to western Uganda and Lake Tanganyika at heights up to 9,200 ft (2,800 m)

HABITAT Woodland and savanna

DIET Mainly vegetation, but also termites, larvae, and other small mammals, sometimes including other primates, such as young baboons and colobus monkeys

SIZE Height of male standing: 47–67 in (120–170 cm); weight: up to 120 lb (55 kg)

LIFESPAN Up to 50 years (in captivity)

FIND OUT MORE | ANIMAL BEHAVIOR | CONSERVATION | GOODALL, JANE | GRASSLAND WILDLIFE | HUMAN EVOLUTION | RAIN FOREST WILDLIFE

M

Higher primates

Mona monkeys live in troops of up to 20 animals.

Red howler monkeys have large mouths to amplify their loud calls.

Bright nose of male

De Brazza's monkeys are shy and live in the forests of Zaïre and Uganda.

Very long tail for balance

Long legs help this monkey to sprint fast.

Crest of black hair

Newborn baby

Semi-prehensile tail

Rufous patas monkeys are also called military monkeys because of their distinguished appearance.

Mandrills are baboons. Mature males have brightly colored noses and buttocks.

Sulawesi crested macaques live in groups with a complex hierarchy.

Black-capped capuchins spend most of the time in the rain forest canopy.

Thick, strong prehensile tail

Large eyes for night vision

Long, white crest

Young are carried on father's back.

Flexible tail curls around branch for support.

Douroucoulis are the world's only nocturnal monkeys.

Cottontop tamarins spend much time grooming each other.

Silvery marmoset young are cared for by their fathers.

Crab-eating macaques live in mangrove swamps.

Squirrel monkeys from South America are agile and acrobatic.

Humboldt's woolly monkeys eat mainly leaves and fruit.

Very long fur

Very long arms

Large hands help orangutan grip branches.

Silver back of mature male

Hamadryas baboons live on the ground in open grasslands.

Lar gibbons live in family groups of two parents and up to four offspring.

This orangutan is a 5-year-old male.

Lowland gorillas often need to walk long distances for food, since there are few nutritious plants on the rain forest floor.

Gorillas walk on their knuckles.

Chimpanzees are the most intelligent of the great apes.

Orangutans are shy, solitary animals. Only close relatives play with and groom each other.

Lower primates

Indris call loudly each morning.

Slender lorises feed on birds, lizards, and insects.

Long hind legs help it leap from branch to branch.

These lemurs have an acute sense of smell.

Head turns 180°.

Coquerel's sifakas live in the forests of NW Madagascar.

Indris, from Madagascar, are the largest of the lemurs.

Slender lorises feed on birds, lizards, and insects.

Eastern tarsiers are nocturnal. Large eyes help them see at night.

Black-and-white ruffed lemurs are superb climbers.

Greater bush babies live in African rain forests.

MOON

A GRAY, DRY, AIRLESS, and lifeless ball of rock – the Moon – is Earth's closest neighbor in space. The Moon is about a quarter of Earth's size and its only natural satellite. It orbits the planet as they travel together around the Sun. It is the only celestial body, apart from Earth, on which humans have walked.

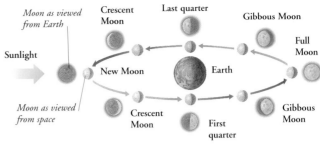

Phases of the Moon

The Moon is lit by the Sun. At any one time, half of the Moon is in daylight and half in darkness. As the Moon orbits Earth, different amounts of the sunlit side are visible. These are the phases of the Moon; each cycle lasts for 29.5 days, beginning at the "New Moon" when the sunlit side of the Moon is not visible from Earth at all.

Lunar surface

Every part of the Moon's surface is made of rock and dust. It is also covered with craters. Most of these craters were formed about 3 billion years ago when meteorites bombarded the Moon. Material thrown out from these meteorites on impact formed mountain ranges, and volcanic lava filled many of the larger craters. The lunar surface has remained virtually unchanged for millions of years.

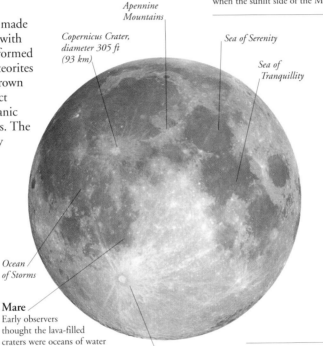

Apennine Mountains

Copernicus Crater, diameter 305 ft (93 km)

Sea of Serenity

Sea of Tranquillity

Ocean of Storms

Moon rock

About 2,000 samples of rock and dust have been brought to Earth from the Moon by American astronauts and Russian robotic spacecraft.

Mare

Early observers thought the lava-filled craters were oceans of water and called them mare, which is the Latin for "sea" (plural maria). The name has stuck even though there is no water on the lunar surface.

Tycho Crater

Eclipse of the Moon

As the Moon orbits around Earth, it is at times farther from the Sun than Earth. Sunlight still reaches it because the Earth is not in perfect alignment between the Sun and Moon. Two or three times a year, the three are aligned directly and the Moon is in Earth's shadow. It is eclipsed; no sunlight reaches the Moon, and it disappears from Earth's view.

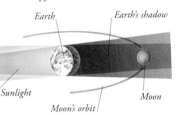

Earth

Earth's shadow

Sunlight

Moon's orbit

Moon

Craters

When a meteorite collides with the Moon it creates a crater. The bigger the impact, the bigger the crater. A rock 0.6 mile (1 km) across, traveling at 60,000 mph (100,000 kmh), would produce a crater about 11 miles (18 km) across. The largest on this picture is 50 miles (80 km) across.

Terminator

The Moon keeps the same side facing Earth because as it orbits Earth it also spins on its axis. From Earth, it is possible to see light areas, which are highland, and darker areas of lowland. More detail can be seen along the terminator, the line separating the sunlit and dark sides of the Moon.

Lunar origins

It is not known for certain where the Moon came from. It may have been captured by Earth's gravity or formed from material left over when Earth was formed. The most popular theory is that an object the size of Mars crashed into the young Earth and dislodged material that then formed the Moon.

Neil Armstrong

In July 1969, American astronaut Neil Armstrong (b.1930) was at the center of one of the most important events in human history. He was the first person to walk on the Moon and became instantly famous. He spent 2 hrs 35 mins on its surface.

Moon landings

Twelve men landed on the Moon between 1969 and 1972, spending almost 80 hours on its surface. They explored 55 miles (90 km) of it on foot or by "moon-buggy," collected rock, set up experiments, and played golf before returning to Earth.

Footprints

When the astronauts left the Moon, they left behind some equipment and their footprints. There is no water, air, or life to erode the footprints, so they could stay for millions of years unless a meteorite destroys them on impact.

FIND OUT MORE   BIG BANG   COMETS   EARTH   PLANETS   SPACE EXPLORATION   SUN AND SOLAR SYSTEM   VOLCANOES

M

MOSQUES

AT THE HEART OF EVERY MUSLIM community is a mosque, the Islamic place of worship. When Muhammad moved to Medina in 622, his house became the model for all subsequent mosques. Devout Muslims pray five times a day, and a mosque's main purpose is to provide a place for prayers. Mosques range from simple places serving the local community or large, beautifully decorated buildings in big cities.

Parts of a mosque

The most important part of a mosque is the prayer hall, where the congregation meets to pray and listen to sermons and readings from the Muslim holy book, the Qur'an. Mosques also usually have a courtyard and a tower called a minaret. Larger mosques may have many more rooms, which are used as schools, hospices, and kitchens to provide food for the poor.

Islamic arch

The horseshoe-shaped arch of this mosque doorway is typical of Islamic architecture. The arch is repeated many times inside the building. Above the door is a richly tiled decoration in abstract patterns. A heavy curtain covers the entrance.

Courtyard

People coming to prayers wash at one of the fountains in the courtyard, then they leave their shoes by the door before entering the prayer hall. There is little furniture inside the hall because Muslims kneel to pray. Separate areas inside the mosque are reserved for men and women.

A mihrab is a niche, often beautifully decorated, that shows the direction of Mecca. Next to it is a mimbar, or pulpit.

Prayer hall

Plain walls with few windows show that this is an inward-looking building, in which people are encouraged to concentrate on their prayers. The minaret and the colorful tiles at the door are the only signs that the austere exterior conceals a sacred place of worship.

Minaret, from where a muezzin calls the faithful to prayer

Mosque decoration

The Islamic religion forbids figurative art on the grounds that the artist must not try to imitate God's creation. Mosques are, therefore, decorated with abstract patterns and beautiful inscriptions. Decoration is often concentrated around doorways and the mihrab.

Tiled decoration

Tiles are used widely in mosques. They can be made into patterns with beautiful, subtle colors, and can create a cool atmosphere, an advantage in the hot Arabic countries where Islam has its roots.

Tile decorated with sacred text

Tiles designed to form wall panels.

Blue often used in tiling

Tiles from a Tunisian mosque

Calligraphy

Quotations from the Qur'an often adorn mosque interiors. These texts are meant to inspire people by their beauty, while also reminding them of the words of Allah.

Islamic architecture

There are two common styles of mosque design. In one, the roof of the prayer hall is supported by numerous decorated columns. In the other, the roof is a large dome.

Great Mosque, Córdoba

This vast Spanish mosque, also known as *La Mesquita*, was begun in 786. Elegant proportions, fine carved decoration, and contrasting use of stone and brick in dozens of arches combine to give the interior a striking appearance.

Córdoba mosque, now a Christian cathedral

Sinan

Sinan (c.1491–1588) was the greatest architect of Ottoman Turkey. He was born into a Greek Orthodox Christian family, but was taken into the Sultan's service and became a Muslim. He trained as a military engineer, and in 1538 Sultan Süleyman I made him chief imperial architect. He designed many buildings, including 79 mosques (among them the famous Süleymaniye Mosque in Istanbul built between 1550–57) and 34 palaces.

FIND OUT MORE | ARCHITECTURE | ISLAM | ISLAMIC | MUHAMMAD | OTTOMAN EMPIRE | PERSIAN EMPIRE | RELIGIONS

MOSSES AND LIVERWORTS

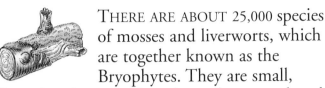

THERE ARE ABOUT 25,000 species of mosses and liverworts, which are together known as the Bryophytes. They are small, flowerless, low-growing plants that reproduce by means of spores. Bryophytes have a distinctly two-stage life cycle. The plant body, or thallus, of a green moss or liverwort produces male and female sex organs. A long-stalked capsule grows from a fertilized female cell. This produces masses of minute spores, each of which can grow into a new moss or liverwort.

Capsule containing spores

Stalk

Tiny leaves

Mosses cling to the ground, rocks, trees, or walls by means of short, rootlike rhizoids.

A common moss (*Bryon* species)

Types of mosses

Mosses are small plants with very tiny leaves. Different species grow in different ways, and their characteristic growth forms help distinguish one from another.

Moss plants growing into a soft, cushion-like clump

Branched stems

As older parts of the stem die, the tips keep growing into new moss plants.

Cushion-forming mosses
Hundreds of tiny moss plants growing very close together make a compact, dome-shaped cushion. Sometimes, the whole cushion will come loose from the ground.

Branched mosses
Some kinds of mosses have stems that branch and spread out over the surface of the ground. They form a loose mass of intertwined leafy stems, or a dense mat.

Tufted mosses
Many of the largest mosses grow as loose tufts of plants that may be branched or unbranched. The largest is an Australasian species that reaches 27 in (70 cm) long.

Sphagnum
Acid-loving sphagnum mosses live in wet, boggy places. They are slow-growing plants that, in cold, wet climates, help form a thick layer that eventually turns into peat. Sphagnum holds an amazing amount of water that keeps the surface of a bog moist, even in summer.

Mosses

There are three groups of mosses: the true mosses, the small group of mountain mosses, and the sphagnum mosses. Mosses are most abundant in damp habitats, but they flourish everywhere except in the sea or in deserts. They can absorb moisture and dissolved minerals all over their surface.

Waxy surface has pores for vital gas exchange.

A thallose liverwort

Liverworts

There are two kinds of liverworts – leafy liverworts and thallose liverworts. They both grow in moist or wet environments, anchored to the ground by means of rootlike cells called rhizoids. The thallose liverworts are plate- or ribbonlike. The leafy liverworts grow in tufts, or form a mat of stems.

Leaves are often cupped to hold water.

Gemmae
Some thallose liverworts reproduce vegetatively by means of budlike growths called gemmae. These develop in small cups on the surface of the liverwort and are splashed out by rain. Each gemma can grow into a new plant.

Gemmae

Leafy liverworts
These delicate liverworts have tiny thin leaves that grow in two or three rows along the stem. The two side rows are easy to see, but the third row of smaller leaves grows underneath the stem.

Ripening moss capsule

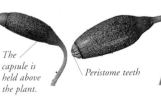

Capsule turns brown as it dries.

The capsule is held above the plant.

Peristome teeth

Open teeth

1 A stemmed capsule called a sporophyte grows. The foot of the stem is embedded in the moss plant.

2 As the capsule ripens, the hood, called the calyptra, falls off, revealing peristome teeth at the tip.

3 Inside each capsule, thousands of minute, dustlike spores are produced. The capsule begins to dry out in fair weather.

4 When the peristome teeth are dry, they flick open to release the spores. These are shaken out and spread over a wide area by air currents.

FIND OUT MORE   MARSH AND SWAMP WILDLIFE   PLANTS   PLANTS, ANATOMY   PLANTS, REPRODUCTION

MOTHER TERESA

IN ONE OF THE POOREST cities in the world – Calcutta, India – a European woman devoted her life to helping the poor and needy. Mother Teresa, an Albanian nun, led the Missionaries of Charity, an international order of nuns dedicated to helping those most in need. When the order was first given the backing of the Catholic Church in 1950, the Missionaries had few resources of their own. But now, thanks to the work of Mother Teresa and her order, money flows in from donors all over the world and is used to alleviate the suffering and poverty of those unable to help themselves.

Early life
Agnes Gonxha Bojaxhiu was born in 1910 into a prosperous family in Albania. Her father, a businessman, died when Agnes was nine, and suddenly she and her family were poor. This first-hand experience of poverty left her with the conviction that she should become a nun and help the poor in India.

Missionaries of charity
Other nuns came to help Teresa in her work with the poor. She formed the Missionaries of Charity to concentrate on this work, and became known as Mother Teresa.

Education

At the age of 18, Agnes joined a Roman Catholic order of nuns, the Sisters of Loreto in India. She served nine years as a novice. On taking her vows in 1937, she took the name Teresa, after St. Teresa of Lisieux, and remained in India.

Sisters of Loreto
Teresa became the Mother Superior of the convent at Entally, Calcutta. She worked there for 11 years, surrounded by poverty. In 1948, she received permission to work outside the convent, setting up a school for poor children and caring for the sick.

Entally Convent, Calcutta

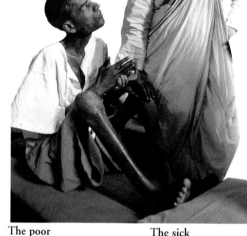

The poor
As she walked through Calcutta, Mother Teresa saw poverty all around her. The poor and sick often had no homes, and lay in squalor in the streets. Teresa provided them with food and clothes, and took unwanted children into her mission to look after them.

The sick
Mother Teresa tried to relieve sick people's pain and, when the end came, help them die in dignity. She also taught people how to recognize the early signs of diseases such as leprosy, so that they could be cured.

Expansion

Gradually, the Missionaries grew in number and strength. The organization expanded across India, and, in 1963, began to admit men. In 1965, the first overseas mission opened in Venezuela. Today, there are more than 4,000 nuns and 40,000 laypeople working for the Missionaries of Charity around the world. The Missionaries even have their own newspaper, *Ek dil* (One Heart), which publicizes their work.

Mobile clinic
In order to take their work to those most in need, the Missionaries of Charity established mobile clinics that toured India to help the poor and heal the sick. These clinics gave hope to many poor people in remote areas. They have also done much to spread the word about the Missionaries, and increase their recognition for doing good works among the poor.

Prizes
In recent years, Mother Teresa received many international awards and prizes. In 1979, she was awarded the Nobel Peace Prize. She used the prize money to expand her work for the world's poor and needy.

Mother Teresa with her Nobel Prize

MOTHER TERESA

1910	Born in Skopje, Albania.
1928	She enters a Convent of the Sisters of Loreto in Skopje.
1928–37	Serves as novice in India.
1937	Becomes head of convent at Entally, Calcutta.
1948	Works outside the convent.
1950	Catholic Church officially backs Missionaries of Charity.
1965	Opens first mission outside India.
1979	Awarded Nobel Peace Prize.
1997	Steps down as head of Missionaries of Charity.
1997	Dies in Calcutta

FIND OUT MORE

CHRISTIANITY　　HOSPITALS　　INDIA AND SRI LANKA　　INDIA, HISTORY OF　　MEDICINE　　MONASTERIES　　RELIGIONS

MOTOR SPORTS

THERE ARE MANY VARIETIES of motor sports, featuring four- or two-wheeled vehicles and taking place on special circuits, regular roads, or rough road tracks. Motor sports on four wheels range from Formula 1 grand prix racing and Indy car racing to karting, which is the sport in which many top drivers first experience motor racing. In between, there are other types of racing including dragster, sports car, and stock car racing, as well as rally driving. The two-wheeled sports range from powerful grand prix motorcycle racing to motocross and speedway. Cars and motorcycles are constantly modified to make them faster and more reliable.

Formula 1

Manufacturers and their drivers compete for world championships throughout the season. There are 16 races run on different grand prix circuits around the world. Races are preceded by practice sessions in which the cars' best times determine their positions at the starting gate. Points awarded to the first six cars that finish are 10, 6, 4, 3, 2, and 1.

Start of a Brazilian Grand Prix

Airfoil pushes the car down.

Williams 1990 car

Slick tires used in dry weather.

Powerful 10-cylinder engine

Streamlined engine cover

Flags
Officials use colored flags to signal to drivers during the race, mostly to warn them of danger or to give them instructions. Drivers want to be the first to see the checkered flag that signals the end of the race.

End of race	Danger	Return to pits
Oil on course	Service car on track	All cars to stop in pits

Formula 1 car
Cars race under categories called formulas to insure that similar machines are matched against each other. There are rules governing bodywork as well as engines. Formula 1 cars are light, single-seater vehicles with a body that fits over a one-piece, or monocoque, chassis.

Formula Three race

Other formulas
Before Formula 1 cars, drivers usually race less powerful models. Formulas have varied, but among the most popular have been Two, Three, Ford, and 3,000. Some have grands prix and national and continental championships.

John Surtees

A British motorcylist who became a race car driver, John Surtees (b. 1934) was world champion at both sports. From 1956 to 1960, he won seven motorcycle world titles at 350 cc and 500 cc. In 1964, he won the World Drivers' Championship.

Pit stops
The pit is an area just off the track where mechanics can work on the cars during a race. Pit stops are important in grand prix racing. The speed with which teams refuel their cars and change tires can make the difference between winning and losing a race.

Indy car racing
This takes place on large oval tracks and twisting road circuits, and competitions run mostly in the United States. The cars are similar to Formula 1 models, and annual championships are decided on the number of points acquired over a number of races. The sport gets its name from the Indianapolis 500, the classic event in American motor car racing.

Indianapolis 500
The oval Indianapolis track is known as the Brickyard because the surface is made of 3.2 million bricks. Its four turns are banked at 9°, and its total length is 2.5 miles (4.025 km). The Indy 500 is raced over 200 laps – 500 miles (805 km).

A top-fueler

Drag racing
In drag racing, pairs of dragsters race side by side along a straight quarter-mile (400-m) track in a series of elimination races. There are several classes of design, engine, and fuel. The fastest – lightweight supercharged top-fuelers – run on rocket fuel and can complete the course in less than six seconds.

Karting
Karting is a sport enjoyed by people of all ages. The simplest karts have a 60 cc or 100 cc engine and no gearbox, and can be driven by boys and girls from about the age of eight. Karts have a low chassis, and the driver sits no more than an inch above the ground.

Kart racing
The 250 cc karts are like race cars in miniature, and reach speeds of 150 mph (240 km/h). In long-circuit racing, which takes place on wide tracks, as many as 60 karts can compete. In short-circuit racing, about 20 karts can compete. Karting has its own world championships.

250 cc karts have sponsors, just like Formula 1 cars.

Rally driving

These are long-distance events over regular roads, with special stages over country roads and tracks. They may be held on one day, or last several days or weeks. Rallies are not strictly races. Drivers aided by navigators set out at intervals in "souped-up" sedans. They lose points for exceeding the time limits between control points.

Monte Carlo Rally

This event made rallying famous. It was established in 1911 to encourage tourists to visit the Principality of Monaco in winter. Motorists set out from all parts of Europe and the final stages center on Monte Carlo.

Le Mans 24-hour race

This famous sports car race is held annually on the 8.5-mile (13.6-km) Le Mans circuit near Paris, France. A team of two or three drivers takes turns at the wheel, driving nonstop through the day and night. The event has become a national institution in France, with shops, amusement parks, and restaurants opening for the huge crowds that turn up to watch.

Motorcycle racing

Motorcycle racing takes place on special circuits. At the professional level, manufacturers and drivers compete in 12 or more grands prix each season for world championships in various classes: 500 cc, 250 cc, 125 cc, and sidecar. Points are awarded for the first 15 home in each grand prix, 25 for first, 20 for second down to one point for 15th.

Riders lean right over at an angle when cornering.

500 cc racing motorcyle

Motorcycle and sidecar molded into one unit.

Stock cars

Stock car racing takes different forms on opposite sides of the Atlantic. In Europe, it is mostly racing on small oval circuits, and cars are driven into each other. In the United States, it features high-speed racing of modified sedans and is a major sport in the south, where it takes place on huge, banked oval tracks.

Land speed record

A land speed record must be the average time of a two-way run over one straight mile or kilometer. The British driver Richard Noble achieved a record 633.5 mph (1,019.5 kmh) in 1983 in his jet-powered *Thrust 2*. He sped along the hard surface of the Black Rock Desert in Nevada.

Rider and machine are covered in sponsors' logos.

Passenger leans out to balance the machine when cornering.

Racing sidecar

Speedway

Most speedway races are run with four riders over four laps of the track. Racing takes place on an oval cinder track. The bikes have no brakes or gears so the riders slide around bends, trailing a leg in the cinders in a move called broadsiding. Three points are awarded for first place, two for second, and one for third. Competitions include team matches and individual events.

Ice speedway

Speedway racing on ice is popular in some northern parts of Europe and the United States. The bikes have special tires with spikes to provide grip on the smooth ice track. There are indvidual and team world championships.

Trials

Best-known as six-day events, trials feature slow sections over difficult natural terrain, including water, mud, loose rock, and steep hills. Riders are penalized for stopping or putting a foot on the ground. The bikes are specially low-geared to allow riders to progess very slowly over the rough course.

Off-road racing

Off-road bikes have chunky tires that provide grip on dirt and in mud. The engines are built higher to avoid damage.

Motocross

Also known as scrambling, motocross takes place over rough country. In big events, as many as 40 riders race over several laps of a winding, muddy, hilly course. World championships are held annually in several categories.

FIND OUT MORE

BICYCLES AND MOTORCYCLES   CARS AND TRUCKS   CYCLING   ENGINES AND MOTORS   TRANSPORT, HISTORY OF

MOUNTAINS AND VALLEYS

THE EARTH'S surface is not flat. In some places, movements of the Earth create gentle hills and sheer, towering mountains. In other places, valleys and gorges are carved into the landscape. Mountains are steep-sided rocks, raised over 2,000 ft (600 m) high by the huge force of the tectonic plates that shift the Earth's crust and make volcanoes erupt. Valleys are elongated depressions eroded slowly from the landscape by rivers, weather conditions, and glaciers (large rivers of slowly moving ice). A few mountains are isolated summits, but most occur in huge mountain ranges, such as the Himalayas in Asia.

Aleutian range
Rocky Mountains
Andes
Brazilian Atlantic Coast Range
Transantarctic Mountains
West Sumatran Javan Range
Tien Shan
Himalaya-Karakoram Hindu Kush
Central New Guinea Range
Great Dividing Range

Mountain systems
Most of the world's mountains are grouped into ranges, like the Jura in Europe. Ranges are often linked together into long chains or cordilleras. Huge mountain systems, such as the Himalayas, include several chains and many ranges.

Mountain building
Mountains are formed in three ways. A few are isolated volcanoes, built up by successive eruptions. Some are huge blocks thrust upward as the Earth's crust cracks. But most mountains are folds, created when the huge tectonic plates that make up the Earth's surface collide.

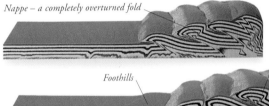

Stages in fold mountain creations

Layers of sand represent layers of crustal rock
First Z-shaped fold forms.
Second Z-shaped fold forms.
New folds begin to form and the first fold becomes more deformed.
Nappe – a completely overturned fold
Fold mountains built up by repeated folding.
Foothills

Fold mountains
When two tectonic plates collide, the Earth's crust buckles, throwing up huge ranges of fold mountains. Mountains are usually created in short mountain-building phases. Most of today's major ranges are less than 50 million years old. Some, such as the Himalayas, are still growing.

Layers of lava build up into a mountain.
One slab of rock is thrust above another.

Volcanic mountain
Isolated mountain peaks are generally volcanoes built up after eruption. But volcanic peaks can also occur within fold mountain ranges, creating some of the world's highest mountains, such as Aconcagua in Argentina.

Reverse fault
Some mountains are created not by the crumpling of the rock, but rather where faults or cracks appear in the Earth's surface. In a reverse fault, plate movements squeeze one block of rock up over another so that one overhangs the other.

Valleys
From rivers and glaciers to heavy rainfall, forces of erosion eat away at the landscape, forming valleys. Mountains are assaulted by the weather as soon as they are raised. Rivers carve out steep, narrow valleys that become broader and gentler as the river and its tributaries wear away the rock. The different formation of a valley determines its type.

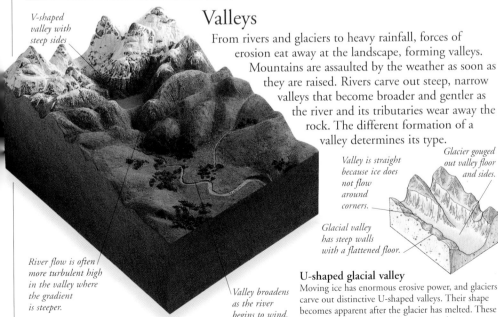

V-shaped valley with steep sides

River flow is often more turbulent high in the valley where the gradient is steeper.

Valley broadens as the river begins to wind.

Mountain and valley range

Valley is straight because ice does not flow around corners.
Glacier gouged out valley floor and sides.
Glacial valley has steep walls with a flattened floor.

U-shaped glacial valley
Moving ice has enormous erosive power, and glaciers carve out distinctive U-shaped valleys. Their shape becomes apparent after the glacier has melted. These valleys are a clear sign of glaciation in the past.

Wadi
In deserts, rainfall is rare. But when it does arrive, it can create huge floods that wash out steep gorges in the dry, crumbly landscape. When the water drains away, it leaves deep, dry channels known as wadis.

Rift valley
When tectonic plates move apart, the stress can create long faults. This allows a belt of land to drop between them, creating a "rift" valley, such as Thingvellir in Iceland, where ravines and cliffs mark the line of the Atlantic Fault.

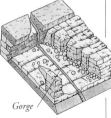

Gorge
In places where there is little surface water – in deserts and in limestone landscapes – valley sides may stay almost clifflike as a river carves down through the landscape. The result is a deep gorge, like the Grand Canyon in the US.

Gorge

FIND OUT MORE — ASIA • CONTINENTS • EARTH • GLACIATION • MOUNTAIN WILDLIFE • OCEAN FLOOR • RIVERS • ROCKS AND MINERALS • VOLCANOES

M

MOUNTAIN WILDLIFE

THE GREAT MOUNTAIN CHAINS of the world are beautiful, but they offer challenging conditions for wildlife. The animals that live in them, such as the alpine ibex, are either exceptionally hardy to cope with steep and rocky terrain or, like the Andean condor, specially adapted to high winds and cold nights in the thin air. In temperate and cold climates, winter is very harsh in the mountains, bringing gale-force winds and deep snow that drive many animals toward shelter. By contrast, in summer, the strong sunshine of high altitudes gives a real boost to life, bringing the buzz of insects and the songs of nesting birds to mountain slopes.

Mountains

Mountains are areas of high land where physical conditions become harsher with increasing altitude. Mountains show a succession of different wildlife habitats from bottom to top. Forests on the lower slopes – rain forest in the tropics or deciduous woodland in temperate regions – gradually give way to a band of stunted "cloud" forests or to hardy conifers. At higher elevation, trees give way to bogs and meadows before plant life dwindles and leaves bare rocks and, on the highest summits, permanent caps of ice and snow.

High, exposed rocky crags

Snow on higher slopes

Timberline – above this level it is too cold for trees to grow.

Dense tree cover and other vegetation on lower slopes

Barren mountains and lush lowlands

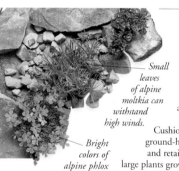

Small leaves of alpine moltkia can withstand high winds.

Bright colors of alpine phlox attract pollinating insects.

Plants
On slopes above the timberline most plants are small and low-growing. Some plants, such as the alpine lily, have supple stems that allow them to bend in the wind without breaking. Cushion plants are compact and ground-hugging to avoid the wind and retain warmth. In some areas, large plants grow above the treeline, such as the 16 ft (5 m) tall lobelia of Africa.

Birds

Birds cope admirably with the hardships of life in the mountains. Well insulated from the cold by their feathers and unaffected by steep terrain, they can search far and wide for food in a habitat where food is scarce. Large, powerful birds such as eagles can ride on the mountain winds with little effort. Many birds migrate to avoid the winter, but some resident mountain species remain, such as seed-eating finches, insectivorous chats, and scavenging vultures.

The Andean condor is the largest flying bird in the world.

Thick feathers for warmth

Mountain dusky salamander
The mountain dusky salamander lives in cool moist areas, such as woodland springs in the mountains of the northeastern US. It is lungless and may grow to up to 4.5 in (14 cm) long. It hunts for insect larvae, worms, and other invertebrates to eat.

Wallcreeper
The wallcreeper inhabits cliffs and crags in the Alps. It uses its curved beak to probe inside rock crevices to catch insects. Strongly gripping claws enable it to scurry up and down vertical cliff faces with ease. In winter, the wallcreeper flies to sheltered and warmer valleys where food is in better supply.

Andean condor
The Andean condor's huge 10 ft (3 m) wingspan enables it to soar effortlessly in the gales that howl around its nesting crags. When searching for carrion to scavenge, a condor can glide long distances across windswept valleys without a single flap of its wings.

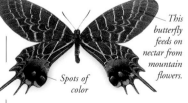

This butterfly feeds on nectar from mountain flowers.

Spots of color

Mammals

Fewer mammals live on mountaintops than in the forests below – those mammals that do have thick fur to protect them from the cold. Rodents and other small mammals vulnerable to the cold, take shelter in burrows and hibernate all winter. Larger mammals such as goats retreat downhill to warmer forests in winter.

Snow leopard
This rare, beautiful creature hunts for mountain goats, sheep, rodents, and birds at heights of up to 16,500 ft (5,000 m) in the mountain ranges of Central Asia. Its thick, pale-colored coat keeps out the cold and provides excellent camouflage against the snow and the gray, rocky landscape. In winter, the snow leopard follows its hoofed prey downhill to forests below the timberline.

Bhutan glory
The Bhutan glory lives in the mountain meadows of central Asia. It flies close to the ground to avoid being swept away by strong winds. Other invertebrates such as spiders and worms also live in the mountains, providing vital food for birds. Some, such as grylloblattid insects, have anti-freezing agents in their bodies for protection against the cold.

Huge horns

Alpine ibex
Ibex have ridges on their hooves that provide them with a remarkably firm grip, even on icy rocks. They can climb steep crags easily and jump between narrow rock ledges. Their thick coats protect them from the cold winter temperatures.

FIND OUT MORE   BIRDS   BIRDS OF PREY   BUTTERFLIES AND MOTHS   LIONS AND OTHER WILD CATS   MAMMALS   MOUNTAINS AND VALLEYS   SALAMANDERS AND NEWTS   SHEEP AND GOATS   TREES

MOZART, WOLFGANG AMADEUS

THE WORLD'S MOST FAMOUS child prodigy, and the finest composer and performer of his time, Wolfgang Amadeus Mozart was born in Salzburg, Austria, in 1756. He wrote his first compositions when he was five, and went on to compose the greatest operas, symphonies, concertos, and chamber music of the Classical period. He produced some of his finest works in Vienna, where he lived from 1781. Although these works were very popular, he never became a rich man. Tragically, illness dogged him throughout his short life, and he died in 1791, just before his thirty-sixth birthday.

Early life
At a very early age, Mozart showed signs of musical genius. His elder sister, Maria Anna, was also a gifted performer, and their father, Leopold, a professional musician, was eager to show off their abilities. The family toured Europe from 1762, giving concerts to appreciative audiences, but it was young Wolfgang's amazing talent that stole the show. During this tour, Mozart wrote his first symphonies.

Mozart played both chamber music and concertos on this violin.

Mozart's violin

Flute of Mozart's time

The composer

Mozart had a steady job as concertmaster to the Archbishop of Salzburg, but he gave it up to make his way by teaching, playing, and publishing his music. Before he left his job, much of his music was rather conventional, but after 1781, he began to write operas and works for orchestra that were soon recognized as masterpieces. He reached the height of his fame in Vienna in the 1780s, both as a composer and performer of his own music.

Concertos
Mozart was a brilliant pianist and violinist, and wrote many concertos in which he played the solo part himself. He composed concertos for other instruments, written for friends of his such as the horn player Ignaz Leutgeb and the clarinettist Anton Stadler. He also wrote several flute concertos for a rich patron, although he did not like the sound of the instrument.

Horn of Mozart's time

Voice and orchestra

Theater was Mozart's passion. His first great opera, *Idomeneo*, was an immediate success, and the three comic operas he wrote to words by the librettist Lorenzo da Ponte (*The Marriage of Figaro, Don Giovanni* and *Così fan tutte*) are still very popular. He also wrote much orchestral music, from dances to symphonies.

Score of Symphony No. 41, the "Jupiter"

Symphonies
Mozart wrote 41 symphonies, developing his skill in writing for the orchestra throughout his life. In 1788, he composed his last three symphonies. These works are very dramatic and expressive, unlike the symphonies by other composers of the time.

Magic flute
Mozart's finest opera was *The Magic Flute,* written in the last year of his life. The opera, a fairy story, tells of an Egyptian Prince, Tamino, who sets out to rescue Pamina, daughter of the Queen of the Night, with a magic flute and a bird-catcher, Papageno. The opera was instantly popular.

Papageno

Stage setting for *The Magic Flute*

Mozart's death

In November 1791, Mozart caught an undiagnosed and terrible fever, and on December 5 he died. After a simple funeral, Mozart was buried in an unmarked grave.

Manuscript of Mozart's *Requiem*

Antonio Salieri
One of the rumors about Mozart's death is that the composer Antonio Salieri (1750–1825), jealous of Mozart's fame and musical ability, poisoned him. Salieri was in fact well respected during his lifetime, and there was no plot to kill Mozart. But the story persists and forms the basis of a modern play, *Amadeus,* by the British writer Peter Shaffer.

Requiem
A few months before he died, Mozart accepted an anonymous commission to write a requiem, or a mass for the dead. A stranger dressed in black came with the request for the work, and Mozart thought this was a bad omen. The caller was a servant of Count Franz von Walsegg, a nobleman who wanted to pass the work off as his own. Mozart never finished his *Requiem*, but left instructions with his pupil Süssmayr to complete it.

WOLFGANG MOZART

1756	Born in Salzburg, Austria.
1762	First public performances; starts European tour.
1769	Appointed concert master to the Archbishop of Salzburg.
1781	Resigns from his Salzburg post after an argument with the Archbishop; settles in Vienna.
1786	*The Marriage of Figaro* performed in Vienna.
1788	Composes symphonies Nos. 39, 40, and 41 (the "Jupiter").
1790	*Così fan tutte* performed in Vienna.
1791	*The Magic Flute* performed; Mozart dies in Vienna.

FIND OUT MORE

BEETHOVEN, LUDWIG VAN   DRAMA   MUSIC   MUSICAL INSTRUMENTS   OPERA   THEATERS

MUGHAL EMPIRE

DURING THE 16TH CENTURY, a new ruling dynasty – the Mughals – came to power in India, bringing a rich, Islamic civilization and uniting the subcontinent for the first time in over 1,500 years. The first Mughal ruler, Babur, came from Persia and was related to the Mongol emperors. He and the later Mughals built an empire that, by 1700, included all of India except its southern tip. The Mughals encouraged the arts, and helped spread Islam across India. In the 18th and 19th centuries, the empire gradually declined as a result of British colonization.

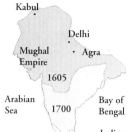

India under the Mughals

Early Mughals
In 1526, Babur defeated the Sultan of Delhi and took over central northern India. But Babur was a poor administrator and the empire began to break up when he died in 1530. By 1600, the emperor Akbar (r.1556–1605) had pulled the empire together and extended it southward.

Akbar and his army cross the Ganges

Rule of Akbar

Akbar (1542–1605) was the greatest of the Mughal rulers. The grandson of Babur, he became emperor in 1556, defeating an Afghan claimant to the throne in the same year and so securing his hold on power. During his long reign, he enlarged the Mughal Empire, patronized the arts, and encouraged religious toleration.

Akbar and the Hindus
Akbar knew that to unite India he would need the help of local Hindu chiefs. So he gave many of these men jobs in his civil service and tried to promote Hindu interests. He introduced a fairer tax system, abolishing the higher taxes that had been levied on Hindus.

Capital cities
At first, Akbar ruled from Agra in north-central India, where he built the famous Red Fort. Later he moved the capital to his new city, Fatehpur Sikri. Here he reorganized the civil service, sent out governors to the provinces, and reformed the coinage and weights and measures.

Red Fort at Agra

Later Mughals

In 1605, Akbar's son, Jahangir, became emperor. He was succeeded by his son, Shah Jahan, who extended the empire southward, and built many great cities and palaces. He and his son, Aurangzeb, showed far less religious tolerance than Akbar, and Aurangzeb destroyed many Hindu temples. After his rule, the empire began to break up.

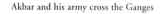

Indian Mughal battle scene, from a 15th-century miniature

Religious tolerance
In the 16th century, India was a country of many religions. Akbar saw that the route to peace was to tolerate all faiths. He built the Ibadat Khana, or House of Worship, as a place where people of different faiths could come to discuss their religious ideas. Muslims, Hindus, Sikhs, and even Christians from Europe were made welcome.

Akbar receives two black-robed Jesuits in the House of Worship

Carvings and murals cover many of the buildings.

Sheikh Salim's tomb, Fatehpur Sikri

Fatehpur Sikri
In 1569, Akbar built the city of Fatehpur Sikri in north-central India. Built to honor the Muslim saint Sheikh Salim, who had foretold the birth of his son and heir Jahangir, the city became Akbar's capital until 1584.

Taj Mahal
One of the greatest Mughal achievements was the magnificent Taj Mahal. It was built as a tomb for Mumtaz Mahal, the beloved wife of Shah Jahan, who died in 1631. The construction took 17 years, and involved hundreds of workers from all over India.

Taj Mahal

Timeline
1504 Babur rules Kabul.

1526 Babur defeats the Sultan of Delhi at the Battle of Panipat.

1530 Babur's son Humayun comes to the throne; the empire starts to split up.

1556–1605 The reign of Akbar: the empire expands and there is a golden age of culture and religious tolerance.

1605 Akbar's son Jahangir comes to the throne; a lover of luxury and heavy drinker, he is a poor ruler.

Breastplate from Mughal suit of armor

1628–57 The rule of Shah Jahan, builder of the Delhi Palace, the Pearl Mosque, and the Taj Mahal.

1658 Aurangzeb seizes power from his brother Shah Shuja. The empire begins to disintegrate.

FIND OUT MORE   ARCHITECTURE   EMPIRES   GUPTA EMPIRE   INDIA, HISTORY OF   ISLAM   MONGOL EMPIRE

MUHAMMAD

MUHAMMAD, A MERCHANT from Medina in Arabia, became the prophet of a new religion, Islam, in the 620s. Followers of Islam believe that Muhammad was selected by God as his prophet. He attracted many followers, and the faith spread rapidly. By the time of Muhammad's death in 632, Islam had been adopted throughout the entire Arabian peninsula. A century later, the Islamic faith was practiced from the Atlantic Ocean in the west to the borders of India in the east, and Islam has affected the lives of millions.

Early life

Muhammad was born in the western Arabian city of Mecca in about 570 AD. He was orphaned soon after birth, and was brought up first by his grandfather and then his uncle, Abu Tâlib, who was head of the Hashim clan. At the age of about 25, Muhammad got a job working for Khadîja, a wealthy widow. Shortly afterward he married her. Muhammad became a merchant, and traveled widely throughout the Arabian peninsula. As he did, he studied the different religions of the local people.

Birth of Muhammad

The mission

In his dream, Muhammad was instructed by the Angel Gabriel to preach a faith centered on the one true God, Allah. The central beliefs of the faith were dictated to Muhammad in a series of visions throughout his life. He began to convert his family and friends in Mecca.

The angel Gabriel appears to Muhammad.

The Revelation

In about 610, Muhammad gave up his daily work as a merchant and went into the local mountains north of Mecca to meditate. In a cave on Mount Hira, he had a dream in which he was told that he had been selected by God to be the prophet of the true religion.

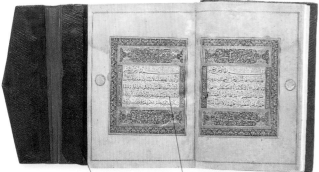

Copy of the Qur'an, made in Turkey

Flap to protect book   *Arabic text written in Naski script*

The Qur'an

Muhammad wrote down the message dictated to him in his visions in a book, the Qur'an (Koran). Muslims believe it contains the direct word of Allah as revealed to his prophet, Muhammad. The Qur'an is one of the most widely read books in the world. Its text is treated with great reverence and is often written out in beautiful calligraphy. Muslims read it in the original Arabic, and most learn to read Arabic by studying the Qur'an.

The Hegira

In Mecca, Muhammad made few converts and many enemies. In 622, he and some 70 followers fled Mecca and moved north to the more welcoming city of Medina. This journey is known as the Hegira (flight).

Medina

Muhammad's reception in Medina was very different from the one he received in Mecca. He attracted many supporters in the city, and established and expanded the first Muslim community there. He also built mosques, in which his followers worshiped.

Mosque

Facing Mecca

In about 624, Muslims in Medina began to face Mecca during prayer. This practice is still followed by Muslims. Niches called mihrabs in mosques show the direction of Mecca, so people know where to face.

Mihrab in mosque

The struggle

While in Medina, Muhammad and his followers regularly ambushed caravans of traders traveling to and from Mecca. In 624, a pitched battle between Muhammad and an armed force from Mecca resulted in victory for Muhammad, giving his new religion great prestige throughout the Arabian world.

The surrender of Mecca

In 629, Muhammad went on a pilgrimage to Mecca and made many converts to Islam. By this time, Muslim missionaries were active throughout the Middle East and as far as Iran and Ethiopia. Muhammad was now strong enough to capture Mecca, which fell without a fight. The entire Arabian peninsula was now ruled by Muhammad and his Muslim followers.

Death of Muhammad

After a final pilgrimage to the city of Mecca, Muhammad died on June 8, 632, in Medina, where he was buried. He was succeeded as leader of the Islamic people by his father-in-law, Abu Bekr, who took the title caliph (successor, or ruler).

MUHAMMAD

c.570	Born in Mecca, modern Saudi Arabia.
594	Marries Khadîja, a wealthy widow.
610	Has a vision, in which he is told to preach the new faith.
622	Leaves Mecca and travels to Medina.
624	His followers defeat the army of Mecca at Battle of Badr.
625	Battle of Uhud against Meccan army ends indecisively.
630	Returns to Mecca and conquers the city.
632	Dies in Medina.

FIND OUT MORE   AFRICA, HISTORY OF   ASIA, HISTORY OF   IRAN AND IRAQ   ISLAM   ISLAMIC EMPIRE   MOSQUES   RELIGIONS   SPAIN, HISTORY OF   WRITING

MUSCLES AND MOVEMENT

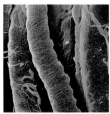

ALL OUR ACTIONS depend on muscles. Muscles are tissues that actively contract, or get shorter, in order to move parts of the body. They use the energy released from the food we eat and convert it into movement. There are three types of muscles: skeletal, cardiac, and smooth. Skeletal muscles move the skeleton under the conscious control of the brain. The other types of muscles work automatically. Cardiac muscle keeps the heart beating. Smooth muscle, or involuntary muscle, is found in the walls of hollow organs such as the intestine and the bladder.

Inside a muscle

Muscles are made up of bundles of long cells called muscle fibers. Each muscle fiber contains many tiny strands called myofibrils that run the length of the fiber. Each myofibril contains two types of protein filament, called actin and myosin, which cause muscle contractions.

Skeletal muscle
The fibers of a skeletal muscle lie parallel to each other. Its actin and myosin filaments are arranged into regular blocks called sarcomeres that are repeated the length of the fiber.

How muscles work
In the relaxed muscle fiber, the myosin and actin filaments overlap a little. If the muscle fiber receives a nerve impulse, the actin and myosin filaments slide over each other. The myofibril shortens, and the muscle contracts.

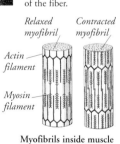

Relaxed myofibril *Contracted myofibril*

Actin filament

Myosin filament

Myofibrils inside muscle

Von Szent-Györgyi
Albert von Szent–Györgyi (1893–1986) was an American biochemist, born in Hungary, who carried out important research into the way that muscles contracted. He discovered the protein actin that forms part of the contraction mechanism in muscles. He was also the first to isolate vitamin C (ascorbic acid), for which he was awarded the Nobel Prize in 1937.

Muscular system

The skeletal muscular system consists of about 620 muscles that make up over 40 percent of body weight. Muscles are attached to the skeleton by tendons. Most muscles are attached at one end to a bone that does not move, and at the other end to a bone that does move. When a muscle contracts, it pulls part of the skeleton in that direction.

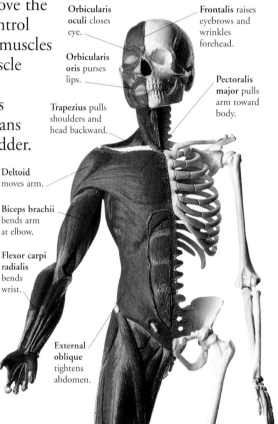

Orbicularis oculi closes eye.

Orbicularis oris purses lips.

Trapezius pulls shoulders and head backward.

Deltoid moves arm.

Biceps brachii bends arm at elbow.

Flexor carpi radialis bends wrist.

External oblique tightens abdomen.

Quadriceps femoris consists of four large muscles that straighten knee.

Tibialis anterior lifts foot.

Extensor digitorum brevis lifts toes upward.

Frontalis raises eyebrows and wrinkles forehead.

Pectoralis major pulls arm toward body.

Sartorius turns thigh outward and bends leg.

Gastrocnemius bends foot downward.

Smiling and frowning
Facial expressions such as smiling and frowning are produced by over 30 small facial muscles. These muscles are unusual because when they contract they pull the skin of the face rather than a bone.

Smiling

Frowning needs more than twice as many muscles as smiling.

Frowning

Movement

Muscles move the body by pulling, not pushing. This explains why many movements are caused by pairs of muscles that produce opposite pulling forces. Each member of the pair is arranged across one side of a joint between bones. When one muscle in a pair contracts, the other relaxes.

Forearm extended
The biceps and triceps are the pair of muscles involved in extending (straightening) and flexing (bending) the forearm. When the forearm is extended, the biceps is relaxed and the triceps is contracted.

Biceps relaxed

Triceps contracted

Forearm half raised
To raise the forearm, the brain sends nerve impulses to the biceps that stimulate it to contract. As the biceps contracts, the triceps starts to relax and lengthen.

Upper arm

Forearm

Forearm flexed
When the forearm is flexed, the biceps is fully contracted and at its minimum length, while the triceps is relaxed and at its maximum length. Other muscles help steady the shoulder and forearm, while the arm bends.

Biceps contracted

Elbow bends

Bodybuilders
Bodybuilders are men or women who greatly increase the bulk of their skeletal muscles. They build up their muscle mass by lifting weights regularly over long periods, using heavy weights that target specific muscle groups.

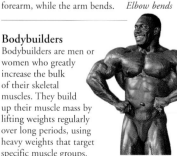

FIND OUT MORE BRAIN AND NERVOUS SYSTEM HEALTH AND FITNESS HEART AND CIRCULATORY SYSTEM HUMAN BODY SKELETON SPORTS

MUSEUMS

MUSEUMS originated in ancient Greece, where offerings to gods or goddesses were displayed in temples. Today, a museum or gallery exhibits works of art or other objects to the public. Museums can cover a range of subjects from vast natural history displays to smaller private art collections. Some museums, such as the *Guggenheim* in New York, are distinctive landmarks that have been specially built for their purpose.

Inside a museum

National museums exhibiting objects bought with public money were set up in the 18th and 19th centuries. In these, the exhibits were simply labeled and displayed inside glass cabinets that protected objects from visitors.

Medieval plate

Interactive museums
Modern museums try to make their exhibits more accessible to the public. They use the latest technology, such as computers and audio cassette guides, to provide information. Many now have interactive exhibits so visitors have a hands-on experience.

At this interactive science museum in Wales, visitors carry out their own experiments at the exhibits.

A museum's role

A museum has specific purposes. The staff is responsible for acquiring works of art or other artifacts. They need to study the collection and make sure it is displayed informatively. Museums also maintain and restore their collections.

This painting has been restored to its original quality.

Adam and Eve Expelled from Paradise by the Italian artist Masaccio (1401-28)

Conservation of paintings
Works of art are often very fragile and have to be carefully displayed. Curators need to monitor levels of humidity and light to ensure they do not damage the paintings.

Restoration of paintings
The restorer removes dirty varnish and fills in areas where the original paint has been lost with paint that matches closely, trying to re-create the artist's intentions.

Private collections
Some small private collections are set up in the collector's home and reflect the particular interests of their founder, such as this collection of over 1,000 bells. Some large national museum collections, such as Prado in Spain, began as private collections and were later bequeathed to the public.

Art galleries

Museums that collect and display works of art are known as art galleries. Some galleries, such as the *Van Gogh Museum* in Amsterdam, the Netherlands, display the work of just one artist. Others, such as the *Louvre* in Paris, France, which has over 5 million visitors a year, show a range of art by a variety of artists.

The Guggenheim Museum, New York, NY

This art gallery was designed by the American architect Frank Lloyd Wright (1867–1956).

The main part of the gallery is the Great Rotunda, where special exhibitions are held.

Natural light enters through the skylight.

Visitors walk down a gentle slope lined with works of art.

Visitors ride an elevator to the top and walk down.

Sculpture is displayed outdoors in a sculpture garden.

Exhibitions in the Small Rotunda show work by 19th- and 20th-century artists.

Main entrance

 FIND OUT MORE ARCHITECTURE • ART, HISTORY OF • DYES AND PAINTS • EDUCATION • GODS AND GODDESSES • GREECE, ANCIENT • PAINTING AND DRAWING • SCULPTURE

MUSHROOMS AND OTHER FUNGI

NEITHER PLANT NOR ANIMAL, mushrooms and other types of fungi form a unique group of organisms of more than 80,000 species. Fungi lack the green, food-making compound found in plants – chlorophyll – and cannot make their own food. Instead, they release enzymes that decompose living, dead, or dying organisms and absorb the nutrients and minerals released. Fungi range from dull gray mushrooms to brightly colored toadstools (a name usually given to more colorful and poisonous fungi).

Life cycle of a mushroom

Mushrooms release spores from their gills or pores. These germinate and produce hyphae that divide to form a mycelium. This may lie hidden in wood, plants, or animals for many years. Gradually, the hyphae spread through the wood and absorb nutrients. When conditions are right, normally in the fall, mushrooms appear on the surface and release more spores.

Spore

Hyphae

Emerging fruiting body

1 Spores are released from mushrooms. They contain small food reserves. Only a few spores find the right conditions to germinate.

2 On germination a single fungal thread, or hypha, grows from the spore. It divides to form the mycelium.

3 As the fungal mycelium expands into its surroundings, it absorbs water and nutrients to build up energy to form the fruiting body.

Features of a mushroom

Mushrooms are the part of a fungus, called the fruiting body, that grows above ground. They contain spores, which enable fungi to reproduce. Spores are produced on the underside of a mushroom and released from flaps called gills, or hollows called pores. Below the fruiting body lies the mycelium, a network of fine threads called hyphae, that are usually hidden within a plant, animal, or soil.

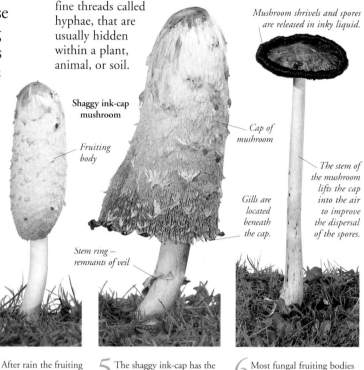

Mushroom shrivels and spores are released in inky liquid.

Shaggy ink-cap mushroom

Fruiting body

Cap of mushroom

Gills are located beneath the cap.

Stem ring – remnants of veil

The stem of the mushroom lifts the cap into the air to improve the dispersal of the spores.

4 After rain the fruiting body enlarges with the rapid uptake of water and becomes a recognizable mushroom, in this case a shaggy ink-cap mushroom.

5 The shaggy ink-cap has the characteristics typical of a mushroom: a stem or stipe, gills on the underside of a cap, and a veil that protects the gills as it pushes up through the soil.

6 Most fungal fruiting bodies release their spores into the air for distribution, but as the ink-cap matures, its cap breaks down to produce a black liquid, in which the spores float away.

Spore dispersal

Fungal fruiting bodies are diverse in shape and color, but all are designed to disperse spores. Many release their spores directly into the air from gills, spines, or pores; other fungi, including stinkhorns, are eaten by animals such as pigs and flies, which disperse the spores in their feces. A few types of fungi, such as the cramp ball, shoot their spores away; puffballs puff out a cloud of spores when hit by a raindrop.

Puffball exploding

Common stinkhorn
Stinkhorn spores are distributed by insects. The fruiting body develops below ground in an egglike structure. When mature, the stem grows rapidly, carrying the cap upward. The cap is covered in a slimy, smelly mass of green spores. Carrion-feeders, such as flies and beetles, are attracted by the putrid smell. They eat the slime and disperse the spores in their feces.

The spaces between spores mirror those between the gills.

Spores are found in slime.

Spore print
A spore print is the pattern that spores make when the cap of a mushroom is placed gillside down on paper. Spores are used to help identify fungi.

Types of fungi

There are many types of fungi. The spores and mycelium of most species are similar in appearance. The main differences occur between the fruiting bodies, which come in many sizes, shapes, and colors. They vary depending on how they reproduce. On this basis, fungi are divided into five groups.

Common morel

Chicken-of--the-woods

Pin mold

Athlete's foot

Potato blight

Sac fungi
Sac fungi, including morels, cup fungi, and truffles, produce spores in a special sac, or ascus.

Club fungi
Club fungi, such as chicken-of-the-woods and puffballs, produce spores on club-shaped fertile cells.

Blights
Blights, such as potato blight and mildew, produce oospores. Many blights live in water.

Molds
Molds have woolly growth and produce zygospores. Pin mold often grows on bread.

Imperfect fungi
Imperfect fungi, such as athlete's foot, ringworm, and thrush, have no sexual stage to their life cycle.

Where fungi live

Fungi grow wherever other living, dying, or dead organisms are found on Earth, mainly in warm, damp conditions. They live in the ocean, in rivers, hedgerows, and lakes, on mountains, and in caves – in fact, in all habitats. They can grow on fruit, bread, cheese, leather, rotting wood, and garden refuse. Warm weather after rainfall offers the perfect conditions for mycelium to produce a crop of fruiting bodies.

These mushrooms grow in woods, parks, and hedgerows.

Shaggy parasols

Woods
Many fungi live in woods and forests, both on the forest floor and directly on the trees. Different types of fungi grow in coniferous forests than in deciduous forests.

Fairy ring fungi

Meadows
Undisturbed grassy meadows are home to many fall mushrooms. Fairy rings are circles of mushrooms created when hyphae spread out in all directions and sprout a circle of mushrooms above.

M

Luminous fungi
The lamp mushroom of Australia and the Jack O'Lantern of North America both have luminous caps. The purpose of the luminescence is still unknown, but their green lights, glowing on the forest floor at night, may attract animals, which help disperse their spores.

Feeding

The majority of fungi live on dead organic matter, breaking it down into a form that they, and other living things, can absorb. These fungi, called saprophytes, play a vital role in recycling nutrients in the environment. Some fungi live on animal dung; others are predatory and trap soil worms. Some fungi get nutrients from paints, gasoline, and plastics. There are also parasitic fungi that live on a live host, and symbiotic fungi that live in harmony with their partner.

Parasitic fungi
Parasitic fungi feed on live animals, plants, or fungi. For example, honey fungus is often found growing on apple trees. Some fungi, such as blights and rusts, harm their plant hosts, but Dutch Elm disease and oak wilt kill theirs. Aspergillus, a fungal lung disease, attacks birds, and ringworm attacks humans.

Symbiotic fungi
Many fungi are found in association with certain plants, such as fly agaric and birch trees. The hyphae penetrate the plant roots to form a partnership, or mycorrhiza, between the plant and fungus; the fungus saps nutrients from the plant, but helps the plant collect water and minerals from the soil. Lichens are fungi that live with algae; the fungi provide protection while the algae provide the nutrients.

Honey fungus on apple tree

Fly agaric fungus by decaying birch tree

Problem fungi

Many fungi cause problems; some are poisonous if eaten, some cause disease, and others may cause structural damage to houses. In the 19th century, many people died in France from the disease called St. Anthony's fire after eating bread infected with ergot fungus. Blue molds, brown rots, and scab cause fruit, such as apples, to rot, while the honey fungus is the most destructive tree parasite, capable of killing whole orchards.

Caps reach 6 in (15 cm) in width.
Stem is white or gray-green.
Death cap

Poisonous fungi
Some fungi are poisonous if eaten. The death cap looks harmless enough, but 1 oz (28 g) can kill a person in just a few hours. Other fungi, such as magic mushrooms, cause hallucinatory effects.

Dry rot
Dry rot fungus lives on damp wood in houses and churches. The mycelium rapidly covers vast areas of timber and damp brickwork. It causes catastrophic decay and weakens the beams, which may eventually collapse.

Ringworm
Ringworm is a fungus that attacks the skin, especially children's scalps. It often causes hair to fall out. A ringworm epidemic occurred in the 1940s in Britain, causing a serious public health problem.

Useful fungi

Many edible forms of fungi are commonly used in cooking, baking, and brewing. Quorn, a fungal meat substitute, is one of the most recent additions to vegetarians' pantries. The chemical industry also uses fungi to produce many products, including citric, gluconic, and oxalic acids, enzymes for detergents, and colorful dyes.

Yeast
Yeast is a type of fungus used in baking to make bread rise and in brewing to turn sugar to alcohol. It is also used to make blood plasma substitutes, extracts high in vitamin B12, and anticoagulants.

Perigord truffle

Edible fungi
Many types of fungi are low in food value but are eaten for their flavor. Commonly eaten fungi include chanterelles, oyster mushrooms, and morels. Truffles grow underground and are considered a delicacy.

Penicillium
Penicillium molds grow on many damp substances. They are often used to flavor cheese. These fungi also produce antibiotics, such as penicillin, which are used to combat bacterial infections.

Shaggy ink-cap

SCIENTIFIC NAME	*Coprinus comatus*
CLASS	Homobasidiomycetes
FAMILY	Coprinaceae
DISTRIBUTION	Australasia, South Africa, Europe, North America, Venezuela
HABITAT	Fields, wasteland, lawns, paths
DIET	Dead organic material in the soil
SIZE	4–14 in (10–35 cm) high
LIFESPAN	Fruiting body present for a few days from April to November

 FIND OUT MORE DISEASES · ECOLOGY AND ECOSYSTEMS · FOOD AND FOOD INDUSTRY · MEDICINE, HISTORY OF · MICROSCOPIC LIFE · WOODLAND WILDLIFE

Mushrooms and other fungi

Club fungi

Common puffballs grow in clusters, mainly in woodland.

Horn of plenty grows in clusters in leaf litter or moss.

Fluted bird's nests disperse their spores when rain falls.

Barometer earthstar curls up its rays in dry weather.

Yellow Spindles grow in moss-rich meadows.

Woolly Milk Caps produce spicy milk when cut.

Dryad's saddles grow out of half-dead trees and stumps.

Amethyst deceivers grow on soil among leaf litter.

Fairy-ring champignons grow in circles on lawns.

Razor-strop fungus grows all year on old birch trunks.

Sulfur tufts are common in temperate woodlands.

Devil's finger was introduced to Europe from Australasia.

Yellow brain fungus is parasitic and grows on hardwood trees.

Many-zoned brackets grow in tiers on the sides of tree stumps.

Meadow coral fungus grows in grasslands and woodlands.

Chicken-of-the-woods often grows high up in trees.

Beefsteak fungus grows on tree trunks. It can make oaks hollow.

Fly agaric toadstools are highly poisonous.

Fine-scaly honey fungus is a deadly tree parasite.

Common hedgehog has short spines on the underside.

Cinnabar brackets grow in sunny sites on tree trunks.

Sac fungi

Orange peel fungus grows on dirt roads, lawns, and between paving.

Candle-snuff fungus grows on tree stumps all year round.

Summer truffles grow below ground among tree roots.

Curly-haired elf cups grow on moss-covered wood.

Scaly earth-tongue grows in grass or moss.

Beech jelly-disks live on the bark of fallen trees.

Jelly babies have a rubbery texture.

Cramp balls forcibly eject their spores.

Orange caterpillar fungus is a parasite on moth larvae or pupae.

Green stain produces a stain inside the wood on which it grows.

Common white saddles grow on woodland soil.

☠ Do not pick wild fungi because many are poisonous.

MUSIC

THE URGE TO MAKE MUSIC is ancient, and it is an essential part of all cultures. Music is thought to be the oldest form humankind has found for expressing its feelings. It can affect emotions, making people dance or cry, or make repetitive work easier to bear. Music is played whenever there is a celebration, from a harvest to a wedding. Essentially, all music is sounds called notes organized into patterns of melody, rhythm, and harmony.

Melody

The basis of any song is its tune, or melody, which consists of a series of single notes. Because most wind and stringed musical instruments normally play one note at a time, the music they play is essentially melodic.

18th-century Japanese musician

The sitar has an exotic, shimmering sound.

Indian classical musicians

Mridangam

The musician sits on the floor to play.

Asian melody
Melody is important in the traditional music of Asia, such as the elegant sounds of Japanese woodwind and string players. The complex chiming sounds of the gamelan, a traditional Indonesian orchestra, are made by a variety of gongs, bells, and xylophones, playing variations on a simple melody.

Ragas and talas
Indian classical music is based on sets of notes called ragas and rhythmic patterns called talas. There are about 130 ragas in common use. Each is associated with a different time of day, and has its own distinctive mood, such as happy, sad, or peaceful. The performer, a vocalist or sitar player, chooses a raga and tala and improvises with them. The performer is accompanied by drums.

Rhythm

Underlying each piece of music is the beat, a pattern that divides music into units of time. The rhythm of a piece of music is determined by how the composer has grouped beats together, by the length of each note, and how notes are accented.

African drum

African musicians

African traditions
Complex, exciting rhythms are central to the many styles of traditional African music. Generally, music is for group performance. Tuned and untuned drums, rattles, and handclaps keep the rhythm. The call-and-response style of solo singer and chorus is important as well. This style was taken by slaves to America, and developed from a simple "field holler" into jazz and the blues.

Harmony

The sound produced when two or more notes are played simultaneously is called harmony. Harmonies accompany the instruments playing the melody and can change the mood of a piece.

Polyphony
Most Western classical music is based on polyphony. Developed by medieval musicians, this is a harmonic style that combines separate melodies. The Italian Giovanni Palestrina (c.1525–1594) composed some of the finest polyphonic music.

Giovanni Palestrina

Gospel music
The rich harmonies and inspirational performances of American gospel choirs have become popular outside the church, too. Gospel music has its roots in a mixture of black American and Protestant evangelical styles.

Gospel choir

Ancient music

Music in ancient civilizations was passed on by listening and repetition; there was no accurate system of writing it down. Some ancient instruments have been found and, together with pictures and descriptions of different periods, they give us an idea of the kinds of music that people played.

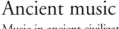

Greece
The ancient Greeks were very concerned with the arts, especially poetry, dance, and music. The philosopher Pythagoras (c.580–500BC) analysed music mathematically, explaining the relationships between series of musical notes and naming the notes with letters of the alphabet.

Lyre player

China
Music and philosophy were linked in ancient China, and philosophers wrote documents on music's place in society. Confucius, a philosopher in the 5th century BC, recognized the power of music and recommended it should be under state control. As a result, *yayue* (elegant music), the music of the ancient style, dominated until the revolution of 1911.

Lute

Model musician, T'ang dynasty

The Middle East
Music was an important part of the cultures of the ancient Middle East. Lyres, harps, flutes, and tambourines were played in Mesopotamian rituals in about 2000 BC. Similar instruments appeared in Egypt 500 years later. Musicians played them in state and religious ceremonies and for entertainment.

Egyptian tomb painting, c.1400 BC

Folk music

Traditional music played by non-professional musicians, especially in rural communities, is known as folk music. Each country has its own folk traditions. There is a huge variety of styles, often using instruments with a strong local association, such as the Scottish bagpipes, or the Russian balalaika. Some professional musicians have taken an interest in folk music, writing down and recording examples for posterity.

Notation

Composers use notation (signs and symbols giving musicians precise instructions about what they should play) to write down the music they create. Monks in the 9th century AD were the first to use notation, and it was fully developed by 1200. It was the basis of Western art music, because it provided a permanent record of the composer's intentions.

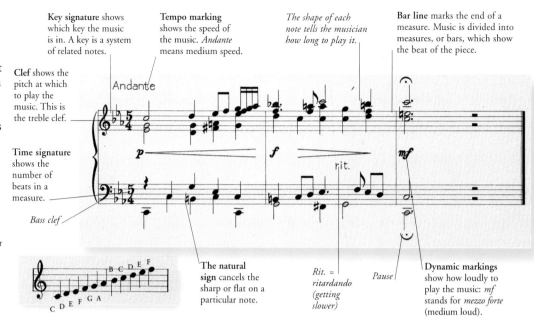

Key signature shows which key the music is in. A key is a system of related notes.

Tempo marking shows the speed of the music. *Andante* means medium speed.

The shape of each note tells the musician how long to play it.

Bar line marks the end of a measure. Music is divided into measures, or bars, which show the beat of the piece.

Clef shows the pitch at which to play the music. This is the treble clef.

Time signature shows the number of beats in a measure.

Bass clef

The natural sign cancels the sharp or flat on a particular note.

Rit. = ritardando (getting slower)

Pause

Dynamic markings show how loudly to play the music: *mf* stands for *mezzo forte* (medium loud).

Scale

The position of a note on the horizontal staff lines indicates its pitch (how high or low the note is). Notes are given letter names from A to G. They can be arranged in ascending and descending sequences called scales. Scales are either major, with a bright sound, or minor, with a darker, more serious sound.

Medieval music

Until the late 11th century, music mainly took the form of simple melodies. Church music was sung in unison (everybody singing the same notes); other music took the form of simple songs. When notation developed, composers could write more complex vocal music in several parts. Meanwhile, early European instrumental music was developing, in dances such as the estampie.

Gregorian Chant

Monasteries were early centers of music-making. The melodies sung by monks during the reign of Pope Gregory (r.AD 590–604) are often called Gregorian Chant, or plainsong. Later, other parts were added to these chants, providing the first examples of harmony. By the 14th century, European composers were writing sophisticated pieces for choirs with several different voices.

Troubadours

In medieval Europe traveling singers entertained at the aristocratic courts. They sang songs of love, accompanied by stringed instruments such as viols and harps. The trend began in France, where the singers, or troubadours, were highly respected as poets and musicians.

J. S. Bach

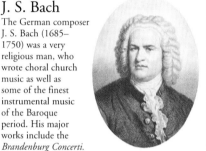

The German composer J. S. Bach (1685–1750) was a very religious man, who wrote choral church music as well as some of the finest instrumental music of the Baroque period. His major works include the *Brandenburg Concerti*.

Baroque music

Western music between 1600 and 1750 was ornate, often using several melodies together in a style called counterpoint. The system of tonality (where music shifts from one key to another) evolved, allowing composers to write works that explored the moods of major and minor keys.

Concerts

Public music-making increased during the 17th century. The first operas appeared in about 1600, and orchestras played the first truly public concerts. George Frideric Handel's (1685–1759) *Music for the Royal Fireworks* was given a spectacular performance.

Renaissance music

In about 1471 in Italy, music printing appeared for the first time. Its arrival helped spread new musical styles through Europe, and encouraged a surge in non-religious music in particular.

Musicians and courtiers in Renaissance France

Madrigal, arranged so the parts can be read and sung by four people seated around a table.

Madrigals

Madrigals are pieces of music for several unaccompanied singers. They developed in 14th-century Italy, but became popular throughout Europe in the 16th century. Generally about love, madrigals were the first choral music to be written for performance in the home.

Court of Burgundy

During the 14th and 15th centuries, Burgundy in eastern France became an influential center for all the arts, including music. The composers Guillaume Dufay (c.1400–1474) and Josquin des Prez (1440–1521) taught there, among others. Josquin is known for music that expressed emotions more directly than earlier styles.

St. Mark's, Venice

Venice, Italy, was at the heart of Renaissance thinking, a mixture of the church and secular society. Andrea Gabrieli (c.1510–1586) and his nephew Giovanni (c.1557–1612) wrote exciting new music to be performed in the cathedral of St. Mark. Their compositions explored the contrasting sounds made by different groups of musicians or singers.

Interior of St. Mark's, Venice

Classical music

Late in the 18th century, composers reacted against the complex style of Baroque music and developed a simpler style. This style is known as Classical music, although the term "classical" is often used loosely for any serious or art music. Composers include the Austrians Haydn (1732–1809) and Mozart (1756–1791), and the German Beethoven (1770–1827). Music was written in forms such as the symphony, and sonatas for the newly invented piano.

Esterháza palace

Beethoven composition

The symphony was the main form of Classical orchestral music.

Patronage
During this period, rich nobles often became patrons to composers. Prince Paul Esterházy employed Haydn as director of music at his palace in Hungary; the composer wrote much of his music here.

Symphony
A symphony is a work usually in four sections, or movements. Each movement is different in character, and the music changes from one key to another within the movements, changing the mood.

Nationalism
Romantic music was largely created by composers from Germany and Austria. Its traditions did not always suit composers in other regions who wanted to express their own national character. Nationalist composers, such as the Norwegian Edvard Grieg (1843–1907), used folk tunes in their music to produce works that summed up the nature of their own countries.

Norwegian fjord

Romantic music

This dramatic style of music emerged during the 19th century. Although composers continued to use Classical forms, such as the symphony and sonata, the mood of Romantic music was more intense, emotional, and individual. Composers also wrote program music that depicted scenes and stories, using the increased range of sounds available from new instruments in the orchestra.

The waltz
This romantic dance first gained popularity in the 19th century. When it first appeared it was considered shocking, because the dancers danced so close together.

Franz Liszt
Recitals of piano music were popular entertainment in the Romantic era. The Hungarian composer and pianist Franz Liszt (1811–86) gained "superstar" status for his dazzling recitals of his own music, such as the *Hungarian Rhapsodies*. Liszt was an innovative and brilliant composer. He invented the form of the symphonic poem, which tells a story through music.

Twentieth century

By 1900 tonality (the use of keys) was stretched to its limits. New styles appeared that moved away from traditional melody and harmony. Russian composer Igor Stravinsky (1882–1971) used jagged rhythms that shocked the musical establishment. Some composers, such as John Cage, introduced random elements into their music.

Arnold Schoenberg

Debussy and Schoenberg
Among the pioneers of early 20th-century music were the composers Claude Debussy (1862–1918) and Arnold Schoenberg (1874–1951). Debussy experimented with unusual sounds and harmonies in his impressionist pieces, such as *Prélude à l'après-midi d'un faune*. Schoenberg wrote music that was atonal, with no feeling of key, as in the *Five Piano Pieces*.

New notation
Much late-20th century music, especially for electronic instruments, cannot be written down in the traditional way. Some composers have developed forms of graphic notation to represent these new sounds.

John Cage
The immensely influential US composer John Cage (1912–1992) wrote music that experimented with noise and chance events, making the listener think again about what music really is. In his highly innovative works, Cage suggested that all sounds, musical or non-musical, are of equal interest. For instance, the famous piece *Imaginary Landscape No. 4* was written for 12 radios, tuned at random.

Broadcasting
The invention of the radio and gramophone brought professional music into the home for the first time. Sales of recordings helped finance musicians, and broadcasting companies often commissioned new works for their orchestras to perform.

Transistor radio, 1940s

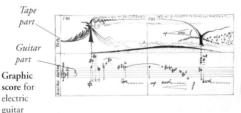
Tape part

Guitar part

Graphic score for electric guitar and tape

Extract, "Caressing Eternity" © Natasha Barrett 1994

Timeline

c.1200 The French monks Léonin and Péotin compose the first properly polyphonic music, based on traditional plainsong melodies.

c.1450 Guillaume Dufay writes the mass *Se la face ay pale (If my face is pale)*, which includes elements of both medieval and the new Renaissance styles.

Medieval stone carving of musician

c.1600 The first concerti, using contrasting groups of musicians, are published in Italy.

1741 Handel completes *The Messiah*, a setting to music of religious texts known as oratorio.

1824 Beethoven's *Ninth Symphony* marks the end of the Classical period, in which the symphony develops into a form that expresses intense human emotions.

1912 Schoenberg composes a set of songs, *Pierrot Lunaire*, in which he abandons tonality.

20th-century recording

1952 John Cage composes *4'33"*, four minutes and 33 seconds of silence.

1993 French composer Pierre Boulez (b.1925) explores computers in art music with a piece called *... explosante fixe*.

FIND OUT MORE · BEETHOVEN, LUDWIG VAN · DANCE · JAZZ · MOZART, WOLFGANG AMADEUS · MUSICAL INSTRUMENTS · OPERA · ORCHESTRA · ROCK AND POP · SOUND

MUSICAL INSTRUMENTS

BY PRODUCING THE SOUNDS we call notes, musical instruments make music to enrich our lives. There are many different instruments throughout the world. Most of them can be grouped into four main families, depending on how they make sound: percussion, wind (including brass and woodwind), strings, and keyboard. Until the relatively recent development of electronic music, all musical instruments were based on these types.

Crash cymbal

Tom-tom drum

Snare drum

Ride cymbal

Floor tom

Bass drum

Percussion

Percussion instruments make sounds by being shaken or struck. The first were probably sticks and bones banged together to accompany people while they sang. Today the huge variety of instruments ranges from drums to rattles or the triangle. Some, such as the xylophone, can be tuned to produce a definite musical note; others accentuate rhythm.

Drums
Drums are found worldwide. They are especially important in traditional African music, which is rhythmically complex and exciting.

Wooden percussion
The short, dry sound of wooden percussion, a feature of South American dance music, is produced by the claves, castanets, maracas, and woodblocks.

Seeds inside hollow shell

Wooden maracas

Gong and bells
Metal percussion instruments produce long, sustained sounds. These vary from crashing cymbals to the exquisite ringing of gongs and bells produced by Indonesian gamelans.

Brass instruments

Brass instruments are long tubes with a mouthpiece. The tubes are bent into coils to make them easier to handle. Most have valves that can be pressed down to open up more of the tube and produce different notes. With their loud, triumphant sound, brass instruments are well suited to outdoor events and grand occasions.

Trumpet player

How they work
Brass players produce sounds by making their closed lips vibrate in the instrument mouthpiece. By changing the tension of the lips, the player produces different notes and can use the valves to complete an entire scale.

Pressing a valve opens side-sections of tubing, and increases the length of the whole tube.

No valve pressed

Longest section of tubing opened

Third valve pressed

Early brass
The first brass instruments were made from conch shells and animal horns. During the Renaissance, the sackbut (an early trombone), the cornett (a wooden trumpet), and the serpent (a bass cornett) appeared. Except for the trombone, these instruments disappeared in the early 1800s, but have been revived.

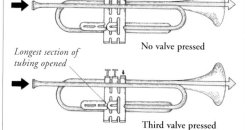

Serpent

Woodwind instruments

Any woodwind instrument is a hollow tube with an arrangement of holes and keys. Blowing into the tube makes a column of air inside vibrate and emit a sound. The musician uses the keys or holes to make the column of air longer or shorter, changing the pitch of the note. The woodwind family includes the flute, pipe, whistle, recorder, clarinet, saxophone, oboe, and bassoon.

Clarinet player

The sheng, a kind of mouth organ, has been played in China for more than 3,000 years.

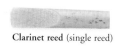
Clarinet reed (single reed)

Oboe reed (double reed)

Bassoon reed

How they work
Blowing across a bottletop makes a note in the same way that the panpipes and flute do. Some woodwinds, such as the clarinet or oboe, have a mouthpiece with a reed (a thin piece of cane). The reed vibrates when the player blows into it; the tube of the instrument modifies the sound produced.

Early woodwind
Once, all woodwind instruments were made of wood, but today they are often made from metal or plastic. The sounds produced by early woodwinds include the loud shawm, the buzzing crumhorn, and the low notes of the racket.

Shofar
The shofar is an unusual instrument made from a ram's horn that produces drawn-out, sobbing sounds. It is played on important Jewish public and religious occasions, such as Yom Kippur, the Day of Atonement.

590

Stringed instruments

The huge family of stringed instruments can be divided into two main groups by the way they are normally played. Most stringed instruments, including the guitar, harp, lute, and sitar, are plucked with the fingers or a pick. Instruments such as the violin and its relatives are usually played by drawing a horsehair bow over the strings to make them vibrate. Many cultures have their own versions of both plucked and bowed instruments.

Moroccan 'ud

Plucked strings
In ancient Egypt and Greece, musicians played the lyre to accompany songs and poetry. Today, plucked instruments are still played as accompaniment. The harp and zither evolved from the lyre. The Arabic 'ud, which dates back 4,000 years, developed into the guitar.

The player's chin and shoulder support the instrument.

Bowed strings
Bowed stringed instruments originated in Arabia, but now are found all over the world. In a modern orchestra, the string section is made up of the members of the violin family – violins, violas, cellos, and double basses. These instruments evolved in Italy during the Renaissance.

Violin player

How they work
When a string is made to vibrate, the sound is amplified by the body of the instrument. The length, thickness, and tension of the string all affect the pitch of the notes produced.

1 Moving a finger up the string shortens the length that vibrates, making the note higher.

2 Strings differ in thickness – thicker, heavier strings produce lower notes.

3 A tightened string vibrates more quickly, so the note it produces is higher.

Stradivari
Italian Antonio Stradivari (1644–1737) is perhaps the best-known and greatest violin-maker of all time. He learned his craft in Italy, placing his own label on a violin for the first time in 1666. The violins and cellos he made between 1700 and 1715 are considered the finest in the world; some are still being played.

Instrument making

In the history of music, the instrument makers are as important as the performers and composers. Instrument making takes years to master and combines art, craft, and science. Makers continually improve the sound of instruments, while Bartolomeo Cristofori (1655–1731), who invented the piano, and Adolphe Sax (1814–94), inventor of the saxophone, added new sounds to music.

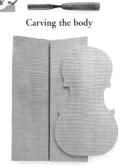

Carving the body

Refining the body

Wood for sides

Adding the ribs (sides)

Complete body

Decorative strip of wood

Mold

Sound holes

Fingerboard glued to neck

Strings

Bridge

Tailpiece

Varnish and dyes

Neck (roughly carved)

Tuning pegs

Chin rest

Making a violin
Months of effort go into shaping, finishing, and assembling a violin. Most of the work is by hand.

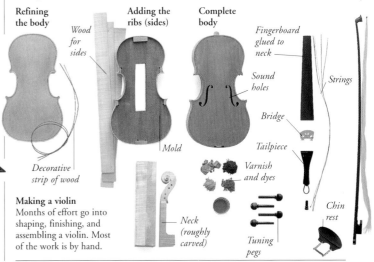

Keyboard instruments

The keyboards are the most expressive of instruments because they are capable of playing many notes at the same time. Pressing a key activates a mechanism inside the instrument. In the harpsichord, the mechanism plucks a string; in the piano, a felt-covered hammer strikes the string. In an organ, the keyboard action sends air through sets of pipes.

Harpsichord
The harpsichord and similar instruments, such as the spinet and virginal, were popular from the 15th to the 18th century, when musicians began to play the newly invented piano.

Spinet, 1550s

Organ
The organ is the largest musical instrument of all and produces a wider range of sounds than any other instrument. It is mainly associated with church music, but is sometimes included in orchestral pieces.

Hundreds of pipes

Piano
This instrument is very expressive, producing a wide range of sounds: players are able to draw notes out, cut them short, or make each one loud or soft. As a result, a great deal of solo music has been written for the piano. The grand piano has a rich, powerful tone and is used for concerts. Upright pianos are smaller and more practical for most homes.

Metal frame on which strings are stretched

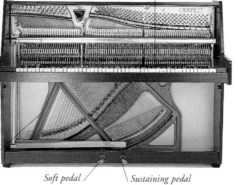

88 note keyboard

Soft pedal *Sustaining pedal*

Display panel

Synthesizer

Electrical and electronic instruments
The first electronic instrument, the Ondes Martenot, had a keyboard but could not play chords. More recent electronic keyboard instruments such as the Hammond organ or the synthesizer are more versatile, producing all kinds of unusual sounds. They often play alongside electrically amplified instruments like the electric guitar.

FIND OUT MORE
BEETHOVEN, LUDWIG VAN   JAZZ   MOZART, WOLFGANG   MUSIC   OPERA   ORCHESTRA   RADIO   ROCK AND POP   SOUND

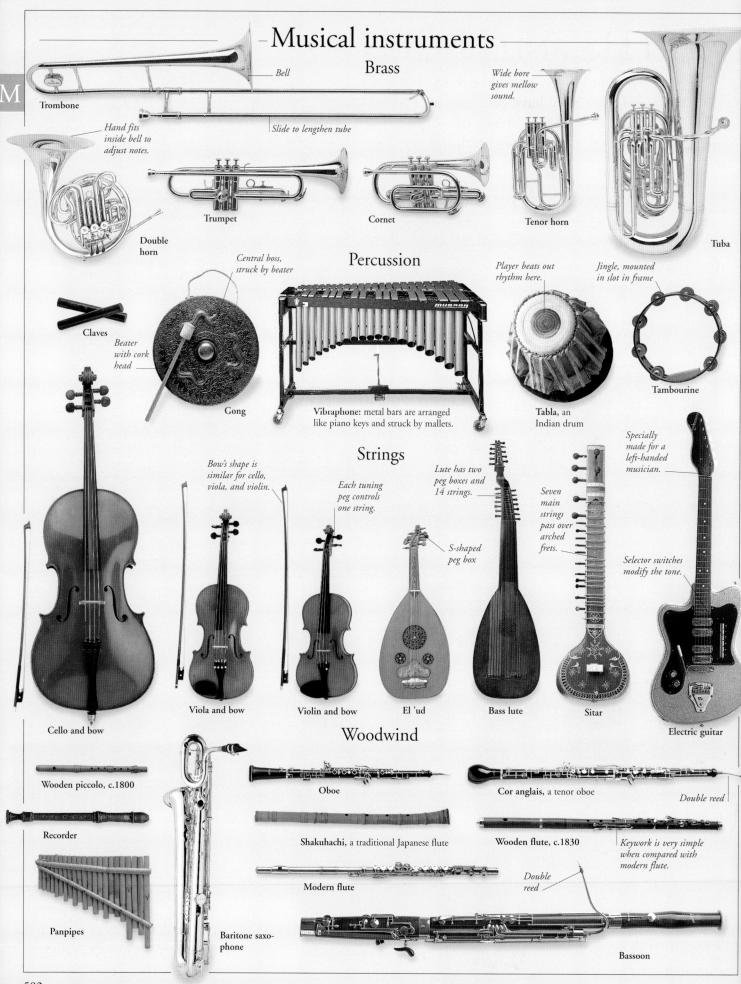

Musical instruments
Brass

Trombone

Bell

Hand fits inside bell to adjust notes.

Slide to lengthen tube

Wide bore gives mellow sound.

Trumpet

Cornet

Tenor horn

Tuba

Double horn

Percussion

Claves

Central boss, struck by beater

Beater with cork head

Gong

Vibraphone: metal bars are arranged like piano keys and struck by mallets.

Player beats out rhythm here.

Tabla, an Indian drum

Jingle, mounted in slot in frame

Tambourine

Strings

Bow's shape is similar for cello, viola, and violin.

Each tuning peg controls one string.

Lute has two peg boxes and 14 strings.

S-shaped peg box

Seven main strings pass over arched frets.

Specially made for a left-handed musician.

Selector switches modify the tone.

Cello and bow

Viola and bow

Violin and bow

El 'ud

Bass lute

Sitar

Electric guitar

Woodwind

Wooden piccolo, c.1800

Recorder

Panpipes

Baritone saxo-phone

Oboe

Shakuhachi, a traditional Japanese flute

Modern flute

Cor anglais, a tenor oboe

Double reed

Wooden flute, c.1830

Keywork is very simple when compared with modern flute.

Double reed

Bassoon

M

MYTHS AND LEGENDS

WHEREVER PEOPLE have lived together they have told stories to explain the mysteries of the universe: of creation and destruction, of how people and animals first came to be, of the characters of the gods and goddesses they worshiped. These tales are called myths, and, with their cast of heroes and monsters, explain how life works. Legends, too, are tales of adventure, but, unlike myths, are thought to have some basis in historical fact. Myths and legends are a record of how ancient people saw the world.

Navajo blanket

Beginnings

In every culture from Asia to the Americas, creation myths exist to explain how the world began, and how the first people came to exist. In Norse mythology, the creator god Odin made the earth from a giant's flesh, and the sky from his skull. One of the Aztec creator gods, Quetzalcoatl, also known as the plumed serpent god, made heaven and earth from the body of a serpent.

King Arthur

The legend of Arthur, king of the Britons, has endured for centuries. Films and books retell the story of the knights of the Round Table at Arthur's court in Camelot. The real Arthur was probably a Romano-British chief who fought against the Saxon invasion in the 6th century.

A scene from the film *Excalibur*

Navajo creation
In Navajo mythology, the cornstalk often symbolizes a creation goddess. Many Navajo blankets, based on the design of sandpaintings, depict healing ceremonies involving the sacred plant.

Ra
The sun god Ra, or Re, was the creator god of ancient Egypt. Ra created all the other gods, and when he cried, his tears became humans. In ancient Egyptian mythology, Ra's granddaughter, the sky goddess Nut, swallows Ra every night, and gives birth to him each morning, creating a new day. During the night, Ra fights the evil serpent Apep. Ancient Egyptians believed that if Apep succeeded in devouring Ra, the world would end.

Yin-Yang symbol
Yang
Yin

P'an-ku
A Chinese myth tells of a cosmic egg formed at the start of time. When the egg hatched, P'an-ku emerged as the first being. He filled the space between the two opposing forces of Yin, which represents the heavens, and Yang, which represents the earth. When P'an-ku died, his eyes became the sun and the moon, his tears became seas, and his fleas became humans.

Legendary animals and plants

Animals and plants play a major role in world legend. Mythical animals include the dragon, the unicorn, and the phoenix, all endowed with special powers. The phoenix, for example, was believed to bring prosperity whenever it appeared, and bad luck whenever it departed.

14th-century imperial seal

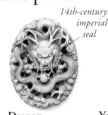

Dragon
The Chinese dragon represented wisdom and goodness, and is still a symbol of good fortune today.

Yeti
For centuries, people have searched for the yeti – an ape-man believed to dwell in the Himalayas.

Mandrake
In medieval times, mandrake was attributed with magical powers. Its roots were thought to resemble human legs, and it was said to scream when uprooted; those people who heard it went insane.

Amaterasu
When Amaterasu, the Japanese sun goddess, was frightened by her brother, Susanowo, the storm god, she hid in a cave. Consequently, heaven and earth were plunged into darkness, and the crops died. The other gods placed a mirror by the cave entrance and lured Amaterasu out with her own reflection, restoring light to the world.

Atlantis

The Greek philosopher, Plato (c.427–c.347 BC), invented a fabulously rich island in the Atlantic – then claimed it was lost beneath the waves during a great storm. People have searched for Atlantis ever since.

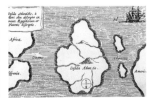

Urban myths and legends

In 1935, the *New York Times* reported that an alligator had been found in the city's sewers. Since then, rumors have spread of a colony of giant white alligators living under New York. The tale of the Vanishing Hitchhiker, told throughout Europe and America, is an example of an old legend adapted to suit modern times. The 19th-century version tells of a traveler who mysteriously disappears during a journey in a horse-drawn carriage; in the modern version, the traveller is a hitch-hiker, and the vehicle is a car.

Fairies
Between 1917 and 1920, two English schoolgirls in Cottingley, England, took a series of photographs, which they claimed were of fairies. Experts believed that the photographs were genuine for many years, until, in later life, the girls confessed that the images were fake.

FIND OUT MORE   EGYPT, ANCIENT   GODS AND GODDESSES   LITERATURE   RELIGIONS   WITCHES AND WITCHCRAFT

NAPOLEON BONAPARTE

BETWEEN 1799 AND 1815, one man dominated Europe. Napoleon Bonaparte was a brilliant military leader who led the French armies to a string of victories over every major European power. As emperor of France, he was also a fine administrator, transforming the government of France and setting up a legal system that survives in Europe to this day. However, he was a controversial figure, because he overturned many of the gains of the French Revolution and ruled his empire with as much authority and power as did the kings of France, whose rule the revolution had ended.

Early life
Napoleon was born in 1769 on the island of Corsica. He had a military education, joined the army in 1785, and won acclaim when he seized the port of Toulon from the British in 1793.

Napoleon's army in Egypt

Bonaparte in Egypt
Napoleon was promoted for his role at Toulon. He defeated the Austrians in Italy in 1797 and the following year set out for Egypt, on the way to invade India and crush the British Empire. He was fascinated by Egypt and took scholars with him to study its ancient civilization.

Emperor
In 1804, Napoleon extended his power by crowning himself Emperor of the French in front of the Pope. As ruler of France, he introduced many reforms. He centralized the state's administration, set up a national school curriculum, and in 1801 made peace with the Roman Catholic church, which had opposed his rule.

The Napoleonic Code
Napoleon introduced a new legal code in 1804 that was based on the principles of the French Revolution. The code protected property rights, established the equality of all people before the law, and allowed freedom of worship. It was carried throughout Europe by French armies, and remains the basis of many European legal systems today.

Court scene from the time of Napoleon

Military campaigns
Napoleon was one of the most brilliant military commanders of all time. He could march his armies speedily across Europe and defeat much larger forces. He had notable victories over Austria, Germany, and Spain, but he was defeated in Russia because of the strength of Russian resistance and the hard Russian winter.

18 Brumaire
Napoleon's rise to power came in several stages. In a coup on November 9, 1799, known by its revolutionary calendar date of 18 Brumaire, the ineffectual Directoire, or committee, governing France was overthrown. Napoleon was one of the three Consuls who were appointed in its place to govern the country. In 1802, he was made First Consul for life.

French officer's czapska

Napoleon's monogram

Napoleon at the head of his Great Army

Invasion of Britain
France ruled mainland Europe, but the British navy ruled the seas. In 1803, Napoleon built up his army to invade Britain, but he needed control of the sea. In 1805, a British fleet led by Nelson defeated a Franco-Spanish fleet at Trafalgar, ending all invasion plans.

Napoleon hoped to invade England in balloons

Joséphine
Napoleon married Joséphine de Beauharnais (1763–1814) in 1796, captivated by her beauty and wit. Her previous marriage had ended in 1794 when her husband was beheaded during the revolution. She already had two children, but when she failed to produce an heir for Napoleon, the emperor divorced her in 1809. Josephine died in retirement.

Napoleon in exile
After his defeat in Russia in 1812, Napoleon gradually lost control of his empire. In 1814, he abdicated the throne and retired to the Mediterranean island of Elba. But he soon left Elba, leading the French army to final defeat at Waterloo in June 1815. He was then exiled to the South Atlantic island of St. Helena, where he died in 1821.

NAPOLEON BONAPARTE

1769 Born in Ajaccio, Corsica.
1785 Joins the army.
1795 Becomes commander of the army of the interior.
1796 Marries Joséphine.
1799 Overthrows the Directoire and becomes First Consul.
1802 Made First Consul for life.
1804 Crowns himself emperor; introduces Napoleonic Code.
1809 Divorces Josephine.
1814 Abdicates and retires to Elba.
1815 Defeated at Waterloo; exiled to St. Helena.
1821 Dies on St. Helena.

FIND OUT MORE | FRANCE, HISTORY OF | FRENCH REVOLUTION | HOLY ROMAN EMPIRE | NAPOLEONIC WARS

NAPOLEONIC WARS

BETWEEN 1797 AND 1815, a series of wars engulfed Europe. Known as the Napoleonic Wars, after Napoleon Bonaparte, they involved France on one side and the old kingdoms of Austria, Prussia, Britain, and Russia on the other. France had been at war since 1792, when its armies fought to protect its revolution. However, wars of defense became wars of conquest as Napoleon extended the boundaries of France to create an empire. By 1808, Napoleon's armies controlled most of western Europe and seemed unbeatable. British supremacy at sea, Napoleon's disastrous Russian campaign, and a general European uprising turned the tide, and by 1815, combined European forces had finally defeated Napoleon.

Battles and campaigns

After his major victories against the Austrians (in 1800 and 1805), the Prussians (in 1806), and the Russians (in 1807), Napoleon amassed the largest empire in Europe since the fall of Rome.

Trafalgar

The victory of Lord Nelson's fleet over Napoleon's forces at Trafalgar (1805) ensured British supremacy at sea. Napoleon was unable to blockade British goods, so supplies reached allied forces in occupied areas.

Napoleon's armies

The French armies were the largest and most powerful in Europe. Most of the soldiers were conscripts (young men forced to fight) either from France, or from occupied countries. Between 1803 and 1815, some two million men were conscripted, and Napoleon regularly commanded forces of 250,000. Napoleon's army was divided into semi-independent corps. Soldiers moved fast and, in battle, fought in massed ranks that broke the enemy lines.

Weapons

Soldiers were constantly drilled, or trained, in the use of their weapons. Drills helped combat nerves and avoid accidents, and taught the men to load and fire quickly. Speedy reloading often made the difference between winning or losing a battle. The most common gun in the French infantry was the musket, and movable muzzle-loaders (front-loading cannon) were used by both sides.

Medicine and food

Napoleon's soldiers lived off the land, finding or stealing whatever food they needed. Medical treatment was primitive; casualties were high. In the Battle of Borodino (1812), Napoleon lost about 30,000 men.

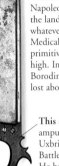

This saw was used to amputate the Earl of Uxbridge's leg in the Battle of Waterloo. He had been hit by a cannonball.

Shako

Plate with imperial eagle and regiment number

Chevron for five years of good conduct

1777-pattern Charleville musket

Muzzle-loader

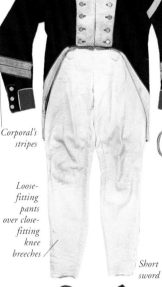

Corporal's stripes

Loose-fitting pants over close-fitting knee breeches

Short sword

Russian campaign of 1812

When Napoleon and 500,000 men invaded Russia, the Russians drew them deeper into the country by retreating, burning food and shelter as they went. The French reached Moscow, but, far from supplies in the harsh winter, thousands starved or froze to death.

Battle of Waterloo

The last major battle of the war took place in 1815 at Waterloo, Belgium. Combined Prussian forces under Blücher, and British forces under Wellington, defeated Napoleon for the last time. This victory led to a period of stability in Europe.

Timeline

1792–95 French Revolutionary Wars: France fights to defend its revolution against hostile European monarchies.

1800 Battle of Marengo results in French victory.

1804 Napoleon becomes emperor. He plans to invade England with an army of 140,000. These plans are canceled after Trafalgar.

1805–1809 Napoleon's victories include Averstädt, Austerlitz, Friedland, Jena, and Wagram. He now controls most of Europe.

1808–14 Peninsular War. British forces and Spanish guerillas fight against France in Spain and Portugal, finally driving the French out of Spain.

1813–14 Wars of Liberation. Austria, Prussia, and Russia defeat France at the "Battle of Nations" in Leipzig.

French flintlock, carried by cavalry

1814 Allied forces enter France. Napoleon exiled to Elba.

1815 Napoleon returns briefly, but is defeated at Waterloo.

Brass buckles

Studs helped shoes last longer.

French corporal's uniform

Uniforms

Morale and efficiency were crucial for success in war. Stylish uniforms made both French and English soldiers proud to be in the army, and taking care of them properly taught the men discipline and obedience.

FIND OUT MORE | ARMIES | FRANCE, HISTORY OF | FRENCH REVOLUTION | NAPOLEON BONAPARTE | WARFARE

NATIVE AMERICANS

PEOPLE FIRST ARRIVED in North America more than 30,000 years ago, when they crossed an Ice Age land bridge that joined Siberia and Alaska. They lived a peaceful existence until Europeans arrived. These new settlers gradually displaced the Native Americans from their homelands and confined them to reservations, where some still live today, upholding their traditions.

Tribes of North America
The climate and local resources shaped the way Native Americans lived. When the Europeans arrived in the 17th century, many tribes lived in the northeast, along the Atlantic coast and fertile shores of the Great Lakes. In the arid southwest, farmers lived in villages, or pueblos. The tribes of the Great Plains were nomadic until Spanish settlers arrived.

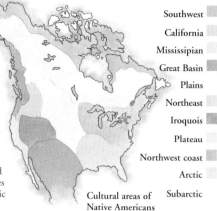

Southwest
California
Mississipian
Great Basin
Plains
Northeast
Iroquois
Plateau
Northwest coast
Arctic
Subarctic

Cultural areas of Native Americans

Homes

Native American homes were designed to provide shelter from a range of climates, from the frozen Arctic to the hot and arid southwest. The homes were often built by women, from locally available materials such as ice, snow, wood, grasses, and animal hides. Some buildings accommodated only one family. Others were built for large groups.

Longhouse
The Iroquois built impressive longhouses of timber and bark that extended up to 200 ft (60 m) in length. They accommodated up to 20 families, who lived in separate compartments along the sides. Shared cooking fires were placed in the central aisle.

Elm-bark covering

Corn is left to dry on storage racks in the roof rafters.

Frame made from wooden poles.

Families shared cooking fires set at intervals along the length of the longhouse. Smoke escaped through the roof.

Igloos
Blocks of snow compressed into ice.

Between October and May, the Inuit of the central Arctic lived in igloos. These could be built in a few hours and were made of blocks of compressed snow, cut with antler or bone knives, and built up in a dome-shaped spiral. A fire was lit inside the igloo, for cooking and keeping warm.

Tepee
Smoke flaps to keep heat in.

The nomadic Sioux, and other hunting tribes on the Great Plains, made temporary shelters called tepees. A framework of long poles was covered with buffalo hides sewn together. The hides were usually decorated with painted designs.

Lodge pins

Door flap

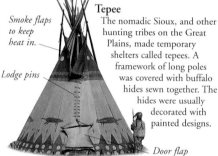

Crazy Horse
Crazy Horse (c.1842–77) was the Sioux chief of the Oglala tribe. He fought against settlers' invasion of the Great Plains, and led his people against US government efforts to build roads through their territories in Montana. He waged constant warfare on the US army until he finally surrendered in 1877. He was imprisoned, and was killed trying to escape.

Domestic life

Most American tribes lived in small villages, securely defended by a wooden fence. They grew crops such as corn, squash, pumpkins, and tobacco.

Ax

Arrows

Hunting weapons
Native Americans revered the animals they hunted, and there were many rituals associated with the hunt. In addition to meat, animals provided hide, hair, horns, and bone, which were used for clothing, ornaments, utensils, and weapons.

Bow   Spear-thrower

Women
In most tribes, women worked much harder than men. They made the clothes and looked after the children and the home. They also prepared food, tended crops, or – if they belonged to hunting tribes – butchered meat.

Modern Native Americans

As Europeans moved west during the 19th century, tribes were forced into reservations. Between 1860 and 1890, resistance to resettlement led to the Indian Wars, but the new settlers overwhelmed the native people. Recently Native American culture, language, and history, long suppressed by the government, have been undergoing a revival.

City life
Between 1950 and 1970, the US government tried to relocate Native American Indians into cities, but many found it difficult to adjust. In the 1980s, the Native Americans opened gambling casinos, creating new jobs.

Reservation life
From the 19th century, the US government tried to enforce a pass system that kept Native Americans confined to reservations. In the 1970s, legal groups helped Indians regain their lost lands, and today about 1.5 million Indians live on reservations that they govern themselves.

FIND OUT MORE   CANADA   CANADA, HISTORY OF   COLUMBUS, CHRISTOPHER   GERONIMO   HOUSES AND HOMES   INCAS   NORTH AMERICA, HISTORY OF   SOCIETIES, HUMAN   WEAPONS

Native Americans

Religion and Ritual

Calumet pipes usually marked the end of fighting.

Soul catchers returned a sick person's spirit to the body.

Grave images were buried alongside bodies.

Snake sticks were symbols of lightning and rain.

Masks represented the spirit world of some Native Americans.

Eagle feathers were used in ceremonial dances.

Totem poles reflected a family's status.

Personal possessions

Deerskin moccasins decorated with colorful glass beads.

An ulu was used for skinning meat

Leather wristband decorated with silver.

Snowshoes worn by subarctic peoples.

Bear claw necklace usually worn by chiefs from the Great Lakes region.

Shawnee cloth bag decorated with appliqué and stitching.

Utensils used for cooking.

Toy horse

Dakota doll in traditional dress

Blankets were woven with intricate patterns and motif designs.

Seminole dolls in traditional costume

Wooden mortar for grinding corn.

Serving bowl and spoon carved in wood.

Creek rattle filled with stones to make sounds.

Whistle played by the tribes of the Northern plains.

Harvesting basket containing dried corn.

Cradleboard made from soft animal skin.

NAVIGATION

WHEN YOU WALK, CYCLE, OR DRIVE from one place to another, you plan your route first, then keep checking you are on course until you arrive at your destination. This process is called navigation. Unless you know the way, you will also need navigational aids, such as maps and a compass. Accurate navigation is especially important at sea or in the air when no landmarks are visible. The first, simple navigational aids, such as lighthouses, allowed early mariners to leave inland waters and navigate their way safely across the oceans.

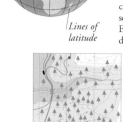

Lines of longitude

Lines of latitude

Latitude and longitude
Maps and charts often show lines of latitude and longitude, imaginary lines criss-crossing the Earth's surface. Navigators use them to help locate their position and to chart their route. Latitude is a north-south division, drawn parallel to the Equator: longitude is an east-west division, drawn from pole to pole.

Maps and charts
A map is a picture of the ground, drawn from above. It shows features on the ground, such as buildings and hills. To navigate, these map features can be matched up with the features on the ground; positions are checked using the lines of latitude and longitude. Charts are more detailed maps, specifically for navigating at sea or in the air.

Map showing landscape detail

Electronic navigation
Modern navigational aids use complex electronics and are very accurate. They detect radio signals sent from fixed radio beacons and use them to determine the receiver's position. The most common and effective equipment is the Global Positioning System (GPS). This detects signals from a network of satellites or spacecraft rather than from Earthbound beacons.

Rotating antennae pick up satellite signals.

Display screen

Different channels

GPS receiver calculates the distance between the satellite and receiver to provide the location of the receiver.

Global Positioning System receiver

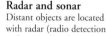

Air traffic control radar scans at airports show the position of all the aircraft in the area.

Navigational aids
For centuries, travelers have used navigational aids. The sextant, which measures the angle between two objects in the sky, such as stars or the Sun, is still used by modern navigators.

Modern sextant

Sight

Magnetic compasses
Because the Earth acts like a huge magnet, a pivotal magnetized compass needle will line up with the Earth's magnetic north and south poles.

Objects are lined up with the "sight" on a hand-bearing compass.

Gyrocompasses
A gyroscope is a device that remains stable while spinning. The gyrocompass needle stays steady, even if it is tilted, making it ideal for accurate navigation.

Gyrocompass

Logs
A log consists of an under-water propeller, or rotator, that spins faster as the ship increases speed. A register counts the number of spins, giving the distance traveled.

Log line

The governor transmits spins to log line.

Register

Rotator

Automatic navigation
Many aircraft have an automatic, computerized navigation system. It consists of a GPS receiver and computerized maps. The aircraft's steering is automatically adjusted to maintain the craft on the correct course. Ships operate with similar systems.

Radar and sonar
Distant objects are located with radar (radio detection and ranging) and sonar (sound navigation ranging). Radar bounces radio waves off objects and detects the reflected waves. Sonar locates underwater objects with sound and echo waves.

Sonar fish finder

Lights and buoys
At sea, a system of visual aids helps vessels navigate safely. Lighthouses and lightships send out a unique pattern of flashing signals. Buoys are floating markers. Their shape and color indicate different hazards, such as the edge of a shipping lane or sandbanks.

North cardinal buoy

Safe water marking buoys

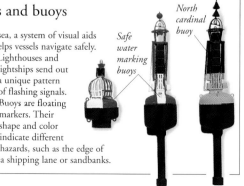

Timeline
11th century Chinese mariners use simple compasses.

14th century The Portuguese develop the astrolabe. Using the Sun and stars, it helps locate a position on Earth.

1569 Flemish geographer Gerardus Mercator (1512–94) publishes the first world map. Mariners use it to navigate.

1762 British inventor John Harrison (1693–1776) wins a prize for building a chronometer, a mariner's clock. It accurately calculates longitude for the first time.

1930s Scottish scientist Robert Watson-Watt (1892–1973) develops the first practical radar system. Radar is used extensively in World War II.

1934 In England, Percy Shaw (1890–1976) nearly drives his car off the road in foggy conditions. He invents cat's eyes, reflecting lights placed in the road to help motorists navigate safely in poor visibility.

FIND OUT MORE ASTRONOMY MAGNETISM MAPS AND MAPPING RADAR AND SONAR

NESTS AND BURROWS

SOME ANIMALS SPEND ALL THEIR LIFE in the open and are always on the move. Others are more like humans. They build homes and use them to shelter from bad weather, and also to bring up their young. Animals make two main types of homes – nests or burrows. Most birds collect building materials and then carefully shape them into a nest. Some fish behave in a similar way. Mammals and insects also make nests, but many of them burrow into the ground instead. A burrow keeps them warm and safe from most of their enemies.

Pied wagtail's nest

Birds' nests

The smallest bird nests can fit into an eggcup; the biggest weigh more than a ton. Many birds use twigs, sticks, and leaves for the frame of their nests, but some birds use mud mixed with saliva. This mixture is soft when wet, but turns hard when it dries.

Social weaver nest
Unlike other birds, social weavers from Africa join together to make giant communal nests. The nests are made of grass and can house several hundred pairs of breeding birds. The nests sometimes get so heavy that they bring down trees.

Each pair of social weavers has its own compartment in the nest.

Mud   Seed heads   Feathers

Leaves   Twigs

Horse hair

Cattle hair

Yarn

String   Metal foil

Moss

Baler twine   Paper

Lichen

Grass

Nest materials
This pied wagtail's nest contains several different kinds of material. Leaves and twigs help create its shape; feathers, yarn, and cattle hair keep it warm; moss and lichen help .disguise it from predators.

Fish homes

Most fish release their eggs directly into the water and do not play any part in raising their young. A few are more careful, and make nests to hold their eggs. Some adult fish make themselves a temporary "home" every night to help keep enemies at bay.

Streambed nest
Small freshwater fish called sticklebacks are skilled builders. The male builds a tunnel-shaped nest from the leaves and roots of water plants, and the female lays eggs inside. The male fertilizes the eggs, then guards the nest.

Fish carries bits of water plant in its mouth.

Nest of foam
A male paradise fish, from southern Asia, blows bubbles near the water's surface to make a floating nest of foam. The female releases her eggs below the foam so that they float upward into the nest. The male guards the nest until the eggs hatch.

Fish prods weeds into place with its snout.

Overnight shelter
As night falls, a tropical parrot fish hides away in a crevice in a coral reef and surrounds itself with a bag of transparent mucus. This slimy cocoon makes it more difficult for predators to attack the fish. In the morning, the fish wriggles out of the mucus.

Nest is sited beneath a small boulder.

1 The male three-spined stickleback looks for a gravel-covered area of the streambed near water plants. He excavates a shallow pit by fanning his fins and by sucking up pieces of grit in his mouth. He then starts to collect the building materials.

2 Leaves, roots, algae, and pieces of twig all help make up the nest. The male collects them in his mouth and piles them up to form a small heap on the gravel base. When he has collected enough nesting material, he sets about gluing it together.

3 The male cements the nest material together using a sticky substance made by his kidneys. Once the nest is firm, he pushes his snout through it to make a tunnel. When the male has completed the nest, the female swims into the tunnel to lay her eggs.

Types of nests

The nests of some large birds, such as eagles and herons, are untidy piles of sticks. By contrast, the nests of many other birds are often carefully crafted.

Bag nest
This Baltimore oriole nest is made of cattle hair interwoven with string. The bird wound some string around a twig for support.

Basket nest
A reed warbler's nest is slung between the stems of reed plants.

Cup nest
The song thrush's nest has an outer cup of twigs and grass and a mud lining. It will last, even in rain, for months.

Insect homes

In the insect world, females often work on their own to build nests for their young. Social insects, which include bees, wasps, ants, and termites, are different because they work together in family groups. Some social insect nests are like miniature cities, complete with their own ventilation systems and stores of food.

Stenogaster wasp nest

Working alone

Stenogaster wasps, from Southeast Asia, make nests out of mud. Each nest is built by a single female and contains just enough room for two or three wasp grubs. The female brings food to the grubs and seals up the nest when they are ready to pupate.

Leaf miners

Some moth caterpillars are so small that they can live inside a leaf. As a caterpillar munches its way through a leaf, it leaves a crooked, transparent trail called a leaf mine. The mine gets steadily wider as the caterpillar grows bigger.

Leaf miner's trail in a blackberry leaf

Mammal nests and burrows

Some mammals make nests above ground; others dig burrows beneath the surface. The burrows often contain special nursery and sleeping quarters, which are lined with dry grass and leaves. Most burrowing mammals come to the surface to feed, but some find everything they need underground.

Naked mole rat's burrow

This African rodent lives in family groups containing about 40 members. The queen produces young, while the others dig tunnels with their front teeth to find food.

Wood mouse burrow

A wood mouse's burrow is less than 0.75 in (2 cm) across. It is small enough to keep out most predators, but it is not totally safe: one predator – the least weasel – can slip inside.

Mole burrow

Moles spend almost all their life underground. They sleep and give birth in a special chamber, and collect food in hunting tunnels that run parallel to the surface. Insect grubs and earthworms drop into these tunnels from the soil, and the moles find them by smell and touch.

Squirrel dray

Small mammals, such as the gray squirrel, lose heat easily, and they often build nests in which to shelter from the worst of the winter weather. A squirrel's nest, or dray, looks like a ball of sticks wedged in high branches. A lining of leaves keeps out the wind.

Dray is in the fork of a tree.

Dormouse's winter nest is made of dry bracken and grass.

Dormouse burrow

In summer, the common dormouse builds a small nest out of grass. In fall, it makes a bigger nest with thicker walls for hibernating. When the nest is ready, the dormouse climbs in, rolls into a ball, and begins its long winter sleep.

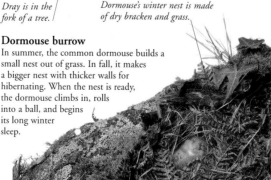

Working together

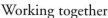

1 Common wasps build their nests with a kind of paper made from wood fibers. The queen begins the nest. She builds walls around a group of cells, each containing one egg.

Common wasp starting her nest

2 When the grubs hatch, the queen brings back food for them. Meanwhile, she starts to expand the nest by adding more layers, in this case made of white wood fibers.

Queen chews wood fibers and mixes them with saliva to make the paper.

New layers are built down and around older layers.

3 The nest is now surrounded by several layers of paper. Paper is a good insulator, so the interior of the nest is warmer than the air outside. This helps the grubs develop.

Small entrance hole keeps the nest warm.

4 When the first batch of grubs have become adult wasps, they join in the building work. They tear down the old inside walls and add new ones on the outside. The queen lays more eggs.

Worker dismantles inner walls.

5 By midsummer, the nest may be as big as a soccer ball and home to hundreds of wasps. The workers all die in late fall, but young queens survive to make new nests the following spring.

Multicolored walls produced by different kinds of wood

Worker ants return with pieces of leaves.

Fungus gardens

Leafcutter ants

In Central and South America, leafcutter ants work together to make a nest underground. A large nest may be several yards across. The ants slice pieces off leaves and carry them back to the nest. In the nest, they chop up the leaves into small fragments and use them to grow a special fungus that they eat. These ants have made a nest in a glass tank so the fungus can be seen.

FIND OUT MORE

ANIMAL BEHAVIOR   ANTS AND TERMITES   BEES AND WASPS   BIRDS   FISH   HEDGEHOGS AND OTHER INSECTIVORES   HOUSES AND HOMES   INSECTS

NETHERLANDS

ALSO CALLED HOLLAND, the Netherlands straddles the deltas of five major rivers in northwestern Europe. The Dutch people say they created their own country because they have enclosed about one-third of the land from sea, swamps, and marshland with earth barriers, or dikes, and drained the water from it. Despite being one of the most densely populated countries in the world, the Netherlands enjoys high living standards. Amsterdam is the official capital, although the government is based at The Hague.

N

NETHERLANDS FACTS

CAPITAL CITY Amsterdam (seat of government The Hague)

AREA 14,413 sq miles (37,330 sq km)

POPULATION 15,800,000

MAIN LANGUAGE Dutch

MAJOR RELIGION Christian

CURRENCY Euro

LIFE EXPECTANCY 78 years

PEOPLE PER DOCTOR 385

GOVERNMENT Multiparty democracy

ADULT LITERACY 99%

Canals
The Netherlands is a land of canals, which drain the land and serve as waterways for people and freight. The capital, Amsterdam, alone has more than 100 canals.

Windmills
For centuries the Dutch landscape was dotted with 10,000 windmills, which powered pumps to drain water from the land. Electric pumps now do this work in the battle to keep the sea back.

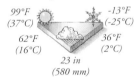

Climate
The Netherlands has mild, rainy winters and cool summers. In winter northerly gales lash the coast, damaging dikes and threatening floods. Frosts sometimes freeze canals.

Physical features
The Netherlands is mainly flat, with 27 percent of the land below sea level. The land is protected from the sea by natural sand dunes along the coast, and by artificial dikes. Wide, sandy plains cover most of the rest of the country, falling into a few, low hills in the eastern and southern parts of the country.

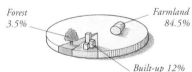

Forest 3.5%
Farmland 84.5%
Built-up 12%

Land use
Almost one-third of the land has been reclaimed from the sea. These areas are known as polders and are extremely fertile. The country has large natural gas reserves in the north, and there is some offshore oil drilling in the North Sea.

Amsterdam
The Dutch capital is built on 70 islands, linked by about 500 bridges that span its many canals. The best way to get around is by bicycle, and about 750,000 people cycle to school or work each day. Today, Amsterdam is a busy center for tourism and diamond cutting.

One of Amsterdam's many canals

People
The Dutch see their society as the most tolerant in Europe, with relaxed laws on sexuality, drugs, and euthanasia. The country has a long history of welcoming immigrants, often from former Dutch colonies. Most immigrants are now assimilated as Dutch citizens. However, members of the small Turkish community, which makes up just one percent, do not enjoy full citizenship.

Street scene, Amsterdam

1,206 per sq mile (466 per sq km)
89% Urban
11% Rural

Farming and industry
The Dutch economy is one of the most successful in Europe. Most imports and exports travel through Rotterdam, the world's biggest port. In addition to high-tech sectors such as electronics, telecommunications, and chemicals, the Netherlands has a successful agricultural industry. Productivity is high, and products such as vegetables, cheese, meat, and cut flowers are significant export earners.

Dutch tulips

FIND OUT MORE · DAMS · EMPIRES · EUROPE · EUROPE, HISTORY OF · EUROPEAN UNION · FARMING · NETHERLANDS, HISTORY OF · PORTS AND WATERWAYS

NETHERLANDS, HISTORY OF

THROUGHOUT THEIR HISTORY, the Dutch have been influenced by the sea. At first they had to reclaim their low-lying land from beneath the North Sea and protect it from flooding. Then they used their maritime skills to create a rich, worldwide trading empire. In the 16th and 17th centuries, cities such as Amsterdam and Rotterdam prospered on the spice trade with the East, and merchants patronized the arts and sciences. Despite a decline during the 18th century, the Netherlands has kept its close relationship with the sea to this day.

Windmill on reclaimed land

Sea

Dutch water engineering
During the 13th century, the Dutch began to reclaim land from the North Sea by building a series of dikes and drainage canals. Dutch engineers became so good at designing drainage systems that their skills were in demand throughout Europe.

William the Silent
Prince William (1533–84) came from Orange, in southern France, but was a major landowner in the Netherlands and resented Spanish rule. In 1576, he became leader of the Dutch United Provinces and proved to be a superb general. He was assassinated before the Dutch won their independence.

William of Orange leading the revolt

Revolt against Spain
In 1556, the Netherlands became part of the Spanish branch of the Hapsburg Empire. The Protestant Dutch resented being ruled by Catholic Spain. A revolt broke out and, in 1581, the seven northern provinces declared independence from Spain. After a long and bloody war, a truce was announced in 1609. Independence from Spain was finally agreed in 1648.

Detail from The Night Watch, by Rembrandt

Golden Age
Freed from Spanish rule, the Dutch state became wealthy. Merchants grew rich on overseas trade, while skilled Jewish and Protestant refugees flooded in, fleeing persecution in Catholic Europe. The openness of Dutch society encouraged a free exchange of ideas. Science flourished and painters such as Vermeer and Rembrandt produced masterpieces for the rich middle classes.

Dutch wars
As the leading maritime trading nation in Europe, the Dutch had to fight to protect their wealth. Commercial rivalry, first with England, and then France in the late 17th century, led to wars that weakened Dutch power.

Tomb of Michiel de Ruyter, admiral killed in French wars

Wealth of empire
The Dutch merchants grew rich on the trade with the East. Although some were based in the capital of the Dutch eastern empire, Batavia (now Jakarta, Indonesia), most built large houses for themselves in Amsterdam. These houses had to be lightweight in construction because they were set on unstable, reclaimed land next to the city's canals. They were therefore built of light materials, such as brick or sandstone, with large windows.

Dutch empire
In the late 1500s, Dutch merchants sailed into the Indian Ocean in search of spices from Asia. In 1602, the Dutch East India Company was set up to exploit this trade. Trading posts were set up in India, China, Japan, and what is now Indonesia. By 1650, the Dutch ruled a vast empire in eastern Asia.

Spice trade
Spices such as pepper, cloves, and nutmeg fetched huge prices in the 16th and 17th centuries. The Dutch defeated the Portuguese and the British to control the spice trade with Europe. They set up an empire in Southeast Asia, where they also grew crops such as coffee.

Fresh peppers

Dried pepper

Nutmeg

Poster for the Social Democratic Party

20th century
The Netherlands was neutral in World War I, but was invaded and occupied by Germany from 1940–45. Since World War II, the Dutch have created one of the most successful economies in Europe. During the government of the Social Democratic Party, a welfare state was introduced. The Netherlands is a keen supporter of closer integration within the European Union.

Timeline
1300–1400s Netherlands is part of Burgundy.

1477 Netherlands becomes part of the Hapsburg Empire.

1555 In the partition of the empire, Netherlands is ruled by Spain.

1568 Revolt against Spanish rule begins.

1579 Seven northern provinces unite in the Union of Utrecht.

1581 The United Provinces declare their independence from their Spanish rulers.

1648 The Treaty of Westphalia recognizes Dutch independence from Spain.

1830 Belgium, its Catholic citizens resenting Protestant rule, at last gains its independence from the northern Netherlands.

1940–45 Netherlands occupied by Germany.

1949 Dutch colony of Indonesia obtains its independence.

1957 Netherlands is a founding member of the European Community (now known as Union).

FIND OUT MORE | ART, HISTORY OF | ASIA, HISTORY OF | EUROPE, HISTORY OF | HOLY ROMAN EMPIRE | SPAIN, HISTORY OF | WORLD WAR II

NEWSPAPERS AND MAGAZINES

NEWSPAPERS PROVIDE PEOPLE with important sources of information on local and international affairs. They cover events in great detail, and are vital in shaping public opinion. They contain up-to-date articles on politics, current affairs, lifestyle, and sports, together with advertising and comic strips. Magazines come out less frequently, and are less concerned with the latest news. They cost more than newspapers, and often use colorful designs.

Early writings
In ancient Rome, news sheets called *Acta Diurna* (Daily Events) were regularly posted to give people news about gladiatorial contests and military successes. Another early newspaper was the *Dibao*, which was distributed to civil servants in Beijing, China, between 618 and 1911.

Types of newspapers
There are many kinds of newspapers. Some support political parties, while others try to remain independent. Some cover world news, while others report local news and events. Still others specialize in areas such as business, or sports. Newspapers can be daily or weekly publications.

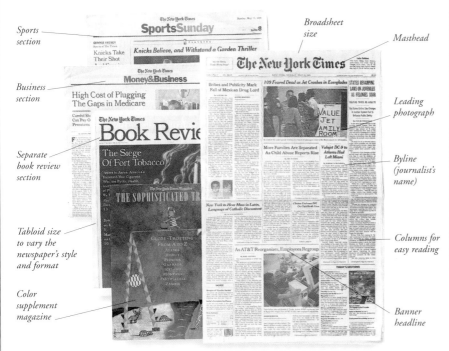

Sports section

Business section

Separate book review section

Tabloid size to vary the newspaper's style and format

Color supplement magazine

Broadsheet size

Masthead

Leading photograph

Byline (journalist's name)

Columns for easy reading

Banner headline

Tabloids
Tabloids cover news events in brief, sensational, and often lurid detail. They attract their readers' interest by printing simple headlines in large type.

Broadsheets
Broadsheets cover important new topics and issues in far more extensive detail than the tabloids, and present a more sophisticated analysis.

Features of a paper
Modern newspapers cover many areas of public interest. Their front section is always devoted to the most important national and international current events, but they may also have separate sections on culture, sports, and business. Sometimes they also include separate supplementary magazines.

New York Times
Founded in 1851 by Henry J Raymond, *The New York Times* is one of the world's greatest daily newspapers, with a global circulation. Renowned for the quality of its writing, and directed at a sophisticated audience, the newspaper covers a wide range of national and international interests in its separate sections.

William Randolph Hearst
William Hearst (1863–1951) was one of the most powerful press owners in the US. He used sensational reporting, brash publicity, and aggressive headlines to achieve record sales. At one point he owned 28 newspapers and lived in a mansion in California.

Making a paper
Putting together a newspaper requires great efficiency. Reporters and photographers send in their copy (stories) and pictures. A desk editor then fits them together accurately on the page. Advertising copy, a major source of revenue, is also placed. The pages are then printed and delivered to outlets by morning.

Paparazzi in action

Paparazzi
Pictures sell newspapers, and editors pay vast sums for controversial photographs. Some photographers, often known as paparazzi, go to any lengths to get exclusive photographs of famous people.

Newsroom
News comes into the newsroom from reporters and news agencies all over the world. Editors must quickly choose the most interesting or important stories for the paper to feature, and assign staff to write and research them.

Inside a newsroom

Page layout on screen

Working on screen
Since the 1980s, editors and designers have assembled newspapers by adjusting text and pictures on computer screens. The pages are automatically sent to the printing presses.

Distribution
Newspapers need large circulations, so an efficient distribution system is required to sell copies. Often printing is carried out in several places at once to make it easier to transport the paper quickly to newsstands across the country.

News kiosk

N

Early magazines
Magazines are descended from cheap pamphlets, which were printed in the 1600s to publicize political or religious views. Magazines covering many kinds of interest became popular in the 1700s. Competition was fierce. In 1821, the editor of *The London Magazine*, a literary periodical, was killed by a rival in a duel.

Turn-of-the-century French magazine

Jazz magazine

Car magazine

Readership for this magazine is fairly specialized.

Magazines

The word "magazine" also means a "storehouse," and all magazines are stores or collections of articles, published at regular intervals. Often magazines' content does not date as quickly as that of newspaper's. Also magazines are generally printed on better paper. Modern magazines cover every imaginable subject and range from the most specialized scientific and trade journals, to more general lifestyle and fashion magazines that are read by millions.

Computer magazine

Women's lifestyle magazine

House-decorating magazine

Scientific magazine

Features
Features are the staple of many magazines. They vary greatly, according to the type of magazine they are published in, but are usually articles that look at a particular subject in depth, often accompanied by photographs and illustrations. In a current affairs magazine, this may mean an analysis of an issue that is making news, or in a homes magazine it may look at how to use a particular color or technique when decorating.

Article features color blue for a strong image on page.

Design makes the subject matter attractive.

Feature has seasonal theme of Easter.

Special photography is commissioned to complement text.

Comics

Comic strips are a series of pictures that tell a story. They may be funny, exciting, or satirical. They first became popular in the 1890s, when American press owners put them in newspapers to attract readers. More than one-third of the world's population reads comics.

Superhero comics
Ever since the 1930s, one of the most popular and enduring forms of American comic has been the superhero strip. Superheroes have amazing powers and fight against threats to humanity. Batman was invented by Bob Kane in 1939, and the adventures have since been transferred to both film and television.

Early Batman comic

Advertising

Newspapers and magazines rely on advertising for income and to keep the publication's cost down. The higher the readership, the more a publication can charge for advertising. Specialist titles with small readerships are useful for targeting specific groups of people. Advertising ranges from the straightforward to subtle messages using humor or strong visuals.

Advertisement page selling cars uses images and descriptions to sell its products.

Timeline

59 BC Handwritten newspapers first produced in Rome.

1615 First printed newspapers published in Germany.

1766 Sweden becomes the first country to guarantee freedom of the press.

American World War II magazine

1815 In Britain, *The Times* prints 5,000 copies daily.

1842 *The Illustrated London News* first to use extensive illustrations.

1854 First war reports on Crimean War for *The Times*.

1939 Batman cartoon published.

Arab newspaper

1989 The Tokyo *Yomiuri Shimbun* newspaper has a circulation of almost 15 million copies a day.

1990s Newspapers begin to publish online.

FIND OUT MORE

ADVERTISING AND MARKETING

BOOKS

CARTOONS AND ANIMATION

DESIGN

DISNEY, WALT

INFORMATION TECHNOLOGY

PAPER

PRINTING

NEWTON, SIR ISAAC

THE BRITISH SCIENTIST and mathematician Isaac Newton was one of the greatest scientists of all time. A leader of scientific thought in England, he figured out how the universe was held together, discovered the secrets of light and color, and invented calculus. Newton did most of this work on his own without any help from assistants or colleagues. However, the great man had his weaknesses. His work was often affected by his furious temper and his inability to take criticism from other scientists. He also spent much of his time dabbling in alchemy (the attempt to turn base metals into gold), and it is thought that his poor health in later life was due to his testing substances by tasting them.

Early life

Isaac Newton was born in 1643 at Woolsthorpe, England. At school he was more interested in making mechanical devices than studying.

Newton's mathematics

At 18, Newton went to Cambridge, but, when the university was closed because of the plague, he went home to study. When he was in his late twenties, Newton invented a method of calculation that studied the rates at which quantities changed. He called this "fluxions"; today, it is known as calculus. The equations Newton developed are still used by mathematicians. As a result of this work, he was made Lucasian Professor of Mathematics at Cambridge when he was only 26.

One of Newton's mathematical manuscripts

Newton's optics

In 1665, Newton began to study the nature of light. After a series of experiments he was able to prove that white was made up of a rainbowlike spectrum of colors. He also tried to make a telescope so that he could study the stars. He found that if he used two lenses, the images he saw through the telescope had colored edges. To avoid this, he invented the reflecting telescope – a telescope that used a lens together with a curved mirror.

Newton studying the Sun's rays coming into the room through a hole in a screen

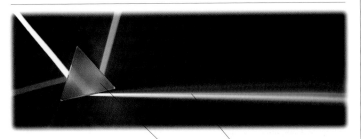

Prism   *White light is turned into spectrum.*

White light

Newton shone a beam of sunlight onto a prism. The light split into a spectrum of colors, that Newton projected onto a board. He then drilled a hole in the board where the red light fell, to make a red beam. When he placed another prism in the path of the red beam, the light changed direction but did not make a spectrum. Newton concluded that white light was made up of different colors.

Newton's drawing of his prism experiment

Newton and gravity

Newton realized that every star and planet in the Universe exerts an attracting force – gravity – that pulls neighboring bodies toward it. He saw that this force keeps the Moon in its orbit around the Earth, and that only the Moon's own movement prevented it from crashing into the Earth. The power of gravity is determined by the amount of matter that makes up the two bodies and the distance between them.

Principia Mathematica

In 1687, Newton published one of the most important science books ever written: *Philosophiae Naturalis Principia Mathematica* (The Mathematical Principles of Natural Philosophy). The book contains Newton's work on the laws of motion, theory of tides, and theory of gravitation. It was also the first book to contain a unified system explaining what happens on Earth and in the heavens.

PHILOSOPHIÆ
NATURALIS
PRINCIPIA
MATHEMATICA

Autore JS. NEWTON, Trin. Coll. Cantab. Soc. Matheseos Professore Lucasiano, & Societatis Regalis Sodali.

IMPRIMATUR
S. PEPYS, Reg. Soc. PRÆSES.
Julii 5. 1686.

LONDINI,
Jussu Societatis Regiae ac Typis Josephi Streater. Prostat apud plures Bibliopolas. Anno MDCLXXXVII.

Title page of Newton's *Principia*

The Royal Society

In 1671, London's Royal Society asked to see the telescope that Newton had invented. They were so impressed that they elected him a fellow of the Society. He became president in 1703, and held this office until his death. In 1696, he became Warden of the Mint and made various changes to British coins.

The original Royal Society building

ISAAC NEWTON

1643	Born in Woolsthorpe, England.
1661	Goes to Cambridge University.
1665	Returns home when the university is closed due to plague.
1665–66	Formulates his three Laws of Motion.
1687	*Principia Mathematica* published.
1672	Newton is elected a Fellow of the Royal Society.
1696	Becomes Warden of the Royal Mint, London.
1703	Becomes President of the Royal Society.
1704	Publishes *Opticks*.
1705	Newton is knighted.
1727	Dies in London.

FIND OUT MORE   GRAVITY   LIGHT   MATHEMATICS   MOON   PHYSICS   SCIENCE, HISTORY OF   SUN AND SOLAR SYSTEM   TELESCOPES

NEW ZEALAND

MIDWAY BETWEEN the South Pole and the Equator, and 990 miles (1,600 km) east of Australia, New Zealand consists of two main islands and a number of smaller islands. As a South Pacific nation, it has developed special ties with Australia, its closest neighbor, and has rapidly expanding trade links with other countries around the Pacific Rim. It is a member of the Commonwealth and the United Nations and was the first country to give women the vote.

Physical features

Both North and South Island have mountains, hills, fertile farmland, forests, and short, swift-flowing rivers that provide a valuable source of hydroelectric power. North Island is volcanically active.

South Island
The Southern Alps form a ridge along South Island. Among them is Mount Cook, New Zealand's highest point at 12,316 ft (3,754 m). To the east are the fertile Canterbury Plains and rolling farmland. The southwest has lakes and glaciers and spectacular fjords.

North Island
New Zealand's North Island is a mixture of green meadows, forest, hot springs, and active volcanoes, such as Mount Ngauruhoe. Geothermal power is generated in this region. The northern peninsula has long, sandy beaches to the west, and islands and inlets to the east.

Climate
The climate in most of New Zealand is generally damp and temperate. However, summers in the far north are warm and subtropical, and winter can bring heavy snow to the Southern Alps. The weather is often changeable.

95°F (35°C) 21°F (-6°C)
60°F (16°C) 46°F (8°C)
51 in (1,300 mm)

Land use
New Zealand's rich pasture is its key resource, and sheep, wool, and dairy products are an important source of income. Energy resources are plentiful, and the country has reserves of coal, oil, gas, gold, and iron.

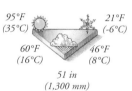

Forest 32%   Barren 5%   Grassland 20%
Built-up 1.5%   Farmland 41.5%

People
The people of New Zealand are ethnically and culturally mixed. About 77 percent are of European origin, and Maoris, the original inhabitants, make up about 12 percent. In recent years, there has also been an influx of non-Maori Polynesians and Melanesians. About three-quarters of the population lives on North Island.

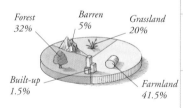

38 per sq mile (15 per sq km)   87% Urban   13% Rural

Young Maori woman from North Island

Farming and industry
New Zealand is one of the world's largest exporters of wool, cheese, butter, and meat. The country has more than 50 million sheep, and its Canterbury lamb, named after the Canterbury Plains of South Island, is world famous. Cattle are also raised for their meat, hides, and milk. In recent years, New Zealand's manufacturing industry has grown and now includes wool products, such as carpets, blankets, and clothing, as well as electronic equipment. Apples, wine, and kiwi fruit are exported worldwide.

Herding sheep

Wellington
One of New Zealand's largest urban centres, Wellington has a population of about 346,500. It is a leading port, and lies at the heart of a manufacturing region. Notable buildings include Parliament House, known as the Beehive because of its shape, and St. Paul's Cathedral, built of wood.

The Beehive

FIND OUT MORE | AUSTRALASIA AND OCEANIA | EARTHQUAKES | MAORIS AND POLYNESIANS | NEW ZEALAND, HISTORY OF | PACIFIC OCEAN | POLYNESIA | UNITED NATIONS | VOLCANOES

NEW ZEALAND, HISTORY OF

IN ABOUT AD 1350, a fleet of Polynesians sailed across a huge expanse of ocean to settle in New Zealand, one of the last places on Earth to be inhabited. They developed a warlike culture that was to remain undisturbed until European settlers arrived in the country in the 19th century. Within a few years, Europeans had taken over the islands, leaving the Maoris to fight for their lives and their land. New Zealand maintained close ties with Britain, but recently the nation has looked more to its Pacific island neighbors and to Asia for its trade and prosperity.

First inhabitants
The first people to settle in New Zealand were Polynesians, who crossed the Pacific Ocean in their wooden dugout canoes in about AD 1000. They took with them sweet potatoes and other island crops, and added fish, game birds, and edible ferns to their diet after they arrived.

Maori chief's staff

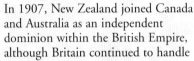

Eyes made of haliotis shell

Decoration of parrot's feathers

Wooden shaft

Carved wooden boat bailer

Hollowed-out scoop for water

Maori battle ax

Whalebone, the usual material for clubs

Ax is made of green basalt stone.

European settlement
After James Cook claimed New Zealand as a British colony in 1769, European traders and whalers regularly visited the islands. In 1840, the first permanent European settlement was founded at Wellington, North Island. All the settlers were colonists sent out from Britain by the New Zealand Company. Within a few years, British settlers outnumbered the Maoris.

Abel Tasman
The first European to see New Zealand was the Dutch navigator Abel Tasman (1603–59), who sighted New Zealand's North Island in 1642. He named the land after Zeeland, a province of the Netherlands.

Maori clubs

Carved wooden decoration

Maori wars
After the Treaty of Waitangi between the British and the Maoris, there was growing Maori opposition to the increasing number of European settlers on their land. In 1860, conflict broke out between Maoris and settlers; it lasted until an uneasy peace was restored in 1870.

Signing the Treaty of Waitangi

Treaty of Waitangi
On February 6, 1840, the Maoris signed a treaty with the British government. The British agreed to protect Maori lands in return for the Maoris recognizing British sovereignty over their country. Today, February 6 is a national holiday in New Zealand.

Independent nation
In 1907, New Zealand joined Canada and Australia as an independent dominion within the British Empire, although Britain continued to handle most of its foreign affairs until 1947. Ties with Britain remained very close and New Zealand troops fought on the Allied side in both world wars.

Welfare state
After a long period of economic depression, a Liberal government was elected in 1890. It created the world's first welfare state, introducing old-age pensions and other reforms. In 1893, New Zealand became the first country in the world to grant women the vote.

Modern New Zealand
Despite a history of economic depression, radical reforms since 1984 have boosted the economy. New Zealand signed the Treaty of Rarotonga in 1986, forming a nuclear-free area in the South Pacific. The 1998 Waitangi Tribunal ordered the return of confiscated ancestral homelands to the Maori people.

Apirana Ngata
Apirana Ngata (1874–1950) was a Maori lawyer who fought for Maori rights all his life. As secretary of the Young Maori political party, he tried to revive Maori society by introducing a national health service and modern farming methods. Ngata was a member of parliament for nearly 40 years, and tried to gain better living standards for his people.

Timeline
c. AD 1000 First Maoris settle in New Zealand.

1642 Dutch navigator Abel Tasman is first European to visit New Zealand.

1769 James Cook claims New Zealand for Britain.

1840 First permanent European settlement established in Wellington, North Island.

1840 Treaty of Waitangi establishes full British sovereignty over the country.

1852–56 New Zealand becomes self-governing.

1893 Women get the vote; other social reforms are introduced.

1907 New Zealand gains the status of an independent dominion.

1914–18 and 1939–45 New Zealand fights with the Allies in both world wars.

1995 The British crown apologizes for historical exploitation of Maori lands and signs Waikato Raupatu Claims Act.

FIND OUT MORE

| AUSTRALIA, HISTORY OF | ECOLOGY AND ECOSYSTEMS | EXPLORATION | POLYNESIA |

NIGHTINGALE, FLORENCE

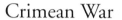

IN THE 19TH CENTURY, nursing was not thought to be a respectable career for women. Most nurses were untrained and worked in appalling conditions. Attitudes were changed by the efforts of one woman – Florence Nightingale. As a nurse in the Crimean War, she experienced the terrible conditions suffered by injured soldiers and dedicated her life to improving them. She campaigned for better training for nurses, and better hospitals. By the time of her death in 1910, the status of nurses had improved and hospital conditions had changed beyond recognition.

Early life
Florence Nightingale was born in Florence, Italy, in 1820 to rich English parents. She seemed destined for the leisured life of an English country lady, but wanted to do something more worthwhile. She decided to become a nurse, an unacceptable job for a woman of her status. But she insisted, did her training, and took a job in a women's hospital.

Crimean War

In 1853, on the Crimean peninsula by the Black Sea, war broke out over the future of the Ottoman Empire. Nightingale persuaded the British Secretary of State for War to allow her to go to the Crimea as a nurse. She left Britain in October 1854, with 37 other nurses, and stayed in the Crimea until war ended in 1856.

Medical knowledge
Medical knowledge was still crude in Florence Nightingale's time. Antibiotics were unknown and surgery crude, and few patients survived a lengthy stay in a hospital. While in the Crimea, she worked hard to improve conditions for the sick and injured, traveling with her personal supply of medicine, and setting new standards for nursing care.

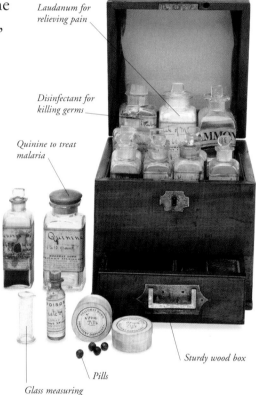

Laudanum for relieving pain

Disinfectant for killing germs

Quinine to treat malaria

Glass measuring beaker

Pills

Sturdy wood box

Florence Nightingale's traveling medicine chest

Scutari Hospital
In the Crimea, Nightingale worked in the Scutari Military Hospital. The conditions in the wards were almost as bad as on the battlefield itself, with no proper medical or nursing care for the injured soldiers. Nightingale cleaned up the hospital, provided basic supplies such as beds and medical equipment, improved the food, made sure proper nursing was available, and even provided a place where soldiers could convalesce before returning to fight.

Lady with the lamp
Florence Nightingale took a personal interest in her patients, touring the wards at night with a lamp to see that all the injured men in the wards were comfortable and free from pain. On her return to Britain, Florence Nightingale was celebrated as a hero, and the image of the lady with the lamp caring for her patients stayed with her for the rest of her life.

Mary Seacole

Mary Seacole was the daughter of a Jamaican mother and a Scottish father. She trained as a nurse in Jamaica, but when she offered to work for Florence Nightingale in the Crimea, she was refused. Ignoring this, she volunteered to nurse soldiers at Balaclava, throwing all her energy and resources into her work. After the war, she returned to Britain in poverty, and wrote a book about her adventurous life.

Mary Seacole tends a wounded soldier

Training the nurses

After the war, Nightingale used her new fame to campaign for better training for nurses. She set up a fund to establish the Nightingale Training Center at St. Thomas's Hospital, London, where nurses could receive proper instruction. She also fought for better conditions for British troops overseas.

FLORENCE NIGHTINGALE

1820 Born in Florence, Italy.

1853 Finishes training as a nurse and takes a job as superintendent of the Institution for the Care of Sick Gentlewomen, a hospital for women.

1854 Goes to the Crimea and nurses soldiers at the Scutari Military Hospital.

1856 Returns to Britain a hero, where she begins to campaign for better standards in nursing.

1860 Establishes a school for training nurses in London.

1907 Awarded the Order of Merit, the highest civilian award in Britain.

1910 Dies at age 90.

FIND OUT MORE   ARMIES   DRUGS   HOSPITALS   MEDICINE, HISTORY OF   OTTOMAN EMPIRE   PASTEUR, LOUIS   WOMEN'S MOVEMENT

NOCTURNAL ANIMALS

AS NIGHT FALLS in the world's forests, grasslands, and gardens, many animals become active. These nocturnal animals sleep or rest by day and emerge at night to hunt and eat. A nocturnal lifestyle gives the animals access to food without having to compete with animals active during the day. Darkness provides camouflage so that some animals can avoid their predators. Many desert animals are nocturnal because it is too hot to emerge during the day. Nocturnal animals are adapted to navigate, find food, avoid predators, and attract mates in the dark.

Large eyes used to see at night

Large ears used to hunt insects

Night eyes

Owls, small primates including bushbabies, aye-ayes, and lorises, and other mammals, such as cats, have large eyes in relation to their body size. The larger the eyes, the more light they are able to gather in dark conditions so that the animal can make sense of its surroundings. Most nocturnal animals have pupils that open very widely at night and allow the maximum amount of available light to enter the eye. They also have a special layer in their eyes, called the tapetum, which helps them see in the dark.

N

Cat's eyes shining at night

Tapetum
This mirrorlike layer in the eye reflects light and makes the eyes more sensitive to dim light. Cats' eyes, for example, are six times more sensitive to dim light than humans' eyes are.

Bushbaby
Huge eyes allow the bushbaby to see in the nighttime darkness of the African forests. Its eyes are also forward-facing, enabling the bushbaby to judge distances accurately, so it can leap in darkness from branch to branch in search of food.

Sensitive ears

Some nocturnal animals use their acute sense of hearing to hunt for prey, or to avoid being eaten by predators themselves. The bat-eared fox swivels its large ears to pick up the faint sounds and location of the insects and scorpions that form most of its diet. Cats use their ears in a similar way, to listen for the rustling sounds made by mice and other prey.

Large hind legs enable the kangaroo rat to hop over large areas each night in search of seeds.

Kangaroo rat
Many desert-dwelling animals are nocturnal. The kangaroo rat, for example, rests in an underground burrow to avoid the daytime heat and emerges at night to feed. It has large eardrums and other modifications inside the ear that make its hearing very sensitive. In most other environments, such acute hearing would deafen the animal, but in the silence of the desert this extra sensitivity is invaluable. The kangaroo rat can even hear the sound of wind against an owl's wings and the rustlings of a rattlesnake's scales moving over sand in time to escape these enemies.

Large ears pick up echoes.

Navigation at night
Nocturnal animals must be able to find their way at night without bumping into objects. Most bats navigate by echolocation. A bat sends out high-pitched sounds through its mouth. The sounds bounce off objects, and the echoes are picked up by the bat's ears and converted by its brain into a "sound picture." Cats navigate with their eyes and whiskers. Whiskers detect slight changes in air pressure when they pass close to an object.

Long-eared bat

Rattlesnake
Snakes have poor eyesight but detect their prey by tasting the air with their tongue or by picking up vibrations made as the prey moves. Rattlesnakes and their relatives have an additional sense – an organ called a heat-sensitive pit on each side of the head between the eye and nostril. The pit is sensitive to infrared radiation and enables the snake to detect heat given off by prey. Even in total darkness, the snake can locate prey and strike accurately.

This is the infrared image of a rat that a rattlesnake can "see" at night.

Acute sense of smell

Some nocturnal animals find food by sensing odors. For example, the gray wolf follows the scent trails of its prey up to 1.5 miles (2.5 km) from their source. Insects can also track smells. Female mosquitoes detect the smells and heat released by warm-blooded animals on whose blood they feed.

Moths
Moths are usually nocturnal and have difficulty finding a mate. Many male moths have feathery antennae to detect attractive smelling chemicals, called pheromones, released by female moths. Moths also avoid bats, by detecting the high-pitched squeaks that the bats make.

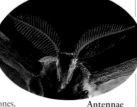

Antennae of North American robin moth

Patterned skin camouflage

FIND OUT MORE

| ANIMAL BEHAVIOR | BATS | CORAL REEFS | DESERT WILDLIFE | MONKEYS AND OTHER PRIMATES | OWLS AND NIGHTJARS | RATS AND OTHER RODENTS | SNAKES | URBAN WILDLIFE |

NORMANS

IN 911, THE FRANKISH KING Charles III (879–929) allowed a group of Vikings to settle on land in France. These settlers were called Normans, because they came from the north, and their new homeland became known as Normandy. They adopted French language and customs, but they were fearsome warriors, and in the 11th century they conquered Sicily and then England. The Normans made a great contribution to the cultures of France, England, and Italy, leaving behind original and beautiful architecture in their castles and cathedrals, a legal system and government, and fine French and English literature.

Territorial control

The Normans built and occupied castles and cathedrals in all their lands. These castles made the territories stable, so culture could flourish – as on the island of Sicily, which became an important scientific center during the 12th century.

Falaise Castle
This castle in Normandy was Duke William's birthplace, and where he made plans to invade England. Many other castles survive in Normandy.

Cefalù Cathedral
The buildings the Normans left behind include this beautiful cathedral in Sicily, established by Roger II.

White Tower
Norman castles always contained large, stone towers for the lord, like this one at the Tower of London.

Conquests

Norman brothers Robert Guiscard and Roger I conquered Sicily between 1060 and 1091. The island became a base for additional conquests in the Mediterranean. Meanwhile, in 1066, Duke William II of Normandy sailed to England, defeated the Anglo-Saxon King Harold II at the Battle of Hastings, and became King William I of England.

Fleet
Like their Viking ancestors, the Normans were skilled ship-builders. They could ship large numbers of soldiers, weapons, and even materials for building castles to the place they had conquered.

Soldiers
Norman soldiers wore pointed helmets and carried kite-shaped shields. Though Vikings fought on foot, Normans copied the use of knights, or mounted warriors, from the French.

Roger II of Sicily

Roger II (1095–1154) was crowned in 1130. He united earlier Norman conquests on Sicily, gained control of parts of southern Italy, and made conquests on the North African coast. He governed wisely and organized the Sicilian government. He believed in religious tolerance, and his court had many links with the Arab world.

Architecture

The Normans loved bold, carved details in their buildings, and their masons invented the pointed "Gothic" style, replacing rounded windows and arches. Although Norman walls looked very thick they were sometimes made of rubble covered by outer "skins" of stone.

Abbey of St. Etienne
Before conquering England, Duke William and his wife Matilda established twin monasteries in Caen – one for monks, one for nuns. St. Etienne was the abbey for monks. It was completed in 1115, long after William's death.

St. Etienne, Caen, France

Durham Cathedral
This beautiful cathedral is one of England's finest Norman buildings. The Normans had two favorite patterns for carving columns: the zig-zag, known as the chevron, and the diamond-shaped lozenge. The Gothic ribbed vault, with its pointed arches, was a major contribution to architecture and was used for the first time in Durham.

Church and state

There was rivalry between monarchs and senior churchmen because both sides wanted ultimate power over the population.

Henry II *Richard I*
King John *Henry III*

Control of the Church
The Church was central to people's lives – to control it was to control the people. Rulers of the 13th century, such as those above, did this by building cathedrals.

St Anselm (c.1033–1109)
Anselm, Archbishop of Canterbury, disagreed with William II and later Henry I, over whether kings or popes had ultimate power within the Church.

Timeline

Coin of William I

911 Rollo the Viking and the Frankish king Charles the Simple agree that Vikings can settle in northern France.

1061 Normans conquer Messina, Sicily.

1066 Battle of Hastings: Normans conquer England.

1086 Domesday Book written.

1087 William I dies. Sons William Rufus and Robert rule England and Normandy.

Seal of William II (Rufus)

1100 Henry I, son of William I, inherits England, and seizes Normandy (1106).

1130 Roger II unites Sicily, Calabria, and Apulia.

FIND OUT MORE | CASTLES | FEUDALISM | FRANCE, HISTORY OF | MEDIEVAL EUROPE | UNITED KINGDOM, HISTORY OF

NORTH AMERICA

NORTH AMERICA includes the countries of Canada, the US, and Mexico, as well as Greenland (the world's largest island), the Caribbean islands, and the narrow isthmus of Central America that joins the continent with South America. Most of the population and industry are concentrated in the northeast, which has a temperate climate. The hotter south and drier west are thinly populated, and few people live in the far north. The US and Canada are powerful, wealthy countries, while Mexico and Central America have weak economies.

Physical features

Northern North America has two main mountain ranges: the Rocky Mountains, which form a huge barrier in the west, and the older, wooded Appalachians in the east. Between them lie the fertile Great Plains, crossed by the Mississippi River. Northern Canada lies within the Arctic Circle, and most of Mexico is in the tropics. Between Canada and the US are the Great Lakes.

Great Lakes
Lying between Canada and the US, the five Great Lakes cover a total of 95,096 sq miles (246,300 sq km) and contain one-fifth of the world's fresh water. Lake Superior is the world's largest freshwater lake; the others are Huron, Michigan, Erie, and Ontario. They are linked to the Atlantic Ocean by the St Lawrence Seaway, which enables ocean-going ships to use inland ports.

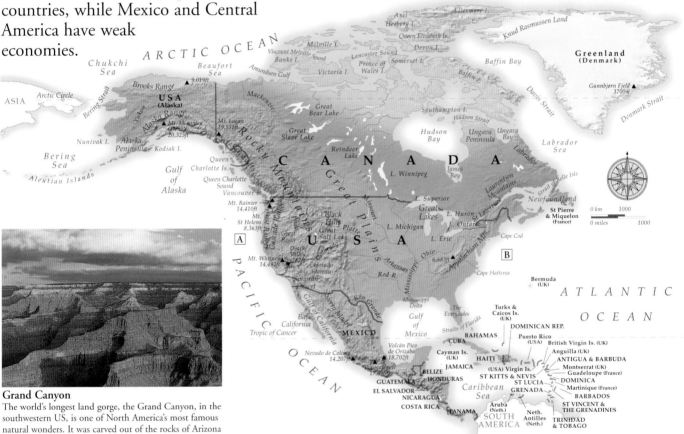

Grand Canyon
The world's longest land gorge, the Grand Canyon, in the southwestern US, is one of North America's most famous natural wonders. It was carved out of the rocks of Arizona over millions of years by the Colorado River and its tributaries. In places it is 1 mile 240 yds (1.8 km) deep.

Cross-section through North America

Travelling from California to the Atlantic coast, the land rises to low coastal mountains and then up to the craggy Rockies. East of the Rockies are the flat, open grasslands of the Great Plains, broken by the Great Lakes. Just before the east coast are the gentle Appalachian Mountains.

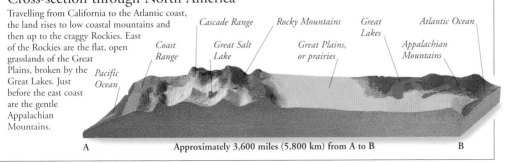

Coast Range
Pacific Ocean
Great Salt Lake
Cascade Range
Rocky Mountains
Great Plains, or prairies
Great Lakes
Appalachian Mountains
Atlantic Ocean

A   Approximately 3,600 miles (5,800 km) from A to B   B

NORTH AMERICA FACTS

AREA	9,357,359 sq miles (24,235,583 sq km)
POPULATION	465,000,000
NUMBER OF COUNTRIES	23
BIGGEST COUNTRY	Canada
SMALLEST COUNTRY	St Kitts and Nevis
HIGHEST POINT	Denali/Mt. McKinley (Alaska) 20,322 ft (6,194 m)
LOWEST POINT	Death Valley (California) 282 ft (86 m) below sea-level
LONGEST RIVER	Mississippi
BIGGEST FRESHWATER LAKE	Lake Superior

Climatic zones

North American climates vary according to latitude, altitude, and distance from the east or west coast. A permanent ice sheet covers Greenland, and cold tundra and taiga extend over the far north. The lush grasslands of the Great Plains enjoy a warm, semiarid climate. In the southwest, the climate turns from snowy mountains to desert.

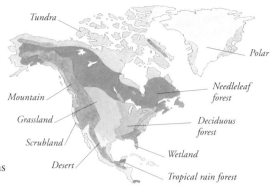

Tundra
Polar
Needleleaf forest
Mountain
Grassland
Deciduous forest
Scrubland
Desert
Wetland
Tropical rain forest

Tundra
The northern parts of Alaska and Canada lie within the Arctic Circle. In the cool, short summers, the land thaws enough to allow flowers to shoot up. Winters are long and bitter, with temperatures dropping below -76°F (-60°C).

Mountain ranges
The Rockies, a comparatively new mountain range, run down the west of the continent from Alaska to Mexico, where they continue as the Sierra Madre. West of the Rockies are the Coast Ranges. The Appalachians run north to south along the east coast.

The Rockies rise up to 6,187 m (20,300 ft).

Needles

Douglas fir

Cone

Rivers often provide the only access to the forest.

Canadian Rockies

Evergreen forest
Vast forests of fir, larch, pine, and spruce trees extend over much of Canada and Alaska, broken only by lakes and rivers. Coniferous forests also cover the slopes of the Rockies. The biggest conifers are the huge redwoods of the US Pacific coast.

Oregon maple leaves

The fall colors of the Canadian forest are a brilliant display.

Deciduous forest
Extensive deciduous (broadleaf) forests cover the area south of the Great Lakes, and both sides of the Appalachians in Canada and the US. Tropical rain forests cloak parts of Central America.

Long grasses of the Prairies

Great Plains
The Great Plains, or prairies, of central Canada and the midwestern US are often called the breadbasket, because much of the world's wheat is grown there.

Deserts
Semidesert and desert regions cover northern Mexico and the southwestern US, experiencing searing temperatures and very little rainfall. They include the Great Basin near the Rocky Mountains, the Mohave Desert, Death Valley, and the Sonoran Desert, which straddles Mexico's border with the US.

Wetland
Covering 2,745 sq miles (7,112 sq km), the Everglades in Florida are the world's largest wetlands. Between Georgia and Florida, the Okefenokee Swamp covers 600 sq miles (1,555 sq km).

Cacti in the Sonoran Desert can survive drought.

People
Most North and Central Americans are descendants of European settlers. About 12 percent descend from black African slaves. Few Native American peoples survive. Recently, many Asians and Hispanics have settled in North America, increasing its variety of cultures.

North America has a multiethnic population.

Resources
North America is rich in resources. It has nearly every important mineral, fertile soil suited to agriculture, huge forests of timber, and access to some fine fishing grounds, although these are in danger of being overfished. Crops include grain, fruit, and vegetables.

Corn

Wheat

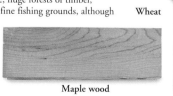

Maple wood

FIND OUT MORE   CLIMATE   CONTINENTS   DESERTS   FORESTS   GRASSLAND WILDLIFE   LAKES   MOUNTAINS AND VALLEYS   NATIVE AMERICANS   NORTH AMERICAN WILDLIFE   TREES   TUNDRA

NORTH AMERICA, HISTORY OF

FOR THOUSANDS OF YEARS, Native Americans developed a series of advanced civilizations that traded and fought with each other over the vast plains and river valleys of the North American continent. Some of these groups constructed complex buildings and developed farming techniques; other groups moved around in search of food and shelter. Yet within a short period of 350 years, European settlers overthrew them all, conquering the entire North American continent from coast to coast and setting up two new independent nations: the United States of America and Canada.

Ice-free corridor
Siberia ASIA *Alaska* *Laurentide ice sheet* *Greenland*
NORTH AMERICA
Route of colonisation
Settlers moved south
Land bridge
Area covered by ice

First people

Until about 15,000 years ago, North America was in the grip of an Ice Age. Because so much water was frozen, sea levels had dropped by about 300 ft (90 m), creating a land bridge to Asia. Before the Bering Strait opened, hunter-gatherers from Asia crossed the land bridge to North America.

Inuit knife made of walrus tusk

Pueblo Bonito

As the first inhabitants of North America moved south and became more established in their new land, they began to build permanent settlements. One of the most impressive of these was at Pueblo Bonito in the Chaco Canyon area of what is now the southwestern United States. It was built by the Anasazi people, who lived there between AD 950 and 1300. At its height, more than 1,200 people lived in the adobe pueblo (large walled village), farming on the cliff tops above the canyon. The dwellings in the pueblo were built one above the other in a structure that rose to four stories in some places. The pueblo was the largest apartment building in North America until the late 19th century.

Ceremonial dress of the Anasazi people

Native American food

The plains and river valleys held abundant food supplies. Fruit and vegetables were plentiful, the land teemed with buffalo and other animals, and the rivers were full of fish.

Squash
Pumpkins and other squash were eaten fresh, or dried for eating in the winter.

Corn
Corn, or maize, was dried and made into porridge, or lightly roasted and eaten with honey, maple sugar, or fat.

Beans
Rich in proteins and vitamins, beans formed an essential part of the daily diet.

Rear wall rose to four stories.
Flat roofs used as open balconies to work on.
Round rooms were for religious ceremonies.
Lower rooms were probably used for storage.

Adena people

The Adena lived by the Ohio River between 1000 BC and AD 200. They hunted and gathered, but also grew some of their own crops. They were the first North American people to build large burial mounds. The Adena mound, near Chillicothe, Ohio, gives the people their name.

Items such as this copper bird were specially made as burial goods.

Hopewells

The Hopewell people were farmers who lived along the banks of the upper Mississippi River from about 300 BC to AD 700. They buried their rulers in large mounds, some 30 of which survive. The mounds were filled with goods made from raw materials gathered from all over North America.

Clay statuette   *Copper bird*

Timeline

c.**20,000** BC Hunter-gatherers from Asia cross the Bering Straits land bridge and begin to move south across the continent in search of food and shelter.

c.**9000** BC Hunter-gatherers begin to hunt bison on the Great Plains.

John Cabot

c.**5000** BC The first farmers grow wheat and other crops in the southwest.

AD **500** Hopewell people build burial mounds along the Mississippi and Ohio Rivers.

700 First pueblos built in the south-western region.

c.**1000** Vikings land on the east coast.

1497 John Cabot, an Italian sailor paid by English merchants, sights Newfoundland and claims it for England.

1534–35 French navigator Jacques Cartier sails up the St. Lawrence River and claims Canada for France.

N

European arrival

After the discovery of land across the Atlantic, many Europeans sailed west. The French sailed up the St. Lawrence River into the interior; the English tried to find a route to Asia around the northern coast; the Spanish moved north from their empire in Mexico.

- ☐ French territory
- ☐ Russian territory
- ☐ Spanish territory
- ☐ British territory

Hernando de Soto

In 1539, Hernando de Soto (1496–1542), Spanish governor of Cuba, set out to explore and conquer North America. He landed on the Florida coast and went northward in search of gold, silver, and jewels, which he failed to find. In 1541, he was the first European to see the Mississippi River, but died before he could return home.

De Soto in Florida

French-style houses

French Canada

After the voyage of the French navigator Jacques Cartier up the St. Lawrence River in 1534–35, French settlers tried but failed to found a colony at Montreal in 1541. Only in 1608 was the first successful French colony in North America founded by Samuel de Champlain at Quebec. In 1663, Quebec became the capital of New France, as the growing French empire in North America was then known.

Lure of the New World

Religious persecution and poverty at home, the lure of exploring and conquering new lands, wealth to be made trading furs and other goods, and the hope of discovering gold and silver, led Europeans to settle in what they called the "New World." By 1750, there were English, French, Dutch, and German colonies in the north and east; the Spanish had settled on the west coast.

Religious persecution

During the 17th and 18th centuries, many religious dissenters fled from persecution in Europe to create their own religious communities in the New World. Puritans, Quakers, Presbyterians, Catholics, and others all established colonies where they could practice their own religion in peace.

Exploration

In 1682, the French trader Robert Cavelier de La Salle (1643–87) sailed down the Mississippi River, naming the land Louisiana after the French king Louis XIV. After Louisiana became part of the US in 1803, the government sent William Clark and Meriwether Lewis to explore it.

Backstaff was used to determine latitude.

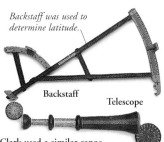

Backstaff   **Telescope**

Lewis and Clark used a similar canoe.

Gold

The discovery of gold in California in 1848 started a rush of prospectors across the continent in search of wealth. New cities such as San Francisco sprang up to house the new arrivals.

Prospecting for gold, US

Fur cap

Gun for hunting and self defense.

Warm, fur-lined clothing

Snowshoes

Fur trapper

Native American hunters were happy to exchange the pelts of wild animals such as foxes, bears, seals, and beavers with the colonists in return for guns, beads, blankets, and alcohol. English fur traders set up the Hudson's Bay Company to exploit this lucrative trade. In Canada, French settlers also traded furs from towns such as Montreal and Quebec.

Otter

Bear

Mink

Cabot and Cartier

While the Spanish and Portuguese explored and colonized Central and South America, England and France explored the North. The Italian navigator John Cabot (c.1450–c.1499) was hired by the English king Henry VII to find a new route to Asia. He was the first European to land in North America, claiming the island of Newfoundland for England. French navigator Jacques Cartier (1491–1557) sailed up the St. Lawrence River in 1534–35, visiting two Huron villages that later became Quebec and Montreal. The Huron word for village, *kanata*, gave the French the name Canada.

Timeline

1607 Jamestown, Virginia, the first permanent European colony in North America, is founded.

1608 French navigator Samuel de Champlain explores Canada and founds the first French colony at Quebec.

The Mayflower

1620 The Pilgrims sail from England in the *Mayflower* to establish a colony at Plymouth, Massachusetts.

1625 The Dutch found New Amsterdam (now New York).

1739 The War of Jenkins' Ear: Spain and Britain fight for control of the waters around North America and the Caribbean.

1759 British capture Quebec.

1763 British take complete control of French Canada.

1776 The 13 British colonies on the east coast declare independence.

1803 The Louisiana Purchase: the US acquires vast tracts of land in the midwest from France.

1867 British colonies in Canada unite to create the independent Dominion of Canada.

FIND OUT MORE   AMERICAN CIVIL WAR AMERICAN REVOLUTION CANADA, HISTORY OF CARIBBEAN, HISTORY OF EUROPE, HISTORY OF EXPLORATION NATIVE AMERICANS US, HISTORY OF

NORTH AMERICAN WILDLIFE

THE VARIETY OF HABITATS found in the huge continent of North America (extending from the Arctic to Mexico, between the Pacific and Atlantic oceans) supports all kinds of plant and animal life, in spite of the pressures imposed by growing human population, larger cities, and habitat destruction. The habitats of North America range from the cold tundra of the north, through large mountain ranges, the northern coniferous forests, the eastern deciduous forests, the prairies and the wetlands, to the deserts of the southwest.

Tundra wildlife

This harsh region in the far north of North America has long, cold winters and brief summers. Sedges, grasses, mosses, and lichens survive in the thin layer that covers the frozen soil. In summer, plants flower, insects emerge, and mammals and birds become more active.

Caribou

Caribou (called reindeer in Europe) live in large herds in the tundra. They migrate north in summer to feed on grasses and sedges, and south in winter to feed on mosses and lichens. Their broad hooves enable them to walk easily in snowy conditions.

Caribou have thick, warm, waterproof coats.

White fur provides camouflage in winter.

Arctic fox

The Arctic fox has very dense fur, enabling it to survive the subzero winds of the tundra winter. The fox is so resilient that it does not begin to shiver until temperatures drop to -94°F (-70°C). It eats almost anything, including berries, birds, rodents, and the carrion left by polar bears.

Sharp talons

Snowy owl

The thick white plumage of the snowy owl, which extends to its toes, keeps the bird warm and acts as good winter camouflage. Snowy owls live in the tundra, but they may migrate south if food is scarce. They hunt by day or night for lemmings, hares, ducks, and gulls. They nest on the ground in the spring.

Wetland wildlife

North American wetlands include lakes, rivers, marshes, and subtropical wetlands, such as the Everglades, swamps, and bogs. Wetlands provide homes for waterbirds, semiaquatic mammals such as beavers and muskrats, frogs, fish, and insects.

American beaver

Beavers are North America's largest rodent. They live by streams and lakes and use their powerful, gnawing incisor teeth to cut down trees and branches for food and to construct dams. In the ponds created by the dams, they build homes, called lodges, with underwater entrances.

American alligator

Alligators live in the subtropical wetlands of the southeastern US. They spend much of the day basking on the muddy shores of swamps and lakes, but forage for food on land or in water by day or night. Alligators eat birds, amphibians, fish, other reptiles, and mammals.

Green tree frog

Green tree frogs live in trees in or near springs, creeks, ditches, lakes, and swamps. Their green color camouflages the frogs among the green of the leaves. They hunt at night, feeding mainly on insects and spiders. In spring, the frogs leave the trees to breed in water.

Body is streamlined when leaping.

Beavers have a streamlined body, flat tail, and webbed feet for swimming.

Saguaro cactus

This giant cactus survives the conditions of the Sonoran Desert by storing water, absorbed by shallow roots, in its ribbed stems. Its flowers, fruits, and seeds provide food for animals; woodpeckers and owls live in holes in its stems.

Saguaros reach up to 65 ft (20 m) in height.

Desert wildlife

Hot, dry deserts, including the Sonoran Desert, are found in southwestern North America. Plants such as cacti are often succulents, with water-storing stems, and small or absent leaves to reduce water loss. Many desert animals shelter from the daytime heat, emerging at night to feed.

Long ears aid heat loss.

Long hind legs enable it to run up to 35 mph (56 kmh).

Black-tailed jackrabbit

Jackrabbits are desert hares. They are active at night, feeding on grasses, cacti, and the bark and buds of shrubs. During the day, they shelter from the Sun's heat.

Roadrunner

The roadrunner rarely flies, but runs with head and tail extended at speeds of 12 mph (20 kmh) to catch prey or avoid enemies.

Desert tortoise

This tortoise shelters from the sun and potential enemies in its long burrow, emerging at dawn and dusk to feed on succulents.

Strong legs dig into dry ground.

N

Mountain wildlife

The Rocky Mountains are one of North America's major mountain ranges. As altitude increases, vegetation changes from coniferous forest and grassland, to tundra and meadow and, higher still, bare rocky crags. Animals found at different levels vary depending on what they eat, and with the seasons.

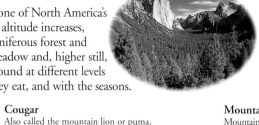

Mountain bluebird
Mountain bluebirds live in western North America. During the summer these small birds live in meadows above 5,000 ft (1,500 m) where they feed on insects caught in flight, or on the ground. In winter, flocks of bluebirds avoid the harsh conditions by migrating to lower altitudes. Females have duller plumage than males.

Males are bright blue.

Cougar
Also called the mountain lion or puma, the cougar thrives in the wilderness of the mountains of western North America at altitudes of up to 15,000 ft (4,500 m). Cougars are powerful, expert hunters; they prey on many mammals, particularly deer.

Mountain goat
Mountain goats are surefooted animals that move easily over rocky crags. In the morning and evening, small flocks may descend from the crags to feed on vegetation in the meadows above the timberline.

Hooves provide good grip.

Whitebark pine
Whitebark pine, a type of conifer growing on the slopes of the Rocky Mountains is found up to 13,000 ft (4,000 m). It provides a home and food, including bark, seeds, and leaves, to many animals.

Temperate forest wildlife

The temperate forests of the US are home to insects, birds, and mammals, especially when summer vegetation carpets the floor. Over 150 species of trees grow here, such as oaks and maples.

Yellow-bellied sapsucker
This species of woodpecker uses its beak to drill holes in the bark of trees such as maples and birches. The sapsucker then flies away, returning later to feed on the sugary sap that has oozed out of the hole. The same holes are returned to, and reopened, year after year.

Monarch butterfly
These butterflies migrate twice a year. In summer, they breed in the forests of northern USA. In fall, a new generation of monarch butterflies migrates to Mexico, spending winter in large groups, returning north in spring.

Coniferous forest wildlife

North America's coniferous forests cover a very large area. Summers are warm; winters are cold and snowy. Forest animals include porcupines and hares, which feed on vegetation, and predators such as lynxes and wolves.

Hooves spread apart on wet ground.

Males use huge antlers to fight in the mating season.

American porcupine
Good climbers, porcupines feed on conifer needles and bark in winter, adding buds, roots, and berries in summer. Their quills can be used for defense.

Spiky quills

Moose
These large deer live in and near coniferous forests and feed on leaves and shrubs. They also stand in water to feed on aquatic plants in streams, lakes, and bogs.

Burrowing owl
This small owl has adapted to a habitat with few trees, by living in a hole in the ground. It shelters and nests in the breeding season in abandoned burrows of rodents such as prairie dogs.

Prairie wildlife

The prairie is a grassland area that used to cover much of central North America. As the area was settled, pronghorn and bison were almost wiped out. However, areas of prairie still survive and are home to animals such as ground squirrels and coyotes.

Buffalo grass
Buffalo grass is dominant in the short grass prairie. This is the region of semiarid plains of the western prairie, where the grasses are adapted to survive drier conditions. Prairie grasses provide food for rodents, insects, and grazing animals, including cattle.

Yellow for camouflage in grass

Pronghorn
Small herds of pronghorns graze on the wide range of grasses and other prairie vegetation. Pronghorns can move fast, at speeds of up to 96 kmh (60 mph) to escape predators. Hunting once drove the pronghorn to near-extinction, but protected herds survive today in and around parks and reserves.

Males have hooked horns.

Sharp claws catch snakes, rodents, and insects.

Lubber grasshopper
These large, robust grasshoppers are found mainly in the western prairies. Lubber grasshoppers live among grasses and other prairie plants and eat their leaves. They are active in the summer and early fall.

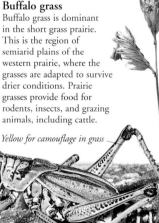

FIND OUT MORE CROCODILES • DEER AND ANTELOPE • GRASSES, RUSHES AND SEDGES • GRASSHOPPERS AND CRICKETS • LIONS AND OTHER WILDCATS • OWLS AND NIGHTJARS • RATS AND OTHER RODENTS • TREES

NORWAY

A LONG, NARROW COUNTRY forming the western part of the Scandinavian peninsula, Norway shares its eastern borders with Sweden, Finland, and Russia. Its north coast is washed by the icy Arctic Ocean, and to the west are the Norwegian and North seas, rich with fish, oil, and natural gas. The small population enjoys equal rights and high living standards. The education system is well developed, and unemployment is consistently low.

N

Physical features

Norway has high, rugged mountains and steep river valleys. Its 13,600-mile (21,900-km) coastline is one of the world's longest, and is noted for its fjords (narrow sea inlets), and about 150,000 rocky islands. The fast-flowing rivers have spectacular waterfalls.

Jostedal Glacier
The largest ice field in western Europe, the Jostedal Glacier in southern Norway covers 188 sq miles (487 sq km). Snow covers the ground three months every year, but in spring it melts into the Utigard waterfall, the third highest in the world at 2,625 ft (800 m).

Fjords
During the Ice Age, glaciers carved steep-sided valleys in the rocks along Norway's west coast. As the ice melted, the North Sea flowed in, creating spectacular fjords. The longest fjord in the country, Sognefjorden can carry large ships more than 124 miles (200 km) inland.

People
Ninety-five percent of the people are ethnic Norwegians. Their ancestors invented skiing for cross-country travel, and now it is the national sport. About 75 percent of Norwegians live in towns. In the Arctic north, the Sami, or Lapps, herd reindeer and have their own language and culture.

38 per sq mile (15 per sq km)

Climate
The warm waters of the Gulf Stream keep Norway's climate mild, and most harbors remain ice-free, even on the Arctic Sea coast. Far north in Norway's more extreme Land of the Midnight Sun, the sun shines all night at midsummer, but hardly rises at all in the depths of winter.

94°F (34°C) -15°F (-26°C)
63°F (17°C) 24°F (-5°C)
29 in (740 mm)

Taking a ski lift

75% Urban   25% Rural

Land use
Only nine percent of Norway's land can be farmed, so livestock farmers combine it with forestry. Like its neighbor Finland, the nation uses its rivers for hydroelectricity.

Built-up 1%   Forest 47.5%
Barren 24.5%
Farmland 9%   Tundra 18%

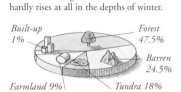

Industry
Norway still depends largely on its abundance of natural resources. North Sea oil and gas are exported globally, and 99 percent of its own electricity needs are met by hydroelectricity. Despite being the world's largest salmon supplier, Norway has to import much of its food. Shipbuilding is important and there is a large merchant fleet.

Oil rig, Stavanger

Oslo
A busy seaport and industrial center, Oslo is Norway's largest city, as well as its capital. It was founded at the head of a fjord in 1050 and blends historic buildings with towering modern blocks. Over 500,000 people live in the suburbs, surrounded by forests and lakes.

Aker Port and City Hall

FIND OUT MORE | COASTS | DAMS | ENERGY | EUROPE, HISTORY OF | FISHING INDUSTRY | GLACIATION | MOUNTAINS AND VALLEYS | OIL | SCANDINAVIA, HISTORY OF | WINTER SPORTS

NUCLEAR POWER

N

AT THE CENTER OF EVERY ATOM is a tiny powerhouse called a nucleus. Strong forces hold particles called protons and neutrons together inside the nucleus. In nuclear reactions, atomic nuclei split apart (fission) or join together (fusion), rearranging the forces between the particles and releasing huge amounts of energy called nuclear power. A nuclear power station harnesses the energy from controlled nuclear reactions in a reactor to generate electricity.

Pumps circulate coolant around the core.

Fission reactor

The heart of a fission reactor is a tough steel container called a core. A continuous series of nuclear fission reactions, called a chain reaction, occur inside the core and produce intense heat. A circulating fluid called a coolant takes heat from the core to steam generators that use the heat to convert water into jets of high-pressure steam. The steam jets drive turbine engines linked to electricity generators.

Pipes carry high-pressure steam to turbines outside the reactor.

Steam generators boil water into steam.

Two walls of reinforced concrete stop radioactive material from escaping.

The core contains about 4,000 rods of uranium fuel.

Fusion reaction

The joining together of two atomic nuclei is called nuclear fusion. Only light elements – those with few protons and neutrons in their nuclei – can take part in nuclear fusion reactions. At very high temperatures, two hydrogen nuclei smash together and form a heavier helium nucleus, releasing energy and expelling a neutron. Fusion reactions occur in the Sun and other stars.

Nucleus of hydrogen-2

Nucleus of hydrogen-3

Nucleus of helium-4 forms.

Neutron is expelled.

Fission reaction

When the nucleus of an atom splits apart it is called nuclear fission. Some heavy elements have unstable nuclei that can be made to split by bombarding them with neutrons. As the nuclei split, they release energy and more neutrons, which may strike other nuclei and start a chain reaction.

The nucleus becomes unstable when struck by the neutron.

The nucleus splits, releasing energy and neutrons.

Neutron

Uranium-235 nucleus

Two lighter nuclei form.

Nuclear fuel rods

Most fuel rods consist of pellets or bars of the isotope uranium-235 held in an alloy casing. Uranium-235 has 235 protons and neutrons in the nuclei of its atoms.

Fuel pellet

Fuel rods

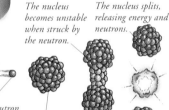

Fast breeder

A reactor that makes, or "breeds," fuel for itself is called a fast breeder. During the chain reaction, some of the uranium changes into plutonium, which can also be used as a nuclear fuel.

Fusion reactor

Scientists have not yet made a practical fusion reactor. This ring-shaped experimental reactor is called a torus. It heats hydrogen gas to millions of degrees so that atomic nuclei can fuse together.

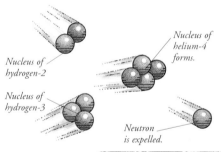

Experimental fusion reactor

Nuclear hazards

The waste from nuclear fuel is dangerously radioactive, so it must be dumped at sea or buried safely underground. Nuclear weapons tests and accidents at reactors can cause long-term health hazards by releasing radioactive material into the air.

Radioactive waste container

Nuclear weapons test

Enrico Fermi

The Italian-born nuclear physicist Enrico Fermi (1901–1954) left Italy in 1938 to live and work in the US. In 1942, he built the first nuclear reactor in an empty squash court at the University of Chicago. Using this reactor, Fermi achieved the first nuclear fission chain reaction.

Timeline

1911 Ernest Rutherford, a New Zealand-born physicist, proposes that each atom contains a small, dense core called a nucleus.

1938 German chemist Otto Hahn and Austrian physicist Lise Meitner discover nuclear fission.

1939 German-born physicist Hans Bethe discovers that nuclear fusion powers the Sun.

1942 In Chicago, Enrico Fermi achieves the first chain reaction.

1945 Nuclear bombs destroy the Japanese cities of Hiroshima and Nagasaki.

1954 Russia's Obninsk reactor is the first to generate electricity.

1986 An explosion at the reactor in Chernobyl, Russia, releases clouds of radioactive material.

1991 In England, the JET (Joint European Torus) project achieves the first controlled fusion reaction.

FIND OUT MORE

ATOMS AND MOLECULES · EINSTEIN, ALBERT · ENERGY · MATTER · MEITNER, LISE · RADIOACTIVITY

NUMBERS

"FIVE, FOUR, THREE, two, one ... liftoff!" is the countdown we hear before a rocket launch. It is natural for people to count, and we use numbers to do so. The simplest way to represent a number is as a series of marks, or tallies, with each tally representing one item. However, it is difficult to write down or read a very large number if it is represented as a collection of tallies. Our own number system, which represents numbers using the digits 0 to 9, enables us to write, read, and manipulate large numbers easily. Arithmetic is the use of numbers in calculations.

Turnstiles in the Paris Metro

Counting

Using numbers to find out how many items there are in a certain place is called counting. The turnstiles at a subway station, for example, count the passengers using the trains. The numbers we use to count (1, 2, 3, 4, and so on) are called counting, or natural, numbers.

Types of numbers

We usually use whole numbers to count items such as cakes. However, if only a part of a cake is present, we must use a part of a whole number, called a fraction, to count it. Other types of numbers prove equally useful in different situations.

Fractions are amounts expressed as one number divided by another. The fraction $3/4$, for example, is equal to 3 divided by 4 (three-quarters).

Powers show how many times a number is multiplied by itself. For example, 10 multiplied by itself 3 times is 10 to the power of 3, or 10^3.

Logarithms (logs) show the power to which a number must be raised to obtain another number. For example, the log of raising 10 to 1,000 is 3, because 10 x 10 x 10 = 1,000.

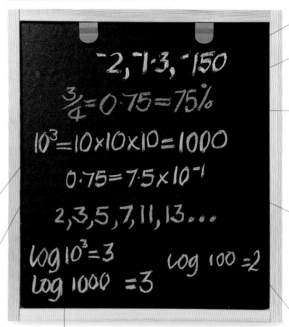

Negative numbers are less than zero.

Percentages are fractions of 100, so 75 percent (%) is the same as $75/100$.

Decimal numbers show values less than whole numbers as digits to the right of a decimal point: 0.75, for example, is seven-tenths-and-five-hundredths.

Scientific notation is a way of writing very large or small numbers using powers of 10. In scientific notation, 0.75 is written as 7.5×10^{-1}.

Prime numbers are whole numbers that can be divided evenly only by 1 and by themselves.

Blackboard showing different types of numbers

Number systems

In a place-value number system, the value of a digit in a written number depends on its position. In the number 22, the 2 on the left is worth ten times more than the 2 on the right. We use a system based on the number 10, but any number can be used as the base for a place-value system. The ancient Babylonians, for example, used a system based on the number 60.

The tablet records figures for crop yields.
Babylonian clay tablet, 2900 BC

1 x 8   1 x 4   0 x 2   1 x 1
These lightbulbs represent the binary number we know as 13. In binary form, the number 13 becomes 1101 (8 + 4 + 0 + 1).

Binary system
The binary system is a place-value number system based on the number 2. The positions of the digits in a binary number represent, from right to left, 1s, 2s, 4s, 8s, 16s, and so on. All binary numbers are made up of the digits 0 and 1.

Denary system
The denary (base 10) system, or decimal system, became common because we first learn to count using our ten fingers and thumbs. Digits in denary numbers represent, from right to left, 1s, 10s, 100s, 1,000s, and so on. A car's odometer records the distance a car travels using a denary counter.

Car odometer

Each wheel turns 10 times faster than the wheel to its left.

Both sides of the equation have the value 6.
Equals sign separates the two quantities.
Equations always balance

Arithemetic symbols
The symbols + (add/plus), - (subtract/minus), x (multiply), and ÷ (divide) represent the four main ways in which numbers can be used in calculations. These symbols are used in equations. For example, the equation 2 + 3 = 15 ÷ 3 is read as: "Two plus three equals fifteen divided by three".

Add (or plus) means to find the sum of two numbers.
Multiply means to make something a number of times larger.
Subtract means to take one number away from another.
Divide means to find out how many times one number goes into another.

Equations

An equation is two groups of symbols and numbers separated by an equals sign (=). The numbers and symbols on either side of the sign must be equal in value, just as the weights in the pans of a balance must be equal for the pans to balance. This means that if you add a number to one side of an equation, you must add the same number to the other side.

John Napier

John Napier (1550-1617), a Scottish mathematician, made many important discoveries about numbers. Napier is most famous for inventing logarithms, which make complex calculations much simpler. Many mathematicians and scientists have used logarithms to solve problems and to devise new theories.

FIND OUT MORE   COMPUTERS   INFORMATION TECHNOLOGY   MATHEMATICS   SCIENCE   WEIGHTS AND MEASURES

OCEAN FLOOR

FAR BENEATH the waves are the mountains, canyons, plains, and valleys that make up the ocean floor. This underwater landscape, which is home to as fantastic a diversity of wild creatures as any continent, covers more than 60 percent of the Earth's surface. New features are continually being added to the ocean floor as molten rock wells up from the Earth's hot interior through gaps in the Earth's crust. Once formed, these features change very little, because they soon become covered by protective layers made of the remains of dead sea creatures that sink to the ocean bottom.

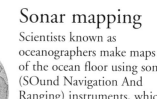

The world's ocean floor — Pacific Ocean, Arctic Ocean, Indian Ocean, Atlantic Ocean, Southern Ocean

Sonar mapping

Scientists known as oceanographers make maps of the ocean floor using sonar (SOund Navigation And Ranging) instruments, which send out pulses of sound that bounce off the seabed and return as echoes. The echoes are used to produce a picture of the ocean floor.

Ocean floor survey

A survey of the ocean floor uses sonar instruments to reveal the general landscape of the seabed. To see certain features in more detail, oceanographers send down camera sleds carrying video and still cameras and powerful lights to pierce the darkness.

Sonar image of mud flows on seabed

Submarine landscape

The ocean floor is really the entire seabed below the low-tide mark, but when people refer to the ocean floor, they usually mean the ocean-basin floor. This is the part of the seabed that lies beyond the continental shelf. Most of the ocean-basin floor is more than 6,500 ft (2,000 m) under the water. It is largely flat, but dotted with huge mountains called seamounts.

Continental shelf is the gently sloping area between the edge of a continent and the deep ocean.

Features of the ocean floor

Submarine canyon

Course of mud river

Continental rise

Guyot (flat-topped seamount)

Seamount

Midocean ridge (gap in ocean floor)

Deep ocean trench, formed where one section of the seabed dips beneath another

Continental crust

Volcanic rock

Abyssal plain – the smooth seabed covered with a thick slime called ooze, largely the remains of sea creatures

Rising magma (molten rock)

Oceanic crust

Hydrothermal vents

Down on the ocean floor are strange, chimney-like structures that gush dark clouds of sulfur-rich hot water from the Earth's interior. These structures are called hydrothermal vents, or "black smokers." The warm water around these vents provides a home for huge quantities of marine life.

Poisonous jets of sulfurous water

Smoker chimneys fused into an arch

Mound of solidified minerals

Mussels and clams up to 1 ft (30 cm) long

Tubeworm tentacles up to 10 ft (3 m) long

Goods from the ocean floor

The seabed is rich in valuable materials, and many people are trying to find ways to extract them. Already 20 percent of the world's oil comes from beneath the seabed, extracted by oil rigs floating on the surface. The rocks of the ocean floor also contain important deposits of diamonds, tin, gold, and billions of tons of manganese nodules (rocky lumps rich in metals). Even the mud on the ocean floor contains silver, copper, and zinc.

Unpolished diamond crystals

Oil

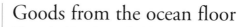

Marie Tharp

American oceanographer Marie Tharp (b.1920) collated the results of a large number of surveys to build up a complete picture of the world's ocean floor. Her painstaking work revealed the existence of long chains of undersea mountains, now known as midocean ridges.

FIND OUT MORE   CONTINENTS   EARTH   OCEANS AND SEAS   RADAR AND SONAR   ROCKS AND MINERALS   VOLCANOES

O

OCEANS AND SEAS

FROM SPACE, PLANET EARTH appears blue because the majority of its surface is covered by oceans and seas. There are five great oceans: the Pacific, Atlantic, and Indian Oceans, which all merge into the Southern Ocean around Antarctica, and the Arctic Ocean. Seas, such as the Mediterranean, Baltic, and Red Seas, are smaller expanses of water, often surrounded by land and connected to the oceans by narrow straits. The waters of the seas and oceans are constantly on the move, driven by the wind and the tides, and by powerful currents coursing through the ocean depths.

Ocean depths

The deepest places on Earth are ocean trenches, where the ocean floor plunges so steeply that the waters above could easily swallow Mount Everest. The first vessel to explore the deep ocean was a cast-iron sphere built in the 1930s by the American Otis Barton. The Frenchman Jacques Cousteau made great advances in the 1960s with his "diving saucer" submersibles.

Oceans and ocean currents

All the world's great oceans are interlinked, forming a continuous expanse of water. Prevailing winds disturb this water and cause surface currents – large flows of water that travel thousands of miles. At a deeper level, differences in the water's temperature and salinity cause vast deep-water currents to circulate.

Seawater

Sea "water" is only 96.5 percent water; most of the rest is dissolved mineral salts. The salt content, or salinity, of oceans and seas is highest in shallow tropical waters, where water quickly evaporates, and lowest in polar regions, where melting ice dilutes the concentration of salts.

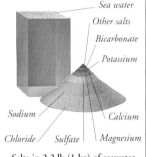
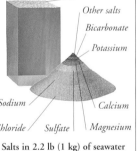

- Sea water
- Other salts
- Bicarbonate
- Potassium
- Sodium
- Calcium
- Chloride
- Sulfate
- Magnesium

Salts in 2.2 lb (1 kg) of seawater

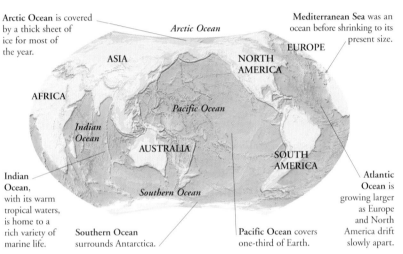

Arctic Ocean is covered by a thick sheet of ice for most of the year.

Arctic Ocean

ASIA

AFRICA

Pacific Ocean

Indian Ocean

AUSTRALIA

Indian Ocean, with its warm tropical waters, is home to a rich variety of marine life.

Southern Ocean

Southern Ocean surrounds Antarctica.

Mediterranean Sea was an ocean before shrinking to its present size.

EUROPE

NORTH AMERICA

SOUTH AMERICA

Pacific Ocean covers one-third of Earth.

Atlantic Ocean is growing larger as Europe and North America drift slowly apart.

Ocean zones

Scientists divide the waters of the oceans into different zones, according to their depth beneath the surface. The relatively light, warm sublittoral zone is where most fish live. Few creatures live in the bleak abyssal zone above the deep ocean floor because it is always icy cold and pitch black, and the water pressure is intense.

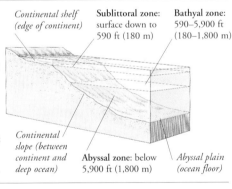

Continental shelf (edge of continent)

Sublittoral zone: surface down to 590 ft (180 m)

Bathyal zone: 590–5,900 ft (180–1,800 m)

Continental slope (between continent and deep ocean)

Abyssal zone: below 5,900 ft (1,800 m)

Abyssal plain (ocean floor)

Tides

The sea rises and floods onto the shore twice each day, and then ebbs away again. These daily changes in sea-level are called high and low tides. The strong gravitational pull among the Earth, Moon, and Sun stretches the Earth into an oval, making the oceans bulge up on either side. As the Earth rotates, these bulges move across the globe, causing tides.

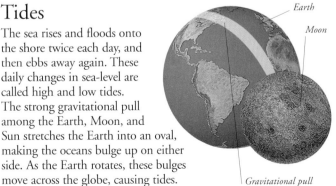

Earth

Moon

Gravitational pull

Tidal range

The difference between the water's height at high and low tide is called the tidal range. This is usually between 7–10 ft (2–3 m) at places on the open coast. In some river mouths and bays, the tidal range may be as great as 56 ft (17 m).

River mouth at high and low tide

FIND OUT MORE · CONTINENTS · EARTH SCIENCES · ENERGY · ISLANDS · MOON · OCEAN FLOOR · OCEAN LIFE · STORMS · WINDS

Deep-sea diving landmarks

JIM diving suit Mark II

Barton's bathysphere: 3,000 ft (915 m)

Cousteau diving saucer: 3,000 ft (915 m)

Deep Submergence Rescue Vehicle: 5,000 ft (1,520 m)

Barton benthoscope: 4,500 ft (1,370 m)

Cousteau diving saucer Cyanea: 11,000 ft (3,350 m)

Argo ROV (remote-operated vehicle) with *Jason*, a small robot equipped with TV cameras and lights

Alvin submarine: 12,500 ft (3,810 m)

Nautile submersible (France): 19,690 ft (6,000 m)

Mir submersible (Russia): 19,690 ft (6,000 m)

Shinkai submersible (Japan): 21,300 ft (6,500 m)

The US Navy's bathyscape Trieste *holds the world record for the deepest dive: in 1960 it reached a depth of 35,797 ft (10,911 m).*

At the bottom of the deepest oceans, the pressure can be equal to more than 140,000 lb pressing on each square inch (10,000 kg per square centimetre).

Mariana Trench 36,161 ft (11,022 m) in the Pacific Ocean, is the world's deepest place.

OCEAN WILDLIFE

THE OCEAN COVERS two-thirds of the Earth's surface. This vast body of water is home to a great variety of plants and animals. On the ocean floor, there are underwater mountain ranges, plains covered with clays and mudlike oozes, deep trenches, and submerged mountains called sea mounts. Animals live in all of these regions and in all depths of the ocean. Generally, food is scarce in the deep sea because there is no light for photosynthesis, which enables plant growth. Plants are restricted to the sunlit waters near the surface, where they either drift in the sea or float, anchored to the seabed. Ocean wildlife is at its richest in the warm, shallow waters of coral reefs.

Oceans

The ocean can be divided into zones. The surface, exposed to the sun and the waves, is a hard place to live. The sunlit waters just below the surface are where life is most abundant. Below that, light begins to fade until, by 3,280 ft (1,000 m), there is no light at all.

A rich variety of marine animals live on coral reefs, from giant clams to brightly colored fish.

Reptiles, such as turtles, have to come to the surface to breathe air.

Most ocean animals, such as fish, breathe by absorbing oxygen from the water.

Plants

The largest plants in the oceans are the seaweeds and sea grasses. The most abundant ocean plantlife are the microscopic organisms, such as diatoms, that drift in the sea. These are called phytoplankton. Phytoplankton get their food through photosynthesis and form the basis of the ocean food chain.

Sargassum weed
This seaweed is not anchored to the seabed. It floats free in tangled mats in the calm waters of the Sargasso Sea in the northwestern Atlantic. Animals like this sargassum crab live among the seaweed.

Sea grasses
Sea grasses grow in shallow coastal waters. They are among only a few flowering plants that live in seawater. They have proper roots that absorb nutrients and help anchor them to the seabed.

Plankton
Tiny animals that drift in the sea are known as zooplankton. These animals feed on the phytoplankton. Some of the animals spend all their lives as plankton; others are the young stages of animals such as crabs.

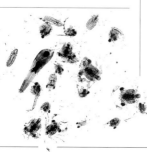

Mammals

Several groups of mammals have colonized the ocean. The most well-adapted to ocean life are the whales and dolphins, which have lost their hind limbs and use their tails to swim instead. Whales and dolphins give birth at sea, unlike seals and walruses, which breed on shore.

Nostrils on the upper part of the snout

Whiskers are sensitive to touch and vibrations in the water.

Large eyes adjust to seeing both in air and water.

Skin gets red when the walrus is hot.

Sea lions
These superb swimmers use mainly their front flippers to "row" through the water. They can also walk on land. Male sea lions are much larger than females. In the breeding season, males have a territory where they keep guard over a group of females.

Walrus
Walruses live in the icy waters of the far north, where they feed mostly on shellfish on the seabed. They haul out on ice floes and along the coast. Walruses have thick blubber to keep them warm. Both males and females have tusks.

Humpback whale
Humpbacks often break through the surface of the water, called breaching. This may be a signal to other humpbacks, and perhaps a method of stunning shoals of fish. It may also dislodge irritating skin parasites.

Sperm whale
The deepest diver of all mammals, the sperm whale can go down even deeper than 3,280 ft (1,000 m). In its head is the spermaceti organ – a huge mass of oily, waxy tissues – that may help to regulate the whale's buoyancy.

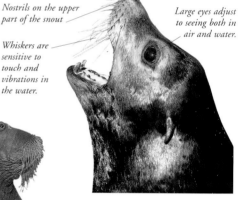

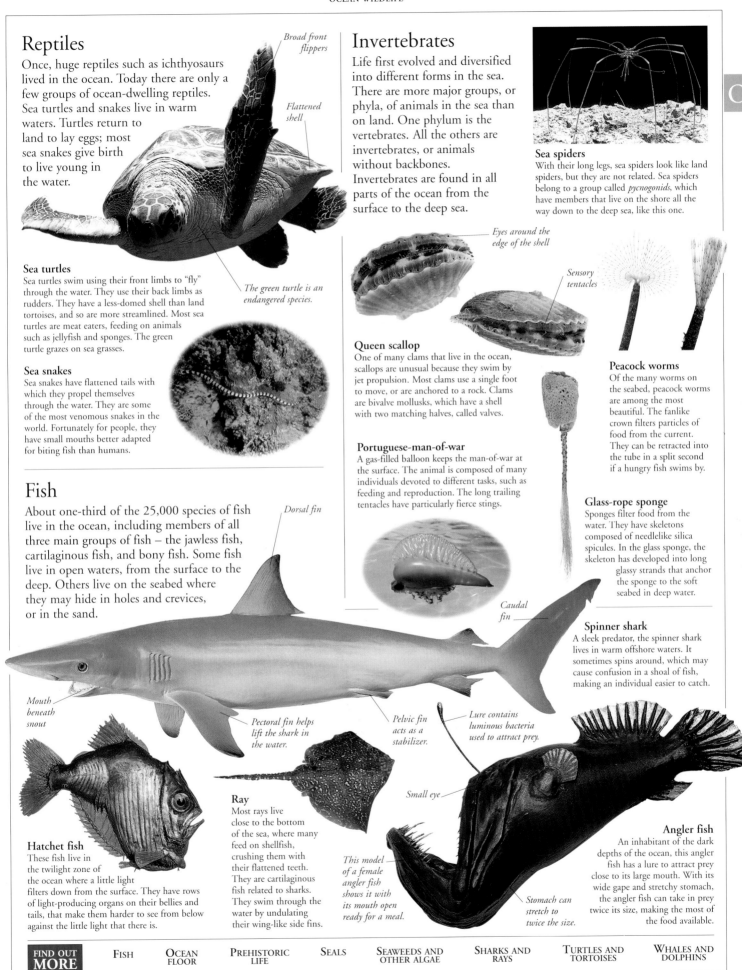

Reptiles

Once, huge reptiles such as ichthyosaurs lived in the ocean. Today there are only a few groups of ocean-dwelling reptiles. Sea turtles and snakes live in warm waters. Turtles return to land to lay eggs; most sea snakes give birth to live young in the water.

Broad front flippers

Flattened shell

The green turtle is an endangered species.

Sea turtles

Sea turtles swim using their front limbs to "fly" through the water. They use their back limbs as rudders. They have a less-domed shell than land tortoises, and so are more streamlined. Most sea turtles are meat eaters, feeding on animals such as jellyfish and sponges. The green turtle grazes on sea grasses.

Sea snakes

Sea snakes have flattened tails with which they propel themselves through the water. They are some of the most venomous snakes in the world. Fortunately for people, they have small mouths better adapted for biting fish than humans.

Fish

About one-third of the 25,000 species of fish live in the ocean, including members of all three main groups of fish – the jawless fish, cartilaginous fish, and bony fish. Some fish live in open waters, from the surface to the deep. Others live on the seabed where they may hide in holes and crevices, or in the sand.

Dorsal fin

Mouth beneath snout

Pectoral fin helps lift the shark in the water.

Pelvic fin acts as a stabilizer.

Caudal fin

Hatchet fish

These fish live in the twilight zone of the ocean where a little light filters down from the surface. They have rows of light-producing organs on their bellies and tails, that make them harder to see from below against the little light that there is.

Ray

Most rays live close to the bottom of the sea, where many feed on shellfish, crushing them with their flattened teeth. They are cartilaginous fish related to sharks. They swim through the water by undulating their wing-like side fins.

This model of a female angler fish shows it with its mouth open ready for a meal.

Small eye

Lure contains luminous bacteria used to attract prey.

Stomach can stretch to twice the size.

Invertebrates

Life first evolved and diversified into different forms in the sea. There are more major groups, or phyla, of animals in the sea than on land. One phylum is the vertebrates. All the others are invertebrates, or animals without backbones. Invertebrates are found in all parts of the ocean from the surface to the deep sea.

Sea spiders

With their long legs, sea spiders look like land spiders, but they are not related. Sea spiders belong to a group called *pycnogonids*, which have members that live on the shore all the way down to the deep sea, like this one.

Eyes around the edge of the shell

Sensory tentacles

Queen scallop

One of many clams that live in the ocean, scallops are unusual because they swim by jet propulsion. Most clams use a single foot to move, or are anchored to a rock. Clams are bivalve mollusks, which have a shell with two matching halves, called valves.

Portuguese-man-of-war

A gas-filled balloon keeps the man-of-war at the surface. The animal is composed of many individuals devoted to different tasks, such as feeding and reproduction. The long trailing tentacles have particularly fierce stings.

Peacock worms

Of the many worms on the seabed, peacock worms are among the most beautiful. The fanlike crown filters particles of food from the current. They can be retracted into the tube in a split second if a hungry fish swims by.

Glass-rope sponge

Sponges filter food from the water. They have skeletons composed of needlelike silica spicules. In the glass sponge, the skeleton has developed into long glassy strands that anchor the sponge to the soft seabed in deep water.

Spinner shark

A sleek predator, the spinner shark lives in warm offshore waters. It sometimes spins around, which may cause confusion in a shoal of fish, making an individual easier to catch.

Angler fish

An inhabitant of the dark depths of the ocean, this angler fish has a lure to attract prey close to its large mouth. With its wide gape and stretchy stomach, the angler fish can take in prey twice its size, making the most of the food available.

| FIND OUT MORE | FISH | OCEAN FLOOR | PREHISTORIC LIFE | SEALS | SEAWEEDS AND OTHER ALGAE | SHARKS AND RAYS | TURTLES AND TORTOISES | WHALES AND DOLPHINS |

OCTOPUSES AND SQUID

Streamlined, torpedo-shaped body

TOGETHER WITH cuttlefish and nautiluses, octopuses and squid belong to a group of mollusks called cephalopods. They live in the sea, floating or moving through the water by jet propulsion, or crawling along the seabed. Cephalopods have a well-developed nervous system and brain. Many can change color rapidly for camouflage, to confuse predators, or to attract a mate.

Cephalopod features

Cephalopods means "head-footed ones": all have a head surrounded by tentacles. The eyes are prominent and often complex. Cephalopods breathe through gills. They have beak-like jaws and a ribbonlike, toothed tongue called a radula.

Squids

In addition to eight arms, squid have two retractile tentacles. These have suckers, often with horny rings for gripping prey. Squid have a horny shell inside the body, called a pen. They have two side fins, which they use as stabilizers.

Tentacles are equivalent to the foot of other mollusks

Baglike body can be reduced in size to squeeze through small spaces

Complex eye resembling a human eye

Suckers can both taste and feel

Arms can be regenerated if torn off

Octopuses

The most familiar octopuses live in shallow water among rocks and coral reefs, but there are also deep sea kinds. Octopuses have a baglike body with eight arms that they use to crawl along the seabed and to hold prey.

Live nautilus

Movement

Octopuses use their arms to crawl. To make a quick escape, they squirt water through a funnel and jet off with their arms trailing behind. Squid use jet propulsion to dart back and forth. Over short distances, squid are among the fastest sea creatures, reaching up to 20 mph (32 km/h).

Defense

The soft-bodied cepahalopods are vulnerable to attack. Many octopuses hide away in holes during the day, coming out only at night to find food. Squid often rise to the surface water at night, when there is less chance of being attacked by daytime predators, such as seabirds.

Decoys

Squirting ink out of its funnel, this cuttlefish may confuse an attacker. Cuttlefish, squid, and octopuses all produce ink from sacs inside their body. Some deep sea squids produce luminous ink.

Color change

Like octopuses, cuttlefish can turn lighter or darker to match the background by contracting or expanding bags of pigment in their skin. Some cephalopods turn vivid colors when irritated or when threatening an attacker.

Cuttlefish becomes lighter

Bites

Cephalopods use their beak-like jaws to bite their prey and to defend themselves. After taking a bite, some inject toxic saliva to subdue their prey. The saliva of the blue-ringed octopus can be strong enough to kill a person.

Cross-section of nautilus shell

Buoyancy control

As a chambered nautilus grows, it adds a chamber to its shell. The new chamber is filled with fluid that is gradually absorbed and replaced by gas. The chambers keep the nautilus centrally buoyant so it does not have to expend energy swimming to stop itself from sinking.

Cuttlefish spend much of the time resting

Hovering

By undulating their side fins, cuttlefish hover in midwater. They have a shell called a cuttlebone inside their body that helps regulate their buoyancy.

Jet propulsion

All cephalopods can move by jet propulsion. Squid usually jet off backward. They take water into the body cavity and expel it through a funnel near their head. They move the position of the funnel to change direction.

COMMON OCTOPUS

SCIENTIFIC NAME	*Octopus vulgaris*
ORDER	Octopoda
FAMILY	Octopodidae
DISTRIBUTION	Atlantic Ocean, Mediterranean and Caribbean seas
HABITAT	Rocky seabed in coastal waters
DIET	Shellfish, such as crabs, and fish
SIZE	Arm span on average between 23–35 in (60–90 cm) long
LIFESPAN	Males up to 15 years

FIND OUT MORE

ANIMAL BEHAVIOR   CAMOUFLAGE   SNAILS AND OTHER MOLLUSKS

OIL

DEEP DOWN IN THE EARTH, trapped by layers of rock, lie pools of the thick, black liquid called oil. It is a fossil fuel, produced from decayed animal and plant life that lived in the seas millions of years ago. Properly termed petroleum, oil has become a vital commodity in the world. Once refined, it is the source of gasoline, kerosene, and diesel fuels. It also yields petrochemicals that are used to make a variety of products, including perfumes and plastics. Close to oil reserves there are often deposits of natural gas that are also produced by the bacterial breakdown of ancient marine life.

Oil reservoirs
Most oil is found underground, but some seeps to the surface, sometimes creating huge lakes. Examples are Guanoco Lake in Venezuela and Pitch Lake in Trinidad. The liquid in these lakes is thick because light substances in the oil have evaporated.

An oil reservoir

Oil exploration

Oil prospectors search for areas that may contain oil and take measurements with instruments such as gravity meters and magnetometers (to measure local magnetism). They carry out seismic surveys that reveal the underground rock structure. If they locate possible rock formations with deposits of oil, they then drill an exploratory well.

Seismic surveying
Oil geologists often search for oil reserves by carrying out a seismic survey. This involves sending shock waves into the ground and recording their echoes which may locate likely reserves. Some geologists also use remote-sensing satellites that can spot details of rock formations in the ground.

Geologists conduct a seismic survey on a glacier in Spitsbergen, Norway.

Drilling

Oil is extracted through boreholes drilled into the ground. Drilling takes place from a rig, notable for its tall tower called a derrick. Beneath the derrick, a rotary table turns the drill pipes, which are added one by one as the hole deepens. A toothed drill bit at the end of the bottom pipe cuts through the rock as it rotates.

Oil production well

Land wells
When oil is struck, the original borehole must be developed into a working well. If the oil flows naturally to the surface under pressure, the borehole steel casing is capped and fitted with valves. If not, pumps are installed to force the oil to the surface.

Sea wells
When oil is struck offshore, the borehole is temporarily capped and the production rig moves in. A production platform is installed from which more boreholes are drilled close to the original strike. Finally machinery is fitted, ready to extract oil from the seabed.

Transporting oil

Two main methods are used to transport oil from the oil fields to the refineries. Oil is usually carried across land by means of a pipeline – for example the US has about 200,000 miles (300,000 km) of oil pipelines. Tankers are used to carry oil cargoes across the oceans.

Tankers
Tankers are among the biggest ships afloat; they may carry more than 500,000 tons of oil. For safety, the crude oil cargo is carried in a series of separate tanks to prevent it surging, which would otherwise capsize the ship.

Pollution
Oil can cause damage to the environment. Oil pipelines may burst and pollute the land, and tankers may collide with other vessels or run aground, spilling their cargo into the sea. Beaches become dirty, and wildlife is threatened.

Burning oil releases poisonous fumes

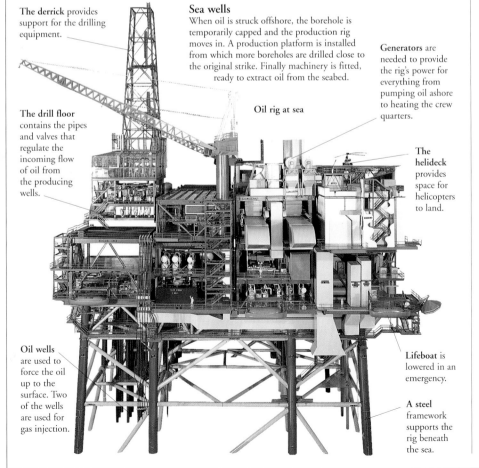

The derrick provides support for the drilling equipment.

The drill floor contains the pipes and valves that regulate the incoming flow of oil from the producing wells.

Sea wells

Oil rig at sea

Generators are needed to provide the rig's power for everything from pumping oil ashore to heating the crew quarters.

The helideck provides space for helicopters to land.

Oil wells are used to force the oil up to the surface. Two of the wells are used for gas injection.

Lifeboat is lowered in an emergency.

A steel framework supports the rig beneath the sea.

Refining

Crude oil is a complex mixture of hydrocarbons and in this form is of limited use. However, oil is easily processed, or refined, into a host of useful products. The major process in an oil refinery is distillation, which splits up the oil into different sets, called fractions, of hydrocarbons.

Oil refinery at Antwerp, Belgium

Cracking

After distillation, cracking is the most important refining process. This chemical reaction breaks down heavy oil fractions into lighter compounds that make useful products such as gasoline. Another product of cracking is ethene, the basis of many plastics and solvents.

Vacuum unit at a catalytic cracking plant

Oil products

The initial distillation process in an oil refinery produces the most familiar oil products, such as kerosene and diesel oil. Cracking and polymerization (building up light fractions) yield a variety of chemicals called petrochemicals. These have become the lifeblood of the chemical industry and are the main compounds used for making products such as as plastics and ethanol.

Collection of perfumes

Ethanol

This is the intoxicating substance found in alcoholic drinks such as beer, wines, and spirits. In industry ethanol is used as a solvent, or dissolving substance, in the manufacture of products such as paints, perfumes, and dyes.

Ski boots   Raincoat

Personal stereo

Plastics

Plastics are used throughout the modern world. They are used in a variety of products from clothing to household items. Three of the most important are polyethylene, polyvinyl chloride (both derived from ethene), and nylon.

Kerosene

Kerosene is an oil fraction that contains heavier hydrocarbons than gasoline does. It has a higher boiling point and vaporizes less easily. It is used as fuel for jet engines. In the home, kerosene is used in portable heaters and was once used in oil lamps. In industry, it is a valuable solvent for paints.

Kerosene lamp

Gasoline

Of all oil products, gas is the most valuable because it powers most car engines. Gas is a mixture of light hydrocarbons that turn easily to vapor. It contains additives that make it burn evenly, including, in leaded gas, lead tetraethyl. Gasoline is also used for making some plastics.

Gasoline pump

Oil nations

Oil deposits are not distributed evenly around the world. The largest deposits are found in the Middle East, the United States, and the countries of the former Soviet Union. Saudi Arabia is the biggest oil producer, with an output of about 8 million barrels a day, about a fifth of the world total.

United States   *Middle East*

South America   *North Africa*

• Principal oil reserves   • Other oil reserves

OPEC

Twelve oil nations from the Middle East, South America, and Africa belong to the Organization of Petroleum Exporting Countries (OPEC). It was set up in 1960 to safeguard members' interests against what they saw as exploitation by western countries.

Natural gas

Natural gas formed millions of years ago beneath the sea. It is called natural gas to distinguish it from manufactured gases such as coal gas. Like oil, natural gas is a mixture of hydrocarbons. It contains methane, butane, propane, and ethane. Major gas producing countries include Russia, the United States, Canada, and Indonesia.

Gas distribution works, Buenos Aires, Argentina

Liquid gas

The butane and propane found in natural gas can be liquified easily under pressure. In this form it is sold as bottled gas, such as that found in camping stoves and cigarette lighters. Natural gas is often liquified by refrigeration in order to transport it in tankers. In this form the gas takes up less space.

Camping stove fueled by liquid gas

Gas impurities

Traces of other gases are found in natural gas as well as hydrocarbons. These include carbon dioxide, sulfur compounds, and helium. These gases may be present in sufficient quantities for industrial use. For example, sulfur can be used to make sulfuric acid, while helium is used to fill balloons and airships.

Balloons filled with helium gas

FIND OUT MORE   AIRSHIPS AND BALLOONS   COAL   CARS AND TRUCKS   CHEMISTRY   GASES   GEOLOGY   GULF STATES   PLASTICS AND RUBBER   ROCKS AND MINERALS   SOVIET UNION

OLMECS

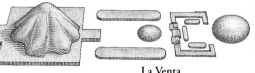

AROUND 1300 BC, in the swampy lowlands of the Gulf of Mexico, one people began to stand out from the rest: the Olmecs. Because they lived mainly from farming, not hunting, they started to live a settled lifestyle. They built towns and created a new kind of civilization. In their major towns, they built ceremonial centers with public buildings, temples, and massive stone sculptures of their rulers. Because of these achievements, Olmec culture is considered one of the first great civilizations of America. They worshipped a jaguar god, and so were known as the "People of the Jaguar."

Olmec centers

The Olmec ceremonial centers were sacred places, with pyramid temples, vast stone heads, and decorated monuments. The biggest ceremonial centers included those at San Lorenzo and La Venta.

Stone relief showing Olmec ruler

Mexico
San Lorenzo • • La Venta

Olmec empire

La Venta

This was the largest Olmec center, in the modern Mexican state of Veracruz. It was built on a small island in coastal mangrove swamps. At its heart were pyramids, altars, long circular mounds, rows of stone columns, and tombs.

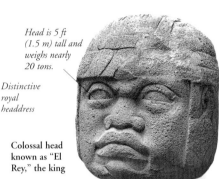

Head is 5 ft (1.5 m) tall and weighs nearly 20 tons.

Distinctive royal headdress

Colossal head known as "El Rey," the king

Colossal heads

The most famous of all Olmec monuments are colossal sculptured heads made of basalt, a dark volcanic rock. These heads represented actual people, probably Olmec rulers. Each head bears a headdress with its own distinctive emblem, a symbol that identified the person's rank and family line.

Worship

Many early American societies believed that when the world was created, a race of part-human, part-jaguar beings was born. In Olmec civilization, these beings were identified with the priest-leaders. The spirit of the jaguar god was thought to live in the priests, giving them strength and agility, and making them Masters of People, just as the jaguar was Master of Animals. There were other gods, including a rattlesnake.

Jaguar spirit

This ceremonial stone ax was carried by an Olmec priest in religious ceremonies. It is carved with the image of the spirit of the jaguar god.

Stone figures

This group of jade and granite figures and tall ceremonial axes was left as an offering in an Olmec temple. It probably represented a group of leaders or priests.

Art

The first Olmec artists produced small statues in clay. The Olmecs were well known for their human figures, often with the faces of newborn babies. Later they mastered stone carving. They produced a wide range of work, from massive stone heads and carved reliefs to small sculptures and jewelry, using materials such as jade, serpentine (a green or brown mineral), and basalt.

Mask made of jade

Jade necklace

Decorative jade mask

Jade masks

The Olmecs were fascinated by the human face and many of their sculptures are stone masks. Sometimes these masks were portraits of real people, such as ball game players, rulers, or nobles. Other masks showed the faces of figures from the stories in Olmec mythology.

Jade necklace

Green stones were valued more than any other in ancient Central America. Jade in particular was favored by the rich as a material for jewelry. This necklace, with its central human head, would have been prized by a member of the Olmec nobility.

Food

The staple food of the Olmecs was corn, which they used to make porridge or baked into pancakes. Olmec farmers also cultivated vegetables such as beans and squash, and the tomato was popular. To vary this diet of vegetables, the Olmecs ate the meat of deer and rabbits.

Squash

Corn

Tomato

Jade fish

Fish were popular in coastal regions and near rivers. They could be caught with nets, hooks, or harpoons.

FIND OUT MORE   AZTECS   CENTRAL AMERICA, HISTORY OF   GODS AND GODDESSES   MAYA

OLYMPIC GAMES

THE MODERN OLYMPIC GAMES, held every four years, are the world's greatest festival of sporting competition. First held in 1896, they were inspired by the ancient Greek Olympics, which lasted for 1,000 years. Thousands of athletes, representing most countries in the world, assemble in a selected city to compete in more than 20 different sports. There are separate Winter Olympics for sports on ice and snow, and Paralympics for the disabled. These games are also held every four years.

Atlanta opening ceremony, 1996

The flame
Before every Games, a flame is lit from the rays of the Sun at the site of the ancient Olympics in Greece. The flame is transferred by a torch relay to the Olympic Stadium, where it burns for the duration of the Games. In 1996, the boxer Muhammad Ali was the final torch bearer.

Olympic sports
Athletics has always been the major Olympic attraction, but other sports, such as swimming, gymnastics, and show jumping, also have huge television audiences. Team games, such as soccer and hockey, are also popular. The Games were originally for amateurs only, but professionals are now allowed to participate.

Opening ceremony
At the opening ceremony, each country's athletes march into the stadium in turn, some teams with hundreds of competitors, others with only one or two. The host city puts on a spectacular show.

Medals
Gold medals are awarded for first place, silver for second, and bronze for third. All members of successful teams receive a medal provided they have taken part in at least one match or heat.

Olympic venues

DATE	VENUE
1896	Athens, Greece
1900	Paris, France
1904	St Louis, USA
1908	London, England
1912	Stockholm, Sweden
1920	Antwerp, Belgium
1924	Paris, France
1928	Amsterdam, Holland
1932	Los Angeles, USA
1936	Berlin, Germany
1948	London, England
1952	Helsinki, Finland
1956	Melbourne, Australia
1960	Rome, Italy
1964	Tokyo, Japan
1968	Mexico City, Mexico
1972	Munich, West Germany
1976	Montreal, Canada
1980	Moscow, USSR
1984	Los Angeles, USA
1988	Seoul, South Korea
1992	Barcelona, Spain
1996	Atlanta, USA
2000	Sydney, Australia
2004	Athens, Greece

Pierre de Coubertin
French scholar Pierre de Coubertin (1863–1937) pioneered the modern Olympics. Inspired in the 1870s by the excavation of ancient Olympia, he founded the International Olympic Committee, the governing body of the Games, in 1894.

1996 gold medal

1996 silver medal

1996 bronze medal

Gold medals are made of silver with a gold coating.

In some sports, both losing semi-finalists receive a bronze medal.

Winter Olympics
The first separate Winter Olympics were staged in 1924 at Chamonix in France. Figure skating had been included in the summer schedule in 1908 and ice hockey was included in 1920. The Winter Olympics were held in the same year as the main Olympics until 1992 but, as from 1994, in Lillehammer, Norway, they are now held midway between the summer Games.

The Olympic rings
Five interlinking rings are the symbol of the Olympic Games. They appear on the Olympic flag on a white background and were designed to represent the coming together of the five "parts of the world" involved in the Olympic Movement when the flag was adopted in 1914.

Winter events
The ice sports are figure and speed skating, and ice hockey. On snow, there is downhill and cross-country skiing and ski-jumping. Freestyle skiing events have recently been added. Sled sports are bobsleigh and tobogganing.

The start of a downhill race

Paralympics
Immediately after the main Olympics, a parallel set of games called the Paralympics is staged for people who have physical disabilities. The events take place at the the same venues as the Olympics. They have been held every four years since 1960. Sport for the disabled was pioneered by Dr Ludwig Guttman, who used it in the treatment of soldiers who had been disabled during World War II.

Paralympic events
There are events in the Paralympics for competitors in wheelchairs, for the blind or partially sighted, for amputees, and for those with cerebral palsy. Seventeen sports are staged, including athletics, swimming, archery, basketball, and tennis.

Tanni Grey, winner of gold in 1992 and 1996

FIND OUT MORE   ATHLETICS   COMBAT SPORTS   GYMNASTICS   HORSE RIDING   SPORT   SWIMMING AND DIVING   WINTER SPORTS

OPERA

AN OPERA IS A MUSICAL DRAMA in which singers act out a story, accompanied by an orchestra. Typically, an opera includes passages of sung dialogue, known as recitative, that move the plot along; solo songs called arias that allow major characters to express their feelings; and scenes that feature a rousing chorus. The earliest operas appeared in Italy and were based on stories from classical mythology. Later, operas also dealt with political and historical subjects.

A scene from *The Marriage of Figaro*

Major singers

Operatic soloists can become internationally famous. Jenny Lind (1820–87) was known as the Swedish Nightingale. The Italian tenor Luciano Pavarotti (b.1935) and the New Zealand soprano Kiri Te Kanawa (b.1944) are stars worldwide.

Jenny Lind

Libretto for *Cosi Fan Tutti*, by Mozart

Recitative

Libretto
The text of an opera is called the libretto. It may be adapted from a play or novel, or written specially for the composer. Only occasionally does the composer write both libretto and music.

Voices

In an opera company the leading female soloist, or prima donna, is usually a soprano, the highest female voice; the leading man often has a high tenor voice. Singers with lower voices, such as the female contralto or the bass (male), may also be used for solos.

Types of operas

There are many different forms of operas. In 18th-century Italy, operas were in the style of either *opera seria* (serious opera) or *opera buffa* (comic opera). Later, composers worked within or around the traditions of these different styles to arrive at new forms – for example, the serious operas of German composer Richard Wagner are known as music dramas.

Grand opera
Grand opera, which featured large choruses, elaborate scores, and spectacular sets, first developed in 19th-century France.

Musicals
Light, small-scale operas developed into the musicals of Jerome Kern (1885–1945) and others in the 1920s, weaving songs and dance around a modern story.

William Tell: grand operas are lavishly staged.

West Side Story: in 1961 a film was made of this 1950s' musical.

Staging an opera

It takes an enormous number of people to stage an opera and make it an exciting musical and dramatic spectacle. In addition to the singers and orchestra, designers and backstage staff are needed to take care of the spectacular sets, costumes, and lighting. A director works closely with the conductor so that the drama and music complement each other.

Ornate interior of opera house

Boxes

Stalls, where the audience sits

Orchestra is positioned in front of the stage.

Bayreuth Festival Theater, Germany, built to house Wagner's operas

Famous opera houses
Early operas were staged in theaters, but soon buildings were made specifically for opera. Now, most major cities have opera houses that present the most lavish productions. Among the best known are Covent Garden, London; La Scala, Milan; and The Metropolitan, New York.

Giuseppe Verdi
The Italian composer Giuseppe Verdi (1813–1901) wrote 27 operas. However, an early opera failed so badly that he almost gave up! Instead, he went on to write *La Traviata, Aïda,* and his masterpiece *Otello,* written when he was over 70.

Timeline

1607 *La Farola d'Orfeo,* by Claudio Monteverdi (1567–1643), one of the first operas, is performed in Italy.

1791 Wolfgang Amadeus Mozart's *The Magic Flute* is first performed.

1637 In Italy, public opera house opens.

1876 Richard Wagner (1813–1883) finishes the series of operas known as *The Ring of the Nibelung,* and sets up the Bayreuth Festival for his work.

1935 *Porgy and Bess,* by US composer George Gershwin (1898–1937), with music influenced by jazz elements, opens in Boston, Mass.

1937 *Lulu,* by Alban Berg (1885–1935), is performed. Written in an experimental, harsh-sounding style, the music suits the violent, tragic story.

FIND OUT MORE   DRAMA   FILMS AND FILMMAKING   JAZZ   MOZART, WOLFGANG AMADEUS   MUSIC   MUSICAL INSTRUMENTS   ORCHESTRAS   SOUND   THEATERS

ORCHESTRAS

THE GLORIOUS SOUND of an orchestra in concert is one of the great thrills of classical music. An orchestra is a group of musicians playing together under the direction of a conductor. The players perform specially composed music that combines specific instruments to achieve a total, balanced sound. The stringed instruments (violin, viola, cello, and double bass) are the basis of every orchestra, but orchestral music includes wind and percussion instruments, too.

18th-century orchestra

Beginnings
Classical orchestras first appeared in Europe during the 17th century. They consisted of about 25 string players, usually with a harpsichord accompaniment. By the mid-18th century, wind instruments and kettledrums were also included. Through the 19th century, orchestras grew rapidly: composers were able to write symphonies for more than a hundred players. This number and range of instruments gave a wider range of sounds.

Sections
The orchestra is divided into four sections by type of instrument: strings, woodwind, brass, or percussion.

Symphony orchestra

The number and type of instruments in an orchestra depend on the style of music being played. Symphonies are written for a full range of musical instruments. Many new instruments have appeared since the first orchestras, particularly in the wind and percussion sections; modern orchestras include most of them. Louder instruments are placed in the back; the quieter instruments in front.

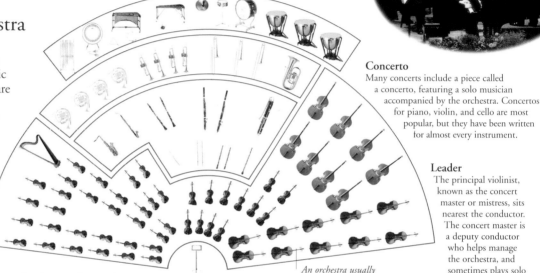

Layout of modern symphony orchestra

Conductor's stand

An orchestra usually contains about 90 musicians.

Concerto
Many concerts include a piece called a concerto, featuring a solo musician accompanied by the orchestra. Concertos for piano, violin, and cello are most popular, but they have been written for almost every instrument.

Leader
The principal violinist, known as the concert master or mistress, sits nearest the conductor. The concert master is a deputy conductor who helps manage the orchestra, and sometimes plays solo parts in concerts.

Chamber orchestra

Some pieces need an orchestra of only about 25 players. Such a group is known as a chamber orchestra. There are only a few performers for each part. They often play early music on authentic instruments.

Chamber music
Classical music written for very small groups of instruments is called chamber music. Such pieces are usually written for between three and eight musicians, with one player for each part; a popular combination is the string quartet, which has two violins, a viola, and a cello.

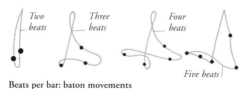

String quartet

Conductor

The conductor's role is to draw the best possible performance of a piece of music from the orchestra. Standing on a raised platform, the conductor beats time, and interprets the mood of the music with gestures and facial expressions.

Conductor's expression tells the violinists to play with delicacy.

Beating time
The conductor's baton traces patterns through the air, indicating the tempo of the music to the orchestra.

Two beats

Three beats

Four beats

Five beats

Beats per bar: baton movements

Thomas Beecham
Sir Thomas Beecham (1879–1961) was a British orchestral and operatic conductor. He was a popular figure who used his own fortune to promote music by financing performances of new works, and founding orchestras and opera companies.

Band
A group of musicians that play wind and percussion instruments only, without a strings section, is known as a band. Military and marching brass bands play outdoors at sports events and ceremonies; dance bands have been popular since the Renaissance. Modern rock and pop groups are also sometimes called bands.

FIND OUT MORE   BALLET   BEETHOVEN, LUDWIG VAN   JAZZ   MOZART, WOLFGANG AMADEUS   MUSIC   MUSICAL INSTRUMENTS   OPERA   ROCK AND POP   THEATERS

OTTOMAN EMPIRE

THE OTTOMAN TURKS were originally a nomadic tribe of Asiatic horsemen with a fearsome reputation. From the 14th to the 17th centuries, these devout Muslim warriors carved out an empire spanning Greece, the Balkans, North Africa, western Asia, and the Middle East. The empire's great success was largely due to its custom of rewarding its people for their talent rather than their noble birth. After 1600, the empire went into a decline because of corruption at the sultan's court. Even so, it staggered on, known as the Sick Man of Europe, until treaties after World War I dismantled it. The sultanate was abolished in 1922.

Expansion of empire
The Ottoman Empire evolved in several stages from a small base in Anatolia (in modern Turkey). In the 14th century, Ottomans expanded into the Balkans; after 1453, their fleet was dominant in the eastern Mediterranean; by the 16th century, with the conquest of Syria, Egypt, and Hungary, the Ottoman Empire was poised to take over the western world.

State and religion
A fierce religious fervor drove Ottoman expansion. The sultans, inspired by their Muslim faith, felt they had a duty to convert their neighbors to Islam and therefore expanded the empire through conquest. Gazis, or frontier-fighters, called themselves "the instrument of God's religion."

House of Islam
To the Ottomans, the world was split between the House of Islam, where there was Muslim government and law, and the House of War, which was inhabited by infidels (non-Muslims). According to Muslim holy law, the Jihad (struggle) between the two Houses had to continue until the House of Islam finally triumphed.

Sultanate
The Ottoman sovereigns and religious leaders were known as sultans. Many of the earlier sultans were men of humble origins who gained power through ability rather than noble birth. This policy was one of the empire's great strengths, until the sultanate became hereditary and some sultans proved lazy and corrupt.

Few portraits exist because Islamic holy law does not encourage artists to depict people.

Steel blade inlaid with verse by the Ottoman poet Nejati.

Semiprecious stones

Ottoman court dagger, 16th century

Sultan Ahmed I as a young man

Warfare
During the 16th and 17th centuries, the Ottoman Empire was constantly at war. As the cavalry (Sipahis) and infantry (Janissaries) conquered each new stretch of land, the sultan split it between them. This system encouraged the soldiers to extend the frontiers.

Janissaries and dervishes
Janissaries were the crack infantrymen of the Ottoman armies. They usually started life as non-Turkish Christian boys from south-eastern Europe. Dervishes – Ottoman holy men – recruited them and sent them to Istanbul for training, where they converted to Islam. If they showed talent in battle, they were well rewarded. This system of meritocracy, or rewarding talent, meant that the sultan could rely on the Janissaries' total loyalty.

Janissary, 16th century

Battle of Lepanto
By 1550, a vulnerable western Europe was torn between warring Protestants and Catholics, and open to sea attack from the Ottomans. However, in 1571, a rare Christian coalition between Spain, Venice, Genoa, and the Papacy thwarted the Ottoman advance at a battle in the Mediterranean and ended Ottoman expansion.

Topkapi Palace
In 1453, Sultan Muhammad II (1451–81) renamed Constantinople Istanbul. He built the magnificent Topkapi Palace, whose gracious courtyards and arcades can still be seen today.

Royal salon, Topkapi Palace

Timeline
1363 Conquests in the Balkans begins Ottoman expansion into Europe.

1453 Capture of Constantinople marks end of Byzantine Empire. The city is renamed Istanbul.

1463 Ottomans defeat Viennese.

1516–17 Ottomans conquer Egypt and Syria.

1526 Battle of Mohács leads to conquest of most of Hungary.

1529 Failed siege of Vienna.

Sixteenth-century Janissaries

1571 Ottoman defeat at Lepanto.

1600 Empire begins decline.

1683 Another failed siege of Vienna.

1909 The last traditional sultan, Abdul-Hamid II, is overthrown and replaced by Muhammad V.

1922 Sultanate is abolished, preparing the way for a new Turkish republic.

Suleiman the Magnificent
The greatest sultan of all was Suleiman I (r.1520–66), called the Lawgiver by his 14 million subjects. Suleiman was also a poet and a patron of the arts. Under Suleiman's rule, the empire's lands reached their greatest expanses, and his advance into Europe was halted only by the failure of a siege of Vienna in 1529. The Ottomans continued as a major sea power for another 50 years.

FIND OUT MORE   ARCHITECTURE   FEUDALISM   ISLAM   ISLAMIC EMPIRE   PERSIAN EMPIRES   WARFARE

631

OWENS, JESSE

OF ALL THE ATHLETES who have performed at the Olympics over the years, few have made more of an impression than Jesse Owens, the young black American who won four gold medals at the 1936 games in Berlin. Nazi leader Adolf Hitler wanted to use the Olyympics to demonstrate his theories about the supremacy of the Aryan race, but Owens showed that such ideas are nonsense. The crowd adored him, for he was a true athlete, whose speed and agility won him admirers wherever he raced.

Early life
Jesse Owens was born in 1913 on a farm in Oakville, in Alabama. His grandparents were slaves, his parents sharecroppers (tenant farmers). Like many poor black families at this time, his parents were forced to leave the land to try and find work in northern cities. The Owens family settled in Cleveland, Ohio. It was at his high school in Cleveland that Jesse Owens' remarkable talent for track and field was first discovered.

Track and field

In high school in Cleveland, Ohio, Jesse distinguished himself in both track and field events. He won major events at the National Amateur Athletic Union meetings in 1934 and 1935, and then broke five world records while competing for the Ohio State University team at Ann Arbor, Michigan, on May 25, 1935.

Owens wins the 100 yards at Ann Arbor

Training and jumping
When he was a young man, Jesse Owens trained with coach Charles Riley, who was one of the first to recognize his athletic ability. Riley helped Owens improve his running style. He also trained Jesse for the long jump. One of the most outstanding records of Owens' career was his long jump at Ann Arbor in 1935, which he made after breaking no fewer than four track records. He made only one attempt at the jump, clearing 26 ft 8 1/4 ins (8.13 m) and setting a world record that was to stand for 25 years.

Berlin Olympics

In August 1936, the Olympic Games were held in Berlin, the capital of Germany. The German leader Adolf Hitler used the games as propaganda for his Nazi regime. He spent lavishly on training the German athletes, and hoped to glorify his racial myth of a superior "Aryan race," the white, northern Europeans. However, Owens' achievements smashed these hopes.

Owens takes the baton in the final leg of the 4 x 100 m relay.

Owens wins the long jump.

Lutz Long
The long jump final in the Olympics turned into a close contest between Owens and the German athlete Lutz Long. Owens eventually won with a new world record of 26 ft 5 3/8 ins (8.07 m), but the two athletes had such respect for each other that they embraced at the end. This gesture annoyed Hitler. He congratulated Lutz Long but completely ignored Owens.

Owens with Lutz Long

Track and field
Owens was the star of the 1936 Olympics, making 12 appearances and winning every heat and event he entered. Although Owens won four gold medals – for the 100 m, 200 m, long jump, and 4 x 100 m relay – and broke two world records, Hitler refused to meet him or shake his hand, as he did white American athletes.

One of Owens' four Olympic gold medals

Spikes on part of sole that touches ground

Entire shoe is made of leather.

Running shoe, worn by Owens

The professional

After the games, Owens had to take part in track meets in Europe to raise money for the American team. Too tired to compete, he pulled out and was suspended by the American Amateur Athletic Union. Later, he entered exhibition races to raise money for his family and for charity, most notably running a race against a horse.

Later life
Owens was secretary of the Illinois Athletics Commission until 1955, and was later active in youth work in the state. As a special envoy for President Eisenhower, he attended the 1956 Olympics in Melbourne, Australia. He also helped publicize the Munich Olympic Games in 1972.

JESSE OWENS

1913	Born in Oakville, Alabama
1933–34	After his family moves to Cleveland, Ohio, wins major track and field events
1935	Breaks world records (100-yard/91.4-m, and 220-yard/201-m sprints; 220-yard/201-m low hurdles; long jump)
1936	Wins four gold medals at the Berlin Olympics (100-m, 200-m, long jump, and 4 x 100 m relay)
1956	Acts as President's special envoy to Melbourne Olympics
1980	Dies at age 67

FIND OUT MORE

GERMANY, HISTORY OF   OLYMPIC GAMES   SPORTS

OWLS AND NIGHTJARS

MOST BIRDS ARE ACTIVE during the day and rest at night. Owls and nightjars usually live the other way around. Both groups of birds come to life at sunset, just when the animals they eat are also on the move, but they feed in quite different ways. Owls snatch up small animals from the ground, using their sharp claws, or talons. They have very good eyesight and even better hearing. Some of them can find prey using their ears alone. Nightjars feed in the air. They also have good eyesight, but instead of using their claws to catch their food, they scoop up moths and other insects in their large beaks.

The owl spreads its wing feathers to control the speed of its approach.

White underparts show when the owl is in flight.

Forward-facing eyes help the owl judge distances.

Feather-covered legs and feet

Barn owl
This silent hunter patrols fields and open ground on slowly flapping wings. If it sees or hears prey, it drops on it silently with talons outstretched. Barn owls can be recognized by their heart-shaped face, which channels sounds to the ears.

The barn owl usually flies just a few yards above the ground.

Soft-edged feathers keep flight silent.

A noise or movement attracts its attention, it prepares to pounce.

The owl's legs swing down, ready to attack.

Nightjars
There are about 80 species of these nocturnal insecteaters, also known as nighthawks. Nightjars have sharply pointed wings, slim bodies, and plumage that camouflages them when they rest on the ground.

Camouflage
Nightjars roost and breed on the ground, or sometimes on a flat roof. They keep very still and their superb camouflage hides them from predators. This European nightjar looks just like a piece of wood.

Whippoorwill
In areas that have cold winters, most nightjars migrate to warmer regions. The North American whippoorwill avoids the cold in an unusual way for a bird. It crawls into a rock crevice and hibernates.

Oilbird
The oilbird of northern South America is a fruit-eating relative of the nightjars. It nests deep inside caves, and, like bats, uses sound to find its way through the darkness.

Barn owl feather

Feathers
An owl's flight feathers have a soft fringe on their front edge. These fringes soften the sounds that feathers normally make when they move through the air.

Fur and bones matted together in a whole pellet

Skulls

Fur

Hip bones

Shoulder blades

Owls
There are 133 species of owls, and they live in almost every land habitat from tropical rainforest to Arctic tundra. Most species hunt after dark, but a few fly by day. Owls' eyes widen inside their heads, and the birds cannot swivel them in the socket. To look around, they twist their necks instead.

Pellets
Owls swallow their food whole. After digesting a meal, they cough up the bones, fur, and feathers in a compact lump called a pellet. This tawny owl's pellet has been pulled apart to show some of its contents. The owl that produced this pellet had been feeding mainly on voles.

Buffy fish owl
Fish owls live in Africa and Asia. The bottom of their toes is covered with sharp spines for gripping fish. Unlike other owls, they do not have fringed feathers.

Elf owl
Only 5.5 in (14 cm) long, this is the smallest owl. It lives in North American deserts and nests in holes in trees or cacti.

BARN OWL

SCIENTIFIC NAME	*Tyto alba*
ORDER	Strigiformes
FAMILY	Tytonidae
DISTRIBUTION	Worldwide, although absent from many islands and cold places
HABITAT	Woodland edges, grassland, farmland, often near buildings
DIET	Mostly small mammals, but occasionally insects, small birds, and amphibians
SIZE	Length including tail: 13 in (34 cm); males slightly smaller than females
LIFESPAN	About 15 years

FIND OUT MORE   BIRDS   BIRDS OF PREY   CAMOUFLAGE AND COLOR   FLIGHT, ANIMAL   MIGRATION, ANIMAL   POLAR WILDLIFE

PACIFIC OCEAN

TWICE AS LARGE as the Atlantic, the Pacific is the world's largest ocean and covers one-third of the Earth's surface. It stretches from the Arctic in the north to the Antarctic in the south, and almost halfway around the globe from the Americas to Australia and Asia. The Pacific is dotted with more than 20,000 volcanic and coral islands, and is ringed by active volcanoes. It is also the world's deepest ocean and drops to 36,197 ft (11,033 m) in the Mariana Trench. Important trade routes cross the Pacific, and some of the world's richest countries lie on its shores.

Physical features

"Pacific" means peaceful, yet the Pacific Ocean has many strong currents that affect climate and weather. These circulate clockwise in the north and counterclockwise in the south.

PACIFIC OCEAN FACTS

AREA	63,800,000 sq miles (165,241,000 sq km)
AVERAGE DEPTH	13,800 ft (4,200 m)
GREATEST DEPTH	36,197 ft (11,033 m) Mariana Trench
NUMBER OF ISLANDS	20,000–30,000
HIGHEST MOUNTAIN	Mauna Kea, Hawaii, 27,605 ft (10,205 m) of which over half is below the ocean's surface

El Niño
Normally a cold current flows from the western coast of South America. However, every few years, in December, a warm current called El Niño flows east towards Peru, causing worldwide weather changes, including severe droughts in Australia.

Ring of Fire
The Pacific is surrounded by deep ocean trenches where the Earth's tectonic plates are pulled downwards. Earthquakes are frequent in these areas, and the many volcanoes form a "Ring of Fire" around the ocean. The Pavlof Volcano on the Alaskan Peninsula is part of this ring.

International Date Line
The world's time zones are based on Greenwich Observatory, England, which is taken as 0° longitude. Halfway around the world at 180° longitude, an imaginary line down the middle of the Pacific Ocean marks one day from the next. So, when it is Monday in New Zealand, it is Sunday in Samoa. In some places the date line has to be moved to avoid dividing countries – it would be difficult if it was Monday in the west of Fiji and Sunday in the east.

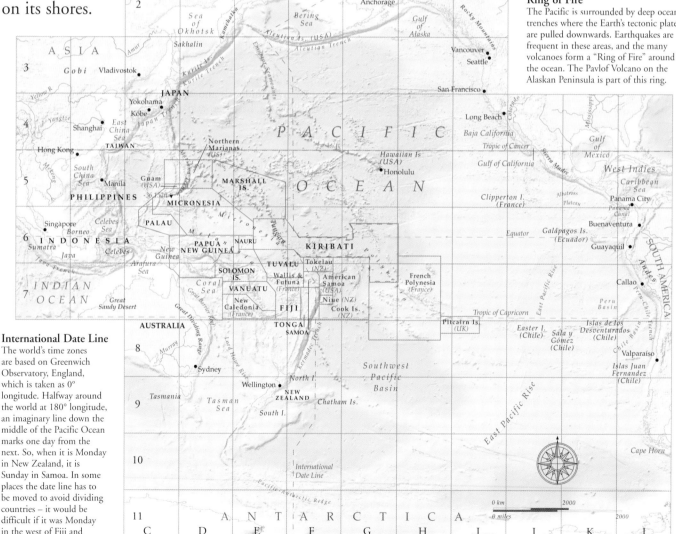

P

Islands

The thousands of islands in the Pacific are scattered over a vast area. They are home to about five million people, whose one great shared resource is the sea. Some islands are mountainous and volcanic in origin, while the lower islands are mostly coral atolls. Most islands are clustered in the southwest Pacific. Others, such as Easter Island and Hawaii, are more isolated – thousands of miles from their neighbors.

Coral islands
The warm waters of the southern Pacific provide ideal conditions for corals, which flourish there. Thousands of the Pacific islands are atolls, coral reefs sitting on the rims of the sunken craters of old volcanoes. Most of the Pacific's coral islands are tiny.

Hawaii
The islands of the US state of Hawaii are not part of the "Ring of Fire," but are hot spot volcanoes that form where magma wells up through weak points in the ocean floor. As the Earth's tectonic plates move, these volcanoes form new islands. Hawaii's two active volcanoes constantly erupt, causing lava to shoot into the air.

Military bases
Several Pacific islands are used as military bases, especially by the US. American bases include Midway, a naval base north of Hawaii, Guam, a naval base in the western Pacific, Wake, an air base, and Johnston atoll, once used for nuclear tests and now a dump for toxic gases and other chemical weapons.

The US naval base on Guam

Bird sanctuaries
Many thousands of Pacific islands, such as the US territories of Baker, Howland, and Jarvis islands, are uninhabited by people but are sanctuaries for millions of birds. Birds such as the Greater Frigate Bird return to the same islands every year to rear their young.

Tropical storms

Trade winds constantly blow across the Pacific, from northeast and southeast of the equator. The trade winds are responsible for the violent tropical storms called either willy-willies in Australia or typhoons, from *tai fung*, which means "great wind" in Chinese.

Pacific trade

Nearly half the world's major shipping routes cross the Pacific. Large cargo ships transport goods between the countries of the Pacific rim, which is the name given to the countries on the shores of the ocean.

Shipping
Huge supertankers and giant bulk carriers carry oil and other raw materials, such as iron ore and copper, from as far north as Alaska to countries along the Pacific rim, such as Japan, the US, Australia, and countries in eastern Asia.

Container ports
Like many Pacific ports, the harbor at Hong Kong has been specially designed to load and unload large numbers of huge cargo ships that arrive every day from all over the world.

Resources

The Pacific's greatest resource is its stock of fish and other seafood. Parts of the ocean floor are covered in small black lumps called manganese nodules that contain many minerals and can be used to make paints, batteries, and steel.

Husk Coconuts

Flesh

Fish farming
Farming fish, often called aquaculture, has been practiced in the Pacific for centuries. China and Korea farm seaweed as well as fish, oysters, and mussels. The endangered giant clam, which grows up to 3.3 ft (1 m), is now bred in the southern Pacific.

Coconuts
Coconut palms flourish along the shores of all the tropical islands of the Pacific. The milky liquid in a coconut is an important drink; its flesh can be eaten fresh or dried as copra, which yields oil. The tough outer fibre can be woven to make ropes and matting for floors.

Giant clam

Fishing
Nearly half the world's fish are caught in Pacific waters. Most of the fish live close to land, particularly along the Asian coasts. During El Niño, weather changes make them desert the South American coast.

Skipjack tuna

Tourists on Santa Cruz in the Galápagos

Tourism
The tourist trade is developing slowly in the Pacific because of the long distances to travel and the shortage of modern hotels. Fiji, Tahiti, American Samoa, and Hawaii are the fastest-growing centers. Islands such as the Galápagos Islands fear tourism will damage the environment.

 FIND OUT MORE   CONTINENTS   CORAL REEFS   FISHING INDUSTRY   ISLANDS   OCEANS AND SEAS   PACIFIC, SOUTH   POLYNESIA   SHIPS AND BOATS   VOLCANOES   WINDS

PACIFIC, SOUTH

THE ISLANDS in the South Pacific are divided into Micronesia and Melanesia, which includes the eastern part of the island of New Guinea called Papua New Guinea. There are only a few large towns on the small islands. Most people live in villages and practice subsistence farming, growing just enough food to support themselves. They export surplus coconut products, bananas, cocoa beans, and sugarcane.

Physical features

Some South Pacific islands are low-lying and easily flooded in stormy weather, while others are volcanic. Several islands have volcanic black sand. Papua New Guinea is highly mountainous and covered in tropical forest.

Volcanoes

Many of the mountainous islands of Micronesia and Melanesia are volcanic. Some island countries, like Vanuatu, have active volcanoes likely to erupt at any time. Others are the rims of extinct volcanic craters, ringed with coral atolls. The combination of volcanic ash and coral results in depleted soil.

Coconuts

Even where the soil is poor, coconut palms manage to survive and are one of the most successful kinds of trees on the Pacific Islands. Washed up on shore, they succeed in sprouting even in saltwater and can thrive in areas with very little freshwater. The Pacific Islanders dry the coconut meat to make copra. The husk is used to make matting.

Regional climate

Melanesia and Micronesia have warm weather year round. Rainfall varies, but the islands all have a wet and a dry season.

64°F (27°C)   64°F (27°C)

72 in (1,819 mm)

Languages

More than one-third of the world's languages are spoken in the South Pacific. Most are spoken in Melanesia, some 750 of them in Papua New Guinea, home to 1,000 different tribes. Micronesians speak 13 different languages, and there are several dialects.

Boys from Papua New Guinea in traditional dress

Papua New Guinea

Papua New Guinea consists of the eastern half of New Guinea Island, plus over 600 islands of the Bismarck Archipelago and surrounding waters. The mainland consists of mountains divided by swampy river valleys and cloaked with tropical forest.

People and languages

Cut off from each other and from the outside world, each of the groups living in Papua's mountain villages has developed very different customs and languages. Great tensions exist between highland peoples that live by hunting and gathering. By contrast, the people in the lowland, coastal areas have frequent contact with the rest of the world.

Mining

Papua New Guinea ranks highly in world gold production and also has natural gas reserves. In recent years, copper mining has led to ecological problems including pollution and landslides.

PAPUA NEW GUINEA FACTS

CAPITAL CITY Port Moresby

AREA 178,700 sq miles (462,840 sq km)

POPULATION 4,800,000

MAIN LANGUAGES Pidgin English, Motu, Papuan, 750 native languages

MAJOR RELIGIONS Christian, traditional beliefs

CURRENCY Kina

Micronesia

The Federated States of Micronesia consist of more than 600 islands stretching over 1,800 miles (2,900 km) of ocean. They are a mixture of hilly, thickly forested volcanic islands and low-lying coral atolls. Most islanders live without electricity or running water. The main source of income is copra and fishing.

MICRONESIA FACTS

CAPITAL CITY Palikir

AREA 270 sq miles (700 sq km)

POPULATION 133,000

MAIN LANGUAGES Trukese, Pohnpeian, English

MAJOR RELIGION Christian

CURRENCY US dollar

Traditional dancers
Although predominantly Christian, the Micronesians follow a traditional way of life, celebrating important occasions with singing and dancing. Women play an important role in society, and the title of chief is passed on through the female line. Although independent, Micronesians rely on US aid for funding.

Marshall Islands

Independent since 1990, this country, consists of five islands, 29 atolls, and 1,150 small islets. People live by selling fish and coconut oil.

Ebeye Island
Most of Ebeye's population was forced to move from Kwajalein in 1947 to make way for a US missile base.

MARSHALL ISLANDS FACTS

CAPITAL CITY Majuro

AREA 70 sq miles (181 sq km)

POPULATION 68,000

MAIN LANGUAGES English, Marshallese

MAJOR RELIGION Christian

CURRENCY US dollar

Nauru

This tiny island, independent from Britain since 1968, has grown rich through its phosphate deposits.

Phosphate mining
Over the last 100 years, the mining of the mineral phosphate for fertilizer has left 80 percent of the island unusable. As supplies run out, Nauru is investing money abroad.

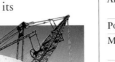

NAURU FACTS

CAPITAL CITY None

AREA 8.2 sq miles (21.2 sq km)

POPULATION 11,800

MAIN LANGUAGES Nauruan, English

MAJOR RELIGION Christian

CURRENCY Australian dollar

Vanuatu

An archipelago of 82 volcanic, mountainous islands, Vanuatu forms a chain 800 miles (1,300 km) long. Many islands have coral reefs and dense rain forest. The people, who mostly live on the 16 largest islands, speak 105 languages.

VANUATU FACTS

CAPITAL CITY Port-Vila

AREA 4,707 sq miles (12,190 sq km)

POPULATION 200,000

MAIN LANGUAGES Bislama, English

MAJOR RELIGIONS Christian, traditional beliefs

CURRENCY Vatu

Carved wood figures
Vanuatu's people are among the most traditional in the South Pacific, and customs are important. They carve unusual wooden figures, similar in style to those on Easter Island, Polynesia.

Solomon Islands

The scene of fierce fighting in World War II (1939–45), the Solomon Islands were a British colony until 1978. There are six large islands and hundreds of islets and coral reefs.

SOLOMON ISLANDS FACTS

CAPITAL CITY Honiara

AREA 11,157 sq miles (28,896 sq km)

POPULATION 444,000

MAIN LANGUAGE English

MAJOR RELIGION Christian

CURRENCY Solomon Islands dollar

Saving trees
In 1998 a new forest policy was introduced to plant new trees to replace the thousands felled as timber for export.

Palau

The Palau Archipelago in the western Pacific consists of more than 300 islands, only nine of which are inhabited. The society is unusual in that the clan chiefs are chosen by the women.

PALAU FACTS

CAPITAL CITY Koror

AREA 188 sq miles (487 sq km)

POPULATION 18,800

MAIN LANGUAGES Palauan, English

MAJOR RELIGIONS Christian, traditional beliefs

CURRENCY US dollar

Rock islands
These strange island mountains, viewed from the air, are thickly forested. Palau's island reefs contain 1,500 species of fish and 700 types of coral.

Fiji

Fiji lies at the eastern edge of Melanesia. It consists of two large islands that are mountainous and volcanic in origin, and more than 800 islets and coral atolls.

FIJI FACTS

CAPITAL CITY Suva

AREA 7,054 sq miles (18,270 sq km)

POPULATION 817,000

MAIN LANGUAGES English, Fijian

MAJOR RELIGIONS Christian, Hindu, Muslim

CURRENCY Fijian dollar

Fijian village
Most Fijians live off the land in rural villages. Many people work on sugar plantations. Sugarcane makes up around one-third of Fiji's exports.

FIND OUT MORE AUSTRALASIA AND OCEANIA · CORAL REEFS · EMPIRES · FARMING · PACIFIC OCEAN · POLLUTION · RAINFOREST WILDLIFE · SCULPTURE · SHIPS AND BOATS · WORLD WAR II

P

PAINTING AND DRAWING

EARLY PEOPLE painted hunting scenes on cave walls using natural pigments. In sixteenth-century Europe, art schools were set up to teach drawing and painting skills. Today, we draw and paint with a variety of materials for a wide range of purposes, from the creation of great works of art to complex and practical architectural drawings and quickly sketched designs.

An artist mixes colors to find the right tone.

An artist's tools
Artists use crayons, paints, brushes, and palettes. These tools have hardly changed over centuries. Paints are made from pigments, which may come from sources such as bark and earth, or from metals.

Charcoal

Watercolors made of water and pigments

Pigments

Pastels

Watercolor paint

Palette
The palette has a central thumb hole so the artist can hold it with one hand and paint with the other.

Drawing

Artists draw with pencils, inks, and crayons. Originally, drawings were done as preparatory sketches for a finished work, such as a painting or sculpture. In the early 16th century, however, artists began creating drawings as finished works of art, as many artists still do today.

Sketches
A quick, rough drawing that captures the impression of a subject is known as a sketch. This black chalk sketch of an elephant is by the Dutch artist Rembrandt van Rijn (1606–69).

Technical drawing
Engineers, architects, and designers need accurate drawings based on precise mathematical calculations to show how to construct objects such as bridges and houses. This skill is known as technical drawing.

Looking at paintings

Paintings can be enjoyed in many ways: for delight in their design; the quality of the light; or the beauty of the color. Sometimes paintings need to be studied to appreciate their complexity.

Artist's model
This detail shows the artist's model dressed as the Muse of history. In Greek mythology, each of the arts and sciences was represented by one of the nine Muses.

The Artist's Studio by Jan Vermeer (1632–75)

The drawn curtain suggests that we are almost spying on a private scene.

Light pours in from the top left of the painting.

In the curtain, Vermeer paints highlights with tiny beads of bright white.

An empty chair in the foreground invites the viewer into the scene, to watch the artist at work.

The many straight lines in the painting, such as the roof beams, give the picture its sense of stability.

The large map shows Holland and Flanders because Vermeer was Dutch.

Jan Vermeer shows himself at work painting details of the model's costume.

The diagonal lines of the floor tiles and the table's edge lead the eye into the painting.

Ways of painting

Art is becoming increasingly experimental as artists try out new ideas, such as imaginative ways of applying paint to a canvas. Painting and drawing may be combined with other techniques such as collage, printing, and papermaking. This combining of techniques is known as mixed media.

The French painter Henri Matisse (1869–1954) combined paper cut-outs with paint.

Textures
Paint has texture as well as color. In this painting, the artist emphasizes texture by painting different colors on patches of material with contrasting textures.

Collage
Materials are cut and then arranged to create a collage. In this collage, vibrant colors and curved shapes are combined to create a sense of dynamism.

Paper
Artists control the color and texture of the surface they paint. They may use a flat canvas or uneven handmade paper, as in this painting.

FIND OUT MORE   ART, HISTORY OF   CRAFTS   DESIGN   DYES AND PAINTS   LEONARDO DA VINCI   MONET, CLAUDE   MUSEUMS   PICASSO, PABLO   RENAISSANCE   SCULPTURE

PAKISTAN

THE COUNTRY OF PAKISTAN was established in 1947 as an independent state for Indian Muslims. The country originally incorporated East Pakistan, formerly Bengal, which broke away in 1971 and became a separate nation called Bangladesh. Pakistan is home to four main ethnic groups. Punjabis make up more than half the population. The rest are Sindhis, Pathans, and Baluch. A military coup in 1999 led to the suspension of democratic elections. Pakistan played a key role in the 2001 US bombing of Afghanistan. Pakistan and India dispute ownership of the largely Muslim state of Kashmir.

PAKISTAN FACTS

CAPITAL CITY	Islamabad
AREA	307,374 sq miles (796,100 sq km)
POPULATION	156,500,000
MAIN LANGUAGE	Urdu
MAJOR RELIGION	Islam
CURRENCY	Pakistani rupee
LIFE EXPECTANCY	60 years
PEOPLE PER DOCTOR	2,940
GOVERNMENT	Military rule
ADULT LITERACY	46%

P

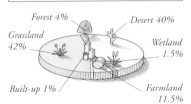

Forest 4%   Desert 40%
Grassland 42%   Wetland 1.5%
Built-up 1%   Farmland 11.5%

Land use
Much of the grassland is used as pasture for sheep. Huge irrigation projects in the Indus Valley enable crops to be cultivated. Opium is grown in the western mountains.

Physical features
The Karakoram and Hindu Kush mountain ranges, dominate the northwest of Pakistan. The Punjab and Sind contain fertile river plains. In the southwest is the dry, rocky Baluchistan plateau, while in the southeast, the Thar Desert extends into India.

Karakoram Mountains
The Karakoram Range lies along Pakistan's northern border with China. It includes K2, the world's second highest peak at 28,253 ft (8,611 m). The Hindu Kush range lies on the Afghan border.

Indus River
From its source in the Himalayas, the Indus flows 1,976 miles (3,180 km) through Pakistan, irrigating the fertile plains of the Punjab and Sind. The ancient Indus Valley civilization thrived here 4,500 years ago.

526 per sq mile (203 per sq km)   36% Urban   64% Rural

People
Nearly 97 percent of Pakistanis follow Islam, a religion that unites the main groups. A class system exists, and the gap between rich and poor is overt. Overpopulation is a problem.

127°F (53°C)   25°F (-4°C)
86°F (30°C)   52°F (11°C)
35 in (900 mm)

Climate
Pakistan has three seasons. Winter (November to March) is warm and cooled by sea breezes on the coast. Summer (April to July) is hot. The monsoon season (July to September) brings heavy rain to hills and mountains.

Fluffy cotton bolls are picked, then spun into thread to make cloth.

Ripe cotton flowers

Young cotton flowers

Cotton
Pakistan is one of the world's largest producers of raw cotton, and cotton textiles and garments are the country's leading exports. The cotton is grown in the fertile Indus flood plains. Farming employs 44 percent of Pakistan's workforce. Wheat is one of the chief crops, and rice, and sugarcane are also grown.

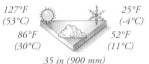

A "line of control" was established in 1972 by Simla Agreement between India and Pakistan

Islamabad
Built in the 1960s to replace Karachi as Pakistan's capital, Islamabad is home to 529,180 people. It is a spacious city with interesting modern buildings and has four areas: business, administrative, diplomatic, and residential. Islamabad also has the world's largest mosque. Karachi, with 9,200,000 people, is the country's largest city and chief port.

Street scene in Islamabad

FIND OUT MORE

ASIA, HISTORY OF   BANGLADESH AND NEPAL   DRUGS   FARMING   INDIA, HISTORY OF   INDUS VALLEY CIVILIZATION   ISLAM   MOUNTAINS AND VALLEYS   RIVERS   TEXTILES AND WEAVING

PANDAS AND RACCOONS

IT IS ONLY RECENTLY that zoologists have sorted out the relationship between pandas and raccoons. Modern scientific techniques now show that the raccoon family is divided into two subfamilies, one including raccoons, coatis, and the kinkajou, the other containing the red panda. The giant panda is related to bears. Apart from the red panda, all members of the raccoon family live in America. The pandas are found only in Asia.

Pandas

The giant panda and the red panda have a number of similar characteristics, such as a false "thumb," so they were once considered to be closely related. It is now thought that the pandas' shared features probably developed as they evolved to survive in similar habitats.

Giant panda
About 5 ft (1.5 m) long, the giant panda lives only in the mountainous forests of southwestern China. Its main food is bamboo. This woody grass is low in nutrients so pandas must eat about 84 lb (38 kg) of it every day to survive.

Paws
Both giant pandas and red pandas have five toes on each foot. They also have a false "thumb" on their forepaws. This thumb developed from the wristbone and the pandas use it to grip bamboo stems.

False thumb

A raccoon often looks for food in streams, feeling underwater for prey with its sensitive paws.

Young raccoons

Raccoons
There are seven species of raccoons. The best-known is the common raccoon with its black mask and ringed tail. This inquisitive animal eats most things, including fish, frogs, insects, small mammals, and fruit. It has adapted well to living near people and will rifle through garbage cans, picking out food with its forepaws.

Red panda
An agile animal, the red panda is about 3.3 ft (1 m) long, including its tail. It lives on the slopes of the southern Himalayas and in parts of China, spending much of the day asleep in a tree. At night, it looks for food on the ground. Bamboo is just part of its diet. Other food includes birds' eggs, chicks, and berries.

Female and young giant panda

Red panda cub

Coatis
These forest animals are at home on the ground and in trees. Females and young form groups and, during the day, forage for food such as insects, lizards, and tubers. They use their forepaws and long, flexible snout to hunt in crevices and on the forest floor.

Kinkajou
The nocturnal kinkajou lives in the forests of tropical Central and South America. It spends almost all its time in trees and is the only American carnivore to have a prehensile tail, which means it can grasp things with it. The kinkajou uses its tail to cling to branches while it feeds – mainly on fruit and nectar. Its back teeth have lost the sharp edges that carnivores need to cut into flesh. Instead, the teeth are blunt and used for crushing fruit.

Young pandas
Giant pandas often give birth to twins, but usually only one cub survives. A newborn cub is hairless and weighs only 3–3.5 oz (90–100 g). The female cradles it constantly for the first three weeks and carries it around for four to five months. Red pandas have up to four cubs that can walk after about three days.

GIANT PANDA
SCIENTIFIC NAME *Ailuropoda melanoleuca*
ORDER Carnivora
FAMILY Ursidae
DISTRIBUTION Southwestern China
HABITAT Forests with bamboo
DIET Bamboo, other plants, and meat
SIZE Length: Up to 5.5 ft (1.7 m)
LIFESPAN Over 20 years (in captivity)

FIND OUT MORE ANIMALS • ASIAN WILDLIFE • BEARS • SOUTH AMERICAN WILDLIFE • URBAN WILDLIFE

PANKHURST FAMILY

WHEN EMMELINE PANKHURST was born in 1858, women had few rights in Britain and were not allowed to vote to change the law. Emmeline and her two daughters devoted their lives to obtaining the vote for women so that they could influence decisions about their lives. They developed new strategies, organizing their supporters into a pressure group, going on protest marches, even chaining themselves to the railings of public buildings to get publicity for their cause. They also produced all kinds of merchandise to gain publicity and raise money. In 1918, after a long, bitter campaign, women aged 30 and over were given the vote in Britain.

The Pankhursts

Emmeline Goulden (1858– 1928) was born in Manchester, England, and went to a women's college in Paris. She married a lawyer, Richard Pankhurst, and had two daughters, Christabel (1880–1958) and Sylvia (1882–1960). Emmeline, a charismatic figure, inspired the WSPU, while Christabel was its leader.

Emmeline Pankhurst

Christabel Pankhurst

Sylvia Pankhurst
A socialist and a feminist, Sylvia built up a mass movement for suffrage among the poor of London's East End and was a pacifist during World War I. In later life, she championed the cause of Ethiopian independence.

WSPU

Emmeline was a member of the Independent Labor Party, but left it because of its resistance to women's suffrage (voting rights). In 1903, she formed the Women's Social and Political Union (WSPU) in Manchester. The WSPU led the campaign for women's suffrage, adopting more militant tactics after the Liberal prime minister refused to support suffrage in 1906.

Suffragettes
Women of all classes and ages joined the women's suffrage movement. Those who favored militant tactics were nicknamed suffragettes. Some risked great personal danger for their cause. In June 1913, Emily Davison threw herself in front of the king's horse at the Derby and was killed. Others risked arrest and imprisonment.

Demonstrations
Women organized demonstrations in Britain's big cities to further the cause of women's suffrage. In June 1908, more than 200,000 people gathered in Hyde Park, London, in the greatest demonstration of all. In addition, individual women performed acts of bravery by heckling and disrupting meetings, attacking prominent politicians, and damaging buildings. Many of these activities led to arrests.

Votes for women
The Pankhursts were highly skilled at attracting publicity. They set up the Women's Press and produced a regular newspaper, *Votes for Women*, sold on street corners and at meetings. They were also among the first to use manufactured items for publicity, producing a range of suffrage-related goods to fund and publicize the cause.

VOTES FOR WOMEN

The War Paper for Women

A VOTE! FOR THE CHILD'S SAKE

Hannah Mitchell
Hannah Mitchell (1871–1956) was born in poverty in rural England. She ran away from home at age 14 and worked as a maid and a seamstress. An active suffragette, Hannah Mitchell became a councillor and a magistrate in Manchester. Her autobiography, *The Hard Way Up*, is a classic account of a woman's rebellion against the unfair circumstances of her life.

Imprisonment

Many suffragettes spent time in prison for their beliefs. They were classed as criminals and subjected to harsh conditions. In protest at not being treated as political prisoners, many suffragettes went on a hunger strike, and were painfully force-fed.

Prison terms
The Pankhurst family was jailed many times. In 1913, Emmeline was jailed and released 12 times under the "Cat and Mouse Act."

Emmeline and Christabel in prison clothes, 1908

THE CAT AND MOUSE ACT
PASSED BY THE LIBERAL GOVERNMENT

THE LIBERAL CAT
ELECTORS VOTE AGAINST HIM!
KEEP THE LIBERAL OUT!

The "Cat and Mouse Act"
In 1913, the British Parliament passed a law under which hunger strikers could be released from prison but would be returned when they regained their health.

PANKHURST FAMILY

1858	Emmeline Goulden born
1880	Birth of Christabel
1882	Birth of Sylvia
1903	Women's Social and Political Union founded
1913	Emmeline sentenced to three years in prison for arson
1918	Christabel runs unsuccessfully for parliament
1918	UK women aged 30 and over given the vote (compared with age 21 and over for men)
1928	Full voting equality obtained when UK women get vote at 21

FIND OUT MORE   CRIME AND PUNISHMENT   EDUCATION   GOVERNMENT AND POLITICS   HUMAN RIGHTS   LAW   WOMEN'S MOVEMENT

PAPER

PAPER TAKES ITS name from "papyrus"– a reedlike plant that the ancient Egyptians used to make the first ever writing material. Today, most paper is made from the pulped wood of trees. Paper has played an influential role in spreading knowledge over the ages, and even in today's computer-based electronic age, more paper is being consumed than ever before. A forest region covering about 174,000 sq miles (450,000 sq km), equivalent to the size of Sweden, needs to be felled each year to support the world's consumption of paper.

What is paper?

Paper is made up of a mass of short, very thin fibers of wood cellulose pressed tightly together. It may also contain certain additives to give color and extra smoothness. If you tear a sheet of paper, you can see the cellulose fibers stuck together.

Cellulose fibers matted together

Uses of paper

One of the biggest uses of paper is for printing newspapers. This relatively cheap paper is called newsprint. Coated papers that use a claylike material to give a smooth effect are used for magazines. High quality writing papers are made from rag and wood pulp. Other paper products are made from different fibrous materials such as hemp, used in manila envelopes, and straw, used to make cardboard packaging.

Watermarked paper

Watermarked paper

When some types of paper are held up to the light, a translucent pattern or wording may be seen. This watermark signifies quality paper. The mark is pressed into the paper by a wire roller on the papermaking machine.

How paper is made

Paper can be made by hand or mechanically. Softwood logs are chopped into pieces and treated with chemicals that convert the wood to a mass of fibers. This "wood pulp" is mixed with water to make paper.

Making paper by hand

1 To make fine handmade paper, the raw material must first be broken down into wood chips and sawdust that are then beaten to a pulp.

Deckle   *Mold*

2 A mold and deckle are lowered into the liquid pulp. A layer of pulp covers the mold, its edges contained by the deckle. The mold is then lifted out and tilted to remove excess water.

3 When drained, the thin layer of paper from the mold is laid on absorbent material. Successive layers are laid on top of each other and pressed. After two hours the sheets are separated and left to dry.

Layers of paper and absorbent material

Finished paper

Paper consumption

In the Western world a person may use – and throw away – up to about 440 lb (200 kg) of paper each year in its many different forms, from note paper to cardboard. Vast areas of forest are cleared to provide raw materials for making paper. This can destroy the landscape and deprive wildlife of precious habitats.

Recycling paper

Paper was the first material to be recycled on a large scale. Recycling helps save resources by reducing the number of trees that are felled each year and some of the chemicals needed in papermaking.

Paper tip at recycling plant

Renewable resource

To maintain future timber supplies for papermaking, trees must be treated as a renewable resource. Over a given period, as many trees need to be planted as are cut down. Some countries, such as Norway and Sweden, already practice sustainable forestry.

Tree plantation, a source of paper

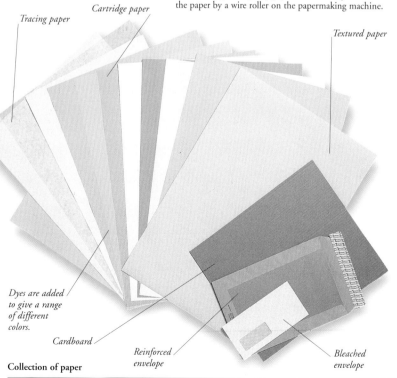

Tracing paper

Cartridge paper

Textured paper

Dyes are added to give a range of different colors.

Cardboard

Reinforced envelope

Bleached envelope

Collection of paper

FIND OUT MORE   BOOKS   DYES AND PAINTS   EGYPT, ANCIENT   POLLUTION   PRINTING   NEWSPAPERS AND MAGAZINES   TREES   WRITING

P

PARASITES

AN ORGANISM THAT LIVES inside, or on, another organism (the host), using it as a source of food, is called a parasite. In a parasitic relationship, the host gets no benefit and is usually harmed in some way by the parasite. In contrast, the parasite gains not only a constant source of food, but also shelter by hiding inside the host or among its fur or scales. Many parasites have hooks, suckers, or claws, which they use to keep a firm hold on their host.

Shaft of hair

Eyes

Claw helps louse grip hair.

Human head louse

Animal parasites

Few animals manage to avoid parasites. Some parasites, such as lice and ticks, live on the outside of their hosts, clinging to their skin or fur, and are called ectoparasites; those that live inside their host's body, such as liver flukes and tapeworms, are called endoparasites. Few parasites are deadly because it is not in their best interest to kill their host; once the host is dead, the parasite will not have long to live either. Many human diseases, such as malaria and elephantiasis, are parasitic in origin.

Fleas and ticks

Many organisms feed on the blood of others, and can spread disease to their host. Fleas are insects that feed on blood once they are adults; their larvae feed on any scraps of organic matter, including the adult fleas' droppings. Ticks, on the other hand, feed from their host throughout their development.

Helmet-shaped head cuts through cat fur.

Cat flea

Reproduction

Parasites often have complex life cycles, involving more than one host at different stages. Because they need to ensure that their eggs reach a suitable host, many parasites produce huge quantities of eggs. For example, the broad tapeworm releases up to 13 million eggs every day within body segments that break off from its rear end.

Tapeworm can reach 33 ft (10 m) in length.

Broad tapeworm

Head hooks

Egg

 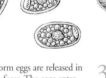

First larval form develops inside water fleas.

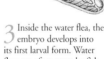

Secondary larvae develop inside fish.

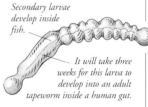
It will take three weeks for this larva to develop into an adult tapeworm inside a human gut.

Life cycle of a tapeworm

1 Tapeworms live in human guts, entering the body through infected fish. They attach themselves to the gut wall with head hooks.

2 Tapeworm eggs are released in human feces. The eggs enter water and hatch into embryos that are eaten by water fleas.

3 Inside the water flea, the embryo develops into its first larval form. Water fleas are often eaten by fish.

4 The larvae penetrate the tissues of the fish to form secondary larvae. If a human eats raw, infected fish, the larvae enter the intestines.

Flatworm

The flatworm *Leucochloridium macrostomum* is a parasite that develops in some snails. The parasite must also get into the guts of birds to complete its life cycle. To do this, it enters the snail's eyestalks where it swells and develops bright bands of color. These attract birds, which mistake the pulsating eyestalks for tasty caterpillars.

Mutualism

Mutualism is a relationship between two organisms in which both benefit, for example, between buffalos and oxpeckers. Buffalos are parasitized by ticks that can make the animal ill. The oxpecker scampers over the buffalo picking off the ticks. In this way, the bird gets a good feed, and the buffalo is cleaned.

Red-billed oxpecker on buffalo's nose

Oxpecker feeds on parasitic ticks on the buffalo.

Plant parasites

Like animals, plants also have parasites. Usually, the parasitic plant attaches its root system to its host and draws off nourishing fluids; others use their host as a means of support. For example, the strangler fig climbs up a tree for support and to get to the light. Eventually, the fig kills the tree, but by this time, its own stem will be strong enough to support it.

Mistletoe

Mistletoe is a parasitic plant that grows on trees. Birds eat its sticky seeds and deposit some on the bark of trees. The mistletoe grows roots that penetrate the bark and extract water and nutrients.

Dodder

The dodder cannot photosynthesize or produce its own food, so parasitizes heath plants such as gorse and heather. It grows long tendrils that swamp the host plant and absorb food.

Useful parasites

Most parasites are harmful, but a few are beneficial to people. In microsurgery the medicinal leech is still used to reduce the amount of damage that small blood clots can cause. Many crops are now sprayed with tiny nematode worms, which are parasites on certain agricultural pests.

Medicinal leech
Leech sucks blood from human.

HUMAN HEAD LOUSE

SCIENTIFIC NAME *Pediculus humanus capitis*

ORDER Phthiraptera

FAMILY Pediculidae

DISTRIBUTION Worldwide, wherever there are humans

HABITAT Attached to hair on head. Larvae live in hair at back of neck

DIET Human blood

SIZE 0.06–1.12 in (1.5–3 mm)

LIFESPAN Adults live for 1–2 months

FIND OUT MORE   DISEASES   MEDICINE   MEDICINE, HISTORY OF   MICROSCOPIC LIFE   PHOTOSYNTHESIS   SNAILS AND OTHER MOLLUSKS   WORMS

PARROTS

WITH THEIR NOISY CALLS and bright colors, parrots are among the most conspicuous of all the world's birds. There are about 330 species, many of which are now threatened by extinction. Most parrots live in forests and woodlands in warm parts of the world. They fly through the trees, or use their feet and their hooked beaks to clamber among the branches. Many live in pairs or flocks and search together for their food of fruits, seeds, nuts, and flowers.

Parrots can hold objects with their toes.

The area of bare skin on the face, is called the cere.

Features

Most parrots are sociable, thickset birds with short necks and large beaks. They have small eyes that are often surrounded by a patch of bare skin. Their feet are short but strong, with four fleshy, clawed toes. Parrots use their toes to grip branches and to pick up food.

Sulfur-crested cockatoo

Yellow-shouldered Amazon
This medium-size parrot lives in forests along the northern coast of South America and on nearby islands.

Two toes pointing forward and two pointing backward

Crests
Types of parrots called cockatoos have feathery crests, which males raise and lower in courtship. They bob and swing their heads at the same time, this makes the crests more obvious, and aims to attract the attentions of a nearby female.

Scarlet macaw
Macaws are the world's largest parrots and live in the forests of Central and South America. They eat fruits, seeds, and nuts, which they crack open with their large beaks.

Diet

Parrots are almost entirely vegetarian. Their beaks are similar but their tongues are shaped to suit different kinds of plant food. Most parrots find their food in trees, but some, such as kakapos and budgerigars, feed mainly on the ground.

Ground feeders
Wild budgerigars live in the dry grasslands of Australia. They often gather in huge flocks of several thousand birds, as they wander the outback searching for seeds to eat and water to drink.

Fruit feeders
The eclectus parrot is a fruit-eating parrot and has a fleshy tongue. The tongue helps the bird to hold the fruit or nut in the top part of its beak, so that it can use the lower part to break up the food.

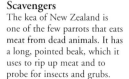

Scavengers
The kea of New Zealand is one of the few parrots that eats meat from dead animals. It has a long, pointed beak, which it uses to rip up meat and to probe for insects and grubs.

Flower feeders
Lories and lorikeets, such as this Duyvenbode's lory, have slender tongues with brush-like tips. Though the parrots have short beaks, they can use their tongues to lap up nectar and pollen from flowers.

Parrots in danger

About a quarter of the world's parrot species are endangered. Some have suffered because they are caught and sold as pets. Others are in decline because their forest home is disappearing. Many are having to face predatory animals introduced by humans.

Powerful jaw muscles for cracking open nuts and seeds.

Long, tapering tail

Beak
The upper part of a parrot's beak is much bigger than the lower part and has a hooked tip. When a parrot opens its beak, both parts hinge against its skull, allowing the bird to bite into large objects.

Trapping
Trading in wild parrots has been banned in many places but it still continues. These macaws will be sold as pets. Many will not survive.

Kakapo
This nocturnal parrot comes from New Zealand. It lives on the ground as it ito too heavy to fly. Sadly its habitat has been invaded by predatory animals brought into the country from outside, and it is now nearly extinct.

SCARLET MACAW

SCIENTIFIC NAME	*Ara macao*
ORDER	Psittaciformes
FAMILY	Psittacidae
DISTRIBUTION	From Mexico south to Brazil and Bolivia
HABITAT	Open forest and forest edges
DIET	Fruit, nuts, and seeds
SIZE	Length: 34 in (85 cm)
LIFESPAN	About 40 years

FIND OUT MORE   BIRDS   CONSERVATION   RAIN FOREST WILDLIFE

PASTEUR, LOUIS

LOUIS PASTEUR WAS one of the greatest scientists of the 19th century. He founded the science of microbiology – the study of organisms not visible to the naked eye. Pasteur believed that science should have practical uses, and that scientists and business people should not live in separate worlds. Much of his work was done in response to requests for help from businessmen. His solutions to problems in the wine and silk industries, and his work in combating life-threatening diseases, such as rabies, made him a hero. Pasteur's method of heating foods to kill harmful bacteria is still used in milk production.

Early life
Louis Pasteur was born in France and brought up in the village of Arbois. At first he did not seem to be a clever student, but his life changed when he went to classes given by a brilliant chemistry teacher. He entered the famous Ecole Normale Supérieure in Paris, and at 32 became Dean of the Faculty of Science at the University of Lille.

Bacteria

Pasteur's greatest discovery was that fermentation and decay were caused by microscopic living organisms – bacteria or germs. People had noticed the tiny organisms in decaying matter, but they thought that the organisms had appeared out of nowhere. Pasteur proved that living things could not simply appear spontaneously without living parent organisms.

Swan-necked flask
Pasteur placed boiled meat extract in a swan-necked flask, that let air in but trapped the dust containing the micro-organisms. The meat extract did not decay and no organisms grew.

Swan neck stops dust and microorganisms from entering flask.

Meat extract is free from micro-organisms.

Yeast
A vinegar manufacturer asked Pasteur to find out why the process of fermentation sometimes went wrong, spoiling the vinegar. The same problem happened with wine. Pasteur noticed that when wine aged properly, it contained round yeast cells; when it spoiled, the cells were long and narrow. He realized that there were two types of yeast, one that helped fermentation and another that spoiled the product.

Objective lens

Stage

Pasteur used this microscope to study yeast cells.

Pasteurization
Pasteur discovered that heating wine to about 140°F (60°C) killed off the unwanted yeast. This method of gentle heating was soon applied to other stored liquids, especially milk. The process became known as "pasteurization," after its inventor. Pasteurization is still used widely today to kill harmful bacteria and help make food and beverages safe for human consumption. One of the most familiar uses of the process is in milk production. Before it is sold in the shops, milk is heated for 30 minutes to kill bacteria that could cause tuberculosis in humans. The protein in the milk is unaffected.

Causes of disease

Pasteur proved that many diseases are caused by bacteria. Vaccination – breeding bacteria in a weak form and placing them in an animal's body – can help the animal develop immunity to the bacteria. Building on the work of British doctor Edward Jenner (1749–1823), Pasteur vaccinated sheep against anthrax.

Cocoon of silkworm

Silkworms
In 1865 Pasteur applied his theory of germs to diseased silkworms. He showed that a parasite was infecting the silkworms and the leaves they fed on. Destroying all the infested worms and leaves wiped out the disease.

Rabies
In 1881, Pasteur began to work on a cure for rabies, a disease that affected both animals and humans and that killed hundreds of people in Europe every year. He found that brain tissue from animals with rabies (below) could be made into a vaccine against the disease. In 1885, he tried out the vaccine on Joseph Meister, a boy who had been bitten by a rabid dog. The boy recovered from the disease.

Pasteur Institute
Pasteur's discovery of a vaccination for rabies made him a hero, and a movement began to collect funds for an institute that would honor him and carry on his scientific work. People from all over the world, including the tsar of Russia and the emperor of Brazil, sent in contributions. The Institute was building was completed in 1895; Pasteur died in the same year and was buried in the Institute.

Pasteur Institute, France

LOUIS PASTEUR

1822	Born, Dôle, France.
1843	Begins his studies at the Ecole Normale Supérieure, Paris.
1849	Marries Marie Laurent.
1854	Becomes Dean of the Faculty of Science at the University of Lille.
1857–65	Studies the fermentation process.
1865–70	Studies pebrine, a disease of silkworms.
1881	Begins work on rabies disease.
1882	Proves the effectiveness of the anthrax vaccine.
1885	Vaccinates Joseph Meister against rabies.
1888	Becomes director of the Pasteur Institute.
1895	Dies; Pasteur Institute building completed.

FIND OUT
MORE

BIOLOGY · DISEASES · FOOD · MEDICINE, HISTORY OF · MICROSCOPES · MICROSCOPIC LIFE · SCIENCE, HISTORY OF

PEACE MOVEMENTS

THROUGHOUT HISTORY, people have engaged in warfare. And every time a war has been fought, some people have joined a peace movement to protest against it. Peace movements contain a wide variety of people: some oppose war for religious reasons or as a matter of individual conscience; others may oppose a particular war for political reasons. Huge demonstrations of thousands of people, and individual acts of courageous protest, contribute to effective campaigns for peace.

The dove is a traditional symbol of peace.

Pacifism

The belief that violence of any kind is wrong is known as pacifism. Pacifists have a principled objection to war and refuse to take part in any behavior that might lead them directly or indirectly to threaten another human life. Pacifists conduct antiwar protests in nonviolent ways (other people use direct action that may harm people and property).

Popular protest

Throughout history, popular protest against war or the threat of war has taken many forms. Individuals have refused to fight or work in war-related industries; groups of people have demonstrated, organized public protests and peace camps, or tried to disrupt war preparations.

White poppy, symbol of Peace Pledge Union

Worn to remember all those who have suffered in war

Antinuclear protest
From the 1950s, popular peace movements have pressured governments to cut their supply of nuclear weapons. Leading groups include SANE and the Nuclear Freeze in the US and the Campaign for Nuclear Disarmament (CND) in the UK.

Greenham Common
There is a long history of women playing a specific part in peace movements. In 1982, a permanent women-only peace camp was set up at the US Air Force base at Greenham Common, England, to protest at the site of US nuclear missiles on British soil.

Objectors in prison, World War I

Conscientious objectors
During World Wars I and II, people on both sides refused to fight on principle. Some took no part at all in war activity; others worked in noncombat areas, such as the medical professions. Many suffered personal abuse or were imprisoned.

Peace Pledge Union
The Peace Pledge Union is a pacifist organization that works for peace. It was set up in 1934, and by 1936, more than 100,000 people had signed the pledge to renounce war as a way of settling disputes between nations.

The CND symbol is a well-known symbol of antinuclear protest.

Greenham Common

Government action

Governments can cause war, but can also contribute to peace by maintaining friendly relations with other nations and by attempting to reconcile international differences through negotiation or diplomacy. Countries prosper in peacetime, because they can trade safely with other nations. However, they also earn money by exporting weapons.

Since 1945, governments and individuals alike have campaigned for nuclear weapons to be banned.

Begin (left) and Sadat (right)

Camp David Accords
To end the historic enmity between their countries, Egyptian President Anwar Sadat (1918–81) and Israeli Prime Minister Menachem Begin (1913–92) signed this peace treaty in 1978. As a result, Sadat was assassinated in 1981.

Disarmament conferences
The first conference to reduce the world stockpile of weapons took place from 1932 to 1934. The talks failed, but since then international negotiations have reduced the nuclear stockpile.

Nobel Peace Prize
Since 1901, the Nobel Peace Prize has been awarded annually to people whose work has promoted peace between nations. The Swedish inventor of dynamite, Alfred Nobel (1833–96), left money in his will to fund the prize.

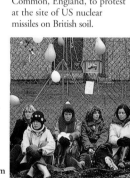

Timeline

1864 Geneva Convention protects the neutrality of noncombatants and medical staff during war.

1901 First Nobel Peace Prize awarded.

The founder of the International Red Cross was awarded the Nobel Peace Prize in 1901.

1915 International Congress of Women meets at the Hague, Holland, with proposals to end World War I. Envoys visit heads of state in 14 countries.

1932–34 World Disarmament Conference meets in Geneva, Switzerland.

1963 US, USSR, and Britain sign the Partial Test Ban Treaty, banning the testing of nuclear weapons in the atmosphere.

1968 Nonproliferation Treaty forbids the export of nuclear weapons.

Polaris nuclear warhead

1972 US and USSR agree to reduce their total number of nuclear weapons in the Strategic Arms Limitation Talks (SALT).

1980s Antinuclear demonstrations throughout Europe at the site of US missiles on European soil.

1988 US and USSR agreed to dismantle all short- and medium-range nuclear weapons.

FIND OUT MORE

COLD WAR · GANDHI, MOHANDAS · UNITED NATIONS · WARFARE · WEAPONS · WOMEN'S MOVEMENT · WORLD WAR I · WORLD WAR II

PENGUINS

THE 17 SPECIES of penguins make up one of the most remarkable families in the entire bird world. None of them can fly, but their streamlined bodies are superbly adapted for swimming. They usually stand upright on land and move by walking or hopping, but on ice they sometimes lie flat and slide along like sleds. They are well adapted for coping with the cold. Penguins are found only in the southern hemisphere, although one species, the Galápagos penguin, lives on the Equator.

Sleek, new plumage

Dense, waterproof plumage

Old feathers ready to molt.

Broad feet with stubby claws

Wings covered with short, hard feathers.

Molting
Every year, penguins molt their old feathers. Unlike other birds, penguins' old feathers do not come out until the new ones have grown, so the bird is always insulated against the cold.

King penguin
Only the emperor penguin is larger than the king penguin. Male and female king penguins look almost identical and they pair up for life. They breed on windswept islands, raising an average of just one chick every two years.

Types of penguins

Macaroni
This penguin breeds on islands around Antarctica. It has long, bright yellow feathers above its eyes.

Humboldt
This species feeds in the cool water of the Humboldt current on the west coast of South America.

Adélie
The most common penguin of Antarctica, the small Adélie nests in huge colonies.

Galápagos
This rare bird lives on the Galápagos Islands near the Equator. The water around there is cold.

Penguin features
Penguins have a large, pointed beak, a streamlined body, and short, stiff wings, which they cannot fold up. Their legs are short, set far back on the body. When standing, they often use their tail as a prop. The birds have short, waterproof feathers all over that keep them streamlined. Under their skin is a layer of fat that keeps them warm in icy water and also acts as a store of food.

Penguin skeleton
Unlike flying birds, penguins have solid bones that make them almost as dense as seawater. Their density allows them to dive easily. Penguins have flexible shoulder joints but their wing bones are firmly locked together so keep their wings stiff.

Skeleton of Rockhopper

Rockhopper penguin

Wings used like flippers.

Feet act as rudders.

Strong chest muscles pull down the wings.

Penguin rises through the water to break through the surface.

Swimming
Some penguins can swim more than 25 mph (40 kmh). They propel themselves forward with their wings and steer with their feet and tail. Many penguins burst through the surface of the water as they swim. This is called porpoising. It gives the penguins' feathers a layer of air bubbles that helps to reduce friction between the penguins and the water.

Breeding
Most species of penguin build nests on the ground or in holes, but the king and the emperor penguin incubate a single egg on their feet under a flap of skin. Emperor penguins breed on Antarctic ice. The female lays one egg in the autumn, then heads out to sea. The male incubates the egg through the winter, when temperatures can drop to below -50°F (-45°C).

Birds take turns to get out of the wind.

Huddling reduces heat loss.

Adult emperor penguins carry small chicks around on their feet.

KING PENGUIN

SCIENTIFIC NAME	*Aptenodytes patagonica*
ORDER	Sphenisciformes
FAMILY	Spheniscidae
DISTRIBUTION	Islands and ocean north of Antarctica
HABITAT	Coasts and open sea
DIET	Fish and squid
SIZE	Length, including tail 37.5 in (95 cm)
LIFESPAN	About 20 years

FIND OUT MORE   ANTARTICA   BIRDS   FLIGHTLESS BIRDS   ISLAND WILDLIFE   POLAR WILDLIFE

PERSIAN EMPIRES

FOR ALMOST A THOUSAND YEARS, immensely powerful Persian rulers controlled three vast empires. The first "King of Kings," as they were known, was Cyrus the Great, who founded the Achaemenid dynasty. This empire was followed by nearly 100 years of Greek rule, which in turn was followed by the long-lived Parthian and Sassanian dynasties. Persian governments employed provincial rulers, or satraps, to keep order and collect taxes. A network of trade routes connected Europe, Arabia, and western Asia with India, Mongolia, and China. In the center of all this, Persia absorbed influences from ancient civilizations, and influenced later ones.

Persian dynasties
The Achaemenid Empire (559–331 BC) was conquered by Alexander the Great in 333 BC. After a period of Greek rule, the Persians regained control, establishing the formidable Parthian dynasty. The final Persian dynasty was the Sassanian (227–651), which glorified its warrior kings in legend and opulent art.

Persepolis

Darius the Great (r.521–486 BC) founded a complex of palaces at Persepolis. It was completed by his son, Xerxes I. Set in lush gardens, its vast audience hall and monumental staircases were designed for magnificent public ceremonies, most importantly the New Year festival on the first day of spring. In 330 BC, Alexander the Great burned Persepolis, possibly in revenge for the razing of the Acropolis in 479 BC by Xerxes.

Staircase to the Tripylon, Persepolis

Square towers

Slender columns

Rosette detail

Carvings of tribute bearers

Lion attacking a bull

Back-to-back bulls often decorated column tops, or capitals.

The king's bodyguards, known as the 10,000 Immortals

Rosette

Stone capital with two bulls, Susa

Wall carvings
Large portraits of kings, courtiers, and attendants were carved on the stone walls. The stairway walls depicted the New Year ceremony. People from all nations of the empire marched past, bringing the king jewelry and tributes. Gifts included live animals, such as bulls.

Monumental staircases were wide enough for eight horsemen abreast.

Darius III being defeated by Alexander the Great at the Battle of Issus, 333 BC

Battle of Gaugamela-Arbela
In 333 BC, Alexander defeated Darius III at the Battle of Issus in Syria. Darius fled. Two years later Alexander beat Darius again at the Battle of Gaugamela-Arbela, farther to the east. This defeat signaled the end of the dynasty and, therefore, the Achaemenid Empire. Darius III, the last of the Achaemenid kings, fled east from Gaugamela-Arbela and was eventually killed by his own cousin. Alexander went on to conquer the great city of Babylon and parts of India.

Trade and tribute

Kings received taxes and tribute from subjects all over the empire and encouraged trade through busy ports on the Persian Gulf. During the Achaemenid dynasty, camels were used to carry goods for the first time, and a Royal Road stretched 1,600 miles (2,500 km) from Susa (Iran) to Sardis (Turkey). Its purpose was to move goods to and from the Mediterranean coast, and it had more than 100 rest stops for travelers.

Arabian camel

Sheep with young

Ivory

Gold

Honey

Greek influence

To consolidate his control of the area, Alexander the Great arranged for his soldiers to marry local Persian women. At the ancient capital of Susa, hundreds of couples were married in one day. After Alexander's death, his general, Seleucus, founded the Seleucid dynasty. The dynasty built Greek-style cities and kept Greek culture alive. In Persian folklore Alexander became a legendary hero called Iskander.

Cyrus the Great
Founder of the Achaemenid Empire, Cyrus II (r.559–530 BC), also known as "the Great," was a just and merciful ruler. After conquering Lydia and Media, he captured the city of Babylon without a battle in 539 BC and told his men not to damage it. One of his first actions was to free the Jews who had been held captive there since 586 BC.

Government

The Achaemenids set up a basic system of government that continued for more than 1,000 years. The king had a council of nobles who represented people from all over the empire. About 20 large provinces, called satrapies, were governed separately. The government spent tax money on public services, such as roads, drainage, and irrigation.

Impression of seal

Sassanian seals were used as symbols of authority.

Satrapies

Retired generals or local princes, known as satraps, controlled the satrapies. The satraps were tolerant: they allowed their subjects to follow their own customs and practice their own religions, as long as they paid tribute to the King of Kings.

Zoroastrianism

Two important prophets came from the Persian Empire: Zoroaster and Mani. Zoroaster (c.620– 551 BC) taught that life was a battle between good and evil, and that a supreme god named Ahura Mazda was the champion of goodness. Each Persian king believed Ahura Mazda chose him to rule others, and that he was therefore protected by the god. Zoroastrianism was the Persian state religion, but following the conquest of the Sassanian Empire by Arab Muslims, most Persians converted to Islam. The Zoroastrians fled to India where they still practice their religion and are known as Parsi (from "Persian").

Modern Parsi priest, India

The magi

In Persia, a class of high priests called magi (singular: magus) performed religious ceremonies involving sacrificial fire. Zoroaster may have been a magus, since the magi accepted his teachings, became leaders in the new religion, and made fire worship a part of it. Magi are often depicted holding barsom – special twigs used to feed sacred flames. Magi were also expert astrologers revered and consulted by the people.

Arts and crafts

Persian artists, particularly the Sassanians, worked skilfully in stone, metal, clay, and textiles. Sassanian kings had valley rock-faces carved with huge images of their royal glory, often using old Achaemenid palace sites. The great care lavished on stone carving was perfectly reproduced in metal work objects, such as the gold and silver temple hoard pulled from the Oxus River in Afghanistan.

Gold Achaemenid drinking horn

Manichaeism

The Persian prophet Mani (216–276) founded a new religion that comprised elements of many faiths. The magi objected and persuaded King Bahram I (r.273–276) to have him tortured and executed. Today, although the religion itself is dead, the influence of Manichaeism is evident in Christianity and Chinese Taoism.

The death of Mani

Figure holding barsom

Metalwork

The Persians were fascinated with animals. Gold, silver, and bronze vessels shaped as lions, eagles, and mythical horned beasts all had symbolic meaning. Sassanian metalwork was particularly highly prized, and huge numbers of valuable cups and serving bowls were used for lavish banquets. Merchants exported silverware along the trade routes to China, and Chinese craftsmen copied Sassanian designs.

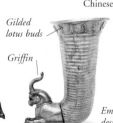

The crown indicates that the figure is possibly a king.

Gilded lotus buds

Griffin

Gold figurine

Embossed design

Silver gilt drinking horn

Inlaid precious stones

Gold bowl, Oxus treasure

Griffin (mythical horned beast)

Gold armlet, Oxus treasure

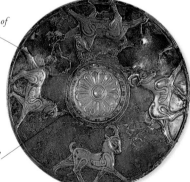

Figures of ibexes

Gold boss

A circular silver shield with gold design

Darius the Great

Under Darius I (521–486 BC), the Persian Empire reached its height. Darius was an energetic military leader and a gifted ruler, with an efficient government at Susa, where he built an elaborate palace before founding Persepolis. Archaeologists have found gold, silver, and stone inscriptions describing Darius's achievements.

Timeline

c.620 BC Birth of the prophet Zoroaster.

559 BC Cyrus II becomes king of Persia.

550 BC Cyrus defeats the Medes, founding the Achaemenid Empire.

539 BC Cyrus II conquers Babylon.

521–486 BC Darius I (the Great) reigns.

333 BC Battle of Issus.

Griffin from gold armlet

331 BC Battle of Gaugamela-Arbela ends Achaemenid Empire.

321 BC Greek Seleucid Empire is founded.

239 BC Beginning of Parthian Empire.

AD 216 Birth of the prophet Mani.

227 Beginning of Sassanian Empire.

651 Sassanian Empire falls to the Arabs.

FIND OUT MORE

ALEXANDER THE GREAT   BABYLONIAN EMPIRE   METALS   RELIGIONS   SAFAVID EMPIRE

P

PHILIPPINES

ACROSS THE CHINA SEA from Southeast Asia are about 7,107 islands of the Philippines, of which only 900 are inhabited. The world's second largest island group, or archipelago, the Philippines lie on the "ring of fire," an arc of volcanoes that circles the Pacific Ocean. Spanish colonization in 1565, and American occupation from 1898 to 1946, have greatly influenced Philippine language and society. The islands are rich in natural resources, but half the population lives in poverty.

PHILIPPINES FACTS

CAPITAL CITY	Manila
AREA	115,860 sq miles (300,076 sq km)
POPULATION	76,000,000
MAIN LANGUAGES	Filipino, English
MAJOR RELIGIONS	Christian, Muslim
CURRENCY	Philippine peso
LIFE EXPECTANCY	69 years
PEOPLE PER DOCTOR	10,000
GOVERNMENT	Multiparty democracy
ADULT LITERACY	95%

Physical features

Most of the large islands are mountainous, with active volcanoes, such as Mount Pinatubo on Luzon, which erupted violently in 1991. Flooding and earthquakes are also common. The islands are thickly forested, and about one-third of the land is used for agriculture.

Terraces
The stunning Banaue rice terraces in northern Luzon are steps cut into the mountain on which large amounts of rice are grown. An ancient water system is used to keep each level moist and limit erosion of the soil. The terraces were built by hand, using stone walls, approximately 2,000 years ago and are now the subject of international research into rice plant breeding and harvesting.

Chocolate Hills
Bohol Island has a central plateau of more than 1,000 mounds, known as the Chocolate Hills, up to 394 ft (120 m) high.

Climate
The climate is hot and humid all year. The rainy season lasts from June to October. About five tropical storms strike the eastern coasts of the islands every year between June and December.

100°F (38°C)   68°F (20°C)
82°F (28°C)   77°F (25°C)
98 in (2,083 mm)

People
The Philippines is the only Christian state in Asia. About 85 percent of Filipinos are Roman Catholics, as a result of the Spanish colonization, and the Church plays an important role in social and cultural life. In the annual 36-hour Moriones festival, held from Good Friday to Easter Sunday, Jesus' crucifixion and resurrection are acted out.

Mock crucifixion during annual Moriones Festival

609 per sq mile (235 per sq km)

54% Urban   46% Rural

Workers must wear hard hats to protect their heads.

Manila
The capital, Manila, is a thriving center for trade and industry, and home to more than ten million people. As a result of population growth and cuts in mass transit, traffic jams are among the worst in the world. Ex US-army jeeps, called jeepneys, left behind after World War II (1939–45), provide one of the main means of transportation.

Traffic jam of jeepneys

Electricity plant of a cement factory

Farming and industry
Most factories use electricity, 40 percent of which is provided by geothermal power from beneath the Earth's crust. Agriculture employs 39 percent of the workforce, although many Filipinos work abroad. Food processing factories export tropical fruits, sugar, coconuts, and tobacco. The islands are rich in minerals, and the waters around them teem with fish, which form the basis of Filipino cuisine.

FIND OUT MORE   ASIA   ASIA, HISTORY OF   CHRISTIANITY   EARTHQUAKES   EMPIRES   ENERGY   FARMING   ISLANDS   STORMS   VOLCANOES

PHILOSOPHY

PHILOSOPHERS TRY TO make sense of the world and of human experiences within it. They seek to understand abstract concepts, such as truth, beauty, right, or wrong, and look for deeper reasons for why we think the way we do. They examine ideas that we might otherwise accept without question. Western philosophy began in ancient Greece, and the word comes from the Greek meaning "love of wisdom." Then, philosophers considered the areas of science, knowledge, and inquiry. Modern philosophers are more likely to examine the nature of language itself, for example, questioning the meaning of words.

Epistemology
This is the study of the theory of knowledge. It asks what knowledge is, how we come to know things, how we can feel sure we know anything for certain, and whether our knowledge is based on reason or experience.

Branches of philosophy

Philosophy is divided into different categories, such as epistemology, logic, metaphysics, and ethics. Philosophers also study areas such as religion, language and the meanings of words, and the methods of science. They examine other fields of thought, such as politics and psychology, and question the methods by which political thinkers and psychologists arrive at their conclusions.

P

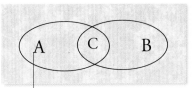

Venn diagrams are a visual way of representing the points of an argument.

Logic
When we discuss or argue, we usually follow basic rules in order to persuade others to agree with us. Logic is the study of these underlying rules: what they are, and why they are important.

René Descartes
French philosopher René Descartes (1596–1650) asked how we can be certain of what we know. He based all knowledge on a central truth: "I think, therefore I am," By this he meant that we cannot doubt the existence of our own thoughts, therefore we must exist.

Metaphysics considers the nature of the Universe.

Metaphysics
Metaphysical problems include the difficulty of explaining how our minds influence our bodies (and vice versa), what it is for something to exist (in reality, in imagination, in the past, present, and future), and how one event relates to another.

Is it always wrong to kill?

Ethics
We believe that certain acts, such as murder, are wrong, and that others, such as kindness, are right. In ethics, philosophers ask what these moral beliefs have in common, and what really makes a particular act right or wrong.

The work of a philosopher

Philosophers do not have any specific methods for proving their theories. They rely on reason and argument to explore ideas. To test statements that other people might think are self-evident, they propose made-up situations and examine them from different angles.

If it is against one's principles ever to kill, then even killing one person to save five becomes a problem.

A runaway train presents a difficult dilemma.

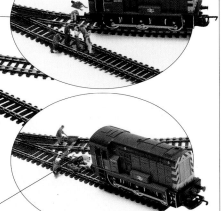

If the woman takes no action, five people will die. Does the absence of action make her responsible for these deaths?

Principles or consequences?
Philosophers examine hypothetical (made-up) situations to explore profound questions. The example shown here was suggested by the British philosopher Phillipa Foot. A woman sees a runaway train approaching a fork in the track. The train is heading for a branch with five people working on it, but the onlooker can divert it to kill one person instead. What is the right course of action to take? There are no easy answers.

The mind

Philosophers discuss the human mind. They ask whether the mind and the soul are the same, or whether the mind is just the sum of millions of electrical signals in the brain. Scientists know that parts of the brain are important for senses and skills, but have yet to explain things such as intention or desire.

Consciousness
Being aware of ourselves and the world around us is called consciousness. It is a central feature of the human mind. Some philosophers ask where this awareness comes from. For example, when I remember a scene, it is as if I project an image onto a screen. If I cannot explain where I am looking at this screen *from,* I cannot explain consciousness.

FIND OUT MORE   BRAIN AND NERVOUS SYSTEM   GREECE, ANCIENT   LANGUAGES   LAW   MATHEMATICS   RELIGIONS   SOCRATES

PHOENICIANS

SOME 3,000 YEARS AGO, expert sailors and merchants known as the Phoenicians controlled trade throughout the Mediterranean. They originated in Phoenicia, a coastal strip at the eastern end of the Mediterranean Sea often known as the Levant and now part of Lebanon, Syria, and Israel. The Phoenicians sailed far and wide, and at their peak in 1250 BC, established trading posts and colonies in Sicily, Malta, Sardinia, and Tunisia, and along the coasts of Spain and North Africa. In 332 BC, Alexander the Great conquered Phoenicia and brought to an end one of the ancient world's greatest trading empires.

Seafaring empire

The Phoenician empire was based on trade. From its ports, fleets of ships laden with trade goods stopped at coastal colonies to exchange luxury items for raw materials. At home in Phoenicia, craftspeople made more goods for trade from the imported materials.

Carthage

According to legend, the African coastal city of Carthage (in modern Tunisia) was founded in 814 BC by a group of Phoenician aristocrats from Tyre, led by Queen Dido. Carthage – meaning "new city" – was built from scratch by the colonists. It became Phoenicia's most prosperous trading port, linking the African interior with the Mediterranean world. By c.600 BC Carthage, the largest African coastal city west of Egypt, gained independence from Phoenicia.

Phoenician dedication, Cyprus, 391 BC

Alphabet
Western scripts are all derived from the Phoenician alphabet. This was used by the ancient Greeks and the Etruscans, whose early civilizations existed at the same time as the peak of the Phoenicians.

Warships
Phoenician warships sailed ahead of the cargo ships to patrol trade routes and protect the cargo from pirates. Warships used both oars and sails and were three times faster than the bulky trading vessels. They were famous throughout the Mediterranean for a revolutionary new weapon – a bronze-tipped ram for piercing the hulls of enemy vessels.

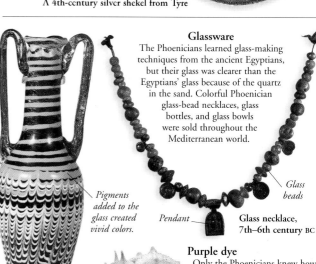

Λ 4th-century silver shekel from Tyre

Glassware
The Phoenicians learned glass-making techniques from the ancient Egyptians, but their glass was clearer than the Egyptians' glass because of the quartz in the sand. Colorful Phoenician glass-bead necklaces, glass bottles, and glass bowls were sold throughout the Mediterranean world.

Trade goods

The Phoenicians traded carvings, glassware, and purple-dyed cloth in return for raw ivory, gold, and precious stones and metals. Trading ports included Tyre, Berytus (modern Beirut), and Carthage.

Ivory carvings
The craftspeople of Tyre used elephant tusks to make beautiful ivory carvings, often decorated with gold leaf and jewels. These carvings were then inlaid in furniture produced by Phoenician carpenters. Carthage was a main trading port for ivory goods.

Gilded ivory furniture panel

Pigments added to the glass created vivid colors.

Glass beads

Pendant

Glass necklace, 7th–6th century BC

Bottle for incense, 3rd–1st century BC

Purple dye
Only the Phoenicians knew how to extract purple dye from murex shells, and the word Phoenicia actually comes from the Greek for purple. For the later Romans and Greeks, purple cloth was highly prized.

Murex seashell

Queen Dido
Roman legend says that when Dido, the King of Tyre's daughter, landed in North Africa, she asked a hostile local ruler for some land. He said that she could have only as much land as one oxhide would cover. Quick-witted Dido had the hide cut into thin strips and laid end to end, thus marking off a large area of land upon which to build the city of Carthage.

Timeline
1500 BC Phoenicians found cities along eastern Mediterranean.

1140 BC Phoenicians found their first North African colony at Utica (modern Utique, Tunisia).

c.1000 BC Trade conflicts between the Phoenicians and the early Greek civilization; and between the Phoenicians and Rome.

c.1000 BC Phoenicians develop an alphabet. This is used later as the model for the Greek alphabet on which all western alphabets are based.

957 BC Phoenician carpenters and stonemasons complete the the first Temple of Solomon in Jerusalem.

Ivory sphinx, 9th century BC

814 BC Phoenicians found the new colony of Carthage on North Africa's coast.

600 BC Carthage breaks away from Phoenician control.

332 BC Alexander the Great conquers Phoenicia. As Greek people move to Phoenician cities, Phoenician culture gradually dies out.

FIND OUT MORE   ALEXANDER THE GREAT   GLASS   GREECE, ANCIENT   ROMAN EMPIRE   WRITING

PHOTOGRAPHY

A PHOTOGRAPH CAN CAPTURE an instant of happiness or record an athlete's record-breaking sprint; it can show the cruelty of war or the beauty of the Earth from space. Photography is more complex than pictures you see in a magazine. Although photography is a relatively new technology, it now influences every part of our lives. X-ray photography can reveal faulty welds in a gas pipeline, or faulty valves in your heart. A process called photo-lithography is used to etch microscopic circuits onto computer chips.

Daguerre's photograph of Paris rooftops

Early photographs
Although French inventor Joseph Niepce (1765–1833) experimented with photography, it was Louis Daguerre (1787–1851) who perfected the process in 1839. Early cameras could only take pictures of perfectly still objects.

Types of photography
Modern cameras have made photography easier, but different types of photography still demand different skills. Great news photographers can anticipate where historic events are about to unfold, while landscape photographers need patience and an artist's skill with composition.

Landscapes
Outdoor scenes offer the photographer infinite variety because the mood of every place alters with changing light, weather, and seasons. Skillful photographs capture atmosphere.

Action pictures
A camera can reveal actions that are too quick to see with the naked eye, splitting a second into 4,000 parts or more. To take good action pictures, a photographer must learn when to trigger the shutter to capture just the right moment.

The people of Berlin pull down the wall that divided their city.

Diffuser spreads light, softening shadows.

White screen positioned to reflect light.

Seamless paper backdrop covers walls and floor.

Studio flash units require heavy power packs.

Three-legged tripod supports camera rigidly.

Spare film in quick change magazines.

A photographer at work
Photography is possible almost anywhere, but taking high-quality pictures is easiest in a specially equipped photographic studio. There, the photographer has complete control over the background, and can quickly change the direction, intensity, and color of the lighting.

Photographic teamwork
Studio photography is complex and needs contributions from many specialists. Besides the model and the assistant, the photographer may also need the help of a hairdresser, makeup artist, and stylist.

Close-ups
Our eyes cannot focus clearly on objects that are closer than a hand's width away. Photography magnifies tiny details so we can look much closer, filling the picture with a flower, or bringing us face-to-face with an insect.

News photography
Television broadcasts show news events as they happen, but photographs in a newspaper can have a more lasting impact. Today, powerful photographs have helped draw attention to the horrors of wars and famines.

Image manipulation
Altering and manipulating photographs has always been possible, but computers now make it easy to do. Merging different images is called photocomposition.

A city backdrop is added on computer.

Eve Arnold
When American Eve Arnold (b. 1913) began her career, most news photographers were male. She photographed scenes where men were excluded, such as the enclosed world of Arab women. She also photographed famous people, but she is best known for her extraordinary pictures of ordinary men and women.

FIND OUT MORE

CAMERAS   CARTOONS AND ANIMATION   COMPUTERS   FILM AND FILM-MAKING   INVENTIONS   PRINTING   TELEVISION

PHOTOSYNTHESIS

PLANTS USE SUNLIGHT to make sugars from water and carbon dioxide. This process is called photosynthesis. It takes place mostly in the leaves, which contain the green pigment chlorophyll. This pigment traps some of the energy in sunlight, using it to drive a sequence of chemical reactions that results in the production of glucose and water. Oxygen is produced as a waste product.

Light energy

Sunlight is a mixture of colored light composed of different wavelengths. The most important wavelength for photosynthesis is that of red light. This is absorbed by the pigment chlorophyll in the plant. The other wavelengths are reflected, making the plant look green.

Sunlight is made up of red, orange, yellow, green, blue, indigo, and violet light.

Energy in sunlight is trapped by chlorophyll in the leaf.

Chloroplasts *Leaf cell*

Chlorophyll

1 The pigment chlorophyll is found inside tiny structures called chloroplasts, which are found in most of a leaf's cells. Each leaf contains millions of chloroplasts. Inside each one there are stacks of membranes that hold the chlorophyll molecules.

Carbon dioxide

2 About 0.03 percent of the air is the gas carbon dioxide. It is breathed out by animals and also released when fossil fuels are burned. For photosynthesis to occur, carbon dioxide enters a leaf through tiny pores called stomata. These are mostly on the underside of the leaf.

Carbon dioxide molecules

Stomata

Oxygen

5 This gas is a by-product of photosynthesis. It passes out of the leaves through the stomata and into the air. Plants produce all the oxygen that animals and plants need for respiration. The plants themselves use only a fraction of the oxygen they make.

Oxygen molecules

Water

3 For photosynthesis to proceed, a plant needs a constant supply of water. It takes the water up from the soil through its roots. The water then travels up the xylem tissue in the stem to the leaves. During photosynthesis, water molecules within the chloroplasts are split apart. This produces hydrogen ions (groups of atoms) and oxygen molecules.

Glucose molecule

Glucose

4 The glucose produced by photosynthesis is a simple sugar. It contains all the energy that the plant needs to grow and reproduce. A plant also uses glucose, together with essential minerals drawn up with water, to produce all the compounds in its make up. These include starch, which acts as an energy store, and cellulose, which builds the plant's cell walls.

Water molecules

Transpiration

Much of the water reaching the leaves is lost through the stomata and evaporates in a process known as transpiration. A plant replaces the water by taking up more through its roots. It also controls the amount transpired by closing its stomata.

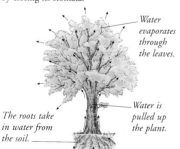

Water evaporates through the leaves.

The roots take in water from the soil.

Water is pulled up the plant.

Xylem and phloem

Water and dissolved minerals pass up the roots, stems, or trunk of a plant in tubes called xylem. These are made of non-living cells with reinforced walls. Sugars formed in the leaves are dissolved in cell sap and are carried to all parts of the plant in living cells called phloem.

Xylem transports water and dissolved minerals.

Phloem transports dissolved sugars.

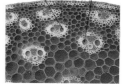

Jan Ingenhousz

The Dutchman Jan Ingenhousz (1730–99) studied physics, chemistry, and medicine. He was one of the first people to study photosynthesis. He followed up the discovery by Joseph Priestley (1733–1804) that plants give off oxygen, and later published a work on gas exchange in plants. He showed that the green part of plants take in carbon dioxide and release oxygen when sunlight falls on them. He also showed that the opposite happens in the dark.

FIND OUT MORE   AIR   ENERGY   FOOD WEBS AND CHAINS   GASES   LIGHT   PLANTS   PLANTS, ANATOMY   PLANTS, REPRODUCTION

P

PHYSICS

PHYSICS IS THE STUDY of energy and matter – from the smallest subatomic particles to the largest galaxies in the night sky. Physics is a basic science that investigates the laws that govern how the Universe works. The broad scope of physics is used to explain concepts in chemistry, astronomy, biology, and other sciences. One of the main tools of the physicist is mathematics. Using mathematics, a physicist can analyze the results of an experiment in order to prove or disprove a scientific theory.

Classical physics

Before the 20th century, physics was limited to the study of electricity and magnetism, force and motion, and light and waves. The accurate theories of that time are today collectively called classical physics. Classical physics began in the 16th century with the study of the flight paths of cannonballs.

Modern physics

Electromagnetic radiation, nuclear reactions, chaos, and relativity are all studied in modern physics. Chaos tries to understand complex systems such as the weather, which can be unpredictable. Chaos can be used to generate complex computerized images called fractals.

Computer-generated fractal

Experimental physics

A physicist who tests theories in a laboratory is called an experimental physicist. For example, a physicist investigating force and motion might carry out the experiment shown here to test a theory that a trolley moving down a slope accelerates at a constant rate. The results may or may not support the theory.

Ticker tape machine

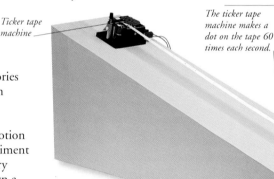

The ticker tape machine makes a dot on the tape 60 times each second.

The ticker tape is attached to the back of the trolley.

The trolley accelerates down the slope, pulling the ticker-tape through the machine.

The steeper the slope, the greater the trolley's acceleration.

Interpreting the results

After the experiment, the tape is cut into strips of two dots. Each strip shows how far the trolley moved in one-thirtieth of a second. The strips are laid side by side to form a graph. The graph's straight line proves that the trolley accelerated down the slope at a constant rate.

Graph of results

Branches of physics

Physics examines the behavior of matter and energy, which, together with empty space, make up the entire Universe. For this reason, the theories and methods of physics can be used in any area of scientific study.

CAT scanner

Biophysics

A biophysicist studies the physical processes and changes that occur in living things and the way they respond to stimuli such as heat and light. Electron microscopes allow biophysicists to see objects too tiny for even optical telescopes to detect.

Dust mite seen in electron microscope

Medical physics

Using the methods of physics to help diagnose and treat sickness is called medical physics. One of the best known tools of the medical physicist is the CAT scanner, which uses X rays to give 3-D images of body organs and tissues.

Particle physics

Matter is made up of more than 200 different types of particles, including electrons, protons, and quarks. Machines called bubble chambers and particle accelerators allow physicists to study these tiny particles and discover new ones.

Particle tracks in a bubble chamber

Earthquake trace on a seismograph

Observatory dome with telescope

Geophysics

A geophysicist studies the physical processes that take place on and within the Earth, including rock formation, the Earth's magnetism, and volcanoes. Devices called seismographs help geophysicists record and predict earthquakes.

Astrophysics

The study of the planets, stars, and galaxies that make up the Universe is called astrophysics. It makes use of data collected by telescopes. Cosmology is the part of astrophysics that attempts to explain how the Universe began.

Physical change

Matter may undergo a physical change if it gains or loses energy. An ice cream bar melts in the sun as it gains heat energy. Physical changes are reversible. The ice cream bar can be cooled until it refreezes.

Timeline

c.400 BC Greek philosopher Democritus teaches that all matter is made up of tiny particles called atoms.

4th century BC Greek philosophers such as Aristotle state that the world must be explained by logical reasoning.

1600 Englishman Francis Bacon argues that scientific theories must be proven by experiment in a process called scientific method.

1680–1710 Englishman Isaac Newton lays the foundations of physics with his work in gravity, light, and mathematics.

1843 James Joule, an English physicist, explains the nature of energy.

1895 Modern physics is born when German physicist Wilhelm Röntgen discovers X rays. Classical physics cannot explain Röntgen's discovery, so scientists start to work on new theories.

1905 German physicist Albert Einstein publishes his Special Theory of Relativity, which states that matter can be changed into energy.

1990s and beyond Physicists look for a single "Unified Theory" that will link all the existing theories and explain the whole Universe.

FIND OUT MORE ATOMS AND MOLECULES · EINSTEIN, ALBERT · ENERGY · MATHEMATICS · MATTER · NEWTON, SIR ISAAC

PICASSO, PABLO

UNCHALLENGED AS THE GREATEST painter of the twentieth century, Pablo Picasso is also known for his sculpture, drawings, and graphics. In all, he produced some 20,000 works. He was one of the inventors of the Cubist style of art, and often shocked the public with his strange, powerful pictures. His work entirely changed our ideas about art. What he saw with his eyes was often only a starting point from which to create pictures. His works can be seen in galleries all over the world, and are widely reproduced.

Early life
Born in Málaga, Spain, in 1881, Picasso learned to draw before he could speak. He hated school and never learned to write well. He often helped his father, a painter, in his studio. When Pablo was 13, his father gave up painting and gave his brushes to Pablo to continue the tradition.

Colors
Soon after Picasso arrived in Paris in 1901, he began to paint entirely in shades of blue, a color he used to depict human misery. In this "Blue" period, he painted mainly beggars and other social outcasts. Later, in his "Rose" period, he portrayed circus performers.

Picasso's palette

Cubism

After his Blue and Rose periods, Picasso invented Cubism. He created images out of shapes such as cubes and cones. He showed objects as if seen from many different angles, so that he could show many aspects of the same object at once.

The Blind Man's Meal, 1903, detail Blue period

Les Demoiselles d'Avignon
The painting *Les Demoiselles d'Avignon* is seen by many as the starting point of many forms of modern art, including Cubism. Picasso worked on it for months before he would show it to his friends. Almost all of them were horrified by the distorted lines of the figures and the angular features of the women's faces. Picasso refused to sell the painting and kept it hidden from public view for many years.

Les Demoiselles d'Avignon, 1907

Ballets Russes

Between 1917 and 1924, Picasso worked for the Ballets Russes, the Russian ballet company based in Paris and run by Sergei Diaghilev (1872–1929). The Ballets Russes dominated ballet in the early 20th century and used the greatest talents of the age as choreographers, dancers, and designers. Composers such as Igor Stravinsky (1882–1971) and Erik Satie (1866–1925) provided the music. Picasso designed stunning sets for ballets such as *Parade*, *Le Tricorne*, and *Pulcinella*.

Parade
The ballet *Parade* was first performed in 1917. The music by Satie included the sounds of typewriters. The first-night audience hissed the ballet, but applauded Picasso's curtain. He also designed Cubist-style backdrops and costumes for the ballet.

Curtain for the ballet *Parade*, designed by Picasso

Guernica

In 1936, the Spanish Civil War broke out. The following year, Picasso painted *Guernica*. It shows the artist's horror at the bombing of the defenseless town by Fascists. It uses the image of a bullfight to depict the horror of war.

Guernica, 1937 | Mother with dead child | Horse, usually a symbol of power, is here a symbol of terror. | Absence of color suits the stark theme

Later work

Picasso experienced great hardship during the 1940s; his art became harsh and somber, often depicting monsters. He also repainted old master paintings in his own style.

Scene from the film *Mystére Picasso*

PABLO PICASSO

1881 Born, Málaga, Spain

1900 Arrives in Paris, where he meets many of the most important modern artists

1901–04 Blue period

1906–07 Rose period

1907 Completes *Les Demoiselles d'Avignon*; the Cubist movement is born

1917 Begins to work as designer for the Ballets Russes

1930s Produces his most important sculptures

1937 Paints *Guernica*

1940s Experiments with different types of prints

1973 Dies in Mougins, France

FIND OUT MORE

ART, HISTORY OF | BALLET | MUSIC | PAINTING AND DRAWING | POTTERY AND CERAMICS | SCULPTURE | SPAIN, HISTORY OF

PIGS AND PECCARIES

A LONG, MUSCULAR SNOUT ending in a round, flat disk is the pig's most distinctive feature. It is used to root around in the soil for food. Other features include tusks, which are used as weapons. The males of some species have large tusks; some are a strange shape. There are 14 species of pigs, ranging in size from the pygmy hog to the giant forest hog. Peccaries are related to pigs but are found only in South and Central America.

Breeding

Pigs produce lots of young, which is one of the reasons they were domesticated. Male wild boars mate after the age of about 4 years; females mate from the age of 18 months. Males join the herd for mating during the winter months. Despite their thick skin, males are often injured during fights to determine who will mate with a female. After 115 days' gestation, a litter of 4–8, but sometimes up to 12, piglets is born.

Wild boars

The wild boar, the direct ancestor of the domestic pig, lives in more areas than any other land mammal – every continent except Antarctica. The wild boar is a powerful animal with a heavy body, short legs, and thick skin that enable it to crash through thick undergrowth. Its straight tail is used to swat flies and also gives an indication of its mood.

Herds

Female wild boars live with their young in herds of up to 50 members. They all share feeding, resting, and wallowing sites. They wallow in mud pools to cool down and for protection from insects. Males live alone except in the mating season.

Feeding

Wild boars, like all other pigs, use their long muscular snouts and their strong sense of smell to root in the ground for food. They are most active at dawn or dusk when they may be heard grunting as they forage. Wild boars are omnivores and will feed on almost anything, including roots, fungi, leaves, fruit, and even small animals. They are particularly fond of wild garlic.

Coarse, bristly coat

Kneeling on front legs to feed

Long snout

Piglets have striped coats for six months.

Types of wild pigs

Babirusa

Restricted to Sulawesi and other Indonesian islands, the babirusa lives in rain forests along the banks of rivers and lakes. It is a strong swimmer and feeds on water plants. The male has antlerlike tusks.

Almost hairless skin

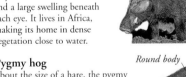

Giant forest hog

The giant forest hog is the largest member of the pig family. It has very coarse black-brown hair and a large swelling beneath each eye. It lives in Africa, making its home in dense vegetation close to water.

Coarse hair

Pygmy hog

About the size of a hare, the pygmy hog is nocturnal and very shy. It was believed to be extinct until it was rediscovered in 1972, on a tea plantation in Assam, India. It lives in a belt of swampy jungle at the foot of the Himalayas.

Round body

Red river hog

The red river hog of West Africa is the most colorful of all pigs. It has a rusty-orange body, black and white markings on its face, long ear tassles, and a white crest running along its spine.

White crest along back

Warthogs

Eyes set high on large head

Broad snout

Curved semi-circular tusks

Protruberances, or "warts", on face protect eyes from injury.

Warthogs live on African savannas south of the Sahara, where they feed on grass, leaves, fruit, and roots. They have poor eyesight but a good sense of smell and hearing and sharp tusks that can cause serious injury. Warthogs live in family groups of a male, female, and their young. Old males may live alone. Warthogs move distinctively – trotting with their tails carried stiffly erect.

Den

Warthogs live in underground dens that they take over from other animals, usually aardvarks. When alarmed, they enter their dens backward to present their tusks to any intruder.

Warthog outside den

Peccaries

There are three types of peccaries: the collared, white-lipped, and Chacoan. All have a small tail and upper tusks that grow down instead of up. The white-lipped and Chacoan peccaries live in large herds. If danger threatens, they stand together to present a row of gnashing tusks. The collared peccary lives in small herds and feeds on fruit, tubers, berries, and small vertebrates.

Collared peccary

WILD BOAR

SCIENTIFIC NAME	*Sus scrofa*
ORDER	Artiodactyla
FAMILY	Suidae
DISTRIBUTION	Continental Europe, North Africa, and much of Asia, eastward as far as Japan, Sumatra, and Java. Introduced to North America and New Zealand
HABITAT	Woodland and forest
DIET	Short succulent grasses, roots, fruit, fungi, and other plant material
SIZE	Height at shoulder: 40 in (100 cm); weight: up to 400 lb (180 kg)
LIFESPAN	Up to 18 years

FIND OUT MORE • AFRICAN WILDLIFE • ASIAN WILDLIFE • EUROPEAN WILDLIFE • FARMING • GRASSLAND WILDLIFE • MAMMALS • NORTH AMERICAN WILDLIFE • SOUTH AMERICAN WILDLIFE • WOODLAND WILDLIFE

PILGRIM FATHERS

ON NOVEMBER 21, 1620, a small ship anchored in the sheltered bay behind Cape Cod, on the east coast of America. The ship, the *Mayflower*, contained 35 religious dissenters who wished to start a new life in America so that they could worship the way they pleased. Sailing with them were 67 other emigrants. Together the voyagers are known as the Pilgrim Fathers. It was their pilgrimage across the ocean that created the first successful European colony in North America. They called their settlement Plymouth, in what is now Massachusetts.

The voyage of the Mayflower

The Pilgrims set sail from Plymouth, England, on September 16, 1620. After a stormy crossing of the Atlantic, they sighted Cape Cod on November 19. They then spent several weeks looking for a suitable place on the coast to land and settle. On December 16, they finally entered Plymouth Harbor. They began to build their first house on Christmas Day.

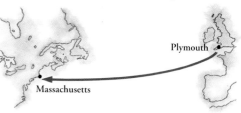

Plymouth

Massachusetts

Separatists and Puritans

A third of the passengers of the *Mayflower* were Separatists. They rejected the pomp and ceremony of the Church of England and wished to practice their own, simpler form of worship. They dressed in plain clothes and disapproved of frivolity and idleness. Later, Puritans (members of the Church of England who wanted to simplify its worship) also came to New England.

New England and the Wampanoag

The area that the Pilgrims first settled became known as "New England." Members of the Wampanoag tribe already lived here. Fortunately, one of them spoke English and, with him acting as a translator, the Wampanoags helped the colonists plant crops and hunt for food. Without their aid, the Pilgrims would not have survived their first year in the new land.

Wampanoag people

The Mayflower

The 177-ton *Mayflower* was originally built to carry wine and other cargoes, not people, and was cramped and uncomfortable. Living quarters for each of the 102 passengers were no bigger than a single bed. Many of the Pilgrims were unprepared for their new life, taking plenty of books and pairs of shoes but no fishing lines or plows. Neither did they take any livestock, such as cows or sheep, to provide food and clothing for their new life. One passenger died and a baby was born on the voyage. However, many did not survive the first winter in America.

Pilgrim settlement

The first houses the Pilgrims constructed were built of roughly cut planks of wood from the local forest. The roofs were coated with bark to keep the rain and snow out. Every Pilgrim had to work hard to help clear the site and plant the crops necessary for their survival. Religious services were held in the open until a church was constructed.

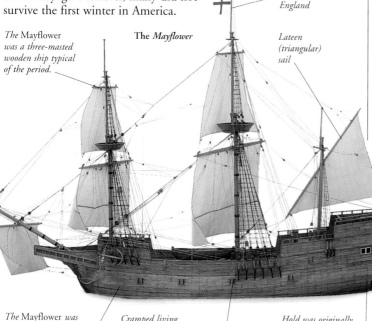

The Mayflower was a three-masted wooden ship typical of the period.

The *Mayflower*

Flag of England

Lateen (triangular) sail

The Mayflower was about 90 ft (30 m) long

Cramped living accommodations below deck

Hold was originally used for carrying wine

Thanksgiving

After a year in America, the Pilgrims celebrated their first successful harvest with a thanksgiving feast. Among the guests were 100 members of the Wampanoag tribe. The celebrations went on for several days. Among the foods the Pilgrims probably ate were pumpkin pie, pecan and apple pies, and roast wild turkey. The first national Thanksgiving Day was proclaimed in 1789. It became a national holiday in 1863.

Pumpkin pie

Roast turkey

Apple pie

Harvard University

The oldest university in America was founded by the colonists in 1636. It was named after John Harvard, a Puritan who emigrated to America and left his fortune to the university.

Timeline

September 1620 The Pilgrims set out from Plymouth, England.

November 1620 The Pilgrims draw up the Mayflower Compact, an agreement about how they will govern themselves.

December 1620 The Pilgrims land and establish a settlement at Plymouth, Massachusetts.

1621 Colonists sign peace treaty with local Wampanoag tribe; the peace lasts for 50 years.

1629–40 20,000 Puritans flee religious persecution in England; they settle in Massachusetts and the surrounding areas.

1691 Plymouth becomes part of Massachusetts Bay Colony.

FIND OUT MORE

EUROPE, HISTORY OF   FESTIVALS   GOVERNMENTS   NORTH AMERICA, HISTORY OF   RELIGIONS   SCHOOLS AND COLLEGES   UNITED STATES, HISTORY OF   WASHINGTON, GEORGE

PIRATES

ON THE WORLD'S OCEANS, robbers have a special name: pirates. Piracy began soon after mariners first sailed the world's waters, and pirates have threatened shipping ever since. In the days of sailing ships, these dangerous criminals piloted the fastest vessels. They swooped in on defenseless ships, stealing their valuable cargo. Some pirate gangs sank the ships they attacked and killed the crews to hide their crimes. The most famous pirates attacked ships in the Caribbean three centuries ago. Novelists glamorized their exciting lives in tales and legends.

Jolly Roger
To scare their victims into surrender, 18th-century pirate ships flew flags that carried symbols of death. The skull and crossbones design, called the Jolly Roger, is the best known, but many pirate captains designed their own emblems. This flag belonged to the English pirate captain Jack Rackham (d.1720).

Pirate hunting grounds
Pirates lurked in places where they could be sure of finding vessels with rich cargoes: on traditional shipping lanes, or where straits and narrows forced ships to sail close to the shore. Pirates considered charts, maps, and surveys – especially of the areas around the Caribbean – to be valuable booty.

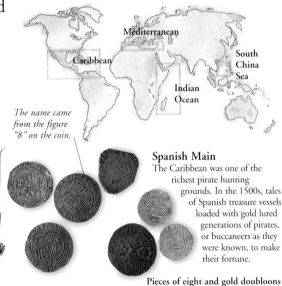

Mediterranean
Caribbean
South China Sea
Indian Ocean

Mediterranean
The Mediterranean Sea has a long history of piracy. Pirates were attacking rich Greek and Roman ships 2,500 years ago. In the 16th century, Maltese corsairs (Christian pirates) clashed with Barbary corsairs (Muslim pirates) from North Africa.

Yard

Maltese corsair galley

Maltese galleys were sleek and speedy like their Barbary counterparts.

The galleys had large sails for use on windy days.

Slaves captured from other ships were forced to row.

Battering ram

Oars

The name came from the figure "8" on the coin.

Spanish Main
The Caribbean was one of the richest pirate hunting grounds. In the 1500s, tales of Spanish treasure vessels loaded with gold lured generations of pirates, or buccaneers as they were known, to make their fortune.

Pieces of eight and gold doubloons

Slaves waxed the hull to maximize speed.

Gold seal ring

Garnet fan holder

Rose sapphire

Jewel necklace

Treasure
After raiding the ship's hold, pirates robbed the passengers. There were especially rich pickings on ships plying the Indian Ocean because all merchant vessels bound for India or China used this route. However, since pirates were often starving or sick, many valued food, medicine, and clothes more than riches.

Blackbeard
The English pirate Edward Teach (d.1718), better known as Blackbeard, plundered shipping off America's coast in the 18th century. Heavily armed and with long, thin candles smoking in his hair and beard, he terrified many crews into submission without even firing a shot. Though his piratical career lasted barely two years, Blackbeard earned a frightening reputation off the shores of Virginia and the Carolinas. According to legend he left fabulous buried treasure – it remains undiscovered to this day.

Women pirates
In a ship's crew, women had an independence that society denied them on land, and some became pirates. Irish pirate Anne Bonney (d.1720) plundered Caribbean ships in the 18th century, and became famous for her courage and fighting skill.

Anne Bonney

Privateers
From the 1500s to the 1700s, warring nations relied on legal and licensed pirates, known as privateers, to supplement their navies. Their job was to plunder enemy shipping.

Sir Francis Drake
English admiral Drake (c.1540–1596) became a national hero fighting Spain as a privateer. His drum, it is claimed, still beats when England is in danger.

Drake's drum, 1596

Modern piracy
Most modern piracy takes place in the South China Sea. The pirates usually attack merchant vessels but in the 1980s, refugees fleeing Vietnam with a few possessions became the targets of brutal piracy.

Vietnamese refugees

FIND OUT MORE
ARMS AND ARMOR · EXPLORATION · FLAGS · MONEY · SHIPS AND BOATS · UNITED KINGDOM, HISTORY OF

PLANETS

THE NINE PLANETS of the Solar System have much in common. Each follows an elliptical orbit around the Sun and each was created from gas and dust left over after the Sun formed. The planets range enormously in size and structure. The four inner ones, including Earth, are spheres of rock. They are tiny compared with the four gas giants, which appear to be spheres of gas although solids and liquids lurk below their thick atmospheres. The most distant planet, Pluto, is also a sphere of rock.

Rocky planets

The four inner planets, in increasing order from the Sun, are Mercury, Venus, Earth, and Mars. Each is a ball of rock, but each has a unique surface. Only two of them, Earth and Mars, have moons. The smallest and most distant of all the Solar System planets is Pluto. It is also a ball of rock, but because of its great distance from the Sun, it is an icy world. It is very unlike its neighbors, the gas giants, and something of a mystery.

Mercury

Closest to the Sun, second smallest, and the fastest moving planet, Mercury orbits the Sun every 88 days. It is a lifeless and dry world covered with craters. Deep below the surface is a large core of iron. The planet's gravity is too weak to hold on to an atmosphere and so heat is lost at night. Differences between day and night temperatures can be 1,080°F (600°C).

Only a third of Mercury's surface has been mapped from space, by *Mariner 10* in 1974–75.

Cratered world
Most of Mercury's craters were formed 3.5 billion years ago when meteorites bombarded the planet. The craters range in size from 3 ft (1 m) to more than 600 miles (1,000 km) in diameter. Here a younger crater (center) about 7.5 miles (12 km) across sits inside an older one.

Venus

Sunlight on the cloud tops makes Venus shine brightly in Earth's sky. As it moves it appears to go through phases similar to those of the Moon. The dense clouds trap the Sun's heat to make it the hottest of the planets. The acid clouds and unbearable pressure make it doubly inhospitable. Beneath the clouds are volcanic plains of hot desert covering about two-thirds of the planet.

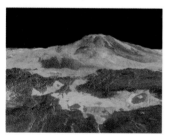

Radar images were used to create this global view of Venus's surface.

Maat Mons

Surface temperature 870°F (465°C)

Beneath the clouds
Radar equipment on board spacecraft have "seen" through Venus's clouds. The most successful craft, *Magellan*, mapped 98% of its surface in the 1990s. About two days of mapping were used to produce this picture of Maat Mons, the largest shield volcano on Venus.

Earth

Largest of the four inner planets, Earth is the only Solar System planet to support life and to have water in abundance. Earth has changed enormously since it was created 4.6 billion years ago. It has developed an atmosphere and gone through climatic and structural change. Internal heat currents push the land masses by up to 3 in (7 cm) a year.

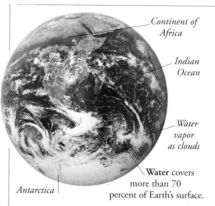

Continent of Africa

Indian Ocean

Water vapor as clouds

Water covers more than 70 percent of Earth's surface.

Antarctica

Mars

The most Earthlike of the planets, Mars is a little over half Earth's size and has polar ice caps. Its red color comes from the iron-rich rock and dust that covers much of its surface, about 40 percent of which is rock desert. Its most dramatic feature is its enormous canyons. Valles Marineris is 2,800 miles (4,500 km) long and up to 4.5 miles (7 km) deep.

Tharsis region

Valles Marineris

Argyre Planitia

Mars is a cold, lifeless planet with a very thin atmosphere.

Olympus Mons
Volcanic activity has changed Mars's surface in the past. There are two main volcanic areas: the Elysium Planitia and the Tharsis region which includes Olympus Mons, the biggest volcano in the Solar System. At 16.4 miles (26.4 km), it is three times higher than Earth's tallest mountain, Mount Everest.

Pluto

This rock and ice planet is a dark and freezing world, more like a moon than a planet. Some astronomers believe it is a large asteroid. No spacecraft have visited Pluto, but astronomers have built up a picture of it from observations. The clearest image of Pluto and its moon was taken by the *Hubble Space Telescope* in 1990.

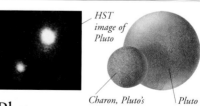

HST image of Pluto

Charon, Pluto's only moon

Pluto

Clyde Tombaugh

The American Clyde Tombaugh (1906–97) was part of a team at the Lowell Observatory in Arizona searching for a planet believed to be disturbing the orbital motions of Uranus and Neptune. On 18 February 1930, he discovered Pluto, but it was too small to affect the orbit of Uranus. Tombaugh spent eight years looking for another planet, but none was found.

Gas planets

There are four gas planets, so-called because of their deep, dense atmospheres. From the Sun, and in order of size, they are Jupiter, Saturn, Uranus, and Neptune. They are the biggest planets, the giants of the Solar System. All that is visible is their gas exterior. Immediately below the gas layer is liquid and in each of their centers is a rocky core. All four have rings and many moons.

Galilean moons
Jupiter's four largest moons are named after the Italian astronomer who discovered them, Galileo Galilei. They are, in order of size, Ganymede, Callisto, Io, and Europa. Ganymede is the largest moon in the Solar System and is bigger than the planets Pluto and Mercury. Jupiter's other 12 moons are tiny in comparison; most are only a few dozen miles in diameter.

Ganymede is the brightest of the moons. Its icy crust has craters and long parallel grooves.

Io has a brilliant orange and red surface because of sulfur compounds ejected by its active volcanoes.

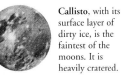

Callisto, with its surface layer of dirty ice, is the faintest of the moons. It is heavily cratered.

Europa has an icy crust with no mountains and few craters. Streaks and cracks crisscross the surface.

Jupiter

Sometimes called the king of the planets, Jupiter is the biggest and most massive planet and has 16 moons. It has a rocky core 10-20 times as massive as Earth. Above this core is metallic and then liquid hydrogen, topped by about 600 miles (1,000 km) of atmosphere, 86 percent of which is hydrogen and 14 percent helium. Jupiter's narrow ring system, discovered in 1979, consists of three rings of dust particles. If it had been 50 times more massive, its core would have been hot enough to fuse hydrogen, and Jupiter would have developed into a star.

North Polar Region

North Temperate Belt

North Tropical Zone

North Equatorial Belt

South Equatorial Belt

Great Red Spot

Trace amounts of phosphorus in the atmosphere give the clouds their red color.

South polar region

Belts and zones
Jupiter's fast spin produces powerful wind systems that divide the atmosphere into bands. The bands are made up of belts and zones running parallel to the equator. The red-brown belts are gases descending and the white-yellow zones are gases rising. The spots, ovals, and streaks in its cloud cover are weather disturbances produced where belts and zones meet.

Great Red Spot
One storm in Jupiter's upper clouds, the Great Red Spot, has been observed for well over 300 years. Over time it has changed color and size. At its biggest, it was about three times Earth's diameter. It is an area of high pressure, above and colder than the surrounding atmosphere. This gigantic storm rotates above the atmosphere, completing one counterclockwise turn every few days.

Saturn

The second largest and sixth planet from the Sun is Saturn. Like Jupiter, it is made chiefly of hydrogen surrounding a rocky core. Its bands are less obvious and contain fewer features apart from white spots caused by weather storms. It has the lowest density of all the planets. Saturn also has an extensive ring system and 20 moons, more than any other planet.

Faint bands in Saturn's atmosphere

The equator bulges because of the planet's rapid rotation.

Cassini division

A Ring

B Ring

C Ring

D Ring

The ring system is up to 1.25 miles (2 km) thick

F Ring

Saturn's rings

Galileo described the rings as Saturn's "ears" when he first observed them in 1610. Their ringlike nature was not explained until 1656.

Titan
More than half of Saturn's moons are small and irregular in shape. The largest by far is Titan, about the same size as Mercury. It is one of three Solar System moons with atmospheres. Titan is a sphere of rock and ice surrounded by a thick mantle of nitrogen.

Giovanni Cassini
There are several gaps in Saturn's rings. The largest is the Cassini division, named after its discoverer, the French astronomer Giovanni Cassini (1625–1712). He was a skillful observer and discovered four of Saturn's moons. His observations of Mars also helped establish the distances in the Solar System.

Ring system
Surrounding Saturn are thousands of ringlets made of billions of ice-covered rock and dust particles. Together they make seven main rings. The particles range in size from a few thousandths of an inch to a few yards across. This enhanced image taken by the *Voyager 2* probe reveals many of the individual ringlets in the system.

Uranus

This planet was discovered in 1781. Twice as far from the Sun as Saturn, it is difficult to observe from Earth. The first close-up views came in 1986 from the probe *Voyager 2*. The atmosphere is predominantly hydrogen but methane in the upper clouds gives Uranus its distinctive blue-green color. It has a ring system and 15 moons.

Clouds of frozen methane ice are the only features visible on Uranus.

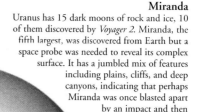

Miranda

Uranus has 15 dark moons of rock and ice, 10 of them discovered by *Voyager 2*. Miranda, the fifth largest, was discovered from Earth but a space probe was needed to reveal its complex surface. It has a jumbled mix of features including plains, cliffs, and deep canyons, indicating that perhaps Miranda was once blasted apart by an impact and then reassembled itself.

Size of Earth compared with Uranus

Axis 98° from the vertical

Sideways planet

Uranus is tilted on its axis as it orbits the Sun. This tilt makes the planet appear to be on its side with its moons and rings circling the top and bottom of the planet. No one knows why the Uranian system is like this – perhaps it is the result of a collision.

Rings of Uranus

The Uranian ring system was discovered in 1977 from Earth. When Uranus moved in front of a star, the star disappeared and then reappeared as each ring blocked the star's light. There are 11 rings, each one dark and narrow and made of lumps of rock roughly 3 ft (1 m) in size.

Uranus is far from the Sun and a cold planet. Its atmospheric temperature measures –378°F (–210°C).

William Herschel

Uranus was discovered by William Herschel (1738–1822), an English amateur astronomer, from his backyard in Bath, England. He became well known and accepted into scientific circles. He was a gifted observer who made his own high-quality telescopes. His later work on double stars, clusters, and nebulae made him one of the most influential astronomers of his time.

Voyager fly-bys

Two identical probes, *Voyagers 1* and *2*, were launched in 1977 to the four gas giants. They both traveled to Jupiter and Saturn, revealing new tiny moons, close-ups of the planets and their larger moons, and the complexity of Saturn's rings. *Voyager 1* then moved off toward the edge of the Solar System, but *Voyager 2* traveled to Uranus in 1986 and Neptune in 1989. At these two planets, it discovered new rings and a total of 16 moons.

Camera and remote sensors

Voyager 1

Communications antenna

Radioactive power source

Magnetic sensor on extendible boom

Neptune

Like Uranus, Neptune is a cold and distant world. It is similar in size and is also blue-green because of methane gas in its hydrogen-rich atmosphere. Belts and zones are just visible in its surface of clouds. Other visible features are white clouds and a dark spot. Neptune was discovered in 1846, but its dark rings – two broad and two narrow – and six of its eight moons were discovered by *Voyager 2* in 1989.

Great Dark Spot

Great Dark Spot

Neptune is the windiest place in the Solar System. Wind speeds of up to 1,370 mph (2,200 kmh) have been recorded. The winds whiz around the planet in a westerly direction in the opposite direction of the planet's spin. The Great Dark Spot is a huge storm with ferocious winds. It is an oval area of high pressure measuring about 7,500 miles (12,000 km) across.

White clouds of methane ice

Great Dark Spot

Triton

Neptune's largest moon is Triton, the coldest place in the Solar System at an icy –391°F (–235°C). Triton has a thin atmosphere, mainly of nitrogen, and is one of only three moons known to have an atmosphere. The surface changes as volcanoes throw out nitrogen and black dust which streak the cracked and wrinkled surface.

Neptune is made of ice and liquid below the thick atmosphere. In the center lies a rocky core.

The Scooter

Neptune looks blue because methane in the upper atmosphere absorbs red light and reflects blue.

Small Dark Spot, an anticyclone storm

FIND OUT MORE ATMOSPHERE · COMETS AND ASTEROIDS · EARTH · EARTHQUAKES · GALILEO GALILEI · MOON · NEWTON, SIR ISAAC · SPACE EXPLORATION · SUN AND SOLAR SYSTEM · VOLCANOES

PLANTS

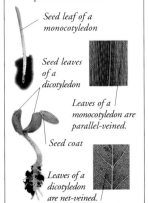

THERE ARE ABOUT 500,000 species of plant, which can be divided into spore-bearing plants and seed-bearing plants. They are food for many animals and are fundamental for life on Earth. Plants vary in size from microscopic algae, to huge sequoia trees more than 26 ft (8 m) across their trunk. Most plants contain a green pigment called chlorophyll that traps the energy in sunlight. The plants use this energy to make their food in a process called photosynthesis. Plants struggle to survive in places where it is very cold, very dry, or very dark.

Seed-bearing plants

Conifers, or gymnosperms, and flowering plants, or angiosperms, reproduce by seeds. Each seed contains an embryo and a food supply, and is encased by a seed coat. A germinating seed is nourished by the food reserves until it can start to make its own food.

Spore-bearing plants

Algae, mosses, ferns, and their relatives all reproduce by means of spores. These are tiny and are produced inside the sporangia in enormous quantities that look like fine dust. Each spore contains a minute amount of essential genetic material in a tough coat.

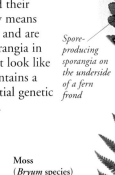

Spore-producing sporangia on the underside of a fern frond

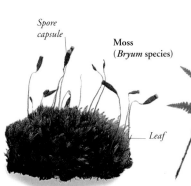

Frond

Green seaweed

Spore capsule

Moss (*Bryum* species)

Leaf

Pinna (leaflet)

Frond of male fern

Algae
The simplest plants are algae. They do not have leaves, stems, or roots. Algae thrive in a moist or wet environment. Many are tiny, single-celled plants, but some seaweeds can be huge.

Mosses and liverworts
Mosses and most liverworts have simple stems and small, thin leaves. Some liverworts are flat and look like seaweed. They live mostly in mild, damp regions, but some survive in the world's coldest places.

Ferns
These are the most-advanced spore-bearing plants. Water and nutrients are carried around the plant. Many ferns grow well in cool, dry places, but the largest ones are found in the hot, damp tropics.

Angiosperms
Angiosperms are the flowering plants. They have seeds that develop inside a ripened ovary, called a fruit. There are at least 250,000 kinds of angiosperm, including most of our food plants.

Delavy's silver fir

Seeds develop on scales inside cones.

Pea plant

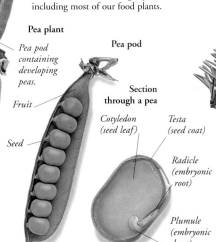

Pea pod containing developing peas.

Pea pod

Fruit

Section through a pea

Seed

Cotyledon (seed leaf)

Testa (seed coat)

Radicle (embryonic root)

Plumule (embryonic shoot)

Gymnosperms
Gymnosperms are plants that have cones instead of flowers. Their seeds develop inside female cones. Most gymnosperms are trees or shrubs. The cones are not as varied as flowers, but they can be brightly colored and attractive.

Cotyledons
Flowering plants have either one or two cotyledons (seed leaves). Monocotyledons (one seed leaf) have floral parts in multiples of three. Dicotyledons (two seed leaves) have floral parts usually in multiples of four or five.

Seed leaf of a monocotyledon

Seed leaves of a dicotyledon

Leaves of a monocotyledon are parallel-veined.

Seed coat

Leaves of a dicotyledon are net-veined.

Oldest plant
Bristlecone pines in Utah, Nevada, and Colorado, are the oldest living plants. Some of these trees are more than 5,000 years old. Scientists study the width of growth rings in the wood of dead trees to see how the world's climate has changed.

Plant lifespans
Plants with non-woody stems (herbaceous plants) have a short lifecycle. Some grow from seed to mature plant in a few weeks, dying when their seeds are shed. Woody plants grow more slowly. Trees may be more than 20 years old before they have seeds, but they may produce them for hundreds of years.

Annuals germinate, grow, have flowers and seeds, and die within one year.

Corn marigold

Biennials produce only foliage in the first year. They then flower, fruit, and die in the second year.

Honesty

Perennials live longer than two years. Some die down in autumn and grow again from a living rootstock the following spring.

Purple monkshood

FIND OUT MORE   FERNS   FLOWERS   FRUITS AND SEEDS   MOSSES AND LIVERWORTS   PHOTOSYNTHESIS   PLANTS, ANATOMY   PLANTS, REPRODUCTION   SEAWEEDS AND OTHER ALGAE   TREES

Plants

Dicotyledons

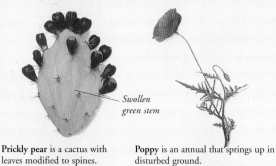

Swollen green stem

Prickly pear is a cactus with leaves modified to spines.

Poppy is an annual that springs up in disturbed ground.

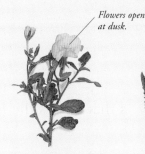

Water lily is an aquatic perennial with floating leaves and flowers.

Flowers open at dusk.

Common evening primrose grows in disturbed soil.

Honesty has flowers that turn into papery fruits.

Michaelmas daisy is a tall, stiff perennial with clusters of flowers.

Hottentot fig is a trailing perennial with fleshy leaves.

Himalayan balsam has fruits that explode when ripe.

Hairy leaves and stems

Common mallow is a sturdy perennial of meadows, roadsides, and hedgebanks.

Marsh marigold grows by ponds and in marshes.

Slightly fleshy leaves

Sea pea is a spreading plant that grows high on stony beaches.

Spring gentian is a perennial often seen in mountain meadows.

Petals are cut into four narrow lobes.

Ragged robin grows in wet grassland and hedgerows.

Wild pansy is a small plant that is often a garden weed.

Bogbean is an aquatic plant that emerges above the water.

Meadow cranesbill is a hairy perennial with deeply lobed leaves and large mauve flowers.

All parts of the plant are poisonous.

Monk's hood is a perennial found in damp woodlands.

Flowers turn into red berries.

Bittersweet is a scrambling plant of ditches and hedgerows.

Sea kale is a coastal plant with thick, gray-green, waxy leaves.

Bell heather is a low-growing evergreen shrub that grows on dry heaths and moors.

Monocotyledons

Star-shaped flowers

Star-of-Bethlehem has leaves that appear before the flower spike.

Waxy flowers

Orchid: this is a rain forest orchid with fragrant flowers.

Stiff, spiny leaves

Urn plant has small flowers surrounded by spiny bracts.

Flowering rush roots in mud at the bottom of ponds.

Large yellow flowers open in early summer.

Yellow flag grows in large dense clumps in wet ground.

P

PLANTS, ANATOMY

THE ANATOMY OF most plants can be divided into roots, stems, leaves, and reproductive organs (the flowers in flowering plants). Some plants have woody stems that let them grow tall. Shrubs have woody stems that branch at ground level. Trees have a single woody stem, the trunk. Wild flowers and other herbaceous plants, have non-woody stems. They die at the end of the growing season. Some plants die back, but store food, which they use to sprout again the following year.

Flowers

A flower is made up of sepals, petals, stamens, and carpels. These are arranged in whorls on the tip of the flower stalk. Flowers contain the reproductive organs of the plant.

The stalk is called the petiole.

Each small leaf is a leaflet.

Compound leaf

The large vein running along the center of the leaf is called a midrib.

Network of finer veins

Simple leaf

Leaves

A plant makes most food in its green leaves. Leaves are usually thin and flat, so they expose a large surface area to the sun to collect energy. A network of veins strengthens the leaf and carries water, sugars, and dissolved minerals.

Flowerhead before it opens

A thistle has prickles as a form of defense.

Magnified view of a maple stem

Corky outer layer

Compound flowerhead

The leaf is covered with a waxy layer to prevent it from drying out.

Stems

A plant's stem supports its leaves, flowers, and fruits. It contains xylem and phloem, called vascular tissues, which carry water and sugars around the plant.

Xylem and phloem

When a tendril touches another stem, the tip coils around it.

Tendrils are sensitive to touch.

Tendrils

Weak-stemmed plants, such as this gourd plant, often have modified leaves called tendrils that twine around other plants for support.

Food stores

Some parts of a plant are swollen with reserves of starches or sugars. This stored food is used the next growing season by sprouting shoots.

Onion bulb

Bulbs
An onion bulb is a swollen bud. It is made up of layers of fleshy scales that contain the stored food.

Roots spread out to hold the plant in the ground.

Stem tissues have reinforced cell walls that give strength and rigidity but allow the plant to bend.

Roots

A plant is anchored in the ground by its roots. Older roots are thick and woody, with a waterproof, corky outer layer. The youngest roots take up water and dissolved minerals from the soil. These enter the root through fine root hairs found just behind each root tip.

Ginger rhizome

Sweet potato tuber

Spear thistle

Rhizomes
The ginger rhizome is a swollen underground stem that grows horizontally.

Tubers
Stem tubers, such as sweet potatoes, are the swollen tips of underground stems.

Breathing roots
All parts of a plant need to breathe, including the roots. Trees that grow in swamps, such as mangroves, have roots that are exposed above the water. These are called pneumatophores. The roots have lenticels (large pores) through which oxygen from the air can enter.

Primary root

The root is part of the plant's transportation system and contains xylem and phloem tissues.

Root hairs

Magnified view of the developing root of a cabbage

Root tip, where the root grows longer

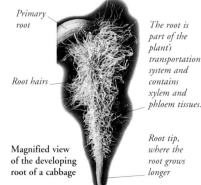

FIND OUT MORE   CARNIVOROUS PLANTS   CELLS   DESERT WILDLIFE   FERNS   FLOWERS   FRUITS AND SEEDS   MOSSES AND LIVERWORTS   PHOTOSYNTHESIS   SOIL   TREES

Plant leaves

Dicotyledons

Leaves can have a blunt or pointed tip.

Toothed leaflets

Asarabacca has a simple, kidney-shaped (reniform) leaf.

Black bindweed has a simple, arrow-shaped (sagittate) leaf.

Lesser spearwort has a simple, spear-shaped (lanceolate) leaf.

Chicory has a simple, spatula-shaped, or spathulate, leaf.

Common lungwort has a simple, oval leaf with white blotches.

Hemlock has a compound leaf with many tiny leaflets.

Leaves grow in whorls of 3 to 5.

Leaf is white underneath, with cottony hairs.

Himalayan balsam has a simple, elliptical leaf with a finely toothed margin.

Balm has a simple, ovate leaf with rounded teeth, described as crenate.

Dusky cranesbill has a simple leaf with spreading lobes, described as palmate.

Slender thistle has a simple, elliptical leaf with spiny-edged lobes.

Chequer bloom has a simple leaf with lobes spread out like a hand.

Croton has a simple leaf. Its shape is described as panduriform.

Leaflets often have a white crescent.

Branched tendrils

Green hellebore has a palmately compound leaf with five to seven segments.

Field scabious has a simple leaf deeply divided into pinnate lobes.

Goat's rue has a pinnate, compound leaf with four to eight pairs of leaflets.

Red clover has a compound leaf in three parts, described as trifoliate.

Garden lupin has a compound leaf with 9 to 16 spear-shaped leaflets.

Broad-leaved everlasting pea has a compound leaf with branched tendrils.

Common holly has a simple, oval leaf with a prickly margin.

Astrophytum cactus is leafless. Its leaves have become protective spines.

Crassula has a simple, oval leaf that is fleshy and can store water.

Spurge-laurel has a simple, oblong leaf that is deep green and glossy.

White poplar has a simple leaf with a thick coat of white hairs underneath.

Kentucky coffee has a large, compound leaf with many ovate leaflets.

Monocotyledons

Leaves have a long stalk.

Leaves have between three and nine curving veins.

Leaves all grow from the base of the plant.

Frogbit grows in ponds and lakes. It has a simple kidney-shaped leaf.

Grape hyacinth has a long, thin leaf, described as linear.

Swiss cheese plant has a large, oval, pinnately lobed leaf.

Lady orchid has a glossy, elliptical leaf with parallel veins and a fleshy feel.

Lords and ladies has a simple, arrow-shaped leaf, often with a wavy edge.

Black bryony has a simple, shiny, heart-shaped leaf.

PLANTS, DEFENSE

THE ROOTS, TRUNKS, STEMS, leaves, flowers, fruits, and seeds of a plant are under constant attack. All herbivorous animals feed on them and can damage the health and reproductive success of a plant. Many plants have evolved strategies that stop animals from eating them. Some have sharp spines, prickles, or stings that make them painful or awkward to eat. Other plants contain poisonous substances that taste horrid and can result in illness, or even death, for the animal.

Chemicals

Acacias grow on the hot African savanna, where there are few other trees. When an animal starts to eat the leaves of an acacia tree, the tree releases unpleasant chemicals. It also gives off a substance called ethylene. This stimulates nearby acacia trees to produce the chemicals, too.

Insects
Some acacias are protected by ants. The ants live in the hollow base of the tree's long, sharp thorns. When another insect or a mammal starts to eat the leaves, the ants rush out and attack them.

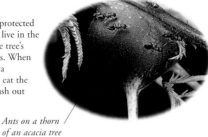

Ants on a thorn of an acacia tree

Acacia trees grow in hot, dry parts of the world.

On the African savanna, acacias are browsed by giraffes.

Spines

Cacti and many other plants survive in arid areas by storing moisture in their stems. Their leaves have become modified into long, hard, sharp spines. These protect the succulent stems and their vital store of moisture from browsing animals. Some plants develop sharp prickles all around their leaf margins to stop animals from eating them.

Cactus

Holly (Ilex sp.) leaves

Stings
Nettles have sharp hairs that can penetrate skin, even through fur, and inject chemicals called histamines. These "stings" are very painful, and animals soon learn not to touch a stinging nettle.

Hairs are borne on the leaves and stem.

Magnified nettle hair

Stinging nettle

Gums
Sticky substances secreted by some plants, such as the horse chestnut, gum up an insect's mouth and legs, and may even trap them.

Horse chestnut

Bud protected by sticky scales

Plant mimicry
Passion flower vines of tropical America contain poisons that deter most creatures from eating their leaves. Postman caterpillars can eat the leaves and the poison builds up in them and makes them poisonous. The butterflies lay eggs only on plants with no other postman eggs. The plant produces false "eggs" on its young leaves and tendrils. These deceive the female butterfly.

Passion flower leaf with false "eggs"

Poisonous plants

Foxglove is poisonous, but drugs prepared from the plant are used to treat humans for some heart conditions.

Poison ivy causes painful blistering and burning of the skin of anyone who brushes against it.

Dumbcane sap causes severe swelling of the mouth and throat.

Castor-oil seeds contain deadly ricin. A tiny amount will kill a human.

Deadly nightshade berries contain the poisonous substance atropine.

Useful drugs are made from a substance in foxglove leaves.

The strong poison is in the sap.

Dumbcane leaves

Poisonous berry

FIND OUT MORE   AFRICAN WILDLIFE   DESERT WILDLIFE   DRUGS   PLANTS   PLANT USES

PLANTS, REPRODUCTION

PLANTS, LIKE OTHER living things, reproduce to ensure the continued existence of the species. They propagate by means of seeds, spores, or plantlets, often in large numbers. Seeds and spores are formed by sexual reproduction involving male and female gametes (sex cells) from different plants. Plantlets are formed by asexual, or vegetative, reproduction, in which a plant produces new plants on its own.

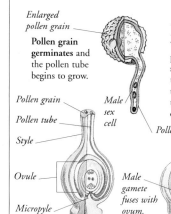

Enlarged pollen grain

Pollen grain germinates and the pollen tube begins to grow.

Pollen grain
Pollen tube
Style
Ovule
Micropyle

Male sex cell

Pollen tube

Male gamete fuses with ovum.

Style and stigma wither.

Testa (seed coat)

Food store

Embryo plant

Fertilization

When a pollen grain lands on a stigma, it produces a tiny tube that grows into the stigma and down the style. Inside the tip of the tube are the male gametes. When the tube reaches the micropyle (a tiny hole in the ovule wall), the male gametes enter the ovule and fuse with the female ovum.

Male gametes reach the entrance to the female ovum.

Fertilization takes place as male and female sex cells fuse.

Ovule begins to develop into a seed.

Sexual reproduction

Seeds are formed by sexual reproduction. This process ensures the mixing of genetic material from different plants. It keeps the species strong and more able to adapt to changes in conditions. If a female sex cell is fertilized by a male one, a seed develops.

Fertile disk of small flowers, or florets

Sterile ray floret for attacting pollinating insects.

Petals are no longer needed.

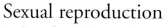

Developing fruits holding seeds.

3 Each fertile ovule develops into a seed. It will be dormant until conditions are right for growth.

4 A seed takes up moisture and begins to grow. This is called germination.

Developing flowerhead

Stem grows thicker and longer.

True leaf

Seed leaf

1 The flowerhead of a sunflower is made up of many small flowers. The large yellow head attracts insects to come to feed on the nectar inside the flowers. These insects bring pollen from another sunflower.

2 When the flowers have been fertilized, the bright yellow petals die away.

Seeds fall to the ground.

Radicle (first small root)

5 The plant uses food from its seed leaves to grow true leaves.

6 Gradually, the plant puts down roots, develops new leaves, and grows taller. The flowers form, eventually producing new seeds.

Asexual Reproduction

Some plants reproduce without the fusion of sex cells. This vegetative reproduction produces plantlets that are all genetically identical to the parent plant. These plantlets are known as clones. Sometimes, the vegetative descendants of one plant cover a large area.

Adventitious buds

The Mexican hat plant develops small adventitious buds around the edge of its leaves. Each bud is a miniature plant with rootlets. The plantlets start to grow as soon as they fall to the ground.

Adventitious buds

Plantlet

Leaf

Runners

Strawberries produce new plantlets on creeping stems called runners. Each runner grows along the ground and produces several new plants. The stem dies once the plantlets have grown their own leaves and roots.

Parent strawberry plant

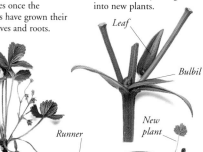

Runner

Bulbils

Some plants, such as this orange lily, produce tiny bulbils on their stems. These fall to the ground where, in the right conditions, they will grow into new plants.

Leaf

Bulbil

New plant

How plants grow

Plants contain hormones that control the way in which they grow. Some hormones make the shoots grow toward the light. Others make the roots grow away from the light into the ground. The movement of parts of a plant toward and away from light is called phototropism.

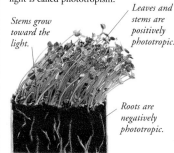

Stems grow toward the light.

Leaves and stems are positively phototropic.

Roots are negatively phototropic.

FIND OUT MORE   FLOWERS   FERNS   FRUITS AND SEEDS   GENETICS   MOSSES AND LIVERWORTS   PHOTOSYNTHESIS   PLANTS   PLANTS, ANATOMY

PLANT USES

ALL HUMAN SOCIETIES are dependent on plants and the products made from them. The use of vegetables and fruit as food is common to all cultures, but plants have a wide variety of other uses. Starchy and spicy roots are used for food and flavorings, plant fibers are woven into textiles and ropes, and trees not only give us timber, but provide the raw materials for rubber, cork, and paper. Perfume, tea, cooking oils, medicine, cosmetics, chocolate, and even chewing gum are all products we obtain from plants.

Food and drink

Starchy plants, such as grains, potatoes, yams, and some grasses, form the basis of most diets. Plants provide tea, coffee, and cocoa, and refreshing, vitamin-rich juices can be squeezed from fruits. Food and drinks are often sweetened with sugar prepared from sugarcane or sugar beet. Wine is made from fermented grapes, and beers from fermented grains.

Spices and flavorings
The aromatic seeds, roots, and bark of some plants are dried to make spices and added to food to enhance its flavor. The nutmeg tree provides nutmeg from its seed, and mace from the flesh around the seed. Other spices include cinnamon and ginger.

Wheat is used to make flour for bread and pasta.

Oats are used in breakfast cereals.

Rice is eaten as a grain and is made into cereals.

Rye is used to make flour.

Barley is used to brew beer.

Millet is ground into flour to make bread and is used in cereal.

Medicine

Some plants produce chemicals that if eaten or touched, can have dramatic effects. These plants may be poisonous if taken in large doses, but in small amounts they often have valuable medicinal properties. Cinchona tree bark is used to make quinine to treat malaria. Digitalin extracted from foxgloves is used as a heart stimulant, and morphine and codeine from the opium poppy are used as painkillers.

Cinchona trees grow in South America.

Cinchona bark is used to make quinine.

Quinine tablets

Wood

Every year, we use almost 106 billion cu ft (3 billion cubic meters) of wood worldwide. The unique properties of wood – its strength, durability, resilience, and appearance – make it ideal for the construction of boats, buildings, furniture, and smaller items such as musical instruments and toys. Resin that oozes from cut conifer trunks provides turpentine and rosin, and is used to make varnishes.

Cork
Cork oak trees have a thick layer of cork below their bark that is stripped from the trees every 8–10 years. Stripping does not harm the trees, because they soon grow a new layer. Cork has many uses – it is waterproof and has good sound and heat-insulating properties.

Untreated cork

Cork tile

Bottle corks

Paper
Books, tissues, and printed items such as newspapers are a few examples of the kinds of paper that we use daily. Paper is made from wood pulp. Some natural forests are still being felled to provide pulp, but now much of the wood needed is grown on plantations of fast-growing trees, such as eucalyptus and poplar.

Cardboard packaging

Tissues

Tea bag

Paper napkin

Rubber
Below the bark of rubber trees is a sticky sap, or latex, that oozes out when the bark is cut. As it dries, the latex becomes stretchy. When treated it turns into rubber. Rubber is used to make shoes and tires, and provides stretch and elasticity in items that need it.

This trunk has been sawed, so the boards keep their shape and have a decorative grain.

Bark is cut at an angle.

Latex is collected by making slits, or punctures, in the bark of the rubber tree.

Fibers

Fibers from the leaves and stems of flax, hemp, raffia, and other plants can be spun into yarns. Some fibers, such as cotton, come from the seed heads. The finer, softer yarns are used to make clothes. Cloth of many colors and patterns is made by weaving threads together on a hand or machine loom. Coarser fibers, from plants such as agave and sisal, are woven into mats, ropes, and baskets.

Raffia cloth made from fibers of the raffia palm

Vats of natural dyes in Morocco

Dyes
Before artificial dyes were invented, most yarns were colored with natural plant dyes. These are made by pounding plants and mixing them with liquid. The color is fixed with chemicals. The colors are quite subtle, but many people prefer them to artificial dyes.

Cosmetics
Plants are an important ingredient in cosmetics. Herbal extracts and fragrant oils, such as jasmine and lavender, are used to scent many cosmetics. Aloe vera and cocoa butter are used in moisturizing lotions, and alginates from seaweeds are used as gelling and stabilizing agents.

Henna plant yields long-lasting hair and skin dyes.

Indian bride's hand painted with henna

Henna powder

Fuel
Coal, oil, and natural gas are all derived from plants that lived long ago. Half the wood cut each year is also burned as fuel. In some countries, such as Ireland, peat – the compressed remains of mosses and sedges – is still dug from the ground and used as fuel.

PLASTICS AND RUBBER

PLASTICS HAVE BECOME one of the most used materials in the world. They come in many forms but have two things in common – their molecules are made up of long chains of atoms and they are easily shaped by heating. Most plastics are synthetic, made from chemicals that are usually extracted from petroleum. Common plastics range from polystyrene and polyethylene, used to make items such as plastic bags, to polyvinyl chloride (PVC) and nylon, used in clothing. Rubber, a gum extracted from trees, is a natural kind of plastic. Synthetic rubber, like plastic, is made using petrochemicals.

Polymers

Polymers are substances that are made up of very long molecules, which consist of a chain of repeated chemical units. Most plastics are polymers, and their chain molecules are built up from smaller molecules (monomers) in a chemical process called polymerization.

Polymers make up PVC used in raincoats

Molding plastic

Impression of channel through which plastic is fed.

Plastics are usually shaped by molding, a process in which molten plastic is injected or blown into a shaped mold. Other methods include extrusion, in which molten plastic is forced through the hole in a die (a shaped block), and vacuum forming, in which a plastic sheet is sucked into a mold by a vacuum.

Injection molding ensures that related parts fit together.

Molded electrical components

Types of plastics

There are a number of plastics in use today, but they all fall into two different classes according to the way they react to heat. Thermoplastics soften and melt each time they are heated, then retain their shape and harden when the temperature falls. Thermosetting plastics will not soften again once they have been heated and set.

Acrylics

Acrylic is an example of a thermoplastic. Its long molecules do not interlink, so when heated the molecules slide over one another and melt. Acrylic is used to make many products, including textiles.

The fur is made from an acrylic fabric.

Epoxies

Epoxies are thermosetting plastics, which have long molecules that cross-link and form rigid structures. An epoxy resin is the resinous material used for molding. A curing agent is then added and the mixture sets into a three-dimensional structure.

Bicycle helmet

Fiberglass is set into a plastic matrix that gives a smooth shiny surface.

Chair

Tennis racket

Carbon fiber frame

Composites

Some plastics are given added strength by reinforcing them with fibers, making a composite. The most common composite is fiberglass plastic. Carbon fiber composites are also used as reinforcements because they are light as well as tough.

Marbled Bakelite

Bakelite hairdryer (c.1930s)

Bakelite

Named after its inventor Leo Baekeland (1863–1944), Bakelite was the first synthetic plastic. Baekeland first produced this material in 1909, by polymerizing phenol and formaldehyde. A thermoset, Bakelite is still used today for its heat and electrical resistance.

Rubber

Rubber may be natural or synthetic. Natural rubber comes from rubber trees cultivated in plantations, particularly in Southeast Asia. It is made by processing the sap, or latex, that is collected from the trees when they are cut. Synthetic rubber is made by polymerization in much the same way as other plastics.

Tapping rubber from a tree plantation, Malaysia

Uses of rubber
Rubber is used for soles of shoes and car tires, because its resilience and elasticity make it a good shock absorber. It is also flexible and waterproof, and therefore is used in protective clothing, such as rubber gloves and rainwear.

Car tire

Rubber dummy

Properties of rubber
When first made from latex, rubber has little elasticity and deteriorates quickly in air. It becomes elastic and hardens when treated with sulfur, a process called vulcanization. A pigment called carbon black is added to make the rubber durable.

Recycling
Since most plastics are made from petroleum chemicals that cannot be replaced, there is a need for recycling. Thermo plastics, such as polyethylene, are easy to recycle because they can be re-melted. Thermosets, such as Bakelite, pose a problem since they cannot readily be broken down.

Plastic ready for recycling

FIND OUT MORE · ATOMS AND MOLECULES · CHEMISTRY · COAL · OIL · POLLUTION · TECHNOLOGY · TEXTILES AND WEAVING

POETRY

AN INTENSE FORM OF LITERATURE, poetry appeals directly to the emotions. In poetry, meaning is condensed to produce strong images, and words are arranged according to the pattern of their sounds. This pattern is like music. It is picked up by the listening ear, and reinforces the thoughts and feelings expressed by the words. Many people are attracted to the rhythms of poetry from infancy, when they learn children's nursery rhymes. All societies preserve great examples of the art, because it can articulate the deepest experiences of life.

Types of poetry

There are three main types of poetry. The oldest is epic poetry, which consists of long narratives with a heroic or profound subject. Dramatic poetry is written in the voices of its characters and can be acted on stage. The third and most familiar type is lyric poetry. Lyric poems are the closest to songs. They are usually short, colorful, and express the poet's feelings deeply and intensely.

Kipling's desk

Kipling's stories were set all over the world.

Rudyard Kipling's study

Gilgamesh

The world's oldest written poem is The *Epic of Gilgamesh*. Discovered in Persia (Iran), it is at least 4,000 years old. The poem tells the Babylonian legend of Gilgamesh, the great king of Uruk in Mesopotamia, who is half-god, half-man. Together with his friend Enkidu the wild man, he slays monsters sent to destroy him. But in the end, Enkidu dies, and Gilgamesh searches for and fails to find a way to live forever. The *Epic of Gilgamesh* is the first example of epic poetry.

William Blake

English poet and artist William Blake (1757–1827) enjoyed neither critical nor commercial success in his lifetime, although he is now regarded as one of the greatest figures of Romanticism. Many of Blake's poems are written from a child's point of view. One of his best known works is *The Tyger* (1794).

Statue of Gilgamesh

Illustration by Blake

Rudyard Kipling

British writer Rudyard Kipling (1865–1936) is now best known for *The Jungle Books* and *Kim,* but during his lifetime he was much more popular for his poems about British soldiers, which were published in *Barrack-Room Ballads* (1892).

Goethe

The German writer Johann Wolfgang von Goethe (1749–1832) published his dramatic poem *Faust* in two parts (1808 and 1832), and it is still regarded as one of the greatest poetic and philosophical works of literature. *Faust* tells the story of a man tempted by the devil.

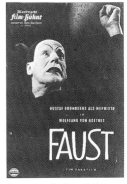

Poster for the film of *Faust*

World poetry

The narrative poem exists in almost every culture. It has various subjects, such as nature, religion, and legend. These are recited on important occasions, as poets are often regarded as divinely inspired. Today, many cultures still use the narrative poem. Others have evolved complex forms, such as the Japanese *haiku,* a poem containing 17 syllables.

Omar Khayyám

One of the most well known Persian poets, Omar Khayyám (1048–1131) was also an architect and astronomer. He wrote many *rubaiyat* – verses in four lines that ponder eternal mysteries, and also celebrate the simple pleasures that life has to offer.

Rubaiyat illustration by Rene Bull

African praise poetry

Praise poems are sung in African communities in celebration of many things, including people, animals, and weapons. In Nigeria, the Yoruba people dress in masks and costumes to recite important poems. The poems are handed down by oral tradition, but a praise poet can also choose to add lines of his own.

Pair of Yoruba tribal masks, Nigeria

War poetry

A new development in the 20th century was war poetry. First associated with World War I (1914–18), war poetry describes the horrors of war. A well known war poet was British soldier Wilfred Owen (1893–1918), whose poetry about the sufferings of soldiers in the trenches was published after his death.

Sylvia Plath

American poet and novelist Sylvia Plath (1932–63) was little known at the time of her death by suicide, but she is now considered an important writer of the 20th century. From childhood she was dedicated to perfecting her art as a poet. Her work shows great skill and poise. Many of her later poems are preoccupied with death.

FIND OUT MORE

BABYLONIAN EMPIRE | BOOKS | DRAMA | LANGUAGES | LITERATURE | WRITING | WORLD WAR I

POISONOUS ANIMALS

POISONOUS AND VENOMOUS animals are often confused with each other. Venomous animals, such as snakes and scorpions, defend themselves by biting or stinging and injecting venom; poisonous animals are those that cause ill effects when eaten or handled. Many venomous and poisonous animals have no need for camouflage and advertise themselves with bright-colored patterns including combinations of yellow, black, and red, which are recognized warning colors. Some harmless species mimic the colors of venomous or poisonous species for protection. For example, harmless milk snakes look like deadly coral snakes.

Pitahui bird
Birds used to be absent from the list of poisonous animals. But recently it was discovered that some species of pitahui bird of New Guinea, such as the black-hooded pitahui bird, have poisonous feathers and flesh. The poison is mild, causing only localized tingling and discomfort when eaten, but may deter its enemies anyway.

Black-hooded pitahui bird

Pufferfish
If eaten, poisonous pufferfish cause lung paralysis and even death. In Japan, pufferfish meat is considered a delicacy. It is prepared so the diner receives just enough toxin for a tingling sensation; even so it causes 50 deaths each year.

Poisonous animals
Poisonous animals – those that cause ill effects if eaten or touched – are poisonous to deter enemies and avoid being eaten. Poisonous skin secretions that make a predator sick or cause its mouth to burn, teach it to avoid such prey in future. The European toad secretes a toxin from parotid glands on its head if touched; the cane toad secretes similar but far more toxic secretions that can even kill a dog.

Poison dart frog
South American poison dart frogs are poisonous to eat and have few enemies. Their diet of insects makes them poisonous. Amerindians use blow-darts tipped with poison from the most toxic species to hunt for monkeys.

Bright-colored stripes indicate that it is poisonous to eat.

Black and red poison dart frog

Scorpion fish
Scorpion fish and lionfish are common in tropical waters. Their enlarged dorsal spines are highly venomous and can give a serious sting. Other venomous fish include freshwater stingrays, the lesser weaver fish of British coastlines, and the ugly stonefish of Australia, probably the most venomous fish in the world. Barefoot bathers are sometimes stung when they accidentally step on weaver fish or stonefish.

Thirteen venomous dorsal spines

Three venomous anal spines

Venomous animals
Venomous animals release toxins in various ways. Some snakes and spiders bite their victims, releasing toxins through fangs. An Amazonian caterpillar has venomous hairs, swarms of killer bees sting and kill people and animals, and beaded lizards chew toxins into their victims. Many venomous animals live in the sea. Cone shells release venomous harpoons, stonefish erect poison-filled spines, and box jellyfish snare and sting swimmers with their tentacles.

Antivenom
Antivenoms are drugs used to save victims of venomous bites or stings. Most snakebite antivenoms are made by giving horses a dose of snake venom. The horses produce antibodies to the venom; blood serum is taken from the horses and used to make antivenom. Some people are allergic to horse serum and scientists are trying to produce antivenoms in sheep.

Snake is milked for its venom.

Duckbilled platypus
Mammals are not normally considered venomous but three kinds are known. The male duckbilled platypus has large venomous spurs on its hind legs and the spiny echidna has small spurs, used mainly for defense. Insectivorous shrews subdue earthworms with a venomous bite.

Sensitive bill

Fangs are used to bite victim and inject venom.

Sydney funnel-web spider
The most dangerous spider to humans is the Sydney funnel-web. The male's bite causes muscle spasms and death. The black widow of Europe and the US and the Australian redback are also deadly.

If alarmed, the blue spots enlarge.

Blue-ringed octopus
The blue-ringed octopus lives in tide pools in Australia and is the most lethal octopus in the world. If handled, it bites and injects tetrodotoxin, the same poison as found in the puffer fish, which causes respiratory paralysis, and, if untreated, death in two hours.

The coils make a warning sound as viper moves.

Carpet viper
Carpet vipers are small snakes common in highly populated areas of Africa and Asia. Their venom is dangerous and may cause kidney failure. Despite their small size, they can easily kill an adult human.

FIND OUT MORE
AUSTRALIAN WILDLIFE   CAMOUFLAGE AND COLOR   FISH   FROGS AND TOADS   JELLYFISH AND SEA ANEMONES   OCTOPUSES AND SQUID   SNAKES   SPIDERS AND SCORPIONS

POLAR EXPLORATION

WHEN EXPLORERS FINALLY REACHED the north and south poles in the early 20th century, their journeys were the last heroic voyages of discovery. Although navigators had always known about the location of the Arctic, the existence of the Antarctic landmass was not proven until 1820. Icy deserts covering both poles make these mysterious places the harshest environments on Earth. Conditions include raging winds, sub-zero temperatures, and a lack of food. Polar explorers needed incredible stamina, resourcefulness, and courage – many died in the attempt to conquer these last frontiers.

Race to the south pole

After the first reliable sighting of the Antarctic in 1820, expeditions from France, the US, and Britain mapped the coastline. Interior exploration did not begin until 1900, but by 1906, a race was on between Britain's Captain Scott (1868–1912) and Norway's Amundsen to be the first to reach the south pole.

Shackleton's attempt on the Pole
Antarctica
Amundsen's route
South pole
Scott's route
Ross Sea ice shelf

Roald Amundsen
Amundsen (1872–1928) and his four companions were the first to arrive at the south pole on December 14, 1911, a month before Scott and his team. Amundsen returned to his Ross Sea base safely, but Scott's team died on the return journey.

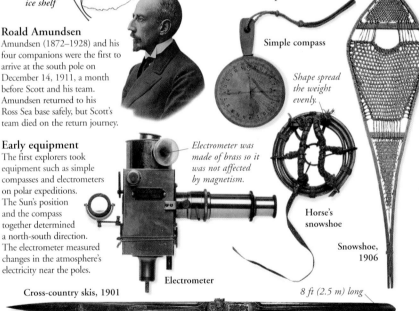

Simple compass

Electrometer was made of brass so it was not affected by magnetism.

Shape spread the weight evenly.

Horse's snowshoe

Snowshoe, 1906

Early equipment
The first explorers took equipment such as simple compasses and electrometers on polar expeditions. The Sun's position and the compass together determined a north-south direction. The electrometer measured changes in the atmosphere's electricity near the poles.

Electrometer

Cross-country skis, 1901

Wooden skis

8 ft (2.5 m) long

Arctic

Native North Americans and Greenlanders have lived on the Arctic's fringes for 5,000 years. European navigators first explored the ice cap 400 years ago, searching for sea routes to the riches of Asia.

Frozen ocean (pack ice)
Alaska
Northwest Passage
Peary's route
Northeast Passage
North Pole
Arctic Ocean
Greenland
Iceland

Peary and Henson
American explorer Robert Peary (1856–1920) and his servant Matthew Henson (1866–1955) are thought to have been the first to reach the north pole. In 1909, they left Greenland with 29 Eskimos and 133 dogs. Some people think that they did not reach it, but the latest research suggests they did.

Robert Peary

Willem Barents (1550–97) seeks the Northeast Passage.

Northeast Passage
In the 1500s, Dutchman Willem Barents tried to reach Asia by sailing northeast from Europe. In 1878–79, Swedish geologist Nils Nordenskjöld (1832–1901) was the first to succeed.

Northwest Passage
English explorer John Franklin (1786–1847) died searching for the elusive route to Asia along Canada's coast, known as the Northwest Passage. His expedition found the entrance, but the Norwegian explorer Roald Amundsen was the first to navigate it in 1906.

Medicine jars

Medicine chest from Franklin's expedition

Modern research

Although the polar regions have now been explored and mapped, multinational stations still conduct scientific research, particularly in the Antarctic.

Scott-Amundsen base

Research stations
Today Antarctica has around 40 permanent and 100 temporary research stations that investigate wildlife, fossils, and minerals. Hundreds of scientists work in the summer at the American Amundsen-Scott base.

Ernest Shackleton
Irish explorer Shackleton (1874–1922) first went to the Antarctic in 1901. During an an expedition in 1914, Shackleton made a heroic 800-mile (1,300-km) journey in an open boat to get help for his stranded team. His bravery earned him a place in history.

Timeline
1611 English navigator Henry Hudson is set adrift to die by mutineers in the northern Canadian bay named after him.

1733 Russian expedition explores Arctic land fringes.

1820 US sealer Nat Palmer sights the Antarctic.

Scott's matchbox

1901–1904 Scott's *Discovery* expedition penetrates Antarctic.

December 1911 Amundsen reaches the south pole.

January 1912 Scott and his team reach the south pole.

1929 First flight over south pole by Richard E. Byrd (1888–1957).

1937 Soviets create Arctic research stations.

1957–58 International Geophysical Year: 12 nations set up about 50 Antarctic bases.

FIND OUT MORE   ARCTIC OCEAN   EXPLORATION   INVENTIONS   NATIVE AMERICANS   NAVIGATION   SCANDINAVIA, HISTORY OF

POLAR WILDLIFE

SUBZERO TEMPERATURES, six months of darkness, hurricane-force winds, and desert conditions make the polar regions some of the most difficult places for wildlife. Only animals and plants specially adapted to the severe conditions can hope to survive. Every animal from the furry nosed reindeer to the thickly blubbered whale is particularly suited to its environment. All wildlife has to be able to breed or flower in the extremely short polar summer. For many animals, the sea, which is rich in plankton and krill, is the key to survival. Most mammals and birds, especially in the south, depend on it for their food.

Emperor penguins in the Antarctic

Polar regions

The Arctic and Antarctic Circles are defined as those parts of the planet that experience 24 hours of daylight and 24 hours of darkness for at least one day in the year. The Arctic and Antarctic are totally different from each other. The Arctic is a frozen sea surrounded by land; the Antarctic is an ice-covered continent surrounded by sea.

Mammals

The Arctic is warmer than the Antarctic and therefore has more vegetation. Some herbivorous land mammals can survive there; other mammals depend on the sea for their food, either directly or indirectly. All the Antarctic mammals are aquatic. Any carnivorous land mammals would create havoc among the millions of penguins that live there.

Polar bear
The polar bear has black skin to absorb heat, and hollow hairs for added insulation. It also has a thick layer of fat beneath its skin and is able to go for long periods without feeding by living on this fat.

Arctic fox
Smaller than the red fox, the Arctic fox changes color from white to gray-brown in the summer. It has a very thick coat and is extremely tolerant of the cold. Its diet is very varied and includes birds' eggs, birds, lemmings, and carrion.

Arctic fox

Pads are covered with fur to save heat.

Strong, partly webbed front paws for swimming.

Polar bear

White fur blends with the snow.

Weddell seal

Seals
Seals are adapted to life in the sea and spend much of their time in the water, often under the ice. They haul out to rest and breed. In the Arctic, seals are hunted by polar bears. Antarctic seals are prey for leopard seals and killer whales.

Arctic hare
The Arctic hare matches its surroundings by changing color from white in winter to brown in summer and is then more difficult for predators to spot. Unusually for hares, it digs burrows and they are often used by its young for shelter.

Colonies of barnacles and lice live on the whale's skin.

Musk oxen
These are not oxen but members of the goat antelope family. They have long black fur that absorbs heat. They are known for forming defensive circles when danger threatens so that predators are faced with a barrier of horns.

Musk oxen

Lemmings
These small vole-like creatures are common in the cold north. In good years their populations can explode, forcing them to migrate. When they come to an obstacle, such as water, large numbers may gather and be drowned.

Whales
The polar regions provide whales with very rich sources of food. The largest whales are the baleen whales, which strain seawater through a series of bony plates and sieve out huge quantities of plankton. The toothed whales hunt fish, seals, and other sea life.

Scratches are from encounters with other whales, sharks, and boats.

Gray whale

Siberian lemmings

Birds

Antarctic birds fall into two main categories. They are either flightless like penguins, or magnificent fliers like albatrosses. The Arctic tends to have greater variety among its birds, which include a large number of migrants. Many wildfowl and waders fly there every year to breed during the short Arctic summer. Some birds of prey, including snowy owls and gyrfalcons, live in the Arctic. They feed on small animals such as lemmings and birds.

Arctic tern
These remarkable fliers travel more than 20,000 miles (31,000 km) a year. They migrate from their Arctic breeding grounds to the Antarctic and back again, enjoying almost continuous summer-time throughout their lives.

Little auk
One of the smallest seabirds, the little auk nests in large colonies on the Arctic cliffs. Like other auks, it has narrow wings and feet set well back on its body. It specializes in diving for its food.

Forward-facing eyes for finding prey

White feathers for winter camouflage

Feathers on legs and feet help keep owl warm

Snowy owl
This large white owl is solitary and active mainly by day. It chases other birds and also takes prey as large as Arctic hares and eider ducks. It perches on low branches to rest or preen, but nests on the ground.

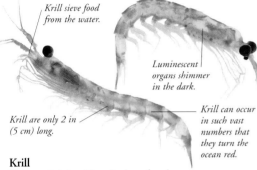

Krill sieve food from the water.

Luminescent organs shimmer in the dark.

Krill are only 2 in (5 cm) long.

Krill can occur in such vast numbers that they turn the ocean red.

Krill
These small shrimp-like animals are found in the sea around the Antarctic and are the staple food of many species, including some whales. Penguin numbers have increased in recent years, probably because the slaughter of whales has left a surplus of krill for the birds.

Plants

It is a real struggle for plants to survive in such extreme climates, and there are only two species of flowering plant in Antarctica. The more maritime climate of the Arctic encourages more plant species. All tend to be low-growing as this gives them shelter from the strong winds. Mosses and lichens are the hardiest plants in polar regions.

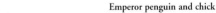

Emperor penguin and chick

Penguins
Several species of these flightless birds breed in their millions in the Antarctic. They are kept warm by their dense plumage and by a layer of fat under their skin. They go without food for long periods while incubating eggs and protecting their young.

Gulls
The only gull that lives and breeds in the Antarctic is the kelp gull, which feeds mostly on limpets and krill. A number of other gull species breed in the Arctic in colonies on the tundra or on the sea cliffs. They fly south to live in warmer climates for most of the year.

Purple saxifrage
This creeping plant is generally found sheltering among rocks in the Arctic. Its beautiful purple flowers bloom almost as soon as the snow has melted, to make the most of the short spring and summer. They add a splash of color to an often drab landscape.

Arctic willow
This is a low-growing shrub that grows in tundra swamps and wet ground. It sends long woody stems along the ground. In the northern spring, it has small catkins that appear out of scale with the rest of the plant. Arctic willow and its close relative Alaska willow are favorite foods of moose.

Hairgrass
This and Antarctic pearlwort are the only two flowering plants found in the Antarctic. Hairgrass grows in low mats and is found only in those areas near the coast from which the snow recedes in spring and where the temperature is sufficiently high.

Lichens
Many species of these hardy plants grow in both the north and south polar regions, where they can thrive in the unpolluted air. Often colorful, they generally occur as encrustations on the rocks. They may be fertilized by droppings from nesting birds.

 FIND OUT MORE   **ANTARCTICA**   **ARCTIC OCEAN**   **MIGRATION, ANIMAL**   **OCEAN WILDLIFE**   **PENGUINS**   **PLANTS**   **SEABIRDS**   **SEALS**   **TUNDRA**   **WHALES AND DOLPHINS**

POLICE

IN EVERY COMMUNITY, LAWS exist to regulate society. Within society, it is usually the police who make sure that these laws are enforced. The police prevent or solve crimes, capture criminals and hand them over for trial, and protect and aid the public. In the course of these duties, the police may undertake many different tasks, such as directing traffic, controlling riots, or investigating murder and other serious crimes. In times of emergency, they may be asked to find shelter and protection for victims of fires, floods, or other disasters.

Bow Street Runner, 18th century

Early police
The first police force was set up in Egypt in about 1340 BC, to protect merchants on the Nile River from pirates. In Britain, the Bow Street Runners were set up in 1750 to capture criminals all over the country; they were replaced in 1829 by the Metropolitan Police, the world's oldest existing police force. In the US, forces similar to the Metropolitan Police were set up from the 1840s on.

Police divisions

In order for the police to carry out their duties effectively, specially trained and equipped divisions exist to deal with specific tasks. Within a police force, a uniformed division patrols the streets, preventing crime or arresting people who are breaking the law. Detective divisions investigate crime; others deal with juvenile crime, drug dealing, or fraud.

Crime prevention
Surveillance work is an important part of crime prevention. Police officers usually work in shifts, patrolling certain areas, and watching people, places of business, and traffic.

Police officer on duty, Hong Kong

Hand signals tell drivers to stop or keep moving.

In summer, the traffic police in Rome wear white uniforms.

Police officers wear uniforms so that the public can recognize them.

Traffic control
Specially trained officers are needed for traffic control, to prevent accidents on congested city streets or highways. Traffic officers promote safety by directing traffic, assisting at accidents, and enforcing parking, speed, and traffic laws, such as seat belt regulations.

Police officer directs traffic, Rome, Italy

Around the world

There is at least one police force in every country, but how they are run and who controls them differ widely. For example, in France the government directly controls a national police force that investigates major crimes, while local forces deal with minor matters. In other countries, such as Australia, separate forces cover different areas.

US law enforcement
In the US, police forces are organized at town, county, city, and state level. A national agency, the Federal Bureau of Investigation (FBI), investigates interstate crime and runs a computerized information system on criminals and stolen property, which is accessible to all US police forces.

FBI emblem

Interpol
To fight international crime such as smuggling, police from more than 140 countries assist each other through the International Criminal Police Organization, known as Interpol.

The Bolshevik secret police were known as the Cheka.

Interpol HQ, outside Paris, France

Identification for Russian secret police officer, 1918

Secret police
Some governments run a secret police force to make sure that people do not speak or act against them. Such forces have a long history; during the 20th century they were used in the Soviet Union, Romania, and other countries.

Detection and investigation

Police officers who specialize in investigating crime are called detectives. Through collecting evidence (proof), interviewing witnesses, and interrogating suspects, detectives try to discover who committed a crime. Once they believe that they have the right person, the police must present a convincing case so that the alleged culprit can be brought to trial in a law court, convicted, and punished.

At a murder scene, officers in the UK wear disposable suits to avoid contaminating any evidence.

Fingerprinting kit

Forensic science
At the scene of a crime, specialized police officers search for clues that will lead them to the criminal and prove in court that he or she is guilty. Finding and interpreting such clues is known as forensic detection. Officers search for fingerprints, fibers, footprints, and even tiny amounts of skin, hair, and blood; all of these can be used to identify people.

1 Lifting fingerprints takes care and skill. Aluminum powder is dusted on an object to detect any print marks.

2 If the prints are clear enough to be used, tape is used to lift them from the object.

3 The fingerprint tape is mounted on a clear plastic sheet and flattened out by a roller.

4 The print is put in a tamperproof evidence bag and sent to a police laboratory for identification.

 FIND OUT MORE | CRIME AND PUNISHMENT | DRUGS | GENETICS | HUMAN RIGHTS | LAW | SOCIETIES, HUMAN | SOVIET UNION

POLLUTION

EVERY DAY, HARMFUL MATERIALS are released into the environment as a result of human activities. These materials are called pollution. Different types of pollution – arising from farming, industry, transportation, and energy use – enter the air, the soil, fresh water, and the oceans. Pollution's effects can be small-scale or global, gradual or dramatic, and include threats to wildlife and health problems for people. Pollution is an important environmental issue – one we can help solve.

Acid rain damages trees by disrupting the chemical balance in the soil around the roots. The first sign of attack is when foliage starts to die back.

Air and streams are cleanest in mountains.

Acid rain
Certain air pollutants, especially sulfur dioxide and nitrogen oxides from vehicle and factory fumes, can mix with water in the atmosphere and fall back to earth in rain. This acid rain seeps into the soil and contaminates lakes and rivers, damaging trees and killing aquatic animals, such as frogs and fish.

Farmers use tractors and aircraft to spray pesticide chemicals on crops. Some of these chemicals enter the soil or are washed into streams.

Smoke and invisible gases released high into the air from power stations and factories, can spread far and wide.

Coaldust particles will be carried into the air.

Plant- and tree-life is reduced in urban and industrial areas.

Harmful waste chemicals from industrial processes, such as mercury compounds used in paper mills, are sometimes discharged into rivers.

Sewage plant

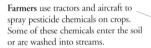

Most of the sewage from our homes is removed from the water at treatment plants, but the leftover waste may be dumped in the ocean.

Garbage is often dumped into holes in the ground called land fill sites. Plastic and metal debris can trap and injure animals looking for food and poisonous liquids can leak out. Buried rubbish may get hot and catch fire. Gases are produced which may explode.

Chemicals from detergents and other household cleaning products pass from homes into the water system.

Pollution types
Pollution enters the environment in many different forms, from different sorts of activity. Gases and smoke from industry and vehicles drift into the air. Household sewage, agricultural sprays, and other liquids are absorbed by the land, the oceans, and rivers. Solids, too, such as refuse and mining waste, are dumped on the ground and into the sea.

The fuel burned in gasoline engines gives off many harmful exhaust fumes, that sometimes produce smog along city streets.

Oil spilled or washed from the holds of tankers rides on the surface of the sea, harming ocean life and contaminating surrounding beaches.

Marine pollution is also caused by tourists when rubbish and debris from beaches and tourist resorts are washed into the sea.

Old, rusting, wrecked ships may steadily release pollutants into the ocean from their cargo holds.

When plantlife at the bottom of the marine food chain is wiped out by pollution, other species in the food chain are affected.

Severe pollution hazards are caused when highly dangerous industrial wastes start to leak from containers buried on land or dumped in the ocean.

Pollution hazards
Some types of pollution pose grave dangers to life. Animals may be directly poisoned or injured by pollutants, or they may suffer indirect ecological effects, such as the reduction of the oxygen supply in polluted water, the killing of food sources or vegetation cover, and the alteration of the climate because of atmospheric pollution.

P

677

Atmospheric pollution

Each year, millions of tons of pollutant gases are sent into earth's atmosphere. Some remain at ground level, fouling the air and causing illness. Some accumulate in the upper atmosphere. They alter the way the sun's heat rays pass to and from the earth.

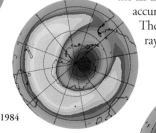

High

1979

Units of ozone

Low

1984

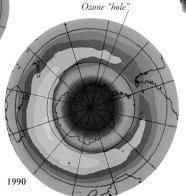

Ozone "hole"

1990

Ozone holes

A natural layer of ozone gas, high in the atmosphere, shields us from harmful rays. Certain pollutant gases, including CFCs (chlorofluorocarbons) and methane, are destroying the ozone. Since 1979, "holes" have appeared in the ozone layer, first near the South Pole and now over the North. These are getting bigger, as can be seen by these satellite pictures of Antarctica. The colors represent different measures of ozone.

Greenhouse effect

Gases naturally present in the atmosphere help keep the earth warm by trapping heat from the sun that would otherwise radiate out into space. The burning of fuel, such as oil in motor vehicles, and coal and wood in factories and homes, produces carbon dioxide and other "greenhouse gases." These are increasing the "greenhouse effect," leading to global warming. Air pollution can be seen easily on this road in Bangkok, Thailand.

Effects on wildlife

Most plants and animals suffer the effects of pollution, but not all to the same degree. Pollution-sensitive species have severely declined in the wild because their habitats have been contaminated. More resistant species have maintained their populations. A few have even increased.

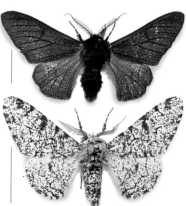

Otters

Pollution has played a large part in the disappearance of otters from many rivers. Industrial waste and pesticides washed into the rivers contaminate the fish on which otters prey. The more fish an otter eats, the more poisons build up in its body, eventually killing it.

Peppered moths

The normally light-colored peppered moth also has a dark form. The dark moths became more common in Britain after the Industrial Revolution of the 18th century. The increase in factories and smoke caused trees in some areas to be coated in soot. The dark peppered moths were well camouflaged and able to avoid more predators. They lived to produce more dark young.

Major incidents

Dramatic pollution incidents make news headlines. They can be the result of a gradual release of pollutants, or of a disastrous event. During the Persian Gulf War, 850 burning oil wells blackened the sky with soot, and an oil slick ruined 285 miles (460 km) of coast.

An oil fire and slick in Kuwait, 1991

Oil slicks

Oil spilled at sea can form an oil slick on the water. The oil slick kills wildlife by weighing down their fur or feathers, or poisoning them when they swallow the foul water. Some are poisoned by swallowing the oil accidentally. A large oil slick, such as the one formed in the Gulf War, or one caused when an oil tanker runs aground, can devastate wildlife.

Organic farming

Some farmers have returned to organic methods of cultivating crops that do not rely on the heavy use of chemical pesticides and fertilizers. Fewer chemicals reduce the amount of pollution from farms, with benefits for land and freshwater wildlife, and for people who eat the crops.

Cleaner cities

Efforts to reduce smog have included promoting unleaded gasoline to avoid the release of lead from car exhaust fumes. The use of electrically powered transportation, such as streetcars, is a further advance, but cyclists use the cleanest energy source of all – muscle power. This car-free shopping street is in Freiburg, Germany.

Reducing pollution

As "green" societies campaign against pollution, people are being made more aware of the harm they are doing. There is a lot we can do to reduce the rate at which we are polluting the earth, but it must be done now. Governments can pass laws to curb some of the worst polluting activities; contaminated habitats can be cleaned up; we can choose to buy products that are less polluting; and we can engage in activities less damaging to the environment.

Using public transportation helps reduce pollution.

FIND OUT MORE   ATMOSPHERE   COAL   CLIMATE   ECOLOGY AND ECOSYSTEMS   FARMING   OIL

POLYNESIA

THE "MANY ISLANDS" that give Polynesia its name are scattered over a vast area of the central Pacific Ocean. Nobody knows how many of these islands there are. Some are just rocks in the sea, but others are inhabited by peoples whose ancestors colonized them thousands of years ago. Today, they include the countries of Kiribati, Western Samoa, Tuvalu, and Tonga as well as many territories. New Zealand also forms part of Polynesia. Many islands remain remote as such vast distances make travel difficult.

Physical features

The islands of Polynesia are the heads of old volcanoes that rise straight from the deep ocean floor. Many of them are topped with coral, forming atolls. The atolls contain sheltered lagoons formed by the volcanic craters and are fringed by coral reefs. Dense tropical rain forest cloaks the mountains of the larger islands. Coconuts grow all over the islands.

Coconuts
Palm-lined beaches set against dramatic mountains are a common sight on some of the larger Polynesian islands, such as Bora Bora in French Polynesia. Many of the trees have sprouted from coconuts that have floated across the ocean and have washed ashore. The Polynesians use all parts of the coconut – the "meat," milk, and husk.

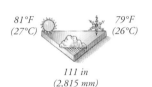

81°F (27°C)   79°F (26°C)

111 in (2,815 mm)

Regional climate
Polynesia lies in the tropics and subtropics so its islands enjoy a warm climate with plenty of rain. However, on many of the islands, vegetation is scant because of the poor quality of the soil, which consists largely of volcanic and coral debris.

People
The Polynesian peoples include Samoans, Maori, Tongans, Tahitians, and Hawaiians. Between them, they speak about 20 native languages, all of which are closely related. Most Polynesians live off the fish they catch and by growing their own food, such as cassava and coconuts.

Native girl wearing flowers, Polynesia

Canoes

The Polynesians are seafaring people. They live off the fish they catch from their small, one-person canoes. They make their canoes by hollowing out a single log to which they attach a balance, or outrigger. Their simple craft are similar to those used by the first Polynesians, who arrived from Southeast Asia thousands of years ago.

Outrigger balances craft in waves.

Canoe is made from a hollowed-out log.

Outrigger canoe

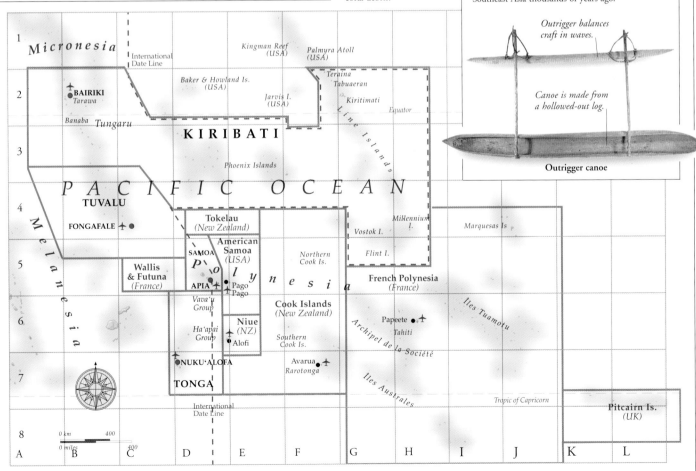

P

Kiribati

Kiribati, pronounced Kiribass, consists of more than 30 islands. Kiribati is the local way of saying Gilbert, the name given to the islands by the British, who ruled them until 1979. Coconuts, copra, and fish are exported.

KIRIBATI FACTS

CAPITAL CITY Bairiki

AREA 274 sq miles (710 sq km)

POPULATION 92,000

MAIN LANGUAGES English, Kiribati

MAJOR RELIGION Christian

CURRENCY Australian dollar

Fishing
Like most Pacific Islanders, the people of Kiribati depend on fish as a source of food and income. This fisherman is setting off with his nets for a day's work in his canoe. His house is thatched with leaves from the pandanus tree.

Samoa

The western half of the Samoan island chain was ruled by New Zealand until 1962. Its nine volcanic islands are forested, and only four are inhabited.

SAMOA FACTS

CAPITAL CITY Apia

AREA 1,097 sq miles (2,840 sq km)

POPULATION 180,000

MAIN LANGUAGES Samoan, English

MAJOR RELIGION Christian

CURRENCY Tala

Fa'a Samoa
The "fa'a Samoa" is the Samoan way of life and is based on the extended family, with many generations living together. Each family is headed by a *matai*, or elected chief. People live in timber-framed houses with roofs but no walls, except screens in wet weather. Clothing is simple.

Tuvalu

Tuvalu is the world's fourth smallest state. This tiny, isolated state in the center of the Pacific was a British colony until independence in 1978. The country is rapidly losing land to rising sea levels caused by global warming and is in danger of vanishing.

TUVALU FACTS

CAPITAL CITY Fongafale

AREA 10 sq miles (26 sq km)

POPULATION 10,800

MAIN LANGUAGE Tuvaluan

MAJOR RELIGION Christian

CURRENCY Australian and Tuvaluan dollar

Stamps
Copra from coconuts is Tuvalu's main export, but these tiny islands increase their revenue from their colorful postage stamps. Without foreign aid, however, they would be unable to survive.

Tonga

There are about 170 islands in Tonga, but people live on only 45 of them. The easterly islands are low and fertile, while those in the west are volcanic. The people live off the land and grow cassava, coconuts, and passion fruit for export. Tonga is the only Polynesian nation to be ruled by a king.

TONGA FACTS

CAPITAL CITY Nuku'alofa

AREA 290 sq miles (750 sq km)

POPULATION 102,200

MAIN LANGUAGE Tongan

MAJOR RELIGION Christian

CURRENCY Pa'anga

Tourism
Tropical beaches, a warm climate, and Tonga's friendly reputation attract more than 35,000 tourists every year, mostly from New Zealand and the US. Tongans are concerned that tourists may undermine the island culture. These elaborate wooden figures have been carved by Tongan people to sell to visiting tourists.

Dependencies

Although many countries in the Pacific have become independent since World War II (1939–45), many people still live under an umbrella of Australia, France, New Zealand, the UK, and the US.

Pitcairn (UK)
This tiny, remote volcanic island of 2 sq miles (5 sq km) has high cliffs and one small bay. It has only about 44 inhabitants.

French Polynesia (Fr)
This group of about 130 islands and atolls covers an area of 1,500 sq miles (4,000 sq km). Most of the people live on Tahiti.

Tokelau (NZ)
These three coral atolls cover an area of 4 sq miles (10 sq km) and have a population of 1,487. Copra and tuna fish are produced.

Niue (NZ)
With an area of 100 sq miles (259 sq km), Niue is the world's largest coral island. Most Niueans live in New Zealand.

American Samoa (US)
This tropical US territory consists of the seven small islands of eastern Samoa and has a total land area of 77 sq miles (199 sq km). The capital is Pago Pago.

Midway (US)
Midway is a US territory. About 450 people live on its two large coral islands and several smaller ones. It is used as a naval air base and wildlife refuge.

Wallis and Futuna (Fr)
Two groups of islands form Wallis and Futuna, an area of 106 sq miles (274 sq km). The 14,375 people live off the land. Fishing licenses are sold to Japan.

Cook Islands (NZ)
These 24 small islands lie 2,175 miles (3,500 km) northeast of New Zealand, with which they have close ties. The population of nearly 14,300 earns a living from clam and pearl fishing, tourism, and banking.

Nuclear testing
Since November 1952, Britain, France, and the US have used the Pacific for testing nuclear weapons. In 1995, France carried out a series of underground nuclear explosions on Mururoa Atoll in French Polynesia, causing a storm of protest among the normally peaceful people who live on these islands.

Anti-nuclear protesters

FIND OUT MORE AUSTRALASIA AND OCEANIA   CHRISTIANITY   CORAL REEFS   EMPIRES   FARMING   ISLANDS   PACIFIC OCEAN   RAIN FOREST WILDLIFE   SHIPS AND BOATS   WEAPONS

PORTS AND WATERWAYS

SHIPS NEED PLACES to load and unload their cargoes. Ports are places on rivers and coasts that provide special facilities for boats to berth and manage passengers and goods. The first ports were natural harbors – places that were sheltered from the wind with water deep enough for ships to sail right up to the shore. Today, large, modern ports can deal with many types of vessels, and have cranes and warehouses for goods and dry docks for repairing ships. Waterways are rivers and canals. They are used to ship goods inland or as a link between two seas.

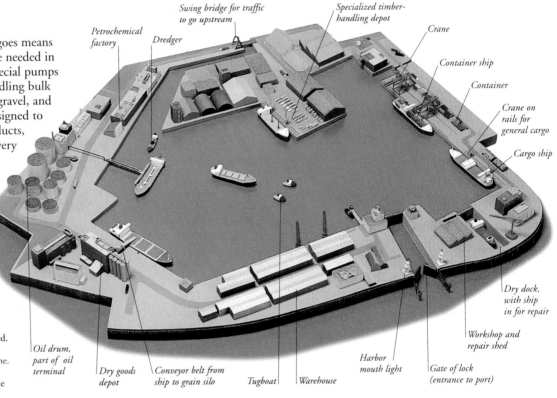

Ancient ports
Many great cities of the ancient world first prospered because they were on or near natural harbors, such as bays and river estuaries. This made them good sites for trade and settlement. Breakwaters of wood or stone were built out to sea to provide extra shelter.

Port of Roman London

Harbor facilities

The variety of modern cargoes means that all sorts of facilities are needed in a port. Some ports have special pumps and conveyor belts for handling bulk dry cargoes, such as sand, gravel, and grain. Oil terminals are designed to handle oil and related products, and are usually built near very deep water because oil tankers are huge ships. Many ports are designed to handle containers – large, standard-size boxes that can be loaded straight off ships and onto trucks or trains.

Swing bridge for traffic to go upstream — Petrochemical factory — Dredger — Specialized timber-handling depot — Crane — Container ship — Container — Crane on rails for general cargo — Cargo ship — Dry dock, with ship in for repair — Workshop and repair shed — Gate of lock (entrance to port) — Harbor mouth light — Warehouse — Tugboat — Conveyor belt from ship to grain silo — Dry goods depot — Oil drum, part of oil terminal

Docking
Every port has places where ships can berth to be loaded and unloaded. Loading platforms, called quays or wharves, are built along the shoreline. In addition there may be piers, structures built at right-angles to the shore where ships can tie up.

Canals

A canal is an artificial waterway. Most are built to transport cargo inland; others take water to dry land. Some, such as the Panama Canal linking the Atlantic and Pacific Oceans across Central America, are built to make journeys shorter.

Holiday barges travel through a lock.

Barges
Transporting cargo by canal is a cheap way of moving goods from place to place. Goods are carried by barge – a narrow, flat-bottomed boat with the capacity to carry a large cargo. Barges were orginally pulled by people or horses, but now generally have their own engines.

Powered barge

Aqueducts
Canals can cross deep valleys on aqueducts – water-carrying bridges that span the valley with tall arches of stone, brick, or metal. Not all aqueducts are navigable; some are used solely to carry water from a river to a town without an adequate water supply.

Locks
A lock allows a canal boat to travel up or down hills. It consists of a section of water with gates at either end. Water is allowed to run in or out of the gates, so that the water–level inside can be raised or lowered to the level of the next stretch of canal.

 FIND OUT MORE | DAMS | INDUSTRIAL REVOLUTION | OIL | PHOENICIANS | RIVERS | ROMAN EMPIRE | SHIPS AND BOATS | TRADE AND INDUSTRY | TRANSPORT, HISTORY OF

PORTUGAL

WITH ITS LONG Atlantic coastline, Portugal occupies the southwestern corner of the Iberian Peninsula. It is the westernmost country on the European mainland. The Azores and Madeira, two self-governing island groups in the Atlantic, are part of Portugal. The country joined the European Union in 1986. It is one of the poorest countries in western Europe, but a stable government and foreign investment are helping improve the situation.

Physical features

Northern Portugal consists of a series of ridges and wide river valleys that cross the country from east to west. The north is mountainous, and the center, south of the Tagus River, gently undulating. The south, the Algarve, is cut off by mountains.

PORTUGAL FACTS

CAPITAL CITY	Lisbon
AREA	35,670 sq miles (92,390 sq km)
POPULATION	9,884,000
MAIN LANGUAGE	Portuguese
MAJOR RELIGION	Christian
CURRENCY	Euro
LIFE EXPECTANCY	76 years
PEOPLE PER DOCTOR	323
GOVERNMENT	Multiparty democracy
ADULT LITERACY	92%

Rio Douro

The Rio Douro, which means "river of gold" in Portuguese, slices across the width of Portugal for 125 miles (200 km) from the Spanish border to Porto on the coast. The mountain terraces that flank the stony sides of the valley are ribbed with vineyards producing grapes for making port wine. Lower down the valley, *vinho verde*, a white wine, is made.

Algarve

The sandy beaches and pretty villages of the Algarve coast attract thousands of vacationers every year. Many travel there from cooler northern European countries to take advantage of the mild winters and beautiful scenery. Other popular coastal resorts are Figueira da Foz and Estoril, near Lisbon, on what is called the Portuguese Riviera.

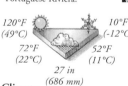

120°F (49°C)		10°F (-12°C)
72°F (22°C)		52°F (11°C)
	27 in (686 mm)	

Climate

The north of Portugal is cooler and wetter than the south, which is generally dry and sunny all year round. Temperatures tend to rise away from the coast toward the border with Spain. Like Spain, Portugal suffers from frequent periods of prolonged drought.

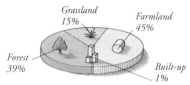

Grassland 15%
Farmland 45%
Forest 39%
Built-up 1%

Land use

Portugal has very few natural resources, and most of the land is used for rearing livestock or for growing crops such as olives, grapes, cork, or eucalyptus. Since the country does not produce its own gas, there are plans to pipe gas into northern Portugal from Algeria, via Morocco and Spain.

Lisbon

Surrounded by hills, Portugal's capital, Lisbon, lies at the mouth of the Tagus River. During the 15th century, it was a major port trading gold and spices. In 1755, a severe earthquake destroyed much of the center, which was later rebuilt on a grid system. The old town, or Baixa, in the east of the city still has many crafts workers such as silversmiths and shoemakers.

View over the rooftops of the Baixa

Map

SPAIN

Minho

A B C D E F

1

2 Viana do Castelo
Braga   Chaves   Bragança
Póvoa de Varzim
Guimarães

3 Matosinhos
Porto   Vila Real
Vila Nova de Gaia
Douro

ATLANTIC
OCEAN   Aveiro   Viseu

4

5 Figueira da Foz
Coimbra
Serra da Estrela
Covilhã

PORTUGAL

6 Castelo Branco
Caldas da Rainha
Tagus
Santarém   Portalegre
7 Barragem do Maranhão
Sintra   Rio Sorraia
Cascais
Serra d'Ossa
LISBON   SPAIN

8 Setúbal   Évora
Alcácer do Sal

9 Sines   Beja
Mira   Guadiana

10 Barragem da Bravura

Algarve
0 km   50
0 miles   50

11 Lagos   Faro   Olhão
Cabo de São Vicente

P

People

About 99 percent of the people are ethnic Portuguese. The remaining one percent are immigrants from Portugal's ex-colonies in Africa, such as Angola. In recent years, lack of opportunity has forced about three million Portuguese to find work abroad.

277 per sq mile
(107 per sq km)

66%
Urban

34%
Rural

Rural communities
About one third of all Portuguese live in rural areas, although more and more are drawn to the cities in search of work. Most Portuguese are Roman Catholics and family life is very important.

Leisure

The Portuguese love watching and playing soccer and have many clubs, such as Sporting Lisbon. They also enjoy tennis, golf, racing, and a wide range of water sports. Bullfights are a part of traditional life, as are bright, colorful fiestas with singing and dancing, usually to celebrate a local saint's day.

Golf
Many Portuguese enjoy a relaxing game of golf. The Algarve has some of Europe's finest golf courses, many of which are set against stunning backdrops of sea and sky.

Bullfighting
The center of Portuguese bullfighting is the province of Ribatejo where the bulls are bred. Fights take place from April to October, usually on Sundays. The bull is not killed in the ring, but sacrificed later.

Farming

About 10 percent of Portugal's labor force is employed in agriculture. Farms tend to be small and rely on traditional farming methods. Crops include olives and figs, wine, cork, and tomatoes. Drought often causes low yields.

Eucalyptus
Portugal and Spain are the only countries in Europe to cultivate eucalyptus, which is grown for its gum, resin, oil, and wood. Eucalyptus trees grow throughout Portugal.

Port
Portugal's most famous wine is port, a fortified drink named after the city of Porto, where much of it is shipped for export. The grapes grow in the Douro Valley.

Sheep
Much of Portugal is hilly or mountainous, providing ideal sheep grazing. Sheep, are bred for their wool, meat, and milk. Most sheep farms are small and family-run. The Portuguese also raise pigs for meat.

Cork
Portugal is the world's leading producer of cork, the thick, spongy bark of the cork oak, used for making wine stoppers and floor tiles. Every nine or ten years, the bark is stripped off, steamed, and pressed into sheets for use.

Men grading quality of cork

Wine cork

Cork floor tile

Industry

Portuguese industry suffers from a lack of natural resources and nearly all gas and oil is imported. Tourism, banking, and textiles are the major sources of income, as well as shoemaking, food, wine, cork, and sardines.

Fishing
Local fishermen mending their nets on the docks are a common sight all along Portugal's coastline. Every day, small boats set out from coastal ports in search of sardines and oysters. Portugal has become a major exporter of canned sardines and pilchards, and has several large fish-processing plants.

Oysters

Sardines

Pottery
Portuguese street markets sell local handicrafts to the thousands of tourists who flock to Portugal throughout the year. Specialties include brightly painted pottery, glassware, silver filigree, porcelain, and embroidery.

Transportation

Highways have developed on a large scale since the 1960s. A main highway links Lisbon with Porto, but there are still few roads that connect with Spain. Portugal also has a small, but efficient railroad system.

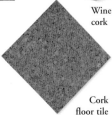

Coastal shipping
Because it's a narrow country, with a long coastline, Portugal relies on coastal shipping to carry much of its freight. However, many of the rivers leading to the interior are blocked by sandbars at their mouths.

FIND OUT MORE | ATLANTIC OCEAN | CHRISTIANITY | EMPIRES | EUROPE | EUROPE, HISTORY OF | EUROPEAN UNION | FARMING | FISHING INDUSTRY | MOTOR SPORTS | SPORTS

PORTUGAL, HISTORY OF

THROUGHOUT ITS LONG HISTORY, Portugal has always looked west to the Atlantic Ocean rather than east to Spain and the rest of continental Europe. Generations of fishermen have made their living from the sea, while explorers and traders created a vast empire during the 15th and 16th centuries. After a period of Spanish rule ending in 1640, Portugal declined, so that by the 20th century it was one of the poorest countries of Europe and slid into a military dictatorship. Today it has shed its colonial and military past and is a thriving democracy.

Roman Portugal
The Romans ruled all of Portugal by the time of Augustus (r.27 BC–AD 14). The country thrived, adopting the Roman lifestyle and Latin language.

Roman bridge at Chaves

Independent Portugal
After the Roman period, the Germanic Visigoth tribe ruled Portugal until 711, when Moors (Muslims) from North Africa conquered the country. In 1143, Alfonso, a local lord, defeated the Moors in battle. Alfonso was then crowned the first king of independent, Christian Portugal.

Lisbon cathedral, built in the reign of Alfonso I

Exploration and empire
In the 15th century the Portuguese began a period of maritime exploration. Sailors traveled south along the west coast of Africa, rounding the Cape of Good Hope in 1488. Soon their trading empire included parts of Africa, Brazil in South America, Goa in India, and Macao on the Chinese coast.

Portuguese empire

Church built by Portuguese settlers in Brazil

Henry the Navigator

Prince Henry the Navigator (1394–1460) encouraged Portuguese exploration of Africa. He set up a navigation school at Sagres and staffed it with the best astronomers and navigators. By the time of his death, Portuguese sailors had explored the entire western African coast.

Lisbon earthquake
On November 1, 1755, Lisbon was struck by a massive earthquake. Two-thirds of the city was destroyed and around 50,000 people were buried in the ruins. Sebastião de Carvalho, later to become Marquês de Pombal, chief minister of Portugal, rebuilt the city, giving it wide boulevards and elegant, classical lines.

Portuguese revolt in 1640
In 1580, Philip II of Spain claimed the vacant Portuguese throne. Portugal was weakened, and other nations seized many of her colonies. In 1640, a revolt led by John of Braganza brought Portugal independence once more.

Brazil
In 1493, Pope Alexander VI proclaimed that the world was divided between Spain and Portugal, giving Spain the west (and therefore all America). However, in 1494, the line was moved westward, giving Brazil to Portugal.

Modern Portugal
In 1910, a revolution overthrew the monarchy and made Portugal a republic. The country was neutral during the two World Wars, but became increasingly poor as it devoted its resources to its colonies in Africa. In the 1970s and 1980s, conditions improved, and in 1986 Portugal joined the European Union.

The 1974 revolution
Opposition to Portuguese rule in its African colonies led the armed forces to overthrow the dictatorship of Marcello Caetano in April 1974. There was turmoil until a failed left-wing coup allowed the socialist Màrio Soares to take control of the country. Free elections were held in 1976.

Left-wing protesters, Lisbon

Antonio Salazar
Economist Antonio Salazar (1889–1970) became finance minister in 1928. In 1932 he became prime minister, ruling as a dictator until 1968 and fighting colonial wars in Africa. In spite of his efforts to improve Portugal's economy, the country became poorer and living conditions worsened under his rule.

Dr. Antonio Salazar

Timeline
1st cent BC–5th cent AD Romans rule Iberian peninsula including Portugal.

711 North African Moors invade Portugal.

1143 Alfonso I defeats Moors.

1498 Portuguese explorer Vasco da Gama reaches the Indian coast.

1500 Portugal claims Brazil. Portuguese Empire founded.

1580–1640 Spain rules Portugal.

1755 Earthquake devastates much of Lisbon.

1822 Under Dom Pedro I, Brazil declares itself independent from Portugal.

1910 Portuguese republic established.

1932 Antonio Salazar becomes prime minister; he changes the constitution to make himself dictator.

1974 Military coup overthrows the ruling dictatorship.

1986 Portugal joins European Union.

FIND OUT MORE   AFRICA, HISTORY OF   ARMIES   EARTHQUAKES   EMPIRES   EXPLORATION   ISLAM   ROMAN EMPIRE   SOUTH AMERICA, HISTORY OF   SPAIN, HISTORY OF

POTTERY AND CERAMICS

CERAMICS ARE OBJECTS that have been shaped from clay or another mineral, then baked hard at high temperatures. This basic technique has been used for thousands of years to produce functional and often beautiful items such as pottery, tiles, and bricks. Today, ceramics are also used to produce ceramic insulators, spark-plugs for car engines, and heat resistant materials for lining the insides of furnaces. Modern scientists have devised methods of making ceramic materials as strong as steel.

Bowl from the Ukraine 3700–3000 BC

Early potters
People first made pots at least 9,000 years ago. Potters shaped clay with their hands, or built up lengths of clay in coils to make larger pots. Baked clay is such a durable material that shards of pottery are now among the most common archaeological finds.

The potter at work

Clay can be molded or pressed into shape, but perhaps the most popular way to shape pottery is on a potter's wheel. The wheel was invented in China in about 3000 BC and later, probably independently, in southern Africa. The potter uses both hands to draw clay into a perfectly round shape while the wheel spins. It takes many years to master this skill.

Prepared clay

Apron protects clothes.
Pressure of potter's hands guides the shape of the jug.
Potter keeps clay centered on the wheel.
Tool helps shape jug.
Bowl of water keeps the potter's hands wet.
Potter presses pedal to operate wheel.

Preparing the clay
The potter begins by kneading the clay to make it soft and smooth and to eliminate air bubbles that could cause the pot to crack during firing.

Shaping
The potter throws the ball of clay on to the middle of the wheel and makes the wheel spin. He pushes his fingers into the center of the clay, forming a pot with low, thick sides. Then he shapes the sides by pressing one hand on the inside and one on the outside of the pot. Once the pot is shaped, the potter trims off excess clay, removing the pot from the wheel with a knife or wire.

Types of pottery

Pottery is usually earthenware, stoneware, or porcelain, depending on the type of clay and the temperature at which it is fired. Earthenware is fired at a fairly low temperature. Stoneware is fired at higher temperatures; the heat damages the more colorful glazes, but makes the pottery strong and waterproof.

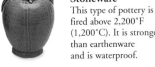

Porcelain
Porcelain is a white clay mixture used to make pottery that is valued for its strength and beauty. It is often called china because it was first made in that country. Porcelain made during the Ming dynasty (1368–1644) is regarded by collectors as artistic treasure.

Earthenware
This type of pottery fires below 2,000°F (1,100°C). When left unglazed, it is porous (not waterproof).

Stoneware
This type of pottery is fired above 2,200°F (1,200°C). It is stronger than earthenware and is waterproof.

Factories
Mass-produced mugs are made in pottery factories by pouring liquid clay (slip) into molds made from plaster of Paris. The plaster absorbs water from the slip, leaving a clay coating inside the mold. The rest of the slip is poured off. Once the molded clay is firm, the mug is taken out and the handle added. Then the pottery is fired and decorated.

Mechanized factory kiln, Holland

Qualities of ceramics

Ceramics are heat resistant and do not conduct electricity. Unlike metals, they do not rust. These qualities make them ideal for use in home and industry.

Ceramic washbasin

Bathrooms
Bathroom fixtures are often made of glazed ceramics since the glaze makes them waterproof and easy to clean.

Space shuttle
The nose of a space shuttle is covered with ceramic tiles capable of resisting the intense heat and pressure caused by reentering the Earth's atmosphere.

Space shuttle

Firing
The dried pot is baked, or fired, in a large oven called a kiln. The temperature must be controlled carefully and will depend on the type of pottery being made, but it must be at least 1,300°F (700°C).

Glazing
To decorate the fired pot and make it waterproof, it is coated with glaze, a glasslike covering. The pot is refired, melting the glaze on to it. A wide range of glaze colors are produced at different kiln temperatures.

Decorating
The methods of decorating a pot include scratching or pressing designs into it, adding underglaze colors, painting on to the unfired glaze, or applying details in liquid clay or enamel.

FIND OUT MORE   CRAFTS   GLASS   ROCKS AND MINERALS   SPACE EXPLORATION

Chinese porcelain
Fine white

Molded design shows dragons.

Dish for ritual use, Yuan dynasty, 14th century

Fish-shaped handle

Ewer, Liao dynasty, 10th or 11th century

Decorated with dragons and floral decoration

Cai Shen, god of wealth, Ming dynasty, 17th century

Copying a design from a silver bottle

Bottle, Tang dynasty, 10th or 11th century

Decoration shows cow gazing at the Moon.

Dish, Jin dynasty, 12th century

Lion handle

Ewer, Liao dynasty, 10th century

Bottle, Liao dynasty, 10th century

Dish, Northern Song dynasty, 11th century

Side view of dish (seen left), showing tapered base.

Handle

Jug, with handles to attach cover, 15th century

Water dropper, probably Liao, 10th century

Iron or copper glaze

Underglaze painted design

Vase, Yuan dynasty, 14th century

Anhua (hidden) dragon design

Bowl, Ming dynasty, 14th century

Pale brown iron glaze

Dish, Ming dynasty, 15th century

Plain copper glaze

Dish, Ming dynasty, early 15th century

Bowl, Ming dynasty, 15th century

Bowl, Ming dynasty, late 14th century

Cobalt underglaze

Dragon motif

Plate, Yuan dynasty, 14th century

Dish, Yuan dynasty, 14th century

Litchi design

Flask, Ming dynasty, early 15th century

Enamels

Trinket box, Ming dynasty, 15th century

Popular phoenix motif

Metal mount adds to value of porcelain.

Jar, Yuan dynasty, 14th century

Dish, Ming dynasty, early 15th century

Covered jar, Ming dynasty, 15th century

Bowl, Ming dynasty, 15th century

Ring handle

Altar vase with ring handles, Yuan dynasty, 14th century

P

PREHISTORIC LIFE

MORE THAN 3,800 MILLION YEARS AGO (mya) as Earth cooled, liquid water produced oceans in which small single-celled organisms evolved. Many believe that this marked the first ever signs of life. These early beginnings are called "prehistory," because they happened before recorded history. Much of our evidence of early life comes from fossils. Using this evidence, paleontologists divided Earth's prehistory into time spans called eras, and eras into periods.

In the beginning
Fossil prokaryotes (simple single cells) have been found in 3.4- to 3.3-billion-year-old rocks in Australia and South Africa. Some of these, such as the blue-green bacteria, formed strings of cells and produced layered mounds called stromatolites.

Fossilized stromatolite

P

Paleozoic era

In the early part of the Paleozoic, the Cambrian period (570 to 510 mya), life was mostly confined to the oceans. By the Carboniferous period (360 to 290 mya), there were large forests of treeferns, and club mosses such as *Lepidodendron*. By the Permian period (290 to 245 mya), much of the land was covered by desert.

Continent distribution, 570 to 245 mya

Lepidodendron, a Carboniferous club moss

Phacops rana, a shelled trilobite

Fossil of *Cephalaspis pagei,* an armored fish

First plants
Until the end of the Silurian period (439 to 408 mya), most plants lived in water. The oldest known plant, *Cooksonia,* developed a rigid stem for carrying water from roots, allowing it to thrive on land.

First shelled animals
The apparent explosion of life at the beginning of the Cambrian period may have been due to environmental changes. These changes allowed shelled skeletons to be preserved in the fossil record.

First fish
The first vertebrates were the jawless fish, which appeared about 470 million years ago. Some of these fish developed heavily armored body plates and lived in shallow marine waters, rivers, and lakes.

Invasion of the land

As plants moved onto land, invertebrate animals followed, evolving to take advantage of the higher oxygen levels and drier conditions. The first were the arthropods. Some, such as *Acantherpestes,* probably survived the same way as millipedes do today, by feeding on decomposing plants. Amphibians and reptiles followed the arthropods.

Modern millipede

Acantherpestes

Mesozoic era

During the Mesozoic era (245 to 60 mya), the supercontinent known as Pangaea moved northward and split into the major continents we know today. A major extinction at the end of the Permian period allowed reptiles to evolve on land, in the air, and in the sea. The end of the era, the Cretaceous period, saw the mass extinction of the dinosaurs.

Continent distribution, 245 to 65 mya

Reptiles
The earliest known reptile is *Westlothiana lizziae,* which dates from 330 million years ago. A reptile such as this gave rise to the giant reptiles and dinosaurs that dominated the Earth during the Mesozoic era. Some adapted entirely to life on land; they were able to stand upright and could easily move around. Some, such as the plesiosaurs, returned to the sea; others, such as pterosaurs, became capable of flight.

Early birds
Birds with feathers developed early in the evolution of dinosaurs, to which they are closely related. Early birds, such as the Jurassic bird *Archaeopteryx,* may have used their feathers for insulation or display, as well as flight.

Modern bird's feather

Fossil feather

The pterosaur *Criorhynchus,* late Cretaceous period

First flowers
Angiosperms (flowering plants) appeared in the Cretaceous period (144 to 65 mya). Before flowering plants, *Ginkgo* (maidenhair tree) was a common leafy tree. This remarkable plant still exists, and is cultivated as a decorative tree.

Hair cover kept in Megazostrodon's body heat.

First mammals
The first mammals to appear developed from the cynodonts, a group of mammal-like reptiles. Some survived the major extinction at the end of the Permian period and developed mammalian characteristics. *Megazostrodon* was one of the first mammals of the late Triassic period (245 to 208 mya).

Model of *Megazostrodon*

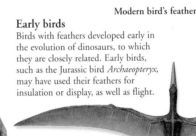

Westlothiana's body was about 1 ft (30 cm) long.

Model of *Westlothiana*

Ginkgo, tree from Jurassic period

P

Cretaceous period

During the Cretaceous period (144 to 65 mya), dinosaurs continued to be the dominant large animals on land. The continents continued to drift apart, and what is now India moved north toward Asia. It is thought that the Cretaceous period probably ended with quite an impact.

Skeleton of the dinosaur *Dromaeosaurus*, c.85 to 70 mya

Tail held rigid by bony rods.

Death of dinosaurs
Dinosaurs became extinct at the end of the Cretaceous period. A popular theory to explain this mass extinction is that an asteroid or a comet hit the Earth about 65 million years ago, throwing large amounts of dust into the atmosphere. This dust is thought to have blocked the sunlight for many months or more, killing off a variety of animals and plants.

Hooked claw to catch prey

Ice ages

Alternating periods of cold and warmth characterize the last 2 billion years of Earth's climate. During cold periods, much of Earth's water was locked up in ice sheets. Animals, such as the mammoth, adapted by growing thick woolly coats. Today, Earth is in a warm, interglacial period.

Thick woolly coat

Hair-covered trunk to keep warm.

Model of *Mammuthus primigenius*, c.1.64 mya

Cenozoic era

During the Cenozoic era (65 mya to present), mammals gradually took over from the dinosaurs. Some reptiles, such as turtles, snakes, crocodiles, and lizards, survived the extinction and still exist today. Birds also survived to become more diverse than either mammals or reptiles today. India eventually collided with Asia, forming the Himalayan mountain range.

Continent distribution, c.65 mya

Wide cheek bone

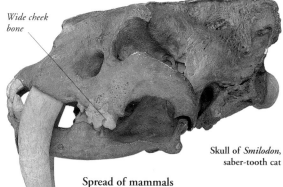

Skull of *Smilodon*, saber-tooth cat

Spread of mammals
Mammals spread quickly across all continents, adapting to most climates because they could maintain a constant body temperature and eat and survive on a variety of both plant material and meat. Marsupials developed first, but placental mammals gradually became dominant.

Canine teeth used to tear animal flesh.

Flying mammals
As birds gradually evolved to take the place of pterosaurs, mammals, such as the bat *Palaeochiropteryx*, also developed flight. This bat was only 3 inches (7cm) long and one specimen that was found had remains of moths in its stomach. Bats are mainly nocturnal, using reflected sound to detect their prey.

Palaeochiropteryx, fossil bat

Extinction

Animals and plants evolving and becoming extinct is a pattern of life on Earth. Mass extinction occurs when many organisms become extinct at the same time. Several such events have occurred throughout Earth's prehistory their cause is not always known.

Dodo
The dodo from Mauritius died out in the late 1700s because of humans. Today, many other plants and animals, such as the African black rhinoceros and the South China tiger, are on the brink of extinction.

Reconstruction of a dodo

First humans
Our first ancestors may have been *Australopithecus afarensis*, a human-like creature that appeared in Africa about 4 million years ago. The earliest true human, *Homo habilis*, probably made and used tools more than 2.5 million years ago. *Homo sapiens* (modern humans) appeared about 100,000 years ago.

Cranium of *Homo habilis*, found in Africa

Timeline

3,800 mya Single-celled photosynthesizing organisms evolve.

550 mya Emergence of hard shells.

c.500 mya Primitive jawless fish appear.

Model of *Ichthyostega*

c.440 mya Plants and animals invade land.

360 mya First tetrapods, such as the amphibian *Ichthyostega*, appear.

c.395 mya Arthropods feed on decomposing plants and other arthropods.

Fossil of Jurassic dragonfly

c.210 mya Dinosaurs start to evolve.

65 mya Mammals take over after demise of dinosaurs.

100,000 years ago *Homo sapiens* appears.

 FIND OUT MORE   COAL   DINOSAURS   EARTH   EVOLUTION   FOSSILS   GEOLOGY   HUMAN EVOLUTION   MAMMALS   PREHISTORIC PEOPLE   STONE AGE

PREHISTORIC PEOPLE

OUR EARLIEST ANCESTORS, the hominids, lived in Africa. As they evolved into an upright posture and learned to make tools, around 100,000 years ago, they became known as "modern people," or *Homo sapiens sapiens*. These people are sometimes called prehistoric, because they lived long before recorded history. From fossil evidence, we know they found food by gathering and hunting, made simple clothes, and built shelters out of local materials. People lived like this for many thousands of years. Around 9000 BC, for the first time, people in western Asia started to produce their food by farming.

Religion

The existence of ceremonial sites, such as stone circles and prepared grounds, show that our earliest ancestors had religious rituals and believed in an afterlife.

Simple marble figurine, c.25,000 to 15,000 BC

Cult figures
Archaeologists have found many figurines in modern-day Greece and the Cycladic Islands. They are thought to represent the gods and goddesses of the prehistoric people who lived there.

Burial of the dead
Prehistoric people were often buried in a fetal, curled up, position. They were usually surrounded by their personal effects for use in the afterlife (grave goods).

Stonehenge
Stonehenge, a stone circle in southern England, was probably built for religious purposes at least 4,000 years ago. On the summer solstice, the sun rises directly over Stonehenge's Heel Stone.

Carnac
Carnac, in France, has the world's largest stone alignment. It contains about 1,100 stones in 11 rows, and stands from east to west. Its creators followed a religion based on the sun.

Food supply

If early people could not find food in one area, they migrated to another. They often followed the seasons, traveling to warmer areas in the winter months. In most societies the women gathered plant material – leaves, fruits, and roots – while the men hunted for meat and fish with weapons such as bows and arrows, clubs, and spears.

Arrowheads of bone were stuck to shafts with glue made from birch resin.

Hunting
Meat was an important food source when green vegetables were scarce. Hunting required co-operation – several men hunted together to track and bring down large animals, such as deer or mammoth.

The flight was made of feathers and helped arrows fly distances.

Fishing
People who lived near the sea, a lake, or a river got most of their nutrition from fish, which they caught using small, simple hooks.

As this stone relief shows, people hunted larger fish with bone or antler harpoons.

Gathering
Early people built up their knowledge about which plants were good to eat and which were poisonous. They ate mainly raw leaves, berries, and roots.

A digger was used to dig up roots and grubs.

Quartz pebble acts as a weight.

Wedge

Food through the seasons

In spring, green vegetables, such as dandelion leaves, were plentiful.

In summer, grapes and other fruits added variety and nutrients to the diet.

In winter, hunters brought home meat to cook and eat with nuts and roots.

In the fall, nuts and berries were gathered and stored for the winter.

Clothes

During the last Ice Age, about 18,000 years ago, people learned to skin animals and wear the pelts to keep warm.

Animal skin clothes

Raw wool

Spindle

Prehistoric people spun wool taken directly from the backs of sheep.

Shelters

Caves made good homes – our early human ancestors were living in caves in Israel at least 100,000 years ago. If there was no natural shelter, prehistoric people made homes from nearby materials, such as wood, stone, or sod.

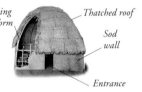

Sleeping platform

Thatched roof

Sod wall

Entrance

Cave shelters
Some caves, such as Silozwane Cave, Zimbabwe, were occupied permanently. Other caves were used as temporary shelters for hunters, or as bases for fishing expeditions.

Temporary shelters
About 18,000 to 12,000 years ago in Central Europe, people built shelters from mammoth bones and skins. A fire kept in a clay and stone hearth heated the shelter.

Permanent shelters
Some early people of North America lived in well-built, permanent houses. They erected a frame made of poles, built a low sod wall, then covered each house with a tall, thatched roof.

Timeline

35 million years ago First true humans, *Homo sapiens*, evolve from primate ancestors in Africa.

2–2.5 million years ago Hominids emerge in Africa.

100,000 BC Modern humans, *Homo sapiens sapiens*, evolve.

50,000 BC First humans arrive in Australia and America.

11,000 BC Humans domesticate animals in western Asia.

10,500 BC Pottery is produced in Japan.

9000 BC Wheat and barley are cultivated in Asia.

6500 BC The first towns develop in western Asia.

FIND OUT MORE   BRONZE AGE   FOSSILS   HUMAN EVOLUTION   STONE AGE

PRESSURE

A STILETTO HEEL can make dents in a hardwood floor, while a hiking boot worn by the same person may not make a mark. This is because the stiletto heel exerts more pressure than the heavy boot. Pressure is a measure of how concentrated a force is. The stiletto heel concentrates the force of the person's weight onto a smaller area than the boot. Fluids – liquids and gases – can also exert pressure.

Blowing over the paper reduces the air pressure above it.

Higher pressure below the sheet pushes paper up.

Moving fluids

Hold a sheet of paper by the edge and it hangs down limply. Blow over the top of the paper and it rises up. The pressure of a fluid is lower when the fluid is moving than when it is still, so the moving air above the paper has a lower pressure than the static air below it. This difference in pressure lifts the paper.

Upthrust

A liquid exerts pressure on any object immersed in it. If you push a table tennis ball underwater, you will feel the water pushing back. This pushing is an upward force called upthrust, and it is caused by the pressure of the water on the ball. The upthrust is equal to the weight of the water pushed aside or displaced as the object is immersed.

Floating and sinking

If the upthrust on an immersed object is equal to the object's weight, then the object floats. In the experiment below, four balls of different weights are placed in a tank of water. Three of the balls sink until they displace enough water to produce an upthrust equal to their weight. The weight of the golf ball is greater than the upthrust from the water, so it sinks to the bottom of the tank.

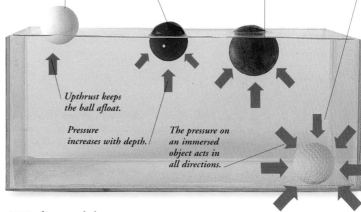

The light plastic table tennis ball floats on water's surface.

The rubber squash ball is heavier than the table tennis ball and floats lower in the water.

Heavier still, the hardwood ball sinks until it is nearly underwater.

The golf ball weighs the most and sinks to the bottom.

Upthrust keeps the ball afloat.

Pressure increases with depth.

The pressure on an immersed object acts in all directions.

Blaise Pascal

In 1646, the French physicist and mathematician Blaise Pascal (1623–62) showed that air pressure decreases with altitude by taking a barometer to the top of a mountain. Pascal was also the first to realize that the pressure exerted by a liquid acts in all directions.

Pressure machines

Fluids in confined spaces exert pressure that can be used to power machinery and tools. Hydraulic machines are powered by high-pressure liquids; pneumatic machines rely on pressurized gases.

Hydraulic brakes

Applying the brake lever of this bicycle squeezes fluid inside the brake cable. The fluid transmits the pressure to the brake pads, which grip the wheel and slow it down.

Pneumatic drill

High-pressure air is pumped into a cylinder inside this drill, where it pushes a piston up and down with great force. The piston hammers the drill into the surface of the hard rock.

High and low pressure

In some situations, solids, liquids, and gases exert a higher or lower pressure than normal. People have found many ways of using such pressure variations to their advantage, but our bodies can withstand only a limited range of pressures. The extreme pressure of the deep ocean can kill a person, while low air pressure at high altitudes makes breathing difficult.

Space suit

In space there is no air. The lack of air pressure would cause human lungs to collapse, so astronauts who leave their spacecraft wear pressurized suits to protect them. They breathe a supply of oxygen at normal earth air pressure.

Safety line connected to spacecraft

Suit's airtight seam can withstand vacuum.

Submersible

At the bottom of the world's seas and oceans, the weight of the water above creates tremendous pressure. Deep-sea explorers travel to the seabed in small vessels called submersibles that are strong enough to withstand such intense pressure.

Power cable

Observation window   *Thruster*

Melted ice lubricates blade and reduces friction.

Ice skate

An ice skate's narrow blade concentrates a person's weight onto a small area. The high pressure under the blade melts the ice, reducing friction so that the skater glides over the ice.

Snowshoe

Snowshoes have long, broad bases that spread a person's weight over a wide area. The shoes reduce the pressure exerted by the feet, so the wearer can walk on soft snow without sinking.

Pressure cooker

A liquid's boiling point can be raised or lowered by increasing or decreasing the pressure acting upon it. Inside a pressure cooker, high pressure raises water's boiling point from 212°F (100°C) to 248°F (120°C). At this temperature, water cooks food more quickly.

High altitude

Lowering the pressure acting on a liquid reduces its boiling point. At high altitudes, it is difficult to make hot drinks or cook with boiling water. The air pressure is much lower, and reduces the boiling point of water to as low as 140°F (60°C).

P

PRINTING

 BEFORE THE 15TH CENTURY, books were copied and illustrated by hand. The development, in the 1450s, of a printing press capable of using movable type caused an information revolution. Large numbers of books and leaflets could now be copied quickly and cheaply, and this led to the rapid spread of learning. Today we are surrounded by printed material, from magazines, flyers, and posters produced by the thousand, to the smaller number of prints made by artists.

Color separations

When a book is printed in color, the paper is inked four times, in black, cyan, magenta, and yellow, to create a complete color image. Each ink is laid on the paper from a printing surface, or plate, made from separate films called color separations. To make the separations, a device called a scanner, linked to a computer, analyses the original color image to produce files in the four separate printing colors.

Color film
The computer files are converted into four colored images on clear film. The film is then used to make printing plates.

Black   Cyan   Magenta   Yellow

The printing process

Printing plates are made by shining light through the color separations, recording their details on to a light-sensitive coating on the plate. Each plate is chemically treated to bring out the print images, then fitted on to a cylinder in the printing press. The inked image on the plate is transferred (offset) on to another cylinder (the blanket cylinder), and from there on to paper.

The printing press
There are many types of printing presses. This modern press uses the offset lithography process, which works because grease attracts ink, while water repels it. The printing image on the plate is greasy, so ink is attracted to it. The non-printing parts are wet, so they do not get inked.

Printing press

Ink rollers keep the plates wet with fresh ink.

Impression cylinder presses paper on to blanket cylinder to transfer the image.

Dampening rollers wet non-image areas of the plate, preventing them from holding ink.

Plate cylinder

Blanket cylinder transfers image to paper.

Four color posters emerge at the end.

Colored inks are added one after another to build up the four color poster.

Johannes Gutenburg

In the mid-1400s, Gutenberg (c.1398–1468), a German goldsmith, devised a system of producing metal type in the form of individual letters. These letters could be arranged to form pages of text and then be printed in a press. After printing, the type could be reused to print another page. Soon presses were set up all over Europe with reusable metal type.

Typography

The design and use of letters printed on a page is called typography. Thousands of type styles, or typefaces, have been designed, from simple types for text to more elaborate ones for newspaper headlines or adverts.

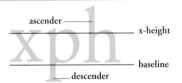

ascender — x-height — baseline — descender

ABCDEFGHIJKLMNO
PQRSTUVWXYZ Times

ABCDEFGHIJKLMNO
PQRSTUVWXYZ Helvetica

roman
italic
bold

Typefaces
Typefaces may be roman, italic, or bold. The last two styles are used for emphasis.

ipsum dolor
consectetuer
adipiscing
ipsum dolor
consectetuer
adipiscing
ipsum dolor

ipsum dolor
consectetuer
adipiscing
ipsum dolor
consectetuer

The space between lines of type is called leading.

9pt type on 9pt leading   **9pt type on 14pt leading**

serif

Serif typeface
The main strokes in some typefaces end in small lines (serifs).

Sans serif typeface
Faces without lines are called "sans (without) serif."

Printing methods

The four printing methods are screen printing, relief printing, the intaglio process, and lithography. These may be used by a commercial printing press to make thousands of copies, or on a smaller scale by an artist to make a very few copies of an original image.

Monoprint
This simple printing method produces just one print. Paper is placed on an inked plate. A design is drawn or scraped onto the paper, then lifted off. The print on the paper is a mirror image of the original design.

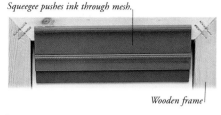
Squeegee pushes ink through mesh.
Wooden frame

Screen printing

In this type of printing, a stencil is attached to a mesh screen. The screen is then laid on the surface to be printed and ink is pushed through the mesh, leaving an image. Screen printing is widely used in business for printing posters and packaging. Prints can be made on many different surfaces, including paper, wood, metal, and fabrics.

Patrick Hughes, **Sea Change**

Fine art screen printing
The fresh, direct quality of the prints make screen printing a popular method with artists. The vividly colored screen print portraits of Marilyn Monroe, by the American artist Andy Warhol, are a well-known example.

Relief printing

With this method, the non-printing areas of a plate are cut away, leaving a raised design, ready to be inked and printed. Letterpress printing, once used to print newspapers, is a type of relief printing.

Wood engraving
Until the 20th century, a popular method of printing illustrations for books was to engrave the design into a block of wood.

End grain woodblock

Inked-up block, engraved design

Wood engraving print

Textiles
When fabric printing began in the 18th century, patterns were printed by hand with wood blocks. For mass-produced printed textiles, a process involving engraved copper rollers was developed in the late 18th century and is still used today. Screen printing is widely used for smaller quantities of textiles.

Printing block

Print

Handprinted textile

Printed image **Etching press** *Rollers force paper and plate together.*

Handle to operate rollers

Inked-up copper plate

Intaglio process

In this process, a reversed design is engraved or etched into a metal plate. The plate is inked and wiped, so that only the grooves are filled with ink. Damp paper is laid on the plate, and both are passed through the rollers of an etching press. The paper is forced into the grooves to take up the ink, printing the design the right way around.

The intaglio process reproduces fine lines and details accurately.

Jock McFadyen, **Annie with a Sun Hat**

Lithography

This printing process works because oil and water do not mix. The printing image on the plate is not raised or engraved, but retains ink because it is greasy. The ink is washed off the non-greasy, non-printing wet areas. When the plate is inked and put into a press, the design prints on to a sheet of paper. Limestone is the traditional material for lithography plates but today metal is often used.

Image drawn on stone   *Mandy Bonnell,* **Crown Gateway 2**

Timeline

868 In China, wood-blocks are used to produce books such as the *Diamond Sutra*, a Buddhist prayer text.

Early composing stick

c.1455 In Germany, Johannes Gutenberg prints about 160 copies of a Latin Bible, the first book printed using movable metal type, oil-based ink, and a wooden hand press.

1796 German printer Alois Senefelder invents the process called lithography.

1800 Charles, 3rd Earl Stanhope, British scientist and politician, develops the all-metal printing press.

1880s The linotype and monotype typesetting systems are introduced and streamline the typesetting process.

1890s Halftone printing is used to print posters and images in color.

1904 US printer Ira W. Rubel develops the offset lithography process, a method which was first patented in England in 1853. The image from a lithographic plate is transferred to a long-lasting rubber cylinder before printing on paper or other materials. This quick, economical method becomes the most popular printing process.

Color bar

1980s Computers are widely used in printing in a range of applications, such as importing text, altering images, and arranging the position of text and images on a page.

Disk

FIND OUT MORE — ART, HISTORY OF   BOOKS   CHINA, HISTORY OF   COLOR   COMPUTERS   NEWSPAPERS AND MAGAZINES

PYRAMIDS

BUILT AS TOMBS for the pharaohs of ancient Egypt, the true pyramid was square at the base and rose steeply to a point, or apex. The triangular outline was significant to the Egyptians – it represented the mound upon which the sun god stood when he created the other gods. Thousands of years later, Central American peoples, such as the Maya, Toltec, and Olmec also built pyramidlike structures. These were made of stone blocks, and featured straight, steep staircases. They were often topped with a temple.

Egyptian pyramids

The Egyptians built their pyramids out of local limestone. The royal burial chamber had granite doors. Passages connected the burial chamber with the outside, and there were often false passages as well, which helped guard against robbers.

Saqqara
The Step Pyramid of the pharaoh Zoser was built c.2950 BC, and is the oldest known pyramid. It takes its name from the series of six steps rising from the base.

Meidum
This 305-ft (95-m) high structure started as a step pyramid, and was later encased in stone to create a true pyramid. It was built under Snefru (c.2920 BC).

Dashur
This pyramid, also built for Snefru, looks "bent" because it started off steep, and then had to be leveled off by builders as cracks began to appear.

Giza
The Great Pyramid is 450 ft (146 m) high, and each side is 756 ft (230 m) at the base – the largest of all the Egyptian pyramids. It dates from c.2567 BC.

Roman pyramid
This striking, steep-sided pyramid is the tomb of Caius Cestius, a wealthy Roman magistrate who died in 12 BC. It took 330 days to build, and is faced in white marble. It was the only European pyramid for centuries.

Inside the Great Pyramid

Made of 2.3 million limestone blocks and taking 20 years to build, Giza's Great Pyramid was the oldest of the Seven Wonders of the Ancient World. The uppermost burial chamber contained Khufu's coffin, but the other chambers may be false. Pyramids like this were usually in a large complex.

Pharaoh's chamber
Abandoned chamber
Grand gallery
Desert bedrock
Entrance
Limestone casing
Small pyramids for Khufu's three chief wives
Mortuary temple
Funerary boat buried in pit

Imhotep

The first known architect, Imhotep, designed the Step Pyramid at Saqqara. He trained as a scribe and became an adviser at the court of Zoser. He was also famous as a healer. His creative talents so impressed the Egyptians that, after his death, they turned him into a god. He was known as the son of Ptah, the Egyptian creator-god.

How an Egyptian pyramid was built

Pyramids were built using massive blocks of limestone – most of the blocks in the Great Pyramid weigh 2.75 tons or more. The Egyptians probably used some form of ramp to raise these blocks into position.

Laborers pull up stone using a simple winch.

Worker uses a sled to drag stone up a ramp.

Transporting the stone
The simplest way to transport the stone was by boat, along the Nile River. Limestone came from nearby quarries, but granite for chamber roofs, doorways, and other features came from Aswan.

On site
Workers dragged blocks on wooden sleds up ramps that were probably made of soil and rubble, topped by wooden boards. Teams of workers could also haul stones up using a simple winch device, consisting of a rope running over a wooden framework.

Central American pyramids

Pyramid-building in Central America reached its height between 300 and 1542. The Maya people favored step pyramids with staircases. They built temples at the top, which sometimes contained tombs.

Temple of the Inscriptions
This temple at Palenque contains writings that compare the Maya Lord Pacal, who was buried here in 683, with the gods.

El Castillo
The Maya built this pyramid at Chichen Itza around a Toltec temple. Its four staircases have 365 steps – to match the number of days in the year.

 FIND OUT MORE | BUILDING AND CONSTRUCTION | EGYPT, ANCIENT | GODS AND GODDESSES | MAYA | MESOAMERICANS | SEVEN WONDERS OF THE ANCIENT WORLD

R

RABBITS AND HARES

RABBITS AND HARES are found almost all over the world. They are not native to Australia and New Zealand, however, the European rabbit was introduced there. The 40 or so species of rabbits and hares belong to the order of animals called Lagomorpha, which also includes 14 species of pika. These ground-dwelling mammals are herbivores – their diet includes grasses, flowers, roots, and the bark of young trees. The European rabbit lives in large groups, but hares and cottontails are mostly solitary animals, usually seen together only in the breeding season.

Prominent bulging eyes give all-round vision.

Rabbits and hares have large ears that help give them an acute sense of hearing.

Strong hind legs are kicked out if the rabbit is attacked.

Mountain hare

Rabbits have a good sense of smell.

European rabbit

Hares
Unlike rabbits, hares do not dig burrows, but live in hollows in long grass called forms. They can run at 45 mph (70 kmh) and will zigzag and leap to escape from a predator. Young hares, called leverets, are able to run within minutes of being born.

Rabbits
Generally, rabbits are smaller than hares, with smaller ears and shorter hind legs. To warn of danger, they thump the ground with a hind leg, then rely on speed to escape. Rabbits produce a large number of young that are helpless at birth.

Rabbit warrens

European rabbits live in large colonies. Each colony inhabits a system of underground burrows called a warren. There is a strict social hierarchy, with the dominant rabbits occupying the best parts of the warren.

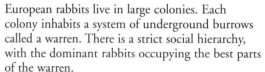

Rabbit's skull

Four incisor teeth

Teeth
All lagomorphs have large incisor teeth that grow continuously. They use these to cut their food, and they can graze very close to the ground. They use their cheek teeth to grind food.

Cottontails
Rabbits are sometimes called cottontails because of the white fur under their tail. This shows clearly when they run, signaling danger to others.

Desert cottontail

The short tail is called a scut.

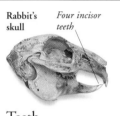

A rabbit can relax if another is watching for possible danger.

Main entrance leads to tunnels only 6 in (15 cm) wide.

Rabbits stand on their hind legs to get a better view of their territory.

Members of the colony graze close to their warren.

A female builds a nest in a side chamber.

A nest is made of grass and fur.

Most tunnels are wide enough for only one rabbit, but passing places are built in some tunnels.

Boxing hares

In the breeding season, hares may be seen "boxing" each other. Male hares, or bucks, gather in the vicinity of a female, or doe, and fights may occur. Females "box" males whose advances are unwelcome. Long chases also occur at this time.

Rivals use their front paws in a fight.

Hares stand on their hind legs to box.

Large ears also aid hearing.

Jackrabbits
Blue-tailed and antelope jackrabbits live in the warmer climates in North America. They have enormous ears that help them to keep cool. Close to the surface of the skin of the ears, front and back, is a network of tiny blood vessels. As blood flows through these vessels it loses heat to the air moving past the ears. The cooled blood then flows back into the body.

Arctic hare
In winter, hares that live in the Arctic and tundra regions grow a white coat instead of their summer brown coat. This fur is thick and keeps them warm and also camouflages them on the snow-covered ground. Hares that live on high mountain slopes also grow a white coat in winter for the same reasons. These hardy hares are active all through the year.

Pikas
Unlike rabbits and hares, pikas have short rounded ears, a rounded body, and no tail. Most live in the mountainous areas of the Pacific Northwest, and central and northeast Asia, where they burrow under rocks. In summer, many pikas store grasses and seeds in a pile to provide them with food for winter.

EUROPEAN RABBIT

SCIENTIFIC NAME	*Oryctolagus cuniculus*
ORDER	Lagomorpha
FAMILY	Leporidae
DISTRIBUTION	Spain, northwest Africa; introduced elsewhere including Europe and Australia
HABITAT	Grassland, pastures, sand dunes, woodland edges
DIET	Grass, leaves, bark
SIZE	Length: 14–18 in (35–45 cm)
LIFESPAN	3–6 years

FIND OUT MORE

ANIMAL BEHAVIOR • CAMOUFLAGE AND COLOR • NESTS AND BURROWS • POLAR WILDLIFE • RATS AND OTHER RODENTS

RADAR AND SONAR

THE HUGE ROTATING DISHES that you can see at any airport are radar antennas. They can detect aircraft hundreds of miles away, even at night and in the worst weather conditions. The word radar stands for RAdio Detection And Ranging. Radar is a type of echolocation, a way of finding the position of an object by bouncing a signal off it and then listening for the echo. Sonar is another form of echolocation used by ships and boats to locate underwater objects. The word sonar stands for SOund Navigation And Ranging.

How radar works

A radar dish, or antenna, sends out pulses of radio waves or microwaves. These waves bounce off any object in their path, and return to the dish, which detects them. The time it takes for the reflected waves to return to the dish enables a computer to calculate how far away the object is.

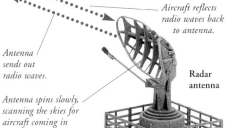

Approaching aircraft

Aircraft reflects radio waves back to antenna.

Antenna sends out radio waves.

Antenna spins slowly, scanning the skies for aircraft coming in different directions.

Radar antenna

Uses of radar

Radar is a useful detection-aid that helps aircraft and ships navigate safely, and police spot motorists driving too fast. Military forces use radar to aim missiles and locate enemy forces, weather forecasters use it to track rainfall, and astronomers use radar to map the surfaces of distant planets.

Air traffic control
In the busy skies above major airports, air traffic controllers use radar monitors to guide aircraft to a safe takeoff or landing.

Navigation at sea
Ships use radar to find their way at sea, especially at night or in fog, when rocks, land, and other vessels may be hidden from view.

Speed trap
Police officers can measure the speed of cars with a handheld radar scanner that fires pulses of microwaves at approaching vehicles.

Robert Watson-Watt

Although research into radar was undertaken in many countries, it was the Scottish physicist Robert Watson-Watt (1892–1973) who developed the first practical radar system in the mid-1930s. In World War II (1939–45), this system was used to give early warning of bombing raids by aircraft.

How sonar works

Echoes bounce back from shoal of fish.

Sound waves transmitted by ship

Echoes from wreck

Beneath a ship's hull, a device called a transponder sends out pulses of high-frequency sound and records the echoes of the pulses as they bounce off the seabed or submerged objects. The time it takes for the echoes to return to the transponder indicates the object's depth and distance from the ship.

Sonar monitor showing ocean floor

Sonar monitor
The transponder detects the echoes returning to the ship and displays them as "blips" or shapes on a monitor screen. By looking at the monitor, the sonar operator can tell how deep the water is and identify underwater objects, such as shoals of fish, submarines, and even shipwrecks.

Echolocation

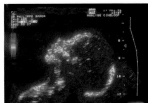

Dolphin

Some animals use echolocation to help them find food or to build up a picture of their surroundings. Dolphins, for example, send out high-pitched squeaks that bounce off anything in their path and return as echoes. The dolphin's brain then analyzes the echoes to form an image.

Ultrasound scan of a baby in its mother's womb

Ultrasound scan
Sound with a pitch above the range of human hearing is called ultrasound. Hospitals examine unborn babies with an ultrasound scanner that sends ultrasonic waves into the mother's womb and then displays the returning echoes as a picture on a screen.

Timeline

1915 Following *Titanic* tragedy, French physicist Paul Langevin pioneers echolocation to detect submarines and icebergs.

1920s British Navy develops early sonar: the Asdic system.

1922 Italian Guglielmo Marconi suggests idea of radar.

1936 Ships begin to use radar for navigation.

1939–45 Radar used to detect enemy aircraft during World War II.

World War II mobile radar

1958 First ultrasound scans of unborn babies.

1970s and 1980s Radar maps surfaces of Venus and Mars.

2000 Sonar readings of Arctic ice thickness give key evidence about global warming.

FIND OUT MORE   AIRPORTS   BATS   MAPS AND MAPPING   NAVIGATION   PLANETS   POLICE   SOUND   WEATHER FORECASTING   WHALES AND DOLPHINS

RADIO

WHENEVER YOU TUNE IN to your radio, you are listening to sounds produced from invisible waves, traveling through space at the speed of light. At any one time, thousands of radio signals are moving through the atmosphere, and from these your radio's receiver picks out the station you want. Before the 1890s, when radio waves were first used to send messages, information took weeks to travel around the world. Now it travels the same distance in a fraction of a second. This ability to transmit and receive information instantly has transformed the world.

1930s' radio set

Early radio
Early radio sets were inconvenient to use. Large, fragile glass tubes amplified the sound: these had to heat up and did not last long. The choice of programs was limited too. Nonetheless, radio provided people in the early 20th century with the first home news and entertainment systems. Listening to the radio became the focus of a family's evening.

How radio works

Radios work by turning sound into electrical signals. The signals are then turned into radio waves that travel through the atmosphere. This is done by a transmitter, using a device called a modulator. The modulator varies a steady radio signal according to the sound content of the broadcast. A radio receiver performs these operations in reverse, changing the signals back into sound.

Uses of radio

Handset

Radio is mainly used to bring information and entertainment into homes. Radio waves carry many different kinds of information, including television pictures and sound, and the signals sent by mobile telephones. Car radio receivers and transmitters allow the emergency services to communicate while on the move. Even smaller radio sets, known as walkie-talkies, are used by contractors on large building sites.

Radio in wartime
Soldiers use portable radios to stay in touch. They radio details of their own and enemy positions back to base, saving time on the battlefield. Radios can save lives in wartime, because details of injuries can be sent quickly, giving medical staff and ambulance crews exact information about the location of the injured.

Handheld radio set, US military, 1990s

Studios
The microphone in a radio studio turns the sound of a presenter's voice into sound signals. Other equipment turns the music on CDs and tapes into sound signals. All the signals are mixed together by an engineer at a mixing desk in an adjoining control room; then the sound signals are sent to a transmitter.

Presenter in radio studio

Transmitters
Radio stations broadcast radio waves from a transmitter. This produces a high-frequency signal that varies according to the content of the sound fed into it from the studio. This varying signal is sent to the transmitter's antenna, which sends the signal into the atmosphere as radio waves.

Radio transmitter

Inside a portable radio receiver

Plastic case

Radio receiver
A radio receiver has its own antenna to pick up radio waves from the transmitter. It contains a tuner that selects the station and a circuit that turns the radio waves into electrical signals. These signals are then amplified (made louder) and fed into a loudspeaker that produces the sounds that you hear.

Tuning control used to select station

Amplifier produces stronger current to send to loudspeaker.

Loudspeaker turns electrical current into vibrations in the air, to produce audible sound.

Printed circuit board

Volume control (variable resistor) adjusts sound level.

Antenna picks up radio waves from transmitter.

Frequencies
Radio waves are waves of electromagnetic energy of different lengths and speeds. Radio stations broadcast their programs on a particular wavelength, or frequency.

Guglielmo Marconi

Italian engineer Guglielmo Marconi (1874–1937) was the first person to patent a method of sending signals by radio, in 1896. Marconi began experimenting with radio waves in his parent's attic while he was a teenager in Italy. By 1901, he sent the first radio signal across the Atlantic Ocean, using Morse code.

Timeline

1888 The German physicist Heinrich Hertz (1857–1894) demonstrates radio waves for the first time.

1896 Marconi patents the first practical wireless telegraphy system.

1901 Marconi sends first transatlantic radio signal.

1906 US: world's first public radio broadcast made.

1954 Transistor radio develops, replacing tubes; radio receivers become much smaller.

1960 The first stereophonic (stereo) broadcasts are made.

1995 Clockwork radio broadcasts to places without electricity and batteries.

late-1990s Digital and Internet radio introduced.

Radio runs on self-generated power.

Clockwork radio

FIND OUT MORE   ELECTROMAGNETISM   ELECTRONICS   SOUND   SOUND RECORDING   TELEVISION

RADIOACTIVITY

ATOMS MAY BE TINY, but they can also be deadly! Some atoms, called radioisotopes, have unstable nuclei that are liable to decay, or break up. If they do, they give out high-energy rays in a process known as radioactivity. Large doses of these rays can kill living cells, but radioactivity can also be used in many positive ways.

Types of radiation

The rays emitted by decaying nuclei are called radiation. There are three types of radiation – alpha, beta, and gamma rays. Gamma rays may accompany the emission of alpha or beta rays, and are sometimes given out on their own. Each type of radiation can penetrate different thicknesses of different materials, although all three types can be dangerous if absorbed by living tissue.

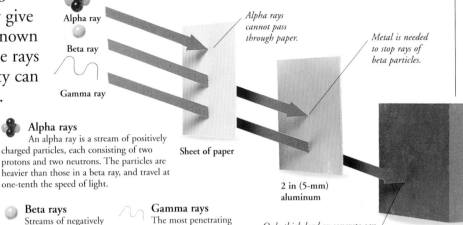

Alpha ray

Beta ray

Gamma ray

Alpha rays cannot pass through paper.

Metal is needed to stop rays of beta particles.

Sheet of paper

2 in (5-mm) aluminum

Only thick lead or concrete can stop the powerful gamma rays.

Thick lead

Radioactive glow
Radioactive objects – such as the fuel rods of a nuclear reactor – are often stored underwater because water absorbs radiation. As the radioactive particles travel through the water, they cause it to glow with blue light.

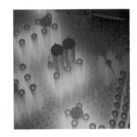

Alpha rays
An alpha ray is a stream of positively charged particles, each consisting of two protons and two neutrons. The particles are heavier than those in a beta ray, and travel at one-tenth the speed of light.

Beta rays
Streams of negatively charged electrons emitted by a nucleus are called beta rays. These particles have hardly any mass and travel at half the speed of light.

Gamma rays
The most penetrating type of radiation is gamma rays – waves of electromagnetic radiation that travel at the speed of light. They have no mass.

Antoine Becquerel

The French physicist Antoine Becquerel (1852–1908) discovered radioactivity in 1896. While investigating X rays, he found that uranium salts fogged a photographic plate wrapped in dark paper. He realized that rays emitted by the uranium had penetrated the paper.

Half-life
The time taken for half of the nuclei in a radioisotope to decay is called its half-life. If you make a pile of coffee beans and remove half the beans every 10 minutes, you will get some idea of how half-life works: over successive half-life periods, the radioactivity falls first to a half, then to a quarter, and so on. Each radioisotope has a different half-life. Uranium-238, for example, has a half-life of 4.5 billion years, but radon-221's is just 30 seconds.

Coffee beans

After 10 minutes

Pile is now half the size of the original.

After 20 minutes

A quarter of the beans are left.

Geiger-Müller counter

Radiation can be detected with a Geiger-Müller counter, which consists of a tube filled with low-pressure gas connected to a meter. If radiation enters the tube, the gas splits into charged particles called ions and causes a pulse of electricity to flow. The more pulses there are, the stronger the radiation is.

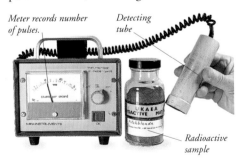

Meter records number of pulses.

Detecting tube

Radioactive sample

Carbon dating
Living things contain the radioisotope carbon-14, which has a 5,730-year half-life. The carbon-14 decays after an organism dies. Scientists can date the remains of dead organisms by measuring the amount of carbon-14 that has decayed. This technique is known as carbon dating.

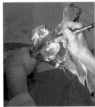

Carbon-dating bones

Uses of radiation

Radiation is used in many branches of medicine for treatment of diseased tissue, for tracing the passage of chemicals through the body, and for sterilizing equipment. It is also to used kill bacteria in food, to check pipes for leakages, and to detect wear on machine parts.

Radiotherapy
Patients suffering from cancer are often treated with radiotherapy. Gamma rays from a radioisotope are focused onto the cancer cells to kill them and stop them from spreading.

Smoke detector
In some smoke alarms, a weak radioisotope emits radiation that causes a small electric current to flow. Any smoke entering the device interferes with the flow of current and sets off a warning alarm.

Film badge
Workers in nuclear power stations wear special badges to record how much radiation they are being exposed to. When the radiation-sensitive film inside the badge is developed, it reveals the radiation levels experienced by the wearer over the previous month.

Timeline

1896 Becquerel discovers radioactivity in uranium.

1898 Polish-born chemist Marie Curie and her husband, French physicist Pierre Curie, discover the radioactive elements radium and polonium.

Marie Curie's flask

1911 New Zealand-born physicist Ernest Rutherford announces that atoms have a dense center called a nucleus.

1908–28 German physicists Hans Geiger and Walther Müller develop a gauge (now called a Geiger-Müller counter) for measuring radioactivity.

Early Geiger-Müller counter

1934 French physicists Irène and Frédéric Joliot-Curie demonstrate that radioactivity can be produced artificially.

1968 Scientists pioneer radiation treatment as a way of preserving food.

FIND OUT MORE | ATOMS AND MOLECULES | CURIE, MARIE | MEITNER, LISE | NUCLEAR POWER | X RAYS AND THE ELECTROMAGNETIC SPECTRUM

RAIN

THE FRESHWATER that makes rivers flow, fills lakes, keeps plants alive, and provides water for us to drink, comes from rain. Like snow, rain is a type of precipitation – moisture falling from the atmosphere to the earth. Raindrops or ice crystals form in a cloud and fall to the ground when they become so heavy that the air can no longer hold them up. Depending on the cloud type and temperature, precipitation may also fall as drizzle (tiny droplets of rain), sleet, or hail, all of different sizes. Too much or too little rain can have a serious effect on plant and animal life.

Mountains force moist air upward.

Air warms and dries as it descends.

Rain falls as moist air is cooled and condenses.

Orographic rain

Types of rain

Rain forms when warm air is swept high in a cloud, cooling the air, and condensing water vapor. Different clouds produce different rain types. Convectional rain is warm, rising air from cumulonimbus clouds. Orographic rain occurs as air is forced up into a cloud over a mountain. Frontal rain is from air rising at weather fronts.

Raindrops

In the warm tropics, clouds are generally warm too. Raindrops form when droplets of water collide and grow so big that the air cannot hold them up. Outside the tropics, raindrops usually start as ice-crystals. High in the clouds, the air is so cold that water turns to ice; ice crystals grow and form snowflakes, which melt and fall as rain.

Precipitation of raindrops

Small droplets of water in the cloud collide to form larger drops.

Large drops break up as they fall.

Freezing level

Small droplets collide again to form large droplets.

Strong air currents carry moisture up through the cloud.

Cumulonimbus cloud

Ice crystals form.

Ice crystals grow as they attract water.

Ice crystals now form snowflakes or hail.

Snowflakes and hailstones melt into raindrops as they fall into warm air.

Warm rain: collision   Cold rain: ice-crystal

Snow

Ice crystals fall from clouds as snow. Moisture freezes on the crystals, which join together as snowflakes. Large snowflakes, formed when the temperature is above freezing fall as wet snow. Dry, powdery snow falls in extreme cold weather cannot stick together well.

Magnified snow crystals

Hailstones

Large pellets of ice fall from a thundercloud as hailstones, more than 0.2 in (5 mm) across. These can form when ice crystals are whirled up and down inside the cloud, acquiring new layers, or when a crystal falls slowly, attracting water that freezes in layers.

Hailstone

Monsoon

Torrential rain hits many tropical areas, such as the southern countries of Asia, for periods of up to six months. Formed by warm air rising over land and drawing in cool, moist air from the sea, monsoon rain can be so fierce that it causes major floods.

Frost

When moisture in the air freezes, it may coat the ground and other surfaces with a layer of sparkling white frost. Spiky needles of hoarfrost form when damp air blows over very cold surfaces. Rime (thick, clear ice) forms when icy air touches a surface. Fern frost (feathery ice trails) forms on cold glass when dewdrops freeze.

Hoarfrost on car

Cloud seeding

In drought areas, airplanes are sometimes used to stimulate rain artificially by seeding thunderclouds with small chemical crystals. These then cause the clouds to release rain.

Snowflakes

Each snowflake is a collection of ice crystals, which are usually hexagonal but may also be needle-shaped or columnar. No two crystals are identical. If snowflakes fall into air that is just above the freezing point, they may melt to form sleet.

Hexagonal crystals form in clouds at 37.4–32°F (3–0°C).

Blizzard

When very heavy snow combines with a strong wind, the result is a blizzard. In a blizzard, visibility drops, and the ground is quickly buried in thick snow, and that snow may be blown by the wind into huge drifts that can engulf a house.

FIND OUT MORE   ATMOSPHERE   CLIMATE   CLOUDS   DESERTS   FORESTS   POLLUTION   STORMS   WEATHER

RAIN FOREST WILDLIFE

THE SCREECHING OF MONKEYS, the buzzing of insects, and the bright color of a bird's wings are common sounds and sights in the world's richest ecosystem, the tropical rain forest. Rain forests provide a home for over half of all plant and animal species. An area of 39 sq miles (100 sq km) can contain 750 types of trees, 400 species of birds, 100 reptile species, and many thousands of insect species. The wildlife is not a random collection of animals and plants, but a complex community in which competition for resources is intense.

Sun conures fly from tree to tree, feeding on fruit, buds, and seeds.

Emergent layer – tall trees rise high above the rest to gain the most light.

Canopy – thick layer of treetops

Liana wound around trunk

Buttress roots

Understory

Ground layer

Emergent layer
This upper layer can reach up to 200 ft (60 m) above the forest floor. Here, the tallest trees of the forest stick out in isolation from the mass of trees below. The emergent layer is home to bats, predatory birds, and fruit eaters, such as the sun conure.

Canopy
Between 100–150 ft (30–45 m) above ground level is the canopy. This dense layer of branches and leaves has the greatest variety of animal life in the forest. Lianas – woody creepers – reach up to the sunlight of the upper canopy.

Understory
Shrubs grow in the understory layer wherever light penetrates through the canopy. Lizards, such as the common iguana, live here, climbing up tree trunks and feeding on insects and vegetation.

Ground layer
There are few plants on the dark forest floor, but many small animals, such as insects, feed on and recycle material that falls from above. Leaf cutter ants use leaves as a compost to grow a fungus they feed on.

Rain forests
Rain forests grow around the equator. The hot, steamy conditions are perfect for plants. In fact, rain forests contain the largest diversity of plant and animal life on Earth; many species are still unidentified. Rain forests form distinct layers, providing homes for animals at all levels.

Harpy eagle
This huge eagle is the major bird of prey of the Central and South American rain forests. It soars over the canopy, watching for prey such as monkeys, sloths, opossums, and snakes. Once it spots them, the harpy eagle swoops through the treetops, snatching animals from the branches with its razor-sharp talons.

Eagle is up to 100 cm (40 in) in length.

Birds
Rain forests contain the richest variety of the world's birds. From the emergent layer, fast-flying predators such as eagles and hawks, descend on forest animals. The canopy is home to birds such as hornbills, parrots, and toucans, which feed on fruit and small animals. On the forest floor, ground-dwelling birds scratch at the soil for insects and plant roots.

Red jungle fowl
Relatives of domestic chickens, Southeast Asian jungle fowl live in small groups on the forest floor, where they nest in grass-lined hollows. They scratch at the ground to unearth invertebrates and plant roots, on which they feed.

Cuvier's toucan
Cuvier's toucan lives in the canopy of South American rain forests. It uses its long beak to reach for fruit and small animals at the ends of branches too thin to bear its weight.

Leaves have a waxy layer to reduce evaporation and channel water down to a mat of roots.

This plant absorbs water from the air through scales on the leaves.

Epiphytic plants

Bromeliad

Plants
Many rain forest trees are tall, with straight trunks and few branches, and are supported by buttress roots. Other plants include epiphytes, such as bromeliads and orchids. Epiphytes use other plants as a support, attaching themselves to branches by their roots to reach the light. They trap water and obtain nutrients from plant material that falls on them. Bromeliads have spiky leaves that channel water, leaves, and fruit into a pool in the center; these rot to provide the bromeliad with nutrients.

Fish
The streams and rivers that flow through rain forests are teeming with fish. Some, such as the pacus from South America, feed on fruit and seeds that fall into the water from overhanging branches; others, such as piranhas, are fierce predators that hunt in packs. They use their sharp teeth and powerful jaws to kill other fish and strip the flesh from larger animals that stray into the water. The electric eel generates electric shocks and fields to stun and detect its fish prey, to deter enemies, and navigate in murky water.

Pacu

Piranha

Sharp teeth line the jaw.

Strangler fig
These tall trees have an unusual life cycle. The seeds, deposited in bird droppings in the canopy branches, grow into plants that send roots down to the ground. The roots thicken and surround the host tree in a latticelike casing. The fig's leaves shade the host tree from the sun. As a result, the "strangled" host tree dies and rots, leaving a freestanding strangler fig, its hollow trunk formed by a network of roots.

R

Reptiles

Many lizards and snakes live in rain forests. Lizards such as iguanas and geckos have long toes and claws adapted for gripping trees; some also have prehensile (grasping) tails. Many forest lizards eat insects; some also feed on vegetation. Rain forest snakes include the boa constrictor and the venomous gaboon viper, which feed on insects, lizards, birds, and mammals.

Brown color camouflages the snake, concealing it as it lies in wait for prey, coiled around a branch.

Tree boa
This South American snake spends most of its life moving between the branches of the understory and canopy of the rainforest, seldom descending to the ground. If small mammals, birds, or lizards come close, the boa strikes and seizes the prey with its fangs. Like other boas, it then constricts, or squeezes, the prey to death, using its strong, muscular coils.

Parson's chameleon
This Madagascan lizard is well adapted for life in the trees. It grips branches and twigs with its toes, aided by its prehensile tail, and will lie in wait for hours for insect prey to come into range. When this happens, the chameleon shoots out its long, sticky tongue to catch the insect. Chameleons have the remarkable ability to change color according to their mood, or to blend with their surroundings.

Dark stripes and spots

Skin is now very dark.

Changing color

1 This Parson's chameleon starts to darken in color to warn off a rival male who has entered his territory.

2 The chameleon darkens farther, and dark purple stripes and spots appear. He becomes more aggresssive and puffs up his body to make himself look bigger.

3 His tail has straightened and his color has intensified. The color is caused by dark pigments released into the skin, triggered by hormones.

Invertebrates

Rain forests contain a huge diversity of invertebrates; many have yet to be identified. On the forest floor, worms, millipedes, beetles, and ants feed on vegetation and dead animals, that fall from the canopy. Spiders also hunt there and in trees for insects, small frogs, and birds. In the understory and canopy, a multitude of insects such as bugs and wasps feed on the prey of other insects or vegetation, and in the canopy colorful, nectar-eating butterflies are common.

Long antenna

Poisonous fangs are below head.

Blue morpho
This butterfly from South America has a wingspan of up to 7 in (18 cm). Invisible to us, and its predators, are beacon-like flashes produced when the wings open and close. These can only be seen by animals, like other morphos, that can detect ultraviolet light. They are used to attract a mate.

Flat body

Leaf insect
This leaf mimic, complete with veins and midrib, lives in Australia and Southeast Asia. To escape detection from birds, its camouflage is enhanced by side-to-side movements, making it resemble a leaf in a breeze.

Giant tiger centipede
This centipede from South America may be up to 8 in (20 cm) long. It eats insects and even small reptiles and mammals. It senses prey with its antennae, then captures and paralyses it with the poisonous fangs below its head.

Amphibians

The warm, moist conditions of rain forests provide ideal conditions for frogs and toads. They defend themselves from larger animals by being camouflaged or distasteful to predators. Some frogs and toads live on the forest floor; others live in trees and have grasping toes that help them climb.

Poison dart frog
The bright colors of these South American frogs warn predators, such as snakes that they are poisonous to eat. Male frogs also use their skin color to deter rivals from entering their territory during courtship.

Ridges look like leaf ribs and veins.

Asian horned toad
This toad's flat body and horns that project over its eyes and snout make it look like a leaf. The effect is enhanced by its color, which matches the dead leaves on the floor where it lives. This camouflage enables it to escape detection by predators and prey alike.

Mammals

Mammals are found at all levels of the rain forest. Numerous insect, plant, and seed eaters live on the forest floor, many emerging at night to avoid predators. Larger forest floor herbivores include tapirs, capybaras, and deer. These mammals are prey for carnivores such as tigers and jaguars. Tree dwellers of the understory include opossums and civets, while in the heights of the canopy live bats, monkeys, and gliding mammals, including flying lemurs that feed on fruit and leaves.

Jaguars may climb trees to lie in wait for prey.

Jaguar
Jaguars are the only large cats found in the Americas. They hunt animals such as deer and peccaries, which they usually stalk through the forest. Their spotted coat provides perfect camouflage in the dappled light of the forest floor, enabling them to get very close to prey before pouncing on it.

Black spider monkey
This highly agile and active monkey lives in the canopy and emergent layer of the South American rain forest. Black spider monkeys move quickly through the branches, making leaps of up to 33 ft (10 m). They live in groups of up to 20 animals that move from tree to tree in search of fruit, rarely, if ever, descending to the forest floor.

Prehensile tail is used to grasp trunks, as an extra hand or foot.

FIND OUT MORE CAMOUFLAGE AND COLOR ECOLOGY AND ECOSYSTEMS FORESTS FROGS AND TOADS INSECTS LIONS AND OTHER WILDCATS MONKEYS AND OTHER PRIMATES REPTILES TREES

R

RATS AND OTHER RODENTS

RODENTS ARE the most numerous and widespread of all the world's mammals. A huge variety of species exist – more than 1,700 in all. The three main types are the mouselike rodents, the cavylike rodents, and the squirrellike rodents. They are found all over the world, from the Arctic to Australia, and occupy all kinds of habitats, from underground tunnels to trees. Between them, rodents have many different lifestyles but most eat plant food and are nocturnal creatures. Rodents are usually small and compact and have sharp gnawing teeth.

The black rat is a skillful climber.

Rats and mice

A typical rodent, the black rat belongs to the mouselike group of rodents, together with mice, voles, hamsters, and gerbils. It has short legs, a long tail, a pointed snout, large eyes and ears, and sensitive whiskers. Agile, alert, and quick to learn, it has adapted so well to living with humans and feeding off their food supplies, that it has spread all over the world from its native Asia. It was first transported from Asia on board the ships of early explorers.

Empty cheek pouches

Extending pouches

Pouches full of nuts

Food

Rodents worldwide eat a huge amount of plant food of all kinds, including underground roots, grass stems, seeds gathered from the ground, and nuts harvested in the treetops. Many also eat worms and insects, and some rodents tackle small mammals and birds. The fish-eating rat, as its name suggests, finds almost all its food in rivers, lakes, and ponds.

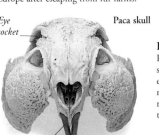
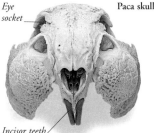

Cavies
The cavylike rodents are large and plump in build compared with rats and mice. They include porcupines, guinea pigs, pacas, chinchillas, and the largest rodent – the capybara. Most are found in South America, although some porcupines live in North America, and the nutria is now found in Europe after escaping from fur farms.

Squirrels
Squirrellike rodents, such as the gray squirrel, are usually larger than rats and mice, and many of them are more active by day than by night. They include tree-dwelling squirrels and chipmunks, burrowers such as marmots and prairie dogs, and water-loving beavers.

Eye socket

Paca skull

Incisor teeth

Rodent teeth
Rodents are equipped with an impressive set of front teeth. These large, sharp incisors enable the animals to gnaw through tough materials, such as nut cases, seed pods, and roots. The incisors grow all the time because they get worn down by continuous use.

Storing food
If they find a good supply of food, many rodents gather more than their immediate needs and store some for later. Hamsters are well known for carrying surplus food in their cheek pouches. It takes this food back to its burrow to use as winter supplies.

Hamster uses its paws to get the nuts out.

Breeding

Rodents breed fast. Some have large litters – hamsters regularly bear 12 young at a time. Others breed several times a year – voles often have four litters per season. These numbers are balanced out because so many are killed by predators or the effects of bad weather. Rodents go to great lengths to protect their young, building special burrow chambers, or nests from grass, leaves, and sticks.

1 At birth, baby mice weigh barely a fraction of an ounce (1 g). They are born naked, blind, and barely able to move.

2 After six days, the young mice in the nest are still helpless and vulnerable to predators. Their fur has begun to grow.

3 After 10 days, most members of the litter have a full coat of fur. Their eyes are open and they can hear, but they still cannot leave the nest.

4 After two weeks, the young mice start to explore. They are almost weaned. They will soon make their own way in the world and begin to reproduce.

R

Beaver lodges

Beavers are famous for the homes called lodges, that they build in rivers. A family of beavers begins its work by constructing a dam of sticks, mud, and stones across a river. This dam stops the river, and in the middle of the still water behind the dam, the beavers build a large conical mound.

Beavers
Found in Europe and North America, beavers can be recognized by their broad, flat, scaly tail. They use their tail as a rudder while swimming, and when danger is near, they slap it on the water to warn their companions.

The family's living quarters are above the water line.

The mound is entered by an underwater tunnel.

Habitats

Rodents occupy a tremendous variety of habitats: from the Arctic tundra to sweltering rain forests; from the driest deserts to waterlogged marshes. Their environment influences both their physical adaptations and the ways they go about finding food and shelter. Some, like the beavers, go to remarkable lengths to make their own shelters.

Mountains
Chinchillas live so high in the Andes Mountains of South America that they have to tolerate bitter cold at night. To help them survive the chill, they have extremely thick fur and take shelter in rock crevices.

A dust bath cleans the fur by dislodging dirt and parasites.

Defense

Rodents are food for many predators. The dangers they face explain why they are nervous creatures, preferring to keep under cover and retreating at the slightest threat. Many rodents have evolved defenses to deter attackers or avoid detection.

Buildings
The house mouse, like the black rat, has colonized human homes and learned to eat food we provide by mistake. It does most of its feeding in the quiet of night, and finds shelter during the day under floorboards and similar out-of-the-way places.

Large ears and eyes for detecting predators.

Deserts
Desert rodents, such as some species of spiny mouse, have to cope not only with a scarcity of water, but also with a poor food supply. They are good at conserving moisture, and breed more freely when rain brings vegetation to life.

Camouflage
Meadow voles live in grassland and woods. They feed on the ground where their brown coloring helps hide them. If danger threatens, they may "freeze," making them difficult to spot.

Mole rats have very poor vision.

Underground
The hairless mole rat is one of several species of rodent that lives underground. They tunnel through the soil, gnawing roots and other food. Since they rarely come to the surface, many species have tiny eyes or are blind.

Spines
The fearsome spines, also known as quills, of porcupines ward off most enemies. If attacked, a porcupine will run into its attacker, leaving spines in its skin. The attacker may die from its wounds.

Largest and smallest

The capybara is the largest rodent. It wallows in pools and swamps in South America. Weighing up to 110 lb (50 kg), it is 10,000 times heavier than the smallest rodent, the pygmy mouse. This tiny mouse scurries through the grass in dry areas of Mexico.

Grooming
Rodents keep their coat in good condition with regular cleaning and grooming to remove dirt, food debris, and parasites. A brown rat may live among garbage, or in sewers, but it meticulously combs through the fur all over its body, using its teeth and paws.

The rat cleans itself with its mouth and front paws.

Claws expertly remove lice.

BLACK RAT

SCIENTIFIC NAME	*Rattus rattus*
ORDER	Rodentia
FAMILY	Muridae
DISTRIBUTION	Worldwide
HABITAT	Around human habitations and buildings, especially near docks and ships
DIET	Varied, but especially cereals and grains
SIZE	Body length 8–10 in (20–26 cm)
LIFESPAN	1–2 years

FIND OUT MORE
ANIMAL BEHAVIOR
ANIMALS
DESERT WILDLIFE
MAMMALS
MOUNTAIN WILDLIFE
RABBITS AND HARES

Rodents

Rats and mice

Dwarf hamsters grow to only 3.3 in (8.4 cm) long.

Field mice can produce up to eight litters a year.

Voles resemble mice, but have rounder faces.

Voles defend themselves by speed and camouflage.

All gerbils have strong back legs and a long tail.

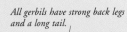

Hamsters groom frequently – their fur traps body heat and keeps them warm.

Gerbils make popular pets; they are gentle and easy to care for.

Chinese hamsters live in grass-lands and deserts in Mongolia, China, Siberia, and Korea.

Pallid gerbils can leap about 1.6 ft (0.5 m) from a standing position. They live in dry, sandy areas, such as the Egyptian desert.

Wood mice are usually nocturnal.

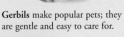

Egyptian spiny mice have stiff hairs in their fur, that stand on end when they are threatened.

Contrary to popular opinion, rats are very clean mammals.

Yellow-necked wood mice feed on plant matter (grain, shoots, and leaves) and animal matter (insects).

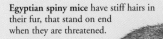

Tails can be shed in danger.

Black-headed rats are less common than brown or black rats.

Black rats carried the fleas that caused bubonic plague epidemics.

Long tails help rats keep balance while climbing.

Squirrels and cavies

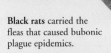

Cheek pouches

Loosely attached spines, or quills, may have barbs attached to their ends.

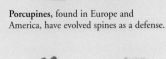

Guinea pigs were raised for food by the Incas of South America.

Porcupines, found in Europe and America, have evolved spines as a defense.

Frequent dust baths help maintain fur.

Chinchillas have luxuriant gray fur, that protects them from the harsh climate of the Andes Mountains of South America.

Chipmunks can manipulate their food with their hand-like forepaws.

Capybaras are the largest members of the rodent family. They live in Central and South America and can grow up to 4 ft (1.2 m) long.

Gray squirrels live in special tree nests, or dreys, in woodland.

REFORMATION

IN THE 16TH CENTURY, Europe's Christians relied on the Roman Catholic church to guide them through their lives on Earth and show them the way to reach Heaven. However many Catholic officials had become rich and corrupt, while ordinary priests were often poor and ignorant. Scholars began to demand reforms that would restore the church's purity. The authorities, however, were slow to respond, so the protesting scholars – backed by certain kings and princes – made their own Reformation by creating an alternative Protestant church, which has existed ever since.

Protestant areas shown in green.

Catholic areas shown in cream.

Catholic and Protestant shown striped.

Christendom, c.1500
When a country's ruler became Protestant, the population usually followed. However, in France and the Netherlands, many ordinary people became Protestant on their own, and were then persecuted by Catholic rulers.

Early protests

Forerunners of the Reformation included the English scholar John Wycliffe (c.1329–84) and the Bohemian (Czech) priest Jan Hus (c.1369–1415). Wycliffe accused the Catholic Church of incompetence and corruption. After his death, many of his followers, known as the Lollards, were put to death for continuing to support his beliefs.

Coin commemorating Hus

Hussites
Hus supported Wycliffe's views, called for reform, and was burned at the stake as a heretic. His followers, the Hussites, proclaimed him a martyr and started an armed struggle against the church. The Hussites were defeated and Bohemia was forced back to Catholicism.

Hus was burned at the stake.

Martin Luther
German university teacher and priest Martin Luther (1483–1546) started the Reformation. From 1517, he challenged aspects of the Catholic Church's teaching and behavior. He wanted people to find their own personal faith in God by individual Bible study. Luther was protected by sympathetic German princes, and his message was spread by the invention of printing.

Protestant division

The Protestant church had divisions within itself as people in different countries followed the teachings of reformers such as Ulrich Zwingli (1484–1531) and John Calvin (1509–64). Calvin greatly influenced the Swiss, Dutch, French, Scottish, and Polish Reformations.

Puritans
English followers of Calvin were called Puritans, after their desire for a "pure" form of worship. Some Puritans wielded great political power and were persecuted; others crossed the Atlantic to establish "godly" colonies in America.

Six Protestant martyrs

Protestantism

Protestants wanted to reform the Catholic church, which, they believed, had slipped away from the Christian ideals set down in the Bible. Their reforms included a return to simple ceremonies, with less emphasis on priestly intervention and more on each worshipper's quest to find God. They also wanted services in native languages, rather than Latin, and an educated, uncorrupted clergy.

Protestant allegory, by Cranach the Younger

Good wine growers represent Protestants.

Martin Luther

Drunk priest

Bad wine growers represent the Catholic church.

Dissolution of the monasteries
In the 1530s, the Reformation reached England. Monastic life had no place in Protestantism, so between 1536 and 1539, King Henry VIII dissolved (shut down) all England's monasteries and took their lands for himself.

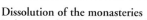

Fountains Abbey, Yorkshire, England

St. Bartholomew's Day Massacre

Huguenots
France's Catholic authorities tried to squash the Huguenots (French followers of Calvin). In August 1572, Catholic mobs in Paris killed 3,000 Huguenots, an event that became known as the St. Bartholomew's Day Massacre. In 1789, the Huguenots won the right to worship freely.

Counter-Reformation

St. Ignatius Loyola

During the 1500s, the Counter-Reformation set out to reclaim Protestant Europe for the church. The Society of Jesus, a major part of this movement, was formed by Ignatius Loyola (1491–1556) in 1534. The Jesuits, as they were called, became famous for foreign missionary work and education.

FIND OUT MORE · CHRISTIANITY · GERMANY, HISTORY OF · HOLY ROMAN EMPIRE · NETHERLANDS, HISTORY OF · RELIGIONS · RENAISSANCE

RELIGIONS

IN ALL SOCIETIES throughout history, people have felt the need for religion. A religion is a set of beliefs that relies on spiritual faith in its followers. Most religions have a god or gods and provide answers to questions such as how the world was created and what happens after death. Religions often have special rituals that act as ways of communicating with the gods or marking major events in a person's life. Finally, religions usually involve an ethical code, a set of rules that believers try to live by.

World religions

There are six major organized world religions – Christianity, Islam, Hinduism, Buddhism, Judaism, and Sikhism – and many smaller religions. For many people, religion provides moral guidance, a sense that life has a meaning, and a feeling of shared values and community. Yet in some places, religious conflict has led to war.

Sikhism
The fifth largest world religion, Sikhism shares elements of Hinduism and Islam. It was founded in India in the 16th century and has one sacred scripture, the *Adi Granth*.

Shinto
The ancient religion of Japan, Shinto, involves beliefs in nature spirits called *kami*, ancestor worship, reverence for certain places and traditions, and respect for military virtues, such as chivalry. It was the state religion of Japan until 1945.

Jainism
Founded in the 6th century BC, Jainism is an Indian religion. Like Hindus, followers of Jainism believe that when people die they are reborn as another being. Nuns may cover their mouths to avoid the risk of harming living things.

Zoroastrians believe that fire is sacred and a flame is always kept burning in temples.

Zoroastrianism
This religion was founded in Asia in the 500s BC. It still survives in parts of Iran and India. Zoroastrians believe that life is a struggle between two forces: good, represented by the god Ahura Mazda, and evil, in the spirit Ahriman. They believe that good will eventually triumph, and Ahura Mazda will establish paradise here on Earth.

Traditional religions

The aboriginal peoples of North America, Australia, and Africa all follow different types of traditional religions. These religions have no written texts – ceremonies and beliefs are handed down from one generation to the next by word of mouth. Many traditional religions involve worship of ancestors or reverence for the forces of nature.

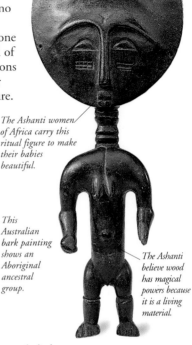

The Ashanti women of Africa carry this ritual figure to make their babies beautiful.

This Australian bark painting shows an Aboriginal ancestral group.

The Ashanti believe wood has magical powers because it is a living material.

Ancestor worship
Most traditional religions have a belief in some sort of afterlife, and the dead person's spirit is often thought to live on among the surviving people. Ancestors may be worshiped through objects that symbolize them, such as the carved totem poles in northwestern North America.

Animism
The belief that spirits inhabit all objects is called animism. These spirits control not only the object itself, but also the lives of people and the natural world. Animism is one of the earliest forms of religion and still exists among people living traditional lifestyles all over the world.

Communicating with the gods

All religions involve rituals, and an important purpose of these ceremonies is to communicate with the gods. At its simplest, talking to a god is a matter of saying a prayer, but more elaborate rituals are also used. Music, dance, readings from sacred books, ceremonies, and meditating are found in different religions to bring the faithful into closer contact with the world of the spirits.

Rosary beads

People pray using rosary beads.

Ancient pot showing human sacrifice

Human sacrifices to the earth gods were made on sacred mountains.

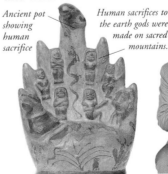

Offerings
In many religions, believers make offerings such as money or food to the gods. In some religions, offerings included human sacrifices.

Music
Music provides a common way of talking to a god. People are brought together in worship by singing hymns or chanting.

Rastafarians play drums in worship.

Crucifix shows Christ on the cross.

FIND OUT MORE   BUDDHISM   CHRISTIANITY   FESTIVALS   GODS AND GODDESSES   HINDUISM   ISLAM   JUDAISM   MUSIC   SHRINES   SIGNS AND SYMBOLS

R

Religions

Holy objects

Miter, or headdress, worn by a bishop

Sikh kirpan, or sword

Jewish baby cloth, worn after baby is circumcised

Hebrew text celebrating the Torah

Headdress worn by a Tibetan monk

Peruvian figure used to guard tombs

Guardian figure used in ancestor worship

Charm necklace used by African healers

Screen showing ancestor spirits, Nigeria

Doll made from sticks, beeswax, beads, and hide

Fertility dolls, Africa

Animist wood carving, Polynesia

Shinto god

Jain shrine

Christian Bible

Islamic lamp

Jain Tirthankara, or guide

Tibetan monk's bell

Holy places

Cathedral window, Britain

Christian church

Islamic window

Zoroastrian temple

Decorative tiles on octagonal base

Islamic mosque, Jerusalem

Christian chapel doorway, France

Dome above gray sandstone octagonal base

Islamic mausoleum, or tomb, India

Minaret on an Islamic mosque

RENAISSANCE

FROM THE 15TH CENTURY, Europe experienced a remarkable growth in the arts and sciences. This era was known as the Renaissance, which in French means "rebirth." From its birthplace in Italy, the Renaissance spread to embrace most of western Europe and deeply affected the way educated people looked at the world and its purpose. Inspired by the study of ancient Greek and Roman society, Renaissance scholars, thinkers, and artists abandoned medieval pessimism and constructed humanism – a new, optimistic outlook for the future, in which men and women played a central role and created a civilized world. Some of our finest art and literature dates from this period.

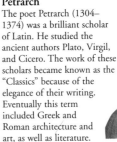
Copy of an ancient Greek bronze

Renaissance origins

The Renaissance began in Italy when the poets Dante, Petrarch, and Boccaccio revived an interest in ancient Greek and Roman civilizations. They believed these societies had experienced a Golden Age of art and literature in the 2nd and 1st centuries BC, and wished to re-create it.

Francesco Petrarcha

Petrarch
The poet Petrarch (1304–1374) was a brilliant scholar of Latin. He studied the ancient authors Plato, Virgil, and Cicero. The work of these scholars became known as the "Classics" because of the elegance of their writing. Eventually this term included Greek and Roman architecture and art, as well as literature.

New order

Medieval thinkers argued that earthly life was less important than the afterlife. In contrast, the Renaissance view was that the mortal world, with all its human achievements, was the most significant part of God's Creation. This inspired explorers, inventors, and astronomers to expand human knowledge.

Age of exploration
Fired by the new spirit of discovery, the Portuguese sailors Bartolomeu Diaz and Vasco da Gama discovered the sea route to India. Ferdinand Magellan set out to sail around the world, though he did not live to complete the trip.

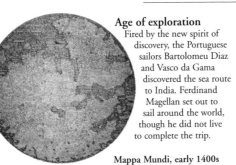
Mappa Mundi, early 1400s

Planisphaerium Copernicum, c.1543

Stars and planets
The astronomer Copernicus was the first to realize that the Universe did not revolve around Earth. Instead Earth revolved around the Sun. Later astronomers, such as Galileo, supported this theory, and formed new ones, using the same system of planetary observation that Copernicus had pioneered.

New ideas
Major Renaissance figures believed that humankind could achieve anything it wanted; enough confidence, education, and faith in God would create a new Golden Age and a better society. One true genius, the artist, engineer, and scientist Leonardo da Vinci (1452–1519), let his imagination run free and produced plans for flying machines about 400 years before they were actually invented.

Thick struts supported the skeleton structure.

Crank and pulley mechanism

Wing span was 36 ft (11 m).

Foot pedals operated the machine

Flying machine by Leonardo da Vinci

Human body

Medieval artists viewed the human form as "a withered fruit stinking in the nostrils of the Lord." The Renaissance overturned this view, and artists such as Michelangelo, Raphael, and Titian portrayed the human figure with beauty and grace. Michelangelo's sculpture the *Pieta* idealizes the human forms to represent their spiritual purity.

Pieta by Michelangelo

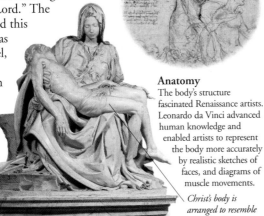

A study by Leonardo da Vinci

Anatomy
The body's structure fascinated Renaissance artists. Leonardo da Vinci advanced human knowledge and enabled artists to represent the body more accurately by realistic sketches of faces, and diagrams of muscle movements.

Christ's body is arranged to resemble a sleeping baby.

Michelangelo

Michelangelo Buonarroti (1475–1564), from Caprese, Tuscany, Italy, was one of the greatest artistic creators of all time. A sculptor, painter, draughtsman, poet, and architect, he was deeply fascinated by the human body and its representation. Sculpture was the art form he loved best. When he sculpted, he believed that he was "releasing" the figures trapped in the stone. His greatest painting is on the ceiling of the Sistine Chapel in the Vatican, Rome.

Hunt in the Forest by Paolo Uccello (1396–1475)

Perspective in painting
The greatest innovation in Renaissance art was the development of perspective. Artists, eager to represent the natural world accurately, learned how to put space and distance in their paintings. Perspective had been missing in the flatter, two-dimensional works of the medieval period.

The Catholic church

By 1400, the church had become wealthy, worldly – and corrupt. The Renaissance directly challenged what was left of church authority, because it emphasized the importance of inquiry. Churchmen ignored any suggestion of reform as, for the first time, cartoons circulated that made fun of the church and its inability to cope with new ideas.

Spread of learning
For centuries, the Church controlled art and learning in Europe. When the Renaissance started, there was an explosion of new ideas and inventions – one of which was printing. For the first time in history, printed books spread the ideas of thinkers and scholars from Italy to people all over Europe. Wealthy rulers such as Lorenzo de' Medici built fabulous libraries – some of which were in cathedrals – to house these books.

Cartoon of the Church, 1497

Interior of San Lorenzo Cathedral, Tuscany, Italy

Humanism

As the Renaissance spread, northern European scholars developed humanism, a philosophy that greatly valued human dignity and moral values. The first humanists were passionate Christians. They studied the ancient Latin, Greek, and Hebrew texts and revolutionized education by teaching the humanities (moral philosophy, grammar, history, rhetoric, and poetry) instead of just learning the Bible by heart.

Desiderius Erasmus
The humanist movement in Europe affected Germany, Holland, and England. Erasmus (c.1468–1536) was a brilliant Dutch humanist who led the revival of learning. He became famous through his religious translations and writings, in which he gently and humorously called for peaceful reform in the church.

Erasmus by Holbein

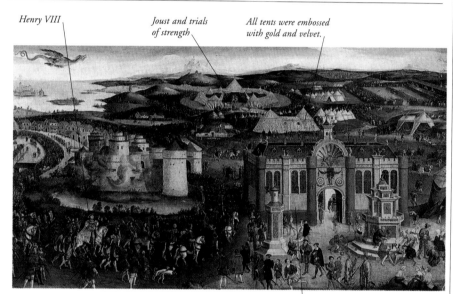

Henry VIII

Joust and trials of strength

All tents were embossed with gold and velvet.

The Field of the Cloth of Gold, 1520

Henry VIII built a temporary palace.

Thomas More's *Utopia*, 1516

Sir Thomas More
England's leading scholar Sir Thomas More (1478–1535) was a humanist. His book, *Utopia*, argued that all political and social evils would be cured by the common ownership of land, the education of both women and men, and religious tolerance. King Henry VIII had More executed for refusing to recognize him as head of the reformed English Church.

Education
Humanists felt that people shaped their own destiny, and that Greek and Roman texts illustrated this. Therefore English humanist educators, such as Sir John Cheke (1514–57) and Nicholas Udall (1505–56), encouraged children to study classic texts so they learned how to serve their society for the common good.

Humanists believed in education for women and men.

La scuola di Signor Buonoventura

Renaissance princes

As the Renaissance progressed, rulers became more sophisticated and ruthless. The political writer Niccolò Machiavelli (1469–1527) described the art of statecraft (methods used by a successful ruler to stay in power) in his book *The Prince* (1532). He formed many of his theories by comparing his own Italian society with that of ancient Rome.

Francis I
King Francis I of France (r.1515–47) regarded himself as a perfect Renaissance prince. An able, quick-witted man, he loved art and learning and was the patron of geniuses such as Leonardo da Vinci and Benvenuto Cellini (1500–91). In June 1520, he vied with the era's other great Renaissance prince, Henry VIII of England, at a magnificent summit meeting at the Field of the Cloth of Gold near Calais, France.

Patronage

As artists' status rose during the Renaissance, rich rulers and noble families were glad to act as their patrons, giving them financial security while they produced their great works. The Florentine Medici family were the patrons of great artists such as Michelangelo.

Artemisia Gentileschi

The Medici of Florence
The Medici banking family rose to power in the early Renaissance and contributed much to the flowering of the arts. They made Florence an artistic and cultural center – all of the great artists went there. Even those who were not supported by the Medicis, such as the Tuscan portraitist Artemisia Gentileschi (c.1590–1642), went to Florence to make contacts and improve their skills.

Albrecht Dürer

Dürer (1471–1528), from Germany, was one of the greatest Renaissance artists. One of 18 children, Dürer was apprenticed to a painter and book illustrator at the age of 15. After four years Dürer began to travel around Europe and picked up new ideas from other artists, including Bellini and Raphael. A true Renaissance man who mastered many subjects from Latin to mathematics, he is mainly remembered for his exquisite engravings and woodblock prints.

FIND OUT MORE

ART, HISTORY OF | GALILEO | GREECE, ANCIENT | EXPLORATION | LEONARDO DA VINCI | PHILOSOPHY | PRINTING | ROMAN EMPIRE | SCIENCE, HISTORY OF

REPRODUCTION

LIKE ALL LIVING THINGS, humans have to reproduce to guarantee the survival of the species. Reproduction is the job of the reproductive system. The female reproductive system lies mainly within the body, while much of the male system is outside the body. Both reproductive systems produce special cells called sex cells. Male and female sex cells are brought together following sexual intercourse. If male and female sex cells meet, they fuse during fertilization into a single cell that develops into a small human being made up of billions of cells.

Female reproductive system

- Ovary produces ova.
- Fallopian tube carries ova toward uterus.
- Urethra
- Labia minora
- Clitoris
- Labia majora
- Bladder
- Seminal vesicle
- Spine
- Uterus is the organ in which baby develops.
- Uterine muscle can expand.
- Cervix is the opening to uterus.
- Vagina leads from uterus to the outside.
- Vaginal opening

Male reproductive system

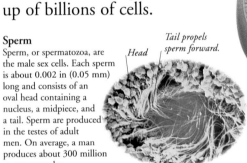

- Prostate gland
- Urethra carries sperm to outside.
- Penis becomes erect during sexual intercourse.
- Epididymis is a coiled tube in which sperm matures.
- Testis is site of sperm production.

Sperm

Sperm, or spermatozoa, are the male sex cells. Each sperm is about 0.002 in (0.05 mm) long and consists of an oval head containing a nucleus, a midpiece, and a tail. Sperm are produced in the testes of adult men. On average, a man produces about 300 million sperm every day.

- Head
- Tail propels sperm forward.

Ova

Ova, or eggs, are the female sex cells. Each ovum is a rounded cell, with a nucleus, about 0.004 in (0.1 mm) in diameter. After puberty, an ovum matures each month and is released from an ovary. This is called ovulation.

An ovum emerging from an ovary

Reproductive systems

In a man, sperm are produced in the testes, nurtured by semen produced in the prostate gland and seminal vesicles, and released from the penis during sexual intercourse. In a woman, ova are released singly from the ovary, travel along the fallopian tube to the uterus, and, if fertilized, develop into a fetus.

Menstrual cycle

The menstrual cycle is a series of changes that takes place in a woman's reproductive system each month. The menstrual cycle lasts about 28 days, and ovulation (part of the ovarian cycle) takes place around day 14. If the ovum is not fertilized, the uterus lining is shed through the vagina. This is called a period.

- Menstrual cycle begins with the period.
- Uterus lining starts to thicken.
- In mid-cycle, an ovum is released.
- Uterus lining thickens further.
- Lining starts to break down.
- Cycle ends and new cycle starts as the uterus lining is shed through the vagina.

Day 1   Blood vessels   Day 14   Blood supply increases   Day 28

Contraception

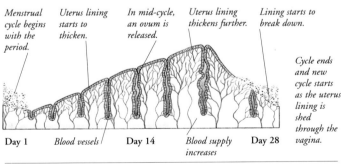

- Contraceptive pills
- Contraceptive pessaries are used with diaphragm.
- A diaphragm is inserted into the vagina.
- Condom

Contraception, or birth control, prevents pregnancy. Types of contraceptives include barrier methods, such as the condom and diaphragm, which prevent sperm from reaching an egg; and hormonal methods, such as the contraceptive pill, which prevent ovulation.

Sexual intercourse

During sexual intercourse, a man pushes his erect penis into his partner's vagina. When he ejaculates, semen carrying millions of sperm spurts into the vagina. The sperm swim into the uterus and to the fallopian tubes, where fertilization may take place. The period from fertilization to implantation is conception.

Fertilization

Fertilization is the joining together of a sperm and an ovum. If an ovum is in the fallopian tube, thousands of sperm cluster around it, trying to break through its outer covering. One sperm succeeds.

Fertilization and implantation

2 Forty-eight hours after fertilization, the fertilized egg has divided into four. From now on, the cells divide about twice a day.

3 Seventy-two hours after fertilization, the egg has become a ball of 64 cells.

4 On about the sixth day, the ball of cells implants in the uterus.

- Fallopian tube
- Egg cell

1 Thirty-six hours after fertilization, the fertilized egg has divided into two cells and is moving along the fallopian tube.

- Uterus
- Ovary
- Thickened lining of uterus
- Vagina

Implantation

The fertilized ovum develops into a hollow ball of cells called a blastocyst. At this stage it is ready to burrow into the lining of the uterus and become an embryo. The embryo will develop into a fetus and then into a baby.

Pregnancy

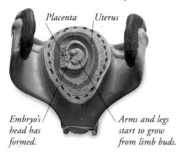

Pregnancy is the time taken for a baby to develop inside a woman's uterus. It begins with conception and ends with birth. On average, pregnancy lasts for 40 weeks. The woman's abdomen gradually swells as the fetus grows inside it. The fetus receives nutrition and oxygen from the mother via the placenta, a flat organ attached to the uterine lining. It floats, protected in a liquid called amniotic fluid, linked to the placenta by the umbilical cord.

Fertilized egg

The fertilized ovum, or egg, divides rapidly as it travels along the fallopian tube toward the uterus, where it will implant.

Egg has divided twice, producing four cells.

Embryo at 6 weeks

The embryo is now just 0.25 in (6 mm) long. Its digestive, blood, and nervous systems are developing, and its heart has started to beat. The beginnings of its ears, eyes, and mouth appear, as do the limb buds from which arms and legs will grow.

Placenta *Uterus*

Embryo's head has formed. *Arms and legs start to grow from limb buds.*

Fetus at 12 weeks

At 12 weeks, the developing baby, now known as a fetus, is about 3 in (7.5 cm) long. It resembles a human being. Fingers and toes have formed, the mouth opens and closes and can suck. Ears and eyelids are present. The external genitals have formed, and the fetus passes urine into the amniotic fluid.

Arms and legs now move.

A layer of fine hair covers the baby's skin.

Fetus at 16 weeks

At 16 weeks the fetus is about 6 in (15 cm) long. The fetus is now fully formed with all its organs in place, and it starts to grow and mature rapidly. The bones are starting to develop, and the muscles are getting stronger.

Baby can move around.

Cervix, or neck of womb

Fetus at 28 weeks

The fetus is about 14.5 in (37 cm) long, and almost fully mature. During the remaining weeks of pregnancy, the fetus will grow plumper as fat builds up. If born prematurely at this stage, the baby could survive in an incubator.

Baby's brain is well developed.

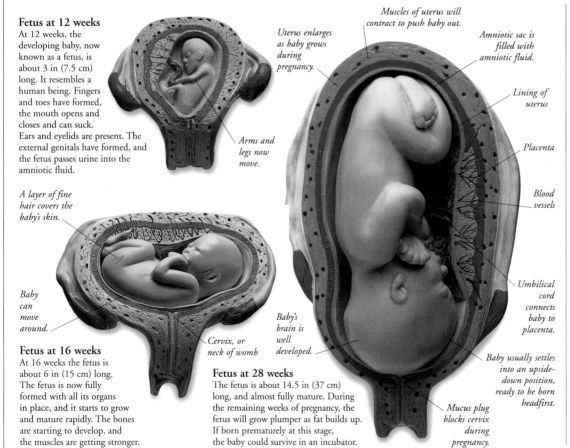

Muscles of uterus will contract to push baby out.

Uterus enlarges as baby grows during pregnancy.

Amniotic sac is filled with amniotic fluid.

Lining of uterus

Placenta

Blood vessels

Umbilical cord connects baby to placenta.

Baby usually settles into an upside-down position, ready to be born headfirst.

Mucus plug blocks cervix during pregnancy.

Infertility

Infertility means the inability in a man or a woman to have a baby. It can be treated in many cases. One treatment is invitro fertilization (IVF). This involves removing eggs from a woman's ovaries, fertilizing them outside her body with sperm, and returning them to the uterus to develop.

Donated semen is stored in a laboratory.

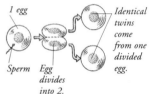

Twins

There are two types of twins, identical twins and fraternal twins. Fraternal twins result when two eggs are released at the same time and are then fertilized by two different sperm. Identical twins develop from just one egg and are much rarer. Having more than two babies is rarer still.

Margaret Sanger

American Margaret Sanger (1883–1966) was a pioneer of contraception. She believed birth control was vitally important to improve living standards for the poor. In 1916, she opened a birth information clinic and was arrested. After her release, she continued to campaign.

Identical twins

Identical twins are produced when a fertilized egg divides into two separate cells, each of which develops into a fetus. Both fetuses share the same placenta. Because they develop from a single fertilized egg, identical twins share exactly the same genes and are always the same sex.

1 egg *Identical twins come from one divided egg.*

Sperm *Egg divides into 2.*

Labor

The sequence of events by which the baby is pushed out of the uterus is known as labor. It has three stages. Changes in the mother's hormone levels start labor. In the first stage, the uterus starts to contract and the cervix widens. In the second stage, the baby is born. Finally, the placenta is pushed out.

Birth

During birth, the muscles in the wall of the uterus contract very strongly. The baby is pushed through the open cervix and into the vagina, from which it emerges normally headfirst. Once outside the body, the baby takes its first breaths. The doctor or midwife cuts the umbilical cord.

FIND OUT MORE

BIOLOGY · GENETICS · GROWTH AND DEVELOPMENT · HORMONES AND ENDOCRINE SYSTEM · HUMAN BODY · MEDICINE · MUSCLES AND MOVEMENT · PLANTS, REPRODUCTION

REPTILES

Crest makes the water dragon more imposing.

Large eyes provide excellent vision.

THE RULING AGE OF THE REPTILES was the dinosaur age, about 200 million years ago, but most modern reptiles evolved much more recently. Dinosaurs and other early reptiles evolved from amphibians that moved onto land and did not need water to breed. Today there are more than 6,000 species of reptile. They have dry skin covered with scales or shields that prevent water loss. They reproduce with internal fertilization, and lay eggs from which the young hatch looking like their parents.

Powerful legs for running and climbing

Tip of the tail has regrown after it was lost, maybe to a predator.

Tail is used for balance when running, as a rudder when swimming, and as a weapon for defense.

Thai water dragon
The water dragon is a type of lizard from Thailand. It lives mainly in trees near water. When on the ground, it may stand up on its hind legs and run along upright for short distances to escape predators. It then climbs a tree or jumps in water and swims.

Thai water dragon

What is a reptile?
Reptiles are cold-blooded vertebrates (animals with a backbone). They are creatures that crawl, their name coming from the Latin *repto*, meaning "to crawl." They breathe with their lungs, and are found in most habitats in the world except cold regions and high mountains. In temperate regions they survive winter by hibernating.

Reptile groups
There are four groups of reptiles: tortoises and turtles, snakes and lizards, crocodilians, and tuataras. Experts disagree about how closely related they are. Some think turtles and tortoises are far removed from other orders, and that crocodilians are more closely related to birds than other reptiles.

Tortoise skeleton cut in half

Tortoises and turtles
There are more than 270 species of these hard-shelled reptiles, which have existed, almost unchanged, for about 200 million years. Tortoises live on land, while turtles live in freshwater or oceans. The hard shell is growing bone attached to the animal's backbone and ribs. It is covered with shields made of keratin.

Python skeleton

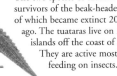
Leopard tortoise

Tuataras
The two species of tuataras are the last survivors of the beak-headed reptiles, most of which became extinct 200 million years ago. The tuataras live on remote rocky islands off the coast of New Zealand. They are active mostly at night, feeding on insects.

Marine iguana

Burmese rock python

Reptiles at sea
Ocean-going reptiles – sea turtles, the saltwater crocodile, sea snakes, and the marine iguana – are adapted to marine life. They have glands that excrete excess salt, and a powerful heart that maintains circulation during deep, rapid dives.

Snakes and lizards
The largest group of reptiles is divided into three suborders: snakes, lizards, and worm lizards. They have scales as opposed to the shields of turtles and leathery skin of crocodiles, and are the most recently evolved reptiles.

Crocodilians cool off by submerging in water.

Spectacled caiman

Crocodilians
This group contains more than 20 species – crocodiles, alligators, caimans, the gavial, and the false gavial. They are survivors from the Jurassic Age of the dinosaurs.

Skin and scales
Its type of skin provides clues to a reptile's life. Tiny geckoes have thin, papery skin; skinks and other lizards and snakes have overlapping scales that allow them to move easily on the ground or up trees. Tortoises have warty skin on the head, tail, and legs – the parts that protrude from the shell. Crocodilians have leathery skin.

Caiman
The skin is thick and leathery. There may be extra toughened areas under the skin.

Chameleon
The texture of the skin is rough and granular. It can change color.

Skink
Small smooth scales help skinks burrow easily into sand or through leaves.

Plated lizard
The scales are large, platelike, and protective. They allow flexibility.

Python
This snake has small scales on top, and large, overlapping belly scales.

R

Growing new parts

Like insects, reptiles shed, or slough, their skin as they grow. Some reptiles also have the ability to lose parts of the body voluntarily to escape predators. For example, some lizards lose their tails. The lost part will regrow in a process known as regeneration.

Broken skin *Back skin* *Belly skin* *Most recent links are nearest the body.*

Slow worm sloughing   **Sloughed skin of a rat snake**

New skin
As snakes and lizards grow, the external layer of their skin gets too small. When a new layer has developed underneath, they slough the old skin, which comes off inside out. A large meal that causes sudden growth or scar damage will also promote skin sloughing.

New rattles
When a rattlesnake sloughs its skin, the bit at the tip of the tail remains and adds a link to the rattle. Since rattles get damaged, and sloughing is not regular, the number of links does not indicate a snake's age.

New tail built on cartilage rather than bone.

New tail
Many lizards lose their tails on purpose to avoid predators. The lizard tenses its tail muscles, and the tail fractures and breaks off. The piece of tail often wiggles to divert the predator from the escaping lizard.

1 This skink voluntarily sheds its tail to avoid being eaten and save its life. The blood vessels in the tail stump have healed to prevent the lizard from losing blood. A new tail will begin to regenerate soon.

2 The new tail is simple. It lacks the complex scales of the original, and its color and patterning will differ. Inside, the bony vertebrae have been replaced by a tube of cartilage.

New tail is fully developed but lacks original color and pattern.

Simple new tail regenerating from the old stump.

3 The tail has grown to its original length. The ability to regenerate its tail diminishes as the lizard gets older.

Breeding

Most reptiles lay eggs. The developing young inside absorb moisture and oxygen through the shell and feed on the yolk. The shells are usually soft and flexible, although some eggs have a hard shell. Some lizards and snakes give birth to fully formed "live" young.

Incubation
Female cornsnakes lay about 12 soft-shelled eggs. They play no part in their incubation, which takes about two months. Female pythons, on the other hand, incubate their eggs in their coils. King cobras build and guard a nest.

Hatchling is alert to danger.

Hatchling cornsnake has a different pattern from adults.

1 A cornsnake is ready to hatch. It makes a slit in the eggshell with a tooth called an egg tooth at the front of its upper jaw.

2 The head emerges, and the hatchling takes its first breath of air. The tiny snake rests frequently and is wary of danger.

3 The hatchling emerges slowly and flicks its sensitive tongue to taste its surroundings. It retreats into its shell if it detects any movement.

4 Following a disturbance, this hatchling retreated inside the egg for almost 24 hours. It eventually emerged through a new slit in the shell. Hatchlings sometimes make several cuts in the shell before leaving the egg.

5 Once free of the egg, the hatchling cornsnake is on its own. It will be sustained for 10 days by the egg yolk it absorbed in the shell and will shed its skin before hunting lizards and baby mice.

Hard-shelled eggs
Tortoises, turtles, crocodilians, and some lizards have hard-shelled eggs. They survive dry conditions better than soft-shelled eggs but are more fragile. They are laid in a nest or underground for protection.

Live young
Boas, such as this boa constrictor, and many vipers are born live. The young are born in a membranous sac that breaks soon after birth. This method of reproduction is ideal for reptiles in colder climates, where eggs would not survive.

Javan garden lizard

Burmese rock python

Soft-shelled eggs
Snakes and many lizards have soft-shelled eggs. These reptiles have soft mouth parts that could not break a hard eggshell. Soft-shelled eggs vary in shape but are often oval or elongated, and may be pockmarked or discolored.

Calabar ground python

Monitor lizard   *Matamata turtle*

American alligator

Reptiles in danger
Many reptiles are threatened with extinction because of trade in their body parts. Snake, lizard, and crocodile skins are used for bags, shoes, and belts; turtle shells become ornaments or combs; turtle meat is used for soup; snake gall or blood is used in Oriental medicine.

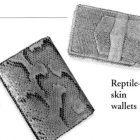

Reptile-skin wallets

FIND OUT MORE AMPHIBIANS CONSERVATION CROCODILES DINOSAURS EGGS LIZARDS SNAKES TURTLES AND TORTOISES

RHINOCEROSES AND TAPIRS

RHINOS' HUGE HORNS and massive bulk make them intimidating animals. There are five species of rhinos: two from Africa and three from Asia. All have poor eyesight and rely on a good sense of smell and acute hearing to detect danger. Other animals help warn of danger – the oxpecker, a bird that feeds on ticks on a rhino's skin, will screech if danger threatens. Rhinos enjoy wallowing in mud pools because the mud keeps them cool and protects them from biting insects. Tapirs are related to rhinos. They are good swimmers and spend much of their time in water.

Feeding
The great Indian and white rhinos graze on grass; but the Sumatran, Javan, and black rhinos browse on twigs and leaves. The black rhino uses its prehensile lip to grasp branches and strip them of their leaves and shoots.

Black rhinoceros
The black, or hook-lipped, rhino from Africa is a large, aggressive animal ready to charge anything that invades its territory. It has very thick, tough, hairless skin and two large horns made of the substance keratin. It uses its prehensile (grasping) upper lip to feed on twigs.

Horn
Nostril
Prehensile lip grasps branch.
Thick, stocky legs
Hooves
Thick gray skin

Rhino horns

Rhinos have been heavily hunted for their horns and all except the white rhino are endangered. The horns are believed to have magical or medical properties. They are also carved into items such as dagger handles.

Types of rhinos

Great Indian rhino

This quiet animal lives in India and Nepal. It has deep skin folds that look like armor plating. Both sexes have a single horn.

Large, single horn

Javan rhino

The Javan rhino is a very rare animal. The few survivors live in a reserve on Java. It has a prehensile upper lip. The males have a single small horn; females are hornless.

Small head

Sumatran rhino
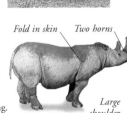
This is the smallest rhino and is very rare. It lives in the forests of Southeast Asia and feeds on twigs and leaves. It differs from all other rhinos because it has a hairy coat when young.

Fold in skin   Two horns

White rhino
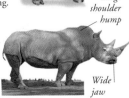
The white, or square-lipped, rhino from Africa is the largest of the rhinos. It has a long head and two horns. It is slightly paler than the black rhino.

Large shoulder hump
Wide jaw

Reproduction
Female black rhinos are ready to breed at 3½–4 years old, and males at 6 years. After a 15-month gestation period, a single calf is born, weighing about 48 lb (22 kg). Within a few minutes of birth, it struggles to its feet to hunt for its mother's teats. The calf is weaned at one year, but remains close to its mother for at least another year.

Young rhino suckling
Tufts on ears
Dried mud from a mud wallow
Large nostrils

Tapirs
There are four species of tapirs, three of which live in the rain forests of South and Central America; the fourth lives in Southeast Asia. Tapirs are shy, solitary animals that prefer to come out at night. The snout is elongated into a flexible proboscis that they use to feed on shoots, twigs, leaves, and water plants.

Thin coat of short hairs
Long, flexible snout
Hooves
Brazilian tapir

Territory
The black rhino lives in a restricted area, or "home range," of several square miles. The home range overlaps with that of other rhinos; they share the same feeding grounds, watering places, tracks, and wallows, but they live independently. The black rhino's way of life, behavior, and habits are adapted to remaining in one place. Even in a severe drought, it will not leave its home to find water elsewhere. To warn other bulls, rhinos may mark their territory with their urine.

Black rhino territory marking

BLACK RHINOCEROS
SCIENTIFIC NAME *Diceros bicornis*
ORDER Perissodactyla
FAMILY Rhinocerotidae
DISTRIBUTION Africa south of the Sahara
HABITAT Thorn scrub and grassland savannahs
DIET Leaves, buds, twigs, and small branches from various shrubs and trees
SIZE Height at shoulder: 5.6 ft (1.7 m) Weight: up to 2,870 lb (1,300 kg) Maximum recorded horn length: 4.5 ft (1.36 m)
LIFESPAN Up to 40 years

 FIND OUT MORE   AFRICAN WILDLIFE   ASIAN WILDLIFE   GRASSLAND WILDLIFE   CONSERVATION   MAMMALS   RAIN FOREST WILDLIFE   SOUTH AMERICAN WILDLIFE

RIVERS

WHEREVER THERE IS ENOUGH RAIN, rivers form, flowing down from mountains to the ocean or into lakes. A river is a natural channel in which water flows downhill. Typically, it begins as a trickle high up in the mountains. As the trickle runs downhill, more rainwater flows in from the surrounding landscape and it swells, first into a stream, and then into a broad river. Aided by sand, boulders, and other debris carried in the water, the river carves out a channel. The river eventually forms a valley and finally, as it nears the sea, a broad plain. A river often winds across this plain in a chain of elaborate loops, called meanders.

River types

Rivers may be permanent geographical features or seasonal, dependent upon rains to keep them flowing. In wet seasons or after snow melts, a river may rise so much that it floods the land.

Ephemeral
In deserts and their edges or on porous rock, a river flows ephemerally, or intermittently. It dries up when there is no rain, leaving behind a gulch or wadi.

Perennial
In wet areas, rivers are usually perennial – that is, they run throughout the year. A steady flow of groundwater lets the river flow between rainstorms.

River features

In its upper level, a river is small and often tumbles down over rapids and waterfalls. Farther downstream, it becomes wider as tributaries bring in more water and silt. Typically, as it nears the sea, it flows across a broad plain formed by silt that is spread across the land in times of flood. It may split into branches, forming a delta, or flow into a wide estuary.

Middle levels
The river's flow is less turbulent as the land becomes less steep at its middle level. Tributaries join it, increasing its volume of water and allowing it to run easily over shallower ground.

Small island

Sea

V-shaped valley with steep sides

Glacier

Tributary

Waterfall

Rapids

Meander

Deposited sediment

Upper levels
In its upper reaches, a river may wind between a series of hills. Valleys formed by the river are narrow and steep-sided. Water is often slowed by the rough riverbed, though there may be fast-flowing rapids and waterfalls.

Oxbow lake
As a river wears away the outside bend of a meander, it makes the meander's neck narrower. Eventually it breaks through the neck, cutting the meander off and stranding the water in an oxbow lake.

Oxbow lake

Delta

Lower levels
By the time it reaches its lower levels, the river has widened enormously. The steeper valleys of its upper and middle sections give way to wider floodplains, often ending in an estuary or delta.

Distributary

Deltas
As a river meets the sea, its flow abruptly slows down. As a result, it may drop its load of sediment in a huge fan of deposits called a delta, and split into many branches or distributaries. Arcuate deltas have a curved, arc-shaped coastline. Bird's foot deltas have a ragged coast, shaped a little like a bird's foot.

Chickahominy River, Virginia

Estuaries
As a river flows into the sea, it often widens, forming a broad inlet called an estuary. Water from the river may become muddy, as saltwater from the ocean causes small particles of clay in the fresh riverwater to clump together. This material sinks to the riverbed, causing sediment build-up, and aids the formation of deltas.

Blackwater estuary, UK

R

Waterfalls

On its course, a river will sometimes wear away soft rock on the riverbed, leaving a sill of hard rock above it. Water falls off this shelf to the soft rock below, forming a waterfall. Rocks and boulders swirl at the base of the waterfall, carving out a deep trough known as a plunge pool.

Rapids

In its upper realms, a river often tumbles over rocky sections that are strewn with boulders. The rocks at this point may be so hard that they are worn away slowly by the river. The slope of the river may be so steep that the river rushes down very quickly and forms rapids.

Hard rock is worn away slowly.

Flow of river is turbulent.

Rapids

Plunge pool

Soft rock is being worn away quickly.

Rocky riverbed

Loads

The material carried by a river is called its load. There are three main types of load. The bedload is stones and other large particles that wash along the riverbed. The suspended load is small particles that float in the water. The solute load is fine material that has dissolved in the water.

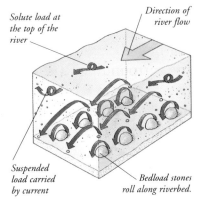

Solute load at the top of the river

Direction of river flow

Suspended load carried by current

Bedload stones roll along riverbed.

Stream erosion

Rivers wear away their channels in several ways. Hydraulic action is wear caused by the pressure of moving water that loosens parts of the riverbed and bank. However, most of the wear is caused by abrasion from boulders and pebbles grinding away the riverbed.

River water sources

All water flowing in rivers comes from snow and rain, but it reaches a river in a variety of ways. Some comes directly from over the ground, but most emerges from underground springs after it has been filtered through the ground. In mountain regions, rivers may emerge from glaciers.

Spring

Like a wet sponge, rock is saturated up to a certain level, called the water table. Where the water table meets the surface, water bubbles out of the ground, forming a spring.

Mountain spring

Meltwater

In cold regions, rainwater is frozen in snow and glaciers for months, years, or even centuries. When conditions warm, the water melts, filling rivers with water.

Glacier with stream

Water on the land

When rain falls on the land, most soaks into the ground or runs off over the surface; the rest evaporates or is taken up by plants. Water that runs off the surface, called overland flow, gathers into rivulets and eventually into streams. When the rain is heavy, the overland flow may flood across the land, forming a sheet of water called sheetwash.

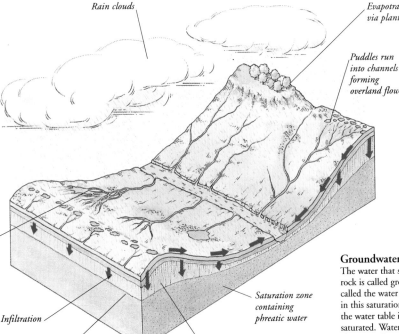

Rain clouds

Evapotranspiration (evaporation via plants) of water from trees

Puddles run into channels forming overland flow

Sheetwash

Infiltration

Water table

Saturation zone containing phreatic water

Aeration zone

Infiltration

When rain falls, most of it soaks into the ground – a process known as infiltration. If the rock is impermeable, water cannot pass through it, so it infiltrates only as far as the soil, which easily becomes saturated.

Throughflow is when water that has seeped into the ground comes to a layer it cannot penetrate and flows through the ground, following rock cracks.

Groundwater

The water that seeps into the spaces and cracks in rock is called groundwater. Up to a certain level, called the water table, rock is always saturated. Water in this saturation zone is called phreatic water. Above the water table is the aeration zone which is rarely saturated. Water here is called vadose water and is always seeping up or down.

Catchment area

Scientists divide the landscape into different areas, according to where the water runs. The area that supplies a river with water is called a catchment area. A drainage basin is a region where several rivers flow into one river.

| FIND OUT MORE | CLOUDS | COASTS | DESERTS | LAKES | RAIN | ROCKS AND MINERALS | SHIPS AND BOATS | SOIL |

ROADS

WITHOUT ROADS, it would be difficult to move people and goods around towns and cities, or from one part of the country to another. There have been roads since ancient times, but modern surfaced roads began to be built in the 18th century to speed up horse-drawn carriages carrying mail and passengers. With the invention of the automobile at the end of the 19th century, road building increased rapidly. Today, more roads are built to keep the ever-increasing numbers of cars moving. Environmentalists want road building to stop and more people to use mass transit instead of their cars.

Ancient roads
Stone paths and roads were built by many ancient civilizations, including the Chinese and the Mesopotamians. In Europe, the Romans developed a huge road network to speed up the movement of troops through their vast empire. By AD 200, people could travel from Spain to the Far East on roads.

Ancient road at Knossos, Crete

Road network
A road network enables people to get from place to place easily and efficiently. It consists of several different types of roads, from urban streets and country lanes to highways and bypasses (which carry traffic around the edge of a city, avoiding the city center). Systems of one-way streets help the traffic flow smoothly during rush hours.

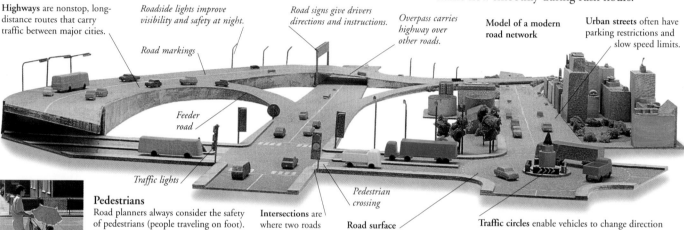

Highways are nonstop, long-distance routes that carry traffic between major cities.

Roadside lights improve visibility and safety at night.

Road signs give drivers directions and instructions.

Overpass carries highway over other roads.

Model of a modern road network

Urban streets often have parking restrictions and slow speed limits.

Road markings

Feeder road

Traffic lights

Pedestrian crossing

Pedestrians
Road planners always consider the safety of pedestrians (people traveling on foot). Sidewalks, pedestrian crossings, and tunnels all help pedestrians move around busy streets. Traffic is banned from some urban centres.

Intersections are where two roads meet: the vehicles on one road have to give way to traffic on the other.

Road surface is Tarmac or concrete over layers of crushed stone and compressed soil.

Traffic circles enable vehicles to change direction without crossing over other lines of traffic.

Road-building machinery in action

Road building
Building a main road is a complex task. It involves creating embankments and cuttings and leveling the site with bulldozers. Then paving machines lay the road surface, and rollers compress the surface to make it smooth. Other machines may be used to build bridges and tunnels.

Traffic
The vehicles that use roads – such as motorcycles, cars, bicycles, buses, trucks, and even wagons and carts – are together known as traffic. Vehicles usually drive on the righthand side of the road, but in some countries, such as the UK, Japan, and Australia, they drive on the left.

Traffic controls
In busy streets, surveillance cameras monitor the flow of traffic. Road markings and signs help control traffic by directing vehicles into the correct lanes, showing how fast they may travel, and warning of hazards ahead. Traffic lights at intersections tell drivers when to stop and go.

Traffic jams
The number of vehicles on the world's roads is rising rapidly. In every major city, traffic jams form in the rush hours as people travel to and from work. Such congestion wastes time and creates pollution as cars stand with their engines running.

Services
At regular intervals on major roads there are service areas where travelers can eat and rest during long trips. Every service area has a garage, so that drivers can buy gas and check the oil in their engines or the air pressure in their tires.

Unsurfaced roads
Tarmac or concrete road surfaces allow rainwater to run off the road quickly, preventing erosion and damage. However, some dirt roads have no such protective surface. They are fine when dry, but during wet weather they become rutted and may even wash away completely.

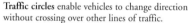

Unsurfaced dirt road, Mbuji-Mayi, Zaïre

| FIND OUT MORE | BRIDGES | CARS AND TRUCKS | CITIES | POLLUTION | ROMAN EMPIRE | TRANSPORT, HISTORY OF | TRAVEL | TUNNELS |

ROBOTS

ROBOTS PLAY AN EVER-INCREASING role in our world. Many people tend to think of robots as the walking, talking, humanlike creations portrayed in science-fiction movies. However, a robot is in fact a mute, automatic machine, with electronic brains programmed to carry out specific tasks. Most robots are used in industry. For example, nuclear scientists use robots to handle radioactive materials. In the 1980s, scientists also began to research the use of robots in routine medical surgery.

Science-fiction robots

The first science-fiction robot was introduced in the play *Rossum's Universal Robots*, written by Czech playwright Karel Capek in 1921. The theme of humanlike robots was developed in the 1926 film *Metropolis*, featuring the divine Maria. More recent moviegoers would probably recognize the comedy duo C3PO and R2D2 from the popular *Star Wars* films. C3PO was an android, while R2D2 was more functionally built – its job was to make repairs on spacecraft.

Humanlike Maria from film *Metropolis*

Uses of robots

Robots are most often used in difficult or dangerous situations to carry out tasks people wish to avoid. Many factories use robots on the production line because they are unaffected by noise, heat, and fumes in the workplace. Robots are also used by security forces in bomb disposal operations and in handling dangerous materials. Space probes are robots used to explore other planets.

Bomb disposal

A mobile robot like this is used by bomb disposal experts to check suspicious objects. It is radio controlled and moves on crawler tracks. It has TV camera eyes and an adjustable arm with a grab attached for gripping.

Industrial robots

The car industry is a major user of robots for welding car components (right), and spraying paint. The robot is programmed to carry out its tasks quickly and accurately.

Robot explorers

Space is a hostile place for humans to explore, but it suits robots involved in exploration. In 1976, American scientists sent two Viking probes to carry out a study of the planet Mars and search for signs of life.

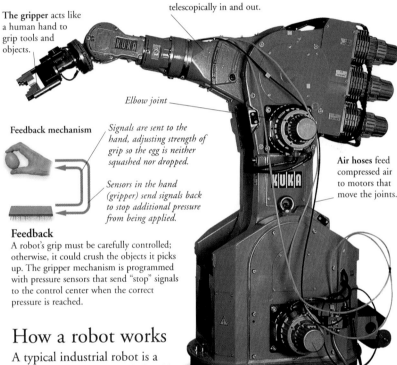

The arm can pivot up and down and also extend telescopically in and out.

The gripper acts like a human hand to grip tools and objects.

Elbow joint

Feedback mechanism

Signals are sent to the hand, adjusting strength of grip so the egg is neither squashed nor dropped.

Sensors in the hand (gripper) send signals back to stop additional pressure from being applied.

Feedback

A robot's grip must be carefully controlled; otherwise, it could crush the objects it picks up. The gripper mechanism is programmed with pressure sensors that send "stop" signals to the control center when the correct pressure is reached.

Air hoses feed compressed air to motors that move the joints.

How a robot works

A typical industrial robot is a one-armed machine with flexible joints equivalent to the human shoulder, elbow, and wrist. It has a gripping mechanism that works as a hand. The robotic arm swivels on its supporting base, and may be moved electrically, or pneumatically, by using compressed air. All movements are controlled by the robot's computer brain.

Swivel joints allow the robot to rotate in a circle.

Isaac Asimov

Science fiction writer Isaac Asimov (1920–96) proposed three laws of robotics to allay fears that one day robots could "take over." These are as follows: a robot must not harm people, or allow them to come to any harm; robots must obey their orders, unless this conflicts with the first law; and a robot must protect itself, unless this conflicts with the other laws.

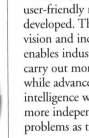

The future

As research into robotics continues, more versatile and user-friendly robots are being developed. Three-dimensional vision and increased sensitivity enables industrial robots to carry out more routine jobs, while advances in artificial intelligence will give robots more independence to solve problems as they arise.

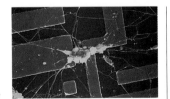

Experimenting with human nerve cells on surface of a silicon chip

Artificial intelligence

The aim of artificial intelligence (AI) is to develop machines that can think and learn, and interact with humans without having to be preprogrammed.

Robots in the home

Robots are good at performing simple, repetitive tasks that people find boring, such as washing and cleaning. However, when analyzed, such household jobs are actually quite complicated. Research is being carried out to make more sophisticated robots that have independent movement and careful co-ordination of "mind," "eyes," and "hands."

FIND OUT MORE   CARS AND TRUCKS   COMPUTERS   FILMS AND FILMMAKING   INFORMATION TECHNOLOGY   SPACE EXPLORATION   TECHNOLOGY

ROCK AND POP

DURING THE 1950S, a new kind of popular music – rock and roll – developed in the United States. It was loud, raucous, and exciting, and soon became popular around the world. Rock, as it is now called, developed from various sources and has influenced most subsequent popular music. Pop music, once just an abbreviated term for all popular music, is now also a recognized musical style. Rock and pop music have been closely linked with the rise of youth culture. They are also big business: record companies make great profits from successful bands.

Blues performer Leadbelly

Early influences
Popular music in the early 20th century included the blues, jazz, and ballads associated with Tin Pan Alley in New York, where music publishers worked. Modern music inherited elements of these styles. The blues influenced rock and roll; the songwriting traditions of Tin Pan Alley continue in many of today's melodic pop songs.

Rock and roll in the 1950s

In the early 1950s, blues musicians in the US discovered the powerful sounds of the new, electrically amplified instruments. These led to the growth of a new kind of music – rhythm-and-blues.

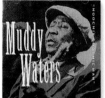
Muddy Waters

Rhythm-and-blues
Unlike the traditional blues, rhythm-and-blues was fast-paced and exciting, stressing the rhythm of the music. Performed by black musicians, it soon became popular dance music. Its greatest performers were Muddy Waters (1915–83), Howlin' Wolf (1910–76), and Chuck Berry (b. 1926).

Rock and roll dance was exuberant.

Rock and roll dancers, 1956

Teenagers
During the 1950s, teenagers on both sides of the Atlantic began to create their own culture. Rock and roll, with its rebellious beats, was their music. Record companies exploited this market, promoting songs about first love, trouble with parents, or tragically early death.

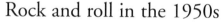
Bill Haley

Rock and roll
When US record companies saw the popularity of rhythm-and-blues, which had begun with black musicians, they brought in white players to sell the music across white America. The music, known as rock and roll, combined rhythm-and-blues with white country music traditions. Bill Haley and His Comets had the first rock and roll hit with *Rock around the Clock*, released in 1955.

Elvis Presley
Elvis Presley (1935–77) was the greatest rock and roll star of all, selling millions of records. His rich, clear voice and moody good looks made the blues harmonies of his music acceptable to white American audiences. He starred in many musical films.

Sounds of the 1960s

During the 1960s, many young people identified with music that expressed their political opinions, as well as their musical tastes. In the US, for example, some songs protested against the Vietnam War.

Beatles fans, 1964

Soul music
Soul music is a development of rhythm-and-blues, which grew during the 1960s. Performed mainly by black musicians, it combines the passion of gospel music with a strong beat. Great soul artists include Aretha Franklin (b.1942).

Tamla Motown
The influential US record company Tamla Motown scored worldwide success during the 1960s and 1970s by promoting black rhythm-and-blues and soul music. Performers on the label included The Supremes, Stevie Wonder (b.1950), and Ray Charles (b.1930).

The Beatles
During the 1960s, rock and roll became known as rock. British bands The Beatles and The Rolling Stones became famous around the world with earthy music that brought an exciting new sound to the rock scene. The Beatles especially attracted hysterical devotion from their young fans.

Reggae
Reggae music developed in Jamaica during the 1960s. It combines elements of US soul with Jamaican and African folk music. It is generally played with an emphasis on the second and fourth beats of the bar, at a relaxed pace. It is closely linked with the Rastafarian religion.

Jamaican musician Bob Marley (1945–1981) was a leading reggae artist. While making political protests with his lyrics, he helped make reggae popular around the world.

Diana Ross (b.1944), later a successful solo star

The Supremes: from 1964 to 1969, this all-girl group had 16 top ten hit records in the US.

Bob Dylan, influential singer and songwriter from the 1960s on.

Folk rock
Rock and folk borrowed heavily from each other in the 1960s. The protest songs of Bob Dylan (b.1941) and Joan Baez (b.1941) expressed the antiwar feelings of many young people.

R

Disco

In the 1970s disco, a dance music with a thumping beat, became the major force in pop music. It was played on records and tapes, rather than by live performers, in crowded nightclubs called discotheques. Leading disco artists included the British group The Bee Gees and US singer Donna Summer (b.1948).

Saturday Night Fever, a movie about the disco lifestyle made in 1977, featured a score by The Bee Gees.

Trends of the 1970s

Concerts during the 1970s were elaborate events, involving large-scale props and light shows. "Glam rock" took this to its limits, with outlandish stage shows by performers such as the British band T-Rex. Fashions reflected musicians' styles; people wore flared pants and grew their hair long. The main movements of the 1970s, however, were disco, funk, and punk.

James Brown

Punks

Lyrics in funk music reflected the strengthening black civil rights movement in America.

Funk

In the late 1960s and early 1970s, the US singer James Brown (b.1933) took soul music in a new, aggressively rhythmic direction. The lyrics of the new style, which was called funk, made strong social comments. Other influential funk innovators included the US group Sly and the Family Stone.

Punk

In 1976, punk music appeared in Britain with The Sex Pistols. Punk was loud and distorted: musicians deliberately played their instruments badly, and their lyrics were offensive. Punks wore ripped, dirty clothes to show that they rejected conventional social attitudes.

1980s and on

Pop music in the 1980s was dominated by catchy melodies, simple harmonies, and unchallenging lyrics. Increasingly since the 1980s, bands have used electronically produced sounds in their music; new styles, such as rap, house, and techno, have emerged. In rap, performers speak over music in rapid rhymes, often with a social comment. In house and techno, artists use samples of sounds, beats, and melodies from other records to create a new dance music.

New technology

Electronic samplers, drum machines, and synthesizers made it possible for dance musicians to isolate and change any tone, beat, or noise, including vocals, from other records, as well as to create their own artificial and unusual sounds, and allowed them to structure their music in surprising new ways.

The band De La Soul mixes other musicians' work in their recordings.

Vinyl record

Electronic music

Much of today's music is made by electronic instruments. When the electronic drum pad, above, is hit with a stick, it produces an electric sound signal that gives an electronic drum sound.

Vinyl records and CDs

During the 1980s, sales of compact discs (CDs) overtook sales of vinyl records, because CDs are longer-lasting, easier to keep in good condition, and give a clearer, purer sound.

With new computer technology, a musician can arrange many different tracks to achieve an original sound.

Mixing desk, to combine different musical tracks

Music industry

Rock and pop music provides a multi-million dollar global market. Performers can make a fortune with just a few chart-topping hits. Music is sold on compact disc, cassette, vinyl, and video. Organizing the marketing and sales of these products is complex and costly. A few major companies dominate the music industry.

Bjork, an Icelandic singer with the One Little Indian label.

Record companies

When a performer has a contract with a record company, the company will promote his or her music, obtain radio airtime, and distribute the records around the world, as well as organize tours and provide recording studios and equipment.

Videos

Videos, short, creative films promoting a record, became widespread in the 1980s. Videos, released at the same time as the song, reach huge television audiences. Good video promotion vastly increases the sales of music.

Madonna

By the late 1990s, the US pop singer and songwriter Madonna Ciccone (b.1958) was the biggest-selling female recording artist in the world. She sustained her popularity by constantly developing her image and musical style, and with spectacular, controversial tours.

Concerts

For most bands, live performances are a central part of their music. Famous bands take over vast stadiums to play to tens of thousands of fans. The massive Live Aid concert (1985), to help African famine relief, featured many of the best-known singers and bands in the world.

FIND OUT **MORE**   BEATLES, THE   CLOTHES AND FASHION   DANCE   JAZZ   MUSIC   MUSICAL INSTRUMENTS   ORCHESTRAS   SOUND   SOUND RECORDING

ROCKETS

GRAVITY KEEPS EARTH'S inhabitants on the planet's surface. A powerful rocket is needed to escape this gravity and to take astronauts, satellites, probes, and other equipment into space. The first rockets were made about a thousand years ago in China, but the first to reach space was the German V2 which, in 1942, achieved a height of 100 miles (160 km). There are two main types of rockets. Tall, thin, pencil-shaped ones are used only once. The space shuttle returns to Earth to be used again. Both are launched pointing up at space and discard their fuel tanks, which fall back to Earth.

Escape velocity

Earth's gravity pulls on a rocket at the launch pad and keeps it on the ground. The rocket needs to move very fast to get away from this pull. When the rocket reaches a velocity of 25,000 mph (40,000 kmh), it can escape the effects of Earth's gravity and enter space. If it fails to reach this velocity, it will be pulled back to Earth.

Rocket's thrust

Earth's gravity

Rocket power

The payload of astronauts or equipment takes up only a small part of the rocket. Most of it contains the fuel needed to launch the rocket into space. Most rockets use liquid fuel with solid fuel for some of the stages.

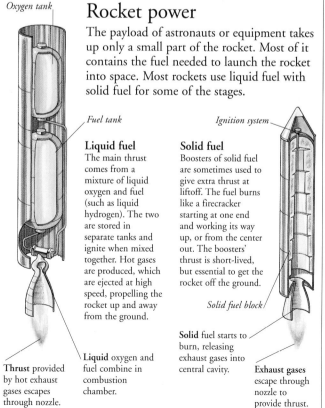

Oxygen tank

Fuel tank

Ignition system

Liquid fuel
The main thrust comes from a mixture of liquid oxygen and fuel (such as liquid hydrogen). The two are stored in separate tanks and ignite when mixed together. Hot gases are produced, which are ejected at high speed, propelling the rocket up and away from the ground.

Solid fuel
Boosters of solid fuel are sometimes used to give extra thrust at liftoff. The fuel burns like a firecracker starting at one end and working its way up, or from the center out. The boosters' thrust is short-lived, but essential to get the rocket off the ground.

Solid fuel block

Thrust provided by hot exhaust gases escapes through nozzle.

Liquid oxygen and fuel combine in combustion chamber.

Solid fuel starts to burn, releasing exhaust gases into central cavity.

Exhaust gases escape through nozzle to provide thrust.

Ariane-5

The European Space Agency (ESA) launches satellites and probes into space with the Ariane series of rockets. The first was launched in 1979: since then, about 90 Arianes have been launched from the Guiana Space Center in Kourou, South America. The latest and most powerful in the series is *Ariane-5*, designed to carry the new generation of heavy satellites into space and also to launch spacecraft with crew aboard. If *Ariane-5* carries crew, Europe will join the Americans and Russians in having rockets that can launch astronauts.

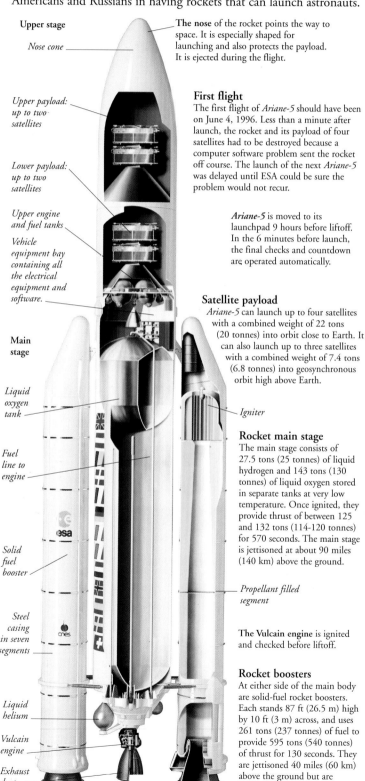

Upper stage
Nose cone

Upper payload: up to two satellites

Lower payload: up to two satellites

Upper engine and fuel tanks

Vehicle equipment bay containing all the electrical equipment and software.

Main stage

Liquid oxygen tank

Fuel line to engine

Solid fuel booster

Steel casing in seven segments

Liquid helium

Vulcain engine

Exhaust duct

The nose of the rocket points the way to space. It is especially shaped for launching and also protects the payload. It is ejected during the flight.

First flight
The first flight of *Ariane-5* should have been on June 4, 1996. Less than a minute after launch, the rocket and its payload of four satellites had to be destroyed because a computer software problem sent the rocket off course. The launch of the next *Ariane-5* was delayed until ESA could be sure the problem would not recur.

Ariane-5 is moved to its launchpad 9 hours before liftoff. In the 6 minutes before launch, the final checks and countdown are operated automatically.

Satellite payload
Ariane-5 can launch up to four satellites with a combined weight of 22 tons (20 tonnes) into orbit close to Earth. It can also launch up to three satellites with a combined weight of 7.4 tons (6.8 tonnes) into geosynchronous orbit high above Earth.

Igniter

Rocket main stage
The main stage consists of 27.5 tons (25 tonnes) of liquid hydrogen and 143 tons (130 tonnes) of liquid oxygen stored in separate tanks at very low temperature. Once ignited, they provide thrust of between 125 and 132 tons (114-120 tonnes) for 570 seconds. The main stage is jettisoned at about 90 miles (140 km) above the ground.

Propellant filled segment

The Vulcain engine is ignited and checked before liftoff.

Rocket boosters
At either side of the main body are solid-fuel rocket boosters. Each stands 87 ft (26.5 m) high by 10 ft (3 m) across, and uses 261 tons (237 tonnes) of fuel to provide 595 tons (540 tonnes) of thrust for 130 seconds. They are jettisoned 40 miles (60 km) above the ground but are recovered, and used again.

R

Launch

The countdown for a rocket launch begins long before the engines are ignited. The rocket undergoes a final thorough testing in the hours before launch. Once everything is ready, the engines are ignited. The rocket leaves the ground when the engines have produced enough thrust, and it gathers speed as it moves skyward. The next few minutes are vital. The rocket has to reach escape velocity. Only when the rocket has reached its target orbit can the launch be regarded as successful.

Rocket stages

A rocket can be made of a varying number of stages. Each stage is like a separate rocket with its own fuel and engine. As a rocket moves away from the ground, it rapidly consumes fuel. As the fuel in one stage is used up, its tank is discarded and the fuel in the next stage ignites, carrying the lighter and lighter rocket on its course. The final stage takes the payload to its orbit. Once the satellite or space probe is launched, the rocket's job is over.

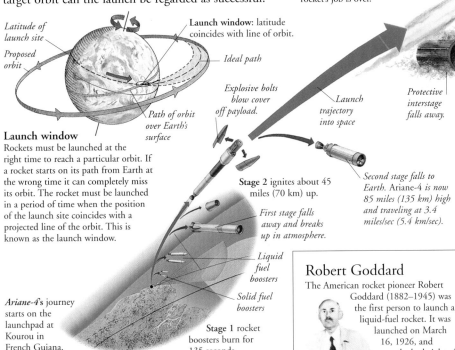

Latitude of launch site

Proposed orbit

Launch window: latitude coincides with line of orbit.

Ideal path

Path of orbit over Earth's surface

Explosive bolts blow cover off payload.

Launch trajectory into space

Protective interstage falls away.

Payload

Cylinder contains a second satellite to be launched later.

Satellite ready to be released.

Stage 3 engines ignite and burn for about 12 minutes until *Ariane-4* reaches target orbit.

Stage 2 ignites about 45 miles (70 km) up.

Second stage falls to Earth. Ariane-4 is now 85 miles (135 km) high and traveling at 3.4 miles/sec (5.4 km/sec).

First stage falls away and breaks up in atmosphere.

Liquid fuel boosters

Solid fuel boosters

Stage 1 rocket boosters burn for 135 seconds.

Launch window

Rockets must be launched at the right time to reach a particular orbit. If a rocket starts on its path from Earth at the wrong time it can completely miss its orbit. The rocket must be launched in a period of time when the position of the launch site coincides with a projected line of the orbit. This is known as the launch window.

Ariane-4's journey starts on the launchpad at Kourou in French Guiana.

Space shuttle

Since the early 1980s, the US has used a reusable launcher to carry astronauts and equipment into space. It is called the space transportation system, or space shuttle. It has three main parts: the orbiter space plane, two large solid-fuel rocket boosters, and a liquid-fuel tank. The boosters are discarded and fall to Earth where they are collected and used again. The launched orbiter travels in orbit around Earth and returns to Earth by landing on a runway like a plane.

Robert Goddard

The American rocket pioneer Robert Goddard (1882–1945) was the first person to launch a liquid-fuel rocket. It was launched on March 16, 1926, and reached a height of 41 ft (12.5 m). The flight lasted 2.5 seconds.

Ground control

A rocket launch is controlled from Earth. A ground control center monitors the spacecraft and any equipment launched until the mission is complete. Radio signals from the spacecraft let the control center know if everything is on track. Tracking stations around the world relay the messages to the center.

Control center

The Mission Control Center in Houston monitors all American space shuttle missions. The mission is supported from the moment of rocket ignition until the shuttle returns to Earth.

Launchpad

Some countries have more than one launch site. Other countries have joined together to share a site. By the late 1990s, nine nations had launched rockets into space from their own launch sites. The launch sites are scattered around the globe. As the Earth spins in a counterclockwise direction, it can give an extra push to a rocket being launched. Many sites are close to the Equator, where this effect is greatest.

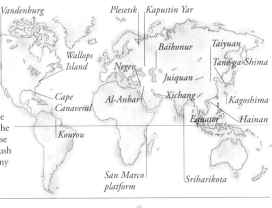

Vandenburg

Wallops Island

Negev

Cape Canaveral

Kourou

San Marco platform

Plesetsk | *Kapustin Yar*

Baikonur

Al-Anbar

Juiquan

Xichang

Taiyuan

Tane-ga-Shima

Kagoshima

Equator

Hainan

Sriharikota

Timeline

1903 Russian schoolmaster, Konstantin Tsiolkovsky, proposes a liquid-fuel rocket for space.

1926 Robert Goddard launches a liquid-fuel rocket.

1942 *V2* is launched, the first mass-produced long-range rocket.

V2 Rocket

1961 Soviet *Vostok* rocket carries first person into space.

Vostok

1961 *Mercury 3* launches the first American, Alan Shepard, into space.

1968 *Apollo 7* is launched – first time the US *Saturn V* carries a crew.

1970 Japan launches a satellite and becomes the fourth nation with a space rocket.

1981 First reusable spacecraft, the American space shuttle, is launched.

1988 World's most powerful rocket, *Energia*, carries the first Soviet space shuttle – into Earth orbit.

1999 First shuttle reaches International Space Station.

US space shuttle

FIND OUT MORE | ASTRONAUTS | ATMOSPHERE | FORCE AND MOTION | GRAVITY | MOON | NEWTON, SIR ISAAC | PLANETS | SATELLITES | SPACE EXPLORATION

ROCKS AND MINERALS

ALTHOUGH IT IS OFTEN HIDDEN under vegetation, soil, and water, every inch of the Earth's surface is made up of rock. Rocks have formed throughout the Earth's history – the oldest rocks date back 3.9 billion years, almost to the beginning of the Earth – and new rocks are still forming. Rocks come in many sizes, shapes, and colors, but they all have a grainy texture because they are made from crystals of naturally occurring chemicals called minerals. The appearance and properties of each type of rock depend on the minerals it contains.

Formation of rocks

Igneous rocks form as magma – molten rock from the Earth's interior – cools and solidifies. Sedimentary rocks form when thin layers of debris on the seabed are compressed over millions of years. Metamorphic rocks form when old rock is crushed by the movement of the Earth's crust or seared by the heat of magma.

Schist

Metamorphic rocks
A metamorphic rock, such as schist, forms when heat and pressure deep below ground alter the mineral content of an existing rock. This change occurs while the rock is still in its solid state.

Gabbro

Igneous rocks
There are two main kinds of igneous rocks. Intrusive igneous rocks, such as gabbro, form when magma cools under the Earth's surface. Extrusive igneous rocks, such as obsidian, form from magma thrown out of erupting volcanoes in the form of lava.

The rock cycle

Eroded rock particles are carried by wind and deposited to form sand dunes.

Waterfall erodes (wears away) rock of mountainside.

Glacier erodes rocks and carries rock particles to river.

Magma emerges as lava flows, which solidify to form igneous rock.

Volcano

Rising magma

River erodes valley floor, carrying rock particles downstream to ocean.

Light rock particles settle on ocean floor as sediment.

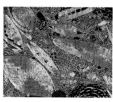

Sandstone

Sedimentary rocks
Most sedimentary rocks, including sandstone, are clastic – that is, made from fragments of eroded rock washed into the sea. Limestone and some other sedimentary rocks are biogenic, which means they are made largely from plant and animal remains.

Compressed sediment layers become cemented together to form sedimentary rock.

Extreme pressure crushes and folds sedimentary rock into new metamorphic rock.

Intense heat of magma transforms the surrounding rock into metamorphic rock.

Mohs' scale of hardness
On this scale, a mineral scratches any mineral with a lower rating (everyday equivalents in brackets).

1 Talc: very soft

2 Gypsum (fingernail)

3 Calcite (bronze coin)

4 Fluorite (iron nail)

5 Apatite (glass)

6 Feldspar (penknife)

7 Quartz (steel knife)

8 Topaz (sandpaper)

9 Corundum

10 Diamond: very hard

Minerals

Some rocks are made of just one mineral; others are a combination of several different minerals, perhaps as many as a dozen. About 98 percent of the rocks in the Earth's crust are made of silicate minerals, which contain the elements oxygen and silica. Geologists classify minerals into two main groups: silicates and nonsilicates.

Magnified rock surface with tiny mineral crystals

Identifying minerals
A mineral can be identified by its color, cleavage and fracture (the way it breaks), luster (how it reflects light), streak (the color of the mark it leaves on a white tile), density, hardness, and how it reacts with acids. Mohs' scale compares the hardness of different minerals.

Silicates
There are more than 500 different types of silicate, including garnet, mica, feldspar, olivine, and the gem beryl. Silicates tend to be hard, transparent or translucent, and insoluble in acids.

Beryl

Garnet

Nonsilicates
The largest group of nonsilicates are the sulfides. Many important metal ores are sulfides, such as galena (lead ore), sphalerite (zinc ore), and pyrite (iron ore). Other key nonsilicate groups include carbonates, oxides, and sulphates.

Charles Lyell
The Scottish geologist Charles Lyell (1797–1875) is known as the founder of modern geology. His book *Principles of Geology*, published in 1830, led to the general acceptance of the idea that the Earth is very old and is constantly being shaped by gradual, everyday processes.

FIND OUT MORE CAVES CRYSTALS AND GEMS EARTH EARTHQUAKES EARTH SCIENCES FOSSILS MOUNTAINS AND VALLEYS VOLCANOES

Rocks

Igneous rocks

Basalt – a dark, extrusive, fine-grained rock – forms from quick-cooling lava.

Andesite is a fine-grained extrusive rock rich in silicon.

Tuff is a rock formed from fragments of hardened volcanic ash.

Rhyolite, fine-grained and intrusive, contains mainly quartz and feldspar.

Diorite is a light-colored, coarse-grained, intrusive rock.

Dolerite has medium-size grains and a mottled look.

Gabbro is an intrusive rock that forms deep underground.

Granite is intrusive and made of quartz, feldspar, and mica.

Syenite may resemble granite, but contains very little quartz.

Trachyte is extrusive, fine-grained, and rich in feldspar.

Peridotite is heavy, dark, intrusive, and coarse.

Sedimentary rocks

Siltstone is a smooth rock with very fine, angular grains.

Sandstone forms when grains of sand become cemented together.

Clay is fine-grained and may become malleable when wet.

Tufa forms when cool, calcite-rich springs evaporate.

Conglomerate contains rounded beach pebbles and other small stones.

Graywacke is a medium-grained rock that forms from ocean sediments.

Shale is a rock that forms from hardened particles of clay.

Limestone's main ingredient is calcite (calcium carbonate).

Chalk is a very pure, white limestone with a powdery texture.

Breccia is composed of fragments weathered and eroded from other rocks.

Arkose usually forms from granite fragments.

Gypsum forms from sediments left behind when saltwater evaporates.

Mudstone is made up of hardened grains of mud.

Carboniferous limestone formed around 360 million years ago.

Metamorphic rocks

Marble is metamorophosed (transformed) limestone that occurs in a variety of colors.

Hornfels forms when hot lava recrystallizes the minerals in mudstone or shale.

Slate forms when mudstone or shale is crushed and baked during mountain building.

Schist forms in a similar way to slate, but at much higher temperatures.

Gneiss has coarser grains than schist; its minerals often separate into distinct bands.

Metaquartzite forms from loose-grained quartz-rich sandstone.

ROMAN EMPIRE

ONE OF THE GREATEST EMPIRES that ever existed, the Roman Empire in its heyday stretched over most of the known world. According to legend, the city of Rome was ruled by kings until 510 BC, when it became a republic. In 27 BC, the first of its emperors, Augustus, took over the republic and created an empire. Emperors ruled for the next 500 years. For much of this period, the empire was peaceful and prosperous, with one legal system, one language, remarkable structures and buildings, and a strong army. The western half of the empire, including its capital, Rome, fell to the barbarians in 476. The eastern half of the empire survived as the Byzantine Empire until 1453.

Expansion
The Roman Empire peaked in the reign of Emperor Trajan (AD 98–117), when it stretched from Asia Minor to Portugal, and from North Africa to Scotland.

Emperors
All rulers chose relatives to succeed them until 98 AD when Emperor Nerva chose his successor on ability. Eventually, after many succession problems, the eastern and western sections of the empire split. The last ruler of a unified empire was Theodosius (379–395).

Emperor Theodosius

Roman lands

After a military conquest, the Romans organized the conquered peoples into provinces. Soldiers and civilians built a "mother city" and then Romanized the surrounding area, usually by example rather than by force. The Romans encouraged a civilized way of life and offered people Roman citizenship. A network of paved roads connected every province to Rome.

Top level showing soldiers from Dacia (modern Romania)

Roman legionaries attacking Dacians

Military camp

Roman standard

Roman guard

Emperor Trajan addressing his troops

Dacian campaign, Trajan's Column

Pax Romana
The 1st and 2nd centuries were the time of a Pax Romana (Roman peace), a system where each province governed itself but was subject to taxation and military control from Rome. The system, which stretched from Persia to North Africa, made much of Europe stable and meant that travel and trade were safe.

The family of Augustus, Altar of Peace, Rome

Divide and rule
Any revolts against Roman rule, such as the Palestine uprising (66–73 AD), were mercilessly crushed. Different tribes rarely helped each other during rebellions. This lack of unity was encouraged by the Romans and always aided their victory.

Army

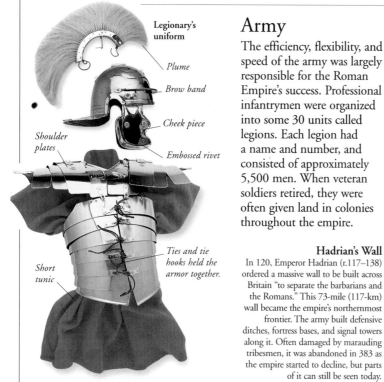

The efficiency, flexibility, and speed of the army was largely responsible for the Roman Empire's success. Professional infantrymen were organized into some 30 units called legions. Each legion had a name and number, and consisted of approximately 5,500 men. When veteran soldiers retired, they were often given land in colonies throughout the empire.

Legionary's uniform

Plume

Brow band

Cheek piece

Embossed rivet

Shoulder plates

Short tunic

Ties and tie hooks held the armor together.

Roman law

Effective and just, Roman law forms the basis of many of today's western codes of law. The first collection of Roman laws was the Twelve Tables of c.450 BC, and the last was Emperor Justinian's *Codex Constitutionum* in 529 AD.

The Senate
Rome's ruling council was the Senate. It consisted of rich landowners (patricians). The lower classes (plebeians) had their own representatives called tribunes. The Senate advised the emperor, who controlled the government. The law was upheld by magistrates, all of whom came from the Senate. In public, magistrates were accompanied by servants carrying a symbol of authority – the *fasces*, an ax in a bundle of rods.

A lictor, or magistrate's servant, carrying the *fasces*.

Hadrian's Wall
In 120, Emperor Hadrian (r.117–138) ordered a massive wall to be built across Britain "to separate the barbarians and the Romans." This 73-mile (117-km) wall became the empire's northernmost frontier. The army built defensive ditches, fortress bases, and signal towers along it. Often damaged by marauding tribesmen, it was abandoned in 383 as the empire started to decline, but parts of it can still be seen today.

Claudius

Claudius (r.41–54 AD) was an able ruler who added Britain and parts of North Africa to the empire. However, there was a lot of murder, madness, and betrayal in his family, and he was poisoned by his fourth wife, Agrippina.

R

Building

The Romans excelled at ambitious public buildings such as the Colosseum, and were also ingenious town planners. Towns were usually divided by straight streets into a series of regular blocks – a grid. Within the grid were luxurious villas, grand tombs, and triumphal arches to commemorate the brave.

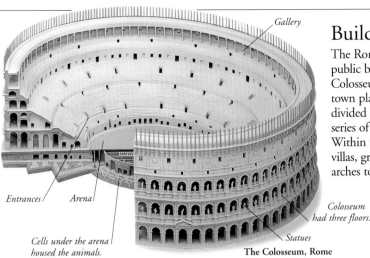

Gallery

Entrances   Arena

Cells under the arena housed the animals.

Colosseum had three floors.

Statues

The Colosseum, Rome

Bathhouses
Public bathhouses in most towns had hot and cold pools where citizens could wash – and meet friends at the same time. Roman engineers also supplied water to wealthy private homes using lead, wood, or pottery pipes.

Pont du Gard
Roman engineers were at their best when they needed to build a practical structure. This aqueduct (canal-carrying bridge) was a superb system that carried fresh water to Nîmes, France, for 500 years.

Gods

The Romans inherited many of their gods from the earlier Greek family of gods. Jupiter, Juno, and Mercury were Roman versions of the Greek gods Zeus, Hera, and Hermes. Many of the older beliefs lived on, even after Christianity became the official religion of the empire. One favorite was Castor, known as the horse tamer, a great warrior who symbolized loyalty. At home, people kept shrines to household spirits, who were known as *lares*.

Castor and Pollux, twin brothers, were favorites with soldiers because they were believed to help the Romans in battle.

Castor, the horse tamer

God-emperor Augustus
The first Roman emperor, Augustus (r.27 BC–14 AD), was deified (declared a god) after his death. After this, the more popular emperors were always deified, and Romans built temples to honor them. People worshiped the emperors as gods – those who refused to do so, such as the Jews and Christians, were persecuted.

Latin

Latin, the language of the Romans, was spoken in the western part of the empire (while Greek was spoken in the east). Latin forms the basis of many modern European languages, for example, Italian, French, and Spanish. Classic Latin literature, such as Cicero's speeches and Virgil's poetry, is still taught and enjoyed today.

The "X" shows that this silver coin was worth 10 copper coins.

Engraved metal plaque

Roman capitals

Roman numerals
The numerals I, II, III, IV, V, VI, VII, VIII, IX, and X were used in Europe for centuries. Roman numerals were eventually replaced by Arabic numerals 1, 2, 3, 4, 5, 6, 7, 8, 9, and 10.

Silver denarius

Constantine the Great
Constantine (c.280–337) succeeded his father, Constantius I, as Emperor of the West in 306. By 324, he reunited the Roman Empire and made himself sole ruler. He built a new capital at Byzantium on the Bosporus and named it Constantinople. In 313, his Edict of Milan stopped the persecution of Christians, and Christianity then became the empire's official religion.

Bronze gladiator

Bust of Hercules

Twist key to lock face guard.

Gladiator's bronze helmet

Games
Roman citizens expected lavish entertainments. Crowds of up to 50,000 watched combat sports in Rome's great amphitheater, the Colosseum, built in 72–80 AD. In arenas all over the empire, gladiators were trained to fight wild animals – or each other – to provide a compelling and bloody spectacle. If they were very lucky, gladiators occasionally survived to win their freedom.

Timeline

753 BC Traditional founding of Rome by Romulus, the first king, and his twin Remus.

509 BC Romans drive Etruscans from Rome; Republic founded.

27 BC Augustus becomes the first emperor.

Hobnailed military sandals

AD 43 Claudius begins Roman invasion of Britain.

66 Palestinian uprising.

98–117 Trajan extends Roman citizenship in his reign.

212 All non-slaves in empire granted Roman citizenship.

285 Diocletian reorganizes empire into two halves.

330 Constantine moves the empire's capital to Constantinople.

395 After a century of compromise, the empire splits permanently into eastern and western sections.

Roman glassware

404 Jerome completes a Latin version of Christian Bible .

410 Visigoths sack Rome.

476 Western Roman empire falls; eastern empire continues.

1453 Byzantine (eastern) Empire falls to Ottoman Turks.

 FIND OUT MORE ARMS AND ARMOR   ARCHITECTURE   BARBARIANS   BYZANTINE EMPIRE   CAESAR, JULIUS   ETRUSCANS   GOVERNMENTS   GODS AND GODDESSES   ITALY, HISTORY OF   SCULPTURE

Roman Empire

Everyday objects

Weighing scales

Bronze inkpot

Pottery inkpot

Faïence inkpot

Reed

Bronze

Pens

Glass table jug

Sewing needles

Sacrifice to Athena

Baking tin

Bronze toga figure

Terra-cotta cloak

Lace-up boot scent bottle

Lekane (bowl)

Bronze food strainer

Cheese grater

Bone pin

Medical objects

Folding knife

Bone saw

Probe

Spatula

Medical instruments

Sports and entertainment

Bronze sistrum, or rattle

Marble

Bone

Crystal

Agate

Dice

Greenstone

Bronze flutes

Glass marbles

Bronze cymbals

Military objects

Slingshot pellets

Catapult bolts

Ivory sword hilt

Religious objects

Winged goddess of victory

Sacrifice to Hermes

Bronze libation bowl

Bronze sacrificial jug

Terra-cotta tablet showing the sacrifice of a bull

Crater (pot) showing a sacrifice

Sacrificial altar knife

ROMANIA, UKRAINE AND MOLDOVA

ROMANIA, UKRAINE, AND MOLDOVA lie in Eastern Europe, southwest of the Russian Federation. Ukraine and Moldova were both members of the former Soviet Union; Romania, which was also communist, remained independent but was closely allied to the Soviet Union. Since the end of communist rule in Romania in 1989, and the breakup of the Soviet Union in 1991, all three countries have struggled to modernize their industries and compete on the world market.

Steppes
The steppes are vast, undulating, grassy plains that extend over much of Ukraine and Moldova. Because of their rich, fertile soils, more than half of the area is devoted to growing barley, corn, oats, and wheat. The rest is used mainly as pasture.

Carpathians
The Carpathian Mountains form a huge arc from northwest to southwest Romania, enclosing the plateau of Transylvania. The highest peak is Moldoveanu at 8,343 ft (2,543 m). Bears and wolves roam through the forests that cover the slopes. The Carpathians are rich in minerals.

Orthodox religion
Most people in the region are Christians and members of the Eastern Orthodox Church, but each country has its own variation. In this way, the different ethnic groups can maintain their own identities.

Eastern Orthodox memorial ceremony in Romania

Physical features
Most of Ukraine consists of a broad grassy plain. Bordered in the south by the Danube River, Romania is mountainous with a central plateau. Moldova has gentle hills and valleys.

Regional climate
Romania has a continental climate, but winters can be bitterly cold. Ukraine and Moldova have a similar climate, with warm summers and mild winters. Ukraine's Crimea has mild winters and hot summers.

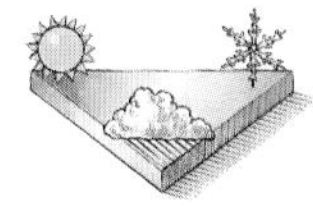

101°F (22°C)   25°F (-4°C)

24 in (597 mm)

Crimea
The Crimea is a peninsula in Ukraine that juts into the Black Sea. Many of its resorts, once popular with communist officials, now cater to western holidaymakers, especially Germans. Local vineyards produce quality wines.

Romania

Long dominated by the Ottoman, Russian, and Hapsburg Empires, Romania became an independent country in 1878. In 1947, it became a communist dictatorship allied to the Soviet Union, and from 1965 was damaged by the harsh rule of Nicolae Ceauçescu. Since 1989, when Ceauçescu was executed, Romania has been struggling to modernize and rebuild its economy.

Bucharest
Home to more than two million people, Bucharest has been Romania's capital since 1861. Modeled on Paris, it is the country's cultural and commercial center, as well as the seat of government. Many people live in huge apartment blocks.

Palace of the People

People
Nearly 90 percent of the people are ethnic Romanians. The rest of the population is made up of Hungarians and Gypsies, also called Romanies, who make up nearly two percent. Most Gypsies no longer have a traveling lifestyle, but live close to towns. Today, Romania's population is decreasing, as many people emigrate in search of work.

Young Gypsy girls

Bran Castle, home of Vlad the Impaler

Transylvania
The rich folklore of the Transylvanian plateau attracts tourists. The story of the bloodsucking Count Dracula is based on a real-life villain, Prince Vlad the Impaler, whose cruelties in the 1400s made his name feared.

ROMANIA FACTS

CAPITAL CITY	Bucharest
AREA	91,700 sq miles (237,500 sq km)
POPULATION	22,300,000
DENSITY	251 per sq mile (97 per sq km)
MAIN LANGUAGE	Romanian
MAJOR RELIGION	Christian
CURRENCY	Leu
LIFE EXPECTANCY	70 years
PEOPLE PER DOCTOR	556
GOVERNMENT	Multiparty democracy
ADULT LITERACY	98%

Ukraine

Ukraine is the second largest country in Europe. It broke away from the Soviet Union in 1991. About 70 percent of the people are Ukrainians and 20 percent are Russian, living mostly in the east. Ukrainian nationalist feelings have created longstanding tension between the two groups. Farming employs 24 percent of the workforce.

Borscht with sour cream

Piroshki

Black bread

St. Georges Church by the Dnieper River

Kiev
Ukraine's capital, Kiev, lies at the meeting point of the Dnieper and Desna Rivers. About a thousand years ago, the Orthodox faith spread from here through Eastern Europe. With beautiful parks and churches, Kiev is a center for culture, industry, and commerce.

Food
Borscht is a traditional Ukrainian soup made from meat stock and beets. It is served with sour cream and *piroshki*, savory patties. Other popular dishes are *varenniki*, dough filled with meat, cheese, or fruit, and *holubtsi*, stuffed cabbage rolls. Food is often accompanied by Crimean wines.

UKRAINE FACTS

CAPITAL CITY	Kiev
AREA	223,090 sq miles (603,700 sq km)
POPULATION	50,500,000
DENSITY	217 per sq mile (84 per sq km)
MAIN LANGUAGES	Ukrainian, Russian
MAJOR RELIGION	Christian
CURRENCY	Hryvna
LIFE EXPECTANCY	68 years
PEOPLE PER DOCTOR	222
GOVERNMENT	Multiparty democracy
ADULT LITERACY	99%

Industry
The Donets'k Basin in eastern Ukraine is rich in coal, iron ore, manganese, zinc, and mercury. Ukraine holds five percent of global mineral reserves. Its factories produce ships, machinery, aircraft, cars, chemicals, processed foods, and consumer goods.

Moldova

Once a part of Romania, in 1940, the small, rural country of Moldova became a Soviet state. It is the most densely populated of the former Soviet republics, and tension exists between the ethnic Moldovan majority and the Ukrainians and Russians who want independence. Food- and leather processing and farming are the main industries.

Wine
Moldova's warm climate is suited to growing vines. The country produces some excellent wines that are stored in large underground vaults burrowed into rocky hillsides. Here the temperature remains cool and constant.

MOLDOVA FACTS

CAPITAL CITY	Chisinau
AREA	13,000 sq miles (33,700 sq km)
POPULATION	4,350,000
MAIN LANGUAGE	Romanian
MAJOR RELIGION	Christian
CURRENCY	Leu

Farming
More than half of Moldova's population lives in the country in small, rural communities. About 65 percent of the land is used to grow grain, fruit, tobacco, beets, and grapes. Pigs, cattle, and sheep are raised for meat.

FIND OUT MORE   CHRISTIANITY   EMPIRES   EUROPE, HISTORY OF   FARMING   GOVERNMENTS AND POLITICS   GRASSLAND WILDLIFE   ROCKS AND MINERALS   RUSSIA, HISTORY OF   SOVIET UNION   TRADE AND INDUSTRY

RUSSIAN FEDERATION AND KAZAKHSTAN

Siberia
Stretching from the Urals to the Pacific Ocean, Siberia covers more than 4,900,000 sq miles (12,800,000 sq km). It contains vast stretches of forest and has around a million lakes, 53,000 rivers, and rich natural resources.

STRETCHING HALFWAY ACROSS the globe and straddling the continents of Europe and Asia, the Russian Federation, usually known as Russia, is the world's largest country. Most people live in the more fertile and industrialized European third of the country to the west of the Ural Mountains. East of the Urals is Asian Russia, called Siberia, which has a harsh climate and is sparsely populated. Kazakhstan, to the southwest of Russia, is a smaller country in Asia. Both countries were part of the former Soviet Union, a world superpower in which Russia played a dominant role.

Women
More than 50 percent of all Russian workers are women. Many do physical jobs, such as working on construction sites or driving heavy vehicles, but increasing numbers of women now train in professions such as medicine and teaching. Working women benefit from good health- and childcare provisions.

Russian woman construction worker, Moscow

Physical features
From north to south, the region is made up of bleak, frozen tundra, the vast forests of the taiga, grassy steppes, and cold desert. Mountains cover much of eastern Russia.

102°F (39°C)   -90°F (-68°C)
66°F (19°C)   16°F (-9°C)
22 in (575 mm)

Climate
Russia has warm summers, bitterly cold winters, and short springs and autumns, with low rainfall. Temperatures in northern Siberia may drop as low as -90°F (-68°C).

Volga River
At 2,190 miles (3,530 km), the Volga is European Russia's longest river. From Moscow to the Caspian Sea, it has been transformed from a fast-flowing waterway to a series of dammed lakes, used for farming, power, and transportation.

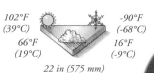

Steppes
The steppes are flat grassy plains that extend across the Russian Federation and Kazakhstan. A large part is treeless and used for grazing, but vast expanses are also cultivated. To the south the steppes gradually give way to semidesert lowlands and mountains.

Russian Federation

Once part of a great empire, Russia is a federation of numerous regions, republics, and territories, many of which are autonomous and self-governing. The dominant element in the former Soviet Union, since the collapse of communism, Russia is today finding its role in the world. It has suffered great damage to its economy and lots of ethnic tension; most recently fighting broke out with the southwestern republic of Chechnya.

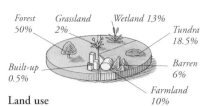

Forest 50% Grassland 2% Wetland 13% Tundra 18.5% Built-up 0.5% Barren 6% Farmland 10%

Land use
Most of Russia's crops are grown in the "fertile triangle" that stretches between St. Petersburg, the Caspian Sea, and Omsk in southern Siberia. Forest provides timber, and coal, oil, and natural gas are mined in Siberia.

People
Most Russians live in small apartments in towns where living standards are low. Since the collapse of communism, crime rates have risen sharply, especially in the cities. Many people are disillusioned by food shortages, and the loss of job security, long-term employment, and guaranteed housing.

Lining up for food in winter

23 per sq mile (9 per sq km) 77% Urban 23% Rural

Ballet
Russia is renowned for its ballet and Moscow's Bolshoi Ballet and the Kirov Ballet from St. Petersburg are world famous. Ballet first arrived in Russia in the 18th century via Paris to St. Petersburg, at the time a cultural center of Europe. During the 19th century, Russian ballet developed its own individual style.

Food
Grain, potatoes, oil, and sugar form the basis of the Russian diet. Famous dishes are *borscht* (hot beet soup served with sour cream), beef *stroganov*, *blinis*, caviar (sturgeon-fish eggs), stuffed cabbage leaves, and *shchi*, a kind of cabbage soup. Russians drink large amounts of *chai*, or tea, served without milk, and vodka often flavored with herbs and spices.

Blinis are small pancakes filled with caviar and served with sour cream.

Blinis **Vodka**

Moscow
With a population of almost nine million, the capital, Moscow, is Russia's biggest city and is linked to the Volga River by the Moscow Canal. The seat of government is the Kremlin, a palace fortress that once belonged to the czars (emperors). It is separated from the old town by the world-famous Red Square. Moscow has fine buildings, theaters, and universities, and a majestic subway system that opened in 1935.

May Day celebrations in Moscow

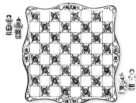

Ceramic chess set

Chess
The ancient game of chess was introduced into Russia more than 1,000 years ago by travelers on the Baltic Sea trade routes. It was quickly adopted as a stimulating way of occupying dark winter evenings. Today, chess is often played outdoors in summer. International competitions are popular.

Russian Orthodox Church
The communist rulers of the Soviet Union discouraged religion, but since the late 1980s, many followers of the Russian Orthodox Church have recovered their church buildings from the state and opened new meeting places. Christmas Day (January 7 in the Orthodox calendar) is now a national holiday.

Russian Orthodox icon of the Madonna and child

Farming
Only one-tenth of the land, mostly in European Russia, is suited to growing crops, yet Russia is a leading world producer of potatoes, oats, and rye. It also ranks highly in milk, butter, and wheat production. Men and women work the fields, often forced by lack of cash to rely on traditional farming methods. Farmers also raise cattle, sheep, and poultry for food.

Timber is sawed into many shapes, each section used for a different purpose.

Timber

Coal

Industry
Russia is one of the world's key producers of natural gas and has rich reserves of oil and coal. Hydroelectric plants generate about 18 percent of power. Leading minerals include tungsten, nickel, mercury, diamonds, gold, uranium, silver, bauxite, platinum, and iron ore. Many raw materials are extracted in Siberia and transported west of the Urals, where most of the manufacturing industries are concentrated. The vast areas of forest yield an almost endless supply of timber.

Trans-Siberian Express
The Trans-Siberian Railroad links European Russia with the Pacific coast across Siberia. It is the world's longest continuous railroad, starting in Moscow and ending 5,777 miles (9,297 km) away in the Pacific port of Vladivostok. The journey takes eight days, and crosses eight time zones. Only one passenger train runs each way daily, but freight trains run every five minutes day and night.

Kazakhstan

 Stretching almost 1,490 miles (2,400 km) from the Caspian Sea in the west to the Altai Mountains in the east, Kazakhstan is the second largest of the former Soviet republics of the USSR. Made up of dry, windswept steppes and mountainous plateaus, it is one of the world's most underpopulated countries. Its rich mineral resources give it great potential for wealth. The need to import most consumer goods has led the government to develop domestic manufacturing industries.

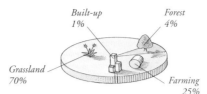

Land use

Much of Kazakhstan's grassland is used for grazing animals, mainly sheep, goats, and cattle. With the help of irrigation, large areas of steppe are cultivated, producing mainly wheat and rice.

KAZAKHSTAN FACTS

CAPITAL CITY Astana

AREA 1,049,150 sq miles (2,717,300 sq km)

POPULATION 16,200,000

MAIN LANGUAGES Kazakh, Russian

MAJOR RELIGIONS Muslim, Christian

CURRENCY Tenge

LIFE EXPECTANCY 64 years

PEOPLE PER DOCTOR 286

GOVERNMENT Multiparty democracy

ADULT LITERACY 99%

People

As a result of the forced settlement of mainly Russians, Ukrainians, and Germans under communist rule, ethnic Kazakhs form only 53 percent of the population. Increasing numbers of Kazakhs are now returning home from neighboring states. Most people live in towns, and only a few Kazakh families still follow a traditional nomadic lifestyle roaming the steppes.

Nomadic Kazakhs live in tents called yurts.

17 per sq mile (6 per sq km)

56% Urban   44% Rural

Caviar

The tiny black eggs of the *beluga* sturgeon, a kind of fish, are salted and eaten as caviar, which is regarded as a delicacy. Some of the world's best caviar comes from fish caught in the Caspian Sea off the coast of Kazakhstan. The people in the region serve caviar as a sign of friendship.

Golden sterlet eggs

Black beluga *eggs*

Caviar served on toast

Almaty

The former capital, Almaty, enjoys a beautiful location between mountains and plains. It is a city of modern architecture, wide streets, cool fountains, parks, squares, and stunning mountain views. A major attraction is Zenkov Cathedral, one of the world's tallest wooden buildings.

Zenkov Cathedral

Religion

Islam is the main religion of the ethnic Kazakh people, and it has continued to grow in popularity since the end of the communist regime. Among the other ethnic groups there is a strong Christian element, largely belonging to the Russian Orthodox Church.

Farming

Irrigation projects set up under communism transformed the dry steppes of Kazakhstan into farmland. The country is now almost self-sufficient in food crops and is a major producer of grain, wool, meat, and fish from more than 48,000 lakes.

Many boats were stranded as the water dried up.

Aral Sea

In 1960, the Aral Sea was the fourth largest lake in the world. Now it is less than half its former size because so much water has been diverted for irrigation from the two main rivers that feed it: the Syr Daria in Kazakhstan and the Amu Darya in Uzbekistan. Unless drastic measures are taken, it will be completely dry in a few years.

Mining

Kazakhstan has plentiful reserves of copper, iron ore, lead, nickel, and uranium, and mining is the country's most important industry. Some of the world's largest oil deposits are located near the Caspian Sea, attracting foreign investment. Gold is a major export, and Kazakhstan is a world leader in chromium production. It is also a major producer of tungsten, zinc, and manganese.

Crude oil

Gold

Oil drill bit

Diamond tips enable drill to cut through rock.

Space center

The former Soviet Union's space program was run from the Baikonur Cosmodrome in the center of Kazakhstan. The world's first artificial satellite and the first person in space were launched from here. The site is still used for Russian space launches.

 FIND OUT MORE ASIA, HISTORY OF · BALLET · CHESS AND OTHER BOARD GAMES · FARMING · OIL · RIVERS · ROCKS AND MINERALS · RUSSIA, HISTORY OF · SOVIET UNION · SPACE EXPLORATION · TRAINS AND RAILROADS

RUSSIA, HISTORY OF

OCCUPYING THE VAST, empty expanses of northern Europe and Asia, Russia has remained on the fringes of both continents for most of its history. Landlocked, and impoverished by its harsh climate, Russia only gained access to the seas to the west in 1721, when it began to play a major part in European history. Over the next two centuries, the country slowly and painfully modernized itself, deposing its czar and emerging under the Union of Soviet Socialist Republics (USSR) as one of the world's major superpowers. After the breakup of the Soviet Union in 1991, modern Russia has struggled to redefine its role on the world stage.

Early Russia

Before about 850, few people lived in what is now Russia. But in the 9th century, Viking raiders from Sweden pushed south in search of plunder and trade. They established a capital at Kyyiv (now Kiev in Ukraine), creating a trading empire in the surrounding area. Small, scattered tribes of farmers and hunters occupied the rest of Russia.

Rus
Russia's Viking settlers were known as the Rus. Their empire, based on trade routes between the Baltic and Black Seas, became the basis of the first Russian state.

Coming of Christianity
At the end of the 10th century, Christian missionaries from the Byzantine Empire arrived in Kyyiv. They converted the people to Greek Orthodoxy and introduced Cyrillic script, both of which survive to this day.

Rise of Muscovy

During the 1330s, the small state of Muscovy, with the city of Moscow, on the northern edge of the Mongol Khanate, at its center began to assert its independence. The Muscovites defeated the Mongols in 1380 and declared their independence a century later. By 1550, Muscovy was the leading state in Russia, expanding its territory into Poland in the west and Siberia to the east.

Ivan IV

Ivan IV (1530–84) became czar in 1533 and ruled until he died 51 years later. He expanded the size of the state and broke the power of the nobility. Ivan was a ruthless ruler, killing many opponents and earning the nickname "Ivan the Terrible."

Peter the Great

Under Peter the Great (1672–1725), Russia became a major European power. Peter traveled in western Europe, returning with new ideas that helped him modernize his country. He reorganized the government and encouraged education.

Hermitage, St. Petersburg

St. Petersburg
To symbolize his new country, Peter built a new capital at St. Petersburg. He brought in architects and craft workers from western Europe to create its streets and palaces. More than 150,000 workers died constructing the city, which was built to rival the palace at Versailles, France.

Kremlin
Every Russian city had a fortified area, known as a kremlin, to protect its civil and religious buildings. The Moscow Kremlin, beside the Movska River in the center of the city, covered many acres and contained fine churches and palaces.

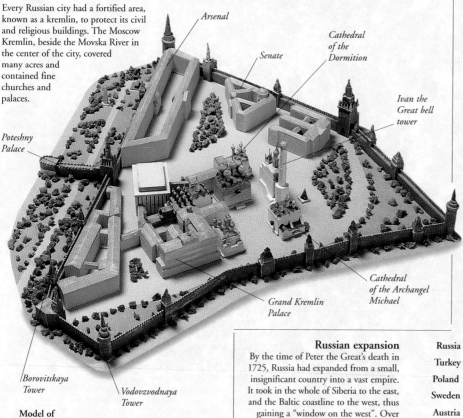

Arsenal

Senate

Cathedral of the Dormition

Ivan the Great bell tower

Poteshny Palace

Cathedral of the Archangel Michael

Grand Kremlin Palace

Borovitskaya Tower

Vodovzvodnaya Tower

Model of the Kremlin

Territory gained from Sweden 1700–1743

Russian expansion 1667-1795

St Petersburg

Territory gained from Turkey 1768–1792

Moscow

Territory gained from Poland 1767–1795

Kiev

Prague

Border shows extent of Russian territory by 1795

Russian expansion
By the time of Peter the Great's death in 1725, Russia had expanded from a small, insignificant country into a vast empire. It took in the whole of Siberia to the east, and the Baltic coastline to the west, thus gaining a "window on the west". Over the next century, further land was gained on Russia's western and southern borders.

Russia	
Turkey	
Poland	
Sweden	
Austria	
Prussia	

R

Imperial Russia

The Romanov dynasty ruled Russia from 1613 until 1917. The royal family kept power firmly in its hands, resisting change, and the serfs, or peasants, remained tied to the land. Agricultural techniques were primitive, and most people lived in conditions of extreme poverty, causing discontent to develop.

Jeweled decoration

Design inspired by the French jewelers to the court of Louis XVI of France

Egg made by Carl Fabergé, goldsmith to the Russian emperors

Emancipation of the serfs

In 1861, long after the rest of Europe, Czar Alexander II liberated the Russian peasants from serfdom (ownership by their landlords). They were allotted land that they had to pay for – a new source of discontent.

Troops beat rebellious serfs.

Catherine the Great

In 1762, Catherine (1729–96) became empress after deposing her husband Peter III. She was an intelligent ruler who encouraged artists from all over Europe to work in Russia. She continued the work of Peter the Great in making Russia into a powerful state.

1905 revolution

In January 1905, troops in St. Petersburg fired on workers who were demonstrating for higher wages and shorter hours. This outrage caused strikes and army mutinies across Russia. Czar Nicholas II granted a constitution and summoned a Russian duma, or parliament, but the reforms were limited and short-lived.

Duma

The Russian duma met on various occasions after 1905, but Nicholas II granted it only limited power. When the members disagreed with the czar, the duma was usually dissolved. Later dumas achieved some limited reforms.

Guns on the streets of St. Petersburg

Early meeting of the duma

Soviet flag

Soviet Russia

In 1917, two revolutions swept away the old imperial government and introduced the world's first communist state. It developed into a major world power and played a pivotal role in defeating Germany in World War II. The state followed the collective principles laid down by Marx and Engels and took over all private land and property.

Modern Russia

In 1991, the Soviet Union collapsed and Russia reemerged as an independent state. Under President Boris Yeltsin, Russia struggled to establish democracy and reform its economy and society along western lines, but it faced huge industrial and environmental problems.

Breakup of the Soviet Union

Mikhail Gorbachev, leader of the USSR from 1985, tried to reform the country. But he was forced to resign after an attempted coup in 1991. Most of the Soviet republics declared their independence, leading to the breakup of the USSR later that year.

Moscow

Key

Russia

Former Soviet states

Soviet legacy

The years of Soviet control left a terrible legacy for Russia. Industry was old-fashioned and inefficient, farms were unable to produce enough food, nuclear waste threatened people's health, and much land was polluted.

Decaying Soviet battleships

Market economy

The Russian economy was reformed along market lines. Reform led to food shortages in the cities and rising prices, but many people still wanted the kinds of goods and services found in capitalist societies.

McDonald's, Moscow

Timeline

800s Viking raiders establish a new state in the Ukraine, based at Kyyiv (modern Kiev).

900s Greek missionaries convert Russians to Orthodox Christianity.

1380 Prince Dimitri of Moscow defeats the Mongols; beginning of the rise of Muscovy.

St. Basil's Cathedral, Moscow

1480 Ivan III of Moscow declares himself czar of all Russians.

1533–84 Reign of Ivan IV (Ivan the Terrible).

1682–1725 Reign of Peter the Great.

1721 Russia defeats Sweden and gains access to the Baltic.

1762–96 Reign of Catherine the Great.

1861 Emancipation of serfs.

1905 Russia defeated in war by Japan; attempted revolution in St. Petersburg.

1914 Russia enters World War I on the side of the Allies. More than a million Russians are killed.

1917 Revolutionaries overthrow Czar Nicholas II, and set up world's first communist state.

1985 Mikhail Gorbachev begins to reform the Soviet Union.

1991 Soviet Union collapses; Russia emerges as independent nation.

Current Russian flag

FIND OUT MORE · ASIA, HISTORY OF · COLD WAR · EUROPE, HISTORY OF · GOVERNMENTS AND POLITICS · MARX, KARL · MONGOL EMPIRE · RUSSIAN REVOLUTION · SOVIET UNION

RUSSIAN REVOLUTION

IN 1917, A REVOLUTION in Russia forced Czar Nicholas II, a Romanov whose family had ruled for over 300 years, to abdicate. As the first revolution to take power in the name of workers and peasants, and because it also inspired later revolutions in China and Cuba, the Russian Revolution is one of the most important events of the 20th century. The revolution began in March 1917, with the formation of a provisional government. This government, not considered radical enough by the people, was overthrown in November, when the Bolsheviks seized power and turned Russia into the world's first Communist state.

Causes of the revolution

By 1917, after years of difficulties, Russia was in crisis. Most Russians – peasants and industrial workers – lived in dire poverty. They were short of food and resented the tyrannical rule of Czar Nicholas II. Russia was also suffering terrible losses against Germany in World War I. Unrest grew as all social groups demanded change.

1917 revolutions

There were two main revolutions in 1917, usually known as the February and October Revolutions. Russia's old-style calendar was 13 days behind the rest of the West, so that the revolutions actually occurred in March and November. Many key events occurred in St Petersburg (formerly called Petrograd), but the revolution affected all Russia, as it moved from a series of small democratic changes, to national social upheaval.

February Revolution
Troops sent to quell food riots in Petrograd disobeyed their orders and joined the workers. Realising he had lost control, Nicholas II (r.1894–1918) abdicated, and a provisional government was formed.

July Days
Soviets (elected councils of workers and soldiers) sprang up all over Russia; they supported the radical Bolsheviks against the provisional government. During the July Days, armed workers and soldiers, calling for "power to the soviets," attempted to seize power. The government brutally suppressed them, and Lenin fled Russia.

October Revolution
Lenin's Bolsheviks stormed the Winter Palace, arrested the leaders of the provisional government, and seized power. Lenin immediately gave control of the factories to the workers, and redistributed land to the peasants. In 1918, the revolutionaries executed the Czar and his family, and Lenin took Russia out of the war.

Lenin sweeping away capitalism

Lenin

Vladimir Ilyich Ulyanov (1870–1924), better known as Lenin, was the architect of the revolution. Born in Simbirsk on the Volga River, he became a revolutionary when his brother was hanged in 1887 for trying to assassinate the Czar. Lenin studied the works of Karl Marx, and became leader of the revolutionary Social Democrats, later the Bolsheviks. He lived mainly in exile until 1917. Following the Bolshevik victory, he ruled the country until his death.

Civil war

In 1918, civil war broke out between the so-called Whites, who were opposed to the revolution, and the Reds, or Bolsheviks. The fighting was bloody, but after three years the Red Army led by Leon Trotsky (1879–1940) was finally victorious.

New Economic Policy
By the end of the civil war in 1921, famine was widespread, and much of the peasant classes had turned against Lenin. In response to this, Lenin introduced a New Economic Policy (NEP) that allowed limited private enterprise, (also known as free trade).

Famine victims

Timeline
1905 Workers' revolution leads to October Manifesto. Czar Nicholas II agrees to a national assembly (duma), but refuses to allow any real changes.

1914 Russia enters World War I. Over three years, some 8 million Russians die or are wounded. Demonstrations against the war break out.

March 1917 (February in old-style calendar). International Women's Day turns into a bread riot in Petrograd. The revolution begins. Nicholas II is ousted from the throne.

Black bread

7 November 1917 (October in old-style calendar). Lenin and the Bolsheviks overthrow provisional government.

1918 Czar Nicholas II and family are executed.

1918–21 Civil war.

1921 Famine in Russia. Sailors mutiny in Kronstadt. Lenin introduces New Economic Policy (NEP), which, by 1925, had improved production levels.

1922 Russia's name changes to the Union of Soviet Socialist Republics (USSR), or Soviet Union.

FIND OUT MORE   CHINESE REVOLUTION   COLD WAR   GOVERNMENTS AND POLITICS   MARX, KARL   RUSSIA, HISTORY OF   SOVIET UNION

SAFAVID EMPIRE

AFTER THE DOWNFALL of its last empire in 651, Persia was under Arab domination for nearly 1,000 years. Then in 1502, a Persian warrior named Ismail founded the Safavid Empire. For more than 200 years, the Safavids ruled an independent land with a distinct national character. Shi'ism, a minority form of Islam, became the empire's official state religion. Shi'ism set Persia against its Muslim neighbors, in particular the Ottoman Turks, but contacts with Europe developed and Persia grew rich through trade. The Safavids, who loved beauty and impressive buildings, created world-famous art and architecture.

Extent of empire
After a series of swift victories against the Arabs, Ismail conquered what is now Iran and parts of Iraq. The Safavids replaced Arabic with Persian as the language of government. Tabriz was their first capital.

Ismail I
The founder of the Safavid Empire, Ismail I (1501–24), was a charismatic religious leader and brave soldier. He named the dynasty after his ancestor, the saint Safi ud-Din. Ismail was only 14 when he conquered Tabriz in modern Iran and declared himself shah, or king.

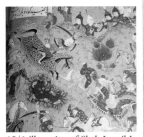

1541 illustration of Shah Ismail I fighting his rival, Alvand

Shi'ism

When Ismail conquered Persia, most people were Sunni Muslims. He invited Arab teachers to spread Shi'ism, and made it the state religion. Ismail's promotion of Shi'ism was seen as an affront to other Muslim countries.

Muslim prayers

Ottoman Turks
The Ottomans were the Safavids' main territorial rivals. As Sunni Muslims, they were also bitter religious enemies. In the 1500s, the great Ottoman ruler Suleiman I waged bloody war against the Safavids.

Sultan Suleiman I's dagger

Muharram
When Muhammad's grandson, Hossein, died in 681, early Shi'ite Muslims felt they had lost the rightful caliph of the Islamic empire. In the 16th century, Safavids began to mark the anniversary of his death with a mass outpouring of grief in the month of Muharram.

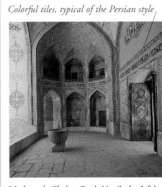

Colorful tiles, typical of the Persian style

Madresseh Chehar Bagh Vestibule, Isfahan

Isfahan
In 1598 Abbas I built a stunning new capital at Isfahan. He had all royal buildings and mosques decorated with dazzling mosaics, and the city became a showcase of the Persian architectural style at its very best. This style greatly influenced other Islamic cities.

The Prophet Muhammad's Ascent to Heaven

Angels

Gold paint

Prophet Muhammad

Buraq, a mythical winged beast

Chinese-style clouds

Decorative Persian writing

Miniatures

Decorated leather-bound books were a major expression of Safavid artistry. Court artists copied classic Persian poetry in elaborate handwriting, and added full-page, colorful illustrations, known as miniatures. Artists used fine brushes and real gold to give a sumptuous effect.

Ascent of the Prophet
Traditional stories, love poems, and legends of ancient Persian kings (the *Book of Kings*) were popular subjects for miniatures. Religious topics were relatively rare, but one 16th-century artist, Aqa Mirak, illustrated the works of the great Persian poet Nezami (1141–1209).

Abbas the Great
Abbas I (r.1587–1629) expanded the empire and founded an efficient administration. Afraid his sons might steal his throne, he killed one and had two others blinded, leaving him without a successor when he died.

Timeline
651 The last ancient Persian (Sassanid) empire falls to the Arabs.

1502 Ismail conquers Tabriz and declares himself Shah.

1524–76 Reign of Shah Tahmasp I; Safavid art peaks, but empire weakens.

1603 Abbas I forces Turks out of all Persian territories. Empire at peak.

1722 Shah Hossein abdicates. Empire begins decline.

1736 Afghan general Nader Qoli Beg deposes Tahmasp III (a child), ending the Safavid dynasty. He declares himself shah.

Pierced metalwork standard

FIND OUT MORE   ARCHITECTURE   ISLAM   ISLAMIC EMPIRE   OTTOMAN EMPIRE   PERSIAN EMPIRES

SAILING AND OTHER WATER SPORTS

BOATS OF ALL KINDS can be found on rivers, lakes, canals, and the ocean, both for leisure and in competition. Individuals and teams row, paddle, and sail in canoes, dinghies, and yachts. They ride on boards, ski across water, and drive powerful motorboats. Racing competitions range from 200-m canoe sprints that last less than a minute to around-the-world yacht races that take months to complete. Sailing, rowing, canoeing, whitewater rafting, and windsurfing have all been included in the Olympic Games.

Sailing

Sailing boats use the power of the wind to drive them through the water. Vessels range from one-person dinghies to oceangoing yachts that have a crew of 12 or more. Boats can sail directly downwind or across the wind, but have to take a zigzag course, called tacking, to sail into the wind.

Mast

Mainsail

The side of the boat farthest from the wind (this side) is called leeward; the side nearest the wind is called windward.

Yacht racing
Yachts race on inshore and offshore courses. Inshore races are held just off the coast, on courses marked with buoys. Offshore races go across the seas. Some races are for yachts of the same design, and other competitions, called handicap races, are for boats of different designs.

Sailing dinghy

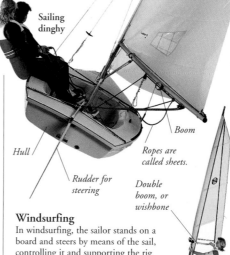

Boom

Hull

Ropes are called sheets.

Rudder for steering

Double boom, or wishbone

Canoeing

The two main types of canoe racing are over calm water and over rough water. There are two types of canoe – kayaks and Canadian canoes. In a kayak, the canoeist sits inside the boat with legs stretched out under the deck and uses a paddle with a blade at each end. In a Canadian canoe, the canoeist sits or kneels and uses a one-bladed paddle.

Canadian canoes

Calm-water racing
There are sprint and long-distance races for singles, doubles, and fours, for both kayaks and Canadian canoes. In long river races, obstacles such as locks and rapids are negotiated by portage; the canoeists have to carry their boats along the riverbank.

Whitewater racing
In slalom races, competitors set out one at a time. They have to negotiate a number of "gates" made from hanging poles, and they incur penalties for mistakes. In whitewater, competitors are timed over a course that includes obstacles such as rocks and rapids.

Kayaks

Windsurfing
In windsurfing, the sailor stands on a board and steers by means of the sail, controlling it and supporting the rig with a double boom. There are several kinds of competitions, including racing around buoys, slalom races, and performing tricks.

America's Cup
The America's Cup is contested by two yachts from different countries. The multicrew vessels compete in a best-of-seven series. An international knock-out competition decides which two countries will contest the Cup. The race is named after the US schooner *America*, which beat the best British yachts in 1851.

Rowing and sculling

Racing boats carry one, two, four, or eight rowers, all on sliding seats, plus sometimes a coxswain to steer. Rowers operate a single oar each in a boat of two, four, or eight; scullers use two oars each and race as singles, doubles, or quadruples. The standard course on nonflowing, or flat, water is 1.24 miles (2 km).

Rowing

Sculling

Steven Redgrave
British oarsman Steven Redgrave (b. 1962) is the first rower to win gold medals in five consecutive Olympics, a feat achieved by only three others in any sport. His medals came in the Games of 1984, 1988, 1992, 1996, and 2000. His career total of 14 gold medals in world championships and Olympics is also a rowing record. He had decided to retire in 1996 for health reasons, but later changed his mind.

Surfing
Surfers paddle out to sea on lightweight boards and ride the waves back to shore. In competition, their moves and routines are judged for style and grace, and the difficulty of the waves they select to ride. Most competition boards have three fins on the tail.

Waterskiing
Water-skiers are pulled behind a motorboat on one or two skis. Competitions have three sections. In slalom, water-skiers negotiate a series of six buoys over increasingly difficult runs. In jumping, they take off from a ramp. In tricks, points are awarded for special maneuvers.

FIND OUT MORE

OLYMPIC GAMES · RIVERS · SHIPS AND BOATS · SPORTS · SWIMMING AND DIVING

SALAMANDERS AND NEWTS

SALAMANDERS ARE AMPHIBIANS with tails. There are many types, including entirely land-living species, species such as newts that return to water to breed, and species that live permanently in water. Most live in the temperate northern hemisphere. Land-living salamanders prefer damp, dark, cool habitats – some live in caves. To avoid the cold of winter, they hibernate in mud or under stones. Species from hot regions live on mountains or in rotten logs in forests and remain dormant during hot, dry periods. Salamanders move in a similar way to lizards, walking with a twisting motion when on land.

Smooth, streamlined head and body

Features of salamanders and newts

Salamanders and newts retain their tails from the larval stage into adulthood. Their skin is permeable to air and water and must be kept moist to avoid drying out. They can breathe through their skin as well as their lungs. Most species have four legs, but these may be very small. Sirens are similar to salamanders, but have front legs only and external gills for breathing.

Salamander
Most salamanders are small, with long bodies and short limbs, but some are huge – the Chinese and Japanese salamanders may grow to 6 ft (1.8 m) long. Salamanders live and breed on land. They usually live in damp areas, near streams. However, some live far from water on mountains, or in woods. There are even cave dwellers, such as the European olm.

Crest grows on male's back in breeding season.

Great crested newt

Four toes on front legs

Five toes on back legs

Tail frill

Spotted salamander

Newt
Newts are salamanders that return to water in the breeding season. They develop filamentous frills on the upper and lower edges of their tails that help them swim. Most newts live in cool water and are found in Europe, Asia, and North America.

Neoteny
Some salamanders and newts, such as the European cave olm, Mexican axolotl, and American mudpuppy, do not develop fully into adults. They retain their gills and remain in the water-dwelling larval form despite being sexually mature and able to breed. This condition is called neoteny.

Red, feathery gills **Mexican axolotl**

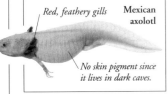

No skin pigment since it lives in dark caves.

Feeding
Larvae that develop in water have horny teeth and feed on invertebrates, smaller newt larvae, or young fish. Land-living adults have sharp teeth to catch prey such as insects and worms. Some salamanders feed on other smaller salamanders. The giant Japanese and Chinese salamanders also feed on animal feces, and some climbing species nibble fungi on tree trunks.

Warts on skin **Mandarin salamander**

Salamander grips earthworm in its teeth.

Reproduction
Most male salamanders lay a sperm sac, or spermatophore, on land that the female takes up into her body through an opening called the cloaca. The eggs are fertilized internally and laid on land. Some species lay eggs that hatch directly into small versions of the adults; others, such as the European fire salamander, bear live young. Newts mate in water; they either lay a single egg or groups of eggs, on plants in the water.

Newly laid egg will be wrapped inside the leaf.

Long, feathery gills

Internal organs

Three pairs of external gills

Small back legs *Long, thin legs*

Development of a great crested newt

1 The female newt lays her eggs singly on underwater vegetation. She folds a leaf around the egg with her feet to protect it inside a sticky envelope. The egg hatches after 3 weeks.

2 The larva is now 5 weeks old. It breathes with external gills. The membranes on the tail and back help it swim in short bursts. It feeds mainly on invertebrates.

3 By 8 weeks, the larva is bigger and stronger. It is now a voracious aquatic predator. By 2–3 months, the gills and tail filaments recede and the legs become stronger. It moves onto land and breathes using lungs. It keeps its tail.

Bright colors indicate it is poisonous.

Defense
Many salamanders and newts hide from their enemies by camouflaging themselves. Some are bright in color and have toxic skin that causes skin irritation and stomach cramps if eaten. Some salamanders, such as American sirens, give a nasty bite; others shed their tails to escape predators. The Pyrenean newt feigns death by lying on its back.

Poison gland

European fire salamander
Fire salamanders have brightly patterned poisonous skin that is powerful enough to kill small mammals that may eat them.

Spines

Iberian ribbed newt
This newt has spines down its side formed by the protruding tips of its ribs. These help deter predators.

GREAT CRESTED NEWT

SCIENTIFIC NAME	*Triturus cristatus*
ORDER	Caudata
FAMILY	Salamandridae
DISTRIBUTION	Europe to central and southern Russia and northern Turkey and Iran in lowlands below 3,300 ft (1,000 m)
HABITAT	Deep water ponds
DIET	Aquatic invertebrates as a larvae; insects, worms, and slugs as an adult
SIZE	Length 6–6.5 in (15–16 cm); tail is 2.75 in (7 cm) of this length
LIFESPAN	25 years (in captivity)

FIND OUT MORE | AMPHIBIANS | CAVE WILDLIFE | HIBERNATION | LAKE AND RIVER WILDLIFE | MARSH AND SWAMP WILDLIFE | MOUNTAIN WILDLIFE | POISONOUS ANIMALS | WOODLAND WILDLIFE

SAMURAI AND SHOGUNS

JAPANESE MILITARY DICTATORS, known as shoguns, seized control of all Japan from 1192 to 1868. Although they ruled in the emperor's name, the shoguns' power was lifelong and hereditary, and the emperors were mere puppets. Through local landowners called daimyos, the shoguns controlled an aristocratic warrior class known as the samurai, meaning "one who serves." Over 700 years these samurai became famous for their bravery and military skill. In their code – the Bushido, or "way of the warrior" – loyalty and honor were the highest virtues, and failure was unforgivable. People regarded the samurai as nobles, but they lived harsh and austere lives.

Origins of the samurai
Samurai first appeared in the early 10th century. Originally samurai bands formed from clans. Later, a feudal system came into effect: mounted samurai fought to the death for their local daimyo, and gained land if successful.

Kamakura shoguns

When Minamoto Yoritimo (1147–99) seized power and established a warrior government at Kamakura, he and his descendants became known as the Kamakura shoguns. After Yoritimo's death, his wife's family, the Hojo, became regents, or caretakers of the shoguns, and held more power than the shoguns themselves. In 1274 and 1281, the Hojo's samurai repelled Mongol invaders, but these campaigns weakened the Kamakura shogunate, which collapsed in 1333.

Minamoto family
The clan's first great chief was Minamoto Yoshiye (1039–1106). He built up the family fortunes to such an extent that the Minamoto could make a bid for power. In 1185, Yoshiye's descendent, Yoritimo, established his court at Kamakura, then in 1192, made himself the first shogun. From that time forward, shoguns were chosen from different branches of the Minamoto family.

Minamoto Yoshiye

Samurai armor
Over 700 years, the 23 pieces in a suit of armor became highly decorative – with gold detail, and colored silk ties – but the basic style remained virtually unchanged.

Kabuto (helmet)
Mempo (face guard)
Sode (shoulder-plate)
Muna-ita (breastplate)
Do (cuirass)
Chain mail kote (arm-plate)
Tekko (hand guard)
Kusazuri (upper thigh guard)
Haidate (lower thigh guard)
Colored ties
Suneate (greave or leg guard)

Samurai armor of the 19th century

Ashikaga shoguns

Ashikaga Takauji defeated the Kamakura shoguns in 1333 on behalf of the emperor, but then made himself shogun in 1338. He established his government in Muromachi, Kyoto. Ashikaga shoguns became interested in the arts, such as the tea ceremony and Noh drama, rather than in warfare. In 1573 a minor chieftain called Oda Nobunaga (1534–82) deposed the last Ashikaga shogun.

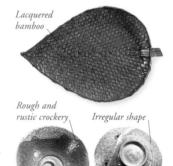

Lacquered bamboo
Rough and rustic crockery
Irregular shape

Tea ceremony
In the 12th century, a Buddhist priest introduced the formal drinking of tea from China. Three hundred years later, the Ashikaga shogun Yoshimasa (1436–90) constructed a special room in his villa for the tea ceremony – Japan's first teahouse. The 16th-century tea master Sen no Rikyu refined and simplified the ceremony. For shoguns and samurai alike, the tea ceremony was a quiet, spiritually refreshing cultural pursuit.

Tea ceremony tray and bowls

Tokugawa shoguns

Tokugawa Ieyasu, a military genius, started as a minor daimyo but, in 1603, became shogun. He and his successors made strict political and economic rules that ensured peace for more than two centuries. In 1868, due to pressure at home and abroad, the last Tokugawa shogun was forced to resign, and the emperor assumed power. This ended 700 years of shogun and samurai rule.

Tokugawa Ieyasu (1543–1616)

Bushido code
The samurai code of service – loyalty, honor, and bravery – extended to ritual suicide (hara-kiri or seppuku) when there was any hint of dishonor. In 1703, 47 ronin (masterless samurai) avenged the death of their lord, Asano, by killing his murderer, then committing hara-kiri to keep their honor.

Lithograph showing hara-kiri, or ritual suicide

Modern samurai
Samurai traditions include kendo (fencing), sumo (wrestling), judo (unarmed combat), and ikebana (flower arrangement). Films, books, plays, and television soap operas based on samurai life attract millions of Japanese. Classic Japanese films, such as *Kagemusha* and *The Seven Samurai*, celebrate samurai traditions.

Scene from *Kagemusha*

FIND OUT MORE | ARMS AND ARMOR | ASIA, HISTORY OF | BUDDHISM | FEUDALISM | JAPAN, HISTORY OF | WARFARE

SATELLITES

CIRCLING EARTH, high above our heads, satellites are messengers and observers in the sky. They relay telephone calls, watch the weather, guide ships and aircraft, and carry out tasks that are impossible on the ground. They travel 10 to 30 times faster than an airliner. A satellite's speed prevents it from falling to Earth and throws it outward. The inward pull of gravity balances this outward force and traps the satellite in an endless path around Earth.

Sputnik could broadcast clear signals even when it was spinning.

Two-thirds of *Sputnik*'s weight consisted of batteries.

Sputnik 1
In 1957, Soviet scientists launched the first satellite, *Sputnik 1*. It was simple, and measured the temperature of the atmosphere, broadcasting the readings as it orbited.

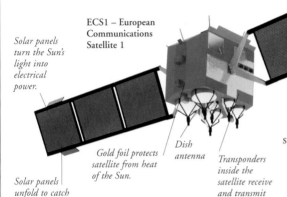

ECS1 – European Communications Satellite 1

Solar panels turn the Sun's light into electrical power.

Solar panels unfold to catch sunlight.

Gold foil protects satellite from heat of the Sun.

Dish antenna

Transponders inside the satellite receive and transmit signals.

Anatomy of a satellite

The main structure is made of aluminum or plastic reinforced with carbon fiber. The satellite must be strong enough to withstand the force of being launched, yet as light as possible because the launch requires enormous amounts of power. There are two or three versions of every system on board so that a failure does not disable the satellite.

Ground station broadcasts signals from dishes pointed at the satellite.

Receiving antenna

Types of satellites
Once satellites were used mainly for spying or to detect the launch of nuclear missiles. Today, satellites are usually used for more peaceful purposes.

Communications
These satellites carry telephone calls and television channels from one continent to another.

Weather
These satellites provide weather forecasters with pictures of cloud formations.

Observation
These satellites can "see" infrared light, so they can monitor vegetation, bare soil and rock, snow and ice, water, and urban areas.

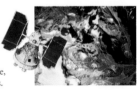

Astronomical
Telescopes above the atmosphere can give astronomers a much clearer view of the Universe.

Orbits

A satellite's orbit is the curved path it follows around Earth. The pull of gravity is stronger closer to Earth, so a satellite in a low orbit must travel faster than one in a geostationary orbit.

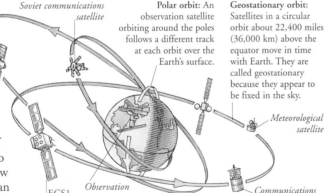

Elliptical orbit: most satellites fly in elliptical orbits like flattened circles.

Soviet communications satellite

Polar orbit: An observation satellite orbiting around the poles follows a different track at each orbit over the Earth's surface.

Geostationary orbit: Satellites in a circular orbit about 22,400 miles (36,000 km) above the equator move in time with Earth. They are called geostationary because they appear to be fixed in the sky.

Astronomical satellite

Meteorological satellite

ECS1

Observation satellite

Communications satellite

Space debris
Since *Sputnik* was launched, eight nations have launched an average of 100 satellites a year. Early launches created tiny pieces of debris, each of which can destroy a satellite. There are more than 7,000 large objects orbiting Earth.

Konstantin Tsiolkovskii
A Russian mathematics teacher Konstantin Eduardovich Tsiolkovskii (1857–1935) is known as "the father of space travel." He was one of the first people to prove that satellites were practical.

Timeline
1687 Isaac Newton describes how to launch an artificial satellite with a cannon.

1945 Arthur C. Clarke proposes a geostationary satellite.

1957 Soviets launch *Sputnik 1*, the first artificial satellite.

1958 US launches first satellite, *Explorer I*.

1962 US sends *Telstar*, the first communications satellite, into orbit.

1963 US launches *Syncom 2*, the first geostationary satellite.

1972 US launches *Landsat 1*, first Earth resources satellite.

1990 *Hubble Space Telescope* launched with a faulty mirror. This is corrected by astronauts in 1994.

1992 USA satellite *COBE* captures temperature data from the afterglow of the Big Bang.

2000 Failed iridium telephone satellite network turned off.

FIND OUT MORE ASTRONOMY EARTH ROCKETS SPACE EXPLORATION TELECOMMUNICATIONS TELESCOPES

S

SCANDINAVIA, HISTORY OF

DESPITE ITS SMALL population, Scandinavia has had a huge impact on European history. The Vikings of Denmark and Sweden raided most European nations in the 9th and 10th centuries, leaving their mark wherever they landed. During the 16th century, Sweden emerged as one of Europe's most powerful nations, creating an empire that lasted for 200 years. In the 20th century, Scandinavian nations led the way in establishing welfare states to support their people, and Norway was the first European nation to give women the vote.

Empire of Canute

In 1016, the throne of England fell vacant. It was seized by Canute, brother of the Danish king. Within a few years, Canute added Denmark, Norway, and southern Sweden to his empire, ruling with great skill until his death in 1035.

Coin of Canute

Coming of Christianity

The nations of Scandinavia became Christian during the 9th to 11th centuries, although remote regions kept their traditional beliefs until much later. In Norway, the first churches were built of wood.

Union of Kalmar

In 1397, in Kalmar, Sweden, Margaret of Denmark persuaded Norway and Sweden to unite. Kings were elected in all these countries, so the union could not be maintained. It collapsed in 1523, when Gustavus I became king of Sweden.

Margaret of Denmark (1353–1412)

Stave church, Gol, Norway

Church is built of vertical pieces of wood called staves.

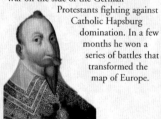

Sweden

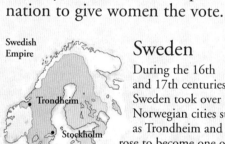

Swedish Empire

Trondheim

Stockholm

During the 16th and 17th centuries, Sweden took over Norwegian cities such as Trondheim and rose to become one of the most powerful states in Europe. The country adopted the Lutheran faith and championed the Protestant cause. A succession of able kings carved out a vast empire that surrounded the Baltic Sea and included Finland and parts of Russia and northern Germany.

Great Northern War

In 1700, Sweden's neighbors joined together to break its stranglehold on the Baltic and its trade. When peace finally came in 1721, Sweden lost its supremacy in the region, and Russia achieved its "window on Europe" by gaining access to the Baltic.

Russia defeated Sweden at the Battle of Hango, 1714.

Gustavus II Adolphus

Gustavus Adolphus (1594–1632) became king of Sweden in 1611. Aided by his chancellor Axel Oxenstjerna, he improved the economy and extended the Swedish empire in northern Poland. In 1630, he entered the Thirty Years' War on the side of the German Protestants fighting against Catholic Hapsburg domination. In a few months he won a series of battles that transformed the map of Europe.

Modern Scandinavia

Norway broke free from Swedish rule in 1905; Finland won independence from Russia in 1917. Later, the Scandinavian nations worked together, setting up the Nordic Council in 1952 to improve relations between them. Denmark, Sweden, and Finland have joined the European Union.

Welfare states

The Scandinavian states were among the first to introduce a strong welfare system. Good child care and facilities for the sick and elderly were provided, and unemployment has been kept low. High taxes are necessary to pay for these benefits.

Modern public housing

Scandinavia in World War II

Denmark and Norway were occupied by Germany from 1940–45; Finland was occupied by the Russians. Sweden stayed neutral. Most people defied the occupying forces – King Christian X and other Danes helped Jews escape to Sweden – but a collaborationist government was set up by fascist politician Vidkun Quisling (1887–1945) in Norway.

Christian X of Denmark (r.1912–47)

Timeline

700s Vikings raid Europe's coasts.

1016 Canute rules Denmark, Norway, and England.

1397 Kalmar Union between Denmark, Sweden, and Norway.

1523 Sweden leaves union and gains independence.

1658 Swedish Empire reaches its greatest extent in Europe.

1700–21 Great Northern War: Sweden fends off an attempted takeover from neighbouring countries.

1814 Norway is transferred from Denmark to Sweden.

1905 Norway gains independence.

1917 Finland gains independence from Russia.

1940–45 Germany occupies Denmark and Norway; Russia occupies Finland.

1967 Denmark joins European Union.

1995 Sweden and Finland join European Union.

FIND OUT MORE | ANGLO-SAXONS | EUROPE, HISTORY OF | HOLY ROMAN EMPIRE | NORMANS | RUSSIA, HISTORY OF | UNITED KINGDOM, HISTORY OF | VIKINGS | WORLD WAR II

SCHOOLS AND COLLEGES

AS YOUNG CHILDREN, most of us first learn how to read and write at school. This is the place where we begin our formal education, which may continue up to college or graduate school. At school, skilled teachers pass on their learning to others and equip them to take their place in society. Until the 1800s, only a privileged few went to school. It is only recently, and in the industrialized nations, that education has become available to all.

Learning to write in ancient Greece

Early education
Schools were first created by the Sumerians c.3500 BC, after the invention of writing. Teachers in the ancient world were often temple priests. Young boys were taught reading and writing, practicing on pieces of flat stone or broken bits of pottery.

Geography workbook, France

Maori school book, New Zealand

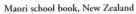

Dinosaur, drawn by 10-year-old Japanese boy

Natural science and math books, Korea

0	sifuri		5	tano
1	moja		6	sita
2	mbili		7	saba
3	tatu		8	nane
4	nne		9	tisa

Schoolbook, Kenya

Writing equipment

Stages of formal education
In the industrialized world, formal education is divided into stages that differ from country to country. In the US, children up to 4 years attend preschool, where they learn through play. From ages 5 to 11, children receive a basic education at elementary school; at high schools, 12-to18-year olds study more specialized subjects. In the developing world, less money is available to provide education for all: school often ends at age 11.

Subjects
At elementary school, children learn to read, write, and do simple arithmetic. In high school, they study core subjects in more detail and are also guided toward subjects in which they show ability, such as sciences, languages, or the arts.

Examinations
At the end of school, many children take final exams to test their knowledge and understanding of the subjects they have studied. Some exams are given nationally; colleges may then select students based on their test scores.

Science in high school

Higher institutes
Pupils who want to continue their studies beyond school, or train for a career, may go on to college or vocational school. Colleges offer a range of subjects and research opportunities; vocational schools offer technical training for job placement.

First universities
In Europe, the first modern-style universities were set up in Italy (Bologna, 11th century), France (Paris, 12th century), and England (Oxford, 12th century).

Seal, University of Paris

Graduation gown

Graduation
When a student successfully completes a period of study, the university or college awards a qualification, or degree: this is known as graduation.

School systems
Most countries provide some free education, although systems vary greatly. Schools are generally compulsory for a number of years. In some places, education is centrally controlled by the government; in others, different regions have their own policies. Schools may be for children of mixed ability, or tracked so that children study with those of similar abilities.

China
All education in China is under the control of the government, and students are taught communist ideas as well as other school subjects. Students who achieve the highest results in national examinations are sent to the schools with the best facilities.

Teacher and child in classroom

Teaching
The chief means of passing knowledge from one generation to the next is teaching, the process by which a person helps others learn. In most countries, people who want to become school-teachers must first attend college. There they learn about the principles of teaching and education, as well as studying one or two school subjects in depth.

Timeline
1088 The first modern-style university, a confederation of student guilds, is established at Bologna, in Italy.

1618 Parts of the Netherlands introduce free village schools.

1697 First Sunday schools started by Congregationalists in Wales.

1837 In Germany, pioneering educator Friedrich Froebel (1782–1852) opens his first kindergarten to help young children learn in a creative way.

1854 First co-educational school opens in London, England.

1945 World War II ends; ambitious to create a better world, industrialized nations expand the opportunities for secondary education.

FIND OUT MORE CHINA EDUCATION MEDIEVAL EUROPE SOCIETIES, HUMAN WRITING

SCIENCE

"EUREKA!" shouted the ancient Greek mathematician and scientist Archimedes when he discovered the principle that explains why objects float in water. The word eureka means "I have found it," and the purpose of science is to find explanations for the things that happen in the world around us. Scientists test their ideas very carefully. If the ideas prove to be wrong, they develop new ones and test those as well. Scientists exchange ideas and the results of their experiments at conferences, through scientific societies, and in articles published in journals or on the Internet.

Scientific method

To find out why a particular event happens, scientists first suggest an explanation called a hypothesis. The hypothesis is tested by conducting an experiment so that the results either support or refute (disprove) the hypothesis. If the results support the hypothesis, the scientists can then develop it into a more detailed explanation called a theory.

Experiment   Control

Cylinder rotates so that light reaches plant from all directions.

Control plant is straight.

Plant from first cylinder is bent.

Leaves need light for growth.

Light reaches plant from one direction only.

Three weeks later

Hypothesis
A houseplant placed near a window will not grow straight upward. The hypothesis that plants always grow toward the light could explain this, but it must first be tested by an experiment.

Experiment
In the experiment, a young plant receives light from one direction only. To check that no other factors are influencing the plant's growth, a "control" is set up, in which an identical plant receives light from all sides.

Observation
After several weeks, the plants are examined. The control plant has grown straight upward, while the plant illuminated from one side only has bent in that direction.

Theory
From the results, the theory is devised that the plants contain a growth-promoting chemical that occurs on the side of a stem or leaf facing away from a light source.

Science and society

John Cockcroft (1897–1967) and Ernest Walton (1903–96)

When English physicist John Cockcroft and his Irish colleague Ernest Walton first split the atom in 1932, few people realized that this achievement could lead to the building of devastating nuclear weapons. Because we often cannot predict how scientific discoveries will shape our future, it is important to analyze the role of scientists in the world and even sometimes to question the way in which they work.

Science in practice

Scientists usually work together in groups and communicate with other groups that share an interest in the same type of research. They write up their work in publications called scientific journals, so that other scientists (their "peers") may check their work. This checking process is known as "peer review."

Laboratory
We often think of a laboratory as a room filled with bottles of chemicals and strange machines. A laboratory can be like that, but any space devoted to experimentation is a laboratory. In fact, laboratories have been set up in tents, airplanes, and even spacecraft.

Working in a biochemistry laboratory

Fieldwork
In some sciences, such as geology, it is vital to go out of the laboratory, to collect samples or data (information), or to make observations. This is called fieldwork. Data and samples collected during fieldwork are taken back to the laboratory and analyzed.

Geologist examining rock samples

Science and technology
The application of science to industry and trade is called technology. In the 20th century, technological developments enabled factories to mass-produce goods cheaply and quickly, and businesses to computerize the records of all their transactions.

Mass-production in a modern factory

Science fiction
In his book *Nova Atlantis*, the English politician and scientist Francis Bacon (1561–1626) foresaw many new technologies, including lasers, telephones, and genetic engineering. The book, like many science fiction novels, made predictions about the future based on the scientific ideas of the time.

NOVA ATLANTIS PER FRANCISCUM BACONUM, Baronem de Verulamio, Vice-Comitem S. Albani.

VLTRAIECTI.

Apud Ioannem à VVaesberge, Anno cIɔ Iɔ c XLIII.

Title page of Bacon's *Nova Atlantis*

Karl Popper

Austrian Karl Popper (1902–94) thought that true science must be able to be tested, so there is always a chance it may be found to be false. This means, for example, that the Big Bang theory of how the universe began is not part of science, as it can never be tested.

FIND OUT MORE   ASTRONOMY   BIOLOGY   CHEMISTRY   EINSTEIN, ALBERT   GENETICS   GEOLOGY   MEDICINE   PHYSICS   TECHNOLOGY

SCIENCE, HISTORY OF

FROM THE TINIEST SUBATOMIC PARTICLE, through all living things, to the Universe itself, the scope of pure science is vast. Science is a quest for true explanations of how the world works. All the scientific knowledge we have today is the result of centuries of careful questioning, research, and observation – known as the scientific method – together with the inspiration of many brilliant minds. Before the scientific method was developed, people made discoveries about the world and developed technologies mainly through guesswork. Over the last four centuries scientific progress has become more rapid, and science has been able to create a more accurate picture of how the world works.

Technological advances

Before science

There were technological advances in very early civilizations, but no real science. After c.3800 BC, people in western Asia learned how to make metal, and this led to a decline in the use of stone tools.

Astronomy
Early people charted the heavens, but believed their gods were responsible for all that they observed. Many civilizations built observatories – huge stone circles – such as Stonehenge in England.

Natural philosophy

The ancient Greeks were perhaps the first to use reasoned argument when looking at the natural world. For the first time, people developed competing theories to explain familiar phenomena. Some of these theories, though untested at the time, are remarkably close to modern ideas. For example, the atomic theory, the idea that all matter is made up of tiny particles, or atoms, was first conceived by Democritus in c.400 BC.

Fire
Earth
Air
Water

Platonic solids
According to the ancient Greeks, four differently shaped types of atom made up the four elements – fire, earth, air, water – from which everything else in the world was made. The word "atom" comes from the Greek "atomein", meaning "indivisible". We now know that many kinds of atoms exist, and that they can be divided.

Medieval science

In medieval Europe, ancient theories prevailed – especially Aristotle's idea that all phenomena had a divine cause. Monks kept their love of learning alive by copying ancient scientific texts. The Islamic world, however, constantly added to the body of knowledge by developing new ideas in mathematics, astronomy, and medicine.

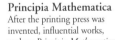

Crucible

The alembic was used to distil liquids.

Alchemists at work

Alchemy
Medieval alchemists, in their quest to make gold and discover the secret of eternal life, discovered much about the properties of metals and other substances. They developed many of the techniques we use today in chemistry laboratories.

Long metal tongs were used to lift the crucible out of the flames.

Renaissance science

By the 15th century, the ideas of the ancient Greeks, along with those of the church, had become dogma (regarded as truth) throughout Europe. During the Renaissance (which means "rebirth"), people began to question this dogma, and experiment in a truly scientific fashion. This new approach took nothing for granted, and used observation, experiments, and argument to develop theories to explain why things happen. Great scientists, such as Galileo and Newton, date from this period.

Scientific instruments
The use of scientific instruments, such as the telescope, made new observations of the Universe possible. Many of these observations challenged the accepted – but untested – ideas of the time. Physical models, such as the armillary sphere, helped to visualize and test the new theories, which now began to replace the old ideas.

This armillary sphere was used to help explain the complex movements of the heavens.

Principia Mathematica
After the printing press was invented, influential works, such as *Principia Mathematica* by Newton (published 1687), became available in great numbers, and helped spread the new scientific method. This book sets out the laws of motion and Newton's theory of gravity.

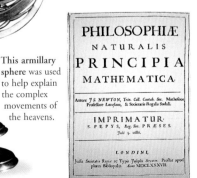

PHILOSOPHIÆ
NATURALIS
PRINCIPIA
MATHEMATICA.

Autore JS. NEWTON, Trin. Coll. Cantab. Soc. Matheseos Professore Lucasiano, & Societatis Regalis Sodali.

IMPRIMATUR
S. PEPYS, Reg. Soc. PRÆSES.
Julii 5. 1686.

LONDINI,
Jussu Societatis Regiæ ac Typis Josephi Streater. Prostat apud plures Bibliopolas. Anno MDCLXXXVII.

Francis Bacon
The English philosopher and statesman Francis Bacon (1561–1626) was the first person to formulate the scientific method. Before this approach became common, explanations of phenomena were accepted without question, but Bacon believed that any ideas about the natural world should be tested thoroughly for truth. In 1605, he published the *Advancement of Learning*, in which he urged people to classify facts about the world using the scientific method. In *The New Atlantis*, published after his death, he suggested the government should employ teams of scientists to conduct research.

Scientific societies

The new enthusiasm for scientific inquiry during the Renaissance gave rise to societies where scientists shared ideas and promoted the study of particular scientific theories. The Royal Society for the Promotion of Natural Knowledge, founded in London, England, in 1660, was one of the first of these organizations. Members met regularly to discuss their experiments – but only in Europe, which still considered itself the center of the world.

The Academy of Science and Fine Art, France

Desaguliers' steam engine, 1740

Mechanical principles

Industry and physical science were firmly linked during the Industrial Revolution. The invention of the steam engine resulted from a growing understanding of what steam was, how it worked – and how it could be harnessed. Steam engines were used to pump water from flooded mines, to drive machines in factories, and eventually to power the first trains.

Nineteenth-century science

Understanding in all the sciences – from the physical to the life sciences – dramatically advanced in the 19th century thanks to better communications, improved scientific instruments, and the possibility of financial reward. Science became less religious, and scientists started to look at the world and everything in it as part of a huge machine, a view that helped them make some of the most important and unifying discoveries in the history of science.

Evolution

The theory of evolution – that species develop according to favorable characteristics – was proposed in the work of English biologist Charles Darwin. His observations led to the conclusion – controversial at the time – that human beings are related to apes and to the rest of the living world.

Handles turn paddles.

Water's movement generates heat, which is measured.

Paddles swirl water.

Forces of Nature

Up until the 19th century, the forces of nature – such as heat, light, electricity, and magnetism – were seen as being completely unrelated. In fact, heat is a form of motion, and the proof of this, along with the discovery of electromagnetism (magnetism produced by electricity), led to the development of the idea of energy during the 1840s. This concept was first recognized by the English physicist James Joule, who gave his name to the "joule" (unit of energy). This paddle wheel apparatus was used in one of his key experiments.

Modern science

By the end of the 1800s, many scientists believed their existing theories could explain everything in the world. Around 1900, however, scientists discovered that our galaxy is just one of millions of similar galaxies that make up the Universe. This and other events caused "classical" physics to give way to "modern" physics, causing new theories to arise. The best-known theories of modern physics are the theory of relativity (developed by the scientist Einstein) and the theory of quantum physics. These two theories have influenced the whole scientific world.

Cosmology

Einstein's theories of relativity, along with increasing knowledge of the Universe, started to give possible answers to the question of how time and space actually began. Most cosmologists now agree that they came into being in a massive explosion called the Big Bang.

Radio map of hydrogen gas, Andromeda Galaxy

Genetics

In the 1850s and 1860s, an Austrian monk, Gregor Mendel, figured out the basic laws of genetics – the study of inherited characteristics. In 1953, scientists finally worked out the structure of the DNA (deoxyribonucleic acid) molecule, a chemical that governs genetics and is found in every cell of every living thing.

DNA molecule

Carbon

Phosphorus

Oxygen

Nitrogen

Computer science

Advances in many fields of study, such as electronics and mathematics, contributed to the development of the electronic computer. Today, not only is computer science an established area of scientific study in its own right, but computers are essential tools for nearly all scientists.

Scientist using a computer

Modern medicine

The development of X-ray photography is just one of the techniques that has advanced modern medicine. Body scanning techniques, such as CAT (computer-aided tomography), along with knowledge from other scientific disciplines, have brought about better understanding of the body and have paved the way for new types of surgery.

Brain scan showing left and right hemispheres.

Subatomic physics

In 1897, the electron became the first known particle smaller than the atom (subatomic particle). Hundreds of other subatomic particles have been discovered during collisions in huge particle accelerators, including protons and neutrons. Such discoveries are fundamental to understanding what matter is, because atomic particles are its building blocks.

Proton-photon collision

Alfred Nobel

Every year, outstanding achievers in physics, chemistry, physiology, and medicine are honored by receiving a Nobel Prize, first awarded in 1901. The prizes are named after Swedish chemist Alfred Nobel (1833–96). Nobel (who invented dynamite in 1867 and gelignite in 1875) left most of his fortune to recognize those whose achievements benefit mankind. In addition to the prizes for scientific achievement, Nobel Prizes are given for literature, peace, and economics.

| FIND OUT MORE | ATOMS AND MOLECULES | COMPUTERS | DARWIN, CHARLES | EINSTEIN, ALBERT | GENETICS | INDUSTRIAL REVOLUTION | MEDICINE, HISTORY OF | NEWTON, SIR ISAAC | SCIENCE |

SCULPTURE

SCULPTURES ARE works of art created in three dimensions. They can be free-standing statues or bas-reliefs, raised pictures on a background. Sculptors have traditionally worked in wood, metal, or stone, using the two main techniques of carving and casting. Carved sculptures are created by gradually taking material away, whereas cast sculptures are made by building material up.

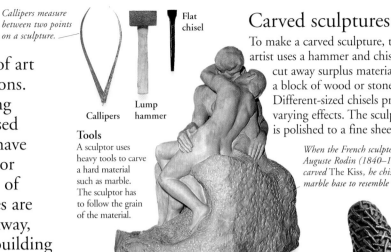

Callipers measure between two points on a sculpture.

Flat chisel

Callipers

Lump hammer

Tools
A sculptor uses heavy tools to carve a hard material such as marble. The sculptor has to follow the grain of the material.

Carved sculptures

To make a carved sculpture, the artist uses a hammer and chisel to cut away surplus material from a block of wood or stone. Different-sized chisels produce varying effects. The sculpture is polished to a fine sheen.

When the French sculptor Auguste Rodin (1840–1917) carved The Kiss, *he chiseled the marble base to resemble rock.*

S

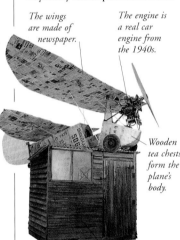

Airplane by Christopher Dobrowolski

The wings are made of newspaper.

The engine is a real car engine from the 1940s.

Wooden tea chests form the plane's body.

A wooden shed is the base.

New materials
A number of contemporary sculptors have experimented with a variety of new materials such as plastics, concrete, and even junk. Some sculptors have also set out to challenge conventional attitudes toward art by using everyday objects to create their work. The sculpture above, for example, is made from objects that are instantly recognizable.

Cast sculptures

Cast sculptures are usually made of bronze. They are almost always hollow, and are therefore light. Bronze casting is a very ancient technique; the earliest examples date from about 5,000 years ago. The sequence here shows the lost-wax process of casting a bronze head.

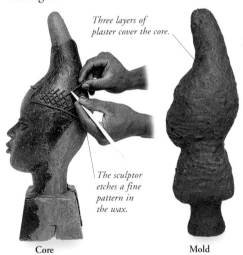

Three layers of plaster cover the core.

The sculptor etches a fine pattern in the wax.

Core

Mold

1 The core of the sculpture is roughly built up out of clay made from soil and water. It is covered with a thin layer of wax that the sculptor carves to add detail.

2 The wax-covered core is covered with a tough, heat-resistant plaster to form a mold. Holes are left at the top and bottom of the mold. It is ready to fire.

The bronze is heated until it is orange-hot, which is hotter than red-hot.

3 Molten metal is poured into the top of the mold. The heat of the metal melts the wax covering and the liquid wax drains out of the bottom, leaving a layer of metal that cools and hardens between the core and the mold.

4 When the metal has cooled, the sculptor breaks open the mold to reveal the sculpture. Its surface is polished to create shine and depth.

The finished replica head of the Queen Mother of Benin

Barbara Hepworth
The British sculptor Barbara Hepworth (1903–75) was one of a group of influential European artists who sculpted traditional materials in a new way. Their goal was to allow the natural properties of a material to dictate the sculpture's final form. Hepworth's works were carved out of wood or stone or cast in bronze, and were normally abstract sculptures.

Modern sculpture

In widening the range of materials they work with, sculptors have moved away from the traditional processes. Modern sculptors are now able to focus more on expressing their artistic ideas than on the technical skills of making a sculpture.

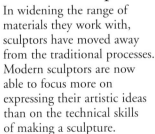

Abstract sculptures
Sculptures that do not represent things realistically are abstracts. This abstract sculpture *Pixel Lunch* is made from plastic lunchboxes.

Figures
This sculpture of two figures rising up out of the grass represents growth and the forces of nature. It is made from concrete and is displayed outside, where, over time, weather will age it.

Two Standing Figures by Federico Assler

FIND OUT MORE | AFRICA, HISTORY OF | ARCHITECTURE | ART, HISTORY OF | BENIN EMPIRE | CHURCHES AND CATHEDRALS | MUSEUMS | PAINTING AND DRAWING | POTTERY AND CERAMICS | RENAISSANCE

Sculpture
Cast sculpture

Egyptian cat goddess, cast in bronze c.600 BC

Bronze equestrian statue of English king William III

Benin bronze cast of king's head, Africa

Viking 10th-century silver figure of a horseman

Bronze bust of a pug dog, France

Dancer, by Edgar Degas (1834–1917)

Carved sculpture

These figures are associated with healing.

Nigerian wood carving of a European missionary

Native North American wooden totem pole

Carved wooden angel, from a medieval church, UK

Nigerian soapstone carving of ancestor figures

Native North American carved clay figurine

Sierra Leone figures, carved in wood

Discus thrower, Roman copy of a Greek original from 450 BC that is now lost

Sculpture captures natural movement of human body.

Central American seated figure of a jaguar deity

Stone dragon, 19th century, London, UK

David, by Michelangelo, 1504

Stone lion, London, UK, 1837

Carving of athlete's muscles and torso looks realistic.

Sweeping curves and sharp lines emphasize this sculpture's three-dimensional quality.

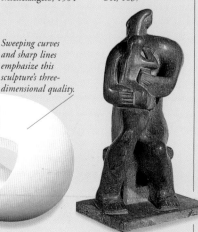

Demon and a Lady of Rank, 13th century, from a cathedral, France

Three Graces, by Antonio Canova, 1813

Oval sculpture, in plaster, by Barbara Hepworth, 1943

Mother and Child, in marble, by Henry Moore, 1932

SEABIRDS

BIRDS THAT SPEND A LARGE part of their lives at sea are called seabirds. There are about 300 species, belonging to 20 different families. They vary in size and shape and also in the way they catch their food. Some seabirds feed by flying close to the surface of the water and snatching their prey. Others plunge beneath the waves and use their wings or feet to swim. Seabirds sometimes travel long distances over the open ocean, but all have to return to land to breed.

Northern gannet

This powerfully built seabird lives in the North Atlantic. It catches fish, such as herrings and mackerel, by diving headfirst into the water and scooping up a fish in its beak. Its head, beak, and body are streamlined to reduce the impact as the bird slams into the water from a height of up to 100 ft (30 m).

Wings are folded back when the gannet plunges into the sea.

Gannets are strong fliers, alternately flapping and gliding.

Feathers
Like other water birds, seabirds cover their feathers with a special oil to keep them waterproof. This oil is made by a gland near the base of the tail.

Salt glands
Seawater is salty, and a seabird's food contains lots of salt, which the birds dispose of through glands in the beak. The glands produce salty water that trickles out through the tip of the beak.

Front-facing eyes pinpoint fish from above.

Feet
All seabirds have webs of skin between their toes. Webbing enables them to paddle through the water. The gannet uses its webbed feet to help it take off after a dive.

It takes five annual molts before young gannets grow the all-white adult plumage.

Seabird features

Seabirds share many features that help them cope with life near saltwater. These include waterproof feathers, webbed feet, and glands that get rid of surplus salt in the body. Most seabirds are good swimmers, but many species rarely settle on the surface of the water.

Feeding

Seabirds live on a wide variety of food, from fish, squid, and jellyfish to small scraps floating on the surface of the water. They use a range of feeding techniques according to the food they are catching. Some rarely catch their own food; they steal it from other birds.

Gulls have a long, hooked beak.

Webbed feet

Cormorant drying
The cormorant does not have fully waterproof feathers so they absorb water. This reduces buoyancy, allowing the bird to dive deeply for fish. After feeding, it has to spread its wings out to dry.

The brown pelican is one of the biggest aerial divers.

Surface divers
Guillemots, puffins, and cormorants swim on the surface, but dive under to pursue their food. Guillemots swim underwater using their wings.

Food thieves
Frigate birds soar over the sea on their long, narrow wings, but hardly ever land on the water. They chase other birds and force them to drop their food.

Surface feeders
Albatrosses, gulls, and storm petrels are surface feeders. Albatrosses and gulls usually snatch food out of the water while flying, but storm petrels patter over the water on their feet.

Aerial divers
Pelicans, gannets, and terns plunge into the water from the air. They have a buoyant body and do not dive deep, but quickly bob up to the surface.

Largest and smallest

The wandering albatross is the largest seabird. It is about 53 in (1.35 m) long with a wingspan of up to 11 ft (3.3 m). The smallest seabird is the least storm petrel, which is about 6 in (15 cm) long.

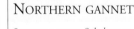

Nesting

Land can be a strange and unfamiliar place to many seabirds. Some spend several years at sea before they visit land to breed. To protect their eggs and chicks, most seabirds nest in large groups in places that land-based predators cannot reach. Some nest in burrows, but many others lay their eggs high up on cliff ledges.

Ground-nesters
Puffins dig clifftop burrows. The females lay a single egg and the chicks spend more than six weeks underground.

Cliff nesters
Kittiwakes nest in huge colonies on cliffs. Each pair makes a nest out of seaweed and raises two to three young.

Ledge nesters
Guillemots lay their eggs on bare ledges. The eggs are pointed at one end so that they roll in a circle and not off the ledge.

NORTHERN GANNET

SCIENTIFIC NAME	*Sula bassana*
ORDER	Pelecaniformes
FAMILY	Sulidae
DISTRIBUTION	North Atlantic
HABITAT	Inshore waters and the open sea
DIET	Fish
SIZE	Length, including tail: 36 in (91 cm)
LIFESPAN	About 20 years

FIND OUT MORE   BIRDS   EGGS   FLIGHT, ANIMAL   OCEAN WILDLIFE   PENGUINS   SHOREBIRDS

SEALS

WITH A STREAMLINED body and four flippers, seals are suited to life in the water. They come on land to rest, mate, and give birth. There are two main groups of seals – true seals and eared seals. Together with the walrus they belong to the order Pinnipedia, meaning "wing foot." Seals live all over the world but are most common in the Arctic and Antarctic where there is plenty of food. They have been hunted for their fur and blubber for hundreds of years and are now threatened by pollution of the oceans.

Eared seal skeleton

Large vertebrae in the neck support powerful muscles for swimming.

Thickened skin under the flippers gives extra grip on land.

Eared seals have a visible ear flap.

On land, eared seals can lift their body clear of the ground.

Californian sea lion

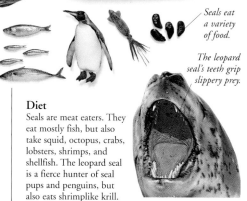

True seal skeleton

Thick layers of fatty blubber under the skin

Gray seal

Nails grip the ground.

Eared seals

The two groups of eared seals – sea lions and fur seals – are more agile on land than the true seals. They can bring their back flippers forward and turn their front flippers outward to walk. The main difference between the two groups is that fur seals have a thick underfur.

True seals

The front limbs of a true seal are smaller than the back limbs and cannot support the seal's weight. True seals move awkwardly on land but are perfectly adapted for life in the water. Before diving for their food, they empty their lungs, and can stay underwater for more than 30 minutes.

Seals eat a variety of food.

The leopard seal's teeth grip slippery prey.

Diet
Seals are meat eaters. They eat mostly fish, but also take squid, octopus, crabs, lobsters, shrimps, and shellfish. The leopard seal is a fierce hunter of seal pups and penguins, but also eats shrimplike krill.

True seal swimming
True seals use their back flippers to push themselves through the water. They press their front flippers against their sides to keep their body streamlined.

Eared seal swimming
An eared seal swims rather like a penguin, using its front flippers to move through the water. Sea lions are more powerful swimmers than fur seals and dive deeper.

Walrus
Found in the Arctic Ocean, near land, walruses are larger than seals, and most closely related to eared seals. They live in groups all year round.

Tusks up to 1 m (3.3 ft) long

Tusks
The upper canine teeth of walruses are long tusks. The animals use these for display, fighting, and hauling themselves out of the water.

Breeding
Seals choose isolated sites, such as rocky islands, to breed because they cannot escape easily from predators. Safe places to breed are rare, so space is often limited.

Elephant seals
Male elephant seals are much larger than females. They make loud calls through their trunklike noses to defend their own group, or harem, of females.

Seal colony
Fur seals gather to breed. Males fight for territory, then the females arrive to give birth. Males then mate with females in their territory.

GRAY SEAL

SCIENTIFIC NAME *Halichoerus grypus*

ORDER Pinnipedia

FAMILY Phocidae

SUB-FAMILY Monachinae

DISTRIBUTION Western North Atlantic, Eastern North Atlantic, and Baltic Sea

HABITAT Ocean, coming on land to mate and give birth

DIET Mainly fish, some sandeels, octopuses, and lobsters

SIZE Length, up to 10 ft (3 m); males are larger than females

LIFESPAN Males 31 years; females 46 years

FIND OUT MORE   MAMMALS   MIGRATION   OCEAN WILDLIFE   POLAR WILDLIFE   WHALES AND DOLPHINS

SEASHORE WILDLIFE

THE SEASHORE IS THE NARROW strip of land around the coast where the land meets the sea. In most places, the tide moves in and out, uncovering the shore twice every 24 hours. During spring tides, at new and full moon, the tides reach farthest up the shore and lowest down the shore. Various animals and plants live at different levels on the shore, called zones, according to how well they tolerate exposure to air or seawater.

Storm waves can pound the seashore, dislodging animals and ripping away seaweeds.

Seashores

Zonation is most clear on rocky shores, where plants and animals live on the surface. Animals cling to rocks or are attached, like barnacles. Seaweeds are anchored by holdfasts. On exposed coasts, zonation is less distinct because spray extends higher up the shore.

The line of washed-up debris is called the strand line.

Sandy shore
There are few clues that animals live on sandy shores because they stay buried in the sand until the tide comes in. Often, the remains of animals, such as shells and the skeletons, or tests, of sea urchins, are washed up.

Tide pools low on the shore are regularly replenished by the tide and contain a rich variety of seashore life.

Tide pools high on the shore have less life, because they suffer greater variation in temperature and salinity.

Plants

A variety of plants that can tolerate salt spray grow in the splash zone – the area that gets sprayed by the waves but does not get covered by the tide. Seaweeds grow from the upper shore to the lower shore, and into deeper water where there is enough light. In some parts of the world, sea grasses also grow on the lower shore.

Mollusks

All mollusks have a soft body surrounded by tissue called the mantle. This secretes the shell of mollusks that have one. Many kinds of mollusks live on the seashore. Most of those on rocky shores crawl around. Most mollusks on sandy shores stay buried in the sand.

Dog whelk
Common inhabitants of the middle shore, dog whelks are predators that feed mainly on barnacles and mussels. They drill a hole in the shell to get at the flesh. If the rock surface dries out, they lose their grip and roll down to damper parts of the shore.

Single foot of limpet, seen from underneath the shell.

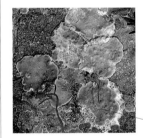

Encrusting algae
Some red seaweeds have chalky tissues. They grow as a crust in tide pools, on boulders, and even on shells, such as limpets.

Red lithothamnion seaweed

Tellins
These clams live buried in the sand on the middle shore and in shallow water. They feed when the tide is in, by extending one of a pair of tube-like siphons over the surface to vacuum up debris.

Mussels
Mussels anchor their shells to rocks with strong strands, called byssus threads. Tiny mussels can move around on their one foot, but they soon attach themselves to other mussel shells.

Limpets
A limpet's large muscular foot allows it to cling tightly to the rocks, both to avoid being washed away and to deter predators. When covered by the tide, limpets crawl around grazing algae from the rock.

Sea slugs
This sea slug gets its name of sea lemon because it looks like a lemon. Lacking a shell, sea slugs are delicate creatures that usually live below low tide. The sea lemon comes onto rocky shores in the summer to lay its eggs.

Seaweed
The largest seaweeds are the brown ones like wracks and kelps. This channelled wrack grows on the upper shore. Red and green seaweeds are smaller and more delicate, often growing in tide pools and on the lower shore.

Lichens
Orange, gray, and black patches on the rocks on the upper shore are lichens. These are made up of algal cells growing in a network of fungal tissue. Lichens tolerate both salt spray and dry conditions.

Crustaceans

There is a great variety of crustaceans, most of which live in the sea. They have a hard outer skeleton, jointed limbs, and two pairs of antennae in front of the mouth. Many crawl, and some swim, while barnacles spend their adult life stuck to surfaces such as rocks.

Narrow pincer for slicing flesh.

First two pairs of legs end in pincers.

Second two pairs of legs end in claws.

Barnacle cemented to lobster's shell.

Heavy pincer for crushing shellfish.

Hermit crabs
Most hermit crabs use a sea snail's shell to protect their soft abdomen. This colorful hermit crab lives on coral reefs. It is found at low tide, hunting among the corals and in rocky crevices for food.

Sea slaters
These relatives of sow bugs live in damp places on the upper shore where there is enough moisture for them to breathe through their gills. They come out from crevices at night to feed on rotting seaweed.

Lobsters
Occasionally, lobsters are found in tide pools on the lower shore. This one has become a home for barnacles, another type of crustacean. Mostly barnacles settle on rocks, but space is limited so some settle on shells. These will lose their home when the lobster molts.

Echinoderms

This group of spiny-skinned sea creatures includes starfish and sea urchins, some of which live on the lower shore under rocks and seaweeds, and in tide pools. Most echinoderms have a five-rayed body plan. They all have tiny tube feet filled with seawater and connected to canals inside their body.

Sand dollars
Sand dollars are sea urchins that are flattened in shape. When alive, they are covered in tiny spines. They live on the surface of the sand, often in warm waters. Bare shells are sometimes washed up on the beach.

Sea potato
The sea potato is a sea urchin. It uses the broader, flatter spines on its lower surface to dig itself down into the sand. It takes in sand, feeding on the film of nutritious material coating the grains.

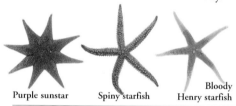

Purple sunstar   Spiny starfish   **Bloody Henry starfish**

Starfish
These starfish live on the lower part of rocky shores and in deeper water. They have a double row of tube feet on the underside of each arm. The tube feet are tipped with suckers, so the starfish can cling to the rocks.

Sea urchins
Like all sea urchins, the common sea urchin has a mouth on its underside. It has five strong teeth with which it scrapes off seaweeds and animals, such as sea mats, from rocks and the long stems of kelps.

Tube feet

Spines

Worms

With their long wriggly bodies, worms look similar to each other, but there are many different groups, which are not all closely related. Among the worm groups that live on the seashore are the peanut worms that do not have body segments, and the bristleworms that do have body segments and bristles.

The body has more than 100 segments.

Ragworms
These bristleworms live under rocks and clumps of seaweed. They crawl using their paddlelike legs, and swim by passing wavelike motions toward the head.

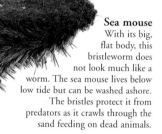

Sea mouse
With its big, flat body, this bristleworm does not look much like a worm. The sea mouse lives below low tide but can be washed ashore. The bristles protect it from predators as it crawls through the sand feeding on dead animals.

Coarse bristles help the worm to move along.

Worm inside its papery tube

Parchment worm
This bizarre bristleworm lives in a papery burrow it constructs in muddy sand on the lower shore and in deeper water. It beats its fan-shaped paddles back and forth to draw water into the burrow, from which it takes in oxygen. Food particles in the water are trapped in a mucus net that the worm then eats.

Peanut worms
Some peanut worms look like peanut seeds when the front part of the body is retracted into the thicker trunk. The mouth is surrounded by a ring of tentacles. Peanut worms burrow in sand or mud, from the shore to the deep sea.

Beadlet anemones
These anemones unfurl their stinging tentacles when covered by water. The anemones use their tentacles to catch small prey and push it into their mouths.

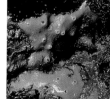

Breadcrumb sponge
Most sponges live in the sea from the shore to the deep sea. This sponge grows under rocks on the lower shore. Sponges are simple animals that usually grow attached to surfaces.

Sea turtle
Female turtles come ashore at night to lay eggs in the sand. Green turtles usually return to the beach where they hatched. They lay about 100 eggs at a time, laying up to five times during the breeding season.

FIND OUT MORE   CRABS AND CRUSTACEANS   JELLYFISH, SEA ANEMONES, AND SPONGES   OCEAN WILDLIFE   SNAILS AND OTHER MOLLUSKS   STARFISH AND SEA URCHINS   TURTLES AND TORTOISES

SEAWEEDS AND OTHER ALGAE

ALGAE ARE THE SIMPLEST of all the plants. They have no waxy layer to prevent drying out, so they live in water or moist places. Algae range in size from minute, single-celled species to seaweeds that can be several feet long. In common with more advanced plants, all algae contain the green pigment chlorophyll. They also contain other pigments that mask the chlorophyll, so algae can be red, purple, or brown, as well as green.

Selection of green, red, and brown seaweeds

Seaweeds
Marine algae are better known as seaweeds. Like other photosynthetic plants, seaweeds need sunlight. Little sunlight penetrates depths greater than 50 ft (15 m), so most seaweeds grow in shallow waters around shores or reefs. Seaweeds provide food for tiny creatures, most of which filter dead particles from the water.

Wrack

Brown seaweeds
These seaweeds include the kelps, gulfweed, and wracks. They are tough, slippery plants. Many of them can survive for long periods out of water.

Channeled wrack

Green seaweeds
Less than 10 percent of the green algae are seaweeds. Green seaweeds are small- to medium-sized plants, often with very thin, delicate fronds. Some such as the sea lettuce, are used as food in parts of the world.

Green seaweed

Red seaweeds
The seaweeds in this group get their red color from a pigment called phycoerythrin. Red seaweeds are small- to medium-sized plants. Some of them are made rigid by a chalky secretion.

Maerl seaweed

Spirogyra
These are threadlike green algae. They are found as a tangled mass in ponds. The ones shown here are magnified 56 times.

Micrasterias
These algae are just visible to the naked eye. They belong to a family of green algae whose single cells are almost divided in two by a "waist." They live in damp, waterside mosses.

Freshwater algae
Many freshwater algae can be seen clearly only under a microscope. They consist of just one or a few cells, or a long, thin line of cells.

Floats
Some species of wrack and kelp have fronds with conspicuous air bladders. These ensure that the fronds stay at the surface of the sea, where the light is brightest, even when the sea is rough.

Holdfast
The holdfast is frequently a many-branched structure that does just what its name suggests – it clings to rocks no matter how much it is pounded by the waves.

Parts of a seaweed
Seaweeds have no roots, leaves, flowers, or seeds. The seaweed plant body is called a thallus. It is divided into a holdfast (hapteron), a stalk (stipe), and a frond. The stalk may be very short – just a few millimeters long – or, occasionally, many meters long. In the sea, seaweeds float gracefully, but they cannot support themselves if taken out of the water.

Giant kelp
This seaweed lives in much deeper water than other seaweeds and can grow to more than 197 ft (60 m) long. Attached to the ocean floor, each plant produces a long stipe that can grow more than three feet in one day to reach light. Sea otters love to float among the fronds.

Lifecycle of a brown seaweed

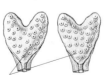

Male and female receptacles

Oogonium

Male sex cells

Male cells come to fertilize female cell

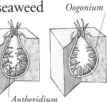

Antheridium

Female sex cells

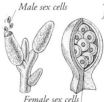

1 Separate male and female reproductive patches, called receptacles, develop at the tip of fronds.

2 Embedded in receptacles are conceptacles, which contain the sex organs – antheridia (male) and oogonia (female).

3 The oogonia split to release female sex cells. Male sex cells swim into the water through pores.

4 Male sex cells are attracted to a female cell to fertilize it by means of chemicals.

 FIND OUT MORE   LAKE AND RIVER WILDLIFE   OCEAN WILDLIFE   PHOTOSYNTHESIS   PLANTS   SEASHORE WILDLIFE

SEVEN WONDERS OF THE ANCIENT WORLD

IN ANCIENT GREEK AND ROMAN TIMES, 2,500 years ago, as people became more interested in the world outside their villages, writers began to celebrate the greatest technological achievements of the age. These writers included the Greeks Herodotus and Antipater, and the buildings and statues they wrote about became known as the Seven Wonders of the World. The wonders ranged from the Pyramids of Giza in Egypt to the Colossus, a statue that towered over the harbor at Rhodes. They showed what the stonemasons, architects, sculptors, metalworkers, and engineers of the ancient world could achieve with the simple tools at their disposal.

The wonders were located around the Mediterranean Sea.

Pharos of Alexandria

This great lighthouse was planned in the reign of Ptolemy I of Egypt and built by c.280 BC, on the island of Pharos just outside Alexandria in Egypt. The light from its fire was visible up to 30 miles (50 km) away and it became the model for many later lighthouses. In 796, the Pharos was damaged by fire and rebuilt, but the original foundations can still be seen.

Mausoleum at Halicarnassus
The tomb of the Persian governor Mausolos was built in Halicarnassus, in present-day Turkey, in the 4th century BC. It was famous for its size and lavishly carved decoration. The Mausoleum was damaged in an earthquake in the 13th century and was later demolished.

Hanging Gardens
The Babylonian king Nebuchadnezzar II built these lush gardens in the 7th century BC to remind his queen, Amytis, of her native Persia. It was a masterpiece of engineering, with small streams flowing along the terraces, bringing water to the plants and trees that grew there.

Great Pyramid
The Pyramids of Giza in Egypt are the only survivors of the Seven Wonders of the World, and are also the oldest. There are three: the Great Pyramid was built as his tomb by Pharaoh Khufu in c.2560 BC. The others were built for two of his successors, Khafre and Menkaure, and are smaller.

Statue of Zeus
In 456 BC, the sculptor Phidias built a 43-ft (13-m) ivory-and-gold statue of Zeus holding a figure of the goddess of victory. A temple was built around the statue at Olympia, Greece, home of the original Olympic Games. In AD 394, the statue was moved to Constantinople (Istanbul), but later destroyed.

Temple of Artemis
This temple was originally built in c.560 BC in the Greek city of Ephesus (Turkey) as a sanctuary for Artemis, goddess of hunting, chastity, and childbirth. The temple was destroyed by the Ostrogoths in AD 263.

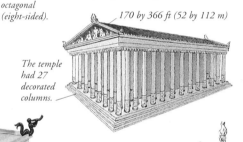
170 by 366 ft (52 by 112 m)
The temple had 27 decorated columns.

Colossus of Rhodes
This huge statue of the Greek sun-god Helios stood near the harbor on the island of Rhodes, Greece. Standing at 110 ft (33 m) and made of cast bronze sections supported on an iron framework, it was the largest statue of its time. An earthquake toppled the Colossus in c.225 BC – only 65 years after it was built to commemorate the end of a seven-year siege.

Statue of Zeus
Pharos tower was 344 ft (105 m) high.
Constantly burning fire of wood or oil.
Metal mirrors to reflect flames
The middle section was octagonal (eight-sided).
The bottom section was square.
A statue crowned the top level.
The base was 126 by 105 ft (38 by 32 m).
Rooms for fuel storage and accommodation
Ancient Egyptians built their pyramids from the center outward.
Base kept tower above sea level.
Each side measured 755 ft (230 m) at the base.

Herodotus
Known as the Father of History, the Greek writer Herodotus (c.484– 425 BC) was born in Halicarnassus, western Asia. He described several of the wonders, particularly the pyramids, in his book, *The Histories*. He also wrote about the Walls of Babylon, which some lists included instead of the Pharos of Alexandria.

FIND OUT MORE — ALEXANDER THE GREAT, BABYLONIAN EMPIRE, HOLY LAND, HISTORY OF, GREECE, ANCIENT, PYRAMIDS

SHAKESPEARE, WILLIAM

THE ENGLISH WRITER William Shakespeare was probably the greatest playwright who has ever lived. In spite of this, few facts are known about his life. Contemporaries who wrote about him described him as a good-looking man who liked a quiet life. Thirty-seven of his plays have survived, although he may have written more that have been lost. He wrote mostly in unrhymed verse, though he also used prose. He was a very successful playwright and actor, and was eventually able to buy a large house in his English hometown, Stratford-upon-Avon. He retired there for the very last few years of his life, and died in 1616.

Shakespeare's birthplace

Early life
Shakespeare was born in 1564 at Stratford-upon-Avon, England. His father was a local businessman. Shakespeare probably went to the town grammar school, where he would have had rigorous study.

Globe Theatre

From 1592, Shakespeare worked as an actor and writer in London. He joined a company called the Lord Chamberlain's Men. In 1599, he and six associates became owners of the Globe Theatre near the Thames. This became the company's home, and many of his plays were produced there.

The Globe no longer survives; this is one possible reconstruction.

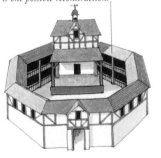

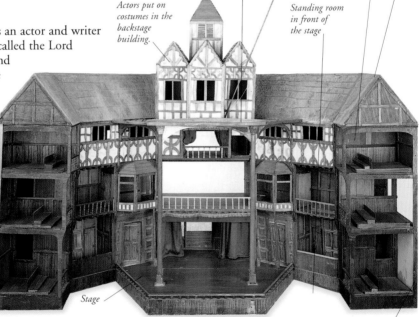

Wooden canopy over stage

Galleries with seats

Thatched roof

Standing room in front of the stage

Actors put on costumes in the backstage building.

Stage

Structure of oak beams

First Folio
Shakespeare did not publish his plays – he wanted to keep the scripts for his company. After his death, his friends John Hemminges and Henry Condell collected the plays and published them in 1623 in a book known as the *First Folio*.

Portrait of Shakespeare on title page of *First Folio*

Shakespeare's works

William Shakespeare wrote his plays with the actors of his company in mind. In addition to comedies (featuring famous comic actor Will Kempe) and tragedies (for leading tragedian Richard Burbage), he wrote a whole series of plays, such as *Henry V* and *Richard III*, about English history. He was one of the most versatile writers of his or any other time.

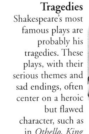

Richard III

Sonnets
Shakespeare wrote 154 fourteen-line poems called sonnets. Some of these are addressed to a young man, others to a woman with dark hair now known as the "dark lady" of the sonnets. It is not known for certain who these two people actually were.

Title page of the first edition of the sonnets

Tragedies
Shakespeare's most famous plays are probably his tragedies. These plays, with their serious themes and sad endings, often center on a heroic but flawed character, such as in *Othello, King Lear, Macbeth,* and *Hamlet.*

Othello

Comedies
Shakespeare's comedies are love stories with amusing twists. They are still among his most popular works. They include *A Midsummer Night's Dream, Twelfth Night,* and *As You Like It.*

Jester in *Twelfth Night*

WILLIAM SHAKESPEARE

1564	Born, Stratford-upon-Avon.
1582	Marries Anne Hathaway.
1592	Writes his first plays in London for the Lord Chamberlain's Men.
1593–94	Plague epidemic forces theaters to close; Shakespeare writes poems such as *Venus and Adonis.*
1594–99	Writes comedies and histories.
1599	Globe Theatre built.
1603	Lord Chamberlain's Men gain the support of King James I; they become the King's Men.
1600–08	Produces many of the great tragedies.
1616	Dies in Stratford-upon-Avon.

FIND OUT MORE   DRAMA   ELIZABETH I   POETRY   THEATERS   UNITED KINGDOM, HISTORY OF

SHARKS AND RAYS

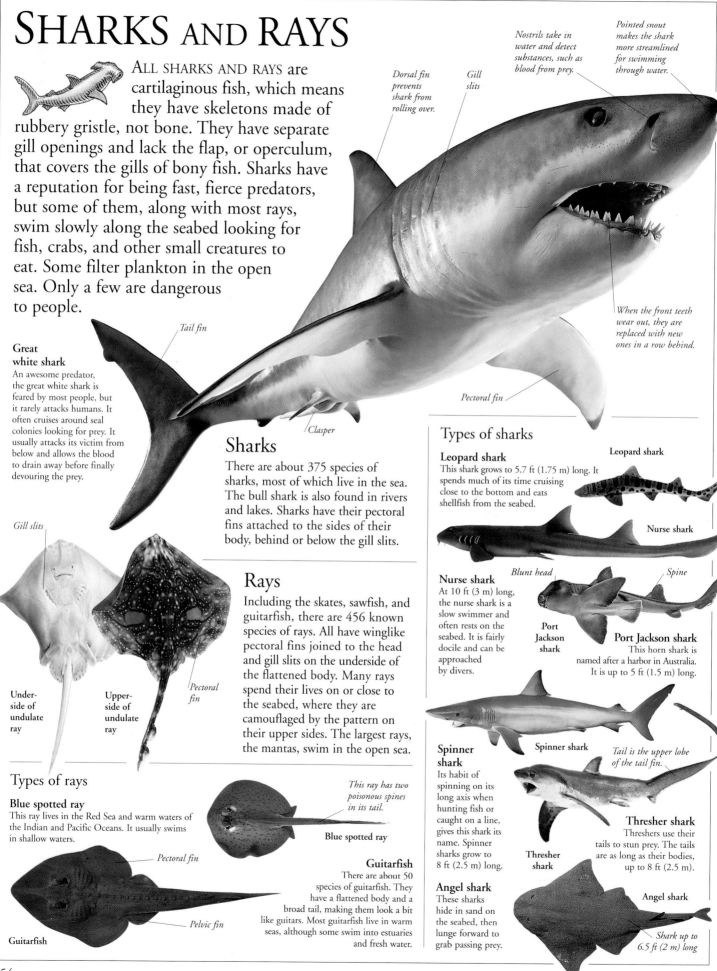

ALL SHARKS AND RAYS are cartilaginous fish, which means they have skeletons made of rubbery gristle, not bone. They have separate gill openings and lack the flap, or operculum, that covers the gills of bony fish. Sharks have a reputation for being fast, fierce predators, but some of them, along with most rays, swim slowly along the seabed looking for fish, crabs, and other small creatures to eat. Some filter plankton in the open sea. Only a few are dangerous to people.

Dorsal fin prevents shark from rolling over.

Gill slits

Nostrils take in water and detect substances, such as blood from prey.

Pointed snout makes the shark more streamlined for swimming through water.

Tail fin

When the front teeth wear out, they are replaced with new ones in a row behind.

Pectoral fin

Great white shark
An awesome predator, the great white shark is feared by most people, but it rarely attacks humans. It often cruises around seal colonies looking for prey. It usually attacks its victim from below and allows the blood to drain away before finally devouring the prey.

Clasper

Sharks

There are about 375 species of sharks, most of which live in the sea. The bull shark is also found in rivers and lakes. Sharks have their pectoral fins attached to the sides of their body, behind or below the gill slits.

Gill slits

Under-side of undulate ray

Upper-side of undulate ray

Pectoral fin

Rays

Including the skates, sawfish, and guitarfish, there are 456 known species of rays. All have winglike pectoral fins joined to the head and gill slits on the underside of the flattened body. Many rays spend their lives on or close to the seabed, where they are camouflaged by the pattern on their upper sides. The largest rays, the mantas, swim in the open sea.

Types of sharks

Leopard shark
This shark grows to 5.7 ft (1.75 m) long. It spends much of its time cruising close to the bottom and eats shellfish from the seabed.

Leopard shark

Nurse shark

Nurse shark
At 10 ft (3 m) long, the nurse shark is a slow swimmer and often rests on the seabed. It is fairly docile and can be approached by divers.

Blunt head

Spine

Port Jackson shark

Port Jackson shark
This horn shark is named after a harbor in Australia. It is up to 5 ft (1.5 m) long.

Spinner shark
Its habit of spinning on its long axis when hunting fish or caught on a line, gives this shark its name. Spinner sharks grow to 8 ft (2.5 m) long.

Spinner shark

Tail is the upper lobe of the tail fin.

Thresher shark
Threshers use their tails to stun prey. The tails are as long as their bodies, up to 8 ft (2.5 m).

Thresher shark

Angel shark
These sharks hide in sand on the seabed, then lunge forward to grab passing prey.

Angel shark

Shark up to 6.5 ft (2 m) long

Types of rays

Blue spotted ray
This ray lives in the Red Sea and warm waters of the Indian and Pacific Oceans. It usually swims in shallow waters.

This ray has two poisonous spines in its tail.

Blue spotted ray

Pectoral fin

Guitarfish
There are about 50 species of guitarfish. They have a flattened body and a broad tail, making them look a bit like guitars. Most guitarfish live in warm seas, although some swim into estuaries and fresh water.

Pelvic fin

Guitarfish

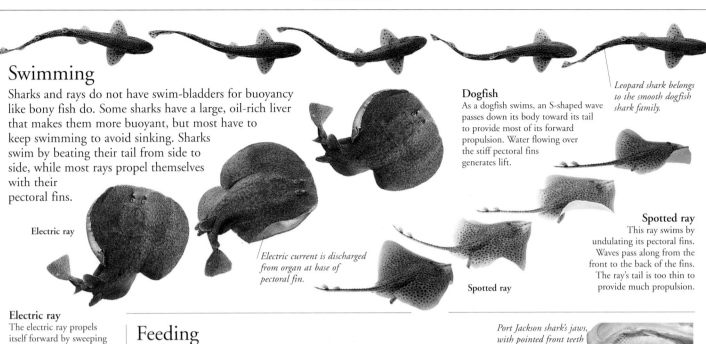

S

Leopard shark belongs to the smooth dogfish shark family.

Swimming

Sharks and rays do not have swim-bladders for buoyancy like bony fish do. Some sharks have a large, oil-rich liver that makes them more buoyant, but most have to keep swimming to avoid sinking. Sharks swim by beating their tail from side to side, while most rays propel themselves with their pectoral fins.

Electric ray

Electric current is discharged from organ at base of pectoral fin.

Dogfish

As a dogfish swims, an S-shaped wave passes down its body toward its tail to provide most of its forward propulsion. Water flowing over the stiff pectoral fins generates lift.

Spotted ray

This ray swims by undulating its pectoral fins. Waves pass along from the front to the back of the fins. The ray's tail is too thin to provide much propulsion.

Spotted ray

Electric ray

The electric ray propels itself forward by sweeping its broad tail from side to side. Undulations passing in waves along the edges of its pectoral fins also help it swim. All electric rays produce electricity and can discharge over 300 volts.

Feeding

All sharks and rays are predators. The fastest sharks, such as makos and great whites, chase and kill fish and other prey. The sluggish sharks, such as nurse sharks and swell sharks, lie in wait for victims on the seabed or feed on slow-moving prey such as clams. Most rays eat shellfish buried in the sand or mud, but manta rays eat plankton that they filter out of the water.

Port Jackson shark's jaws, with pointed front teeth and crushing back teeth

Tiger shark tooth has a sharp point and a serrated cutting edge.

Gill rakers

Gill arch

Teeth

The shape of a shark's teeth indicates what it eats. Sharp curved teeth grip fish; serrated teeth cut flesh; a fused row of flattened teeth crush shellfish.

Electrosense

Sharks can detect small amounts of electricity generated by their prey. They pick up signals from pores on their snout. They also appear to navigate by detecting changes in their electric field in relation to the Earth's magnetic field.

Whale shark

Largest and smallest

The largest shark, also the largest fish, is the whale shark, which reaches lengths of at least 39 ft (12 m) long. Like other ocean giants, it strains food out of the water using gill rakers, however, it also eats quite large fish. The lantern sharks are the smallest sharks. They grow to less than 8 in (20 cm) long.

Lantern shark

Gill rakers

Inside the basking shark's huge mouth are gill arches lined with rows of bristles called gill rakers. The rakers create a sieve through which water is strained before it flows out through the gill slits. Tiny animals called plankton, drifting in the water, are caught in the rakers and then swallowed.

Sawfish "saw"

Sawfish are types of rays that have a row of teeth on each side of a long snout. The sawfish uses its "saw" to probe the mud for prey such as mollusks and crustaceans. The "saw" may also be used to kill fish by slashing at them when the sawfish swims through a shoal.

Reproduction

In both sharks and rays, the male passes sperm directly into the female with an organ called a clasper, so the eggs are fertilized inside her. Most sharks and rays give birth to live young, but some, such as dogfish, lay eggs with horny cases. Compared to bony fish, some of which lay millions of eggs at a time, sharks and rays produce relatively few eggs or young at a time – from one to 300.

Dogfish hatching

1 A dogfish embryo takes about nine months to develop before it is ready to hatch.

2 When the young dogfish breaks out of its egg case, it looks like a small version of its parents.

Tendrils anchor the egg to seaweed.

3 The dogfish swims free and must fend for itself immediately. It will soon start to feed on small prey.

Live birth

A lemon shark pup is born tail-first. Inside its mother, it was nourished by blood passing through a placenta, like a human baby. This birth is unusual. Most shark pups develop from large yolky eggs inside the mother.

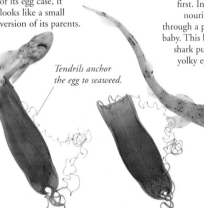

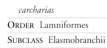

GREAT WHITE SHARK

SCIENTIFIC NAME *Carcharodon carcharias*

ORDER Lamniformes

SUBCLASS Elasmobranchii

CLASS Chondrichthyes

DISTRIBUTION All oceans

DIET Fish, seals, dolphins, and whale carcasses

SIZE Up to 19.5 ft (6 m) long

 FIND OUT MORE   EGGS   FISH   OCEAN WILDLIFE   POLAR WILDLIFE   REPRODUCTION   WHALES AND DOLPHINS

SHEEP AND GOATS

WITH THEIR THICK COATS and ability to tackle rough terrain, sheep and goats can survive under harsh conditions, ranging from mountain cold to desert heat. Sheep and goats are closely related and belong to a group of mammals that also includes antelope and cattle. There are many types of sheep and goats. They live in western North America, northern Africa, Europe, and Asia, spending the summer at high altitude, descending to the foothills and valleys in winter.

Features of sheep and goats

Sheep and goats are agile creatures with cloven, or split, hooves that allow them to scramble over the craggiest of rocks. They have keen eyesight, good hearing, and coats of wool or hair. All rams (males) have horns. Goats have beards, and the males give off a pungent smell; sheep are beardless. Sheep graze on grass; goats browse mainly on shrubs. Both animals regurgitate their food and chew the cud.

Bighorn sheep
Bighorns live in the Rocky Mountains of North America. They take their name from the large horns of the rams. The horns grow backward, then curve around to point forward at eye level in older animals.

Corkscrew horns

Rams' horns can reach 36 in (91 cm) in length.

Goats' foreheads curve outwards

Sheeps' foreheads curve inwards

Woolly coat

Mane

Cloven hooves

Markhor
Markhors live in the Hindu Kush and nearby mountains in Afghanistan. Males and females have beards and manes that run along the chest, throat, neck, and back. The male's corkscrew horns may reach 5 ft 5 in (1.65 m) along the curve.

Types of horns
The males of all wild sheep and goats have curved horns. Females of some species, such as barbary sheep and ibex, also have horns.

Himalayan ibex of both sexes have large, heavy, gnarled horns.

Mouflons, Europe's only wild sheep, have spiral horns with tips pointing inward.

Argalis, the largest of all sheep, may have horns up to 6 ft (1.83 m) long.

Bharal, or blue sheep, from central Asia, have horns that curve backward and inward.

Reproduction

Female sheep and goats mature by 2 years; males by 3–4 years. Mature males live apart from the females, but rejoin the herd in the rutting season to find a mate. In spring, after 5–7 months' gestation, females give birth to one kid, or sometimes twins. The young can walk almost at birth and follow their mother, who protects them.

Family groups
Most sheep and goats live in small herds of females and young. Old rams are solitary and live apart for most of the year. Young rams form separate bachelor groups. Sheep and goats feed in the early morning and evening and rest among rocks during the heat of the day. The herds are extremely wary; several females act as guards and either stamp or give a warning whistle if danger threatens.

Chamois live in herds of up to 30 animals.

Family group of chamois

Female watches for danger.

Huge horns

Ram rears and will charge head on.

Alpine ibex fighting

Fighting
During the breeding season, males frequently fight to establish dominance. They kick and paw with their forel legs, then charge head on. They often rise up on their hind legs, lowering their heads at the last moment to meet with a skull- splitting crash that can leave them dazed. Rams may also strike each other from the side.

Adaptation to habitat

Most sheep and goats are exceptionally hardy and live in highland regions. Agile species, such as the chamois, have special hooves that grip rock and cushion the shock of heavy landings, enabling them to move easily over sheer rock faces. Rocky Mountain goats can negotiate the steepest of inclines with ease, and can jump down vertical rock walls onto narrow ledges. The ability to thrive in harsh conditions makes sheep and goats suitable for domestication.

Dense white fur for warmth in the mountains

Rocky Mountain goats

BIGHORN SHEEP

SCIENTIFIC NAME *Ovis canadensis*

ORDER Artiodactyla

FAMILY Bovidae

DISTRIBUTION North America, from British Columbia to Mexico

HABITAT Craggy, often precipitous slopes extending above the timber line

DIET Primarily grazes on grass, but also eats berries, lichen, and bark in winter, and shoots and spruce in summer

SIZE Male – height at shoulder: 3.5 ft (1.06 m); weight: 300 lb (136 kg)

LIFESPAN Up to 15 years

FIND OUT MORE   ANIMALS   DEER AND ANTELOPE   EUROPEAN WILDLIFE   FARMING   MAMMALS   MOUNTAIN WILDLIFE   NORTH AMERICAN WILDLIFE

SHIPS AND BOATS

THROUGHOUT HISTORY, ships and boats have provided an important means of transportation. Early boats were simple, made from hollowed-out logs or bundles of reeds. Over the years the design of ships and boats improved as nations began to trade and fight for supremacy at sea. Although there are similarities between a boat and a ship, a boat is in fact much smaller and lighter. It is usually a single-decked craft propelled by either a sail, a pair of oars, or an outboard motor. A ship, however, is a large, ocean-going vessel, powered by many engines. Unlike a boat, it can carry large cargoes and passengers across the seas.

Types of ships and boats

There are many different types of ships and boats. Most are designed to carry out a specific function, such as fishing, carrying goods and people, fighting, or leisure. As a result, there are differences in the shape of the hull, the size of the engine, and the equipment that is carried on board.

Sport and leisure boats
Boats used for pleasure are designed for a variety of purposes, such as racing and cruising. They range in size from lightweight jet skis to large luxury motor cruisers and yachts.

Fishing boats
Fishing boats are sturdy vessels designed to withstand rough seas. Various types of boats are used to catch different sorts of fish. A trawler, for example, is equipped to catch deep sea fish. Today, most fishing boats are motorized.

Service vessels
Working boats have a variety of uses. For example, a tug tows larger ships in and out of harbors. In Arctic countries, icebreakers are used to crush through the ice and clear a path for other ships.

Warships
Warships are operated by the world's navies to patrol the seas and oceans. The largest is the aircraft carrier. Frigates protect aircraft carriers and search for enemy submarines.

Cruise liners

Cruise liners are large ships that carry travelers around the world. A liner is similar to a luxury hotel on water, and is a popular form of travel with many vacationers. Before long-distance air travel became common in the 1960s, passenger liners such as the *Queen Mary* were the only way for most people to travel between the continents.

How ships float
A ship's hull pushes through water, and the water pushes back on the ship with a force called upthrust. The upthrust balances the weight of the ship and keeps it afloat.

Upthrust from water pushing upward

Sections of a liner
The inside of a liner is divided into decks, separating the sleeping areas from the rest of the ship. All outdoor activities take place on the upper decks, while entertainment rooms and cabins are located on the lower decks.

Sun deck   *Entertainment deck*

Passenger cabins   *Medical quarters*   *Crew's quarters*

Captain
The captain of a ship is responsible for the safety of the passengers and crew on board. From the control room, the captain maintains contact with other ships in the surrounding waters and with onshore control centers.

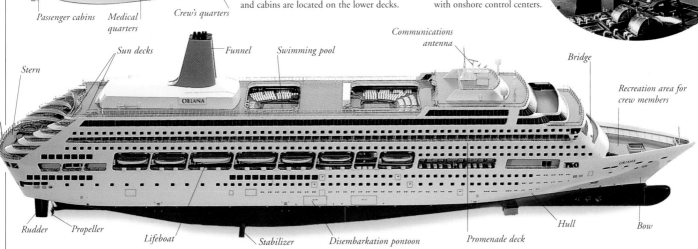

Stern — *Sun decks* — *Funnel* — *Swimming pool* — *Communications antenna* — *Bridge* — *Recreation area for crew members*

Rudder — *Propeller* — *Lifeboat* — *Stabilizer* — *Disembarkation pontoon* — *Promenade deck* — *Hull* — *Bow*

Hull shapes

Ships and boats have different hulls that make the vessel more efficient at moving through the water and carrying cargo. The shape also determines how far the vessel sinks into the water, or how stable it is against rolling.

Keeled boat
A sailboat has a rounded hull to help control the boat in strong winds. The keel is filled with a heavy ballast, such as concrete, to stop the sailboat from tipping over.

Keel

Cargo ship
In the middle of a cargo ship, the hull is as large as possible so that it can contain heavy loads. The hull is more V-shaped toward the bow, and rounder at the stern.

Central hull

Speedboat
The shape of a speedboat's hull helps keep air between the boat and the water. As the boat speeds up, the hull starts to skim across the water instead of cutting through it.

Flat V-shape

Catamaran
A catamaran has two separate hulls, joined together with strong crossbeams. This shape is very stable because it is so wide.

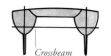

Crossbeam

Engines

Engines provide the power to push a ship or boat through the water. They normally turn one or more propellers under the stern of the vessel. The propellers bite into the water, forcing the ship along. Most ships burn diesel fuel to produce gas or steam to turn the turbine engines. Some ships use nuclear energy. An outboard motor usually powers leisure boats.

Ship engineer checking machinery

Engine room
Situated on the lower decks of a ship, the engine room houses all the engines and electricity generators needed to make the ship function. Regular maintenance checks ensure that all the equipment is in order and safe to use. Many engine rooms on large ships are controlled by computers.

Outboard motor engine
Small boats are often powered by an outboard engine attached to the stern. A throttle is used to start up the engine and the boat is steered using the tiller.

Throttle

On the bridge
The main control room of a ship is called a bridge. Located on the upper deck, toward the front of the vessel, it has large windows to give good all-around visibility. It houses the ship's steering and navigational instruments, such as radar, as well as controls for the engine room.

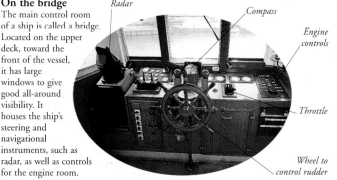
Radar · Compass · Engine controls · Throttle · Wheel to control rudder

Shipbuilding

Building a large ship is a major engineering project, requiring hundreds of expert workers. Although the basic structure of ships has not changed since the first wooden ships were built, materials such as steel and plastic are now used. Today, many ships are built in sections, which are then fastened together.

1 The first part of a ship to be built is the keel, followed by the stern and hull. Scaffolding is used to support the hull and keel so they will not tip over. The ship is usually built on a metal slipway.

2 Once the structure of the ship is complete, the upper decks of the hull start to take shape. Skilled workers start to work on the rest of the ship. The ship is then launched as an empty shell, where it is equipped for a lifetime at sea.

Sailboat

Sailboats use wind for propulsion. They do not have to have the wind behind them – they can travel in almost any direction by adjusting the position of their sails. Most modern sailboats have two sails, arranged in a "Bermuda" rig. Some also have an engine, in addition to the sails.

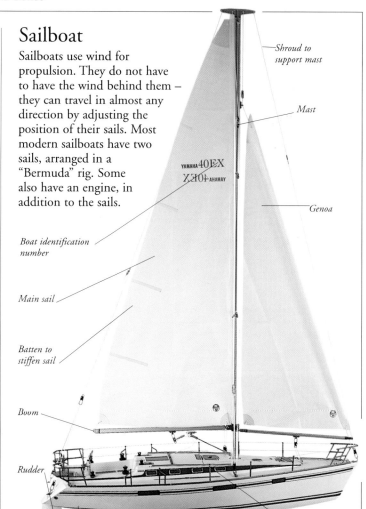
Shroud to support mast · Mast · Genoa · Boat identification number · Main sail · Batten to stiffen sail · Boom · Rudder · Fiberglass reinforced plastic hull. · Cabin · Keel

Passenger services

Despite the growth of airlines, ships still carry thousands of passengers to their chosen destinations. Modern passenger ships include ferries, hovercrafts, and hydrofoils. New designs mean that ships are faster, safer, more economical to maintain, and more environmentally friendly.

Hovercraft
A hovercraft reduces water resistance by riding just above the surface on a cushion of air. The cushion is made by large fans blowing air under the hovercraft. The air is held in place by a flexible "skirt." The hovercraft is pushed along by propellers in the air. Hovercraft can travel onto land for loading and unloading.

Hydrofoil
All boats are slowed down by the resistance of the water on their hulls. Hydrofoils have winglike foils under the hull. As the boat speeds up, the foils lift the hull completely out of the water, and the boat skims across the surface. This allows the hydrofoil to travel much faster than other boats.

Ships and boats
Merchant ships

Tramp steamers are cargo vessels with no fixed route.

Oil tankers are specially constructed to carry vast quantities of oil.

Liberty ships were mass-produced steel cargo ships. They were made by the US during World War II.

Containers

Container ships are designed to stow and transport large freight containers efficiently.

Cruise liners do not take freight containers, and are equipped with passenger entertainments and facilities.

Large freight containers park on deck.

Drive-on-drive-off ferries allow trucks and passenger cars to drive on and off without unloading.

Fighting ships

Torpedo tubes

Torpedo boats are swift, small warships that carry torpedoes and other weapons.

Ship is controlled from bridge.

Flight deck

Aircraft carriers are huge warships with large landing strips to allow aircraft to take off and land.

Minesweepers drag the water to remove undersea mines.

Utility craft and fishing vessels

Dredgers clear shipping channels, keeping them free from obstructions.

Police riverboats patrol waterways, sometimes in search of smugglers.

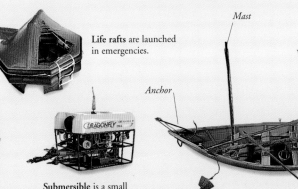

Life rafts are launched in emergencies.

Anchor

Submersible is a small underwater craft.

Mast

Oar

Grapnel

Trawler often diesel powered

Deep-sea trawlers drag nets to catch fish.

Small fishing boats are used to catch fish with rod and line.

Pleasure craft

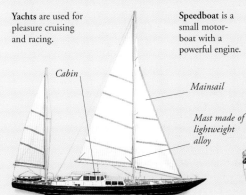

Yachts are used for pleasure cruising and racing.

Cabin

Mainsail

Mast made of lightweight alloy

Speedboat is a small motor-boat with a powerful engine.

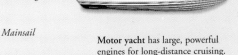

Motor yacht has large, powerful engines for long-distance cruising.

Sailing dingy is used to teach young people to sail.

Sprit

Boom

Mast

Hull

Wooden rudder

Rutterboard

SHOPS

BUILDINGS DEVOTED TO BUYING and selling, shops allow customers to buy small amounts of what they need. They are the end of a chain that sees products travel from a manufacturer to a consumer, and shopping is a vital part of any national economy. Historically, shops such as butchers and bakers stocked only one sort of product. Today, shopping is big business; global chain stores sell a variety of goods. Customers can also buy from 'online shops' on the Internet and have the goods delivered.

Butcher's shop in ancient Rome

Early shops

Early nomadic peoples traded goods wherever they wandered. Shops began when people first settled in towns and were common by 3000 BC. They did not replace outdoor trading at fairs and in markets. The huge 16th-century market at Tlaltelolco, Mexico, astonished Spaniards who came and conquered the Aztec Empire.

Shopping centers

Increasingly, many different items are sold under one roof. Department stores are large shops, each department specializing in a different kind of item. The first opened in Paris, France, in 1865. Shopping malls began in 19th-century Europe as arcades linking downtown streets. The first modern-style mall opened in Kansas City, MO, in the 1920s.

Harrods' merchandise

Supermarkets

A supermarket is a self-service food store. The first was opened in 1916 in Memphis, Tennessee. The invention of the shopping cart in 1937 allowed shoppers to buy more than they could carry, and ensured the success of the supermarket. By the 1950s, supermarkets were popular across the US and had spread throughout Europe.

Shopping mall, Kuala Lumpur, Malaysia

Department stores

Some department stores are world-renowned for the variety of luxury items they offer, and have become tourist attractions. They include Bloomingdales in New York; GUM in Moscow; Au Bon Marché in Paris; and Harrods in London.

Malls

In addition to shops, a mall may contain banks, movies, offices, and restaurants. The covered streets of a mall are traffic-free. They are often built in out-of-town sites, accessible only by car, so that planners must include enough parking spaces.

F. W. Woolworth

US tycoon Frank Winfield Woolworth (1852–1919) made his fortune from discount shops that priced everything at either 5¢ or 10¢. The company he set up in 1879 now has 9,000 branches around the world.

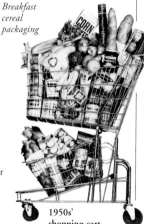

Breakfast cereal packaging

Packaging

Food in supermarkets is generally pre-packaged for speed and convenience, to keep food fresh, and to identify ingredients.

1950s' shopping cart

Bar codes

A bar code identifies the contents of a package. A computer at the checkout scans the code, adds the item's price to the bill, and orders more of the product from the manufacturer when stock is low.

ISBN 0-7513-6034-1

9 780751 360349

Bar code

Markets

Malls may offer economy and convenience, but they lack the character of traditional markets everywhere in the world where people gather to buy and sell their wares.

Fresh vegetables

Shopping from home in the 1930s

Selling spices in a Moroccan souk

Souks and bazaars

The roof of a souk (Arab marketplace) shades shoppers from the burning sun. Some are vast: the Grand Bazaar in Istanbul covers an area the size of 700 tennis courts.

Floating market

In Venice, Italy, where the canals are the quickest transportation routes, shops that are at the water's edge are convenient.

Mail order and online shopping

Catalog shopping is especially useful for disabled people, and those in remote areas. The British Army and Navy Cooperative Society printed the first catalog in 1872, and the Sears Roebuck catalog began in the US in 1894. Today, TV shopping channels and ordering goods over the Internet offer a more versatile and modern version of the mail order catalog.

FIND OUT MORE — ADVERTISING AND MARKETING • MONEY • TRADE AND INDUSTRY

SHOREBIRDS

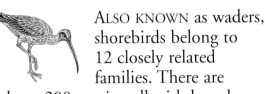

ALSO KNOWN as waders, shorebirds belong to 12 closely related families. There are about 200 species, all with long legs and slender beaks with which they probe for food in wet sand, soft ground, or mud. Some use their beaks to hammer open shells; others pull up worms or catch swimming animals. Many waders live on the shore, but others are found everywhere from riverbanks and woods to waterlogged hillsides.

Shorebird features

Shorebirds have specialized beaks for reaching a particular food. Some swim to find food, but most wade through water or walk over the ground on their long legs. They have good eyesight for watching out for danger.

Eyes face sideways for all-around vision.

Strong beak is used to smash open shells.

Eurasian Oystercatcher

Oystercatchers
Like most shorebirds, an oystercatcher lays camouflaged eggs directly on the ground. If a predator approaches, a parent bird tries to lure it away from the eggs.

Feeding

Shorebirds eat a wide range of animals, from clams and snails to worms and shrimps. Many shorebirds live on creatures that are normally hidden in mud or cloudy water. The birds can catch these without being able to see them, because they can feel for them with the sensitive tip of their beaks.

American avocet

Oystercatcher hammers shells with the blunt end of its beak.

Slender, upturned beak

An avocet holds its beak open while looking for food.

Curlew

A curlew's beak is up to 7.5 in (19 cm) long.

Hammering beak
Some oystercatchers have a blade-like tip on their beaks, which they use to hammer open shells or pry them apart. Others have a pointed beak and eat worms.

Sweeping beak
An avocet sweeps its unique upturned beak from side to side, just below the water's surface. When the beak touches suitable prey, the avocet snaps it shut, trapping the animal inside.

Probing beak
The curlew uses its curved beak to probe deep into mud and damp grass. It can collect worms and mollusks that are beyond the reach of other birds.

Jacanas are also called lily-trotters.

Shield above the base of the beak

Jacanas
These waders live mainly in the tropics, on ponds and lakes with floating plants. Their weight is spread over their huge toes, allowing them to walk on plants without sinking.

Long legs

Inland waders

Waders are found in many places inland. They live where the ground is damp enough for them to search for food, and where there are safe places for them to nest and raise their chicks.

Riverbank waders
The blacksmith plover lives in southern Africa, and usually stays close to water. It gets its name from its alarm call, which sounds like a blacksmith hammering a piece of metal.

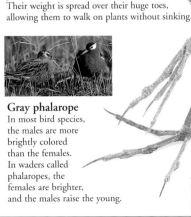

Gray phalarope
In most bird species, the males are more brightly colored than the females. In waders called phalaropes, the females are brighter, and the males raise the young.

Slender toes with long claws

Woodland waders
Woodcocks are shy woodland birds. They feed mainly after dark, when they probe the ground for worms. Their plumage provides them with superb camouflage.

Marshland waders
Northern lapwings are common in marshes and grasslands in Asia and Europe. They are acrobatic fliers, and the males do aerial displays in the breeding season.

OYSTERCATCHER

SCIENTIFIC NAME	*Haematopus ostralegus*
ORDER	Charadriiformes
FAMILY	Haematopodidae
DISTRIBUTION	Europe, Asia, Africa
HABITAT	Rocky and muddy coasts
DIET	Mollusks, worms
SIZE	Length: 17 in (43 cm)
LIFESPAN	About 5 years

FIND OUT MORE BIRDS   DUCKS, GEESE, AND SWANS   HERONS, STORKS, AND FLAMINGOS   MARSH AND SWAMP WILDLIFE   SEABIRDS

SHRINES

A SHRINE IS A SACRED PLACE dedicated to the memory of a person or event, or to a spirit god. Shrines range from tiny roadside structures housing pictures or statues to huge, richly decorated churches or temples. Sometimes special rocks, trees, or springs are also venerated as shrines. People visit shrines to pray and give offerings, hoping for good health or fertility.

Prayer flags flutter in the wind at a Buddhist shrine in Tibet.

Buddhist shrines

The Buddhist faith has many shrines and places of pilgrimage. These range from large and elaborate temples, adorned with statues of the Buddha, to simple hilltop sites. Some shrines are linked to the Buddha; others are associated with Bodhisattvas, outstanding people who help others along the Buddhist path of enlightenment. Flags often fly at Buddhist shrines. A prayer is written on each flag so that the words can waft toward heaven as the flag flutters in the wind.

Spirits of nature

Many traditional religions worship nature spirits that reside in sacred trees, springs, or rocks. When a shaman (priest) performs holy rituals at these shrines, his followers believe he actually becomes the nature spirit.

Well dressing

In some parts of England, ancient wells are decorated once a year with Christian designs of seeds, flowers, and other natural materials. They are often dressed at midsummer, indicating that the custom has survived from pagan times.

Decoration shows Jesus calling his disciples

A well in Derbyshire, England, with traditional decoration

Many of the standing stones in Brittany, France are aligned in long avenues.

Fertility stones

Ancient standing stones of northern Europe are often placed so the Sun rises over them on Midsummer's Day, June 24. They were probably erected by people who wanted the Sun to ripen their crops. Women still visit the stones, hoping the stones will help them conceive.

Pilgrimages

Making a pilgrimage, a journey to a shrine, is important in many religions. Pilgrims hope their journey will bring them closer to God.

Santiago de Compostela is dedicated to St. James.

Santiago de Compostela in northern Spain has been a popular pilgrim destination with Christians for centuries.

Cockle shell, symbol of St. James

Small shrines

In many countries people build small shrines wherever they want to pray or feel close to God at a spot with a beautiful view, beside the road, and in the home. Such shrines are treated with great reverence, and often decorated with pictures and flowers.

Roadside shrines

Small shrines by the side of the road are common throughout Greece. They often commemorate the life of a local person, or mark a spot where someone died. They sometimes contain a statue or picture.

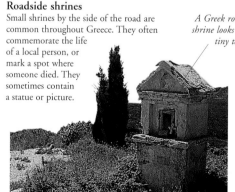

A Greek roadside shrine looks like a tiny temple.

A homemade shrine in a Chinese kitchen

Household shrines

Many Chinese houses contain a small homemade shrine dedicated to one of the traditional Chinese gods or to the family's ancestors. The shrine may be made of wood and decorated with colored cloth and beads. It opens to reveal a little statue of the deity. The family prays and makes offerings to their household shrine, especially when they have problems or are making important decisions about their lives.

FIND OUT MORE | ART, HISTORY OF | BUDDHISM | CHRISTIANITY | HINDUISM | ISLAM | PREHISTORIC PEOPLE | RELIGIONS | SCULPTURE

SIGNS AND SYMBOLS

LOOK UP FROM THIS BOOK, and you will probably see a sign or a symbol nearby. Both are means of communication, but in different ways. A sign is an object, gesture, or idea that points to something else, giving information clearly and quickly. A road sign, for example, advises drivers of conditions ahead; a trade mark guides shoppers to a product. A symbol is less direct; it usually represents something other than its image to convey a hidden, deeper meaning.

Luck

Some people believe that certain symbols bring good luck. The eye is a common example. Portuguese fishermen paint eyes on their boats for luck; Chinese sailors believe a ship will lose its way without eyes to see. In the Mediterranean, people carry glass magic eye charms to turn away the intentions of evil-wishers.

Magic eye charm

Information signs

Signs must be concise and easy to understand, even for people who do not read or speak the language. For immediate impact, the most important information signs avoid words. An exclamation mark in a triangle spells "Danger!" in any language.

Picture signs help overcome language barriers in an international airport.

"To parking lot"

"Airplane departures"

"Men's, women's, disabled toilets"

"This way"

"Checked baggage"

"Airport hotel"

Arrows

Signs work only when everybody agrees on their meaning. To most people, the sharp end of the arrow sign points the direction, just as a real arrow fired from a bow leads to its target.

Trade marks

Manufacturers may mark the products they make with symbols called trade marks. A trade mark links a company's reputation to a product. The trade mark may be the main difference between competing products, so companies protect trade marks closely.

Brand names

The best known brand in the world is probably Coca-Cola. Its distinctive symbol has become as much a symbol of American culture as of the drink itself. The trade mark was created by a bookkeeper who worked for the Pemberton Chemical Company, which invented Coca-Cola.

Hallmarks

Hallmarks are tiny signs and symbols stamped into gold and silver items to show the purity of the metal. In some countries, they are required by law. In the US, the symbols are not used: instead, the words "coin" or "sterling" are stamped into silver.

Officially tested in London

Year of testing (1986)

Some hallmarks and their meanings

Maker's mark

Made in UK

22-carat gold

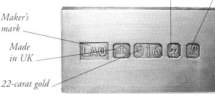

Seals and belonging

Signs and symbols act as a focus to unite people who belong to the same country, family, or organization, or who share the same beliefs. Some symbols have had the same meaning for centuries; others are modern, reflecting changes in society.

Seals and badges

Seals are raised images pressed into wax, which governments once attached to documents to prove they were genuine. The image represented an aspect of the organization. Modern seals and badges often continue this tradition.

Space shuttle crew members designed this badge

AIDS ribbon

The folded, pinned red ribbon represents the fight against the disease AIDS. The wearer shows support for sufferers, and for research to find a cure for the disease.

State seal of Florida

Space camp badge

Shop signs

Until street numbers began in the 18th century, shops hung out signs so customers could find them. Roman taverns, for example, hung out a bush to signal they sold wine. Some British public houses are still called the Bush, continuing the ancient tradition.

Religious symbols

A symbol may act as a focus for religious rituals. The symbol may stand for god, or may itself be holy. The Sikh religious community has five outward symbols.

The red ribbon, a symbol of the fight against AIDS since 1991

Kangha (comb) **Kara** (steel bangle)

Kirpan (sword)

The bat may symbolize death.

Symbolism

Artists, writers, and musicians use symbolism to subtly introduce a theme or an idea in their work, without actually showing it. For instance, western authors sometimes use bats to symbolize darkness, chaos, or impending doom. However, symbolic meanings are not necessarily the same worldwide. In China, the bat symbol represents good luck and happiness.

Three of the five Sikh symbols

FIND OUT MORE   ADVERTISING AND MARKETING   CODES AND CIPHERS   FLAGS   LANGUAGES   SHOPS

Signs and symbols
Religious signs and symbols

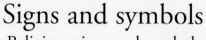

Om, a sacred syllable in the Hindu faith

Swastika, an emblem of the Hindu deity Vishnu

Star of David, the main symbol of Judaism

The sacred lamb, a Christian symbol for Jesus Christ

Animal symbols

The octopus is sometimes a symbol of fickleness.

Crocodile tears are a sign of hypocrisy.

The frog is associated with healing and wealth in China.

The camel, which kneels to receive a load, symbolizes humility.

The bald eagle is a national US symbol.

The whale is a symbol of death and rebirth.

Warning and prohibitive signs

A line through a red circle indicates that a certain action is not allowed.

Flammable

Radioactive
A triangle is a warning sign.

Toxic/poisonous

No cycling

Not suitable for drinking
A red circle is a warning sign.

No smoking

General information

Post office

Tourist information

Disabled access

Telephone

Women's bathroom

Men's bathroom

Weather symbols
International symbols used by meteorologists

Astronomical symbols

      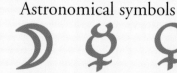

Wind calm | Fog | Drizzle | Rain | Snow | Showers | Sun | Moon | Mercury | Venus | Mars

Thunderstorm | Rainbow | Hail | Windspeed 18–22 knots | Cumulonimbus cloud, anvil top | Jupiter | Saturn | Uranus | Neptune | Pluto

SKELETON

THE BODY IS SHAPED and supported by a framework of bones called the skeleton. An adult skeleton consists of 206 bones that protect internal organs, such as the brain and lungs, and provide anchorage for the muscles. The skeleton can be divided into two main parts. The axial skeleton forms the axis of the body and consists of the skull, vertebral column (backbone), and ribcage. The appendicular skeleton consists of the bones of the arms and legs and the shoulder and hip girdles.

Ancient bones

If a person dies and is buried, the body tissues gradually break down and then disappear. However, the hard mineral salts that make up the bones remain and can retain their original shape for several thousands of years. The existence of ancient skeletons enables archaeologists to gather information about early people.

Movement

The skeleton is a flexible framework because bones meet at joints where they can move in relation to one another. Muscles are attached to the bones across joints so that when a muscle contracts, movement occurs. The body can perform a wide range of movements.

Arm movements help the body balance and move faster during running.

Leg straightens at knee as the foot pushes against ground to propel body forward.

Leg bends at knee before pushing down and back for next stride.

Flexion is a movement that reduces the angle of a joint. This skeleton flexes, or bends, the left leg and the right arm.

Extension is a movement that increases the angle of a joint. This skeleton extends, or straightens, the right leg and the left arm.

Cranium surrounds and protects the skull.

Skull consists of the cranium and the facial bones.

Facial bone forms part of the face.

Vertebra is one of the bones that make up the backbone.

Scapula (shoulder blade)

Clavicle (collarbone)

Humerus (upper arm bone)

Sternum (breastbone)

Rib

Backbone (vertebral column)

Radius

Ulna

Pelvis

Carpal is one of eight wrist bones.

Metacarpal is one of five palm bones in the hand.

Femur (thighbone) is the largest bone in the body.

Phalanx is one of 14 finger bones (phalanges) in the hand.

Tibia (shinbone)

Patella (kneecap) protects the knee joint.

Metatarsal is one of five bones forming the arch and ball of the foot.

Fibula

Phalanx is one of 14 toe bones (phalanges) in the foot.

Tarsal is one of seven anklebones.

Backbone

The backbone, or vertebral column, is the body's main support structure. It consists of short bones called vertebrae. A backbone has 24 separate vertebrae and nine vertebrae that are fused together. Between the separate vertebrae are joints that are slightly movable, which make the backbone strong but flexible. Pads between the vertebrae called intervertebral disks are made of cartilage tissue. These disks cushion the vertebrae against jolts.

Sacrum

Coccyx

Pelvic girdle is made up of two hipbones joined at the front and at the sacrum.

Pelvis is narrow.

Male pelvis

Hip-bone

Pelvis is broad and shallow.

Pelvic inlet is wider in females for giving birth.

Female pelvis

Male and female pelvises

The pelvis is the bony girdle that links the legs to the backbone, and supports the abdominal organs. It is made up of the two hipbones, or coxae, which together form the pelvic girdle along with the sacrum and coccyx, the bones that make up the end of the backbone. In the center of the pelvis is an opening called the pelvic inlet. Male and female pelvises are different shapes.

Imaging bones

Doctors use X rays to look inside a patient's body for signs of damage or disease without surgery. X rays are a type of radiation that passes through the body's soft tissue but not through bone. An X ray machine produces a negative photograph called a radiograph, in which only the bones show up.

False-color radiograph of a broken arm bone

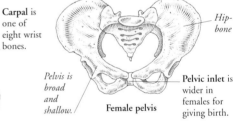

765

Bones

Bones are made of a hard, living, self-repairing tissue that is supplied with blood vessels and nerves. Bone consists of widely spaced osteocytes (bone cells) and the matrix that lies between them. The matrix is made up of fibers of collagen, which give bone its flexibility, and mineral salts, mainly calcium phosphate, which give bone its strength. Surrounding all bone is a layer of hard, compact bone. Within the compact bone is a layer of lighter, spongy bone. The spaces within spongy bone are frequently filled with red marrow.

Structure of compact bone

Haversian canal is a space that runs down the center of the osteon, carrying blood vessels and nerves.

Blood vessel supplies bone cells with oxygen and food.

Lamella is one of the tubes of bone surrounding a Haversian canal.

Lacuna is a space that contains an osteocyte (bone cell).

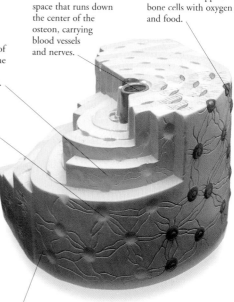

Red marrow is the site of red and white cell production.

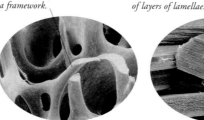
Struts link to form a framework.

Each osteon consists of layers of lamellae.

Bone marrow
Bone marrow is a jellylike material found inside bones. Red bone marrow inside the hip, skull, collarbone, sternum, and backbones is the site of blood cell production.

Spongy bone
Spongy bone is a "honeycomb" layer that lies beneath compact bone. It forms a light but strong framework that reduces the bone's weight but not its strength.

Compact bone
Compact bone forms the outer part of bone. After teeth enamel, compact bone is the hardest material in the body. It is made up of parallel cylinders called osteons.

An osteon is a small piece of compact bone made up of tiny bony tubes called lamellae arranged in circular layers around a central Haversian canal.

Joints

Joints occur where bones meet. The majority of joints move freely, and are known as synovial joints. They make the skeleton flexible, so that when muscles pull on bones, a part of the body moves. There are several different types of synovial joints, each of which allows a different range of movements. These include ball and socket, saddle, and hinge joints.

Movement in many directions

Ball and socket
This joint consists of a ball-shaped head that fits into a cup-shaped socket. It is the most flexible type of joint and allows movement in the most directions. It occurs in the hip joint and in the shoulder joint.

Movement in two planes

Saddle
In a saddle joint, the end of each bone is saddle-shaped. This allows movement forward and backward, from side to side, and, in a limited way, around and around. There is a saddle joint at the base of the thumb.

Joint allows movement in one plane.

Hinge
In a hinge joint, the cylindrical surface of one bone fits into the curved surface of the other, so the bones can only be moved up and down. Hinge joints are found in the elbow and knee.

Femur (thighbone)

Knee joint is a hinge joint between tibia and femur.

Ligament is a tough strap that holds the joint together.

Fibula

Tibia (shinbone)

Frontal bone   *Parietal bone*

Edge of frontal bone forms suture with edge of parietal bone.

Skull
The skull is made up of 22 bones, 21 of which are held together by immovable joints called sutures. Only the mandible (lower jaw) is freely movable. In a suture, the edges of bones fit tightly together and are prevented from moving, to protect the brain.

Skull is "exploded" to show component parts.

Giovanni Ingrassias

Giovanni Ingrassias (1510–80) was one of the first doctors to study in detail the structure of bones. He was a physician and anatomy professor in Naples until 1563, when he returned to Palermo in his native Sicily. Among his achievements, Ingrassias discovered the stapes (stirrup), the innermost of the tiny ossicles in the ear and the smallest bone in the body.

Bone fractures

A fracture, or break, happens when a bone is exposed to a sudden force that it cannot withstand. There are two types of fractures. In simple or closed fractures, the broken bone ends remain below the skin; in compound or open fractures, they stick out through the skin and often cause damage to surrounding tissues. Fractured bones mend themselves.

Casts
A cast is used to immobilize a limb so that the broken ends of a bone are lined up in the right position. A cast is applied by wrapping wet bandages dipped in plaster of Paris or plastic around a limb. When dry, the plaster hardens.

1 A blood clot forms where bone is broken.

2 Spongy bone forms between broken ends.

3 Fracture has healed and bone returns to its original shape.

FIND OUT MORE   FOSSILS   GROWTH AND DEVELOPMENT   HUMAN BODY   HUMAN EVOLUTION   MEDICINE   MEDICINE, HISTORY OF   MUSCLES AND MOVEMENT   TEETH AND JAWS   X RAYS AND THE ELECTROMAGNETIC SPECTRUM

SKIN, HAIR, AND NAILS

COVERING THE OUTSIDE of your body is a protective layer that consists of your skin, hair, and nails. Skin is the body's largest organ and it has several functions. It waterproofs the body and forms a barrier against bacteria, viruses, and the harmful effects of sunlight. Skin also contains sensors that detect pressure, pain, heat, and cold, enabling you to feel your surroundings. Nails and hair are extensions of the skin.

Dead cells flake from the top layer of epidermis.

Hair follicle

Hair shaft

Basal cell layer is at base of epidermis.

Sebaceous gland produces an oil called sebum, which lubricates skin and hair.

Epidermis is the outer part of the skin, which protects the dermis.

Dermis is the inner part of the skin that contains blood vessels and nerve endings.

Arrector pili muscle pulls hair upright in cold conditions.

Blood vessels supply skin with oxygen and food.

Sweat duct carries sweat to the skin's surface.

Sweat gland produces sweat.

Artery *Vein*

Sensory receptor detects pressure and vibrations.

Fat layer helps insulate the body and keep it warm.

Hair root

Skin

Skin consists of two layers: the epidermis and the dermis. The epidermis is the thin, but tough, outer protective part of the skin. It has a number of layers. The inner, thicker dermis contains sensory nerve endings, blood vessels, hair follicles, and sweat glands.

Pigmentation
Cells in the epidermis make a pigment called melanin, which protects the body against damage by strong sunlight. People with darker skin produce more melanin than those with lighter skin.

Temperature control
Skin helps the body maintain an even temperature of about 98.6°F (37°C). If your body gets too hot, glands release sweat and blood vessels widen to give off heat. To cool the body, blood vessels get narrower.

Sweat pore releases sweat on the skin's surface.

Epidermis
The upper layer of epidermis consists of dead cells packed with a tough protein called keratin, that are constantly being worn away and replaced. Cells in the lower epidermis divide and push new cells toward the surface to replace the lost ones. As they move upward, these cells fill with keratin.

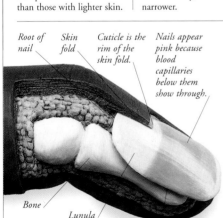

Root of nail *Skin fold* *Cuticle is the rim of the skin fold.* *Nails appear pink because blood capillaries below them show through.*

Bone

Lunula

Nail structure
Nails are made of the tough protein keratin. They are colorless but appear pink because they rest on a bed served by blood vessels. They grow from active skin cells under skin folds at their base and sides. An opaque crescent called the lunula at the base of each nail contains many of these active cells.

Nails

Nails are hard coverings that protect the ends of fingers and toes. Cells in the root of the nail divide constantly, pushing the nail forward over the nail bed. Finger-nails grow at a rate of about 0.2 inches (5 mm) each month, but toenails grow more slowly.

Nail protects sensitive skin.

Fingerprints
The undersides of your fingers are covered with tiny epidermal ridges that, together with a sticky film of sweat and natural oils, help you grip objects. When you touch an object, some of the film sticks to the object so that you leave behind a fingerprint.

No two people, not even identical twins, share the same fingerprints.

Hair structure
The shaft of a hair consists of three layers. The cuticle forms overlapping scales on the surface of the hair. Below the cuticle, the cortex forms the main part of the shaft and the medulla is the tough core. Cells in the follicle divide and push upward to form the shaft of the hair.

Hair

Millions of hairs cover your body. There are two types of hair. Fine vellus hair grows over most of the body. Thicker terminal hair grows on the scalp, and makes up the eyebrows and eyelashes. Hairs grow out of pits in the skin called follicles. Hairs on your head grow about 0.4 inch (1 cm) a month.

Dense curly hair *Straight hair* *Wavy hair*

Types of hair
Whether the hairs on your head are straight, wavy, or curly depends on the shape of the hair follicles they grow from. Round follicles produce straight hair; oval follicles produce curly hair; and curved follicles produce wavy hair.

| FIND OUT MORE | CELLS | CRIME AND PUNISHMENT | DISEASES | GENETICS | GROWTH AND DEVELOPMENT | HEAT | HUMAN BODY | HUMAN EVOLUTION | MUSCLES AND MOVEMENT | SKELETON |

S

SLAVERY

THE PRACTICE OF SLAVERY, the ownership of one person by another, goes back to ancient times, when the Sumerians, Egyptians, Romans, and Greeks kept slaves. From the 15th century a huge slave trade developed when Europeans began selling captured Africans for profit and shipping them across the sea to work in European colonies. This trade in humans lasted until the 19th century, and greatly affected African and American cultures. Today, slavery is illegal, although it still exists in some parts of the world.

Ancient world
Slavery in ancient times reached its height in the Greek world and Roman Empire. Slaves made most of the goods, and worked in the home and on farms. They had few rights, but some gained freedom, and even high social status.

Slave trade

The Portuguese began the Afro-European slave trade in about 1440, but it reached its height under the English, who shipped vast numbers of Africans across the Atlantic to work as slaves on cotton and tobacco plantations in their American colonies.

More than 7 million Africans were transported from Africa to lives of misery in the Americas. The trade brought huge profits to European and African traders, and devastated some African kingdoms. It also changed the population of the Americas; by 1800, half of Brazil's population was African in origin.

Traders
Traders sailed to West Africa from English ports and exchanged goods for Africans who had been captured and marched to the coast. Slaves were branded like cattle and shipped to the Americas.

Slave ships
Between 1701 and 1810, more than a million Africans died from suffocation, disease, or starvation on the journey across the Atlantic, which could take up to 10 weeks. Slaves were chained to prevent them from jumping overboard, because the loss of a slave meant a loss of profit.

Branding iron

Markets
In the Americas, traders auctioned Africans to plantation owners at slave markets. To traders and buyers, Africans were no longer people, only property. Families were usually separated forever.

Ankle fetter

Model of the English slave ship *Brookes*

Women's area | Men's area

Slaves survived on rice, corn, yams, seeds, and rootstock.

Men and boys were kept at the front of the boat, and girls at the back; most slaves were between 16 and 45 years old.

Plantation slavery

Slaves worked long hours on cotton plantations in the southern United States, or they worked indoors cooking and cleaning. They lived in huts and slept on floor mats. The black people had no rights; they were the property of the plantation owners. Because of this oppression, more than 250 slave revolts took place.

Abolitionists
From the late 18th century, there were English and American movements to abolish slavery. *Uncle Tom's Cabin* (1851) by Harriet Beecher Stowe was a major anti-slavery novel. In 1833, Britain ended its slave trade, but slavery continued in the United States, particularly in the south, until after the Civil War in 1865.

Timeline

73–71 BC Spartacus leads revolt of slaves in the Roman Empire. After the defeat of the slaves, 6,000 are crucified.

1100s Arab traders send West African slaves to Asia and Arabia.

1619 First shipload of African slaves arrives in Virginia.

1780–86 Some northern states pass manumission (freedom from slavery) acts.

1831 Nat Turner leads slave uprising, Virginia. All involved are hanged. Slave codes prohibit literacy.

1833 British abolish their slave trade.

1857 Dred Scott case: Supreme Court rules that African-Americans are not citizens.

1863 Emancipation Proclamation frees slaves in the South.

1948 Declaration of Human Rights from the United Nations prohibits slavery and trade in slaves.

Harriet Tubman

Born into slavery in Maryland, Harriet Tubman (c.1820–1913) escaped in 1849. She then helped some 300 slaves to freedom on a secret escape route from the South to the North known as the Underground Railroad. During the Civil War, Tubman worked for the North as a nurse and spy.

FIND OUT MORE | AFRICA, HISTORY OF | AMERICAN CIVIL WAR | CARIBBEAN, HISTORY OF | EGYPT, ANCIENT | GREECE, ANCIENT | HUMAN RIGHTS | ROMAN EMPIRE

SMELL AND TASTE

THE AIR THAT WE BREATHE IN, and the food that we eat, contain chemicals that can be detected by our senses of smell and taste. Both senses depend on chemoreceptors, which are sensors that react to the presence of certain chemicals by sending nerve impulses to the brain. Chemoreceptors in the nose detect smells, or odors, while those on the tongue detect tastes. Smell and taste work together. Your sense of smell is about 20,000 times more sensitive than your sense of taste.

Nose and mouth

The smelling part of the nose is the nasal cavity, which is divided into two halves, each served by one nostril. Smell receptors are found in the upper part of each nasal cavity. Taste receptors are found inside the mouth, on the surface of the tongue, and in the lining of the mouth cavity.

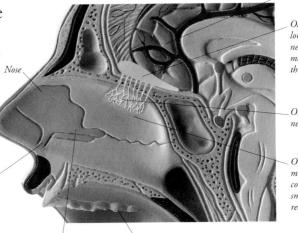

Brain

Olfactory lobe carries nerve messages to the brain.

Olfactory nerves

Olfactory membrane contains smell receptors.

Nose

Nostril is one of two openings to the nasal cavity.

Nasal cavity

Mouth

Smell

Your sense of smell operates when you breathe in through your nose. Chemicals carried by the air dissolve in the layer of mucus covering the olfactory membrane. The dissolved chemicals cause the olfactory cells to send nerve impulses to the olfactory lobes. From here, the nerve impulses are carried to the brain, where they are interpreted as smells.

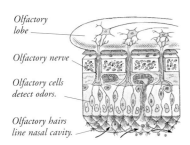

Olfactory lobe

Olfactory nerve

Olfactory cells detect odors.

Olfactory hairs line nasal cavity.

Olfactory membrane
The moist olfactory membrane covers an area the size of a postage stamp in the upper part of each nasal cavity. The membrane contains chemoreceptors called olfactory cells that detect odors.

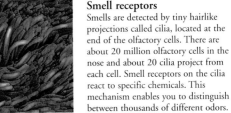

Smell receptors
Smells are detected by tiny hairlike projections called cilia, located at the end of the olfactory cells. There are about 20 million olfactory cells in the nose and about 20 cilia project from each cell. Smell receptors on the cilia react to specific chemicals. This mechanism enables you to distinguish between thousands of different odors.

Taste

Your tongue can detect only four basic tastes: sweet, salty, sour, and bitter. The tongue is divided into different taste areas, each containing taste buds that are sensitive to one of these tastes. There are over 10,000 microscopic taste buds on the tongue, and these are located on or between tiny projections called papillae.

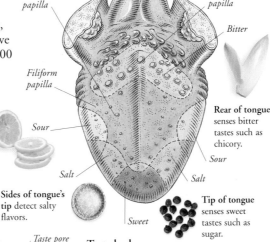

Tongue

Epiglottis

Fungiform papilla

Circumvallate papilla

Bitter

Filiform papilla

Sour

Salt

Sweet

Salt

Sour

Rear of tongue senses bitter tastes such as chicory.

Tip of tongue senses sweet tastes such as sugar.

Edges of tongue detect sour flavors such as lemons.

Sides of tongue's tip detect salty flavors.

Tongue papillae
Your tongue is not smooth. Its upper surface is covered by papillae that make it rough so it can grip and move food during chewing. Papillae also allow you to lick food such as ice cream. Taste buds are found in pores on and between some of the papillae.

Inside a taste bud

Taste pore

Taste hair

Taste cell

Nerve fiber

Taste buds
Each taste bud contains a cluster of chemoreceptors (taste cells). When food is chewed, chemicals dissolve in saliva and pass into the taste bud through the taste pore. The chemicals stimulate taste hairs on the chemoreceptor cells. These send impulses along nerve fibers to the brain's taste area, where the impulses are interpreted as salty, sour, sweet, or bitter tastes.

Sense of smell
Our sense of smell is poor compared to that of some other animals. Dogs, for example, have an olfactory membrane ten times more extensive than a human's. This enables them to detect much weaker smells and a wider range of odors than humans can. Dogs can be trained to sniff out drugs or explosives.

Detecting flavors

Your senses of smell and taste work together to enable you to detect many flavors. For example, when you eat food, information from the chemoreceptors in your nose and mouth is processed by your brain so that you can sense the flavor of the food. Some people use their very good senses of smell and taste to make a living as, for example, wine tasters and perfume blenders.

The durian is a very unusual fruit. It has a revolting smell but a delicious taste.

FIND OUT MORE   BRAIN AND NERVOUS SYSTEM   CHEMISTRY   DIGESTIVE SYSTEM   DOGS   FOOD AND FOOD INDUSTRY   FRUITS AND SEEDS   HUMAN BODY   TEETH AND JAWS

SNAILS AND OTHER MOLLUSKS

THESE SOFT-BODIED animals all have a single muscular "foot," a gut, and a mantle cavity. Most produce a protective calcium-based shell, although some species have lost their shells altogether. The 80,000 or so living snails and mollusk species are divided up into bivalve, cephalopod, chiton, gastropod, and tusk shell groups. They have colonized almost all areas of the world.

Gastropods

Snails and slugs belong to a group called gastropods. All gastropods move on a flat, muscular foot and are equipped with tentacles and a rasping mouthpart called a radula. Most have a protective shell. Marine snails have gills. Many freshwater and land snails have adapted their gills to form lungs.

Snail

Shells protect snails from enemies and drying out, and are colored to blend in with their environment. Snails have a mouth with a radula (tongue), and two pairs of tentacles, the longer of which has simple eyes. They are hermaphrodites (that is, they contain both male and female reproductive organs). They lay large eggs in warm, damp soil that hatch into young snails.

Shells normally coil in a right-handed spiral.

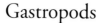

Radulas are tonguelike organs consisting of a ribbon of teeth that rasps food into small pieces.

Tail

Tentacle

Head

Eyes

Giant African snail

Foot produces slime.

Emerging from shell

1 The snail's body is curled up inside the shell, sealed with a layer of mucus for protection.

2 In a special kind of twisting known as torsion, the snail's head emerges first from the shell, followed by the tail.

3 The long tentacles emerge last, and the eyes become visible. The snail's muscular foot can now lie flat on the ground.

Cone shell

Cone shell

The beautiful but deadly cones are well adapted for catching and killing their food. They attack their prey – usually small fish – with a single poison-filled tooth. Fish are swallowed whole; humans usually survive – although in 1960, an adult man died two hours later.

Slug

Slugs are snails with no shell, or a very tiny one. Without the protection that a shell can offer, slugs rely on their slime, which is sticky and offensive to predators. Some snails are carnivorous, but most land-living slugs are herbivores.

Head

Foot

Bivalves

Bivalves (meaning two-shelled) include clams, mussels, and cockles. Bivalves that dive underwater have gills for breathing and a foot, like the gastropods. Some bivalves cement themselves to rocks using thin threads called byssus strands. Most bivalves have two tubes, or siphons. One takes in water and food, and the other expels waste. Bivalves such as the giant Pacific clam can grow to more than 4 ft (1.2 m) across.

Queen scallop

Black-lipped oyster

Scallop

The beautifully colored scallop swims by rapidly opening and closing its hinged valves. Scallops have a fringe of tentacles around the edge of the shell. This is interspersed with tiny, light-sensitive eyes that can detect moving objects. Its main predator is the starfish.

Oyster

The oyster is one of the best-known bivalves. An oyster lays up to 50 million eggs in a single spawning season, but in its natural environment only a few reach adulthood. A popular food, oysters are cultivated commercially in marine oyster beds in America, Australia, Asia, and Europe.

Chiton

Chitons, also known as coat-of-mail shells, are small mollusks with eight flattened shell plates held together by a protective leathery girdle. A chiton's internal structures are simple, and it lives off algae. Chitons range in size from 0.1 in (2 mm) to 12 in (30 cm) and live on rocky shores.

Jointed shell plates

Girdle

Eye

Cephalopods

Cephalopods are also mollusks, but their "foot" has evolved into a set of tentacles on the animal's head. Cephalopods swim by pushing jets of water through a funnel under the body. Some produce a cloud of ink as a protective device. The largest-ever recorded cephalopod was a 65-foot (20-m) squid.

Tentacles on head

Cloud of ink

Cuttlefish releasing ink

Tusk shells

The marine bivalves known as tusks are so-called because they look like elephant's tusks. The broad end of the tusk is buried in sandy mud and contains the head and foot of the animal. The narrow end, where respiration takes place, projects into the water. Tusks search for food with slender retractable tentacles, and some live at great depths.

GIANT AFRICAN SNAIL

SCIENTIFIC NAME	*Achatina achatina*
ORDER	Sigmurethra
SUPERFAMILY	Achatinacea
DISTRIBUTION	Africa, America, and Asia
HABITAT	Forests, gardens, and cultivation
DIET	Plants
SIZE	Shell can grow up to 5.9 in (15 cm) long
LIFESPAN	25 years (in captivity)

FIND OUT MORE

OCEAN LIFE • SEASHORE WILDLIFE • URBAN WILDLIFE

Snails and other mollusks
Gastropods

Land snails' color and banding depends on whether their habitat is woodland or grassland.

Shells normally coil in a right-hand spiral.

Snails grow by adding new material to the open end of the shell.

Partula snails are close to extinction.

Posterior tentacle

Anterior tentacle

Brown-lipped snails live mainly on chalk lowland.

Garden snails need to remain moist to survive. In dry conditions they seal themselves inside their shells to hibernate.

Apple snails are used in aquariums to keep the glass clean.

Thin shell

Spine used to lever apart barnacle plates

Whelks are sea snails that live just below the tide line.

Bubble shells appear to "fly" through the water.

Gills absorb oxygen from sea water.

Pond snails can live in very stagnant water.

Dog whelks are carnivorous and live on barnacles.

Common periwinkles move on a muscular "foot" like the land snail.

Lettuce slugs are brightly colored and taste unpleasant.

Sea slugs, or nudibranchs as they are also known, live in tide pools.

Slugs are mollusks without shells. They tend to be more drab in color than sea slugs.

Bivalves

Mantle

Shell halves are called valves.

Giant clams live on coral reefs and have soft, colorful mantles. Barnacles often grow on the shells.

Spiny oysters are also known as chrysanthemum shells because they resemble the flower.

Hinge

Queen scallops have two perfectly matched shell halves that are connected by a hinge.

Oysters live in the sea, buried in sand or attached to rocks.

Green mussels use tough threads called byssus to attach themselves to rocks.

Cephalopods and other mollusks

To swim, an octopus takes water into its body cavity and forces it out through a funnel.

Eye is similar to a human eye.

Tentacles grasp food as it floats by.

The beaklike jaw has a poisonous bite.

Squid have a tube-like internal shell.

Suckers

Squid, among the most common animals in the ocean, swim in shoals. Sperm whales feed on them.

Octopuses feed mainly on shellfish. Their name comes from their eight tentacles.

Chambers contain gases that help the nautilus float.

Nautiluses live in the deep waters of the South Pacific.

Cuttlefish have a hard internal shell instead of an external shell.

SNAKES

SNAKES ARE LONG, scaly, legless reptiles. There are about 3,000 species of snakes, 600 of which are venomous. Snakes are found on all continents except Antarctica, and also in the Pacific and Indian Oceans. They are believed to have evolved from lizards that lost the use of their legs. Snakes are successful predators – some, such as mambas, kill their victims with a venomous bite; others, such as pythons, suffocate their prey to death. Snakes are feared around the world – they cause up to 100,000 human deaths every year.

Features of a snake

Snakes are legless reptiles, but boas and pythons have remnants of hind legs called spurs. Snakes are covered in an outer skin that they shed, often in one piece, as they grow. They have no eyelids, but a spectacle called a brille, covers the eyes. They lack ears and are deaf, but can sense vibrations.

Forked tongue
The snake's tongue is a highly sensitive organ of taste, smell, and touch. It is used to find prey or a mate, to detect a threat, and to follow trails. The tongue collects scent particles that are analyzed on the roof of the mouth in a structure called the Jacobson's organ.

Snakes have smooth, muscular, streamlined bodies.

Red-tailed racer

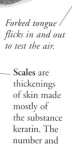

Nostril

Forked tongue flicks in and out to test the air.

Scales are thickenings of skin made mostly of the substance keratin. The number and arrangement of scales vary among species.

Wagler's temple pitviper

Special pit detects heat from other animals.

Heat-sensitive pits
Boas, pythons, and pitvipers have thermo-sensory receptors to locate warm-blooded prey. In pythons and boas, the pits form a series of slits in the lip scales, but pitvipers have a single large pit between the nostril and the eye. These receptors are very sensitive and enable tree boas to capture bats in flight.

Movement
Most snakes move on land or in water using a twisting motion, but heavy snakes such as large anacondas move in straight lines. Some desert vipers move diagonally across loose sand by moving sideways, or "sidewinding," leaving a J-shaped trail.

Sidewinding viper

Feeding

No snakes are herbivores; some kill their prey by biting and injecting venom, other nonvenomous snakes kill their prey by constriction. Most snakes feed on frogs, lizards, small mammals, and birds. Some also eat termites, crabs, and birds' eggs. King cobras eat other snakes.

Fangs and venom
When a snake, such as a rattlesnake, bites its prey, venom is injected through hollow teeth called fangs. Venom kills prey by affecting the nervous system, muscles, heart, or blood. It also starts the snake's digestion process. Spitting cobras primarily use venom for defense, causing intense pain or blindness.

Fangs of a rattlesnake

Boa constrictor eating a rat

Prey is eaten headfirst.

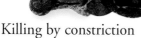

Coils squeeze the prey to make it easier to swallow whole.

Tail of the rat

Killing by constriction
1 The boa constrictor uses its sharp teeth to grasp its prey, in this case, a rat. Once the rat is secure within its mouth, the boa wraps its powerful coils around the victim's body.

2 The coils tighten until the prey cannot breath and it suffocates. When the prey is dead, the boa starts to devour its meal. The two halves of the lower jaw are not connected, so they can articulate (expand) to swallow prey much wider than the the boa's head.

3 The boa's skin stretches as it swallows its prey. A muscular windpipe enables a snake to breathe during swallowing. Huge meals such as pigs or deer, eaten by large pythons, last for many months.

Reproduction
Most snakes, such as cobras and pythons, lay eggs. They normally bury the eggs in rotting vegetation or soil and leave them to incubate. King cobras build a nest that they guard; pythons coil around and incubate their eggs. A few snakes, such as boas, give birth to live young.

Green tree python guarding eggs

Habitat

Snakes live in most habitats, including deserts, rain forests, temperate forests, swamps, savannas, cultivated land, estuaries, rivers, and even oceans. They do not live in areas of high altitude or latitude, where it is too cold. Most snakes live on land. They range from desert vipers, with rough scales that help them grip and move along rocky terrain, to burrowing blindsnakes with smooth scales that allow them to slip easily through soil.

Slender body coils around branch.

Prehensile tail grasps branch.

Sea krait

Water snakes
Sea snakes and sea kraits have flattened tails for swimming huge distances. Sea kraits can move onto land and even climb cliffs; sea snakes are helpless on land.

Ornate flying snake

Tree snakes
Prehensile tails and ridged belly scales give tree snakes extra grip when climbing trees. Strong vertebrae allow them to bridge wide gaps.

RED-TAILED RACER

SCIENTIFIC NAME	*Gonyosoma oxycephalum*
ORDER	Squamata
FAMILY	Colubridae
DISTRIBUTION	Southeast Asia, from Thailand to Indonesia and the Philippines
HABITAT	Rain forests
DIET	Rodents and birds
SIZE	Length 5 ft (1.75 m)

FIND OUT MORE   DESERT WILDLIFE   EGGS   LIZARDS   MONGOOSES AND CIVETS   POISONOUS ANIMALS   RAIN FOREST WILDLIFE   REPTILES   WOODLAND WILDLIFE

Snakes

Invertebrate eaters

This snake hunts for its prey at night.

Ringed snail-eating snakes live in trees. They are experts at pulling snails out of their shells.

These snakes can burrow into leaf litter or forest topsoil.

Small head and smooth scales help this snake burrow.

Ground snakes have tiny mouths and feed mainly on earthworms and insect larvae.

Black-banded snakes are mildly venomous. They are thought to eat only tropical centipedes.

This snake is almost invisible in the bushes.

Smooth green snakes from North America feed on insects and spiders.

Vertebrate eaters

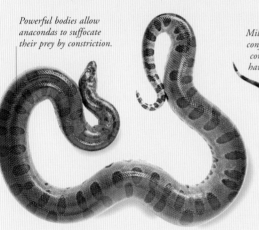

Powerful bodies allow anacondas to suffocate their prey by constriction.

Green anacondas, the largest, heaviest, and strongest snakes in the world, feed on waterbirds, caimans, and sometimes humans.

Milk snakes are often confused with deadly coral snakes as they have similar colored bands.

Common milk snakes from North and Central America feed on small mammals, lizards, and other snakes.

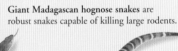

The snake must writhe around to crack the eggshell.

African egg-eating snakes have no teeth. They swallow bird eggs whole and cough up the shell.

This snake has an upturned snout for burrowing in leaf litter for food.

Giant Madagascan hognose snakes are robust snakes capable of killing large rodents.

Bones in the neck spread out to form the hood.

Gaboon vipers from Africa are huge and can capture rats from ambush.

Mottled skin for camouflage

Monocled cobras are from Thailand. They are highly venomous and eat rats.

Brown saddles (wide irregular markings) act as camouflage in woodlands.

Copperheads live in woodlands in North America. They use their heat-sensitive pits to locate mice.

This snake shows a variety of patterns from bands to saddles.

Gray-banded king snakes from the deserts of Western Texas hunt for lizards at night.

Corn snakes are common around houses in the southeastern USA, where they hunt mice.

If threatened, this snake can ooze blood-stained liquid from its cloaca.

Western long-nosed snakes of North America feed on lizards and their eggs.

Thick, muscular body allows python to squeeze and suffocate large animals to death.

Jaws can expand to swallow prey three times wider than the head.

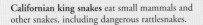

Californian king snakes eat small mammals and other snakes, including dangerous rattlesnakes.

This snake is banded, but others have stripes along their bodies.

Burmese rock pythons are powerful snakes capable of killing large animals, such as deer and pigs, by constriction.

SOCIETIES, HUMAN

SINCE PREHISTORY, and in every culture, humans have organized themselves into groups, or communities, and have established "rules" of living. A society is the name we give to the customs and organization of such a community. Certain things are found in every society, such as the family, kinship, the division of work by gender or age, marriage, the sharing of food, and the idea of ownership. But the customs that govern behavior at work, in the home, and in other social institutions and organizations vary greatly worldwide.

The study of people

Both anthropology and sociology are social sciences that study the origins and development of human societies and customs. They have revealed universal features of human societies and explained the emergence of important differences.

Sociologists collect data to study social behavior, whether in crowded cities or rural communities.

Anthropology
Anthropologists examine humanity in terms of evolution and development. They also study the customs, religions, and laws of a specific people at a given time, and consider the differences among cultures.

Sociology
Sociology is concerned with how human beings behave in groups: how they organize themselves, and how one group relates to another. Sociologists may try to develop solutions to social problems such as crime.

Families

The family is a basic social unit and exists in every culture. Most of us are born into one and first learn about the wider world through it. Later, we may start a family of our own. Nuclear and extended families are perhaps the two best-known family types, but family structures vary widely among, and within, societies as they are affected by such things as increasing divorce, and changing social attitudes.

Extended families
Families share responsibilities such as bringing up children, providing food, and performing domestic tasks. Many societies have a wide concept of the family group, with duties extending over several generations who all live together. This type of family is often found in small, traditional communities, where shared property and kinship ties form a bond.

Not only their parents, but also aunts, uncles, and grandparents care for young children.

Adult children live with their parents.

Extended family of four generations

Nuclear families
The term "nuclear family" usually refers to a core family of just two parents and their children. It is the most widespread family type in industrialized nations, although today, single-parent families are also becoming more common.

People are now more financially independent than before and can choose to live alone.

Single-person household

One type of family structure

Nuclear family

Households
A household refers to the people who live under one roof. Single-person households are becoming more common as individuals either choose to live alone, or find themselves on their own.

Where people live

The jobs and available resources determine where people live. In early societies, people lived in hunter-gatherer communities of 80 to 150 people. As work patterns changed and populations grew, societies adapted in different ways.

Kinship
Kinship is the recognition of blood or family ties between individuals. It is the binding force in families, clans, or tribes; some societies have strict rules governing kin relations.

Sister gives brother a raksha of coloured threads.

In India, the Raksha Bandan festival celebrates the kinship between sister and brother.

Cities
Half the world's people live in cities and this number is increasing. These large, crowded settlements offer the most job opportunites. Although the rise of cities has brought benefits, it has also created health problems, overcrowding, and pollution.

Shortage of housing is a problem in cities; high-rise apartments are one solution to lack of space.

High-rise apartment building, Moscow, Russia

Nomads
Where food, water, and grazing were scarce, people could not build fixed settlements, but moved their animals between grazing areas. Peoples who still live this nomadic lifestyle include the Bedouins in North Africa and the Mongols of the Asian steppes.

Bedouin tent in the desert

Social stratification

Sociologists have shown that all societies are stratified: they are divided into different strata, or layers. Stratification may be based on various factors, such as caste, class, gender, race, or even age. As a result of the layering, some people will have greater advantages or status than others, and this often leads to divisions in society.

Brahmans (priests) are the highest Hindu caste and have great social prestige.

Privileged pupils at a private school

Black woman worker

Race and gender

Within a society, a peoples' status may be affected by the ethnic group they belong to, or whether they are a man or a woman. They may earn less and not be able to own property or even do certain jobs. During the 20th century, racism and sexism were challenged – for example, by civil rights groups and the women's movement. Laws were passed to make discrimination illegal.

Caste

This is an ancient social hierarchy that still exists among Hindus in India. It is inherited and fixed. There are four main levels, with the Brahmans supreme, and 36 lower levels, members of which are seen as inferior.

Class

People are said to belong to a social class depending on the property they own or their occupation. There may be some movement between classes; education helps people improve their class status.

Residents at a home for the elderly

Female plumber (traditionally a male job)

Age roles

Depending on their age, society gives people different status. Youth is generally seen as an advantage; old people may be discriminated against or venerated, depending on the culture in which they live.

Ceremonies and rites

In every society, people come together to mark or celebrate certain occasions or events that are meaningful to the larger community. Such ceremonies are shared events that may involve traditional words, music, or dance, or include special ritual actions or costumes. The ceremonies linked to birth, marriage, and death often have a symbolic meaning: they mark the different phases in an individual's status in society.

Some people receive a key on their 21st birthday, a symbol of their entry into adulthood.

Gifts are given in celebration.

Margaret Mead

Pioneering and outspoken US anthropologist Margaret Mead (1901–78) studied social behavior in Samoa, New Guinea, and Bali, writing on rites of passage and childrearing. She also analyzed US society and was an early advocate of women's rights.

Marriage

When a man and woman marry, they make a formal commitment to spend their lives together; they agree to share their property and set up a new household; and their families are also linked to each other. This great change in social status is celebrated in wedding ceremonies worldwide, often of a religious nature.

Birth

Birth, when a new member arrives in a community, is marked in different ways. In Christian ceremonies a baby's head is dipped in, or touched, with water. Male Jewish infants are circumcised eight days after birth. In western countries, an individual's 18th or 21st birthday is celebrated as a time when he or she becomes an adult, or "comes of age".

Work

People spend most of their lives working, producing goods or services to support themselves and their families and create wealth for their community. People also work for social status, intellectual satisfaction, or company.

Hindu wedding ceremony

Death

Death, when a loved and valued member leaves a community forever, is marked by rituals in most societies. In China, for example, Taoist mourners at funerals traditionally cover themselves to show their respect for the dead.

Mourners wear veils made of rough burlap.

Taoist mourners

Leisure

In western societies, work tends to happen in a certain place, for a set amount of time. Time away from work is sometimes known as leisure time. During this time, people may choose enjoyable activities, such as sport. In some countries, leisure is big business. In less wealthy societies, less time may be available for leisure.

FIND OUT MORE CRIME EDUCATION FESTIVALS GOVERNMENTS HUMAN RIGHTS LAW PHILOSOPHY POLICE RELIGION WOMEN'S MOVEMENT

SOCRATES

THE GREEK THINKER Socrates, who lived 2,400 years ago, was one of the most important people in the history of philosophy. He wrote no books, and we know little about the events of his life, but Socrates still has a strong influence on Western thought. He believed strongly that philosophy should concern itself with the conduct of everyday life, not with abstract ideas. He valued human intelligence, reason, and open discussion, and through his teachings showed people how to live a good and virtuous life.

S

Early life
Socrates was born in Athens, Greece, in 469 BC. Very little is known about his background, but it is thought that his mother was a midwife and his father, Sophroniscus, was a stonemason and sculptor. As a young man, Socrates probably followed his father's trade. He later served in the Athenian army as a hoplite (foot soldier), before turning to philosophy during his middle years.

Later life of Socrates

In middle age, Socrates studied the teachings of other great thinkers, developed a philosophy of his own, and debated regularly with other philosophers. Most of what we know about his philosophy comes from the writings of two of his pupils, the philosopher Plato and the historian Xenophon.

Plato's dialogues
Plato (c.428–347 BC) wrote a series of books called dialogues, in which he sets out the arguments of Socrates in the form of conversations with other thinkers. Plato records that the oracle of Delphi considered Socrates to be the wisest man in Greece. Socrates was puzzled by this acclaim, until he realized that while other people claimed to be intelligent without acknowledging their ignorance, he at least recognized his own ignorance.

Xenophon
Unlike Plato, who describes the philosophy of Socrates, Xenophon (c.430–354 BC), in books such as his *Memoirs* and *Anabasis*, draws a more practical picture. In his book *Oeconomicus*, for example, Xenophon describes a discussion between Socrates and another man about managing a household and a farm.

Philosophy of Socrates

Socrates believed that philosophy should be applied to the events of daily life. To lead a good life, we must, therefore, understand what virtue means. According to Socrates, "virtue is knowledge." He, therefore, stressed the importance of self-knowledge, and told his pupils to question every statement to test its truth.

Raphael's painting, *The School of Athens*

Greek philosophers assemble for discussions.

"Know thyself"
Socrates believed that before commenting on the outside world, he should understand his own beliefs. This would give him the confidence to know what was best for others. The importance of self-questioning in philosophy began with Socrates.

Socratic method
Socrates's philosophical method was known as dialectic. When Greek philosophers gathered for discussions, Socrates asked a series of questions about each statement to find out if it was true. By questioning every assumption made in a statement, Socrates believed it was possible to arrive at the truth. In order to do this, he pretended ignorance of the subject under discussion.

SOCRATES

469 BC Born in Athens, Greece.

c.420 BC Socrates marries Xanthippe.

399 BC Put on trial and sentenced to death in Athens.

387 BC Plato founds the Academy, the world's first formal philosophical school, to carry on Socrates's work.

NOTE Little is known of the life of Socrates, although the development of his philosophy was well described by his pupils, particularly Plato and Xenophon.

Trial of Socrates

During his life, Socrates made enemies because of his teaching. In 399 BC, he was brought to trial on a charge of "introducing strange gods" – in other words subversion – and for corrupting the young. He was found guilty and sentenced to death by drinking hemlock, a deadly poison. His death is recorded in Plato's dialogue, *Phaedo,* and in a painting, *Death of Socrates,* by the 18th-century French artist Jacques-Louis David.

Socrates

FIND OUT MORE GREECE, ANCIENT PHILOSOPHY RELIGIONS SOCIETIES, HUMAN WRITING

SOIL

MUCH OF THE WORLD'S land surface is covered in decaying matter – soil. Soil is a layer of weathered rock fragments, rotting plants, and animals that coats the ground everywhere, except for deserts, polar regions, steep slopes, and artificial environments. Although soil is made from decaying material, it is far from dead; it is a living, ever-changing system. Tiny gaps in the soil are filled with water or air, in which live myriad bacteria, algae, and fungi. These microorganisms speed up the process of decay, making the soil a good home for plant roots, insects, worms, and other creatures.

Soil type

A soil's texture, or average grain size, varies with the nature of the bedrock beneath. Soils are divided into three main types, according to their texture – clay, sandy, and loamy. However, there are many other soil types, which depend on climate, vegetation, and landscape. Soils are also classified by their acidity, or pH. They need to have the right pH to be fertile.

Clay

Sand

Chalk

Clay soils
In clay soil, most grains are fine clay or silt (medium-sized grains). Fine grains often stick together in clumps. When dry, the soil is hard and likely to crack. When wet, it is sticky and waterlogged.

Sandy soils
Sandy soils contain coarse sand-sized grains. Sandy soils are well-aerated, warm, and are easy to work or dig. However, they can be very dry, and their nutrients are quickly washed out.

Chalky soils
Chalky soils are thin and stony, and drain water quickly. Their high pH content makes them very alkaline, and therefore not very fertile.

Loam

Peat

Loam
Loams are the best soils for plant growth. Loams are a mixture of clay, silt, and sand, which make them fertile and easy to work.

Peat
All soils contain rotting organic matter, but peat is made of nothing else. Its dark brown mass consists of rotten plants. Gardeners may add peat to other soils to boost their organic content.

The soil provides nutrients for plant and shrub growth.

Humus

Soil profile

Soils develop from a layer of loose weathered rock fragments, called a regolith. Chemicals released by rotting organic matter – anything derived from plants or animals – slowly transform the regolith into soil. As this happens, the soil forms distinct horizons, or layers.

Humus
The top coat is a thin dark layer of humus – rotting organic matter. Humus is crucial to maintaining the balance of minerals and nutrients needed for plant growth.

A horizon

Topsoil
The topsoil, or A horizon, is the uppermost layer of soil. This is where plants grow and creatures burrow. It is usually rich in both humus and minerals.

B horizon

Subsoil
The subsoil, or B horizon, contains more weathered rock fragments than organic matter. It is poor in humus but rich in minerals, leached (washed down) from above.

C horizon

C horizon
Weathered rock fragments with little or no organic content make up the C horizon.

D horizon

Bedrock
Beneath the soil is the D horizon. This is usually solid, weathered "parent" rock. It can also be the loose material deposited in huge quantities by rivers, glaciers, and wind.

Life in the soil
The soil provides the conditions for giving life to plants but is itself teeming with life, from ants and termites to earthworms and rodents. Earthworms play a vital role in improving the soil's texture by passing it through their digestive tracts and excreting it as worm casts.

Plants thrive in fertile soils.

Slugs and snails burrow in the soil.

Earthworms improve soil fertility: their burrowing mixes and aerates the soil.

Erosion
Damaged soil is infertile and unable to support plant or animal life. Erosion, a natural weathering process in which rain and wind erode soil from the land, causes such damage. Human activity, for example over-farming, can also cause soil damage.

Salinization
In hot, dry places, dissolved mineral salts leave a salty crust, as water evaporates from the surface of the soil.

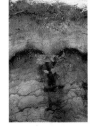

Leaching
In some places, water washes soil minerals down through the soil, depleting the top-soil of nutrients.

Lessivage
In wet areas, clay particles may be washed through the soil, coating the grains beneath and dampening the soil.

Soil creep
On steep slopes, soil often creeps slowly downhill over the years. Hill-side trees show the soil's movement.

FIND OUT MORE — FORESTS — MICROSCOPIC LIFE — PLANTS — ROCKS AND MINERALS — WORMS

SOLIDS

THE PHRASE "SOLID AS A ROCK" makes us think of something that is very hard and rigid. But rock is only one example of a solid, and some solids are weaker or more flexible than others. A solid is any piece of matter that has a definite shape and volume and does not flow like a liquid or a gas. When a solid gets hot, it may turn into a liquid: the heat of a volcano can turn even the hardest rock into liquid lava.

Solid structure

Inside a solid, tiny particles of matter called atoms or molecules are packed together in orderly patterns, like bricks in a wall. The particles are "cemented" firmly in place by forces called chemical bonds.

Solid particles
Although solid particles are held close to their neighbors and cannot move away, they vibrate within fixed positions.

A certain amount of force is needed to break or change the shape of a solid.

Strong forces bind the particles together in granite, making it a very hard rock.

Melting

When heated, a bar of chocolate turns into a runny liquid. The change of a solid to a liquid is called melting. Heating a solid gives its particles energy and makes them vibrate more vigorously. At a temperature called the melting point, the particles are able to break free from their fixed positions and the substance flows as a liquid.

Melting chocolate

Plumes of iodine gas rise up as the crystals sublimate.

Iodine crystals are heated from below.

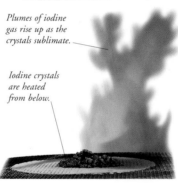

Sublimation
When heated, most solid substances will first melt to form a liquid, and then boil to form a gas. However, a few solids, such as iodine crystals and dry ice (frozen carbon dioxide), transform directly from a solid to a gas as they get warmer. This change is called sublimation.

Crystalline solids
Many solids, especially rocks, minerals, and metals, have crystalline structures. They are made up of crystals, which are geometrically shaped pieces of solid matter with smooth surfaces, straight edges, and symmetrical corners. The atoms in a crystal are arranged in a regular, repeating pattern. It is this pattern that determines the shape of the crystal.

Sulfur crystals

William Henry Bragg
The English physicist William Henry Bragg (1862–1942) and his son William Lawrence Bragg (1890–1971) discovered that if a beam of X rays passes through a crystal, it makes a pattern of dots on photographic film. This pattern shows how the atoms are arranged inside the crystal.

Properties of solids

Solid materials are often described in terms of their strength, elasticity, and hardness, and how easily they can be shaped. Such properties help scientists, engineers, architects, and designers decide how to use the materials, and choose the most suitable material for a particular task.

A scratch test determines the hardness of two materials.

Nail scratches slate.

Hardness
Dragging a nail across a slate makes scratch marks on the surface of the slate, but leaves the nail unmarked because the nail is harder than the slate. The ability of a material to resist scratching is called hardness. The particles in the iron nail are bound together more rigidly and tightly than those in the slate.

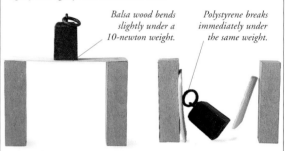

Balsa wood bends slightly under a 10-newton weight.

Polystyrene breaks immediately under the same weight.

Strength
A strip of polystyrene breaks more easily than a similar strip of balsa wood because the balsa wood is a stronger material. The strength of a material is its ability to resist forces that act upon it. The more powerful the forces between the particles in the material, the greater is its strength. Steel and concrete are extremely strong materials, which is why they are widely used in building and construction.

Elasticity
When you pull a spring and then let it go, it leaps back to its original size. Elasticity is the ability of a material to regain its size and shape after being stretched or squeezed. Most materials are elastic only up to a certain point, called the elastic limit. If too much force is applied, the material reaches its elastic limit and will not regain its shape.

Steel spring

Spring is stretched by weights.

Heavier weights stretch the spring to its elastic limit.

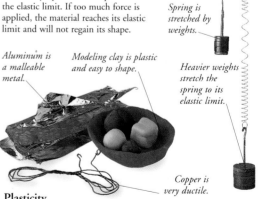

Aluminum is a malleable metal.

Modeling clay is plastic and easy to shape.

Copper is very ductile.

Plasticity
Modeling clay will not return to its original shape once it has been squeezed. A material that can be reshaped permanently when force is applied to it is said to be plastic. Most metals are plastic, but considerable force is needed to reshape them. A ductile metal is one that can be drawn out into fine wire. A metal that can be beaten or rolled out into thin sheets is said to be malleable.

| FIND OUT MORE | ATOMS AND MOLECULES | BUILDING AND CONSTRUCTION | CRYSTALS AND GEMS | GASES | LIQUIDS | MATTER | METALS | ROCKS AND MINERALS | VOLCANOES |

SONGBIRDS

ALMOST HALF THE WORLD'S bird species are songbirds – a name given to the passerines, or perching birds. There are more than 4,000 species and they are found all over the world. The males of most species sing loudly during their courtship season, although some can only croak harshly. Females usually do not sing. Songbirds feed on insects or seeds according to the shape of their beak. Most are blind and helpless when they hatch.

Small head has a powerful beak.

Female has a paler chest than the male.

Hind toe is larger and stronger than front toes.

Songbird features

Songbirds are varied, but most are quite small with a compact body and a small beak. They have small feet, with four slender toes. Their toes lock around twigs or branches enabling them to perch, even when they are asleep. The male and female of a species sometimes look identical.

Gouldian finches
These brilliantly colored seedeaters from northern Australia are typical songbirds. They spend most of their time in tall grasses or bushes, but come to the ground to drink.

Perching feet
A songbird's feet have three toes pointing forward, and one pointing backward. When the bird rests its weight on its feet, its toes automatically close.

Syrinx
The syrinx is a songbird's voicebox. It is located at the base of its windpipe, or trachea. It has thin walls that vibrate to make complex sounds.

Lungs
Trachea
Syrinx
Lungs

Bullfinch

Buds
The bullfinch eats buds in spring and seeds in summer.

Thick beak for removing buds.

Seed-eaters
Seedeaters, such as bullfinches, crossbills, and goldfinches, specialize in feeding at different types of plants. They have beaks shaped to extract the seeds and crack them open. Many of these birds also eat berries and buds, and occasionally insects.

Cones

Cross-tipped beak extracts seeds from cones.

Crossbill

Teasels

The spotted flycatcher darts out from a perch to catch passing insects.

Goldfinch

Slender beak can reach into teasel flower heads to extract the seeds.

Spotted flycatcher

Beaks and diet

The shape of a songbird's beak provides important clues to what it eats. For example, those with short, stubby beaks usually feed on seeds. Those with long, narrow beaks feed on insects, or on a range of food. Insect-eating songbirds often migrate to warm places when winter approaches, because insects are hard to find in cold weather.

Insect-eaters
Insect eaters usually feed on their own. They use their beaks either to probe into crevices for hidden insects, or to catch flying insects in midair. Some eat their food in flight, but others take it back to a perch.

Starling

A starling's sharp, straight beak probes grassy ground.

General feeders
Starlings, thrushes, and crows are songbirds that have a varied diet. They feed on a mixture of seeds, worms, and insects, and sometimes on the remains of dead animals.

Using tools
The woodpecker finch from the Galápagos Islands is one of the few animals in the world that uses tools. It picks up cactus spines and then uses them to pry insects out of cracks in the bark of trees.

Feeding underwater
One of the few songbirds that ventures into water is the dipper. It jumps into fast-flowing streams and walks or swims beneath the surface, picking up insect grubs in its beak from the riverbed.

Nectar eaters
Only a few songbirds feed on nectar, but their beaks are specially adapted for reaching inside flowers. Sunbirds, which live in Africa and southern Asia, have slender beaks with a downward curve. They suck up the liquid food using their tongue like a straw.

Sunbird

S

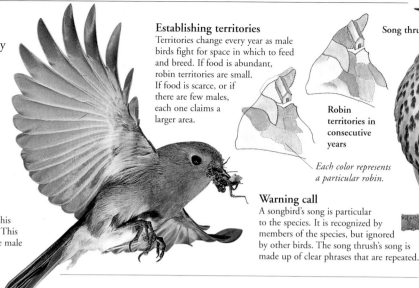

Courtship

During the breeding season, many male songbirds claim a small patch of land called a territory. They keep other males out of their territory, but encourage females to enter so that they can mate and raise a family. A male's song announces that he has a territory and will defend it against his rivals.

Attracting a mate

When a male robin has drawn a female into his territory, he often gives her presents of food. This is called courtship feeding. By doing this, the male encourages the female to mate and lay eggs.

Establishing territories

Territories change every year as male birds fight for space in which to feed and breed. If food is abundant, robin territories are small. If food is scarce, or if there are few males, each one claims a larger area.

Robin territories in consecutive years

Each color represents a particular robin.

Song thrush

Warning call

A songbird's song is particular to the species. It is recognized by members of the species, but ignored by other birds. The song thrush's song is made up of clear phrases that are repeated.

Raising young

Most songbirds are expert nest builders. They make their nests above the ground, usually in trees or dense vegetation. During the breeding season, the adults are kept extremely busy building nests and feeding the young. Once their first nestlings are ready to look after themselves, many female songbirds lay another clutch of eggs. Some species may raise up to five families a year.

Nest-building

Songbirds usually make cup-shaped nests. They collect twigs, leaves, and other materials and press them into shape with their breasts. Some species finish their nests with a smooth lining of mud.

Feeding a family

Most songbird nestlings are completely helpless when they hatch. They rely on their parents to feed them and to keep them warm until they develop feathers. In most species, the male and female share the task of finding food and bringing it to the chicks in the nest.

Hatching

The blue tit is a typical small songbird. It lays between six and 12 eggs, and the female starts to incubate the eggs immediately after the last one has been laid. The eggs hatch after about two weeks, and during the following two weeks, the nestlings grow and develop their feathers, or fledge.

Feather tract on the back

Flight feathers on the wings

Flight feathers almost fully formed.

1 At the age of just four days, the nestlings are still naked, and their eyes have not fully formed. They beg noisily when their parents approach the nest with food.

2 By six days, the nestlings' feathers are beginning to grow. They form in special patches called feather tracts. Some of these are on the body, and some along the wings.

3 At nine days, the nestlings' flight feathers emerge from their tube-like sheaths. Shorter feathers begin to cover the rest of the nestlings' bodies.

4 At 13 days, the nestlings are almost fully fledged. They will leave the nest in another four or five days, and will follow their parents as they learn how to feed.

Types of songbirds

House sparrows are originally from Africa and Asia. This small songbird now lives all over the world.

Blue-faced honeyeater has a harsh call. This large Australian bird feeds on insects, fruit, and nectar.

Nightingales are known for their song, which can be heard during the day and night.

Northern oriole is a common North American bird. It belongs to a family of songbirds with sharply pointed beaks.

Golden-crowned kinglet

Kinglets are among the smallest songbirds. The Golden-crowned kinglet is 3.5 in (9 cm) long.

Scarlet tanager

Tanagers usually live in the American tropics and subtropics, but the Scarlet tanager lives as far north as Canada.

Red-billed queleas

These small African songbirds are probably the world's most abundant birds. They eat mainly seeds, and feed in flocks that are sometimes more than one million strong. In the whole of Africa. there are at least one and a half billion of these birds.

 FIND OUT MORE

ANIMAL BEHAVIOR   **BIRDS**   **EGGS**   **NESTS AND BURROWS**

GOULDIAN FINCH

SCIENTIFIC NAME	*Chloebia gouldiae*
ORDER	Passeriformes
FAMILY	Estrildidae
DISTRIBUTION	Tropical northern Australia
HABITAT	Open woodland, grassland, and scrub
DIET	Seeds of grasses and other plants
SIZE	Length from the tip of the beak to the end of the tail: 5 in (13 cm)
LIFESPAN	About 5 years
MIGRATION	Non-migrant
PLUMAGE	Females are slightly paler
NEST	Dome of grass, usually in a hollow in the ground

SONGHAI EMPIRE

ONE OF THE LARGEST empires of 16th-century West Africa was that of the Songhai. Tradition has it that the Songhai kingdom was founded in the 7th century by al-Yaman, a Christian, but in the 11th century, its rulers converted to Islam. In the 14th century, the Mali Empire ruled the Songhai kingdom, but in 1464 a warrior-king named Sonni Ali rose up and conquered the Mali capital of Tombouctou, making Songhai independent once again. The Songhai Empire then continued to grow in wealth and power until internal divisions coupled with a Moroccan invasion brought the empire to an end in 1591.

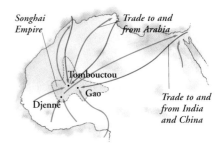

Boundaries of the empire
The Songhai Empire, which flourished from 1464 to 1591, initially occupied the same area as the previous West African empire of the Mali. Gao was the capital of the Songhai, and from here they expanded farther eastward, invading the territories of the Hausa states in modern northern Nigeria.

Songhai rulers

Gilded tent

Mythical Songhai ruler

The two greatest Songhai rulers were Sonni Ali (1464–1492) and the statesman Askia Muhammad (1493–1528). After Sonni Ali founded the Songhai Empire by a series of conquests, Muhammad consolidated and expanded it.

Askia Muhammad
When Sonni Ali died in 1492, his son, Sonni Baare, succeeded him. However, Baare was a weak ruler and Askia Muhammad, a former general in Sonni Ali's army, overthrew him in 1493. Muhammad expanded the empire to its greatest area by controlling trade routes to North Africa. He founded an efficient administration and protected all he had gained with a standing army and a fleet of war canoes.

Trans-Saharan trade
From trade centers in the Songhai Empire, such as the oasis town of Walata, goods traveled across the Sahara Desert on camel trains to countries in North Africa, especially Morocco, Algeria, and Libya. From there, they transported goods by ship to Europe, Arabia, and China.

River Niger

Trade goods
Africa has always been rich in natural resources, such as copper, salt, and gold. The Songhai based their empire on their gold trade with Arabia and Europe. Songhai merchants also traded other home-grown goods, such as figs, dates, kola nuts (a stimulant), and ivory. In return they bought ceramics, silk, beads, and cowrie shells.

Niger River
The Niger River crossed the Songhai Empire from east to west. It was crucial to the success of the empire, as it had been in the 12th to 15th centuries when the Mali Empire was dominant. Merchants had fleets of canoes to transport goods between different trading centers along the Niger River, such as Djenné, Tombouctou, and Gao.

Religion and education
Songhai boasted great scholars, including Ahmad Baba (b.1556), who wrote more than 50 books on Islamic tradition and a huge dictionary. The empire's most important religious and educational center was Tombouctou.

Islamic writing

Tombouctou
Known as the "holy town" of the Sudan, Tombouctou had three great mosques – the Jingereber, the Sidi Yahya, and the Sankore; all contained many superb copies of the Qur'an. It also had a university and 180 schools.

Page from a 16th-century Qur'an

Trade goods

Dried figs | Copper | Salt | Kola nut

Dates | Gold | Ivory

Decline of empire

Moroccans wanted to control the source of West African gold. In 1591, Ahmad al-Mansur (1578–1603), the Sultan of Morocco, sent a powerful army to conquer the Songhai Empire. The Moroccans conquered Tombouctou, which they ruled for more than 100 years. Shortly afterward, Morocco absorbed the rest of the empire.

Moroccan coins

Timeline
1464 Sonni Ali conquers Tombouctou, the former center of the Mali Empire.

1473 Sonni Ali conquers the trading town of Djenné.

1492 Sonni Baare, Sonni Ali's son, refuses to convert to Islam.

1493 Civil war; Sonni Baare is overthrown by the Muslim Askia Muhammad.

1496 Askia Muhammad's Mecca pilgrimage.

1528 Askia Muhammad is deposed by his eldest son Musa.

1588 Civil war erupts as Askia's descendants fight over the succession.

1591 The Moroccan army defeats the Songhai army at the Battle

Cowrie shells

FIND OUT MORE

AFRICA, HISTORY OF | TRADE AND INDUSTRY | MALI EMPIRE | MONEY

S

SOUND

FROM THE ROAR of city traffic to the quiet rustle of the wind in the trees, the world is full of sounds. A sound is a form of energy produced by vibrating objects, such as a person's vocal cords or a drum. When sound travels through a material such as air, molecules in the material vibrate and bump into other molecules, passing on their energy. Sound cannot travel in a vacuum.

Echoes

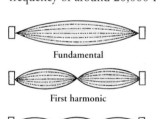

Sound can reflect off hard surfaces and return to its source as an echo. If you stand some distance away from a wall and shout or clap, you may hear an echo a short while later. The farther from the wall you stand, the longer the echo takes to reach you. Most of the sounds we hear are a mixture of the original sound and echoes from nearby objects.

Frequency and pitch

The pitch of a sound (whether it is high or low) depends on its frequency. Frequency is measured in hertz (Hz) – 1 Hz is one vibration per second. The lowest-pitched sound audible by most people has a frequency of about 40 Hz, and the highest has a frequency of around 20,000 Hz.

Fundamental

First harmonic

Second harmonic

Harmonics

Most sounds are made by objects that vibrate at several different frequencies at once. The sound consists of one main frequency, called the fundamental, mixed with several higher frequencies called harmonics.

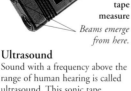

Display

Sonic tape measure

Beams emerge from here.

Ultrasound

Sound with a frequency above the range of human hearing is called ultrasound. This sonic tape measure sends out beams of ultrasound that bounce off an object and return to the device. The time the sound takes to return reveals the distance to the object.

Speed of sound

Sound travels at about 1,080 ft/s (330 m/s) through air. This is far slower than the speed of light, which is why lightning is seen before thunder is heard. The time lapse between a lightning flash and a thunderclap tells you how far away a storm is – that is, about 1 mile (1.6 km) away for every 5 seconds that pass.

Compressions
The air molecules are squeezed close together, so the air density and pressure increase.

Sound waves

Our ears detect sound traveling through the air as vibrations called sound waves. As this tuning fork vibrates, its prongs move outward and squeeze the air around them, creating high-pressure areas called compressions. As the prongs move back, the air expands and creates low-pressure areas called rarefactions. These pressure vibrations spread out from their source as sound waves.

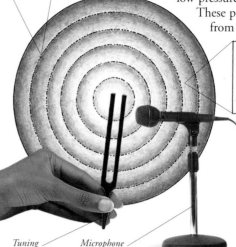

Rarefactions
The air molecules spread apart, giving the air a lower density and pressure than normal.

Electrical signal is sent to oscilloscope.

Tuning fork

Microphone changes sound into electrical signal.

Oscilloscope displays waveform on screen.

Waveforms
The shape of a sound wave as displayed on the screen of an oscilloscope is called its waveform. The peaks and troughs of the waveform correspond to the areas of high pressure and low pressure in the sound wave. Sounds are defined by their frequency and amplitude. The frequency of a sound wave traveling through the air is the number of pressure changes per second. The amplitude is the size of the pressure changes.

Oscilloscope
A sound wave cannot be seen, but a device called an oscilloscope can be used to give a visual representation of the sound wave. The sound wave's pressure changes are displayed as a wavy line on the oscilloscope's screen.

Soft sounds have a small amplitude and waveforms showing little difference between areas of high and low pressure.

Loud sounds have a large amplitude, and their waveforms show a greater difference between high- and low-pressure areas.

Low-pitched sounds have a low frequency, which means that there are fewer sound waves per second and they are farther apart.

High-pitched sounds have a high frequency, so there are more sound waves per second and they are closer together.

Loudness
The louder a sound is, the more energy its sound waves carry. Loudness is measured in decibels (dB). Sounds of 0 dB are just audible to the human ear, while sounds of 130 dB or more cause pain. Listening to loud music on a personal stereo for too long can damage your hearing. Although the stereo is not very powerful, almost all the sound goes directly into the ears, creating high levels of sound energy inside the ear.

Headset

Christian Doppler

The pitch of a sound from a moving source, such as the siren of a speeding fire engine, changes from high to low as the object passes you. The Austrian physicist Christian Doppler (1803–53) explained this effect in 1842. He showed that it is caused by the way sound waves bunch up ahead of the moving object and spread out behind it, changing the frequency of the sound. This effect is now known as the Doppler effect.

FIND OUT MORE

EARS AND HEARING   ENERGY   MUSICAL INSTRUMENTS   SOUND RECORDING

SOUND RECORDING

COMPACT DISCS (CDs) enable us to listen to the past. The information stored on the disc allows a CD-player to recreate sounds made at another time and in another place. Sound consists of vibrations that travel as waves of varying air pressure. A microphone makes a copy of these vibrations as an electrical sound signal, which can be stored in a number of different ways, including on CDs, magnetic tape, and vinyl records. The stored signal may be a direct representation of the original sound (analog recording), or it may be translated into electronic pulses (digital recording).

Recording studio

Sound recordings are often made in a recording studio, which normally consists of two adjoining rooms. In one room, people make music, sing, or speak. The sounds of the different voices and instruments are converted to electrical signals by microphones, and each is recorded separately. The separate signals are then added together again in the control room.

Recording studio

Performers speak or sing into microphone in soundproof booth.

TV screen for matching sound to screen actions.

Loudspeakers allow engineer to hear the sound from the booth.

Reel-to-reel tape machine can record sound from booth or add backing sound to new recordings.

Mixer takes the signals from the tape and the microphones and "mixes" them together to produce the desired sound.

Digital editing and recording system

Sound engineer controls the quality and "mix" of the sound.

Microphone

Diaphragm
Wire coil
Magnet

A microphone contains a wire coil attached to a thin sheet called a diaphragm. Sound waves cause the diaphragm and coil to vibrate within the force field of a magnet. This movement produces a fluctuating electric current, called an analog sound signal, that copies the vibrations in the sound waves.

Digital sound

In digital recording, the analogue sound signal produced by a microphone is measured, or "sampled", thousands of times every second. These measurements, which are in the form of numbers, are then converted into binary code – that is, into a series of on-off pulses of electricity. This is known as a digital sound signal.

Electrical copy of sound wave

Samples record shape of sound wave

3 5 6 6 4 2 1 2 — *as numbers.*

Recording formats

Analog formats store sound as wavy grooves or varying magnetic patterns that copy the changes in the analog sound signal. Digital formats store the binary-code information of a digital sound signal as magnetic patterns or a series of tiny holes.

Vinyl records (analog) record the vibrations of sound waves as undulations in a spiral groove cut into a vinyl disk.

Compact discs, or CDs, (digital) are metal and plastic disks that store sound as tiny pits on a spiral track.

Magnetic tape (analog) records sound as changing patterns in magnetic particles on a plastic tape.

Digital audio tape, or DAT, works like magnetic tape, but stores sound information digitally.

Minidiscs (digital) store sound signals as a spiral pattern on a magnetic disk.

MP3 player

The MP3 was launched in the 1990s as a high quality digital file format for storing music. MP3 files, created on a computer, are very small and can be transferred over the Internet or saved onto a portable music device, called an MP3 player. The MP3 player can hold several hours' worth of music that can be updated regularly.

With headphones this device works like a personal stereo.

Portable MP3 player

Emile Berliner

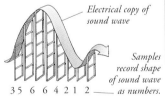

German-born Emile Berliner (1851–1929) invented the gramophone, which could replay sound recorded on flat discs. He also devised a method of reproducing hundreds of these discs from a single master copy.

Timeline

1876 The microphone is invented by Scottish-born Alexander Graham Bell, who uses it in the first telephone.

1877 Thomas Edison, an American inventor, makes the first sound recording – the words "Mary had a little lamb" – on to tin foil.

1887 Berliner invents the gramophone.

1898 Danish inventor Valdemar Poulsen makes magnetic recordings of sound on to steel piano wire.

1887 Magnetic tape is used to record sound.

Poulsen's telegraphone

1948 The first vinyl disks are produced.

1964 The cassette tape becomes available.

1980s Compact discs become the main medium for sound recording.

1992 The Sony Corporation of Japan introduces the minidisc.

2001 Internet site Napster is banned from swapping MP3 files for free because it infringes artists' copyright.

FIND OUT MORE   EDISON, THOMAS   ELECTROMAGNETISM   LASERS AND HOLOGRAMS   MUSIC   SOUND   TELECOMMUNICATIONS   TELEPHONES   VIDEO

SOUTH AFRICA

LYING AT THE SOUTHERN TIP of the African continent, South Africa is bordered by both the Atlantic and Indian Oceans. Two small, independent countries, Lesotho and Swaziland, are enclaves within South Africa and depend on it heavily. Racism dominated politics for many years, and from 1948, the white minority ruled the land and enforced apartheid, a system of racial segregation. In 1994, the country held its first multiracial elections and, with the end of apartheid, Nelson Mandela became South Africa's first black president, ruling until 1999.

SOUTH AFRICA FACTS	
CAPITAL CITIES	Pretoria, Cape Town, Bloemfontein
AREA	471,443 sq miles (1,221,040 sq km)
POPULATION	40,400,000
MAIN LANGUAGES	Afrikaans, English, Ndebele, North Sotho, South Sotho, Swazi, Tsonga, Tswana, Venda, Xhosa, Zulu
MAJOR RELIGION	Christian
CURRENCY	Rand
LIFE EXPECTANCY	54 years
PEOPLE PER DOCTOR	1,667
GOVERNMENT	Multiparty democracy
ADULT LITERACY	85%

Physical features

South Africa is a land of contrasts. The steep cliffs of the Great Escarpment separate the flat-topped plateau hills from the low-lying, sandy coastal regions. The arid Namib and Kalahari deserts, to the northwest, contrast with the lush forests of the northeast.

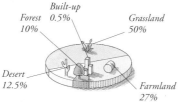

Built-up 0.5%
Forest 10%
Grassland 50%
Desert 12.5%
Farmland 27%

Land use
Although much of the country is high ground, the majority is used for grazing livestock and growing crops, including sugar, corn, and grain. South Africa has vast mineral resources, such as gold and coal.

Drakensberg
The dramatic Drakensberg, or Dragon Mountains, are a vast range located in the southeast of South Africa and Lesotho. They rise out of the eastern rim of the high plateau land to form a steep escarpment. The highest peak measures 11,424 ft (3,482 m) above sea level, at Thabana Nrlenyana, formerly known as Champagne Castle.

Climate
Generally, South Africa's climate is warm, sunny, and dry. The east receives about three times as much rain as the north and western desert regions. Winters are short, between June and August, and mild, although the Drakensberg and Cape mountains often have snow. The Cape Province has hot, dry summers from October to April.

107°F (42°C)
70°F (21°C)
16°F (-9°C)
52°F (11°C)
31 in (785 mm)

Veld
The grassy plateau, or tableland, that covers most of South Africa is known as the *veld*. In many places, it is more than 3,900 ft (1,200 m) above sea level. The central plateau is dry savanna, with scattered trees. Rolling grassland and subtropical woods with a wide variety of flora and fauna make up the northeastern *Lowveld*; sheep and cattle graze on the western *veld*.

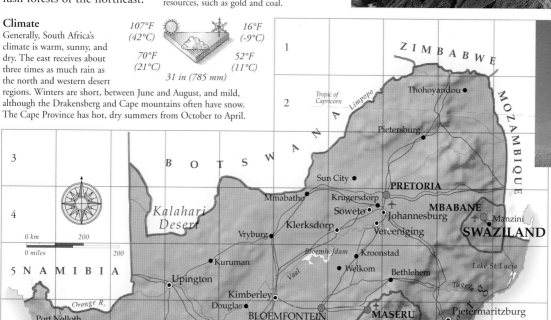

Three capital cities
South Africa has three capital cities. Most important is Pretoria, the center of administration. The government is based in Cape Town, which is situated at the foot of Table Mountain, and the lawcourts are in Bloemfontein.

Cape Town and Table Mountain

People

Most South Africans are black and belong to the Zulu or Xhosa groups. About ten percent are Coloreds, of mixed race, and the remainder are whites, of British origin, or Afrikaners of Dutch origin. Efforts are being made to create harmony between the races.

93 per sq mile
(36 per sq km)

55% Urban   45% Rural

Townships
Under apartheid, black South Africans had to live in planned communities, and most still live there. Soweto, near Johannesburg, is a complex of 29 towns with a total estimated population of two million. Houses range from luxury to shacks, and many people line up for water.

Farming

A warm climate and fertile soils mean that South Africa can grow nearly all its food, as well as a surplus for export. Farming accounts for seven percent of the country's economic activity. Corn, wheat, fruit, and tobacco are leading crops.

Lime

Orange

Lemon

Citrus fruits
Lemons, limes, and oranges grow well in tropical regions of South Africa, as do apples and pears, grown for export in the Cape area. A successful fruit juice industry has grown up in South Africa.

Vineyards
South African wines, made in the western and southern Cape, have been made in the region since 1662, and are known worldwide for their quality and flavor. Stellenbosch is a major winemaking center.

Leisure

Many South Africans are sports lovers, especially of outdoor games such as cricket, rugby, and soccer. Since the end of apartheid, the country has rejoined international events.

Rugby
South Africa's national sport, Rugby Union soccer, is widely played and watched. In 1995, South Africa hosted its first Rugby World Cup, won by its own international team, the Springboks.

Housepainting
Ndebele women of the Transvaal are known for their brightly decorated homes. Every spring, women renew the paint, passing on their skills to younger girls. Older wall patterns are geometric, but modern symbols such as airplanes and cars are now portrayed in the designs.

Industry

The South African economy is based on its mineral wealth. The iron and steel industries are important, but manufacturing, mainly in Durban, Johannesburg, Cape Town, and Pretoria, now forms the largest sector in the economy.

Diamond mines sprawl over large areas.

Gold
South Africa leads the world in the production of gold. Its Johannesburg mines provide about 30 percent of the world total, and most is used in jewelry and electronics.

Krugerrand

Mining
One of South Africa's main employers, the mining industry forms the backbone of the country's economy. There are vast reserves of diamonds, manganese, chromium, and lead.

Lesotho

Lesotho is a tiny, mountainous monarchy surrounded by South Africa, on which it depends for work. Farming is the main activity for 86 percent of the people. A new hydroelectric project is being developed, which will create energy.

Women dig a road by hand.

LESOTHO FACTS

CAPITAL CITY Maseru

AREA 11,718 sq miles (30,350 sq km)

POPULATION 2,200,000

MAIN LANGUAGES English, Sesotho

MAJOR RELIGION Christian

CURRENCY Loti

Women
Many women endure hardship and undertake labor in the community because three-quarters of the men leave their homes to work in South African mines. Women in Lesotho have Africa's highest literacy rate.

Swaziland

Bordered by South Africa and Mozambique, Swaziland is a small kingdom perched on a series of plateaus. The country's mineral resources include bauxite and diamonds. Farming employs 40 percent of the labor force. Citrus fruit and pineapples are grown in plantations, and sugarcane is the main export crop.

SWAZILAND FACTS

CAPITAL CITY Mbabane

AREA 6,703 sq miles (17,360 sq km)

POPULATION 1,000,000

MAIN LANGUAGES Siswati, English

MAJOR RELIGIONS Christian, traditional beliefs

CURRENCY Lilangeni

Swazis
Most of the people are Swazis, who follow a traditional clan lifestyle. The clans settle in rural, scattered homesteads, run by a chief and his mother. Swazis have a rich history of poetry and folktales.

FIND OUT MORE   BALL GAMES   CRYSTALS AND GEMS   DESERTS   FARMING   GRASSLAND WILDLIFE   MANDELA, NELSON   MOUNTAINS AND VALLEYS   ROCKS AND MINERALS   SOUTH AFRICA, HISTORY OF

SOUTH AFRICA, HISTORY OF

FROM C. AD100, SOUTH AFRICA was increasingly populated by Bantu-speaking farmers. In the 1600s, Dutch settlers founded farms in Cape Colony, forcing African farmers off the land. British settlers followed the Dutch, and both groups clashed ferociously with the black majority, particularly the Zulus. By the 1800s, the British and the Dutch – now called Boers – were competing with each other to control South African wealth. By 1950, an all-white government was in power that deprived black South Africans of the vote. In 1991, this policy was reversed. South Africa's first democratic elections took place in 1994.

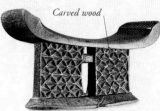
Carved wood

Head-rest

Bantu
Two thousand years ago, Iron Age Bantu-speaking farmers from the northeast settled South Africa's east coast and the savanna areas of the Transvaal. They were the ancestors of most of South Africa's black population. Today, most people speak some form of Bantu dialect.

European settlers

In 1651, Dutch farmers founded settlements in the Cape Colony. The settlers were called Boers (from the Dutch for "farmers"), and their descendants are today called Afrikaners. From 1795, as Dutch power faded, the British started to control more South African land.

Great Trek
In 1806, British settlers seized the Cape Colony from the Boers. To escape British control, the Boers migrated inland in large numbers. This became known as the Great Trek (1836–45). The Boers then formed two independent republics – the Orange Free State and the Transvaal.

Rest stop for a Boer family

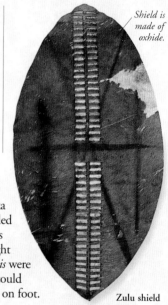
Shield is made of oxhide.

Anglo-Boer Wars
From 1880, the British attempted to take control of the Boer republics. They failed in the first Boer War (1880) but, after the discovery of gold and diamonds in the Transvaal in 1886, they redoubled their efforts. A second bloody war in 1899 finally led to a Boer surrender in 1902.

Boer War commemorative fan

Zulus

By 1818, a Zulu chief named Chaka (d.1828) had formed an empire called Zululand in northeastern Natal. His well-organized *impis* (warriors) fought both the Boers and the British. *Impis* were fierce and strictly disciplined: they could travel up to 40 miles (64 km) a day on foot.

Zulu shield

Union of South Africa

In 1910, British and Boer minorities formed the Union of South Africa, with the British in charge. There followed decades of repression of South Africa's non-whites.

Apartheid
Under the Apartheid (separateness) Policy of 1948, all South Africans were classified according to race. Black South Africans lost the right to vote, own land, travel, or work without permits. Asian and "colored" South Africans were allowed to vote, but not to use the same facilities as white South Africans. Whites reserved for themselves the best housing, jobs, and schools.

ANC flag

African National Congress
The African National Congress, or ANC (founded 1912), was the only political party representing the interests of black South Africans. Its main goal was the abolition of apartheid. South Africa's government outlawed it, but finally accepted its legality in 1990, just before Nelson Mandela's release.

Non-whites' post office entrance

New South Africa
In 1990, after spending 28 years in prison, one of the ANC's leaders, Nelson Mandela, was released. He immediately met President FW de Klerk to discuss political change in South Africa. Following their talks, apartheid was abolished and the first free, multiracial elections took place. For the first time, "Asians," "Blacks," and "Coloreds" gained full voting rights. The country elected Nelson Mandela president of a new, democratic South Africa.

Election queue, Katlehong

Stephen Biko
Biko (1946–77) was an opponent of apartheid who founded the South African Students Organization (SASO) and co-founded Black Consciousness. In 1977, he was arrested and beaten unconscious by police. Six days later he died; his death caused an international outcry. No one was charged with his murder, but investigations into it were reopened in 1997.

Timeline

1852 Boers create their independent republics.

1910 Union of South Africa formed, including Cape Province, Natal, Orange Free State, and Transvaal.

1931 South Africa gains independence.

Goatskin apron

1948 National Party (NP) is elected to government and passes Apartheid Policy. It establishes poor residential areas called Homelands for black majority.

1976 Police fire on a student march in Soweto; widespread demonstrations follow.

1970s World community imposes economic sanctions on South Africa.

1990 ANC deputy Nelson Mandela released from prison.

1991 Apartheid is abolished.

1994 First non-racial general election is held.

FIND OUT MORE   AFRICA, HISTORY OF   EMPIRES   EXPLORATION   HUMAN EVOLUTION   MANDELA, NELSON

SOUTH AMERICA

THE FOURTH LARGEST CONTINENT, South America ranks only fifth in population. Its 12 independent countries were once colonies of European powers, particularly Spain and Portugal, whose languages, culture, and religion have greatly influenced the region. Many South Americans are farmers who grow their own food. Three-quarters of the continent's population lives in large, overcrowded cities, often in squalid conditions. Many countries suffer huge foreign debts.

Physical features

Landscapes in South America range from the volcanic peaks of the Andes to the lush, tropical forests of the Amazon Basin in the east and center. Farther south are the rolling grasslands of the Chaco and pampas. In the west is the hot, dry Atacama Desert; the cold Patagonian desert lies in the extreme south.

Andes
Stretching 4,970 miles (8,000 km) down South America's Pacific coast from Venezuela to Chile, the Andes form the longest mountain chain in the world. The peaks are volcanic and subject to earthquakes. The highest point is Aconcagua in Argentina at 22,835 ft (6,960 m).

Amazon
The world's longest river, the Amazon stretches 4,040 miles (6,500 km); ships can navigate approximately 2,300 miles (3,700 km). The mouth of the Amazon, where it joins the Atlantic Ocean, is 90 miles (150 km) wide. It is estimated that about 20,900 gallons (95,000 litres) of water flow out each second.

Patagonia
Constant gales sweep the bleak southern plateau of Patagonia. With no more than 10 in (25 cm) of rain a year, much of Patagonia is cold desert, or semidesert with scant, gray vegetation of scrub and tussock grass. A few sheep are raised in the north.

Map labels

Caribbean Sea
19,030ft
CENTRAL AMERICA
VENEZUELA
Apure
Orinoco
Angel Falls
3,215ft
French Guiana (France)
Guiana Highlands
GUYANA
SURINAME
Ruiz 17,717ft
COLOMBIA
19,689ft
Equator
ECUADOR
Caquetá
Rio Negro
Amazon
Amazon Delta
Ilha de Marajó
Chimborazo 20,674ft
Marañón
Amazon Basin
Juruá
Madeira
Tapajós
Represa de Tucuruí
Cabo de São Roque
Huascarán 22,206ft
BRAZIL
Xingu
Araguaia
Tocantins
São Francisco
Represa de Sobradinho
P E R U
Lake Titicaca
BOLIVIA
Mato Grosso
Brazilian Highlands
6,670ft
Sajama 21,392ft
Guallatiri 19,883ft
Gran Chaco
Pantanal
Paraguay
9,144ft
Serra do Mar
Tropic of Capricorn
Atacama Desert
PARAGUAY
Paraná
6,193ft
Serra do Mar
Ojos del Salado 22,588ft
Cerro Bonete 22,546ft
Salinas Grandes
Uruguay
Lagoa dos Patos
Mercedario 22,212ft
Laguna Mar Chiquita
Aconcagua 22,831ft
URUGUAY
Río de la Plata
ATLANTIC OCEAN
PACIFIC OCEAN
CHILE
ARGENTINA
Pampas
Villarrica 9,318ft
Colorado
Bahía Blanca
Isla de Chiloé
Golfo San Matías
Salinas Grandes -131ft
Archipiélago de los Chonos
Chubut
Península Valdés
Golfo San Jorge
Lago Buenos Aires 12,159ft
Deseado
Isla Wellington
Patagonia
Bahía Grande
Falkland Is. (UK)
Lago Argentino
Tierra del Fuego
Strait of Magellan
Cape Horn

0 km 1000
0 miles 1000

Cross-section through South America

From the Pacific coast, the land rises steeply to the Andes, which separate into two parallel chains divided by a dry, grassy plateau called the Altiplano. East of the Andes is the steamy, forested Amazon basin. In the east, the plateau of the Guiana Highlands rises, then drops to the Atlantic.

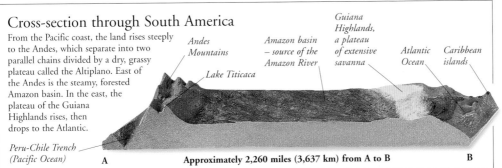

Andes Mountains
Lake Titicaca
Amazon basin – source of the Amazon River
Guiana Highlands, a plateau of extensive savanna
Atlantic Ocean
Caribbean islands
Peru-Chile Trench (Pacific Ocean)

A   Approximately 2,260 miles (3,637 km) from A to B   B

SOUTH AMERICA FACTS

AREA	7,177,259 sq miles (18,589,118 sq km)
POPULATION	385,000,000
NUMBER OF INDEPENDENT COUNTRIES	12
BIGGEST COUNTRY	Brazil
SMALLEST COUNTRY	Suriname
HIGHEST POINT	Aconcagua (Chile) 22,835 ft (6,960 m)
LOWEST POINT	Salinas Grandes (Argentina) 131 ft (40 m) below sea level
LONGEST RIVER	Amazon (Peru/Colombia/Brazil)
BIGGEST FRESHWATER LAKE	Lake Titicaca (Bolivia/Peru) 3,200 sq miles (8,288 sq km)

Climatic zones

The tropical rain forest that occupies the Amazon basin is intensely hot, humid, and wet all year. It has an average temperature of 70°F (21°C) and an annual rainfall of more than 79 in (2,000 mm). Much of the south of the continent has hot summers and cool winters, and there are wide grasslands with some semiarid areas. In the Andes, the climate becomes cooler and drier toward the peaks, which are snowcapped all the time.

Tropical rain forest

Mountain

Desert

Grassland

Scrubland

Wetland

La Gran Sabana, Venezuela

Grassland
Temperate grassland covers vast areas of South America, such as the Pampas of Argentina and the Gran Chaco of Paraguay and Bolivia. In the north, close to the equator, tropical grassland, or *llanos*, covers Venezuela's La Gran Sabana in the Guiana Highlands, the Brazilian Highlands, and the Mato Grosso plateau.

Large expanses of tropical grassland can be used for grazing.

Waxy leaves

Ulmo

Flowers appear in spring.

This tree's other name is monkey puzzle because of its twisted branches.

Cone

Chilean pine

Tropical rain forest
Dense, impenetrable rain forest crossed only by rivers covers the vast Amazon basin in northern South America. This region contains about 30 percent of the world's remaining forest and holds 20 percent of the world's fresh water. The Amazon and its many tributaries drain 40 percent of South America – an area of 2,702,700 sq miles (7,000,000 sq km).

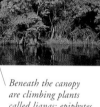

Beneath the canopy are climbing plants called lianas; epiphytes attach themselves to the branches.

Dry woodland
In northeastern Brazil, down into Paraguay, central Chile, and northern Argentina, there are large areas of dry, open woodland and savanna. The vegetation here includes trees such as the Chilean pine and shrubs such as ulmo, whose evergreen leaves thrive during long periods without water.

Columns of eroded rock stick up from the bare Atacama desert. Very few plants can live here.

The forest in southern Brazil extends down to the Atlantic coast.

Small cacti grow in the hot sun along the coastlines.

Hot and cold deserts
South America has two deserts – the cold Patagonian desert in Argentina, and the hot Atacama desert, the world's driest, in northern Chile. The Atacama runs for about 600 miles (965 km) along the coast. Rain has not fallen on some parts of the Atacama for hundreds of years.

Deciduous rain forest
Parts of southern Brazil and northern Uruguay are covered in deciduous rain forest. Unlike the equatorial Amazonian rain forest, where rain falls almost all year round, these forests have a distinct dry season when many of the trees lose their leaves. There are fewer species of trees here than in the tropical forests.

Mediterranean scrubland
Chile's Central Valley has a warm, Mediterranean-type climate with hot, dry summers and mild, damp winters. Small, thorny shrubs, stunted trees, cacti, and tough grass cover coastal cliffs. This region is famous for its fine wines, produced from grapes grown on the rich, fertile soils, watered by the melting snows of the Andes.

People
Only two percent of the population is descended from the Native Americans who settled in South America thousands of years before Europeans arrived. The majority are *mestizos* – of mixed American and European descent, and South Americans, who descended from Africans who either escaped from slave ships in the Caribbean or worked plantations on the mainland.

Brazilian girl **Bolivian boy** **Argentinian boy**

Resources
Rich volcanic soil provides some of the best farmland in the world, yielding wheat, corn, fruit, coffee, and tomatoes and potatoes, which originated in South America. The rain forests are a treasure trove of medicinal and other valuable plants. The continent is rich in minerals, especially oil, natural gas, gold, copper, tin, and precious stones.

Coffee beans **Orange**

Emerald

FIND OUT MORE CONTINENTS DESERTS DESERT WILDLIFE GRASSLAND WILDLIFE MOUNTAINS AND VALLEYS NATIVE AMERICANS RAIN FOREST WILDLIFE RIVERS SOUTH AMERICAN WILDLIFE

SOUTH AMERICA, HISTORY OF

SOUTH AMERICA was the home of many Native American civilizations until the first Europeans arrived in the 1520s. From that time on, Spanish and Portuguese conquerors took over, claiming the entire continent and its people and ruling there for 300 years. In the early 19th century, the area won its independence, but the new South American countries were poor and unstable. Today, the nations of South America have a vibrant culture that includes local, European, and African elements.

Early civilizations
The Native Americans were ancient peoples, whose civilizations flourished for thousands of years, particularly in the Andes Mountains. At the time of the European conquest, much of South America formed part of the most important of these civilizations – the Inca Empire of Peru.

Inca pot in the shape of a human face

Spanish rule

After the conquests of Francisco Pizarro (1475–1541) and other Spanish *conquistadores*, much of South America was ruled from Spain. Later, the Spanish kings sent officials called viceroys to govern the area, raise taxes, and run the courts. In the 18th century, the Viceroyalty of New Granada ruled what are now Colombia, Ecuador, Panama, and Venezuela.

El Dorado
Rumours were rife among the early Spanish explorers that beyond the Andes lived a people so rich in gold that the king covered himself in gold dust every year. This Man of Gold – "El Dorado" – was never found, but the legend spurred on many Spanish adventurers in their quest for gold.

Quest for silver
In 1545, the world's largest silver deposits were discovered at Potosí, Bolivia. Silver was carried in great quantities to Seville, Spain, and it fuelled both European and transatlantic trade. However, conditions in the mines were terrible: four out of five Native American workers died in the first year of mining.

Silver mine, Potosí

Bolivian silver

Francisco Pizarro

Native peoples
The native peoples of South America suffered badly from the conquest. They had very poor resistance to the diseases introduced from Europe, and were badly treated by the conquerors. The population of South America dropped from 16 million to about 4 million in the hundred years after the conquerors arrived in the 16th century.

Catholic Church

Native temples and religious statues were nearly all destroyed during the Conquest. Most people were converted to Roman Catholicism, although many continued to hold on to traditional beliefs. Churches were built in the Spanish style but were often adorned with native-style works of art.

Scene from the film, *The Mission*

Bartolomé de las Casas
Dominican friar Bartolomé de las Casas (1474–1566) argued that the Spanish conquest was illegal, and that Native Americans were free. He campaigned against their mistreatment by Spanish settlers, and laws were enacted to protect the native peoples. But the laws were often not observed, and came too late for many.

Jesuit missions
The Roman Catholic order known as the Society of Jesus, or the Jesuits, founded missions in Paraguay among the Guaraní and Tapes peoples. By the mid-18th century, there were 30 missions. They were farming villages in which the land and animals were owned by the people as a whole. In the 1770s, the Jesuits were expelled from Spanish and Portuguese territories and thousands of Native Americans were enslaved or killed.

Jesuit missionary

Local villagers

Churches
In order to protect the Native Americans from exploitation by Portuguese settlers, the Jesuits built their missions, with their Baroque-style churches, in the jungle, thus isolating themselves from the outside world.

Many of these Jesuit churches were simple stone buildings.

S

Independence

In the early 1800s, the French invaded Spain and replaced the king with Joseph Bonaparte (1768–1844), brother of the emperor Napoleon. At first, the colonies remained loyal to the king, but soon independence movements began in South America. The campaign for independence was led by "creoles," Spaniards born in South America. The most important of these leaders was Simón Bolívar. He dreamed of a united continent, but the different populations could not agree, and South America divided into many different nations.

Brazil

During the Napoleonic Wars, the king of Portugal, John VI, fled to Brazil and ruled from there. The country became rich, but the threat of revolution took the king back to Portugal. His son, Dom Pedro, declared Brazil independent in 1822.

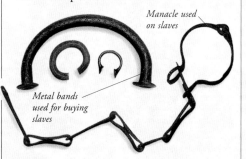

Manacle used on slaves

Metal bands used for buying slaves

Slavery
There were no large settled native populations in Brazil before the conquest, so the Portuguese colonists brought slaves from West Africa to work on plantations and in mines. Runaway slaves formed settlements known as quilombos: the most famous was at Palmares, where several thousand runaway slaves lived in towns and villages.

Spanish colonies

British, Dutch, and French colonies

Portuguese colony

• Lima

• Santiago
• San Fernando

Bernardo O'Higgins
O'Higgins (1778–1842) was the son of an Irishman who was governor of Chile. He became governor himself in 1814, but was removed by the Spaniards for his republican beliefs. He fought for Chile's independence and, in 1817, became the country's first head of state.

Red, white, and blue feathers symbolize liberty.

Bernardo O'Higgins

José de San Martín
General José de San Martín (1778–1850) was born in Argentina, where he led the movement that brought independence to the colony in 1816. He then marched to Chile, where he defeated the Spanish and restored the patriot leader Bernardo O'Higgins. In 1821, he went to Peru, took Lima, and declared Peru independent.

José de San Martín

Modern South America

In the 19th century, the new nations of South America relied on income from growing crops such as coffee. In the world depression of the 1930s, there was a sudden drop in demand for these products. Factories were set up, and thousands of people came to the cities to work there. Most South Americans still live in cities today.

Rubber
The rubber tree grows naturally in South America. There was an increasing demand for rubber in the 19th and early 20th centuries, and plantations were set up in Brazil. In 1900–14, there was a "rubber boom," when many plantation owners made large fortunes. Demand slackened in the 1930s.

Latex (sap) is tapped from the trees and left to harden.

The twin towers of Brasília's Congress Building

Brasília
In 1960, the capital of Brazil was moved from Rio de Janeiro to the new city of Brasília, with its modern government offices, national museum, and university.

Salvador Allende
Allende (1908–73) was elected president of Chile in 1970. His socialist policies antagonized his right-wing opponents who had the backing of the US. He died in a coup.

Falklands War
In 1833, British settlers occupied a group of islands in the South Atlantic and named them the "Falkland Isles." Argentina disputed British sovereignty and invaded the islands in 1982. Britain sent troops to recover the islands, and Argentina surrendered, but the disagreement over sovereignty continued into the 1990s.

Eva Perón
Born in poverty, Eva ("Evita") Duarte (1919–52) was a radio actress. She married politician Juan Perón, who became Argentine president in 1946. Adored by the poor of her country, she ensured Perón's re-election in 1952, but died of cancer in the same year.

Timeline

900–1476 Chancay culture develops on the west coast of South America.

1438–1532 The powerful Inca civilization flourishes in Peru and the surrounding area.

Chancay figurine

1530s Portuguese settlers arrive in Brazil.

1530s–1560 Spain completes the conquest of most of South America.

1532 The Spaniards, under Pizarro, conquer the Incas.

1717 Spain sets up the Viceroyalty of New Granada to govern most of South America, except for the Portuguese colony of Brazil.

1767 Spanish king Charles III expels the Jesuits from Spain and its colonies.

1808 South American colonies begin to mount campaigns for independence.

Opera House, Manaus, Brazil

1825 The struggle for independence ends with the creation of the new state of Bolivia.

1900–14 Rubber boom in Brazil.

1955 Military coup in Argentina ousts Juan Perón.

1976–82 Thousands of Argentinians disappear, probable victims of the military rulers' death squads.

1982 Britain and Argentina at war after Argentina invades the Falkland Islands.

FIND OUT MORE

BOLIVAR, SIMON   CENTRAL AMERICA, HISTORY OF   CHAVINS   EXPLORATION   MAYA   INCAS   PORTUGAL, HISTORY OF   RELIGIONS   SPAIN, HISTORY OF

SOUTH AMERICA, NORTHERN

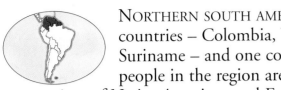

NORTHERN SOUTH AMERICA is made up of four countries – Colombia, Venezuela, Guyana, and Suriname – and one colony – French Guiana. The people in the region are ethnically mixed, but most are *mestizos,* of Native American and European origin. Along the coast are small settlements of black Africans, descendants of slaves who were brought in by colonial masters to work the plantations of sugar-cane and coffee. Polarization of rich and poor, highly overcrowded cities, and trade in illegal drugs are a problem in the area, which has a reputation for violence.

Physical features

The Andes dominate western Colombia and Venezuela. Lush lowlands surround Lake Maracaibo and the plain of the Orinoco River. Dense tropical rain forests cover much of the interior of Suriname and Guyana, both of which have a marshy coastal strip.

Northern Andes
The northern Andes are divided into three ranges by the valleys of the Cauca and Magdalena rivers. Most Colombians and many Venezuelans live on the lower slopes of the mountains.

Angel Falls
The spectacular Angel Falls on the Churún River in eastern Venezuela are the world's highest at 3,215 ft (980 m). The longest unbroken drop is 2,648 ft (807 m). Thousands of tourists visit the falls each year.

Shantytowns
Many South American countries have young, rapidly growing populations, with most people living in the towns and cities of the north. Unable to find adequate housing, many end up living in rough *barrios*, shantytowns, around modern urban centers. Services such as running water and sanitation are poor.

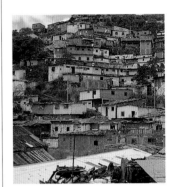

Housing for poor people in the Pro Patria district of Caracas

68°F (20°C) 70°F (21°C)

279 in (7,090 mm)

Regional climate
Lowlands in northern South America are mostly hot and humid, but the Maracaibo coast is hot and dry. Temperatures in the Andes are much lower.

Rain forest
Dense tropical rain forests cover the southern regions of Colombia and Venezuela and most of Suriname, Guyana, and French Guiana. Untouched by modern life, isolated groups of Native Americans still live in some of the most inaccessible areas.

Colombia

Divided from north to south by the Andes, Colombia has coastlines on both the Caribbean and the Pacific. The country is economically one of the strongest in South America, but trade in illegal drugs poses a serious problem. With help from the US, the government is waging a constant war against the "drug lords."

Colombian folk dancing

Cumbia
The *cumbia* is the most popular dance along Colombia's Caribbean coast. It is a blend of the region's Spanish, Native American, and African influences. Men in white, and women with long skirts, dance to flute music and drums.

81 per sq mile
(31 per sq km)

70% Urban   30% Rural

COLOMBIA FACTS

CAPITAL CITY Bogotá

AREA 439,733 sq miles (1,138,910 sq km)

POPULATION 42,300,000

MAIN LANGUAGES Spanish, Indian languages, English Creole

MAJOR RELIGION Christian

CURRENCY Peso

LIFE EXPECTANCY 71 years

PEOPLE PER DOCTOR 909

GOVERNMENT Multiparty democracy

ADULT LITERACY 92%

Bogotá
Founded by the Spanish in 1538, Colombia's capital and largest city, Bogotá, lies 8,560 ft (2,610 m) up in the Andes. Home to 6,700,000 people, it is the country's industrial, financial, and commercial center.

Modern buildings in Bogotá

Barren 1%   Grassland 16%   Wetland 1%
Forest 48.5%
Built-up 0.5%
Farmland 33%

Land use
Colombia's lush, fertile lowlands enable a wide range of crops to be grown all year round. Rain forest covers the east.

Emerald
Calcite

Mineral resources
Colombia produces about 60 percent of the world's emeralds. It also has large reserves of gold and coal. The recent discovery of oil allows Colombia to be self-sufficient in energy.

Farming
Colombia is one of the world's largest producers of coffee, which is grown on thousands of small farms. Other leading crops include sugarcane, rice, corn, plantains, bananas, sorghum, cotton, and cut flowers. Farmers raise cattle, vicuñas, pigs, and sheep. Farming accounts for more than half of the country's export earnings.

Venezuela

Drained by the Orinoco River, Venezuela's vast central plain is home to five million cattle. Despite its oil wealth and fertile lands, the country has been plagued by corruption, which led to crisis in the late 1990s, and a large devaluation of currency. Venezuelans in urban areas have suffered as a result.

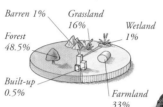

Oil and minerals
Venezuela ranks highly in world oil production, which provides 80 percent of export earnings. The richest reserves are to be found along the Orinoco River. Emphasis on the oil industry, however, has held back the development of the rest of the economy. Venezuela also has large reserves of coal, diamonds, bauxite, gold, and iron ore.

VENEZUELA FACTS

CAPITAL CITY Caracas

AREA 352,143 sq miles (912,050 sq km)

POPULATION 24,200,000

MAIN LANGUAGE Spanish

MAJOR RELIGION Christian

CURRENCY Bolívar

Guyana

Apart from a coastal strip, where most people live, Guyana is covered by rain forest. Its economy is based on bauxite, gold, rice, and sugar. Half the population is descended from Asians and 38 percent from African slaves, both of whom the British brought to work the sugar plantations.

Georgetown
The Dutch were the first Europeans to settle in Guyana, and the capital, Georgetown, still has old Dutch wooden buildings. The city sits on the bank of the Demerara River. It has wide streets, botanical gardens, and a university.

St. George's Cathedral

GUYANA FACTS

CAPITAL CITY Georgetown

AREA 83,000 sq miles (214,790 sq km)

POPULATION 861,000

MAIN LANGUAGE English

MAJOR RELIGIONS Christian, Hindu, Muslim

CURRENCY Guyana dollar

Suriname

Bauxite and aluminum, produced with hydroelectric power, are Suriname's main exports. In recent years, civil unrest has damaged the economy and about one-third of the people of this former Dutch colony have moved, in search of work, to the Netherlands.

Fishing
Sea fish, particularly shrimps, are among Suriname's chief exports. They are caught in the coastal waters of the Atlantic Ocean, off the Suriname coast.

SURINAME FACTS

CAPITAL CITY Paramaribo

AREA 63,039 sq miles (163,270 sq km)

POPULATION 417,000

MAIN LANGUAGE Dutch

MAJOR RELIGIONS Christian, Hindu

CURRENCY Guilder

French Guiana
South America's only remaining colony, French Guiana has been an overseas department of France since 1946. It covers 35,000 sq miles (91,000 sq km), and has a population of about 157,000. The European Space Agency has its rocket launching site on the colony.

Ariane rocket

FIND OUT MORE   CRYSTALS AND GEMS   DANCE   EMPIRES   FARMING   FISHING INDUSTRY   NATIVE AMERICANS   OIL   SOUTH AMERICA, HISTORY OF   SPACE EXPLORATION

SOUTH AMERICAN WILDLIFE

SOUTH AMERICA'S habitats include tropical forests of the north, grasslands of the center and south, tributaries of the Amazon River, the Andes mountains in the west, deserts fringing the west coast, and the wetlands of Brazil. South America is rich in wildlife, much of it found in the rain forests. The distinctive animals of South America, including anteaters, sloths, opossums, and New World monkeys, evolved when South America was separate from North America and isolated from the rest of the world.

Rain forest wildlife

South America's rain forests, including that of the Amazon basin (the largest rain forest in the world), contain a huge diversity of wildlife; many species are yet to be classified. The humid climate encourages rapid plant growth. Trees provide homes and food for insects, amphibians, reptiles, birds, and mammals.

Hoatzin
Relatives of cuckoos, these birds live in small flocks in trees bordering streams and swamps. Hoatzins are poor fliers that glide from tree to tree, then clamber up by using two hooked claws on each wing. Young hoatzins leave the nest soon after hatching and climb through the branches using their wings.

Two-toed sloth
The sloth spends most of its life upside-down in the trees, descending to the ground occasionally to defecate. It moves slowly along branches to find leaves to feed on.

Sloth feeds on leaves.

Margay
These small cats are perfectly adapted for life in the trees. They grip onto branches with their claws and, unlike other cats, can run down tree trunks head-first. Margays are solitary hunters that stalk prey such as tree frogs, lizards, birds, and small monkeys. The margay's coat provides camouflage in the dim forest light.

Hard-walled fruits contain nuts.

Margays spend most of their time in trees.

Sloths hang from branches by their long, curved claws.

Brazil nut tree
The brazil nut tree is one of many species of tree found in the Amazon tropical forest. The tree reaches a height of more than 45 m (150 ft). It produces hard-shelled fruits that fall to the ground and break open to reveal 8–24 hard shelled nuts, or seeds, arranged like the segments of an orange. The canopy of the brazil nut, and neighbouring trees is home for many species of insects, birds, and mammals.

Pectoral fins

Hatchet fish
These small fish are one of many species of fish that live in the rivers that flow through the rain forest. The hatchet fish leaps from the river and beats its long pectoral fins noisily like wings, to "fly" for short distances above the water. It catches insects and crustaceans on, or above, the river's surface.

Very deep body

Wetland wildlife

There are two major areas of wetland in South America. Many streams flow into the Amazon River and flood the tropical forest floor. The streams are rich in animals, which feed on forest products that fall into the water. The Pantanal in southern Brazil is the world's largest wetland. It is an important habitat for water birds such as spoonbills.

Suriname toad
This toad lives in slow-moving tropical streams. It forages in mud for invertebrates, which it senses through touch organs on its fingers. The female lays eggs which the male presses into the skin on the female's back. The eggs hatch into tadpoles and develop under the skin, protected from predators. Later the pouch opens and the young emerge.

Streamlined body, flat tail, and webbed feet help the otter swim.

Eggs are covered in skin pockets on female's back.

Giant otter
This large, powerful otter lives in tropical lagoons and shallow creeks. It catches catfish and other fish, which it clasps in its front paws and eats head first. It also eats mammals and water birds, and animals caught on land.

Roseate spoonbill
Roseate spoonbills live in marshes, lagoons, coastal waters, and mangrove creeks. They find food while wading, by sweeping their spoon-shaped bills from side to side through the water, and grasping any small crustaceans, fish, or plants they come into contact with. Spoonbills nest in small colonies in trees or reeds.

Spoon-shaped bill

Webbed feet used for swimming

Yacare caiman
Caimans are related to alligators. They live in swamps, or on the banks of slow-moving rivers and backwaters with muddy bottoms. Caimans are strong swimmers and feed on fish, crustaceans, and other animals caught in the water. They also catch water birds and small mammals, pulling them underwater to drown them, before eating them. Female caiman lay their eggs in nests, that they build and guard themselves.

Caiman has sharp teeth for crushing prey.

Wood stork
These large, long-legged wading birds live in flocks in wooded marshes and swamps, near pools. They rest and nest together in trees. Wood storks feed by standing in water, sometimes up to the belly, and moving their large, open bill from side to side. When they encounter prey, such as fish, frogs, or crustaceans, they snap their bills tightly shut.

Very long legs for wading in water.

S

Mountain wildlife

The Andes form a spine that runs down the western side of South America. The western side of the Andes has low rainfall and little wildlife; the eastern slopes have humid forests and a greater diversity of species. Mountain animals, such as the vicuña, are adapted for life at high altitudes.

Andean condor
The Andean condor is the world's largest bird of prey with a wingspan of more than 10 ft (3 m). Condors feed mainly on carrion, but also attack animals that are old or wounded, and take eggs from seabird colonies on the Peruvian coast.

Condors soar for hours at high altitude, above mountain summits searching for food.

Dense fur for warmth in the mountains.

The vicuña's movable toe pads help it walk easily over all types of terrain.

Vicuña
The vicuña is the smallest member of the camel family. Small herds of vicuña graze on grasses in the high altitude grasslands of the central Andes between 12,500–16,500 ft (3,800–5,000 m). Once hunted to near extinction for its wool and meat, the vicuña is now protected in national parks.

Vicuñas have very fine, soft wool.

Spectacled bear
The spectacled bear is the only species of bear found in South America. It lives in the humid forests and grasslands of the northern Andes. The spectacled bear gets its name from the pale circles of fur around some of the individuals' eyes. An adult male weighs up to 286 lb (180 kg); females are about half this size. It is a good climber, and will climb trees in search of fruit and other vegetation. It also eats insects and carrion, and sometimes deer and vicuña.

Lesser rhea
This large flightless bird feeds among the tall grasses and shrubs on roots, plant seeds, insects, and other small animals. It nests in a hollow in the ground; the eggs, laid by several females, are incubated and guarded by just one male.

Rheas can run at speeds of up to 30 mph (50 kmh).

Giant anteater
Living in grasslands and open woodlands, the giant anteater feeds almost exclusively on ants and termites. It has a long, flexible snout and an acute sense of smell for detecting food. It uses its powerful front legs and large claws to open a termite or ant nest, then flicks its 2 ft (60 cm) long sticky tongue into the nest about 150 times per minute, to extract its food.

Long snout and tongue

Grassland wildlife

Grassland and scrub cover much of central, eastern, and southern South America. The best known area is the pampas of Argentina and Uruguay, now used for farming. Plants that grow there include grasses, sedges, and shrubs. In the west, the grasslands are hot and dry; in the east, they are wetter.

Long legs for running through long grass.

Hooked beak

Crested caracara
This ground-dwelling member of the falcon family uses its long toes and claws to turn over stones and scratch the ground, in search of prey, as well as for grasping prey. The crested caracara catches insects, frogs, lizards, snakes, young birds, and small mammals. It also flies low over grasslands in search of carrion.

Long legs for walking through the long grass.

Maned wolf
Maned wolves hunt at night by stalking prey and then pouncing on it. Their prey includes rabbits, rodents, armadillos, reptiles, and insects, as well as eggs and fruit.

Desert wildlife

South America's main deserts are the Patagonian Desert in Argentina, and the Atacama in Peru and Chile. The Atacama is the driest desert on Earth, but sea mists from the Pacific provide some moisture within a "fog zone," allowing some wildlife such as cacti, lizards, and rodents to survive.

Cardon
The cardon is a cactus found in Monte, a region of desert east of the Andes mountains in Argentina. Cacti are flowering plants adapted for surviving in hot, dry areas. The cardon has an extensive shallow root system that gathers water rapidly whenever it rains. Scarce water is stored within the ribbed, expandable stem. The cactus provides food and shelter for desert animals.

Chilean racer
This snake is found on the southern fringes of the Atacama Desert, southward into the drier parts of Chile, from sea-level up to 5,000 ft (1,500 m) into the Andes. The Chilean racer hunts for prey by day, feeding mainly on lizards. It may climb into scrub when looking for its prey.

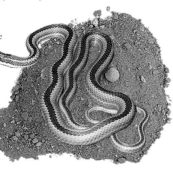

Spotted monitor tegu
This is one of several species of lizard found in the fog zone of the Atacama Desert and in dry regions on the western slopes of the Andes. It forages for prey, including insects and smaller lizards, during the day, and stores food reserves, in the form of fat, in its tail. It grows to 20 in (50 cm) in length.

Spotted skin camouflages lizard against the rocks.

Water is stored in expandable stems.

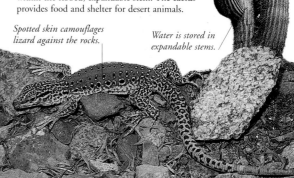

FIND OUT MORE   ANTEATERS, SLOTHS, AND ARMADILLOS   BEARS   BIRDS OF PREY   CAMELS   CROCODILES   FLIGHTLESS BIRDS   LIZARDS   SNAKES   WOLVES AND OTHER WILD DOGS

SOVIET UNION

BORN OUT OF the chaos of the 1917 Russian Revolution, the Union of the Soviet Socialist Republics, or Soviet Union, was the world's first communist country. During its 75-year history, the Soviet Union became one of the world's most powerful states, playing a leading role in world politics and achieving huge technological advances. But the Soviet Union failed to deliver prosperity or liberty to its subjects. Efforts to reform the communist system failed, and the republics finally split up in 1991.

Five Year Plans
During the 1920s and 1930s, Soviet leader Joseph Stalin produced a series of long-term plans to steer the country's economy. Known as Five Year Plans, they covered areas such as heavy industry, agriculture, manufactured goods, defense, and arms production.

Propaganda poster showing Soviet workers

Soviet state
The Soviet Union was made up of several republics, which were governed by soviets (councils). Every aspect of Soviet life was rigorously controlled by the state. Industry and agriculture were taken over by the state, the press was censored, and cultural life was directed toward the glorification of the communist system. A vast secret police force (known as the KGB) kept control of the population and removed all dissent.

Joseph Stalin
Stalin (1879–1953) was born in the Russian state of Georgia. A communist from an early age, he seized control of the party in 1923, and took over the Soviet Union in 1924. He held absolute power, torturing and killing opponents and dissidents. This type of ruthless dictatorship is now known as "Stalinism."

USSR at war
On June 22, 1941, 79 German divisions invaded the Soviet Union, bringing it into the war on the same side as Britain and, later, the US. Although the Germans soon occupied huge tracts of the western Soviet Union, they failed to capture Moscow before winter set in and were heavily defeated at Stalingrad (now Vologard) in January 1943.

Siege of Leningrad
In September 1941, German forces surrounded Leningrad. The city held out for 900 days until supplies finally arrived in January 1944. Bombardment, hunger, and cold caused the deaths of thousands of citizens.

Consequences of war
Much of the western half of the country was destroyed in the war and more than 20 million people lost their lives. To stop this from happening again, Soviet troops occupied much of Eastern Europe after 1945, setting up a buffer zone of communist governments.

Show trial of Stalin's opponents, Moscow

Show trials
In the 1930s, Stalin removed opposition to his rule in a series of show trials. Dissident leaders were shot or imprisoned, and hundreds of thousands of Soviet citizens were condemned to forced labor in Siberia or the Arctic lands.

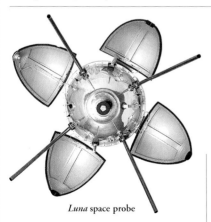

Luna space probe

Space race
In 1957, the USSR became the first nation to launch an artificial satellite into space, and sent the first astronaut – Yuri Gagarin – into space in 1961. Soviet space successes promoted a massive space race with the US.

Superpower
The USSR emerged from World War II as a superpower. It competed with the US in scientific and military affairs, using its first nuclear weapon in 1949. Direct armed conflict between the two sides did not break out in the so-called Cold War, but the Soviets supported nations such as Vietnam in conflicts with the US.

Timeline
1917 Russan revolution, under leaders such as Trotsky, establishes communism.

1918–20 Russian Red Army wins civil war.

1924 Joseph Stalin takes over after revolutionary leader Vladimir I Lenin dies.

1928 First Five Year Plan.

1941–45 USSR fights in World War II, sustaining horrendous losses.

1945 Russian troops occupy much of Eastern Europe.

1953 Death of Stalin.

Revolutionary leader Leon Trotsky 1879–1940

Perestroika
In 1985, Mikhail Gorbachev became leader of the USSR. He began to reform the communist system through *perestroika* (restructuring) and introduced *glasnost* (openness). Gorbachev resigned in 1991 after an attempted coup.

Mikhail Gorbachev

1956 New leader Nikita Khrushchev denounces excesses of Stalin's rule.

1964 Khrushchev replaced by Leonid Brezhnev.

1985 Mikhail Gorbachev becomes leader and begins reforms.

1991 Gorbachev resigns and the USSR breaks up.

FIND OUT MORE | COLD WAR | EUROPE, HISTORY OF | GOVERNMENTS AND POLITICS | MARX, KARL | POLICE | RUSSIA, HISTORY OF | RUSSIAN REVOLUTION | WORLD WAR II

SPACE EXPLORATION

THE SPACE AGE BEGAN IN 1957 with the launch of the first satellite. Since then astronauts and robots have flown from Earth to explore space first hand. Twelve astronauts have landed on the Moon. Many more have conducted experiments in space while orbiting Earth. Spacecraft equipped with robotic equipment have visited all the planets except Pluto, many moons, two comets, and two asteroids.

Galileo's **journey:** 1989, launched from space shuttle *Atlantis*; 1989–1992, circled Earth and Venus to gain momentum; 1995, reached Jupiter.

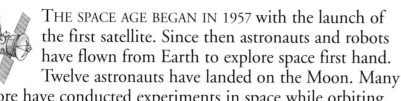

Galileo's route — Earth — Sun — Venus — Jupiter

Space probes

Robotic spacecraft have been used since 1959 to make long-distance journeys to the planets and their moons. The first flew past their targets; orbiters and landers came later. The real work starts when the craft reaches its target. Equipment switches on and collects data that is transmitted to Earth for analysis.

Radioactive power source

Attitude control thrusters inside protective shields

Sensing instruments

Antenna

Galileo space probe

Main antenna

Gravity assist

A space probe can fly by a planet to reach its target planet. It uses the planet's gravitational field to change direction and speed. The *Galileo* probe used this technique to reach Jupiter: it passed by Earth twice and Venus once to gain speed, before heading toward Jupiter.

Galileo probe

This was the last great space probe of the 20th century, and the first to investigate the atmosphere of a giant planet by sending a mini-probe into it. As *Galileo* approached Jupiter in July 1995, a smaller probe separated from the main craft. They both reached Jupiter in December 1995. The small probe descended into the planet's thick atmosphere of hydrogen, helium, and other gases. It collected data for 57 minutes before it stopped working.

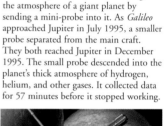

Fly-by probes

Some probes simply fly by a planet. At a preplanned distance, the instruments switch on and start to record data. Once the probe has passed the planet, they switch off again.

Low-gain antenna

Heat shield protects the atmosphere probe.

Atmosphere probe

The *Galileo* probe was designed to orbit Jupiter and its moons 11 times and send data back to Earth for about two years.

Radioactive power source

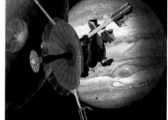

Mariner 10
The only space probe to visit Mercury, *Mariner 10* was also the first to go to more than one planet. Between 1974 and 1975, it flew by Venus once and Mercury three times.

Mariner 10

Cameras

Sensor

Solar panel

Giotto
Ten instruments on *Giotto* investigated Halley's Comet in 1986. The probe flew within 400 miles (600 km) of the nucleus.

Orbiters

When some space probes reach their target, they follow a preset route that puts them into orbit around the planet. The orbiter may stay in orbit forever. It will transmit data back to Earth until it is shut down or stops working.

Magellan probe
In 1990, the *Magellan* space probe entered into orbit around Venus. Its radar equipment "saw" through the planet's clouds to produce detailed maps of the surface. *Magellan* completed six surveys before being destroyed as it plunged into the planet's atmosphere.

Dish emits radar signals that bounce off the surface.

Magellan

Radio signals show height.

Reflected radar signals

Venus's surface
Magellan mapped almost 99 percent of Venus's surface. Impact craters, canyons, lava flows, and volcanoes were revealed. This *Magellan* image shows the mountain region called Ishtar Terra.

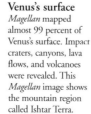

Landers

Probes put into orbit around a planet may release a smaller probe to land on the planet. Landers have touched down on Venus, Mars, and the Moon. The data they collect is transmitted to the orbiter and from there to Earth.

Viking lander
In July and September 1976, two *Viking* probes parachuted onto the surface of Mars. They took pictures of the landscape and carried out a series of experiments. Tests of the soil to establish any sign of life on the planet were inconclusive.

Viking lander

Antenna

Cameras

Robot arm to take soil samples

Atmosphere sensors

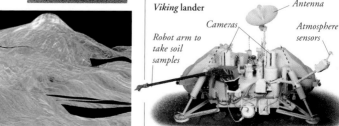

Wernher von Braun
Born in Germany, Wernher von Braun (1912–77) developed the *V2* rocket in 1942. He later became an American citizen and developed rockets for the USA. His *Saturn V* rocket took astronauts to the Moon in the 1960s. In the early 1970s, he was in charge of planning NASA's future in space.

Space stations

A permanent spacecraft in orbit around Earth can act as a base for astronauts to live and work in and as a station for beginning journeys into space. Russia and the US have both launched space stations. A team of about 18 nations is working together to build *Alpha*, a space station for the 21st century.

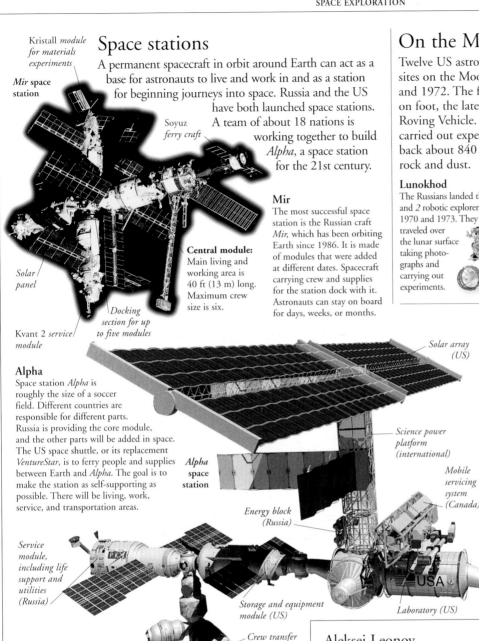

Kristall module for materials experiments

Mir space station

Solar panel

Soyuz ferry craft

Docking section for up to five modules

Kvant 2 *service module*

Mir

The most successful space station is the Russian craft *Mir*, which has been orbiting Earth since 1986. It is made of modules that were added at different dates. Spacecraft carrying crew and supplies for the station dock with it. Astronauts can stay on board for days, weeks, or months.

Central module: Main living and working area is 40 ft (13 m) long. Maximum crew size is six.

Alpha

Space station *Alpha* is roughly the size of a soccer field. Different countries are responsible for different parts. Russia is providing the core module, and the other parts will be added in space. The US space shuttle, or its replacement *VentureStar*, is to ferry people and supplies between Earth and *Alpha*. The goal is to make the station as self-supporting as possible. There will be living, work, service, and transportation areas.

Solar array (US)

Science power platform (international)

Mobile servicing system (Canada)

Alpha space station

Energy block (Russia)

Service module, including life support and utilities (Russia)

Storage and equipment module (US)

Laboratory (US)

Crew transfer vehicle (US)

Skylab

The only American space station, *Skylab*, was used by three teams of visiting astronauts between May 1973 and February 1974. They carried out experiments in the laboratory and used it as an observatory for looking out to space and down to Earth. In 1979, it burned up in Earth's atmosphere.

Aleksei Leonov

In 1965, the Russian cosmonaut Aleksei Leonov (b.1934) became the first person to "walk" in space. On his second space trip, in 1975, his *Soyuz* spacecraft docked with an American *Apollo* spacecraft to make the first international space hook up.

On the Moon

Twelve US astronauts landed at six sites on the Moon between 1969 and 1972. The first crews explored on foot, the later ones in a Lunar Roving Vehicle. They set up and carried out experiments and brought back about 840 lb (380 kg) of Moon rock and dust.

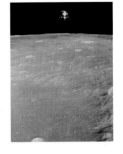

Lunokhod

The Russians landed the *Lunokhod 1* and *2* robotic explorers on the Moon in 1970 and 1973. They traveled over the lunar surface taking photographs and carrying out experiments.

Lunar module

The *Apollo 12* capsule carried two astronauts to the Moon's surface on November 19, 1969. They walked to the *Surveyor 3* spacecraft that had landed in 1967 and retrieved materials from the craft for analysis.

Space missions

Space journeys are planned years in advance. An international team works to build a probe to conduct specific experiments. Some are part of a series, such as the *Apollo* lunar missions. Others, such as *Cassini*, are single missions.

Cassini

When the *Cassini* probe, scheduled for launch in 1997, reaches Saturn in 2004, it will make 23 fly-bys in a four-year study of the planet, its atmosphere, rings, and some of its moons. A smaller probe, *Huygens*, will separate from the main craft and head for the largest moon, Titan. It will make a three-hour descent through the thick atmosphere to Titan's surface.

Earth's messages

Space probes carry messages from Earth in case aliens ever find them. Plaques and disks on board the probes identify Earth and its life forms with maps, pictures, and, in more recent craft, sounds.

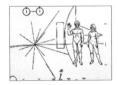

The plaque on *Pioneers 10* and *11* that identified Earth and its inhabitants.

Timeline

1962 *Mariner 2* flies by Venus, the first spacecraft to visit another planet.

1966 *Luna 9* makes the first successful landing of a craft on the Moon.

1971 *Salyut 1*, the first space station, is launched.

Venus

1973 *Pioneer 10* flies by Jupiter, the first craft to cross the asteroid belt and reach one of the giant planets.

1986 *Giotto* takes the first images of the nucleus of a comet.

1987 Astronauts on *Mir* start the first permanent manned space station.

1989 *Voyager 2* flies by Neptune three years after it flew by Uranus.

1993 *Hubble Space Telescope* is repaired. First detailed photographs of outer space objects sent back to Earth.

1998 *Lunar Prospector* discovers ice on the surface of the Moon.

FIND OUT MORE | ASTRONAUTS | COMETS AND ASTEROIDS | EXPLORATION | MOON | PLANETS | ROCKETS | SATELLITES | SUN AND SOLAR SYSTEM | TELESCOPES | UNIVERSE

SPAIN

SEPARATED FROM the rest of Europe by the Pyrenees in the north, and from Africa by the Strait of Gibraltar to the south, Spain shares the Iberian Peninsula with Portugal. Spain is the fourth largest country in Europe and, on average, also one of the highest. Once reliant on farming and fishing for its income, Spain has experienced rapid economic growth since becoming a member of the European Union in 1986. Today, it is a major industrial nation with a large agricultural sector and a booming tourist trade.

Physical features

Spain is a land of contrasts, with mountains in the north, center, and south, an arid plateau, the *Meseta*, at the center, green valleys in the northwest, and warm plains on the Mediterranean coast.

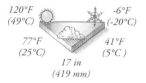

120°F (49°C)   -6°F (-20°C)

77°F (25°C)   41°F (5°C)

17 in (419 mm)

Climate

The *Meseta* has hot, arid summers; in winter snow blizzards are common. The coast and Balearic Islands have periods of drought in summer, and mild, damp winters.

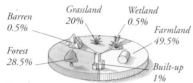

Barren 0.5%   Grassland 20%   Wetland 0.5%

Farmland 49.5%

Forest 28.5%

Built-up 1%

Land use

Spain has very few natural resources, including water. With the help of irrigation, half of the land is used for growing crops such as grains, olives, citrus fruits, and grapes. About one-fifth is pasture for grazing animals, mainly sheep.

Balearic Islands

Majorca, Minorca, and Ibiza are the largest of the Balearic Islands. They lie to the east in the Mediterranean, and have a total area of 1,935 sq miles (5,011 sq km); 700,000 people live there. The islands, which are governed by Spain, are famous for wine, fishing, and tourism. Thousands of vacationers visit each year.

Pyrenees

Separating Spain from France are the imposing Pyrenees. This mountain range runs from the Mediterranean to the Atlantic coast and contains many peaks more than 9,800 ft (3,000 m) high. It is a wild area, where bears and wolves still roam.

Meseta

The vast, dry plateau known as the *Meseta* covers most of central Spain. Hills and low mountains break into the plateau, through which rivers run, although many dry up in the summer heat. There is little rain, and farmers rely on irrigation to water crops.

Madrid

King Philip II made Madrid the capital of Spain in 1561 because he liked the climate and location in the center of the country. Home to around five million people, it has many fine buildings, including the Prado, one of Europe's leading art galleries. The city is a center for finance, government, and industry.

Gran Via

People

The Spanish are divided into regional groups, each with their own language and culture. About 16 per cent are Catalan, Galicians make up seven per cent, and just two per cent are Basques. Most of the rest are Castilian Spanish, which is the official dialect taught in schools.

205 per sq mile
(79 per sq km)

78% Urban   22% Rural

Urban life
Over three-quarters of Spaniards live in cities, where young people move in search of work. Barcelona, home to about four million people, is Spain's center of finance and government. Most people who live in rural areas are elderly. The status of women is rising quickly.

Leisure

Many Spaniards enjoy watching or playing soccer, and the teams of Real Madrid and Valencia are well known internationally. The warm climate makes eating outdoors practical and relaxing.

Fiestas
Most Spaniards are Roman Catholic, and fiestas, often to celebrate a local saint's day, include a procession of people in traditional costume, music, and dancing. Over 3,000 fiestas take place each year in Spain.

Flamenco
This traditional Spanish dance was developed by the gypsies of Andalusia in the 15th century. Men in black and women in bright dresses dance to flamenco music played on a guitar.

Industry

Spain's major industries are textiles, fishing, metals, shipbuilding, cars, and tourism. Since the 1980s, many high-tech industries have been established. Although Spain has few mineral resources, it is a major world producer of mercury.

Sherry
Spain is famous for producing sherry, a fortified wine made by adding alcohol to wine during fermentation. It is named after the town of Jerez de la Frontera, where it is produced. Sherry production is a major industry because of the demand for this popular aperitif.

Olives
The warm climate and terraced slopes of the mountains, particularly in the south and east, are ideal for cultivating olives. Spain is second only to Italy's olive production. Some of the fruit is processed for eating, but most of the crop is made into olive oil.

Olives are often eaten as an appetizer.

Farming

Poor soil and lack of water make agriculture difficult, but farmers use every available bit of land. They grow barley, corn, sorghum, and wheat. Sheep are the main animals raised. People also keep lots of pigs and smaller numbers of cattle and goats.

Oranges and lemons
The climate of the Mediterranean coast is ideal for growing citrus fruit. Spain is a major producer of oranges and lemons. The bitter oranges grown in the area around the city of Sevilla are the best for making marmalade.

Food

One of Spain's best-known dishes is *paella*, a tasty mixture of chicken, pork, shellfish, beans, tomatoes, peas, and rice. Food is often eaten with wine, such as Rioja from the north, or sangria, a blend of red wine, citrus fruit, lemonade, and brandy.

Prawn

Mussel *Chicken* *Rice*

Tourism
Sandy beaches, beautiful cities, and hot, sunny days attract about 48 million visitors a year. Tourism employs ten percent of Spain's workforce and is a major source of income. The Costa Blanca on the southwest coast is popular with British and German vacationers.

Car manufacturing
Spain ranks highly in world car production. However, following the demise of once-famous national makes such as the Hispano-Suiza and the Pegaso, it is restricted to manufacturing foreign cars under license. This Seat is being produced in Spain for the Italian company Fiat.

Andorra

Lying high in the Pyrenees, Andorra is a tiny country between France and Spain. Tourism is the main source of income and it has few resources. Divorce is illegal.

Landscape
Andorra is a country of mountains and valleys that attract large numbers of visitors to ski and sightsee. Duty-free goods draw summer shoppers.

ANDORRA FACTS

CAPITAL CITY Andorra la Vella

AREA 181 sq miles (468 sq km)

POPULATION 66,800

MAIN LANGUAGES Catalan, Spanish

MAJOR RELIGION Christian

CURRENCY Euro

ADULT LITERACY 99%

FIND OUT MORE   CARS AND TRUCKS   CHRISTIANITY   DANCE   EUROPE   EUROPE, HISTORY OF   EUROPEAN UNION   FARMING   FESTIVALS   SOCCER   SPAIN HISTORY OF

SPAIN, HISTORY OF

FOR MUCH OF ITS HISTORY, Spain has been ruled by foreign powers. Greeks, Romans, Visigoths, and Moors all left their mark on the country. In 1492, Spain was finally united. It became powerful and acquired a vast empire in the Americas. However, the effort of holding this huge empire together weakened Spain – by 1700, the country was exhausted. The ailing monarchy was finally overthrown in 1931 and, after a vicious civil war, a Fascist government under General Franco took power. The monarchy was restored in 1975.

Roman Spain

In 133 BC, Spain was conquered by the Romans, who united the country and brought peace, prosperity, and, later, Christianity. Roman rule lasted for more than 500 years until Germanic invaders overran the country in the 5th century.

Roman carving

Moorish Spain

In 711, Moors (Muslims from north Africa) invaded Spain, driving the Christian rulers into the mountains of the north. For 700 years, the Moors ruled much of Spain. They introduced Islam, but allowed Jews and Christians to worship freely. They were known for their scholarship and fine buildings.

Ceiling at the Moorish palace of the Alhambra, Granada

Queen Isabella of Castile

King Ferdinand of Aragon

Ferdinand and Isabella and their army

Ferdinand and Isabella

In 1479, the two main Christian kingdoms of Spain were united when Ferdinand of Aragon married Isabella of Castile. By 1492, the Moors were expelled from Spain, and the Christian "reconquest" was complete. Spain was a single country for the first time since the Romans.

Cleansing of the Temple by El Greco

Golden Age

In the 16th and early 17th centuries, Spain was one of the most powerful countries in Europe, controlling much of Italy and the Netherlands, as well as a vast American empire. Gold and silver from mines of the Americas flooded into the country, creating huge wealth. Artists such as El Greco, Murillo, and Velásquez made Spain one of the artistic centers of Europe.

Civil War 1936–39

In 1936, civil war began between the Nationalists, whose leaders included army officers and who supported Fascist political policies, and the Republicans, who wanted to curb army power and return to a socialist government. Fascist Italy and Nazi Germany backed the Nationalists, and after three years of fighting and one million deaths, Nationalist leader Francisco Franco seized power.

Republican soldiers

Basques

The Basques of northern Spain are a distinct people with their own language and culture. In 1936, they sided with the Republicans. In response, German bombers supporting Franco attacked the town of Guernica, killing many.

EXPO '92

Juan Carlos

Franco died in 1975 and power passed to Juan Carlos (b.1938), grandson of the last Spanish king. Under his rule, Spain became a multiparty democracy, reaching world prominence with events, such as Expo 92.

Philip II

Philip II (1527–98) ruled Spain, southern Italy, and the Netherlands from 1556. Son of Charles V, Holy Roman Emperor, he continued his father's war against France, and drew England into the conflict. A revolt by the Dutch after 1568 weakened his rule and led him to send an ill-fated armada to invade England in 1588. His chief success was the conquest of Portugal in 1580.

Timeline

201–133 BC Romans rule Spain.

AD 300 Spain becomes Christian.

711 Moors invade Spain and establish Islamic rule.

1479 Kingdoms of Aragon and Castile are united.

1492 Moors expelled; Columbus sails the Atlantic, beginning Spain's American empire.

1556–98 Reign of Philip II.

1808–14 Napoleon's armies seize Spain.

1816–28 Spain loses empire in South and Central America.

General Franco

1936–39 Civil War leads to a Fascist dictatorship by General Franco.

1975 Franco dies and is succeeded by King Juan Carlos.

1986 Spain joins European Union.

FIND OUT MORE | CENTRAL AMERICA, HISTORY OF | COLUMBUS, CHRISTOPHER | HOLY ROMAN EMPIRE | SOUTH AMERICA, HISTORY OF

SPIDERS AND SCORPIONS

WITH THEIR LONG LEGS and silent movements, spiders can approach prey without warning. Scorpions also give little notice before they sting. However, only a few species of spiders and scorpions are dangerous to humans. Both are arachnids – a group of mainly solitary, carnivorous, land-living invertebrates. Included in the group are 30,500 species of mites and ticks, and 4,500 species of harvestmen, or daddy-longlegs.

Fangs
Between the pedipalps of all spiders lie hollow fangs called chelicerae. They are connected to a venom gland that pumps venom into prey, when the spider bites its victim.

Irritant hairs may be kicked at predators.

Opisthosoma

Cephalothorax

Chelicera

1st leg

4th leg

2nd leg

3rd leg

Pedipalp

Spinnerets

Red-kneed tarantula

Features of a spider
There are 40,000 species of spiders. All have four pairs of legs, with spans ranging from 0.8 in (2 mm) in money spiders to 12 in (30 cm) in goliath spiders. They lack antennae, but frontal appendages called pedipalps are used as sense organs, and, in males, to transfer sperm. Spiders' bodies are made up of a fused head and thorax, or cephalothorax, and an abdomen, or opisthosoma. Most spiders have 4, 6, or 8 eyes.

Spinnerets
Three pairs of tiny organs called spinnerets lie at the base of the opisthosoma. They produce silk for making webs and cocoons. The silk is made from protein. It is very elastic, and stronger than steel wire of the same thickness.

Silk and webs
Spiders spin silken webs to catch their prey. Each strand of a web may be made of several strands of silk. Some spiders make messy webs called cobwebs. Trap-door spiders lay silk trip lines near their burrows and strike if prey touches one. Silk is also used to make cocoons, or spun into nets to drop on prey, and wrap up food. Money spiders use silk as a parachute.

Spinning a web
1 The spider makes a Y-shaped structure of silk, then spins the radii, or spokes, of the web.

2 The spider has now spun a spiral of non-sticky web. It uses this spiral as a platform to spin the sticky spirals.

3 The spider now spins dense concentric spirals of special sticky silk, which it will use to trap prey.

4 Having finished spinning, the spider now waits in the middle of its web to catch its first meal.

Feeding
Spiders are carnivores and kill prey such as insects. Most trap their victims in webs; some, such as wolf spiders, hunt for prey. Spiders cannot eat solid food. They inject venom to paralyse the prey, and enzymes to dissolve its internal organs. Once prey is liquefied, the spider sucks the fluids from its victim, leaving a crumpled external skeleton, in the case of an insect.

Wolf spider eating a fly

Reproduction
A female spider may mistake a male for prey as he approaches her to mate. To prevent this, male orb-web spiders pluck at the edge of the web in a specific way; other spiders present the female with gifts of food, or tie her up with silk while mating. Despite taking precautions, the male is still often eaten by the female after mating has taken place.

Black widow with cocoons

Cocoons
Many spiders, such as black widows, wrap their eggs in silk cocoons to protect them while they develop. Cocoons keeps the eggs together and prevent eggs drying out The spiderlings hatch from the eggs and cut their way out of the cocoons.

Defense
Spiders have a range of defenses: many hide to avoid enemies; others disguise themselves as ants. Some tarantulas flick irritant hairs at attackers to blind them. Australian red-backs have bright colors that warn that they are venomous – but if attacked they, and funnel-webs, inject venom into their enemies.

Raised legs in defense posture.

Sydney funnel-web spider

Fangs

Scorpions
Most scorpions live in warm regions, hiding in crevices or below rocks by day. They are carnivorous and emerge at night to hunt their mainly insect prey. Scorpions use their pincers and the venomous sting in their tail to kill prey and for defense. Some, including fat-tailed scorpions, can kill humans. There are 2,100 species of scorpions; the largest is 7 in (18 cm) long.

Reproduction
Scorpions mate with care because of their stings and pincers. They grasp each other's claws and perform a ritual called the scorpion dance. The male pulls the female forwards to guide her over a packet of sperm until it slots into her genital pore.

Sting

Pincer

Young sit on mother for two weeks.

Imperial scorpion

RED-KNEED TARANTULA

SCIENTIFIC NAME	*Brachypelma smithii*
ORDER	Araneae
FAMILY	Theraphosidae
DISTRIBUTION	Mexico
HABITAT	Dry srubland and woodland, especially in areas of rocky ground covered by thick vegetation
DIET	Large insects, other spiders, small reptiles, and occasionally small mammals
SIZE	Legspan: up to 6.3 in (16 cm)
LIFESPAN	Males live for 7–8 years; females live for 20–30 years

FIND OUT MORE   ARTHROPODS   CAVE WILDLIFE   DESERT WILDLIFE   MARSH AND SWAMP WILDLIFE   POISONOUS ANIMALS

S

Spiders

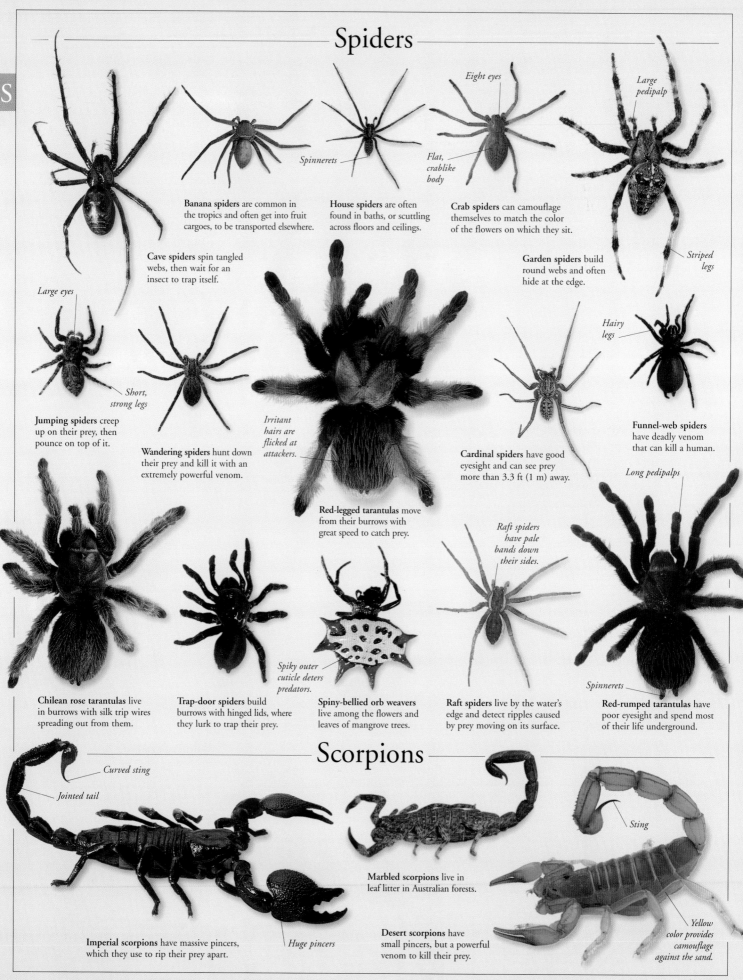

Banana spiders are common in the tropics and often get into fruit cargoes, to be transported elsewhere.

Spinnerets

House spiders are often found in baths, or scuttling across floors and ceilings.

Eight eyes

Flat, crablike body

Crab spiders can camouflage themselves to match the color of the flowers on which they sit.

Large pedipalp

Cave spiders spin tangled webs, then wait for an insect to trap itself.

Garden spiders build round webs and often hide at the edge.

Striped legs

Large eyes

Short, strong legs

Jumping spiders creep up on their prey, then pounce on top of it.

Wandering spiders hunt down their prey and kill it with an extremely powerful venom.

Irritant hairs are flicked at attackers.

Hairy legs

Cardinal spiders have good eyesight and can see prey more than 3.3 ft (1 m) away.

Funnel-web spiders have deadly venom that can kill a human.

Red-legged tarantulas move from their burrows with great speed to catch prey.

Long pedipalps

Raft spiders have pale bands down their sides.

Chilean rose tarantulas live in burrows with silk trip wires spreading out from them.

Trap-door spiders build burrows with hinged lids, where they lurk to trap their prey.

Spiky outer cuticle deters predators.

Spiny-bellied orb weavers live among the flowers and leaves of mangrove trees.

Raft spiders live by the water's edge and detect ripples caused by prey moving on its surface.

Spinnerets

Red-rumped tarantulas have poor eyesight and spend most of their life underground.

Scorpions

Curved sting

Jointed tail

Marbled scorpions live in leaf litter in Australian forests.

Sting

Imperial scorpions have massive pincers, which they use to rip their prey apart.

Huge pincers

Desert scorpions have small pincers, but a powerful venom to kill their prey.

Yellow color provides camouflage against the sand.

SPORTS

SINCE ANCIENT TIMES, people have taken part in sports, either for recreation or for the thrill of competition. In ancient Greece, for example, men regularly visited gymnasiums to relax and to keep fit; some also participated in the more formal ancient Olympics. Today, there is an impressive range of sports to choose from, including activities as diverse as athletics, archery, and horseback riding. Sports can be enjoyed for their own sake, as leisure or health pursuits, or at a competitive level.

Sports today

Sports is a thriving industry, with billions of dollars poured into it every year by television companies, sponsors, and the public. People pay to watch major events, and also buy sports equipment for their own use. There is now a growing concern for health and fitness and new trends in sports are always emerging.

Thousands of people watch events such as this international in Hong Kong, China.

Professionalism
Top sports stars, such as US tennis star Venus Williams, can earn a huge amount of money. With so much money in sports, even the main stronghold of amateurism – the Olympics – now allows professionals to take part.

Sponsorship
Companies sponsor teams, individuals, and competitions. They pay to promote their products on clothing and around stadiums at key matches.

International soccer match

Types of sports

Most sports can be classified under one or more of the following categories: air, athletic, ball, combat, equestrian, racket, target, water, wheel, and winter sports. These categories can be further divided into individual and/or team sports, and contact or non-contact sports.

Athletics
Athletics is probably one of the most popular groups of sports. It includes running, hurdling, jumping, and throwing. Running may range from jogging for health and fitness to more gruelling cross-country events.

Running for fun

Winter sports
Although many sports are played in winter, those known specifically as winter sports are performed on ice and snow, such as skiing, snowboarding, or ice hockey. Skating can be enjoyed all year on indoor ice-rinks.

Snowboarding

Inline skating
Inline skating evolved from rollerskating during the 1980s. Inline skates allow high speeds and complex tricks. Although this sport is also called "rollerblading" that is in fact the trademarked name of just one manufacturer of inline skates.

Mountain biking   **Inline skating**

Cycling
Cycling is very popular around the world. It is a great way to keep fit, as well as a cheap and non-polluting means of transportation. "Mountain bikes", first designed for offroad cycling, are now common in cities too.

Wind surfing

Soccer

Water sports
Water provides the means for gentle activity or vigorous exercise. People enjoy sailing and rowing in boats, and swimming, which is enjoyed in indoor pools as well as outdoors.

Ball games
Controlling a ball with a hand, foot, stick, or bat is a satisfying experience. Ball games include team sports, such as soccer and basketball, and individual sports, such as golf.

Gymnastics
Young people can excel at the highest level in this sport. It combines agility, grace, and physical discipline. Rhythmic gymnastics combines elegance with entertaining juggling skills.

Rhythmic gymnastics

Combat sports
Many of today's combat sports evolved from fight-to-the-death contests in ancient times, but the rules of sports such as judo, karate, and wrestling are designed to prevent injury and reward skill. Boxing is controversial because its aim is to inflict damage on the opponent.

Judo

Racing kart

Motor sports
People can take part in motor racing sports at various levels. In grand prix racing, sponsors' money and a large back-up team are needed to support the competitors.

Racket sports
Sports played with rackets need hand-eye co-ordination. Many people play tennis, badminton, squash, and table tennis for recreation. At the highest level, the games require great skill, fitness, and stamina.

Tennis

Horse riding
Riding can be an exhilarating pastime, enhanced by the necessary understanding between horse and rider. Young people enjoy competing in gymkhanas, and top-class show jumping and eventing are thrilling spectator sports.

Tacking up for riding

FIND OUT MORE   ATHLETICS   BALL GAMES   COMBAT SPORTS   CYCLING   GYMNASTICS   HORSE RIDING   MOTOR SPORTS   SWIMMING AND DIVING   TENNIS AND OTHER RACKET SPORTS   WINTER SPORTS

STAMPS AND POSTAL SERVICES

EVERY DAY, MILLIONS OF PEOPLE send and receive mail. The sender sticks a postage stamp to the envelope or package to show that he or she has prepaid the cost of postage, then mails the item at the post office or a mailbox, confident that it will reach its final destination. Every country operates a postal service. It remains a vital means of national and international communication, despite the growth of electronic systems, such as e-mail and the fax machine.

Postal services

Services to collect and deliver mail have existed since ancient times. A major reform came with postage stamps, used regularly around the world from 1840. Previously, the recipient had paid on delivery for his or her mail; now, the sender pays in advance for postage by attaching a stamp. Today, the cost of postage is determined by the weight, destination, and priority of a letter. Mail is first collected from a mailbox, and taken to a central sorting office.

Philately

Philately (stamp collecting) began in the 1840s. Since there were few stamps in existence, early philatelists collected many of the same kind, and stuck them on walls or furniture for decoration. Today, a stamp album may include different stamps from every nation of the world. Because governments often use stamp designs to mark special political events or to honor individuals, stamp collections can be interesting documents of social history, reflecting social attitudes and priorities in different nations.

Starter pack

Stamps from different countries

Collectors mount stamps in specially designed albums.

Perforation gauge

Protective sheet keeps stamp collection clean.

Tweezers, for handling stamps with care

Reproduction of rare stamp appears on modern stamp.

Magnifying glass

Color key, to match against stamp shades

Stamp collections

Some of the equipment a collector may need is shown here. Most important, when beginning a collection, are the stamp album and starter pack of assorted stamps. Collections can be organized in many ways: by country, shape, or theme. Stamps need not be rare or expensive, just interesting to the person collecting them.

Sorting office

Sorting

At a sorting office, an operator marks mail with phosphor dots, according to the zip code of the address. The dots are read by an automatic sorting machine that determines priority and nonpriority mail, then cancels every stamp so that it cannot be reused.

Transporting airmail

Delivery

Mail is transported by road, rail, or air as quickly as possible. To speed the process some railroad stations are also post offices. The mailsacks are then taken to the sorting office near their destination, sorted according to area, and delivered.

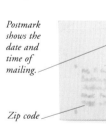

Postmark shows the date and time of mailing.

Zip code

Phosphor dots are read by the sorting machine; such machines sort mail eight times faster than by hand.

Phosphor dots

The name of the issuing country appears on every postage stamp, apart from those issued in the UK.

Queen Victoria

Airmail stationery is made from lightweight paper.

British Guiana One Cent appears on stamp from 1967

Valuable stamps

The world's rarest stamp is the 1856 British Guiana One Cent, because only one copy exists. It was found by a schoolboy in British Guiana in 1873. In 1980, a US millionaire bought it for $850,000.

Timeline

500 BC Cyrus the Great, Emperor of Persia, sets up mail route. Messengers on horseback carry royal commands across the empire.

1840 In Britain, the Penny Post introduces the first regular use of postage stamps, with the issue of the Penny Black and Twopence Blue. The sender pays the cost of postage.

Penny Black

1874 The Universal Postal Union is set up by international agreement to provide a uniform system for the exchange of mail between nations.

1919 First regular international airmail service begins.

1977 US introduces Express Mail for overnight delivery of priority post.

FIND OUT MORE   CODES AND CIPHERS   INFORMATION TECHNOLOGY   PERSIAN EMPIRE   TELECOMMUNICATIONS   TRADE AND INDUSTRY

Stamps and postal services

Stamp collections: the natural world

Orchids,
Algeria

Orchids,
Belize

Giant anteater,
Guyana

Dahlia,
Japan

Shell duck,
Soviet Union

Red deer,
Belarus

Love birds,
US

Transportation and sports

Naval frigate,
Chile

Commemorates a European soccer tournament

Soccer,
Albania

Space shuttle,
US

Yachting,
Japan

Ferrari

Race car,
Belgium

Celebrates the Olympic Games

Javelin throwing,
Monaco

Golf,
Kenya

Rare or unusual

Marks the centenary of the Universal Postal Union
Island-shaped stamp,
Norfolk Island

Bananas are an important crop in Tonga.

Banana-shaped,
Tonga

Printed in 1913

Rare stamp with no watermark, Japan

Circular,
Singapore

Valuable for its unusually good condition

1861 3 cent,
US

Printed on metallic paper

Kidney-shaped,
Bahamas

Cricket is a popular sport on the island.

Triangular,
Sri Lanka

Famous people

Hungarian activist
Flora Martos
(1897–1938)

Italian astronomer
Galileo Galilei
(1564–1642)

US film star
James Dean
(1931–55)

US president Richard
Nixon (1913–94)

US film star
Grace Kelly
(1929–82)

Chilean poet
Pablo Neruda
(1904–73)

Chilean leader
Salvador Allende
(1908–73)

Mailboxes

France

Initials of reigning monarch at time mailbox was put up.

United Kingdom

Standard delivery mailbox

United States

The Netherlands

Box has one slot for local mail and one for all other destinations.

Italy

Express mailbox guarantees next day delivery.

United States

S

STARFISH AND SEA URCHINS

ON THE SEABED lurk many spiny-skinned animals, including starfish and sea urchins. They, along with sea lilies, feather stars, brittlestars, and sea cucumbers, belong to a group of invertebrate animals – the echinoderms. The 6,000 species of echinoderms all live in the sea, moving slowly along the seabed by extending their tube feet. They have chalky plates, radially symmetrical bodies, and a water pumping system used for movement.

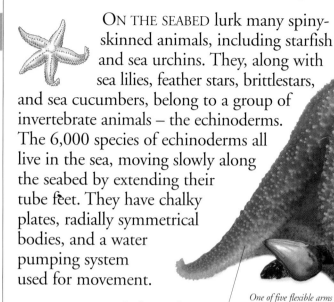

Anus is on upperside of central area.

Starfish

A starfish's body consists of five "arms" that radiate from a central area that contains the mouth on the underside and the anus on the upperside. The arms will often grow again if bitten off by predators. The underside of the body is covered in rows of suckerlike tube feet that enable the starfish to move and hold on to surfaces; chalky plates embedded in the spiny skin protect the upper side.

Feeding

Many starfish are active predators. They feed on shellfish, which try to clam up, but the starfish wraps its arms around the shell and pulls until the shellfish can resist no longer. Once the shell is open, the starfish pushes its stomach through its mouth to digest the flesh of the shellfish.

Common starfish feeding on mussels

Small spines and pincers cover the starfish's upper surface.

One of five flexible arms

Tube feet

Tube feet tipped with suction pads

Movement
Rows of tube feet line the underside of a starfish's arms and form part of the hydraulic vascular system common to all echinoderms. These tiny, water-filled tubes are elastic and have a bulb-shaped swelling at the base and a suckerlike disk for attachment at the end. Muscles squeeze the bulbs, pushing water through the tubes and extending them. This propels the starfish forward.

Tube feet of a common starfish

The starfish has started to turn itself over.

Two lower arms are attached to the seabed.

Three arms reach out to find a surface to grip.

The starfish is now right side up.

How a starfish turns over

1 Starfish are often overturned by waves and water currents and are then vulnerable to attack with their soft undersides exposed.

2 Two arms stiffen and fix themselves to the seabed. The body rises and the tube feet on the other three arms feel for a surface to grip.

3 The three arms in the air are lowered to the seabed, where the tube feet grab hold. Some species of starfish may take an hour to turn over.

4 The whole body is now right-side up. A variation on the basic somersault method involves arching the body, and then toppling over.

Sea urchins

Most sea urchins are about 3 in (8 cm) in diameter and live in shallow seas on the seabed. They are like starfish with the arms folded up to make a ball. Their outer skeleton is covered in spines and tube feet, used for movement. Some species, such as the sand dollar, are flat in shape and have special spines for burrowing into sand; others can tunnel into rock.

Anus and genital openings on upper side

Spines

Tube feet

Mouth is on the lower side.

Defense
Slow-moving sea urchins need good protection. Spines, varying from long, sharp needles to short, stout clubs, cover their bodies. Muscles allow the spines to move during locomotion and for protection. Some sea urchins have poison-tipped spines; others have pincers that secrete a poison and are used to paralyze small animals.

Feeding
Most sea urchins eat algae and dead animal matter. Their tube feet push food into the mouth, where teeth chop it up before it enters the long gut. The teeth are set within a frame of chalky plates connected by muscles – a structure called Aristotle's lantern.

Aristotle's lantern

Feeding tentacles

Sea cucumbers
These soft-bodied creatures look like large slugs with feeding tentacles around the mouth. They live on the seabed in deep water where they move along on rows of tube feet. Some sea cucumbers can also burrow; others can swim.

Brittlestars
Brittlestars, so-called because their arms easily snap off, are the most numerous echinoderms, with over 2,000 species. They are covered with chalky plates and spines and have long, slender, occasionally branched arms clearly distinct from the body. The arms are used both for movement and feeding. Most brittlestars are filter feeders, but some are scavengers.

Common brittle star

Feather stars
Feather stars and sea lilies have flexible arms for filter feeding. Sea lilies grow on stems attached to solid surfaces. Feather stars use rootlike arms to swim or hold on to surfaces.

Yellow feather star

COMMON STARFISH

SCIENTIFIC NAME	*Asterias rubens*
ORDER	Forcipulata
FAMILY	Asteriidae
DISTRIBUTION	At depths of 3–650 ft (1–200 m) in the Atlantic ocean and the NW European continental shelf
HABITAT	Rock surfaces and stony sand sediment surfaces on seabeds
DIET	Shellfish; a serious pest on oyster and scallop beds
SIZE	Diameter: up to 12 in (30 cm)
LIFESPAN	2–4 years

FIND OUT MORE

ANIMALS   CORAL REEFS   OCEAN WILDLIFE   POISONOUS ANIMALS   SEASHORE WILDLIFE

STARS

THERE ARE MORE STARS than any other object in the Universe. Each is a spinning ball of hot, luminous gas. Most stars are made mainly of hydrogen and helium. As these gases are converted to heavier elements, energy is produced. A star has a life cycle of billions of years that takes it through many changes. The mass of the star, however, dictates how it will develop and die.

Nucleosynthesis

Chemical elements are created inside stars by nuclear reactions. The process, called nucleosynthesis, starts by converting hydrogen to helium. A sequence of reactions at higher and higher temperatures produces heavier and heavier elements. The heaviest produced is iron. Most stars complete only part of the process in their lifetime.

Four hydrogen nuclei (protons) are smashed together. Two positive particles escape, converting two protons into neutrons.

Positively charged proton

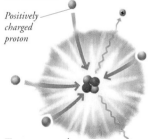

Two protons and neutrons combine to form helium nucleus. *Positive particle released*

Formation and development of a star

A protostar condenses, nuclear reactions start, and energy is produced.

Hydrogen is turned to helium in the star's core. The star has begun its main sequence of stellar development.

The Sun is halfway through its main sequence period of 10 billion years.

Stars expand as the hydrogen is used up. Their surfaces cool and get red.

Stars become red giants and leave the main sequence of stellar development.

The outer layers of a red giant become unstable. Most stars shed these layers and become white dwarfs.

More massive stars explode as supernovas.

Star birth

Stars are created from clouds of gas and dust. The cloud spins, and the material inside condenses and splits to form smaller clouds. These in turn spin and condense. Each is a protostar, a star in the making. Once material in the core of a protostar has reached a critical density and temperature, nuclear reactions start and energy is produced. The star is born. As the energy reaches the surface, the star shines. The stars created from the original large cloud make a star cluster.

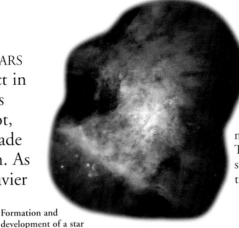

Orion Nebula: an interstellar cloud of gas and dust producing new stars. Left of center are four young and bright stars known as the Trapezium.

Double stars

About half the stars are in a double-star system. Both were created together from the same cloud of material, and the force of each other's gravity keeps them together.

Star clusters

Groups of stars living together are called clusters. A group may contain anything between a few or many thousands of stars, all created from the same cloud of gas and dust. The stars will be roughly the same age, but each develops in its own way.

Pleiades cluster

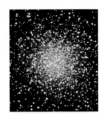

Globular cluster

Older stars are densely packed in globular clusters that are spherical in shape. The Hercules globular cluster contains several hundred thousand stars.

Hercules cluster

Open cluster

Young stars are loosely bound in open clusters and will disperse eventually. The stars in the Pleiades cluster are still surrounded by cloud material left over from their formation.

Star death

After billions of years, a star uses up its gases in the nuclear reactions taking place at its core. The star starts to die, but death can still be millions of years away. The mass of a star dictates how it dies. A star like the Sun gradually sheds material from its outer layers. One with eight times the Sun's mass can end its life in a gigantic explosion called a supernova because the explosion looks like a bright new star.

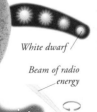

White dwarf

Beam of radio energy

Pulsar

Neutron star

White dwarf

Stars with less than eight solar masses end their lives as white dwarfs. Some of their material has been thrown off; the rest condenses to form a compact star about twice the size of Earth.

A matchbox of material from a white dwarf would weigh as much as an elephant.

Neutron stars and pulsars

After a massive star explodes as a supernova, gravity forces the core to collapse with incredible force. The material is so densely packed that it is compressed into neutrons. The result is a neutron star, perhaps only 8-12 miles (10-15 km) across. Pulsars are neutron stars that spin rapidly, sending out beams of radio energy.

A pinhead of pulsar material would weigh more than the biggest supertanker.

Brightness

A star's luminosity is the amount of light it produces; the true brightness. If all stars were the same distance from Earth, their luminosity could be compared easily. But a star may appear bright because it is close rather than because it is truly bright. Astronomers use two scales – apparent and absolute magnitude – to measure the brightness of stars. Each allocates a number to indicate brightness; the higher the number, the fainter the star.

Apparent and absolute magnitude

The apparent scale describes how bright a star is when viewed from Earth. Stars up to 6 are visible with the naked eye. Stars of 7 and above need an optical aid to be seen. The absolute scale describes the true brightness of stars by comparing how bright they would appear if viewed at a standard distance of 32.6 light-years (ly) from Earth. On both scales, each step in magnitude means a star is 2.5 times brighter or fainter than its neighbor.

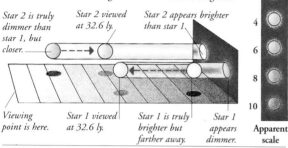

Star 2 is truly dimmer than star 1, but closer.

Star 2 viewed at 32.6 ly.

Star 2 appears brighter than star 1.

Viewing point is here.

Star 1 viewed at 32.6 ly.

Star 1 is truly brighter but farther away.

Star 1 appears dimmer.

−2
0
2
4
6
8
10

Apparent scale

Constellations

The sky is divided into 88 areas, or constellations, based on the patterns of stars that early astronomers used. Many are named after animals and figures from Greek mythology. Twelve constellations, known as the zodiac, form the backdrop against which the Sun and planets move.

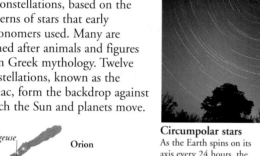

Circumpolar stars
As the Earth spins on its axis every 24 hours, the stars seem to circle a point directly above the north or south pole. These are the circumpolar stars.

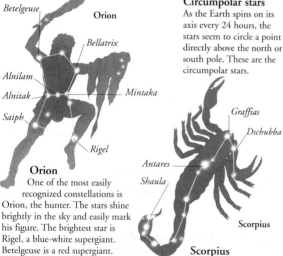

Betelgeuse
Orion
Bellatrix
Alnilam
Alnitak
Mintaka
Saiph
Rigel

Orion
One of the most easily recognized constellations is Orion, the hunter. The stars shine brightly in the sky and easily mark his figure. The brightest star is Rigel, a blue-white supergiant. Betelgeuse is a red supergiant.

Graffias
Dschubba
Antares
Shaula
Scorpius

Scorpius
A red supergiant star, Antares, marks the center of the scorpion's body and dimmer stars outline his tail. He is said to be the creature that stung Orion to death.

Star names: Astronomers identify the prominent stars by a Greek-alphabet letter and the constellation name. Many of these stars also have their own name.

Star types

Stars are classified into groups according to the characteristics of their spectrums. A spectrum provides information on a star's color, temperature, and chemical composition. There are seven main types of stars, each assigned a letter. They are, from hottest to coolest: O, B, A, F, G, K, and M.

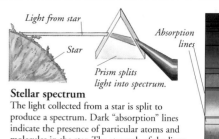

Light from star
Star
Absorption lines
Prism splits light into spectrum.

Stellar spectrum
The light collected from a star is split to produce a spectrum. Dark "absorption" lines indicate the presence of particular atoms and molecules in the star. The strength of the lines indicates the temperature of the star. Blue-white stars classified A, for example, have hydrogen lines dominant, yellow G stars such as the Sun have ionized calcium dominant.

Star spectrum

Astronomers can deduce the color of a star from its temperature, or vice versa. Blue stars, at left, are the hottest, and red stars, at right, are the coolest.

The brightest stars are at the top, and the dimmest are near the bottom.

Main sequence stars are those that are converting hydrogen to helium.

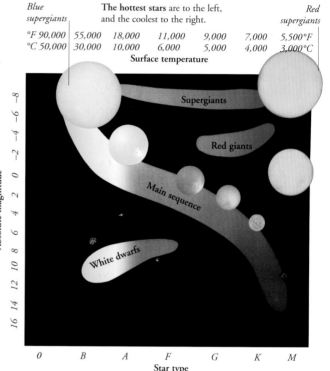

Blue supergiants	**The hottest stars** are to the left, and the coolest to the right.					*Red supergiants*
°F 90,000	55,000	18,000	11,000	9,000	7,000	5,500°F
°C 50,000	30,000	10,000	6,000	5,000	4,000	3,000°C

Surface temperature

Supergiants
Red giants
Main sequence
White dwarfs

Absolute magnitude: −8 −6 −4 −2 0 2 4 6 8 10 12 14 16

Star type: 0 B A F G K M

Hertzsprung-Russell diagram
If the absolute magnitudes of stars are plotted on a graph against their temperatures, the stars form groups that represent the stages in a star's life. Most stars fall within a narrow band, the main sequence, which runs from top left to bottom right. The star moves from one position to another on the graph as it develops. As the hydrogen is used up, the star dims and then moves off the main sequence. Giant stars are found above the main sequence and dwarf stars below. Astronomers have used the graph, called a Hertzsprung-Russell diagram, since 1913 to help them understand stars, the relationship of their properties, and how a star changes. It is named after the two astronomers who created it.

The Sun is a type G star in the main sequence group of stars. From here, it will move to the red giants and then to the white dwarfs.

Cecilia Payne-Gaposchkin

A British-American astronomer, Cecilia Payne-Gaposchkin (1900–79), spent her working life studying stars. When she started, one of the main problems taxing astronomers was the composition and structure of stars. She established the surface temperatures for each of the different types of stars and that the main sequence stars are made mainly of hydrogen and helium gas. She also found that the cycle time of a Cepheid star is related to its brightness.

Variable stars
The properties of some stars, such as brightness, vary in regular intervals that can last for minutes or years. In some stars, the dimming and brightening may be caused by a second star regularly eclipsing it. In other stars, the brightness varies because the star is pulsating: its outer layers alternately expand and contract and the star dims and brightens.

Cepheid stars are yellow supergiants that change physically in size and temperature. As they alternately expand and contract, their brightness varies. They take between one and about 50 days to complete one cycle of change.

FIND OUT MORE — ASTRONOMY • BIG BANG • BLACK HOLES • GALAXIES • SUN AND SOLAR SYSTEM • TELESCOPES • UNIVERSE • X RAYS AND ELECTRO-MAGNETIC RADIATION

STONE AGE

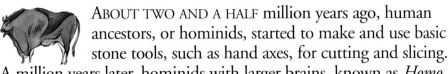

ABOUT TWO AND A HALF million years ago, human ancestors, or hominids, started to make and use basic stone tools, such as hand axes, for cutting and slicing. A million years later, hominids with larger brains, known as *Homo erectus* (upright people), made more complicated stone tools, such as arrowheads and small blades. This period is known as the Old Stone Age, or Paleolithic Age. With these sharp tools, hominids carved bone and antlers, made clothes from animal skins, and chopped wood for fire and shelter. Later, in the Neolithic, or New Stone Age, humans created beautiful paintings and sculptures. In Europe, the period between the Old and New Stone Ages was called the Mesolithic, or Middle Stone Age.

Types of stone and bone tools

When ancient flintworkers realized they could predict the size and shape of flint chips coming off a flint core, they began to use the chips, or microliths, as blades, and then as arrowheads. This way of working has become known as the Levallois Technique. Tools became more specialized and people began to make stone knives and scrapers. They began to make tools of other materials – hammers, needles, and harpoons were made of antler or bone.

Hand ax
The sharp points and twin edges of hand axes made them useful for all sorts of chopping and cutting jobs, from butchering meat and making clothes to cutting down branches for shelter.

Harpoon
Ancient people mounted bone harpoon heads on wooden shafts and used them to spear fish.

Rounded head of hammer

Antler hammer
An antler or bone hammer was used for hitting flint rocks and detaching small flakes, which could then be used as blades.

Scraper
Flint tools with one curved sharp edge could be used to prepare animal skins for clothing. People probably used this example more than 35,000 years ago.

Arrowhead
Hunters tied finely worked flint arrowheads to wooden shafts to make useful weapons.

Hand ax

Point for boring holes
Sharp edge for cutting

Burin
This type of pointed tool could have been used for making engravings on cave walls. This burin is more than 35,000 years old.

Art and sculpture

Humans produced some superb paintings and sculptures in the Stone Age. Often, these works were made in deep, dark caves. Archaeologists think that they were decorations for special ceremonial centers or secret religious shrines used by Stone Age priests.

Portable art
An artist in France carved this stylized mammoth from an animal's shoulder blade more than 10,000 years ago. Artists often portrayed the quarry of the local hunters, hoping that this would bring them good luck when hunting. Mammoth meat was popular food.

In-situ sculpture
Sometimes sculptures were "built-in" to caves. These clay bison form the centerpiece of a small, low chamber in a cave at Tuc d'Audoubert, France.

Cave and rock painting
Some of the finest Stone Age paintings have been found in the caves of Europe and the rock shelters of Australia. This painting of hunters or warriors comes from Valltorta in Spain, and may be 10,000 years old.

Making a hand ax
Simple pebbles were the very first tools, but then Stone Age people learned to make better tools by striking one piece of stone against another, a process known as flint-knapping. They could then turn a core tool, like the one below, into a hand ax.

Core tool
Flintworkers first trimmed a suitable piece of flint into a core tool by striking it with a stone hammer, such as a quartzite pebble. The tool was then roughly the right shape to be worked into a hand ax.

Flake tool
The flintworkers learned to predict how the stone would break when sharply hit with the stone hammer. They then sliced off long flakes from the underside of the core tool. This gave the ax a sharp, strong edge.

Underside

Pressure flaking
The flintworker finished the ax by hitting its edge with a bone or antler hammer to remove small flakes of stone. This made it very sharp.

Crafts
People used clay, reeds, and wood to produce cooking and carrying utensils. Few wooden objects have survived, though a plank at least 50,000 years old has been discovered in Japan.

Pottery
The first pots were made in Japan 12,500 years ago by rolling clay into a long sausage shape and coiling it in a spiral. The sides of the vessel were then smoothed down.

Bowl

Basket-making
Stone Age people wove twigs, reeds, grass, and canes to make containers. Impressions of basketwork in ancient mud floors in western Asia show that baskets date back 10,000 years.

Basket

Timeline
2–2.5 million years BC Hominids start to use crude pebble tools.

1.3 million years BC Hand axes are developed, followed by finely shaped tools in Africa.

460,000 BC First evidence of hominids using fire, Zhoukoudian, China.

100,000 BC Modern humans evolve.

60,000 BC Flint-knapping spreads to Europe.

9000–8500 BC Neolithic Age begins in western Asia.

6500 BC Neolithic Age begins in Europe.

3000 BC Metal weapons and tools start to replace stone.

Microliths

FIND OUT MORE | ART, HISTORY OF | BRONZE AGE | CRAFTS | HUMAN EVOLUTION | PREHISTORIC PEOPLE

STORMS

TORRENTIAL RAIN, THUNDER, lightning, and gales can bring turmoil and devastation. To most of us, a storm is a spell of severe weather, with strong winds and heavy rain. Meteorologists – people who study the weather – define a storm as a wind blowing persistently at more than 64–72.7 mph (103–117 kmh). Storms form in areas of low pressure, where air is warm and less dense than the surrounding air. In certain conditions more powerful storms can develop. These are known as typhoons, cyclones, hurricanes, or Willy-Willy in different parts of the world.

Hurricanes

These huge storms can measure about 400 miles (650 km) in diameter. Hurricanes develop as clusters of thunderstorms over warm tropical seas. They tighten into a spiral, with a calm central ring of low pressure called the eye. They sweep westward with heavy rain and winds up to 220 mph (350 kmh). As they pass over cool water or land, their intensity lessens.

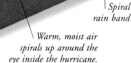

Ice crystals form on the top of the clouds.

Air billowing from the top of the storm causes the clouds to spread out.

Slice through a hurricane

The strongest winds are found beneath the eye wall, immediately outside the eye.

Eye wall

Air descends into the calm eye, leaving it free of cloud. Winds are less than 16 mph (25 kmh).

Winds in excess of 100 mph (160 kmh) occur beneath the storm.

Warm, moist air spirals up around the eye inside the hurricane.

Spiral rain band

The heat in the warm ocean provides the energy needed to drive the storm.

Hurricane damage
Violent winds cause the most hurricane damage, flattening whole buildings and uprooting trees. There may also be a sudden rise in sea level, called a storm surge, that can bring widespread flooding. Hurricane Andrew in Florida (above) killed 15 people and left over 50,000 homeless in 1992.

Tornadoes

Small but ferocious, tornadoes are whirling masses of wind spiraling beneath a thundercloud. They roar past in minutes, bringing winds of up to 250 mph (400 kmh) that leave a trail of destruction. Air pressure at the center is so low that air rushes in at enormous speed, sucking up people, cars, and even whole trains.

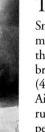

Waterspouts
When a tornado passes over water, it sucks water up into a column called a waterspout. These usually develop over shallow water in summer. Waterspouts tend to last longer than tornadoes, but their wind speed is often less than 50 mph (80 kmh).

Dust devils
In deserts, there is so much loose, light, dusty material that tornadoes create columns of dust – dust devils. These are caused by columns of hot air whirling up, carrying debris from the ground.

Thunderstorms
Created from huge cumulonimbus clouds, thunderstorms bring heavy rain, thunder, and lightning. They are made by strong updrafts along a cold front or over ground warmed by summer sun. Air expanding quickly causes thunder, the rumbling that follows lightning.

Lightning
Air currents in a thundercloud hurl water drops together so violently that the cloud bristles with electrical charge. The charge is unleashed in a dramatic flash of lightning.

Clement Wragge
Popular myth has it that the idea of naming hurricanes came from Australian Clement Wragge (1852–1922). It is said that he decided to give hurricanes the names of women he particularly disliked. Today, hurricanes are named according to an alphabetic list, created each year, of alternating men's and women's names.

FIND OUT MORE   AIR   CLIMATE   CLOUDS   DESERTS   FRANKLIN, BENJAMIN   OCEANS AND SEAS   RAIN   WEATHER   WEATHER FORECASTING   WINDS

STRAVINSKY, IGOR

IGOR STRAVINSKY WAS one of the greatest composers of the 20th century. He was born in Russia in 1882, but later lived in Paris and the US. He first found fame with *The Firebird*, a ballet based on old Russian stories. Much of his work had its roots in Russian traditional music, but his style evolved throughout his life to produce exciting and sometimes shocking musical effects.

Ballets Russes

Stravinsky wrote three of his best known works – *The Firebird*, *Petrushka*, and *The Rite of Spring*, – for this ballet company run by Russian impresario Diaghilev. Stravinsky was still a young man when he wrote these nationalistic Russian ballets, and they took Paris by storm. The success of *The Firebird* made Stravinsky famous all over the world.

Sergei Diaghilev

Diaghilev
Sergei Diaghilev (1872–1929) was an active promoter of the arts in his native Russia before moving to Paris in 1908. The following year he founded the Ballets Russes, which commissioned music by the young Stravinsky and other notable composers to accompany the dancers.

The Rite of Spring
This ballet tells the story of a sacrificial maiden dancing herself to death. Its jagged rhythms and violent harmonies were too much for some of the audience at the first performance. Fights broke out between those for and against the music, and the ballet ended in chaos. The piece launched modernism in music.

Characters from The Rite of Spring

Early life
Stravinsky was born near St. Petersburg, where his father was a singer. As a young man he trained as a lawyer, but in 1902, he met the composer Rimsky-Korsakov and decided to devote his life to music. He studied with Rimsky-Korsakov, and the influence of the great Russian composers can be heard in his early music.

Firebird
Stravinsky's first score for the Ballets Russes, *The Firebird*, debuted in 1910. The Russian story suited Stravinsky's colorful orchestral style. Although he lived in Western Europe, Stravinsky still wrote music on Russian themes.

Brightly colored costumes were a hallmark of the Ballets Russes.

Costume design for The Firebird

Neoclassicism
Soon after World War I, Stravinsky's style began to change. He rediscovered the music of 18th-century Europe and adapted it to create the new, clear-sounding style now known as neoclassicism.

The Soldier's Tale
One of Stravinsky's most popular pieces is *The Soldier's Tale* (1918), a fairy tale for musicians, narrators, and a dancer. This piece of "music theater" also shows the influence of popular musical forms such as ragtime.

Performance

Stravinsky was a highly respected conductor as well as composer, noted for his very precise conducting style. He gave numerous concerts, particularly of his own works, and made many recordings of his music. These records, still available today, give us a clear idea of how he intended his music to be played.

Robert Craft
Later in life, Stravinsky took on an assistant, the American musician Robert Craft (b.1923), to help when ill health prevented him from conducting. Together, they also wrote several books about music, and Craft has written about their collaboration.

Stravinsky with Robert Craft

Date on which Stravinsky completed the composition.

Stravinsky's manuscript score of The Rite of Spring

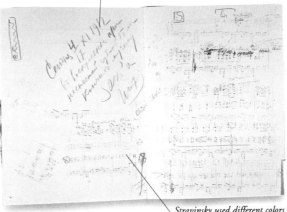

Stravinsky used different colors for different instructions.

Manuscript scores
Stravinsky's beautifully handwritten scores show how meticulous he was. He worked very precisely and carefully to achieve just the right effect, giving little room for a performer's or a conductor's own interpretation.

IGOR STRAVINSKY

1882	Born near St. Petersburg, Russia
1910	*The Firebird* first performed
1913	*The Rite of Spring* first performed, provoking a riot
1920	Moves to Paris; neoclassical ballet *Pulchinella* first performed
1926	Rejoins Orthodox church
1930	Completes *Symphony of Psalms*
1939	Moves to US
1951	Completes the opera *The Rake's Progress*
1957	Completes *Agon*, ballet score using twelve-tone techniques
1971	Dies in New York

FIND OUT MORE BALLET DANCE MUSIC OPERA ORCHESTRAS

SUBMARINES

THE ABILITY TO STAY hidden deep under the waves makes the submarine a powerful and effective warship. To travel underwater, a submarine needs a strong hull to resist high water pressure, and engines for both surface and underwater use. Submarines were used effectively as deadly weapons for the first time in World War I. Today, there are two main types of military submarines in operation. A patrol submarine searches for and attacks enemy vessels. A missile submarine carries long-range nuclear missiles.

Anatomy of a submarine

A submarine is encased in a strong steel hull. On top is a conning tower that stands above the water when the submarine is on the surface. Inside the submarine, rooms are arranged on two or three decks. Bulkheads separate the submarine into several sections that can be shut off from each other in case of leaks in the hull.

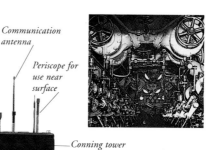

Engines
Submarines have engines that run on nuclear power or on a combination of electric and diesel motors. The engines drive a propeller that pushes the submarine through the water.

Communication antenna

Periscope for use near surface

Conning tower

Hull

Senior officers' mess (living quarters)

Torpedo tube

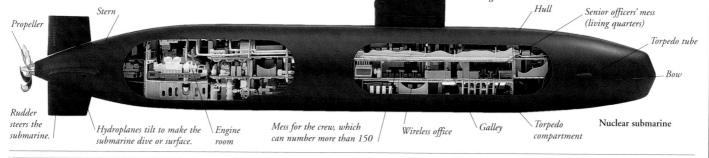

Propeller

Stern

Bow

Rudder steers the submarine.

Hydroplanes tilt to make the submarine dive or surface.

Engine room

Mess for the crew, which can number more than 150

Wireless office

Galley

Torpedo compartment

Nuclear submarine

Diving and surfacing

On the surface, a submarine floats like a normal ship. To dive, valves let water fill the large ballast tanks on either side of the hull. The extra weight causes the ship to descend. When submerged, the submarine moves up or down using its rudderlike hydroplanes. To surface, the water is blown out of the tanks.

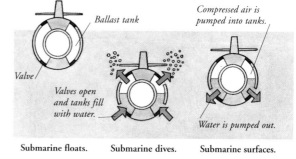

Ballast tank

Compressed air is pumped into tanks.

Valve

Valves open and tanks fill with water.

Water is pumped out.

Submarine floats.   Submarine dives.   Submarine surfaces.

Submersibles

Civil (non-military) submarines are called submersibles. They are smaller than military submarines and are used for carrying out specialized tasks deep underwater, from maintaining ocean pipelines to carrying out salvage operations or marine research. Submersibles are submerged only for a few hours.

Deepest dives
Most military submarines can dive to depths of about 2,500 ft (750 m). The deepest dive was by a US Navy submarine that achieved a depth of 3.7 miles (6.2 km).

Nuclear submarines
The most powerful submarines are those that carry nuclear missiles and run on nuclear energy. Each missile can destroy a large city, killing thousands of people. Nuclear engines allow a submarine to stay submerged much longer than other submarines, which have to return to the surface to recharge their batteries.

Torpedoes
Military submarines carry underwater missiles called torpedoes. They are launched from tubes in the submarine's bow or stern. Homing systems, or signals from the submarine, guide modern torpedoes to their targets.

Timeline

1776 David Bushnell's *Turtle* is a waterproof wooden barrel, operated by hand and foot pedals.

The Turtle

1864 The human-powered, iron submarine *Hunley* is the first submarine to sink a ship. Its explosive charge is carried on a long pole.

1901 *The Holland VI* is the first submarine with both gasoline and electric engines.

1939–45 German submarines (U-boats) hunt Allied ships in packs, sinking ships with torpedoes.

1954 The first nuclear-powered submarine is the US *Nautilus*.

1986 Crew on the US *Alvin* photographs wreckage of *Titanic*.

2000 The "unsinkable" Russian *Kursk* sinks.

 FIND OUT MORE | ENGINES AND MOTORS | NUCLEAR POWER | PRESSURE | WARSHIPS | WORLD WAR I | WORLD WAR II

SUMERIANS

IN ABOUT 5000 BC, the Sumerians settled Mesopotamia, the fertile land between the Tigris and Euphrates rivers. They founded farming settlements, which, by 3200 BC, had grown into the world's first cities. As these cities flourished, the Sumerians developed the first known writing system. The Sumerian cities, linked by waterways, developed into a civilization based on a shared language, religious beliefs, art forms, and building styles. The cities traded with each other, but also fought for dominance. In c.2000 BC, eastern desert tribes in search of fertile land moved into the region, and the Sumerian civilization collapsed.

Shrine or temple

Ziggurats were pyramids built with two to seven layers of bricks.

Square bottom tier

The triple staircase at Ur was the first of its kind.

City life

Sumerian cities consisted of brick houses, palaces, and temples enclosed by a large wall. Every day, people left home to farm the surrounding land or fish the rivers. Many worked for the king or the temple. As food production increased, more people were free to work with stone or metal, produce textiles, or make the thousands of bricks necessary to build ziggurats and temples.

The city of Ur
This ziggurat dominated the city of Ur, which was dedicated to the moon god Nanna. There were hundreds of gods in the Sumerian religion, and each city had its own special patron.

War
Competition between cities for farmland and materials led to almost endless warfare. The Standard of Ur, an elaborately decorated wooden box, shows the ruler leading his soldiers against an enemy. The soldiers are equipped with copper helmets, felt cloaks, spears, and axes.

Gold necklace

Gold helmet

Gold bull on a lyre

Art objects
Sumerian artists were highly skilled. They decorated palace and temple walls with shell and stone inlays. Their craftworkers used imported stone to make statues of humans, animals, and gods. Metalworkers made exquisite jewelry of gold, silver, and rare stones, such as blue lapis lazuli and red cornelian, which they shaped into delicate animals and flowers.

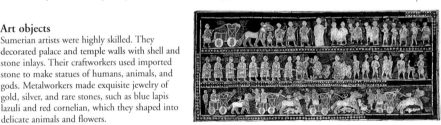

Cuneiform script

The Sumerians invented writing, using a cut reed to draw signs on damp clay. The signs, representing sounds, were combined to form words. The impressions gradually became more cuneiform (wedgelike).

Symbol for day three *Symbol for a commodity* *Symbol for 10 units*

Farming and fishing
Farming communities developed in Mesopotamia between 6000 and 5000 BC. Food was easy to grow in the fertile soil of the marshes. Outside the marshes, the settlers gradually banded together and built canals to irrigate the land. They cultivated the soil, and kept sheep, cattle, and pigs. Today, the Marsh Arabs of Iraq farm in a similar way to that of their predecessors, the Sumerians.

Marsh soil produced wheat, barley, and date palms.

Sargon
Legend tells how the baby Sargon was left in a basket on the Euphrates, and the goddess Ishtar gave him an empire. In fact, Sargon of Akkad (2000s BC) was the first conqueror of Sumer and most of Mesopotamia, and the first ruler to unify these territories into an empire.

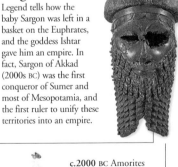

Timeline

5000 BC Farmers and fishermen settle the Fertile Crescent of southern Mesopotamia.

3200 BC Large cities develop, such as Uruk.

3100 BC Sumerians invent writing.

2700 BC Kings, such as the legendary Gilgamesh of Uruk, rule independent cities.

2600 BC Sumerians trade their produce for luxury items, such as metal and precious stones.

c.2350 BC Sargon of Akkad unites Sumerian cities into an empire.

c.2300–2100 BC Sargon's empire fades. Political power shifts from city to city.

c.2100 BC Ur-Nammu of Ur controls the whole of Sumer, helped by his civil service.

c.2000 BC Amorites from the Syrian desert invade the region, and Sumerian slowly ceases to be spoken. However, people continue to use Sumerian cuneiform script for monumental and religious inscriptions.

Lapis lazuli
Goat statue, Ur

FIND OUT MORE | ASSYRIAN EMPIRE | BABYLONIAN EMPIRE | CITIES | FARMING, HISTORY OF | HITTITES | WARFARE | WRITING

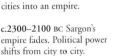

SUN AND SOLAR SYSTEM

THE SUN IS A STAR – a huge ball of spinning gas – that is about 5 billion years old. It is important to us because it is the most massive and influential member of the Solar System. Its gravity keeps Earth and eight other planets, more than 60 moons, and millions of comets and asteroids orbiting around it. Together they make up a disk-shaped system that is billions of miles across. They share a past and a future dependent on the Sun.

The Sun's face

Earth is 93 million miles (149.6 million km) from the Sun but still close enough for observers to make out surface features. Energy generated in the core takes millions of years to reach the surface, the photosphere, where some of it breaks through as sunspots, flares, and prominences.

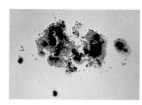

Sunspots

Disturbances in the Sun's magnetic field produce dark, cooler patches – sunspots – in the photosphere. Sunspots follow an 11-year cycle: they first appear at high latitudes and then increase in number, forming nearer and nearer the equator during the cycle.

Sunspots are purple and black in this false-color picture.

Inside the Sun

The Sun is an incredibly hot sphere of gas that is generating energy. Its core is particularly hot and dense. Here nuclei of hydrogen collide and fuse to form helium. This reaction produces energy that, among other things, lights and heats the Solar System. The energy passes through the radiation and convection zones to the surface (photosphere), then through the atmosphere (chromosphere) into space.

Core 27 million°F (15 million°C)

Photosphere 9,900°F (5,500°C)

Chromosphere 90,000°F (50,000°C)

Life of the Sun

The Sun is a middle-aged star. As it ages, its appearance will change. In about 5 billion years, the hydrogen in its core will have been converted into helium and the outer layers will swell. It will expand to more than 150 times its present size, becoming a red giant. Mercury will be engulfed and life on Earth will cease. Eventually, the outer layers will drift off and the remains will shrink to become a white dwarf.

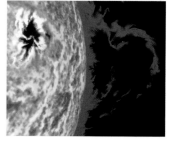

A solar prominence forms a loop.

Flares and prominences

An explosive release of energy from the Sun is a flare. A jet of material shoots out from the photosphere, is brilliant for a few minutes, and fades in about an hour. Longer-lived jets are prominences. They may last several months and be 125,000 miles (200,000 km) long. Some shorter-lived prominences form a loop where ejected material is returned to the Sun.

Solar movement

The Sun spins on its axis. Different parts of it take different lengths of time to complete one turn. The equatorial regions move the fastest, completing a turn in about 25 days. The polar regions take 35 days.

Ecliptic

The position of the Sun does not change in the Solar System but it appears to move across Earth's sky. As Earth spins, the Sun rises at the start and sets at the end of each day. The Sun's path, called the ecliptic, is measured against the more distant background stars. From Earth, the other planets and the Moon are seen to cross the sky close to the ecliptic.

Solar corona

Beyond the photosphere are the chromosphere and the corona; the Sun's inner and outer atmospheres. They are only visible during a solar eclipse, when the Sun's face is obscured by the Moon. The corona extends for more than 600,000 miles (1 million km).

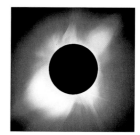

Arthur Eddington

Present knowledge of the nature of stars owes much to an English astronomer, Arthur Eddington (1882–1944). His understanding of the internal structure of stars became the basis of future stellar work. He also produced the first proof for general relativity.

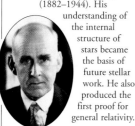

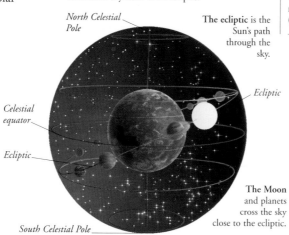

North Celestial Pole

The ecliptic is the Sun's path through the sky.

Celestial equator

Ecliptic

Ecliptic

The Moon and planets cross the sky close to the ecliptic.

South Celestial Pole

Moon's orbit

Sunlight

Umbra

Penumbra

Earth

Moon

Moon's shadow

Solar eclipse

When the Moon is directly between the Sun and the Earth, it covers the Sun's face. The Sun is eclipsed. From the part of Earth covered by the umbra (the darker, inner shadow), the Sun appears totally eclipsed. For those people in the penumbra (the outer shadow), the Sun is only partially eclipsed. The eclipse is possible because the Sun and Moon appear to be the same size in Earth's sky. The Moon is 400 times smaller than the Sun, but it is 400 times closer to Earth.

The Sun, the nearest star to Earth, is a sphere of gas. About 70 per cent of its mass is hydrogen and 28 per cent helium.

Inner planets
Venus   Mars

Mercury   Earth

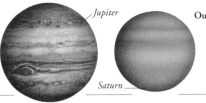

Jupiter

Saturn

Outer planets
Neptune

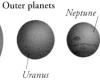

Uranus   Pluto

The planets
Nine planets orbit the Sun. The four inner ones are made of rock. The four largest, known as the gas planets, consist of large amounts of gas. The most distant, Pluto, is icy rock.

Solar System

Almost 99% of the mass of the Solar System is in the Sun. It is not only the most massive but the largest object – 109 Earths could fit across its face. Next is Jupiter, 11 Earths across. The smallest objects are tiny specks of dust. Each one of these objects spins on its axis and follows an orbit around the Sun. The Sun was created about 5 billion years ago, followed by the planets and smaller bodies.

Sun's gravity
The mass of the Sun gives it the most gravitational pull and keeps the planets and other objects orbiting it. They move fast to prevent being pulled into the Sun. The closest planets orbit the fastest. The more distant planets, where the gravitational pull is weaker, move more slowly.

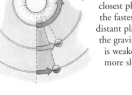

Biggest planet
Jupiter is the most massive planet. It is made of the most material – 318 times the amount of material that makes Earth. It is also the biggest: it would take 1,330 Earths to fill Jupiter's space.

The axis of Venus is tilted by 178°.

Venus spins backward, and takes 243 days to turn once.

Backward spinner
Each planet spins on its axis as it orbits the Sun. The planets are not upright – their axes are not at right angles to their orbital path. Earth is tipped by 23.5° and spins counter-clockwise as viewed from above the North Pole. Venus, Uranus, and Pluto are tipped over so far they spin on their axes in the opposite direction.

Neptune's orbit
Pluto's orbit
Neptune

Uranus's orbit

Saturn's orbit

Jupiter's orbit

Mars's orbit

Mercury
Earth
Jupiter

Uranus

Pluto

Venus
Mars
Saturn

Orbits

The planets and asteroids all travel around the Sun in the same direction (counter-clockwise if viewed from above the North Pole) but at different speeds. The orbits are elliptical (oval) and on approximately the same plane. Pluto's is the most inclined, tilted at 17°. Comets can orbit the Sun clockwise or counterclockwise.

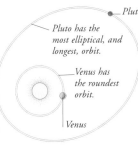

Pluto

Pluto has the most elliptical, and longest, orbit.

Venus has the roundest orbit.

Venus

Days and seasons
As Earth spins once every 23 hours 59.6 minutes, any one part of it alternately receives and is hidden from the Sun's light. At the same time, it is orbiting the Sun once every 365.25 days, and different amounts of sunlight are received at different places on its orbit. These differences produce the seasons of a year. They occur because the Earth's axis is tilted by 23.5° as it orbits the Sun. If its axis were at right angles to its orbital path, day and night would always be the same length and there would be no seasons.

The seasons

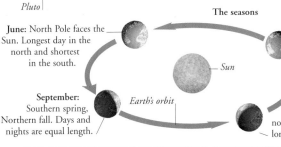

June: North Pole faces the Sun. Longest day in the north and shortest in the south.

March: Northern spring, southern fall. Day and night are equal length.

Sun

Earth's orbit

September: Southern spring, Northern fall. Days and nights are equal length.

December: South Pole faces the Sun. Shortest day in the northern hemisphere and longest in the south.

Origins

The Sun and all the objects orbiting it came from the same cloud of gas and dust. The spinning cloud condensed to form the young Sun surrounded by a disk of leftover material. Mercury, Venus, Earth, and Mars formed from the dust nearest the Sun. Farther out, where it was colder, snow and gas joined with dust to form Jupiter, Saturn, Uranus, and Neptune.

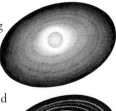
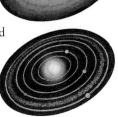

Asteroid belt
Smaller bodies in the Solar System, including Pluto and the planetary moons, were formed from material not swept up into the planets. Between Mars and Jupiter is the asteroid belt, made of millions of rocky pieces. The gravity of Jupiter prevented this material from staying together and forming one planetary object.

Johannes Kepler
The first accurate model of the Solar System was produced by the German astronomer Johannes Kepler (1571–1630). He developed three laws to describe the relative distances, speeds, and shapes of the planets' orbits. From then on, it was accepted that the planets follow elliptical orbits around the Sun.

FIND OUT MORE   BIG BANG   COMETS AND ASTEROIDS   EARTH   GALAXIES   GALILEO GALILEI   GRAVITY   MOON   PLANETS   ROCKS AND MINERALS   STARS   TIME

SWEDEN

THE FIFTH LARGEST COUNTRY in Europe, Sweden occupies the eastern half of the Scandinavian peninsula, which it shares with Norway. The Gulf of Bothnia separates most of Sweden from Finland, and the Baltic Sea surrounds the jagged southeastern coastline. About 25 percent of the country lies in Lapland, in the Arctic Circle. Sweden is a prosperous, environmentally conscious country, boasting one of the world's most efficient welfare systems to support its small population.

SWEDEN FACTS

CAPITAL CITY	Stockholm
AREA	173,730 sq miles (449,960 sq km)
POPULATION	8,900,000
MAIN LANGUAGE	Swedish
MAJOR RELIGION	Christian
CURRENCY	Swedish krona
LIFE EXPECTANCY	80 years
PEOPLE PER DOCTOR	323
GOVERNMENT	Multiparty democracy
ADULT LITERACY	99%

Physical features

About half of Sweden is covered by the Inner Norrland, a region of gentle hills, dense forests of spruce and pine, and more than 100,000 lakes. The bitterly cold, mountainous north includes part of Lapland, shared with Finland, which makes up one-quarter of Sweden's land area.

Sarek National Park
Conservation is a key issue in Sweden, and there is much concern about forest damage from acid rain. Sarek, Europe's first national park, was set up in 1909 and forms part of its largest protected area.

95°F (35°C)   -36°F (-38°C)
60°F (16°C)   24°F (-4°C)
25 in (622 mm)

Climate
Northern winters are bitterly cold, with six months of snow and only a few hours of sunlight. The south has a much milder climate, with only two snowy winter months.

Lakes, rivers, and waterfalls
This peaceful scene epitomizes Arctic Sweden's vast wilderness. Its long rivers rise on the Norwegian border and flow through many lakes to the Baltic Sea, generating hydroelectricity along the way. Sweden's largest lake is Vänern, at 2,156 sq miles (5,584 sq km).

People
Most of Sweden's small population lives in the south, enjoying a comfortable lifestyle and equal rights for all. Women constitute half of the workforce, and men share childcare. Swedes have Europe's highest life expectancy because of their good diet and healthcare.

Built-up 2.5%   Forest 70%
Farmland 17.5%
Tundra 4.5%   Barren 5.5%

Land use
Less than nine percent of the land is available for farming, but small areas of the fertile south are cooperatively used for crops and animals. Sweden is 70 percent forest, and paper and wood products account for 16 percent of exports. The country ranks highly in world softwood production.

Swedish family in local costume for midsummer festival, Dalarna

56 per sq mile (22 per sq km)   84% Urban   16% Rural

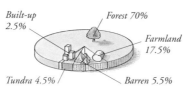

Volvo car

Farming and industry
Milk, beef, and pork are the main products of the small farming sector. Much larger are the growing technology industries, including Volvo and Ericsson, which have earned Sweden a reputation for design and reliability.

Stockholm
Sweden's capital is a harbor city, built partly on 14 islands that are linked by 50 bridges. At the heart is Gamla Stan, the Old Town, founded in 1250. Its narrow, cobbled streets are lined with traditional craft and antique shops. The city also has more than 50 museums.

Central Stockholm

FIND OUT MORE — ARCTIC OCEAN · CARS AND TRUCKS · CONSERVATION · DAMS · DESIGN · ENERGY · EUROPE, HISTORY OF · FORESTS · PAPER · PORTS AND WATERWAYS · SCANDINAVIA, HISTORY OF

SWIFTS AND HUMMINGBIRDS

JET-BLACK SWIFTS AND JEWELLIKE hummingbirds belong to the same group of birds. They both have tiny feet and curved bladelike wings and are agile fliers. Swifts eat insects, which they catch in midair, often twisting and turning with amazing speed to catch their prey. They hardly ever walk on the ground, and make their nests in attics and chimneys, or in caves. The main food of hummingbirds is sugary nectar from flowers. They dart from plant to plant, and hover in front of flowers while they drink. Despite their small size, hummingbirds are noisy and fearless. They often fight over the best places to feed.

Swifts

There are 92 species of swifts, some of which spend most of their life in the air. Swifts often feed, mate, and even sleep on the wing. Many land only to breed. Swifts are found in many parts of the world, but they often migrate to warmer countries in winter when the supply of flying insects dries up.

Flight

Swifts can beat each wing at a different speed. This unusual ability makes them very agile, and they can twist and turn in the air at high speed.

Narrow wings reduce friction at high speed.

Hummingbirds

There are about 300 species of hummingbirds, and they are found only in the Americas. Hummingbirds are the most agile fliers in the bird world. In addition to flying normally, they can hover in one place to feed at a flower, and can even fly backward.

Male

Brilliant metallic colors change as the bird moves.

Feather "boots"

Female

Booted racket-tail

In most hummingbird species, the male is much more colorful than the female, and takes almost no part in raising the young. This male racket-tail has two long tail feathers. They create an impressive display as he tries to attract a mate.

The sword-billed hummingbird's beak is longer than its body.

Hummingbird beaks

The shape of a hummingbird's beak varies according to the flower it feeds at. The sword-billed hummingbird feeds on deep flowers, and its beak is straight. Some hummingbirds have curved beaks, and feed on curved flowers.

This hummingbird is 10 in (25 cm) long, including its beak.

Swift nests

Swifts do not land to collect nesting material. Instead, they make their nests out of saliva and material that they snatch up in the beak or break off with their claws.

Cave swiftlet nests

Chimney swift

This North American swift makes its nest from saliva and tiny twigs. It often glues it to the inside of a tall chimney or ventilation shaft.

How hummingbirds hover

Wings can beat up to 90 times a second.

Joints inside the wing stay straight.

Wing muscles make up one third of the hummingbird's weight.

1 The bird sweeps its wings backward until they touch. This creates a downdraft that pushes the bird upward.

2 The wings rotate on very flexible shoulder joints as the bird starts to bring them forward again.

3 The forward stroke also creates a downdraft. The moving air again pushes the bird upward.

4 The wings swing backward for the next stroke. The movement is usually too fast to be seen.

COMMON SWIFT

SCIENTIFIC NAME	*Apus apus*
FAMILY	Apodidae
ORDER	Apodiformes
DISTRIBUTION	Europe and Asia (summer); Africa (winter)
HABITAT	Open air, often above towns and cities
DIET	Flying insects
SIZE	Length, including tail: 7 in (18cm)
LIFESPAN	About 15–20 years

FIND OUT MORE   BIRDS   FLIGHT, ANIMAL   FLOWERS   MIGRATION   NESTS AND BURROWS   SONGBIRDS

SWIMMING AND DIVING

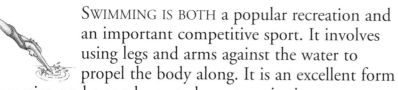

SWIMMING IS BOTH a popular recreation and an important competitive sport. It involves using legs and arms against the water to propel the body along. It is an excellent form of exercise, and a good way to learn to swim is to use buoyancy aids, such as water wings, when practicing strokes. Diving, in which a person enters the water head first, is fun too, although at competitive levels it calls for great agility. In competition, divers perfom about 10 dives from a choice of more than 80 dives recognized by the governing body.

Types of stroke

The four competitive strokes are freestyle (invariably front crawl), backstroke, breaststroke, and butterfly.

Knees begin to bend and part slightly.

Arms stretch out in front.

Breaststroke
This is the slowest stroke. Arms and legs move symmetrically underwater, the legs providing most of the thrust. The arms circle from an outstretched position, pulling through the water, around, and under the chin. At the same time, the legs move with a frog-like kick.

Preparing for the powerful arm stroke

Butterfly
Purely a competitive stroke, butterfly was invented when swimmers began to bend the breaststroke rules. The arms move symmetrically from above the water with an explosive pull. The legs kick up and down together.

Backstroke
Swimmers lie on their backs in backstroke. The stroke requires alternate arm pulls, windmill style, and a flutter kick, in which the legs move up and down in the water.

Gertrude Ederle

First woman to swim the Channel in 1926

Cross-Channel swimming
Of all the long-distance sea swims, the Channel between England and France – 21 miles (34 km) minimum – has always provided the greatest challenge.

Front crawl
This is the fastest stroke, so it is used in freestyle races, but it may also be performed slowly. It is a popular recreational stroke and is used in long-distance swimming. The swimmer lies face down in the water. Both arms and legs move alternately – the arms pull down through the water from an outstretched position, and the legs move up and down.

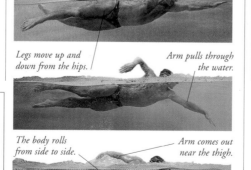

Legs move up and down from the hips.

Arm pulls through the water.

The body rolls from side to side.

Arm comes out near the thigh.

Mark Spitz
American swimmer Mark Spitz (b. 1950) set an an unprecedented record when he won seven gold medals at one Olympic Games. At Munich in 1972, he won the 100- and 200-m freestyle and butterfly, and swam in three winning US relay teams, with world records in all events.

Swimming
Swimming is a major Olympic sport. Before going on to championship meetings, children can compete in their own age groups in swimming contests. Other aquatic sports involving swimming include water polo and synchronized swimming. The former is a seven-a-side ball game; the latter is a kind of underwater ballet.

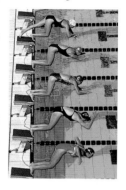

Racing
Races are started from blocks, and electronic touch pads at the end of the pool enable major events to be timed to one thousandth of a second. Olympic-size pools are 164 ft (50 m) long.

Diving
There are two standard diving events – the springboard, 10 ft (3 m) above the water, and the fixed platform, or highboard, 33 ft (10 m) high. The diver performs aerial maneuvers such as twists and somersaults before entering the water. Points are awarded for technique and style.

Cliff diving
Cliff diving is a popular show for tourists in some Hawaiian and Mexican resorts, such as Acapulco, shown here. Divers plunge 115 ft (35 m) or more into water perhaps only 13 ft (4 m) deep, avoiding projecting rocks as they do so.

Types of dive
There are six main types of dive: forward, backward, twist, inward, reverse, and handstand.

Handstand dive
Handstand, or arm stand, dives are performed from the highboard. The diver goes into a steady handstand on the edge of the board before proceeding with the dive.

Backward dive
In the starting position for a backward dive, the diver must keep a straight body, with head up. The arms are swung upward just before takeoff from the platform or springboard.

Forward dive
Forward dives may be performed with a run-up as well as from a standing position. As with all dives, the body should enter the water straight, with legs, arms, and hands extended.

FIND OUT MORE

HEALTH AND FITNESS   MEXICO   OLYMPIC GAMES   SAILING AND OTHER WATER SPORTS   SPORTS

SWITZERLAND AND AUSTRIA

MOUNTAINOUS AND LANDLOCKED, Switzerland and Austria sit in the heart of Western Europe, with the tiny principality of Liechtenstein tucked in between them. This central position, and some of Europe's longest rivers, have enabled the three countries to take advantage of trading routes between east and west, and north and south. Switzerland's lack of raw materials has led to the development of specialized high-tech industries, which have made the country rich. Austria's mineral resources supplement its income from farming, and the picturesque lakes and mountains of all three countries attract millions of tourists.

Communications

Treacherous mountain passes were the only routes through the Alps until tunnels and high bridges were engineered. Switzerland's St. Gotthard traffic tunnel, the world's longest road tunnel, stretches for 10 miles (16 km). Rivers have provided links for centuries. The river port of Basel on the Rhine connects Switzerland to the North Sea, while the mighty Danube joins Austria to the Black Sea.

Train on a high mountain bridge, Switzerland

Physical features

The highest mountains in Europe, the Alps, cover 75 percent of Austria, 70 percent of Switzerland, and much of Liechtenstein. Dense coniferous forest dominates Switzerland and is scattered around Austria and Liechtenstein. Two great rivers, the Rhine and the Danube, provide access to the north and south.

Alps

Forming a vast, rocky barrier between northern and southern Europe, the Alps are some of the most impressive mountains in the world. They range across western Europe and are at their most dramatic on the Swiss-Italian border, where the icy Matterhorn rises to 14,691 ft (4,478 m). The Alps are fragile, and tourism is regulated.

Matterhorn

Regional climate

66°F (19°C)   30°F (-1°C)

32 in (813 mm)

In Switzerland, Austria, and Liechtenstein, alpine regions are cooler and wetter than the valleys, and have a lot of snow. Switzerland's climate varies, and south-facing mountains are much warmer than northern slopes. On the plateau, summers are warm and dry winds often bring high winter temperatures. Austria has a high rainfall in the west.

Austrian plains

Broad, fertile plains surrounding the Danube and its tributaries cover part of northeastern Austria. The small, privately owned farms keep Austria self-sufficient in potatoes, sugar beets, and cereals. Surplus crops are exported. Cattle graze on mountain slopes.

Swiss lakes

Switzerland has some of the most scenic and famous lakes on the European continent, including the two largest lakes in Western Europe, Geneva and Constance. Pollution is affecting some of the more popular lakes, such as this tranquil area of Lake Silser, near St. Moritz.

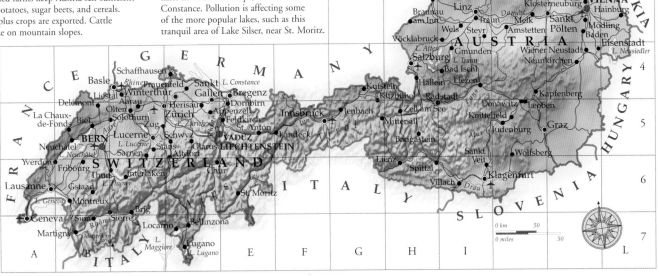

S

Switzerland

Switzerland is a land of isolated valleys, divided into 26 provinces. A united confederation since 1291, Switzerland has a strong central government. The country has a long history of neutrality in war, and now many international organizations have their headquarters in Geneva. Successful banking and high-tech industries have made Switzerland the world's wealthiest country.

Bern

Home to more than 130,000 people, Switzerland's ancient capital, Bern, dates from the 11th century. Its streets mix historic medieval buildings with modern factories and offices. The bear is a city symbol and its namesake market is a colorful scene.

A panoramic view of Bern

People

Swiss people are the richest in the world, but their costs of living are high. The most multilingual of all European countries, Switzerland has three main languages, with German most used. The Swiss people vote on all major political issues, but two conservative cantons did not grant women the vote until 1989.

Industry

About 35 percent of the labor force works in manufacturing, one of the highest levels in Europe. The Swiss have a world-wide reputation for their precision engineering, especially for making clocks and watches. In 1968, they invented the quartz watch. Other important industries include making optical instruments and the growing chemical and pharmaceutical sector that employs about ten percent of the workforce.

Tag Heuer watch

Drug capsules

Dairy farming

Arable land is scarce in Switzerland, but mountain cattle grazing has turned the country into a leading exporter of dairy products. Milk from the cows is used to make a wide range of cheese and chocolate, invented by Henri Nestlé (1814–90).

Banking

Financial stability, political neutrality, and strict secrecy laws combine to make Switzerland a major banking center. Foreign investors are attracted by low taxes and few government regulations.

SWITZERLAND FACTS

CAPITAL CITY Bern

AREA 15,940 sq miles (41,290 sq km)

POPULATION 7,400,000

MAIN LANGUAGES German, French, Italian, Romansch

MAJOR RELIGION Christian

CURRENCY Swiss franc

LIFE EXPECTANCY 79 years

PEOPLE PER DOCTOR 526

GOVERNMENT Multiparty democracy

ADULT LITERACY 99%

Austria

Once the center of the Austro-Hungarian Empire and a major European power, Austria today is a small, industrialized republic. It has close ties with Switzerland and its powerful northern neighbor, Germany, with which it shares many aspects of language and culture. Nearly 94 percent of the people are ethnic Austrians.

Vienna

One of the most beautiful cities in Europe, Vienna was once the capital of the Holy Roman Empire. Many of its historic buildings, including St. Stephen's Cathedral, survived the bombs of World War II (1939–45). Others, such as the Opera House, were rebuilt.

St. Stephen's Cathedral

Skiing

Austria's winter sports bring in one-third of the country's tourist income; more than 10 million people flock to the Alps every year. Skiers enjoy premier alpine resorts, such as St. Anton, attracted by heavy snow, breathtaking views, and modern facilities.

Music

Many great composers were Austrian, including the Strauss family, which composed the Viennese waltzes. Spring's Festival of Vienna hosts concerts, balls, operas, and theater performances.

Hydroelectric power

With limited fossil fuels, Austria has to rely on its fast mountain streams to provide power for its steel and manufacturing industries. The Danube has also been harnessed to provide 40 percent of power used.

AUSTRIA FACTS

CAPITAL CITY Vienna

AREA 32,375 sq miles (83,850 sq km)

POPULATION 8,200,000

MAIN LANGUAGE German

MAJOR RELIGION Christian

CURRENCY Euro

LIFE EXPECTANCY 78 years

PEOPLE PER DOCTOR 333

GOVERNMENT Multiparty democracy

ADULT LITERACY 99%

Liechtenstein

Nestled between the Rhine and the Alps, this tiny principality has close economic ties with Switzerland. A busy financial center, its economy is highly industrialized. Liechtenstein is known for fine vineyards, forested nature reserves, and postage stamps.

Lifestyle

The people of Liechtenstein enjoy a high standard of living and traditional family life. Most are ethnic Liechtensteiners, but about 35 percent are Swiss and German. The majority disagree with equal rights for women, who only got the vote in 1984.

LIECHTENSTEIN FACTS

CAPITAL CITY Vaduz

AREA 62 sq miles (160 sq km)

POPULATION 32,200

MAIN LANGUAGE German

MAJOR RELIGION Christian

CURRENCY Swiss franc

FIND OUT MORE   CHURCHES AND CATHEDRALS   DAMS   EMPIRES   EUROPE, HISTORY OF   EUROPEAN UNION   FARMING   HOLY ROMAN EMPIRE   MONEY   MOUNTAINS AND VALLEYS   MUSIC   WINTER SPORTS

SYRIA AND JORDAN

SYRIA, JORDAN, AND LEBANON together form part of a region called the Middle East that lies between Europe, Africa, and the rest of Asia. The majority of people are Muslim, sharing a common environment and culture. By contrast, the nearby island of Cyprus has strong ties with Europe and its people are mostly Christian. Politics in the region are volatile. The three mainland countries lie on important ancient trade routes, and Syria and Jordan have modern trade links through their pipelines that carry oil from countries farther east for shipment to Europe and beyond.

Physical features

The mainland countries of this region are dominated by dry deserts, with strips of fertile land along the Mediterranean coast and in the Jordan Valley. The Jordan River flows 200 miles (320 km) from its source on the border between Syria and Lebanon down to the Dead Sea. Cyprus has fertile plains, mountains, and sandy beaches.

Wadi Rum
In southern Jordan, the towering sandstone mountains of the Wadi Rum – an ancient watercourse that is now dry – rise sharply out of the sand to create one of the world's most spectacular desert landscapes. Now a national park, Wadi Rum is home to several Bedouin tribes that live in scattered camps throughout the area.

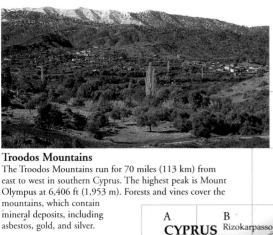

Troodos Mountains
The Troodos Mountains run for 70 miles (113 km) from east to west in southern Cyprus. The highest peak is Mount Olympus at 6,406 ft (1,953 m). Forests and vines cover the mountains, which contain mineral deposits, including asbestos, gold, and silver.

80°F (27°C)   50°F (10°C)

17.5 in (444 mm)

Regional climate
Summers throughout the whole region are hot and dry and winters cool, with moderate rainfall. Below sea level, the Jordan Valley has warm winters and scorching summers. In the mountains of Lebanon and Cyprus, winters are colder and wetter with frequent snow.

Bedouins
Nomadic Bedouin peoples and their animals have roamed the deserts of the Middle East for centuries. Living in tents, family groups move around exploiting the limited water and grazing their animals on a seasonal basis. Some Bedouin are camel herders; others keep sheep and goats. Today, their way of life is under threat as governments urge people to settle in towns and cities.

Bedouin people in tent, Jordan

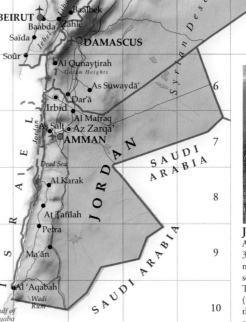

Jebel Liban
Almost half of Lebanon lies more than 3,000 ft (900 m) above sea level. Two mountain chains run from north to south down the length of the country. The Jebel Liban run for about 100 miles (160 km) along the west coast, and in the east are the lower Jebel esh Sharqi, or Anti-Lebanon Mountains. The fertile Bekaa Valley lies between the two ranges.

821

S

Syria

Inhabited for tens of thousands of years, Syria has a rich cultural history. Only one-third of the land is cultivated and oil is the main source of income. About 20 percent of Syria is desert, some of which can be grazed. Most Syrians are Muslim Arabs, with a small Kurdish minority who live in the north. The leading political force is the ruling Ba'ath Party.

Cotton

Syria's main cash crop is cotton, grown mainly in the north of the country on land watered by the Euphrates and Orontes Rivers. Wheat, barley, fruit, and vegetables are also grown. Sheep and goats are raised for meat and milk.

Sacks of cotton ready for processing

Damascus

Syria's capital, built about 5,000 years ago on the Barada River, is the world's oldest inhabited city. The most important building is the 7th-century Umayyad Mosque, which contains parts of a former Christian church. Nearby, the booths of the Al-Hamidiyah bazaar sell all kinds of craftwork. Small shops sell fresh fruits grown in the orchards outside the city.

Lebanon

This small country on the Mediterranean coast was home to Phoenician traders around 1200 BC. From 1975 until 1991, Lebanon was shattered by civil war between Christians and Muslims. One-third of the land is cultivated, yet farming employs one in five Lebanese workers. The country produces fine wines.

Pickled chilies

Pickled rutabaga

Kibbeh

Pastry

Lebanese food

The national food of Lebanon is *kibbeh,* made of lamb or fish pounded to a fine paste with *burghul* (cracked wheat) and served raw or baked in flat trays or rolled into balls and fried. The Lebanese also love pastries filled with nuts and dates and covered with honey.

Beirut

Lebanon's ancient capital, Beirut, lies at the meeting point of three continents. The city is home to more than one million people and is a center of culture, trade, and tourism. It is now being rebuilt after war damage.

Jordan

Apart from a short strip of coast on the Gulf of Aqaba, Jordan is landlocked. Since Eastern Jordan is desert, most people live in the more fertile northwest, close to the Jordan – the main source of water. At 1,312 ft (400 m) below sea level, the Dead Sea is the world's lowest point on land. Most Jordanians are Muslim and speak Arabic. Jordan plays a peacekeeping role between Israel and its Arab neighbors.

Farming and industry

Jordan receives most of its income from phosphate mining, light industry, and, increasingly, tourism. Although water is in short supply, Jordan grows tomatoes, cucumbers, eggplant, citrus fruit, and wheat.

Minaret for calling Muslims to prayer

Mosque overlooking Amman

Amman

Although Amman has been Jordan's capital only since 1921, the city dates back to biblical times when it was built on seven hills. Today, Amman is a mix of old and new buildings, including museums and art galleries. The central *souk* (market) is a lively and colorful reminder of the city's ancient origins. Amman holds about one-third of Jordan's population.

Petra

The city of Petra was built 2,000 years ago by Nabatean Arabs who cut tombs, dwellings, and temples into the solid rock. Set in a valley surrounded by red stone cliffs, Petra is reached through the *Siq,* a narrow entrance. Petra is now a great tourist attraction.

Cyprus

Cyprus is the largest island in the eastern Mediterranean. Following Turkish and British rule, it became independent in 1959. The majority of Cypriots is Greek- or Turkish-speaking. In 1974, increasing hostilities led to a split between the Greek south and Turkish north.

Tourism

Sun, sand, spectacular mountain scenery, and ancient Greek and Roman ruins lure more than 2 million tourists to Cyprus each year. Tourism in the southern part of the island increased greatly in the 1980s.

FIND OUT MORE

ASIA, HISTORY OF   CRUSADES   DESERTS   FARMING   IRAN AND IRAQ   ISLAM   ISLAMIC EMPIRE   MOSQUES   OIL   PHOENICIANS   WARFARE

TECHNOLOGY

THE SCIENCE OF PUTTING inventions and discoveries into practical use is known as technology. A scientist discovers scientific principles, properties, and processes, while engineers use that knowledge to build machines and structures. Technology began in prehistoric times, but did not have a major impact until the 18th and 19th centuries. Then a host of new technologies sprang up, spawning a revolution in industry and at home. Today, it is information technology that is bringing about another major revolution.

Early technology
Prehistoric people pioneered technology when they made the first tools. They smashed pebbles to produce sharp cutting pieces, then later shaped flints into specialized tools such as hand axes, knife blades, and weapons. Tools continued to be made from stone until about 5000 BC, when copper was first smelted and used in the Middle East. In about 3500 BC, metal technology spread with the discovery of bronze. The Bronze Age was then followed by an Iron Age from about 1500 BC.

Stone-Age flint hand ax carefully worked to produce a sharp cutting edge.

Modern technology

The foundations of modern technology were laid in the 1700s, at the beginning of the Industrial Revolution. Inventions transformed traditional craft-based industries into factory-based ones. Key inventions, such as the spinning jenny (1764) and Watt's steam engine (1775), provided the materials, machines, and power necessary for technology to develop.

Quorn is a meat substitute made from mycoprotein – a protein derived from fungi.

Freeze-dried food is light, but still retains nutrients. This type of food is used by astronauts in space.

Tray to hold space foods

Food technology
One of the most important aspects of food technology is preservation. Methods such as salting meat have been practiced for thousands of years to stop food from spoiling, while canning and refrigeration are more recent. Modern methods include freeze-drying, which helps preserve food structure better, and the use of additives. Food technology also includes the manufacture of synthetic substitutes such as TVP (textured vegetable protein).

Materials technology
A range of materials is used for manufacturing goods, machines, and structures. Plastics, for example, are popular because they are cheap and easy to shape. They are used in solid form, as synthetic fibers for textiles, film for packaging, and in composites such as fiberglass. Metals such as iron and aluminum are strong and continue to be important for building machines and structures. Concrete, usually reinforced, or strengthened, is the prime material for building massive structures such as dams, bridges, and skyscrapers.

Reinforced concrete

Information technology
Information technology, or IT, encompasses the revolution in communications and the exchange of information brought about by the widespread use of computers. One aspect of IT is the creation of the Internet, a global network that provides access to "sites" containing a range of information, and allows communication between network "surfers" (users).

Portable, or laptop, computers allow users to work anywhere.

Laptop computer

Engineering

Engineers make technology work. They design and mend machinery and electrical equipment, as well as build a range of structures, mines, and chemical plants. The five main categories of engineering are mechanical, civil, mining, chemical, and electrical engineering.

Civil engineering
Civil engineers are involved in construction engineering projects, which provide a range of structures that are beneficial to the public. These include roads, bridges, dams, tunnels, and skyscrapers. One of the most impressive engineering structures is the 31-mile (50-km) long Channel Tunnel under the English Channel connecting France with the UK.

Glen Canyon dam, Arizona

Appropriate technology
An appropriate technology can be defined as one which serves local needs, using local resources. Many developing countries cannot afford to develop large projects, so they tend to upgrade and manage existing technologies on a community level. They might make small water turbines to generate power, build irrigation schemes, or produce renewable energy sources, such as wind and solar power.

Irrigation pumps on wheat field

Research biochemist experiments in a sterile environment

Chemical engineering
Chemical engineers build and operate chemical manufacturing plants, such as those used in the petrochemical industry. They develop large-scale processes that research chemists have produced on a small scale in a laboratory. Their approach is to break down the manufacturing operation into a series of steps.

Service engineer

Design and maintenance
A team of engineers is responsible for developing a new product. Design engineers decide how to make it, and what materials to use. Detailed plans are then passed to production engineers who devise its manufacture. After sale, service engineers are on call to carry out maintenance and repairs.

| FIND OUT MORE | BRIDGES | BUILDING AND CONSTRUCTION | DAMS | DESIGN | FOOD | INDUSTRIAL REVOLUTION | INFORMATION TECHNOLOGY | INVENTIONS | PLASTICS AND RUBBER |

TEETH AND JAWS

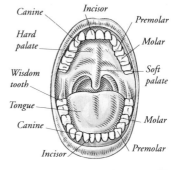

BEFORE FOOD CAN BE SWALLOWED, it must be cut up into small pieces so it can travel down the esophagus and into the stomach. The job of cutting and grinding is carried out by the teeth. These are small, hard structures embedded in the upper and lower jaw bones that grip, bite, slice, and crush food into a paste ready for swallowing. Different types of teeth are adapted to perform particular functions. As a child grows, his or her jaw bones increase in size, until by the end of adolescence they can accommodate a set of 32 adult teeth.

Types of teeth
Each adult jaw contains 16 teeth: four incisors, two canines, four premolars, and six molars. Incisors, at the front of each jaw, are cutting teeth that slide past each other to slice up food. Canines grip and tear food. Premolars and molars have flattened crowns to crush and grind food.

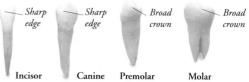

Incisor · Canine · Premolar · Molar

Growth of teeth and jaws
We have two sets of teeth during our lifetime. The first set are called primary, or milk, teeth and they gradually appear in babies until a set of 20 is in place. At about the age of six, the roots of some milk teeth loosen and they start to be pushed out and replaced by the permanent or adult teeth.

Milk teeth in gums
Maxilla (upper jaw)
Mandible (lower jaw)

A newborn baby has no visible teeth. Within the upper jaw and lower jaw, however, the milk teeth are developing. These start to erupt at around the age of six months.

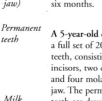

Jaw bone grows
Permanent teeth
Milk teeth

A 5-year-old child has a full set of 20 milk teeth, consisting of four incisors, two canines, and four molars in each jaw. The permanent teeth are developing and will push out.

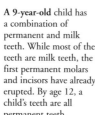

First permanent molars
Permanent incisors
Milk teeth still in place

A 9-year-old child has a combination of permanent and milk teeth. While most of the teeth are milk teeth, the first permanent molars and incisors have already erupted. By age 12, a child's teeth are all permanent teeth.

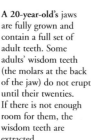

Jaw bone has reached adult size.
Full set of permanent teeth
Roots of teeth

A 20-year-old's jaws are fully grown and contain a full set of adult teeth. Some adults' wisdom teeth (the molars at the back of the jaw) do not erupt until their twenties. If there is not enough room for them, the wisdom teeth are extracted.

Structure of a tooth
Every tooth is made up of three basic layers. Enamel forms a hard cap that protects the tooth. Dentine forms the bulk of the tooth and extends into the root along the root canal. The pulp contains blood vessels and nerves that allow you to detect pressure when chewing.

Crown is the upper visible part of the tooth.

Gum is soft tissue covering jaw bone.

Blood vessels

Root anchors tooth in jaw bone.

Root canal contains pulp.

Blood capillary supplies tooth with food and oxygen.

Enamel is a very hard material that covers the crown.

Dentine is a living, bonelike material inside the tooth.

Pulp cavity contains pulp.

Cement and peridontal ligament hold root in socket.

Nerve ligament

Jaw bone

Brushing your teeth regularly helps get rid of plaque.

You brush the plaque away from your gums.

Tooth decay
Food leaves behind a sticky residue on your teeth called plaque. Bacteria in plaque release acids that eat away at the enamel. This can expose the inner parts of the tooth, causing tooth decay.

Chewing and biting
The first stage in digestion is chewing, which breaks food up into small particles ready for swallowing. Chewing is controlled by three pairs of muscles that move the lower jaw. The temporalis and masseter muscles pull the lower jaw upward to crush food. The pterygoid muscles move the lower jaw from side to side, and slide it forward, to grind food.

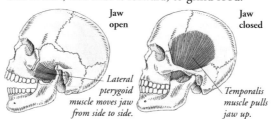

Jaw open
Jaw closed
Lateral pterygoid muscle moves jaw from side to side.
Temporalis muscle pulls jaw up.

Dentistry
In the past, a decaying tooth would have been extracted, but dentists now treat tooth decay by removing affected parts of a tooth and filling the cavities with hard materials. Artificial crowns can be screwed into a tooth to replace the real thing. Dentists are also concerned with the prevention of tooth and gum disease.

FIND OUT MORE DIGESTION FOOD GROWTH AND DEVELOPMENT HUMAN BODY HUMAN EVOLUTION MEDICINE MUSCLES AND MOVEMENT SKELETON SMELL AND TASTE

TELECOMMUNICATIONS

THE WORLD SEEMS TO BE shrinking thanks to modern telecommunications, which enables us to send messages across the globe in an instant. Telecommunications is the use of technology to send and receive information – such as speech, music, pictures, and documents – over long distances. The devices that make this possible include telephones, radios, satellites, televisions, and computers. The forerunner of modern telecommunications was the telegraph, which sent messages by electrical wires.

Network

Telecommunications devices send information across a network of links that create a pathway between the sender and receiver. The information travels as electrical pulses along copper cables, as flashes of light along optical fibers (thin strands of glass), or as radio or microwave signals between dishes on towers, buildings, and satellites.

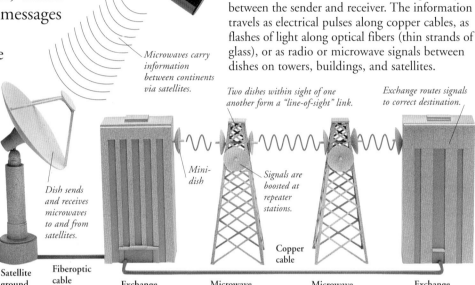

Satellite

Microwaves carry information between continents via satellites.

Two dishes within sight of one another form a "line-of-sight" link.

Exchange routes signals to correct destination.

Mini-dish

Signals are boosted at repeater stations.

Dish sends and receives microwaves to and from satellites.

Copper cable

Satellite ground station

Fiberoptic cable

Exchange building

Microwave repeater station

Microwave repeater station

Exchange building

Samuel Morse

American Samuel Morse (1791–1872) devised a telegraph system that used a type of modulation called Morse code. Letters and numbers represented by dots and dashes were sent along wires as long and short pulses of electricity.

Modulation

Telecommunications information must be modulated (coded) in some way before it is sent across a network. Radio and television programmes are broadcast by coding the information into a "carrier" radio wave that is sent through the air to a receiving aerial. The aerial sends an electrical signal to a radio or television set, where it is demodulated.

AM carrier wave

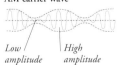

Low amplitude   High amplitude

FM carrier wave

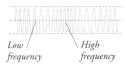

Low frequency   High frequency

Amplitude modulation
In amplitude modulation (AM), the information is carried by changes in the amplitude, or size, of the carrier wave.

Frequency modulation
In frequency modulation (FM), information is represented by changes in the carrier wave's frequency (the number of waves per second).

Messaging technology

Until recently, a fax machine was the best way to send a written message quickly. However, e-mailing from a computer now allows all kinds of information to be sent instantly around the world, including large computer files. Text messaging via mobile phones is another new technology that is rapidly evolving.

Screen used to read and manage e-mail account

Control panel

Keypad for dialling numbers

Telephone handset

Telephone/e-mail machine

E-mail
E-mail works by sending images and words down a telephone line over the Internet. Most people e-mail from a computer, but e-mail is also becoming available on other devices, including telephone/e-mail machines, such as the one pictured, mobile phones, and even televisions with a digital connection and a keyboard.

Mini keyboard for typing

Fax machine
A fax machine sends and receives facsimiles, or copies, of documents and pictures via the telephone line. The machine scans a document and sends the information down the line as electrical signals. The receiving fax machine decodes the signals and prints a copy of the original document.

Keypad for dialling numbers.

A document is sent down an ordinary telephone line.

Telephone handset

Liquid crystal display

Documents to be sent are fed in here.

Heat-sensitive paper prints documents received from other fax machines.

Telephone/fax machine

Timeline

1793 Frenchman Claude Chappe invents the semaphore, which sends messages using moving arms on towers.

1844 In the US, Samuel Morse builds the world's first telegraph line.

Early Bell telephone

1876 Scottish-born Alexander Graham Bell invents the telephone.

1878 First telephone exchange opens in New Haven, US.

1901 Italian inventor Guglielmo Marconi astounds the world by transmitting a radio signal across the Atlantic Ocean, from England to Canada.

1956 Undersea telephone cable installed in Atlantic.

1962 Satellite is first used to make telephone calls.

1977 Optical fibers are used for telephone calls.

1990s E-mail gains mass appeal around the world.

FIND OUT MORE   COMPUTERS   ELECTRICITY   LIGHT   RADIO   SATELLITES   SOUND RECORDING   TELEPHONE   X-RAYS AND THE ELECTROMAGNETIC SPECTRUM

TELEPHONES

"I'LL GIVE YOU A CALL", we often say to our friends, but we rarely wonder how it is that, only a few seconds after entering a number on a keypad, we can be speaking to a friend many miles away – even on the other side of the world. A telephone is a device that transforms a person's voice into an electrical signal made up of varying electric currents. This signal travels along copper cables to reach its destination. Sometimes, it is changed into pulses of light and sent along thin glass strands called optical fibers. The signal can also be transmitted as radio waves or microwaves.

Mobile phone

Mobile phones allow the freedom to make calls from almost anywhere because they are not physically connected to the telephone network. They send and receive calls as radio wave signals. Mobile phone technology is fast evolving so that the handheld devices can now also send text messages, emails and video images, as well as connect to the Internet.

Aerial inside receives radio waves from mobile phone exchange.

Designs have become more compact over the years.

Mobile phone

Receiving a text message

Text messaging
Mobile phones allow users to send instant text messages to other mobile phones. Pressing specific combinations of buttons converts the numeric keypad into a text keypad for spelling out words.

Videophone
Videophones are telephones that allow users to see each other. A tiny camera captures the image of the caller as a signal. The signal is sent to the receiving phone, where it is decoded to display the caller's face. A videophone can be either a mobile phone or a fixed-line telephone.

Alexander Graham Bell
In 1875, the Scottish-born inventor Alexander Graham Bell (1847–1922) made the first successful transmission of the human voice along an electrical wire. The first words he spoke were to his colleague, Thomas Watson. Bell patented the telephone the following year, beating his American rival Elisha Gray (1835–1901) by just two hours.

How telephones work

Once two telephones are linked via the telephone network, the sounds of the speakers' voices are picked up by microphones in the handsets. Loudspeakers reproduce and amplify (boost) these sounds, so that each caller can hear what the other is saying.

Switch hook opens line circuit when handset is down.

Circuit boards contain electronic components.

Keypad
To make a telephone call, the caller picks up the handset, which switches on an electrical circuit. Pressing the keys on the handset sends a sequence of electrical pulses or different tones to an exchange. Each telephone number has a different sequence, so the exchange can easily route the call to the right number.

Earpiece

Earpiece
The earpiece contains a loudspeaker. When the telephone receives an electrical signal from the network, it causes a diaphragm in the loudspeaker to vibrate and recreate the sound of the person's voice at the other end.

Keypad

Caller speaks into the mouthpiece.

Mouthpiece
Inside the mouthpiece is a microphone that contains a thin plastic disk called a diaphragm. The sound of the caller's voice causes the diaphragm to vibrate. As it vibrates, it generates an electrical signal that passes down the telephone line to the receiving telephone.

Handset

Telephone network

Every call reaches its destination via a network of communications links. A local exchange can make connections with any telephone in the caller's area. Long-distance connections are made via national or international exchanges, or even satellites. Cellular exchanges handle the radio signals that carry calls to and from mobile phones.

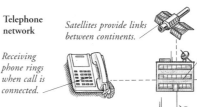

Telephone network

Satellites provide links between continents.

National or international exchange selects best route for call.

Caller dials number by pressing keypad.

Receiving phone rings when call is connected.

Cellular exchange can connect to mobile phones.

Local exchange can connect call to local numbers or send call to larger exchange.

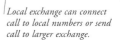

Exchange
An exchange is a building containing equipment that recognizes dialled pulses and tones. It sends calls to the correct destination, represented by a unique telephone number. This process is called switching and is controlled by powerful computers inside the exchange.

Communications satellites
Long-distance telephone calls are often sent as microwave signals via satellites orbiting above the Earth. The satellite strengthens the signal and sends it back to Earth.

FIND OUT MORE ELECTRICITY   ELECTROMAGNETISM   ELECTRONICS   LIGHT   SOUND   SOUND RECORDING   TELECOMMUNICATIONS   VIDEO

Telephones

Dials

Metal dial, pre-World War I (1914–18)

Colored plastic dial from the 1930s

Black dial from 1920s Swiss-designed phone

Development of the telephone

Speaking and listening cone

Alexander Graham Bell's box telephone, 1876

Dials

Lightweight plastic dial, 1963

Alphanumeric dial, 1960s, with both letters and numbers

Phone engineer's dial, 1960s

Mobile phones

Portable phone, mid-1980s: like all mobile phones, it contains a built-in radio transmitter and receiver.

Picking up the earpiece connected caller to the operator.

Hook for second earpiece if hard of hearing.

Crank handle

Candlestick phone, 1905: users asked the exchange operator to dial the number they wanted to call.

Crank handle telephone, 1890s: user turned the crank to contact the operator in order to make a call, and again to tell the operator that the call was finished.

Early car phone, mid-1980s

Handset

Mobile phones

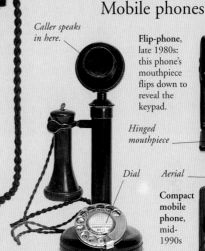

Caller speaks in here.

Hinged mouthpiece

Dial

Candlestick phone with dial, 1930s, allowed user to call without going through operator.

Flip-phone, late 1980s: this phone's mouthpiece flips down to reveal the keypad.

Aerial

Compact mobile phone, mid-1990s

Liquid crystal display

Walnut-veneer phone, 1920s, molded in Bakelite plastic to look like wood.

Colored phone, 1930s: new plastics allowed different colored phones.

Compact table phone, 1967, designed for use in the home.

Self-contained keypad phone, 1970s: early models had a separate box for the keypad.

Memory keys

Modern phone, mid-1990s: this phone stores frequently called numbers in its electronic memory.

Novelty telephones

Mickey Mouse phone, 1980, based on the popular Walt Disney character

Trim phone, 1960s, had a luminous dial and electronic ringer.

Bell housing

Separate-bell telephone, 1977: the long cord allowed the caller to move around while talking.

Earpiece

Mouthpiece

Marble phone, 1984

One-piece desk phone, 1970s

Bells

Transparent phone, 1950s, showed the internal workings of the phone.

Leather-bound phone, 1980s

Snoopy phone, 1980, features the character from the cartoon "Peanuts."

TELESCOPES

THE TINIEST OBJECT in the sky can become clearly visible when viewed through a telescope. An optical telescope forms a magnified image of a distant object by altering the path of light rays using lenses and mirrors. There are two main types of telescopes. A refracting telescope forms an image by bending, or refracting, light rays using lenses. A reflecting telescope bounces, or reflects, light rays off mirrors so that they form an image. Powerful telescopes allow astronomers to see incredible distances into space. Radio telescopes form images from radio waves emitted by distant stars and galaxies.

Bringing things closer
Seen with the naked eye, the Moon looks very small because it is far away. A telescope can magnify (enlarge) this image, making the Moon seem larger and much closer. A telescope's magnifying power is shown by the symbol "x." A telescope with a magnification of 100x, for example, makes objects seem 100 times larger.

Naked eye image   Telescope image

Refracting telescope
As light rays from an object enter the telescope, a convex lens (the objective) bends them to form an upside-down image of the object. A second lens (the eyepiece) bends the rays again, magnifying the image.

Chromatic aberration
Light consists of many different colors. When light from an object passes through a lens, each color bends at a different angle, creating a spectrum of colors around any image that forms. This is called "chromatic aberration." It can be eliminated by adding another lens.

Cutaway of a refracting telescope

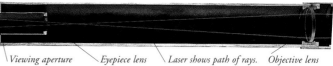

Viewing aperture   Eyepiece lens   Laser shows path of rays.   Objective lens

Galileo's telescope
The Italian scientist Galileo Galilei (1564–1642) was the first to use a telescope to systematically study the night sky. He made many important discoveries about the planets and stars.

Sliding tube for focusing   Objective lens

Eyepiece lens   Galileo's telescope (replica)

Reflecting telescope
A concave (inward-curving) mirror collects light rays from an object and reflects them onto a flat, angled mirror, which forms an image of the object. A lens (the eyepiece) then magnifies the image for the viewer. Using more than one mirror increases the power of the telescope.

Cutaway of a reflecting telescope

Viewing aperture

Eyepiece lens

Image forms here.

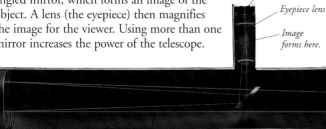

Concave mirror   Reflected light   Flat mirror   Light enters here.

Binoculars
A pair of binoculars consists of two compact refracting telescopes joined together. Each telescope uses two prisms to reflect light rays from the objective lens to the eyepiece lens. The image is focused by adjusting the position of the eyepiece lenses.

Eyepiece lens   Focusing mechanism

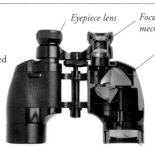

Prisms "fold up" the path of the light rays, enabling each telescope to be very compact.

Objective lens

Keck telescope
Many large telescopes are built on mountaintops, where the sky is clear and cloudless. The largest optical telescope, the Keck, is on Mauna Kea volcano in Hawaii. Its collecting mirror consists of 36 hexagonal mirrors, totaling 108 ft² (10 m²).

Sliding doors

Incoming starlight

Secondary mirror

Light reflects between mirrors.

Third mirror directs light to viewer.

Viewing position

Collecting mirror

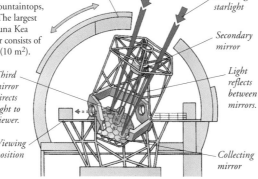

Radio telescope
A radio telescope detects radio waves emitted by stars, galaxies, nebulae, and other astronomical objects. It uses a large dish to focus the waves onto an aerial. The aerial changes the waves into electrical signals, from which a computer generates an image of the object.

Arecibo radio telescope, Puerto Rico

Timeline
10th century The Chinese discover that light rays can be bent by curved pieces of glass.

1608 Dutchman Hans Lippershey invents the telescope.

1673 Englishman Isaac Newton makes a reflecting telescope.

William Herschel's telescope

1789 British astronomer William Herschel designs one of the first large telescopes.

1880 The prism binoculars are invented.

1917 The Mount Wilson telescope is erected in California.

1931 American engineer Karl Jansky discovers that radio waves reach Earth from space.

1937 Grote Reber, an amateur US astronomer, builds the first radio telescope.

1948 The huge Hale reflecting telescope on Mount Palomar, California, is completed.

1970 The Very Large Array of radio telescopes is set up in New Mexico.

1990 Launch of the Hubble Space Telescope, an optical telescope orbiting 310 miles (500 km) above the Earth.

Hubble Space Telescope

2002 Giant telescope with 64 radio dishes planned in Chile.

FIND OUT MORE   ASTRONOMY   GALAXIES   GALILEO GALILEI   LIGHT   MOON   NEWTON, SIR ISAAC   STARS   X RAYS AND THE ELECTROMAGNETIC SPECTRUM

TELEVISION

TELEVISION WAS ONE OF THE most significant inventions of the 20th century; it completely transformed society. Television works by converting pictures and sound into signals, and sending them out by transmitters, satellites, or along underground cables. Television was first developed in the 1920s; it spread rapidly and by the 1980s, almost every US home contained a TV set. By bringing information and entertainment directly into the home, television altered daily life. Today, new advances in television technology, including digital and broadband access, mean that TV can also provide interactive services such as email, shopping, and information.

Early television
The first television service began in the UK in 1936. By the 1950s, many families had TV sets, especially in the US. People who could afford an expensive early receiver wanted to stay at home to be entertained. They were impressed by the up-to-date news coverage and the fact that they could see celebrities in their own homes.

Early TV screens were tiny, and the pictures were black-and-white.

Inside television

A television receiver (TV set) picks up the signals broadcast by a TV station and turns them into images using a picture tube (known as a cathode-ray tube). The tube produces a series of black-and-white or color images in rapid succession, creating the illusion that the picture is moving. The set also contains electronic circuits which enable viewers to tune in to the channel of their choice.

Widescreen TV

Electron guns
The television screen is just one part of the picture tube. Behind the screen, an electron gun fires three beams of electrons (parts of atoms) at the screen. These beams correspond to the three colors used in television – red, blue, and green. Mixed together, they produce full-color images.

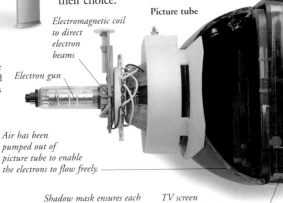

Electromagnetic coil to direct electron beams

Picture tube

Electron gun

Air has been pumped out of picture tube to enable the electrons to flow freely.

Shadow mask ensures each electron beam only strikes one color of phosphor.

TV screen coated in tiny phosphor dots

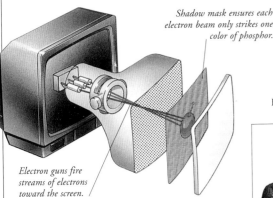

Early electron gun

Electron guns fire streams of electrons toward the screen.

Producing a color picture
The screen is coated with thousands of tiny dots of phosphor. When the electrons hit these dots, they cause them to glow and produce a red, green, or blue image, depending on the kind of phosphor. The strength of each electron beam varies according to the intensity of color needed. Because 25 to 30 images are produced on screen every second, TV pictures appear to move.

Uses of television

Television broadcasts cover every area, from drama to documentary. TV informs, educates, and entertains us, depending on what we choose to watch. And, with audiences in the millions, the information is spread farther than ever before.

Millions watch the soccer World Cup live on TV.

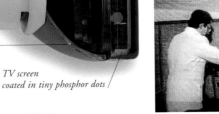

Sponsorship
To raise awareness of their products, some companies sponsor television programs or advertise during commerical breaks. Many TV programs and events are underpinned by sponsorship money. Popular sports such as football have gained, with some benefits passed on to sports fans, such as funds for safer stadiums.

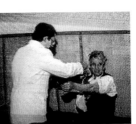

The revolution that overthrew Romanian dictator Nicolae Ceauçescu (1918–89) was shown live on television.

Current affairs
Thanks to television, we can now watch history as it is made, anywhere in the world, and are better informed than ever before. Satellites beam television signals around the world in seconds. Viewers can watch news events as they happen.

Vladimir Zworykin
Russian-born scientist Vladimir Kosma Zworykin (1889–1982) did most of his work in the US. In 1923, he patented the iconoscope television camera tube, the device that made electronic television possible. He followed this with other improvements in television systems.

Ernie

Bert

Educational television
Television provides educational programs for children and adults. Programs are part of correspondence learning up to college level, being accessible to people in remote areas, or to those with limited time.

Sesame Street is a program that helps young children learn to read.

Producing a newscast

Before a newscast appears on your screen, it is carefully produced (planned and put together). Newscasts are planned only hours before airing. The news team meets to decide which of the day's stories to include; these are researched, and a script is prepared. A news broadcast may also include location reports – stories filmed outside the studio.

Light, portable video camera

Houses of Parliament, London, UK

Reporter

On location

Only one person is needed to work a video camera, so a reporter and camera operator can easily produce a simple news report on location. The operator is careful to include an identifiable scene in the background.

Original tape

New tape to be broadcast

Editing equipment

Editing room

An editor gathers together the camera operator's videotapes and copies the best sections from each onto another tape, in the order they will be broadcast. This is done in an editing room, where videotape recorders, monitor screens, and vision mixers are linked together with a computer.

In the studio

The live news broadcast *Newsround* is made for younger viewers by the BBC in the UK. It is broadcast five days a week. As with most newscasts, it is made inside a TV studio. The anchor stands in front of a highly graphic, brightly lit set, reading the day's news stories from the TelePrompTer.

TelePrompTer

The TelePrompTer enables the anchor to see the script while looking directly at the camera. A small computer screen just below the camera lens displays the words and reflects them onto a diagonally mounted sheet of glass in front of the camera. Although the anchor can see the words, they are invisible to both camera and viewer.

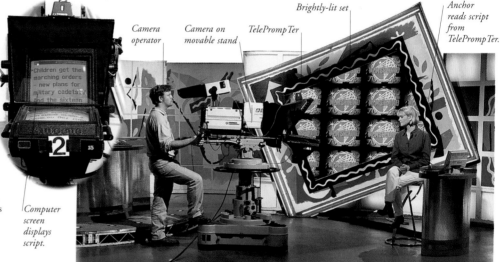

Computer screen displays script.

Camera operator

Camera on movable stand

TelePrompTer

Brightly-lit set

Anchor reads script from TelePrompTer.

Clock, to check the timing of each part of the broadcast

Mixing desk, where video, sound, and graphics are mixed together

The rows of buttons on a mixing desk are known as buses and banks.

The team in the studio and gallery talk to one another via microphones.

The gallery

The gallery (control room) is where the material to make the news broadcast is coordinated during transmission. This includes sequences from the studio cameras, outside broadcasts, music, and graphics. Monitors (videoscreens) display the different material.

Mixing desk

Different shots are prepared for transmission by a vision mixer, seated at a computerized mixing desk. The vision mixer combines the different elements, fading, jump-cutting, or blending from one sequence to another.

TV staff

The director and vision mixer sit in the gallery during the live broadcast. The director decides what image should appear on the screen, and for how long. He or she instructs the vision mixer. The producer has overall control.

Timeline

1923 Vladimir Zworykin begins to develop electronic camera tube.

1926 Scottish inventor John Logie Baird (1888–1946) demonstrates his mechanical television system.

1929 Experimental television transmissions begin in England, using Baird's TV system.

1936 World's first regular TV broadcasts begin in England, using electronic system.

1951 US: first color broadcasts.

1960 Japanese firm Sony introduces all-transistor TV receivers.

1962 *Telstar* satellite relays television signals across the Atlantic.

1979 Flat-screen pocket television.

1990s Digital and broadband TV.

FIND OUT MORE ADVERTISING AND MARKETING CARTOONS AND ANIMATION DRAMA ELECTRONICS INFORMATION TECHNOLOGY INVENTIONS RADIO TELECOMMUNICATIONS

TENNIS AND OTHER RACKET SPORTS

LAWN TENNIS is the most popular and widely played of the racket sports – those in which rackets are used to strike balls of various shapes and sizes across a net or against a wall. Other racket sports are: squash, played in a walled court; badminton, played across a high net; and table tennis, played on a table. Real tennis is an ancient game still played in a few places, and the relatively new sport of racquetball is popular in some parts of the United States.

T

Server stands perpendicular to the net with feet slightly apart.

Racket arm is bent behind the neck as the ball is thrown up.

Eyes on the ball

Racket arm is fully outstretched when hitting the ball.

Server puts power into the serve using the leg muscles.

Serving the ball to start a point

Lawn tennis

In tennis, players hit a ball over a net into the opponent's court so that it cannot be returned. When they win a point they score 15, then 30, 40, and game. A player with six games, two ahead of the opponent, wins a set. Tennis is played as singles with two opponents, or doubles with opposing pairs.

Real tennis
Real, or royal, tennis was played by French and English royalty in the Middle Ages. The few courts around the world are bounded by open windows and doors and sloping roofs.

Tennis racket and balls

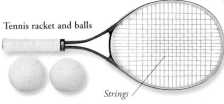

Strings

Tennis balls
White or yellow, tennis balls are 2.5 in (6.5 cm) across. They weigh about 2 oz (57 g) and must conform to a specific standard. In major tournaments, the balls are changed every nine games.

Tennis racket
The frame is of a racket is made of wood, metal, or other material, such as carbon graphite. It must be evenly strung. The racket may not be more than 81.3 cm (32 in) long and 12.5 in (31.75 cm) wide.

Tennis court

Tennis court
Tennis is played on a court 78 ft (23.77 m) long. It is 36 ft (10.97 m) wide for doubles, and 27 ft (8.23 m) wide for singles.

Andre Agassi
US tennis star Andre Agassi (b.1970) is one of the few players to have won six Grand Slam titles in his career. He also won an Olympic gold medal in 1996. The player has a reputation as a rebel on court due to his loud dress sense.

Squash

Mainly a singles game, squash is played in an enclosed court with four walls. The players use the same floor space. The object is to hit the ball against one or more walls, provided one is the front wall, so that the opponent cannot return it before it has bounced twice on the floor.

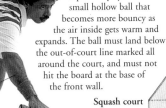

Taking a low ball

Squash ball and court
Squash is played with a small hollow ball that becomes more bouncy as the air inside gets warm and expands. The ball must land below the out-of-court line marked all around the court, and must not hit the board at the base of the front wall.

Squash court

Racquetball racket and ball

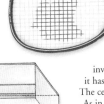

Racquetball
This game was invented in 1950 in the US, where it has overtaken squash in popularity. The ceiling is used as well as the walls. As in squash, the ball must always hit the front wall and may bounce only once on the floor.

Badminton

The aim of badminton is to hit a feathered shuttlecock over a high net into the opponent's court. The shuttle must be returned before it touches the ground. Matches are usually the best of three games, with a game being won by the first player to reach 11 or 15 points, two ahead of the opponent.

Shuttlecocks

Badminton racket

Badminton equipment
Shuttlecocks may be plastic, but most players prefer to play with shuttles made of a "skirt" of goose feathers fixed in a cork base. Rackets, made mostly of metal or carbonfiber, are extremely light.

Badminton court

Table tennis

Players aim to hit a ball over a net so that an opponent cannot return it. The ball must bounce before being hit. For service, it must bounce on the server's side first. The first player to score 21 points, wins.

Ball

Bat

Table

Table tennis
The small ball is made of light plastic. The blade of the wooden bat may be covered in pimpled rubber on both sides. The net is 6 in (15.25 cm) high. The table measures 9 x 5 ft (2.74 x 1.52 m) and is 30 in (76 cm) high.

FIND OUT MORE | BALL GAMES | HEALTH AND FITNESS | MEDIEVAL EUROPE | OLYMPIC GAMES | SPORTS

TEXTILES AND WEAVING

A TEXTILE IS ANY MATERIAL that has been made from fibers linked together. For thousands of years, all textiles were made from natural fibers, obtained from either animal or plant sources. In the 20th century, chemical processes produced synthetic (artificial) fibers as well. Most textiles are made by weaving (textile comes from the Latin *texere*, meaning to weave), but they can also be made by knitting or binding together in other ways. Finished textiles are made into a wide variety of goods, including clothing, furnishings such as curtains and carpets, string, rope, and parachutes.

Jacket, made from oil: mixture of nylon and other artificial fibers; is designed to keep the wearer dry and not too hot.

Nylon rucksack: durable and waterproof

T-shirt: a mix of natural cotton and synthetic polyester fibers; polyester helps the T-shirt keep its shape.

Denim, a tough fabric, is made from woven cotton.

Waterproofed textiles, such as those used in these sneakers, have been coated with a thin layer of resin.

Spinneret and cooling nylon filaments

Wool
Wool comes from the fleece of sheep, goats, camels, and llamas. It is popular for making clothes, carpets, and upholstery, because it is warm, strong, stretchy, and absorbent.

Fibers
Natural fibers include wool and silk from animals, and cotton, flax, and hemp from plants. Synthetic fibers, such as polyesters and acrylics, are made from wood, coal, or oil. Each fiber has different qualities; manufacturers may combine two or three kinds to produce an "ideal" fabric.

Undyed fleece

Woven rug

Spun wool

Main wool producers are Australia, New Zealand, South Africa, and Argentina.

Crude oil

Nylon
Nylon, a synthetic fiber, is made from chemicals found in crude oil. When the chemicals are heated, they form a liquid, which is forced through a spinneret and cooled to form filaments. These are then spun into a yarn.

Making yarn
Before a fiber is made into cloth, it must be spun into yarn (thread). Most natural fibers are very short and must be spun into longer, stronger yarn. Artificial fibers are produced as a continous thread and are spun to make them stronger, rather than longer, or are spun to combine them with natural fibers.

Spinning cotton
Cotton can be spun by hand or by huge factory machines. The machines first squeeze the cleaned fibers together between rollers, into a mat. This is then divided and twisted together into finer and finer threads.

A cotton boll (a clump of fibers) may comprise 500,000 short, white fibers.

Spinning cotton by hand in India

Weaving
Once produced, yarn can be made into cloth. One of the most common means of making cloth is weaving. This is an ancient craft; the earliest evidence of weaving dates from 5000 BC. Most weaving is carried out on a frame called a loom; these can be either massive, machine-powered factory looms, or hand looms.

Weaving a rug by hand

Warp threads must be very strong.

Shuttle

Hand loom

Mechanized looms in a textile factory

The loom
A set of parallel threads, called the warp, are stretched lengthwise on the loom. The threads that run widthwise are called the weft. The weft is carried over and under the warp by a device called a shuttle. This process interlaces the weft and warp to make fabric.

Textile industry
Until the 18th century, weaving was a craft practiced in the home on a small scale. The advances in technology made during the Industrial Revolution massively increased the amount a weaver could produce. Mechanical looms now produce thousands of yards of fabric in a day.

FIND OUT MORE AUSTRALIA CHEMISTRY CLOTHES AND FASHION DYES AND PAINTS FARMING FURNITURE INDUSTRIAL REVOLUTION OIL SHEEP AND GOATS TRADE AND INDUSTRY

THAILAND AND MYANMAR

LYING SIDE BY SIDE in the west of mainland Southeast Asia, Thailand and Myanmar (formerly Burma) resemble each other in many ways. Both countries have mountains and forests in the north, fertile river valleys, similar mineral resources, and a shared religion – Buddhism. However, their governments and economies differ greatly. Thailand is a wealthy, democratic monarchy; Myanmar is isolated and undeveloped with a poor human rights record.

Physical features

The densely forested mountains in the north of Thailand and Myanmar give rise to many rivers, such as the Chao Phraya and the Irrawaddy, that cut through the fertile countryside on their way to the coast. The western coast on the Andaman Sea is dotted with many islands.

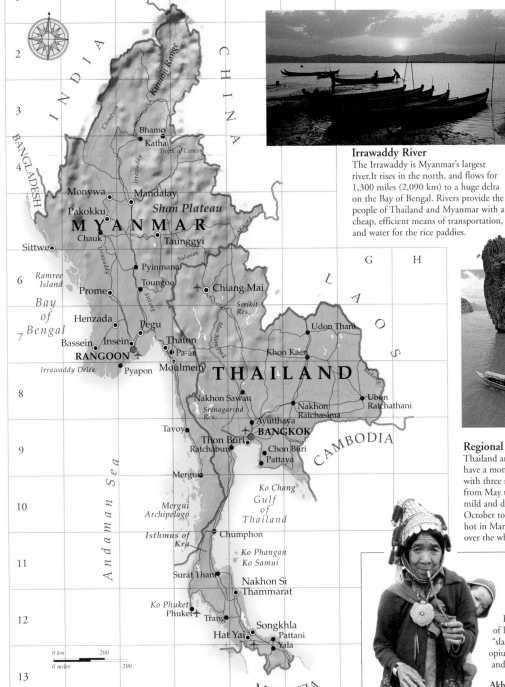

Irrawaddy River
The Irrawaddy is Myanmar's largest river. It rises in the north, and flows for 1,300 miles (2,090 km) to a huge delta on the Bay of Bengal. Rivers provide the people of Thailand and Myanmar with a cheap, efficient means of transportation, and water for the rice paddies.

Monsoon rain forest
The border between Myanmar and Thailand is covered in thick, impenetrable monsoon rain forest. In the 1980s, the destruction of large areas of forest to provide timber, especially teak, for export led to serious flooding. As a result, in 1989, the Thai government banned logging.

Andaman Sea
To the west of the narrow strip of Burmese land at the top of the Malay Peninsula lies the Andaman Sea, which is part of the Indian Ocean. It is bordered by mangrove swamps, which help prevent coastline erosion. Dotted with hundreds of tiny, remote islands, this area is a growing tourist attraction.

Regional climate
Thailand and Myanmar have a monsoon climate with three seasons: rainy from May to September, mild and dry from October to February, and hot in March and April. In the south, rainfall is spread over the whole year. The average temperatures are high.

80°F (27°C)   77°F (25°C)

79 in (2,008 mm)

Hill tribes
The mountainous and largely forested region where Thailand, Myanmar, and Laos meet is known as the Golden Triangle. Here, poor hill tribes live in villages, farming small plots of land that have been cleared of trees using the "slash-and-burn" technique. They also cultivate opium poppies, which are used to make heroin and other drugs for the illegal drug trade.

Akha tribeswoman with opium pipe

Thailand

Bordered by Myanmar, Laos, Cambodia, and Malaysia, the kingdom of Thailand, once called Siam, was established in the 13th century, and the country has remained independent for much of its history. It was the only country in mainland Southeast Asia never to be colonized. Its name in the Thai language is Muang Thai, meaning "land of the free." Modern Thailand has one of the world's fastest growing economies, although there is still great poverty in rural areas, where 80 percent of the people live. Bangkok, the capital and only big city, is very crowded.

Ethnic Thais
Most Thais are descended from people who began migrating south from China nearly 2,000 years ago. As a nation, they are traditional Buddhists. About 12 percent of the population is ethnic Chinese.

King of Thailand
Thailand's ninth king, Bhumibol Adulyadej, came to the throne in 1946. His family, the Chakris, have ruled Thailand since 1782. The king has immense personal prestige and criticism of him is frowned upon.

THAILAND FACTS

CAPITAL CITY	Bangkok
AREA	198,116 sq miles (513,120 sq km)
POPULATION	61,400,000
MAIN LANGUAGE	Thai
MAJOR RELIGIONS	Buddhist, Muslim
CURRENCY	Baht
LIFE EXPECTANCY	70 years
PEOPLE PER DOCTOR	2,500
GOVERNMENT	Multiparty democracy
ADULT LITERACY	96%

Rice
About a quarter of Thailand is used for farming, mostly for growing rice in the fertile river valleys. Every year, 21,428,906 tons (19,440,000 tonnes) are produced. Rice is the basis of all main meals, usually accompanied by at least five other dishes, flavored with fish sauce and coriander.

Industry
Although only 15 percent of Thai workers are employed in industry, manufacturing is increasingly important. In recent years, American and Japanese companies have set up factories in Thailand, which is now a leading producer of electronic goods. Other manufactures include rubber and jute products. Thai mines produce tin, other metals, and precious stones.

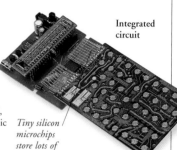

Integrated circuit

Tiny silicon microchips store lots of information.

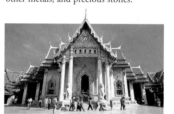

Tourism
Thailand's ornate Buddhist temples and cultural heritage draw thousands of tourists every year. New golf courses are being built to attract Japanese visitors, and the northern hill villages, island resorts, and pristine beaches are also popular holiday destinations.

Crops
More than half of Thailand's workers are employed in farming. Important crops include cassava, a root that is the source of tapioca, sugarcane, and pineapples. Thailand is the world's biggest exporter of canned pineapple, and a leading producer of natural rubber. Thais also grow bananas, coconuts, jute, and cotton.

Pineapple

Cassava

Bangkok
Thailand's capital was originally built on a network of canals, many of which are still used for transporting goods. For a city of over six million people, Bangkok has relatively few major roads and limited public transportation, giving it the world's worst traffic jams. Many commuters equip their cars as offices so they can work on the move.

Floating market on a Bangkok canal

Sugarcane

Myanmar (Burma)

When Myanmar became independent in 1948, it adopted a policy of political and economic isolation that reduced this once wealthy nation to one of the poorest on Earth. Revolts by hill peoples and a military government have kept out foreign influences.

Teak logging
In 1990, Myanmar had about 70 percent of the total world reserves of teak. Selective logging of teak using elephants is not often practiced, and today vast areas are cleared by machine. Deforestation has caused erosion, and replanting is rare.

Rubies
The rubies mined in the northeast of Myanmar are considered to be the world's finest, prized for their glowing, deep red color. Myanmar is also rich in silver, copper, jade, lead, zinc, and tin, and has extensive reserves of natural gas and oil.

Fishing
Fish served with vegetables forms an important part of the Burmese diet. Shrimps and saltwater fish are caught the off the coast. To harvest the freshwater fish that abound in the rivers, people build fishing huts on stilts over the water.

MYANMAR FACTS

CAPITAL CITY	Rangoon (Yangon)
AREA	262,200 sq miles (676,550 sq km)
POPULATION	45,600,000
MAIN LANGUAGE	Burmese
MAJOR RELIGIONS	Buddhist, Christian, Muslim
CURRENCY	Kyat

FIND OUT MORE ASIA, HISTORY OF   BUDDHISM   CONSERVATION   CRYSTALS AND GEMS   GOVERNMENTS AND POLITICS   RAIN FOREST WILDLIFE   ROCKS AND MINERALS   TRADE AND INDUSTRY   WINDS

THANKSGIVING see PILGRIM FATHERS

THEATERS

THROUGHOUT THE AGES, theaters have provided two essentials: somewhere for performers to act, and a place for an audience to watch them. A theatre may be a purpose-built environment, such as the Paris Opera House, or it may be as simple as an open-air stage. Either way, theaters provide the setting for performances of all kinds, from plays to opera, and from puppet shows to dance. Most modern theaters have a huge pool of workers including craft workers, prop-makers, set designers, scene painters, make-up artists, and costumiers, as well as the actors themselves.

Roman amphitheater

History of theaters

The earliest surviving theaters were ancient Greek amphitheaters, where audiences sat in a semicircle around a pillared stage. The Romans copied the Greek design, but from then until the Renaissance, theaters tended to be temporary wooden stages.

The rich sat in the galleries; the poor stood in the courtyard.

Theaters through the ages
During the Renaisssance, theaters were once again permanent structures, but with simple interiors. Shakespeare's theater, the Globe in London, had three enclosed galleries but retained an open-air courtyard.

Modern theaters
During the 19th century, theaters became very ornate, but they simplified in design during the 20th century. Today theaters, such as the National in London, are often built in complexes that contain stores or movie houses.

Globe Theatre, UK   National Theatre, UK

Features

In the 1800s, drama became more realistic, with elaborate scene changes. Theater structure reflected its functions. There were four main features in every theater: stage, backstage, front of house, and auditorium.

Lighting grid

Central dome is supported by iron girders.

Auditorium has five tiers and seats 2,000 people.

Backstage area contains the "green room," where performers wait for their cue.

Stage and orchestra pit
The Paris Opera House (built 1862–75) covers 3 acres (1.2 hectares) and was designed by Charles Garnier. The stage is 175 ft (53 m) wide and 85 ft (26 m) deep. It slopes upward toward the back to let the audience see the action more clearly. The orchestra pit, where the musicians play, is located beneath the front of the stage.

Grand foyer features a mosaic ceiling.

Garnier Opera House, Paris, France

Fly tower, with pulley system, hoists heavy pieces of scenery.

Below-stage scenery storage

Stage at the Paris Opera House can hold up to 400 people.

Grand staircase

Lobby
The audience enters through an area known as the lobby. It provides a space for people to meet before going into the performance, and also houses the box office, where tickets are sold. The lobby of the Paris Opera House is one of the world's grandest. It includes a staircase (needed in theaters because seating is on different levels) and balconies, where 19th-century society's opera-goers could be seen arriving, as was the fashion.

Grand staircase, Paris Opera House, France

Auditorium
The auditorium, such as that at London's Theatre Royal Haymarket, contains seating on different levels: stalls, tiered "circles" of seats, and private boxes. The stalls have the best view of the stage; they and the private boxes contain the most expensive seats. The dress circle above the stalls, and the upper circle above that, have cheaper seats. The upper circle (sometimes known as "the gods") has the poorest view.

Theatre Royal, Haymarket, London, UK

Production

Many people are involved in the production of a play – director, actors, designers, makeup, stage managers, lighting, and sound engineers. Rehearsals (meetings held to work out the production) may run over weeks and end in a full dress rehearsal before the play is performed.

Bill Alexander, theater director

Director

The director interprets the play and "directs" the action. He or she works with the actors to decide how they should play the characters and speak the lines. The actors read through the script and learn the words. They write notes on their copies concerning movements, cues, and props.

Props

Articles used on stage that are not costume or scenery are known as properties, or "props". Props are numerous and are the responsibility of the stage manager, who manages them between performances and makes sure they are left out – often on tables – backstage, where the performers can find them quickly when they are needed.

Audiences cannot see wear and tear.

Papier-mâché crown

Original 1920s' telephone

Simple fastening

Plastic jam

Iron ball and chain

Jam dish

Makeup

Under bright theater lights, unmade-up faces look pale and flat. Makeup is therefore an essential part of theater. It defines the performers' facial features, and brings characters to life.

Transformation

Theatrical makeup can be used to change the appearance of a face, for example, making actors look older than they really are. Another use of makeup is to produce an obviously unrealistic effect, such as the white face traditionally worn by clowns.

Black and white makeup and red-rimmed eyes give the actor a haggard look.

A stick-on gray beard immediately makes the actor appear older.

Final touches ensure that the makeup stays on under the hot lights.

Lighting

Direct lighting creates dramatic shadows and builds atmosphere; spotlights pick out individuals. Multiple lighting produces a "natural" effect and allows parts of the stage to be dimmed or lit more brightly if necessary. There are special technical rehearsals for lighting.

Spotlight highlights individual performers.

Bank of lights

Production of *Jesus Christ, Superstar*

Kabuki

Kabuki is a traditional theatrical form in Japan. In Kabuki, the all-male cast wears makeup according to 17th-century rules that have remained virtually unchanged. Each character has a distinctive masklike makeup the audience identifies.

Kabuki actor, Uzaemo Ichimura

Orson Welles

The American actor, director, and filmmaker Orson Welles (1915–85) is best known for his classic film *Citizen Kane* (1941). It was his theater career that established him as a leading director of his day. One of his first productions was a version of *Macbeth* (1936) that used an entirely black cast – the first time this was ever done.

Ruff, a 16th-century fashion

Velvet hat

Hat with feathers

Bright colors

Braiding

Leather shoes

Elizabethan man's costume

Original handmade shoes

1940s' women's costume

Costumes and sets

Most theater productions need historical costumes and stage sets. Theaters usually employ a person in wardrobe. He or she takes care of the costumes and helps the performers change between scenes.

Stage model, *Dream King*

Set designers

Set designers design and create the stage set. First they construct a model. When this is approved, they work with scene painters and carpen to build the set.

FIND OUT MORE

DRAMA   ELIZABETH I   FILM   GREECE, ANCIENT   JAPAN, HISTORY OF   OPERA   RENAISSANCE   ROMAN EMPIRE   SHAKESPEARE, WILLIAM

TIME

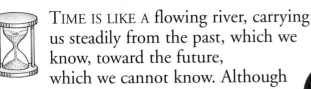

TIME IS LIKE A flowing river, carrying us steadily from the past, which we know, toward the future, which we cannot know. Although we are unable to control time, we can record its passing using measuring devices such as clocks and watches, and calendars that help us organize and plan our lives. However, time is not constant, and in certain situations it can slow down. Some scientists think that time may even come to a stop inside black holes in deepest space.

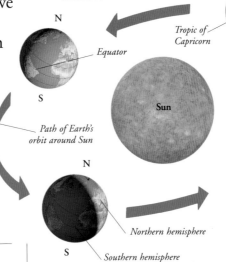

Day
One full day is the time it takes for the Earth to spin once on its axis. Each day contains 24 hours, each hour is made up of 60 minutes, and each minute contains 60 seconds.

Equator

Tropic of Capricorn

Tropic of Cancer

Sun

Path of Earth's orbit around Sun

Northern hemisphere

Southern hemisphere

Earth's axis

Year
A year is 365 days long. This is based on the time it takes for the Earth to orbit the Sun, which is 365 $\frac{1}{4}$ days. The $\frac{1}{4}$ day is impractical, so every four years – except 2000 and other century years – the $\frac{1}{4}$ days are added together to make up one extra day, giving a "leap" year of 366 days.

Seasons
The phases of weather we call seasons are caused by the fact that the Earth's axis is not at right angles to the Sun, but tilts at an angle of 23.5°. This means that, as the Earth travels around the Sun, each hemisphere leans first toward the Sun, giving longer, warmer days, and then away from it, giving shorter, colder days.

Time in modern physics

Scientists had to revise their ideas about the nature of time when the German physicist Albert Einstein (1879–1955) published his theories of relativity. The theories showed that time slows down for objects traveling close to the speed of light. Research has shown that this is true even for slower-moving objects: astronauts who spend a year in orbit age by one-hundredth of a second less than people on Earth.

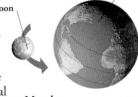

Astronauts in space

Time on Earth

The passage of time on Earth is measured in terms of the motion of the Earth and the Moon. The rotating Earth turns us toward the Sun, giving day, and then away from the Sun, giving night. Day and night are of equal length during the equinoxes – the two occasions in the year when the Sun is directly overhead at the equator. At the two solstices, when the Sun is directly overhead at one of the tropics, one hemisphere has its longest day, while the other has its longest night.

Moon

Earth

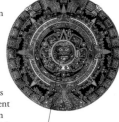

Months
There are 12 months in a year. Months last between 28 and 31 days. They were originally based on the time it takes for the Moon to go through all its phases as it orbits the Earth, which is 29½ days

Glass shatters into tiny fragments.

Time's arrow
How can we be sure that time does not go backward? The proof lies in the increasing disorder of the Universe. For example, when a glass smashes, its orderly arrangement breaks into disordered fragments. Broken glass never reassembles itself, proving that time can move only forward, from the present to the future.

Each month is named after an animal.

Calendars
The Western world uses the 365-day Gregorian calendar. This is based on the Earth's orbit of the Sun, so the Sun appears in the same place in the sky on the same date each year. Many other calendars have been devised throughout history. The traditional Hindu, Chinese, Muslim, and Jewish calendars are based on the Moon's cycles. The Chinese calendar has 12 months and is 354 days long. The ancient Aztec calendar was solar, like the Gregorian calendar, but consisted of 18 months of 20 days, and five extra days that were considered unlucky.

Chinese calendar

Aztec calendar

At the center of the calendar is the Aztec sun god.

Time and speed

To understand how fast an object moves, we need to know how far it travels and how long it takes to travel that distance. The graph below shows the relationship between distance and time for a car journey: the steeper the graph's slope, the faster the car is moving.

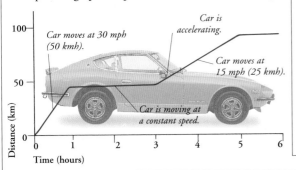

Car is accelerating.

Car moves at 30 mph (50 kmh).

Car moves at 15 mph (25 kmh).

Car is moving at a constant speed.

Distance (km)

100

50

0

Time (hours)
0 1 2 3 4 5 6

Time zones

To make it easier to set clocks, the world is divided into 24 regions called time zones, each of which is about 15° of longitude wide. These time zones ensure that wherever you are in the world, the Sun is directly overhead at 12 noon. The map shows what time it is around the world when it is 12 noon at Greenwich, England.

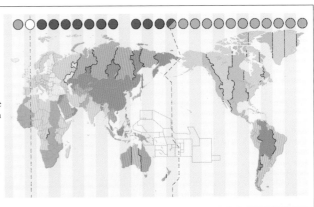

Early time measurement

To tell the time, ancient peoples used the changing shadows cast by the Sun as it moved across the sky during the day, and the movement of stars at night. Later, timekeeping devices such as sundials, hourglasses, clock candles, and star dials were developed. The invention of mechanical clocks made these methods redundant.

Sundials
As the day progressed, a shadow cast by the Sun moved slowly around a dial marked with hours.

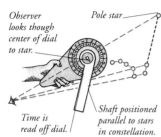

Observer looks though center of dial to star.
Pole star
Time is read off dial.
Shaft positioned parallel to stars in constellation.

Clock candle
A candle ringed with notches recorded the passing of the hours as it burned down.

Star dial
A device called a star dial was used to find the time from the position of familiar stars and constellations in the night sky.

Hourglass
Sand flowed from the top of the glass to the bottom in a fixed amount of time.

Quartz watch

Most modern clocks and watches are controlled by a thin slice of quartz crystal. Electricity supplied by a small battery makes the crystal vibrate and give out pulses of current at a precise rate, or frequency. A microchip then reduces this rate to one pulse per second. This control signal goes to an electric motor that turns the hands or changes the numbers on the digital display. Most quartz clocks and watches are accurate to within about 15 seconds per year.

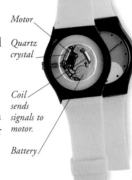

Motor
Quartz crystal
Coil sends signals to motor.
Battery

Quartz watch

Atomic clock
The most accurate of all clocks are atomic clocks because they lose or gain just one second every 300,000 years. Atomic clocks measure time by recording the natural vibrations of atoms, usually of the element cesium. The second – the basic scientific unit of time – is defined as the time it takes a cesium atom to vibrate 9,192,770 times.

Clock weighs about 66 lb (30 kg).
Cesium clock

Mechanical clocks and watches

Early all-mechanical clocks were made in European monasteries and cathedrals in the 13th century. They were powered by falling weights linked to a mechanism called an escapement. Clocks became more accurate when pendulums were used to regulate the escapement. The invention of the mainspring made smaller clocks possible and led to the development of the watch. Early watches were worn around the neck on a chain. Later designs were small enough to fit into a pocket or be worn around the wrist on a strap.

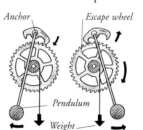

Anchor
Escape wheel
Pendulum
Weight

Escapement
Many pendulum clocks are driven by a falling weight linked to an escape wheel. As the pendulum swings, it rocks a lever called the anchor, causing it to grip and release the escape wheel with a regular motion. One tooth of the wheel escapes with each swing, moving the clock's hands.

Hour hand
Hours in Roman numerals
Minute hand

Clock face
There are twelve hours marked on a clock face, so the hour hand moves around the clock face twice each day. The minute hand revolves once every hour. Many clocks also have a second hand that circles the clock face once every minute.

Falling weight drives the clock mechanism.
This weight acts as a counterbalance.

Each back-and-forth swing is called a period.

Pendulum
A pendulum is a weight that swings back and forth on a fixed string, rod, or wire. Each back-and-forth movement takes the same amount of time, and it is this regular motion that makes it useful for timekeeping. In a clock, a pendulum controls the escapement.

Mainspring
In the 16th century, springs began to replace falling weights as the energy source for clocks. The energy stored by winding the spring up with a key is then slowly released by the escapement to drive the hands.

Twenty-four-hour clock
Timetables give arrival and departure times using the twenty-four-hour clock. In this system, midnight is 0000 and noon is 1200. Times after noon are given as numbers greater than 1200. For example, 4:00 p.m. is 1600.

14.29	Kölner Rheintzug	FRANKFURT
14.28	Köln Bonn Mainz	STUTTGART
14.30	Dortmund Köln	HANNOVER
14.31	Köln Bonn Mainz	MÜNCHEN
14.33	Haan	KÖLN
14.36	Köln Dortmund	KIEL
14.37	D-Zug Köln	DÜREN
14.39	Wuppertal Rheintal	HAGEN
14.44		METTMANN
14.50	Leverkusen Köln	KÖLN
14.51	Leverkusen Mülheim	DORTMUND

Christiaan Huygens

The Dutch physicist Christiaan Huygens (1629–95) built the first practical pendulum clock in 1657. Huygens also found the mathematical rule that links the duration of a pendulum's swing to its length: the longer the pendulum, the longer its swing. Huygens gave the first accurate description of Saturn's rings and was the first to suggest that light travels as waves.

Timeline

c.2600 BC The Chinese develop a primitive form of sundial.

c.1400 BC The Egyptians use water clocks, which measure time by the flow of water through a vessel with a hole in it.

Chinese water clock

c.890 Clock candles appear in England.

c.1300 Mechanical clocks are built in Italian and English monasteries.

1581 Italian scientist Galileo Galilei observes the regularity of a pendulum's swing.

Pendulum clock designed by Galileo

1657 Huygens builds the first pendulum clock.

1759 Englishman John Harrison makes a marine timekeeper, or chronometer, that has less than one minute of error after five months at sea.

Harrison's chronometer

1884 The time at Greenwich, London, UK, is adopted as the standard time for the whole world.

1905 Einstein's Special Theory of Relativity gives a new understanding of the concept of time.

1929 Warren Morrison, an American, invents the quartz clock.

1948 The atomic clock is developed in the US.

1965 US physicists Arno Penzias and Robert Wilson provide evidence that time began with the Big Bang.

FIND OUT MORE | ATOMS AND MOLECULES | AZTECS | BLACK HOLES | CHINA, HISTORY OF | CRYSTALS AND GEMS | EINSTEIN, ALBERT | GALILEO GALILEI | FORCE AND MOTION | PHYSICS | SUN AND SOLAR SYSTEM

Time

Early timepieces

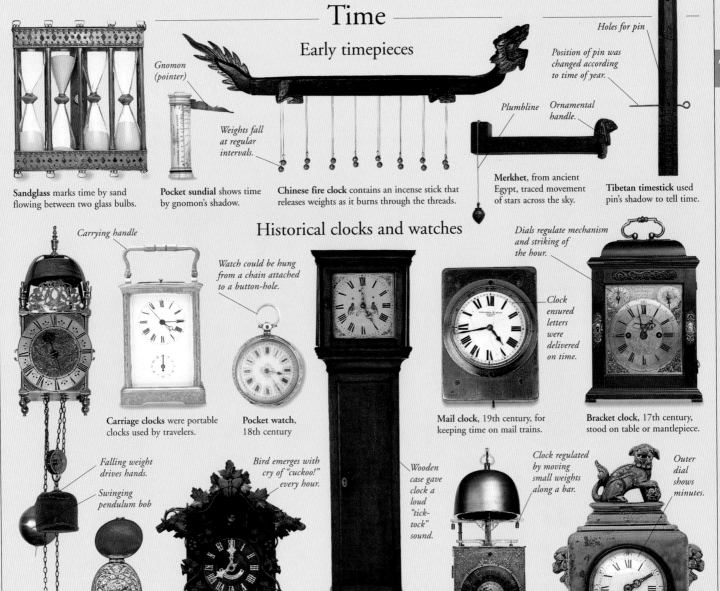

Sandglass marks time by sand flowing between two glass bulbs.

Gnomon (pointer)

Weights fall at regular intervals.

Pocket sundial shows time by gnomon's shadow.

Chinese fire clock contains an incense stick that releases weights as it burns through the threads.

Plumbline

Ornamental handle.

Merkhet, from ancient Egypt, traced movement of stars across the sky.

Holes for pin

Position of pin was changed according to time of year.

Tibetan timestick used pin's shadow to tell time.

Historical clocks and watches

Carrying handle

Watch could be hung from a chain attached to a button-hole.

Dials regulate mechanism and striking of the hour.

Clock ensured letters were delivered on time.

Carriage clocks were portable clocks used by travelers.

Pocket watch, 18th century

Mail clock, 19th century, for keeping time on mail trains.

Bracket clock, 17th century, stood on table or mantlepiece.

Falling weight drives hands.

Swinging pendulum bob

Bird emerges with cry of "cuckoo!" every hour.

Wooden case gave clock a loud "tick-tock" sound.

Clock regulated by moving small weights along a bar.

Outer dial shows minutes.

Verge watch, driven by a coiled spring

Pendulum clocks were controlled by the swing of a suspended weight.

Cuckoo clocks were invented in Germany around 1730.

Grandfather clocks housed pendulum in a long case.

Lantern clocks were named after their lanternlike shape.

Japanese ornamental clock, made out of the gemstone turquoise.

Modern clocks and watches

Braille watch used by people who are blind or partially sighted.

Start/stop control

Dial shows diver's time under the water.

Friendly panda

Talking watch speaks the time to the wearer.

Second hand

Rubber strap

Display shows time as digits.

Upside-down face

Stopwatch can measure time in fractions of a second.

Mechanical alarm clock rings bells at preset time.

Waterproof watch for use by divers

Child's clock has large hands and clear numbers.

Digital alarm clock controlled by a tiny quartz crystal

Nurse's watch hangs from nurse's uniform.

TRADE AND INDUSTRY

ANY SORT OF ACTIVITY that is done to create wealth is known as industry. The term also describes a group of businesses that produce a similar service or provide a similar product. Trade is the process of buying and selling such products. The thousands of different industries do many things, such as mining, advertising, construction, farming, and broadcasting. Many industries change raw materials into products. Others provide services, from haircuts to health care.

Coal is an important fuel in industry; most of the world's supply is mined in Asia.

Primary industry
Coal, oil, stone, grain crops, and timber are among the products of primary industry, which is concerned with extracting raw materials from the Earth. Such products may be used just as they are, or processed by the manufacturing industries into something else.

Types of industry

When most people talk about industry, they are thinking of the factories and assembly lines involved in manufacturing. In fact, there are three basic types of industry: primary, manufacturing, and service industries. In the developing countries, most people work in primary industry. Any country where most people work in the manufacturing and service industries is known as an industrialized nation.

Car manufacture

Manufacturing
The manufacturing, or secondary, industries make products either from raw materials or from other manufactured goods. Much modern manufacturing is heavily automated: machines carry out the heavy, repetitive tasks.

Service
The service, or tertiary, industries do not produce anything, but offer a service, such as banking. In some highly industrialized countries, more people work in service industries than in either of the other industries.

Service industries include restaurants, shops, and tourist businesses.

Restaurant in Paris

What industry needs

In order for an industry to produce anything, it must have certain basic assets: money, machinery, labor, and raw materials. The aim of any industry is to make a profit. If the basic assets are abundant and inexpensive, then the industry produces a more profitable product or service. An industry also needs a market: if nobody wants to buy a product, the money and effort spent in making it is wasted.

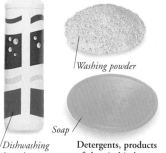

Washing powder

Soap

Dishwashing liquid

Detergents, products of chemical industry

Violin maker

Cottage industry
Cottage industry is where workers produce goods on a small scale, generally in the home or a small workshop. The workers may sell the goods themselves, or to an employer who pays per finished piece. The system may be abused by unscrupulous employers who pay low wages for long hours.

Energy and materials
Both the primary and manufacturing industries must have materials to work with, and fuels and energy to power machines. In some countries, large industrialized regions, such as the Ruhr in Germany, develop near areas of raw materials, such as coal or iron.

Coal mines

Oil

Timber

Steel

Raw materials and fuels

The service industries depend most heavily on labor.

Stages in production
In the manufacturing industry, most products go through basic stages before they can be sold to the public. Once the product is designed, the design is checked to ensure that the product works and is affordable. The product is made from raw materials; finally, it is tested, to make sure there are no faults.

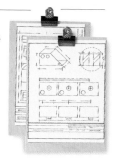

Product designs

Factory premises

Capital
Capital means money, which industries need to buy machinery, pay staff, and build or rent a factory or other premises. It also means the equipment that will help to manufacture a product over a period of time. Machines are regarded as capital, but the raw materials from which products are made are not.

Factory

Labor
Many industries are set up close to cities, so they can have a ready supply of workers, or labor. The labor supply must include management, accountants, and research and development staff among others, plus bluecollar workers.

Communications
Good communications are vital for the growth of industry. Efficient road systems, railroads, air and sea routes, and global telecommunications allow some industries to make their goods in parts of the world where property prices and wages are lower.

T

Trade

The process of exchanging the goods or services produced by industry is known as trade. It is a vital part of modern life. Even the richest nations do not have the resources to produce everything their people need or want; by trading surplus goods with others, countries earn the money to buy the things they need. Trade between different countries is called foreign trade. So-called domestic trade takes place within the boundaries of a country.

Market traders, 15th century

History of trade
Trade has an ancient history. From about 3000 BC, the Phoenicians traded metals, cloth, and animals with Mediterranean peoples. From 300 BC, traders traveled the Silk Road from China to Europe, a famous early trade route. Trade between different peoples led to the exchange of ideas and culture, as well as goods. Trade between different countries grew steadily from medieval times on, when merchants traveled the globe with goods.

Distribution

The movement of goods or services from the manufacturer to the consumer (the person who wants to buy them) is known as distribution. Distribution between producer, wholesaler, and retailer relies on efficient, economical transportation systems. Foreign trade has grown steadily, in part thanks to advances in transportation – for example, the arrival of the railroads, air freight, and refrigerated cargo ships.

Refrigerated warehouse

Wholesalers
Many small shops rely on wholesalers to deliver products to them when needed. A wholesaler is a business that buys large quantities of goods directly from the manufacturers. It stores them in huge warehouses, ready to sell in smaller amounts at higher prices to retail outlets, or stores. Warehouses are found near major roads or railroads, to ensure rapid, economical transport of the products.

Retailers
Retailers are businesses that buy products from wholesalers and sell them at a higher price. Most stores are part of the retail trade – outlets where consumers can buy the goods they want. As such, stores are the end of a long chain of trading.

Buying jeans from a store

Imports and exports

The goods or services one country buys from another are called imports; the goods a country sells to others are called exports. To earn the money to pay for imports, a country must export its own produce.

Imports   Exports
Goods coming in   *Goods going out*

Balance of payments
The payments a country makes to others for imported goods, and the payments it receives from other countries for exports within the same period of time, are together known as the balance of payments. If a country does not export enough goods, it must borrow money to pay for imports.

Tariffs and customs

Some countries tax imported goods. This tax is known as a customs duty, or tariff. Such duties are a way of making money for the government, or of protecting the country's industries by raising the price of imported goods, which might otherwise be cheaper than those produced locally.

World trade
International trade is regulated by the World Trade Organization, set up in 1995. It works to reduce trade barriers and tariffs between nations. It succeeded the General Agreement on Tariffs and Trade (GATT), set up in 1948 under the auspices of the United Nations.

World Trade Organization building

Factory chimneys

Industrial pollution

Industry provides us with clothing, food, shelter, labor-saving devices, and medicines. But it has harmful side effects. Many industrial processes cause pollution in the form of smoke from factories and waste products dumped in the sea, rivers, and lakes. The rapid growth of industry threatens to exhaust the world's supplies of oil and natural gas.

Werner von Siemens

German engineer Werner von Siemens (1816–92) helped the growth of the communications industry, by his improvements to the telegraph. The electrical manufacturer AG Siemens, which trades in more than 125 countries, evolved from a company originally established by the Siemens family.

Timeline

c.3000 BC Phoenicians trade with other countries around the Mediterranean.

c.1500 Commercial Revolution begins; merchants start trading around the globe.

Newcomen's engine

1705 English inventor Thomas Newcomen (1663–1729) builds a simple steam engine that contributes to the 18th-century Industrial Revolution in Great Britain.

1871 Trade Union Act makes trade unions legal in Britain.

1913 US industrialist Henry Ford (1863–1947) introduces assembly-line procedures to produce his Model-T cars, stimulating mass-production.

20th century Transport and communications developments spur growth of foreign trade.

Model-T

1968 The European Economic Community (EEC) abandons trade tariffs between member nations, establishing a "Common Market."

1990s US, Japan, and European nations are the world's major traders.

FIND OUT MORE   ADVERTISING AND MARKETING   FARMING   FISHING INDUSTRY   INDUSTRIAL REVOLUTION   MONEY   PORTS AND WATERWAYS   SHOPS   TRANSPORTATION, HISTORY OF   UNIONS, TRADE

TRAINS AND RAILROADS

WHEN YOU SEE a sleek express train whizzing by, you may find it hard to believe that the first railroads were iron tracks with wooden wagons pulled by horses. The first steam railroads were opened in the 1820s, allowing people and goods to travel at undreamed-of speeds. The new form of transport spread rapidly across the world. Today's trains are a very efficient method of transportation – they use less fuel and produce less pollution than cars and trucks, and carry much larger freight. Many people believe trains are the best form of transport for the future.

Early trains

Wheels are driven by steam-powered pistons

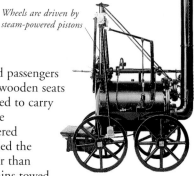

The first train provided passengers with a bumpy ride on wooden seats in open wagons designed to carry coal. At the front of the train was a steam-powered locomotive, which pulled the wagons not much faster than walking pace. Some trains towed wagons onto which the passengers attached their own carriages.

"Catch Me Who Can," built in 1808

Modern trains

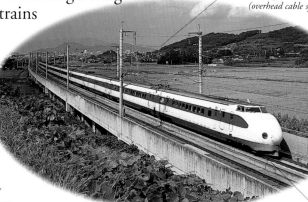
Electric locomotive gets its electricity via a catenary (overhead cable system).

Bullet trains first ran in 1965.

Electricity and engines powered by diesel make modern trains move. In an electric locomotive, electric motors turn the wheels. The electricity comes from the track or from overhead cables. In a diesel-electric locomotive, a powerful diesel engine turns an electric generator. This creates electricity, which in turn drives electric motors. Modern trains give a smooth, comfortable ride and are air-conditioned. They have automatic locking doors for the safety of their passengers.

Bullet train

Japanese Shinkansen, or "bullet" trains, travel along specially built high-speed tracks. They average speeds up to 140 mph (225 kmh). Other countries have also opened new lines designed for high-speed electric trains, including France, where the TGV train holds the world speed record of more than 310 mph (500 kmh).

Tracks

Overhead cables for electric locomotives

Gantries support cables and signals.

Points are intersections in the rails that move trains onto a new section of track.

Railroad tracks have two parallel steel rails supported on wood or concrete sleepers that spread the weight of passing trains into the ground. Rails are often welded into a continuous track to allow trains to run smoothly. Points direct trains left or right on to diverging tracks. Most railroads have different tracks for opposite directions.

Signals keep trains a safe distance apart.

George Stephenson

British railroad engineer George Stephenson (1781–1848) established his locomotive works in 1823 and built the very first public railroad, from Stockton to Darlington, England, in 1825. He also built many steam locomotives, working with his son Robert.

Streetcars

Many cities, especially in Europe, have a streetcar system. Streetcars run on railway tracks laid in the streets. They are usually powered by electricity from overhead wires.

Types of trains

A train consists of locomotives and rolling stock (passenger and freight cars). Commuter trains and local trains, which make many stops and starts, often have combined locomotives and passenger cars, called multiple units. Sleeper trains travel long distances and have bunk beds for passengers.

Passenger express

Express trains usually have a separate locomotive at the front. The rolling stock often includes a buffet car for snacks and drinks and a dining car, as well as normal carriages with seats. Some high-speed trains have a locomotive at each end.

Freight train

A long freight train can have hundreds of freight cars, and sometimes more than one locomotive. Some are designed to hold specific cargos, such as oil tankers.

Hong Kong streetcars

Double-decker streetcars have been running through the streets of Hong Kong for many decades. They provide a clean form of transport that is needed in a crowded city. Streetcars were taken out of some cities in the mid-20th century, but efficient new systems are now being built in their place.

FIND OUT MORE | CARS AND TRUCKS | ENERGY | ENGINES AND MOTORS | FORCE AND MOTION | INDUSTRIAL REVOLUTION | TRANSPORT, HISTORY OF | TRAVEL

TRANSPORT, HISTORY OF

FROM SIMPLE, PREHISTORIC rafts to the arrival of supersonic passenger flight, transportation has a long history. For centuries, the only way to move around on land was to walk or to use animals as beasts of burden. The invention of the wheel around 3500 BC, and the ensuing development of wheeled vehicles, revolutionized transportation. Also important was the arrival of powered vehicles, with the development of steam engines in the 18th century, and the internal-combustion engine in the late 19th century.

Cast-iron spokes with wooden rim

Wire spoked wheel

Strong and light metal alloy wheel

Wheels
The most important invention in transportation history was the wheel. Draft animals could pull wheeled vehicles with heavy loads for longer than they could drag or carry the same load. Wheels were solid wood until spokes were developed in about 2000 BC. Tires were originally made from iron. Pneumatic tires, filled with air and made of rubber to cushion the ride, appeared in the 1890s.

Carts and carriages
People traveled on early roads in two-wheeled carts and four-wheeled wagons or carriages. These were pulled by horses or oxen. "Horseless carriages" – carriages powered by steam engines – were first made in the 18th century.

Road transportation
Roads began as footpaths that often meandered around the contours of the countryside. Then 2,000 years ago, Roman engineers built a vast network of straight roads that allowed people, goods, and troops to move quickly across their empire. Few new roads were built until the 18th century, when they were needed for mail coaches. In the 20th century, roads carrying several lanes of traffic crisscrossed the landscape as car ownership became widespread.

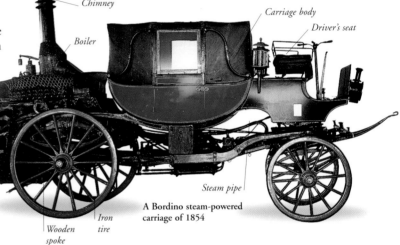

Chimney

Boiler

Carriage body

Driver's seat

Steam pipe

Wooden spoke

Iron tire

A Bordino steam-powered carriage of 1854

Cars

Experimental automobiles were built soon after the invention of the internal combustion engine, compact enough to be carried around, in 1876. In 1886, the first practical car was demonstrated to the public. Today the car is the most common form of transportation in many countries.

The Toyota 2000GT, Japan; launched 1966; top speed 128 mph (206 kmh); a classic small sports car.

Trucks
The first trucks appeared in the 1890s. Powered by steam engines, they began to replace heavy, horse-drawn carts for road haulage. Most modern trucks have powerful diesel engines. There are many specialized trucks for carrying different types of cargo, such as cars, liquids, or refrigerated foods.

Modern articulated truck

Kiichiro Toyoda

Japanese engineer Kiichiro Toyoda (1894–1952), established the Toyota Motor Corporation in 1937. He devoted much of his life to producing affordable automobiles, and to building up a vast manufacturing company.

Rail transportation
An important development in transportation history came in 1804, when the first steam locomotive was built to run on rails. Passenger railroads opened in the 1820s – the first fast form of land travel. Steam power lasted until the mid-20th century, when it was replaced by electric motors or diesel engines.

Modern trains
Electric current to power trains comes from the tracks or overhead cables. High-speed, long-distance trains are sleek and give a smooth, comfortable ride in air-conditioned cars: an example is the Eurostar, which travels from London, England to Paris, France in a few hours. Local commuter trains carry thousands of people into and out of towns and cities every day.

Bicycles
The first type of bicycle was the Draisine of 1817. It had no pedals, but was pushed along by the rider's feet. Pedals attached to the front wheel appeared in 1839 and were improved upon in 1865. The modern-style bicycle, where the pedals drive the back wheel with a chain, was developed in the 1880s. Bicycles are a popular form of transportation, but in many countries they are now used mainly for leisure. In some parts of the world, such as China, most people still travel by bike.

Early trains
Passengers on early trains traveled in uncomfortable open wagons pulled by slow, puffing steam locomotives. Steam engines gradually got more powerful and rolling stock more comfortable. By the end of the 19th century, steam locomotives were pulling express trains at more than 93 mph (150 kmh).

An electric-powered Eurostar express train waiting to leave its London terminus

Modern mountain bike

Water transportation

Traveling on water is one of the oldest forms of transportation. The earliest craft were simple rafts made of logs lashed together. In the ancient civilizations of Egypt and Mesopotamia, people built boats from bundled reeds to travel up- and downriver. They also built wooden seagoing ships and used them for trading. Until the advent of the railways in the 1800s, boats and ships were the only way of transporting heavy goods over long distances. Today there are various types of boats and ships made from many materials, from bark and animal skins to plastic, fiberglass, iron, and steel.

Wooden masts support sails

Cloth sails stiffened with thin wooden spars

Queen Elizabeth II ocean liner

Sail

The first sailing ships, built in about 3500 BC, had simple square sails. They were well suited for sailing with the wind behind, but oars were needed to go against the wind. From the 1600s, ships had both square and triangular sails. The triangular sail, or lateen, could be used for tacking – sailing in a zigzag pattern to make headway into the wind. The sailing ship ushered in an age of worldwide exploration and trade.

Steam and iron

In the 1800s, steam power began to replace sail. This freed ships from relying on the wind. At the same time, shipbuilders began to use huge plates of iron riveted together to construct hulls. This allowed them to build much bigger ships than was possible with wood. Huge luxurious passenger liners were built, which rivaled the best hotels on land.

Ferdinand de Lesseps

French entrepeneur Ferdinand de Lesseps (1805–94) was a great canal builder. His major achievement was the Suez Canal, opened in 1869, to link the Mediterranean and Red Seas.

Traditional bargeware is still to be seen on today's pleasure barges.

Chinese junk with lateen sails

Decorated bargeware used on canal boats in the 19th century

Hull of wooden planking

Canals

Before the development of trains and trucks, heavy goods were transported from place to place via networks of specially built waterways, called canals. Cargo was carried by flat-bottomed boats, called barges. Some shipping canals, such as Suez and Panama, were built to shorten sea routes by cutting across narrow strips of land. Today, though barges are still used for transporting goods, they are also popular for leisure trips.

Sternpost rudder for steering

Air transportation

The first powered airplane flight was made in 1903. Airmail and passenger services began after World War I. Air travel has since developed into a form of transportation for passengers and goods.

Passenger travel

The first airliners were converted World War I bombers. Long-distance air travel really took off in the 1920s and 1930s with the development of all-metal airliners and huge flying boats driven by piston engines. Jet-powered airliners, such as the Boeing 707, were put into service in the 1950s, making air travel faster, quieter, and cheaper. The introduction of the wide-bodied jet in 1970 makes international jet travel commonplace.

Balloons and airships

The first manned flight was made in a hot-air balloon; but balloons are blown by the wind, and cannot be steered. By the 1920s, airships powered by engines carried passengers across the Atlantic. Filled with hydrogen, they were at terrible risk from fire.

Helicopters

Developed by many aircraft engineers through the 20th century, helicopters were first produced in large numbers in the 1940s. Unlike most other aircraft, they do not need a runway for takeoff and landing, and can hover over the same spot. This makes them invaluable for fast transportation to inaccessible places, and for rescue, police, and military work.

The helicopter's rotors are powered by a turboshaft jet engine.

Timeline

1804 Richard Trevithick builds first steam-powered railroad locomotive.

1825 Stockton to Darlington Railway in England is the first public railroad to start operations.

The Ordinary bicycle, nicknamed the "penny farthing"

1874 In Britain, the Ordinary bicycle is invented. It has a massive front wheel, to make it as fast as possible, and a small rear wheel for balance.

1838 The steamship *Great Western* begins a regular transatlantic passenger service.

1886 In Germany, the first gas-powered car – a three-wheeled vehicle – makes its first public run.

Henry Ford's Model-T

1903 In the US, the Wright brothers make the first successful airplane flight in their *Flyer*.

1908 Introduction of the Model-T Ford, the first small economy car to be mass-produced.

1952 Jet-powered passenger services begin in the De Havilland Comet operated by British airline BOAC.

FIND OUT MORE   AIRCRAFT   AIRSHIPS AND BALLOONS   BICYCLES AND MOTORCYCLES   CARS AND TRUCKS   EXPLORATION   FLIGHT, HISTORY OF   PORTS AND WATERWAYS   SHIPS AND BOATS   TRAINS AND RAILROADS

TRAVEL

PEOPLE HAVE BEEN on the move since prehistoric times: initially to find food or land, and then for trade, exploration, and pleasure. Some have traveled great distances to escape danger or oppression. However, it is only since the 19th century, with the development of more efficient transportation, that mass travel has become widely available. In 1990, there were 425 million tourists worldwide.

Early travel
The ancient Romans visited thermal spas for their health, medieval pilgrims traveled great distances to reach religious shrines, and in 18th-century Europe young aristocrats made the "Grand Tour," visiting sites of classical antiquity. Travel at the time was a grueling experience. People covered vast distances on foot, often across lonely, wild landscapes, and were vulnerable to attacks from bandits and wild animals. Only the rich could afford to travel in comfort.

Thermal bath, England

Tourism

Tourism has become the world's biggest industry as more and more people travel away from home for short periods of time. Although most people go to see family and friends, or to explore a new country, others take short breaks to health spas, or to take part in study tours. People also travel to attend business meetings.

Beach vacations
In 18th-century England, trips to the beach were a pastime taken up by the wealthy. By the 1840s better social conditions made beach vacations affordable to the working class, who flocked to the seaside by train. Today, Europeans and North Americans take the most vacations to beach resorts around the world.

Travel agents
The first travel agency opened in the 1850s. Since then, a large industry has developed devoted to organizing tours, booking tickets and hotels, and insuring vacationers.

Thomas Cook
An English preacher, Thomas Cook (1808–1892) started a career in tourism in 1841, when he set up a train service for a party of missionaries. By 1855, he was organizing trips to the Paris Exposition, running the "Grand Tour" of Europe, and establishing the world's first travel agency.

Migration

Over the centuries people have been leaving their country of origin, searching for a better life, escaping famine, warfare, or hardship. Between 1892 and 1954, the United States saw the greatest wave of migration ever, when nearly 17 million people arrived in New York before settling in other parts of the country. Other popular destinations for people seeking a new life include Australia.

Statue of Liberty welcomes new arrivals to New York

Refugees
Famine, war, and conflict have displaced millions of people, driving them from their homes. They are forced to find asylum, or refuge, in other countries, and if they fail to do so, may remain stateless. Often refugees have to leave their homes quickly and only take the personal possessions they can carry on their backs. During the 1980s, the plight of refugees was highlighted by the Vietnamese boat people who fled their country in fear of persecution.

Ecotourism
Regions that have interesting wildlife, such as Antarctica, have become holiday destinations for nature lovers, or ecotourists. Specialized travel companies provide organized tours to these remote parts of world, little seen by other tourists. However, this kind of tourism can have a terrible impact on fragile ecosystems. The 1990s has seen a move toward responsible ecotourism, protecting the rare environments on which it depends.

A knapsack can hold everything a backpacker needs, such as a sleeping bag and camping equipment.

Vacations today

Vacation packages that offer flights and hotels at bargain rates are extremely popular. Increasingly, people are looking to remote corners of the globe to find undiscovered vacation destinations, while tour operators compete to meet this demand.

Tourists visiting pyramids in Egypt

Backpacking
Many people prefer independent travel to organized tourism, especially young people traveling on a tight budget for long periods of time. Backpackers like to take very little lugguage, and they travel cheaply by using local transportation, camping, and buying food in local stores. In this way it is possible to explore remote and exotic regions that have not seen reached by other tourists.

FIND OUT MORE | AIRPORTS | CAMPING AND HIKING | ECOLOGY AND ECOSYSTEMS | EXPLORATION | SEVEN WONDERS OF THE ANCIENT WORLD | TRANSPORT, HISTORY OF | UNITED NATIONS

TREES

TREES HAVE FLOURISHED on Earth for more than 210 million years. The earliest trees were giant, woody, spore-producing plants, the ancestors of modern ferns and club mosses. Today's trees are large seed-producing plants with an upright woody stem called a trunk. Trees help balance the atmosphere, stabilize the soil and supply all kinds of other organisms with food. They also provide timber for building and fuel. There are three main groups: conifers, broad-leaved trees, and palms. Many species survive for 200 years or more – bristlecone pines can live for 4,000 years.

The top of a tree is called the crown.

How a tree grows

Each year the tree's crown grows a little taller and broader. The twigs and side shoots grow longer only from their tips. The branches and trunk become thicker as the layer of cells called the cambium divides. This process is called secondary thickening. A ring of growth called an annual ring is formed each year.

Tree trunks

Most of the tree trunk consists of wood, a very tough, durable material. Wood is strong yet so flexible that the tree trunk can support the weight of the crown and sway in the wind without snapping.

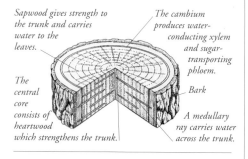

Sapwood gives strength to the trunk and carries water to the leaves.

The cambium produces water-conducting xylem and sugar-transporting phloem.

The central core consists of heartwood which strengthens the trunk.

Bark

A medullary ray carries water across the trunk.

Bark

Covering the trunk and branches is a layer of corky, waterproof bark. Beneath the bark there is a layer of living phloem. The bark helps to protect the phloem from extremes of temperature, and it also helps prevent insects and fungi from damaging the tree.

Poplar bark is cracked into vertical ridges.

River birch bark peels off the trunk in uneven flakes.

Himalayan birch peels in long, horizontal strips.

Parts of a tree

A tree consists of a trunk that supports a crown of branches, and roots that anchor the tree into the ground and absorb water and minerals from the soil. Water passes up the trunk from the roots, and sugars are carried to the roots from the leaves. The branches bear leaves, flowers, fruits, or cones.

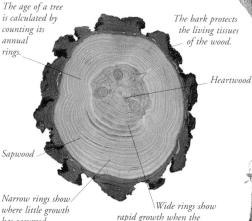

The age of a tree is calculated by counting its annual rings.

The bark protects the living tissues of the wood.

Heartwood

Sapwood

Narrow rings show where little growth has occurred.

Wide rings show rapid growth when the conditions were good.

Tallest trees

The tallest living coniferous tree in the world is the "National Geographic Society" coast redwood in North America, which has reached more than 364 ft (111 m) high. The tallest broad-leaved species of tree is the Australian mountain ash. This has been known to grow up to 370 ft (113 m) high.

Each spring, twigs, leaves, and flowers develop from buds.

As a tree grows taller, many twigs are shed, and only a few grow into branches.

Higher up the tree, the bark is often smooth and pale in color.

The bark is thicker and darker near the base of the trunk, and is cracked into ridges, called plates.

The tangled network of roots spreads out horizontally as well as down into the soil.

Profile of an oak tree

Coniferous trees

All conifers are either tall trees or woody shrubs, and they are almost all evergreen. They belong to a group of flowerless plants called gymnosperms. The seeds of conifers are not enclosed inside fruits. Instead, they develop between the woody scales of cones, or they are embedded in a fleshy cup or scale.

Cones open in warm weather to release their seeds.

Cones
Female pine cones are woody, and some are extremely hard, with sharp prickles at the tip of each scale. Male cones produce large amounts of pollen, then fall from the tree. The pollen is carried to the female cones by the wind.

Cone shapes
Cones may be round, ovoid, or cylindrical. They range in size from the 0.4 in (1 cm) cones of some cypresses to the 24 in (60 cm) long cone of the sugar pine. The heavy cones of the big cone pine tree may weigh up to 5 lb (2.27 kg).

Norway spruce cone

Douglas fir cone   Redwood cone

Pine trees
There are about 80 species of pine tree. All except one grow in the northern hemisphere. Pine trees are typical conifers. Their seeds develop inside hard pine cones. Pine leaves are narrow needles that grow in clusters and give off a pleasant, distinctive smell.

Pine tree

Needles
Pine trees have long, narrow, spiky needles that stay on the tree for at least two years. These needles are arranged in bunches of two, three, or five.

Conifers in winter
Evergreen conifers keep their needles all winter. A thick, waxy outer layer on the needles prevents frost from harming them. The branches of conifers curve downward so that snow slides easily off their crowns.

Resin
The roots, leaves, and trunk of conifers ooze sticky resins when the tree is cut or damaged. This resin helps seal the wound, keeping out harmful insects and fungal spores. Resin can be tapped and used to make turpentine.

Tree shapes
Each type of tree has a certain shape. Broad-leaved trees usually have a spreading crown, whereas conifers often have a spire shape. Palms usually have a tuft of large, feathery leaves.

Broad-leaved tree   Conifer   Palm

Broad-leaved trees

This is the largest group of living trees, with more than 10,000 different species. Broad-leaved trees have thin, flat leaves on a spreading crown of irregular branches. Many broad-leaved trees are deciduous, shedding their leaves each fall.

Each acorn sits in a little cup.

Acorns
The fruit of an oak tree is a one-seeded nut called an acorn. A large oak may produce thousands of acorns in a single season. Only a small amount germinate, and even fewer survive to grow into trees.

Oak trees
Oaks are typical broad-leaved trees. There are about 800 species. Oak wood is very hard and durable, so many types of oak tree are commercially important, providing valuable timber for building and furniture making.

Buds
Tightly folded inside each bud are the soft leaves of the next season's growth. Tough scales protect these buds and are shed as soon as the bud starts to open.

Leaves are grouped in clusters at the tips of the twigs.

Leaves
Broad, flat leaves have a large surface area that makes them efficient at producing food for the tree. They are also easily damaged by wind and insects because they are thin. To deter insects, these leaves often contain unpleasant tasting substances, such as the bitter tannins in oaks.

Oak tree

How trees lose their leaves

1 Chlorophyll in the leaf starts to break down, and the tree reabsorbs nutrients.

2 Waste products enter the dying leaf, which provides a useful disposal system for the tree.

3 These chemical changes make the leaf change color, creating the brilliant reds and golds of fall.

4 Before a leaf is shed, a corky layer forms across the base of the leaf stalk. The leaf snaps off at this point, leaving a scar.

Leaf scar

Bud

Palm trees
Most palm trees grow in tropical or sub-tropical regions. Many have a tall, woody trunk without branches. The large leaves, called fronds, grow in a fanlike tuft on the upper part of the trunk.

The sago palm tree has a seed that is enclosed in a corky fruit covered with overlapping scales.

FIND OUT MORE   FORESTS   FRUITS AND SEEDS   FURNITURE   PHOTOSYNTHESIS   PLANTS   PLANTS, ANATOMY   PLANT USES   RAIN FOREST WILDLIFE   WOODLAND WILDLIFE

Trees
Conifers

Male cone

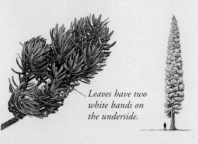
Leaves have two white bands on the underside.

Cone consists of six overlappping scales.

Scalelike leaves

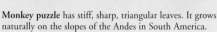

Monkey puzzle has stiff, sharp, triangular leaves. It grows naturally on the slopes of the Andes in South America.

Plum-fruited yew is a South American tree, not related to true yews. Its seeds are encased in an edible fleshy scale.

Incense cedar is a tall, narrow tree from North America. Its wood has a pleasant smell.

Egg-shaped upright cone

Giant fir is a 164 ft (150 m) tall tree of the damp coastal forests of the Pacific Northwest.

Stone pine grows all around the Mediterranean region. It has large, heavy cones full of edible seeds.

Japanese larch is one of the few deciduous conifers. It is an important tree for the timber industry.

Broad-leaved trees

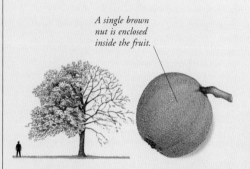
A single brown nut is enclosed inside the fruit.

Leaves have ten or fewer pairs of veins.

Bristly fruit husk

Black walnut has large edible seeds and provides one of the most highly valued timbers in the world.

Silver birch is a graceful, white-barked tree. It quickly grows in open spaces. Flowers are borne in catkins.

Common beech is a valuable timber tree, with dense foliage that provides thick shade.

Fruit, called an acorn, is held in a rough cup.

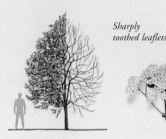
Sharply toothed leaflets

Leaves turn yellow to orange or red in fall.

White oak has large, lobed leaves that turn a brilliant purplish red in fall. It grows in eastern North America.

Mountain ash has clusters of small flowers followed by orange-red berries much loved by birds.

Sugar maple is also known as rock maple. It is tapped for its sap, which is then refined into maple syrup.

Cider gum is one of about 600 different kinds of eucalyptus trees from Australia.

Indian bean tree grows in moist places in the southeastern US. It has long narrow seedpods.

White poplar has foliage so thickly covered with cottony down when it is young that the leaves look white.

TRUTH, SOJOURNER

IN THE 19TH CENTURY, most black people in America were slaves and black women had no rights at all. One remarkable woman dedicated her life to changing this situation. Sojourner Truth was born a slave, but was freed and spent her free life campaigning against slavery and fighting for women's rights. Her speeches and actions gave heart to all those who fought to abolish slavery, and inspired many early feminists.

Early life
Isabella Baumfree was born the daughter of two slaves in upstate New York State in about 1797 – her owner did not record the year. Her parents died in 1809 and she was bought and sold several times. In 1826, she escaped from her owners, and was freed from slavery on July 4, 1827, when all slaves in New York who had been born before July 4, 1799 were freed. Isabella took the name Sojourner Truth in 1843.

Campaigns

As soon as she gained her freedom in 1827, Isabella Baumfree (as she was then known) began to fight against slavery. She gave support to the antislavery Union in the Civil War, especially to the black soldiers who fought in the war. She also cared for freed slaves, nursing them when they were ill, and educating them. Throughout her life she traveled around the country, preaching the word of God, campaigning against the evils of slavery, and speaking in support of women's rights. She set an example that has been followed by black activists to the present day.

Speaking and preaching
Truth spent much of her life as a traveling preacher, paying her way by doing domestic work for the people who came to hear her speak. Although she could neither read nor write, she knew much of the Bible by heart. She was an electrifying platform performer and became a household name in the US.

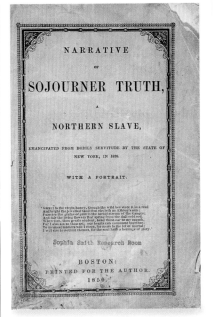

Narrative

In 1850, Sojourner Truth published her autobiography, *Narrative of Sojourner Truth*. This was a rare accomplishment for a black woman at that time, especially since Truth had never learned to read or write. She had to dictate the book to a friend. The book was successful and sold many copies, giving Sojourner Truth an income that she used to travel around the country on her campaigns against slavery.

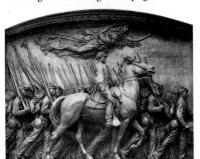

FREE LECTURE!
SOJOURNER TRUTH.

Poster for lecture

Meeting of women's rights campaigners

Women's rights
As a black woman, Sojourner Truth had to face extreme prejudice on account of both her race and her sex. But this only reinforced her conviction that she was the equal of any man, and therefore she campaigned for women to be given equal status in American society. Although there were numerous campaigns for women's rights in the US in the 19th century, most of them were organized by white women, some of whom did not accept Sojourner Truth, a black ex-slave, as their equal.

The war effort
During the American Civil War of 1861–65, Sojourner Truth toured the midwest to get support for the antislavery Union cause. She met with great hostility in some of the places she visited. In one town, an antiwar group threatened to burn down the hall where she was speaking. The threat did not deter Sojourner Truth. She retorted to the protesters: "Then I will speak upon its ashes."

Cavalry officer / Infantrymen of the 58th Regiment

Memorial to black Civil War regiment

Truth and Lincoln
Sojourner Truth was afraid of no one, even visiting the White House in 1864 to meet President Lincoln to persuade him to support her various causes. When she said that she had not heard of him before he was president, he replied that he had heard of her years ago.

Truth with Lincoln

SOJOURNER TRUTH

c.1797	Born in Hurley, New York.
1809	Parents Betsy and James die.
1826	Escapes from her owners.
1827	Granted her freedom on Freedom Day.
1843	Takes the name Sojourner Truth.
1850	*Narrative of Sojourner Truth* published.
1862	Supports the antislavery Union side in US Civil War.
1883	Dies at Battle Creek, Michigan.

FIND OUT MORE   AMERICAN CIVIL WAR   HUMAN RIGHTS   KING, MARTIN LUTHER   SLAVERY   SOCIETIES, HUMAN   UNITED STATES, HISTORY OF   WOMEN'S MOVEMENT

TUNDRA

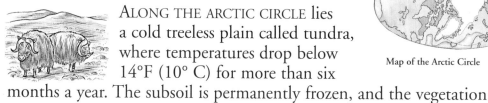

ALONG THE ARCTIC CIRCLE lies a cold treeless plain called tundra, where temperatures drop below 14°F (10° C) for more than six months a year. The subsoil is permanently frozen, and the vegetation is restricted to mosses, lichen, sedges, and rushes, with occasional flowers and small deciduous shrubs, such as hazel and alder. Animals include the Arctic fox and snowshoe rabbit. Worn flat by the vast ice sheets of the past, the tundra is now an open landscape of shallow lakes, bare rock outcrops, and small hummocks.

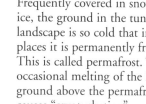

Map of the Arctic Circle

Tundra regions
Tundra exists mostly within the Arctic Circle. There are also tundra regions in the far north of Alaska, Canada, Scandinavia, and Siberia. It is widest in North Siberia, on the Kara Sea, and reaches as far south as the Kamchatka peninsula.

Tundra

Tundra landscape

Frequently covered in snow and ice, the ground in the tundra landscape is so cold that in many places it is permanently frozen. This is called permafrost. The occasional melting of the ice in the ground above the permafrost level causes "cryoturbation", a stirring up of the ground that creates a unique range of landforms.

Periglacial activity

The landscapes bordering ice sheets are periglacial (near glacial). The bitterly cold conditions produce a distinctive environment. All tundra is periglacial, as are nunataks and hills in ice sheets. In winter, the temperature never rises above freezing, and often drops to -58°F (-50°C). Short, mild summers allow the ice to melt.

Periglacial landscape

Stone stripes
In periglacial areas, water freezing in between stones in the ground heaves the stones upward in places, creating stone patterns – stone stripes and rings called stone polygons.

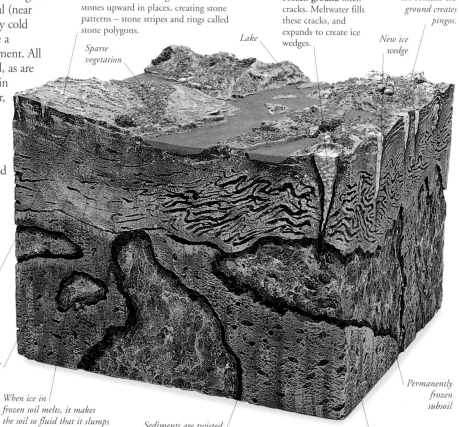

Sparse vegetation

Lake

Frozen ground often cracks. Meltwater fills these cracks, and expands to create ice wedges.

Ice beneath the ground creates pingos.

New ice wedge

Topsoil defrosts during short summer months.

Mother rock

When ice in frozen soil melts, it makes the soil so fluid that it slumps down the gentlest of slopes.

Sediments are twisted by cryoturbation into buckled layers called involutions.

Permanently frozen subsoil

Ice wedge filled with gravel.

Nunataks
Conditions and landforms on nunataks, upland areas protruding above the ice sheet, are very similar to those in the tundra. However, nunataks are cut off by vast seas of ice, so they are often completely bare of vegetation and animal life, and the ground is unprotected.

Mammoth
Permafrost has been frozen for thousands of years. It sometimes contains the perfectly preserved remains of long extinct animals, including complete carcasses of mammoths that died out over 10,000 years ago. This mammoth was found frozen in Siberia.

Pingos
These are mounds up to 160 ft (50 m) high that have been raised by the freezing and expansion of their ice core. The ice core may once have been a shallow lake that filled up with sediment, or it may be frozen groundwater. As the core melts, the pingo collapses.

Permafrost

Unfrozen ground

Permafrost forces ground water upward.

Surface cracks appear.

Collapsed pingo

Lake

Ice core

Ice core

FIND OUT MORE   ARCTIC   CLIMATE   GLACIATION   LAKES   MOUNTAINS   SOIL   WEATHER

TUNNELS

HIDDEN AWAY UNDER STREETS, hills, mountains, rivers, and seas are many thousands of miles of tunnels. Some carry roads, railroads, canals, and subways, making transportation quicker and safer. Others carry services, such as water supplies, sewage, or communications cables. Using only hand tools, the ancient Greeks and Romans built the first tunnels to supply water to their cities. Modern tunnels are dug by special machines or blasted with explosives. Most tunnels are close to the surface, but mountain tunnels may be hundreds of feet underground.

Building tunnels

The method used to build a tunnel depends on the type of rock (either hard or soft) through which the tunnel will run and how deep under the ground the tunnel needs to go. In deep tunnels, digging takes place at the tunnel face. The waste rock is removed along the tunnel.

Cut and cover
The simplest tunnel-building method is cut and cover, used for tunnels just below the surface, such as subways. Engineers dig a trench, build the tunnel inside it, and then cover over it.

Rock blasting
Tunnels are blasted through hard rock by placing high explosives in holes drilled into the rock face. Most hard-rock tunnels are strong enough to support themselves.

Pit props
Narrow tunnels are dug ro reach layers of coal or mineral ore far below the surface. The roof of each tunnel is held up by steel or wooden supports, called pit props.

Model of tunnel boring machine (TBM)

Conveyor belts move lining segments to the tunnel face.

Concrete tunnel-lining segments

Gripper shoes hold rock and thrust TBM forward.

Control cabin

Rotating head cuts through rock.

Tunnel boring
A tunnel boring machine, or TBM, digs through the soft rock (such as chalk) underneath rivers and seas. The TBM creeps slowly forward as its spinning cutting-head digs at the rock. The TBM lines the tunnel with concrete as it moves along.

Parts of a tunnel

A tunnel usually consists of a concrete, steel, or brick lining that supports the roof and makes the tunnel waterproof. Many "tunnels" – such as the Channel Tunnel, which runs under the English Channel and links Britain and France – are actually tunnel systems made up of several separate tunnels running parallel with each other. The tunnels are linked by cross passages.

Cross-section of the Channel Tunnel

Fire-fighting equipment

Relief duct stops air pressure building up in tunnels.

Drainage pipes

Communication cables carry train signals, telephone messages, and computer data.

Cooling pipes carry chilled water to absorb heat given off by the trains.

Electricity cables supply power to the trains, and to lighting, signaling, and ventilation equipment.

Service tunnel is used by engineers and emergency services.

Cross passages link tunnels.

Running tunnels, lined with tough concrete, carry high-speed trains traveling in each direction.

Tunnel safety

Modern tunnels are equipped with safety devices to warn of fire, flooding, and other dangers. In the past, miners and tunnel diggers took caged canaries underground. If a canary collapsed, it was a sign that there were poisonous or explosive gases in the air.

Canary

Ventilation
Road and subway tunnels must be well ventilated to provide passengers with fresh air. In long tunnels, particularly where cars emit toxic exhaust gases, there are ventilation shafts leading to the surface, or huge ventilation fans that create a flow of fresh air through the tunnel.

Timeline

1st century AD Romans build an aqueduct that travels through 19 miles (25 km) of tunnels dug with picks and shovels.

1818 British engineer Marc Isambard Brunel invents the tunneling shield – a device that makes underwater tunnlling safer.

Pick

1867 Rock tunneling becomes easier when Swedish chemist Alfred Nobel invents the explosive dynamite.

1871 The Mont Cenis (or Fréjus) tunnel beneath the Alps is the first to be built using compressed-air drills.

1988 Japan's underwater Seikan Tunnel opens – at 34 miles (54 km), it is the world's longest tunnel.

1994 The Channel Tunnel opens between Britain and France.

FIND OUT MORE

BIRDS · BRIDGES · COAL · PRESSURE · ROADS · ROMAN EMPIRE · TRAINS AND RAILROADS · TRANSPORT HISTORY OF · WEAPONS

TURKEY

SPLIT BETWEEN Europe and Asia, Turkey has a strategic influence over the Black Sea, Mediterranean, Middle East, and Central Asia, and is divided in two by a huge plateau. The European part has adopted western cultures and supports modern industry and cosmopolitan cities. Asian Turkey is the country's rustic heartland, steeped in Islamic tradition, and home to farmers and nomads. Following the collapse of the Ottoman Empire in 1913, Turkey underwent a policy of modernization.

Physical features
European Turkey joins the tip of the Balkan Peninsula. In Asian Turkey, coastal plains border the Anatolian plateau, which is enclosed by the Pontic and Taurus Mountain ranges. The mountains converge in a vast region, where the Euphrates and Tigris rivers rise.

Farmland 43.5%   Barren 4%   Desert 28%   Built-up 1%   Forest 23.5%

Land use
Anatolia's western plateau is used mainly for grazing animals, while the broad, fertile valleys of the Aegean and Mediterranean coasts form the main farming region. About one-third of the land is isolated desert or rocky mountain.

Coastal regions
Turkey is bordered on three sides by long coastlines. The sandy beaches and turquoise seas of the Aegean and Mediterranean coasts give way to fertile plains inland. The pristine Black Sea coast also has long, sandy beaches but is more rugged, with mountainous forests and a changeable climate.

Anatolian plateau
Nearly 97 percent of Turkey is raised, flat-topped land known as Anatolia. The western plateau is dry with few river valleys, while the smaller eastern plateau is rugged, with ocher-red plains, fertile valleys, and rocky caves. Central Anatolia has low mountains and grassy plains.

Ankara
Built in central Anatolia on an ancient site, Ankara replaced Istanbul as the capital of Turkey in 1923. The city is dominated by the Mausoleum of Atatürk, the nationalist who liberalized Turkey in the 1920s and 1930s. Giant stone monuments cover more than 0.6 miles (1 km) in area.

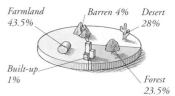

Atatürk's Mausoleum

Lake Van
Turkey's largest lake, Lake Van has an area of 1,453 sq miles (3,736 sq km). It lies in the east of the country near Mount Ararat, and is 5,400 ft (1,650 m) above sea level.

Tenth-century Armenian church on Akdamar Island, Lake Van

109°F (43°C) 73°F (23°C) -33°F (-36°C) 32°F (0°C) 14 in (367 mm)

Climate
The Aegean and Mediterranean coastal regions have hot summers and mild winters. The Anatolian plateau and the mountains have mild or warm summers and cold, snowy winters.

People

About 70 percent of the people are ethnic Turks. About 20 percent are Kurds, who live in the extreme east, and there are also Armenians, Arabs, Greeks, and refugees from former Soviet states.

224 per sq mile (87 per sq km)   **74% Urban**   **26% Rural**

People
Most Turks live in western Turkey. Many have moved from poor countryside areas to cities to try and make a living at the bustling market stalls, or bazaars. Almost all Turks are united by their shared religion, Islam, which plays a key role in history and culture.

Leisure

Most Turkish leisure pursuits are not considered appropriate for women, though as mothers they may attend family outings. Soccer and greased wrestling are both popular games for men and draw huge crowds.

Turkish coffee-pot

Coffeehouses
Turkish men meet regularly in coffeehouses, or *kiraathanes*, to drink Turkish coffee, which is thick, strong, and sweet. While drinking, men play backgammon and smoke pipes.

Turkish delight – rose- or lemon-flavored jellies.

Wrestling
Greased wrestling is the national sport of Turkey. Men smear their bodies with olive oil to resist the grip of their opponents. An annual wrestling feast called *kirkpinar* is held every spring.

Farming

About 38 percent of Turkey's labor force works in farming. The country's varied climate allows a wide variety of crops to be grown. Cotton, which supports a thriving textile industry, and tobacco, grown on the central plateau, are the main export crops.

Sheep and goats
On the pastures of eastern and western Turkey, sheep and goats graze. Goats provide angora wool, named after Turkey's capital, Ankara, originally called Angora.

Rice pilaf

Food
Rice and yogurt are the base of many Turkish dishes. Lamb or mutton are commonly served, most frequently in a *shish kebab*, in which cubes of meat are grilled on a skewer with onion, peppers, and tomatoes. Fish such as swordfish, shrimps, and mussels, caught off the 8,300 km (5,160 miles) of coastline, are a speciality. *Baklava*, a sweet pastry stuffed with honey and nuts, is a treat.

Roasted pieces of lamb   *Yogurt sauce*

Crops
Turkey grows its own food as well as grain and specialized crops such as grapes, dates, and eggplants. Hazelnuts and tea are cultivated along the Black Sea coast. Peaches, melons, and figs, of which Turkey is the world's largest producer, flourish on the warm coasts.

Hazelnuts

Figs

Peach

Transportation
Bordering the sea on three sides, Turkey has many fine harbors and a merchant fleet of nearly 900 ships. Ferries and two bridges link the Asian and European parts of the country. Turkey also has a railroad network, 1,072 miles (12,000 km) long that provides links between its principal cities.

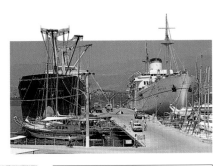

Industry

Turkey has more than 30,000 factories, mainly in the west of the country, which produce processed food, textiles, iron and steel, chemicals, machinery, and vehicles. Mining is concentrated in the east. Turkey has a rapidly expanding tourist industry.

Kilims
Knotted-pile carpets, called *kilims*, are made throughout Turkey. Every year, the country makes about 474,000,000 sq ft (44,000,000 sq m) of carpet. Each region has its own individual designs and colors, and the *kilims* are sold at bazaars in every town and city.

Tourism
More than nine million tourists flock to Turkey every year, attracted by its wealth of historic sites, pleasant climate, and fine beaches. The Aegean coast is dotted with the remains of Greek and Roman cities. Pamukkale, a popular resort since Roman times, draws locals and visitors to its cascading, mineral-rich thermal pools, set on a chalky hillside.

At Pamukkale, calcium deposits form remarkable shapes.

Istanbul
The world's only city to be split between continents, Istanbul lies partly in Europe, partly in Asia. Once called Constantinople, it was Turkey's capital from AD 330–1923. Today, it is Turkey's largest city, home to 8,000,000 people. It has a mix of colorful bazaars, elaborate mosques, and modern shops.

Sunset over Istanbul

FIND OUT MORE   ASIA, HISTORY OF   COASTS   EUROPE, HISTORY OF   FARMING   ISLAM   OTTOMAN EMPIRE   ROMAN EMPIRE   SEVEN WONDERS OF THE ANCIENT WORLD   SHIPS AND BOATS   TEXTILES AND WEAVING

TURTLES AND TORTOISES

APPROXIMATELY 250 SPECIES of turtles and tortoises exist today. They are reptiles with hard shells and can be found from the tropics to temperate regions. Those that live in water are called turtles; those that live on land are called tortoises. They lack teeth but have sharp horny lip shields. All reproduce by laying eggs, females laying from one to more than 100 eggs in loose soil or sand. Many tortoises and sea turtles are endangered, the result of trade in their shells and meat, and theft of their eggs.

Carapace covers the back.

Plastron covers the belly, and protects against stones and twigs.

Sea turtles

There are seven species of sea turtles. The largest is the leatherback, which grows up to 6 ft (1.8 m) long and weighs 1,500 lbs (680 kg). Other species include the hawksbill and the loggerhead turtle. Turtles migrate long distances from their feeding grounds to mate near traditional nesting beaches. The females lay up to 160 eggs in pits that they dig in the sand.

Shells
A tortoise or turtle shell is made up of many small plate-like bones and is part of their skeleton. The flat underneath is called the plastron; the domed upper part is called the carapace. The shell is covered by either hard horny plates or leathery skin, and provides protection when the animal withdraws inside.

Tortoises

Most tortoises have stumpy legs and a high, rounded upper shell, although the crevice-dwelling pancake tortoise has a flattened upper shell, giving it its name. The largest tortoises are the giant Galápagos and Aldabra tortoises of the Pacific and Indian oceans. Both these species can weigh more than 550 lb (250 kg) and live for more than 150 years.

Hingeback tortoises
There are three species of hingeback tortoises, all living in Africa and Madagascar. They can close the hind section of their carapace to give added protection to their legs and tail from predators. The plates on this part of the carapace gradually get worn.

Starred tortoise
Adult starred tortoises have a pattern of pale lines radiating over a darker background. As the tortoise ages, the pattern may fade. Young may be entirely yellow with black markings only between the shell plates.

Hinge allows back of shell to bend downwards for added protection.

Head, legs, and tail are pulled into shell.

Swimming
Sea turtles have flipperlike legs for swimming. They can dive to considerable depths and hold their breath underwater for long periods.

Back pair of flippers used as rudders to steer turtle along.

Turtle shell is stream lined for gliding through water.

Powerful flippers propel the turtle through the water.

Green turtle swimming

Head and neck are about 5.5 in (14 cm) long.

Snake-necked turtle
With its long neck, this carnivorous Australasian turtle can snorkel for air from deep water, forage for food in deep holes, and defend any part of its body with a vicious bite. It must turn its head sideways to withdraw it under the carapace.

Freshwater turtles

Sometimes called terrapins, river- and swamp-dwelling turtles are found all over the world. Mostly small, like the 11 in (28 cm) red-eared slider, freshwater turtles also include giant Amazon river turtles, leathery soft-shelled turtles, and snapping turtles such as the 31 in (80 cm) alligator snapping turtle found in the southeastern US.

Legs rather than flippers allow the turtle to walk on land.

Turtles have a flatter carapace than tortoises.

Leopard tortoise hatching

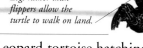

1 The hatchling tortoise begins to crack the egg with a projection on its lip.

2 The eggshell cracks as the baby tortoise moves around inside.

3 The hatchling learns to use its lungs to breathe for the first time.

4 When the yolk has been absorbed, the hatchling leaves the egg.

STARRED TORTOISE

SCIENTIFIC NAME	*Geochelene elegans*
FAMILY	Testudinidae
ORDER	Testudines
DISTRIBUTION	Central and southern India and Sri Lanka
HABITAT	Dry and wet forests
DIET	Vegetation
SIZE	Length 10 in (25 cm)

FIND OUT MORE

CONSERVATION   EGGS   MARSH AND SWAMP WILDLIFE   MIGRATION, ANIMAL   OCEAN WILDLIFE   REPTILES

Tortoises

Starred tortoise from India and Sri Lanka has a star pattern on its shell.

Leopard tortoise is from dry parts of Africa. It has a spotted pattern.

Red-legged tortoise from South America has large red scales on its front legs.

Characteristic red scales

Stumpy front feet with short toes for walking

Hinged rear section of shell.

Hinge-back tortoise from Africa has a flexible section of shell that hinges downward to protect its rear quarters.

Herman's tortoise lives in areas in south and southeastern Europe where summers are hot. It hibernates in winter.

Pattern of radiating lines

Radiated tortoise from Madagascar has been known to live for at least 137 years.

Turtles

Red stripe easily identifies this species.

Yellow-bellied slider is a close relative of the red-eared slider. This one is a newly hatched juvenile.

Leathery shell lacks the characteristic hard scutes of other turtles.

Male red-eared sliders have long front toenails used in courting females.

Red-eared slider of North America is commonly kept as a pet.

Spiny softshelled turtle lies buried in the sand of lakes or riverbeds in North America, ready to ambush passing prey.

Shell color is often hidden by growths of algae.

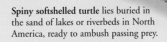

Large head with a strong beak cannot be retracted fully into the shell.

Mississippi mud turtle is known as a sawback when young because of the ridge down its shell.

Common snapping turtle is a voracious American turtle with a powerful bite.

Big-headed turtle from Southeast Asia is a poor swimmer, but a good climber.

Painted turtle has a brightly patterned shell.

Neck as long as or longer than the body

Smooth, dark-colored shell

Snake-necked turtle from Australia actively hunts for aquatic animals. It sleeps with its long neck tucked sideways underits shell.

Shell is used for tortoiseshell products.

White-lipped mud turtle has a double-hinged plastron that allows it to close up like a box.

European pond terrapin is the most widespread European turtle.

Big-headed mud turtle has a large head and powerful jaws. It is known locally in Belize as "toe-biter."

Green sea turtle is endangered because it is the source of turtle soup. It also drowns in fishing nets.

Alligator snapping turtle is the largest American freshwater turtle.

Razor-sharp lips

TWAIN, MARK

MILLIONS OF READERS, young and old, have enjoyed *The Adventures of Huckleberry Finn*, the story of an unconventional boy and a runaway slave as they travel down the Mississippi River on a raft. But behind the book is the amazing story of its author, Mark Twain. Born in 1835, Twain lost his father when he was 12. He worked as a printer, publisher, and river-boat pilot, using his experiences of life on the frontier in a series of books that changed American literature through their humor and use of everyday speech.

Samuel Clemens

Mark Twain was born Samuel Langhorne Clemens in 1835 in Florida, Missouri. After the death of his father in 1847, Clemens was apprenticed to a printer in Hannibal, on the banks of the Mississippi River. Here he began his writing career, working on a newspaper owned by his brother.

Lecturer

When the American Civil War broke out in 1861, most traffic on the river stopped and Twain lost his job. He began writing for the *Virginia City Examiner* and later joined a newspaper in San Francisco. He began to publish humorous stories under the name Mark Twain and traveled widely, lecturing about his exploits to appreciative audiences.

Innocents abroad
After his return from a trip to the Mediterranean and Holy Land in 1869, Twain wrote of his journey in a book, *The Innocents Abroad*. The success of the book established Twain as an author, as well as beginning an American literary obsession with the "Old World."

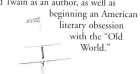

Mississippi steamer

Steamboat pilot
In 1857, Clemens traveled south to New Orleans to seek his fortune in South America. But he never left the city; instead, he became a riverboat pilot on the Mississippi. While working on the river, he adopted the pseudonym Mark Twain. "Mark Twain" is the pilot's call marking water two fathoms deep. Many of the sights he saw and people he met in his journeys along the river appear in Twain's later novels and short stories.

Clemens's pilot's license

Charles Webster and Co.

In the 1870s, Twain set up his own publishing company to print and publish his own novels and stories. He wrote a stream of books, including *A Tramp Abroad* (1880), inspired by a walking tour in Germany; *The Prince and the Pauper* (1882), a historical fantasy set in England; and *Life on the Mississippi* (1883), an autobiography of Twain's time as a riverboat pilot. By this time, Twain had become one of America's most celebrated authors.

Connecticut Yankee
Twain's *A Connecticut Yankee in King Arthur's Court*, published in 1889, is a disturbing satire mixing historical and present-day characters. Twain contrasts the common sense of the American character with the superstition of the British court, and comments on the vast differences between the societies.

The Connecticut Yankee

Tom Sawyer and Huckleberry Finn
Two books by Twain have made him one of the best-loved authors of all time – *The Adventures of Tom Sawyer* (1876) and its sequel, *The Adventures of Huckleberry Finn* (1885). Both books draw on Twain's childhood in Hannibal and paint an unforgettable picture of frontier life on the Mississippi River. Although full of humor, both of these books make profound moral comments on American life, focusing in particular on the institution of slavery.

Bankruptcy
In 1894, most of Twain's business ventures had failed and he was deeply in debt. To pay off his debts, he embarked on lengthy lecture tours and wrote books and stories designed to cash in on his famous name.

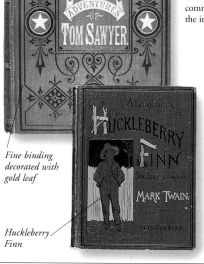

Fine binding decorated with gold leaf

Huckleberry Finn

Later life
In his later years, Twain toured the world giving lectures. He was awarded honorary degrees from universities all over the world, such as Oxford, England. His last years were marked by tragedy. By 1904, two of his three daughters had died, followed, after a lengthy illness, by his wife. In 1906, his own death was reported while he was still alive, forcing him to cable the Associated Press agency stating that "the report of my death was an exaggeration."

Twain's Oxford gown

MARK TWAIN

1835	Born in Florida, Missouri.
1857–61	Works as riverboat pilot.
1867	*The Celebrated Jumping Frog of Calaveras County*, a collection of short stories and sketches.
1869	*The Innocents Abroad.*
1876	*The Adventures of Tom Sawyer.*
1883	*Life on the Mississippi.*
1885	*The Adventures of Huckleberry Finn.*
1895–96	Series of lecture tours.
1910	Dies in Redding, Connecticut.

FIND OUT MORE   BOOKS   LITERATURE   UNITED STATES, HISTORY OF   WRITING

UNIONS, TRADE

AROUND THE WORLD, the response of working people to poor conditions or low pay has been to organize themselves into trade unions. Trade unions are formed and run by their members to represent their interests and may sometimes conflict with employers or governments. In Britain and the US, unions are organized by craft, with unions of miners and engineers, while in the rest of Europe they are organized by industry, with unions of workers in the car or chemical industries.

Tolpuddle Martyrs
In 1834, six English farm workers from the village of Tolpuddle in Dorset, England, were deported to Australia for seven years for daring to organize a trade union. After a big campaign, they were pardoned in 1836.

Inside trade unions

A trade union is run by and for its members. The members elect the leading officers, who run the union's administration, and meet regularly to decide union policy and debate issues of common concern. Because of their large size, most unions are organized on a local factory or workplace basis, coordinated regionally and nationally.

Membership pins

Membership papers

Membership
Traditionally, trade unions have recruited male manual, or "blue-collar," workers. Today, many clerical and professional people, known as "white-collar" workers, as well as many more women, are union members. White-collar workers include civil servants, teachers, and journalists.

Workers in a car factory in Germany, where trade unions are organized by industry.

Services
Trade unions offer a wide range of services to their members in addition to their work of negotiating employment conditions. Banking, insurance, pensions, credit cards, loans, and many other financial and personal services are all provided to support existing members and to encourage new members to join.

International unionism

Two international organizations exist to support trade unions around the world: the Communist-led World Federation of Trade Unions, set up in 1945, and the International Confederation of Free Trade Unions, established in 1949.

What unions do

Trade unions exist to support their members at work. They campaign for better pay and improved conditions, negotiate pay raises and other benefits, and represent individual members at hearings and on health and safety issues.

Hard hat

Ear protectors

Strike
The ultimate weapon of any trade union is to call its members out on strike – that is, to refuse to work. Although strikes can be an effective weapon in achieving what unions want for their members, they can cause considerable hardship as workers lose their pay and possibly their jobs.

Collective bargaining
Trade unions bargain with the management to improve their members' working conditions. The two sides negotiate until they reach a deal that gives them both what they want. Without a trade union, individual workers must do this for themselves.

Industrial boards
In Sweden and some other European countries, trade unions sit on the management boards of companies and work with government and employers to help tackle national industrial and economic problems.

Lech Walesa
The Polish trade unionist Lech Walesa (b. 1943) was fired from the Gdansk shipyards in 1976 for leading a strike. Walesa then set up a trade union called Solidarity, in opposition to the government unions. It was formally recognized in 1980. After Communism's fall, he became President of Poland in 1990.

Timeline

Early 1800s Industrial Revolution and the growth of factories leads to the formation of the first trade unions in Europe and the US.

1850s Trade unions are formed in most European countries.

1868 First meeting of the Trades Union Congress (TUC) held in Manchester, UK.

1881 American Federation of Labor (AFL) set up.

1919 International Labor Organization (ILO) set up and affiliated to the League of Nations.

1926 General Strike causes state of paralysis in Britain.

1946 ILO affiliates with the UN, to improve workers' conditions through international agreement.

1955 AFL merges with the more militant Congress of Industrial Organizations (CIO).

FIND OUT **MORE** | EUROPE, HISTORY OF | GOVERNMENTS AND POLITICS | INDUSTRIAL REVOLUTION | MONEY | TRADE AND INDUSTRY | UNITED NATIONS

UNITED KINGDOM

THE UNITED KINGDOM consists of England, Wales, and Scotland, which make up the islands of Great Britain, Northern Ireland, and hundreds of smaller islands. Great Britain is separated from mainland Europe by the English Channel and the North Sea. Highly urbanized and densely populated, the UK is one of the world's leading industrial economies and one of its oldest monarchies. The Isle of Man and the Channel Islands are self-governing dependencies: the UK government handles their international affairs.

UNITED KINGDOM FACTS

CAPITAL CITY London

AREA 94,550 sq miles (244,880 sq km)

POPULATION 58,800,000

MAIN LANGUAGE English

MAJOR RELIGIONS Christian, Muslim, Hindu, Sikh, Jewish

CURRENCY Pound sterling

LIFE EXPECTANCY 78 years

PEOPLE PER DOCTOR 588

GOVERNMENT Multiparty democracy

ADULT LITERACY 99%

Physical features

The rolling green fields of southern England contrast with the flat, marshy fens in the east. Scotland, Wales, and northern England have craggy mountains and windswept moors and fields. Northern Ireland has undulating pasture and low coastal mountains.

Coastline

The UK has more than 3,000 miles (5,000 km) of coast. The rocky inlets and cliffs of the Cornish coast in southwestern England contrast with the broad, sandy beaches in the southeast. The English Channel coast is characterized by the distinctive chalky "white cliffs of Dover."

Countryside

Viewed from the air, the English countryside forms a neat patchwork of color that reflects generations of farming and cultivation. The pattern is broken only by farms, villages, and country roads. Fields are traditionally separated by hedgerows, many of which mark ancient boundaries. The hedges also provide a valuable refuge for wildlife.

Climate

The UK has a generally mild climate, but the weather is changeable. Rainfall is highest in the north and west, and lowest in the extreme southeast. Winter snow is common in northern and mountainous areas.

Land use

More than two-thirds of the UK is used for cultivating crops and rearing livestock. The most built-up region is southeastern England. Scotland is five times less densely populated than the rest of the UK.

93°F (34°C)
64°F (18°C)
1°F (-17°C)
41°F (5°C)
24 in (600 mm)

Farmland 71%
Barren 4%
Built-up 11%
Forest 14%

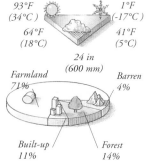

London

Capital of the UK, the largest city in Europe and home to about seven million people, London is the hub of British business and government. Founded by the Romans as a center for trade with the rest of Europe, London is an exciting, bustling city. Every year, thousands of tourists visit its historic buildings, museums, galleries, and shops, and ride on traditional double-decker buses.

Big Ben and the House of Commons

U

People

The English, Scottish, Welsh, and Irish each have their own customs, traditions, and even languages. British society is still divided by a class system based on heredity and wealth. The standard of living is good, but poverty exists in some inner-city areas.

89% **11%** **622 per sq mile**
Urban **Rural** (240 per sq km)

Multicultural society
Since the 1950s, thousands of people have settled in the UK from former colonies in Asia, Africa, and the Caribbean. The result is a multicultural society with a wide range of food, art, music, religions, and festivals, such as London's colorful Notting Hill Carnival.

Leisure

The British are great sports fans and enjoy playing and watching soccer, rugby, cricket, golf, snooker, and tennis. Fishing, walking, and cycling are popular outdoor pursuits. Many people, however, prefer to go to the theater or movies, or relax at home with the TV or a good newspaper.

Gardening
The British are avid gardeners and spend many hours out of doors creating colorful seasonal displays. Thousands of people flock to flower shows. Garden centers selling a wide variety of plants, books, and equipment are big business.

Cricket
A summer cricket match on the village green is a traditional English scene. The English invented the game in the 1300s, and it is now played in many counties.

Farming

British farming is highly mechanized and produces 66 percent of the UK's food, but only one percent of the labor force works on the land. Most farms are small and are often run on a part-time basis, employing only one or two workers. Farming of both animals and crops is common.

Dartmoor sheep

Hereford bull

Crops
Wheat, barley, sugar beets, and potatoes are Britain's most widely grown crops. Kent, in the southeast, is famous for its hops for making beer. Large farms in eastern England produce cereals and vegetables such as peas and beans.

Livestock
Beef and dairy cattle are raised in areas of lush pasture. Sheep are raised in hilly, more rugged areas. Chicken and pigs are raised intensively in sheds as well as free-range pens.

Food

The British are best known for their cooked breakfasts, roast dinners, and afternoon teas. Fast food and takeouts probably started here, with fish and chips, the sandwich – a British invention – and Cornish pasties. The UK also produces a wide range of cheeses, such as Cheddar and Stilton. The national drinks are tea, beer, and Scotch whisky.

A typical cooked English breakfast

Industry

Until recently, Britain had thriving coal, iron, and steel industries. Today, oil and natural gas from the North Sea have replaced coal, and light engineering and financial and service industries have become the mainstay of the economy. Reduced fish stocks have caused a decline in the fishing industry.

Banking
Dominated by glossy office buildings such as the Lloyds Building, the City of London is one of the world's leading financial centers. Situated strategically between Tokyo and New York City, more currency changes hands here than in any other city.

The Lloyds Building by Sir Richard Rogers

Cars
Britain ranks highly in world car production and produces about 1,300,000 vehicles a year. The skilled workforce has attracted investment from US, German, and Japanese manufacturers. Vehicles make up ten percent of exports. Famous makes include Rolls Royce and Rover.

Tourism
More than 25 million tourists visit Britain every year. Many are drawn by the history and culture of cities such as London and Edinburgh, while others are attracted by the wild scenery of Scotland, Wales, and the Lake District.

Transportation

Large container trucks transport nearly all Britain's freight over an extensive network of roads and highways. The British drive on the left. Intercity trains are generally fast, comfortable, and efficient. Britain is also an international gateway for air and sea traffic.

Channel Tunnel
The Channel Tunnel, Britain's first rail link with continental Europe, opened in 1994. High-speed Eurostar trains make the journey from London to Paris and Brussels in three hours. The tunnel is 31 miles (50 km) long, and 75 percent runs underwater.

Heathrow Airport
Situated within easy reach of the city, Heathrow is the largest of London's three airports. It handles 62,000,000 passengers and 480,000 flights annually. Plans for a new terminal, the fifth, are underway.

FIND OUT MORE AIRPORTS • BALL GAMES • EMPIRES • EUROPE, HISTORY OF • EUROPEAN UNION • FARMING • FESTIVALS • GARDENS • MONEY • TUNNELS • UNITED KINGDOM, HISTORY OF

UNITED KINGDOM, HISTORY OF

THROUGHOUT THEIR HISTORY, the British Isles have been subject to frequent invasions. In turn, Celts, Romans, Anglo-Saxons, and Vikings invaded the islands and established their rule. In 1066, the Normans invaded and subjugated England. Thereafter, England emerged as the strongest nation, conquering first Ireland, and then Wales, before joining with Scotland in 1603. The United Kingdom thus formed the leading industrial and colonial power in the world, maintaining a supremacy that was to last into the present century.

Ancient British harness mount

Ancient Britain

The earliest inhabitants of Britain were nomadic hunter-gatherers, who moved from place to place in search of food. In about 4000 BC, people began to settle in villages, farm the land, and raise animals.

Roman Britain

Julius Caesar invaded Britain in 54 BC to stop local Celtic tribes from helping the Gauls in France to undermine the Roman Empire. In AD 43, England and Wales were conquered and made part of the empire. The Romans built many towns and roads, and encouraged trade.

Roman towns

The Romans built a network of towns as centres of trade and local government. Among these were Londinium (London) on the Thames River , and Aquae Sulis (Bath) in the west of England.

Roman baths in the city of Bath

Anglo-Saxon invasions

After the Romans left in 410, Germanic Anglo-Saxons from northern Europe began to invade Britain. By 613, the Anglo-Saxons had conquered all of England, dividing it into seven kingdoms.

Christ is offered a sponge soaked in vinegar to quench his thirst.

Anglo-Saxon relief of the crucifixion, Daglingworth, England

St. Augustine

Under Roman rule, most of Britain was Christian, but the Anglo-Saxons had their own gods. Christian missionary St Augustine came to Canterbury in 597 and began to convert the area to Christianity.

Norman England

In 1066, William Duke of Normandy invaded England to claim the throne. Near Hastings, he defeated the English army led by King Harold, and conquered the country. The Normans built castles to enforce their rule, and provided England with strong central government.

Bayeaux tapestry, showing the Norman victory

Magna Carta

Under Norman rule, arguments frequently occurred between the king and his most powerful lords. In 1215, at Runnymede in Surrey, King John signed the Magna Carta, a document drawn up by senior lords. It laid down the responsibilities and rights of citizens and the Church in relation to the crown. The Magna Carta is one of the major constitutional documents of modern English government.

William I

William I (c.1027–87) was a descendant of Vikings who had settled in Normandy in northern France. As king of England, he was a strong ruler who brought stability to the country. He died after falling from his horse at Nantes, France.

Magna Carta

Vikings and Cnut

In 787, Viking sailors made their first raid on the English coast, and soon controlled the north and east of the country. In 1013, they seized the entire kingdom; under King Cnut, England was part of a Viking empire called the Danelaw that included much of Scandinavia.

King Cnut

Royal seal of King John

Modern Houses of Parliament

Parliament

In 1265, Henry III called representatives of the towns, lords, and clergy to the first parliament in London to advise the government. Within a century, parliament had the right to make laws and levy taxes.

Wales

England tried to rule Wales from Saxon times, but the Welsh princes resisted. In 1282, Edward I conquered the country, and built many castles to keep the Welsh subdued. An Act of Union in 1536 formally joined Wales to England. The Welsh language was suppressed for centuries afterwards.

Dolbadarn Castle, Wales

U

Tudors and Stuarts

Henry VII, the first Tudor king, seized power in 1485. He curbed the power of the lords, restored royal finances, and ruled strongly. The Tudors ruled until 1603. They were followed by the Stuarts, under whom England tried to keep its leading role in Europe, despite a bitter civil war.

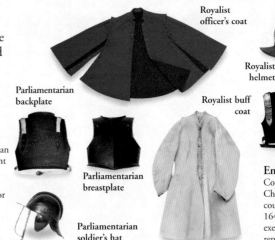

Royalist officer's coat

Royalist helmet

Royalist buff coat

Royalist armor

Royalist backplate

Parliamentarian backplate

Parliamentarian breastplate

Parliamentarian soldier's hat

Dissolution of the monasteries
In 1534, Henry VIII broke with the Roman Catholic church because it refused to grant him a divorce. He created the Church of England, with him as its supreme head, dissolved the monasteries to get money for his court, and seized Church lands.

Henry VIII, the second Tudor king, painted by Hans Holbein

English Civil War
Conflicts between parliament and Charles I over the government of the country broke out into open war in 1642. The king was defeated and was executed in 1649. England became a republic until 1660.

Scotland
Scotland first became a kingdom in 843, and remained independent for centuries despite constant invasions by England. In 1603, the Scottish king, James VI, inherited the English throne from the Tudor queen Elizabeth I; in 1707, the two countries were formally united.

Crown of Scotland

Industrial England

In the 18th century, Britain became the world's first industrialized country. Millions of people moved from the countryside to the towns to work in new factories and workshops. Canals and railroads moved raw materials and finished goods around the country. By 1850, Britain was the "workshop of the world."

Chartist demonstration

Victorian England
During the reign of Queen Victoria (1837–1901), Britain became the world's richest country, with an empire that covered one-quarter of the globe. Despite this wealth, living conditions were poor for many people in the cities.

Crystal Palace, site of the Great Exhibition of 1851

Chartists
In the early 19th century, demands grew for better representation of working people in government. In the 1830s and 1840s, groups such as the Chartists campaigned for reform. They were named after the People's Charter, drafted by William Lovett in 1838. Reforms were finally granted later.

Modern Britain

During the 20th century, Britain underwent many changes. It granted much of its empire independence, lost control of most of Ireland, and struggled to cope with economic decline. In the late 20th century, Britain became a more multicultural society, as many immigrants arrived from the country's former colonies in Africa, Asia, and the Caribbean.

Wartime Britain
In 1940, Britain stood alone in the fight against Nazi Germany. British fighter pilots fought off a planned German invasion during the Battle of Britain, but British cities were heavily bombed throughout World War II.

Londoners take shelter in the subway during air raids.

Free school milk

Items provided by the welfare state

Welfare state
In the early 20th century, Britain introduced national pensions and insurance schemes to protect workers against poverty, poor health, and unemployment. In 1948, a national health service established free medical treatment.

Low-cost eyeglasses

Forms for free medical prescriptions

Prescription for free medicines

Entry into Europe
After a referendum of the adult population, Britain joined the European Community (now called the European Union) in 1973. Membership brought many benefits, but the role of Britain in Europe has remained one of the most controversial issues for British political parties.

European referendum poster

YES ✓
DO SOMETHING POSITIVE FOR YOUR COUNTRY'S FUTURE
Vote YES to keep Britain in Europe

Timeline
54 BC Julius Caesar leads exploratory invasion of England.

AD 43–410 England and Wales are part of the Roman Empire.

613 Anglo-Saxons complete their invasion of England.

787 Vikings begin to raid coastline.

1016–35 Cnut rules England as part of large Scandinavian Empire.

1066 Battle of Hastings: Normans rule England under William.

1455–85 Wars of the Roses: the Houses of York and Lancaster, with the white and red rose respectively as their emblems, fight for the English throne.

1603 James I (James VI of Scotland), the first Stuart king, comes to the English throne, uniting the English and Scottish thrones.

Domesday Book, the Normans' complete survey of England

1707 The Act of Union between England and Scotland creates the United Kingdom of Great Britain.

1800 Union between Great Britain and Ireland.

1837–1901 Reign of Queen Victoria. British Empire at its height.

1922 Most of Ireland gains its independence from Britain and is called the Irish Free State.

1973 United Kingdom joins European Community, later called the European Union.

FIND OUT MORE — ANGLO-SAXONS · ELIZABETH I · EMPIRES · EUROPE, HISTORY OF · EUROPEAN UNION · INDUSTRIAL REVOLUTION · IRELAND, HISTORY OF · VIKINGS · WORLD WAR I · WORLD WAR II

UNITED NATIONS

AT THE HEIGHT OF WORLD WAR II, the 26 Allied countries fighting Germany, Italy, and Japan pledged as the "United Nations" not to make a separate peace with the enemy. From this declaration grew the UN, a new international organization that aimed to keep world peace and bring warring nations closer together. Today the UN includes almost every state in the world as a member. Its main success has been to act as an international forum where issues can be discussed and often resolved.

The League of Nations
Set up in 1919 after World War I, the League of Nations was designed to preserve peace and settle disputes by arbitration. However, the league had no armies of its own to enforce its decisions and relied instead on sanctions against offending nations. The absence of the US and other important nations weakened the league, which collapsed during World War II. It was replaced by the UN.

Secretariat building, where the daily administration is carried out.

Flags of member nations fly in front of the UN complex.

International Court of Justice
International legal disputes between nations are settled at the International Court at The Hague in the Netherlands. The court consists of 15 judges elected by the Security Council and the General Assembly and makes its decisions by a majority vote.

General Assembly

The main forum in the UN is the General Assembly. Every member state sends one delegate to the assembly, which meets for four months a year. Decisions are made by a simple majority vote, unless they are so important that they require a two-thirds majority. The assembly has few powers, but it does serve as an international parliament in which member states can discuss issues of mutual concern.

The Conference Building houses meeting rooms for several UN councils.

Security Council

The Trusteeship Council is responsible for trust territories placed under its supervision by member states.

Economic and Social Council

Visitors' entrance

The UN headquarters is in New York, USA. This site is an international zone and has its own stamps and post office.

Peace garden has 25 varieties of rose.

Security Council
The most powerful part of the UN is the Security Council. The council has a membership of 15, comprising five permanent members – US, Russia, China, UK, and France – and 10 members elected for two-year terms by the General Assembly. The council can meet at any time and can call on the armies of member states to enforce its decisions.

Economic and Social Council
The 54 members of the Economic and Social Council monitor the economic, social, cultural, health, and educational affairs of member states and work to ensure human rights throughout the world. The council reports to the General Assembly.

Peacekeeping statue outside UN headquarters

Let Us Beat Swords Into Plowshares

Secretariat
The day-to-day administration of the UN is in the hands of the Secretariat. The staff of the Secretariat comes from every nation and works both in the headquarters of the UN in New York and in any country in the world where the UN is active.

Secretary General
The most powerful person in the UN is the Secretary General, who is elected for a five-year term by the General Assembly. Boutros Boutros-Ghali (b. 1922), shown here, was the UN Secretary General from 1992–96. As Secretary General, he mediated in international disputes, and played a role in international diplomacy. However, the Secretary General can act only if the Security Council members reach a joint agreement on policy.

U

Specialized agencies

Much of the detailed work of the UN is carried out by 15 specialized agencies affiliated with the UN. Some of the agencies, such as the International Labor Organization (ILO), were set up before the UN was founded; others are more recent. The organizations cover such areas as international aviation control, trade union and labor affairs, maritime law, and aid and development.

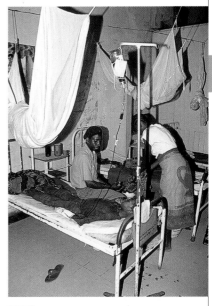

UNICEF
The United Nations Children's Emergency Fund (UNICEF) works for children around the world. It provides health care and health education in many developing countries and plays a vital role in looking after children orphaned or injured by war.

UNESCO
The United Nations Educational, Scientific, and Cultural Organization (UNESCO) was set up in 1946 to promote international cultural collaboration. Its broad range of activities includes restoring sites of cultural value, such as the Angkor Wat temple in Cambodia.

IMF

The International Monetary Fund (IMF) was set up in 1944 to promote international monetary co-operation and stability and the expansion of world trade. The IMF advises member nations on their economic and financial policies.

WHO
The World Health Organization (WHO) works to improve standards of health and combat disease around the world. Its most important achievement was the complete eradication of smallpox from the world by 1980. Other successful campaigns have been waged against polio and leprosy.

The work of the UN

The UN and its agencies are active in almost every country of the world, paying most attention to the poorer, less-developed nations and to areas of the world affected by war, civil strife, drought, or famine. The UN can offer its own technical assistance and advice, but relies on the support of member nations to provide the necessary funds, personnel, and, in case of war, army troops.

Peacekeeping sculpture outside UN headquarters

Peacekeeping
The UN tries to keep the peace between warring nations or sides in a civil war. The famous blue berets of UN troops have been in operation in most of the world's trouble spots, including the Middle East and former Yugoslavia. At the start of 2002, UN peacekeeping missions operated in 15 nations, deploying 47,000 troops.

Humanitarian aid
The UN plays an important role in providing humanitarian aid to people in distress. The UN High Commissioner for Refugees, based in Geneva, Switzerland, provides food and shelter for refugees fleeing war, famine, or drought, while other UN agencies work to improve water supplies or local health and education provision.

Environmental role
The UN has taken a major role in environmental issues as concern rises about threats to the world's ecology. In 1992, it convened a major conference in Rio de Janeiro, Brazil, on the environment and development. The conference, known as the Earth Summit, committed world nations to reduce pollution in order to prevent global warming.

A UN conference in 1996 votes to ban all nuclear testing.

Dag Hammarskjöld
The Swedish politician Dag Hammarskjöld (1905–61) became UN Secretary General in 1953. He was a skilled diplomat who raised the prestige of the UN through his impartial handling of international crises, such as the invasion of Suez in 1956. In 1961, Hammarskjöld was killed in a plane crash. He was awarded the 1961 Nobel Peace Prize after his death.

Timeline

1945 San Francisco Conference drafts the UN Charter, which is ratified at the first meeting of the UN in London in October.

1946 Trygve Lie of Norway becomes the first UN Secretary General.

Permanent members of the Security Council

1950–53 UN sends troops to South Korea to repel invasion by North Korea.

1953 Dag Hammarskjöld becomes Secretary General.

1960–64 UN intervenes in civil war in the Congo (Zaïre).

1961 U Thant of Burma becomes Secretary General.

1964 UN sends troops to keep the peace in Cyprus.

1971 Taiwan expelled from UN and its place taken by China.

1972 Kurt Waldheim of Austria becomes Secretary General.

1982 Javier Pérez de Cuéllar of Peru becomes Secretary General.

1992 UN troops are deployed in Bosnia after civil war erupts in the states of the former Yugoslavia.

1992 Boutros Boutros-Ghali of Egypt becomes Secretary General.

1997 Kofi Annan of Ghana becomes Secretary General.

FIND OUT MORE   ARMIES   COLD WAR   ECOLOGY AND ECOSYSTEMS   EUROPE, HISTORY OF   GOVERNMENTS AND POLITICS   MEDICINE   MONEY   PEACE MOVEMENTS   POLLUTION   WARFARE

UNITED STATES OF AMERICA

THE WORLD'S WEALTHIEST COUNTRY, the United States of America (US) is also the fourth largest and the third most populated. It is made up of 50 states, 48 of which occupy the central part of North America. Alaska, the 49th state, lies in the northwest of North America and Hawaii, the 50th state, is a chain of Pacific islands. The US is a major industrial and economic force; since 1945, it has also played a leading role in world affairs.

UNITED STATES OF AMERICA FACTS

CAPITAL CITY	Washington DC
AREA	3,681,760 sq miles (9,372,610 sq km)
POPULATION	281,400,000
MAIN LANGUAGES	English, Spanish
MAJOR RELIGION	Christian
CURRENCY	US dollar
LIFE EXPECTANCY	77 years
PEOPLE PER DOCTOR	370
GOVERNMENT	Multiparty democracy
ADULT LITERACY	99%

Physical features

A vast flat plain lies between the high Rocky Mountains in the west and the weathered Appalachians of eastern US. The Mississippi River flows south across the plain. Thick forests grow in the northwest.

135°F (57°C) -80°F (-62°C)
77°F (25°C) 34°F (1°C)
42 in (1,064 mm)

Climate
Summers are hot and humid; subtropical in Florida and tropical in Hawaii. Winters are snowy, and notably bitter in Alaska and the mountains. Storms, hurricanes, floods, and droughts are frequent.

Monument Valley
In the arid desert of Arizona is Monument Valley, where giant rocks up to 1,000 ft (300 m) have eroded from red sandstone. The Mittens, so-called because they look like hands, are a striking feature.

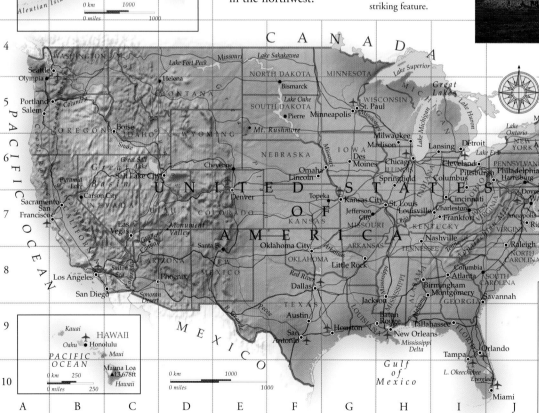

Washington DC
Named after the first US president, the capital, Washington, lies between Virginia and Maryland. The center of federal government, its green parks and marble buildings are home to 572,000.

The Capitol Building

Land use
The US has huge forests, which serve a large timber and wood-pulp industry. On the vast fertile plains, or prairies, farmers cultivate wheat and half of the world's corn.

Built-up 0.5%
Forest 37.5%
Wetland 2.5%
Barren 3.5%
Desert 12%
Farmland 29.5%
Grassland 9.5%
Tundra 5%

80 per sq mile (31 per sq km)

77% Urban 23% Rural

People
The US has a diverse, multiracial population. Throughout its history, waves of immigrants have arrived from Europe, Africa, Asia, and South America.

U

Northeastern states

One of the first regions to be settled by European immigrants, the northeastern states have a rich historical and cultural heritage, and are a melting pot of peoples and cultures. Thanks to rich mineral resources, and many good harbors and rivers, this area has become the most industrialized and heavily populated part of the US. Busy cities, such as Boston, New York City, Pittsburgh, and Philadelphia, contrast with the unspoiled rural farmsteads of New England.

At the end of October, city markets sell giant pumpkins for Halloween.

New York City
Covering an area of 301 sq miles (780 sq km), New York City is the largest city in the US and a leader in the arts, business, and finance. Wall Street's Stock Exchange is the world's biggest, while Broadway is the heart of theater land. More than 19 million people live and work in the New York metropolitan area, which stretches into New Jersey and Connecticut, enjoying its rich social and cultural mix and vibrant customs and festivals.

Fishing
The North Atlantic coastal waters are rich in fish such as cod, herring, and clams. Maine alone has 2400 miles (3,840 km) of coast, and the state is famous for its lobsters.

Tourism
More than 50 million people visit the US every year, and many come to the northeastern states, attracted by the rolling countryside and rich autumn colors of New England, as the maple leaves turn bright red and gold. Tourists flock to New York City and Niagara Falls, on the border with Canada. Fishing, rafting, hiking, and skiing are popular in this region.

Newspapers
More than 1,700 daily and 7,500 weekly newspapers are produced in the US. Most newpapers are local, with the exception of the *Wall Street Journal*, which has a national circulation of 2,200,000, *USA Today*, which covers the diversity of life across the US, and the *New York Times*. The newsprint media is facing increasing competition from satellite and cable television and the Internet.

Cranberry farming
On meticulously cultivated water fields, cranberries are grown in large quantities. The scarlet berries are made into a sauce that is served with turkey at Thanksgiving, juiced, or used as a filling in pancakes.

Great Lakes states

The six states of Minnesota, Wisconsin, Illinois, Indiana, Michigan, and Ohio lie on the shores of the Great Lakes. Ocean ships serve lake ports that are linked to the Mississippi River, whose trade routes to the Gulf of Mexico have boosted the region's agricultural and manufacturing industries. Vast natural resources, such as coal, iron, copper, and wood, and the fertile land of the prairies have brought this area much prosperity.

Motown records

Motown records
The US has produced some of the most important popular music forms. In 1959, record producer Berry Gordy founded the Tamla Motown record label in Detroit, known as the "Motor Town." He promoted many black singers, including Stevie Wonder and Diana Ross.

Hamburgers
The US is a giant in the production and consumption of fast food – 200 burgers are eaten every second in the US. The hamburger originated in Hamburg, Germany, and was brought across the Atlantic by German immigrants. Now, burgers are enjoyed worldwide.

Car industry
Detroit is the center of the US's car industry and General Motors, Chrysler, and Ford together employ about ten percent of the city's workforce. More than five million cars are produced annually.

Chicago
America's third largest city, with a population of 2,900,000, Chicago is often called the "Windy City" because of the breezes that sweep in from Lake Michigan, and its colorful politicians. Chicago is a centre of architectural innovation and competing skyscrapers. The 110-story Sears Tower, 1,707 ft (520 m), was built in 1973.

Sears Tower, world's second tallest habitable building

Chicago has 27 miles (43 km) of beaches.

Hamburger

Sailing
The five Great Lakes of North America form the world's largest area of fresh water, and attract millions of visitors each year. Marinas line their shores, and behind them are hundreds of vacation homes.

Central and mountain states

The ten central and mountain states run from Montana, on the Canadian border, down to Oklahoma in the south. In this region of contrasts, the vast, open fields of the Great Plains, watered by the Mississippi and its tributaries, meet the steep Rocky Mountains. Tornadoes are common in the spring. Most of the people who live here are employed in the booming farming and mining industries.

Yellowstone National Park
Opened in 1872, Yellowstone, in northern Wyoming, was the first American national park. Covering 3,471 sq miles (8,991 sq km), the park's natural habitat is home to black and grizzly bears, and many species of animals and birds. It has hot springs and more than 200 geysers, including Old Faithful, which erupts, on average, every 73 minutes.

Grain
The large farms of the Midwest are highly mechanized and efficient. Iowa is often called "the corn state", because it grows 20 percent of America's corn, and its grain factory at Cedar Rapids is the world's largest.

Cowboys
Modern American cowboys tend beef cattle on luxury family-run ranches on the plains. Increasingly, they are abandoning their traditional horseback lifestyle and keeping watch on the herd with the use of helicopters and pickup trucks.

Traditional high-crowned Stetson

Carved heads of presidents Washington, Lincoln, Jefferson, and Roosevelt

Western saddle

Mount Rushmore
It took more than 14 years to create the faces of four US presidents in the granite cliffs of Mount Rushmore, South Dakota. Carved by Gutzon Borglum, whose son finished them in 1941, the heads stand 60 ft (18 m) tall and attract thousands of tourists.

Gold
Since gold was discovered in South Dakota in 1874, its Homestake Mine, the USA's largest, has been one of the world's main gold producers. About 330 tons (300 tonnes) of gold are mined every year.

Southern states

Three regions characterize the 14 southern states: the Appalachian Mountains in the center, the fertile plains of the south and west, and the tropical Gulf of Mexico. The states' mixed fortunes were established in the 19th century by cotton plantations worked by African slaves. Now, the region has a prosperous and varied economy that runs on farming, oil, coal, manufacturing, and tourism. Many people are devout Christians.

Mouthpiece with single reed

Jazz
Originating in New Orleans around the beginning of the 20th century, jazz music developed from the ragtime style played by black musicians at funerals and street parades. It gradually spread north to Chicago and New York City. The "Original Dixieland Jazz Band," a group of white musicians, were the first band to make jazz recordings.

New Orleans
Founded by the French in 1718, New Orleans is a major port and one of the largest metropolitan areas in the south, home to more than 500,000 people. Half are African Americans, but French influences remain, notably in the vibrant Mardi Gras (Shrove Tuesday) Festival.

Cotton
The US is the world's second largest producer of cotton, most of which grows in the south. Founded in the days of slavery, the cotton industry is now highly mechanized and large-scale. The cotton fabric is used to make towels, sheets, and clothes. Denim is woven to make jeans.

Jazz saxophone is accompanied by drums, piano, and double bass.

Disney World
One of America's top attractions, with more than 20,000,000 visitors a year, Walt Disney World opened in Orlando, Florida in 1971. The fantasy complex based on cartoon characters is a myriad of color and music in a world of hotels and restaurants. The nearby Epcot Center exhibits future technology.

Farming
The southern states grow soybeans, tobacco, and half the country's supply of peanuts, much of which is used to make peanut butter. Florida is the world's second largest orange grower, and produces 75 percent of the nation's supply.

Peanut butter

Peanuts

Denim jeans

U

Southwestern states

Made wealthy by the discovery of oil, the six southwestern states share an arid landscape including part of the Rockies. Close links with Latin America have given this area the largest concentration of Native Americans in the US, as well as many people of Spanish and *mestizo* descent. Houston, Texas is America's fourth largest city, and is the center of the US space program.

Navajo people

About 150,000 Navajos live in Arizona, Utah, and New Mexico on America's largest Native American reservation that covers 24,000 sq miles (70,000 sq km). Formerly a nomadic people, Navajos are farmers, growing corn, beans, and squashes. They are skilled potters, weavers, and silversmiths.

Distinctive Navajo geometric design

Navajo rug

Beef

Cattle ranching began in the mid-19th century to meet the food demands of growing cities on the east coast. Today, it is still a successful business, and cattle are raised on the vast plains throughout Texas, New Mexico, and eastern Colorado.

Oil workers use a horizontal drilling method.

Las Vegas

Filled with glittering neon signs that lure people into nightclubs and casinos, Las Vegas is an opulent urban creation devoted to gambling. Situated near the Grand Canyon, in the middle of Nevada's desert, Las Vegas attracts about 30 million visitors every year.

Oil industry

Since the discovery of oil in 1901, Texas is America's top oil producer alongside Alaska. One of the country's wealthiest cities, Houston is the heart of the industry, with its vast refineries.

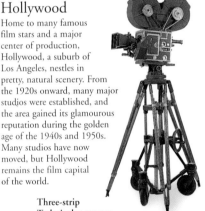

Pacific states

The three states of Washington, Oregon, and California have a long Pacific coastline. The scenery varies from the mountains, volcanoes, and forests of the north, to the arid desert and Sierra Nevada range of California. All three states enjoy thriving economies. California is the most populated and attracts many tourists.

Logging

One-third of America's softwood comes from the vast cedar and fir forests of Oregon and Washington. Most is used to make paper. The world's tallest living trees are California's coast redwoods, growing up to 363 ft (111 m).

Hollywood

Home to many famous film stars and a major center of production, Hollywood, a suburb of Los Angeles, nestles in pretty, natural scenery. From the 1920s onward, many major studios were established, and the area gained its glamourous reputation during the golden age of the 1940s and 1950s. Many studios have now moved, but Hollywood remains the film capital of the world.

Three-strip Technicolor camera

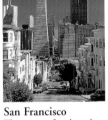

San Francisco
The center of trade and shipping for the West Coast, San Francisco lies on a natural bay. The hilly, green city endures frequent earthquakes, but its skyscrapers are built to withstand them. About six million people have made San Francisco and its suburbs their home.

CD disc

Silicon Valley

The Santa Clara Valley, south of San Francisco, has been dubbed "Silicon Valley," because more than 3,000 computer and other electronics firms are based there. It is a center of high-tech innovation and thrives on the development of new ideas, often working in partnership with nearby Stanford University.

Avocado   Grapes   Almonds

Peach

Farming

Fertile soils and a warm climate enable California to produce about half of all America's fruit and vegetables, including avocados, peaches, and almonds. One-third of the country's apples are grown in Washington, but the main crop is grapes.

Alaska

Lying beyond Canada in northwestern North America, Alaska was bought from Russia in 1867. It is the largest of the states, and much of it is forest or snowy tundra with long, dark winter days. The discovery of oil in 1968 made it one of the US's greatest assets, and oil drilling, fishing, and forestry are the main activities. The population is sparse, but many Inuit still live here.

Hawaii

This chain of 8 volcanic islands and 124 islets in the Pacific Ocean became the US's 50th state in 1959. Palm-fringed beaches have earned Hawaii a reputation as a tropical paradise; tourism along with farming and US military bases provide most state income. Most Hawaiians descend from Polynesian, European, American, Chinese, and Japanese immigrants.

FIND OUT MORE   DISNEY, WALT   EARTHQUAKES   FARMING   FILMS AND FILMMAKING   FORESTS   JAZZ   LAKES   NATIVE AMERICANS   NEWSPAPERS AND MAGAZINES   NORTH AMERICA, HISTORY OF   OIL

UNITED STATES, HISTORY OF

JUST OVER 200 YEARS AGO, the British colonies on the east coast of America became the first colonies in the world to achieve independence from European rule. One hundred years later, they had created a nation that spanned the continent. Many Americans trekked westward to settle on the prairies; others went farther to California to find gold. Millions of people came to America from Europe to escape poverty and persecution and begin a new life. Today, the United States is the world's richest nation, its people drawn from all over the globe.

Declaration of Independence, 1776

Birth of a nation

The 13 British colonies on the east coast of America resented paying high taxes without being represented in the British parliament. In 1775, colonists rose up against Britain. The next year the 13 colonies declared their independence. After five years of fighting, they forced the British to surrender in 1781.

US Constitution
In 1787, representatives of the American states drew up a constitution. They set up a federal system, sharing power between the states and central government.

Wagon trails

In 1862, the US government passed the Homestead Act, which gave farmers 160 acres (65 hectares) of land west of the Mississippi after they had cultivated it for five years. People headed for the plains in covered wagons. Some took the Oregon Trail over the Rockies to the northwest; others went south to California.

Waterproof canvas held up by iron hoops

Wooden wheel with iron rim

Wagon contained everything a family needed.

Expanding nation
Within 65 years of independence, the 13 original states on the east coast had expanded the territory of the US across the whole continent.

	1776
	1783
	1803
	1845
	1846
	1848

Expansion of the United States

Wooden frame houses

Shantytowns
In order to exploit the mineral wealth of the country, workers lived in shantytowns around the mines. In 1848, gold was discovered in California, and many thousands of prospectors arrived in the area.

Coast to coast
Until the 1860s, most of the railroads were in the eastern part of the country, and the only way to travel west was on horseback or by covered wagon. On July 10, 1869, the first transcontinental railroad was completed, linking the two coasts for the first time. Six further transcontinental railroads were completed by 1909.

Immigration
Irish fleeing famine, Jews fleeing persecution, Italians and others fleeing poverty – all made their way across the Atlantic Ocean to start a new life in the US. In one decade – the 1890s – the total population rose by 13 million to 76 million people. By 1907, more than 1 million people were arriving in the country each year from Europe. The US became a melting pot of different languages and cultures.

Immigrants arrive in New York

Gettysburg

In 1861, civil war broke out between the northern and southern states over the issue of slavery. Fighting lasted for four years. One of the turning points was the Battle of Gettysburg in July 1863. At Gettysburg, the advance of the southern army northward was finally halted in a battle in which thousands lost their lives. The north eventually won the war, ensuring the abolition of slavery.

North and South clash at Gettysburg

Timeline

1783 United States of America founded.

1787 Constitution of the US is drawn up .

1789 George Washington is elected first president of the US.

1861–65 Civil war between southern and northern states.

1890s US becomes major industrial power.

1903 President Roosevelt acquires right to build Panama Canal.

Theodore Roosevelt

U

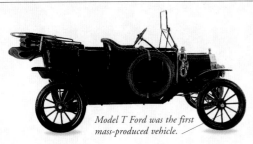
Model T Ford was the first mass-produced vehicle.

Industrialization

Between 1870 and 1914, industrial output in the US tripled, making it a powerful economy. In 1912, Henry Ford introduced mass production into the car industry.

Pearl Harbor

When war broke out in Europe in 1939, the US stayed neutral. But on December 7, 1941, Japanese aircraft bombed the US fleet at anchor in Pearl Harbor, Hawaii. The US joined the war against Germany, Italy, and Japan, fighting on many continents until victory in 1945.

The Jazz Age

Following World War I, the American economy boomed. The 1920s became known as the Jazz Age, after the music of the time. In 1920, the American government introduced Prohibition – a ban on alcohol. Crime rose as gangsters fought for control of the black market.

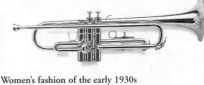
Women's fashion of the early 1930s

J.F. Kennedy

Born in Massachusetts, John F. Kennedy (1917–63) was the 35th US President. He took office at the age of 43 – the youngest man to do so. His youth and vigor attracted many people, but he faced enormous problems. At home, he tried to tackle racial discrimination, as black Americans demanded the same rights as whites. Abroad he faced the threat of Soviet nuclear missiles in Cuba, which were removed after a tense period of negotiations in October 1962. Before completing his reforms, Kennedy was assassinated in Dallas, Texas.

Great Depression

In 1929, the New York Stock Exchange collapsed, causing a massive economic depression. By 1932, over 12 million Americans were out of work; soup kitchens were set up to feed the hungry.

Vietnam War

Between 1965 and 1973, Americans fought in South Vietnam in an attempt to prevent the unification of the country under commmunist North Vietnamese control.

Postwar society

Between 1945 and 1970, American science and industry flourished. The US economy almost quadrupled, and the real income of the average family doubled. Today, the nation still remains a major power, and is a world leader in technology and space research. However, this success does not extend to the living standards of the whole population. Many major cities suffer from mass unemployment and contain large areas of sub-standard housing, and millions of Americans continue to live in conditions of near poverty.

The 1950s

The 1950s were a period of rising wealth. Car ownership became common, and most families could afford to equip their homes with new electric appliances such as washing machines.

Consumerism

In the 1950s, shopping malls opened across the country as rising prosperity allowed people to spend more on consumer goods. Americans were also able to take vacations abroad for the first time.

Woodstock

In the 1960s, a new youth culture grew up based on rock music. More than 300,000 people attended the Woodstock music festival in August 1969, one of the most successful music events of all time.

Wall Street

During the 1980s, the US continued to prosper, and many people became wealthy by investing on Wall Street. But in 1987, the stock market crashed again, with $500 billion wiped off share values in one day. Irresponsible trading was blamed.

September 11, 2001

On September 11, 2001, the worst terrorist attack in history took place in the US. Terrorists flew a hijacked passenger plane into the World Trade Center in New York City, resulting in an explosion that demolished its twin towers and killed almost 3,000 people. Other synchronized attacks on the day included a plane flown into the Pentagon in Washington, D.C. The US retaliated with the bombing of Afghanistan, believed to harbour the key perpetrators of the crime, including the head of al-Qaida, Osama bin Laden.

Firemen battled bravely to find survivors.

1917 The US enters World War I and fights alongside Britain and France.

1920–33 Prohibition laws ban the sale and manufacture of alcohol in the US.

1929 Wall Street Stock Exchange crashes in New York.

News of Wall St. crash

1929–39 Great Depression causes mass poverty.

1933 President F.D. Roosevelt promises a "New Deal" to get the US out of economic slump.

1945 The US drops atomic bombs on Japan, ending World War II.

1945–89 "Cold War" between US and the Soviet Union.

1954 Supreme Court prohibits racial segregation in schools.

1965–73 Over 50,000 US troops killed in Vietnam.

1960s and 1970s Black people fight for equal rights.

Ronald Reagan and Mikhail Gorbachev

1969 American Neil Armstrong is the first person

1989 Presidents Reagan and Gorbachev sign Nuclear Forces Treaty.

1991 Operation Desert Storm is launched against Iraq in the Gulf War.

2001 Terrorist attacks in the US lead to the bombing of Afghanistan.

FIND OUT MORE   AMERICAN CIVIL WAR   AMERICAN REVOLUTION   COLD WAR   GREAT DEPRESSION   KING, MARTIN LUTHER   NORTH AMERICA, HISTORY OF   PILGRIM FATHERS   TRADE AND INDUSTRY

UNIVERSE

EVERYTHING THAT EXISTS makes up the Universe, from the smallest particles to the biggest structures, whether on Earth or in space. It includes everything that is visible, much that is invisible, everything that is known, and more that is unknown. Over time, humans have had different ideas of what the Universe is and how it works, how it started, and what its future is. Today, scientists know more than ever before, but there is much still to be learned.

Structure of the Universe

The most common object in the Universe is the star. There are billions and billions of them. At least one of these, the Sun, has planets. One of these planets, Earth, has life. On the face of it stars, planets, and humans are very different, but they do have things in common. They are all made of the same chemical elements, or compounds of them, and they are all affected by the laws of science, such as gravity and the electromagnetic force. By studying the constituents of the Universe and understanding the laws, scientists can construct a picture of the Universe and discover its past and predict its future.

A large star dies as a supernova.

Galaxies contain billions of stars.

Great Wall
The largest structures in the Universe are long threadlike filaments made of thousands of galaxies. They surround huge, empty voids. Here a computer simulation shows the view from an imaginary spacecraft traveling above one such filament, known as the Great Wall.

The Universe was created 15 billion years ago in the Big Bang. Since then, matter has come together to form stars, galaxies, planets, and life.

Interstellar material
Gas and dust are found in the vast spaces between stars and make up about 10 percent of the Universe. In places, the gas and dust is so thinly spread that it is like a vacuum; in other places they make enormous clouds. Gas and dust can form new stars and be replenished by material from dying stars. Gas and dust are also found between the galaxies.

The Sun, an ordinary middle-aged star

Clusters of stars

Cloud of gas and dust

Comet

Planets – balls of rock, gas, or ice

Apparent position of star

Real position of star

Path of light rays

Ptolemy
Once the Earth was thought to be the center of the Universe with the other celestial objects moving around it. This idea is the Ptolemaic view, named after Claudius Ptolemy, an Egyptian. In the 2nd century AD, he brought together the astronomical ideas of the ancient Greek world in his work the *Almagest*.

Dark matter
Scientists have calculated how much material the Universe contains: the answer is about 90 per cent more than has been detected. This gas cloud, with a cluster of galaxies embedded in it, may contain some of the missing material.

Gravity
A star's gas is held together by gravity. Everything in the Universe is affected by gravity. Earth's gravity keep things on its surface, the Sun's gravity keeps the Solar System together, and the stars in the Milky Way are held together by gravity. In general, the more massive a body is, the more gravitational pull it has.

General relativity
Early in the 20th century, gravity was shown to affect not only objects but space itself. Massive objects, which have immense gravitational pull, curve space. This pull is seen when the light from a star, instead of following a straight path through space, falls into the curved space created by the Sun. This law is called the general theory of relativity.

Looking at the Universe

Everything known about the Universe has been learned from Earth or close to it. Telescopes collect information by picking up electro-magnetic radiation, transmitted in a range of wavelengths, by every object in the Universe. By analyzing different wavelengths, it is possible to construct a picture of the Universe.

Infrared
Andromeda Galaxy as recorded at infrared wavelengths. Infrared images can help astronomers locate cooler objects and regions not visible at optical wavelengths.

Visible light
The Andromeda Galaxy at optical wavelengths. It is the largest of the galaxies close to the Milky Way. It has two smaller companion galaxies, also visible in this image.

X rays
An X ray image of the Andromeda Galaxy. X rays are short wavelengths with high energy. They pinpoint "hot spots" or areas of intense activity in space.

Edge of the Universe
As telescopes have improved, astronomers have been able to see farther and farther. With present instruments, they can see almost to the edge of the Universe, 15 billion light-years away. This quasar, one of the most distant objects visible, is 12 billion light-years away.

Each wavelength gives different information about an object.

Long wavelengths

Radio waves   *Microwaves*   *Infrared*   *Visible light*   *Ultraviolet*   *X rays*   *Gamma rays*   **Short wavelengths**

U

Scale of the Universe

Earth is tiny compared with other objects in space and the overall Universe. Distances on Earth are measured in miles or kilometres, but distances in space are so great that these measuring units become unwieldy. Astronomers use astronomical units (au) in the Solar System and light-years (ly) outside it. The distances are always changing because the Universe itself is getting bigger. It has been expanding ever since it was created by the Big Bang.

Earth to the Sun

Earth does not stay a constant distance from the Sun but moves closer and farther away as it orbits the Sun. The average distance is 93 million miles (149.6 million km), or 1 au. Light from the Sun takes 8.3 light-minutes to reach Earth.

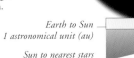

Earth to Sun
1 astronomical unit (au)

Sun to nearest stars
270,000 astronomical units

Sun to nearest star

The nearest star to the Sun is Proxima Centauri, 4.2 ly away. A light-year is the distance light travels in one year (9.46 million km/5.88 million miles). Less than 10 stars are within 10 ly.

Sun to nearest stars 10 ly

Milky Way 100,000 ly wide

Distance across Galaxy

The Milky Way Galaxy is about 100,000 ly across, and is made up of billions of stars. On average, the stars are 4 ly apart. The Solar System is about 27,700 ly from the center.

Milky Way 100,000 ly wide

Milky Way to nearest galaxies 2.25 million ly

Milky Way to Andromeda Galaxy

The largest of the nearby galaxies is the Andromeda Galaxy at 2.25 million ly away. The Milky Way and Andromeda Galaxy are part of the Local Group cluster, which consists of about 30 galaxies.

Distance across the Universe

By measuring the distance to the most distant galaxies, astronomers can calculate the size of the Universe. The radius is believed to be 15 billion ly.

Measuring the Universe

The nearest celestial objects to Earth are the Moon and the planets. Their distance is measured by radar. The closest stars, those up to about 1,600 ly away, are measured by parallax. The distance to more remote stars and galaxies is calculated by analyzing the object's light or by comparing it with an object of known distance.

Redshift

Light from stars and galaxies travels in a wave and tells us if an object is moving away from or toward Earth. The light is split to produce a spectrum. If the object is moving away, the wavelength will be stretched toward the red end of the spectrum – a redshift. If the object is moving towards Earth, waves are squeezed and shift toward the blue end of the spectrum.

Apparent movement of star A
Apparent movement of star B
Star A
Star B
Earth's position in June
Earth's position in January
Earth orbits the Sun.

Light waves from a galaxy moving toward Earth are squeezed or blueshifted.

Light waves from a galaxy moving away from Earth are stretched or redshifted.

Parallax

The parallax method requires a star to be observed twice, six months apart. In this time, the star appears to have shifted against the background of distant stars. The angle of shift, the parallax of the star, indicates the distance. The greater the angle, the nearer the star.

Universe through history

People have always tried to make sense of their surroundings, and different ideas of the Universe evolved as people discovered more. First, they struggled to explain the mechanics of the Solar System. Then, as they discovered more distant objects, the size of the Universe grew. Discoveries of new types of objects brought new questions to be answered.

Babylonian

Gods played an important part in the Babylonian view of the Universe 3,500 years ago. They had placed the Sun, Moon, planets, and stars in heaven, and Earth was a large, round, hollow mountain resting on water and supporting the domed sky.

Ptolemaic

The ancient Greeks saw Earth as the center of the Universe. The Sun, Moon, and the five known planets moved around it. The sphere of fixed stars lay beyond.

Copernican

Devised in the 16th century, this system is the basis of today's understanding of the Universe. Earth rotates on its axis once a day and orbits the Sun in one year. Earth is no longer at the center; it is just one of the planets.

Copernicus

The work of the Polish astronomer Nicolaus Copernicus (1473–1543) marks a change in the understanding of the Universe. He proposed that the Sun and not the Earth was at the center of the Universe. His theories were not generally accepted until the mid-17th century, when astronomers provided the proof that Earth and the other planets orbited the Sun.

Today

Astronomers in the 20th century learned much about the structure, scale, and history of the Universe. The Milky Way is not the only galaxy: there are millions of them. The Universe is believed to have been created in a giant explosion, the Big Bang, 15 billion years ago. It has been evolving and expanding ever since.

FIND OUT MORE   ASTRONOMY   BABYLONIANS   BIG BANG   BLACK HOLES   FORCE AND MOTION   GALAXIES   GRAVITY   GREECE, ANCIENT   STARS   TELESCOPES   X-RAYS

URBAN WILDLIFE

THE MAN-MADE LANDSCAPES of our towns and cities may seem an odd setting for wildlife, but a variety of animals, from foxes to cockroaches, have made their homes there. Some animals live among the shrubs and weeds of forgotten street corners and re-create wild habitats; others have colonized artificial structures – even the most sterile concrete buildings harbor life. For species such as rats, adaptable enough to try new foods, explore new places for shelter, and withstand congestion, the urban environment can be an attractive habitat free of many predators, and full of opportunities.

This raccoon is foraging through the litter in search of food.

Types of urban habitat

The typical city offers wildlife an amazing assortment of habitats, from the concrete and tarmac of city centres to the ornamental greenery of parks and suburban gardens. Office blocks harbour insects, monkeys often linger around African market squares, and rubbish tips in North America may be visited by animals as large as polar bears. Railside verges, playing fields, waste ground, and reservoirs alike all have their typical animal residents.

Raccoons often tip over dustbins to make their search for food easier.

Railroad tracks
Undisturbed land alongside railroads provides a refuge through the heart of cities for wild plants and wild animals such as foxes.

Houses and buildings
Many creatures live below floorboards, in attics, and on roofs. Some live in our houses; others raid our food supplies.

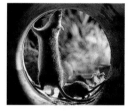

Life underground
Burrowing animals, such as brown rats, live in sewer systems where they can take shelter, eat waste matter, and breed freely.

Raccoons are found scavenging from dustbins in towns in the US

Ultimate adapters

Cockroaches colonized in Britain after being carried accidentally in imported food from the warmth of the tropics. They now thrive wherever there is artificial heating and food to plunder. They are common in bakeries and restaurants, as well as many houses.

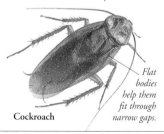

Cockroach

Flat bodies help them fit through narrow gaps.

Source of food

Urban habitats offer rich pickings for scavengers of refuse, waste matter, and the food stored in kitchens, shops, and warehouses. City residents even encourage animals into their gardens and parks by feeding them. These areas also provide plentiful food for non-scavenging animals. Insects feed on the nectar from flowers, birds eat berries, and weasels feed on nesting birds and mice.

Hedgehogs often visit gardens where food may be left out for them deliberately.

Re-created habitats

Many of the habitats that exist in urban areas re-create the types of habitats found in the wild. A garden pond, for example, serves as a miniature wetland, while a well-weathered wall resembles a rugged hillside. Buildings are often clifflike on the outside, while their unlit recesses are similar to caves. It is little wonder that animals used to such habitats have moved in.

Swallows used to nest mainly on cliffs and crags under overhanging rocks. Many now build their mud nests below the eaves of houses.

Neatly made mud nest

Frogs and toads have found refuge in garden ponds, because their natural wetlands have receded.

Many frogs now live in garden ponds.

City warmth

The heating of buildings and the heat generated by machines, motors, and ovens all create extra warmth for urban wildlife. Some birds, such as pigeons and starlings, roost in downtown areas on winter nights because it is normally a few degrees warmer there than in the suburbs. Artificial heating has also enabled tropical insects to colonize buildings in cold climates.

Starlings roosting on ledges of a cathedral

FIND OUT MORE

CITIES, TOWNS AND VILLAGES   GARDENS   INSECTS   PANDAS AND RACCOONS   RATS AND OTHER RODENTS

URINARY SYSTEM

URINATING IS SOMETHING we do every day without really thinking about it. Urine is a waste liquid produced by the urinary system, which consists of the kidneys, ureters, bladder, and urethra. The two kidneys regulate water levels inside your body and filter waste substances from the blood. As blood passes through the kidneys, waste is extracted from it to make urine. Two long tubes called the ureters carry urine to the bladder, where it is collected and then passed out of the body through the urethra.

How the kidney works

Each kidney is divided into an outer cortex and a middle medulla where urine is produced. Each cortex and medulla contain about one million tiny filtration units called nephrons. Nephrons filter fluid from blood as it passes through the kidney, and then process it. Useful substances pass back into the bloodstream and unwanted substances form urine.

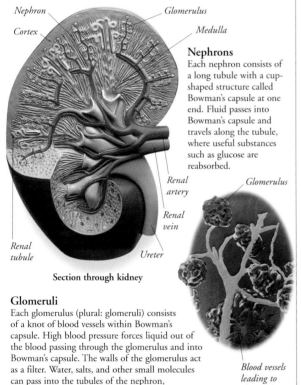

Nephron
Cortex
Glomerulus
Medulla
Renal artery
Renal vein
Renal tubule
Ureter

Section through kidney

Nephrons
Each nephron consists of a long tubule with a cup-shaped structure called Bowman's capsule at one end. Fluid passes into Bowman's capsule and travels along the tubule, where useful substances such as glucose are reabsorbed.

Glomerulus

Glomeruli
Each glomerulus (plural: glomeruli) consists of a knot of blood vessels within Bowman's capsule. High blood pressure forces liquid out of the blood passing through the glomerulus and into Bowman's capsule. The walls of the glomerulus act as a filter. Water, salts, and other small molecules can pass into the tubules of the nephron, while blood cells cannot.

Blood vessels leading to glomeruli

Carl Ludwig
The German physiologist Carl Ludwig (1816–95) fully explained the workings of the kidney. He determined that, once inside the kidney, blood was filtered through the glomeruli into Bowman's capsule before being concentrated in the long tubules of the nephron to form urine, which was then expelled from the body.

Kidneys and bladder

The two kidneys are reddish-brown, bean-shaped organs, each about 5 in (12.5 cm) long, attached to the back wall of the abdomen. The ureters gently squeeze urine from the kidneys to the bladder where it is stored. The bladder opens to the outside of the body through the urethra.

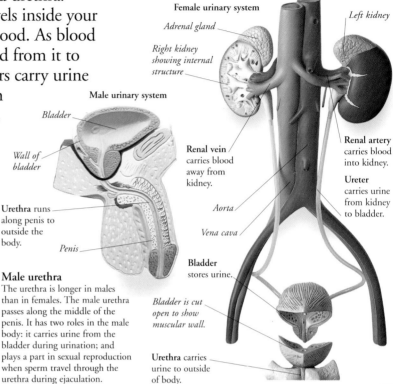

Female urinary system
Adrenal gland
Right kidney showing internal structure
Left kidney

Male urinary system
Bladder
Wall of bladder
Urethra runs along penis to outside the body.
Penis

Renal vein carries blood away from kidney.
Renal artery carries blood into kidney.
Ureter carries urine from kidney to bladder.
Aorta
Vena cava
Bladder stores urine.
Bladder is cut open to show muscular wall.
Urethra carries urine to outside of body.

Male urethra
The urethra is longer in males than in females. The male urethra passes along the middle of the penis. It has two roles in the male body: it carries urine from the bladder during urination; and plays a part in sexual reproduction when sperm travel through the urethra during ejaculation.

Bladder

Urine is produced continuously by the kidneys. The bladder stores urine until it is convenient to release it. At the base of the bladder, guarding the exit to the urethra, there are two rings of muscles called sphincters. As the bladder fills, the sphincters contract to prevent any leakage.

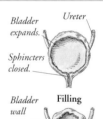

Bladder expands.
Ureter
Sphincters closed.
Filling
Bladder wall contracts.
Sphincters open.
Emptying

Controlling bladder
You can decide when you want to urinate. One of the sphincter muscles only relaxes when you tell it to. We learn to control our bladders in childhood.

Renal dialysis
If someone's kidneys stop working properly, poisonous waste products can build up in the blood, making that person very ill. Kidney failure can be treated by renal dialysis; this uses an artificial kidney or kidney machine to clean the blood.

Water balance

Over half of your body is water. In order to work properly, your body must keep its water content at a constant level. However, water is constantly being lost from the body as urine and in other ways (see right). To balance these daily losses, we must take in more water by drinking regularly.

Sweat 7 oz
Feces 7 oz
Skin 14 oz
Lungs 14 oz
Urine 42 oz

FIND OUT MORE   DIGESTION   HUMAN BODY   LIQUIDS   MEDICINE   MUSCLES AND MOVEMENT

VESALIUS, ANDREAS

DURING THE 16TH CENTURY, physicians followed the methods laid down by ancient Greek doctors more than 1,500 years before. One Flemish doctor, Andreas Vesalius, challenged these teachings. He dissected human corpses to discover how the body worked, and then published his findings in a book, giving physicians the first reliable guide to human anatomy. By basing his conclusions only on research, Vesalius set new standards for medicine that have survived until today.

Early life
Andreas Vesalius was born in 1514 in the Flemish city of Brussels. His father was a pharmacist and encouraged his son to study medicine. Andreas began his studies in Paris. Vesalius learned about anatomy from the books of the Greek writer Galen. He later moved to Louvain near Brussels and then to Padua, Italy, where he took his medical degree at the university in 1537. The authorities at Padua recognized his talent and made him a professor of anatomy.

Early work
Vesalius was fascinated by anatomy, but was frustrated at the primitive knowledge of most anatomists. In the 16th century, it was almost unheard of for a doctor to dissect a human corpse to find out how the body worked. Vesalius wanted to do this, but he knew he would face opposition from the Roman Catholic Church, whose priests thought that cutting up a dead body was wrong.

Galen
Galen of Pergamum (129–199) was a Greek medical scientist. He experimented on animals, such as pigs and apes, to find out about their anatomy. Galen and his followers assumed that the inner organs of humans were similar to those of pigs and apes. Galen also established the importance of diagnosis and observation in treating disease.

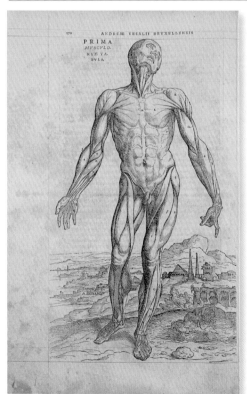

Structure of the human body
In 1543, Vesalius published *De Humani Corporis Fabrica (On the Structure of the Human Body)*. The book contained many woodcut illustrations by the German artist John Stephen, depicting the results of the dissections that Vesalius had carried out. Vesalius challenged many earlier teachings, recognizing that Galen's beliefs rested on a knowledge of animals rather than humans. For the first time, an accurate guide to the human body was available.

Dissection
In spite of the objections of other doctors backed by the Church, Vesalius continued dissecting corpses. As he worked, he made careful drawings of the different functional systems of the body – such as the blood vessels, muscles, and digestive system. These detailed, first-hand studies put him in the forefront of medical science.

Arteries
In his book, Vesalius made a detailed study of the blood vessels, showing how the veins and arteries linked together in the body. With this work, he prepared the way for William Harvey, the 17th-century English scientist who correctly proposed that blood is pumped around the body by the heart, and not produced by the liver, as Galen had thought.

Woodcut of Vesalius's dissection of a human body

Human arteries

Shows bloodflow of the body

Vesalius's dissecting tools

Controversy
After his book was published, Vesalius continued to dissect corpses, and he published a revised version of the work in 1555. But his work attracted such controversy from other doctors that he resigned his post at Padua and became personal physician to the emperor Charles V and later to Charles's son Philip II of Spain.

Holy Roman Emperor Charles V

ANDREAS VESALIUS

1514	Born in Brussels.
1530s	Studies in Paris and Louvain.
1537	Gains his medical degree from Padua University, where he becomes a professor.
1453	Publishes *De Humani Corporis Fabrica*.
1550s	Works as physician to Charles V and then Philip II of Spain.
1555	Publishes revised edition of *Fabrica*.
1563	Goes on pilgrimage to Jerusalem.
1564	Dies in Greece on his way back from Jerusalem.

FIND OUT MORE

MEDICINE, HISTORY OF

SCIENCE, HISTORY OF

VIDEO

ALL THE EXCITEMENT of a sports event or the happy memories of a birthday party can be captured using video. Video is the recording and playing back of television (TV) signals. A television signal is an electric current or digital transmission produced by a television camera. The signal carries both picture (video) and sound (audio) information that can be used to recreate a moving scene on a TV screen or computer. Videocassette recorders can record TV signals on to magnetic tape, and then play them back on a TV screen. Nowadays, much video technology is digital.

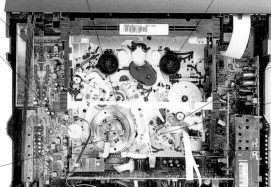

Videocassette recorder with top removed
Loading pole engages tape.
Circuitry
Tape cassette is inserted here.
Capstans rotate to feed tape through machine.
Erase head wipes off any previous recording from tape.
Guide roller ensures that tape runs smoothly through the machine.
Audio record/play-back head
Electric motor
Video-head drum spins 50 times every second.
Signals from TV aerial enter here.

Camcorder

A camcorder is a combined videocamera and recorder in a handheld unit. Until recently, most camcorders were analog, which means that the image signal is captured electrically on tape. Today, digital camcorders are more popular because they have the advantage of producing a high-quality image that can be replayed over time without deteriorating. The digital image signal is recorded on tape using a binary computer code.

Compact design
Digital zoom
Playback monitor
Lens
Camera also takes digital photos.
Digital camcorder
Rechargeable battery
LCD screen can be adjusted to any angle.

Videocassette recorder (VCR)

A videocassette contains a reel of magnetic tape that stores a TV signal as changing patterns of magnetism. Inside a VCR, the tape moves past a video-head drum, which converts the patterns back into a video signal. The audio signal is picked up by a separate audio head. The signals are then sent to a TV set, which recreates the sounds and pictures. The audio and video heads can also record signals fed into the VCR via an aerial.

Diagonal scanning
The VCR records the information in the video signal as a series of diagonal tracks across the magnetic tape. To read the tracks, the video-head drum is set at an angle, so that it scans the tape diagonally. The audio information is recorded along the edge of the tape.

Using a camcorder
A camcorder is very simple to use: just point it at the scene you want to capture and press the "record" button. You can zoom in for a close-up or zoom out for a wider view, and use the controls to get the best lighting conditions. A playback screen allows you to view what you have recorded.

Digital video types
The two types of digital video format are Digital8 and the smaller MiniDV. Both produce crystal-clear images that can be edited easily on a home computer.

Plastic cards hold data in binary code.

Digital memory card
Some analogue camcorders can be partially upgraded to digital quality by recording the signal on to a plastic card instead of a tape. The card stores the signal digitally, as binary numbers made up of the digits 0 and 1. This produces better quality sound and pictures overall.

Digital memory cards

Uses of video

Video recording brings us news from around the world in an instant. The VCR makes it possible to record TV shows when we are doing something else, and watch films at home after release at theatres. Videocameras in shops and banks also help deter criminals.

Home entertainment
Most towns have stores where people can rent or buy videocassettes or digital video discs (DVDs). DVDs have superior image quality.

Broadcasting
All the different elements of a TV show are pieced together and recorded on to videotape. The tape is then played back to viewers over the TV network.

Security
Stores, banks, and many other buildings install videocameras to catch thieves. The pictures the cameras produce can be used in court to help identify criminals.

News gathering
Reporters send video pictures of world events back to TV stations by cable or by radio waves, bringing news to the viewers almost as it happens.

FIND OUT MORE   CAMERAS   ELECTRONICS   FILMS AND FILM-MAKING   LIGHT   PHOTOGRAPHY   SOUND RECORDING   TELEPHONES   TELEVISION

VIETNAM, CAMBODIA, AND LAOS

THE COUNTRIES OF VIETNAM, Cambodia, and Laos form the eastern half of the Southeast Asian peninsula and for many years were known as Indochina. People from China migrated there about 2,000 years ago. The French colonized the area during the 1800s as French Indochina. Japan occupied Indochina in World War II (1939–45) and urged the people to seek independence. The French resisted this move, but were defeated in a war that raged from 1946 to 1954, when all three countries gained their independence.

Physical features

The region is a mixture of rugged, forested hills and fertile river valleys. The only large lake is the Tonlé Sap in Cambodia. For seven months of the year, it feeds the Mekong River, but in the monsoon, the Mekong drains into the lake, making it ten times larger.

Ha Long Bay
A legend says that the fantastic limestone rocks and thousands of islands and caves of Ha Long Bay on Vietnam's Red River Delta were formed when a dragon smashed up the coast.

Mekong River
The world's tenth longest river, the Mekong rises in Tibet and flows for 2,600 miles (4,180 km) through China, Burma, Laos, and Cambodia, ending in a vast delta in South Vietnam. Many people live in riverside towns and villages and use the water to cultivate rice.

Forests
Dense rain forest covers much of the region, particularly the hilly areas. These forests are home to scattered groups of hill people who clear small areas for farming. Hardwoods, such as teak and rosewood, are a significant resource in both Cambodia and Laos.

Regional climate
Cambodia, Laos, and southern Vietnam have a tropical climate with high temperatures all year round. The dry season ends in May with the arrival of the monsoon rains, which last until October. Northern Vietnam and Laos have cooler, more humid winters.

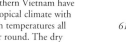

83°F (28°C)   70°F (21°C)

61 in (1,618 mm)

Rice
Rice is the staple food of Southeast Asia, where the warm, humid weather and plentiful water make it easy to grow. Vietnam is the world's fifth largest producer of rice, and one of the largest exporters. The most important growing areas lie in the deltas of the Mekong and Red rivers.

Rice picker, Phnom Penh, Cambodia

Vietnam

For 18 years, Vietnam was torn by a vicious war between the communist north and US-backed south, which devastated the economy. In 1975, the north won the war, and the country was unified. Today, Vietnam is slowly reestablishing its industrial strength and has close trade links with Japan, Eastern Europe, and Southeast Asia.

VIETNAM FACTS

CAPITAL CITY Hanoi

AREA 127,243 sq miles (329,560 sq km)

POPULATION 79,800,000

MAIN LANGUAGE Vietnamese

MAJOR RELIGIONS Buddhist, Christian

CURRENCY Dông

V

Boat people
After the end of the war, about a million Vietnamese set sail for Hong Kong, Singapore, and Malaysia, hoping to find refuge in the West. Crowded into tiny boats in appalling conditions, thousands died on the journey. Most were sent home, but some still live in Hong Kong.

Transportation
Few Vietnamese families can afford cars, and people rely on scooters and bicycles to get to work, to school, or to the stores. Rush hour is dominated by thousands of cyclists ringing their bells and shouting warnings. Heavy freight is transported mostly on the rivers.

Fishing
Seafood and fish are an important part of Vietnamese cooking. Thousands of people earn their living by fishing off the long coastline and in the river deltas. They catch more than a million tons of lobsters, fish, squid, and shrimps every year.

Cambodia

Once at the center of the Khmer Empire, Cambodia was ravaged by war during the 20th century. From 1975 to 1979, the country was terrorized by the communist Khmer Rouge led by Pol Pot. More than a million people were killed, many of them intellectuals. Today, a democratic government is slowly rebuilding the shattered economy.

CAMBODIA FACTS

CAPITAL CITY Phnom Penh

AREA 69,000 sq miles (181,040 sq km)

POPULATION 11,200,000

MAIN LANGUAGES Khmer, Chinese, Vietnamese

MAJOR RELIGION Buddhist

CURRENCY Riel

Minefields
More than three million active mines were left in the ground after the wars in Cambodia. As a result, thousands of people have been maimed or disabled.

Classical dance
The highly stylized classical dance of Cambodia is based on religious dances originally performed in the 12th-century temple complex of Angkor Wat. The dancers spend years perfecting the graceful movements, and wear costumes that are so tight they must be sewn on before each performance.

Khmers
About 90 percent of Cambodians are Khmers, an ancient people who had a flourishing kingdom two thousand years ago. Most live in small rural villages, where houses are often built on stilts to avoid floods during the monsoon rains.

Laos

Surrounded by land on all sides, Laos has rich reserves of tin, lead, and zinc as well as iron, coal, and timber, yet it remains one of the world's least developed nations. About 80 percent of the people work on the land, growing just enough food for themselves. Since 1975, Laos has been under communist rule.

LAOS FACTS

CAPITAL CITY Vientiane

AREA 91,428 sq miles (236,800 sq km)

POPULATION 5,400,000

MAIN LANGUAGES Lao, Miao, Yao

MAJOR RELIGIONS Buddhist, traditional beliefs

CURRENCY Laotian New Kip

Buddhism
More than half of the people in Laos are Theravada Buddhists, a branch of Buddhism that originated in Sri Lanka. Theravada means the way of the Elders and encourages followers to reduce suffering in the world.

Friendship Bridge
The Mekong River forms a natural border between Laos and neighboring Thailand. Since 1988, there has been increased trade between the two countries, and in 1994, with Australian backing, a "Friendship Bridge" was built across the river's lower reaches. It connects Vientiane with the Thai town of Nong Khai, and gives Laos access to Thai ports.

Hill tribeswoman

Kha peoples
The Kha, the many hill peoples of Laos, were the country's first inhabitants. For centuries the Lao have treated them like slaves. The Kha live in scattered villages, and speak many different languages. They use traditional slash-and-burn farming methods to grow crops and opium poppies for the drug trade.

 FIND OUT MORE   ASIA   ASIA, HISTORY OF   BRIDGES   BUDDHISM   DANCE   EMPIRES   FARMING   GOVERNMENTS AND POLITICS   KHMER EMPIRE   UNITED STATES, HISTORY OF

VIKINGS

FROM THE 8TH to the 11th centuries, the powerful Vikings emerged from their homelands in Norway, Sweden, and Denmark, and swept across Europe. They were superb shipbuilders and navigators, and they used these skills to travel as far afield as the eastern coast of North America and the eastern Mediterranean. Vikings had a reputation for raiding wherever they landed, and many of their leaders grew wealthy from plunder. However, they were not all raiders – some established peaceful colonies.

Greenland
Homelands
River routes
Iceland
Vinland
Constantinople

Prow carved in the shape of a snake's head

Longships were streamlined and fast-moving, so they were used for battle and long-distance travel.

Mast

Square sail

Steering oar, which could be detached in shallow water

Oars could row the ship when there was no wind.

Exploration

Traveling by sea from Scandinavia, the Vikings raided and settled along the coasts of Europe, and crossed the Atlantic to Iceland, Greenland, and Newfoundland. They also sailed the rivers of Europe to Russia and Constantinople.

Single square sail

Ropes, known as shrouds

Room for cargo

Shallow in depth, these ships could sail upriver.

A knarr, or full-bellied ship, took settlers to Greenland.

Ships

All Viking ships had a keel, matching prow and stern, and were built with overlapping planks. Long, fast ships were used for raiding trips, while fatter vessels, with a large capacity, were used for carrying cargo.

Raiders

In 793 a group of Vikings raided the monastery of Lindisfarne, northern England. The attack was the first of many raids along the coasts and up the rivers of Europe. Houses and churches were plundered, people were taken as slaves, and the Vikings demanded money before they would leave.

Warriors
Each warrior provided his own armor. Some could afford strong mail armor, others made do with a leather tunic. But most wore pointed iron helmets and carried a round, wooden shield.

Double-edged blade

Weaponry
Most Viking warriors fought with swords or axes, although spears and bows were also used. Iron swords were the most important weapons.

Conquests
The Vikings defeated some of the most powerful people in Europe, such as King Edmund of East Anglia, who was tortured and killed when he refused to give up Christianity.

Traders

Viking traders brought items such as furs, whalebone, walrus ivory, and timber to Britain and the Mediterranean. They brought back wheat and cloth from Britain, and pots and wine from the Mediterranean.

Furs
The Vikings traded animal products that could only be found in the north. Walrus hide could be turned into ropes and leather. The fur of animals such as brown bears and wolves made warm clothes.

Weights
The Vikings developed a system of weights and measures. These five pieces would have been used to weigh small items, such as jewelry made from precious metals. The largest weighs around 1.4 oz (40 g).

Arts and jewelry

Rich people wore brooches, armbands, rings, and gold or silver pendants. Poorer people wore bronze or pewter jewelry.

Gripping beast brooch

Silver spiral arm ring

Coins

Most Viking traders worked by barter – exchanging goods from their homeland for items they wanted. Then coins came into use and, by the end of the 10th century, they were widely accepted.

 Brown bear

 Gray wolf

 Seal

Iron weights

Leif Eriksson

In about the year 1000, Leif Eriksson (born c.970) sailed to North America, and explored the coast, spending the winter in a place he named Vinland (wine land) from the grapes he found there. He was following up the accidental discovery of North America in 986 by a fellow Viking, Bjarni Herjolfsson, who was blown off course on a voyage from Iceland to Greenland.

FIND OUT MORE   ARCHAEOLOGY   EXPLORATION   NORMANS   SCANDINAVIA, HISTORY OF   SHIPS AND BOATS

Vikings
Everyday objects

Glass counters *Wooden counters*

Wooden board

Hnefetafl was a popular Viking board game.

Leather board

Wooden counters

Nine men's morris is still played today in some places.

Glassware was used only by the richest Vikings because it was so difficult to get. Many jugs and cups were found in graves in Sweden.

Leather half-moon pouch on a belt

Whetstone

Dagger and sheath with runes

Comb and case with runes engraved into it

Purses and pouches were an everyday necessity.

V

Weapons and body armor

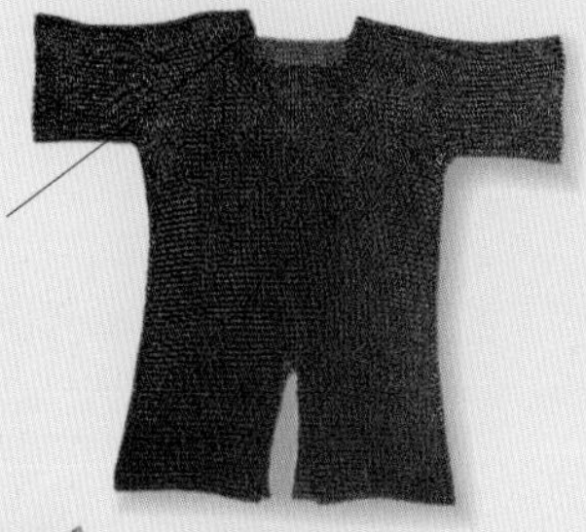

Anglo-Saxon square neck

Chain-mail shirt

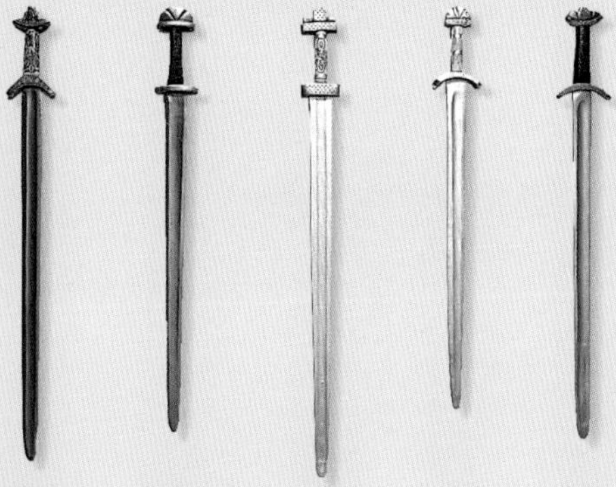

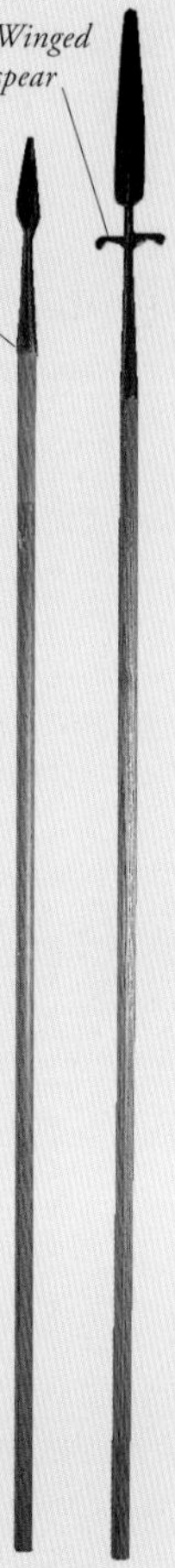

Winged spear

Straight spear

Dagger points

Chain-mail shirt

Painted wooden shields

Painted wooden shields

Steel rivets

Dragon design

Swords and scabbards

Image of warrior on nose guard

Leather trim to protect the shield

Dane axes

Helmets

Nose guard

Spears

Jewelry

Gripping beast brooch

Trefoil brooch

Swedish disk brooch

Oval brooch

Brooches were mainly used to fasten cloaks.

Disk pendant

Comb pendant

Cross pendant

Dwarf pendant

Pendants were often made of gold and silver for the rich, and bronze and pewter for the poor.

Thor's hammers

Amber and glass beads

Boar's tusks

Men's jewelry, such as this necklace, was often highly decorative.

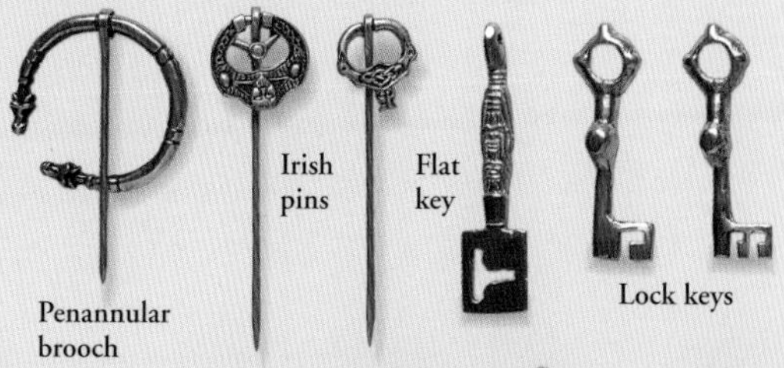

Penannular brooch

Irish pins

Flat key

Lock keys

Birka man

Odin's head

Valkyrie

Birka crucifix

Pendants could show pagan symbols, such as Odin's head or the Valkyrie, or Christian, such as the crucifix.

VOLCANOES

THE ERUPTION OF A volcano can be one of nature's most terrifying events. A volcano is a vent or fissure where magma (molten rock) from the Earth's hot interior emerges onto the surface. In some places, the molten rock, called lava once it has emerged onto the surface, oozes out slowly and gently. But in others, the eruption is a violent explosion, flinging out molten lava, red-hot lumps of rock, scorching ash, and clouds of steam that spread for miles.

Clouds of ash, steam, and rock fragments are hurled into the air.

Volcanic phases

All volcanoes, on land and under the ocean, are at different stages in their life cycles. Some volcanoes are very active, erupting year after year. Others are dormant (sleeping) and erupt only once in a while. Many more are extinct – meaning they have stopped erupting altogether. Vulcanologists monitor active and dormant volcanoes to try to predict future eruptions.

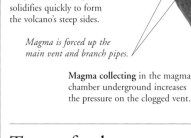

Vent often becomes blocked by congealed magma.

Lava flow

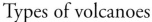

Thick, slow-moving lava, called andesite, solidifies quickly to form the volcano's steep sides.

Magma is forced up the main vent and branch pipes.

Magma collecting in the magma chamber underground increases the pressure on the clogged vent.

Magma chamber

Cone built up by successive layers of lava and ash.

Explosive volcanoes fling out large amounts of volcanic material during eruptions. This material cools to form their distinctive cone shapes.

Volcanic eruptions

Volcanoes erupt violently when the build-up of magma in the magma chamber below creates enough pressure to blast through the clogged vent. This sudden release of pressure causes a rapid expansion of carbon dioxide gas in the magma. This expansion creates fountains of lava that stream out from the volcano's vent and cover the surrounding land.

Extinct
Once a volcano is extinct, it begins to be eroded by wind and weather. All that remains of this extinct volcano in Le Puy, France, is the hard plug of material that once clogged the volcano's vent.

Active
Some volcanoes erupt almost continuously, while others erupt very violently but only at infrequent intervals. Each year there are about 25 major volcanic eruptions on land and thousands of minor ones.

Types of volcanoes

Volcanoes are different shapes and sizes depending on the thickness of their lava and the shape of their vents.

Shield volcanoes are broad, shallow cones made of very runny lava that flows easily.

Fissure volcanoes are long cracks in the ground through which the magma oozes up gently.

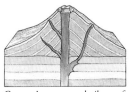

Composite cones are built up of alternate layers of lava and ash. Cones can be made of ash alone.

Ash and cinder volcanoes have concave-shaped cones made of the solid fragments ejected by eruptions.

Katia and Maurice Krafft

French vulcanologists Maurice Krafft (1946–91) and Katia Krafft (1947–91) were legendary for working consistently closer to erupting volcanoes than any other vulcanologists. They obtained unique data, amazing film footage, and close-up photographs of eruptions. Sadly, their bravery led to their deaths. In 1991, they were engulfed by a Japanese volcano. Their bodies were never found.

V

Types of lava

Lava is the molten rock thrown out by a volcano. The most common forms of lava are basalt, which is thin and runny and cools to a heavy black rock, and rhyolite, a thick, pale-colored lava. How a volcano erupts depends on the lava's thickness.

Acidic
Very viscous lava flows, such as this one, are usually linked to acidic magma, which contains a high proportion of the mineral silica.

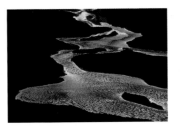

Aa
In Hawaii, where Mauna Loa is erupting almost all the time, lava that solidifies into sharp, jagged chunks is known as aa, or block lava. Lava in this part of the world is basic, which means it is non-acidic.

Pahoehoe
Lava may cool quickly to form a skin tough enough to walk over. If lava continues to flow underneath, the surface wrinkles into ropelike coils. In Hawaii this is called pahoehoe, or corded lava.

Pyroclastic debris

When an explosive volcano blasts out the plug of volcanic material in its vent, the plug is shattered into an array of fragments. These fragments are known as pyroclasts, which means "fire-broken."

Ashfalls
Big volcanic eruptions can fling vast clouds of ash and dust high into the sky. These can often fall like snow, covering the ground for miles around in a thick, gray blanket.

Bubbles of air caught in the stone.

Tephra
Tephra are chunks of pyroclastic rock that are thrown high into the air during an eruption and rattle down on the slopes below.

Volcanic bombs
Pyroclastic fragments over 1.26 in (32 mm) across are known as volcanic bombs. They take various forms including "breadcrust bombs" (above).

Lapilli
Lapilli are smaller chunks of tephra. Sometimes they are foamlike magma fragments; sometimes they are more solid lithic (rock) pieces.

Pele's hair
Lava in Hawaii is so fluid that it forms long strands as it is flung out. This is known as Pele's hair after the Hawaiian goddess of volcanoes.

Volcanic landscape

In volcanic areas, underground heat may create other effects on the surface besides volcanoes. Hot gases may billow out through fissures, for instance, while the heat of rocks underground may be enough to boil groundwater, creating jets of water or bubbling mud pools.

Superheated groundwater, rich in dissolved limestone, cools to create cascading terraces of a deposit called travertine.

Geysers are small vents that spout a fountain of boiling water heated underground by magma.

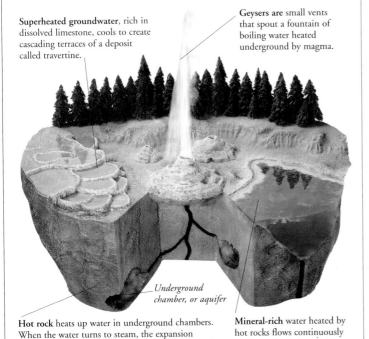

Underground chamber, or aquifer

Hot rock heats up water in underground chambers. When the water turns to steam, the expansion pushes water above up through vents in the ground.

Mineral-rich water heated by hot rocks flows continuously to the surface in hot springs.

Volcanic features

Volcanoes and volcanic activity leave behind all kinds of distinctive features in the landscape to bear witness to their ferocity and heat – sometimes relics of the outpouring of lava, sometimes relics of their effect on landscape features.

Calderas
Calderas are saucerlike craters at the tops of volcanic cones, created by the collapse of the cone during a huge explosion. Smaller calderas can occur when the top of a volcano is blown off by an eruption.

Giant's Causeway
The extraordinary hexagonal, basaltic columns that make up the Giant's Causeway in Co. Antrim, Northern Ireland, are formed from lava cooled after ancient volcanic activity.

Cones
The most distinctive volcanic relic is a cone-shaped mountain, formed when lava pours out from the vent and is then covered by ash. This process continues in successive eruptions.

FIND OUT MORE

CONTINENTS   EARTH   EARTHQUAKES   FOSSILS   MOUNTAINS AND VALLEYS   ROCKS AND MINERALS   ROMAN EMPIRE

WARFARE

WHEN PEOPLE DISAGREE about land, property, religion, or politics, one person may end the argument with violence. When nations cannot agree, the violence takes the form of warfare. If one nation is very strong, warfare can seem like an easy way of winning land or resources. But battles kill so many people, and cost so much, that nations usually start fighting only when diplomacy has failed. Peacekeeping organizations, such as the United Nations, try to keep diplomacy working and stop wars before they begin.

Ancient warfare

Battles are part of every country's history. Some past civilizations glorified war as a way to make their nations strong. However, ancient wars were often smaller and less destructive; without modern industry and transportation, it was more difficult to supply a huge army with weapons and food.

Stirrups
Technology decided the winner in ancient wars, as it does today. From at least the 4th century AD, Chinese horsemen were equipped with stirrups. Well-balanced in the saddle, they easily defeated enemies without stirrups.

Tomb figure of a warrior

Modern warfare

As science and industry flourished and farms grew more food in the 19th century, European nations devised more awful forms of war. Inventions such as the machine gun could kill more soldiers; with better transportation, armies could fight in more distant regions; food surpluses meant troops rarely starved. In this "total war," everyone who could either fought or supplied troops.

World war
During the 20th century, warfare became truly global for the first time. World Wars I and II involved almost every nation. Countries taking part made military service compulsory and poured all their resources into the conflicts. Beyond the armed forces, each side waged war against civilians and economic targets in order to break down the will to fight on.

Allied bombs devastated Dresden, Germany, in February 1945.

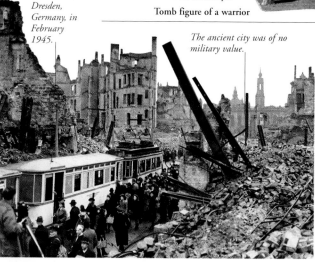

The ancient city was of no military value.

Civil war
In a civil war, groups within the same state fight each other. They battle for racial or religious reasons, or to control the government. Since the end of World War II in 1945 most wars that have broken out have been civil wars.

Civil war in El Salvador killed more than 70,000 people.

Guerilla organization flag, Cameroon

Guerilla war
Troops who occupy enemy lands may face guerilla (little war) soldiers. Guerillas often succeed despite poor equipment and little training because they know the countryside and have the support of local people.

US soldiers in Vietnam

Limited war
Some modern wars, such as the Vietnam War (1957–75) or the Iran-Iraq conflict (1980–88), are confined to a small region. These limited wars may not spread, because allies of the warring nations have little to gain by joining in, and much to lose.

Where war happens

A military leader must choose the battlefield with care. Each side's weapons, communications and logistics (their ability to keep fighters fed, clothed, and armed) decide what makes a favorable battlefield for them and a bad one for the enemy.

Infantry soldiers

On land
A major goal in war is to occupy the territory of a neighbor, so most wars are fought partly on land. However, because of the power of modern aircraft, armies must now control the skies before they can advance on the ground.

Karl von Clausewitz
Von Clausewitz (1780–1831) was a Prussian general. His influential book *On War* set out his theories on the nature of war and the tactics needed to win. It defined war as "an act of violence intended to compel our opponent to fulfill our will."

At sea
When all long-distance transportation was by ship, warring nations battled to control the seas. Air travel has now made naval battles less important. Battleships and aircraft carriers are easy targets for missiles, so navies hide much of their power beneath the waves in submarines.

German U-boat shells a merchant vessel, World War II.

Stealth bomber

In the air
War first spread to the air in World War I (1914–18). Radar and missile systems now provide defenses against bombers and fighter planes, but methods of attack have also improved: the "stealth" bomber cannot be detected by radar.

The rules of war

Formal rules to protect ordinary soldiers and civilians during war were first attempted in 1863, when the German-American scholar Francis Lieber (1800–1872) wrote *Code for the Government of Armies in the Field*. His work recognized the need to ban weapons that caused unnecessary suffering, and to protect the wounded and prisoners of war; it influenced later international agreements about the conduct of warfare.

Nürnberg

After World War II, Nazi leaders were tried at a special court at Nürnberg, Germany, for the murder of more than six million people (mostly Jews). The court convicted 22 Nazis of breaking international treaties and the rules of war, and of crimes against humanity.

Prisoners of war

In the past, prisoners of war (POWs) became slaves or bought their freedom, but the Geneva Convention now protects them. An army that captures uniformed enemy soldiers must move them away from the battlefield and imprison them in reasonable conditions until the war ends.

Boer women as prisoners of war

Geneva Convention

Henri Dunant (1828–1910), a Swiss citizen, founded the Red Cross to relieve the suffering of war wounded. In 1864, a Convention protecting them and those treating them was signed in Geneva by European nations; later treaties have extended its protection.

International Red Cross logo

The cost of war

In war, each side fears defeat so much that no price seems too high to pay for victory. Though the defeated side generally suffers more, the cost of winning can also be disabling. War costs are measured not just financially, but also in the loss of natural resources and human lives. During the 20th century, more than 100 million soldiers and non-combatants have been killed in wars.

The Unknown Soldier

Burying the body of an unidentified soldier in a special Tomb of the Unknown Soldier created a memorial to all the nameless war dead.

Refugees

When wars drive civilians across borders to seek asylum (a place of safety), they become refugees. They have no rights, and often no money or possessions. For food, water, shelter, and medical care, many depend on the country sheltering them, or on organizations such as the United Nations.

In the 1990s, war forced 4.5 million Sudanese to leave their homes.

Environmental damage

Wildlife and the natural environment always suffer in and around a battle zone. Sometimes, nations may use environmental damage as a weapon: in the Vietnam War, US forces deliberately killed crops and jungle to deprive their enemy of food and cover. Weapons testing, and the pressure that refugees put on the land as they try to survive, also severely damage the environment.

Bomb damage

War dead

War kills and injures huge numbers of servicemen and women; during World War I about 8.5 million servicemen died. But the changing nature of warfare meant that by World War II, more civilians were killed than soldiers. In war today, bombs and bullets kill some; hunger and disease kill many more.

World War I graves in France

Government war bonds promise interest on loans.

Paying for war

War consumes a huge share of a nation's wealth: in 1944, for example, the British government spent 60 percent of its people's earnings on World War II. Governments may pay for war with borrowed money, which later generations repay.

Timeline

1096–9 European Christian knights win control of Palestine, (The Holy Land) in the first, and most successful, Crusade (holy war) against the Arab world.

1240 Mongol warriors from central Asia capture Kiyyev (Kiev), Ukraine, in one of a series of wars that give them control of much of Asia and eastern Europe.

Mongol quiver

1861–5 In a bloody Civil War, northern and southern American states fight with modern weapons and supplies. The north wins; more than 600,000 people die.

1914–18 Thirty countries fight for control of Europe. Many millions die in World War I; the treaties that end it bring peace for just 21 years.

1939–45 In World War II, more fighters (17 million) die than in all previous wars put together.

1957–75 US fights a damaging war in Vietnam against communist forces.

During World War II, the Nazis forced Jews to wear identity badges.

1967 The Six-Day War is fought between Israel and Arab forces. Israel wins.

1990–91 US-led Persian Gulf War against Iraq.

2001–02 September 11 terrorism leads to US-led war on Afghanistan.

FIND OUT MORE ARMS AND ARMOR COLD WAR GUNS HOLOCAUST PEACE MOVEMENTS UNITED NATIONS WARSHIPS WARPLANES WEAPONS WORLD WAR I WORLD WAR II

WARPLANES

AIRPLANES WERE first used in warfare during World War I (1914–18). They have been vital elements of armed combat ever since. Warplanes range from fast, nimble, jet-powered fighters to battlefield helicopters or tankers for in-flight refueling. Between them, they find and destroy enemy aircraft and targets on the ground. Warplanes also help transport troops and equipment to and from the battlefield. In peacetime, military transport aircraft often help with emergencies and famine relief.

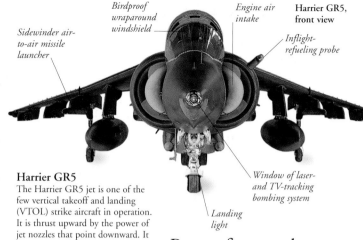

Birdproof wraparound windshield

Sidewinder air-to-air missile launcher

Engine air intake

Harrier GR5, front view

Inflight-refueling probe

Window of laser- and TV-tracking bombing system

Landing light

Harrier GR5
The Harrier GR5 jet is one of the few vertical takeoff and landing (VTOL) strike aircraft in operation. It is thrust upward by the power of jet nozzles that point downward. It does not need a runway, so can be hidden near to a battlefront.

Parts of a warplane
Fighters and fighter-bombers are highly sophisticated aircraft. On-board computers help the pilot fly and navigate the aircraft and operate the weapons. Warplanes carry air-to-air weapons (guns and missiles) for attacking other aircraft, and air-to-ground weapons (missiles and bombs) for attacking targets on the ground and at sea. They also have self-defense systems, including electronic beams and flares for confusing missiles fired at them.

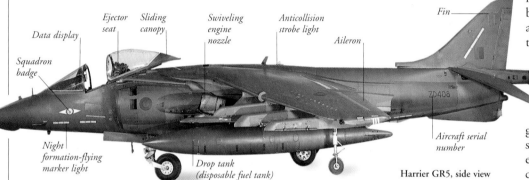

Data display

Ejector seat

Sliding canopy

Swiveling engine nozzle

Anticollision strobe light

Aileron

Fin

Squadron badge

ZD408

Night formation-flying marker light

Drop tank (disposable fuel tank)

Aircraft serial number

Harrier GR5, side view

Types of warplane
Warplanes are either combat aircraft or noncombat aircraft, which support other military forces. Combat aircraft include fighters (also called interceptors), which win superiority in the air, so other aircraft can operate over a battlezone, bombers, and fighter-bombers. Noncombat aircraft carry out reconnaissance, or carry troops and equipment rapidly to a battle zone.

Rockwell B-1B

Heavy bombers
Heavy bombers are large aircraft, often as big as passenger airliners. They fly high above the battlefield and release bombs, which fall to the ground. Several crew members are needed to operate the aircraft.

Air forces
An air force is much more than just a collection of aircraft and their crews. There are thousands of ground staff, too, including the engineers who service the aircraft. Most air forces are divided into sections called squadrons. The first organized air force was the British Royal Air Force (RAF), formed in 1918.

Flying helmet

Oxygen mask

Life-jacket

Personal Equipment Connector

Anti-G pants

Attack helicopters
A cross between helicopters and fighter aircraft, these destroy enemy targets on the battlefield with a cannon, rockets, and missiles.

Heavy lift aircraft
Heavy lift aircraft (right) carry hundreds of fully equipped military personnel from home bases to a war zone.

Cobra Venom AH-1W

Lockheed C5 Galaxy: a heavy lift aircraft

Reconnaissance aircraft
Keeping track of enemy positions is the job of reconnaissance aircraft (left). Some fly low and fast, taking photographs. Others fly high, using powerful radar to detect other aircraft.

Boeing E3-A

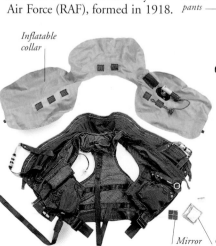

Uniform, jet crew member, British RAF

Jet crews wear lifejackets with survival aids in case they need to eject from a plane.

Inflatable collar

Mirror

Code booklet

| FIND OUT MORE | AIRCRAFT | AIRSHIPS AND BALLOONS | ARMIES | ENGINES | FLIGHT, HISTORY OF | WARFARE | WEAPONS | WORLD WAR I | WORLD WAR II |

WARSHIPS

SEVERAL DIFFERENT TYPES OF SHIP are involved in modern warfare, from small, fast patrol boats to massive aircraft carriers. Each type carries out a particular job, such as protecting merchant ships from attack or searching for enemy ships and submarines. A modern warship is crammed with sophisticated navigation and weapon systems. Warships normally operate together in groups called fleets. They are supported by naval auxiliary ships, which deliver supplies such as fuel and food.

Parts of a warship

Warships are designed to be fast and easy to maneuver. They have lightweight aluminum hulls and powerful gas turbine engines. Inside, each ship is divided into watertight sections that can be sealed off if the hull is punctured in an attack. Here are the crew's quarters, storerooms, and control rooms. Above the deck are weapons and communication equipment. Warships carry several different types of weapons, including guns, missiles, and torpedoes.

Frigate
A frigate is a medium-sized, light, fast warship. Frigates normally escort aircraft carriers, protecting them from attack. They carry antiaircraft and antiship missiles, and submarine hunting equipment.

The frigate was developed during World War II to protect convoys from submarine attack.

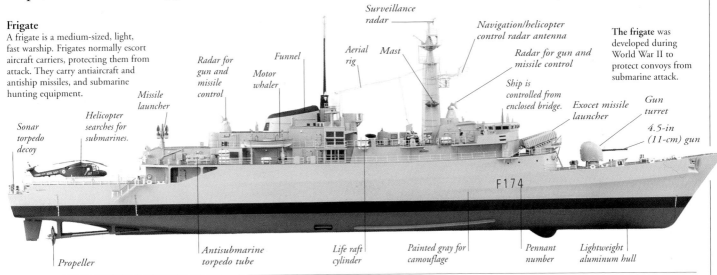

Surveillance radar

Navigation/helicopter control radar antenna

Aerial rig

Mast

Radar for gun and missile control

Radar for gun and missile control

Funnel

Motor whaler

Missile launcher

Ship is controlled from enclosed bridge.

Exocet missile launcher

Gun turret

4.5-in (11-cm) gun

Helicopter searches for submarines.

Sonar torpedo decoy

F174

Propeller

Antisubmarine torpedo tube

Life raft cylinder

Painted gray for camouflage

Pennant number

Lightweight aluminum hull

Types of warship

Warships are either surface warships or submarines. The most important surface warship is the aircraft carrier. Other types of surface ships defend carriers and attack enemy ships. Submarines are either hunter-killers, which search for and destroy enemy ships, or ballistic missile submarines, which stay hidden in the oceans for months.

German navy minesweeper

US Navy aircraft carrier

Aircraft carriers
The aircraft carrier is the largest of all warships. It is a floating air base: in addition to runways for takeoffs and landings, it has hangars where planes are serviced, and a control tower to communicate with pilots. The largest aircraft carriers carry up to 100 airplanes and a crew of more than 2,000 sailors, plus a flying crew of more than 1,000.

Mine warfare vessels
Minehunters search for mines (explosive charges) submerged beneath the sea; minesweepers have special equipment to locate and destroy surface mines. These warships have wood or plastic hulls because magnetic mines are set off when a steel hull comes near them.

Helicopter cruisers
Cruisers are large warships, armed with guns, missiles, and torpedoes. A helicopter cruiser has a deck at the rear where helicopters land, and hangars where helicopters are stored.

US Navy helicopter cruiser

Navies

In wartime, a navy's job is to keep a nation's sea-lanes open, protect merchant and other ships at sea, hunt and destroy enemy ships, and support armies and air forces. In times of peace, they help with disaster relief and rescue work, and make visits to foreign countries to promote goodwill.

Uniforms
This uniform from the Soviet Navy is in a traditional style. Many nations have a similar uniform.

Sailor's badge

Trade badge

Sweater, shirt, collar

Boots

Pants

Cap

FIND OUT MORE | ARMIES | RADAR AND SONAR | SAILING | SHIPS AND BOATS | SUBMARINES | TRANSPORTATION, HISTORY OF | WARFARE | WEAPONS | WORLD WAR II

WASHINGTON, GEORGE

AS LEADER OF THE AMERICAN forces that won the Revolutionary War against the British and as the first president of the new nation, George Washington is known as the "Father of his Country." He learned his military skills fighting for the British in the 1750s, and used those skills to good effect against them 20 years later. A fine politician and administrator, he worked hard to unite his new country and to reconcile conflicting interests. His honesty and moderation made him a symbol of his nation.

Early life
Washington was born in 1732 into a landed family in Virginia. When he was 11, his father died, and he went to live with his half-brother Lawrence. George wanted to go to sea, but was persuaded to train as a surveyor. A practical man, he succeeded despite his limited education.

Musket from the French-Indian War

French-Indian War
In 1753, French armies from Canada occupied the Ohio River Valley. George Washington fought for the British against the French and their native American allies. He was promoted quickly for his military and organizational skills.

Mount Vernon
When his half-brother Lawrence died in 1752, George inherited the family's large estate at Mount Vernon, Virginia. He made many changes there and experimented with new crops. In 1759, he married Martha Custis, a wealthy widow, and entered Virginia politics. Throughout Washington's life, Mount Vernon was a welcome retreat, and he retired there at the end of his life.

Delegates at the Continental Congress

Continental Congress
Washington was an early champion of American independence. In 1774 and 1775, he served as a delegate from Virginia to the Continental Congresses held to organize the 13 colonies' struggle against the British. When the Revolutionary War broke out in 1775, the Congress appointed Washington commander-in-chief of the colonial army.

Washington Crossing The Delaware by Emanuel Leutze

Commander-in-chief
When war broke out in 1775, Washington took command of a disorganized, ill-equipped army incapable of beating the professional, well-equipped British. Despite interference from Congress, he turned the colonial troops into an efficient force able to outwit and defeat the British in 1781.

Trenton
In the first two years of the war, American troops were outmaneuvered by the British. On December 25, 1776, Washington and his troops crossed the frozen Delaware River near Trenton, New Jersey. They captured the surprised British army the next day at the Battle of Trenton.

Valley Forge
The American army spent the winter of 1777–78 in Valley Forge, Pennsylvania. The winter was severe and food and clothing were scarce, but despite desertions and the threat of mutiny, Washington showed his grit and determination, holding his army together. In the spring, the army emerged prepared for battle.

President of the United States
After American independence was assured in 1783, Washington withdrew from politics. But conflicts between the states forced him to take a leading role. In 1787, he presided over the convention that drafted the Constitution, and in 1789 he was unanimously elected president of the new country. He served two four-year terms before retiring in 1797.

Thomas Jefferson
The author of the American Constitution, Thomas Jefferson (1743–1826) became secretary of state under Washington and led the Democratic-Republicans, who favored individual and state rights. Washington tried to keep aloof from party politics, but favored the Federalists, who wanted a stronger national state. Party conflicts caused many problems during Washington's presidency.

Whiskey Rebellion
In 1794, rioting broke out against the imposition of a national tax on alcoholic drink. The American government tried to enforce the law, but in the end Washington was forced to use troops. This, and other troubles, meant that Washington decided against running for a third term as president.

GEORGE WASHINGTON

1732	Born in Virginia.
1743	On the death of his father, goes to live with his brother Lawrence.
1754–59	Fights in the British Army against the French.
1759	Enters Virginia politics.
1774–75	Delegate at two Continental Congresses.
1775	Appointed commander-in-chief of Colonial forces.
1783	US wins independence from Britain.
1789–97	Serves two terms as President of the US.
1799	Dies at Mount Vernon.

FIND OUT MORE AMERICAN REVOLUTION GOVERNMENTS AND POLITICS LAW UNITED STATES, HISTORY OF

WEAPONS

STRENGTH AND SKILL decide the winner in a fight without weapons, but in armed combat, the fighter with the better killing tool may win. Ever since people began to compete for land or food, warriors have sought weapons of increasing power. Changing technology supplied them: metals were used to make swords; nuclear power was first used in bombs. This arms race has now led to weapons so powerful that a nation that used them might win the war, but would destroy everything in the conquered lands.

Early weapons

Early warriors fought with clubs and short blades. Lances and spears kept the enemy farther away; missiles such as the boomerang allowed warriors to attack anyone within throwing distance. To launch missiles farther still, fighters used slingshots or bows.

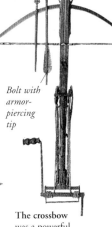

Bolt with armor-piercing tip

The crossbow was a powerful weapon used in medieval warfare.

Blade could be stone, bronze, or iron.

The dagger, used in hand-to-hand fighting, was one of the first weapons.

Gunpowder

Gunpowder

The most far-reaching development in weapons technology came in the 14th century with the invention of firearms. These weapons were powered by gunpowder, an explosive. Although feeble at first, firearms were soon capable of firing missiles great distances. Battles could be fought at long range, instead of face-to-face.

Nikolaus von Dreyse

German gunsmith Dreyse (1787–1867) designed a more effective weapon for the battlefield: a rifle that fired twice as fast as earlier guns. Troops loaded bullets near the trigger so they could shoot lying down, safe from enemy fire. The Prussian army began using the gun in 1840.

Bombs and missiles

A bomb is a container filled with explosive material and a detonator to make it explode. The explosion causes a lethal blast, scattering deadly bits of the bomb casing far and wide. Missiles are weapons that are propelled toward a target; they allow a warring nation to destroy an enemy nation without risking the life of a single soldier.

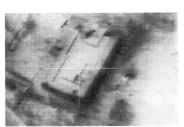

Smart bomb approaches target.

Smart bombs

Smart bombs are missiles in which a warhead is guided directly to its target by a laser-aiming device or on-board computer map. Some contain video cameras in their noses.

Booby traps

Seemingly harmless objects or areas can be unexpectedly deadly. Guerilla fighters may capture or wound enemies with trip wires or spike-filled holes. Most modern traps rely on explosives. Buried antitank mines explode when vehicles crush them; smaller antipersonnel (AP) mines blast people stepping on them. Aircraft can drop huge numbers of AP mines very quickly.

Mine victims, Kurdistan, 1993

How an AP mine works

When someone steps on an AP mine, the pressure sets off a process that detonates an explosive charge. The force of the explosion travels upward, causing terrible injuries. Such mines are designed to maim rather than kill, as a wounded person needs more care than a dead one, draining enemy resources.

Explosive material stored here

Metal fragments to cause severe harm

Pin

Box, 6 in long

AP mine, World War II

Aerial bombing began in World War I: bombs were originally dropped by hand.

Gravity bombs

Dropped from aircraft, gravity bombs contain high explosives. Most explode when they hit the ground. Modern types may separate into many "bomblets" to blast a wider area.

Mass destruction

The most powerful weapons can destroy a city or poison the land of a whole nation. These weapons are so dangerous that there are international treaties that intend to outlaw their use in war and reduce their numbers.

Nuclear weapons testing, 1995

Respirator protects the lungs.

Special suit protects skin from gas.

Nuclear weapons

In an atomic bomb, a piece of uranium the size of a sugar cube has the same destructive power as a block of conventional explosives the size of a house.

Chemical weapons

Chemical and biological weapons spread poisons or epidemic diseases, so they kill or injure the enemy without damaging property. Casualties die slowly, overwhelming an enemy's medical facilities.

FIND OUT MORE

| ARMS AND ARMOR | GUNS | HUNDRED YEARS' WAR | NUCLEAR POWER | PEACE MOVEMENTS | WARFARE | WORLD WAR I | WORLD WAR II |

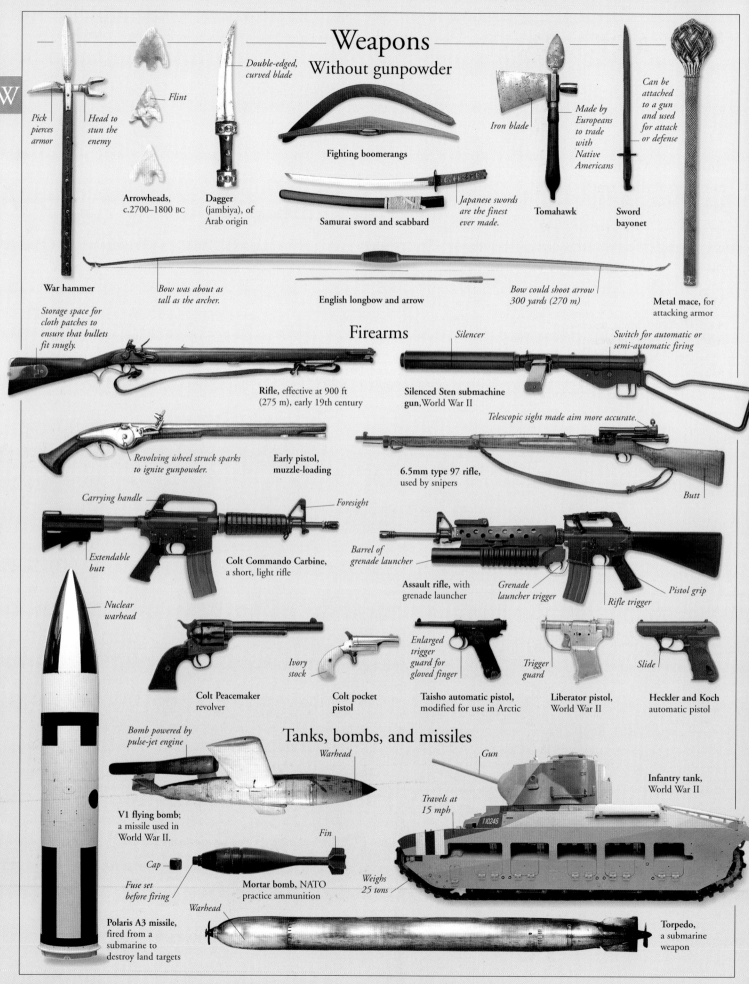

Weapons
Without gunpowder

Pick pierces armor

Head to stun the enemy

Flint

Arrowheads, c.2700–1800 BC

Double-edged, curved blade

Dagger (jambiya), of Arab origin

Fighting boomerangs

Japanese swords are the finest ever made.

Samurai sword and scabbard

Iron blade

Made by Europeans to trade with Native Americans

Tomahawk

Can be attached to a gun and used for attack or defense

Sword bayonet

War hammer

Bow was about as tall as the archer.

English longbow and arrow

Bow could shoot arrow 300 yards (270 m)

Metal mace, for attacking armor

Firearms

Storage space for cloth patches to ensure that bullets fit snugly.

Rifle, effective at 900 ft (275 m), early 19th century

Silencer

Switch for automatic or semi-automatic firing

Silenced Sten submachine gun, World War II

Revolving wheel struck sparks to ignite gunpowder.

Early pistol, muzzle-loading

Telescopic sight made aim more accurate.

6.5mm type 97 rifle, used by snipers

Butt

Carrying handle

Foresight

Extendable butt

Colt Commando Carbine, a short, light rifle

Barrel of grenade launcher

Assault rifle, with grenade launcher

Grenade launcher trigger

Rifle trigger

Pistol grip

Nuclear warhead

Ivory stock

Enlarged trigger guard for gloved finger

Trigger guard

Slide

Colt Peacemaker revolver

Colt pocket pistol

Taisho automatic pistol, modified for use in Arctic

Liberator pistol, World War II

Heckler and Koch automatic pistol

Tanks, bombs, and missiles

Bomb powered by pulse-jet engine

Warhead

Gun

Infantry tank, World War II

V1 flying bomb; a missile used in World War II.

Travels at 15 mph

Fin

Cap

Fuse set before firing

Mortar bomb, NATO practice ammunition

Weighs 25 tons

Warhead

Polaris A3 missile, fired from a submarine to destroy land targets

Warhead

Torpedo, a submarine weapon

WEASELS AND MARTEN

SMALL AND SLENDER mammals, weasels and marten are some of the most efficient hunters. They are aggressive and, on their own, can kill prey much larger than themselves. With their excellent senses of smell, hearing, and sight, they track down their prey, then pounce, and kill it with a lethal bite. Different species occupy habitats from the polar regions to the tropics. Some live in trees, others in burrows or among rocks or tree roots.

Weasels

Stoats, polecats, mink, weasels, and ferrets are all types of weasels. They have long, sinuous bodies, long necks, and short legs. Mostly nocturnal hunters, they can move extremely fast and run, climb, and swim after their prey.

Young weasels
Weasels breed in the spring, producing litters of up to eight young. The baby weasels stay in the safety of the den in the first weeks of life and are looked after by their mother alone. After about two months, the young begin to hunt for themselves.

Common weasel
One of the most numerous weasels is the common weasel. It weaves through the undergrowth searching for small rodents, such as mice and voles, and is small and lithe enough to pursue them into their burrows. Males may be twice as big as females, so they chase larger prey down larger burrows. Each weasel has its own territory, that may cover several acres.

Weasels have a flexible spine and strong back muscles.

Weasels are particularly good at hearing high-pitched sounds, such as a mouse squeaking.

Short legs allow the weasel to maneuvre in small burrows.

All weasels stand up on their back legs to look around.

Stoat
The stoat, seen here tracking its prey by scent, looks similar to the common weasel, but it has a black tip on its tail and is a little bigger than the weasel. It can tackle prey as large as a hare. In the northern, colder parts of its range, the stoat's coat turns white in winter to camouflage it against snow. It is then known as ermine.

Least weasel skull
The least weasel is the smallest carnivore in the world, only 6.8 in (17.5 cm) long. Its strong jaws and sharp stabbing teeth are typical of all weasels.

Polecats are solitary animals, as are all weasels.

Polecats
Like most weasels, polecats are versatile hunters, eating rodents, rabbits, frogs, birds, and lizards. They patrol their territory at night, marking it with their scent.

Minks
These weasels are good swimmers, helped by their partly webbed feet. They usually live by rivers, lakes, and marshes, taking their prey of fish, frogs, and birds from the water.

Minks have thick, oily, waterproof fur.

Marten

There are eight species of marten inhabiting forests in Europe, Asia, Canada, and Alaska. They are larger than weasels, and their slightly longer limbs make them better climbers. They readily catch prey in trees, though they also hunt on the ground, eating squirrels, birds, eggs, insects, and plant food such as berries.

Pine marten
An extremely agile climber, the pine marten is able to run and leap along branches. It has a bushy tail that helps with balance, and long claws and large paws that grip bark. It is the largest Eurasian marten.

Fisher
Despite its name, the fisher feeds largely on the flesh of birds and small mammals such as rabbits. It is known for its ability to kill porcupines, whose quills it avoids by attacking the unprotected face and belly.

Wolverine
A giant among weasels and martens, the wolverine weighs up to 55 lb (25 kg). It is powerful enough to kill and eat a reindeer. It catches its prey not by stalking, but by pouncing in ambush, often from a tree.

Zorilla
Widespread in Africa, the zorilla's vivid stripes act as a warning to larger predators not to attack. If the warning is ignored, the zorilla will raise its tail and spray a noxious fluid at the attacker.

COMMON WEASEL

SCIENTIFIC NAME	*Mustela nivalis*
FAMILY	Mustelidae
ORDER	Carnivora
DISTRIBUTION	Europe, most of Asia, northwestern Africa
DIET	Rodents, moles, rabbits, birds
SIZE	Length 8–11.5 in (21–29 cm)

FIND OUT MORE
ANIMAL BEHAVIOR
BADGERS, OTTERS, AND SKUNKS
FOOD WEBS AND CHAINS
MAMMALS

W

WEATHER

WIND, RAIN, SNOW, fog, frost, and sunshine are all signs of the constant shifting of the lowest level of the atmosphere. This continual change is what we call the weather. Weather changes in four main ways: its movement, which can bring winds; its temperature, which can cause anything from frosts to heat waves; its moisture content, which can bring rain and fog; and its pressure, which can cause anything from sunny days to fierce storms. The average weather in one particular area is known as the climate.

Highs
These are caused by blocks of denser air in the upper atmosphere. The density of the air makes it heavy, and creates a high pressure region. With very little water vapor in it, a high creates a clear and cloudless day.

Depressions and fronts
The atmosphere often forms into blocks of air, or air masses, over an area where conditions are similar. A front is the boundary between two air masses. Where a warm and cold air mass meet, lighter air rises up over the cold, creating a low pressure area, or depression, which brings storms as it drifts eastward.

High-level cirrus clouds precede the warm front.

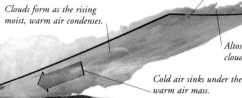

Clouds form as the rising moist, warm air condenses.

Rain falls from nimbostratus clouds.

Altostratus cloud

Cold air sinks under the warm air mass.

Warm front

The mass of cold air dips sharply beneath the warm air.

Some of the moisture in the cloud tops turns to ice.

After the heaviest part of the storm, light showers may still occur.

High-level winds blow the cloud tops into wedge shapes.

Rising warm air

Cold front

Advancing front

Strong winds and heavy clouds occur along the cold front.

Warm front
In a depression, the front often breaks into two – a warm front and a cold front. As the depression passes, the warm front is usually ahead of the cold. The warm air slides gently up over the cold, bringing soft, steady rain.

Cold front
After the warm front has passed, there is generally a brief pause. The cold air then drives sharply under the warm, forcing it upward, and creating huge clouds that bring heavy rain and thunderstorms.

Formation of a depression

1 A polar front is where warm, tropical air meets cold, polar air.

2 A depression begins to form where warm air bulges over the cold air.

3 Cold air chases under the warm air and the front splits into two – warm and cold fronts.

4 The cold front may lift the warm front off the ground, to form an occluded front.

Air pressure
The force of molecules (groups of atoms) moving in the air creates air pressure. The more molecules are in motion, the greater the pressure. Warm air expands, making it less dense and reducing pressure. Cold air contracts, raising pressure. Pressure variations cause changes in the weather.

Barometer
Barometers measure air pressure and show changes in pressure on a dial. A dramatic fall in pressure usually means that a storm is on its way.

Aneroid barometer

Isobars
Air pressure is measured in millibars and is shown on weather maps by isobars (lines). Each isobar links points of equal pressure. The closer together the isobars are, the sharper the difference in air pressure.

Weather map showing isobars

Air temperature
Air temperature largely depends on the sun's heat. Air temperatures are highest in the tropics, where the sun is strongest. Meteorologists place thermometers in the shade, when measuring air temperatures, for an overall reading.

Double-ended thermometer records the daily maximum and minimum temperatures.

Humidity
Humidity is the moisture content of clouds. Moisture is present as vapor in the air almost all of the time, but is invisible. However, when the air gets cold, the vapor condenses into water drops, and forms clouds, fog, or rain.

Wet and dry hygrometer uses a scale to show humidity.

FIND OUT MORE   AIR   ATMOSPHERE   CLIMATE   CLOUDS   RAIN   STORMS   TIME   WEATHER FORECASTING

WEATHER FORECASTING

FROM FARMERS TO ICE-CREAM makers, different communities, businesses, and individuals want to know what the weather is likely to be. Weather forecasting is the prediction of weather conditions over an area, either for days (short-range) or for months (long-range). Every three hours, 10,000 weather stations world-wide simultaneously record observations of weather conditions. These data, called synoptic values, feed huge computers in the 13 main weather centres of the World Meteorological Organization. Meteorologists – people who study the weather – produce weather forecasts based on the computers' calculations plus satellite and radar images.

Weather charts

Some of the first weather forecasts were printed in the London *Daily News* in 1848. These reports were crude and very short-term compared to today's sophisticated predictions. Technology now enables satellite images of the weather to be taken from high above the Earth. A computer applies different colors to the map to indicate variations in temperature, humidity, clouds, and atmospheric pressure.

Color spectrum shows temperatures, with red denoting the hottest and violet the coolest.

Orange and red tinting indicates very hot weather.

Swirl of cloud indicates a severe storm over the British Isles.

Images are taken from hundreds of miles above ground level.

Dark gray cloud shows heavy rain.

Colors show that it is generally warmer inland than on the coast.

Patchy cloud cover

Ocean is dark blue to reflect cool temperature.

Satellite image of Europe and North Africa taken in 1997

Weather stations

Ships at sea, city roofs, and mountain-tops all provide sites for the world's weather stations. Most stations are equipped with thermometers and hygrometers to show temperature and humidity, anemometers to record wind speed, rain gauges to collect rainfall, and mercury barometers to monitor changes in air pressure.

Stevenson screen
Air temperature readings are taken in the shade. A white box, called a Stevenson screen, shields thermometers from direct sunlight. Ventilation slats keep air flowing freely.

Radiosondes are filled with helium.

Weather balloon
Every day around the world, at noon and midnight GMT (Greenwich Mean Time), balloons, known as radiosondes, are launched into the atmosphere to measure conditions such as air pressure, temperature, and humidity at heights up to 12 miles (20 km).

Weather planes
These provide detailed information about conditions high in the atmosphere, especially around storms. Weather planes are equipped with a range of monitoring devices to record anything from the ice content of clouds to the presence of gases.

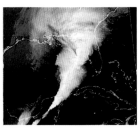

Weather satellites
The first weather satellite, launched by the USA in 1960, orbited 531 miles (850 km) above the North and South poles. In the 1970s, geostationary satellites were made to travel up to 25,000 miles (40,000 km) away.

Lewis Richardson

British mathematician Lewis Richardson (1881–1953) devised a system called numerical forecasting. This system forecast the weather, by feeding millions of simultaneous measurements of atmospheric conditions into giant computers.

Natural weather forecasters

Natural signs are still used to help forecast the weather. Many plants and animals react to moisture changes in the air, and so may indicate that rain is coming.

Closed pine cone scales warn of rain.

Wool shrinks and curls up in dry air.

Seaweed becomes limp in moist air.

Radar
Radar (which stands for Radio Detection And Ranging) signals reflect off water present in the air, such as snow and rain. Radar can be used to generate computer images of depressions and other systems to give a clear indication of where rain is falling, and how much.

A depression over the United Kingdom

FIND OUT MORE   AIRSHIPS AND BALLOONS   ATMOSPHERE   COMPUTERS   RADAR AND SONAR   SATELLITES   TREES   WEATHER

WEIGHTS AND MEASURES

IN ANCIENT EGYPT, the cubit was the main unit used to measure length. It was based on the distance from a person's elbow to his or her fingertips. Because different people have arms of different size, it eventually became necessary for the Egyptians to define a standard length for the cubit, so that the cubit was the same throughout the country. In the same way, our modern systems of measurement, such as the metric and imperial or customary systems, are based on standard units. The quantities we measure include length, area, volume, weight, and mass.

Measuring space

When we measure length, area, or volume, we are measuring space. Length is the amount of linear space between two points. Area is a measurement of the two-dimensional space of a surface such as a wall. Volume is the amount of three-dimensional space occupied by a solid object or an amount of liquid or gas.

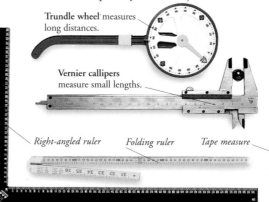

Trundle wheel measures long distances.

Vernier callipers measure small lengths.

Right-angled ruler   *Folding ruler*   *Tape measure*

Metal metre rule

Retractable steel rule

Length and distance

All devices designed to measure length or distance measure space along a line. The word length is used when measuring how long an object is; distance refers to the space between two places. Units of length or distance include the foot (ft), meter (m), mile (mi), and kilometer (km).

Measuring weight

We usually describe an object's "weight" in grams and kilograms, or ounces and pounds. However, these are really units of mass – that is, the amount of matter in an object. In science, weight refers to the force of gravity pulling an object downward. Scientists measure weight in different units, such as newtons and poundals.

Digital scales

Scales and balances

To weigh things accurately, we must use scales or a balance. Digital scales use electronic components to find the weight of an object. A balance consists of two linked pans. The object to be weighed is placed in one pan, and standard weights are added to the other. The two pans will balance when they are carrying the same weight.

Flour   **Simple balance**   *Weights*

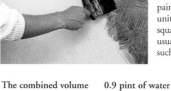

Area

To ensure you buy enough paint to cover a wall, it is important to know the area of the wall you are gong to paint. Area is measured in square units, such as square feet (ft^2) or square meters (m^2). Land areas are usually measured in different units, such as acres (ac) or hectares (ha).

The combined volume of the bricks equals the volume of the water.

0.9 pint of water

Ten bricks, each 2.6 in^3 volume

Volume

Solid volume is measured in cubic units, such as cubic inches (in^3) or cubic centimeters (cm^3). Capacity units, such as pints (pts) or litrers (l), measure liquid volume. Gas volume is measured in either cubic units or capacity units.

Standard units

Today, there are two major systems of standard units. The metric system, which is decimal, is the most common and is used by scientists worldwide. Some countries, such as the US, use the older imperial or customary system. In other countries, such as the UK, people use the metric and imperial systems side by side.

Metric system

Units in the metric system include the centimeter (cm), meter (m), gram (g), kilogram (kg), liter (l), and hectare (ha). Prefixes such as milli- and kilo- denote smaller or larger units. For example, one-thousandth of a meter is a millimeter (mm) and 1,000 metrer is one kilometer (km).

Imperial system

The inch (in), foot (ft), ounce (oz), pound (lb), pint (pt), and acre (ac) are all imperial units. Unlike metric units, which are all based on the number 10, imperial units do not all have the same number base: a foot is divided into 12 inches, but a pound contains 16 ounces.

Non-standard units

Parts of the body were once used as measuring units. The hand, for example, was used to find the height of horses. Such units were non-standard, because people's bodies are never the same. A horse could be 18 hands high to one person, but only 16 to another. The hand has now been standardized to a length of exactly 3.94 in (10 cm).

Thread (length): 26 ft; 8 m

Ribbon (length): 10 in; 25 cm

Oil (volume): 2.1 pt; 1 l

Cereal (mass): 9 oz; 250 g

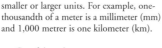

Flour (mass): 1.1 lb; 0.5 kg

Rug (area): 64 ft^2; 6 m^2

Grapes (mass): 7 oz; 200 g

A hand was 4 fingers wide.

FIND OUT MORE   DYES AND PAINTS   EGYPT, ANCIENT   FOOD   GRAVITY   HORSES   MATHEMATICS   MATTER   NUMBERS   SCIENCE

WHALES AND DOLPHINS

OF ALL MARINE MAMMALS, the best adapted to life in the sea are the whales. Underneath their thick, smooth skin is a layer of blubber that insulates them against the cold. Like all mammals, they are warm-blooded, air-breathing animals and give birth to live young. Whales, including dolphins and porpoises, form the order Cetacea, and most probably evolved from four-legged mammals. They are separated into two groups – the toothed whales, of which there are about 80 species, and the baleen, or whalebone whales, of which there are about 12 species. The only other entirely aquatic mammals are the Sirenians.

Whale's body encrusted with barnacles

Grey Whale

Baleen whales

The baleen, or whalebone, whales are the giants of the ocean. They feed by swimming through a shoal of shrimp-like krill with their mouths wide open. When they close their mouths, the water is forced out through the baleen plates suspended from their upper jaws, leaving the krill trapped on the inside. Adult blue whales can swallow a huge quantity of krill in a single mouthful.

Teeth
A whale's teeth are all the same shape. A killer whale has stout, conical teeth that curve backward.

Powerful jaws

Baleen
Plates of baleen are made from keratin. This is the same material that makes up human hair.

Toothed whales

Dolphins, porpoises, sperm whales, beaked whales, and the killer whale are all species of toothed whales. The unusual narwhal and beluga also belong to this group. The toothed whales have as many as 260 teeth or as few as a single pair. The whales use their teeth to catch and hold, but not to chew, their prey which includes fish and squid. Instead they swallow food whole.

The baleen of right whales grows longer than that of other whales.

Aerial view of a whale "blowing"

Blowholes
In the course of evolution, the nostrils of almost all whales have moved to the top of the head. This position makes it possible for the animals to breathe without having to expose their bodies above the surface of the water. Toothed whales have one blowhole; baleen whales have two. When a whale surfaces, it "spouts" by blowing moist air out through its blowhole. Then it breathes in, closes its blowhole, and submerges again.

Gray whale
A baleen whale, the gray whale feeds on crustaceans living on the seabed. It uses its snout to stir up sediment that it strains through short baleen plates. Each year, the California gray whale migrates from its feeding grounds in the Arctic Ocean to its calving lagoons in southern California and Mexico.

A narwhal's tusk is a greatly enlarged left upper incisor tooth.

A tusk can grow to 9 ft (2.75 m) long.

Until 17th century tusk was thought to be unicorn horn

Killer whale
A powerful and ruthless predator, the killer whale eats mainly fish, penguins, and seals. It is particularly efficient when hunting for food as a pack. Even a large whale stands little chance against a pack of killer whales.

Narwhal skull and tusk

Narwhal
Male narwhals have a long, spiral-shaped tusk growing from the upper jaw. A narwhal's only other tooth rarely grows beyond the gums. Narwhals are found only in Arctic waters, where they live in herds of about 12 animals.

The entire body comes out of the water.

Porpoising
Dolphins are renowned for their ability to make spectacular leaps out of the water. This is called porpoising, but, strangely enough, porpoises do not leap.

Dolphins and porpoises

Both dolphins and porpoises are toothed whales. They eat fish, cuttlefish, and squid. Most dolphins are larger than porpoises, which have rounder bodies and foreheads.

Common dolphin
Found in warm and temperate oceans, the common dolphin sometimes travels in schools of several hundred. It feeds on fish and is itself often caught in nets. As a result, its population has greatly reduced.

Dolphin enters the water headfirst.

Dolphin rises at high speed.

Fluking

A whale's tail is horizontal and flattened. It provides the whale with its means of propulsion and generates enormous power. Before beginning a deep dive, some whales lift their tail flukes into the air to help them get into position for a steep descent – a movement known as fluking. The way a whale flukes tells us what kind of a whale it is. This sperm whale brings its tail so high into the air that the underside can be seen. Other whales keep the flukes turned down.

Threats

The great whales have few natural enemies except for the killer whale. Smaller whales are threatened by sharks. Whales are still hunted by humans, and many species are on the verge of extinction. Even dolphins and porpoises are killed. A great number of whales are caught in fishing nets and drown.

Beaching

These pilot whales have become stranded on a beach in Tasmania, Australia. No one is sure why whales do this. One theory is that they rely on the Earth's magnetic field to navigate and sometimes become confused, for example, during a magnetic storm. Some people think pollution of the seas weakens the whales' resistance to disease.

Toothed whales use echolocation to find prey.

Echolocation

Toothed whales have developed an extremely sophisticated sense of hearing. Like bats, whales use a system of echolocation to detect other things in the water. They emit an almost non-stop stream of "clicks" that cannot be detected by the human ear. The clicks bounce off objects in the water around them and are picked up by the whales' receiving mechanisms.

Sirenians

The four species of Sirenians – three manatees and one dugong – are, like the whales, entirely aquatic mammals. Often called sea cows, they are all herbivorous, feeding mainly on sea grasses. Manatees live in tropical coastal waters on both sides of the Atlantic, entering large rivers and estuaries and rarely venturing into the open sea. The dugong lives around the edges of the Indian and western Pacific oceans.

Whiskers are used to find food on the riverbed.

Manatees can weigh up to 1.76 tons.

West Indian manatee

Schools

Most whales live in communities. They associate in groups, called schools when referring to dolphins, or pods when referring to larger toothed whales such as these killer whales. The groups vary in size from a male, several females, and their calves, to thousands, as sometimes happens with pilot whales.

Mother and calf stay close to each other.

Flukes are up to a quarter of the body length.

A newborn blue whale weighs 2.3 tons and is more than 23 ft (7m) long.

Throat grooves allow the mouth to expand.

Blue whale

By far the largest animal the world has ever seen, the blue whale grows up to 105 ft (32 m) long and weighs up to 176 tons. Its tongue alone weighs 4.4 tons – almost as much as a full-grown elephant. It can grow this size only because its huge bulk is supported by water. Blue whales live mainly in cold water and open oceans throughout the world.

Largest and smallest

The blue whale is the largest of the Cetaceans. The smallest is the vaquita, also called the Gulf of California harbor porpoise. An adult is about 4-5 ft (1.2-1.5 m) long. Large numbers have been caught in fishing nets, but this species is seldom seen and is believed to be rare.

Breeding

Whales usually give birth to one calf after a gestation period of 10-12 months. When the calf is born, the female guides it to the surface so that it can take its first breath. A mother whale takes good care of her calf, and may nurse it for several years.

GRAY WHALE

SCIENTIFIC NAME	*Eschrichtius robustus*
ORDER	Cetacea
FAMILY	Eschrichtiidae
DISTRIBUTION	Pacific coasts of North America and Asia
HABITAT	Shallow coastal waters
DIET	Crustaceans

FIND OUT MORE   BATS   MAMMALS   MIGRATION   OCEAN WILDLIFE   POLAR WILDLIFE   SEALS   SHARKS AND RAYS

Whales and dolphins

Toothed

No dorsal fin

Baird's beaked whale is one of 18 species of beaked whales.

Lower jaw protrudes beyond the upper jaw.

Powerful jaws with conical teeth

False killer whale is black all over. It is closely related to the killer whale.

Narwhal – only the male has a long tusk, which is one of two teeth.

Tusk can grow up to 9 ft (2.75 m) long.

Sperm whale is the largest toothed whale. Males are up to 59 ft (18 m) long.

Head is full of an oily substance called spermaceti oil.

Killer whale is the fastest marine mammal. It can move at up to 34 mph (56 km/h).

Rounded flippers

Slender body

Amazon river dolphin is the largest of the river dolphins.

Small eyes

Long-snouted spinner dolphin performs spectacular aerial displays.

Hector's dolphin is one of the smallest of all cetaceans.

La Plata dolphin lives in the sea, preferring shallow water.

Dusky dolphin lives in groups and also likes the company of other species.

Dall's porpoise lives in deep ocean waters.

No beak

Long beak

Harbor porpoise is also known as the common porpoise.

Yangtze River dolphin is also known as the baiji.

Baleen

Pygmy right whale is the smallest baleen whale.

Areas of rough, horny skin

Humpback whale is easy to recognize by its long flippers.

Knobs on head and lower jaw

Bowhead whale is one of the right whales.

Upper jaw curves to hold long baleen.

Right whale has a huge head with up to 270 pairs of baleen plates.

Paired blow-holes

Minke whale has a sharply pointed snout.

White flipper band on some whales

Concave dorsal fin

Blue whale is the largest animal that has ever lived. It weighs up to 175 tons.

Bryde's whale is inquisitive and will sometimes swim alongside boats.

WINDS

THE AIR AROUND us is rarely still. When air moves in a continuous stream, it becomes wind. Winds are caused by air moving from areas of high pressure to areas of low pressure. Rising air does not exert great force, thereby creating an area of low pressure. Sinking air exerts more force, thereby creating an area of high pressure. Dramatic pressure differences generate strong winds, such as hurricanes. The strength of wind is measured from 0 to 12 on the Beaufort scale. Winds are part of a global circulation pattern that keeps temperature patterns in balance.

Cold air sinks over forests.

Air rising over warm areas creates a return air flow at high altitude to complete the air circuit.

Warm air rises over cities.

Air sinks over cool sea.

Area of low pressure as air is warmed by reflection of the Sun

Cold air under high pressure moves to an area of lower pressure.

Wind generation

Low pressure areas are created where the Sun warms the Earth's surface. High pressure areas are created where the air is cooler. The extra pressure in these zones (anticyclones or highs) pushes air toward low pressure zones (depressions or lows). At ground level, low-level winds blow from high to low; higher up, winds spread out above low pressure areas.

Local winds
Some winds only blow in certain places and at particular times, such as North America's Chinook. Cattlemen in the Rocky Mountains like the Chinook as this warm, dry wind rapidly removes snow cover.

Approach of strong winds

Prevailing winds

Winds are described by the direction from which they blow. A wind blowing from west to east is called a westerly or west wind. In most places, the wind usually blows from one direction most of the time. This is known as the prevailing wind.

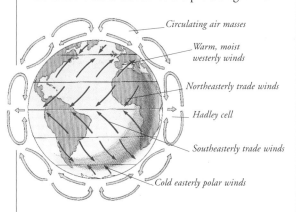

Circulating air masses

Warm, moist westerly winds

Northeasterly trade winds

Hadley cell

Southeasterly trade winds

Cold easterly polar winds

Hadley cells
Prevailing winds are the ground level part of huge cells of circulating air. For every wind at ground level, there is a turning high level wind. The cell in the tropics is called a Hadley cell, after English meteorologist George Hadley (1685–1768).

Coriolis effect
The Earth's rotation stops winds from blowing straight from high to low pressure areas. Instead, it deflects winds sideways. This is known as the Coriolis effect. In the northern hemisphere, winds are deflected to the right, and in the southern to the left.

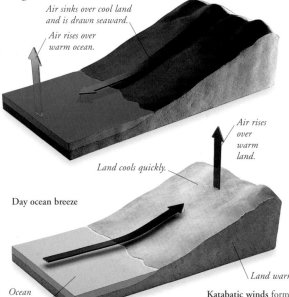

Night land breeze

Air sinks over cool land and is drawn seaward.

Air rises over warm ocean.

Land cools quickly.

Day ocean breeze

Air rises over warm land.

Ocean warms slowly.

Land warms quickly.

Mountain winds
Mountains often generate their own local winds. At night, cool air flows down into valleys, creating katabatic winds. In the day, sun-warmed air rises out of the valleys, creating anabatic winds.

Down-valley wind

Land and ocean breezes

The land heats up faster than the water, so warm air rises over the land during the day as it is warmed by the Sun. At certain times of year, this can create an ocean breeze, which is a gentle breeze blowing in to the land off the cold ocean. At night, the land cools faster than the ocean, reversing the air flow. This creates a land breeze that blows out over the ocean.

Katabatic winds form in mountains as cool air sinks at night.

Anabatic winds form in valleys as warm air rises during the day.

Up-valley wind

Jet streams

At high altitudes, there are narrow rivers of air that roar steadily around the world at speeds of 230 mph (370 kmh) or more. This photograph shows a jet stream high over the Sahara in Egypt.

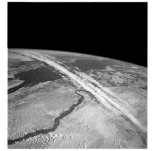

Rossby wave
Between the westerly winds and the polar easterlies, a jet stream runs eastward. It meanders around the world in four to six giant waves, called Rossby waves, that form cyclonic storms below.

1 A Rossby wave develops as a major bend forms in the polar front of the stream.

Warm air

Cold air

2 The Coriolis effect makes the wave deeper and more pronounced.

Wave deepens.

3 Caught in the loops, warm and cold air may detach to form cyclones.

Air is trapped.

FIND OUT MORE AIR   ATMOSPHERE   COASTLINES   ENERGY   KITES   MOUNTAINS AND VALLEYS   OCEANS AND SEAS   SAILING AND OTHER WATER SPORTS   SHIPS AND BOATS   WEATHER

WINTER SPORTS

THE TERM WINTER SPORTS refers to sports that take place on snow and ice. Keen competition has grown up around them, and the Winter Olympics are held every four years. There are two main types of skiing: Alpine skiing, which features downhill and slalom racing; and Nordic skiing, which is a cross-country sport, that also includes ski jumping. A new type of skiing, freestyle, is about performance rather than speed. In sled racing, riders hurtle down special runs. Skating includes figures, ice hockey, and racing.

Mittens

Alpine boot

Bindings automatically release the boot in the event of a fall.

Ski bindings

Skiing

Alpine racing is about speed and technique; Nordic, more about stamina. The two disciplines use different equipment. Alpine skis are wider and heavier than Nordic skis, and the boots are attached to the skis with safety bindings. Nordic boots are like sneakers, and the heel lifts free with each stride.

Ski jumping
In ski jumping, competitors take off from the end of a chute on a ski tower. They aim to fly gracefully, perfectly balanced and still in the air before landing smoothly. Judges award points for style as well as distance jumped.

Nordic racing
Cross-country courses have no steep slopes or sharp turns. Races range from 3 to 30 miles (5 to 50 km), with skiers starting at 30-second intervals. Placings are decided on time. There are relays, combined events, and the biathlon, which includes shooting at targets.

Ski poles   Skis

Downhill racer

Alpine racing
In downhill racing, skiers take the fastest line down a set route, taking off into the air where necessary. In slaloms, skiers weave in and out of pairs of flags, or "gates." Both races are decided on time.

Sled racing

Any snowy slope is a site for sled racing, but for major competitions, special steep, twisty runs are made from ice and snow. The art is to shift the bodyweight to make the sled go the fastest way down, letting gravity do the work. Riders go one at a a time and the winner is the one with the lowest total time from up to four runs.

Skating

Figure skating takes place on an indoor ice rink. There are four events – men's and women's singles, mixed pairs, and ice dancing. Long-track speed skating usually takes place outdoors and skaters race against the clock. Short-track is held indoors, with elimination heats. Ice hockey, on indoor ice rinks, is a major sport in North America and parts of Europe.

Speed skating
Long-track racing is held on a 436-yd (400-m) track with two skaters in separate lanes. There are no lanes in short-track racing, and four to six skaters jockey for position around a tight oval track.

Short-track racer

Arm held out for balance.

Racers lean right over on the tight turns.

Skater is allowed to touch the ice with a hand.

Luge
The luge is a one- or two-person toboggan with no brakes or steering. The riders, or sliders, use their legs and shoulders to guide the vehicle. The luge is ridden face up, in a sitting or lying position.

Bobsled
Two- or four-man bobs have metal runners, steering, and brakes. In a four, the two middle men help to guide the bob by shifting their weight on turns. A brake man uses the brakes only for correcting skids or for stopping.

Toboggan
The skeleton toboggan is so-called because it has no structure above the runners. The rider lies face down, uses toe pieces for braking, and steers by shifting weight. The only major competitions are on the Cresta Run at St. Moritz in Switzerland.

Sonja Henie
A Norwegian figure skater, Sonja Henie (1912–69) turned professional in 1936 after winning three Olympic gold medals and 10 world championships. With her theatrical performances and short skirts, she revolutionized the sport. She toured the US with her own ice show, became an American citizen, and made several films.

Figure skating
Skaters perform set routines and free programs to music, featuring spins, jumps, and, in pairs, lifts. Judges award marks out of six for artistic impression and for technical merit. Ice dancing is less athletic, with more emphasis placed on interpretation of the music.

Referee drops the puck to restart the game.

Ice hockey
Ice hockey is played six-a-side with substitutes allowed at any time. The object is to propel a hard disk, the puck, into the opposition's goal. There are three 20-minute periods. Players serve time penalties for foul play.

FIND OUT MORE   BALL GAMES   HEALTH AND FITNESS   MOTOR SPORTS   OLYMPIC GAMES   SPORTS

WITCHES AND WITCHCRAFT

THE BELIEF IN WITCHES – people with supernatural powers – is ancient and universal. No one knows whether witches do actually have special powers, but from earliest times, people in all cultures have believed that some men and women can use rituals, spells, and other magical means to influence events of good or evil. Definitions of witchcraft vary, but it is always associated with magic. Uniquely, however, in Europe from the 15th to the 18th centuries, witchcraft was associated with devil worship and was punishable by death.

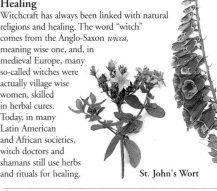
Foxglove

Healing
Witchcraft has always been linked with natural religions and healing. The word "witch" comes from the Anglo-Saxon *wicca*, meaning wise one, and, in medieval Europe, many so-called witches were actually village wise women, skilled in herbal cures. Today, in many Latin American and African societies, witch doctors and shamans still use herbs and rituals for healing.

St. John's Wort

Magic

Magic, or sorcery, is the attempt to use supernatural or natural forces to influence events. Belief in magic has a long history – evidence of magic spells has been found in prehistoric cave paintings – and it continues today in many cultures, either as a superstition or as a religion. In some cultures, magic is considered to be sacred and is practiced by specially skilled people.

Carving of African shaman

Familiars
Identifying witches was difficult because they looked like any member of society. However, medieval people believed that true witches could fly – usually on a broomstick – and were accompanied by a "familiar," such as a cat, which was really a demon in disguise.

Torture
Suspected witches were savagely tortured in order to make them confess and also to name accomplices. Methods of torture included whipping, branding with red-hot irons, stretching on the rack, thumbscrews, and the gouging out of eyes. Most people confessed to almost anything just to stop the torture.

Eye gouger

Thumbscrews

European witch-hunts

In early medieval Europe, belief in witches was a natural part of everyday life. However, from the 12th century, the Christian church redefined witchcraft as heresy, or treason against God. Witches were described as evil devil-worshipers, and the Church set up massive witch-hunts in which anyone suspected of witchcraft was rounded up, tried, and often executed. The witch-hunts lasted some 300 years, and at least 300,000 innocent people, mostly women, were put to death. Historians have put forward various reasons for the witch-hunts. These include a general persecution of women, and the rise of medical science.

Witch burning
Proving witchcraft was a difficult matter, and various tests were devised. One of these was throwing a bound person into water. If she was guilty, she floated; if innocent, she sank. Death was the usual penalty for witchcraft, particularly burning at the stake, on the grounds that this punishment mirrored the fires of hell. Many thousands were put to death this way, including Joan of Arc the French heroine who was accused of being a witch by the English and burned at the stake in 1431.

Witch trials
Persecution of supposed witches reached its height between 1580 and 1660, when trials occurred throughout western Europe. As hysteria mounted, thousands were brought before Church and civil courts. Anyone old, alone, or eccentric could be accused, including elderly women, village midwives, and herbalists. Their persecution was fueled by gossip and rumors, which were used as evidence in court.

Malleus Maleficarum
In 1486, two Dominican monks, Heinrich Krämer and Jacob Sprenger, published the *Malleus Maleficarum* (Hammer of the Witches). This book included the pope's definition of witches as "anti-Christian," and set out rules for identifying, prosecuting, and punishing witches. The book quickly spread throughout Europe, and was used as the essential witch-hunter's reference.

Salem trials
The earliest English settlers took their fear of witches to the American colonies. In 1692, a series of notorious witch trials took place in Salem, Massachusetts. In all, 27 people were tried and convicted; of these, 19 were hanged, and one man was stoned to death. The trials were later condemned and the convictions overturned.

Halloween
Originally a Celtic festival for the dead, Halloween falls on October 31. It was once believed that on this night, witches and warlocks flew abroad, and bonfires were lit to keep spirits away. Trick-or-treating has replaced witches' pranks today.

FIND OUT MORE | CRIME AND PUNISHMENT | EUROPE, HISTORY OF | HUNDRED YEARS WAR | MEDICINE, HISTORY OF | RELIGIONS

WOLVES AND WILD DOGS

THE FAMILY CANIDAE, the dog family, contains about 34 species, which can be divided into three main groups. The lupine (meaning wolflike) group contains wolves, jackals, the coyote, wild dogs, and domestic dogs, many of which hunt in packs. The second group contains the vulpine (meaning foxlike) foxes. The third group contains the south American foxes, or zorros. Canids are mainly carnivorous. Alert, hardy mammals, they are able to catch and kill animals as large as or larger than themselves. They can travel long distances without tiring, keeping up a steady trot on long legs and large paws.

Foxes have light builds for better agility.

The fox catches a small animal by pouncing on it like a cat and pinning it to the ground with its front paws.

Foxes

There are about nine species of vulpine foxes, of which the red fox is the largest and the most numerous. This agile animal owes its success to its intelligence and adaptability. It is able to thrive equally well in towns and in rural areas. Foxes do not form packs; they live alone or in small family groups.

Wolves

There are two species of wolves – the gray wolf and the red wolf. The red wolf is an endangered species and the gray wolf is nearly extinct in much of its former range. Wolves are social animals that live in packs led by a top male and female. The pack marks the boundary of its territory with urine and howls to tell other packs to stay away.

Most of the adults in a pack go on hunting trips.

Thick, short underfur and long outer guard-hairs insulate the wolf against freezing temperatures.

The wolf has excellent hearing, eyesight, and sense of smell.

Wolves have pale undercoats, with darker fur on the body, ears, and tail to match their habitat.

Long legs have four toes on the hind feet and five on the front feet.

In the snow, each wolf walks in the leader's tracks.

Raccoon dog with a white coat

Member of the fox species

Carnassials

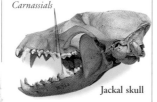

Jackal skull

Jackals form pairs for life.

Jackals

The four species of jackals are closely related to wolves. As with most canids, they have two sharp carnassial teeth used for cutting meat, located where the jaws exert greatest force. Their long pointed canine teeth are for gripping and killing prey.

Mottled coloration gives African hunting dogs an effective camouflage.

Hunting

The most specialized pack hunters are African hunting dogs. They hunt as an organized team, but they often lose a kill to stronger predators. Human persecution and introduced diseases have reduced their numbers drastically.

Red fox cubs do not forage with the adults until they are about 12 weeks old.

Learning skills

Cubs will not survive to adulthood unless they learn to kill and defend themselves. They learn these skills through playing, chasing, and pouncing upon each other. Social canids learn hunting skills from the adults in their pack.

Wild dogs

The African wild dog, the dhole, and the dingo are known as wild dogs, often hunting in packs over huge areas. The maned wolf, the bush dog, and the raccoon dog are distantly related canids. The raccoon dog is a timid, solitary creature that lives in dense undergrowth and feeds on fruit, insects, and small animals. It stays underground in harsh winter weather.

RED FOX

SCIENTIFIC NAME	*Vulpes vulpes*
ORDER	Carnivora
FAMILY	Canidae
DISTRIBUTION	North America, Eurasia, North Africa, Australia
HABITAT	Everywhere except deserts
DIET	Meat, insects, and fruit
SIZE	Length: about 42 in (110 cm)
LIFESPAN	3 years in wild

FIND OUT MORE	ANIMAL BEHAVIOR	AFRICAN WILDLIFE	DESERT WILDLIFE	DOGS	HYENAS	MAMMALS	POLAR WILDLIFE	URBAN WILDLIFE

Wolves and wild dogs

Bush dog is a strong swimmer and hunts other aquatic animals.

Raccoon dog has a varied diet, and large cheek teeth for grinding up fruits and seeds.

African hunting dog has a pattern of brown, dun, and white on its body, with a white-tipped tail.

Golden jackal shares parental duties with its mate.

An adult wolf needs to eat up to 13 lb (6 kg) of food every day.

A maned wolf is about 31 in (80 cm) tall.

Gray wolf is the largest wild dog. Although once widespread, it is now extinct or nearly extinct in many parts of its range.

Rounded ears

Dingo is a wild dog from Australia. It was probably introduced there about 7,000 years ago.

Indian dhole has a coat that ranges from sandy brown to orange red.

Maned wolf needs a large grassland territory. It lives in eastern South America.

Large ears can pick up the sounds of insects.

Bat-eared fox feeds on beetles and other invertebrates.

Ruppell's sand fox lives in North Africa and the Middle East.

Fennec fox is the smallest member of the family.

Like all dogs, foxes have an acute sense of smell.

Erect ears help the fox tell from which direction a sound is coming.

Paws are well furred to save heat.

Red fox has adapted to live in suburbs and towns.

Gray fox is a good climber and will make its den in large trees up to 30 ft (9 m) above the ground.

Arctic fox has a pale winter coat and a dark summer coat.

WOMEN'S MOVEMENT

FOR THE LAST 200 YEARS, women have fought for their rights. Their struggle is sometimes called the women's movement, although the term includes different campaigns. The first wave of organized feminism – the fight for women's rights – appeared during the 1800s, and was concerned with legal rights and the right to vote. During the 1960s, a new wave of protest – the women's liberation movement – appeared that made women's rights a global issue. By the 1990s, the women's movement had gained many victories and changed society.

Early stirrings
In the 18th century, women had no rights – they were the property of their husbands or fathers. Inspired by the French Revolution, women began to challenge this situation.

Mary Wollstonecraft
In 1792, an Englishwoman, Mary Wollstonecraft (1759–97), wrote *Vindication of the Rights of Women*. She deplored the fact that married women were kept at home "confined in cages, like the feathered race," and called for an end to their oppression.

Mary Wollstonecraft

First wave
During the 1800s, middle-class women, such as Englishwoman Madame Bodichon (formerly Barbara Leigh Smith), campaigned for a married woman's right to keep her own property, and for the right to education and meaningful work.

Madame Bodichon (1827–90)

Votes for Women poster

Fight for the vote
From the 1840s, American and British women focused on fighting for the vote, because they believed that only by voting could they improve their situation. The Cause, as it became known, was a long struggle involving hundreds of thousands of women.

National Union of Women's Suffrage Societies (NUWSS) banner

Women's liberation movement
In the late 1960s, the women's liberation movement exploded onto the political scene. Increasing numbers of women around the world challenged oppression and traditional female roles. They demanded an end to all forms of sexual discrimination, and campaigned around issues such as equal pay, job opportunities, healthcare, childcare, reproductive freedom, violence toward women, and racism.

Miss World contest, 1970
Women on strike, 1977

Equal rights
During the 1970s, the women's liberation movement was a major political influence in many countries. It forced the introduction of legislation that ensured equal rights for women by banning sex discrimination at work and in education. Although this legislation established women's rights to equal opportunities, inequalities still existed.

Demonstrations
In 1970, feminists demonstrated at the Miss World beauty contest, protesting that it degraded women. The contest continued on a stage covered in flour and other debris thrown by the protesters. After this event, which was televised worldwide, more women began to meet in groups to discuss how sexism affected their lives, and to plan changes.

International Women's Day
In 1908, socialists in the United States set aside one day for women's suffrage demonstrations. In the 1970s, feminists revived the idea, and today women worldwide celebrate March 8.

Silver wattle, the Women's Day emblem

Timeline

1830s Antislavery campaign stimulates growth of women's movement, US.

1848 First ever women's rights convention, Seneca Falls, US.

1869 Susan B. Anthony and Elizabeth Cady Stanton form National Woman Suffrage Association, US.

WSPU enamel badge

1893 New Zealand women are the first to gain the vote.

1968 Women workers at Ford, UK, strike for equal pay.

1970 Australian Germaine Greer writes *The Female Eunuch;* it calls for women's liberation.

1975 Equal rights laws passed, UK.

Simone de Beauvoir
French philosopher Simone de Beauvoir (1908–86) was a major figure in modern feminism. In 1949, she wrote *Le Deuxième Sexe (The Second Sex),* in which she drew on history, art, literature, and psychology to show how men had consistently denied women's identity. Her book was very influential, and de Beauvoir herself campaigned actively for women's rights.

 FIND OUT MORE   CURIE, MARIE   FRENCH REVOLUTION   HISTORY   PANKHURST FAMILY   HUMAN RIGHTS   TRUTH, SOJOURNER

WOODLAND WILDLIFE

IN TEMPERATE REGIONS, where there is lots of rain, woodland is the natural form of vegetation. In some areas, only one species of tree grows. Other woodlands have a mixture of needle-leaved conifers, broad-leaved trees, evergreens that keep their leaves all year, and deciduous trees that shed leaves in winter. Some woods are open to the sky; in others, tree crowns mingle to create a closed canopy. All woodlands are rich habitats for wildlife. While there are few large animals, such as boars, there are many species of insects and birds.

Canopy

Shrub layer

Field layer

Leaf litter

Layers of the woodland

Woods are usually described as having five layers, each with its own characteristic vegetation and wildlife. A natural woodland offers a rich mix of living spaces for wildlife, both on the ground level that consists of clearings and streams, and in the layers that exist from the treetops down to the ground.

Canopy
The canopy consists of the crowns of the tallest trees. Branches and twigs sprout a luxuriant layer of leaves that trap most of the incoming sunlight. Here, well above ground level, the canopy provides protection from most predators for insects, birds, and tree-climbing mammals, such as squirrels.

Shrub layer
Beneath the canopy grow woody plants, including shrubs and bushes, such as hazel and hawthorn, and young trees that have not reached their full height. They form an often densely foliaged layer, that provides nest sites for birds and plentiful insect food.

Field layer
Wildflowers, ferns, mosses, and other low-growing vegetation grow on the ground and are called the field layer. They have adapted to shade because so much sunlight is trapped by the trees above. These plants provide food for insects and snails and cover for small animals, such as rodents.

Leaf litter
The slow decay of fallen leaves creates a layer of leaf litter on the ground. Mixed with fallen twigs, nuts, and berries, this layer harbors its own wildlife community. Millipedes and beetles live here and supply food for foraging mammals, ground birds, and lizards.

Soil
Plants take root in soil that is richly supplied with nutrients from decaying leaf litter above. Moles tunnel through soil and other mammals make their burrows here. Soil also provides food for beetle larvae and earthworms.

Earthworm

Mammals

Seldom seen because of their secretive or nocturnal habits, woodland mammals signal their presence in various ways – in the rustle of leaves made by a mouse in the undergrowth, in the fresh earth around the entrance to a fox's burrow, or in a track of hoof prints made by deer across fresh snow. Many mammals forage or hunt on the woodland floor; others climb into the trees to find food and shelter.

Chipmunk feeding

Eastern chipmunk
This chipmunk from North America moves easily through the layers of a woodland. It climbs branches, forages for seeds and nuts on the woodland floor, and makes its home in a burrow in the soil.

Roe deer
Foliage from the field layer up to the lower shrub layer provides food for the shy roe deer, which lives either alone or in small groups. Unable to climb or burrow, deer rely on their keen senses, inconspicuous coloring, and speed to avoid danger. When alarmed, the white hairs on the roe deer's rump fluff out.

Roe deer within deep foliage

Badger at entrance of burrow

European badger
Extensive family burrows, or setts, dug out with strong claws, are the hallmark of European badgers. Each sett has a series of underground chambers, a network of tunnels, and several entrances from the woodland floor. Badgers emerge at night to rifle through leaf litter in search of worms, grubs, fruit, and nuts.

Birds

Woodland birdlife is wonderfully diverse. There are ground foragers, such as pheasants, species good at scaling tree trunks, berry-eaters of the shrub layer, such as blackbirds, songsters in the treetops, and menacing birds of prey such as the golden eagle. Summer is the busiest time; when fall comes, many birds migrate to warmer climates far away.

Dappled brown feathers help conceal the owl by day.

Well-camouflaged nightjar

Tawny owl
The tawny owl hunts at night. It rests in the canopy and scans the ground for prey, with huge eyes and sensitive ears that are alert for the slightest movement from a shrew or rodent. Then, with a silent, agile swoop, the owl pounces on its victim.

Green woodpecker
Woodpeckers are famous for hammering rapidly into tree trunks with their sharp beaks to excavate nests. The green woodpecker climbs trunks to dig insect larvae out of the bark, but it also forages on the ground where it breaks into ants' nests to feast on the occupants.

Common nightjar
The common nightjar visits temperate woodlands to breed in summer, but migrates to Africa in winter. It lives at the edge of the forest, and in more open woods where it darts through the air at night chasing moths. By day, it rests on branches or on the ground, camouflaged by its mottled plumage.

Reptiles

Most woodlands are inhabited by lizards and snakes. They usually make their home on the ground, underneath logs and rocks, or in hollow tree trunks; others live in shrubs and hunt for insects and birds. The world's most northern woods are too cold for most species of reptile, which spend the winter in hibernation.

To escape from predators, the tail can break off.

Lizard can change the color of its skin.

Anole lizard
With their long toe pads for gripping branches, anoles are among the most adept tree climbers of all lizards. The green anole of North America hunts for insects and spiders among foliage, where its body color provides effective camouflage. When the lizard scurries down a trunk or crosses the woodland floor, however, it changes to a brown color within seconds.

Rat snake
Living in the woodlands of North America, the rat snake preys on small mammals, birds, and lizards. In many areas, the cold winter weather forces the snake into hibernation. Hiding deep in leaf litter or in a hollow log, the snake can remain dormant for several months.

The rat snake can grow up to 8 ft (2.5 m) in length.

Tongue

Amphibians

Although amphibians usually live in or near water, many species find the humid conditions they need in woodlands – near streams and in the cool shade beneath a mature canopy. Toads and salamanders spend much of their lives crawling through damp leaf litter and undergrowth, snatching invertebrates to feed on. A few species of frogs are adapted for foraging up into the trees themselves.

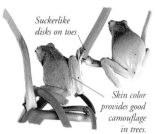

Suckerlike disks on toes

Skin color provides good camouflage in trees.

North American tree frog
Tree frogs live in warmer areas of woodland across the world, where they snap up insects and spiders among the leaves of trees. They have loose belly skin and suckerlike toe disks that enable them to climb vertical surfaces. Tree frogs camouflage themselves by changing their skin color to match their surroundings.

Spotted salamander
Salamanders are numerous in the damp mountain woods of the eastern US. The spotted salamander spends most of its time hidden within leaf litter and soil, hunting for invertebrates such as worms and slugs. Instead of being camouflaged, it is brightly colored, warning predators that it is poisonous to eat.

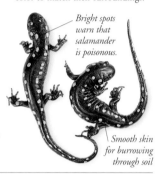

Bright spots warn that salamander is poisonous.

Smooth skin for burrowing through soil

Insects

During spring, when eggs have hatched and any larvae or adults have emerged from dormancy, a woodland is alive with insects. From the sunlit treetops to the perpetual darkness of the soil layer, insects are busy gathering nectar, hunting each other, munching leaves and wood, and processing debris.

Worker ants hunt for food.

Antennae can detect chemicals produced by other ants.

Wood ant
Wood ants live in huge colonies on the ground where they build domed nests of twigs and leaves or pine needles. The queen ant produces batch after batch of young, while worker ants go out in search of food for the colony.

Cardinal beetle
The grubs of this brightly colored beetle are among many beetle larvae that bore their way under tree bark. Here they remain safe from most predators, but they may still be plucked from hiding by woodpeckers.

Antenna

Tree wasp
Tree wasps live in large colonies. They make nests of paperlike material that they suspend from the branches of trees and shrubs. Workers make the paper by scraping off and chewing fragments of wood from trees with their strong jaws, and mixing it with saliva.

Huge jaws used when fighting

Stag beetle
The stag beetle lays its eggs in rotting wood on the woodland floor. Male stag beetles use their impressive jaws not for feeding, but to brandish at rival males. During a fight, two rivals use their jaws like antlers to grapple and wrestle with one another. Stag beetles are the largest British beetle and may reach 2.8 in (7 cm) in length.

Dark wings help conceal the moth on trees.

Old lady moth
Adults of the old lady moth appear only in mid-summer, flying at night, but hiding during the day in hollow trees. The larvae, or caterpillars, relish the leaves of some woodland shrubs. The larvae live longer than the adults, first emerging from eggs in late summer and spending the winter in hibernation.

Plants and fungi

Tall trees dominate woodlands, but many other types of vegetation exist with them, such as shrubs, creepers, mosses, and ferns. Wildflowers often bloom early in spring, taking advantage of the light available before new leaves on trees have grown. Most of these plants are adapted to grow in shade and can extract the energy they need for growth from the sunlight that filters down to their leaves. Fungi and some orchids do not need light. They obtain their energy directly from other plants.

Oak galls
Galls are abnormal growths caused by gall wasps, which lay their eggs in the leaves of oak trees. When the grubs hatch, they cause the plant tissue to grow in a protective, food-rich ball around them.

Oak gall

Bracket fungus
Many types of fungi live near the shady woodland floor. Bracket fungus often sprouts from old tree trunks. Using fine, rootlike structures, fungi draw energy and nutrients from the plant matter on which they grow.

Pinecone seeds

Pinecone
Pine trees have needlelike leaves that animals do not eat. Their cones, however, offer seeds that squirrels and other creatures find nutritious. Some animals break open the cones to extract the seeds; others wait for the cones to split open.

Ferns
Ferns are simple plants that produce spores instead of flowers. They are common in the humid shade of woodlands, where they grow along the ground like a carpet. In warmer climates, ferns can grow so big they form part of the shrub layer.

Ferns unfurl as they grow.

FIND OUT MORE   AMPHIBIANS   BEETLES   CAMOUFLAGE AND COLOR   FORESTS   HIBERNATION   INSECTS   MUSHROOMS AND OTHER FUNGI   PLANTS   REPTILES   SOIL   TREES

WOODPECKERS AND TOUCANS

THEY LOOK DIFFERENT, and also feed in different ways, yet woodpeckers and toucans are close relatives. They live in forests and woodlands, and most of them spend nearly all their time in trees, making their nests in holes in the trunks. Woodpeckers usually feed by chiseling their way into wood to reach burrowing insects. Toucans clamber around the treetops and use their huge colorful beaks to collect food.

Woodpeckers

There are about 200 species of woodpeckers, and they live in every continent except Australasia and Antarctica. Instead of perching on branches, woodpeckers cling to tree trunks with their sharp claws. They use their strong beaks to bore holes in trees for nesting. They also use them to communicate with each other by hammering on dead wood.

Flight
When a woodpecker flies, it flaps its wings a few times, then keeps them closed for a few seconds. This makes the bird rise and fall.

Tail
The woodpecker uses its short tail to brace itself against tree trunks. Each of its tail feathers ends in a stiff point.

Claws
Woodpeckers have short but powerful legs, and feet that work like clamps. They lock themselves into position with their claws before they start to feed.

Acorn woodpecker
In western North America, the acorn woodpecker uses trees as pantries. It pecks hundreds of holes in them and stores an acorn in each one for future food supply.

Green woodpecker
This bird lives in trees, where it is well camouflaged, but it usually flies down to the ground to feed. It has a harsh laughing call that can be heard for miles.

Toucans

There are 33 species of toucans, found only in South and Central America. The family includes toucans, toucanets, and aracaris. Most have a large beak – up to two-thirds as long as their body. When feeding, a toucan juggles its food in its bill and then tosses its head back before swallowing.

The beak contains lots of air-filled spaces that make it lighter than it looks.

Toucan beaks
Toucan beaks are often brightly colored, this may help birds identify their own species. The size and color might also be to frighten away other birds.

Slender tongue

Glossy black beak

Beak much larger than the head

Chestnut-eared aracari
This bird's beak is long and narrow, and gently curved. Both parts have a distinctly serrated edge.

Ariel toucan
Found in the southern part of the Amazon rain forest, this toucan feeds on small animals as well as fruit.

Toco toucan
This toucan has one of the largest beaks. It can use it to reach fruit on twigs that cannot take its weight.

Red-billed toucan
The Red-billed toucan eats fruit, insects, spiders, and other animals, such as lizards and small birds. It lives in northern South America in the high branches of the rain forest. It usually occurs singly or in pairs.

Red-billed toucan

Toucan nests
Toucans nest in tree trunks. They use either a natural hole where the wood has rotted away, or a hole that has been made by a woodpecker. Some species line the hole with leaves, but most leave it bare. Female toucans lay two to four shiny, white eggs. Both parents take turns incubating the eggs and bringing food to the young chicks. After about three weeks the naked chicks will open their eyes, and by about six weeks they will be able to begin to survive on their own.

Tongue curled around skull

Tongue
A woodpecker's tongue can be three or four times as long as its beak, and it has a sticky or spiny tip. The woodpecker flicks it out and uses it to probe for insects. When not in use, the tongue curves around the back of the skull, just beneath the skin.

GREEN WOODPECKER

SCIENTIFIC NAME	*Picus viridis*
ORDER	Piciformes
FAMILY	Picidae
DISTRIBUTION	Europe and western Asia
HABITAT	Woodland and grassy places
DIET	Ants and other insects
SIZE	Length, including tail: 12 in (30 cm)
LIFESPAN	About 7 years

FIND OUT MORE   BIRDS   EGGS   FLIGHT, ANIMAL   KINGFISHERS AND HORNBILLS   NESTS AND BURROWS   WOODLAND WILDLIFE

W

WORLD WAR I

FOR MORE THAN FOUR years, the world was engaged in a war of a ferocity and on a scale never seen before. The conflict, known then as the Great War and today as World War I, arose out of the economic, colonial, and military rivalry of the European empires. The assassination in 1914 of the heir to one of those empires – Austria-Hungary – was the spark that ignited the rivalries. Within months, fighting had broken out in Europe, Africa, and Asia. By the time the war ended in 1918, the old empires were in ruins, their place taken by a new world power – the United States.

Neutral states

Central powers
Austria-Hungary

Central powers
Ottoman empire

Allies (1914 on)

Allies (1915 on)

Western Front

The German plan was to sweep through Belgium and northern France to capture Paris and knock the French out of the war within weeks. This plan was thwarted by the French army at the Marne River. Both sides then dug lines of defensive trenches that stretched from the English Channel to the Swiss border, to protect their positions.

Troops submerged in mud at Passchendaele

The Battle of Passchendaele

Outbreak of war
On June 28 1914, the heir to the Austrian throne was killed in Serbia. Austria invaded Serbia, Russia came to Serbia's aid, and Germany supported Austria. Fearing war on two fronts, Germany invaded Belgium and France. Britain then declared war on Germany.

Recruitment
At first, regular troops were reinforced by thousands of volunteers. But as casualty rates soared, governments had to bring in conscription (compulsory military service) to keep up the strength of their armies.

South African recruitment poster

Trenches at the Somme

The Somme
On July 1 1916, Allied troops (those on the British and French side) tried to break through German lines near the Somme River, France. By the end of the four-month battle, the Allies had advanced just 5 miles (8 km). One million men were killed.

Passchendaele
In July 1917 the Allies tried again to get through German lines, this time near the village of Passchendaele, Belgium. Bad weather turned the area into a sea of mud, over 300,000 Allied troops lost their lives, and hardly any advance was made.

Eastern Fronts

The war in eastern Europe, between Germany and Austria-Hungary on one side, and Russia on the other, was more fluid than in the west. Most battles were in open country, across what is now Poland and in the eastern Mediterranean. The war expanded into Asia when Turkey attacked Russia at the end of 1914, and the Allies launched the ill-fated Gallipoli campaign. Turkey also posed a threat in Syria and Palestine and so Allied troops were sent from Egypt to defend the region.

British troops in Palestine

Uniform of British Private, Scottish Battalion was kaki-colored to blend with the mud.

French infantryman's equipment included spare ammunition and food supplies.

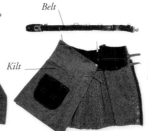

Cap

Sporran

Belt

Kilt

Cartridge pouch

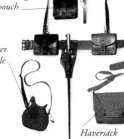

Water bottle

Doublet

Haversack

Manfred von Richthofen

The most famous pilot of the war was the German airman Manfred von Richthofen (1892–1918). He is said to have destroyed 80 Allied aircraft before he was killed when his aircraft was shot down over France. He was known as the Red Baron because of his bright red Fokker triplane.

Timeline
June 1914 Archduke Franz Ferdinand, heir to the throne of Austria-Hungary, is assassinated; Serbia is blamed.

July 1914 Austria-Hungary invades Serbia in retaliation; France, Germany, and Russia mobilize their armies in preparation for war.

August 1914 Germany declares war on Russia and France and invades Belgium; this brings Britain into the war; Germany pushes back Britain at Mons, Belgium; Germany defeats Russia at Tannenberg.

September 1914 German advance halted by the British and French at the Marne River.

German infantryman

October 1914 Turkey enters the war on the German side; in France a line of defensive trenches is dug stretching along the Western Front.

April 1915 Germans use poison gas for first time at Ypres, Belgium; Allies try to force Turkey out of war by invading Gallipoli peninsula.

May 1915 Italy joins the war on the Allied side.

The civilian war

The huge armies of World War I needed a massive force of back-up workers to provide them with weapons, food, and other supplies. The entire civilian workforce was directed toward war work, producing arms and ammunition, growing food, and keeping industry and commerce going at home while millions of soldiers fought at the front.

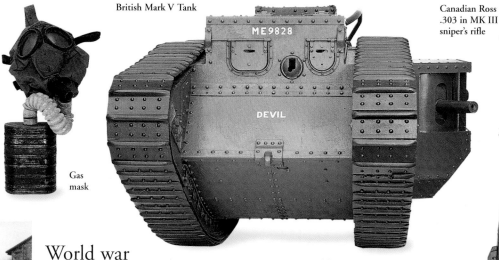

Gas mask

British Mark V Tank

Canadian Ross .303 in MK III sniper's rifle

Women ambulance drivers at the front

Women at war

Before 1914, women traditionally worked in jobs men did not want. During the war, women were required to do jobs normally done by the men fighting at the front. Across Europe, women worked in factories and offices, drove buses and trains, dug fields, and even joined the police forces.

Propaganda

To stiffen morale and weaken the enemy's resistance, both sides used propaganda. People were made to believe the worst of the other side, with leaflets, posters, and radio broadcasts all used for propaganda. Those who refused to fight were given white feathers, a sign of "cowardice."

White feathers

World war

World War I was the first truly international war in history. People from every continent took part in the fighting. In Africa and Asia, the Turkish Empire and former German colonies were overrun by British Empire troops. There was also fighting in the Middle East and in the Pacific. The entry of the US into the war in 1917 marked the end of European dominance of world affairs.

New weapons

The main weapons used in the war were the rifle (with its bayonet), the machine gun, and the artillery shell. In April 1915 the German army introduced a new weapon – gas – which both sides later used to deadly effect. The British first used tanks at the Somme in September 1916, and both sides made more and more use of aircraft – at first for reconnaissance, later for bombing.

End of the war

In mid-1918, fresh US troops arrived to fight on the Allied side, and there was increasing hunger and discontent among the German soldiers. The Allies broke through the German lines in August 1918. Austria-Hungary and Turkey collapsed in October, and the Allies finally forced Germany to make peace on November 11, 1918.

The Treaty of Versailles

The peace treaty was signed on June 28, 1919, in the palace of Versailles, France. Germany lost territory, and had to limit the size of its army as well as pay compensation to the Allies. Subsequent treaties redrew the map of eastern Europe.

Signing of the treaty

The cost of war

No-one knows how many people died in the war. About 9 million soldiers and possibly 13 million civilians were killed. A further 20 million died in the influenza epidemic that swept Europe during 1918–19. Poppies, which grew on the fields of France, became the symbol of those killed in the war.

Poppies

War art

The horrors of the war inspired painters and poets on both sides. The old romantic idea of war as a great cause was replaced by the realization of its cruelty and destructive force. Many young artists and writers fought at the front; some, such as the British poet Wilfred Owen (1893–1918), were killed in the fighting.

War Landscape by British artist Paul Nash

February 1916 German forces try to capture French fortress of Verdun in a 10-month battle.

May 1916 British and German fleets fight inconclusive Battle of Jutland, off Denmark.

French infantryman, 26th Regiment

July–November 1916 Battle of the Somme; tanks used for first time.

April 1917 US enters war on Allied side.

July–November 1917 Battle of Passchendaele.

March 1918 Germany and Russia make peace at Brest-Litovsk.

March 1918 German forces make massive advances on the Western Front.

July 1918 German advance halted.

August 1918 With the help of American forces, Allied troops make the decisive break through German lines.

Handpainted camouflage coat

October 1918 Italy defeats Austria-Hungary; both Austria-Hungary and Turkey ask for peace.

November 1918 Armistice signed between Germany and the Allies.

June 1919 Peace treaty signed at Versailles, France. The conditions imposed on Germany became a major cause of World War II.

FIND OUT MORE   AFRICA, HISTORY OF   ARMIES   EMPIRES   EUROPE, HISTORY OF   FRANCE, HISTORY OF   GERMANY, HISTORY OF   UNITED KINGDOM, HISTORY OF   WORLD WAR II

WORLD WAR II

WORLD WAR II WAS the most devastating war in history. For the first time ever in warfare, more civilians than soldiers lost their lives. In total, more than 50 million people were killed, including 20 million Russians, 6 million Poles, and 6 million Jews. The war, which lasted from 1939–45, involved every continent, and few countries or people remained untouched by the carnage. In Europe, the strength of the Russian and American armies was required to defeat Germany. In Asia, atomic warfare was used for the first time to defeat Japan.

How war began

Adolf Hitler took control of Germany in 1933 and set out to restore German power in Europe. He built a strong army and air force, and began to expand German territory in central and eastern Europe. On September 1, 1939, German troops invaded Poland. In response, Britain and France declared war on Germany.

German Messerschmitt Bf 109E fighter

British Hawker Hurricane Mark 1 fighter

Blitzkrieg
The German army moved tanks quickly into enemy territory, supporting them by aerial bombardment. This strategy, called Blitzkrieg, (lightning war), was successful in 1939–40.

Battle of Britain
For four months in 1940, British aircraft fought many battles against the German air force. After heavy casualties, Germany canceled its plans to invade Britain.

World war

In June 1941, German troops invaded Russia. Six months later, Japanese aircraft bombed the US naval base at Pearl Harbor, bringing the US into the war. By the end of 1941, an international alliance of the US, Russia, and Britain confronted the Axis powers of Germany, Italy, and Japan.

War in Europe

Norway
Sweden
Britain
Soviet Union
Atlantic Ocean
France
Germany
Ukraine
Spain
Italy
Bulgaria
Greece
Turkey
Algeria
Mediterranean Sea
Jordan
Libya

- ☐ Axis states
- ☐ Areas controlled by Axis
- ☐ Allied states
- ☐ Areas controlled by Allies
- ☐ Neutral states
- --- Extent of German military occupation

China
Korea
Japan
Hong Kong
Pacific Ocean
Philippines
Singapore
Australia

War in the Pacific

Japanese-controlled area by 1942
--- Extent of Japanese occupation

Pearl Harbor
On December 7, 1941, Japanese planes launched a surprise attack on the American Pacific Fleet stationed at Pearl Harbor in Hawaii, and also invaded the Philippines, Hong Kong, and Malaya. The US then declared war on both Japan and Germany.

Bombing of the American fleet at Pearl Harbor

German tank, 1941

Operation Barbarossa
On June 22, 1941, 79 German divisions invaded Russia in the biggest military operation in history. At first they made good progress, but Russian resistance meant that they failed to capture Moscow and Leningrad.

Turning point

By mid-1942, the Germans occupied most of Europe and northern Africa, and the Japanese controlled most of the Pacific. Three battles turned the tide: Midway, where the US stopped the Japanese; El Alamein in North Africa; and Stalingrad, where the Russians began to push back the occupying forces.

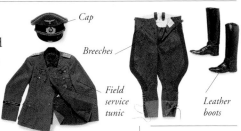

Cap
Breeches
Field service tunic
Leather boots

Items from a German officer's uniform

Adolf Hitler
Hitler (1889–1945) became German Chancellor in 1933. He quickly took dictatorial powers and ruled until his death in 1945. His spellbinding oratory convinced many people that he could restore German pride and greatness lost after World War I.

El Alamein
In 1942, German and Italian troops led by Field Marshal Rommel advanced across North Africa toward Egypt and the Suez Canal. In a lengthy battle, the British 8th Army led by General Bernard Montgomery defeated Rommel at El Alamein on the Egyptian border.

Rommel in North Africa

Timeline
March 1936 German troops occupy Rhineland, expanding Germany's territory.

October 1936 Germany and Italy become allies, forming the Rome-Berlin Axis.

November 1936 Germany and Japan become allies.

March 1939 Germany occupies Czechoslovakia.

Major General, German army

September 1939 Germany and Russia invade Poland; Britain and France declare war on Germany.

April 1940 German troops overrun Denmark and Norway.

May 1940 German troops invade and capture the Netherlands, Belgium, and France.

July–October 1940 British air force defeats Germany in the Battle of Britain, preventing Germany's invasion.

Occupied Europe

Life in German-occupied Europe was hard. Food was rationed, newspapers and radio were censored, and everyone was put to work producing supplies for the German war effort. Jews lived in fear of their lives, as more and more of them were rounded up and sent to their deaths in concentration camps, such as Auschwitz and Treblinka.

Resistance

Across Europe, individual people fought to rid their countries of German occupation. In the Netherlands and Denmark, families sheltered Jews in their houses, while in France and Yugoslavia, armed fighters fought a spirited war against the occupying armies.

French resistance fighters

Incendiary bombs

Civilians at war

For the first time, war was brought into the homes of people far away from the battlefield. Bombing of towns and cities meant that civilians became the targets of enemy action and often had to take refuge in shelters. At sea, submarine warfare stopped ships bringing in food and other supplies, causing severe shortages.

Rationing

Shortages all over Europe led to many foods being rationed. Everyone was given a ration card stating what food they were able to buy each week. People with gardens grew their own food.

Weekly food ration, British adult, 1941

Bacon: 4 oz (113 g)

Meat: 10 cents worth

Tea: 2 oz (56.5 g)

Sugar: 8 oz (226 g)

Margarine: 4 oz (113 g)

Butter: 2 oz (56.5 g)

Lard: 2 oz (56.5 g)

Cheese: 1 oz (28 g)

1 egg

Dresden, after the 1945 air raid

Air raids

During 1940–41, the German air force bombed many British cities, and many civilians lost their lives. As the war progressed in favor of the Allies, German cities came under attack. In February 1945, the Allied forces bombed Dresden, and more than 50,000 people were killed.

Winston Churchill

Churchill (1874–1965) became prime minister of Britain in May 1940. A fine orator whose speeches boosted British morale during the Battle of Britain and the rest of the war, Churchill led Britain to victory in 1945, but lost power in July 1945. He was elected prime minister in 1951–55.

Labor camps

In Germany, millions of Jews, gypsies, and prisoners of war were incarcerated in camps. Some camps held slave laborers, who produced munitions and other supplies; others were concentration camps to exterminate Jews and other "undesirables." Conditions were inhumane, and many died of ill-treatment and starvation. Prisoners of war (right) were also often kept in appalling conditions.

End of the war

By 1944, the war had turned in the Allies' favor. Italy had surrendered and the Russians were making slow progress toward Berlin. In June 1944, the Allies invaded France, opening up a new western front. The Russians entered Berlin in April 1945, and Germany surrendered in May 1945.

D-Day

On June 6, 1944, more than 100,000 Allied troops, supported by thousands of ships and aircraft, crossed the English Channel and landed on the beaches of France. At first they met fierce German resistance, but by August 25 the Allies had liberated Paris. By the end of the year, they had retaken the whole of France.

Troops landing on D-Day

Hiroshima

The war against Japan seemed likely to continue as the Japanese fought hard to protect their country. On August 6, 1945, the US air force dropped an atomic bomb on the Japanese city of Hiroshima, and a second on Nagasaki on August 9. The Japanese surrendered five days later.

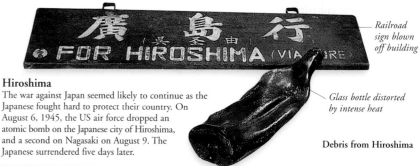

Railroad sign blown off building

Glass bottle distorted by intense heat

Debris from Hiroshima

December 1941 Japan bombs US Pacific Fleet, leading to US entry into the war.

US serviceman's novel

1942 US fleet stops Japanese advance across the Pacific at the Battle of Coral Sea and the Battle of Midway.

November 1942 British defeat German forces at El Alamein in North Africa.

January 1943 German siege of Stalingrad (Volgograd) broken.

June 1943 Allies invade Italy.

July 1943 Italian fascist dictator Mussolini resigns.

June 1944 D-Day landings: the Allies invade France.

June–August 1944 Russian armies reach Warsaw, Poland, and eastern Prussia.

US serviceman's ration kit

April 1945 Adolf Hitler commits suicide, as the Russian army reaches Berlin.

May 1945 Germany surrenders.

August 1945 Atomic bombs are dropped on the Japanese cities of Hiroshima and Nagasaki; Japan surrenders.

FIND OUT MORE | ARMIES | ASIA, HISTORY OF | EUROPE, HISTORY OF | FRANCE, HISTORY OF | GERMANY, HISTORY OF | HOLOCAUST | UK, HISTORY OF | UNITED STATES, HISTORY OF

WORMS

WORMS ARE ANIMALS that have an elongated, tubelike body, and no legs. The body of a worm can be cylindrical, flattened, or leaflike in shape. Worms vary enormously in size and can grow up to 100 ft (30 meters); they include segmented, ribbon, roundworms, and flatworms. We tend to think of these animals as the English naturalist Charles Darwin did – "little plowmen" worming their way through the soil. However, worms also live in the sea, in freshwater, and as parasites of plants and animals.

Short antennae help the worm find food.

Tentacles

Flat body can squeeze into cracks.

Segmented worms

There are three groups of segmented worms. The first group includes the ragworm. The second group includes earthworms and bloodworms (small red freshwater worms living in polluted waters worldwide). The third group includes leeches, which survive by sucking blood from an animal host.

Ragworm

The omnivorous ragworm is a scavenger and a predator, and lives in shallow seashore burrows. Its clearly defined head has tentacles (which grow back if they are cut off), eyes, and a mouth with strong, pincer-like jaws. Bristled, paddle-like flaps along each side give it the appearance of a tattered strip of rag. The ragworm moves by swimming or wriggling over surfaces. It is unisexual and usually dies shortly after mating.

King ragworm

Earthworms

The earthworm lives below ground in a burrow. By moving through the soil, eating as it goes, an earthworm aerates the ground and distributes plant nutrients. When breeding, it produces a cocoon that protects its eggs until they hatch into tiny worms. Thirty five cubic feet (1 cubic m) of grassland may contain 500 worms.

Cocoons, or egg capsules, have up to 20 eggs inside, but usually only one worm develops fully and emerges.

Peacock worms

These worms live on the shoreline, in tubes made of mud or sand. They have a fan of feathery tentacles around their heads that withdraw into the tube when they are threatened. One group of peacock worms can create reefs with their sandy tubes.

Gills for breathing and catching food

Mouth is in center of gills.

How an earthworm moves

1 The earthworm has a set of circular muscles around its body. When contracted (squeezed), they propel the front half of the worm forward.

2 Muscles running down the length of the worm's body drag the worm's tail after its head. A mucus covering aids this movement.

Saddle

Tail end

Earthworm

Roundworms

Roundworms are unsegmented, spindle-shaped, and usually microscopic. Some roundworms live in the earth – the top 3 in (7.5 cms) of 2.5 acres (a hectare) of soil contains up to 7,500 million round- worms. Other round- worms are parasitic, such as the filariasis worm. A single female roundworm can produce up to 200,000 eggs a day.

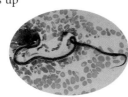

Filariasis worm

Elephantiasis

The roundworm *Wuchereria* causes the filariasis group of diseases. One of these diseases causes grossly enlarged human tissues, and is known as elephantiasis. Elephantiasis occurs when mosquitos infested with the *Wuchereria* larvae bite humans, infecting them with the larvae. The larvae then grow to adult worms within the body. They produce tiny young that they release into the lymph fluid. The larvae block the lymph vessels, and this causes the swelling.

Leg affected with disease

Ribbon worms

Parasitic forms of ribbon, bootlace, or horsehair worms lay their eggs in freshwater. When the eggs hatch, the larvae infect and feed on an insect host until the host dies.

Ribbon worm, foraging for food

Worms can grow to 100 ft (30 meters).

Flatworms

There are three groups of flatworms: planarians, flukes, and tapeworms. The primitive planarians grow into new worms when cut into pieces. The best-known member of the second group is the liver fluke, which infests mammals, snails, and other vertebrates. The third group – tapeworms – includes the human gut tapeworm, which can grow to 60 ft (18 meters).

Human gut tapeworm   *Sections of tapeworm*   *Head*

Suckers attach worm to gut wall.

Rosette of hooks

Sucker

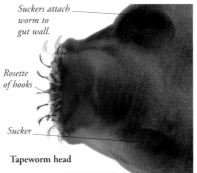

Tapeworm head

KING RAGWORM

SCIENTIFIC NAME	*Nereis diversicolor*
CLASS	Aclitellata
FAMILY	Nereidae
DISTRIBUTION	Seas around western Europe, the Baltic, and Finland
HABITAT	Sandy, muddy, or rocky shores.
DIET	Omnivorous, feeding on worms, dead, and dying animals
SIZE	Usually 10 in (7–25 cms), but can grow up to 35 in (90 cms)
LIFESPAN	Up to a year, but often die after spawning

FIND OUT MORE   DARWIN, CHARLES   DISEASES   OCEAN WILDLIFE   PARASITES   SEASHORE WILDLIFE

WRITING

COMMUNICATING BY USING MARKS on a surface to represent spoken language is called writing. Its vital importance lies in its power to preserve thoughts and ideas that would otherwise be lost. Thousands of scripts have been invented, each expressing a different language or adapted to a particular surface, be it clay, wood, stone, or paper. Writing not only conveys meaning – it can also be beautiful in itself. The art of fine script is called calligraphy.

Chinese passage skillfully written on silk

Writing implements

Throughout history, writers have used many different kinds of tools, each one suited to the most commonly available writing surface. The kind of mark each tool makes profoundly affects the nature of the script.

Stick and clay
The first writing was devised by the Sumerians 5,000 years ago. They used sticks called styluses to make triangular marks in soft clay, which was then baked hard.

Stylus

Pen and ink
For centuries, people wrote on paper using pens repeatedly dipped in ink. Early pens were trimmed goose quills. Later pens had metal nibs.

Early pens

Ballpoint pens
A ballpoint is a disposable pen that has a small ballbearing as a writing point, and an internal ink supply. One of the world's most-used ballpoint pens is the biro, patented in 1943.

Biros

Monumental inscription in Latin

Roman alphabet
The ancient Romans evolved a new alphabet to write Latin. The alphabet had 21 characters, and each represented a different sound. It was written in either uppercase (capital) or lowercase (small) letters. Today, the influence of the Roman Empire can be seen throughout Europe. Most of the languages of western Europe, such as English, are written in the Roman alphabet, now with 26 characters.

Scripts

All writing consists of a series of marks, or characters, that make up a script. In some scripts, such as Chinese, each character carries the meaning of a spoken word. In alphabetic scripts, such as Latin or English, each character represents a sound, and must be fitted with others to make a word.

Chinese
Chinese has the longest history of all current writing systems, stretching back to at least 1500 BC. Each character represents a different word, so many thousands must be learned before even simple passages can be read. Traditional Chinese is written with brush and ink on paper.

The fluent lines of Arabic give beauty to each word.

Arabic
Arabic has 17 basic characters, written from right to left. Dots are added to create the 28 letters of the Arabic alphabet. The letters are joined with curved strokes, and there are additional bold strokes at the end of each word. This gives Arabic an urgent sense of movement from right to left. The Qur'an, the holy book of Islam, teaches that writing is a gift from God. As well as using writing practically, to provide information, it is also used as decoration (like Chinese, Arabic calligraphy is a prized art form). Texts from the Qur'an are inscribed on mosque walls.

Unknown scripts

There are many ancient scripts that are no longer understood. Language experts work for years trying to decipher them. No one could read Egyptian hieroglyphics until the Frenchman Jean-François Champollion (1790–1832) deciphered them in 1824.

Mayan glyphs carved in stone.

Rounded, stylized symbols

Mayan glyphs
Between AD 300 and 1500, the Mayans of Central America produced thousands of carved stone inscriptions. Many of the 850 characters, or glyphs, clearly represent animals and objects, but others are abstract symbols. Very little Mayan writing was deciphered until the 1960s, when the life histories of Mayan rulers were first translated. About 85 per cent of glyphs can now be understood.

Shorthand
Words are spoken much faster than they can be written, and for people such as reporters it is useful to learn a quick way of jotting them down quickly and accurately. Shorthand systems replace words and phrases with brief marks, that can be read and understood later. Today, shorthand has largely been superceded by tape recorders and dictaphones.

Timeline
c.3100 BC Sumerians develop first writing system using pictograms (picture symbols of people, animals, and objects.)

Pictograms

3000 BC Egyptians develop hieroglyphics.

1800 BC Chinese characters, similar to those in use today, are written on tortoise shells.

c. 1000 BC Greeks invent the first alphabetic script, where each character (letter) represents a sound, and letters combine to form words.

c.63 BC A Latin form of shorthand (a kind of speedwriting) is invented: it is used for 1,000 years.

1905 After 5,000 years, linguists produce the first modern translation of the Sumerian writing system.

FIND OUT MORE

EGYPT, ANCIENT   LANGUAGES   MAYA   ROMAN EMPIRE   SIGNS AND SYMBOLS

X RAYS AND THE ELECTROMAGNETIC SPECTRUM

INVISIBLE WAVES OF ENERGY called X rays allow doctors to see through the soft tissues of the human body, enabling them to diagnose disease and injury without resorting to surgery. X rays are a type of wave energy called electromagnetic radiation. They form one part of a whole range of electromagnetic radiation called the electromagnetic spectrum, which also includes radio waves and light.

Electromagnetic radiation

The true nature of electromagnetic radiation still puzzles scientists, because it travels as waves of energy but also seems to be made up of tiny energy particles. Radiation can travel through many types of matter, and also through a vacuum.

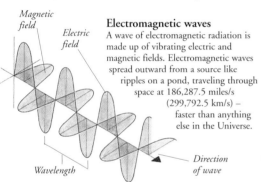

Magnetic field

Electric field

Electromagnetic waves
A wave of electromagnetic radiation is made up of vibrating electric and magnetic fields. Electromagnetic waves spread outward from a source like ripples on a pond, traveling through space at 186,287.5 miles/s (299,792.5 km/s) – faster than anything else in the Universe.

Wavelength

Direction of wave

Photons
Scientists think that the energy carried by electromagnetic waves is split up into particlelike units called photons. They are often described as "wave packets." An electromagnetic wave probably consists of a stream of photons.

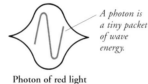

A photon is a tiny packet of wave energy.

Photon of red light

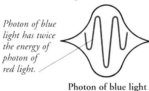

Photon of blue light has twice the energy of photon of red light.

Photon of blue light

Electromagnetic spectrum

Each type of electromagnetic radiation has a different wavelength and frequency (number of waves per second). Waves with the shortest wavelengths and the highest frequencies have the most energy.

Wavelength (in meters)

Gamma rays
The nuclei (centers) of radioactive atoms give out gamma rays during nuclear reactions and explosions. These high-energy rays are very penetrating and can damage human cells as they pass through the body.

Nuclear bomb explosion

10^{-14}

10^{-12}

X rays
An X-ray photograph shows the denser parts of the human body as light areas on a dark background. X rays can pass through flesh, but are blocked by teeth, bones, and some organs.

X-ray photograph

10^{-10}

Ultraviolet
A substance that absorbs the energy of ultraviolet waves and immediately releases it again as visible light is called a fluorescent. A fluorescent rock glows in the dark when exposed to ultraviolet waves.

Fluorescent rock

10^{-8}

Visible spectrum
Light is the only type of electromagnetic radiation visible to human eyes. Light includes all the colors of the rainbow, which together are called the visible spectrum.

Human eye

10^{-6}

Infrared
All warm objects give out infrared rays. Photographs called thermographs record these rays and show the warm and cool parts of an object as different colors, from yellow (hottest) to blue (coldest).

Infrared photograph

10^{-4}

Microwaves
Microwaves are actually short-wavelength radio waves. A microwave oven uses microwaves to cook food that contains water. The water molecules absorb the energy of the microwaves and vibrate faster, heating up the food.

Microwave oven

10^{-2}

1

Radio waves
Electromagnetic waves with the lowest energy are called radio waves. They can have wavelengths of thousands of miles. These waves are easy to produce using an electrical device called an oscillator. Radio waves are used to transmit radio and television programs.

Radio masts

10^{2}

James Clerk Maxwell
The Scottish physicist James Clerk Maxwell (1831–79) was the first to realize that light is a form of electromagnetic radiation. In 1864, he used mathematical equations to prove the existence of the electromagnetic spectrum. Maxwell is also famous for his work on the movement of molecules in gases.

Solar radiation
The Sun gives out a wide range of electromagnetic radiation that travels through space and reaches the Earth. Most of this radiation is absorbed by gases in the Earth's atmosphere, but radio waves, the visible spectrum, and some infrared and ultraviolet are able to pass through.

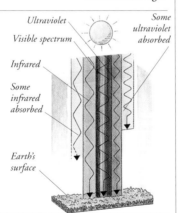

Ultraviolet

Visible spectrum

Infrared

Some infrared absorbed

Some ultraviolet absorbed

Earth's surface

Timeline

1667 English scientist Isaac Newton splits white light into the visible spectrum.

1800 William Herschel, a German-born astronomer, discovers infrared rays.

1801 German physicist Johann Ritter discovers ultraviolet radiation.

1864 Maxwell proves that the electromagnetic spectrum exists, and that electromagnetic radiation is caused by the link between electricity and magnetism.

1887 German physicist Heinrich Hertz makes radio waves artificially.

1895 German physicist Wilhelm Röntgen discovers X rays.

1896 First medical X ray taken by American scientist Michael Pupin.

1900 French physicist Paul Villard is the first to detect gamma rays.

1901 Italian inventor Guglielmo Marconi sends the first radio signal across the Atlantic.

1947 Microwave ovens on sale in the US.

FIND OUT MORE   COLOR   ELECTRICITY   ELECTROMAGNETISM   ENERGY   HEAT   LIGHT   MAGNETISM   RADIOACTIVITY

10^{4}

ZOOS

HUMANS HAVE ALWAYS been fascinated by animals and their lifestyles. Since ancient times, animals have been kept in captivity. Today, many cities have a zoo, or zoological garden, where animals are exhibited. In recent years, zoos have been criticized by those who believe it is wrong to keep animals in captivity. However, others argue that zoos can play a part in conservation.

Zoo history

Humans have kept animals for at least 25,000 years. Possibly the first animals kept solely out of curiosity were pigeons in Iraq over 6,500 years ago. The first animal collection was probably that of the ancient Egyptians over 4,000 years ago. It contained 100 elephants, 70 big cats, and thousands of other mammals. Rulers in China also established a huge zoo, called the Gardens of Intelligence, about 3,000 years ago. In the past, animals were often taught to perform for visitors; this rarely happens today.

London Zoo
In 1828, a small corner of Regent's Park was set aside for the use of the Zoological Society of London. The society's goal was to "interest and amuse the public." However, the zoo soon took on more serious scientific work concerned with living animals.

The role of a zoo

Zoos have three main goals: education, conservation, and research. Least important is entertainment for the public. In this way, zoos protect animals and do not exploit them. Organizations such as Zoo Check, in the UK, make sure the animals are given proper care, monitoring their diet, enclosures, and physical and mental health.

Children watch rabbits from "rabbit hole."

Snow leopard under anesthetic before surgery

Penguin wears tracking device to monitor its movements in Antarctica.

Education
Many people do not have access to the wild, so zoos are the only place that they have contact with rare, endangered, and exotic animals. Zoos educate children to appreciate animals and the dangers they face.

Animal welfare
The health of zoo animals is very important. Animals are encouraged to behave as they would in the wild. For example, chimps are given logs containing crickets for them to extract. Without this stimulation, animals get bored and start behaving abnormally.

Conservation
Because their habitats are being destroyed, many animals avoid extinction by being bred in captivity. Many species from rhinos to crickets have been bred in zoos and successfully returned to the wild.

Research
Zoos carry out research, such as developing pregnancy test kits for rhinos, treating illnesses, artificially inseminating animals, and tracking animals in the wild.

Greenhouse for growing food for locusts and other invertebrates.

These rain forest trees are found in the animals' natural habitat.

Glass sides for all around visibility

Breeding units for endangered species

Model of proposed new invertebrate house for London Zoo

Twilight world – dark cave setting for nocturnal invertebrates

Layered walkways allow animals to be observed at all levels of the trees.

Zoo of the future

With changing attitudes toward animals in captivity and advances in technology, zoos are becoming more sophisticated. New enclosures simulate the animals' natural habitats, both for the animals' welfare and so visitors can see animals in their natural surroundings. The combination of species, vegetation, temperature, and humidity are all considered. Food is hidden to encourage animals to forage, as they would in the wild.

Wildlife parks

Many people disagree with keeping animals behind bars. Most city zoos do not have enough space to keep animals in more natural settings; as a result, wildlife parks were developed. One of the first was Whipsnade Park Zoo, in the UK. With over 567 acres (230 ha), large animals can roam around in herds in more natural settings. Animals from the same country are often put together, making them feel more at home and giving the visitor a better idea of what they look like in the wild.

Giraffes in safari park

Aquariums
Aquatic animals need very special care, so specially designed aquariums have been built. In many of these centers, people get to touch certain marine animals, something that is almost impossible in the wild. Aquariums primarily concentrate on displaying marine animals local to the area in which they are situated. However, some aquariums also have more exotic or endangered animals. Many people are unhappy about keeping large marine animals, such as dolphins and the orca, in captivity.

Killer whale in aquarium

| **FIND OUT MORE** | ANIMALS | ANIMAL BEHAVIOR | CONSERVATION | ELEPHANTS | GIRAFFES | PENGUINS | RHINOCEROSES AND TAPIRS | WHALES AND DOLPHINS |